Personal Injury Limitation Law

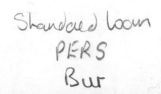

To our wives

Caroline Reid

and

Catherine Roy

Personal Injury Limitation Law

Third edition

Frank Burton BA, PhD, QC
Barrister

Andrew Roy MA, LLB
Barrister

Bloomsbury Professional

Bloomsbury Professional Ltd
Maxwelton House
41–43 Boltro Road
Haywards Heath
West Sussex
RH16 1BJ

British Library Cataloguing-in-Publication Data
A CIP Catalogue record for this book is available from the British Library.

ISBN 978 1 84766 984 1

Typeset by Phoenix Photosetting, Chatham, Kent
Printed and bound in Great Britain by CPI Group (UK) Ltd, Croydon, CR0 4YY

Preface to third edition

Since the publication of the second edition of this book at the start of 2007, there have been numerous significant developments in the law of personal injury limitation and related areas such as service.

The House of Lords in *A v Hoare* overturned *Stubbings v Webb*, thereby bringing claims for intentional torts such as physical and sexual abuse within the general personal injury limitation regime. Simultaneously, the House gave important guidance as to how this impacted upon the approach to both knowledge under section 14 and discretion under section 33. The Supreme Court (as it had since become) in *B v Ministry of Defence* (the 'atomic veterans litigation') further refined the restrictive approach to knowledge. Meanwhile, the Court of Appeal has clarified the need for a defendant to show forensic prejudice to succeed on section 33 (*Cain v Francis*) and confirmed the death of *Walkley v Precision Forgings Ltd* by holding that, following *Horton v Sadler*, a service failure is no longer an automatic bar to a claim proceeding (*Aktas v Adepta*).

As we see it, the overall trend and effect of these cases has been to enable the courts to take a less technical approach that focuses upon the substantive justice of whether or not a claim should be allowed to proceed, and thus to strike a balance of fairness as between claimants and defendants. This has manifested itself in three ways: first, in a more restrictive approach to date of knowledge, which requires the courts to balance factors previously relevant to knowledge in the discretionary exercise; secondly, in a widening of the circumstances in which the section 33 discretion is available; and, thirdly, in a broader and less technical approach to the exercise of this discretion.

Aside from these landmark cases, there have been a plethora of more fact-specific ones, ever more so as the number of judgments available online increases. As with previous editions, we have sought to include all such as have the potential to prove useful.

The law relating to service has undergone an even more radical overhaul, with a very different set of rules governing the service of proceedings with effect from 1 October 2008. Our chapter on service has been substantially re-written as a result.

Limitation law does not, of course, exist in a vacuum. It is applied in the context of the overall litigation landscape. Whilst we await the impact of the Jackson reforms of civil costs and funding (which, we would tentatively and respectfully suggest, will not necessarily lead to time limits being missed less frequently than before), it is right to note that court resources are, at present, very thinly stretched indeed. They will undoubtedly become more so as public spending cuts take their toll. The days of being able to walk up to the counter of the local court and have the claim form issued there and then are long gone in most areas; proceedings generally have to be sent to County Court Bulk Centres, and it often takes weeks for the court to process and issue them. Strong anecdotal evidence suggests that this is a source of considerable concern and confusion amongst practitioners facing a limitation deadline. In light of this, we have included a new section within the service chapter explaining how to ensure that proceedings can be brought in time, despite such difficulties.

In preparing this book, we have received assistance from many people. We are grateful to them all, and in particular to Kiran Goss of our publishers, whose tireless (and merited) urgings have prompted us to provide our copy only a few months after the agreed deadline, and who indulged us when we did so (happily, this particular time limit proved to be a flexible one).

Finally, it will be noted that the co-author of the first two editions, Rodney Nelson-Jones, is now enjoying a very well-earned retirement. We would emphasise that his work remains a large and integral part of this book.

The law is stated as at 1 January 2013.

Frank Burton QC
Andrew Roy

Preface to second edition

Since the publication of the first edition of this book 13 years ago, the legal and civil procedural landscape has changed significantly. The introduction of the CPR and with it the court's powers to actively manage cases has rendered the esoteric principles of striking out for want of prosecution an historical anachronism. This has allowed us to remove one whole chapter from the first edition. There has been, however, a steady stream of new limitation cases which have required us, with the assistance of an additional author Andrew Roy, to digest and add numerous cases to Part 2 and completely rewrite Part 1. We have kept the same format, as feedback from practitioners indicated they found the layout of the text very accessible. The only change is that, with the new cases added to Part 2, authorities are cross-referenced with the body of the reports rather than immediately following them. This was felt preferable in light of the increased density of case law that has built up.

Since the first edition the Human Rights Act 1998 has come into force, and we look at the challenges made to limitation law through the Act which, so far, has had surprisingly little impact. Of more significance have been two decisions in the House of Lords. In *Horton v Sadler*, the rule in *Walkley v Precision Forgings* was abolished and with it a complex set of exceptions as to when a section 33 application could and could not be made in circumstances where a second set of proceedings had been issued. In *Adams v Bracknell Forest Borough Council*, the House provided much needed clarification over the test to be applied in considering constructive knowledge.

The Law Commission Report 270 was published with July 2001. It recommended that the decision in *Stubbings v Webb* be reversed to permit a section 33 application to be made in cases of assault. This has yet to be done and limitation case law concerning sexual and physical abuse, described as seriously deficient and incoherent by the Master of the Rolls in *A v Iorworth Hoare*, continues to produce anomalous judgments. We have included these and many other cases in Part 2 and have discussed their significance in Part 1.

Many people have assisted us in the preparation of this edition and we are grateful to them all, in particular our publishers Sarah Thomas and Lesley Whitbourn who have worked tirelessly on our behalf.

The law is stated as at 1 January 2007.

Rodney Nelson-Jones
Frank Burton QC
Andrew Roy

Preface to first edition

This text is designed to act as a practitioner's guide to the complex principles and extensive case law concerning limitation issues in personal injury actions. There are a number of competent books on limitation generally, notably McGee *Limitation Periods* and Prime & Scanlan *The Modern Law of Limitation* which have useful chapters on personal injury cases. There is, however, at the time of writing, no text available dealing exclusively with personal injury actions despite the vast increase in the number of reported decisions in personal injury limitation law. Stephen Todd's *Limitation Periods in Personal Injury Claims* is an excellent book but is now over 12 years old, and largely limited itself to a short exposition of the principal sections of the Limitation Act 1980.

Limitation problems can create difficult questions of statutory construction. To simplify the exposition of the 1980 Act this book has adopted a tripartite structure. Part 1 is an analysis of the principles of limitation law with a number of chapters specifically dealing with various sections of the 1980 Act. Part 2 contains a summary of over 330 of the most important cases governing personal injury limitation law. We believe this to be a unique archive of cases. The summaries are designed to give easy access to the increasing number of both reported and unreported cases. The Appendix provides the reader with the relevant statutory material and rules of court discussed in both Part 1 and in the cases in Part 2.

In addition to limitation issues, the text has also included chapters in Part 1 and cases in Part 2 on a number of time-related procedural matters which are of crucial relevance to the practising lawyer. The chapters on service of proceedings, renewal of process, and striking out are designed to analyse the problems which can arise in civil litigation and which are inextricably connected with limitation questions. This is an area of the law which few texts, apart from the White and Green Books, address and where the practitioner is frequently left to the vagaries of experience to educate him to recognise the perils that exist in civil procedure.

The emphasis on cases and examples adopted throughout this book is an attempt to simplify the complexity of the subject-matter.

Many people have contributed to this book in a number of ways. We would like to thank Toby Hooper and John Finch who read and commented constructively on earlier drafts of the book. Valuable research assistance was provided by Jane Wycherley, Maria Cordina and Deborah Nadal. Patient and industrious secretarial help was given by Amelia Plaza. The law is stated as at 18 February 1994.

Frank Burton and Rodney Nelson-Jones

Contents

Table of statutes

Page references printed in **bold** type indicate where the provision is set out in part or in full.

Table of statutory instruments

Page references printed in **bold** type indicate where the provision is set out in part or in full.

In the Civil Procedure Rules 1998, Part 6 has been substantially replaced. The old service rules are indicated by *italics*.

Table of EC and international material

Page references printed in **bold** type indicate where the provision is set out in part or in full.

Table of cases

Page references printed in **bold** type indicate where a case summary is set out.

S

X

Y

Z

Part 1

1 History and policy
(Limitation Acts 1623–1980)

Introduction

All personal injury lawyers are required to be familiar with the operation of a complex and technical code concerning limitation law contained in the Limitation Act 1980. They also require more than a passing knowledge of the extensive case law that has arisen in interpreting both this statute and the earlier statutes of limitation. This text is designed to give a practical outline of the current principles in operation concerning the legal time limits imposed on actions for damages arising out of personal injury. Its specific emphasis is to give an ease of access within **Part 2** to the summaries of the most important cases.

Because the 1980 Act is a consolidating statute, it is desirable to trace its legislative history so as to provide a firmer grasp of the conceptual and procedural problems that limitation law has been designed to deal with and which it has also created. Running through the statute and case law is the ancient tension between the conflicting interests of claimants and defendants, on the one hand, and the legislature's and court's attempts to strike a balance of fairness between litigants, on the other. An injured person who alleges that damage has been caused by a breach of duty has long had an enshrined right to recourse to law, but that right has also long been restricted as being exercisable only within a defined period of time during which the legislature has determined the action as being reasonably defendable.

The Limitation Act 1623

Although most of the earlier cases arising out of the first major Limitation Act of 1623 (21 JAC 1 C16) and the earlier Act of 32 Henry VIII C2 concerned actions in respect of land and debts, the judicial interpretation of the policy behind the statute is capable of generalisation to all forms of action. Early juristic formulations emphasised that the policy of limitation was to create certainty and finality. Claims if they had merit should be brought within a reasonable period of time and a limitation period imposed on claimants an obligation of reasonable diligence. The court recognised that some delay might be inevitable before an action could be brought, because, for example lack of funding might require a litigant to save so that he could pursue his action. The 1623 Act imposed a limitation period of six years in respect of causes of action which basically concerned simple contract and tort. A claimant lost the right to bring an action in court after this period. Limitation law is accordingly a creature of statute not common law. The cause of action itself was not extinguished by the statute. If there remained other ways of recovering, for example a debt, such as having a lien over property or enforcing a security, then a claimant would not be entirely remediless. However, for most actions concerning personal injury, prohibiting the right to bring an action effectively amounted to extinguishing the cause of action.

The effect of imposing a certain period of limitation protected potential defendants against procedural prejudice. This could take the form of witnesses disappearing or dying or the probity of their oral recollections weakening due to the passage of time. In addition the stipulation of the latest date at which legal proceedings could be initiated has the benefit of limiting potential liability on a defendant so that he could reasonably alter his position after that time without the fear of having to pay damages and without the prospect of having to attempt to defend a stale claim. The very earliest of the reported cases on limitation tend to emphasise the interests of certainty and finality. Later there is detectable, both in the legislation and in the case law, an historic shift to looking in a more particular way at actual procedural prejudice that might occur after the passage of time. In *Scales v Jacob* ((1826) 3 Bing 638, 11 Moore CP 3553) the court was concerned with an action for the price of meat and whether the claimant could bring his case six years after the sale but within a six-year period from when the defendant had promised to pay him as soon as he could. The court emphasised the policy of the 1623 Act and held the claim as statute barred:

'It might perhaps have been as well if the letter of the Statute had been strictly adhered to: it is an extremely beneficial law; on which it has been observed, the security of all men depends, and it is therefore to be favoured. And although it will now and then prevent a man from recovering an honest debt, yet it is his own fault that he has postponed his action for so long, besides which permitting the evidence of promises and acknowledgement within the six years seems to be a dangerous inlet to perjury … I come next to the statute. If the language of that is clear we are especially bound to adhere to it … it has been argued, that the object of the statute was to protect those who have lost the evidences of their payment. This I deny. The title of the Act is proof of the contrary: "An Act for Limitation of Action, and for avoiding suits in law", and the preamble is "for quieting men's estates and avoiding of suits" … it is not a statute to protect parties against loss of evidence but to quiet claims. To sue a Defendant when he has slept six years over his rights, when time and misfortune may have disabled the debtor from discharging his obligations is at once iniquitous and antichristian.' (page 645.) (See also *A'court v Cross* (1825) 3 Bing 329, 11 Moore CP 198.)

In an action for land (*Tolson v Kaye* (1822) Brod & Bing 217), an issue arose as to whether proceedings could be brought within 20 years after title had first fallen to an heir or whether each successive heir had 20 years to bring a claim. The court emphasised that the statute had been enacted because the earlier Act of 32 Henry VIII C2 was found to be insufficient for quieting possession. Accordingly the court held that the statute should be given a beneficial construction so that it could achieve its object described by Lord Kenyon as a statute of repose:

'It has been the endeavour of the jurisprudence of all civilised countries to give repose to the possession of property, and the question is whether we shall not give the best effect to this statute by holding that the time specified begins to run from the period when the first title descends or falls. It has been urged, that the Plaintiff's case is entitled to the indulgent consideration of the Court, but I think that the indulgence ought to incline the other way; for unless the limit pointed out by statute be observed, no man is safe but may be reduced to poverty after long and undisputed possession. I agree in the observation ... that the preamble of the statute settles this question, how shall we quieten men's estates if we acceded to the arguments advanced on the part of the Defendants.' (Park J at 224–5) '... the statute of limitation was intended to quiet possessions, particularly as to land and property; and we are to carry into effect the object of a statute; now, if men were permitted to lie by till deeds and evidences were lost, no-one could be safe and they might lie by to any length of time if they could exceed the time described by the statute.' (Burroughs J at 225)

Nearly 200 years later, the same principles were invoked in *D v Harrow and others* (p394), although within a very different statutory framework which allowed the court to exercise a discretion to permit a stale claim to proceed. Mr Justice Eady, in considering whether the case concerning historic allegations of sexual abuse on a child when aged between 8 and 14 could be brought (at a time when the claimant was nearly 42) against a local authority, stated:

'35.   Although the discretion is unfettered, and must be addressed in the light of all the individual circumstances of the case, the court should never lose sight of the public policy considerations underlying the legislative regime governing limitation periods. Public authorities, as well as commercial entities and individuals, should not remain exposed indefinitely to the threat of litigation based upon historic allegations. Fairness requires a balancing of all relevant factors and their interests have to be taken into account. There is a public interest in certainty and finality and such considerations must not be lightly discounted, especially not on the basis of sympathy for an individual litigant – even where there is, or might be, a strong case on liability and causation.

36.   No doubt most people involved in this case will feel disquiet and frustration as to the plight suffered by this Claimant over the years. Yet, when everything is taken into account as it must be, the conclusion has to be that there is no sufficient justification for imposing on this Defendant a trial relating to historic allegations in respect of which its information has been significantly depleted.'

See also the reasoning in *Cain v Francis* (p360) per Lady Justice Smith at paras 64–69, and the historical review of Lord Wilson in *B v Ministry of Defence* (p312) at para 6.

The legislature did, however, recognise in the 1623 Act that fixed periods could cause injustice to certain classes of litigants who were unable to sue because of disability. Section 7 of the Act accordingly provided that time would not run against a claimant who was not capable of suing because of a disability, which was then defined not only in the modern senses of minority (then under 21, now under 18) and mental capacity but also in cases of *feme covert,* imprisonment or where a claimant was beyond the sea. This section allowed time to run only after the claimant was of full age, of sane memory, discovert, at large and returned from beyond the sea. The section was amended, so as to remove disabilities in respect of imprisonment and absence overseas, by the Mercantile Law Amendment Act 1856.

The amended s 7 did not avail a Kentish farmer, Mr Harnett, in the celebrated case of *Harnett v Fisher* (p462). Mr Harnett, through a jury decision, established that he had been wrongly certified as insane by Dr Fisher and forcibly committed to an asylum on 10 November 1912. Mr Harnett was only able to escape from the asylum in October 1921. He brought proceedings against the doctor in May of 1922. The court held that because the claimant was never insane he never was under a disability within the meaning of s 7 of the 1623 Act. Accordingly, time did not stop running when his cause of action accrued in 1912 when he was wrongfully detained. As he only had six years from the date to bring an action, his claim was held to be statute barred. Mr Harnett, acting in person, made a series of eloquent submissions to the House of Lords. He contended that at the date of his cause of action he had the status of a lunatic and could not therefore sue. It should not now lie in the defendants' mouth to say that he was not a lunatic when in fact the defendant certified him as such and deprived him of his liberty. He argued that the defendants should be estopped from making such a claim and that time should not run against him when he was physically detained. However, the House of Lords felt restrained by the Act:

> 'The object of the Act is to protect defendants against belated claims not merely those defendants who have a good defence and to that extent need no protection, but those also who have not or owing to the lapse of time, can no longer count on making out a sufficient answer … the question is not as the Appellant put it, of the status of a lunatic, imposed on him after the making of the reception order, but of his mental condition of sanity or insanity and this has been finally disposed of in his favour by the verdict (of the jury that he was sane) … I am not concerned to justify what the Legislature has enacted or to regret that it has gone no further to assist persons in the Appellant's position.' (Viscount Sumner at 581–2)

Only one of their lordships expressed criticisms from which it might be implied that certainty could be brought at too high a price:

> 'If it be the function of an appropriate limitation period to hold the scales evenly between the plaintiff and the defendant, the statute of James seemed to be singularly unsuited to a claim like the present … the statute must, if, applicable, bring in not a few similar cases, dire results in its train.' (Lord Blanesburgh at 597)

Fortunately, Mr Harnett's position should not reoccur today, as s 38(4) of the Limitation Act 1980 provides that a person shall be conclusively presumed to be of unsound mind while he is liable to be detained under the Mental Health Act 1983.

From the Limitation Act 1939 to the Limitation Act 1980

THE LAW REFORM (LIMITATION OF ACTIONS ETC) ACT 1954

Although the Limitation Act 1623 was repealed in part by a number of statutes, few amending enactments affected the six-year period governing simple contract and tort which founded most personal injury actions. (See Real Property Limitation Act 1833, Civil Procedure Act 1833, Real Property Limitation Act 1824 and Civil Procedure Act 1883.) One substantial change was to impose a six-month limitation period in respect of an action against a public authority through the Public Authorities Protection Act 1893. This Act caught a large number of personal injury claims brought against councils, dockyards, passenger transport boards and other public utilities and led to a number of obvious injustices. For example in *Freeborn v Leeming* [1926] 1 KB 160 a medical officer negligently failed to diagnose a claimant's injury and the correct diagnosis was only made six months after the negligent act. By that time the cause of action was statute barred (see also *Nelson v Cookson* [1940] 1 KB 100). Actions on behalf of dependants of a deceased person under the Fatal Accidents Act 1846 were also restricted to a short period of limitation namely one year from the date of death. A two-year period of limitation was imposed by the Maritime Conventions

Act 1911 in respect of personal injury or death arising out of fault between vessels used in navigation.

The Limitation Act 1939 consolidated all interim enactments. It came into force on 1 July 1940 and remained the primary Limitation Act until 1980. The 1939 Act preserved the six-year period for actions founded on simple contract or tort but retained the privileged position of public authorities although it did extend against them the limitation period from six months to one year from the date when the cause of action accrued.

Criticism of the one year period in respect of public authorities was reviewed in 1946 by the Departmental Committee of Alternative Remedies which was set up to investigate the effects of new social insurance legislation on personal injury actions, particularly those arising at the workplace (Cmd 6860, Chairman Lord Monckton). In its final report, the Committee proposed abolishing the privileged position of public authorities. It also recommended a fundamental alteration in the limitation period by cutting it from six to three years in respect of personal injury actions. The report stated that:

'In our opinion six years is too long for a period of delay before the commencement of an action. Once the action has been commenced the defendant can get it dismissed if it is not prosecuted with reasonable speed by the plaintiff, but a person who has merely been threatened with an action cannot of himself take proceedings to get the claim disposed of as he can if the claim is for compensation under Workman's Compensation Acts. It seems clearly unreasonable that a prospective plaintiff should have the power to keep the threat of an action hanging over the employer or third party for so long a period as six years. On the other hand injustice will be done unless adequate time is given to the injured person or his dependents before they are compelled to commence proceedings. For example some time may elapse before the extent and effect of the injury can be ascertained or before the injured person has secured sufficient funds to launch an action which may involve heavy costs ... for those reasons we recommend that in employment cases ... the time limit for commencing an action should be three years.' (para 107, p 47)

The Committee's view that six years was 'clearly unreasonable' in personal injury cases appears not to have been supported by any detailed reasoning and may well have been influenced by the perceived increase in industrial personal injury actions that would accompany the abolition of the Workman's Compensation Acts. It is not, for example, immediately obvious as to why other actions in tort and contract which might also depend on the oral recollection of witnesses should retain the six-year period.

Nevertheless this major proposal came to be enthusiastically endorsed by the 1949 Report of the Committee on the Limitation of Actions chaired by Lord Justice Tucker (Cmd 7740). Like the 1946 Committee, it criticised the privileged position of public authorities. It recommended a two-year period of limitation in personal injury cases on the grounds that such actions should be started while evidence is fresh in the minds of the parties and the witnesses. The Committee did, however, further recommend a procedure whereby leave could be granted by the court to bring an action after the expiry of two years if the judge thought it was reasonable in all circumstances to do so, with the proviso that there would be a longstop of six years after which no claim should be brought. The recommendation of a two-year period was perhaps a little surprising. The Committee had evidence before it from the Scottish Motor Tractors Company Limited, as to what their claims history was like in Scotland where there was a 20 year period of prescription. The company indicated that, over a five-year period, 10% of claims against it were raised within nine months, 50% within nine months to a year, 30% within one to two years, 9% within two to three years, and only 1% after more than three years.

The 1949 Committee also recommended that the two-year period ought to be the time limit for all personal injury actions not just employment cases, but specifically emphasised that it should not include those actions for personal injury which arise out of trespass to the person, false imprisonment or malicious prosecution (paragraph 23). The House of Lords in *Stubbings v Webb* (p677) relied on this recommendation in formulating its decision that intentionally inflicted injuries such as sexual abuse were governed by a six-year limitation period and were excluded from the limitation regime affecting all other personal injuries.

However, in *A v Hoare* (p287) the House of Lords invoked its *Practice Statement (Judicial Precedent)* [1966] 1 WLR 1234 to reverse *Stubbings v West*, acknowledging that unsatisfactory decisions in the higher courts had created uncertainty as the lower courts tended to distinguish them on inadequate grounds. The House of Lords considered that *Stubbings* had placed more weight on the Tucker Committee and Hansard than they could properly bear, and restored the reasoning in *Letang v Cooper* (p533) and *Long v Hepworth* [1968] 1 WLR 1299 which treated intentional assaults as personal injury actions (per Lord Hoffmann at paras 1–25).

Parliament also acted on some of the other proposals from the 1946 and 1949 Committees by passing the Law Reform (Limitation of Actions, etc) Acts in 1954. This reduced the period for instituting proceedings in claims of personal injuries to three years and abolished the one-year rule favouring public authorities. The 1954 Act, which came into force on 4 June 1954, did not enact any postponement of the running of time until an injury was discoverable or give the court any discretionary power to extend the limitation period. The right to bring a claim in respect of personal injuries, which had remained six years for over three centuries, was halved.

THE LIMITATION ACT 1963

The fact that a certain period even of six years in personal injury claims was capable of causing manifest injustice was graphically illustrated in the cases of imperceptible injury, most notably in the House of Lords' judgment in *Cartledge v E Joplin & Sons Ltd* (p366). In *Cartledge*, nine steel dressers had been wrongly exposed to silica dust for periods from 1939 to 1950 which had caused them to contract pneumoconiosis before 1950. None of the men had been diagnosed or indeed had been capable of being diagnosed as suffering from the disease until dates between 1950 and 1955. The men or their personal representatives commenced an action on 1 October 1956 which was held to be statute barred because their cause of action had accrued six years before the date of the proceedings (the 1939 Act applied). A cause of action was held to accrue in personal injury cases when damage which was more than minimal had occurred even though that damage had been done on a date before the men knew or before medical science could have discovered that the men were in fact injured. Lord Reid was of a clear view that the law required urgent amendment:

'It appears to me to be unreasonable and unjustifiable in principle that a cause of action should be held to accrue before it is possible to discover any injury and therefore before it is possible to raise any action. If this were a matter governed by common law I would hold that a cause of action ought not to be held to accrue until either the injured person had discovered the injury or it be possible for him to discover it if he took such steps as were reasonable in the circumstances.' ([1963] AC 758 at 772)

All the speeches in the judgment expressed concern at the harshness of the decision which was necessarily imposed by the provisions of the Limitation Act 1939. The Limitation Act 1954 only served to aggravate the decision. Lord Pearce's speech specifically referred to a 1961 committee chaired by Sir Edmund Davies. This committee had been appointed to look into the *Cartledge* case following the decision in the Court of Appeal. Lord Pearce expressed hope that the recommendations in the report would be enacted. The committee (Report of the Committee on the Limitation of Actions in Personal Injury 1962, Cmnd 1829) did not restrict its deliberations to cases of imperceptible injury where there was an insidious onset of disease or a delayed manifestation of symptoms. The committee also looked at cases where the injured person was unaware of the cause of his injury, namely so-called concealed causation cases (see para 9). The committee was satisfied that although the number of cases precluded by the application of the Limitation Acts was small the hardship and injustice caused in those few cases required a change in the law. Instead of listing diseases and latency periods which would be exempt from the provisions of the Limitation Act the committee proposed that time should run either from the date of the injury or from the time when the claimant had knowledge of the existence of the injury and the cause of it. The committee recommended a procedure whereby the claimant would be required to have leave from the court on an ex parte application where the initial three-year period had expired. This would involve the claimant persuading a judge that he could not reasonably have been expected to discover the existence or cause of his injury within the primary limitation of three years. The claimant would also have to demonstrate that he had commenced proceedings within one year from the earliest date on which he could reasonably have been expected to have discovered his injury.

The Limitation Act 1963, which came into force on 31 July 1963, sought to resolve some of the criticisms that had arisen in the *Cartledge* case and to enact some of the recommendations of Lord Edmund Davies' committee. The 1963 Act provided that an action was not to be statute barred if:

(a) The claimant was in a state of justifiable ignorance for more than two years of the normal three-year limitation period; and
(b) he instituted proceedings within 12 months of his date of knowledge.

The claimant's date of knowledge referred to either actual or constructive knowledge. His action would only be allowed to commence after the three years if the claimant could demonstrate that material facts of a decisive character were outside his knowledge within the three-year period. Section 7 of the Act sought to define material facts of a decisive character as those which a reasonable person, having obtained appropriate advice would have regarded as giving him a reasonable prospect of succeeding in an action for damages. The same section attempted to define actual or constructive knowledge as those facts which were known or which were capable of being ascertained by taking reasonable actions to discover them, including those facts which could be ascertained with advice which it was reasonable for the claimant to take whether this was medical legal or other advice.

THE LIMITATION ACT 1975

The Limitation Act 1963 was reviewed in 1970 by the Law Commission (Law Commission 35: Cmnd 4532). Two fundamental changes were introduced by the

Law Reform (Miscellaneous Provisions) Act 1971. The first extended the time for bringing an action in the so-called state of ignorance cases from one year to three years from the date of knowledge. The reasoning was that a claimant might have difficulty preparing an affidavit for his ex parte application for leave to proceed and to prepare a statement of claim within the one year from his date of knowledge. The Law Commission recommended that a full three-year period should be allowed from the date of knowledge, as they did not anticipate that it would significantly inconvenience defendants. A similar recommendation was made by the Scottish Law Commission. The Committee also recommended that in fatal accident cases the date of knowledge of the actual claimant as well as that of the deceased should be considered. They recommended that both the personal representatives and the dependents should also have a three-year period to bring an action from the date of death or alternatively from the date of their own relevant knowledge whichever was later. The Law Reform (Miscellaneous Provisions) Act 1971 had therefore the effect of reversing the decision of *Lucy v W T Henleys Telegraph Works Co Ltd* [1970] 1 QB 393. In that case a widow's claim was held to be statute barred even though she did not have and could not have acquired knowledge of the material facts within the period allowed for her claim to proceed.

The Limitation Act 1963 was further reviewed by a Law Reform Committee chaired by Lord Justice Orr set up in December 1972. The committee's recommendations on personal injury issues was published in 1974 (Inquiry Report on Limitation of Actions in Personal Injury Claims 1974, Cmnd 5630). The committee attempted to grapple with the uncertainty that had been generated by case law concerning the concept of knowledge as defined in the 1963 Act. A major problem of construction had arisen as to whether time should run against a person when he knew not only those facts which allowed him to realise he had suffered an injury caused by the defendants but also whether he also needed know whether he had a case in law that is in negligence, nuisance, breach of contract or statutory duty. The committee expressed the view that the law had been left in a state of uncertainty by the House of Lords' decision in *Central Asbestos Co Ltd v Dodd* [1973] AC 518 because whether a claimant needed to know he had in law a worthwhile cause of action before time began to run had been left unclear. Following a careful and interesting review of the history of limitation enactments and the policy behind limitation, the committee recommended that knowledge that the claimant had a cause of action in law should *not* be required before time started to run against him. The reasoning was that ignorance of the law should never constitute a legitimate excuse and stale claims could extract a nuisance value from insurers who in turn needed some degree of protection. The committee was also concerned that open ended liability might restrict the insurability of certain risks and some degree of sanction was necessary to ensure that claims were prosecuted diligently. In coming to its recommendations, the committee examined the parliamentary proceedings in respect of the 1963 and 1971 Acts. These satisfied it that Parliament had not deliberated on whether time should not run until the claimant knew that he had a worthwhile cause of action.

The committee further considered whether knowledge should be construed objectively or subjectively and endorsed the judgment of Widgery LJ in *Newton v Cammell Laird & Co Ltd* (p581):

'In my judgment when one has to consider constructive notice under section 7(5)(c) [of the Limitation Act 1963] it is necessary to look at all the circumstances of the particular individual concerned to see whether, when all those circumstances are looked at in the round, it can be said that his failure to take advice was reasonable. The court must consider the period of time during which it was open for him to seek advice, the state of his health, the availability of facilities to him, and many other matters.'

However, the most radical recommendation from the committee was not in its redrafting of the concept of date of knowledge but its recommendation that the court should have a discretion to disapply the primary limitation period in personal injury cases. Part of the reason why the committee had rejected the view that a claimant should have knowledge that he had a worthwhile cause of action was because, if that was so, the claimant would get an automatic extension of time without any mechanisms for considering the particular difficulties or prejudices which the defendant might have been caused. This led the committee to the proposal that in those cases where delay had arisen because of the claimant's ignorance of his legal rights the court should have an opportunity to investigate the particular prejudices to which the defendant might be exposed if an action was allowed to proceed:

'We have asked ourselves why in a residual class of cases the court should not have the discretion to weight the prospective actual hardship ... the question arises ... whether ... there should not be vested in the court a residual discretion which would cover all such cases, to extend the time where on consideration of all the circumstances including the respective hardship actually involved to the plaintiff if time is not extended and to the defendant if it is, if it is considered equitable to do so. The virtue of such a provision is that it would enable the court to do what the existing law does not permit, namely to investigate the actual hardship arising on each side, in the circumstances of each particular case and to try and strike a fair balance between them.' (para 56)

The Limitation Act 1975 enacted many of the Orr Committee's recommendations. It clarified the concept of knowledge to make it clear that ignorance of a legal cause of action did not prevent time running. It also abolished the need to obtain the leave of the court to initiate proceedings outside the primary limitation period. More importantly, the 1975 Act also gave the power to the court to disapply the primary limitation period if in all the circumstances of the case it was thought equitable to do so. This fundamental reform represents the high watermark in the development of limitation law away from the jurisprudential concepts of finality and certainty. Instead of giving to potential defendants a certain period, on the basis that after its expiry they would have suffered some degree of unspecified and generalised prejudice, the Limitation Act 1975 empowered the court to look specifically at the actual prejudice of any particular defendant if an action was allowed to proceed outside the primary limitation period and outside the period given by the date of knowledge.

THE LIMITATION ACT 1980 AND THE CONSUMER PROTECTION ACT 1987

The Limitation Act 1980, which came into force on 1 May 1981, consolidated all interim limitation legislation from 1939 and contains the major legislative code in respect of personal injury actions. A significant amendment has been made to the 1980 Act by the Consumer Protection Act 1987. This created a statutory cause of action for damages, including those arising out of personal injury, due to unsafe products. Any such action has to be brought within three years of the cause of action accruing or from the date when the claimant knew or could with reasonable diligence have discovered the existence of his cause of action (Limitation Act 1980, s 14(1A)). In addition the 1987 Act innovatively provided a longstop proviso which prohibited any action brought after 10 years from when the product in question was last supplied

(Limitation Act 1980, s 11A). The 1987 Act therefore provides an example of a cause of action being extinguished after 10 years rather than the remedy being barred.

The legislative history of limitation law in personal injury cases is no longer governed by a simple concept of certainty. The statutory framework is now characterised not only by the concept of an accrual of a cause of action but also concepts such as the date of knowledge of the claimant and the court's equitable discretion to disapply the primary limitation period.

The following chapters look at the concepts of the accrual of the cause of action, the date of knowledge and the discretion to extend the primary limitation period to analyse how the case law has developed and how ss 11, 14 and 33 of the Limitation Act 1980 have been judicially interpreted.

Accrued defences

Notwithstanding the purposes behind the 1963 and 1975 Acts there persists, however, a class of case which will still remain statute barred under the 1939 Act. In *Arnold v Central Electricity Generating Board* (p306) the House of Lords held that, where a cause of action had accrued before the coming into force of the 1954 Act, namely 4 June 1954, any limitation defence that had been available to the defendant at that time remains. Accordingly the 1963 Act provisions as to date of knowledge and the 1975 Act discretion to waive time limits are not applicable. Mr Arnold had been employed by the Birmingham Corporation in a power station between 1938 and April of 1943. As a result of his exposure to asbestos he contracted mesothelioma which was diagnosed in 1981 and which caused his death in 1982. His widow sued the successor in title of the occupiers of the power station, the Central Electricity Generating Board, who pleaded that the relevant limitation period was applicable under s 21 of the Limitation Act 1939. This preserved the privileged position of public authorities and limited the time in which an action could be brought to one year. Accordingly the claim was statute barred by April 1944. The House of Lords held that, although s 21 was repealed by the Law Reform (Limitation of Actions etc) Act 1954, s 7(1) of that Act preserved the right to plead any accrued limitation defence. The court went on to hold that the 1963 Act , which brought in the right to bring an action based on a date of knowledge, also preserved by s 1(4)(a) any existing limitation defence. However the 1975 Act was apparently intended to apply to causes of action which had accrued before its coming into force as well as those which accrued afterwards and did not contain any provision for a saving of limitation defences. In particular, s 2(1) of the 1975 Act provided:

> '(1) The provisions of this Act shall have effect in relation to causes of action which accrued before, as well as causes of action which accrued after, commencement of the Act, and shall have effect in relation to any cause of action which accrued before the commencement of the Act notwithstanding that an action in respect thereof has been commenced and is pending at the commencement of this Act.'

Notwithstanding this provision Lord Bridge in the leading speech examined the legislative history and relied on the report of the Law Reform Committee Cmnd 5630 to hold that the 1975 Act did not retrospectively revive the claimant's cause of action. Lord Bridge further held that paragraph 9 of Schedule 2 to the Limitation Act 1980 provided that nothing in the 1980 Act would enable any action to be brought which was barred by the Limitation Act 1939. McGhee has subjected this decision to sustained criticism (see *Limitation Periods* (4th edn, 2004, paras 1–021).

Accordingly, the effects of *Cartledge* (p366) are not yet entirely a matter of history. There will be some claimants who have, for example, been exposed to asbestos prior to the coming into force of the 1954 Act who will be unable to sustain an action if it is demonstrated that they have suffered damage due to that exposure before the coming into force of the 1954 Act on 4 June 1954. However, whether they have in fact suffered damage or not by that date will be a matter for medical evidence. In cases of mesothelioma such damage would not in fact have occurred until well after the exposure and certainly well after 4 June 1954 (cf *Keenan v Miller Insulation & Engineering Ltd* (p515), *McCaul v Elias Wild & Sons Ltd* (p547)).

The House of Lords had an opportunity to revisit *Arnold* in *McDonnell v Congregation of Christian Brothers Trustee* (p549) but affirmed the correctness of its decision. This case concerned an action for damages arising out of alleged physical, emotional and sexual abuse between 1941 and 1951 when the claimant was attending the defendant's school. Proceedings were issued on 9 August 2000. The primary limitation period was six years after the claimant reached his majority (then 21) pursuant to s 2 of the Limitation Act 1939, namely on 6 January 1963 (the claimant had been born on 6 January 1936) (see *Stubbings v Webb* (p677)). The claimant's cause of action accordingly accrued before the coming into force of the 1954 Act on 4 June 1954 but was not time barred because of the extended period of limitation afforded by his disability as a minor. The defendants contended that the claimant's claim was statute barred by 6 January 1963 because the subsequent legislative changes concerning date of knowledge and judicial discretion were not retrospective. The claimant contended that the effects of the 1963 and 1971 Acts were retrospective and *Arnold* was distinguishable on the grounds that, inter alia, it turned on the narrow point of s 21 of the 1939 Act concerning public authorities and further that Mr McDonnell's case, unlike the position in *Arnold*, was not statute barred before the coming into force of the 1954 Act. The House of Lords in *McDonnell* unanimously rejected the claimant's submissions, although Lord Bingham, who gave the leading speech, accepted that a different position might have been reached in *Arnold*:

'24. I would accept that a different conclusion might have been reached by the House in *Arnold*. The provision in section 1(1) of the 1963 Act that section 2(1) of the 1939 Act "shall not afford any defence" could, as Ms Gumbel argued, have been interpreted more expansively. The decision has been the subject of measured but penetrating criticism by McGee in the *Statute Law Review* in 1988, pp 130–134 and McGee *Limitation Periods*, 3rd edn (1998), pp 8–13. It is arguably anomalous to treat six-year and three-year claims differently, since if a cause of action expired before a plaintiff can reasonably be aware of it the potential injustice is as great in the one case as in the other. But *Arnold* was a unanimous decision of the House which has now stood for 16 years. It may doubtless have been relied on and applied to defeat other claims. Parliament could, if it wished, have reversed the decision, but has not done so. The decision is not plainly wrong, even if one were inclined to disagree with it, and the House has made plain that "it requires much more than doubts as to the correctness of [a considered majority opinion of the ultimate tribunal] to justify departing from it" (*Fitzleet Estates Ltd v Cherry* [1997] 1 WLR 1345, 1349). Sympathy for the possible injustice suffered by the appellant must be tempered by recognition of the almost impossible task the respondents would face in seeking to resist a claim of this kind after the lapse of half a century.'

McGee has remarked on this decision in *McDonnell*:

> 'It is a cause of regret that the House of Lords should more or less acknowledge that their earlier decision was wrong and yet decline the opportunity to correct it. There would without doubt have been serious difficulties in conducting a fair trial of the action after so long a lapse of time, but that is a point which could potentially have caused difficulties for both sides. In any event, it cannot be a proper ground for ignoring the correct construction of an Act of Parliament.'
> (*Limitation Periods* (4th edn, 2004),1st Supp, paras 1021–1025)

The Human Rights Act 1998

Following the coming into force of the Human Rights Act 1998 (Royal Assent received in November 1999, implemented in full 2 October 2000) practitioners have had to consider whether the provisions of the Limitation Act 1980 are compatible with convention rights. Section 3 of the Act requires that, insofar as it is possible to do so, primary and subordinate legislation must be read and given effect in a way which is compatible with such rights. Specifically, Article 6, the right to a fair trial, Article 8, the right to respect for private and family life, and Article 14, prohibition on discrimination of the convention rights, are likely to be engaged. The United Kingdom Parliament permitted individuals to petition the Court in Strasbourg from 1996 and the leading case concerning limitation law occurred before the Human Rights Act in the case of *Stubbings v United Kingdom* [1997] 23 EHRR 213. The House of Lords in *Stubbings v Webb* (p677) held that cases involving the infliction of deliberate harm, such as in sexual abuse claims, were subject to a non-extendable six-year period of limitation under s 2 of the 1980 Act. This meant that unlike claims based on a breach of statutory duty, contract or negligence involving personal injuries, the date of knowledge provisions within ss 11 and 14 and the court's discretion in s 33 to waive the three-year time limit was not applicable. In *Stubbings v United Kingdom*, the European Court considered four cases of sexual abuse in childhood, all of which were brought six years after the claimants' 18th birthdays. This limitation period could not be waived or extended as the House of Lords held that torts concerning intentional trespass to the person did not arise from any breach of duty within the meaning of s 11 of the 1980 Act. The European Court declined to find that this categorisation violated the claimants' right to a fair trial (Article 6, the right to family life), Article 8 or was discriminatory with respect to convention rights under Article 14.

The court's reasoning took into account the legislative history of limitation law in the United Kingdom and the policy behind legislative restrictions (paragraphs 28–34). The court recognised that contracting states have no uniformity with regard to limitation periods or the date from which the period was calculated but each state was entitled to enjoy a margin of appreciation in such matters, as long as they were in pursuit of legitimate aims and were proportionate. With reference to the claim under Article 6, the European Court held that the very essence of the applicants' rights of access to courts had not been impaired:

> '(50)   The Court recalled that Art 6(1) embodied the "right to accord" of which the right of access, that is, the right to institute proceedings before a Court in civil matters, constitutes one aspect. However, this right is not absolute, but may be subject to limitation; these are permitted by implication since the right of access by its very nature calls for regulation by the State. In this respect, the Contracting States enjoy a certain margin of appreciation although

the final decision as to the observance of the Convention's requirements rests with the Court. It must be satisfied that the limitations applied do not restrict or reduce the access left to the individual in such a way or to such an extent that the very essence of the right is impaired. Further, a limitation will not be compatible with Art 6(1) if it does not pursue a legitimate aim and if there is not a reasonable relationship of proportionality between the means employed and the aim sought to be achieved (see *Ashingdane v United Kingdom* (1985) 7 EHRR 528, para (57) and, more recently, the *Belet v France* judgment of 4 December 1995, Series A No. 33-B, p41, para (31)).

(51)   It is noteworthy that limitation periods in personal injury cases are a common feature of the domestic legal systems of the Contracting States. They serve several important purposes, namely to ensure legal certainty and finality, protect potential defendants from stale claims which might be difficult to counter, and prevent the injustice which might arise if Courts were required to decide upon events which took place in the distant past on the basis of evidence which might have become unreliable and incomplete because of the passage of time.

(52)   In the instant case, the English law of limitation allowed the applicants six years from their 18th birthdays in which to initiate civil proceedings. In addition, subject to the need of sufficient evidence, a criminal prosecution could be brought at any time and, if successful, a compensation order could be made (see paras 38–42 above). Thus, the very essence of the applicants' right of access to a court was not impaired.

(53)   The time limit in question was not unduly short; indeed, it was longer than the extinction period for personal injury claims set by some international treaties (see para 48 above). Moreover, it becomes clear that the rules applied were proportionate to the aims sought to be achieved (see para 51 above) when it is considered that if the applicants had commenced actions shortly before the expiry of the period, the Courts would have been required to adjudicate on events which had taken place approximately 20 years earlier ...

(55)   The Contracting States properly enjoy a margin of appreciation in deciding how the right of access to Courts should be circumscribed. It is clear that the UK legislature has devoted a substantial amount of time and study to the consideration of these questions. Since 1936 there have been four statutes to amend and reform the law of limitation and six official bodies have reviewed aspects of it (see paras 28–34 above). The decision of the House of Lords, of which the applicants complain ... fixed six-year periods should apply in cases of intentionally caused personal injury, was not taken arbitrarily, but rather followed from the interpretation of the Limitation Act 1980 in the light of the report of the Tucker Committee upon the Act had been based .'

With respect to Article 8, the court concluded that the restriction upon suing beyond age 24 did not violate the positive obligation on the state to respect private and family life:

'(62)   It is to be recalled that although the object of Article 8 is essentially that of protecting the individual against arbitrary interference by the public authorities, it does not merely compel the State to abstain from such interference: there may, in addition to this primary negative undertaking, be positive obligations inherent in an effective respect for private or family life. These obligations may involve the adoption of measures designed to secure respect for private life, even in the sphere of the relations of individuals between themselves (ibid para 23).

(63)   There are different ways of ensuring respect of private life and the nature of the State's obligation will depend upon the particular aspect of private life that is in issue. It follows that the choice of means calculated to secure compliance with this positive obligation principle falls within the Contracting State's margin of appreciation (ibid para 24).

(64)   Sexual abuse is unquestionably an abhorrent type of wrongdoing, with debilitating effects on its victims. Children and other vulnerable individuals are entitled to State protection, in the form of effective deterrents, from such grave types of interference with essential aspects of their private life …

(65)   In the instant case, however, such protection was afforded. The abuse of which the applicants complain is regarded most seriously by the English criminal law and subject to severe maximum penalties … provided sufficient evidence could be secured, a criminal prosecution could have been brought at any time and could still be brought … Indeed the Court notes that a charge of indecent assault was brought against the applicant BS' father, to which he pleaded guilty.

(66)   In principle, civil remedies are also available providing they are sought within the statutory time limit. It is nonetheless true that under domestic law, it was impossible for the applicants to commence civil proceedings as against their alleged assailants after their 24th birthdays … However, as noted above (para 62) Article 8 does not necessarily require the State to fulfil their positive obligation to secure respect for private life by the provision of unlimited civil remedies in circumstances where criminal law sanctions are in operation.'

The applicants also complained that they were disadvantaged in comparison with those who suffered non-intentional assaults or negligent injuries because they could not avail themselves of the date of knowledge provisions or discretionary remedies. The court, however, did not accept that this was discrimination within the meaning of Article 14:

'(73)   It is to be recalled that the applicants complain that they were treated less favourably than both the victims of negligently inflicted harm and the victims of other forms of intentional injury which did not lead to psychological damage, preventing them from understanding its causes (see paragraph 69 above). The Court observes, first, that as between the applicants and the victims of other forms of deliberate wrongdoing with different psychological after effects, there was no disparity in treatment, because the same rules of limitation are applied to each group. Secondly, the victims of intentionally and negligently inflicted harm cannot be said to be in analogous situations for the purposes of Article 14. In any domestic judicial system, there may be a number of separate categories of claimant, classified by reference to the type of harm suffered, the legal basis of the claim or other factors, whilst subject to varying rules and procedures. In the instant case, different rules have evolved within the English law of limitation in respect of the victims of intentionally and negligently inflicted injury, as the House of Lords observed with reference to the report of the Tucker Committee (see para 15 above). Different considerations may apply to each of these groups; for example, it may be more readily apparent to the victims of deliberate wrongdoing that they have a cause of action. It would be artificial to emphasise the similarity between these groups of claimants and to ignore the distinctions between them for the purposes of Article 14 ...'

The effect of this decision was that the victims of sexual, physical and emotional abuse sought to avoid the six-year limitation period with respect to intentional trespass by relying upon collateral causes of action based on negligence which came within the provisions of s 11 of the Limitation Act 1980, see *C v D* (p359), *H v (1) N and (2) T* [2004] EWCA Civ 526, *C v Middlesbrough Council* (p359), *KR v Bryn Alyn Community Holdings Ltd* (p505), and *Catholic Care (Diocese of Leeds) and another v Young* [2006] EWCA Civ 1534. The need for the lower courts to revert to anomalous decisions in sexual abuse cases was removed when the House of Lords invoked its Practice Statement in *A v Hoare* (p287) and finally reversed *Stubbings v Webb*.

In *Dobbie v United Kingdom* (28477/95) the European Commission on Human Rights concluded that the provisions of ss 11, 14 and 33 did not affect 'the very essence' of the claimant's right of access to the courts (see *Dobbie v Medway Health Authority* (p411)).

In *Young v Western Power Distribution (South West) plc* (p733), the Court of Appeal considered whether the rule in *Walkley v Precision Forgings Ltd* (p705), which prior to the House of Lords overruling the decision 26 years later in *Horton v Sadler* (p482), prohibited the use of the exercise of the court's discretion within s 33 of the Limitation Act 1980 in respect of second actions where a first valid action has been discontinued or struck out, was compatible with Article 6. The court relied upon some of the reasoning in *Stubbings v United Kingdom* to hold that the rule performed a legitimate and proportionate aim, and was consistent with the United Kingdom's margin of appreciation, despite the criticism that had been made of the rule over many years:

'(51)   Plainly, if the House of Lords' construction of Section 33 were to operate incompatibly with the respondent's right of access to the Court under Article 6 then, consistently with the Court's duty under Section 3 of the Human Rights Act 1998, we must construe it afresh in such a way as not to bar her action. It would clearly be "possible to do so" within the meaning of Section 3. Indeed, it would not be in the least difficult having regard to the criticisms made of *Walkley* over recent years. But, of course, there can be no question of this Court declining to follow *Walkley* unless we were to conclude that the principle for which it stands does indeed breach Article 6 ...

(53)   Tempting though it is to succumb to these submissions, I feel unable to do so. To my mind, *Stubbings v United Kingdom* [1997] 23 EHRR 213 is fatal to their success ...

(55)   True it is, as Arden LJ noted in paragraph 26 of her judgment in *Piggott (the Estate of Aulton deceased)* [2003] EWCA Civ 24), that the Law Commission's report on limitation of actions has recently recommended an end to the *Walkley* principle and that the Government have accepted that recommendation in principle and stated in Parliament that it will introduce legislation when a suitable opportunity arises. It by no means follows, however, and I cannot accept, that whilst the *Walkley* principle continues to hold good under domestic law, the UK are to be regarded as violating the Article 6 rights of those affected by it ... it seems to me for Parliament or the House of Lords rather than for this Court by reference to Article 6 to reverse the law.' (per Simon Brown LJ)

In *Horton v Sadler* (above), the House of Lords invoked its *Practice Statement (Judicial Precedent)* [1966] 1 WLR 1234 to overrule the decision in *Walkley* on the basis that the previous House's decision wrongly construed the statute by precluding the court's discretion to disapply the primary limitation period in second actions. Lord Bingham did, however, indicate that he would have needed much persuasion that an alternative argument from the claimant that the rule was a breach of Article 6 was made out as the claimant had had untrammelled access to the court for three years after his injuries and there was accordingly no violation of convention rights (per Lord Bingham at para 36).

In *Rowe v Kingston-upon-Hull City Council* (p633), the Court of Appeal, also following *Stubbings v United Kingdom* (p678), determined that s 3 of the Human Rights Act did not apply retrospectively (before 2 October 2000) and did not avail a claimant suing in respect of injuries occurring before that date (per Mummery LJ at paras 45–7). Similarly, in *A v Iorworth Hoare* [2006] EWCA Civ 395, the Court of Appeal held it was bound by *Stubbings v Webb* in dismissing an action by A against a defendant who raped her in 1988 and who was imprisoned in 1989. The defendant won £7m in the national lottery in 2004 and the claimant then issued proceedings as he was now able to satisfy a judgment. The court further held that the Human Rights Act 1998 came into force after the accrued limitation defence and accordingly was inapplicable. The court stated that the law in this area was unsatisfactory and invited the House of Lords to revisit these issues; which, as indicated above, it did by reversing *Stubbings v Webb* in *A v Hoare* (p287).

Reform of limitation law

The Law Commission produced a lengthy and authoritative report on limitation law (Law Com Report No 270) following a detailed consultation paper (Law Com 151). The Commission has suggested that a uniform period of limitation should be three years and time should not start to run until a claimant knows or ought reasonably to know that he has a cause of action (the date of discoverability). The date of discoverability should be defined as the date when the claimant had actual knowledge that he had a cause of action against the defendant which was sufficiently serious to justify bringing proceedings on the assumption that the defendant would not dispute liability. In its initial proposals in Law Com 151, the Commission thought that there should be a longstop 30-year period and that the judicial discretion to waive the primary limitation period should be abolished. Following a number of concerns by consultees over the effect that this would have on personal injury claims, the report itself accepted that there should be no longstop and that the court should retain its discretion in personal injury cases only to waive the primary limitation period.

A radically different set of proposals was raised by Lady Hale (at paras 162–175) in *B v Ministry of Defence* (p312) where she considered that the current law of limitation concerning s14 was 'complicated and incoherent' and opined that, in policy terms, the world might be a more sensible and predictable place if the court only had the discretion in s33 without the discoverability provisions in ss11 and 14 and, better still, if time simply ran from the date of the wrongful act or omission rather than the date of damage.

However, the core proposals contained within Law Com 270 do not alter the basic structure of the existing law in personal injury cases. The Law Commission did, however, recommend (at para 3.166) abolishing the rule in *Walkley*, which the House of Lords has done through invoking its 1966 *Practice Direction (Judicial Precedent)* in the case of *Horton v Sadler* (above). The Commission also stated (at para 3.162) that it would like to see the reversal of the House of Lords' decision in *Stubbings v Webb*, which the House of Lords subsequently did in *A v Hoare*.

2 The primary limitation period (sections 2, 5 and 11)

Introduction: Section 11 of the Limitation Act 1980

The Limitation Act 1980, which came into force on 1 May 1981, is structured into three Parts. Part I (ss 1–27) lays down specific time limits for different causes of action, Part II (ss 28–33) deals with extensions and exclusions to those primary time limits. Part III (ss 34–41) is concerned with a number of general matters.

For actions in respect of the vast majority of wrongs causing personal injury, the primary limitation period is governed by s 11 which provides, by s 11(4), a three-year period from the date upon which the cause of action accrued or, if later, the date of knowledge of the injured person. In respect of claims resulting from wrongful death, the period for the estate to bring a claim under the Law Reform (Miscellaneous Provisions) Act 1934 is three years from the date of death or three years from the date of the personal representatives' knowledge (s 11(5)). A similar period is laid down for the dependants to initiate proceedings under the Fatal Accidents Act 1976, namely three years from the date of death or three years from the date of knowledge of the person for whose benefit the action is brought, whichever is later (s 12(2)). The distinction with non-personal injury actions brought into law through the Law Reform (Limitation of Actions etc) Act 1954, imposing a three-year period in which to bring personal injury actions, persists in the consolidating 1980 Act. Section 2 of the 1980 Act provides a six-year period for non-personal injury actions founded on tort and s 5 provides a six-year period for non-personal injury actions based on simple contract. Confusing a s 11 claim with a s 5 or s 2 claim is a fundamental error likely to lead to a summary judgment against legal practitioners who fail to consider the provisions of s 11 (*Bond v Livingstone & Co* (p337)).

This chapter examines the ambit of ss 2, 5 and 11 of the 1980 Act in respect of the primary limitation period. It then discusses more general matters concerning the way in which time is computed, the burden of proof in limitation cases and waiver of limitation rights. **Chapter 3** examines the concept of the date of knowledge in ss 11 and 14. **Chapter 4** looks at the special provisions concerning disability and concealment. **Chapter 5** considers the court's discretion within s 33 of the 1980 Act to disapply the primary period. **Chapter 6** deals with actions arising out of wrongful death.

Section 11(1) applies to:

'… any action for damages for negligence, nuisance or breach of duty (whether the duty exists by virtue of a contract or of provision made by or under a statute or independently of any contract or any such provision) where the damages claimed by the plaintiff for the negligence, nuisance or breach of duty consist of or include damages in respect of personal injuries to the plaintiff or any other person.'

Section 11(2) provides that the time limits in the preceding sections of the Act do not apply to s 11 cases.

1 'Negligence, nuisance or breach of duty': intentional and unintentional assaults

The vast bulk of personal injury claims fall within causes of action founded upon negligence, nuisance or breach of duty where the breach of duty arises under contract or pursuant to statute. Prior to the House of Lords' decision in *A v Hoare* (p287), the only significant exception concerned those injuries arising out of trespass to the person caused by deliberate assaults, including rape and indecent assault. This was due to the prior determination by the House of Lords in *Stubbings v Webb* (p677) that such actions fell outside the ambit of s 11 of the 1980 Act in that they did not constitute any breach of duty. The effect of this ruling was to extend the primary limitation period for those torts to six years; but it thereby took the actions outside the provisions of s 14 (with respect to the assaulted person's date of knowledge) and s 33 (concerning the discretion of the court to extend the primary limitation period).

Prior to *Stubbings v Webb*, the courts had viewed both intentional and unintentional trespass to the person as falling within s 11 of the 1980 Act. In *Letang v Cooper* (p533), Mrs Letang was inadvertently run over by a car while she was sunbathing and it was conceded that her writ was issued outside the limitation period for negligence. She claimed, however, to also have an action founded on trespass to the person. Elwes J found that there did exist such a cause of action which was not statute barred because the primary limitation period was six years. The Court of Appeal allowed the defendant's appeal on the basis that no such action in trespass existed because, when an injury was unintentionally inflicted, the true cause of action was based on negligence and not trespass to the person. In addition, Lord Denning and Lord Diplock were of the view that, in any event, the words 'breach of duty' were wide enough to include unintentional trespass and thereby to restrict the primary limitation period to three years.

Similarly, in *Long v Hepworth* [1968] 3 All ER 248, Cooke J found that a deliberate throwing of cement at Mrs Long which caused her injury did involve a 'breach of duty'. In *Halford v Brookes* (p453) the Court of Appeal determined that a civil action arising out of the murder of the claimant's daughter was governed by s 11 of the 1980 Act and, accordingly, the court was able to apply the provisions of both ss 14 and 33.

Such cases were effectively overruled by the House of Lords' judgment in *Stubbings v Webb* which accepted, some 50 years later, Lord Justice Tucker's Committee's recommendations (1949 Committee on Limitation of Actions, Cmd 774) that the limitation period should be different for torts involving trespass to the person, false imprisonment and malicious prosecution from ordinary personal injury actions. The House of Lords' decision in *Stubbings* survived an attack, subsequently mounted on it, that it was contrary to Articles 6, 8 and 14 of the European Convention on Human Rights (see *Stubbings v United Kingdom* (p678)).

(For applications of the rule in *Stubbings*, see *Rogers v Fine Modern Ltd and Walker* (p630) and *Parchment v Secretary of State for Defence* (p593).)

The rule in *Stubbings* created anomalies. In clinical negligence cases, for example, an allegation that treatment was negligently performed might also be accompanied by an allegation that the treatment was done without consent (see *Wilding v Lambeth,*

Southwark & Lewisham Area Health Authority (p716)). The rule in *Stubbings v Webb* leads to a position whereby the cause of action based on lack of consent, that is assault, had a limitation period of six years pursuant to s 2 of the Limitation Act 1980, but the action based on negligence fell within s 11 and was limited to three years (subject to the claimant's date of knowledge as defined in s 14 and open to the court's discretionary power to disapply the primary limitation period under s 33). In *Dobbie v Medway Health Authority* (p411), at first instance, and before the House of Lords' decision in *Stubbings v Webb*, the trial judge held that a three-year period applied to a clinical claim based on a failure to obtain consent. On appeal, however, Lord Bingham, then Master of the Rolls, confirmed that s 11 did not apply to actions in trespass for which a six-year non-extendable period was applicable.

In sexual abuse cases, litigants sought to avoid the effects of *Stubbings v Webb* by contending that they had a collateral claim based on negligence. In *S v W* (p636), the claimant, who was born on 5 November 1965, suffered sexual abuse from her father until 1983. Her mother was broadly aware of the child's predicament. In 1985 the father was jailed for incest. The claimant sued both her parents in 1992. The claim against the father was held to be statute barred with time expiring six years after the end of her minority in 1989, based, as it was, on intentional assault. However, the claim against the mother was based on a breach of a common law duty of care to protect her from her father and was held to be subject to s 11 and therefore ss 14 and 33 of the Act. This approach was followed in the consolidated actions brought by 14 claimants against the owners of a children's home for sexual and physical abuse perpetrated on them by the defendant's employees (*KR v Bryn Alyn Community Holdings Ltd* (p505)). The court held that the deliberate assaults perpetrated by the staff fell into essentially three categories. The first type of assaults were those which were outside the extended definition of vicarious liability as set out in *Lister v Hesley Hall Ltd* (p535) and the employer was not therefore vicariously liable. The second type of assaults did give rise to vicarious liability in that the acts were sufficiently closely connected to the 'carer's' employment. These assaults being deliberately intentional acts were restricted to a non-extendable six-year limitation period ending six years after the children reached their majority. However, most of the assaults could also be characterised as involving a breach of a duty of care by the employer delegated or entrusted to the employee (category three). The court held that these duties of the employer gave rise to a separate cause of action based on systemic negligence and therefore imposed a direct liability on the employer. The third category of assaults were therefore subject to the provisions of ss 11, 14 and 33 (see paras 97–108 of the judgment). This analysis resulted in most of the cases falling within the personal injury limitation regime. The Court of Appeal endorsed the Law Commission's recommendation that claims for personal injury including trespass to the person should have the same core limitation regime as other personal injury claims:

> 'For what it is worth, we warmly commend such a proposal. Early statutory implementation of it would obviate much arid and highly wasteful litigation turning on the distinction of no apparent principle or other merits.' (per Auld LJ at para 100)

The House of Lords decided in *A v Hoare* (p287) to invoke the *Practice Statement (Judicial Precedent)* [1966] 1 WLR 1234 and reverse *Stubbings v Webb*.

Hoare concerned six conjoined appeals raising the question as to whether claims for sexual assaults and abuse which took place many years before the commencement of proceedings were statute barred because of s 2 of the Limitation Act 1980, due to the rule in *Stubbings*.

Lord Hoffmann noted that the wording of s 2(1) of the Law Reform (Limitation of Actions etc) Act 1954 did not mirror the Tucker Committee's recommendations by specifically excluding trespass to the person, but spoke of 'actions for damages for negligence, nuisance or breach of duty ... where the damages ... consist of or include damages in respect of personal injuries'.

Lord Hoffmann referred to the case of *Billings v Reed* [1945] KB 11 where a similar wording had been construed as including trespass to the person and endorsed the reasoning in *Letang v Cooper* (p533) and *Long v Hepworth* [1968] 1 WLR 1299. Lord Hoffmann stated that *Stubbings* had put more weight on the Tucker Committee and Hansard than they could properly bear (para 17). After analysing the anomalies that *Stubbings* created, and recognising that unsatisfactory decisions of the higher courts lead to uncertainty because the lower courts tend to distinguish them on inadequate grounds, he concluded:

'I therefore think it would be right to depart from *Stubbings* and reaffirm the law laid down by the Court of Appeal in *Letang v Cooper* [1965] 1 QB 232.' (para 26)

This decision accordingly achieved the Law Commission's recommendations without the need for legislation and permits all personal injury actions to be subject to ss 11, 14 and 33 of the 1980 Act.

2 'Consists of and includes damages in respect of personal injuries to a plaintiff or any other person'

Section 38 of the 1980 Act defines personal injuries to include:

'any disease and any impairment of a person's physical or mental condition and "injury" and cognate expressions shall be construed accordingly.'

This definition clearly includes so-called nervous shock actions founded on recognisable psychiatric syndromes. The definition is also broad enough to include the failure to mitigate the effects of constitutional dyslexia (see *Adams v Bracknell Forest Borough Council* (p292), *Phelps v Hillingdon London Borough Council* [2002] 1 AC 619, and *Anderton v Clwyd CC* [2001] AC 619). A claimant suffering from dyslexia which is not recognised and dealt with due to a negligent failure by an education authority and who subsequently fails to achieve their full potential will have a claim 'in respect of personal injuries'. What is of particular interest is that the personal injury for this purpose does not need to amount to a recognised psychiatric condition. A negligent failure to improve the consequences of dyslexia by appropriate treatment causes the continuation of the injury analogous to a negligent failure to treat a physical injury (*Adams v Bracknell Forest Borough Council* per Lord Hoffmann at para 20).

In *Robinson v St Helens Metropolitan Borough Council* (p628), the Court of Appeal confirmed, following *Phelps* and *Anderton* above, that emotional and psychological damage resulting from a failure to ameliorate dyslexia was a personal injury although it fell short of a psychiatric injury (see Stuart Smith LJ at para 21, Brooke LJ at para 36).

Conversely, where a negligent misinterpretation of two biopsies led to a misdiagnosis of coeliac disease, no personal injury was sustained where the claimant suffered distress less than a psychiatric injury. The claimant's case was that she had unnecessarily been required to eat a gluten-free diet and, although this had not caused her physical harm, it did cause her psychological upset. The court held that her claim was one of economic loss based on negligent misstatement and was governed by s 2 of the Act and not s 11 (*Younger v Dorset and Somerset SHA* (p734).

The definition was also found, unsurprisingly, not to include damage to stored sperm held by a hospital. The court stated that it would be fictional to find that damage to a substance generated by a person's body, inflicted after its removal, amounted to an injury (see *Yearworth v North Bristol NHS Trust* (p730)).

The extended definition of the impairment of a mental condition would probably not include actions seeking general damages based on injured feelings, mental distress, vexation, frustration and annoyance as, for example, found in holiday cases or housing disrepair cases, being subject to the provisions of s 11 of the Act, as cases of this type have not previously been considered as personal injury actions (see *Jackson v Horizon Holidays* [1975] 1 WLR 1468 and *Haywood v Wellers* [1976] QB 446).

A claimant will not ordinarily be able to circumvent the time limit within s 11 by framing a claim as an economic loss of a partnership, firm or company if in fact the true nature of the loss is a loss of income or profit arising out of personal injury occasioned to a partner, proprietor or director. In *Howe v David Brown Tractors (Retail) Ltd* (p483), the Court of Appeal held that a claim for loss of a partnership's profit which arose directly out of personal injury sustained by the claimant when injured whilst using agricultural equipment supplied by the defendant, was an action 'consisting of or including damages' in respect of personal injury. As such, it was properly governed by s 11 of the 1980 Act, and was not one to which a six-year period of limitation applied pursuant to s 2 or s 5 of the 1980 Act.

Similarly, in *Walkin v South Manchester Health Authority* (p705), the Court of Appeal held that an unplanned for pregnancy caused by a negligent failure to sterilise leading to the birth of a healthy child constituted a personal injury. The court further held that this gave rise to only one cause of action. This had the effect of overruling *Allen v Bloomsbury Health Authority* [1993] 1 All ER 651 where Brooke J had held that in such cases two causes of action existed, one for personal injury and one for pure economic loss. The injury in question in failed sterilisation cases was the impairment to the mother's condition which occurred at conception. The court doubted that there was any valid distinction to be drawn between a failed sterilisation and a failed vasectomy as set out in *Pattison v Hobbs* (1985) Times, 11 November. *Pattison* held that s 2 rather than s 11 applied in a case where a claim was restricted to the financial loss of the upkeep of the unplanned for child resulting from a failed vasectomy. Auld LJ stated in *Walkin* (page 1552) that the injury in both failed sterilisation and vasectomy cases is the mother's unwanted pregnancy as both were caught by the words of s 11(1) 'damages in respect of personal injuries to the plaintiff *or any other person*'.

Walkin was followed in *Godfrey v Gloucestershire Royal Infirmary* (p443) where a mother sued in respect of the death of her daughter on 15 February 2003 due to brain damage caused by cerebral palsy which had been apparent since her birth on 1 March 1995. Proceedings were issued on 25 April 2002. The claimant's case was based upon an allegation that a pre-natal ultrasound scan showed abnormalities but she was not properly advised of the significance of the scan and accordingly elected to continue the pregnancy rather than to undergo a termination. The defendants alleged that as no claim for personal injury was advanced the claim if it existed was for pure economic loss and limited to a six-year period and was statute barred. The defendants relied upon the House of Lords' decision in *McFarlane v Tayside Health Board* [2000] 2 AC 59 which held that a claim for the upkeep of a healthy child as a result of a failed vasectomy was invalid. The defendants contended that this meant that *Walkin* was no longer good law and relied upon the Court of Appeal's remarks in *Greenfield v Flather* [2001] Lloyds LR Med 143. Leveson J held that Mrs Godfrey's claim was in respect of personal injuries to her and he remained bound by *Walkin*. This meant the claim fell within s 11 and permitted the application of a s 33 dispensation which was granted.

The precise ambit of *Walkin* and *Howe v David Brown Tractors (Retail) Ltd* (p483) has still to be defined. In *Walkin*, Lord Justice Neil echoed with approval Lord Justice Nicholls' remarks in *Howe* that a claimant cannot 'step outside the three-year limitation period prescribed by s 11 by abandoning any claim for damages in respect of the physical injury and claiming damage in respect of loss of earnings' or in *Walkin*'s case the cost of upkeep of the unplanned for child.

This approach was adopted by Singer J in *Oates v Harte Reade & Co* (p585) in a case where the claimant sued her solicitors over their handling of her divorce and ancillary relief claim. Mrs Oates included a claim for stress and anxiety consisting of memory lapses, slurred speech, and debility caused by an imbalance to her thyroid condition which was precipitated by the stress generated by the solicitors' alleged incompetence. The defendants contested that the case was statute barred as it was governed by s 11 and relied upon *Bennett v Greenland Houchen & Co* (p329) in which a professional negligence claim against a solicitor for failing to defend the case properly and which was said to have caused the claimant depression was found to be a personal injury case. In *Oates*, Singer J agreed that Mrs Oates' stress and anxiety amounted to a personal injury. He further took the view that although he retained a discretion to sever off the personal injury claim so as to allow the economic loss claim to continue, he would not exercise his discretion because it would deprive the defendants of their limitation defence.

However, in *Shade v The Compton Partnership* (p646), the Court of Appeal took a different position and stated that they found the reasoning in *Oates* as 'less than fully satisfactory'. The court also distinguished *Bennett v Greenland*. Mr Shade instructed the defendants to act for him against another firm of solicitors who he claimed had failed to act competently over a series of conveyancing transactions. The claimant sought not only economic losses but also contended that he had suffered severe psychiatric and physical injuries as a result of the defendant's negligence. The defendant accordingly sought to have the claim struck out as statute barred claiming it was a s 11 case and brought out of time. The master severed off the personal injury claim as statute barred but allowed the rest of the claim to proceed. An appeal to the judge resulted in the whole of the claim being struck out. The Court of Appeal found, however, that the claimant should have been allowed to sever off his personal injury claim because if he wished to, he could still bring a claim for his other losses as he was still within the six-year period governed by s 2. The Court of Appeal distinguished *Walkin*:

> '*Walkin* was a case of a claim for damages in respect of an unwanted pregnancy which followed after an unsuccessful operation for female sterilisation. The whole claim, both as to pain and as to economic loss, followed solely from the effects of the unsuccessful medical treatment upon the plaintiff's physical condition. The fact that a second Writ was issued in that case claiming economic loss only could not alter the character of that particular and unusual type of claim. The observations which Auld LJ made on page 1549 of the report must be read in that light.
>
> In the course of argument, my Lord suggested three different types of cases in which such a problem might arise. At one extreme my Lord suggested a case in which a plaintiff had a claim for £3 m for economic loss for her solicitors'

negligence in pursuing an indisputable liquidated liability, coupled with an additional claim for, say, £500 for the cost of a single psychiatric consultation and the supply of tranquillisers to the plaintiff who had suffered stress on learning of his huge economic loss. It would be quite extraordinary in a case like that if the claim, which was very largely a claim for economic loss, could not, if necessary by amendment, be afforded the six-year limitation period which it would be expected to have.

At the other extreme is the *Walkin* type of case in which the plaintiff has suffered physical injury of some sort, although the claim is not only for pain and suffering and disability, but also for economic loss. I can well understand that in a case of that sort there may be real difficulties about permitting an amendment to limit the scope of the claim. *Walkin* itself is an authority to that effect. The present case appears to fall within those two extremes. Mr Shade's suggestion that his claim is worth more than £1m seems to me inflated. The figure mentioned to the Court suggested that his maximum claim might be approximately one quarter of that. It is by no means obvious that his claim for psychological injury is the lion's share of that sum of the order of £0.25m which quantifies his claim at present.

In these circumstances, although the position might be different in a case where the plaintiff has actually suffered personal injury, which has also caused economic loss, there is no reason either in the statutory provisions and, in the rules of court, or in commonsense, to stand in the way of paragraphs 7 and 8 alone of the prayer for relief being struck out so as to leave the rest of the claim to proceed in accordance with the directions for preparation for trial already given by Master Eyre.' (per Robert Walker LJ at 225G–226E)

It would therefore seem permissible for a claimant in certain circumstances where the personal injury claim is not very substantial and where the injury itself has not directly caused economic loss to sever off that part of the claim to avoid the three-year primary limitation period.

Where a claimant suffers not only personal injury but also damage to property, for example his home or where his car is damaged in a road traffic accident in which he was also hurt, he has two distinct causes of action, one based on personal injury and one based on property damage (*Brunsden v Humphrey* (1884) 14 QBD 141). If the same claimant sues in respect of both causes of action simultaneously the provisions of s 11 would apply (see for example *Mills v Ritchie* (p560)). However, if the claimant sued after three years in respect of the property damage only, his cause of action would not be statute barred if brought within the six-year period provided by s 2 of the 1980 Act. Similarly, if, after litigating the personal injury action alone, he subsequently sued after three years from the accident but within the six-year period sued for the property damage as a matter of limitation law the cause of action would be valid. However, such an action would most probably be caught by the doctrine of res judicata (issue estoppel/action estoppel) as applied in *Talbot v Berkshire County Council* [1993] 4 All ER 9. In *Crawford v Dalley and The Royal Marsden Hospital* (p391) the claimant sued in respect of radionecrosis and was held to caught by the principles in *Talbot* from advancing her claim. Mrs Crawford received radiotherapy for breast cancer as a private patient in the defendant's hospital. She failed to settle the defendant's invoice as she was dissatisfied with the treatment because it caused her significant damage to her right shoulder and arm. The hospital sued for its fees and the claimant in that action counterclaimed for expenses incurred due to the hospital's treatment of her. That counterclaim and her defence was subject to a debarring order with which she failed to comply and judgment was entered without a hearing of the issues for the hospital. Subsequently the claimant became seriously ill with radionecrosis and issued her own proceedings. The court found that her counterclaim in the hospital's action and the claim in her own action were the same claim and the latter was prohibited by the doctrines of cause of action and issue estoppel from proceeding and was struck out.

In disease cases where it is possible to assess the cumulative progression of the effects of the disease, as in industrial deafness and asbestosis claims, a claimant may be restricted to that damage which falls within the limitation period as occurred in *Berry v Stone Manganese & Marine Ltd* (p331). Where, however, it is not possible to determine on the medical evidence what part of the injury has been caused in the non-statute barred period from that which has occurred in the statute barred period as, for example, in the case of an indivisible injury such as mesothelioma, then a claimant is likely to recover all of the damages so long as he proves that the events occurring within the non-statute barred period materially contributed to his disease. (See *Fairchild v Glenhaven Funeral Services Ltd* [2003] 1 AC 32, *Barker v Corus (UK) plc* [2006] UKHL 20 and s 3 of the Compensation Act 2006, *Clarkson v Modern Foundries Ltd* (p376), *Bonnington Castings Ltd v Wardlaw* [1956] AC 613, *McGhee v National Coal Board* [1973] 1 WLR 1). Where, however, the injury is truly divisible (for example pneumoconiosis, asbestosis, deafness) damages are likely to be apportioned so that no damages are recoverable if they resulted from exposure outside the limitation period (*Holtby v Brighan & Cowan (Hull) Ltd* [2000] 3 All ER 421, *Cartwright v GKN Sankey Ltd* [1972] 2 Lloyds' Rep 242).

An action for professional negligence or breach of contract based upon the loss of a chance to recover damages in an accident for personal injury lies outside the ambit of s 11 of the 1980 Act. If, for example, a claimant sues a solicitor who failed, on his behalf, to issue a claim form in time in respect of a claim for personal injuries, the time limit for the professional negligence action is six years under ss 2 and 5 and not three years (see *Jones v GR Smith & Co* (p500)). If, however, a claimant sues a solicitor not only for the lost opportunity of obtaining damages for a pre-existing personal injury claim but also contends that a further personal injury has been caused as a result of the stress induced by the negligence of the solicitor the claim might be characterised as one consisting of or including damages in respect of personal injuries (see the cases of *Oates* (p585), *Bennett* (p329) and *Shade* (p646) discussed above).

In *Ackbar v C F Green & Co Ltd* (p291) a claimant sued his insurance broker for failing to effect passenger liability insurance on his lorry. He was held to have a limitation period of six years rather than three years. The claimant himself was a passenger in his lorry when it was involved in a road traffic accident and he sustained personal injury. Croom-Johnson J held that the damage sued for in the action against the broker did not 'consist of or include damages in respect of personal injuries' because the claim was based upon the contractual loss of a chance to recover damages from his own insurance company and the personal injury was the measure of the loss only.

A parallel form of reasoning is to be found in the Scottish case of *McGahie v Union of Shop Distributive and Allied Workers* (p552) where the claimant sued her union for failing to prosecute an action against her employer in respect of an accident at work which caused her personal injury. That action became statute barred. In her claim against the union, it was contended on their behalf that her claim included one for damages in respect of personal injury. The court held that the true nature of her claim was for the loss of her right to sue her employer and that loss did not of itself cause her personal injury.

In *Howe v David Brown Tractors (Retail) Ltd* (p483) the Court of Appeal considered *Ackbar* and *McGahie*. Mr Howe traded with his father as a farming firm. In August 1982 the firm purchased agricultural equipment which caused him severe injuries in January 1985. His writ for damages in respect of his personal injury was issued out of time in July 1988 but the defendants consented to a s 33 dispensation. However, in November 1989 the claimant sought to add his father and the firm to the action to claim for the whole of the firm's loss of profit arising from the claimant's inability to work. The Court of Appeal held that the firm's claim, if it existed in law, was one to which s 11 of the 1980 Act applied because it related to a claim for damages 'in respect of personal injuries to the plaintiff or to *any other person*', the firm/father being the 'other' person. Nicholls LJ gave three examples of contractual arrangements which brought a personal injury action within s 11. The first was a straight forward medical malpractice claim based on private treatment. The second concerned a defective product brought by a claimant against the supplier. The third, as in *Howe*, extended the section to cases where injury had been caused to an 'other' person. So, for example, if an employer buys a defective tool which injures his employee and the employee obtains damages against him, any action which the employer brings against the supplier/manufacturer in contract would be one to which s 11 applies. This would mean that the contractual limitation would no longer be six years under s 2. Additionally it would mean that the employer could take the benefit of ss 14 and 33. This would amount to a surprising extension to the concept of date of knowledge and discretionary dispensation. Sections 14 and 33 would not be available to a defendant seeking a contribution not on the basis of a contract but under the Civil Liability Contribution Act 1978, as s 10 of the Limitation Act 1980 provides for a two-year period for such an action from the judgment or settlement of the claim brought by the claimant, and s 10(5) of the 1980 Act specifically excludes s 33.

Nicholls LJ affirmed that professional negligence actions against solicitors who fail to issue personal injury actions in time will be governed by s 2 or s 5. The reasoning, as in *Ackbar*, was because the failure did not cause any personal injury.

However, in *Norman v Ali and Aziz* (p582) the Court of Appeal distinguished *Ackbar* when it held that a claim under the principles laid down in *Monk v Warbey* [1935] 1 KB 75 is one to which s 11 applies. Such cases concern actions based on breach of statutory duty whereby the owner of a vehicle allows a person to drive his vehicle knowing that the person is not covered by a certificate of insurance. If the driver causes injury to a person whilst driving, the injured person may also bring an action against the owner of the vehicle. The court distinguished *Ackbar* on the basis that in that case the breach of duty to effect insurance was independent of the accident. The court held:

'The breach of contractual duty by the brokers (in *Ackbar*) to their client occurred prior to the accident. It was independent of the accident. Consequently the injuries sustained in the accident were "only the measure of damages now claimed". In a *Monk v Warbey* case the breach of duty by the owner towards the person injured arises only when the person is in fact injured, viz in the accident itself. Where an accident for personal injuries against the original tortfeasor is struck out because of the claimant's solicitors' breach of duty, different considerations arise. The breach of duty by the solicitor to his client arises subsequent to the personal injuries occurring. Moreover, as Mr Stewart succinctly put it, "the breach by the solicitor of his duty is to his client qua client not to his client as a person who has suffered personal injury". The breach of duty (as distinct from the measure of damages) does not consist of or include damages in respect of personal injuries within Section 11.'

In *Norman v Ali and Aziz* there was no prospect of a s 33 discretion being applied, as previous proceedings had been issued against the car owner and the rule in *Walkley v Precision Forgings Ltd* (p705) then prevented a s 33 application in the second action. Different considerations would now apply since the abolition of the rule in *Walkley* by the House of Lords in *Horton v Sadler* (p482).

In *Clarke v Barber* (p376) at first instance the court held that a claim for personal injuries under s 2(2) of the Animals Act 1971 was not a claim caught by s 11, as the Animals Act imposed strict liability and the claim was not in respect of breach of duty. This case was not subject to appeal and is at risk of an appeal court finding such claims do result from a breach of statutory duty.

SUMMARY

In summary, the vast majority of personal injury cases will fall within s 11 of the 1980 Act. These will include, since the decision in *A v Hoare* (p287), both intentional and unintentional assaults, such as clinical cases alleging an absence of consent. They will also include mixed claims where there are two separate causes of action brought at the same time where one includes a claim for personal injury. In certain circumstances, however, the court will permit a severing off of the personal injury claim to achieve a longer limitation period where the personal injury claim is not very substantial and is not the direct cause of a more substantial economic loss claim. Section 11 will also govern claims brought in contract by employers seeking to recover damages they have paid or are liable to pay to injured employees against suppliers or producers of defective products.

Section 11 will not apply to cases such as in *Ackbar* concerning a failure to insure. Section 11 will, however, govern *Monk v Warbey* claims against the owner of a vehicle who allows it to be driven knowing it is uninsured contrary to s 143(1) (b) of the Road Traffic Act 1988. An action against insurers under the Third Parties (Rights against Insurers) Act 1930 is one to which a six-year period applies pursuant to s 9 of the Limitation Act 1980, as it is an action for a sum recoverable by statute (*Lefevre v White* (p533)). Similarly, claims brought against the government for so-called *Francovich* damages for failure to implement an EC Directive will be governed by the six-year period in s 2 of the 1980 Act (see *Spencer v Secretary of State for Work and Pensions, Moore v MIB* (p669)). Cases brought under the Human Rights Act 1998 are restricted to the statutory one-year period under s 7(5), which may be extended by the court (see *Rabone v Pennine Care NHS Foundation Trust* (p616).

Accrual of cause of action: Section 11(4)

This subsection provides:

'(4)   Except where subsection (5) below applies, the period applicable is three years from –

(a)   the date on which the cause of action accrued; or
(b)   the date of knowledge (if later) of the person injured.'

(Subsection (5) is concerned with fatal claims.)

Time begins to run against a claimant, in most cases of simple personal injury, as soon as his cause of action accrues, because that is frequently simultaneous with his date of knowledge. Even in those cases where a court is concerned with determining the claimant's date of knowledge under ss 11 and 14 of the Act or is considering disapplying the primary limitation period under the provisions of s 33 of the Act, an analysis is always required as to when the cause of action arose. A cause of action consists of the existence of every fact which it would be necessary to prove, if contested, to found a right to judgment (*Read v Brown* (1888) 22 QBD 128, *Coburn v Colledge* [1897] 1 QB 702). As a general rule, only one action can be brought in respect of any cause of action, and the court will scrutinise any second action to determine if it is subject to action estoppel, issue estoppel or amounts to an abuse of process (cf *Fitter v Veal* (1701) 12 Mod Rep 542, *Darley Main Colliery Co v Mitchell* (1886) 11 App Cas 127, *Johnson v Gore Wood & Co* [2001] 1 All ER 481, *Stanway v Attorney-General* (1999) Times, 25 November).

Section 34(1) of the 1980 Act makes provision that the Act is applicable not only to court proceedings but also to arbitration.

In the overwhelming majority of personal injury actions, the cause of action arises in negligence, breach of statutory duty or nuisance, all of which are torts which require proof of damage. A cause of action based on these torts is complete when it is established that there is in existence a duty of care, a breach of that duty and that more than minimal damage has been caused by the breach. Such torts differ from the tort of trespass to the person, now also within the provisions of s 11 of the 1980 Act, which does not require proof of damage and is actionable per se. Those actions for personal injury which arise out of breach of contract are complete upon the breach of contract and not when the claimant has suffered damage or when the claimant is aware of the breach (cf *Lynn v Bamber* [1930] 2 KB 72). Theoretically, there is, accordingly, a distinction between those torts which require proof of damage and an action based on breach of contract. For example, a claimant who is a private hospital patient may have concurrent causes of action in both contract and tort in a case where clinical negligence is alleged. The different causes of action might be subject to different dates of accrual. A negligently performed private sterilisation which, for example, failed to clip the fallopian tube, would give rise to a breach of contract immediately following the lack of care during the operation. Conversely damage in the form of a subsequent pregnancy would only arise after conception. On the completion of such damage the accrual of a cause of action in tort would occur. Practically, however, the difference is unlikely to be pertinent because the provisions of s 14 of the 1980 Act have the effect of extending the limitation period in contract to that date when the claimant first knew that she had suffered damage, namely when she was diagnosed as being pregnant. Conflicting judicial opinions as to whether a claimant is able to sue concurrently in both contract and tort have been resolved in the case of *Henderson v Merrett Syndicate* [1994] 3 All ER 506. The House of Lords has determined that, where a defendant assumes responsibility for professional services which are relied upon by a claimant, a duty of care in tort arises even when there is also a concurrent contract between the parties.

The knowledge provisions within the limitation statutes were first enacted to mitigate the harshness that a cause of action could accrue even before it was known or indeed knowable that damage had occurred (*Cartledge v E Joplin & Sons Ltd* (p366)). However, precisely when damage occurs remains of practical significance in a residual class of disease cases. In *McCaul v Elias Wild & Sons Ltd* (p547) a claimant was diagnosed in 1987 as suffering from asbestos induced pleural thickening due to industrial exposure to asbestos by the defendants between 1943 and 1950. The claimant issued proceedings in October 1988 and the defendants contended, relying on *Arnold v Central Electricity Generating Board* (p306) that the action was statute barred pursuant to the provisions of s 2 of the Limitation Act 1939 because the claimant's cause of action was complete before the coming into force of the Law Reform (Limitation of Actions etc) Act 1954. If that contention was correct a limitation defence would have been available to the defendants, because the claimant's action would not have attracted the benefits of the retrospective effects of the Limitation Acts 1963 and 1975. The claimant, however, contended that a cause of action in tort for breach of duty or for negligence did not arise until damage which was more than minimal occurred (cf *Cartledge v Joplin* (p366), *Brazier v Ministry of Defence* (p342)). The claimant adduced medical evidence that he had no actionable damage prior to the coming into force of the 1954 Act (namely 4 June 1954) because, although his lungs would have been contaminated by asbestos fibres at that time, they would not have caused disease but merely a latency which manifested injury later. These submissions were accepted by the trial judge and the action was found not to be statute barred. A similar form of argument has been accepted in the case of *Keenan v Miller Insulation & Engineering Ltd* (p515). It is now likely that in the few remaining cases of pre-1954 exposure to asbestos the effects of *Arnold v Central Electricity Generating Board* may be neutralised, providing a claimant can adduce medical evidence supporting the proposition that damage had not occurred in his lungs by the coming into force of the 1954 Act (see also *Guidera v NEI Projects (India) Ltd* (p451)). Where, however, damage has been caused prior to 1954 the action will remain statute barred (see *Parish v Imperial Chemicals Industry plc* (p594)).

In *Rothwell v Chemical and Insulating Co / Grieves v FT Everard & Sons* [2006] EWCA Civ 27, the defendants in the so-called 'pleural plaques litigation' failed at first instance to establish that symptomless pleural plaques did not constitute actionable damage. The court found that a cause of action for asbestos-induced injuries was complete when the claimant developed pleural plaques. This was because the condition, when taken with the anxiety generated by the diagnosis together with assessable risks of the future onset of other symptomatic asbestos illnesses, caused by the exposure to asbestos but not by the plaques, amounted to more than minimal damage to complete the cause of action. On appeal, the Court of Appeal by a majority disagreed and allowed the defendants' appeal finding that it was impermissible as a matter of policy to aggregate the plaques themselves with future risks and/or anxiety so as to cross the threshold of actionability. The House of Lords upheld the Court of Appeal's decision and, accordingly, time will not run against a claimant diagnosed with pleural plaques as these are not considered injuries in law. Time will only start running when another asbestos-induced condition occurs causing more than minimal injury such as pleural thickening, asbestosis, mesothelioma or asbestos-induced lung cancer. For an application of the *Rothwell* decision, leading to what the Court of Appeal called a 'litigation disaster', see *Preston v BBH Solicitors* (p609).

Continuing torts and 'the injury in question'

Where a defendant continues a form of conduct which causes continuing harm, such as in persistent exposure to noise, dust, skin irritants, vibration or repetitive strain, a fresh cause of action arises constantly as long as the breach of duty persists (*Darley Main Colliery v Mitchell* (1886)11 App Cas 127, HL). As indicated in *Berry v Stone Manganese & Marine Ltd* (p331), a claimant may be statute barred in respect of some but not all of the damage caused if that damage is capable of pro-rated assessment pre- and post- the expiry of the limitation period.

In certain disease or sexual abuse cases, it may also be necessary to consider the inter-relationship of the accrual of a cause of action and the *injury in question* within s 14(1)(a). In *McManus v Mannings Marine Ltd* (p555) the Court of Appeal was concerned with a case where a claimant had worked for the defendant for 12 days in June 1989 and for a further 14 days in January 1990. In September 1992, he submitted a claim for vibration white finger to the Department of Social Security. The injury at that time being in two fingers of the left hand. The claimant then resumed employment with the defendants from August 1993 to November 1999 and his condition worsened to the point that it affected all his fingers and thumbs. He issued proceedings on 2 December 1999 and at first instance his case was found to be statute barred on the basis that he had suffered earlier injury in 1992. The Court of Appeal allowed the claimant's appeal and remitted the case for re-hearing. The court held that the claimant's claim was not for the vibration white finger that had been caused before 1993 but, rather, for the additional injury that had occurred since. The *injury in question* therefore, within the meaning of s 14, was the exacerbation of the VWF that had occurred and which had been contributed to by the later exposure within the period 1993 to November 1999. Some of that period of employment may have caused the exacerbation and accordingly there was a continuing cause of action so that part the damage was not statute barred.

In the sexual abuse cases of *KR v Bryn Alyn Community Holdings Ltd* (p505) the court determined that the injury in question was not the initial acts of abuse on the children, whether physical or sexual, but the later psychiatric reaction to the abuse. The court went on to determine that the initial injuries were not significant within the meaning of s 14 and, accordingly, time was postponed until the claimants' date of knowledge that their injury in question, namely the psychiatric reaction to the abuse process, was significant. However, *Bryn Alyn* must now be read in the light of *A v Hoare* (p287), which reversed the rule in *Stubbings v Webb* and thus permits the court to consider all assaults as personal injuries subject to ss 14 and 33, thus obviating the reasoning in *Bryn Alyn*. Subsequent decisions concerning sexual abuse have emphasised the significance of the first acts of abuse. In *Albonetti v Wirral Metropolitan Borough Council* (p298), the court accepted that the 'injury in question' is the immediate effects of the abuse, namely the pain, distress and humiliation experienced and remembered at the time, and time runs from this date (per Smith LJ at para 21). (See also *B v Nugent* (p315).)

In *Shepherd and others v Firth Brown Ltd* (p647), 16 claimants sued in respect of contracting vibration white finger which was induced by vibration from carborundum sticks which had to be held against a grinding wheel. The exposure occurred over years prior to the issue of proceedings in 1977. Many of the claimants continued to work for the defendants doing the same work until the date of the trial in 1985. The judge found that there had not in fact been any breach of duty until after the spring of 1979, and by that time, the writs had been issued. This meant that the cause of action had occurred after the institution of proceedings and the judge found that the claimants were not entitled to any damages because no negligence had been found prior to 1977. The judge held that a fresh cause of action accrued daily while the breach of duty persisted but the claimants could not recover damages for harm done after the issue of the writ in circumstances where the breach of duty also post-dated the issue of proceedings. The judge indicated that to prevent the fresh causes of action being time barred, fresh writs would have to be issued every three years. The technicality of this position might have been overcome if the claim had been pleaded as a continuing tort with continuing post-writ damage. Any damage which occurred after the issue of proceedings but which arises from the accrued cause of action, is recoverable to the date of trial. In any ordinary case where pain and suffering and special damages were still continuing, there is no difficulty in the case of assessing damages to the date of the trial and thereafter for damages for future loss and continuing disability. The particular difficulty in *Shepherd* was that no liability was established for the period prior to the issue of proceedings and that a continuing tort had not been pleaded.

Where there is only one cause of action, rather than consecutive or continuing causes of action, only one set of proceedings may be brought. If an injured person brings an action for general damages and consequential losses and is compensated but subsequently develops further injury or losses then, unless the award was for provisional damages, the subsequent losses are not recoverable because the cause of action has been extinguished (*KR v Bryn Alyn Community Holdings Ltd* (p505) at para 37).

To complete a cause of action, there must be a party which is capable of being sued (*Thompson v The Lord Clanmorris* [1900] 1 Ch 718 at 729). Accordingly, time was held not to run against a company which was not in fact in existence at the time when the cause of action would otherwise have accrued because the company had been dissolved (*Re Russo-Asiatic Bank* [1934] Ch 720). Where, however, a cause of action accrues against a company in existence, time does not cease to run even though the company is subsequently dissolved. In these circumstances, if insurers can be identified, it is worthwhile restoring the company to the register pursuant to s 651 of the Companies Act 1985 as amended by s 141 of the Companies Act 1989. The court has extensive powers to resurrect companies by declaring a dissolution to have been void. The normal two-year period within which an application should be made does not apply to actions in personal injury damages or to fatal accident actions which may be made at any time (Companies Act 1985, s 651(5)). The court has a power under s 651(6) to direct that time between the dissolution and restoration should be disregarded for the purposes of limitation. Prior to the case of *Smith v White Knight Laundry* (p663), the court frequently exercised this power to disregard the time that had elapsed during the dissolution for the purposes of limitation if a creditor had a personal injury claim which was not statute barred at the date of dissolution (see *Re Advance Insulation Ltd* (p294), *Re Donald Kenyon* (p412), *Re Regent Insulation Company Ltd* (p619), *Re Huntingdon Poultry Ltd* (p486)). However, *in Smith v White Knight Laundry* the Court of Appeal analysed the precise effect of restoring a company to the register and laid down guidelines as to the procedure to be adopted. In *Smith* the deceased had worked for the defendant in the period 1950–1956 and was exposed to asbestos which had caused mesothelioma from which he had died on 6 February 1995. The defendant company was dissolved in 1963 but restored to the register on 28 January 1998 under s 651 of the Companies Act 1985 as amended by the Companies Act 1989 to pursue a claim on behalf of the widow and his estate. The restoration ordered that the period of time during dissolution should not count for limitation purposes. Proceedings were issued on 14 April 1999. The defendant pleaded that the claim was statute barred on the basis either that the deceased's date of knowledge occurred three years prior to his death or the claimant had commenced proceedings more than three years after her husband's death and a s 33 direction was not appropriate. The claimant contended that the effect of the order was to prevent limitation being raised at all as the period of dissolution did not count and accordingly opposed the defendant's application for an order of a preliminary trial on limitation. The defendants obtained such an order and the claimant appealed that order to the judge. The judge confirmed the need for a preliminary trial on limitation and went further by setting aside the direction that time should not run during the period of dissolution. The claimant appealed this decision. The Court of Appeal dismissed the claimant's appeal, finding:

1.   The true effect of the restoration order was as if the dissolution had never occurred. This meant that the defendant did exist as a party and could be sued

and time did run against the claimant (*Re Dixon C W Ltd* [1947] 1 Ch 251 affirmed).

2. Granting an order that time should not run during the period of the company's dissolution under s 651 was equivalent to the effect of granting a s 33 dispensation. The court, following *Re Workvale Ltd* (p726) held that such an order should only ever be done if the court has all the relevant evidence, the notice has been served on interested parties and the application was bound to succeed (see para 60).

The computation of time

Time runs against a claimant in a personal injury action either from the date of accrual of the cause of action or from the date of knowledge, whichever is later. Time stops running when proceedings are issued either from the High Court or a county court and not *from when proceedings are served*. The proceedings in the High Court or a county court are begun by the issuing of a claim form under CPR 7. Claims may also be initiated by the alternative procedure set out in CPR 8 in circumstances where the claim is unlikely to involve a substantial dispute of fact or where other rules of court require the Part 8 procedure to be used. The Part 8 procedure is suitable for claims brought by patients or children which settle before the issuing of proceedings but which require the court's approval or where a claim for provisional damages or periodical payments has been agreed but a consent judgment is required. The relevant date for the issuing of proceedings is the date entered on the form by the court pursuant to CPR 7.2(2). A defendant accordingly does not know unless he has been informed by the claimant that time has ceased to run until proceedings are served. The general rule is that a claim form is served on the defendant when the claimant completes the step required by CPR 7.5(1) before 12 midnight on the calendar day four months after the date of issue of the claim form, or six months when the claim form is to be served out of the jurisdiction (CPR 7.5(2)). If the defendant is aware that a claim form has been issued against him, he can serve a notice on the claimant requiring the claimant to either serve the claim form or discontinue the action. If after 14 days from that notice the claimant has not complied, the defendant may make an application to the court. On such an application, the court may dismiss the claim or make any order that it thinks fit (CPR 7.7).

If a claim form is sent by post to a county court office and is received before the day it is actually issued by the court, the proceedings will be deemed to be brought on the day of the receipt by the court not the date of issue (CPR 7 PD 5.1). In *Barnes v St Helens MBC* (p321), the court confirmed that, once the claimant had delivered his request for the issue of a claim form to the court office, he had 'brought' his action (see also *Page v Hewetts Solicitors* (p592).

CPR PD5A, para 5.2 requires that particulars of the date of delivery at a court office of any document for filing must be entered on the court record. Issuing out of the wrong county court will nevertheless stop time running (*Sharma v Knight* [1986] 1 WLR 757).

In calculating the period of limitation, the day upon which the cause of action arose is excluded (*Marren v Dawson Bentley & Co Ltd* (p543)). In *Marren* a cause of action that accrued on 8 November 1954 was held to be brought in time although proceedings were issued on 8 November 1967.This method of calculating time is broadly in accordance with the so-called 'corresponding date' rule espoused by the House of Lords in *Dodds v Walker* (p411) applied to an annual period. This method of calculation has the convenience of ignoring fractions or parts of any day by leaving out of the reckoning the actual day of the accident. Under the rules of court prior to the coming into force of the Civil Procedure Rules 1998, a writ or summons was valid for four months only which included the day of issue (RSC Ord 6 r 8(1); cf *Trow v Ind Coope (West Midlands) Ltd* [1967] 2 QB 899). In *Trow* a writ issued on 10 September 1965 was deemed to be valid for precisely one year and accordingly expired on 9 September 1966. By contrast, the current rule in CPR 7.5 provides that the claim form is served if the steps taken in the rule (posting, delivering faxing, e-mailing) are done before 12 midnight on the calendar day four months after the date of issue of the claim form, and the day of issue of the claim form will be excluded. This effectively gives the claimant one more day to serve than under the old rules (see *Smyth v Probyn* (p664)).

Conversely, service of the particulars of claim, if it has not been served with the claim form, must be served within 14 days (see CPR 7.4(1)(b); see also CPR 2.8(3)(iii)).

If process cannot be issued because the court office is closed, as on a weekend or on a public holiday, the limitation period will be extended until the next date upon which the court is open for business (see CPR 2.8(5)). In *Pritam Kaur v F Russell & Sons Ltd* (p613), a case under the old rules, a widow sued in respect of the death of her husband who was killed when crushed by a skip whilst working in a foundry pit on 5 September 1967. Proceedings were issued on Monday 7 September 1970. The third anniversary of the death fell on 5 September 1970 which was a Saturday. The next open day for court business was on Monday 7 September. The Court of Appeal held that in those circumstances proceedings had been brought in time. Similarly, in a case where proceedings were required under the Hague Rules to be initiated within a year an action was held to be brought in time when that year expired on a Sunday and proceedings were started the following day (*The Clifford Maersk* (p377)). The practical reasoning behind extending the limitation period in this way is that if a claimant cannot comply with statutory requirements without the co-operation of the court in issuing process then it is reasonable that the court should be available to give such co-operation.

The burden of proof and limitation

The general effect of statutes of limitation in English law, with noticeable exceptions in respect of actions for the recovery of land and theft and conversion, is that the remedy of suing in court is barred rather than the right being extinguished. Such a distinction is of little significance in personal injury cases because there will rarely be available an alternative remedy to enforce a claim for damages. One practical effect of this distinction is, however, that the court will regard limitation as a procedural rather than a substantive matter and will not, of its own motion, take a limitation point. A limitation defence must therefore be pleaded (see CPR 16 PD 13.1, *Rodriguez v Parker* (p628), *Ronex Properties Ltd v John Lang Construction Ltd* [1983] 1 QB 404). Further, a late amendment during the final stages of the trial seeking to plead a limitation defence will not ordinarily be allowed (*Ketteman v Hansel Properties Ltd* (p517), *Lewis v Hackney LBC,* April 9 1990, unreported, CA).

Once a limitation point is taken in a defence, the general weight of the authorities is that the claimant has the burden of proving that the case has been brought in time (*Ketteman v Hansel Properties Ltd* (above), *London Congregational Union v Harriss and Harriss* [1988] 1 All ER 15, CA). In a personal injury case in *Clarkson v Modern Foundries Ltd* (p376), Donovan J inclined to the view that it was for the defendants to prove a limitation defence. In *Beer v London Borough of Waltham Forest* (p327) Hodgson J, dealing with an application under s 33 of the Limitation Act 1980, to disapply the primary limitation period, determined that the claimant had the burden of proof in seeking to persuade the court to disapply the provisions of s 11 (see also *Thompson v Brown Construction (Ebbw Vale) Ltd* (p690)). In *Driscoll-Varley v Parkside Health Authority* (p416), Hidden J held that once pleaded the preliminary burden of establishing whether an action was brought in time rested on the claimant. If, however, the defendant contended that the cause of action accrued earlier because the claimant should be fixed with constructive knowledge, then the burden effectively passed to the defendant. Hidden J drew directly from the speech of Lord Pearce in *Cartledge v E Joplin & Sons Ltd* (p366) and the judgments of Lord Justices Gibson and Buckley in *London Congregational Union v Harriss and Harriss* (above) to support the proposition that there was an evidential burden shifting to the defendant when there is a positive averment that a cause of action accrued earlier that the claimant's contention. The Court of Appeal expressed a similar view in *Nash v Eli Lilly & Co* (p568). However, in a thorough review of this case law, Mance J held in *Crocker v British Coal Corporation* (p392) that the legal burden remains on the claimant throughout to establish that the action is not statute barred, both in respect of when the cause of action accrued and when the claimant's date of knowledge occurred. An evidential burden on the defendant may arise with respect of the issue of constructive knowledge under s 14(3):

> 'The legal burden rests throughout on the plaintiff, whether the issue is when the cause of action accrued or when the plaintiff first had knowledge of the facts in the sense identified in section 14. The concept which the authorities have called "constructive knowledge" is by definition in section 14(3) one aspect of "knowledge". The date of first knowledge depends as much on knowledge which the plaintiff might reasonably have been expected to acquire from (a) facts observable or ascertainable by him or (b) ascertainable (subject to the proviso) by him with the help of medical or other appropriate expert advice as it does on actual knowledge. An issue arising under section 14(3) is, however, apt to involve an evidential burden on a defendant, at all events if there is nothing in the plaintiff's own case or evidence to raise the issue, although in some respects, for example in relation to the words "so long as he had taken all reasonable steps to obtain (and, where appropriate, act upon) that advice" in the proviso where they became material, it may be easy to envisage both the legal and evidential burden on the plaintiff.'

[*Crocker* was quoted with approval by the Supreme Court (per Lord Walker at para 48) in *B v Ministry of Defence* (p312) and by the Court of Appeal in *KR v Bryn Alyn Community Holdings Ltd* (p505), and was followed in the case of *Smith v NHSLA* (p662).]

Waiver of limitation rights and estoppel

Parties are at liberty to agree to exclude the statute as in *Abouchalache v Hilton International Hotels (UK) Ltd* (p290) where the defendants undertook not to plead a limitation defence provided that proceedings were issued by a certain date. In addition, in certain circumstances, an admission of liability may be held to amount to a waiver of the defendant's limitation defence. In *Lubovsky v Snelling* [1944] KB 44 an agreement by the defendants not to contest liability was held by the Court of

Appeal to also exclude them from taking a limitation defence in respect of a writ which was issued to determine quantum only (see also *Sauria* [1957] 1 Lloyd's Rep 396). A similar position was reached in two older cases where the defendants had admitted liability and the court held that an unambiguous admission of liability precluded the defendant from raising a limitation defence (see *Wright v John Bagnall & Sons Ltd* [1900] 2 QB 240 and *Rendall v Hill's Dry Docks & Engineering Company* [1900] 2 QB 245). However, in *Cotterell (Executors of Reeve deceased) v Leeds Day* [2001] WLR 435, Parker J doubted whether a mere admission could prevent a limitation defence from being raised. The court held that the admission was subject to an implication that proceedings would be issued within the limitation period. For an admission to be effective, there should be a clear agreement that the defendants will not rely on any limitation they might otherwise have had.

The mere fact that negotiations had been ongoing will not stop time running but circumstances may be created where waiver or estoppels can be raised (see *Rowan v Lambert Eggink Offshore Transport Consultants (No 2)* [1999] 2 Lloyds Rep 443, *Kammins Ballrooms Company v Zenith Investments Ltd* [1971] AC 850, *Paterson v Glasgow Corporation* [1908] 46 SLR 10, *Kaliszewska v J Claque & Partners* (1984) 5 Con LR 62). A claimant will normally have difficulty establishing an estoppel except in very clear cases. For example, in *Bytheway v British Steel Corporation* (p358), the Court of Appeal found that the defendants had not waived their limitation rights in a case brought for industrial deafness. Thousands of claims had been dealt with by the defendant's insurers under a scheme which included an agreement not to take any limitation point if a claimant settled on the basis of damages as calculated by the scheme rather than at common law. The insurers ended that agreement in 1993 and the claimant issued proceedings in 1994. The issue arose as to whether the claimant's claim and other claims which were already being dealt with under the scheme could now rely on the agreement over limitation. The Court of Appeal reversed the first instance judge's decision that the insurers had waived their limitation rights. The Court of Appeal held that the insurers were entitled to end the agreement and that the waiver of limitation only applied to scheme claims and not common law claims. In addition, the Court of Appeal held that it would not be appropriate to grant a s 33 dispensation (see also *Ace Insurance v Seechurn* [2002] EWCA Civ 67, [2002] 2 Lloyd's Rep 390). Further case law confirms that there needs to be a clear and unequivocal representation that the claimant has relied on to his detriment before an estoppel can be created (see *Law Society v Sephton & Co* [2004] EWHC 544, [2004] PNLR 27).

The court, prior to the House of Lords decision in *Horton v Sadler* (p482), had taken a similar view in cases where claimants contended that the rule in *Walkley v Precision Forgings* (p705) should not apply because the defendants, by their conduct, should be estopped from relying on the limitation defence (see *Deerness v John R Keeble & Son (Brantham) Ltd* (p408), *Forward v Hendrick* [1997] 2 All ER 395, *Clay v Chamberlain* (p377) and *Young v Western Power Distribution (South West) plc* (p733)). The court held in this context that the exceptional circumstances referred to in *Walkley* for the rule not to apply should amount to an estoppel. *Horton* abolished the rule in *Walkley*, and the court is now permitted to exercise a s 33 discretion in a second action (for such examples, see *Cain v Francis* (p360), *McDonnell v Walker* (p550) and *Williams v Johnstone's Estate* (p719).

3 The claimant's date of knowledge (section 14)

Introduction

Section 11(4) of the Limitation Act 1980 provides a three-year primary limitation period for personal injury actions running from either the date of the accrual of the cause of action or alternatively, if later, from the date of knowledge of the injured person. In many cases, these dates will coincide when an obvious injury results directly from a straightforward accident and there is an immediately identifiable wrong-doer. In a significant minority of actions, however, there is no simple injury or no straightforward causation between the injury and the wrong. For example, in disease cases, the onset of symptoms may be insidious and might also be characterised by a long latency period between the wrongful exposure to a product or a system of work and the subsequent development of the disability. In clinical negligence actions or product liability cases against drug manufacturers, a claimant's injury may require a specialist opinion to differentiate between the presenting symptoms of a disease or condition and the consequences of the doctor's treatment or the effect of a drug. In these types of case, the accrual of the cause of action arises in tort when damage which is more than minimal occurs, or in contract when the breach occurred. Accordingly, the date of accrual of the cause of action may be years before a claimant is able to establish a factual causal connection with his symptoms and the alleged wrongdoer. Such a position frequently arises in claims based upon mishandling birth where the injured claimant does not find out that his injuries might be attributable to clinical negligence until long after his minority has ended.

As was discussed in **Chapter 1**, the concept of a claimant's date of knowledge was introduced by the Limitation Act 1963 and was subjected to substantial modification by the Limitation Act 1975. These reforms were designed to deal, predominantly, with cases of imperceptible injury and concealed causation which had given rise to manifest injustice by becoming statute barred even before a claimant knew that he had an injury or before he knew who was responsible for causing it (cf *Cartledge v Jopling* (p366)). The concept of a claimant's date of knowledge within s 11(4) and as defined by s 14 of the 1980 Act is largely a re-enactment of the changes introduced by the 1975 Act. Further modifications have been introduced into s 14 by the Consumer Protection Act 1987 which by s 14(1A) inserts broadly parallel provisions for dealing with a person's date of knowledge in cases of personal injury arising out of defective products. The major difference between ordinary personal injury actions and those brought under the Consumer Protection Act 1987 is that the latter contains no equivalent provision to s 14(3) concerned with so-called constructive knowledge. Additionally, pursuant to s 11A(3), a longstop period prevents the bringing of an action after 10 years.

Further, a new section has been inserted into the 1980 Act, namely s 14A, by the Latent Damage Act 1986. This section is not concerned with personal injury actions but introduces analogous provisions concerning a date of knowledge for non-personal injury actions based on negligence where facts relevant to the cause of action are not known at the date of accrual. This provision was enacted to deal with concern over cases in negligence, often associated with damage to buildings, which might become statute barred before the damage that has occurred was discoverable (cf *Pirelli General Cable Works Limited v Oscar Faber & Partners* [1983] 2 AC 1). In such non-personal injury actions based on negligence including those under s 2 discussed in **Chapter 2**, the primary six-year period is now supplemented by an alternative three-year period from the date of knowledge. However, by s 14B a longstop of 15 years prevents the bringing of an action after that period similar to the 10-year longstop under the Consumer Protection Act 1987.

It can be seen that the general law of limitation concerning a claimant's date of knowledge within the tort of negligence has followed the direction first forged by the 1963 and 1975 Limitation Acts concerning personal injury cases. The existing case law under s 14 of the Limitation Act 1980 is of direct relevance to cases falling within s 14A concerned with a non-personal injury action including professional negligence cases arising out of negligently conducted personal injury claims (see *Oakes v Hopcroft* (p585)). Similarly, the leading case on s 14A (*Haward v Fawcetts* (p469) was endorsed by Lord Walker, in the Supreme Court in *B v Ministry of Defence* (p312), as containing the most authoritative judicial exposition of s 14(1) (a) concerning personal injury actions.

Section 14, leaving aside s 14(1A) concerning defective products, has three subsections which define and expand the meaning of date of knowledge. The section uses the concepts of knowledge, significance, attribution, identity and constructive knowledge and each have received considerable judicial attention. This chapter will discuss the particular statutory constructions of these concepts in the existing case law. It is of interest to note that the Law Commission in its Final Report on Limitation Periods in Civil Procedure (Law Com 151) advocates a general three-year period of limitation for all causes of action running from the date of discoverability namely when a claimant knows or ought reasonably to know that he has a cause of action. Lady Hale in *B v Ministry of Defence* (p312), at paras 162–175, considered the current law of limitation concerning s 14 as 'complicated and incoherent' and opined that, in policy terms, the world might be a more sensible and predictable place if the court only had the discretion in s33, without the discoverability provisions in ss11 and 14, and better still if time simply ran from the date of the wrongful act or omission rather than the date of damage. The following sections deal with the law as it currently is.

Section 14(1)

This subsection provides that:

'Subject to subsection (1A) below, in sections 11 and 12 of this Act references to a person's date of knowledge are references to the date on which he first had knowledge of the following facts–

(a)   that the injury in question was significant; and
(b)   that the injury was attributable in whole or in part to the act or omission which is alleged to constitute negligence, nuisance or breach of duty; and

(c)   the identity of the defendant; and

(d)   if it is alleged that the act or omission was that of a person other than the defendant, the identity of that person and the additional facts supporting the bringing of any action against the defendant;

and knowledge that any acts or omissions did or did not, as a matter of law, involve negligence, nuisance or breach of duty is irrelevant.'

1   Actual knowledge: belief may be sufficient

Section 14(1):

'... the date on which he first had knowledge of the facts ...'

For time to run against a claimant, s 14(1) requires the claimant to have knowledge of the four factual matters listed. The section does not seek to statutorily define what the courts have called actual knowledge. Section 14(3) gives some assistance in what the courts have called constructive knowledge by permitting the court to 'fix' a claimant with knowledge he might reasonably have acquired from facts observable or ascertainable by him or with the help of medical or other expert advice which he ought reasonably to have sought. What constitutes *actual* knowledge has been determined by the courts as being a reasonably firmly held belief sufficient to warrant the taking of preliminary steps to the issuing of proceedings, such as submitting a claim to the defendant, taking legal advice and collecting evidence. This definition of actual knowledge within s 14(1) was endorsed by the Court of Appeal in *Nash and others v Eli Lilly & Co and others* (p568), *Spargo v North Essex District Health Authority* (p667), *Haward v Fawcetts* [2006] 1 WLR 652 and by the majority in the Supreme Court in *B v Ministry of Defence* (p312). On the issue as to what condition of mind constitutes knowledge, the Court of Appeal in *Nash* followed the reasoning of the then Master of the Rolls Lord Donaldson in *Halford v Brookes and another* (p453).

Prior to *Halford* and *Nash*, the court had made a distinction between knowledge and belief, derived from Lord Justice May's judgment in the case of *Davis v Ministry of Defence* (p405). In *Davis* the Court of Appeal declined to define knowledge but indicated that it was an ordinary English word with a clear meaning to which full effect had to be given, and reasonable belief or suspicion was not enough to start time running against the claimant. Mr Davis first issued proceedings in October 1973 in respect of a serious attack of dermatitis which both he and his general practitioner believed was caused by his working conditions as a welder and which first manifested itself in a localised form in 1969. A first set of proceedings was allowed to lapse because medical opinion failed to support any causal link between the claimant's disease and his working conditions. New proceedings were issued in 1981 following supportive medical opinion, and the defendant sought to have the proceedings struck out as being statute barred. The Court of Appeal declined to dismiss the action, drawing upon a distinction between the claimant's belief, albeit a firm belief, that his disease was connected to his working conditions and actual knowledge that it was. What the claimant needed to know was that his dermatitis was capable of being attributed to his work conditions and was not constitutional. *Davis* also impliedly indicated that if a claimant believed his work conditions had caused the disease but a first expert instructed by him said in fact they did not, time did not run against him until a subsequent expert said that in fact the work conditions did cause the disease.

This distinction between knowledge and belief was noted again by the Court of Appeal in *Wilkinson v Ancliff* (p718) some six months after *Davis*. A differently constituted Court of Appeal laid greater emphasis upon a claimant only requiring a broad knowledge of causation, particularly in a case like *Wilkinson* which involved a general allegation of a failure to provide a safe system of work. The difference between knowledge and belief was further emphasised in *Stephen v Riverside Health Authority* (p676), where a state of anxiety by a claimant founded on a suspicion that an overdose of radiation during a breast x-ray could give rise to an increased risk of cancer was held not to amount to a state of knowledge. This was particularly so in the circumstances where experts were initially denying that any negative effects could arise from the particular level of exposure thought to have occurred. Auld J found that:

'There is no doubt that right from the start, and throughout, Mrs Stephen has believed or at the very lease suspected that she received an overdose in the mammography significant to cause the erythema, the moist spots and an increased risk of cancer. This was a belief or suspicion to which she held despite all the contrary medical opinions that she had received. However, as Lord Justice May pointed out in *Davis v MOD* [1985] CA Transcript 413 and as Lords Justices Slade and Croom-Johnson agreed in *Wilkinson v Ancliff* ([1986] 1 WLR 1352), knowledge is what is required in section 14(1), suspicion or belief or even reasonable belief is not enough.' ([1990] 1 Med LR 261 at 266)

This relatively clear distinction between knowledge and belief was, however, substantially eroded by the Court of Appeal in *Halford v Brookes* (p453). *Halford* concerned a case brought by the mother of Lynn Siddons, who was murdered in April 1978, against two defendants, one of whom had been indicted but acquitted of the murder. By the time the claimant had heard the evidence in the criminal trial in November 1978 she had formed a firm belief that both the defendants in the civil action were involved in the murder of her daughter. Lord Donaldson, the Master of the Rolls, expressed caution in relying on the 'highly unusual' facts of *Davis v Ministry of Defence* and held that knowledge within the meaning of the section would in fact normally mean a state of mind based upon reasonable belief:

'The word has to be construed in the context of the purpose of the section which is to determine a period of time within which a plaintiff can be required to start any proceedings. In this context "knowledge" clearly does not mean "know for certain and beyond possibility of contradiction". It does, however, mean "know with sufficient confidence to justify embarking on the preliminaries to the issue of a writ such as submitting a claim for the proposed defendant, taking legal or other advices and collecting evidence". Suspicion, particularly if it is vague and unsupported, will indeed not be enough, but reasonable belief will normally suffice. It is probably only in an exceptional case such as *Davis v Ministry of Defence* that it will not, because there is some other countervailing factor.' ([1991] 3 All ER 559 at 573J)

Accordingly, the claimant in *Halford* was fixed with a date of knowledge from the date of the criminal trial in November 1978.

The continued retreat from *Davis v Ministry of Defence* was underlined in *Nash v Eli Lilly* (p568). These actions concerned preliminary trials on limitation in respect of claims arising out of the side effects of the drug Opren such as eye and skin sensitivity, abnormal hair growth and liver and kidney failure. The drug, which was prescribed to relieve arthritic pain, was withdrawn in the United Kingdom in August 1982 with considerable publicity. The Court of Appeal, before analysing each claimant's case individually, laid down a number of principles governing the interpretation of both ss 14 and 33 of the 1980 Act. With respect to the concept of actual knowledge the court adopted the Master of the Rolls' formulation in *Halford*. Giving the judgment of the court Lord Justice Purchas said this:

'We do not, of course, intend to lay down a definition of the word "knowledge" for the purposes of a statute in which Parliament left the word to speak for itself. In applying the section to the facts of these cases we shall proceed on the basis that knowledge is a condition of mind which imports a degree of certainty and that the degree of certainty which is appropriate for this purpose is that which, for the particular plaintiff, may reasonably be regarded as sufficient to justify embarking upon the preliminaries to the making of a claim for compensation such as the taking of legal or other advice.' ([1993] 4 All ER 383 at 392b–d)

The court also expressed the view that whether any claimant has such a degree of mental certainty will depend upon the information available to him, the extent to which he paid attention to that information, and his capacity to comprehend it. Moreover the court emphasised that the date of knowledge is the first date when the claimant has this condition of mind because of the clear wording of the statute ('the date at which he *first* had knowledge …'). The Court of Appeal in *Nash* accordingly regarded as unarguable the contention that if a claimant had 'knowledge' but is then told by an expert, incorrectly, that he is wrong, that this has the effect of stopping the running of time. Time runs from when the claimant had his reasonably certain belief and not from when a second or subsequent expert confirmed his belief. Negative expert advice does not therefore have any consequence on the running of time in circumstances where the claimant irrespective of such advice has already formed a reasonably certain belief. The court found that there was a false antithesis between knowledge and belief and did 'not find any great deal of assistance from the judgment of May LJ in *Davis v Ministry of Defence*'.

A period of limitation therefore begins to run against a claimant when it can first be said that he has knowledge of the nature of his injury to justify him taking preliminary steps for the institution of proceedings against the person whose act or omission he reasonably believes has caused the injury.

There is however a proviso for those claimants who, although they might firmly believe their condition is related to the act or omission of the defendant, also feel that they need reassurance or conformation by an expert. In this category of case, the court in *Nash* thought that a firm but suspended belief will not be enough to start time running:

'It is to be noted that a firm belief held by the plaintiff that his injury was attributable to the act or omission of the defendant, but in respect of which he thought it necessary to obtain reassurance or confirmation of an expert, medical or legal or otherwise, would not be regarded as knowledge until the results of his enquiries are known to him, or if he delayed in obtaining that confirmation, until the time at which it was reasonable for him to have got it.' (at 396c–d)

However, this contention that a firm but suspended belief will not set time running has been the subject of further Court of Appeal authority. In *Spargo v North Essex District Health Authority* (p667), a case concerned with knowledge of attribution within the meaning of s 14(1)(b), the court sought to distil some of the principles to be found in *Nash* and subsequent cases. Lord Justice Brooke said this:

'What, then, does the law require in order that actual knowledge is established?

This branch of the law is already so grossly over-loaded with reported cases, a great many of which have been shown to us or cited by Counsel, that

I see no reason to add to the overload by citation from early decisions. I have considered the judgments of this Court in *Halford v Brookes* [1991] 1 WLR 443; *Nash v Eli Lilly & Co* [1993] 1 WLR 782; *Broadley v Guy Clapham* [1993] 4 All ER 439; *Dobbie v Medway Health Authority* [1994] 1 WLR 1234; *Smith v Lancashire Health Authority* [1995] PIQR 514; and *Forbes v Wandsworth Health Authority* [1996] 7 Med LR 175. From these decisions I draw the following principles:

(1)   The knowledge required to satisfy s 14(1)(b) is a broad knowledge of the essence of the causally relevant act or omission to which the injury is attributable;

(2)   "Attributable" in this context means "capable of being attributed to", in the sense of being a real possibility;

(3)   A plaintiff has the requisite knowledge when she knows enough to make it reasonable for her to begin to investigate whether or not she has a case against the defendant. Another way of putting this is to say that she will have such knowledge if she so firmly believes that her condition is capable of being attributed to an act or omission which she can identify (in broad terms) that she goes to a solicitor to seek advice about making a claim for compensation;

(4)   On the other hand, she will not have the requisite knowledge if she thinks she knows the act or omission she should investigate but in fact is barking up the wrong tree: or if her knowledge of what the defendant did or did not do is so vague or general that she cannot fairly be expected to know what she should investigate; or if her state of mind is such that she thinks her condition is capable of being attributed to the act or omission alleged to constitute negligence, but she is not sure about this, and would need to check with an expert before she could be properly said to know that it was.'

(See also *Whitfield v North Durham Health Authority* (p713), *Gregory v Ferro GB Ltd* (p448), *O'Driscoll v Dudley Health Authority* (p588) and *Roberts v Winbow* (p627).)

Ali v Courtaulds Textiles (p301) illustrates a case where a two-judge Court of Appeal determined that time did not run against a claimant in a deafness case until he received an expert opinion that his deafness was noise induced rather than constitutional and due to the ageing process. This was so even though the claimant had been told, by a community worker, to consult a solicitor, which he did, as he might have a claim against his employers. The Court of Appeal thought that the case fell within category 4 of the *Spargo* exception.

However, in *Sniezek v Bundy (Letchworth) Ltd* (p664) a differently constituted three-judge court doubted *Ali* and reaffirmed that firm belief in attribution which takes a claimant to a solicitor for advice is likely to be regarded as actual knowledge (*O'Driscoll v Dudley Health Authority* affirmed). Whether a case falls within category 3 or category 4 of *Spargo* will require a close factual analysis. Simon Brown LJ said this in *Sniezek*:

'6.   Now it seems to me one thing to say that a mere believer in attributability who "realises that his belief requires expert confirmation" does not have knowledge of that attributability; arguably another to say that a firm believer who, for example, nevertheless wants legal advice (say to reassure him that he has reasonable prospects of success) is not to be regarded as having the requisite knowledge. Why should not time have started running in the case of the latter? Why should he be entitled to his solicitor's reassurance before the three year limitation period ever begins? I do not think that he is and nor do I think that the Court in *Nash v Eli Lilly* were intending to suggest otherwise: and that surely is evidenced from the final sentence in paragraph 5.

7.   In short, it seems to me that the real contrast being struck in *Nash v Eli Lilly* is between on the one hand the mere believer whose situation is described in the first passage in the judgment, and on the other hand the firm believer sufficiently certain of his case to have clearly in mind (although always, of course, subject to the taking of appropriate advice and the preparation of evidence) the making of a compensation claim …

8.   Having regard to these considerations and having regard to the underlying purpose of this legislation – to postpone the three year period allowing for the investigation and institution of a specified claim until the claimant knows enough to make it reasonable to set time running – I find it difficult indeed to imagine a case where, having consulted a solicitor with a view to making a claim for compensation, a claimant could still then be held lacking in the requisite knowledge.

9.   In short, I adhere to what I said in *O'Driscoll* and in the result confess to some difficulty both with the reasoning and, I have to say, with the result in the subsequent case of *Ali*. True it is that when Mr Ali went to his solicitor he knew only that his deafness might have been caused by his conditions of work in a cotton mill rather than (as he had earlier assumed) by a natural aging process. But that seems to me sufficient knowledge of attributability given, as stated in the second of the *Spargo* principles, that in this context a real possibility of establishing causation constitutes attributability … Mr Ali, therefore, seems to me to have come strictly within the second category outlined in *Nash v Eli Lilly*; he was someone "obtaining advice about making a claim for compensation"; he had, indeed, already obtained a legal aid certificate for the purpose, albeit one initially limited to obtaining the necessary ENT report.'

The whole of this jurisprudence was subjected to critical analysis by the Supreme Court in *B v Ministry of Defence* (p312), with the majority supporting the *Halford* definition of actual knowledge as amounting to no more than reasonable belief (per Lord Wilson at para 11).

In *B v Ministry of Defence*, 10 individual cases were selected from approximately 1,011 claimants (in a group action started on 23 December 2004) who contended that they had sustained disparate injuries all due to exposure to radiation from experimental explosions in the atmosphere carried out by the Ministry of Defence in Australia and the South Pacific when serving as soldiers, sailors and airmen in the period from October 1952 to September 1958. Some claimants joined the action later, between 16 November and 29 September 2008. Limitation was ordered to be determined on generic issues. The claimants were hampered in the action by the absence of any cogent evidence that their injuries were caused by ionising radiation. The Ministry of Defence denied that the veterans were in fact exposed to levels of radiation capable of causing their injuries or that their injuries were caused by radiation. The Ministry of Defence relied on studies by the National Radiological Protection Board in 1988, 1993 and 2003 that there was no general increase in mortality on the part of veterans, either generally or from cancer, and other epidemiological studies concluding that there was no disproportionate incidence of injuries among veterans. It was common ground that radiation can cause injury either if an individual was so close to a nuclear explosion to be affected by 'prompt' radiation from the powerful but short-lived effect of gamma rays or, alternatively, from fall-out of alpha and beta particles which can be carried some distance and ingested by breathing and swallowing and which can produce a cumulative effect by continuing to radiate.

The claimants alleged exposure to both prompt and fall-out radiation, but abandoned the claim in respect of prompt radiation on the morning of the 10-day hearing at first instance. In addition, it was accepted that none of the claimants had a conventional case on causation, as the highest they could contend was that the exposure to fall-out had increased the risk of them sustaining injury which, to succeed, would require the court to extend the *Fairchild v Glenhaven Funeral Services* [2002] UKHL 22 principle beyond mesothelioma cases – a distinctly unlikely proposition, given the subsequent decision of *Sienkiewicz v Grief* [2011] UKSC 10.

The claimants' case was substantially based upon the Rowland Report shown to the group in 2007 (that is, after issue of most of the claims) that some of the blood samples taken from 50 New Zealand veterans showed abnormal incidences of chromosomal changes indicative of exposure to ionising radiation. The study, however, made no claims about the health of the veterans, and therefore did not support the contention that the veterans had sustained any injury as opposed to some chromosomal abnormality.

At first instance, the judge indicated he would, if unconstrained by authority, have found the veterans had no knowledge that radiation was capable of causing their injuries until the Rowland Report and that they had been barking up the wrong tree because of their firm but mistaken belief they were exposed to prompt radiation. This was because he would have preferred the test of knowledge to be reasonably based on fact. Applying the test he believed as formulated in *Spargo* (p667) and *Sniezek v Bundy* (p664), he found five of the ten claimants to have a sufficiently strong belief that their illnesses were caused by radiation to amount to knowledge. With respect to those that were statute barred, he exercised his discretion to allow them to proceed under s33.

The Court of Appeal allowed the defendants to appeal and found all but one of the cases statute barred. The Court of Appeal reversed the judge's exercise of discretion on the basis that the claimants had no reasonable prospect of success on causation, and noted that this was the reason why the earlier case of *Pearce v Secretary of State for Defence* [1988] AC 755 was discontinued. The Court of Appeal found the judge had set the bar for actual knowledge too high. At paras 91–92, the court stated that the test is whether the claimant had such a degree of belief that it was reasonable to expect him to commence investigating whether or not he had a viable case. Crucially, the court went on to state:

> '93. We note in *Halford*, Lord Donaldson MR suggested that a belief would have to be reasonable before it could amount to knowledge. With great respect, we do not think that the belief needs to be objectively reasonable. We think what matters is the claimant's state of mind. If a claimant comes to believe that there is a causal connection between his condition and the matters complained of, it will matter not from where he has derived his belief, even if it were from an incompetent expert adviser or from a newspaper article which is not based on sound research. If the belief were of such a strength that it was reasonable to expect him to start investigating his claim, it would amount to knowledge within section 14.'

The Supreme Court, by a majority of 4 to 3, upheld the Court of Appeal in dismissing nine of the test cases as statute barred and declined to exercise s 33 discretion in their favour. The court held that it was heretical and a legal impossibility for a claimant to lack knowledge of attributability at a time after the date of issue of his claim, as the veterans' contention that they lacked knowledge until receipt of the Rowland Report in 2007 necessitated. Lord Wilson asserted that this must be so in part due to the statement of truth in the claim form that the claimants believed the facts stated were true.

The majority endorsed Lord Donaldson's approach in *Halford v Brookes* (p453) confirming that a claimant will have knowledge of the required facts when he first came to believe them with sufficient confidence to embark upon the preliminaries to the issue of proceedings. There was a distinction between this subjective belief, that the claimant had a real possibility of a claim, and the assembly by him with the help of legal and expert assistance of justifying the commencement of proceedings with a prospect of success. What mattered was the strength of the claimant's belief. It did not automatically follow that a claimant had such knowledge by the time he consulted a solicitor, but such an inference might be justified. The date upon which a claimant first consulted an expert was not likely to assist in determining the date of knowledge; of more importance was the degree of confidence the claimant had in his case and the content of the expert's report and its effect on him.

Lord Walker endorsed Lord Phillips' description of the categorisations made in *Spargo* as a valiant attempt, but cautioned that it should not be treated as if they were statutory texts and recommended Lord Nicholls exposition of similar provisions in *Haward v Fawcetts* [2006] 1 WLR 682 at paras 8–15 as most authoritative. He further added (at para 68) that, in a complex case, it was important to remember that constructive knowledge in s 14(3) was an essential part of the statutory scheme, not an occasional add-on, and that the date of a claimant's visit to a solicitor was, without more information, of little significance in most cases.

In summary, time will run against a claimant if he has a firm enough belief to warrant the taking of preliminary steps for the institution of proceedings. If those steps fail at first to confirm his belief but subsequently his belief is confirmed, time will have run from the first date at which he had belief, irrespective of the initial non-confirmation. If, however, a claimant has a suspicion or a relatively uncertain belief which requires expert or other opinion to establish whether he has suffered any injury and, if so, whether it was due to any act or omission of a possible defendant, time may not run until that belief is confirmed. In cases concerning injury to the claimant during birth, the court has emphasised that the knowledge in question is the knowledge of the claimant himself and not the knowledge, actual or constructive, of his parents (see *Appleby v Walsall Health Authority* (p305), *Parry v Clwyd Health Authority* (p596), *Bates v Leicester Health Authority* (p324) and *Mirza v Birmingham Health Authority* (p562)). Obviously, however, if the parents discuss the birth with the claimant, the claimant may have actual knowledge or the court may impose constructive knowledge (see *O'Driscoll v Dudley Health Authority* (p588).

The court, having refused to define knowledge, has created a pragmatic theory of knowledge based upon a condition of mind which would warrant the initiation of preliminaries to making a claim. The practical effect of this approach is to require a detailed examination of the claimant's state of mind in the light of the information he has available to him, and the distinction between knowledge and belief for these purposes has been substantially eroded. For actual knowledge, *as opposed to constructive knowledge*, the test was, until the cases of *A v Hoare* (p287) following *Adams v Bracknell Forest BC* (p292), thought to be entirely subjective, namely that the personal characteristics of the claimant, and the effects, if any, of the injury upon him, were relevant in considering what facts were observable and ascertainable by him, given his intellect and other characteristics.

However, Lord Walker in *B v Ministry of Defence* (p312), at para 47, confirmed that what was within the claimant's actual knowledge is undoubtedly a subjective question but considered that, post *Hoare* and *Adams*, the policy of the law is for the date of knowledge to be ascertained in the same way for all claimants.

Accordingly, once the court is satisfied that the claimant has a reasonably firmly held belief, it will not consider the subjective characteristics of the claimant as to how he should have acted on the belief in ascertaining the date of knowledge, because such personal factors are now to be taken into account when exercising discretion under s 33. This is the effect of the House of Lords' decision in *Hoare*, which emphasised the essentially objective nature of knowledge within the whole of the section, following its decision in *Adams v Bracknell Forest BC* (p292). These principles are discussed below.

2   Significance

Section 14(1)(a):

'... that the injury in question was significant'

Section 14(2):

'For the purposes of this section an injury is significant if the person whose date of knowledge is in question would reasonably have considered it sufficiently serious to justify his instituting proceedings for damages against a defendant who did not dispute liability and was able to satisfy a judgment.'

For time to start running against a claimant, he must 'know', in the sense of having a reasonably certain belief, that the injury in question was significant, was attributable to an act or omission of the defendant and who that defendant is. With respect to the first of these facts, namely that the injury was significant, the effect of s 14(2) is to make most injuries significant, even relatively trivial ones, because the test implies that a defendant will be able to pay damages without liability being an issue. In *Bristow v Grout* (p345) the Court of Appeal confirmed Jupp J's finding that a claimant's facial injuries sustained in a road traffic accident constituted a significant injury so that time ran from the date of the accident. Accordingly, the later discovery of a more serious hip injury also sustained in the accident was statute barred. (The court had taken a similar position under the 1963 Act see *Goodchild v Greatness Timber Company Ltd* (p445), *Miller v London Electrical Manufacturing Company Ltd* (p559).) Similarly, in *Brooks v J & P Coates (UK) Ltd* (p350) a claimant who had left his place of work at a cotton mill in 1965 because of wheezing, coughing and shortness of breath was fixed with a significant injury at that date and not when a later diagnosis of byssinosis was made in 1979. In *Roberts v Winbow* (p627) the Court of Appeal held that a claimant's significant injury ran from the onset of acute symptoms caused by a reaction to a drug (known as a Stevens-Johnson Syndrome) and was not postponed until a later and more serious injury of oesophageal stricture was found to be also drug related. Hale LJ noted that the court's approach in emphasising the low threshold of significance was in accord with the Law Commission Report No 151, Consultation Paper on Limitation of Actions 1998 (see paras 3.38–43, 12.39–41). Similarly in *Dobbie v Medway Health Authority* (p411) the Master of Rolls, Sir Thomas Bingham, emphasised that the question of significance went only to the issue of quantum:

'The requirement the injury of which a Plaintiff has knowledge should be "significant" is, in my view, directed solely to the quantum of the injury and not to the Plaintiff's evaluation of its cause, nature or usualness. Time does not run against the Plaintiff, even if he is aware of the injury, if he would reasonably have considered it insufficiently serious to justify proceedings against an acquiescent and credit worthy defendant, if (in other words) he would reasonably have accepted it as a fact of life, or not worth bothering about. It is otherwise if the injury is reasonably to be considered to be sufficiently serious within the statutory definition: time then runs (subject to the requirement of attributability) even if the Plaintiff believes the injury to be normal or properly caused.'(at p12)

In *Briggs v Pitt-Payne* (p344) the Court of Appeal emphasised that, in assessing whether an injury caused by a drug regime was significant, there was no need for a complicated analysis of whether the side effects of the drug outweighed its benefits (see also *Rowe v Kingston Upon Hull City Council* (p633)).

From these cases, it is apparent that a claimant must be careful not to delay bringing an action on the basis that he would sooner wait until the full effects of his injuries have manifested themselves because he is most likely to be fixed with a date of knowledge based on the initial symptoms of the injury or disease. Occasionally, the court has been willing to sanction a 'wait and see' attitude, particularly in back injury cases where a claimant may be held to have acted reasonably by delaying to see if a strain or an ache sustained in an accident would spontaneously resolve. In *Devonport v A V Wright (Builders) Ltd* (p409) a back injury sustained at work in January 1980 resulted in two periods of hospital treatment and a course of physiotherapy over a five-month period. When the physiotherapy failed, the claimant then thought that his injury might be more serious than he first believed. Webster J held that the claimant would not reasonably consider the injuries sufficiently serious to justify instituting proceedings until May 1980 and his writ was held to be issued in time. A similar view was taken in *Pacheco v Brent & Harrow Area Health Authority* (p591) where a state-enrolled nurse, whilst lifting a patient, felt a sharp stabbing pain on 13 March 1978 which prevented her from working after 15 March 1978. A preliminary diagnosis of a ricked back and sciatica with possible disc involvement was made over the next two months. Eventually, traction was ordered for a disc problem on 26 May 1978. Comyn J said that, taking into account the claimant's position as a Spanish speaker with imperfect control of English, the injury did not fall to be considered as significant until 26 May 1978, and her writ issued on 22 May 1981 was accordingly in time (see also *Harding v People's Dispensary for Sick Animals* (p458). In *Platt v Quaker Oats Ltd* (p606) the trial judge indicated that he would have been willing to postpone a date of knowledge for approximately one year in respect of a back injury that required an initial two week period off work in January 1984. However, the judge held that the claimant by 1985 required further time off work and had intermittent pain throughout the year and it would have been apparent to him that by then it would be reasonable to issue a claim and accordingly found that his claim was prima facie statute barred. Conversely the 'wait and see' approach did not avail the claimant in *Collins v Tesco* (p383). The claimant hurt her shoulder using a metal cage to move stock in 1996. In January 1998, the physiotherapist told her that her injury was caused by heavy lifting and proceedings were issued in 2001. The Recorder found that the injury was not significant until the meeting with the physiotherapist and the 'wait and see' attitude as to whether the pain would settle was reasonable. The Court of Appeal disagreed and found the injury was significant before that meeting and was statute barred:

'13. The test is not an easy one to apply. It is set out in section 14(2) of the Act … That definition must be read, in my judgment, in the context for the purpose of the statute. The limitation period for an action such as this is normally one of three years. The Act provides relaxations, with one of which the Court is concerned. It allows a claimant with a lack of knowledge to bring a claim beyond the three-year period from when the cause of action arose. At the same time it must be borne in mind that the defendant is entitled to the protection of the limitation defence which the statute provides and that section must, in my judgment, be read as striking a balance between fairness to a claimant who lack knowledge and fairness to a defendant who, because of the statute and in the public interest, is entitle to be free of claims unless they are brought within an appropriate time.

14.   In my judgment, an over elaborate approach to the question is inappropriate. A possible elaboration is introduced with the "no risk" litigation contemplated in the section. That does not introduce into the test the consideration of the readiness with which particular injured person may resort to litigation. Such elaboration is, in my judgment, inimical to the intention of the statute in this respect. The word "significant" has to be approached in a common sense way, and a common sense way based upon the evidence in a particular case. While in some circumstances the effect on a particular Plaintiff may be a factor, the test appears to me to be an objective test as, in my judgement, Lord Justice Geoffrey Lane in effect recognised. If, by introducing the concept of wait and see, the Judge was suggesting that a relevant consideration when considering the significance of the injury is the degree of robustness or stoicism which a claimant has, in my judgement, it is an elaboration which is not appropriate to the test and I would respectfully disagree with this approach. However sympathetic one would wish to be to a claimant who may be slow to resort to the courts and who is prepared to adopt the wait and see attitude as to whether the injury is significant, these factors cannot be crucial to whether an injury is significant, although in some circumstances, they may throw light on whether or not it is.' (per Pill LJ)

The reference in *Collins* to Lane LJ is to the test that was espoused by him in *McCafferty v Metropolitan Police Receiver* (p546):

'... it is clear that the test is partly a subjective test, namely: would this Plaintiff have considered the injuries sufficiently serious? And partly an objective test namely: would he have been reasonable if he did not regard it sufficiently serious? It seems to me that (the) subsection ... is directed at the nature of the injuries known to the Plaintiff at the time. Taking that Plaintiff with that Plaintiff's intelligence would he have been reasonable in considering the injury not sufficiently serious to justify instituting proceedings for damages.'

The Court of Appeal in *Nash v Eli Lilly* (p568) confirmed the *McCafferty* test and made a distinction between the normal or expected side effects of a drug and the injurious and unacceptable consequences which may not have been immediately apparent to any particular claimant. The limit of that approach for drug-induced injuries was further explained and clarified in *Briggs v Pitt Payne* (p344).

That the test for significance has a degree of subjectivity within it was further confirmed by the Court of Appeal in *KR v Bryn Alyn Community Holdings Ltd* (p505). Applying the so-called *McCafferty* test in *Young v GLC & Massey* (p733) had the effect of postponing for three years the claimant's date of knowledge. Mr Young sustained what was thought to be a minor whiplash injury to his neck in April 1981 which required some time off work at regular intervals during the three years after the accident. In May 1984, however, he was declared permanently unfit for his work as a foreman. Owen J found it reasonable for that particular claimant not to sue prior to May 1984 because he reasonably did not think it worthwhile or proper to do so. In *Woods v Attorney General* (p725), McPherson J indicated that a claimant should not necessarily be considered as essentially litigious and willing to issue proceedings for the slightest of injuries. In *Stephen v Riverside Health Authority* (p676), Auld J felt it reasonable that a claimant did not sue in respect of erythema and anxiety because she did not consider this sufficiently serious to warrant proceedings, and that knowledge of how significant the injury was only came later when she knew that the overdose of radiation she had been subjected to might cause her cancer.

However, in *Catholic Care (Diocese of Leeds) and another v Young* [2006] EWCA Civ 1534 the Court of Appeal held that the test in s 14(2) is objective. This was on the basis that, since *Bryn Alyn*, the House of Lords in *Adams v Bracknell Forest BC* (p292) determined that the test for constructive knowledge in s 14(3) was objective and that the presence of the word 'reasonably' in both sections required a similar construction (per Dyson LJ at para 45).

Young was heard together with *A v Hoare* (p287) and three other abuse cases by the House of Lords, who agreed with the Court of Appeal in *Young* that the test of whether an injury was significant was objective and disapproved both *McCafferty* and *Bryn Alyn*.

Lord Hoffmann stated:

'33.   The question which has arisen is whether the definition of significance in section 14(2) allows any (and if so, how much) account to be taken of personal characteristics of the claimant, either pre-existing or consequent upon the injury which he has suffered. This question was first considered in *McCafferty v Metropolitan Police District Receiver* [1977] 1 WLR 1073, 1081, soon after the 1975 Act had come into force. After reading the then equivalent of subsection 14(2), Geoffrey Lane LJ said:

"[T]he test is partly a subjective test, namely: 'would this plaintiff have considered the injury sufficiently serious?' and partly an objective test, namely: 'would he have been reasonable if he did not regard it as sufficiently serious?' It seems to me that the subsection is directed at the nature of the injury as known to the plaintiff at that time. Taking that plaintiff, with that plaintiff's intelligence, would he have been reasonable in considering the injury not sufficiently serious to justify instituting proceedings for damages?"

34.   I respectfully think that the notion of the test being partly objective and partly subjective is somewhat confusing. Section 14(2) is a test for what counts as a significant injury. The material to which that test applies is generally "subjective" in the sense that it is applied to what the claimant knows of his injury rather than the injury as it actually was. Even then, his knowledge may have to be supplemented with imputed "objective" knowledge under section 14(3). But the test itself is an entirely impersonal standard: not whether the claimant himself would have considered the injury sufficiently serious to justify proceedings but whether he would "reasonably" have done so. You ask what the claimant knew about the injury he had suffered, you add any knowledge about the injury which may be imputed to him under section 14(3) and you then ask whether a reasonable person with that knowledge would have considered the injury sufficiently serious to justify his instituting proceedings for damages against a defendant who did not dispute liability and was able to satisfy a judgment.

35.   It follows that I cannot accept that one must consider whether someone "with [the] plaintiff's intelligence" would have been reasonable if he did not regard the injury as sufficiently serious. That seems to me to destroy the effect of the word "reasonably". Judges should not have to grapple with the notion of the reasonable unintelligent person. Once you have ascertained what the claimant knew and what he should be treated as having known, the actual claimant drops out of the picture. Section 14(2) is, after all, simply a standard of the seriousness of the injury and nothing more. Standards are in their nature impersonal and do not vary with the person to whom they are applied.

36.   In *KR v Bryn Alyn Community (Holdings) Ltd* [2003] QB 1441, 1459 the Court of Appeal ventured even further into subjectivity. That too was a case of claims by victims of sexual abuse. In giving the judgment of the Court, Auld LJ said that victims of such abuse may regard such conduct by persons in authority as normal. It might be unreal to expect people with such psychological injuries to commence proceedings. Therefore, he said, at para 42, at p 1459:

> "However artificial it may seem to pose the question in this context, section 14 requires the court, on a case by case basis, to ask whether such an already damaged child would reasonably turn his mind to litigation as a solution to his problems?"

37.   This approach treats the statute as if it had said that time should run from the date on which it would have been reasonable to expect the claimant to institute proceedings. If it had said that, the question posed in *Bryn Alyn* would have been correct. But section 14 makes time runs from when the claimant has knowledge of certain facts, not from when he could have been expected to take certain steps. Section 14(2) does no more than define one of those facts by reference to a standard of seriousness.

38.   The Court of Appeal said that there was some "tension" between the *Bryn Alyn* test and the recent decision of the House of Lords in *Adams v Bracknell Forest Borough Council* [2005] 1 AC 76. I suppose that this is true in the sense that the House in *Adams* said that one had to take words like "reasonable" and "reasonably" seriously and the *Bryn Alyn* test does not. But *Adams* was dealing with section 14(3), which is very different in its purpose from section 14(2). The test for imputing knowledge in section 14(3) is by reference to what the claimant ought reasonably to have *done*. It asks whether he ought reasonably to have acquired certain knowledge from observable or ascertainable facts or to have obtained expert advice. But section 14(2) is simply a standard of seriousness applied to what the claimant knew or must be treated as having known. It involves no inquiry into what the claimant ought to have done. A conclusion that the injury would reasonably have been considered sufficiently serious to justify the issue of proceedings implies no finding that the claimant ought reasonably to have issued proceedings. He may have had perfectly good reasons for not doing so. It is a standard to determine one thing and one thing only, namely whether the injury was sufficiently serious to count as significant.

39.   The difference between section 14(2) and 14(3) emerges very clearly if one considers the relevance in each case of the claimant's injury. Because section 14(3) turns on what the claimant ought reasonably to have done, one must take into account the injury which the claimant has suffered. You do not assume that a person who has been blinded could reasonably have acquired knowledge by seeing things. In section 14(2), on the other hand, the test is

external to the claimant and involves no inquiry into what he ought reasonably to have done. It is applied to what the claimant knew or was deemed to have known but the standard itself is impersonal. The effect of the claimant's injuries upon what he could reasonably have been expected to do is therefore irrelevant.'

The law on s 14(2) is now clear, and the test as to whether an injury is significant is an objective one, namely what a person in the claimant's position would reasonably have considered as serious enough to sue in circumstances where liability was not in issue and the judgment could be satisfied.

The test as clarified was applied in *Albonetti v Wirral Metropolitan Borough Council* (p298). The claimant sued in 2001 in respect of sexual abuse, including anal rape, whilst at the defendants' care home when aged 15 in 1970. At first instance, the trial judge applied the test in *Bryn Alyn* and found that the claimant was unaware that his psychiatric symptoms were attributable to the abuse until he saw a psychiatrist in 2001, and that the psychiatric effects constituted the significant injury in question; and his action was accordingly brought within the three-year period from the date of knowledge that the injury was significant. The appeal was stayed, pending the decision of the House of Lords in *A v Hoare*. The Court of Appeal, in applying *Hoare*, found that the initial rape constituted the significant injury, and proceedings should have been brought within three years from the date of the claimant becoming 18.

'INJURY IN QUESTION'

In some cases where an initial injury has occurred before a later more serious injury or deterioration, the courts have circumvented the low threshold of significance within s 14(2) by permitting time to run from the later manifestations on the basis that the latter constitute 'the injury in question' within s 14(1)(a). The two classes of case where this approach has been considered are disease and sexual abuse actions, but both have to be read in the light of the House of Lords' decision in *Hoare*.

In *McManus v Mannings Marine* (p555) the claimant developed vibration white finger in his left hand in the 1980s and made a claim for benefit to the Department of Social Security in 1992. His condition was due to working in the ship building industry including a short period with the defendants in 1989 (12 days) and 1990 (14 days). The claimant was told in 1993 that his condition would deteriorate. His application to the DSS was rejected in September 1992 as was a separate application to an industry wide scheme. The claimant resumed employment from August 1993 to November 1999 with the defendants. His condition did worsen and spread to both hands. He issued proceedings in September 2002. At first instance, the judge held, conventionally, that the claimant's claim was statute barred as his date of knowledge was 1992. The Court of Appeal reversed this decision stating that 'the injury in question' was the injury for which the action was brought, namely the exacerbation of his condition since 1993. The question, therefore, with respect to significance, was when was this exacerbation significant? In the Court of Appeal, it became common ground that the judge should have not have dismissed the claim in respect of any exacerbation within the three-year period from 2 December 1996 to 2 December 1999 (when proceedings were issued) as this would have been in time because the tort was a continuing one. Lady Justice Hale said this:

'12. In my judgment, the judge did take the wrong approach to this question. Section 14(1) clearly refers back to section 11 which refers to an action for "damages in respect of personal injuries". When, therefore, section 14(1)(a) talks about "the injury in question" it must mean the injury in respect of which the action is brought. This appellant is not bringing an action in respect of any injury that he may have suffered in the two very short periods of employment with this respondent before 1993. This action is in respect of exacerbation since then. The respondent accepts that there was a continuing cause of action arising day by day as and when the appellant continued to be affected by any negligence or breach of duty which may eventually be proved against the respondent.

13.   I conclude that the judge must have approached this matter wrongly. He should have asked himself when, within the meaning of the Act, did this claimant know that the injury in question, that is the exacerbation of his condition in this employment, was significant?'

The case was remitted back for a final hearing on both liability and limitation. No authorities were cited in the judgment. This case is of interest because the court is not saying that the initial injury was insignificant (owing to the fact that the claimant went to the solicitor, made a claim for state benefit and to an industry scheme) but the exacerbation is the significant injury in question. The claimant was, therefore, effectively permitted to abandon part of his personal injury as statute barred but was able to continue to sue in respect of the exacerbation. This case is perhaps best understood as one where a fresh injury is caused during the post-1993 employment because a new cause of action was arising daily (see also the judgment of Keene LJ). Construed in this way, the decision probably survives the ruling in *Hoare*.

The second class of case to adopt this approach was in the sexual abuse actions in *KR v Bryn Alyn Community Holdings Ltd* (p505). This case concerned a consolidated action by 14 claimants for damages arising out of physical and sexual abuse suffered by them when residents at children's homes run by the defendant. The abuse was substantial and included buggery and sexual intercourse with respect to some of the children. The Court of Appeal found, however, that the so-called impact injuries of the initial assaults were not significant in the meaning of s 14 and were not, in any event, the 'injury in question'. The significant injury in question was the long-term psychiatric harm created by the abusive experience rather than the immediate assaults. At first instance, the court had found that all claims were statute barred but a s 33 discretion was exercised. The Court of Appeal's decision was a remarkable one. None of the claimants, except one, sought to challenge the judge's findings with respect to their date of knowledge on a cross-appeal. It was not until the Court of Appeal had started to write its judgment that it effectively took the point on the date of knowledge of its own motion, and found that the initial injuries were not significant and the claimants could sue for both the impact injury and the later psychiatric consequences.

This approach to sexual abuse cases concerning children, as laid down in *Bryn Alyn*, was followed in the subsequent case of *H v (1) N (2) T* [2004] EWCA Civ 526. However, the reasoning does not survive the House of Lords' decision in *Hoare* and, in sexual abuse cases, the initial assault is most likely to be found to be the significant injury. Lady Justice Smith indicated this in *Albonetti* where she said, injecting a degree of realism back into this area of law:

'24.   ... In my view, a person who has been raped whether vaginally or anally must know that she or he has suffered not only a grave wrong but also a significant injury. That was the view expressed *obiter* by Lord Griffiths in *Stubbings v Webb* [1993] AC 498 HL at page 506B and I respectfully agree. He drew a distinction between an allegation of rape and lesser forms of sexual abuse, such as fondling, which might not amount to a significant injury. Here, the allegation of anal rape by more than one man on more than one occasion cannot in my view sensibly be regarded as anything other than a significant injury ...

31.   The first question we have to answer is whether the respondent knew of his own knowledge that he had suffered a significant injury. Applying the objective test, as we must now do, on the assumption that the respondent's allegations are true, I have no hesitation in holding that he knew at all times after it had occurred that the abuse amounted to a significant injury. He would not know of his own knowledge whether it was worth bringing an action but he would at least know enough to make it reasonable to expect him to consult a solicitor. Had he done so, he would have discovered (from a reasonably competent solicitor) that substantial damages could in theory be awarded for such abuse. I accept that he might well have been advised not to proceed but that would have been for other reasons, not that he had not suffered a significant injury.

32.   For the avoidance of doubt, I wish to make it plain that I am not suggesting that, in every case of abuse, the victim must be taken to have known at the time that he has suffered a significant injury. I quite accept that, where the abuse is of a less obviously intrusive nature, a different conclusion might be reached.'

Following remission back to the trial judge to determine whether a s 33 dispensation should be given, the case was dismissed on the basis that a fair trial was no longer possible (*Albonetti v Wirral Metropolitan Borough* (p298)).

In certain types of case, particularly in clinical negligence and disease/deafness actions, a claimant may not have knowledge that an injury is significant until he is informed of the fact by a medical practitioner. For example, in noise-induced deafness cases where the onset of the hearing loss is gradual, it may be difficult to pinpoint when the loss became significant, and in respiratory cases a loss of lung function may present initially as insidious (for deafness cases, see *Field v British Coal Corporation* (p431); *Furniss v Firth Brown Tools Ltd* (p439); *Milner v Hepworth Heating* (p561), but note the position is different where the claimant knows he has serious hearing loss, as in *Mackie v Secretary of State for Trade and Industry* (p539) and *McCoubrey v Ministry of Defence* (p548); for asbestos-related examples, see *Guidera v NEI Projects (India) Ltd* (p451), *Sir Robert Lloyd & Co Ltd v Hoey* (p652) and *Preston v BBH Solicitors* (p609)).

3   Attribution

Section 14(1)(b):

'that the injury was attributable in whole or in part to the act or omission which is alleged to constitute negligence, nuisance or breach of duty ...

... and knowledge that any acts or omissions did or did not as a matter of law, involve negligence, nuisance or breach of duty is irrelevant.'

Once a claimant knows that he has a significant injury, the court must next enquire as to whether the claimant knows that his injury was attributable to the acts or omissions of the defendant. Attribution here refers only to factual causation, as the clear wording of the statute stipulates that it is irrelevant whether the claimant knew he had a case in law. The proviso that knowledge of law was irrelevant was introduced by the 1975 Act, which finally laid to rest the ambiguity that was epitomised in the House of Lords speeches in *Central Asbestos Company Ltd v Dodd* [1973] AC 518.

Precisely what detail the claimant needs to know about the act or omission of the defendant was analysed by Slade LJ in *Wilkinson v Ancliff (BLT) Ltd* (p718). This case involved a tanker driver developing asthma due to the inhalation of chemicals he was transporting. Drawing on May LJ's judgment in *Davis v Ministry of Defence* (p405), the Court of Appeal held that in a case:

'... where the acts and omissions on the part of the defendants which are complained of are, in broad terms, their failure to take reasonably proper steps to protect him from such conditions, I think that the employee who has this broad knowledge may well have knowledge of the nature referred to in section 14(1)(b) sufficient to set time running against him, even though he may not yet have the knowledge sufficient to enable him or his legal advisers to draft a fully and comprehensively particularised statement of claim.' ([1986] 2 All ER 427 at 438)

The court further agreed with the proposition that attributable meant 'capable of being attributed'. This approach was reaffirmed in *Nash v Eli Lilly* (p568). Attribution was there interpreted as meaning knowing the essence of the case against the defendants rather than the specific particulars of negligence or breach of duty which could later be formulated:

'It was not in our judgment the intention of Parliament to require for the purposes of section 11 and section 14 of the Act proof of knowledge of the terms in which it will be alleged that the act or omission of the defendant constituted negligence for breach of duty. What is required is the essence of the act or omission to which the injury is attributable.' (Purchas LJ at 368)

In formulating this construction, the court drew upon the Court of Appeal's judgment in *Guidera v NEI Projects (India) Ltd* (p451), where it was determined that attribution meant a cause or connection which was possible not necessarily probable:

'The stark strength of the word "knowledge" does not stand alone. It is knowledge that attribution is merely possible, a real possibility not a fanciful one, a possible cause as opposed to a probable cause of the injury. It is that sense that I use the word throughout this judgment.' (Sir David Croom-Johnson)

In *Nash v Eli Lilly* (above) the Court of Appeal confirmed the trial judge's view that the attribution required in that case was knowledge that drugs had been provided which were unsafe because they could cause photosensitivity and further knowing that the defendants failed to disclose this so as to protect their patients.

Many cases concerning attribution involve clinical negligence actions. In some of these cases attribution is conventionally established when the claimant knows his injury, in relatively broad terms, as being caused by a clinical act or omission. For example, in *Dobbie v Medway Health Authority* (p411) a claimant had a mastectomy during surgery because the surgeon considered that he had found a pre-cancerous lump. Subsequent analysis of the tissue indicated that in fact the lump was benign. Otton J found that time ran against the claimant when she was informed about the laboratory analysis of the lump as, at that time, her injury was capable of being attributed to the defendant's fault. The Court of Appeal agreed with Otton J's decision but emphasised that there was no need for the claimant to have knowledge of fault. All the claimant needed to know was that the breast had been removed:

'She knew of this injury within hours, days or months of the operation and she at all times reasonably considered it to be significant. She knew from the beginning that the personal injury was capable of being attributed to, or more bluntly was the clear and direct result of, an act or omission of the Health Authority. What she did not appreciate until later was that the Health Authority's act or omission was (arguably) negligent or blameworthy.' (per Bingham LJ)

In more complex cases, the court may well require a greater degree of specificity which is frequently established by the report of a medico-legal expert.

In *Davis v City & Hackney Health Authority* (p403) a claimant who was suffering from cerebral palsy was held not to have been aware of the act alleged to have caused his condition until he received a medical report some 23 years after his birth. This report from an expert alleged that an injection of Ovametrin into his mother while she was pregnant was responsible for his condition. In *Doughty v North Staffordshire Health Authority* (p414) the claimant had 12 operations in attempts to remove a facial birthmark between 1957 and 1974. In 1974 she was told by her surgeon's successor that no improvement was possible and he had doubted whether such a prolonged course of surgery should in any event have been embarked upon. That information was held to provide the claimant with knowledge of attribution. In *Driscoll-Varley v Parkside Health Authority* (p416), following a careful review of *Davis v Ministry of Defence* (above) and *Wilkinson v Ancliff (BLT) Ltd* (above), Hidden J found that the claimant did not know of the attribution of her failed medical treatment concerning a leg fracture until she was told some 17 months later that a part of the dead bone was floating in her leg and causing her infection. Similarly, in *Hendy v Milton Keynes Health Authority* (p472), time was held to run against the claimant in terms of attribution when she was told nine months after her operation, in general terms, that her right ureter had been damaged.

In *Broadley v Guy Clapham & Co* (p345) the Court of Appeal reaffirmed that knowledge of attribution, even in clinical negligence actions, need only be in relatively broad or general terms. Knowledge of the detailed act or omissions such as would be necessary to draft particulars of negligence was not required. To contend otherwise would be to assert that knowledge of a cause of action in law was required. In *Broadley* the claimant underwent an operation in August 1980 to remove a foreign body from her knee. Unfortunately she developed a nerve palsy creating a left foot drop which was noted on 18 August 1980. In June 1983 she instructed solicitors and was seen by a surgeon in July who said the operation may have been performed negligently. The solicitors failed to prosecute a claim and on 17 August 1990 she issued proceedings against them. The defence alleged her claim against them was statute barred in that it occurred earlier than six years before she issued proceedings pursuant to s 5 of the 1980 Act. For that contention to be evaluated the court needed to investigate when the claimant's cause of action against her treating surgeon was statute barred. Her primary period of limitation against him would have expired in August 1983 unless a date of knowledge was later. The preliminary issue was to ascertain whether her date of knowledge was before or after 19 August 1981. If it was before, her claim against the solicitors would have accrued before 18 August 1984 and therefore over six years before she issued proceedings against them. The trial judge fixed the claimant with constructive knowledge of attribution before August 1981 on the basis that the foot drop had not got better as the surgeon said it would and it would have been reasonable for the claimant to ask her GP or the surgeon what had gone wrong. In fact she took no such steps until much later. The claimant contended in the Court of Appeal that her date of knowledge should be when she had knowledge of:

'some act or omission which could adversely affect the safety of the operation or proper recovery from the operation, such as unreasonable interference with the nerve or failure reasonably to safeguard it from damage, or failure properly to investigate and/or repair the nerve lesion in time.' (transcript, page 12A–B)

This submission followed a similar and successful submission by the claimant in *Bentley v Bristol & Western Health Authority* (p328) a case where a sciatic nerve was damaged in a hip replacement operation. The trial judge, Hirst J, accepted in *Bentley* that time would run only from when Mrs Bentley knew that there had been a failure to carry out the operation safely and specifically that her injury might be due to excessive traction of the nerve. The Court of Appeal, however, rejected such an analysis in *Broadley*, and held that *Bentley* was wrongly decided. To require knowledge of such detail was to require knowledge of all matters to establish negligence or breach of duty and was in contravention of the final words of s 14(1), which stated that knowledge that the acts or omissions constituted negligence or breach of duty was irrelevant. The broad knowledge that Mrs Bentley needed to acquire for the purposes of s 14 was held to be:

'That her injury had been caused by damage to the nerve resulting in something which Mr Lowy (the treating surgeon) had done or not done in the course of the operation.' (per Hoffmann LJ at 4B–G)

Attribution must, of course, relate even in general terms to the act or omission complained of (that is, it must be causally relevant). In *Ogunsanya v Lambeth Health Authority* (p590) the claimant was rendered paraplegic following a gallstone operation which resulted in extensive internal bleeding. The cause of the paraplegia was thought to be attributable to a low dose of subcutaneous heparin which caused the bleeding. It was not until a medical report from a neurologist, indicating that the paraplegia was due to a delay in treating the bleeding, that attribution was established. Similarly, in *Scuriaga v Powell* (p645), time was held not to run against the claimant in respect of a claim arising out of a failure to terminate a pregnancy, until she received a medical report indicating that it was a lack of care on the part of the surgeon which had caused the failure. The treating surgeon had in fact told the claimant that his failure to terminate the pregnancy was due to a structural defect in her which she believed until a medico-legal expert contradicted it. In *Khan v Ainslie* (p520) a claimant's blindness was thought by him to have been caused when his medical practitioner administered eye drops which caused him pain. Nearly six years later, he finally received a medical opinion indicating that the cause of his blindness was in fact delay in treating his condition of glaucoma. The receipt of this report was held to be the date of attribution and the claimant's date of knowledge.

In *Stephen v Riverside Health Authority* (p676), although a claimant suspected she was at an increased risk of cancer following an overdose of radiation, she was not fixed with actual knowledge until nearly eight years later when, in conference with her own counsel and her medical expert, she learned that the overdose might not have been in the order of only 34 roentgen, as claimed by the defendant, but could possibly have been in the order of hundreds or thousands of roentgen. This case was of added interest in that the claimant herself had some experience of radiology, having been an unqualified radiographer 24 years before her own x-rays. The judge found that that in itself was not sufficient to constitute making her an expert to set off against the chorus of negligent expert advice she had received until that stage concerning attribution.

In *Forbes v Wandsworth Health Authority* (p434) the Court of Appeal confirmed in clinical negligence cases that there must be knowledge of some causative link between the treatment or lack of it and the claimant's condition. Mr Forbes was operated on in 1982 for a bypass. The operation failed and a second operation was carried out the next day. That operation was unsuccessful and the claimant was told that he needed to have his leg amputated to prevent gangrene and this was done on 5 November 1982. Subsequently, the claimant obtained a report in 1992 which alleged that the medical practitioners had been negligent not to perform the second operation sooner. The defendant contended that all that was needed for attribution was knowledge that there was a period of time between the first and second operations, that the second operation was not successful and as a result the claimant had his leg amputated. The Court of Appeal found, however, that the claimant did not know that the loss of his leg was capable of being attributed to the actual omission of the defendant until the receipt of an opinion by a vascular surgeon. The court held that in many clinical negligence cases the claimant would not know that his injury was attributable to the act of the defendant until he also learned that there had been negligence. That, however, did not mean that there was no distinction between causation and negligence, the first being relevant to s 14 and the second irrelevant.

A similar approach was taken in the case of *Smith (Michael John) v West Lancashire Health Authority* (p657). Mr Smith injured his right hand on 12 November 1981 and attended hospital for emergency treatment where a diagnosis of an uncomplicated fracture to the ring finger was made. In January 1982, an operation was necessary as the conservative treatment had not worked. In 1989, Mr Smith was dismissed from his job as a labourer due to loss of function in the right hand. In 1991, an expert medical report said that there had been a failure in November 1981 to treat the finger properly which had resulted in degenerative changes that now meant loss of function in the hand. The Court of Appeal held that the claimant did not have the requisite knowledge on which to found his claim until 1991 because although he was aware that the first treatment had not worked that did not imbue him with the knowledge of an omission on the part of the treating physicians.

For other cases where knowledge of attribution has been postponed because it was unclear whether the persisting problems facing a claimant were extensions of a pre-existing condition or due to a medical mishap see *Hind v York Health Authority* (p476), *Jones v Liverpool Health Authority* (p500), *O'Driscoll v Dudley Health Authority* (p588), *Rowbottom v the Royal Masonic Hospital* (p632), *Skitt v Khan and Wakefield Health Authority* (p654) and *Smith v NHSLA* (p662).

Similar principles were adopted by the Court of Appeal in *Oakes v Hopcroft* (p585), a case of professional negligence concerning a medical expert's alleged incompetence which led to an under-settlement of a personal injury claim. The court were concerned with the provisions of s 14A of the Limitation Act 1980 but applied the principles derived from personal injury cases under s 14 and as also set out in *Hallam Eames v Merrett Syndicate* [1995] 7 Med LR 122. In *Hallam Eames* Hoffmann LJ had emphasised the need for the causal relevance of the act or omission:

> '... If all that was necessary was that a plaintiff should have known that the damage was attributable to an act or omission of the defendant, the statute would have said so. Instead, it speaks for the damage being attributable to "the act or omission which is alleged to constitute negligence". In other words, the act or omission of which the plaintiff must have knowledge must be that which is causatively relevant for the purposes of an allegation of negligence.'
> (pp 125–6)

In *Haward v Fawcetts* (p469) the House of Lords, in a professional negligence action against an accountant, approved *Hallam Eames*.

In *Oakes v Hopcroft* (p585), Clarke LJ considered in detail *Hallam Eames v Merrett Syndicates* [1995] 7 Med LR 122, *Broadley v Guy Clapham* (p345) and *Dobbie v Medway Health Authority* (p411) and concluded:

'52 ... If one asks what is it that the claimant is essentially complaining about, it is that the defendant failed to diagnose her condition correctly and to advise her that the accident had caused a severe traction injury to the brachial plexus and damage to the radial artery and that her condition would not improve. It was only when she knew both what injuries had been caused by the accident and, importantly, that they would not improve so that she would not (as it were) get better, that, to my mind, it can fairly be held that she knew that the omission of the defendant to give her that advice caused her damage. The damage was the loss she sustained because she settled for too little. The claimant could not know that she had settled for too little as a result of any failure on the part of the defendant until she knew that she would not get better because it was that fact, namely that her condition would not improve, which essentially caused the settlement to be too low. That is because the essential reason that the settlement is said to have been too low is that it did not include anything to compensate her for not being able to work in future as a result of the accident.'

In *Spargo v North Essex District Health Authority* (p667) the Court of Appeal took the opportunity to review some of the leading authorities in an area of law which is described 'already grossly overloaded with reported cases'. The Court of Appeal drew the following principles:

'(1) The knowledge required to satisfy s 14(1)(b) is a broad knowledge of the essence of the causally relevant act or omission to which the injury is attributable;

(2) "Attributable" in this context means "capable of being attributed to", in the sense of being a real possibility;

(3) A plaintiff has the requisite knowledge when she knows enough to make it reasonable for her to begin to investigate whether or not she has a case against the defendant. Another way of putting this is to say that she will have such knowledge if she so firmly believes that her condition is capable of being attributed to an act or omission which she can identify (in broad terms) that she goes to a solicitor to seek advice about making a claim for compensation;

(4) On the other hand she will not have the requisite knowledge if she thinks she knows the act or omission she should investigate but in fact is barking up the wrong tree: or if her knowledge of what the defendant did or did not do is so vague or general that she cannot fairly be expected to know what she should investigate; or if her state of mind is such that she thinks her condition is capable of being attributed to the act or omission alleged to constitute negligence, but she is not sure about this, and would need to check with an expert before she could be properly said to know that it was.'

In *Sniezek v Bundy* (p664) the court, in considering the question of significance, discussed the difficulties which can arise concerning the last sub-category of point 4 in *Spargo* (namely, knowledge that required expert confirmation). The court doubted whether the decision in *Ali v Courtauld* (p301) had been correct in this respect (this issue is further discussed above under 1: Actual knowledge). (See also *Farraj and Farraj v Kings Healthcare NHS Trust* (p427).)

In *Haward v Fawcetts* (p469) the House of Lords was concerned with a professional negligence action and accordingly s 14A of the Limitation Act rather than s 14. However the House indicated that the observations on s 14A applied also to s 14 and approved *Broadley, Spargo* and *Nash* on attribution.

This case law was revisited in the 'atomic veterans' action by the Supreme Court (*B v Ministry of Defence* (p312)), the facts of which are set out in the discussion above under 1: Actual knowledge. Lord Walker's analysis treated the issue of attributability as the 'what' question (namely, what a claimant has to know to start time running) and, after considering the issue before the 1980 Act, stated:

'30. The new legislation also has produced difficult problems for the courts. They can be roughly grouped under two general heads. First, what is it that the claimant has to know at the date of knowledge ("the what? question"). Secondly, how must the claimant know what he has to know – that is, what state of mind, assessed subjectively or objectively or by a mixture of the two, amounts to knowledge for this purpose ("the how? question"). The what? question depends on the interpretation and application of section 14(1) of the 1980 Act, and in particular (since it gives rise to most of the problems) section 14(1)(b), which relates to the fact "that the injury was attributable in whole or in part to the act or omission which is alleged to constitute negligence, nuisance or breach of duty". The how? question depends partly on the interpretation and application of section 14(3) of the 1980 Act …

31. Almost all of the many authorities cited to the Court in this appeal are concerned with one or both of these questions. My perception is that the case law has made more progress in clarification of the what? question than of the how? question. That may be because in some of the leading cases the House of Lords or the Court of Appeal has been able to reach a conclusion on actual knowledge and has not found it necessary to consider constructive knowledge. For instance in *Haward v Fawcetts* [2006] 1 WLR 682 the defendants (a firm of accountants) relied only on the actual knowledge of the claimant, and the House of Lords found that his actual knowledge of the financial state of the business in which he had invested was sufficient to make it reasonable for him to consider whether his accountants' advice had been flawed. The case was concerned with section 14A of the 1980 Act, added by the Latent Damage Act 1986, but the same principles apply. So the difficulties of constructive knowledge do not feature in Lord Nicholls' admirably brief statement of the relevant principles at paras 7 to 15.

32. In *Spargo v North Essex District Health Authority* [1997] PIQR P235, P242 Brooke LJ referred to this branch of the law being already "grossly over-loaded with reported cases". That was fifteen years ago, and the overload has increased. But this appeal requires the Court, in the context of heavy group litigation, to grapple with some unresolved difficulties. In view of the differences of opinion in the Court I wish, while conscious of adding to the overload, to set out my reasons in my own words. I start with some observations on the what? question and then address the how? question.

The what? question

33. The case law on the concept of "attributable" has developed in a coherent way. It is not without its difficulties, especially in cases involving specialised and technical areas of expertise (discussed by Lord Mance in *Haward v Fawcetts* [2006] 1 WLR 682 at paras 114 to 121). But on the whole the case law is consistent and provides a workable test.

34.   In *Smith v Central Asbestos Co Ltd* [1973] AC 518, 543 Lord Pearson quoted the Oxford English Dictionary definition of "attributable" ("capable of being attributed or ascribed, especially as owing to, produced by") and stated that "attributable" refers to causation. This view has been consistently followed in later authorities on the legislation in its present form. In *Haward v Fawcetts* [2006] 1 WLR 682, para 45, Lord Scott quoted a passage from the judgment of Hoffmann LJ in *Hallam Eames v Merrett Syndicates Ltd* [2001] Lloyd's Rep PN 178, 181, which conveniently sets out some of the most important cases:

> "In other words, the act or omission of which the plaintiff must have knowledge must be that which is causally relevant for the purposes of an allegation of negligence ... It is this idea of causal relevance which various judges of this court have tried to express by saying the plaintiff must know the 'essence of the act or omission to which the injury is attributable' (Purchas LJ in *Nash v Eli Lilly & Co* [1993] 1 WLR 782, 799) or 'the essential thrust of the case' (Sir Thomas Bingham MR in *Dobbie v Medway Health Authority* [1994] 1 WLR 1234, 1238) or that 'one should look at the way the plaintiff puts his case, distil what he is complaining about and ask whether he had in broad terms knowledge of the facts on which that complaint is based' (Hoffmann LJ in *Broadley v Guy Clapham & Co* [1993] 4 Med LR 328, 332)."

35.   In this context, therefore, "attributable" has been interpreted by the courts as directed to a real possibility of a causal link: Lord Nicholls in *Haward v Fawcetts* at para 11, citing *Nash v Eli Lilly & Co* at pp 797–798. In that case Purchas LJ (who gave the judgment of the Court) quoted with approval some observations of Hidden J in his second judgment on the preliminary issue:

> "The stark strength of the word 'knowledge' does not stand alone. It is knowledge that attribution is merely possible, a real possibility and not a fanciful one, a possible cause as opposed to a probable cause of the injury."

36.   At this point the what? question and the how? question come into close proximity, since confident knowledge that there may be some causal link between two events is not dissimilar from a less confident belief that there is indeed a causal link between them. So the way in which "attributable" has been interpreted in the case law eases the Court's task in deciding whether "knowledge" includes more or less firmly held belief. But it does not remove all the difficulties, as this appeal shows.

37.   *Broadley v Guy Clapham & Co* [1994] 4 All ER 439 was an unusual case because it involved a double limitation point. Mrs Broadley had a complaint against a surgeon who had operated on her in August 1980, but she did not consult a solicitor (the defendant) until June 1983. The solicitor arranged for her to see a specialist in July 1983, who gave a favourable oral opinion. But for some unexplained reason nothing was done to pursue the claim and in August 1990, having taken other legal advice, Mrs Broadley sued the solicitor whom she had consulted in 1983. He pleaded that the claim against him was statute barred, because (as he contended) her claim against the surgeon became statute barred in August 1983, and so that was when any cause of action against him arose. So there was an issue as to whether the standard three-year period applied to her original claim against the surgeon, or was to be treated as extended under sections 11 and 14 of the 1980 Act.

38.   In his judgment Hoffmann LJ used a colloquial expression, "barking up the wrong tree", which has been repeated in some later cases. He said ([1994] 4 All ER 439, 449):

> "Ordinarily it will suffice that he knows that the injury was caused by an act or omission of the defendant. But there may be cases in which his knowledge of what the defendant did or did not do is so vague and general that he cannot fairly be expected to know what he should investigate. He will also not have reached the starting point if, in an unusual case like *Driscoll-Varley v Parkside Health Authority,* he thinks he knows the acts and omissions he should investigate but in fact he is barking up the wrong tree."

Driscoll-Varley v Parkside Health Authority [1991] 2 Med LR 346 is mentioned a little earlier in the judgment. It was a case in which the plaintiff thought that an injury to her leg had been caused by a surgeon's negligence, but later discovered that the real cause was not the operation but the removal of the leg from traction during subsequent treatment. It seems a rather marginal example of barking up the wrong tree, since the plaintiff's misapprehension was in relation to the causative event in a single course of treatment, although the real complaint was about the after-care rather than the operation itself.

39.   The point is relevant in this appeal because Mr Dingemans QC put in the forefront of his case the submission that those of his clients who thought they had been exposed to ionising radiation were barking up the wrong tree, because they were focusing on "prompt" (gamma ray) radiation. Foskett J was inclined to accept that submission (para 515, in the course of the discussion of his "preferred view"). The Court of Appeal (para 86) rejected this, having observed in the previous paragraph that the claimants' contention on this point demonstrated a fundamental misunderstanding of the concept of knowledge for limitation purposes.'

Accordingly, the majority in *B v Ministry of Defence* have broadly endorsed the previous case law on attribution. Lord Walker concluded with some further reflection:

> '68.   Our judgments on this appeal will not, I fear, be an ideal source of guidance to lower courts which regularly have to deal with these difficult problems. There are two reasons for that: the extreme complexity of this group litigation, and the division of opinion in the Court. For my part I would suggest that short summaries like that of Brooke LJ in *Spargo* (which Lord Phillips rightly describes as a "valiant attempt") may be unhelpful if treated as if they were statutory texts. The words of the 1980 Act themselves must be the starting-point, illuminated where necessary by judicial exposition, of which the opinion of Lord Nicholls in *Haward v Fawcetts* [2006] 1 WLR 682, paras 8 to 15, is the most authoritative. To that guidance I would tentatively add two points. In a complex case section 14(3) is an essential part of the statutory scheme, not an occasional add-on. And the date of a claimant's first visit to a solicitor is (without more) of very little significance in most cases.'

ATTRIBUTION: SUMMARY

In summary, attribution will be established when the essence of the case against the defendant is known by a claimant, so that the act or omission complained of is possibly capable of being attributed to the defendant in broad terms rather than with the degree of precision which a pleaded particulars of claim would require; in short, where there is a real possibility of a causal link. In some circumstances often arising out of acts and omissions in clinical negligence cases, attribution may be postponed until a causal connection between the injury and the act or omission said to constitute negligence is established. This is not the same as knowledge of fault, which is not required, but in practice it can be, because knowledge of cause and knowledge of fault may be simultaneous. In such cases, attribution may be delayed until an expert opinion establishes a causal connection between the injury and the act or omission. Difficulties may arise in determining whether, in any particular case, the certainty of the belief of attribution is sufficient to start the running of time or whether a belief remains uncertain until expert confirmation.

4 Identity

Section 14(1):

'(c)   the identity of the defendants; and

(d)   if it is alleged the act or admission was that of a person other than a defendant, the identity of that person and the additional facts supporting the bringing of an action against the defendant.'

The final fact the claimant must know, after significance and attribution are established, is the identity of the defendant who may be personally liable (s 14(1)(c)) or vicariously liable (s 14(1)(d)). These provisions have not generated any complex problem of construction and remain relatively straightforward. The subsections are designed to deal with cases where it may be difficult to ascertain immediately who was responsible for the injury, such as in a road traffic accident where a driver fails to stop. In other cases, particularly accidents on construction sites, there may be a complex division of labour and division of responsibility, making it initially difficult for a claimant to identify who in the chain of contractors was responsible for the particular act of negligence or breach of statutory duty which led to his injury. Often in such cases there will be an averment in the defence that the defendants sued are not responsible for the particular act complained of, which was caused by another named party.

For example, in *Davies v Reed Stock & Company Ltd* (p401) a claimant sued his employers when he tripped on a step leading to his office. The employers initially admitted in their defence that they were occupiers of the premises but subsequently by an amendment alleged that Lovell Shipping & Transport Group Ltd were the landlords and occupiers responsible for the steps. The claimant accordingly sought to add Lovell outside the primary limitation period and the Court of Appeal held that time did not run against the claimant in respect of a cause of action against Lovell until they were implicated by the employers in the amended defence (see also *Fowell v National Coal Board* (p437) and *Ryan v Carr and Marples Ridgeway & Partners* Ltd (p634)).

In *Foster v Mall Builders Ltd* (p436) a claimant was injured in July 1978 when he stepped on rubble left by contractors in a house where he was working and which was then owned by Hammersmith Borough Council. His solicitors were told by the council that the contractors responsible were Contract Services Ltd who were subsequently sued. Contract Services Ltd said in turn that they were not involved but the property had been purchased by the Notting Hill Housing Trust who indicated that the contractors at fault were Mall Builders Ltd. A fresh writ was issued outside the primary limitation period and the trial judge held that the actual identity of the defendants was not known until September 1981. In addition the judge did not fix the claimant with an earlier constructive date of knowledge (see below).

In *Leadbitter v Hodge Finance Ltd* (p529) a claimant was injured in a road traffic accident in September 1976 which caused him post-traumatic amnesia. He sued the suppliers and manufacturers of his motor vehicle and also the hire purchase company through which he was purchasing the vehicle, all within the primary limitation period, on the understanding that there was a defect in the vehicle which caused the accident. Subsequently he sought to join, outside the primary limitation period, a fourth defendant in the form of the Highway Authority which was allegedly responsible for a large pool of water that caused flooding on the road. The fact of this flooding was recorded in a police report which the claimant did not receive until October 1979. By August 1980 the claimant had established the fourth defendants who were responsible for the flooding. The judge held that the actual date of identity was August 1980 but fixed the claimant with an earlier constructive date of knowledge being the time when the police report should reasonably have been obtained namely the end of July 1979. That earlier date still meant that proceedings had been brought in time. A similar decision was reached in *Copeland v Smith and Goodwin* (p387). However, in *Henderson v Temple Pier Co Ltd* (p471) a claimant was fixed with a date of constructive knowledge of the identity of the owner of a ship upon which she slipped outside the three-year period, as her solicitors could reasonably have ascertained the owner's name within the limitation period.

Ascertaining the precise legal identity of a defendant may be difficult where a complex corporate structure exists with connected companies with similar names. In *Simpson v Norwest Holst Southern Ltd* (p648) a claimant carpenter hurt his leg at work and notified the claim to Norwest Holst Ltd who he believed were his employers. The claimant's pay slips indicated 'Norwest Holst' as the employers and his contract of employment was with 'Norwest Holst Group'. The defendant's replied through their insurers, after the claim had been made, with a heading indicating that the defendants were Norwest Construction Company Ltd. The correct name of Norwest Holst Southern Ltd was not confirmed by the insurers until shortly before the expiry of the primary limitation period and proceedings were not started until shortly after the expiry of the primary limitation period on 17 August 1979. The Court of Appeal had no difficulty in finding that the claimant did not know the identity of his employers before 17 August 1976 because they had effectively hidden behind the rubric 'Norwest Holst Group' and, accordingly, his action was not statute barred. For an earlier decision under the 1963 Act, see *Re Clark v Forbes Stuart (Thames Street) Ltd* (p375).

In *Cressey v E Timm & Son Ltd and E Timm & Son Holdings Ltd* (p391), the Court of Appeal affirmed *Simpson v Norwest Holst Southern Ltd*. The claimant had worked as a fork-lift truck driver for the second defendant but his pay slips were in the name of an associated company, the first defendants, whom he believed he was employed by. The claimant was injured on 2 December 2000 and sued the first defendant on 27 November 2003 within time. The claim form was not, however, served in time and a second claim form against both companies was issued on 30 March 2004. The second defendants only sought to strike out the claim. The court confirmed the first instance decision that the claimant did not know, within the three-year period prior to 30 March 2004, who the identity of his employers were, the earliest possible date being 30 April 2000 when the solicitors learnt of the existence of the second defendant:

'28. On the particular facts of this case, I do not think that the right answer is hard to reach. It is likely that in most cases in an accident at work, the employee will there and then have knowledge of the identity of his employer, and therefore of the defendant. However, in a minority of cases, where the identity of the employer is uncertain, as in *Simpson*, or even wrongly stated to the employee, as here, the date of knowledge may well be postponed. How long it will be postponed by will depend on the facts of such cases. In general I do not believe that it can be postponed for long: only as long as it reasonably takes to make and complete the appropriate enquiries. But if such enquiries are met by misinformation, or a dilatory response, again as in *Simpson*, then it is not possible to be dogmatic about the right conclusion. In *Simpson*, the court only had to cover a period of about two weeks after the accident and therefore did not have to go further into the facts.

29. In the present case, I agree with the submission that the facts are in their way stronger than in *Simpson*.' (per Rix LJ)

Where a number of connected defendants are sued simultaneously and others, also connected, are sought to be added later, dicta in *Nash and others v Eli Lilly and others* (p568) by the Court of Appeal indicate that the court might well fix a claimant with constructive knowledge in respect of the additional defendants on the basis that all identities within a group structure should be reasonably ascertainable:

'It is also a clear requirement of section 14(1)(c) that the plaintiff must have knowledge of the identity of the defendant. However, in a case of corporate entity, such as those with which these appeals concern, the law applicable to the operation of such corporations may be expected to provide, and do provide, that the true position of the individual members of the corporate structure are ascertainable. These details as facts would therefore fall within section 14(3)(c).'

Conversely, in an action against drug manufacturers where more than one unconnected company has produced a drug, it may be very difficult to ascertain precisely which manufacturer was responsible for the actual drug ingested by any particular claimant. For an illustration of the difficulties facing claimants seeking to sue in respect of a synthetic hormone which was manufactured by many defendants during the period 1947 to 1971, see Redmond-Cooper, 'Product Liability – Problems of the Unknown Defendant', (1986) Sol Jo 621.

Section 14(1)(d) is principally designed to meet a case where a claimant learns later that the person who committed the tort or breach of duty was also acting in the course of his employment or acting as an agent for a principal. As a matter of law, such a relationship will provide the claimant with a separate cause of action against the employer or principal because of the doctrine of vicarious liability. The claimant's knowledge of those legal principles is irrelevant but knowledge of the facts which would give rise to such a legal relationship is directly pertinent. A good illustration of this principle is found in *Stevens v Nash Dredging & Reclamation Co Ltd* (p676). This case involved a claimant who was working in Swedish waters as a grease-man on a tug directly employed by the defendants. He was severely injured on 16 July 1975 due to the act or the omission of his captain whilst manoeuvring an anchor and a buoy. Insurers for the defendants indicated in 1976 that the captain was employed by the defendants' Dutch parent company. It was not until March 1979 that Dutch lawyers acting for that Company told the claimant's solicitors that in fact the captain was seconded to the defendants. That fact set up an arguable case on vicarious liability for which the claimant issued proceedings on 31 July 1980.

Leonard J held that although the claimant had always known of the identity of the defendants, he did not learn of the 'additional facts supporting the bringing of an action against the defendant' until March 1979, namely when the employment status of the captain was ascertained and accordingly his claim was not statute barred.

5　Constructive knowledge

Section 14(3):

'For the purpose of this section a person's knowledge includes knowledge which he might reasonably have been expected to acquire–

(a)　from facts observable or ascertainable by him; or

(b)　from facts ascertainable by him with the help of medical or other appropriate expert advice which it is reasonable for him to seek;

but a person shall not be fixed under this sub-section with knowledge of a fact ascertainable only with the help of expert advice so long as he has taken all reasonable steps to obtain (and, where appropriate, to act on) that advice.'

This sub-section affords a good deal of protection to prospective defendants. A claimant cannot simply close his mind and wilfully or even unintentionally ignore the commonsense reality of his position. The claimant must act reasonably in using information he has or could ascertain to establish knowledge of the significance of his injury, attribution to the act or admission by the defendants and the identity of the defendant. It is, accordingly, extremely important to emphasise that at each step in considering significance, attribution or identity, the court will first ask the question 'What did the claimant actually know?', and then, if necessary, 'What should the claimant have reasonably known?'. Only if both his actual and his constructive knowledge, as fixed by the court, are within the three-year period prior to the issue of proceedings, will his action not be time barred. The subsection, therefore, requires that the claimant is both mentally active in comprehending the facts of his accident and injury and also physically active in obtaining expert and other advice and opinions. It is for the claimant to establish that his actual date of knowledge is within time but, if a defendant contends for an earlier constructive date of knowledge, the evidential burden *may* shift to the defendant to establish that fact (see **Chapter 2** and *Crocker v British Coal Corporation* (p392), *Smith v NHSLA* (p662), *KR v Bryn Alyn Community Holdings Ltd* (p505) and Lord Walker at para 48 of *B v Ministry of Defence* (p312)).

5.1　SECTION 14(3)

'… which he might reasonably have been expected to acquire …'

If construing what is reasonable, the courts initially adopted the same approach used in construing whether a claimant reasonably felt his injury was significant. This was to qualify the objective criteria of reasonableness with the particular qualities of the actual claimant:

'The standard of reasonableness in connection with the observations and/or the effort to ascertain are therefore finally objective but must be qualified to take into consideration the position and circumstances and character of the plaintiff. Turning to subsection (3)(b), this subsection deals with facts ascertainable with the help of advice from outside expert sources which, in the circumstances of the case, it is reasonable for the plaintiff to seek ... In considering whether or not the inquiry is, or is not, reasonable, the situation, character and intelligence of the plaintiff must be relevant.' (*Nash v Eli Lilly* at 399C–E)

(See also the judgment of Widgery J in *Newton v Cammell Laird & Co Ltd* [1969] 1 WLR 415 and the House of Lords' decision in *Smith v Central Asbestos Co Ltd* [1973] AC 518 per Lord Reid at 530.)

This approach is illustrated in *Davis v City & Hackney Health Authority* (p403), where a claimant suffering from cerebral palsy had an actual date of knowledge of attribution determined on the receipt of a medico-legal report nearly 23 years after his birth and approximately two years outside the primary limitation period. Jowitt J had to consider whether that actual date of knowledge ought to be replaced with a constructive date of knowledge based upon the claimant's failure to take legal advice earlier than he did. The judge held that taking into account the claimant's age, his disability and his dependence upon his parents, who discouraged him from making a claim, that the claimant had not acted unreasonably in delaying. Similarly, in a case concerning constructive knowledge of the identity of a defendant, Beldam LJ held in *Foster v Mall Builders Ltd* (p436) that it was reasonable for a young claimant to delay in making inquiries as to who it was who had left rubble over which he tripped during his course of his employment. The claimant had a natural optimism that his injury would clear up, he never in fact returned to the site of the injury and had gone on to engage in studies. In a case concerning constructive knowledge of attribution, *Atkinson v Oxfordshire Health Authority* (p308), a claimant who suffered from deafness, double vision and difficulty in balance sued 22 years after an operation which was said to be unnecessary and/or improperly performed. In the interim years the claimant and his mother had instructed four sets of solicitors and had received much negative legal advice. The judge found that the claimant, given his difficulties and disabilities, should not be fixed with an earlier constructive date of knowledge. See also *Hall v Eli Lilly* [1992] 3 Med LR 233 and *Cockburn v Eli Lilly* (p378).

However in *Forbes v Wandsworth Health Authority* (p434), the Court of Appeal emphasised the primarily objective nature of the test to be applied in s 14(3). Mr Forbes received surgery in 1982 for a heart bypass operation which was unsuccessful so a second operation was carried out the next day. That operation was also unsuccessful and the claimant's leg had to be amputated. He later received in October 1992 a medical opinion alleging negligence against the clinical practitioner for not performing the second operation sooner than it was. Proceedings were issued on 10 December 1992. Part of the delay was due to the implicit trust the claimant had in his surgeon. The judge said that the claimant's claim was not statute barred as he had neither actual nor constructive knowledge until 1992. The Court of Appeal agreed with the judge on actual knowledge, as the claimant did not know until he was told by a vascular surgeon that the loss of his leg was capable of being attributed to an act or admission of the defendant. However, the Court of Appeal (Roch LJ dissenting) fixed him with constructive knowledge, saying that it was reasonable to allow the claimant 12 to 18 months to get over the shock of the amputation, take stock of his situation and then take advice. The court therefore considered that the claimant had constructive knowledge in 1994. The court went on to express the view that the claimant's individual characteristics were not relevant to s 14(3) and doubted *Nash v Eli Lilly* on this point (Roch LJ dissenting, holding that *Nash* was binding). Stuart-Smith LJ considered the passage from Purchas LJ in *Nash v Eli Lilly* (quoted above), but said this:

'... I have difficulty in seeing how the individual character and intelligence of the plaintiff can be relevant in an objective test ... It does not seem to me that the fact that the plaintiff is more trusting, incurious or indolent resigned or uncomplaining by nature can be a relevant characteristic, since this too undermines any objective approach.' (pp 19/20)

Lord Justice Evans agreed, stating that the claimant's situation is relevant but not his character and intelligence. *Forbes* was followed in *Parry v Clwyd Health Authority* (p596). However, difficulties of having two conflicting Court of Appeal decisions soon arose. In *Smith v Leicester Health Authority* (p659) the Court of Appeal considered the conflicting decisions in *Nash* and *Forbes* and felt free to decide which to follow. They opted for the objective *Forbes* approach:

'We are prepared to accept, for the purposes of this appeal, that the proper approach to this question is "What would the reasonable man have done, placed in the situation of the plaintiff?" and that the answer in each case must depend on its own facts ... We accept that the plaintiff's individual characteristics which might distinguish her from the reasonable woman should be disregarded. Thus her fortitude, her lack of any bitterness at becoming a tetraplegic and the determination and devotion she has shown to making herself as independent and a useful member of her family and society as she can, which has surpassed what might be expected, are to be put on one side.'

The court in *Smith* did, however, state that *Forbes* was not authority for the proposition that, when a patient is severely disabled following an operation, they have 12 to 18 months to decide whether to investigate the claim. The court reversed the trial judge on constructive knowledge and found that the claim was not statute barred and in any event would have exercised a s 33 discretion in her favour. But, on the issue of whether it is reasonable for a claimant to seek advice, the court was of the view that it would depend on the facts and circumstances in each case, excluding the character traits of the individual claimant.

However, in *Ali v Courtaulds Textiles Ltd* (p301) a differently constituted Court of Appeal relied on *Nash v Eli Lilly* to find that:

'The temporal and circumstantial span of reasonable enquiry will depend on the factual context of the case and subjective characteristics of the individual (claimant) involved.'

In *Fenech v East London Health Authority* (p429) the claimant had experience of severe perineal pain following the birth of her child in 1960. This pain continued and was apparent after sexual intercourse, but she did not mention that fact to her male GP due to embarrassment. Investigation of her hips eventually found a needle fragment in the perineum in 1991 and she was told about this in 1994. She issued proceedings on 24 January 1997. The court fixed the claimant with constructive knowledge by the early 1960s. Lord Justice Simon Brown said:

'For my part I think it unnecessary on the present appeal to attempt any final reconciliation of the authorities or solution of the difficulties presented by the section. It is sufficient to recognise that some degree of objectivity at least must be required in determining when it is reasonable for someone to seek advice – otherwise the proviso could never apply save only when a person acts out of character – and to conclude, as I do, that on any sort of objective approach ... this claimant should have sought medical advice on her injury long before she did, indeed in the early 1960s at latest.'

(See also *O'Driscoll v Dudley Health Authority* (p588).)

In *Bates v Leicester Health Authority* (p324), Dyson J, after reviewing the disparity between *Nash* and *Forbes*, approached the question of constructive knowledge:

> '... by asking what knowledge it was reasonable to expect to be acquired by a plaintiff of average intelligence and without unusual personal characteristics. The personal characteristics which I believe the Court of Appeal in *Forbes* were saying should be left out of account were personality traits such as those mentioned at the end of the passage that I quoted from the judgment of Stuart-Smith LJ (trusting, incurious, indolent, resigned and complaining). I do not think that the Court of Appeal was saying that in applying the objective test, one should ignore the fact that as in the present case, a plaintiff has great difficulty of communication, and that the potential source of knowledge is a parent who is trusted and is heavily relied upon by the plaintiff in all the important areas of her life. As Evans LJ said, (in *Forbes*): "The reasonable man must be placed in the situation that the plaintiff was".'

The conflict between the authorities received the House of Lords' attention in *Adams v Bracknell Forest Borough Council* (p292) which determined that *Forbes* should be preferred over *Nash* and that the test was objective. Mr Adams suffered from severe dyslexia and sued an education authority for negligent failure to ameliorate his condition whilst at school between 1977 and 1988. He issued proceedings in 2002, after having spoken to an educational psychologist at a social event in 1999. At first instance the judge found he did not have constructive knowledge and the Court of Appeal refused the defendant's appeal. The House of Lords found that there was no evidence in Mr Adams' case to support the judge's finding that the claimant, because of his dyslexia, could not reveal his problems to his doctor. Neither was it established that extreme reticence about the problem of dyslexia was standard behaviour for dyslexics. The claimant was found to be of normal intelligence and there was no reason why the normal expectation, that a person suffering from a significant injury should not be curious about its origins, should not apply to dyslexics. Constructive knowledge was fixed well before the three-year period before proceedings were started.

The route which led Lord Hoffmann to his decision was partially based on policy and the recognition that the court did have a discretionary power to extend the primary limitation period. Lord Hoffmann reviewed the subjective element in the test, as set out in *Newton v Cammell Laird & Co Ltd* (p581) and *Smith v Central Asbestos Co Ltd* (p658), but preferred the reasoning of the Court of Appeal in *Forbes*:

> '45. I find this reasoning persuasive. The Court of Appeal did not refer to the decisions of the 1963 Act which had taken a more subjective view. While it is true that the language of section 7(5) of the 1963 Act was not materially different from that of section 14(3) of the 1980 Act, I think that the Court of Appeal in *Forbes* was right in saying that the introduction of the discretion under section 33 had altered the balance. As I said earlier, the assumptions which one makes about the hypothetical person to whom a standard of reasonableness is applied will be very much affected by the policy of the law in applying such a standard. Since the 1975 Act, the postponement of the commencement of the limitation period by reference to the date of knowledge is no longer the sole mechanism for avoiding injustice to a plaintiff who could not reasonably be expected to have known that he had a cause of action. It is, therefore possible to interpret section 14(3) with a greater regard to the potential injustice to defendants if the limitation period should be indefinitely extended.

46. I, therefore, think that Lord Reid's dictum in *Smith v Central Asbestos Co Ltd* [1973] AC 518, 530 that the "test is subjective" is not a correct interpretation of section 14(3). The same is true of the dictum of Purchas LJ and *Nash v Eli Lilly & Co* [1993] 1 WLR 782, 799 …

47. It is true that the plaintiff must be assumed to be a person who has suffered the injury in question not some other person. But, like Roch LJ in *Forbes* [1997] QB 402, 425 I do not see how his particular character or intelligence can be relevant. In my opinion, section 14(3) requires one to assume that a person who is aware that he has suffered a personal injury, serious enough to be something about which he would go and see a solicitor if he knew he had a claim, will be sufficiently curious about the causes of the injury to seek whatever expert advice is appropriate.'

However, Baroness Hale, although concurring with the decision, took 'a slightly different view' and emphasised that she would not want to rule out that a claimant's personal characteristics may be relevant to what knowledge can be imputed to him under s 14(3). Baroness Hale reviewed the leading authorities and the Law Commission Report 151 and expressed the opinion that:

'88. I wonder, therefore, how much difference there is in practice between the two approaches. We are not here concerned with knowledge that the claimant might reasonably have been expected to acquire from facts observable or ascertainable by him. We are concerned with knowledge that he might reasonably be expected to acquire with the help of medical or other advice which it is reasonable for him to seek. The question is when is it reasonable to expect a potential claimant to seek such advice? Objectively, it will be reasonable to seek such advice when he has good reason to do so. This will depend upon the situation which the claimant finds himself, which includes the consequences of the accident, illness or other injury which he has suffered. Rarely, if ever, will it depend upon his personal characteristics. If, faced with the situation which is reasonable to seek advice, a person fails to do so, then the fact that he was reluctant to make a fuss, or embarrassed to talk to his doctor, while understandable, does not take him outside this subsection.

89. Mr Forbes was faced with the amputation of his leg after an unsuccessful bypass operation. This was clearly a significant and unexpected injury connected with the medical treatment he had been receiving. It is not clear why he took no further action at the time, although in the end he did so reluctantly later. But it was reasonable to expect him to seek a second opinion then and there. Mrs Fenech was faced with years of pain after giving birth to her first child, when she was told that the needle used to stitch up an episiotomy had broken. She was embarrassed to talk about these matters, even to her doctor. But of course it was reasonable to expect her to do so. In contrast, Miss Smith underwent numerous operations during her childhood because of her spina bifida, one of which resulted in her becoming tetraplegic. There was no reason for her to think that this was anything other than a consequence of her disability (another example is *Mellors v Perry* [2003] EWCA Civ 89, where the claimant had endured a childhood of renal problems with three kidney transplants but had no reason to think that this was anything other than a consequence of her congenital disability) …

91. In my view, all the cases to which we have been referred are explicable on the basis that the law expects people to make such enquiries or seek such

professional advice as they reasonably can when they have good reason to do so. Their motive for not doing so will generally be irrelevant. But I would not want to rule out that their personal characteristics may be relevant to what knowledge can be imputed to them under section 14(3). There is a distinction between those personal characteristics which affect the ability to acquire information and those which affect one's reaction to what one does know. A blind man cannot be expected to observe things around him, but he may sometimes be expected to ask questions. It will all depend upon the circumstances in which he finds himself. As McGee & Scanlan have suggested, in an attempt to reconcile the authorities, a factor or attribute which is connected with the ability of the claimant to discover facts which are relevant to an action, should be taken into account: but a factor in his make-up which has no discernible effect upon his ability to discover relevant facts should be disregarded: see "Constructive knowledge within the Limitation Act" (2003) 22 Civil Justice Quarterly 248, at 260. They go on to suggest that qualifications, training and experience may have such an affect whilst intelligence may not. It will all depend upon the facts of the case.'

Lord Walker also expressed caution about any simple formula put forward to cover every case that might occur (see paras 76–78)

The House of Lords in *A v Hoare* (p287) extended the objective nature of s 14 by also applying an impersonal test to the concept of significance. Lord Hoffmann drew a difference between the two sub-sections, however, and echoed Lady Hale's qualification in *Adams*:

'38.   The Court of Appeal said that there was some "tension" between the *Bryn Alyn* test and the recent decision of the House of Lords in *Adams v Bracknell Forest Borough Council* [2005] 1 AC 76. I suppose that this is true in the sense that the House in *Adams* said that one had to take words like "reasonable" and "reasonably" seriously and the *Bryn Alyn* test does not. But *Adams* was dealing with section 14(3), which is very different in its purpose from section 14(2). The test for imputing knowledge in section 14(3) is by reference to what the claimant ought reasonably to have *done*. It asks whether he ought reasonably to have acquired certain knowledge from observable or ascertainable facts or to have obtained expert advice. But section 14(2) is simply a standard of seriousness applied to what the claimant knew or must be treated as having known. It involves no inquiry into what the claimant ought to have done. A conclusion that the injury would reasonably have been considered sufficiently serious to justify the issue of proceedings implies no finding that the claimant ought reasonably to have issued proceedings. He may have had perfectly good reasons for not doing so. It is a standard to determine one thing and one thing only, namely whether the injury was sufficiently serious to count as significant.

39.   The difference between section 14(2) and 14(3) emerges very clearly if one considers the relevance in each case of the claimant's injury. Because section 14(3) turns on what the claimant ought reasonably to have done, one must take into account the injury which the claimant has suffered. You do not assume that a person who has been blinded could reasonably have acquired knowledge by seeing things. In section 14(2), on the other hand, the test is external to the claimant and involves no inquiry into what he ought reasonably to have done. It is applied to what the claimant knew or was deemed to have known but the standard itself is impersonal. The effect of the claimant's

injuries upon what he could reasonably have been expected to do is therefore irrelevant.'

The effect of the more stringent test has been to restrict the date of knowledge and require claimants to rely more frequently on s 33 discretion. In *Smith v Liverpool CC* (p660) and *Smith v Hampshire CC* [2007] EWCA Civ 246, cases concerning failures to deal with dyslexia, the court applied *Adams*, and this resulted in both claimants being fixed with constructive knowledge and in each a s 33 discretion was declined. In the vibration white finger cases of *Kew v Bettamix Ltd* (p518), *Norton v Corus UK Ltd* (p583) and *White v Eon* (p713), all claimants were fixed with constructive knowledge and only one (Kew) received a s 33 dispensation. Similarly, in *Johnson v Ministry of Defence* (p497) the Court of Appeal also applied a tougher objective test on constructive knowledge in a deafness case where the claimant knew he had hearing problems in 2001 but did not issue until 2009 on the basis of an expert's report attributing the problem to working conditions between 1965 and 1979. The claimant had asked his GP in 2006, when he was 66, if he had wax in his ears, and was told he did not and the problem was probably due to ageing. The court held that, following Lord Hoffmann's speech in *Adams v Bracknell Forest BC* (p292), any person with a significant injury should be reasonably curious to find out its cause unless there were reasons why a reasonable person would not have done so. Although the case was said to be close to the line, the claimant was fixed with constructive knowledge by 2002, giving him one year after onset to find out the cause of his deafness at the relatively early age of 61. There was no appeal against the trial judge's decision to refuse a s 33 dispensation, and so the claimant's action was dismissed.

In *Whiston v London Strategic Health Authority* (p710) a claimant born in 1974 suffering from cerebral palsy sought to sue in October 2006 following a dramatic deterioration in his condition in 2005. Mr Whiston had poor balance and some slurring of speech but had achieved a PhD and worked as a quantitative analyst. His mother had concerns over the management of the birth but her approach was to deal with his disability and get on with life. However, as a result of having to become a wheelchair user and his speech and swallowing deteriorating, the claimant investigated the circumstances of his birth. He had known for years that he was delivered by forceps and sustained hypoxia causing his cerebral palsy. He came to learn from his mother that a junior doctor had tried for too long to deliver him before obtaining assistance. At first instance, using a partly subjective approach to constructive knowledge, the judge found the action was brought in time. The Court of Appeal disagreed and found that a reasonable person in his position should have asked his mother, who was a midwife, about the circumstances of his birth by about 1998 and fixed him with constructive knowledge. The matter was remitted back to the judge for re-consideration of a s 33 dispensation.

TEST FOR CONSTRUCTIVE KNOWLEDGE: SUMMARY

The test for constructive knowledge within s 14(3) is objective. However, this will require the court to consider the objective situation in which the claimant finds himself in including the effects of the injury itself. If the injury itself would reasonably inhibit him from seeking advice, that is a factor which must be taken into account (*Adams*, per Lord Hoffmann at para 41, Lord Scott at para 71 and Lady Hale at para 88; *Hoare*, per Lord Hoffmann at para 38). The norms of the behaviour of persons in the situation in which the claimant is should be the basis for the test (*Adams*, per Lord Scott at para 71). For example, a brain injury to the frontal lobe might not be not sufficiently serious to make a claimant a protected party , but it may well inhibit him from making decisions, being able to concentrate or being able to comprehend information that would be relevant to what was objectively reasonable for him. If, however, that claimant was in his character and personality stoical, or forbearing, or too embarrassed to ask questions, those traits would not be relevant. In addition, pre-accident characteristics which affect an individual's ability to discover and comprehend facts would be relevant. To this extent, a pre-accident 'subjective' characteristic may be pertinent, as in the case of a blind man.

5.2   SECTION 14(3)(a)

'… from facts observable or ascertainable by him.'

Given the claimant's situation, he will be fixed with facts that are observable and ascertainable by him which it would be reasonable for him to acquire. In the Opren litigation, several claimants were fixed with knowledge which they had been exposed to and had gleaned from newspaper and television coverage of the drug's withdrawal and its possible side effects (see 'Mrs Eaton' and 'Mrs Higgins' in *Nash & others v Eli Lilly & others* (p568)). A claimant may also be fixed with knowledge which would have been easily ascertainable from a witness to his accident. In *Napper v National Coal Board* (p567), an action brought by a son in 1988 in respect of his father's death in a coal mining accident in 1957 was dismissed as statute barred on the basis that the statement taken in 1985 from a material witness could reasonably have been taken much earlier. In *Leadbitter v Hodge Finance Ltd* (p529), the claimant was fixed with a constructive date of knowledge by the court as to when he ought, through his solicitors, to have learned of the identity of a further defendant by ascertaining facts from a full police report. A claimant is most likely to be fixed with facts ascertainable with the help of his solicitor. In determining when such facts might have been available the date when it was reasonable for a solicitor to have been consulted will be evaluated (see *Hills v Potter* (p474), *Nash v Eli Lilly* (p568)). In *Henderson v Temple Pier Co Ltd* (p471) a claimant was fixed with constructive knowledge in circumstances where her solicitor acted dilatorily in acquiring the name of the owner of a ship upon which she slipped, as this did not require any particular expertise and the proviso in s 14(3)(b) did not apply (see below).

5.3   SECTION 14(3)(b)

'from facts ascertainable by him with the help of medical or other appropriate expert advice which it is reasonable for him to seek.'

In *Fowell v National Coal Board* (p437), the Court of Appeal held, obiter, that a claimant's solicitor was not an expert in the meaning of this subsection. Hidden J, at first instance, in *Nash v Eli Lilly* ([1991] 2 Med LR 169 at 182) concluded, after a detailed analysis of *Fowell*, that there was no binding authority on the point as to whether solicitors came within the ambit of s 14(3)(b) but he doubted whether in most ordinary circumstances they did. Hidden J did emphasise, however, that:

'… suffice it to say that I am satisfied for the purposes in section 14, a plaintiff's knowledge of facts include knowledge which he might reasonably have been expected to acquire from facts ascertainable by him through the services of a solicitor.' (at 182)

The Court of Appeal in *Nash v Eli Lilly* saw no reason to depart from Hidden J's approach but also emphasised:

> 'Of course, as advice from the solicitor as to the legal consequences of the act or omission is not relevant, his contribution can only consist of factual information. Moreover, where constructive knowledge is under consideration through the channel of the solicitor this can only be relevant where it is established that the plaintiff ought reasonably to have consulted a solicitor at all. Thus it is for the defendant to establish not only that a solicitor whom the plaintiff might consult might have the necessary knowledge but also that it was reasonable to expect the plaintiff to consult him.' ([1993] 1 WLR 782 at 800)

In *Henderson v Temple Pier & Co Ltd* (p471), the Court of Appeal decided that advice given by a solicitor could only fall within s 14(3)(b) if it related to a matter of fact on which expert advice was required. In that case, the obtaining of the identity of the owners of the ship upon which the claimant fell was a relatively simple matter not requiring expert advice:

> 'Having given her solicitors general responsibility for the conduct of her claim, actions are taken and knowledge is acquired on behalf of the plaintiff. If solicitors fail to take appropriate steps to discover the person against whom that action should be brought, she cannot take refuge under section 14(1)(c) because on the face of it the occupier of the St Katherine and the gangway was knowledge which she might reasonably have been expected to acquire from facts obtainable or ascertainable by her. Even if the solicitor is to be regarded as an appropriate expert, the facts were ascertainable by him without the use of legal expertise. The proviso is not intended to give an extended period of limitation to a person whose solicitor acts dilatorily in acquiring information which was obtainable without particular expertise.' (per Bracewell J at 1545)

In *Copeland v Smith & Goodwin* (p387), decided four and a half months after *Henderson*, *Henderson* was applied in the Court of Appeal and the claimant was, in principle, to be fixed with the action and inaction of her legal advisers. The Court of Appeal indicated its concern that *Henderson* had not been brought to the attention of the trial judge, who had expressed surprise that the matter was said to be free from authority:

> '... it is quite essential for advocates who hold themselves out as competent to practice in a particular field, to bring and keep themselves up-to-date with recent authority in their field. By "recent authority" I am not necessarily referring to authority which is only to be found in specialist reports, but authority which has been reported in the general law reports. If a solicitor's firm or barrister's chambers only take one set of the general reports, for instance, the Weekly Law Reports as opposed to the All England Reports ... they should, at any rate, have systems in place which enable them to keep themselves up-to-date with cases which have been considered worthy of reporting in the other series. If this is not done, judges may be getting the answer wrong through the default of the advocates appearing before them. The English system of justice has always been dependent upon the quality of the assistance that advocates give to the bench ... It is, of course, the duty of an advocate under the English system of justice to draw the judge's attention to authorities which are in point, even if they are adverse to that advocate's case.' (per Brooke LJ)

It is, of course, frequently the case that experts are only instructed after a solicitor is instructed. The type of solicitor that is instructed may well, therefore, be relevant. Invidious as it may seem, a claimant who consults a specialist firm in personal injury with expertise in spinal, brain injury or disease work might be fixed with an earlier date of constructive knowledge than one who seeks the advice of a non-specialist.

Clearly, simply contacting a solicitor will not start time running if the claimant is seeking to ascertain expert evidence to support a mere suspicion that his injury may be connected to an act or omission of the defendant. In *B v Ministry of Defence* (p312), Lord Walker thought that the first date of contacting a solicitor was, without more, of little significance. After reviewing some of the authorities, principally on what constitutes knowledge, he stated:

'54.   That is a formidable line of authority. But still there is no clear consensus. Most strikingly, in *Sniezek v Bundy (Letchworth) Ltd* [2000] PIQR P213, Judge LJ (at P229) rejected the notion that time automatically starts to run against a client who has taken legal advice, whereas Simon Brown LJ (at P 234) found it "difficult indeed to imagine a case where, having consulted a solicitor with a view to making a claim for compensation, a claimant could still then be held lacking in the requisite knowledge".

55.   I respectfully but unhesitatingly prefer the view of Judge LJ. The typical scenario for a claim for personal injury sustained from a bad working environment (exemplified by *Ali v Courtaulds Textiles Ltd* (1999) 52 BMLR 129) is for the potential claimant to go for medical advice to his general practitioner. The overworked GP is naturally more interested in diagnosis and treatment than in aetiology, unless his patient presses him. It is often a trade union representative (or in Mr Ali's case a community worker) who at some later date advises the claimant to take legal advice, which at that stage can be no more than preliminary; it generally results in a referral to a medical specialist who is asked to advise on the likely cause of the trouble, as well as on the seriousness of the injury and its prognosis. The facts of *Sniezek*, as recounted in detail by Bell J at P216 to P217, show how protracted and uncertain that process can be. Mr Sniezek first consulted his union solicitors in 1990; it was 1994 before he obtained favourable medical advice linking the hyposensitivity of his aerodigestive tract with polymer exposure; and further investigations postponed the issue of the writ until 1998 (the reference to 1988 on P217 of the report is one of several obvious errors in editing).

56.   So in practice a claimant's first visit to a solicitor may do no more than initiate the process of obtaining expert medical advice. That process may take years, with the solicitor's function limited to the collation of medical and other technical evidence (such as the nature of the polymer in *Ali*, or the nature of the pesticide in *Griffin v Clwyd Health Authority* [2001] EWCA Civ 818, [2001] PIQR P31).'

Whether it is reasonable for a claimant to seek the advice of a solicitor or another expert will also depend on the precise circumstances of the case (see *Adams v Bracknell Forest Borough Council* (p292)). In *Bates v Leicester Health Authority* (p324) a claimant's birth resulted in tetraplegia due to cerebral palsy in 1968. The claimant alleged his birth had been mismanaged. His parents told him that he could not sue the hospital. In 1993 he instructed a solicitor after his care worker suggested, following his father's death, that he might have a claim. The judge found that the claimant did not have actual knowledge of an omission of failing to intervene in the birth until receipt of an expert's report in 1994. The court also refused to fix the claimant with constructive knowledge as the defendant had not demonstrated that if the claimant had pressed his parents it would have made any difference to the knowledge he received. Relevant to this claimant's particular situation was his difficulty in communication and his substantial reliance on his parents.

In *Guidera v NEI Projects (India) Ltd* (p451), McCullough J at first instance fixed a claimant with constructive knowledge by finding that he acted unreasonably by ignoring the advice of his chest physician in 1982 to make a second application to the Pneumoconiosis Medical Panel for benefit in respect of his asbestos related disease. However, the judge further held that even if the claimant had taken such a step, inevitably time would have elapsed before the medical panel reported and in those circumstances the defendant had not discharged the burden of establishing that the claimant should be fixed with a constructive date of knowledge outside the three years prior to the issue of proceedings. The Court of Appeal, however, fixed the claimant with an earlier constructive date of knowledge as it found he acted unreasonably in failing to answer the chest physician's earlier question put to him in 1976.

In *Khan v Ainslie* (p520), Waterhouse J refused to fix the claimant with constructive knowledge in respect of the cause of his blindness in the circumstances where his solicitor had received a negative medical opinion. Given the tenor of the report, the solicitors had not acted unreasonably in failing to put supplementary questions to the medical expert. Similarly, in *Jeffrey v CMB Speciality Packaging UK Ltd* (p495) the Court of Appeal allowed a claimant's appeal against the finding of constructive knowledge by the trial judge. The judge found that the claimant, in a deafness case, should have made further enquiries of medical staff who provided him with the results of his hearing test. The claimant was told that a natural cause of his tinnitus was being investigated by his consultant. The Court of Appeal found that it was not reasonable to require the claimant to go behind this until 1991 when a further report expressed concern over his hearing loss.

Section 14 does not define who is an expert but singles out, appropriately, medical experts who can range from a general practitioner to treating hospital physicians or medico-legal experts instructed by his solicitors. In *Nash v Eli Lilly* (above) the Court of Appeal held that certain claimants would be fixed with the knowledge of their GP's providing it was reasonable for the claimant to have sought the advice of their doctor and reasonable to ask him what information the doctor had concerning the drug and its negative side-effects. In *Stephen v Riverside Health Authority* (p676) the claimant, with a limited knowledge of radiography, was held not to be an expert in her own case particularly when much medical expertise directly conflicted with her own suspicions concerning the possible consequence of a radiation overdose.

If a claimant fails to take expert advice but relies on non-expert opinion he may nevertheless escape being fixed with constructive knowledge that would have been available from an expert if his action in going to non-experts was reasonable. In *Smith v Central Asbestos Ltd* (p658) the House of Lords indicated that workmen had acted reasonably in relying on erroneous advice given by their works manager. Similarly in *Howell v West Midlands Passenger Transport Executive* [1973] 1 Lloyd's Rep 199 the Court of Appeal held that the claimant in her circumstances had acted reasonably in relying on the opinions of unqualified people. Both these cases arose under the 1963 Act and concerned advice over a matter of law which is no longer relevant under the 1980 Act. However, the cases do indicate the approach the court is likely to take, as it did in *Knipe v British Railways Board* [1972] 1 Lloyd's Rep 122, where it was considered reasonable that a claimant took advice from his trade union.

'but a person shall not be fixed under this sub-section with knowledge of a fact ascertainable only with the help of expert advice so long as he has taken all reasonable steps to obtain (and, where appropriate, to act on) that advice.'

This proviso helps a claimant who instructs an expert who through oversight or incompetence, or even in the case of a treating doctor on therapeutic grounds, fails to provide the claimant with relevant facts concerning significance, attribution or identity. This principle is well illustrated in the case of *Marston v British Railways Board* (p545) where an engineer had been instructed by the claimant's solicitors to examine a hammer which had caused Mr Marston's carotid artery to be severed when a chip from the hammer flew off whilst he was striking a metal sett. Both Mr Marston, before his death, and other employees believed that the hammer was in fact new. The expert reported that the hammer was satisfactory in terms of its hardness, but he failed to mention the fact that the hammer was neither new nor in good condition. At the trial, one expert thought the hammer fractured because of poor manufacturing while another thought it was due to previous misuse. The fact that the hammer was in poor condition did not emerge until cross-examination of the claimant's experts. Croom-Johnson J held that the claimant, the widow, was not to be fixed with the knowledge of the hammer's defect, because all reasonable steps had been taken to obtain that knowledge which the expert had not in fact revealed. Similarly, when a doctor fails to establish attribution, a claimant will not be fixed with constructive knowledge of attribution providing it was reasonable for the claimant to rely upon the practitioner's advice (see *Newman v Bevan Funnell Ltd* (p580) obiter). Nor will a claimant be fixed with constructive knowledge when a medical adviser withholds facts from a claimant on the grounds that is not in his medical interest to be informed of them (see *Newton v Cammell Laird & Co Ltd* (p581) where a man dying of an asbestos-related cancer was not told that he only had a short expectation of life which may, in turn, have influenced his decision about seeing a solicitor).

The proviso itself would rarely avail a claimant who relies upon a solicitor's advice not to pursue a witness or avenue of inquiry and, thereby, fails to uncover some relevant knowledge, because as indicated a solicitor is normally not an expert within the meaning of s 14(1)(b) (see *Fowell v National Coal Board* (p437), *Nash v Eli Lilly* (p568), *Halford v Brookes* (p453), *Henderson v Temple Pier Co Ltd* (p471)). If, of course, a solicitor is in possession of relevant knowledge but advises a claimant that he has no case in law, that is entirely irrelevant on the clear wording of the section and time will continue to run against a claimant with relevant knowledge of significance, attribution and identity.

In *Jones v Bennett* [1976] 1 Lloyd's Rep 484, Widgery LJ held that a claimant had constructive knowledge from the date when it was reasonable for her to seek advice. The case concerned the claimant's inability to pay for her solicitor's advice so no detailed advice was given. Many other cases, however, have indicated that the date of constructive knowledge would, in fact, be when the advice was actually received or was likely to have been received following the instruction of the solicitor or of an expert (see *Guidera v NEI Projects (India) Ltd* (p451), *Nash v Eli Lilly* (p568), *Bentley v Bristol & Western Health Authority (No 1)* (p328)). This approach appears to be eminently reasonable because frequently when a report is commissioned from an expert, substantial time will elapse before the report is produced and delivered to the solicitors and its details are disclosed to the actual claimant.

6 The Consumer Protection Act 1987

The Consumer Protection Act 1987 incorporated s 14(1A) into the 1980 Act but appears to have produced a truncated version of the existing provisions of s 14 of the 1980 Act where a case concerns a defective product. There is, however, no equivalent provision within s 14(1A) of s 14(3) concerning constructive knowledge.

Defendants in cases concerning defective products under the Consumer Protection Act 1987 may not be able to fix an injured claimant with a constructive date of knowledge. Whether the claimant knew or not that the injury was significant, attributable and related to the identity of the defendant sued will be a matter of actual knowledge. A claimant in such circumstances may not be fixed by facts which are observable or ascertainable by him with or without expert help, and the manufacturers or suppliers of the defective products will have to deal with the claimant's actual date of knowledge alone. However, any such cause of action is extinguished after 10 years because of the longstop provisions contained within s 11A(3).

4   Disability and concealment (sections 28 and 32)

The scheme of the Limitation Act 1980 is that the ordinary time limits which it provides are contained in Part I. Those relating to personal injury cases have been considered in **Chapters 2** and **3**.

By s 1(2) the ordinary time limits in Part I are subject to extension or exclusion in accordance with the provisions of Part II. Extension arises in cases of disability (s 28) and fraud, concealment and mistake (s 32), and is considered in this chapter. Discretionary exclusion, which is permitted under s 33, is discussed in **Chapter 5**.

1   Disability

DEFINITION OF DISABILITY

Section 38(2) of the Limitation Act 1980, as amended by the Mental Capacity Act 2005, states that: 'For the purposes of this Act a person shall be treated as under a disability while he is an infant, or lacks capacity within the meaning of the Mental Capacity Act 2005 to conduct legal proceedings'. Thus, there are just two types of disability: infancy and incapacity. No other possible disability qualifies for this purpose. The classification of dermatitis as a disability in *Pilmore v Northern Trawlers Ltd* (p606), although made in the context of a finding under s 33(3)(d), is therefore misconceived. Nevertheless it appears that there are conflicting judicial dicta on this point. In *Bater v Newbold* (p323), Parker LJ, whilst ruling that the claimant's loss of memory in that case did not constitute a disability within s 33(3)(d), stated:

> 'The disability in that paragraph, although it is not necessary finally to decide it, appears to me not to be a disability as defined in section 38, which refers, as I see it, to section 28, which prevents, in the event of the defined disability, the time running until the disability ceases. If that be the case, it does not appear to me that the disability referred to in sub-paragraph (d) of subsection (3) can be that form of disability: it could be something less.'

This seems inconsistent with Lord Diplock's statement in *Thompson v Brown Construction (Ebbw Vale) Ltd* (p690) that: 'Paragraph (d) is restricted to cases where plaintiffs have been under a disability, a class of persons that equity has always been zealous to protect'. Since s 38 begins with the words 'For the purposes of this Act', and not 'For the purposes of section 28', the authors in the first edition of this book (1994) preferred the interpretation that disability in s 33(3)(d) solely referred to infancy and incapacity, described in the pre-2005 Mental Capacity Act as 'unsoundness of mind'.

This view has been supported by two subsequent Court of Appeal decisions. In *Yates v Thakeham Tiles Ltd* (p729), both Nourse LJ and Wall J held that the trial judge had erred in taking account of the claimant's physical disability (a back injury) under s 33(3)(d) and that 'disability' in this subsection is strictly limited to unsoundness of mind although, in rejecting the defendant's appeal, each added that the judge was entitled to have regard to the physical disability as a circumstance of the case.

It is submitted that the matter has been settled by the Court of Appeal decision in *Thomas v Plaistow* (p687). Referring to the 20th Report of the Law Reform Committee, Cmnd 5360, on whose recommendations this part of the Limitation Act 1980 was based, Hirst LJ stated:

> 'I have to declare an interest since I was at the time a member of the committee and a signatory of the report. The report shows clearly, as the respondent accepts, that the committee intended the "disability" in section 33(3)(d) to have the same meaning as in section 28, ie as defined in section 38(2) and (3). The rationale for this, as the report shows, was that while section 28, which I have quoted, conferred the mandatory extension of time in the case of *existing* disability, supervening disability should be no more than one of the factors relevant to the exercise of the court's discretion: the reason for that was that it would be difficult to frame a coherent rule which would take into account all the various possible circumstances and timing of a supervening disability (see paragraphs 95 and 148(7) of the report). Parliament eventually enacted almost, if not exactly word for word, the committee's draft recommendations on this topic.'

Infancy is simply defined. A person is under a disability until reaching the age of 18, the age of majority fixed by s 1(1) of the Family Law Reform Act 1969. No case law has been needed to clarify the concept of infancy which, unlike incapacity, lasts for a set period and can never recur.

In *Byrne v Motor Insurers' Bureau and Secretary of State for Transport* (p357) the absence of an equivalent provision in the 1972 MIB Untraced Drivers' Agreement of s 28 meant that an infant had to bring a claim under the Agreement within three years, as time was not suspended during minority. The court held this to be a breach of the relevant EC Directive 84/5, which provided for an equivalence between rights against traced drivers and untraced drivers and was a sufficiently serious breach to expose the UK government to a claim for *Francovich* damages.

Incapacity, unlike 'unsoundness of mind', is no longer defined in the Limitation Act following the repeal of ss 38(3) and (4) by Schedule 7 to the Mental Capacity Act 2005. The definition of incapacity is accordingly as found in s 2(1) of the 2005 Act:

'2   People who lack capacity

(1)   For the purposes of this Act, a person lacks capacity in relation to a matter if at the material time he is unable to make a decision for himself in relation to the matter because of an impairment of, or a disturbance in the functioning of, the mind or brain.'

Section 3 further defines the inability to make a decision as:

'3   Inability to make decisions

(1)   For the purposes of section 2, a person is unable to make a decision for himself if he is unable–

(a)   to understand the information relevant to the decision,

(b)   to retain that information,

(c)   to use or weigh that information as part of the process of making the decision, or

(d)   to communicate his decision (whether by talking, using sign language or any other means).

(2)   A person is not to be regarded as unable to understand the information relevant to a decision if he is able to understand an explanation of it given to him in a way that is appropriate to his circumstances (using simple language, visual aids or any other means).

(3)   The fact that a person is able to retain the information relevant to a decision for a short period only does not prevent him from being regarded as able to make the decision.

(4)   The information relevant to a decision includes information about the reasonably foreseeable consequences of–

(a)   deciding one way or another, or

(b)   failing to make the decision.'

The courts are developing case law on these new provisions in personal injury actions where disputes arise as to whether a claimant is a protected party and, accordingly, needs to sue via a litigation friend and/or whether after the litigation will become or remain a protected beneficiary requiring the Court of Protection and a deputy to manage his affairs (see *Masterman-Lister v Jewell* [2002] EWCA Civ 1889; *Saulle v Nouvet* [2007] EWHC 2902 (QB)).To date, no cases have been litigated concerning the effects of the new definitions of incapacity in the context of personal injury limitation law, and it should be borne in mind that the following cases were decided under different statutory frameworks.

Under the unamended Act, unsoundness of mind was defined as a person being unable to administer their property and affairs due to a mental disorder as defined by Mental Health Act 1983.

In *Dawson v Scott-Brown* (p406), although the claimant was invalided out of the Royal Navy on the grounds of mental ill-health, he continued to be capable of managing his affairs. Accordingly, he was not held to be unsound of mind.

Winn LJ observed in the case of *Kirby v Leather* (p521) that mere unconsciousness or delirium does not of itself constitute unsoundness of mind. He said that care must be taken not to confuse the court's favourable decision in that case with the proposition advanced in argument:

'that there can be a suspension of the running of the statutory limitation period during such time as an injured person is unconscious or ill or in a state of delirium without more being shown. In this case I am satisfied, as are my lords, that from the moment when David Kirby suffered these injuries to his head, he then became, and thereafter at all times remained, of unsound mind in the sense in which my Lords have defined that term for the present purpose. Had he merely been unconscious, as indeed he was for some three weeks, unable to recognise any member of his family, as indeed he was for some six weeks, but had there been lacking cogent and convincing medical evidence that throughout that period of unconsciousness and amnesia his mental powers had been so affected as to make him in the relevant sense of unsound mind, I would not have thought that there would have been any suspension of the running of the statutory period of limitation.'

The new definition is broader and a state of unconsciousness is most likely to be included in 'impairment of, or a disturbance in the functioning of, the mind or brain' (as per s 2(1) of the Mental Capacity Act 2006).

In any event, unconsciousness immediately after an accident will always defer the date of knowledge under ss 11(4) and 14(1) of the 1980 Act.

In *Penrose v Mansfield* (p600), the court held that the onus was on the claimant to prove disability over the whole of the relevant period. The writ of the claimant, who was seriously injured in a car accident on 10 November 1965, was not issued until 12 December 1968. The supporting evidence of a neurologist who examined him in 1967 was fatally undermined by two neurological opinions dated 26 and 29 November 1965, found in the contemporary hospital records, to the effect that, by then, the claimant was conscious and rational and capable of making business decisions. His case was held to be statute barred.

In *Rogers v Finemodern Ltd and Walker* (p630), the claimant sustained a fractured skull. In the months after the injury however, he returned to work for a short period, visited solicitors, reported the incident to the police and lodged a claim with the Criminal Injuries Compensation Board. Medical evidence showed that in the period after regaining consciousness he had 'virtually no neurological abnormality'. Although the evidence as to whether he was incapable of managing his affairs was divided, Garland J held that he had not proved himself to be so incapable in the months following the incident. Accordingly, s 28 did not apply.

In *Maga v Birmingham Roman Catholic Archdiocese Trust* (p541) a claimant who suffered from epilepsy and learning difficulties, and whose IQ was assessed at 70, was found to be suffering from a disability within the meaning of the unamended s 38(3). Accordingly, his case for damages arising out of sexual abuse by a Catholic priest was held not to be statute barred. However, the court dismissed his case on the basis that the defendant was not vicariously liable for the priests' abuse. On appeal, this finding was reversed and the claim succeeded. The defendant's cross-appeal on the issue of capacity failed. The Court of Appeal's analysis is instructive (per Lord Neuberger, then Master of the Rolls) and the reasoning will also inform the court's future approach to the new definition of incapacity under the 2005 Act:

'16.   Section 28(1) of the Limitation Act 1980 provides that, if on the date on which a cause of action accrues, a person is "under a disability", the action may be brought at any time up to six years after he ceases to be under a disability. Section 38(2) defines under a disability as meaning being an infant or "of unsound mind". At the relevant time for present purposes, section 38(3) provided that a person is of unsound mind "if he is a person who, by reason of mental disorder, is incapable of managing and administering his property and affairs"; it went on to explain that "'mental disorder' has the same meaning as in the Mental Health Act 1983". (The Mental Capacity Act 2005 replaced the central part of the definition in section 38(2) with "if he lacks capacity (within the meaning of the Mental Capacity Act 2005) to conduct legal proceedings"; and section 38(3) was repealed, as "lacking capacity" was itself defined in section 2(1) of the 2005 Act.)

17.   In order to decide whether the claimant could rely on section 28(1), the Judge obtained guidance as to the appropriate approach to adopt from two decisions of this court, *Kirby v Leather* [1965] 2 QB 367 and *Masterman-Lister v Brutton* [2003] 1 WLR 1511, as well as from two first instance decisions, *White v Fell*, unreported, 12 November 1987 and *Lindsay v Wood* [2006] EWHC 2895. He concluded that, at least in the present case, he needed to consider only one question, namely whether the claimant was able to conduct

the instant proceedings, in the sense of being "able to deal rationally with the problems which … will arise in the course of it", as, if he was not, it was common ground that his inability was by reason of mental disorder (paragraphs 28 and 53 of the judgment).

18.   There is some doubt in my mind whether this was precisely the right formulation, butI do not think that it would be right to go into that question. Miss Gumbel QC, who appeared for the claimant, as she does on this appeal, was recorded by the Judge as identifying "the issue [as] the claimant's ability to conduct the litigation"; and Mr Faulks QC, who also appears here as he did below, was quoted by the Judge as saying that there was no difference in practice in this case between the two issues, which he propounded, namely capacity to conduct proceedings and capacity to commence proceedings. (The discussion is in paragraph 27 of the judgment). As the parties were agreed that this was the issue, and as that was the approach the Judge adopted, it seems to me that, as there are no exceptional facts to justify an appellate court taking a different approach, we should not consider determining a reformulated issue on this appeal – not least because I am far from convinced that the Judge adopted the wrong formulation.

19.   Having identified the issue, the Judge then considered whether the claimant, on whom the burden lay, had established that he could not deal rationally with the problems which would arise in this litigation. He first considered the claimant as a witness. He said that the claimant had difficulties in understanding contradictions and in giving evidence generally, concluding that "his evidence suggests a considerable intellectual disadvantage" (paragraph 30). He then turned to the claimant's history and referred to the fact that the claimant had settled a road traffic accident claim at the first figure offered, and then had given the £2,500 to a moneylender simply "because he was being pressed" and even though he did not know how much he owed (paragraph 32). The Judge also said that the claimant's psychiatric notes suggested that he was inconsistent as to whether he wanted to manage his own affairs (paragraph 34) and that two psychiatrists were recorded as independently noting that he needed help with his finances (paragraph 35). In connection with the appointment of the Official Solicitor as his litigation friend, his GP had recorded that the claimant could not read or write, and needed looking after (paragraph 38).

20.   The Judge then considered the evidence of the expert witnesses in paragraphs 40 to 48. The statements prepared before the hearing presented a somewhat unsatisfactory picture because Dr Shapero and Professor Murphy did not appear to have addressed the precise question which the Judge identified as having to be decided, and because their understanding of the question which required answering seems to have changed, so that their answers at different times appeared mutually inconsistent. As a result of their cross-examination, it appears that, when faced with what the Judge had identified as the correct question, Dr Shapero thought that the claimant could not conduct the litigation, whereas Professor Murphy thought he could.

21.   In paragraph 51, the Judge said that he did not find the issue of capacity "straightforward". This is underlined by the fact that the Judge changed his mind on this issue between the circulation of his draft judgment and the handing down of the final version. In my judgment, the fact that a Judge changes his mind, particularly on a difficult issue such as the claimant's capacity in this case, suggests that he has given the issue really serious consideration. I accept,

however, that it also can be said, as Mr Faulks argues, to indicate that the case is near the borderline, and therefore may merit particularly careful scrutiny on an appeal.

22.   In paragraph 52, the Judge said that he had to take into account "what he knew about the claimant's abilities from the evidence I have heard about his life", "the expert evidence", and "the impression the claimant made on me, bearing in mind the conditions". In paragraph 53, he reached the conclusion that the claimant lacked capacity under section 38(2) of the 1980 Act. He said that he considered that this conclusion was "supported by the aspects of the history" set out in the judgment, and "the concern which I would have if it were the claimant who was responsible for making the decisions in the litigation rather than the Official Solicitor". He also said that "in the end, I prefer Dr Shapero's view on this to that of Professor Murphy".

23.   Mr Faulks, for the Archdiocese, contends that the Judge reached the wrong conclusion on section 28(1) for a number of reasons – (a) failing to take into account the claimant's manipulative ability, (b) failing to allow sufficiently for the privilege which incapacity confers in the limitation context, (c) accepting Dr Shapero's final view when it was against the weight of the expert evidence, (d) the claimant's ability to understand that he might recover a large sum; (e) the fact that the claimant had previously brought a claim, apparently without a litigation friend; (f) the fact that his solicitor had certified that the claimant understood the contents of his witness statement, (g) the fact that he had his own bank account and could remember his pin number, (h) the fact that the claimant could understand concepts such as confidentiality and legal advice, (i) the fact that he understood, and expressed views about, the function of the Court of Protection, and (j) the fact that he had taken part in a radio interview where he had referred to "making a civil claim against the Catholic church".

24.   As to (a), the Judge accepted in paragraph 37 of his judgment, and obviously took into account, that the claimant was manipulative; how he took it into account was very much a matter for him. (b) It is true that a person who can bring himself within section 38(2) of the 1980 Act on a permanent basis is given a very great advantage, but that is a matter for the legislature not the courts, save that it serves to emphasise the care which has to be applied when deciding the issue.

25.   The expert evidence, raised under (c), was, as already mentioned, somewhat confused, and it seems quite likely that neither expert was entirely consistent in his opinion, which is not an adverse criticism: I suspect that the inconsistencies are attributable partly to the changing nature of the question put to them, and partly to the difficulty of resolving the issue in this case. However, in the end, each expert expressed a view on the issue which the Judge had to decide; although there were good reasons for doubting Dr Shapero's ultimate view, there were also good reasons for doubting Professor Murphy's ultimate view. Further, the recorded views of the psychiatrists who had cared for the claimant, and indeed those of his GP, seem to support the Judge's conclusion.

26.   As to (d), the claimant cannot possibly have been told that he would recover £750,000 which is what he was recorded as saying that he had been advised, so, at best, that factor cuts both ways. Similarly, the evidence relating to the road traffic accident claim, (e), at best cuts both ways from the Archdiocese's point of view, as the Judge said in paragraph 50. The claimant was able to

bring an action, through Claims Direct with the help of the Citizens' Advice Bureau, but the way he dealt with the offer and the proceeds tends to support the Judge's conclusion. I do not think (f) takes matters further: much more important was the Judge's ability to see the claimant as he gave evidence. (g) is more than outweighed by the fact that the claimant could not manage his finances, despite the fact that they are handled by Social Services. As to (h), (i) and (j), consideration of the whole of the evidence in relation to each item appears to me to provide some support for each side. Thus, the transcript of the radio interview suggests that the claimant confused the abuse perpetrated by Father Clonan with that he suffered subsequently at school.

27. The Judge set out the relevant evidence on the section 28(1) issue fully and helpfully, including almost all the points which are now relied on by the Archdiocese. However, it would have been better if he had spent a little more time explaining why he came to the conclusion that he did; in particular why he preferred the evidence of Dr Shapero to that of Professor Murphy. Nonetheless, it is quite possible to discern his reasons, at least in general terms, for reaching his conclusion. The difficulty involved in, and the effort that he gave to, deciding the issue may well have resulted in the Judge concentrating more on reaching a conclusion than spelling out his reasons, which is understandable. Further, this is very far from being a case where no reasons have been given for the Judge's conclusion.

28. As the Judge indicated, this was very much of a borderline case on the question of whether section 28(1) applied. The issue is certainly not one of discretion; nor is it an issue of primary fact. It is a matter of judgment, and one which is primarily for the first instance tribunal. There may, in an Aristotelian sense, be only one right answer to the question whether a claimant was able to conduct the litigation, but in this imperfect world, it must, in some cases, be an issue on which reasonable and fully informed Judges could differ. In such cases, and this is, in my view, such a one, an appellate court should not interfere with the Judge's conclusion unless he has relied on irrelevant evidence, ignored relevant evidence, or misunderstood some evidence. I do not consider that Jack J has committed any such oversight in this case. Accordingly, I would dismiss the Archdiocese's cross-appeal on this issue.'

Prior to its repeal by Sch 7 to the Mental Capacity Act 2005, s 38(4) conclusively presumed unsoundness of mind if the claimant was detained or receiving treatment in hospital for his mental health.

Those provisions, if in force at the time, would have rescued the unfortunate claimant in the case of *Harnett v Fisher* (p462). Mr Harnett was a sane Kentish farmer who, in November 1912, was certified as a lunatic by a country doctor who observed him in the street for a few minutes. Consequently he was immediately confined to a lunatic asylum and houses for lunatics until escaping in October 1921. The House of Lords, whilst appreciating the immense forensic skill with which he conducted his own case, found itself compelled to rule that his court action commenced against the country doctor in May 1922 was statute barred: since the claimant had never been insane, time ran against him throughout. Under s 38(4), however, unsoundness of mind would have been conclusively presumed in respect of the period between November 1912 and October 1921, up to the escape, so that the court action would have been commenced in time within a mere seven months of cessation of the disability. With the abolition of this presumption, a claimant will have to prove an inability to make a decision in terms of formulating his claim throughout the whole of the period from the accrual of the cause of action without any such presumption. A contemporary Mr Harnett would, however, have the prospects of a s 33 dispensation.

CONSEQUENCES OF DISABILITY

Section 28(1) provides for the limitation periods under the 1980 Act to be extended in cases of disability:

'Subject to the following provisions of this section, if on the date when any right of action accrued for which a period of limitation is prescribed by this Act, the person to whom it accrued was under a disability, the action may be brought at any time before the expiration of six years from the date when he ceased to be under a disability or died (whichever first occurred) notwithstanding that the period of limitation has expired.'

Section 28(1) is subject to s 28(6):

'If the action is one to which section 11 or 12(2) of this Act applies, subsection (1) above shall have effect as if for the words "six years" there were substituted the words "three years".'

The combined effect of these provisions is that, in the standard personal injury (including fatal) case, the limitation period in cases of disability at the date of accrual is usually three years from the cessation of disability or death, whichever first occurs. Where the disability is infancy, which ceases on the minor's eighteenth birthday, that means that the limitation period expires three years later on his twenty-first birthday.

Antenatal injuries are covered by this rule. By s 1 of the Congenital Disabilities (Civil Liability) Act 1976, a child can sue in respect of injuries sustained before birth. Section 4(3) of this Act provides that such a pre-birth injury is to be treated as having been sustained by the child immediately after its birth. Therefore, whether an injury is sustained before birth or during childhood, the limitation period can never expire before the age of twenty-one.

Where the disability is incapacity, the limitation period expires three years after capacity is first regained. If incapacity is permanent, time will only begin to run on death. The two disabilities of infancy and incapacity can overlap, with the result that a child who is badly and permanently brain damaged at birth will never be subject to a limitation period in the whole of its life.

This is illustrated by the case of *Headford v Bristol and District Health Authority* (p470) in which the claimant, who was born in October 1963 and suffered a cardiac arrest and subsequent severe permanent brain damage in an operation in the defendant's hospital in September 1964, finally started court action in July 1992. Rejecting the defendant's application for the statement of claim to be struck out and the action to be dismissed as an abuse of process due to alleged prejudice to the defendants resulting from the 28-year delay, Lord Justice Rose in the Court of Appeal observed:

'Firstly, that section 28 contains no provision comparable to that in section 33 for the carrying out of a balancing exercise as to prejudice in relation to the disapplication of time limits prescribed by sections 11 and 12. Section 28 does not refer to prejudice at all.

Secondly, section 28(1) contains no provision comparable to that in section 28(4) for a timeous longstop or cut-off point.

Thirdly, in permitting an action to be started within six years of the end of a disability, Parliament has expressly contemplated, by section 28(1), that, in the case of one well-known and substantial group of persons under a disability, namely minors, an action may not be started until 24 years after the conduct of which complaint is made.'

Consequently, the Court of Appeal held that the issue of a properly pleaded first court action, within the time limit permitted by Parliament, was 'unlikely to be capable of being categorised as an abuse of process'. Prejudice arising to the defendants was immaterial. The Court of Appeal distinguished its earlier decision in *Hogg v Hamilton* (p479) on the grounds that in *Hogg* there had been an earlier court action (albeit against a different defendant) that had been struck out.

The effects on action to dismiss for want of prosecution have been considered in the cases of *Tolley v Morris* (p693) and *Turner v W H Malcolm Ltd* (p696). In both cases, despite delays of many years on the part of the claimants, it was held that it would be fruitless to dismiss the actions since they would be entitled under s 28(1) of the Limitation Act 1980 to start fresh actions on the same causes. Accordingly, it was stated that such applications to dismiss should not be granted, save in exceptional circumstances such as disobedience to a pre-emptory order. This issue is discussed in greater detail in **Chapter 10**.

Section 28(1) refers to 'the date when any right of action accrued', not the date of knowledge as defined by s 14. Thus it is on the date of accrual, not the date of knowledge, that the disability must exist. If an adult person is still sound of mind immediately after a car accident, time will not be prevented from running against him merely because he has become mentally ill by the time he learns the driver's identity.

The next reference in s 28(1) is to a right of action 'for which a period of limitation is prescribed by this Act'. This excludes actions for which a limitation period is fixed under any other statute, eg s 8 of the Maritime Conventions Act 1911. Thus the disability provisions of s 28 do not apply, for instance, to the strict two-year limitation period in aviation actions against airline carriers laid down by Article 29 of the Warsaw Convention as amended at The Hague, and incorporated into English law by the Carriage by Air Act 1961. (See **Chapter 8** for the applicability of ss 28 and 32 to other Acts.)

Section 28(1) applies when, on the date that the right of action accrued, 'the person to whom it accrued was under a disability'. The disability need not result from the cause of action: indeed, infancy will, and unsoundness of mind may, exist independently of it. However, the disability must have existed on the date when the right of action accrued, eg by the end of the day on which an accident occurred.

The classic example of this arose under s 22 of the Limitation Act 1939, the predecessor of s 28 of the 1980 Act, in the case of *Kirby v Leather* (p521). There the claimant, who was thrown off a scooter onto his head in a road accident in May 1959, was unconscious for several days and badly affected mentally ever after, so much so that, when he went to a firm of solicitors in August 1963 to ask if they could help him to trace his scooter, he could not even remember that the accident had occurred. His court action commenced by writ in October 1963 was held not to be statute barred.

The same principle applies to cases of overlapping disability. In the 1871 case of *Borrows v Ellison* (1871) LR 6 Exch 128 before the end of the claimant's infancy she contracted another then disability (marriage, described as the 'disability of coverture'!). Holding her adult court action to be maintainable, Martin B in the Court of Exchequer stated that: 'The party never at any time being free from disability, the disability, though due to different causes, must be looked on as one continued thing'.

It is submitted that the same principle would apply under s 28(1) to unsoundness of mind commencing before the end of a claimant's infancy.

The situation is otherwise in cases of a subsequent disability which only arises after the right of action accrued. In the early case of *Purnell v Roche* (p613), the claimant's cause of action for enforcement of a mortgage accrued by 1903 and she became unsound of mind in 1907; her court action commenced in 1926 was dismissed as statute barred. Where comparable facts arise in a modern personal injury case, the court is enjoined under s 33(3)(d) of the 1980 Act to have regard to 'the duration of any disability of the plaintiff arising after the date of accrual of the cause of action' and is entitled under s 33(1) to allow the action to proceed if it would be equitable to do so.

Section 28(1) and (6) next provide that, in personal injury cases, 'the action may be brought at any time before expiration' of three years from cessation of disability or death. This allows an injured person to start court action while still under a disability. In that event, RSC Ord 80 r2 requires that the action must be brought through a next friend acting by a solicitor who must certify that the next friend has no interest in the case that is adverse to that of the claimant under disability.

Section 28(1) states that time begins to run 'from the date when he ceased to be under a disability or died (whichever first occurred)'. Once time begins to run, nothing on the claimant's side can interrupt it. Therefore, in a case of intermittent disability, where a claimant is unsound of mind at the date of an accident, time begins to run when this disability ceases and does not stop running if he again becomes unsound of mind. The court retains a discretion to resolve any undue harshness which this rule may create by disapplying the limitation period under s 33.

Section 28(2) provides that: 'This section shall not affect any case where the right of action first occurred to some person (not under a disability) through whom the person under a disability claims'. In other words, if the right of action first accrues to a sane adult, it matters not that the person claiming through him is an infant. By s 38(5) '... a person shall be treated as claiming through another person if he became entitled by, through, under, or by the act of that other person to the right claimed'.

Section 28(3) governs accrual on death. 'When a right of action which has accrued to a person under a disability accrues, on the death of that person while still under a disability, to another person under a disability, no further extension of time shall be allowed by reason of the disability of the second person'. Under s 28(1), time starts running on the death of the original claimant under disability. Section 28(3) means that it is not prevented from running by the disability of the subsequent claimant.

Special provisions for product liability actions governed by the Consumer Protection Act 1987 are to be found in s 28(7) of the 1980 Act. First, it is stated that any action under Part I of the 1987 Act is governed by the three-year limitation period from the end of the disability set out in s 28(1). Second, it is confirmed that this extended limitation period is subject to the overriding 10 year longstop period created by s 11A(3) of the 1980 Act as amended. Therefore a child injured by a defective product supplied on her fifth birthday must sue under the Consumer Protection Act 1987 by her fifteenth birthday, even though her infancy has not expired and even though any other action in tort or contract based on the same injury can be brought until the age of 21.

Another example of s 28 applying to, but not ultimately governing, a case arises where the date of knowledge under s 14 is later than the date on which the extended limitation period would otherwise expire under s 28(1). For instance, in *Atkinson v Oxfordshire Health Authority* (p308) where the claimant was suing in respect of two unsuccessful operations performed in 1967 when he was 17, the extended period under s 28(1) and (6) would normally have expired in 1971. However, it was held that he did not acquire the relevant knowledge within the meaning of s 14 before July 1986, so his writ issued in July 1989 was not statute barred. Thus, the extended period under s 28 is always subject to the potentially longer limitation period allowable by ss 11 and 14. Cases vary on their facts as to whether s 14 or s 28 produces the later expiry date.

Section 33(8) of the 1980 Act stipulates that: 'References in this section to section 11 (or 11A) include references to that section as extended by any of the preceding provisions of this Part of this Act ...'. This confirms what has already been observed, namely that any extended limitation period created under s 28 can be disapplied altogether in the exercise of the court's discretion under s 33(1).

2 Concealment

Section 32 of the Limitation Act 1980 provides for the postponement of the limitation period in cases of fraud, concealment or mistake. Only concealment is potentially relevant to personal injury cases.

By s 32(1):

'subject to subsections (3) and (4A) below, where in the case of any action for which a period of limitation is prescribed by this Act, either:

(a)   the action is based upon the fraud of the defendant; or
(b)   any fact relevant to the plaintiff's right of action has been deliberately concealed from him by the defendant; or
(c)   the action is for relief from the consequences of a mistake;

the period of limitation shall not begin to run until the plaintiff has discovered the fraud, concealment or mistake (as the case may be) or could with reasonable diligence have discovered it.

References in this subsection to the defendant include references to the defendant's agent and to any person through whom the defendant claims and his agent.'

In *Beaman v A R T S Ltd* [1949] 1 All ER 465, the claimant sued the defendants for conversion and pleaded under s 26 of the Limitation Act 1939, the predecessor of s 32 of the 1980 Act, that the limitation period had been postponed by the defendants' fraud. The Court of Appeal held that, as proof of fraud was not an essential ingredient in an action for conversion, the action was not 'based upon the fraud of the defendant'. Since fraud is not a necessary ingredient in a personal injury action, it follows that s 32(1)(a) does not apply to personal injury cases.

Similarly, in *Phillips-Higgins v Harper* [1954] 1 All ER 116, the claimant sued in 1951 for an account in respect of past profits and, since the earlier years from 1938 were outside the limitation period, pleaded under s 26 of the 1939 Act that the period should be postponed as there had been a mistake over the amount of profits payable. Pearson J rejected this plea, holding that s 26 only applied where mistake was an essential ingredient of the cause of action. Since mistake is not a necessary ingredient in a personal injury action, s 32(1)(c) of the 1980 Act does not apply to personal injury cases either.

This leaves concealment under s 32(1)(b), where any fact relevant to the plaintiff's cause of action has been deliberately concealed from him by the defendant. The concealment must be of facts that are relevant to the cause of action. Concealment of evidence that relates merely to the proving of a case is not sufficient (*Frisby v Theodore Goddard & Co* (1984) Times, 7 March).

Section 32(2) states that, 'For the purposes of subsection (1) above, deliberate commission of a breach of duty in circumstances in which it is unlikely to be discovered for some time amounts to deliberate concealment of the facts involved in that breach of duty'. For s 32(1) to apply, it is necessary for there to have been some deliberate commission of breach of duty as above or other act of deliberate concealment. Silence alone will not suffice. A clear example of deliberate concealment is that of builders covering up defective foundations, as in *Kijowski v New Capital Properties* (1987) 15 Con LR 1.

The period of limitation does not begin to run until the plaintiff discovers the concealment or could with reasonable diligence have discovered it. The meaning of reasonable diligence was considered by Webster J in *Peco Arts v Hazlitt Gallery Ltd* [1983] 3 All ER 193. He concluded:

> 'first of all, that it is impossible to devise a meaning or construction to be put on those words which can be generally applied in all contexts ... In the context to which I have to apply them, in my judgment, I conclude that reasonable diligence means not the doing of everything possible, not even necessarily the using of any means at the plaintiff's disposal, not even necessarily the doing of anything at all, but that it means the doing of that which an ordinarily prudent buyer and possessor of a valuable work of art would do having regard to all the circumstances ...'

There are exceptions and limitations to even the theoretical application of s 32 to personal injury cases. By s 12(3), s 32 shall not apply to any action under the Fatal Accidents Act 1976. Section 32(4A) provides that it will not be permitted to override the 10-year maximum limitation period from the relevant date of supply set down by s 11A(3) for product liability actions brought under Part 1 of the Consumer Protection Act 1987.

Matters occurring before the right of action occurred cannot amount to concealment under s 32. In *Skerratt v Linfax Ltd* (p654), before using and getting injured at the defendant's go-karting track, the claimant signed a disclaimer form that was invalid under the Unfair Contract Terms Act 1977. There was no evidence that the defendants realised this. Dismissing the claimant's appeal, Waller LJ stated (at para 20) that:

> '20. ... in my view it is difficult to conceive of a case of concealment unless that concealment takes place either at the very time that the cause of action is occurring, or unless it takes place after the cause of action was accrued, ie unless the defendant is taking some steps to deliberately conceal a fact relevant to the cause of action.
>
> 21. ... I, for my part, have some doubt whether the existence or otherwise of a cause of action is a fact relevant to the claimant's right of action on any view. *Johnson v Chief Constable of Surrey*, the transcript of which is with our papers dated 19 October 1992, makes clear that a fairly narrow construction is to be placed on section 32(1)(b). The court is strictly concerned with facts relevant to the cause of action. It is not concerned, for example, with the suppression of evidence that might be relevant to the proof of the cause of action. Mr Clifford Darton submits that this disclaimer was relevant to the question whether there was a breach of duty at all. Thus he submits that it falls outside the decision of *Johnson v Chief Constable of Surrey*. I have to say I have serious doubts about that, but it is unnecessary to finally decide that aspect having regard to the other points that I have made. As it seems to me, the District Judge, who dealt with this aspect as the first point in his judgment, was clearly right that there was no concealment within section 32.'

In practice, the main restraint on the application of s 32(1)(b) to personal injury claims is that it will very often be otiose. The reason is that, in a case of deliberate concealment by a defendant of facts relevant to a right of action, the claimant will seldom have acquired the required knowledge within the meaning of s 14 so as to set time running under s 11(4)(b) or (5)(b). Therefore, s 32(1)(b) can only apply to a personal injury case when the deliberately concealed fact is not one of those listed in s 14(1). A possible example is a misleading negative answer by a defendant to a question by a claimant which, if correctly answered, might establish the claimant's right of action to sue for negligence, nuisance or breach of duty.

There is no corresponding restraint on the applicability of s 32(1)(b) to a professional negligence action arising out of a misconducted personal injury claim.

Section 38(5) specifically states that, 'Sections 14A and 14B of this Act shall not apply to any action to which subsection (1)(b) above applies'. Accordingly, where s 32(1)(b) applies, the special limitation periods incorporated as a result of the Latent Damage Act 1986 are excluded. In such a case, the extended limitation period is simply six years from the date when the claimant discovers the concealment or could with reasonable diligence have discovered it.

Consequently, the case of *Kitchen v R A F Association* (p522) continues to be good law. In May 1945, Mr Kitchen was electrocuted at home and died. In May 1946 the solicitors acting for his widow culpably allowed the one-year limitation period then applicable to expire. In October 1946 they reached and implemented an agreement with the electricity company to pay £100 on condition that it would be sent to the widow without her knowing its origin. When she sued the solicitors for damages for professional negligence in September 1955, the Court of Appeal upheld the trial judge's finding in her favour that the solicitors' concealment had postponed the running of the limitation period.

Section 32(1)(b) was directly applied to the professional negligence case of *Williams v Fanshaw Porter & Hazelhurst* [2004] EWCA Civ 157 which arose out of a failed medical negligence action against a doctor at the claimant's general practice. In 1994 the defendant solicitors consented to the court proceedings against the doctor being struck out, without the claimant's knowledge or consent, and also decided not to tell the claimant at the time of their unsuccessful application to re-join the doctor to the action. The Court of Appeal held that time against the defendant solicitors only started to run from the date during 1995 in which they finally informed the claimant of the facts, with the result that her court action against them commenced in December 2000 was in time. Explaining this decision, Park J made four observations on the wording of s 32(1)(b):

'(i)   The paragraph does not say that the right of action must have been concealed from the claimant: it says only that a fact relevant to the right of action should have been concealed from the claimant.

(ii)   Although the concealed fact must have been relevant to the right of action, the paragraph does not say, and in my judgment does not require, the defendant must have known that the fact was relevant to the right of action. In most cases where s 32(1)(b) applies, the defendant probably will have known that the fact or facts which he concealed were relevant, but that is not essential. All that is essential is that the fact must actually have been relevant, whether the defendant knew that or not. The paragraph does of course require that the fact was one which the defendant knew, because otherwise he could not have concealed it. But it is not necessary in addition that the defendant knew that the fact was relevant to the claimant's right of action.

(iii) The paragraph requires only that *any* fact relevant to the right of action is concealed. It does not require that *all* facts relevant to the right of action are concealed.

(iv) The requirement is that the fact must be "deliberately concealed". It is, I think, plain that, for concealment to be deliberate, the defendant must have considered whether to inform the claimant of the fact and decided not to. I would go further and accept that the fact which he decides not to disclose either must be one which it was his duty to disclose, or must at least be one which he would ordinarily have disclosed in the normal course of his relationship with the claimant, but in the case if which he consciously decided to depart from what he would normally have done and to keep quiet about it.'

By s 33(8) of the 1980 Act, any postponed limitation period arising under s 32(1) may be disapplied altogether in the exercise of the court's discretion under s 33(1) where it would be equitable to allow the action to proceed.

5 Discretion to disapply limitation periods (section 33)

Introduction: the ambit of discretion

This chapter examines the court's power to allow a personal injury action to proceed even though it is statute barred. This remarkable inroad into the certainty of limitation law was first established by s 1 of the 1975 Limitation Act through the insertion of s 2D into the 1939 Limitation Act. Section 33 of the 1980 Limitation Act follows precisely s 2D of the 1939 Act. Most of the legal reform committees charged with investigating the workings of the Limitation Act 1939 rejected submissions made to them that the court should have a residual discretion to allow a time barred action to proceed (cf Cmnd 5334: Revision Committee's 5th Interim Report (Statute of Limitation) December 1936, Cmnd 1829: Report of Committee on Limitation of Actions in Cases of Personal Injury, September 1962). The notable exception was the Tucker Committee (1949 Report of the Committee on the Limitation of Actions Cmnd 4770) which recommended a two-year primary limitation period but with the power to extend up to a maximum of six years in the case of personal injury actions. However, in 1974 the Orr Committee (Cmnd 5630: Law Reform Committee 20th Report (Interim Report on Limitation of Actions in Personal Injury Claims), May 1974) did recommend empowering the court with a discretion to override the limitation period in what they described as *a residual class of case* (para 56). This class of case was principally envisaged to be those where delay had occurred because the claimant did not know that he had a worthwhile cause of action in law. The recommendation was to counter balance the committee's expressed view that ignorance of the law was not to prevent time running when calculating a claimant's date of knowledge. The committee thought that the benefit of introducing a judicial discretion into the limitation statutes would be to allow the court to analyse the potential prejudices suffered by each party and then to determine whether a case should be allowed to proceed or not.

As enacted, the 1975 Limitation Act provisions have been construed by both the Court of Appeal and the House of Lords as providing a wide and general discretion which, on its clear wording, is not restricted to any residual category of case. Accordingly, s 33 of the 1980 Act is as applicable to road traffic and factory accidents as it is to long-maturing insidious diseases and cases of childhood abuse. The discretion may also be applied to those actions where solicitors have simply failed to issue proceedings in time, as well as to those cases where the injured person was ignorant of the fact that he had a worthwhile cause of action in law. Interestingly, a member of the Orr Committee, Griffiths J, did initially construe s 2D of the 1939 Act as not being intended to deal with straightforward running down cases but only there to determine the occasion hard case (*Finch v Francis*, 21 July 1977, unreported). The Court of Appeal, however, in *Firman v Ellis* (p433) was emphatically opposed to such a restricted construction. Lord Denning said:

> 'Although the Committee did not accept the proposal for a general discretion, nevertheless, when Parliament passed the 1975 Act, it did give the court a general discretion. Section 2D, as I read it, gives a wide discretion to the court which is not limited to "residual classes of case" at all. It is not limited to "exceptional cases". It gives the court a discretion to extend the time to all cases where the three year limitation has expired before the issue of the Writ ... it confers on the court an unfettered discretion to extend the three year period in any case where it is equitable to do so. The granting of the discretion is a revolutionary step. It alters our whole approach to time bars. I do not regard it as a retrograde step. In former times it was thought that judges should not be given a discretionary power. It would lead to too much uncertainty ... these days are now passed.' ([1978] QB 886 at 905 C–F)

In *Firman v Ellis* the court was considering combined appeals arising out of circumstances the Orr Committee may not have considered, namely cases where there had been negotiations for settlement but the claimant's solicitors by 'the merest slip' allowed time to run out. Ormrod LJ emphasised how there was a disjunction between what the Orr Committee had intended and what Parliament had enacted. He dealt with propositions that the Act should be construed in restricted terms in the following manner:

> 'The reasons put forward to support the argument that the court should apply the Section restrictively, in the interests of public policy, were twofold: first the loss of certainty which would inevitably arise if the discretion was freely used and, second, the loss of a valuable sanction over plaintiffs and their solicitors to discourage delay in the bringing of proceedings, and, in particular, over solicitors by allowing them to avoid liabilities to their clients for negligence. So far as the first point is concerned Parliament has now decided that uncertain justice is preferable to certain injustices, or in other words that certainty can be brought at too high a price, as these four cases vividly demonstrate. If insurance companies through their customers choose to take wholly unmeritorious technical points to avoid liability, they cannot complain if ultimately their ability to take them is severely restricted. To retain a highly formulistic procedure, the real effect of which is simply to transfer liability from the original tortfeasor's insurers to the plaintiff's solicitors insurers, is not very impressive, as a piece of public policy.' (911E–G)

Similarly, Lane LJ (at 915D) opposed fettering the new discretionary power which he indicated gave 'to the court as wide a discretion as could well be imagined'.

This interpretation of the wide discretion given by the 1975 Act was endorsed by the single speech of Lord Diplock in the House of Lords three years later in *Thompson v Brown Construction (Ebbw Vale) Ltd* (p690). This case concerned a claimant who sued 37 days out of time and in which he had, but for the limitation defence, a clear case against the defendant as well as a clear case against his solicitors for negligence. Lord Diplock agreed with the wide ambit of the court's discretion which, being unfettered, gave the court a power to allow a time-barred action to proceed even when a claimant had a cast-iron case against his own solicitors for negligence (see also *Conry v Simpson* (p385) and *Donovan v Gwentoys Ltd* (p412)).

In *KR v Bryn Alyn Community Holdings Ltd* (p505) the Court of Appeal stated that the s 33 discretion was fettered only to the extent that the section provides a non-exhaustive list of circumstances to which the judge should have regard (cf para 68). However, this court chose to emphasise that the exercise of the discretion was not determined by simply assessing comparative scales of hardship but requires consideration of whether it was equitable to disapply the limitation period (cf *Long v Tolchard and Son Ltd* [2001] PIQR 18). The court went on to state:

> 'The burden of showing that it would be equitable to disapply the limitation period lies on the claimant and it is a heavy burden. Another way of putting it is that it is an exceptional indulgence to a claimant, to be granted only where equity between the parties demands it.' (per Auld LJ at para 74(ii))

In *Horton v Sadler* (p482) the House of Lords reaffirmed that the discretion was unfettered and approved Lord Denning's exposition of the statutory language in *Firman v Ellis*. The description of the exercise as exceptional is, accordingly, potentially misleading (cf *AB v Nugent Care Society* [2009] EWCA Civ 827 at para 20, and *Sayers v Chelwood (deceased) and another* (p642) at paras 53–56). In *Horton*, the House invoked its Practice Statement [1966] 1 WLR 1234 to reverse the major fetter that had been put on the discretion for 26 years by its earlier decision in *Walkley v Precision Forgings Ltd* (p705). To understand the significance of the decision in *Horton*, it is necessary to examine how the rule in *Walkley* shaped personal injury limitation law for a generation.

Cases prior to *Horton v Sadler* to which s 33 did not apply: the *Walkley* exceptions

Section 33 discretion was not applicable in the years 1979–2006 to those cases where a claim form had already been issued during the primary limitation period but not served or not lawfully renewed and a second claim form was issued out of time. In addition, the discretion was inapplicable to those cases where proceedings have been served but had been allowed to elapse through discontinuance or had been struck out. In these circumstances, if a claimant issued a second set of proceedings he was normally unable to rely on a s 33 discretion. This was because, in *Walkley v Precision Forgings Ltd* (p705), the House of Lords held that the court has no power in such circumstances to invoke a s 33 discretion (then a s 2D discretion under the 1975 Act). In *Walkley* the claimant was employed as a grinder between 1966 and 1971 and in 1969 developed Raynauld's disease which he was told was attributable to his work. A writ was issued and served in 1971 but then proceedings went no further due to negative advice from counsel. A second writ was issued in 1976, which the defendants claimed was statute barred. The claimant sought to reply upon the court's discretion to disapply the limitation period. The House of Lords held that no prejudice in these circumstances arose from the provisions of the Limitation Act because the first action had been brought in time. Prejudice arose from failing to proceed with the first action. Accordingly, the court said it had no discretion to disapply the time limit. The only possible exception would be those cases where a first action, brought in time, was discontinued due to misrepresentation or improper conduct on the part of the defendant. Otherwise, Lord Diplock considered, the failure to proceed with the first action, whether through a failure to serve a writ or to proceed after it had been served, was a self-inflicted wound:

> 'The provisions of section 2A caused him no prejudice at all; he was able to start his action. The only cause of the prejudice to him in the case of dismissal

for want of prosecution is dilatoriness which took place after the action started whether on his own part or on the part of his legal advisors. In the case of discontinuance the only cause of prejudice is his own act ... the only exception I have been able to think of where it might be proper to give a direction under section 2D, despite the fact that the plaintiff had previously started an action within the primary limitation period but had subsequently discontinued it would be a case in which the plaintiff had been induced to discontinue by a misrepresentation or other improper conduct by the defendant.' ([1979] 2 All ER 548 at 559)

Walkley effectively overruled the decision in *Firman v Ellis* (above) where the solicitor's errors had been in failing to extend the period of validity of the writ or in failing to serve the writ in time. The effect of excluding the ambit of the court's discretion under the 1980 Act, in a case where a valid claim form has been issued, was to put a defendant in a better position if a claim form has been issued but not served in time than if one had not been issued at all. It also made a solicitor who negligently failed to issue less likely to suffer the consequences of his own negligence than one who issues in time but forgets to serve or to renew. This anomaly was referred to by Lord Diplock in *Thompson v Brown Construction (Ebbw Vale) Ltd* (p690) which he attributed to:

'a consequence of the greater anomaly too well established for this House to abolish that, for the purposes of the limitation period an action is brought when a writ or other originating process is issued by the Central Office High Court and not when it is brought to the knowledge of the defendant by service on him.' ([1981] 1 WLR 744)

The effect of *Walkley* was considered soon after in *Chappell v Cooper* (p369) by the Court of Appeal who quickly dispensed with the submission that *Walkley* only applied to its particular facts. The Court of Appeal emphasised that, when an action was discontinued after service or where a writ was never in fact served through decision or default, a claimant could not rely on the court's powers to disapply the primary limitation period. Rather ruefully, Ormrod LJ in *Chappell* referred to his own judgment in *Firman v Ellis*:

'I was foolish enough in the course of giving judgment in *Firman v Ellis* to think that at a third attempt Parliament had succeeded in reforming this part of the law. Now it is apparent that a fourth attempt will be necessary, if the law on this topic is to be rationalised ... the result (of *Walkley*) is that the game will continue to be played between defendants' insurance companies and solicitors' insurance companies ... the House of Lords having adopted a restricted construction of section 2D there is no alternative but to accept the consequences which are as I said: the old game will continue.' ([1980] 2 All ER 463 at 470F–J)

In *Deerness v John Keeble and Son (Brantham) Ltd* (p408) the so-called 'game' was again played out to the House of Lords. Their Lordships were given an opportunity to consider what might constitute exceptional circumstances so that even when an action had been initiated a second action might take the benefit of a s 33 discretion. Miss Deerness was rendered paraplegic in a road traffic accident, and if her claim had been presented timeously she was bound to succeed. The defendant's insurers had entered into negotiations and had made an interim payment. The writ, though issued, was not served during its period of validity by oversight and a second writ was issued which the defendants claimed was statute barred. Comyn J at first instance found that the case fell into Lord Diplock's category of exceptional circumstances as set out in *Walkley*. The judge emphasised the case was otherwise bound to succeed because the driver pleaded guilty to driving without due care and attention, there had been prolonged negotiations and correspondence with the defendants' insurers who had made an interim payment and the defendants had suffered no prejudice. The Court of Appeal said regretfully that no such exceptional circumstances existed and allowed the defendants' appeal indicating that the judge allowed his heart to rule his head. Lord Diplock agreed with the Court of Appeal:

'My Lords I share the regret (of the Court of Appeal) but with heart unmoved. The plaintiff herself has not suffered: she has already received £100,000 pursuant to a condition which an Appeal Committee of this House imposed on granting leave to appeal. She should now receive the balance. The solicitor's insurers will have to pay out for a risk they insured and for which they charged a premium, so they have suffered no injustice. Cornhill (insurers of the defendants) have had the good luck to escape having to pay out for a risk that they had insured and for which they too had charged a premium, but in liability insurance business, as between two insurers where the only question is which of them has to pay a claim, one cannot blame either insurer for taking advantage of his own good luck … No question arises in the instant case as to the possible exception to the general rule laid down in *Walkley*'s case that was alluded to in my speech.' ([1983] 2 Lloyd's Rep 260 at 264)

Lord Diplock further defined what he meant by exceptional circumstances. He stated that the example he had given in *Walkley* of exceptional circumstances (where a claimant was induced to discontinue by a misrepresentation or other improper conduct) could more accurately be characterised as an estoppel from relying on s 11 of the Act. Whether a defendant was estopped was a matter of fact and not a matter of discretion (at 262). (For other examples where *Walkley* had been applied, see *Whitfield v North Durham Health Authority* (p713) and *Forward v Hendricks* [1997] 2 All ER 395.)

In *Young v Western Power Distribution (South West) plc* (p733) the Court of Appeal applied *Walkley* to a fatal claim both under Fatal Accidents Act 1976 and the Law Reform (Miscellaneous Provisions) Act 1934. Mr Young had been exposed to asbestos by the defendants and was diagnosed in December 1993 as having mesothelioma, an asbestos induced malignancy. He issued proceedings in his lifetime on 6 January 1995. However, both a treating physician and the defendants' medico-legal expert thought that the diagnosis was more compatible with adenocarcinoma which was not related to asbestos exposure. Mr Young's own medico-legal expert remained sceptical and said the diagnosis could not be properly determined until after post mortem. Because Mr Young was unable to prove his case on causation, he discontinued proceedings. Mr Young died on 2 March 1999 and a post mortem revealed that, in fact, he did have mesothelioma. His widow subsequently issued further proceedings on 22 May 2002, that is, outside the three-year anniversary of his death, and would have needed a s 33 dispensation in any event. The defendants, however, further contended that the second action was caught by the principle in *Walkley* and no discretion under s 33 was available to the widow. The court at first instance held that *Walkley* did apply to the second action but the facts brought it within the exception of estoppel or something close to it. The Court of Appeal disagreed and allowed the defendants' appeal. Expressing the view of the court (with no particular enthusiasm), Simon Brown LJ (para 38) held that *Walkley* did apply to both the widow's claim under the Fatal Accidents Act 1976 and the estate claim under the Law Reform (Miscellaneous Provisions) Act 1934. The deceased could not have brought a second action in his own lifetime, had a more definitive diagnosis of mesothelioma been possible and the court held that the claimant could be in no better position. Further, on the facts of the case, no estoppel arose. The court also found that the *Walkley* principle did not offend against Article 6 of the European Convention on Human Rights, as English limitation law pursued a legitimate aim and each contracting state had a margin of appreciation as set out in *Stubbings v UK* (p678). Lord Justice Simon Brown added that it was for Parliament or the House of Lords to reverse this rule and noted that the Law Commission Report 270 had recommended the abolition of the rule. (See paragraph 3.166 of the Law Com Report.)

The courts were not astute to extend the *Walkley* principle and distinguished several classes of cases where the rule was not to be applied. These were cases where the first claim form was issued out of time itself, where the claim form was a nullity or was defective and where the second action was against a different party. This led to a series of case where there was no principled distinctions but much judicial creativity to avoid an unpopular rule.

In *Adam v Ali* [2006] EWCA Civ 91 a simple road traffic accident was issued one week out of time and, because no particulars of claim were served, was struck out by the court on its own motion. A second claim form was issued and the claimant sought to rely on a s 33 discretion. The defendant relied on *Walkley* and the judge agreed that the principle applied and he had no discretion to allow the claim to proceed (and, even if he did, he would not have exercised it in the claimant's favour). The Court of Appeal allowed the claimant's appeal contending that the anomalies of *Walkley* should be carefully confined (per Ward LJ at para 24) and restricted its ambit to those cases where the first action had been brought in time. In addition, the court exercised its discretion in the claimant's favour as the errors had been due to her solicitors rather than to her.

The court further held that, if s 33 was to be excluded from consideration, there must have been not only a claim form physically issued but it must be a valid claim form. So where, for example, a writ had been issued without leave against a company in compulsory liquidation, the process was wholly ineffective and a nullity. In *Wilson v Banner Scaffolding Ltd* (p722) the claimant issued such a writ against a company in liquidation without leave of the court as was then required by s 231 of the Companies Act 1948. Subsequently, after the expiry of the limitation period and after leave was given to issue proceedings, an amendment was allowed to the writ and Milmo J held that the defendants could not rely on the principle in *Walkley* because the initial writ was a nullity and he therefore retained a discretion under s 33 of the 1980 Act. This he applied in the claimant's favour. The Court of Appeal subsequently came to the same view in *Rose v Express Welding Ltd* (p631).

Similarly, *Walkley* was held not to apply where a defendant company had ceased to exist because it had been dissolved and struck off the register. If a claim form was issued against it, because it was a non-existent legal entity the process was invalid. The court, therefore, retained the discretion to use the provisions of s 33 of the 1980 Act in a case where subsequently the same company was restored to the register under the provisions of s 651 of the Companies Act 1985, as amended by s 141 of the Companies Act 1989. This occurred in *Re Workvale Ltd (No 2)* (p726), where Scott LJ held:

'... The present case is not on all fours with *Walkley v Precision Forgings Ltd*. The action that was started with in the primary limitation period in the present case was not an effective action. Unknown to the plaintiff and his advisers the defendant did not exist. The facts relevant to the defendants' corporate existence did not become known to the plaintiff or his advisers until after the primary limitation period expired. So, as it seems to me, the plaintiff in the present case has been prejudiced by the three year limitation period.' ([1992] 2 All ER 627 at 635)

(In *Re Philip Powis Ltd* (p603) and *Smith v White Knight Laundry* (p663) the Court of Appeal subsequently approved *Re Workvale Ltd*.)

In *Smith v White Knight Laundry* (above), the court emphasised that the true effect of the restoration order was as if the dissolution had never occurred. That being so, the court should not grant an order that time should not run during the period of the company's dissolution under s 651, as this was equivalent to granting a s 33 dispensation. The proper procedure was for the applicant to seek to restore the company to the register and thereafter take out an application under s 33 which would have the benefit of having been served on all interested parties.

The Court of Appeal further limited the *Walkley* restriction in *White v Glass* (1989) Times, 18 February by holding that *Walkley* did not apply to a case where the writ was defective as well as where the writ was a nullity. Mr White sought to sue an unincorporated football club in its own name. These proceedings, which were issued within the primary limitation period, were defective because the club itself was not a legal entity. After the limitation period expired, he issued fresh proceedings against the correct defendant and sought to rely on s 33 of the 1980 Act. The defendants contended that the court had no power to invoke its discretion but the Court of Appeal held that the action did not come with the ambit of *Walkley*. The first action was deemed not to be a properly constituted action and the fact that it could have been remedied was 'neither here nor there'. A similar approach was taken by the Court of Appeal in *McEvoy v AA Welding & Fabrication Ltd* (p551) where proceedings were issued without leave against a company in liquidation. Although the court recognised that there were conflicting authorities on the question as to whether leave given after the commencement of proceedings could validate the proceedings retrospectively, the court did not apply *Walkley*. Lady Justice Arden in a later case, *Piggott v Estate of Aulton decd* [2003] EWCA Civ 24, said that this was because:

'The plaintiff's solicitors believed that proceedings were a nullity and started new proceedings. This court held that there were exceptional circumstances within the *Walkley* principle because the reasonable belief that the original proceedings were a nullity.' (para 8)

(See also Lord LJ Simon Brown at paragraph 32 in *Piggott*.)

Finally the rule in *Walkley* did not apply where the second action was against a different party. In *Shapland v Palmer* (p646) the claimant first sued an employer of a driver whose negligence caused the claimant's whiplash injury. This action was struck out because his solicitors failed to serve the claim form in time. A second action was initiated against the driver himself in a personal capacity, and the Court of Appeal held that *Walkley* did not apply as the parties were not the same and, accordingly, a s 33 discretion was available to the court which was exercised in the claimant's favour. Similarly, in *Piggott v Aulton* (above) the Court of Appeal held that, where proceedings had been brought against the estate of a deceased person but no person had been appointed to represent the estate, *Walkley* did not apply to subsequent proceedings against nominated personal representatives. The second set of proceedings were not against the same party and *Walkley* could be distinguished (cf *Clay v Chamberlain* (p377), affirmed on different grounds).

The abolition of the rule in *Walkley*: *Horton v Sadler*

In *Horton v Sadler* (p482) the House of Lords put an end to this complex jurisprudence by simply accepting that the previous decision in the House in *Walkley*, as confirmed in *Thompson v Brown Construction (Ebbw Vale) Ltd* (p690) and *Deerness v Keeble* (p408), was simply wrong. In *Horton* the claimant was injured in a road traffic accident on 12 April 1998 but, because the defendant was uninsured, made a claim against the MIB. The claimant's solicitors did not comply with a condition precedent of the MIB's liability, as they failed to inform the MIB of notice of the proceedings. The MIB took this point in their defence and sought the return of an interim payment. The claimant's solicitors issued a second set of proceedings and gave proper notice to the MIB but did so outside the primary limitation period, on September 2001. The court in the second action felt bound by *Walkley* but the trial judge indicated that, if he had a discretion, he would have exercised it in the claimant's favour as liability was not in issue, there was no prejudice to the defendant save the loss of the limitation defence and there was some prejudice to the claimant in having to bring an action against his solicitors. The judge considered but rejected the MIB's submission that the loss ought to fall on the solicitors' insurers, who had received a premium, rather the MIB who had not. As *Walkley* bound the Court of Appeal, the matter was dismissed in the Court of Appeal without argument. In the House of Lords the claimant succeeded on three grounds. First, it was accepted that the claimant was prejudiced by the provisions of s 11 and that the reference in s 33 to it being equitable for the action to proceed referred to the action in issue, namely the second not the first action. Lord Diplock and Lord Wilberforce had therefore been wrong to construe the equivalent provision in the 1975 Act as referring to the first rather than the second action. Secondly, the House accepted that the fine distinctions made in the subsequent case law were irrational and lacking in principle. Finally, the court accepted that the discretion in the provision was in fact, on a proper construction, unfettered and in subjecting it to technical rules and not permitting it to be applied to second actions subverted the intention of Parliament. The House therefore felt compelled to apply the Practice Statement of 1966 and departed from its previous decisions. Lord Bingham stated:

'... I feel bound to conclude that the reasoning of the decision was unsound, that it has given rise to distinctions which disfigure the law in this area and that the effect has been to restrict unduly the broad discretion which Parliament conferred.' (para 28)

Lord Hoffmann expressed similar views:

'My Lords, it is with a reluctance verging on disbelief that one is driven to conclude that the deliberate opinions of Lord Wilberforce and Lord Diplock were quite wrong.' (para 39)

Lord Carswell's nail in the *Walkley* coffin was that he had long viewed the decision in Walkley as based on flawed logic and being capable of causing signal unfairness (para 51). Lord Brown, who had grappled with many of the intractable problems thrown up by *Walkley* when sitting in the Court of Appeal, stated:

'the curious but plain fact is that in *Walkley* Homer nodded: an impossible and illogical construction was put upon the section ... In stating ... that a plaintiff who has already brought a first action in time "has not been prevented from starting *his action*" (emphasis added), Lord Diplock appears to have confused or conflated the two separate sets of proceedings: it is not the first action in which the plaintiff is prejudiced by the time bar but the second; and it is the second action for which the plaintiff seeks the favourable exercise of the court's discretion....' (para 63)

It is now, therefore, open to the court in any time-barred personal injury action to consider whether a s 33 discretion should be exercised. In *Richardson v Watson* (p621) the principles in *Horton* were soon applied and the Court of Appeal allowed the claimant to proceed in a second action against the MIB pursuant to exercising a s 33 discretion. In *Richardson*, the claimant was the widow whose husband was killed in a road traffic accident and the court was influenced in part by the fact that the MIB had in any event to deal with child dependency actions which were not statute barred, having an extended limitation period. In *Leeson v Marsden* (p530), the court gave a dispensation in a second action where the first action concerning a clinical negligence case had not been served in time .The court also rejected the defendant's argument that permitting a second action was an abuse of process, a view upheld in the subsequent case of *Aktas v Adepta* (p296). The rest of this chapter examines the principles governing how the s 33 discretion has been exercised.

1 Prejudice

Section 33(1) provides:

'If it appears to the court that it would be equitable to allow an action to proceed having regard to the degree to which–

(a) the provisions of section 11 or 11A or 12 of this Act prejudice the plaintiff or any person whom he represents; and

(b) any decision of the court under this subsection would prejudice the defendant or any person whom he represents;

the court may direct that those provisions shall not apply to this action, or shall not apply to any specified cause of action to which the action relates.'

This subsection requires the court to examine separately the respective prejudices that will occur to the claimant if the claim remains statute barred and to the defendant if it is allowed to proceed. In determining the type and the amount of prejudice, the court is required by s 33(3) to look at all the circumstances of the case with particular reference to the six specified factors. After undertaking this inquiry the court is required to exercise its discretion on the basis of what is equitable. The subsection probably confers the widest possible ambit of discretion that it is possible to create requiring fairness and justice between the parties.

The court has declined to lay down firm guidelines as to how the discretion should be exercised. Lord Diplock in *Thompson v Brown Construction (Ebbw Vale) Ltd* (p690) thought it inappropriate that the House of Lords, with minimal experience of such applications, should enumerate guidelines for first instance judges who have great familiarity with the typical type of circumstances that arise. He did, however, indicate that the Court of Appeal if necessary might lay down such principles. In *Ramsden v Lee* (p618) the Court of Appeal was asked to consider giving such guidance by the defendant's counsel, who suggested that, in the absence of any fault on the part of the defendant, the limitation period ought to be enforced against a claimant unless the delay was minimal and particularly if the claimant had a good claim over against his solicitors. However, Dillon LJ indicated:

'To my mind there is a considerable danger in laying down guidelines where the need for guidelines has not been made entirely apparent. The risk is that then more and more cases will come which are treated as matters of law on the application not of the statute but of the guidelines.' ([1992] 2 All ER 204 at 209)

The court went on to state that any guidelines would be likely to generate more litigation and, in any event, it would be difficult to construe guidelines which were not inconsistent with the statutory requirement to look at all the circumstances of a case. Nevertheless, in *Hartley v Birmingham District Council* (p465), Parker LJ, in view of the House of Lords' indication in *Thompson v Brown* that the Court of Appeal might provide such guidelines, did indicate 'some general observations' on the nature of prejudice but, beyond that, did not consider 'it either useful or desirable to attempt to lay down guidelines where circumstances are infinitely variable' ([1992] 2 All ER 213 at 224). In *KR v Bryn Alyn Community Holdings Ltd* (p505) the Court of Appeal was concerned with cases of longstanding psychiatric injury alleged to have resulted from sexual and/or physical abuse in children's homes. This court stated that, given the width of the discretion, the extent to which any court could give general guidelines on the exercise of it was limited (para 70). The court did, however, go on to set out eight starting points for the exercise of discretion (para 74) and made three observations of a general nature (in para 80). Lord Justice Auld, giving the judgment of the court, stated:

'74.   We take the following to be well-established and/or uncontroversial starting points for the exercise of the discretion:

   (i)   In multiple claims of this sort, a judge should consider the exercise of his discretion separately in relation to each claim: *Nash v Eli Lilly & Co* [1993] 1 WLR 782, 808–810, per Purchas LJ.
   (ii)   The burden of showing that it would be equitable to disapply the limitation period lies on the claimant and it is a heavy burden. Another way of putting it is that it is an exceptional indulgence to a claimant, to be granted only where equity between the parties demands it; … *Thompson v Brown* [1981] 1 WLR 744, 750, 752 …
   (iii) Depending on the issues and the nature of the evidence going to them, the longer the delay the more likely, and the greater, the prejudice to the defendant.
   (iv)   Where a judge is minded to grant a long "extension" he should take meticulous care in giving reasons for doing so: *Mold v Hayton, Newson* [2000] MLC 207.
   (v)   A judge should not reach a decision effectively concluding the matter on the strength of any one of the circumstances specified in section 33(3), or on one of any other circumstances relevant to his decision, or without regard to all the issues in the case. He should conduct the balancing exercise at the end of his analysis of all the relevant circumstances and with regard to all the issues, taking them all into account: *Long v Tolchard & Sons Ltd* [2001] PIQR P18, 26, per Roch LJ.
   (vi)   Wherever the judge considers it feasible to do so, he should decide the limitation point by a preliminary hearing by reference to the pleadings and written witness statements and, importantly, the extent and content of discovery … It may not always be feasible or produce savings in time and cost for the parties to deal with the matter by way of preliminary hearing, but a judge should strain to do so wherever possible.

(vii) Where a judge determines a section 33 issue along with the substantive issues in the case, he should take care not to determine the substantive issues, including liability, causation and quantum before determining the issue of limitation and, in particular, the effect of delay on the cogency of the evidence. Much of such evidence, by reason of the lapse of time, may have been incapable of being adequately tested or contradicted before him. To rely on his findings on those issues to assess the cogency of the evidence for the purposes of the limitation exercise would put the cart before the horse. Put another way, it would effectively require a defendant to prove a negative, namely, that the judge could not have found against him on one or more of the substantive issues if he had tried the matter earlier and without the evidential disadvantages resulting from delay.

(viii) Where a judge has assessed the likely cogency of the available evidence, that is, before finding either way on the substantive issues in a case, he should keep in mind in balancing the respective prejudices to the parties that the more cogent the claimant's case the greater the prejudice to the Defendant in depriving him of the benefit of the limitation period. As Parker LJ showed in *Hartley v Birmingham City District Council* [1992] 1 WLR 968, 979, such a finding is usually neutral on the balance of prejudice ... (However, the) ... remarks of Parker LJ ... were qualified in *Nash v Eli Lilly & Co* [1993] 1 WLR 782, 804E, where this Court said that there could be instances of weak claims where disapplication of the limitation provision could cause the Defendants considerable prejudice in putting them to the trouble and expense of successfully defending them and then not being able to recover costs against impecunious claimants.'

Further, the court continued at paragraph 80:

'... for the reasons we give in the following paragraphs, we consider:

 (i) that, as a general rule of thumb, the longer the delay after the occurrence of the matters giving rise to the cause of action the more likely it is that the balance of prejudice will swing against disapplication;

 (ii) that in cases of this nature, where issues of liability causation and quantum can be so difficult with or without delay, the permissible delay in each case is likely to be highly sensitive to the prejudice it causes to the defence notwithstanding good reasons of the claimant for its length; and

(iii) that, if the date of knowledge test in Section 14 is properly applied so as to provide a claimant with an extension of the period by reference to it, the weight to be given to his reasons for delay thereafter should, in normal circumstances be limited ...'

The court finally sought to endorse a more liberal approach to the interpretation of s 14 on the claimant's date of knowledge and a more restrictive approach to s 33:

'96.   Some of these difficulties may be partly mitigated if there is legislation to implement the Law Commission's recommendation in paragraphs 3.45–50 of its Report for the amendment of section 14 to substitute a more subjective definition of the date of knowledge. As the Law Commission observed in paragraph 3.164 of its Report, that should in turn encourage courts to confine to truly exceptional cases those in which a further "extension" is sought through the medium of disapplication under section 33:

"We have considered whether any restriction should be placed on the use of such a discretion. When the Law Reform Committee first recommended that discretion to disapply the limitation period be introduced in personal injury cases, they intended the discretion to apply only to exceptional cases. However, it has in practice become generally available. It is arguable that under the regime we recommend this will be unnecessary. The core regime will relax the definition of the date of knowledge in favour of the claimant, by incorporating a more subjective definition of constructive knowledge. In addition, the primary limitation period running from the date of knowledge will be the only limitation period applying to personal injury claims. The claimant will therefore have had three years from the date on which he or she should have discovered the relevant fact, whenever that was, to bring proceedings against the defendant. Once the time limit has expired, it should only be in the most exceptional cases that the court will be justified in allowing a claimant a more generous time period within which to bring a claim.'"

Regrettably, however, for litigants and practitioners seeking consistency of interpretation of the statute, this guidance was very soon subjected to major modification following the House of Lords' decision in *A v Hoare* (p287) to interpret the law on ss 14 and 33 in precisely the opposite direction to that advocated by the Court of Appeal in *Bryn Alyn*.

As has been discussed in **Chapter 3**, the House of Lords in *Hoare* and conjoined cases determined that s 14 should be construed restrictively so that victims of abuse would be judged by the objective standards applicable to persons in their position, and this would mean ignoring the subjective effects that the abuse had on them in considering when they had actual or constructive knowledge of a significant injury. This meant that it would usually be the injury when they were first abused, as opposed to any subsequent psychiatric condition caused by the abuse that started time running.

Lord Hoffmann emphasised that the proper place for consideration of the subjective factors which may have inhibited a claimant from suing earlier was in a s 33 application:

'44. This does not mean that the law regards as irrelevant the question of whether the actual claimant, taking into account his psychological state in consequence of the injury, could reasonably have been expected to institute proceedings. But it deals with that question under section 33, which specifically says in subsection (3)(a) that one of the matters to be taken into account in the exercise of the discretion is "the reasons for … the delay on the part of the plaintiff".

45. In my opinion that is the right place in which to consider it. Section 33 enables the judge to look at the matter broadly and not have to decide the highly artificial question of whether knowledge which the claimant has in some sense suppressed counts as knowledge for the purposes of the Act. Furthermore, dealing with the matter under section 14(2) means that the epistemological question determines whether the claimant is entitled to sue as of right, without regard at any injustice which this might cause to the defendant. In my view it is far too brittle an instrument for this purpose. There are passages in the judgement of Buxton LJ which suggest that, had he not been bound by *Bryn Alyn*, he would have shared this opinion.

46. This approach would, I think, be in accordance with the recommendations of the Law Commission in the Report (Law Com No 270) to which I have

referred. In its Consultation Paper No 151, Limitation of Actions (1998) para 12.44, the Commission had proposed that the test of significance should take into account "the plaintiff's abilities". But they abandoned this position in their final report and recommended (at para 3.24) that the test of significance should be entirely objective: "only claims in respect of which a reasonable person would have thought it worthwhile issuing proceedings will qualify as 'significant'".

47.   In paras 4.27–4.28 of their final report the Law Commission considered whether victims of sexual abuse should be subject to a special regime. It had been submitted that no limitation period should apply to sex abuse claims because victims commonly suffered from 'dissociative amnesia', a recognised mental disorder which produced an inability to recall traumatic events or at any rate an unwillingness to be reminded of them. The Law Commission said that so far as dissociative amnesia was a "mental disability" within a fairly broad definition proposed by the Commission (see paras 3.123–3.124), it would (if their proposals were implemented) stop time running while the disability persisted. But they rejected (in para 3.125) any specific provision for the psychological incapacity suffered by victims of sexual abuse because they said that it would be very difficult to define.

48.   If the Commission thought that the "psychological incapacity suffered by victims of sexual abuse" (para 4.28) was too uncertain and indefinite a concept to be used for suspension of the limitation period on grounds of incapacity, I can see no advantage in relying upon the same uncertain concept to give an artificial meaning to the concept of knowledge in section 14. Until Parliament decides whether to give effect to the Commission's recommendation of a more precise definition of incapacity, it is better to leave these considerations to the discretion under section 33.

49.   That brings me, finally, to the approach of the judge and the Court of Appeal to the exercise of the discretion. In *Bryn Alyn* [2006] QB 1441 the Court of Appeal said, at para 76, that the judge in that case had gone wrong in giving undue weight to his conclusion that "the claimants' reasons for delay were a product of the alleged abuse ... and that, accordingly, it would be unjust to deprive them of a remedy". These matters, said the Court of Appeal, were more appropriately considered under section 14. *I am of precisely the opposite opinion, and if your Lordships share my view, the approach to the discretion will have to change.* In *Horton v Sadler* [2007] 1 AC 307 the House rejected a submission that section 33 should be confined to a "residual class of cases", as was anticipated by the 20th Report of the Law Reform Committee (Cmnd 5630) (1974) at para 56. It reaffirmed the decision of the Court of Appeal in *Firman v Ellis* [1978] QB 886, holding that the discretion is unfettered. The judge is expressly enjoined by subsection (3)(a) to have regard to the reasons for delay and in my opinion this requires him to give due weight to evidence, such as there was in this case, that the claimant was for practical purposes disabled from commencing proceedings by the "psychological injuries which he had suffered".' (emphasis added)

Lord Carswell noted that the effect of *Hoare* was to require a more liberal approach to s 33:

'70.   If, as I think to be the case, section 14 should be construed in this manner, which is less favourable to a claimant, there requires to be a more liberal approach to the exercise of discretion than has always been the case. For the reasons which my noble and learned friends and I have set out, that less favourable construction of section 14 is correct in principle, but it must follow that the favourable factors which have hitherto been taken into account in reaching a conclusion under section 14 should form a part, and in appropriate cases a very significant part, of the judge's determination in exercising his discretion under section 33.'

Lord Brown indicated how the approach to discretion would change in sexual abuse cases:

'84.   With regard to the exercise of the court's discretion under section 33 of the 1980 Act, however, I would make just three brief comments – not, let it be clear, in any way to fetter a discretion which the House in *Horton v Sadler* [2007] 1 AC 307 recently confirmed to be unfettered, but rather to suggest the sort of considerations which ought clearly to be in mind in sexual abuse cases in the new era which your Lordships are now ushering in, firstly, by departing from *Stubbings v Webb* and, secondly, by construing section 14(2) so as to transfer from that provision to section 33 consideration of the inhibiting effect of sexual abuse upon certain victims' preparedness to bring proceedings in respect of it.

85.   First, insofar as future claims may be expected to be brought against employers (or others allegedly responsible for abusers) on the basis of vicarious liability for sexual assaults rather than for systemic negligence in failing to prevent them, they will probably involve altogether narrower factual disputes than hitherto. As Lord Hoffmann suggests, at para 52, that is likely to bear significantly upon the possibility of having a fair trial.

86.   Secondly, through the combined effects of *Lister v Hesley Hall Ltd* and departing from *Stubbings v Webb*, a substantially greater number of allegations (not all of which will be true) are now likely to be made many years after the abuse complained of. Whether or not it will be possible for defendants to investigate these sufficiently for there to be a reasonable prospect of a fair trial will depend upon a number of factors, not least when the complaint was first made and with what effect. If a complaint has been made and recorded, and more obviously still if the accused has been convicted of the abuse complained of, that will be one thing; if, however, a complaint comes out of the blue with no apparent support for it (other perhaps than that the alleged abuser has been accused or even convicted of similar abuse in the past), that would be quite another thing. By no means everyone who brings a late claim for damages for sexual abuse, however genuine his complaint may in fact be, can reasonably expect the court to exercise the section 33 discretion in his favour. On the contrary, a fair trial (which must surely include a fair opportunity for the defendant to investigate the allegations – see section 33(3)(b)) is in many cases likely to be found quite simply impossible after a long delay.

87.   Hitherto the misconstruction of section 14(2) has given an absolute right to proceed, however long out of time, to anyone able to say that he would not reasonably have turned his mind to litigation (more than three years) earlier (the *Bryn Alyn* test described by Lord Hoffmann at paragraph 36). It is not to be supposed that the exercise of the court's section 33 discretion will invariably replicate that position.

88. My third and final comment relates most directly to A's appeal and it is this. The definition of "significant injury" in section 14(2) refers to the justifiability of bringing proceedings against a defendant "able to satisfy a judgment". That surely is unsurprising. It would not ordinarily be sensible to sue an indigent defendant. How then should the court approach the exercise of its section 33 discretion in a case like A where suddenly, after many years, the prospective defendant becomes rich. The House is not, of course, itself exercising this discretion. I would, however, suggest that it would be most unfortunate if people felt obliged (often at public expense) to bring proceedings for sexual abuse against indigent defendants simply with a view to their possible future enforcement. (Judgments, although interest-bearing for only six years, are enforceable without limit of time.)

89. For the purposes of these appeals, my comments are, of course, essentially by the way. Your Lordships were, however, invited by the Bar (indeed, those representing the interests of both claimants and defendants) to give such broad assistance as we felt able to regarding the exercise of discretion under section 33.'

The jurisprudential U-turn necessitated by *Hoare* on both ss 14 and 33 is well illustrated in the abuse cases brought against the Nugent Care Society, which produced further modification to the *Bryn Alyn* guidelines. Prior to the handing down of the House of Lords' decision in *Hoare*, Mr Justice Holland ([2006] EWHC 2986) found three test cases concerning inmates' allegations of sexual abuse statute barred and exercised a s 33 discretion in only one of the cases. The other two cases appealed ([2008] EWCA Civ 795) and the Court of Appeal referred the matter back to the judge for a reconsideration of the exercise of his discretion, because of the change in the law, which they summarised as:

'4. The impact of the decision in *A v Hoare* is two-fold. First it was decided, departing from *Stubbings v Webb* [1993] AC 498, that section 11 of the 1980 Act extends to a claim for damages in tort arising from trespass to the person, including sexual assaults. Previously the understanding was that this was not so, so that a claim for damages which was outside a six–year limitation period was unextendable. This means that claimants may not be limited to claims in negligence but can claim that an employer is vicariously liable for the assaults of an employee. This in turn may feed through to have an effect on any section 33 decision. I pause to say that each of the claimants present before the court now has the benefit of that first part of the *Hoare* decision, their cases heretofore not having been framed in vicarious liability of the assaults, sexual or otherwise, which they allege. Secondly the House of Lords decided that, in applying section 14(2) of the 1980 Act, the court was not to ask whether a claimant's psychological state in consequence of the injury was such that he could not reasonably be expected to bring proceedings, that the correct approach was to ascertain what the claimant knew about the injury he had suffered and any knowledge about the injury which was to be imputed to him under section 14(3) of the Act, and then ask whether a reasonable person with that knowledge would have considered the injury sufficiently serious to justify instituting proceedings with any question as to the effect of psychological factors on the claimant's knowledge of injury or his ability to issue proceedings being a matter for consideration under section 33 of the Act; and that, accordingly, since the nature of the assaults which the claimant alleged to have suffered was such that on a true construction of section 14(2) his date of knowledge would have arisen upon his discharge from the third defendant's detention centre in 1977, his claim was liable to be barred under section 11 but would be remitted to the judge for a fresh consideration under section 33.'

The Court of Appeal refused to consider exercising its own discretion, as it had not heard the evidence from the claimants which Holland J had, and declined to give guidance on how such an exercise should be conducted.

The cases were then remitted to Irwin J as Mr Justice Holland had in the interim retired. Irwin J also heard two other cases involving the defendant's care homes. The judge produced a model exegesis of the history of limitation law ([2009] EWHC 481 (QB) at paras 6–38) and found all cases statute barred, but exercised his discretion to allow two to proceed. His approach to s 33 is set out in para 39:

'39. To summarise: the discretion in these cases has to be exercised individually. It does seem clear in the speeches in *Hoare*, that some real significance has been attached to the specific factor arising in sex abuse cases, namely, that the tort inflicted by the abuser and for which the defendants are now vicariously liable, has itself the tendency to inhibit the victim from complaining, reporting or suing, even where the consequences do not include frank psychological and psychiatric injury. Such an effect was acknowledged by the defendants during the hearing before me. In an appropriate case, that must be a proper factor in the exercise of discretion. I take that to be an important part of what was meant when their Lordships recommended a more liberal approach to the exercise of the discretion under Section 33.'

The cases, together with an additional case, went back to the Court of Appeal ([2009] EWCA Civ 827). Both the appeals and cross-appeal were dismissed but the court gave further guidance substantially modifying the *Bryn Alyn* approach. Lord Clarke MR, after a careful review of the applicable legal principles, considered the effect of *Hoare*:

'10. We consider the correct approach to knowledge further below but will consider first the principles relevant to the exercise of the discretion under section 33. In that regard the critical point is that the effect of the decision of the House of Lords is to transfer the relevance of the question whether the actual claimant, taking into account his psychological state in consequence of the injury, could reasonably have been expected to institute proceedings from the enquiry whether he had sufficient knowledge for the purpose of section 14 to the consideration of the question whether the court should exercise its discretion to extend time under section 33. As Lord Hoffmann put it at [44] and [45], section 33(3)(a) expressly says that one of the matters to be taken into account in that regard is "the reasons … for the delay" on the part of the claimant and section 33 enables the judge to look at the matter broadly.

11. Before *A v Hoare* the leading case on the correct approach both to knowledge for the purposes of section 14 and to the exercise of the discretion under section 33 in this type of case was *KR v Bryn Alyn Community (Holdings) Ltd* [2003] EWCA Civ 85 and 783, [2003] QB 1441. The approach to knowledge in that case has now been replaced by the approach in *A v Hoare* and it is not necessary to consider it here. However, its approach to the exercise of the discretion under section 33 remains valid, subject to appropriate amendment in the light of *A v Hoare*.

12. In *Bryn Alyn* the judgment of the court, which comprised Auld, Waller and Mantell LJJ, was given by Auld LJ. At [74] of the judgment it set out the relevant starting points, which it said were well-established or uncontroversial. We reproduce them, in the main without reference to the authorities stated in them:

"(i) In multiple claims of this sort, a judge should consider the exercise of his discretion separately in relation to each claim.

(ii) The burden of showing that it would be equitable to disapply the limitation period lies on the claimant and it is a heavy burden. Another way of putting it is that it is an exceptional indulgence to a claimant, to be granted only where equity between the parties demands it.

(iii) Depending on the issues and the nature of the evidence going to them, the longer the delay the more likely, and the greater, the prejudice to the defendant.

(iv) Where a judge is minded to grant a long 'extension' he should take meticulous care in giving reasons for doing so.

(v) A judge should not reach a decision effectively concluding the matter on the strength of any one of the circumstances specified in section 33(3), or on one of any other circumstances relevant to his decision, or without regard to all the issues in the case. He should conduct the balancing exercise at the end of his analysis of all the relevant circumstances and with regard to all the issues, taking them all into account.

(vi) Wherever the judge considers it feasible to do so, he should decide the limitation point by a preliminary hearing by reference to the pleadings and written witness statements and, importantly, the extent and content of discovery. (See further below)

(vii) Where a judge determines the section 33 issue along with the substantive issues in the case, he should take care not to determine the substantive issues, including liability, causation and quantum, before determining the issue of limitation and, in particular, the effect of delay on the cogency of the evidence. Much of such evidence, by reason of the lapse of time, may have been incapable of being adequately tested or contradicted before him. To rely on his findings on those issues to assess the cogency of the evidence for the purpose of the limitation exercise would put the cart before the horse. Put another way, it would effectively require a defendant to prove a negative, namely, that the judge could not have found against him on one or more of the substantive issues if he had tried the matter earlier and without the evidential disadvantages resulting from delay.

(viii) Where a judge has assessed the likely cogency of the available evidence, that is, before finding either way on the substantive issues in the case, he should keep in mind in balancing the respective prejudice to the parties that the more cogent the claimant's case the greater the prejudice to the defendant in depriving him of the benefit of the limitation period. As Parker LJ showed in *Hartley v Birmingham City District Council* [1992] 1 WLR 968, CA, at 979G–H, such a finding is usually neutral on the balance of prejudice:

'... in all, or nearly all, cases the prejudice to the plaintiff by the operation of the relevant limitation provision and the prejudice which would result to the defendant if the relevant provision were disapplied will be equal and opposite. The stronger the plaintiff's case the greater is the prejudice to him from the operation of the provision and the greater will be the prejudice to the defendant if the provision is disapplied ... as the prejudice resulting from the loss of the limitation defence will always or almost always be balanced by the prejudice to the plaintiff from the operation of the limitation provision the loss of the defence *as such* will be of little importance. What is of paramount importance is the effect of the delay on the defendant's ability to defend.'

We should not leave those remarks of Parker LJ without noting that they were qualified in *Nash v Eli Lilly & Co* [1993] 1 WLR 782 at 804E, where this Court said that there could be instances of weak claims where disapplication of the limitation provision could cause defendants considerable prejudice in putting them to the trouble and expense of successfully defending them and then not being able to recover costs against impecunious claimants."

We return below to the extent to which those principles must be revisited in the light of *A v Hoare*.

13.   In *Bryn Alyn* the court had earlier stressed these points under the heading of the nature of the discretionary exercise:

"(i)   The discretion of a judge under section 33 is fettered only to the extent that it provides a non-exhaustive list of circumstances to which he should have regard. However, the matter is not determined simply by assessing comparative scales of hardship. The overall question is one of equity, namely, whether it would be 'equitable' to disapply the limitation provisions having regard to the balance of potential prejudice weighed with regard to all the circumstances of the case, including those specifically mentioned in section 33(3). See [68].

(ii)   The width of the discretion is such that an appellate court should not intervene save where the judge was so plainly wrong that his decision exceeded the ambit within which reasonable disagreement is possible. That includes the exercise of wrong principles, taking account of irrelevant factors, ignoring relevant factors or the making of a decision that is 'palpably' or 'plainly' wrong. If the court intervenes on any of those grounds, it should treat the matter as at large and exercise its own discretion in accordance with section 33. See [69].

(iii) Given the width of the discretion, the extent to which the court can give general guidance on the exercise is limited. The task for a judge is particularly difficult and onerous in cases where he has to decide whether he should attempt to determine and evaluate what happened many years before, often on little more than the uncorroborated and uncheckable assertion of a complainant. Where, as in the appeals in *Bryn Alyn*, there is a history of pre-care abuse supplemented by a post-care lifestyle each, individually or cumulatively, capable of causing or aggravating psychiatric harm, the further difficulty of determining the fact of injury and its extent and causation is formidable. See [70].

(iv) Many claimants, before being taken into care, have had troubled backgrounds, including sexual and/or violent abuse, and arrive in the homes in a highly disturbed state. And, often, after leaving them, their lives deteriorate into alcohol and drug abuse and crime. Stripping away legal niceties, the question for the judge under section 33 was whether, given the delays, he could fairly try claims that the first defendant had culpably failed to improve the claimants' physical and/or mental condition and/or had culpably caused it to worsen. See [71].

(v) The nature of the prejudice either way and the equity in allowing the action to proceed may vary from issue to issue. See [72]."

14. It is in our opinion important to note the distinction between the questions being considered in *Bryn Alyn* and those being considered since *A v Hoare* and thus in the instant appeals. There are two critical points of distinction to which we have already referred. The first is that previously it was necessary for the evidence to cover the whole system being operated in the relevant home over a long period and for the court to consider whether there was a relevant breach of duty. Now no such analysis is required. In order to succeed the claimant has to show the following: (1) that he was assaulted, that is that the alleged abuse occurred; (2) that the defendant was vicariously responsible for the abuse: (3) that the abuse caused the alleged psychological or psychiatric damage; and (4) quantum.

15. In our opinion the difficulties of establishing those matters can be overstated. On the claimant's side the fact of the abuse depends largely, if not entirely, upon the evidence of the claimant and must be set against any evidence available to the defendant. The effect of *Lister* is that in most cases, once abuse by an employee of the home is established, vicariously liability will follow. As to causation, it will be necessary to consider other possible causes of the state of the claimant, including his condition and lifestyle before and after the abuse but it seems to us that in many cases it will be possible to reach reasonable conclusions with appropriate medical assistance. If the claimant succeeds on (1) to (3), quantum should not present too much of a difficulty.

16. The second point of distinction is that the exercise under section 33 is significantly different from before. We have already referred to the speech of Lord Hoffmann in *A v Hoare*. Thus at [44] he said that the right place to consider the question whether the claimant, taking into account his psychological state in consequence of the injury, could reasonably have been expected to institute proceedings is under section 33. This consideration was previously treated as relevant to knowledge and not to the exercise of the discretion: see *Bryn Alyn* at [76]. At [49] Lord Hoffmann expressly treated this part of the reasoning in *Bryn Alyn* as wrong. As he put it, sub-section 3(a) requires the judge to give due weight to evidence that the claimant was for practical purposes disabled from commencing proceedings by the psychological injuries he had suffered. Lord Carswell said much the same at [69] and [70].

17. There was some debate in the course of the argument as to whether it is now easier for a claimant to persuade a court to exercise its discretion under section 33 in his or her favour. Mr Maxwell QC submitted that the answer

was yes, whereas Mr Faulks QC submitted that the answer was no. As we see it, as ever, all will depend upon the circumstances. The effect of the two changes to which we have referred is likely to make it easier for claimants in two respects. First, it is no longer necessary to establish systemic negligence, whereas previously it was, and allegations of systemic negligence presented particular difficulties for defendants after the passage of time, whereas the same may be less true of the allegations of abuse, which was previously only one aspect of the facts to be considered. Secondly, evidence of the claimant that he or she was inhibited by the abuse, is now relevant to the exercise of the discretion, whereas previously it was not: see per Lord Hoffmann at [49] referred to above. This is an important point because it stresses the broad nature of the discretion and that it does not focus solely on whether there has been prejudice to the defendant. It was this that Lord Carswell had in mind when he said at [70] that there now requires to be a more liberal approach to the exercise of the discretion than had been the case.

18.   On the other hand, it remains to be seen what overall effect the changes have had. The relevant date of knowledge is now much earlier than it was previously thought to have been. Further Lord Brown expressed some caution at [84] to [87]. Lord Hoffmann described those paragraphs at [52] as being particularly valuable and Lord Walker said at [53] that he was in complete agreement with both Lord Hoffmann and Lord Brown. The judge described Lord Brown's paragraphs as containing valuable guidance. We agree. They read as follows:

> "84.   With regard to the exercise of the court's discretion under Section 33 of the 1980 Act, however, I would make just three brief comments – not, let it be clear, in any way to fetter a discretion which the House in *Horton v Sadler* [2006] UKHL 27, [2007] 1 AC 307 recently confirmed to be unfettered, but rather to suggest the sort of considerations which ought clearly to be in mind in sexual abuse cases in the new era which your Lordships are now ushering in, first, by departing from *Stubbings v Webb*, and secondly, by construing consideration of the inhibiting effect of sexual abuse upon certain victims' preparedness to bring proceedings in respect of it.
>
> 85.   First, so far as future claims may be expected to be brought against employers (or others allegedly responsible for abusers) on the basis of vicarious liability for sexual assaults rather than for systemic negligence in failing to prevent them, they will probably involve altogether narrower factual disputes than hitherto. As Lord Hoffmann suggests, at paragraph 52, that is likely to bear significantly upon the possibility of having a fair trial.
>
> 86.   Secondly, through the combined effects of *Lister v Hesley Hall Ltd* and departing from *Stubbings v Webb*, a substantially greater number of allegations (not all of which will be true), are now likely to be made many years after the abuse complained of. Whether or not it will be possible for defendants to investigate these sufficiently for there to be a reasonable prospect of a fair trial will depend upon a number of factors, not least when the complaint was first made and with what effect. If a complaint has been made and recorded, and more obviously still if the accused has been convicted of the abuse complained of, that will be one thing. If, however, a complaint comes out of the blue with no apparent support for

it (other perhaps than that the alleged abuser has been accused or even convicted of similar abuse in the past), that would be quite another thing. By no means everyone who brings a late claim for damages for sexual abuse, however genuine his complaint may in fact be, can reasonably expect the court to exercise the section 33 discretion in his favour. On the contrary, a fair trial (which must surely include a fair opportunity for the defendant to investigate the allegations – see section 33(3)(b)) is in many cases likely to be found quite simply impossible after a long delay.

87. Hitherto, the misconstruction of section 14(2) has given an absolute right to proceed, however long out of time, to anyone able to say that he would not reasonably have turned his mind to litigation (more than three years) earlier (the *Bryn Alyn* test described by Lord Hoffmann at paragraph 36). It is not to be supposed that the exercise of the court's section 33 discretion will invariably replicate that position."

19. As we see it, since there is no disagreement expressed by any of the members of the appellate committee with the approach of Lord Hoffmann and Lord Brown recognised the narrower nature of the enquiry, the relevance of the claimant's inhibitions to the exercise of the discretion and the broad nature of the discretion, we do not think that he was disagreeing that the effect of the two changes to which we have referred is likely to make it easier for claimants in the two respects identified above. He was simply sounding a cautionary note, which will be of particular relevance on the facts of some cases. In any event it cannot be in doubt that the judge had his views in mind in this case.

20. In the light of the considerations in *A v Hoare* to which we have referred we conclude that the "starting points" taken from [74] of *Bryn Alyn* and quoted above remain valid subject to these considerations. As to ii), it is correct to describe the exercise of the discretion as an exceptional indulgence to the claimant because, but for the exercise of the discretion, his claim will be time barred. But it is only exceptional for that reason. The cases stress that the discretion is wide and unfettered.

21. As to vi), we think that there are now likely to be many cases in which a judge will consider that it is not feasible to decide the issues simply by reference to the pleadings, written witness statements and the extent and content of discovery. He or she may well conclude that it is desirable that such oral evidence as is available should be heard because the strength of the claimant's evidence seems to us to be relevant to the way in which the discretion should be exercised. We entirely agree with the point made at vii) that, where a judge determines the section 33 application along with the substantive issues in the case he or she should take care not to determine the substantive issues, including liability, causation and quantum before determining the issue of limitation and, in particular, the effect of delay on the cogency of the evidence. To do otherwise would, as the court said, be to put the cart before the horse.

22. That is however simply to emphasise the order in which the judge should determine the issues. When he or she is considering the cogency of the claimant's case, the oral evidence may be extremely valuable because it may throw light both on the prejudice suffered by the defendant and on the extent to which the claimant was reasonably inhibited in commencing proceedings. Thus, if the claimant's case is beset by inconsistencies and the claimant shows himself in evidence to be unreliable, the court may conclude that the delay is

likely to prejudice the defendant in the way contemplated in *Eli Lilly*, namely by being put to the trouble and expense of successfully defending proceedings and then not being able to recover costs against impecunious claimants. In those circumstances, viewing the matter more broadly, as *A v Hoare* enjoins the courts to do, it may well be that it would not be equitable to allow the claimant to proceed. On the other hand, if the evidence of the claimant is compelling and cogent that the abuse occurred, and it is said that it was the abuse that inhibited him from commencing proceedings, that is surely a compelling point in favour of the claimant.

23.   In this regard Irwin J expressed some doubt about point viii) in [74] of *Bryn Alyn* quoted above. Having set it out as we have done, Irwin J said this at [29]:

> "29. With great diffidence, I do have some difficulty in following how the cogency of a claimant's case can be held to be neutral. An incoherent and weak case from an impecunious claimant will be likely to prejudice a defendant, who will probably defend successfully, but not recover the cost of doing so. That is easy to follow. However, it seems to me that a cogent and well supported case for a claimant must usually argue at least to some degree in favour of the extension of discretion, since such a case would tend to carry the promise of a potentially fair trial, and since the implication would also usually be that a case which remains cogent and well supported after a lapse of time, would always have been more difficult to defend. I find it hard to think that it is usually equitable to refuse to extend the discretion because the claimant's case is weak, whilst it is also usually equitable to bear in mind how valuable is the limitation defence when the claimant's case is strong."

What Parker LJ meant has been fully explored in the judgments of Smith LJ and the Chancellor in *Cain v Francis* and *McKay v Hanlani* [2008] EWCA Civ 1451. All he was intending to say was that the prejudice to the defendant of losing a limitation defence is not the relevant prejudice to be addressed. The prejudice to be addressed is that which affects the defendant's ability to defend. Clearly the strength of the claimant's case is relevant and was relevant to the decision of Parker and Leggatt LJJ in *Hartley*. If the action in a case, where liability has been admitted, is commenced a day late but the defendant is in no way prejudiced in defending the claim, the limitation defence would be a windfall and so as in *Hartley* the discretion will be exercised in favour of the claimant.

24.   As the Chancellor put it at paragraphs 80 and 81 of his judgment in *Cain v Francis*:

> "80. The consequence of the disapplication of s. 11 will be that there may be a trial of the claimant's claim on its merits notwithstanding the delay in commencing the proceedings. Has that delay caused prejudice to the defendant in its defence? If so, does it outweigh the prejudice to the claimant of being denied a trial at all? In addition the court will need to consider all the circumstances of the case and in particular to the other aspects of the case enumerated in subsection (3).

> 81. In that context it does not appear to me that the loss of a limitation defence is regarded as a head of prejudice to the defendant at all; it is merely the obverse of the disapplication of s. 11 which is assumed. It

is this consideration which, in my view, accounts for and justifies the marked reluctance of the courts, as demonstrated by the judgments to which Smith LJ has referred in detail, to have regard to the loss of a limitation defence."

This echoes Smith LJ's own formulation, which we believe to be consistent with our approach in paragraph 73:

"73. It seems to me that, in the exercise of the discretion, the basic question to be asked is whether it is fair and just in all the circumstances to expect the defendant to meet this claim on the merits, notwithstanding the delay in commencement. The length of the delay will be important, not so much for itself as to the effect it has had. To what extent has the defendant been disadvantaged in his investigation of the claim and/or the assembly of evidence, in respect of the issues of both liability and quantum? But it will also be important to consider the reasons for the delay. Thus, there may be some unfairness to the defendant due to the delay in issue but the delay may have arisen for so excusable a reason, that, looking at the matter in the round, on balance, it is fair and just that the action should proceed. On the other hand, the balance may go in the opposite direction, partly because the delay has caused procedural disadvantage and unfairness to the defendant and partly because the reasons for the delay (or its length) are not good ones."

25.   In considering the exercise of his or her discretion under section 33 the judge must consider all the circumstances including of course any prejudice to the defendant. That involves considering what evidence might have been available to the defendant if a trial had taken place earlier or it had learned of the claim earlier. We accept Mr Faulks' submission that it is not sufficient for the court simply to hear the evidence of the claimant, and indeed any other evidence now available, and to decide the issue of limitation on the basis of it, without considering what evidence would or might have been available at an earlier stage. We return to this point below.

26.   We only add that, where a claimant gives evidence for the purposes of a preliminary issue on limitation, and where the judge exercises the discretion of the court to permit the claim to continue, every effort should be made to make sure that the claimant does not have to give oral evidence again on the issue of liability. We would hope that this can ordinarily be achieved by ensuring, so far as possible, that the same judge will hear the trial as determined the preliminary issue of liability. Indeed, it may well be appropriate to decide the preliminary point and then either stop or continue with the trial.'

Irwin J subsequently applied the guidance in further cases involving the defendant ([2010] EWHC 1005 (QB)). For illustrations in respect of other sexual abuse actions, see *Raggett v Society of Jesus Trust 1929 for Roman Catholic Purposes* (p617), *Albonetti v Wirral Metropolitan Borough* (p300), *EB v Haughton* (p418), *EL v Children's Society* (p419), *RAR v GGC* (p615) and *D v Harrow LBC* (p394).

SUMMARY

The extensive case law that has developed under s 33 has to be viewed in the light of the general reluctance to issue guidelines and the limited success that generalised propositions from the appellate courts have achieved. Primacy must be given to the statutory requirement to look at all the circumstances of the case. Nevertheless, certain principles of construction may be extracted from the case law indicating the likely approach the court will adopt without treating such cases as precedents. The effect of the leading cases on date of knowledge (namely, *Adams v Bracknell Forest BC* (p292), *A v Hoare* (p287) and *B v Ministry of Defence* (p312)) has been to push back a claimant's date of knowledge much closer to the date of breach of duty and first injury than was previously thought to be the case. The consequence of transferring to section 33 considerations of the claimant's subjective reasons for the delay in issuing proceedings, including many of the effects that the tort has had on the claimant, should result in a more liberal exercise of discretion. However, unfettered as the discretion is, the exercise will always be fact specific to all the circumstances of the case. The effects of the delay on the cogency of the evidence, and whether it is still possible to have a fair trial on the issues of breach of duty, causation and quantum, will be highly significant in considering whether it would be equitable to allow an action to proceed. Although lack of prejudice to the defendant on an issue of liability or quantum will not trump all other considerations, it will always be given considerable weight (see *EB v Haughton* (p418) and *Roberts v Commissioner of Police of the Metropolis* (p624)).

1.1 PREJUDICE TO THE CLAIMANT

The obvious prejudice to the claimant is being precluded from suing to obtain damages. Accordingly it is relevant for the court to consider, though not necessarily in the greatest of detail, the strength of the claimant's case on liability. If the claimant has such a weak case, limited only to a nuisance value, then little or no prejudice is likely to be caused to him by refusing to allow the claim to proceed, because if litigated the case would probably fail on liability (*Thompson v Brown* above, per Lord Diplock at 301). The degree of prejudice will vary with the claimant's prospects of success in a contested trial on liability and causation. In simple cases this may be a conclusive factor such as where a claimant trips, possibly on a paving stone and the irregularity is only in the order of half an inch (see *Mann v Bournemouth District Council* (p542)). Both the trial judge and the Court of Appeal in *Mann* had no difficulty indicating that the action was most likely to fail in any event. In *Freeman v Home Office (No 1)* (p438), Shaw LJ stated that the existence of a good arguable case was a sine qua non of allowing a time-barred action to continue. However, the court when exercising a s 33 discretion is normally doing so on a preliminary basis rather than at the trial on liability and only a broad view on liability needs to be taken. So, for example, in another tripping case in *Beer v London Borough of Waltham Forest* (p327) the trial judge allowed an action to continue because everything under s 33 was in the claimant's favour save for the strength of her case. A claimant might therefore in certain circumstances have a weak case on liability but nevertheless the court will exercise discretion in the light of all the other circumstances. In *Jeffrey v Bolton Textile Mill Co plc* (p495) a widow was given leave to proceed in respect of an action concerning the death of her husband from byssinosis, even though it was said she had an uphill though not impossible task to establish liability. Similarly in *Woods v Attorney General* (p725) a High Court judge allowed a claimant to proceed after weighing both sides' prejudices, which included a remark that if the claimant wished to proceed knowing that her case was more difficult to establish because of the delay then that was 'her funeral'.

However, in *B v Ministry of Defence* (p312), the majority of the Supreme Court agreed with the Court of Appeal that the 'atomic veterans' case on causation was so weak and would require a substantial modification to the law on causation that it failed the broad merits test. Lord Wilson stated:

'27.   It is undesirable that a court which conducts an inquiry into whether a claim is time-barred should, even at the stage when it considers its power under section 33, have detailed regard to the evidence with which the claimant aspires to prove his case at trial. But the ten claims placed before Foskett J were of particular complexity; and the nature of the submissions made to him on behalf of the appellants about the meaning of knowledge for the purpose of section 14(1) of the 1980 Act led him to undertake, over ten days of hearing and expressed in 885 paragraphs of judgment, a microscopic survey of the written evidence available to the parties, in particular to the appellants, in relation to causation. At all events the result was to yield to the Court of Appeal an unusual advantage, namely a mass of material which enabled it with rare confidence to assess the appellants' prospects of establishing causation. It expressed its conclusion in terms of the "very great difficulties" which confronted the appellants in that regard. But, in line with the realistic concession made by Mr Dingemans in this court, the fact is that, for the reasons set out by Lord Phillips in paras 156 to 158 below, their claims have no real prospect of success. In my view it would have been absurd for the Court of Appeal to have exercised the discretion to disapply section 11 so as to allow the appellants to proceed in circumstances in which the next stage of the litigation would be likely to have been their failure to resist entry against them of summary judgment pursuant to CPR 24.2(a)(i). In this regard I do not share the view of Lord Phillips, at para 160 below, about the relevance of the fact that, at least until that next stage, the action brought by the late Mr Sinfield, together no doubt with other actions in the group which do not fall foul of section 11, are to proceed.'

In *Mutua v Foreign and Commonwealth Office* (p565), Kenyan nationals brought actions in 2009 for personal injuries sustained in the 1950s by mistreatment and torture perpetrated while the colonial administration was in power. The claimants' case was that the UK government was jointly or vicariously liable for their injuries. The trial judge permitted the cases to proceed, indicating that the law on vicarious liability as illustrated in the sexual abuse cases (eg *JGR v The Trustees of the Portsmouth Roman Catholic Diocesan Trust* [2012] EWCA Civ 938) was in a continuous state of development and the formulation of the claimants' case could not be described as weak and passed the broad merits test.

Conversely, just because a claimant has a strong case, it does not automatically mean that discretion will be granted because that will only be one factor and the court has emphasised that the exercise of discretion has to be equitable. In *Long v Tolchard and Son Ltd* (p537) a claimant had failed to disclose relevant documents and had not given a true account of his previous medical history. The court said that the fact he had a strong case was an important factor but did not determine the issue and held that it would not be equitable in the circumstances to allow the claim to proceed. More recently, the court has introduced the concept of proportionality when considering the strengths of the claimant's case. In *Adams v Bracknell Forest BC* (p292) the House of Lords confirmed the approach taken to the exercise of s 33 discretion in cases arising out of negligent failures to diagnose and treat dyslexia. The Court of Appeal had stated in *Robinson v St Helens Metropolitan Borough Council* (p628) that:

'The question of a proportionality is now important in the exercise of any discretion, none more so than under section 33. Courts should be slow to exercise their discretion in favour of a claimant in the absence of cogent medical evidence showing a serious effect on the claimant's health or enjoyment of life and employability. The likely amount of an award is an important factor to consider, especially if, as is usual in these cases they are likely to take a considerable time to try.' (per Sir Murray Stuart-Smith)

Lord Hoffmann stated in *Adams* (para 55) that observations of that nature from judges with considerable experience in exercising and overseeing the s 33 jurisdiction should be given great weight. Similarly, in *McGhie v British Telecommunications plc* (p553) the Court of Appeal applied the concept of proportionality by looking at the merits of the case, the value of the case and the costs of bringing and defending the proceedings. Mr McGhie sued in respect of the acceleration of back symptoms caused by an injury at work said to be worth in the region of £10–20,000. His proceedings were brought approximately two years after his date of knowledge and at first instance he was given a s 33 dispensation. The defendant appealed on the basis that the judge failed adequately to consider the strengths of the claimant's case and to consider the concept of proportionality as applied in *Adams*. The Court of Appeal agreed and allowed the defendant's appeal. Lord Justice May on the issue of proportionality said:

'35 ... The question of proportionality is, in my judgment, in the first place, a proportionality between the size of the claim and the legal and other costs of running it. The question of proportionality also has an eye, in my judgment, to the strength of the claimant's claim. In my judgment, taking the matters in the round, it would be a great prejudice to a claimant who was very badly injured and likely to suffer the consequences of that injury for many years to come if, what would otherwise be a very large claim, based upon very strong evidence, were to be lost through a refusal to exercise the discretion under section 33.'

On the facts of this case, the court found that there was very little to put in the claimant's favour and the appeal was allowed. For a case where the Court of Appeal considered the issue of proportionality and refused to interfere with the trial judge's exercise of discretion in the claimant's favour in a vibration white finger case, see *Kew v Bettamix Ltd* (p518); see also the sexual abuse cases in *AB v Nugent Care Society* [2010] EWHC 1005 (QB) and vibration syndrome cases in *Cairns-Jones v Christie Tyler South Wales West Division* (p363).

It is therefore apparent that, in cases where the defendant has no defence save for limitation and the claimant has no claim over against the solicitor, the claimant's prejudice is probably at its highest. If, added to these factors, the claim is of high value and there is no overt costs disproportionality, the claimant's prospects are considerably enhanced. It is axiomatic that a tetraplegic who is statute barred will suffer greater economic prejudice than a claimant who has a minor whiplash injury; for other cases on this issue, see *Pavan v Holwill's (Oils) Ltd* (p598), *Common v Crofts* (p384), *Platt v Quaker Oats Ltd* (p606), *Davis v Jacobs and Camden Islington Health Authority et al* (p404), *Gaud v Leeds Health Authority* (p440), *Roberts v Winbow* (p627), *Smith v Donelan & Co Ltd* (p659), *Bates v Leicester Health Authority* (p324), *Briggs v Pitt-Payne & Lias* (p344) and *Connelly v RTZ Corporation* (p384).

An important judicial analysis of the nature of prejudice is to be found in Parker LJ's 'general observations' in *Hartley v Birmingham City District Council* (p465). Emphasis was laid by the Court of Appeal on the actual effect the delay had on the defendant's ability to defend the claim on its merits. Lord Justice Parker considered that the prejudice referred to in s 33(1) was likely to be equal and opposite, and the real focus of prejudice should be on evidential prejudice, effectively the separate issue contained within s 33(3)(b). Mrs Hartley's case concerned the issuing of proceedings one day out of time in respect of action to which the defendants had no defence, save on limitation, and in which no allegations of contributory negligence were made. In addition, the claim had been properly notified to the defendant and the defendant's ability to defend the claim on the merits was not 'in the slightest degree affected by the fact that the writ instead of being issued in the afternoon of 11 December was issued in the morning of 12 December'. Equally, however, the claimant had a cast-iron action over against her own solicitors. The judge at first instance refused to allow the action to proceed, a decision which Parker LJ found:

'... plainly wrong. If in this case the discretion is not to be exercised in favour of the plaintiff I find it difficult to envisage circumstances in which it could ever be exercised.'

The Lord Justice then proceeded to become the first appellate judge to make general observations on the question of prejudice:

'It appears to me to be apparent that in all, or nearly all, cases the prejudice to the plaintiff by the operation of the relevant limitation provisions and the prejudice which would result to the defendant if the relevant provisions were disapplied will be equal and opposite. The stronger the plaintiff's case the greater is the prejudice to him from the operation of the provision and the greater will be the prejudice to the defendant if the provision is disapplied. Likewise the weaker the case of the plaintiff the less he is prejudiced by the operation of the provision and the less is the defendant prejudiced if it is disapplied. This might lead one to suppose that the prejudice referred to in section 33(1)(b) was not the deprivation of the fortuitous defence as such but prejudice to the defence on the merits caused by the delay. Both Lord Denning MR and Ormrod LJ appear to have assumed so in (*Firman v Ellis*). That this was the parliamentary intent appears to be indicated by the fact that as Lord Diplock pointed out only section 33(3)(a) and (b) appear to go to prejudice and both are dealing with the merits. The decisions of their Lordships (in *Thompson v Brown, Donovan v Gwentoys Ltd*) preclude such construction of the section. In my view, however, as the prejudice resulting from the loss of the limitation defence would always or almost always be balanced by the prejudice to the plaintiff from the operation of the limitation provision the loss of the defence as such will be of little importance. What is of paramount importance is the effect of the delay on the defendant's ability to defend. The specific example in section 33(3)(b) so indicates. Next it appears to me that if it is, as it is, legitimate to take into account, when considering prejudice to the plaintiff, that he will have a claim against his solicitors, it must in my judgment follow that it is legitimate to take into account that the defendant is insured. If he is deprived of his fortuitous defence he will have a claim on his insurance. Finally I would add to the item of prejudice which a plaintiff will suffer even if he has a cast-iron claim against his solicitors and which were indicated by both Lord Diplock and Ormrod LJ, the fact that if the plaintiff has to change from an action against a tortfeasor, who may know little or nothing of the weak points of this case, to an action against his solicitor, who will know a great deal about them, the prejudice may well be major rather than minor.'

Lord Justice Parker concluded by indicating that the balancing exercise required considering what was equitable, namely what was fair and just, and indicated that if the delay resulted in a windfall defence only but did not seriously affect the evidence, the power to allow the action to proceed will generally be exercised ([1992] 2 All ER 213 at 224C–225C).

However, a year after *Hartley*, a differently constituted Court of Appeal in *Nash v Eli Lilly* (p568) suggested that Lord Justice Parker's principles were not truly general:

'The principles stated cannot in our judgment be regarded as of universal application and we do not accept that in every case when the ability of a defendant to defend on the issue of liability has not been affected by the delay, the benefit of the limitation defence must be regarded as a "windfall" ... If it is shown that the claim is a poor case lacking merit, there may be significant relevant prejudice to the defendant if the limitation provisions are disapplied.' ([1993] 4 All ER 383 at 403j)

The specific prejudice in *Nash* concerned proportionality namely the potential disproportion between the level of costs the defendant would incur to defend a poor case and the likely level of damages a claimant might recover in any event which would make an action uneconomic to defend. This would be particularly so when a claimant was legally aided and the defendant's costs were irrecoverable:

'The defendants in short assert that it is or may be inequitable to secure to a dilatory plaintiff who had let the limitation period pass without action, the power to claim from the defendants a sum in settlement of a poor claim which sum would reflect as much or more the risk in cost to the defendants as the fair value of a claim. In general we agree with this submission.' (*Nash* at 407f)

In *KR v Bryn Alyn Community Holdings Ltd* (p505) the Court of Appeal specifically approved Parker LJ's remarks in *Hartley*, but with the caveat espoused by the Court of Appeal in *Nash* (see para 74).

In *Horton v Sadler* (p482) the House of Lords again declined to give guidance on the exercise of the court's discretion (see Lord Bingham at para 33). However, Lord Carswell did make some general observations (at para 53) which included approving Lord Justice Parker's remarks in *Hartley*.

In *Cain v Francis* (p360), the claim was just one day out of time and liability was admitted. At first instance the trial judge refused to exercise his discretion principally because of the substantial damages that the defendant would be liable for if the limitation defence was denied him which he regarded as obvious prejudice. In a conjoined appeal with *Cain v Francis*, *McKay v Hamlani*, liability was also conceded, the delay was approximately one year and the judge allowed the action to proceed principally because the limitation defence was a windfall and no evidential prejudice to the defendants arose. The same insurers were on risk for both defendants and they sought clarity as to the proper approach in such cases. The court permitted both cases to proceed, emphasising that a critical issue was whether the delay had caused a fair trial to be no longer possible because the cogency of the evidence on liability or quantum had been affected. It was also of the clear view that the financial prejudice of the defendant having to pay damages was an irrelevant consideration. Smith LJ reviewed the authorities, including *Hartley*, and stated the law:

'57.   It appears to me that there is now a long line of authority to support the proposition that, in a case where the defendant has had early notice of the claim, the accrual of a limitation defence should be regarded as a windfall and the prospect of its loss, by the exercise of the section 33 discretion, should be regarded as either no prejudice at all (see *Firman*) or only a slight degree of prejudice (see *Gwentoys*). It is true that, in *Thompson*, Lord Diplock said that the accrual of the defence might be regarded as a windfall only where the delay in issuing proceedings was short. However, with great respect, it does not seem to me that the length of the delay can be, of itself, a deciding factor. It is whether the defendant has suffered any evidential or other forensic prejudice which should make the difference.

58.   If the House of Lords were not prepared to disturb this long-established jurisprudence which runs from *Firman v Ellis* in 1978 to *Horton v Sadler* in 2007, it does not seem to me that Mr Burton has or should have much prospect of persuading this Court that the practice has been wrong and should now be changed. I regard the matter as settled. Moreover, although the discretion given by the statute is unfettered, it must be exercised consistently with the broad guidance given by the higher courts, otherwise, as I have said earlier, applications for a direction will be a lottery.

59.   Having said that, it does appear that, although the authorities all lead to the same result, they do not speak with one voice as to the underlying rationale. In the citations above, I have italicised the passages in which the judges have explained their reasoning. The reasons differ. In *Firman,* Lord Denning MR thought that it was a matter of simple justice that it was the tortfeasor's insurers who should pay the damages and not the insurers of the solicitor who had made a minor slip, which had not caused any prejudice. Ormrod LJ said that, in those cases, the procedural mistake had not caused any inconvenience let alone prejudice. So, it seems that they thought that the direct financial prejudice flowing from the loss of the limitation defence was not relevant to the balancing exercise. It was only the forensic prejudice which mattered and, in those cases, there was none.

60.   In *Thompson,* Lord Diplock thought that the prejudice to the defendant in the making of a direction clearly included the loss of the accrued limitation defence which would mean that the defendant would have to pay damages which he would otherwise avoid. That prejudice would be at its highest where the defendant had no defence on the merits. But, he said, to my mind rather cryptically, that where the delay was short, the loss of an accrued limitation defence might be regarded as a windfall. As I have noted, he did not say why that meant that it should either not count as prejudice at all or not count as heavily as the loss of a defence which was not a windfall. One possible and rational explanation was that, if the delay was short, there could not be any (or much) forensic prejudice to the defendant. But did that mean that the judge should ignore the direct financial prejudice which would result from the loss of the defence? It is not clear.

61.   In *Donovan v Gwentoys,* Lord Griffiths thought that prejudice arose where a defendant did not have notice of a claim until it had become stale and there was only slight prejudice where a defendant had been notified promptly and had had every opportunity to investigate the claim. He was of the view that what mattered was the prejudice to the defendant in the conduct of the action, which of course included investigating the circumstances of the accident. He did not consider whether the loss of the limitation defence was, per se, prejudice which was to be taken into account.

62.   Finally, in *Hartley,* Parker LJ grappled, as it seems to me somewhat uneasily, with the conflict between Lord Diplock and Lord Denning MR. He said that the prejudice to the claimant from the operation of section 11 and

the prejudice to the defendant from the loss of its accrued limitation defence are equal and opposite; they cancel each other out. He must have meant the direct financial prejudice. But that balancing exercise ignores the effect of the claimant's claim against his solicitor, which appears to be at least one of the circumstances of the case. However, the balancing exercise as envisaged by Parker LJ led him to suppose that the prejudice referred to in section 33(1)(b) was not that kind of financial prejudice but the prejudice to the merits of the defendant's case as the result of the delay. It seems that Parker LJ was saying that the section was not concerned with direct financial prejudice at all, only forensic prejudice caused by the delay.

63.   As I have said, the authorities all arrive at the same result but by different reasoning. I believe that it would be helpful to judges if some rational explanation for the authorities could be advanced. I have searched for some coherent explanation of Parliament's intention within the words of the section itself but did not for myself find one. However, having now read the Chancellor's judgment, I agree with his analysis of section 33(1)(b). I do not think one can infer much from the six factors in section 33(3) which, as Lord Diplock said, are "a curious hotchpotch". I agree with the Chancellor that the phrase "it would be equitable to allow the action to proceed" is at the heart of the section. Equitable here means "fair and just". With that in mind, I think that the rationale underlying the provision must be found in a consideration of the background to limitation law as a whole.

64.   It is fundamental precept of the common law that a tortfeasor should compensate the victim of the tort. At common law, the victim, now the claimant, could sue the tortfeasor at any time, without limitation. It is also a fundamental precept that any person who is sued in respect of a tort should have a fair opportunity to defendant himself. In 1623, a uniform limitation period of six years was introduced for all actions. The rationale behind the limit was to protect defendants from stale claims. It was not fair and just to impose liability on a defendant who had not had a proper opportunity to investigate the allegations against him and to assemble the evidence necessary to defend himself. There may have been other policy reasons for the provision, such as the desirability of finality but, as between the parties, the reason was to protect the defendant from a stale claim.

65.   The effect of the limitation provision was not to extinguish the claimant's right of action, only to bar his remedy. The Act did not provide a defence on the merits; the defendant was *ex hypothesi* still a tortfeasor; but he could not be sued. The six year period must have been Parliament's best estimate of when it would be unfair or unjust to the defendant to allow the claimant to enforce his right of action.

66.   So far as personal injury actions were concerned, the limit remained at six years until the Limitation Act 1954, when it was reduced to three. I infer that Parliament must have thought that, in the context of that kind of action, unfairness to the defendant was likely to arise at an earlier date than in other actions.

67.   Any limitation bar is arbitrary. It cannot always be fair and just to permit a claimant to proceed with his action if he commences it two years and 364 days after the relevant injury. Significant prejudice and unfairness might already have arisen, even long before the expiry of three years, for example by the

death of an important witness. But the rule is that the claimant can proceed, notwithstanding any unfairness to the defendant. On the other hand, the expiry of the three year term does not automatically create unfairness. Yet what was deemed fair on Tuesday is deemed unfair on Wednesday. There might be no unfairness to the defendant even if he is required to answer the claim, say, five years after the accident. The three year limit is Parliament's best guess as to when prejudice can be expected to have arisen such that it is unfair to expose the defendant to the claim. The imposition of an arbitrary limit could only ever hope to do rough justice.

68.   In 1975, in response to recommendations in the Law Commission's paper, mentioned above, Parliament introduced further provisions, designed principally to improve on those introduced in the Limitation Act 1963 and to assist a claimant who was suffering from a disease which had developed slowly over many years to pursue a cause of action which, under the old law, had become time-barred before he even knew of its existence. Those "knowledge" provisions were contained in sections 2A to 2C of the Act of 1975 and are now to be found in sections 11 to 14 of the Act of 1980. But in addition, Parliament introduced section 2D, now section 33 of the 1980 Act, which was not related to the knowledge provisions and which applied to all personal injury actions, even where knowledge was not a problem. The only rationale which could have underlain the introduction of this provision was a desire to refine the rough justice of the old arbitrary provision. Instead of a limitation rule of thumb, the courts would be required to consider what was fair and just in all the circumstances of the individual case.

69.   In my view, the words of section 33 must be construed against that background. The context is that the claimant had the right to pursue his cause of action which he has lost by the operation of section 11. The defendant, on the other hand, had an obligation to pay the damages due; his right was the right to a fair opportunity to defend himself against the claim. The operation of section 11 has given him a complete procedural defence which removes his obligation to pay. In fairness and justice, he only deserves to have that obligation removed if the passage of time has significantly diminished his opportunity to defend himself (on liability and/or quantum). So the making of a direction, which would restore the defendant's obligation to pay damages, is only prejudicial to him if his right to a fair opportunity to defend himself has been compromised.

70.   Thus, although on a literal construction of section 33(1), it appears to be relevant to the exercise of the discretion that the defendant would suffer the financial prejudice of having to pay damages if the arbitrary time limit were to be disapplied, Parliament cannot have intended that that financial prejudice, as such, should be taken into account. That is because, in fairness and justice, the defendant ought to pay the damages if, having had a fair opportunity to defend himself, he is found liable. If having to pay the damages is not a relevant prejudice under section 33(1), it cannot be relevant either as one of the circumstances of the case.

71.   I accept that some judges appear to have thought that this financial prejudice, as such, was relevant to the exercise of the discretion. In particular, Lord Diplock appears to have thought so and the rest of the House agreed with him. I must say, with hesitation and great respect, that I think he was wrong. I comfort myself with the knowledge that his remarks were not essential to the

ratio of the decision in *Thompson*. Apart from Lord Diplock's, all the other judicial utterances are broadly consistent with the reasoning I have advanced.

72. A claimant's position is different. He has a substantive right, his cause of action, but he cannot proceed with it because of the operation of section 11. He has therefore been prejudiced by the loss of the right to enforce his cause of action. That prejudice is greatly reduced if he has a good claim over against his solicitor. In a case where the defendant has suffered some forensic or procedural prejudice, which will diminish his ability to defend himself, it will be relevant to consider that the claimant has another remedy. But the fact that the claimant has a claim over will not necessarily mean that the direction should be refused. It might still be fair and just that the defendant remains in the frame. It is the defendant who has, *ex hypothesi,* committed the tort and, as Lord Denning MR pointed out, it is his insurer who has received the premiums in respect of the relevant risk. So the fact that the claimant will not suffer financially in the end is relevant but not determinative.

73. It seems to me that, in the exercise of the discretion, the basic question to be asked is whether it is fair and just in all the circumstances to expect the defendant to meet this claim on the merits, notwithstanding the delay in commencement. The length of the delay will be important, not so much for itself as to the effect it has had. To what extent has the defendant been disadvantaged in his investigation of the claim and/or the assembly of evidence, in respect of the issues of both liability and quantum? But it will also be important to consider the reasons for the delay. Thus, there may be some unfairness to the defendant due to the delay in issue but the delay may have arisen for so excusable a reason, that, looking at the matter in the round, on balance, it is fair and just that the action should proceed. On the other hand, the balance may go in the opposite direction, partly because the delay has caused procedural disadvantage and unfairness to the defendant and partly because the reasons for the delay (or its length) are not good ones.

74. Although the delay referred to in section 33(3) is the delay after the expiry of the primary limitation period, it will always be relevant to consider when the defendant knew that a claim was to be made against him and also the opportunities he has had to investigate the claim and collect evidence: see *Gwentoys*. If, as here, a defendant has had early notification of a claim and every possible opportunity to investigate and to collect evidence, some delay after the expiry of three years will have had no prejudicial effect.'

The Chancellor agreed and added an insightful interpretation of the statute, explaining why the financial prejudice to the defendant of having to pay damages was irrelevant:

'78. In cases to which s. 11 Limitation Act 1980 applies an action may not be brought after the expiration of the periods prescribed by subsections (3) and (4). In any such case there will be no trial on the merits. The purpose of s. 33 is to enable the court to review the position in the light of the facts of individual cases. The object of the exercise is to consider the circumstances of individual cases in order to determine whether the action should proceed to trial. That this is the purpose is confirmed by the material words in subsection (1) which pose the indirect question whether "... it would be equitable to allow the action to proceed ...".

79. The action can only proceed in cases to which s. 11 applies if the provisions of that section are disapplied by a direction to that effect made by

the court under s. 33. By subsection (1)(b) the court is required to have "regard to the degree to which – [such a decision] ...would prejudice the defendant ...". Thus the prejudice is to be ascertained on the assumption that the provisions of s. 11 have been disapplied by an order made under s. 33. The subsection does not direct the court to have regard to the prejudice the defendant would suffer from the very act of disapplication.

80. The consequence of the disapplication of s. 11 will be that there may be a trial of the claimant's claim on its merits notwithstanding the delay in commencing the proceedings. Has that delay caused prejudice to the defendant in its defence? If so, does it outweigh the prejudice to the claimant of being denied a trial at all? In addition the court will need to consider all the circumstances of the case and in particular to the other aspects of the case enumerated in subsection (3).

81. In that context it does not appear to me that the loss of a limitation defence is regarded as a head of prejudice to the defendant at all; it is merely the obverse of the disapplication of s. 11 which is assumed. It is this consideration which, in my view, accounts for and justifies the marked reluctance of the courts, as demonstrated by the judgments to which Smith LJ has referred in detail, to have regard to the loss of a limitation defence.'

This formulation was applied in *B v Nugent Care Society* (above) as the explanation for Parker LJ's formulation in *Hartley*, that the prejudice to the plaintiff by the operation of the relevant limitation provisions and the prejudice which would result to the defendant if the relevant provisions were disapplied, will be equal and opposite, as meaning no more than the prejudice to the defendant was not the loss of the defence per se but the ability to defend the case on the merits and on quantum. (See also *EB v Haughton* (p418) and *Roberts v Commissioner of Police of the Metropolis* (p624).)

It would therefore appear that, apart from those cases where a claimant's case is weak on liability, causation or quantum, and when the matter of costs is a pertinent factor, the Court of Appeal has not sought to distinguish *Hartley* in respect of the general principles laid down for the majority of cases. As is apparent from *Hartley* and confirmed in *Cain*, the existence of even a cast-iron case against the claimant's own solicitors for failing to issue proceedings does not preclude the claimant from relying on s 33 or from demonstrating that he is in fact still prejudiced. Such view is supported by Lord Diplock in *Thompson v Brown* (above) when he held:

'But, even where, as in the instant case and as in *Browes* (*Browes v Jones & Middleton* (1979) 123 Sol Jo 489), if the action were not allowed to proceed the plaintiff would have a cast-iron case against his solicitor in which the measure of damages would be no less than those that he would be able to recover against the defendant if the action were allowed to proceed, some prejudice, although it may only be minor, would have been suffered by him. He will be obliged to find and instruct new and strange solicitors; there is bound to be delay; he would incur personal liability for costs of the action up to the date of the court's refusal to give a direction under section 2D, he may prefer to sue a stranger who is a tortfeasor with the possible consequences that may have on the tortfeasor's insurance premiums rather than sue his former solicitor with corresponding consequences on their premium.' (at 301j–302a)

As indicated, Lord Justice Parker added to this prejudice the fact that the former solicitors may well know of potential weaknesses in the claimant's case, whether on liability or quantum, and was of the view that, in such circumstances, the prejudice may be more than minor.

Where a claimant's claim over against his solicitors is doubtful, little or no weight is likely to be attached to it (see *Deeming v British Steel Corporation* (p407), *Grenville v Waltham Forest Health Authority* (p449), *Reynolds v Spousal* (p620), *Stannard v Stonar School* (p673), *Atha v ATV Network* (p308), *Wasley v Vass* (p708), *Thompson v Edmeads* (p692) and *Siodlaczek v Hymatic Engineering Co Ltd* (p652)). Where a claimant has already started proceedings against his solicitor and there is a prospect that certain of his heads of damage, such as an overdraft cost which the solicitors were aware of, might be more readily recoverable against them than the original tortfeasor, little prejudice is likely to arise (see *Mills v Ritchie* (p560), *Constantinides v C Birnbaum & Co* (p386), and *Straw v Hicks* (CA 13 October 1983)).

1.2   PREJUDICE TO THE DEFENDANT

Lord Diplock in *Thompson v Brown Construction (Ebbw Vale) Ltd* (p690) found that prejudice will always occur to a defendant if a case is allowed to proceed:

> 'A direction under the section must ... always be highly prejudicial to the defendant, for even if he also has a good defence on the merits he is put to the expenditure of time and energy and money in establishing it, while if, as in the instant case, he has no defence as to liability he has everything to lose if the direction is given under the section. On the other hand, if, as in the instant case, the time elapsed after the expiration of the primary limitation period is very short, what the defendant loses in consequence of a direction might be regarded as being in the nature of a windfall.' (p 301e–g)

As seen in *Nash v Eli Lilly* (p568) the Court of Appeal emphasised the economic prejudice that might occur to a defendant, particularly in complex litigation, in the form of the amount of costs required to resist a weak claim. In *Donovan v Gwentoys Ltd* (p412) the House of Lords further emphasised that, although a defendant can only rely under s 33(3)(b) on prejudice subsequent to the expiry of the limitation period, the court is permitted to examine 'under all the circumstances of the case' the effect that the passage of time has had prior to that date:

> 'The argument in favour of the proposition that dilatoriness on the part of the plaintiff in issuing the writ is irrelevant until the period of limitation has expired rests on the proposition that since the defendant has no legal grounds for complaint if the plaintiff issues his writ one day before the expiry of the period, it follows that he suffers no prejudice if the writ is not issued until two days later, save to the extent that, if the section is disapplied, he is deprived of his vested rights to defend the plaintiff's claim on that ground alone. In my opinion that is a false point. A defendant is always likely to be prejudiced by the dilatoriness of the plaintiff in pursuing his claim. Witnesses' memories may fade, records may be lost or destroyed, opportunities for inspection and report may be lost. The fact that the law permits the plaintiff within prescribed limits to disadvantage the defendant in this way does not mean that the defendant is not prejudiced. It merely means that he is not in a position to complain of whatever prejudice he suffers. Once the plaintiff also allows the permitted time to elapse the defendant is no longer subject to that disability, and in a situation where the court is directed to consider all the circumstances of the case, and the balance of prejudice to the parties the fact that a claim has as a result of

the plaintiff's failure to use the time allowed to him become a thoroughly stale claim cannot in my judgment be irrelevant.' ([1990] 1 All ER 1018 per Lord Oliver at 1025b–e)

The delay in *Donovan* was five and a half months outside an extended primary limitation period because Miss Donovan was a minor at the time of her injury. The trial judge, supported by the majority of the Court of Appeal, held that the proper test was to examine the prejudice that had occurred after the expiry of the primary limitation period. The House of Lords overturned that construction and held that in weighing prejudice to the defendant it was always relevant to consider when the defendants first had notification of the claim. Lord Griffiths, in emphasising that the defendants in *Donovan* were unaware of a claim until five years after the accident, held that, in those circumstances, it would be absurd if this could not be taken into account by a judge in the exercise of his discretion:

> 'In weighing the degree of prejudice suffered by a defendant it must always be relevant to consider when the defendant first had notification of a claim and thus the opportunity he will have to meet the claim at the trial if he was not to be permitted to rely on his limitation defence. To the extent that the decision in the Court of Appeal in *Eastman v London Country Bus Services Ltd* [p420] appears to cast doubt on this proposition it should not be followed.' (at 1024g–j)

(See also *Hands v Coleridge-Smith & Horsburgh* (p457).)

The speeches in the House of Lords in *Donovan* opened up for consideration the prejudice suffered by the defendants both pre- and post-expiry of the primary limitation period. This leads to a position in which, when examining evidential prejudice under the specific provisions of s 33(3)(b), the court is only concerned with prejudice after the expiry of the limitation period (per Lord Diplock's construction in *Thompson v Brown*), but under the general rubric of 'all the circumstances of the case' the court may look at the pre-expiry limitation period prejudice.

As discussed above, in *Cain* the Court of Appeal has excluded the economic prejudice to the defendant of having to pay damages as a factor to be taken into account, describing it as merely the obverse of the effect of the disapplication.

In *Davies v Secretary of State for Energy and Climate Change* (p401) the defendant successfully resisted applications for s 33 dispensations by showing evidential prejudice in a post-*Cain* case concerning group litigation in respect of miners' claims for knee arthritis due to chronic exposure to principally poor road conditions in the mines. The eight representative cases were all statute barred, with dates of knowledge agreed or found to be between 1984 and 1991 in respect of employment in the mines from 1954 to 1983. The actions were brought both in negligence and breach of duty on the basis that, although it was accepted that normal mine working imposed strains on the knees, there were systemic failures to prevent chronic bumps, trips and knocks which caused avoidable arthritis of the knees due to mainly poor road conditions affording access to the coal face. The cases were between 10 and 23 years out of time, with the average period being 15.6 years.

At first instance, the judge had refused to grant any of the cases a dispensation on the basis that the defendant had suffered evidential prejudice in defeating the claim on the merits. The Court of Appeal agreed, and dismissed the claimants' appeal. The judge accepted that the claimants had shown a prima facie breach of s 34 of the Mines and Quarries Act 1954 and had not therefore misapplied the broad merits test set out in the 'atomic veterans' action (*B v Ministry of Defence* (p312)). However, the prima facie breach highlighted the defendant's difficulty in making out the defence of impracticability under s 157 in circumstances where the documentary evidence was mainly limited to major traumas, where there was a shortage of willing defence witnesses on the actual conditions, and where the passage of time had affected recollections. The case was distinguished from most other industrial disease actions, where the issue was usually directed to the degree of exposure of one noxious agent as opposed to a consideration of what road conditions were inevitable, given the geology of the mines, and what were avoidable. The court also refused to accept that the reason for the delay, insofar as it related to the miners' unions failing to bring claims, could inure to the benefit of the men themselves, as they could not be in a better position simply because of delay by their unions.

In *Jones v Secretary of State for Energy and Climate Change* (p503), s 33 dispensations were granted to eight lead claimants who were exposed to polycyclic aromatic hydrocarbons during the production of Phurnacite in the period 1948–1991. The defendant's contention, that they were prejudiced on account of witnesses being unavailable, was not accepted by the trial judge, who found the attempts to identify and trace witnesses as superficial and that, as well as 30 witnesses being available, there was ample documentary evidence to permit a fair trial of the action. The judge also accepted, as a good reason for the delay, the need to proceed by way of a group litigation order (GLO), as unitary funding of individual actions was difficult to fund.

In *Sayers v Chelwood (deceased) and another* (p642) the claimant appealed against the court's refusal to grant a dispensation in respect of noise-induced deafness arising out of the use of machinery when employed as a gardener by Lord and Lady Chelwood. The Court of Appeal accepted that the judge had been wrong to impose a test described as a 'heavy burden' following the *Bryn Alyn* case, and the appropriate test was as indicated in *B v Nugent* (p315). However, applying the test that the burden was on the claimant and the discretion was unfettered, the court refused a dispensation on the grounds that a fair trial was not possible. It did so in part on the basis that the surviving defendant was 90 years old and could no longer trace liability insurance for the whole of the employed period. The claimant's offer to limit the damages to the insured proportion was not accepted by the court, as she still suffered prejudice with respect to 100% of the costs.

For a post-*Cain* case where the defendant did show evidential prejudice on the issue of quantum and liability was not in issue, see *McDonnell v Walker* [2009] EWCA Civ 1257. In addition to the costs spent in defending an action and evidential prejudice, a defendant may also in certain circumstances suffer personal prejudice based on the strain of the proceedings and the effect it may have on an individual's reputation or his business. In *Dobbie v Medway Health Authority* (p411) a claimant sued in respect of physical and psychiatric injury following an unnecessary mastectomy undertaken some 16 years prior to proceedings. Otton J refused to disapply the limitation period on the grounds, inter alia, that both the hospital and the surgeon would be prejudiced by the action hanging over them indefinitely. In doing so he followed a similar principle espoused by the then Master of the Rolls Lord Denning in *Biss v Lambeth, Southwark and Lewisham Area Health Authority* (p336). In *Birnie v Oxfordshire Health Authority* (p335), the Damoclean sword hanging over an allegedly negligent physician in a case brought nearly three years outside the primary limitation period was not, however, enough to stop the court exercising its discretion in favour of that claimant. A different outcome occurred in *James v East Dorset Health Authority* (p493).

The fact that a defendant is insured may be a relevant consideration, particularly in those cases where the court has to balance the prejudice to a claimant who has a claim over against his solicitors who will also be insured. (See *Firman v Ellis* (p433), *Hartley v Birmingham City District Council* (p465), *Jeffrey v Bolton Textile Mill Co plc* (p495), and *Bradley v Hanseatic Shipping Co Ltd* (p340).) In *Reynolds v Spousal (London) Ltd* (p620) the absence of insurers was a critical factor where one but not the other three defendants were allowed to take advantage of their accrued limitation defence on the basis that those particular defendants had been in liquidation for many years and there appeared to be little or no relevant insurance (see also *Jeffrey v Bolton Textile Mill Co plc*). However, in *Kelly v Bastible* (p515) the Court of Appeal emphasised that ordinarily the insured and the insurer should be considered as a composite entity when considering prejudice. In *Kelly* the judge at first instance felt constrained by Lord Justice Parker's judgment in *Hartley* (above) to draw a distinction between the defendant doctor himself and his insurers the Medical Defence Union. The judge reluctantly granted the dispensation on the basis that there was no personal prejudice to the doctor as the prejudice occurred to his insurers. The Court of Appeal stated that Lord Justice Parker's observations in *Hartley* did not preclude insurers from being entitled through the defendant to rely on any point which might demonstrate evidential prejudice:

> 'Clearly, in relation to the question of evidential prejudice or considering whether or not there can be a fair trial, it seems to me that the approach of considering the insurer and the defendant as a composite unit must always be the right approach, and indeed is supported by the cases to which I have referred. It is always right in weighing prejudice against one side to prejudice against the other for a judge to recognise that the plaintiff has no alternative remedy against his solicitor, and he will as a matter of reality be aware that the defendant is insured. However, if the conclusion has been that treating the defendant and insurer as a composite unit that delay has severely prejudiced their ability to defend, and if the court would not allow the action to continue if the defendant was *not* insured (taking account at that stage of the fact that the plaintiff has no claim against his solicitor if he is not allowed to proceed with his claim) the weight to be given to the mere fact that the defendant is insured, ought in my view to be nil. I say that first because a claim against a solicitor cannot really be equated with a claim under a policy of insurance for which the defendant has paid, and second because insurers are entitled to expect, when fixing their premiums, that they will not be penalised by being made to fight claims that their insured would not have been held bound to fight simply because they are insurers.' (per Waller LJ)

The approach of the Court of Appeal in *Kelly* was influenced by the decision in *Davis v Saltenpar* (p405) where the court held that the Motor Insurers' Bureau, as the effective insurers in a road traffic accident against an uninsured defendant, were entitled to have their position taken into account and it was appropriate that the insurer and the defendant for the purposes of prejudice should be considered as a composite unit and this would include the MIB (see also *Straw v Hicks* CA, 13 October 1983).

2 Section 33(3)(a)

'In acting under this section the court shall have regard to all the circumstances of the case and in particular to–

(a)   The length of, and reasons for, the delay on the part of the plaintiff; ...'

The six factors singled out which the court is required to consider in s 33(3) do not operate in isolation from one another, and the exercise of discretion is based on the totality of the evidence and circumstances in the case. Further, the wide ambit of 'all the circumstances of the case' as seen in *Donovan v Gwentoys Ltd* (p412) has the effect of allowing the court to look at prejudice which has occurred before the expiry of the limitation period. The six factors are accordingly exemplary and not exclusive. Nevertheless, trial judges sensibly tend to treat the six factors in turn and it is of some analytic benefit to consider each factor individually and how the case law has developed in relation to each particular factor.

The length of, and reasons for, the delay here refers specifically to the delay since the expiry of the limitation period. This proposition was determined by Lord Diplock in *Thompson v Brown Construction (Ebbw Vale) Ltd* (p690) and was reiterated in a number of cases such as *Deeming v British Steel Corporation* (p407), *Eastman v London Country Bus Services Limited* (p420) and again reaffirmed in the House of Lords in *Donovan v Gwentoys Ltd* (p412). In considering the period of delay, the court is required to consider when the actual or constructive date of knowledge was and to allow three years after that date. This, of course, may be significantly later than when the cause of action accrued. There is no 'out of time' limit on the period of delay and the Law Commission in its most recent report did not advocate any longstop provision. Cases concerning the insidious onset of diseases, the sexual or physical abuse of children and actions concerning a failure to diagnose or treat dyslexia can result in extensive periods of delay even from the extended period permitted through minority and from when the date of knowledge occurred.

2.1   THE LENGTH OF THE DELAY

In *Buck v English Electric Co Ltd* (p353) a claimant delayed 12 years from his date of knowledge before proceedings were issued in a pneumoconiosis case. The trial judge held that the extreme delay did not exclude the exercise of the court's discretion but a delay of five years created a rebuttable presumption that the delay was excessive. In *Buck* the reasons for the delay were that the claimant was initially able to continue to work being only 20 per cent disabled and in addition he had received a disability pension. Mr Buck took the view that, if he sued his employer as well as receiving a pension, it might be seen as sponging. However, his disability gradually rose to 100 per cent and he was forced to give up work. The court held that he had acted reasonably and indeed in the best tradition of a dignified workman, and allowed his claim to proceed, particularly as the defendants had suffered little evidential prejudice. In *KR v Bryn Alyn Community Holdings Ltd* (p505) the Court of Appeal doubted whether it was correct to speak of a presumption of delay after five or six years:

> '79.   We do not consider it would accord with the broad discretion conferred on the court by section 33 and the fact-sensitive nature of the exercise to suggest some form of tariff for cases such as these. For example, we could not justify in this context a proposition similar to that of Kilner Brown J in *Buck v English Electric Co* [1997] 1 WLR 806, 810b–c, drawing on the then pattern of decisions in cases of strike-out for want of prosecution, that where there has been a delay of five or six years there is a rebuttable presumption that the defendant will suffer prejudice. Although such a presumption might be thought to be more readily applicable in section 33 limitation cases, where the onus is on the claimant, than in strike-outs for want of prosecution, where

the onus is on the defendant, it would, in our view, impermissibly cut down the wide discretion in such cases. For the same reason, we would not go so far as Mr Faulks (defendant's counsel) in his suggestion that, except where there has been "a fairly minimal period of delay", the limitation period should not be dis-applied.'

Nevertheless, the Court of Appeal in *KR v Bryn Alyn* did accept as a general proposition that the longer the delay, the more likely it was that the balance of prejudice would swing against a disapplication; and this part of the guidelines has survived the criticisms made of *KR v Bryn Alyn* in *A v Hoare* (p287) and *B v Nugent Care Society* (p315).

There are, however, several examples of where the court has been minded to grant a dispensation in disease cases after substantial delay. In *Jeffery v Bolton Textile Mill Co plc* (p495) a widow was given leave in 1989 to proceed in respect of an action based on exposure to dust to her husband during his working life with the defendants from 1919 to 1957. In *McLaren v Harland and Wolff Ltd* (p555) a widow sued in 1989 in respect of her husband's exposure to asbestos between 1953 and 1960 where an asbestos-related disease was diagnosed in 1983. In exercising its discretion under s 19A of the Prescription and Limitation (Scotland) Act 1973 (similar but not identical to s 33 of the Limitation Act 1980), the Scottish court expressed the view that the fact the deceased was unaware that he had a claim against the defendants was not unreasonable as he had left the shipyard where he was exposed to asbestos some 28 years before his death.

In *Lea v Armitage Shanks Group Ltd* (p528) a delay of 19 years was held not be fatal to a claim for pneumoconiosis in a case where it was once again emphasised that there was an important distinction to be made between an accident which involved witnesses recollecting an event and cases where the recollection of a system of work only was required.

In *Reynolds v Spousal (London) Ltd* (p620), permission was given to proceed against certain defendants in respect of the death of the claimant's husband in 1980 from mesothelioma due to exposure to asbestos. The court was of the view that there was unlikely to be any substantial issue on liability. The deceased had a date of knowledge in 1966 and the writ was not issued until 19 years later. The delay was largely due to negative legal advice. Similarly, in *Smith v Ministry of Defence* (p661) a claim for mesothelioma on behalf of a widow was permitted following a six-year delay after her husband's date of knowledge in respect of exposure some 32 years earlier. In *Whittaker v Westinghouse Brake and Signal Holdings* (p715) a widow was also permitted to bring a claim in respect of her husband's death from silicosis-induced lung cancer 31 years after he had been diagnosed as suffering from silicosis on the basis that at no time was the deceased aware that he could bring a claim (see also *Hall v John Laing Plc* (p455), *Harding v Richard Costain Ltd* (p459), *Parsons v Warren* (p597) and, for a case going against the claimant, *Hinchcliffe v Corus UK Ltd* (p475)).

Not all disease cases are treated so sympathetically. In cases of long delay arising out of deafness claims, the Court of Appeal has emphasised the prejudicial nature to the defendants of having to face very stale claims, even when many other cases may have been dealt with by the same defendant (*Price v United Engineering Steels Ltd* (p612); see also *Lennon v Alvis Industries plc* (p532), *Barrand v British Cellophane Ltd* (p326), *Beattie v British Steel plc* (p327) and *Mackie v Secretary of State for Trade and Industry* (p539). Similarly, cases arising out of a failure to diagnose and to treat dyslexia have met with a degree of judicial reluctance to exercise a s 33 dispensation in the claimant's favour (see *Adams v Bracknell Forest Borough Council* (p292), *Robinson v St Helen's Metropolitan Borough Council* (p628), *Rowe v Kingston Upon Hull City Council* (p633), *Meherali v Hampshire County Council* (p556) and *Sullivan v Devon County Council* (p679)). This reluctance has principally been on the basis of long delays causing evidential prejudice and the court looking at the issue of proportionality between the value of the claim and the costs of prosecuting and defending it.

In cases of sexual abuse, the gravity of the wrong itself may be a relevant factor (*C v D* (p359)), but the court would probably consider this under all the circumstances of the case rather than raising it to a matter of public importance that allegations of grave wrongs should to be litigated as this is more the function of the criminal rather than the civil law. Irwin J in *B v Nugent Care Society* [2009] EWHC 481 (QB) stated:

'49.   Finally, I turn to the argument advanced by Mr. Maxwell that there is a public interest in having allegations of this kind tested in civil proceedings. I reject that. There is a definite public interest in having sex abuse or physical abuse investigated, and where appropriate, prosecuted. However, it does not seem to me that there is any identifiable public interest in civil proceedings going ahead. Civil proceedings are by definition private litigation between the parties. There is a very strong public interest in having a system by which private grievances can properly be tried, both at common law and within the terms of the European Convention of Human Rights. However, that is a different matter from any public interest in a particular class or description of proceedings, and even more so from a public interest in any particular case going ahead by means of a specific exercise of discretion.'

(See also the remarks of McCombe J in *Mutua v Foreign and Commonwealth Office* (p565) at paras 150, 157–158 in the context of abuse amounting to torture.)

Following *A v Hoare*, it is clear that, in cases concerning sexual abuse, the subjective effects of the abuse in accounting for the length of the delay because of psychological factors (such as fear of the abuser, embarrassment and denial) are to be specifically considered under s 33 rather than under s 14. Irwin J in *B v Nugent Care Society* [2009] EWHC 481 (QB) at para 39 stated:

'It does seem clear in the speeches in *Hoare*, that some real significance has been attached to the specific factor arising in sex abuse cases, namely, that the tort inflicted by the abuser and for which the defendants are now vicariously liable, has itself the tendency to inhibit the victim from complaining, reporting or suing, even where the consequences do not include frank psychological and psychiatric injury.'

For further examples of abuse cases, see *Albonetti v Wirral* (p298), *EB v Haughton* (p418), *D v Harrow LBC* (p394) and *RAR v GAC* (p615).

2.2   THE REASONS FOR THE DELAY

What constitutes an acceptable period of delay and an acceptable reason for the delay will obviously depend on the particular facts of any one case. In general, the court will be looking for either a good or reasonable explanation for the delay, or at least one that does not involve direct criticism of the claimant himself. In *Coad v Cornwall and Isles of Scilly Health Authority* (p378) the Court of Appeal held that the test to be applied under s 33(3)(a), as opposed to the test under s 33(3)(e), was a subjective not an objective one. Mrs Coad sustained injury to her back in the course of her employment as a nurse whilst she was attempting to lift a tetraplegic patient who had sustained a fall. Her injury occurred in 1983 but she did not issue proceedings until January 1993 and was approximately six and a half years out of time. Her case was that she did not know that she could bring a claim all the time that she continued to be employed and thought that a claim could only be made if she lost her job. The defendants contended that that was objectively an unreasonable belief. The Court of Appeal held that s 33(3)(a) did not contain any reference to reasonableness and, accordingly, the test was subjective. The trial judge found that the claimant had a genuine belief that she did not have a legal right until she lost her job and given that there was no challenge to this her ignorance of the law was a reason that the court could take into account in exculpating the delay. The defendants' appeal accordingly failed, although two of the Lord Justices expressed a view that, had they been trying the matter at first instance, they may not have exercised the discretion in the same way that the trial judge had.

The courts have tended to look reasonably favourably on those claimants whose delay has been due to a non-litigious attitude. In *McCafferty v Metropolitan Police District Receiver* (p546) the court was impressed by a combination of reasons given by the claimant which had led to a delay of some six years from his date of knowledge before proceedings were issued. These included a desire to preserve good relations with his employer and an attempt to dismiss a developing deafness as merely an irritating nuisance. Similarly, in *Buck v English Electric Co Ltd* (p353) a deceased's reluctance to sue during his lifetime was partially based on the belief that he might be sponging if he sued his employers while he was working and also in receipt of a disability pension.

However commendable such an attitude might be, it obviously has to be balanced against the other factors listed in s 33(3). So, for example, in *Woolnough v G & M Power Plant Co Ltd* (p726) the Court of Appeal allowed a defendant's appeal in a case of a six-year delay arising out an accident at work. The delay was because the claimant took the view that his employers were good to him and he did not want to seek compensation while he was receiving a wage. The appeal was allowed primarily on the basis that the defendants had suffered evidential prejudice, in respect of both where the accident occurred and the manner in which it had occurred. A different outcome was achieved in *Hart v British Leyland Cars Ltd* (p464) where a claimant delayed for nearly nine years from his date of knowledge before issuing proceedings in an action arising out of his contraction of contact dermatitis. Lawson J found that the reason for his delay, namely that he had lost little time off work until he was made redundant in 1980, was not adverse to his case. Because the case involved a system of work and because there was no significant evidential prejudice, he allowed the action to continue.

A court might also look favourably on a delay due to a deterioration in the claimant's condition. In *Miller v London Electrical Manufacturing Co Ltd* (p559) a claimant who contracted dermatitis in 1967 sought to sue in 1974 after he developed a serious deterioration in his condition. The case was held to be statute barred under the Limitation Act 1963, which gave the court no power to disapply the limitation period. The then Master of the Rolls, Lord Denning, indicated that this was perhaps the type of case where, if the court did have discretion, it might exercise it. Similarly, in *McCafferty v Metropolitan Police District Re*ceiver (p546) the court accepted that some of the reasons for the delay were due to the claimant's deafness developing from an irritating nuisance through to a disability which necessitated medical retirement. In *Davis v Union Insulation Co Ltd* (p406) a s 33 dispensation was granted to a claimant whose asbestos disease progressed to cause disabling symptoms. Mr Davis was diagnosed in 1990 with pleural thickening, and solicitors had advised him to bring proceedings. Mr Davis rejected that advice because he was suffering no symptoms and did not change his mind until his condition materially altered. Although the court indicated that the matter was finely balanced, the claimant was allowed to proceed five and a half years after his date of knowledge. Conversely, in *Buckler v Sheffield Forest Borough Council* (p354) where a claimant erroneously believed that his asbestos-related condition worsened, the Court of Appeal allowed a defendant's appeal. Mr Buckler was diagnosed in April 1991 with pleural thickening (in fact, the correct diagnosis should have been for pleural plaques) and was informed that he could make a claim but chose not to do so as the condition was causing no symptoms. In 1999 the correct diagnosis of pleural plaques, also symptomless, was made. Mr Buckler brought a claim on the basis that he thought his condition had deteriorated. The Court of Appeal accepted that the claimant may have been under a misapprehension in believing that his condition had worsened but they did not find that this was cogent enough a reason to allow the claim to proceed as he had previously made a conscious decision not to sue. Similarly, where only a moderate aggravation occurred to a back injury and the claim was brought 18 years after the accident, the court unsurprisingly refused to exercise its discretion to allow the action to continue (see *Cooper v National Coal Board*, unreported, Cardiff 6 February 1979).

Ignorance that a claimant has a cause of action, although specifically excluded from preventing time running under s 14, is an important consideration under s 33. In *Halford v Brookes* (p453), Russell LJ accepted that a claimant did not know that murder might give rise to a civil cause of action as well as a claim from the Criminal Injuries Compensation Board:

> 'For my part I can detect no legitimate criticism of this plaintiff. It is not suggested that she was ever aware that a civil remedy was open to her until she consulted her new solicitors ... the reality of the case is that she did not know of the existence of a remedy and this I find entirely understandable in one, with her background, who is not versed in the law.' ([1991] 3 All ER 559 at 567a–c)

The Court of Appeal confirmed this approach in *Coad v Cornwall and Isle of Scilly Health Authority* (p378).

In *Lea v Armitage Shanks Group Ltd* (p538), 19 years passed in a pneumoconiosis case due to the claimant being unaware that he could claim damages. The action was allowed to proceed. However, in *Cotton v General Electric Co Ltd* (p388) a shorter period of delay in a silicosis case brought by a widow was held to be statute barred. The deceased believed, wrongly, that the claim could not be brought during his lifetime. The delay, however, had caused considerable difficulty in establishing the precise cause of his lung disease. Similarly, in *Casey v J Murphy & Sons* (p366) a claimant who sued in 1979 in respect of dermatitis contracted in 1973 failed to persuade the court to exercise its discretion in his favour. The Court of Appeal acknowledged that the fact that the claimant was ignorant that he had a claim in law until 1979 was pertinent but, given the fact that he was a trade unionist who had access to legal advice and the claim itself was not so unusual, the court would not exercise its discretion in his favour (see also *Hart v British Leyland Cars Ltd* (p464)).

In *Common v Crofts* (p384) a short delay of five months, based on the mistaken belief that a claimant could not sue in a civil action arising out of a road traffic accident where he had been criminally prosecuted for his driving, was found to be reasonable, and the Court of Appeal upheld the judge's decision to allow the matter to proceed.

Negative advice from a lawyer or delay caused by legal and other advisers is usually the basis of absolving a claimant of any personal criticism. In *Doughty v North Staffordshire Health Authority* (p414) there was a delay of effectively nine years in a case relating to medical treatment received over a period of up to 25 years before proceedings were started. The action was allowed to continue even though the treating surgeon was no longer able to testify because of his infirmity. The judge held that, notwithstanding the defendant's prejudice, since the medical records were still intact, it was possible to have a fair trial. He accepted that the reasons for delay were partly due to discouraging expert opinion followed by negative legal advice leading to a discharge of the claimant's legal aid certificate.

In *Das v Ganju* (p398) the Court of Appeal stated that there was no rule of law that a solicitor's fault leading to the delay had to be attributed to the claimant. Mrs Das gave birth to a severely disabled child in October 1978 due to congenital rubella syndrome. She received inaccurate advice from her first counsel and solicitors and did not issue proceedings until 17 December 1996. The court found her blameless and allowed her action to proceed. In dismissing the defendant's appeal the Court of Appeal found dicta in *Whitfield v North Durham Health Authority* (p713), insofar as they contended that there could be no separation of the claimant's acts and omissions from that of her advisers, to be irreconcilable with other authority. Having found that the claimant had struggled against legal and medical misfortune for 20 years, Sir Christopher Staughton stated:

> 'But are they to be criticised for the fault of their lawyers? On this topic we were referred to *Whitfield v North Durham Health Authority* [1995] 6 Med LR 32. There Waite LJ said at 35:
>
>> "In a discretionary jurisdiction where the court is required to have regard to 'all the circumstances of the case' it would clearly be inappropriate to look for hard and fast rules, but counsel were agreed in this court that the section must be read as incorporating one underlying principle. In the process of assessing equity and balancing prejudice which the section enjoins, a party's action or inaction cannot be divorced from the acts or omissions of his legal representative. The principle in that respect is analogous to that applying in cases of striking-out for the prosecution".
>
> If that passage means that in a matter of law anything done by lawyers must be visited on the client, it cannot in my view be reconciled with other authority. It appears to have been a concession which the court accepted. The other authority is *Thompson v Brown* [1981] 1 WLR 744 and the speech of Lord Diplock at 750 and 752, which I do not set out for fear of lengthening this judgment even further. I would also return to *Halford v Brooks*, where again it is said that it is no reproach to the plaintiff that he received the wrong legal advice.'

A differently constituted Court of Appeal in *Corbin v Penfold Metalising* (p387) expressed the same view; see also *Steeds v Peverel Management Services Ltd* (p674) and *Adam v Ali* [2006] EWCA Civ 91.

However, in *Horton v Sadler* (p482), Lord Carswell made some general observations on s 33 which included the following comments on *Das* and on *Corbin*:

> 'In *Das v Ganju* [1999] Lloyd's Rep Med 198 at 204 and *Corbin v Penfold Metallising Co Ltd* [2000] Lloyd's Rep Med 247 the Court of Appeal expressed the view that there was no rule of law that the claimant must suffer for his solicitor's default. If this is interpreted, as it was in *Corbin*, as meaning that the court, is not entitled to take into account against a party the failings of his solicitors who let the action go out of time, that could not in my view be sustained and the criticism voiced in the notes to the reports of

Das and *Corbin* would be justified. The claimant must bear responsibility, as against the defendant, for delays which have occurred, whether caused by his own default or that of his solicitors, and in numerous cases that has been accepted.' (para 53)

Nevertheless, in *Horton* the House of Lords declined to interfere with the judge's exercise of his discretion in favour of the claimant where the fault was that of the solicitors and the claimant had a good case over against the solicitors in negligence.

Conversely, in *Cyster v Council of the City of Manchester* (p394) the court declined to extend the limitation period. The claimant had failed to obtain disclosable medical opinion, despite six sets of solicitors, and part of this was considered the claimant's personal fault. Moreover, through the delay of some seven and a half years the defendant suffered considerable evidential prejudice in the form of losing contact with witnesses and in losing records.

In *Stannard v Stonar School* (p673), part of the delay was due to a possible misunderstanding with the claimant's solicitors who had not acted on the claimant's instructions to prosecute his claim and that was held not to be adverse to his case. In *Newman v Bevan Funnell Ltd* (p580) a delay in instituting proceedings was due to a misdiagnosis. Although this probably would have been sufficient to prevent knowledge of causation being established, there was no appeal on the judge's finding concerning the claimant's date of knowledge. The Court of Appeal, however, upheld the judge's decision to disapply the limitation period on the basis that the cause of the delay was attributable to inaccurate medical advice through a misdiagnosis.

In *Lewis v Poulton* (p534) a claimant sought to sue in respect of an injury sustained in a road traffic accident which occurred in 1970. She first consulted solicitors in 1973 who told her directly that her case was now statute barred. In 1977 she learnt that a discretion to disapply the limitation period had been brought in by the 1975 Limitation Act and she promptly instructed further solicitors. These solicitors and subsequently doctors instructed by them failed to report quickly. The court did not find the claimant culpable for that delay and because she personally had acted promptly once she knew of the new legal remedy open to her the court allowed the case to proceed. This is an interesting example, because it demonstrates that a change in the law may well be a good reason for allowing a time barred action to proceed, whether due to a change in the common law or as in the case of *Lewis* a change of statute. Following the abolition of the rule in *Walkley v Precision Forgings* (p705), in *Horton v Sadler* many second claims were brought out of time seeking the court's discretion, and some of these were successful (see *Leeson v Marsden* (p530), *Richardson v Watson* (p621) and *Aktas v Adepta* (p296). A similar flurry of actions followed the House of Lords' decision in *Stubbings v Webb* which permitted assaults to be brought within s 11, and therefore s 33, rather than governed by a fixed six-year period.

In *Ward v Foss* (p708) a change in the law did not assist a defendant. This action was started in November 1989 on behalf of dependent children and the estate of a couple who had died in a road traffic accident in July 1982. The children's claim under the Fatal Accidents Act 1976 was brought in time, but the estates action under the Law Reform (Miscellaneous Provisions) Act 1934 required a s 33 dispensation. The defendants argued that it would be inequitable to allow the Law Reform Act claim to continue because it would take the benefit of the law as it was before the coming into force of the Administration of Justice Act 1982 which applied to causes of action after 1 January 1983. This Act abolished the estate's claim for loss of income in the so-called lost years which could in some cases generate a degree of double recovery. The Court of Appeal allowed the estate's action to proceed stating that s 33 did not ask whether the claim per se was inequitable but whether it was equitable to allow it to proceed. The defendants failed to establish any convincing evidence of prejudice (for other examples of the interaction of the Fatal Accidents Act claims with the Law Reform (Miscellaneous Provisions) Act claims and s 33, see **Chapter 6**).

In *Grenville v Waltham Forest Health Authority* (p449) an administrative error by the court office in failing to issue proceedings properly led to an action becoming statute barred. The Court of Appeal granted a s 33 dispensation principally on the grounds that the claimant did not have in those circumstances a good claim over against her solicitors.

In *Skitt v Khan and Wakefield Health Authority* (p654) the impecuniosity of a claimant during his lifetime which prevented him from investigating whether a cancer he was suffering from was caused by a cut to his leg he received at work in 1977 was held not to be a sufficient reason to permit his widow to bring a claim out of time. The Court of Appeal held that the deceased claim was statute barred and it would not be equitable even bearing in mind the financial circumstances of the deceased to allow his claim to proceed. This was so even in circumstances where he had been refused legal aid.

In *Khairule v North West Strategic Health Authority* (p518) a claimant aged 25 sued in March 2006 for injuries sustained at birth causing him athetoid cerebral palsy with preservation of intellect. The court fixed him with actual and constructive knowledge that his injuries were capable of being attributable to an act or omission of the defendant by 2002. In exercising the discretion in favour of the claimant, the court was in part influenced by the fact that the claimant had been told little of the circumstances of his birth, had struggled with a severe disability in the context of a difficult home life, and did not have access to the internet permitting him to research his condition until 2002. These personal and particular subjective circumstances weighed in his favour and, notwithstanding the loss of the birth CTG trace, it was still possible to have a fair trial on the remaining available evidence.

3   Section 33(3)(b)

'the extent to which, having regard to the delay, the evidence adduced or likely to be adduced by the plaintiff or the defendant is, or is likely to be, less cogent than if the action had been brought within the time allowed by section 11, by section 11A or (as the case may be) by section 12.'

In *Hartley v Birmingham City Council* (p465), the court elevated the question of evidential prejudice to the most significant factor that ought to be borne in mind when exercising its discretion. Of paramount importance was the effect, if any, on how the delay had weakened the defendants' ability to resist the claim on the merits. Parker LJ formulated the proposition that, if the delay did not seriously affect the evidence, the power will generally be exercised in the claimant's favour. This approach was endorsed by Lord Carswell in the House of Lords in *Horton v Sadler* (p482). However, a differently constituted Court of Appeal in *Nash v Eli Lilly* (p568) sought to qualify this statement of principle by saying it was not of universal application and, in particular, it would not apply to those actions where the claimant's case was weak on liability and the defendants would be put to expense disproportionate to the value of the claimant's claim in defending, particularly when the claimant was legally aided. The Court of Appeal in *KR v Bryn Alyn Community*

Holdings Ltd (p505) affirmed the view of Parker LJ in *Hartley* but also endorsed the *Nash* proviso. In *Cain v Francis* (p360) the Court of Appeal again elevated the effects of the delay on the cogency of the evidence as a critical factor:

> '73.   It seems to me that, in the exercise of the discretion, the basic question to be asked is whether it is fair and just in all the circumstances to expect the defendant to meet this claim on the merits, notwithstanding the delay in commencement. The length of the delay will be important, not so much for itself as to the effect it has had. To what extent has the defendant been disadvantaged in his investigation of the claim and/or the assembly of evidence, in respect of the issues of both liability and quantum? But it will also be important to consider the reasons for the delay. Thus, there may be some unfairness to the defendant due to the delay in issue but the delay may have arisen for so excusable a reason, that, looking at the matter in the round, on balance, it is fair and just that the action should proceed. On the other hand, the balance may go in the opposite direction, partly because the delay has caused procedural disadvantage and unfairness to the defendant and partly because the reasons for the delay (or its length) are not good ones.'

In the end, the exercise of discretion is always a matter of what is equitable, but it is unsurprising that there are very few reported cases where, once the defendant has established a significant loss of cogency in the evidence that can be produced (as opposed to the evidence that would have been capable of being produced if the case had been brought in time), the action has been allowed to proceed (cf *Brooks v J & P Coates (UK) Ltd* (p350), *Doughty v North Staffordshire Health Authority* (p414), *Pavan v Holwill's (Oils) Ltd* (p598), *Farthing v North Essex District Health Authority* (p429) and *Colley v Bard Ltd* (p380)). The position may be otherwise where it can be said the loss of evidence is due to a defendant failing to preserve documents (x-rays) where a claim had been intimated in time but brought out of time, as occurred in *Hammond v West Lancashire Health Authority* (p456). Similarly, in *S v Camden London Borough Council* (p635) a claim brought 11½ years out of time against a local authority for failing to take the claimant into care and therefore prevent physical, emotional and sexual abuse by her mother was permitted to proceed out of time as the defendant's loss of a file was found to be its own fault. Additionally, the defendant had delayed, despite requests, in providing to the claimant documents that it still retained.

The period within this subsection, as in s 33(3)(a), is that which has passed after the expiry of the limitation period and not the passage of time since the claimant's cause of action accrued. A distinction needs therefore to be drawn between prejudice to a defendant which occurred during the primary limitation period and that which has occurred after. Section 33(3)(b) is concerned only with the latter. However, the effect of this distinction has been largely negated by the House of Lords ruling in *Donovan v Gwentoys Ltd* (p412) which permits consideration of the whole of the defendant's prejudice since the accrual of the claimant's cause of action under the injunction in the preamble to s 33(3) to examine 'all the circumstances of the case'.

Evidential prejudice under s 33(3)(b) will frequently take the form of having lost contact with witnesses or witnesses becoming infirm or dying. In addition, all recollections are generally accepted as becoming less cogent, particularly in respect of an accident, after a significant passage of time. Documents can also be mislaid or lost or destroyed and where this has had a detrimental effect on the cogency of the evidence, a defendant is likely to be able to demonstrate significant prejudice. There are many cases that illustrate the particular importance the court attaches to the loss of cogency of the defendant's evidence.

In the following examples, the defendant succeeded in resisting the court's exercise of discretion predominantly on the basis of evidential prejudice. In *Bater v Newbold* (p323), a claimant sued seven years out of time in respect of an accident on a building site. The defendants were by then unable to trace the scaffolders or their witnesses, and in any event alleged the proper defendant was a dissolved company. Moreover, the foreman had died and the claimant himself could not remember the precise circumstances of the accident. Clearly the prejudice to the defendant was held to make a fair trial impossible (see also *Woolnough v G & M Power Plant Co Ltd* (p726), and *Gregory v Ferro (GB) Ltd* (p448)).

In *Bailey v T J Frames* (p319) a claim brought 20 months out of time was held as statute barred because the defendants were no longer able to identify the particular staple gun which had been used by the claimant when inadvertently a staple had been fired into his knee. In addition, the trial judge emphasised the difficulty of witnesses recalling events some six years later when the trial was likely to be heard.

In *Davies v British Insulated Callendar's Cables Ltd* (p400) a claimant fell at work in 1970 and did not issue proceedings until 1976. The court not only found it difficult to comprehend that the claimant did not know that he could sue his employers, but it also indicated that it was difficult to pinpoint precisely when a back injury occurred, particularly in a case where the claimant had not reported the accident and no witness statements had been taken.

In *Freeman v Home Office* (p438) a prisoner sued in both negligence and trespass to the person in respect of forcible injections of tranquillisers while in Wakefield prison between 1972 and 1974. He issued proceedings in 1979, by which time the doctor who administered the drug had died. The Court of Appeal accordingly found that the clinical negligence action, based upon a failure to give simultaneously a drug to mitigate the side effects of the tranquillisers, should not proceed because of the evidential prejudice. However, the assault action was allowed to continue because the prison staff, who held the claimant down while the injections were administered, were still available.

In *Wilding v Lambeth, Southwark and Lewisham Area Health Authority* (p716) a late amendment to add a new cause of action in trespass was refused in a clinical negligence case, where it was sought at the trial of the action to allege lack of consent to a dental operation. The judge refused the application and refused to exercise his discretion under s 33 on the basis that it would not, some eight years later, be satisfactory to have a trial on the oral statements made by the medical practitioners at the time of the claimant's operation.

An extensive delay in *Pilmore v Northern Trawlers Ltd* (p606) resulted in a claimant being shut out in respect of the claim based upon his contraction of dermatitis in 1970 which made him unfit to work on trawlers by 1972. By the time proceedings were issued in 1984 the defendants had sold the fishing vessel that the claimant had worked on, had lost the pertinent documents and the gloves and barrier cream had long since been unobtainable. In addition, the crew had dispersed.

A destruction of the Pneumoconiosis Medical Panel's records in *Cotton v General Electric Co Ltd* (p388) made the apportionment of a claimant's respiratory disability between constitutional bronchitis and tortious silicosis difficult to evaluate. The Court of Appeal accordingly upheld the judge's refusal to allow the widow's claim to proceed out of time. Further, although this was a case which involved a system of work rather than an accident, the defendants had not had similar claims made against them and the working conditions of some 11 years before might be difficult to recollect.

Except in very clear cases where the defendants concede liability or accept that that they suffered no prejudice (cf *Hendy v Milton Keynes Health Authority* (p472),

Hills v Potter (p474)), it is normally possible for a defendant to demonstrate some prejudice. The issue for the court is to weigh the effect of the prejudice, and the claimant may be given leave to proceed when the degree of prejudice caused by the delay does not seriously affect the cogency of the evidence.

In *Conry v Simpson* (p385) the claimant was injured in a road traffic accident in 1973 and promptly notified his claim to the defendants. Proceedings were not issued until 1977, during which time the defendants' insurers had destroyed the file, and a medical report they had obtained, because they reasonably believed the case was not going to proceed, had also been destroyed. The Court of Appeal took the view that, on the facts, no severe prejudice had been caused to the defendants because they were still in a position to have the claimant examined, and the prognosis in respect of his condition would now in fact be clearer.

In *Birnie v Oxfordshire Health Authority* (p335) a specialist in pain relief carried out in 1972 a procedure called a barbotage which left the claimant permanently paralysed. The claimant developed depression and attempted to commit suicide. Following a period of hospitalisation after a suicide attempt, the claimant developed bed sores and gangrene which led to the amputation of one of his legs in 1975. Proceedings were issued in 1979. The trial judge found that there was prejudice to the surgeon who had had the claim hanging over his head and in respect of the recollection required concerning the barbotage. However, substantial documentation was still available, and the judge allowed the action to proceed. Similarly, the presence of hospital notes and the fact that a statement had been taken from two surgeons, availed the claimant in *Bentley v Bristol & Western Health Authority* (p328). The trial judge held that he would have allowed the action to proceed under s 33, had he not found that the claim in fact was brought within the claimant's date of knowledge. Generally speaking, clinical negligence actions primarily based upon expert opinions on preserved medical and nursing notes and tests are more likely to be permitted to proceed, as opposed to those cases which raise issues concerning consent and warning about risks, which turn upon oral evidence. In *Rogers v East Kent Hospitals NHS Trust* (p629) a High Court judge allowed a claimant's appeal from a Circuit judge on her date of knowledge concerning a failed operation to correct a foot deformity in a claim brought nine years after amputation of a toe. The judge also indicated that, if necessary, he would also have allowed a s 33 dispensation refused by the judge because the relevant treating doctors had been traced, the notes preserved and the claimant's medico-legal expert felt no difficulty in supporting a claim in negligence on the available material.

In *Briody v St Helens & Knowsley Health Authority* (p344) a claimant was permitted to proceed on one set of allegations concerning a failure to perform a caesarean section which, on the evidence, was not particularly time sensitive. She was, however, refused permission to proceed on allegations concerning the precise management of the labour which did turn more on oral recollection.

In *Farthing v North Essex District Health Authority* (p429) the claimant sued in 1995 in respect of damage to her right urethra caused during a hysterectomy in 1981. Despite one doctor having died, one emigrating and one having no recollection, the Court of Appeal agreed that the claimant's case should proceed as the evidence would turn on available contemporaneous records. A similar approach was endorsed in *Appleby v Walsall Health Authority* (p305), *Roberts v Winbow* (p627), *Brewer v North Tees NHS Trust* (p343) and *Smith v Leicester Health Authority* (p659) because the evidential primacy of written records prevailed over deficiencies in the availability and efficacy of witness recollections.

By contrast in *Forbes v Wandsworth Health Authority* (p434), because operation notes could no longer be found, the Court of Appeal indicated that this was likely to cause significant prejudice and was one factor in not permitting a s 33 dispensation. In *Whitfield v North Durham Health Authority* (p713) the Court of Appeal took a different view to the first instance judge on the significance that cytological slides were still available. At first instance, the judge permitted a s 33 dispensation but the Court of Appeal allowed the defendants' appeal on the basis that, inter alia, cytological expert evidence would still be hampered by the delay in bringing the case.

In *Brooks v J & P Coates (UK) Ltd* (p350) a byssinosis claim was allowed to proceed 15 years out of time despite the fact that real prejudice to the defendants had occurred because the workforce had been dispersed, the mill where the exposure to cotton dust had occurred had been closed and records were no longer available. The judge was satisfied that, because the action concerned a system of work rather than a particular incident, a fair trial was still possible. (For other cases involving a system of work, see *Allen v British Rail Engineering and RFS Industries Ltd* (p301), *Fletcher v Containerbase (Manchester) Ltd* (p434), *Buck v English Electric Co Ltd* (p353), *McCafferty v Metropolitan Police District Receiver* (p546), *Reynolds v Spousal (London) Ltd* (p620), *McLaren v Harland & Wolff Ltd* (p555) and *Middleditch v Thames Case Ltd* (p558).)

Occasionally, even in an accident case, a claimant may be given leave despite considerable delay, if the loss of cogency is not of high degree (see *Cornish v Kearley & Tonge Ltd* (p388)). The claimant's chances of being allowed to proceed may increase if the accident was a particularly memorable one (cf *Stannard v Stonar School* (p673)).

In *Waghorn v Lewisham & North Southwark Area Health Authority* (p703) a claimant sued in 1984 in respect of alleged substandard surgery in 1977. In the interim, but after the expiry of the prime limitation period, the claimant had two further operations which obscured the initial surgery. The judge was satisfied that the surgery's effect on the evidence was only marginal and allowed the action to proceed.

Although it is rare, a claimant may on occasion be given leave to proceed even when the cogency of the evidence has been significantly affected, providing that a fair trial is still possible. In *Doughty v North Staffordshire Health Authority* (p414), a claimant had undergone twelve facial operations in an attempt to remove a port wine birthmark. The operations had taken place between the ages of 5 and 17 from 1962 to 1974. The claimant was fixed with a date of knowledge in 1974 and her writ was issued some 13 years later, mainly due to negative advice and legal aid restrictions. The surgeon who had undertaken the operation had a stroke in 1989 and was unable to testify. The medical records were still available. Despite the prejudice to the defendants, the judge considered that a fair trial was possible and allowed the action to proceed, in which the defendant was subsequently found to have been negligent.

Loss of cogency can also affect the claimant's prospects of succeeding. The court will look at how far the passage of time has reduced the quality or quantity of the evidence the claimant is likely to adduce. In *Jeffrey v Bolton Textile Mill Co plc* (p495), Garland J indicated that the long delay of nearly 13 years made the claimant's task an uphill one but it was not impossible, and he allowed the case to proceed emphasising that the onus was on the claimant to prove her case (see also *Adam v Ali* [2006] EWCA Civ 91). In *Woods v Attorney General* (p725), MacPherson J was satisfied that a fair trial was still possible and allowed an action to proceed, commenting that, if the passage of time had made the evidence the claimant wished to adduce more troublesome, that was the claimant's funeral.

In *Nash v Eli Lilly* (p568) the Court of Appeal rejected an argument that prejudice to the claimant in respect of cogency of evidence could somehow inure to her benefit and accordingly prejudice the defendant. The trial judge had been persuaded by an argument that, in the Opren cases, evidence was likely to come from claimants who would be suffering an obvious loss of cogency due to their age or because they were taking other drugs for a variety of conditions. Hidden J accepted that such an explanation might be a basis for explaining contradictions in their evidence:

'In my view ... a lack of cogency in the case of a plaintiff – and there were frequent instances of this in the cases before me – especially when that plaintiff is elderly, may often be used to the advantage of that plaintiff. It may in particular be used in an attempt to explain away or at least mitigate the effect of omissions or contradictions which emerge during the evidence. In assessing the effect of delay upon cogency, I have to consider the totality of the matter.' ([1991] 2 Med LR 169 at 201)

The Court of Appeal, however, was not persuaded by that reasoning and stated:

'While we understand what the learned judge had in mind we regret to have to say that in our view this is logically unsustainable. It depends upon the assumption that the trial judge will not be able properly to assess the evidence led on behalf of the plaintiff.' ([1993] 4 All ER 383 at 406j)

Finally, it is important to recognise that cogency may not only affect the evidence adduced on liability but also on causation, such as diagnosis of a condition, and on quantum in respect of calculating, for example, loss of earnings (cf *Smith v Leicester Health Authority* (p659), *McDonnell & anor v David Walker (Executor of the Estate of Richard Walker, deceased)* (2009), *Cooper v National Coal Board* (Cardiff, 5 February 1979, unreported) and *Hayes v Bowman* (p468) (a dismissal for want of prosecution case)).

4   Section 33(3)(c)

'the conduct of the defendant after the cause of action arose including the extent (if any), to which he responded to requests reasonably made by the plaintiff for information or inspection for the purposes of ascertaining facts which were or might be relevant to the plaintiff's cause of action against the defendant.'

Deliberate stone walling tactics by a potential defendant or his insurers or solicitors designed to frustrate the formulation of an action will not stop time running against a claimant. However, such activity is precisely the third factor which the court will be required to consider, in determining whether such behaviour played any part in accounting for the claimant's failure to issue proceedings in time. As is clear from the wording of the subparagraph, the defendant's conduct is to be looked at from the time when the cause of action accrued and not from the date of the claimant's knowledge which may be later or from the expiry of the limitation period. In *Thompson v Brown Construction (Ebbw Vale) Ltd* (p690) the House of Lords indicated that the ambit of the defendant's conduct included his insurers and solicitors:

'The reference in this paragraph ... recognises an obligation on a potential defendant not to be obstructive in enabling a potential plaintiff to establish relevant information though not imposing any obligation to volunteer such information ... the conduct of the defendant must, I think, be understood as including the conduct of his solicitors and his insurers.' ([1981] 2 All ER 296 at 302, [1981] 1 WLR 744)

Accordingly, the view of Leonard J in *Stevens v Nash Dredging and Reclamation Co Ltd* (p676), that the unintentional misleading by a defendant's insurers of the claimant's solicitors was not something which could be held against the defendant, is probably wrong.

In *Halford v Brookes* (p453), a case concerning a civil action for murder, the Court of Appeal determined that the provision was concerned with purely procedural matters where the forensic tactics of the defendant might lead to delay. This put outside the ambit of the subparagraph previous conduct of a defendant who had given perjured evidence at a criminal trial and who had allegedly coerced another defendant into giving a statement to the police. The then Master of the Rolls Lord Donaldson stated:

> 'Paragraph (c) is directed at the case of a road traffic accident where the defendant obstructs the plaintiff in his quest for knowledge of the circumstances of the accident or of the identity of those responsible. Where the essence of the claim is that the defendants had been guilty of very serious criminal offences is not to be held against them that they are less than cooperative.' ([1991] 3 All ER 559 at 575c)

Such dicta are, however, unlikely to avail an employer who, as well as causing injury or death to an employee, simultaneously commits a criminal offence, whether under the Factories Act 1961 or the Health & Safety at Work etc Act 1974 or indeed a corporate manslaughter.

Delay in dealing with requests for documents concerning social services records relevant to a failure to take a child into care weighed against the defendant in *S v Camden London Borough Council* (p635).

In *Atkinson v Oxfordshire Health Authority* (p308) the court stated that, had it been required to exercise its discretion under s 33, it would have done so in the claimant's favour because a large part of the delay was a failure by the defendant to tell the claimant's mother precisely what had happened to him during an operation to evacuate a tumour. Similarly, in *Scuriaga v Powell* (p645), Watkins J found that an action had been brought within three years from the claimant's date of knowledge in respect of a failed abortion which led to the birth of a child. Had the judge needed to, however, he would have exercised his discretion under s 33 in the claimant's favour because the doctor in question had deliberately misled the claimant into believing that the abortion had failed due to a structural defect in her rather than due to negligence by him.

In *Sniezek v Bundy (Letchworth) Ltd* (p664) a claimant suffered a burning sensation on his lips and throat in 1984 which became severe in 1989 and which he believed was due to exposure to chemical dust at his place of work. It was not, however, until a third expert was instructed in 1994 that a possible link with exposure at work was posited with the dust acting as a sensitizer. The defendants obstructed pre-action disclosure which meant that it was not until 1997 that proof of the link between the dust and the injury was established. The Court of Appeal held that the claimant had knowledge since 1989 and that his case was statute barred. However, the delay in initiating proceedings was principally due to negative advice but also due to the failure of the defendants to disclose documents and accordingly a s 33 dispensation granted to him by the first instance judge was upheld.

The court, however, will not only look at activity deliberately designed to slow the case down, such as in protracted negotiations, resisting pre-trial disclosure, refusing facilities for inspection, or failing to respond reasonably quickly to enquiries. On some occasions the court will look at innocent behaviour that has also contributed to delay. In *Marston v British Railways Board* (p545) the trial judge held that maintaining an honest but mistaken defence, namely that a hammer which fractured and caused a serious injury was in fact a new hammer when it was not, was conduct relevant to the sub paragraph. Similarly, in *Marshall v Martin* (p545), Mustill J held that it was proper within the subsection to consider what effect an interim payment had had on the claimant's belief that the claim was going to be settled.

A clear indication that liability is not an issue might create an estoppel to prevent a defendant relying on a limitation defence. Behaviour and activity amounting to less than an estoppel, but which lulled a claimant into a false sense of security that a claim was to be compromised, may be relevant in respect of an application under s 33. A dispute as to whether an agreement not to take a limitation defence may not, however, suffice. In *Wasley v Vass* (p708) the defendants admitted liability but the court held that there was a misunderstanding as to whether the defendants' insurers in a telephone conversation with the claimant's solicitors had also agreed not to take a limitation defence. The Court of Appeal upheld the judge's finding that there had been no agreement and that the claimant's solicitors were at fault for not following up the conversation with confirmatory correspondence.

In *Mutua v Foreign and Commonwealth Office* (p565) the claimant contended that part of the delay in bringing an action in respect of Kenyan nationals suffering mistreatment and torture was due to the destruction of documents and/or difficulties in tracing surviving documents. The trial judge acknowledged that the Colonial Office had permitted the destruction of embarrassing documents but many were preserved, including some 294 boxes containing 1,500 files found in 2011, not all of which had yet been considered. The true effect of the loss of documents would have to be assessed at the trial but the judge was satisfied, for the purposes of s 33(3)(c), that there was no question of conduct against the defendant.

In *AB v Nugent Care Society* [2009] EWHC 481 (QB) the court rejected a submission that failure to promptly investigate allegations of sexual abuse by a defendant amounted to conduct in the meaning of the subsection but it might be relevant to the general exercise of discretion if the defendant's evidential difficulties arose partly out of their own delay in investigating allegations. Conversely, in the first instance decision in *Maga v The Trustees of the Birmingham Archdiocese of the Roman Catholic Church* [2009] EWHC 780 (QB), a case which failed to establish vicarious liability, Jack J (after a detailed analysis of the Church's response to sexual abuse allegations) was satisfied that conduct was made out:

'I conclude from this review of the conduct of the defendant Church after the cause of action arose favours the extension of the limitation period because the Church did not make enquiries and take steps, which, given its position, it should reasonably have taken.' (para 76)

5 Section 33(3)(d)

'the duration of any disability of the plaintiff arising after the date of the accrual of the cause of action.'

Disability, as defined under s 38(2) of the 1980 Act, refers to infancy or incapacity. An infant is able to bring a claim in time three years after the age of majority is reached. Accordingly, infancy is of no relevance to a s 33 application in respect of disability because infancy cannot arise after the accrual of a cause of action. Disability might therefore reasonably be thought to refer in this subparagraph to incapacity, previously defined as unsoundness of mind. If a claimant suffers from incapacity, so that he is unable to make a decision for himself in relation to the matters in the litigation because of an impairment of, or a disturbance in the functioning of, the mind or brain, he will be able to rely on the provisions of s 28 of the Limitation Act 1980, provided that the disability pre-dated the injury or was caused directly by it at the time of the injury. In such cases the claimant has three years after the disability ceases to bring a claim. Subparagraph (3)(d) might logically, therefore, be thought to refer to cases of so-called supervening mental disability within the meaning of the Mental Capacity Act 2005, which occur after the cause of action has accrued or after the claimant's date of knowledge. Obviously, an inability to make decisions in the litigation, including whether to sue, would have a potentially disastrous effect upon prosecuting a cause of action that had accrued prior to the onset of the debilitating mental illness.

It was therefore somewhat surprising that, in 1991, the Court of Appeal in *Bater v Newbold* (p323) stated, obiter, that disability for the purposes of this subparagraph did not mean disability as defined in s 38(2). Indeed, in the earlier case of *Pilmore v Northern Trawlers Ltd* (p606) the trial judge refused to disapply the limitation period in a dermatitis case, but he did indicate that dermatitis could be a disability within the meaning of this subsection. Such a wide interpretation would have meant that any illness will be relevant under s 33(3)(d). This construction of the subsection was specifically rejected by the Court of Appeal in 1997 in *Thomas v Plaistow* (p687). The court here confirmed that disability in this subsection was limited to disability within the meaning of s 38 and that the remarks in *Bater* were obiter. The court in *Thomas* looked at the 20th Report of the Law Reform Committee (Cmnd 5360) on whose recommendations this part of the 1980 Act was based. This showed that disability in s 33(3)(d) was meant to have the same meaning as in s 28 and therefore s 38(2) and (3). The court confirmed that the purpose of the subsection was to deal with cases of supervening disability in the same way that s 28 dealt with existing disability (see also *Yates v Thakeham* (p729)). These decisions concur with Lord Diplock's remarks in *Thompson v Brown Construction (Ebbw Vale) Ltd* (p690):

> 'Paragraph (d) is restricted to cases where Plaintiffs have been under a disability, a class of person that equity has always been zealous to protect.' ([1981] 1 WLR 744 at 751G)

6   Section 33(3)(e)

> 'the extent to which the plaintiff acted promptly and reasonably once he knew whether or not the act or omission of the defendant, to which the injury was attributable, might be capable at that time of giving rise to an action for damages.'

One of the major reasons for recommending a discretionary power to disapply the limitation period by the Orr Committee (Cmnd 5630) was to mitigate the effect that ignorance of the law should not stop time running against the claimant. A claimant will be faced with actual or constructive knowledge, irrespective of his appreciation that he had a cause of action in law. Where, however, the claimant did not realise that he could sue, that is a pertinent matter for the judge in determining why the claimant in fact delayed. Similarly, once the claimant finds out that he has a cause of action in law, the court will be concerned to ascertain whether from that date he acted promptly and reasonably. An investigation is therefore required by the court under this subparagraph to determine, in the first place, when in fact the claimant personally knew that he had a claim in law. This date may well be much later than the date of knowledge which a court may fix him with under s 14.

In *Eastman v London Country Bus Services Ltd* (p420) a claimant struck his head on 24 November 1978 whilst bailing out an inspection pit. The trial judge found that the date of knowledge was 28 February 1979 and, accordingly, proceedings issued in September 1982 were approximately seven months out of time. The judge went on to find that the claimant acted neither promptly nor reasonably, even looking at it from the claimant's perspective, from his date of knowledge. The Court of Appeal emphasised that the pertinent date for considering the promptness and reasonableness of the claimant's behaviour was in fact potentially later than the date of knowledge, and accordingly found that the trial judge had misdirected himself by conflating the relevant date within s 33(3)(e) with the date of knowledge within s 14.

Once the date of *personal* knowledge had been ascertained, the court will examine whether any subsequent delay occurred and, if so, whether it was reasonable. In *McCafferty v Metropolitan Police District Receiver* (p546) the court looked favourably on a claimant who desired to preserve good relationships with his employer and not to sue in respect of what was at first an irritation but which later became disabling deafness. Similarly, in *Buck v English Electric Co Ltd* (p353) the court accepted the claimant's reluctance to sue until the disease became extremely serious, indicating that he acted in the best tradition of dignified and responsible workmen (see also *Cornish v Kearley & Tonge Ltd* (p388)).

Conversely, in *Casey v J Murphy & Sons* (p366) the Court of Appeal was less impressed with the claimant who knew the nature and causes of his dermatitis even if he did not know that he had a claim in law. Because the claimant had access to trade union advice, even though he did not take it, the court thought it would be inequitable to allow the action to proceed.

In *Dale v British Coal Corporation (No 2)* (p396) the Court of Appeal held that the test when considering whether a claimant had acted reasonably within this subsection was an objective one (cf *Coad v Cornwall & Isle of Scilly Health Authority* (p378), where the test under s 33(3)(a) is a subjective one). In *Dale* the claimant brought an action for the amputation of his left leg 15 years after it had occurred. Mr Dale was a trade union member and the court held that, in considering what a reasonable man in the claimant's position would have done, it would usually be held reasonable to follow the advice of the union (see also *Thompson v Garrendale Ltd* Current Law 2000/528).

In *Hunt v Yorke* (p485) an estate worker was injured in January 1980 when a shed collapsed on him. He issued proceedings nine months out of time following a deterioration of his back condition which led him to be dismissed in January 1983. The judge found that the claimant had been reasonable in relying on the defendant's assurances that he always looked after his workers and, accordingly, the claimant did not issue proceedings until he lost not only his job but also his tied cottage.

In *Thompson v Brown Construction (Ebbw Vale) Ltd* (p690), Lord Diplock stated that:

'In contrast to paragraph (c) I think it is apparent that paragraphs (e) and (f) are referring to the conduct of the plaintiff himself, as well as that of his lawyers after he had consulted them the first time. If he has acted promptly and reasonably it is not to be counted against him, when it comes to weighing conduct, that his lawyers have been dilatory and allowed the primary limitation to expire without issuing a writ. Nevertheless when weighing the degrees of prejudice the plaintiff has suffered, the fact that if no direction is made under section 2D he will have a claim over against his solicitor for the full damages that he could have recovered against the defendant if the action had proceeded must be a highly relevant consideration.' ([1981] 1 WLR 744 at 752C–D)

Accordingly, although the 'plaintiff' within sub-paragraph (e) may include the actions or inactions of his advisers, he is unlikely to be tarnished with their dilatoriness.

In *Doughty v North Staffordshire Health Authority* (p414) the claimant's solicitors failed to act promptly. The trial judge found that the claimant, who had a number of difficulties herself including looking after a handicapped daughter, could not be blamed for failing to chivvy them into activity. In *Davis v Jacobs and Camden & Islington Health Authority* (p404) the Court of Appeal did, however, state that, in construing s 33(3)(e), it was concerned only with the conduct of the claimant (see para 86, column 2). Perhaps the better view is that, although the claimant will be fixed with the actions and behaviour of his lawyers as well as himself, he will not necessarily be blamed for his lawyers' delays (see *Adam v Ali* [2006] EWCA Civ 91, *Das v Ganju* (p398), *Corbin v Penfold Metalising* (p387), *Whitfield v North Down Health Authority* (p713), and *Steeds v Peverel Management Services Ltd* (p674), but cf *Young v Chief Constable of Northumbria* (p732)).

However, in *Horton v Sadler* (p482), Lord Carswell (para 53) reaffirmed that the claimants' solicitors' delay was a matter which the court had to have regard to and that the claimant must bear the responsibility as against the defendant for his solicitors' delay. The lawyers' delays may be highly significant in considering whether the claimant has a cause of action over against his own solicitors.

In *Obembe v City & Hackney Health Authority* (p586) a couple sued in July 1988 for alleged medical malpractice at the birth of their son in July 1979. They included a claim for themselves which alleged that they, as well as their child, had suffered personal injury, presumably psychiatric injury. The court found that they had not acted reasonably in failing to prosecute their own claim which they were advised existed in law in July 1984. It was not a good reason for delaying that they had 21 years to prosecute their son's action. The court found that the defendants had sustained prejudice because witnesses had gone missing, and so it refused the application to proceed out of time.

In *Rihani v J Wareing* (p622) the claimant worked in a noisy environment for 23 years and sued his employees in respect of occupationally induced deafness in 1997, some 11 years after he was advised by his doctor to bring a claim. The claimant said that he feared being victimised if he brought a claim, not least because he had been subject to racial abuse at work. The Court of Appeal upheld the trial judge's refusal to allow the claim to proceed, stating there was no evidence that anyone had ever been sacked or disciplined for bringing a claim. The claimant had failed to do anything in 11 years and fell foul of the subsection.

7   Section 33(3)(f)

'the steps, if any, taken by the plaintiff to obtain medical, legal or other expert advice and the nature of any such advice he may have received.'

Lord Diplock in *Thompson v Brown Construction (Ebbw Vale) Ltd* (p690) described as a curious hotchpotch the six matters which the court had to have particular regard to when exercising its discretion. With respect to subparagraph (f), he was of the view that it appeared chronologically to be in the wrong order insofar as obtaining legal advice was concerned, because until a claimant did that he was unlikely, in many cases, to know whether he had a cause of action, and accordingly subparagraph

(f) might need to be considered before subparagraph (e). Either way, the court will be concerned to establish precisely what advice the claimant did seek and, if the claimant failed to seek any advice at all, whether that was reasonable or not in the circumstances. If a claimant does take advice and receives negative advice, the court is likely to be reasonably sympathetic. Negative legal advice does not stop time running under s 14 but will have an obvious effect on the progression of potential litigation, particularly if it leads, in clinical negligence cases, to a Legal Services Commission funding being discharged (see *Bentley v Bristol & Western Health Authority* (p328), *Waghorn v Lewisham & North Southwark Area Health Authority* (p703), *Thompson v Edmeads* (p692), and *Burke v Ash Construction* (p356)).

In *Halford v Brookes* (p453), Lord Donaldson MR emphasised that the claimant, although she was interested in pursuing financial compensation arising out of the death of her daughter, was told by her solicitors that the only civil remedies she had was an application to the Criminal Injuries Compensation Board. In the light of that advice, he indicated:

> 'She cannot be blamed for accepting this advice or failing to ask other solicitors or counsel for a second opinion. When, for some reason, she consulted new solicitors in July 1985 and they advised her that there was another civil remedy, she immediately applied for Legal Aid and upon this being granted at once issued her writ.' ([1991] 3 All ER 559 at 575j)

Negative non-legal advice may prevent time running if it inhibits the claimant's knowledge of significance, attribution, or identity. However, failing to take such advice can lead to the court imposing a constructive date of knowledge. Similarly, failing to take reasonable steps to obtain expert evidence may well act against a claimant under s 33 if the court thinks it reasonable to have done so (cf *Casey v J Murphy & Sons* (p366), where a claimant failed to use facilities open to him to consult his trade union, and *Dale v British Coal Corporation (No 2)* (p396)). The court will also have regard to the steps taken to obtain expert evidence after a claimant knows that he has a claim not only in attempting to prove liability but also in attempting to quantify the value of the claim.

The clear wording of the subparagraph indicates that it is relevant for a court to consider what the advice was and, in particular, whether there has been the discovery of fresh evidence or developments in knowledge which may have made that advice outdated. In *Jones v G D Searle & Co Ltd* (p499) a claimant sued in respect of a thrombosis she sustained in 1966 allegedly due to taking the oral contraceptive pill. The decision to sue, out of time, was largely due to leading counsel giving positive advice following expert evidence on causation linking the pill to thrombosis which only became available shortly before proceedings were issued. The defendants wished to know whether the previous legal advice was negative or not and sought leave to administer an interrogatory to ascertain this. The claimant claimed that, if she answered the interrogatory, it might be interpreted as waiving legal professional privilege in respect of advices so as to make those disclosable documents. The Court of Appeal held that the interrogatory, which was restricted to whether the previous advice was favourable or not, should be answered because the words 'the nature of the advice' clearly made the issue relevant within the meaning of the subparagraph. The court, however, indicated that, as a consequence of giving the answer to the interrogatory, it did not follow that counsel's opinions were liable for disclosure.

The Court of Appeal further considered the relationship of legal professional privilege and the disclosure of advice that the claimant had received in *Tatlock v G P Worsley & Co Ltd* (p683). Here, a claimant sued in respect of lung damage induced by inhaling steel dust in 1978/9. Proceedings were issued in 1985 following a favourable medical report indicating that Mr Tatlock's condition was work related.

The claimant had, in 1980, consulted his trade union, and a medical report obtained by solicitors instructed by them in 1983 was negative. The defendant sought discovery of various documents, including part of the claimant's proof dealing with the question of date of knowledge and the 1983 negative medical report, as well as the correspondence with the medical expert. The Court of Appeal held that s 33(3)(f) did not override the rules of legal professional privilege, save in the restrictive sense of requiring a claimant to indicate the nature of the advice only. There was, however, no statutory removal of legal professional privilege, although as a matter of tactics and evidence a claimant may need to waive privilege if he was to rely effectively on the contents of the documents in issue.

8   Section 33(3)

> 'In acting under this section the court shall have regard to all the circumstances
> of the case ...'

The six factors singled out in s 33(3) need to be addressed individually, but the exercise of discretion will require that they are looked at not in isolation but in the context of the case as a whole. Moreover, the factors are not exclusive because of the wider injunction to have regard to 'all the circumstances of the case'. As has been indicated, the House of Lords in *Donovan v Gwentoys Ltd* (p412) emphasised that, although subparagraphs (a) and (b) required the court to look at the delay after the expiry of the limitation period, the general proviso of looking at all the circumstances of the case allowed the court to consider what prejudice had occurred within the primary limitation period. In particular, the court was concerned in *Donovan* that the defendants had not had the opportunity to deal with the claim until five years after the accident occurred, even though the claim was only five and a half months outside the primary limitation period because of the extended period due to the claimant's minority. Accordingly, one of the most important circumstances of the case will be when in fact the claim was first indicated to the potential defendant (see *Hands v Coleridge-Smith and Horsburgh* (p457)).

Circumstances can, of course, be infinitely variable and it is not possible to establish principles in advance as to what weight should be given to any particular matter. There is, in any event, likely to be a substantial overlap between considering 'all the circumstances of the case ' in s 33 and the weighing of the prejudices under s 33(1) (a) and (b). Earlier cases suggest the court is likely to have regard to the strength of the claimant's or the defendant's case on the merits or on quantum (cf *Nash v Eli Lilly* (p568), *Mann v Bournemouth District Council* (p542)). This has evolved into a consideration of whether the claimant's case succeeds in passing a broad merits test. In *B v Ministry of Defence* (p312) the claimants failed to obtain a s 33 extension because the appellate court thought the prospects of establishing causation were very weak. Conversely, in *Mutua v Foreign and Commonwealth Office* (p565) the court did not regard the prospect of the claimants establishing that, as a matter of law, the United Kingdom government was jointly or separately liable with the colonial government as so weak as to not warrant a s 33 extension.

In *McGhie v British Telecommunications plc* (p553), the Court of Appeal stated that it was relevant to consider the question of proportionality in the sense of considering the size of the claimant's claim, the costs of prosecuting it and the strength of the claimant's case. This was further endorsed in *Robinson v St Helens Metropolitan*

Borough Council (p628) and approved by the House of Lords in *Adams v Bracknell Forest BC* (p292). Lord Hoffmann stated:

'54.   In *Robinson v St Helens Metropolitan Borough Council* [2003] PIQR P128, P139–140 Sir Murray Stewart-Smith said:

"32. The Limitation Acts are designed to protect defendants from the injustice of having to fight stale claims especially when any witnesses the defendants might have been able to rely on are not available or have no recollection and there are no documents to assist the court in deciding what was done or not done and why. These cases are very time consuming to prepare and try and they inevitably divert resources from the education authority to defending the claim rather than teach. Under section 33 the onus is on the claimant to establish that it would be equitable to allow the claim to proceed having regard to the balance of prejudice.

33. The question of proportionality is now important in the exercise of any discretion, none more so than under section 33. Courts should be slow to exercise their discretion in favour of a claimant in the absence of cogent medical evidence showing a serious effect on the claimant's health or enjoyment of life and employability. The likely amount of an award is an important factor to consider, especially if, as is usual in these cases, they are likely to take a considerable time to try. A claim that the claimant's dyslexia was not diagnosed or treated many years before at school, brought long after the expiry of the limitation period, extended as it is until after the claimant's majority, will inevitably place the defendants in great difficulty in contesting it, especially in the absence of relevant witnesses and documents. The contesting of such a claim would be both expensive and likely to divert precious resources. Courts should be slow in such cases to find that the balance of prejudice is in favour of the claimant."

55.   Peter Gibson and Brooke LJJ agreed. Their Lordships think that these observations from judges with considerable experience of exercising and overseeing the section 33 jurisdiction carry great weight. As in *Phelps*, where the plaintiff recovered £12,500 general damages and about £32,000 special damages (mostly an estimate of loss of earnings), the uncertainties of causation and quantification mean that in the event of success an award is likely to be relatively modest. The council is in a very difficult position and there are no special features about the reasons why Mr Adams left his claim so late which tilt the balance in his favour.'

This passage was applied by the Court of Appeal in *AB v Catholic Care Society* [2009] EWCA Civ 827 at para 63. In *Lye v Marks & Spencer plc* (p538) the court thought it relevant to consider whether a claimant was legally aided. Since the effective abolition of Legal Services Commission funding in personal injury cases, the court has been asked to consider whether conditional fee agreements (CFAs) may in certain circumstances constitute prejudice because defendants are liable to pay a successful claimant's costs and a percentage uplift on costs up to 100 per cent. In *Smith v Ministry of Defence* (p661), Silber J was willing to assume without specific evidence that delay resulting in litigation being pursued by a CFA ,as opposed through a legal aid certificate, if the claim had brought timeously might amount to prejudice. However, it did not avail the defendant in that case and a dispensation was granted. However, in *Clack v Thames Television Ltd* (p374) the court held that the fact that a defendant was potentially liable for an uplift on CFA costs could not assist the defendant. It could in the alternative be argued that the withdrawal of legal aid discouraged certain claims and CFA agreements allow defendants, if successful, to obtain costs which they could not routinely do if the claimant was legally aided.

Earlier cases such as *Firman v Ellis* (p433) and *Bradley v Hanseatic Shipping Co Ltd* (p340) thought it pertinent to consider whether the defendant was insured. In *Kelly v Bastible* (p515) the court emphasised that for the purposes of limitation the defendant and his insurers should be treated as a composite entity and nil weight should be given to the basic fact that the defendant was insured.

Alterations in insurance relationships may be relevant. In *Whitfield v North Durham Health Authority* (p713) the defendants contended that changes in the funding of payments for clinical negligence caused them prejudice due to the claimant delaying in initiating his action. The trial judge thought that this did not amount to prejudice because NHS patients would altruistically accept that diminutions in NHS resources was a reasonable price to pay for compensation to the victims of medical accidents. The Court of Appeal disagreed and found this to be a misdirection. In *Smith v Leicester Health Authority* (p659) the court found at first instance that changes in insurance and funding arrangements meant the defendants themselves had had to bear something over £100,000 more than if the action had been brought in time. The Court of Appeal, however, noted that the prejudice to the claimant if the action was not allowed to proceed would have been approximately ten times that amount. In addition the court had power to restrict the award of interest on any part of the judgment which gave the defendant some limited protection.

The existence of a good claim over against the claimant's solicitors will always be a relevant consideration (see *Thompson v Brown Construction (Ebbw Vale) Ltd* (p690) and *Taylor v Taylor* (p685)). In *Liff v Peasley* [1980] 1 WLR 781 the possibility of a judgment being satisfied by the Motor Insurers' Bureau was also found to be relevant. In *Horton v Sadler* (p482), where the claimant sued an uninsured driver and the judgment was liable to be satisfied by the MIB, the House of Lords declined to interfere with the court's exercise of discretion against the MIB. The claimant had a good cause of action over against the solicitors who had failed to give the MIB proper notice within the primary limitation period. The MIB submitted that it was more appropriate that the solicitor's insurers should bear the loss as they had received a premium rather than the MIB who had not (an argument successfully advanced in the unreported case of *Morris v Lokass* (2003)). The court considered this a relevant factor but permitted the claim to be continued against the MIB as the claimant had some prejudice in starting a new action against his solicitors. *Horton* was followed in *Richardson v Watson* (p621).

9   Procedure

A district judge or a master in addition to a judge is empowered to exercise discretion under s 33 of the Limitation Act 1980 pursuant to CPR 2.4. If the defendants believe that they have an extremely strong case, they may issue an application to strike out the claimant's claim, but this is unlikely to be successful if the claimant has any arguable merit at all. The normal procedure adopted is to issue an application to determine the limitation issue at an interlocutory hearing. If, however, it is desirable to call evidence, or where there is a need for extensive discovery of documents, it is better to have a preliminary trial on the issue of limitation. Any such preliminary trial may take place immediately before the trial of the main action or it may be at an earlier date. If the preliminary trial requires a rehearsal of many or most of the issues likely to be raised in the main trial, there is no great saving in costs by having the preliminary issue on limitation tried on a different date to the substantive hearing. In *KR v Bryn Alyn Community Holdings Ltd* (p505) the Court of Appeal emphasised that limitation issues should be decided as preliminary issues if practicable. If the limitation issue is tried at the main trial, it should be done before determining the substantive issues. However, in *AB v Catholic Care Society* [2009] EWCA Civ 827, this part of the *Bryn Alyn* guidance (found at para 76(vi)) was modified:

> 'As to vi), we think that there are now likely to be many cases in which a judge will consider that it is not feasible to decide the issues simply by reference to the pleadings, written witness statements and the extent and content of discovery. He or she may well conclude that it is desirable that such oral evidence as is available should be heard because the strength of the claimant's evidence seems to us to be relevant to the way in which the discretion should be exercised.'

The court went on to state:

> '26. We only add that, where a claimant gives evidence for the purposes of a preliminary issue on limitation, and where the judge exercises the discretion of the court to permit the claim to continue, every effort should be made to make sure that the claimant does not have to give oral evidence again on the issue of liability. We would hope that this can ordinarily be achieved by ensuring, so far as possible, that the same judge will hear the trial as determined the preliminary issue of liability. Indeed, it may well be appropriate to decide the preliminary point and then either stop or continue with the trial.'

In *Raggett v Society of Jesus Trust 1929 for Roman Catholic Purposes* (p617) the Court of Appeal further qualified *Bryn Alyn* (para 76(vii)) in respect of the guidance that a s 33 exercise should always be undertaken before deciding the issue of liability, as to do otherwise was to 'put the cart before the horse'. The Master had ordered a split trial on limitation and liability separate from the issues of causation and quantum. The trial judge heard the claimant's evidence on the sexual abuse allegations and found that the abuse occurred, determined the case was statute barred under s 14 and then exercised her discretion in favour of the claimant. The defendants appealed on the basis that this was procedurally incorrect and contrary to *Bryn Alyn*. The Court of Appeal dismissed the appeal finding that the judge had properly considered whether the delay had affected the evidence that the defendants might have produced if the claim had been brought in time. The court stated:

> '13. In approaching this contention, it is easy to confuse form over substance. As all the cases make clear, the judge's discretion is unfettered. What an appellate court is concerned to see is whether the judge has approached the exercise of discretion in accordance with principle and come to a decision within the ambit of the discretion open to the decision maker. It is not, in my judgement, appropriate for an appellate court to ascribe a format for the delivery of a judgment or to decide the issue on the form of the judgment and the order in which the issues are set out.
>
> 14. The judge was quite properly asked to decide the issues of limitation and liability together, as the issue of limitation could not be decided without hearing evidence. The task facing the judge was one which presented the judge with the necessity of asking the right logical questions; whilst an appellate court must be sure that the correct questions were asked and

properly addressed, it should not, in my view, prescribe the format in which the decisions on those questions must be recorded or the order in which they must be recorded …

16.   Only after all those matters which she dealt with in the first 83 paragraphs of her judgment, did the judge turn at paragraph 84 to the issues on limitation. She then dealt first with the question of s 11 and s 14 of the Act and made the findings to which I have briefly referred that his knowledge for the purposes of s 14 dated from the time the abuse had occurred. It was only then at paragraph 111 of her judgment that she turned to the question under s 33.

(v) Conclusion

17.   Although, as is apparent from the description of the order of the judgment, findings that the abuse had occurred were made prior to the discussion of and decision on the limitation issue under s 33, what matters, in my view, is an analysis of the way in which she approached the exercise of the discretion under s 33. In the part of her judgment in which she considered the issue under s 33 the judge first set out the respective contentions of the claimant and the Governors. It is clear from the recitation of those submissions that the matters to which the judge was directing her attention at this stage of the judgment were not the findings which she had made about the happening of the abuse, but to the cogency of the evidence, the claimant's submission that the evidence was overwhelming and the Governors' submission as to prejudice and in particular the impossibility of the court ascertaining the effects of the abuse.

18.   The judge then carried out a careful analysis of the cogency of the evidence. At paragraph 123 she set out the key features of the evidence upon which the claimant relied and in particular that this was a case where the allegations did not bear the hallmarks of exaggeration and where the claimant had not jumped on a bandwagon of other similar complaints; that there was evidence to support the allegations from a number of contemporaries, one of whom had seen Father Spencer filming the claimant; that despite the delay six witnesses had come forward spontaneously shortly before the trial started. She concluded:

> "In the face of evidence such as this, the defendants were always going to experience great difficulties in persuading a court that the claimant's allegations were untrue or exaggerated."

She then carefully analysed the prejudice, particularly that caused by the death of Father Spencer and the difficulty in finding other members of the staff at the College.

She concluded:

> "I regard it as highly unlikely that the availability of other members of the staff of the school would have improved the school's prospect of succeeding on the issue of liability."

She then considered the effect of delay on the cogency of the evidence relating to the psychiatric effect of the abuse on the claimant. I will return to that at paragraphs 23 and following below. She concluded at paragraph 129:

> "To the extent that there is any prejudice in relation to the issue of causation, it is likely to operate to the detriment of the claimant since he will bear the burden of proving his loss."

19.   In my view, this part of her judgment was an analysis of the factors relevant to s 33, namely an assessment of the reasons for the delay, the cogency of the claimant's case against the prejudice likely to be caused to the Governors and other relevant considerations. She did not adopt the approach which is the foundation of the contention of the Governors that she was satisfied that Father Spencer had in fact sexually abused the claimant and therefore there could be no prejudice. In accordance with the decision in *A v Hoare* the judge took into account her findings that knowledge dated from the time that the abuse was alleged and the reasons for the delay in bringing the claim, but her analysis was throughout based not on a finding that the abuse had occurred but on the cogency of the evidence of that abuse and the prejudice to the Governors.

20.   When this court observed that the judge must decide the issue on the exercise of the discretion under s 33 before reaching the conclusions on liability, it was enjoining a judge to decide the s 33 question on the basis, not of the finding that abuse had occurred, but on an overall assessment, including the cogency of the evidence and the potential effect of the delay on it. It was not seeking to prescribe a formulaic template for the construction of a judgment; it was leaving the judge to decide the best way to write the judgment which would expound the analysis that the law required.

21.   In the circumstances of this case, it is clear from an analysis of the judgment that the judge approached the issue under s 33 entirely in accordance with principle. She reached a decision that was plainly open to her in the circumstances of the case; the evidence against Father Spencer was strong, particularly in the light of the evidence of the claimant's contemporaries at the College; it is important to note the observation of the judge at paragraph 66:

> "Despite these criticisms of the claimant's evidence, [the Governors] did not seriously dispute the fact that Father Spencer had been guilty of some abuse, in the form of filming the claimant naked and fondling him sexually. However, they did not accept that the abuse was as long-lasting or as severe as the claimant had described."

In contrast there were ample grounds for concluding that the prejudice to the Governors, particularly the death of Father Spencer, the inability of Father Edwards to give evidence and the general effects of delay, had not materially affected the ability of the Governors to defend the action.

22.   There is, in short, no basis for concluding that the order in which the judge approached the issues in any way affected the substance of the way in which the discretion under s 33 was exercised or the decision reached.'

(See also *J v Birmingham Roman Catholic Archdiocese Trustees* (p492).)

A pertinent distinction between having an interlocutory trial and having a trial on limitation immediately before the trial of the main action was thought to be at one stage that if a claimant failed on an interlocutory hearing leave was not required to appeal to the Court of Appeal but if a claimant failed at trial of the preliminary limitation point immediately before the substantive hearing no leave was required. However, the Court of Appeal in *Dale v British Coal Corporation (No 1)* [1992] 1 WLR 964 stipulated that whatever procedure is adopted a judge's determination is deemed to be a final one and at the time of that ruling pursuant to the then RSC Rules no leave was required. (See *Hughes v Jones* (p485) and *Pavey v Ministry of Defence* (p599).) Under the CPR provisions the distinction between an interlocutory and a final order is not pertinent to the issue of permission, as permission is now required pursuant to CPR 52.3. The destination of an appeal is now determined by the Destination of Appeals Order 2000 as amended by Civil Procedure (Modification of Enactment) Order 2003 and Practice Direction 52PD. The general principle is that an appeal lies to the next level of judge in the court's hierarchy. However, the normal rule will not be followed in a case where the court's decision is a final one in multi-track claims. In these cases, s 14 and s 33 appeals would lie to the Court of Appeal (see *Tanfern Ltd v Cameron-MacDonald* [2000] 1 WLR 1311). This does not apply to those cases not in the multi-track.

The onus of persuading the court to disapply the primary limitation period lies on the claimant (*Thompson v Brown Construction (Ebbw Vale) Ltd* (p690)).

Practitioners have been divided as to whether the proper pleading practice is for a claimant to particularise the facts and circumstances which he intends to rely on in seeking to persuade the court to exercise s 33 in his favour in the particulars of claim or whether it should be pleaded in a reply following the defendant raising limitation in the defence. In that limitation is not a bar to a case but is a defence, it would seem that there is no need to anticipate the defence. It might be preferable to wait and see if the defendant takes the point (see *Ogunsanya v Lambeth Area Heath Authority* (p590)). Alternatively, in a clear case where the claimant is obviously out of time, it may be sensible for the claimant to plead the particulars intended to be relied upon for a s 33 dispensation so to assist the court in fulfilling the overriding objective and clarifying the issues between the parties pursuant to the spirit of the CPR. A limitation defence must be pleaded and, if a s 33 application is required and the pleading has not been contained in the particulars of claim, there must be a reply.

Appeals to the Court of Appeal are not infrequent, as the number of cases referred to in this chapter illustrates. Because the discretion of the judge is unfettered, the Court of Appeal has indicated that it will be slow to overturn a first instance decision recognising that judgments over what is equitable in all the circumstances will necessarily lead to a variation of judicial opinion (*Conry v Simpson* (p385)). Where, however, the judge has failed to exercise his discretion at all or has exercised it erroneously or on wrong principles, the court has not infrequently reversed a trial judge's decision. The Court of Appeal will not interfere merely because its own discretion might have been exercised in a different way (*Bradley v Hanseatic Shipping Co Ltd* (p340) and *Carlisle v Associated British Ports* (p365)). In *Nash v Eli Lilly* (p568), Lord Justice Purchas stated:

'Subject to acting judicially the discretion of the Court is unfettered. The specific matters set out in subsection (3) are exemplary not definitive. Thus the Court of Appeal will be very slow to interfere with the exercise of that discretion under this section: See *Conry v Simpson* [1983] 3 All ER 369. Where, however, it is established that the judge either took into account factors which he should have ignored or ignored factors which he should have taken into account, or was plainly wrong, then this court is under a duty to interfere and in appropriate cases to substitute a decision based upon its own discretion. On the other hand, provided that it is relevant to the circumstances of the case, the judge may take into account a factor not specifically mentioned in the sub-paragraphs of subsection (3), but on the other hand, if it is established that the judge failed to take into account any of the matters in subparagraph (3) which were relevant to the carrying out of the balancing exercise, then his judgment is susceptible to attack. It should however be mentioned that a judge is not under a duty specifically to refer to each and every fact which he has found and upon which he has exercised his discretion.' ([1993] 4 All ER 383 at 402)

In *KR v Bryn Alyn Community Holdings Ltd* (p505) the Court of Appeal confirmed this approach by indicating that a judge's s 33 discretion could only be disturbed if it was outside the ambit of reasonable disagreement. This included the exercise of wrong principles, taking into account irrelevant factors, ignoring relevant factors or making a decision that was plainly wrong. If the appeal court intervened on any such ground the matter should be treated as at large and the discretion exercised afresh.

Where a claimant restores a dissolved company to the Register in order to bring proceedings under s 651 of the Companies Act 1985, the restoration order should not usually include a provision that the period of dissolution should not count for limitation purposes. In *Smith v White Knight Laundry* (p663) the Court of Appeal held that such an order, that the period of dissolution was to be discounted, should only be made where: notice of the restoration was served on all parties that could be expected to oppose it; the court was satisfied that it had all the evidence that the parties would wish to adduce for an application under s 33; and any such application was bound to succeed. Otherwise, as will be the case in most proceedings, the claimant should seek relief under s 33 in the normal manner.

6 Fatal cases (sections 11, 12 and 13)

Introduction

At common law, an injured person's cause of action terminated when he died, so it did not survive for the benefit of his estate or his dependants. Two statutes have altered this: the Law Reform (Miscellaneous Provisions) Act 1934 provides that the deceased's cause of action survives for the benefit of his estate; and the Fatal Accidents Act 1976 gives a right of action to his dependants. The damages awarded under these two statutes are cumulative, in the sense that they are additional to each other.

Section 1(1) of the Law Reform (Miscellaneous Provisions) Act 1934 states that:

> 'Subject to the provisions of this section, on the death of any person after the commencement of this Act all causes of action subsisting against or vested in him shall survive against or, as the case may be, for the benefit of, his estate ...'

If the injured person had already started proceedings, rules of court (CPR 19.8) permit the personal representatives to carry on these proceedings. If no action had been started by the deceased during his life, new proceedings can be instituted. In personal injury law, damages for the estate under the Law Reform Act only arise where the death following the tort is not instantaneous. In such cases, the main heads will be general damages for pain and suffering and loss of amenities plus damages for any loss of earnings or other financial loss during life. Funeral expenses may be added.

Section 1(1) of the Fatal Accidents Act 1976, as amended by the Administration of Justice Act 1982, provides that:

> 'If death is caused by any wrongful act, neglect or default which is such as would (if death had not ensued) have entitled the person injured to maintain an action and recover damages in respect thereof, the person who would have been liable if death had not ensued shall be liable to an action for damages, notwithstanding the death of the person injured.'

By s 1(2):

> '... every such action shall be for the benefit of the dependants of the person ('the deceased') whose death has been so caused.'

'Dependants' are defined in the rest of s 1. Such claims are usually brought on behalf of a widow(er) and dependent children. The main heads of damages are (a) bereavement damages, (b) the income dependency on the deceased's earnings or pension, and (c) the services dependency on such services the deceased may have provided, such as DIY, gardening, driving, housework and looking after the children.

The Limitation Act 1980 deals separately with each of the statutory causes of action. Section 11(5)–(7) covers Law Reform Act claims, and s 11A(5)–(8) contains corresponding provisions for product liability actions brought under the Consumer Protection Act 1987. Sections 12 and 13 apply to Fatal Accidents Act claims. Both causes of action are governed by the specific knowledge provisions in s 14 of the 1980 Act. They are both also subject to the court's discretion under s 33 to disapply the primary three-year limitation periods.

As will be seen, a distinctive feature of claims involving death is that in effect two separate limitation periods are involved. Under the Law Reform (Miscellaneous Provisions) Act 1934, these are the deceased's limitation period and the personal representative's limitation period. Under the Fatal Accidents Act 1976, these are the deceased's limitation period and the dependant's limitation period. If either is exceeded, the case is prima facie statute barred. In that event, it can only be saved by favourable exercise of the court's discretion under s 33. This general concept of dual limitation periods underlies much of the specific analysis that ensues.

1   Law Reform Act claims

(A)   SECTION 11(4) AND 11(5)

As seen in **Chapter 2**, s 11(4) of the Limitation Act 1980 states that:

'Except where subsection (5) below applies, the period applicable is three years from:

(a)   the date on which the cause of action accrued; or
(b)   the date of knowledge (if later) of the person injured.'

Section 11(5) then states:

'If the person injured dies before the expiration of the period mentioned in subsection (4) above, the period applicable as respects the cause of action surviving for the benefit of his estate by virtue of section 1 of the Law Reform (Miscellaneous Provisions) Act 1934 shall be three years from:

(a)   the date of death; or
(b)   the date of the personal representative's knowledge;

whichever is the later.'

Section 11(4) creates what may be termed the deceased's limitation period. If that has been exceeded before his death, the case is prima facie statute barred. If it has not been exceeded, s 11(5) comes into play by giving the estate a primary limitation period of its own: three years from whichever is the later of (a) the date of death and (b) the date of the personal representative's knowledge.

The combined operation of section 11(4) and 11(5) may be illustrated by the following examples.

(B)   EXAMPLES

(a)   The deceased is killed instantaneously in a work accident on 3 May 2002. His personal representative learns of this (and other material facts within s 14) on the same day. Obviously the deceased's own limitation period under s 11(4) has not been exceeded. Time expires under s 11(5) on 3 May 2005.

(b)   The deceased has sustained serious injuries in a road accident on 8 September 2001. She dies of these on 29 September 2001. Although acting reasonably, her personal representative only ascertains the identity of the defendant and other material facts on 11 December 2001. Obviously the deceased's own limitation period under s 11(4) has not expired by the date of her death on 29 September 2001. The personal representative's limitation period under s 11(5) starts to run from the date of his knowledge on 11 December 2001. Time expires under s 11(5) on 11 December 2004.

(c)   The deceased learns of his asbestosis and other material facts in March 1996. He does not claim damages before his death on 16 March 2003. His personal representative promptly commences proceedings on 10 June 2003. The deceased's limitation period under s 11(4) had expired in March 1999, well before his death. Accordingly his case is prima facie statute barred, and s 11(5) does not apply.

(d)   The deceased learns on 24 February 2000 that he has an industrial cancer due to his work. He does not claim damages and dies on 24 August 2002. His personal representative already knows all of the material facts. The deceased's own limitation period under s 11(4) had not expired at his death. Accordingly time starts to run from the date of death on 24 August 1992 and expires on 24 August 2005.

This last example demonstrates how, in a Law Reform Act case, time may not expire under s 11(5) until almost six years from the date on which time originally started to run. The deceased knew the relevant facts for two and a half years before his death, but did not become statute barred under s 11(4). His personal representative then had a further three years under s 11(5). An overall total of five and a half years was thus created. It is therefore important to avoid the fallacy of advising a personal representative in such a case that the limitation period simply expires three years after the deceased's date of knowledge. In example (d), any lawyer advising a personal representative in 2004 that the limitation period had expired on 24 February 2003 would be guilty of negligence, if the consequence of the erroneous advice was to cause the personal representative not to pursue an otherwise valid claim.

(C)   PERSONAL REPRESENTATIVES AND SECTION 14

Section 11(6) provides that:

'For the purposes of this section "personal representative" includes any person who is or has been a personal representative of the deceased, including an executor who has not proved the will (whether or not he has renounced probate) but not anyone appointed only as a special personal representative in relation to settled land; and regard shall be had to any knowledge acquired by any such person while a personal representative or previously.'

Thus 'personal representative' includes an executor, whether or not the will has been proved. Furthermore it includes an executor, whether or not he had renounced probate; accordingly there is nothing to be gained by attempting to substitute an executor who has lacked knowledge of material facts for one who possessed such knowledge at the outset. The personal representative also includes the administrator of an estate. Since grants of letters of administration are customarily only made months or sometimes even years after the death, it is specifically provided that the administrator's pre-grant knowledge is relevant. If, following a death in March 2003, the personal representative acquires knowledge of all the material facts within s 14 by June 2003 and letters of administration are granted in September 2003, the limitation period under s 11(5) runs from the date of knowledge in June 2003, not the date of the grant in September 2003.

Under s 11(5), the court needs to enquire into the personal representative's date of knowledge in a case where proceedings have not been issued within three years after the death. If death occurs on 10 January 2001 and proceedings are not commenced until 20 January 2005, the case will be prima facie statute barred unless it can be established that the personal representative did not acquire knowledge of the material facts before 20 January 2002. In such a case, the court has to enquire into the personal representative's date of knowledge of each of the material facts stipulated in s 14(1). Moreover, s 14(3) also applies, so for the purposes of the section the personal representative's knowledge includes knowledge which he might reasonably have been expected to acquire (a) from facts observable or ascertainable by him or (b) from facts ascertainable by him with the help of medical or other appropriate expert advice which it is reasonable for him to seek.

Section 11(7) states that:

'If there is more than one personal representative, and their dates of knowledge are different, subsection (5)(b) above shall be read as referring to the earliest of those dates.'

This provision is more likely to apply to cases where the deceased leaves a will, since often two or more executors are appointed, than cases where there is no will since it is relatively rare for letters of administration to be granted to more than one administrator. In cases involving two or more personal representatives, it is the date of knowledge of the earliest to possess it that sets time running. If a death occurs in June 2001, and one personal representative acquires all the relevant knowledge in July 2001 but the other only acquires it in November 2001, the limitation period will expire in July 2004. Consequently, once one executor acquires the relevant knowledge, the ignorance of any other executors becomes immaterial.

Where there is no will and therefore no executor, an estate with a Law Reform Act claim which has failed to start proceedings within three years from the date of death might attempt to circumvent the primary limitation period by appointing as an administrator (where none has already been appointed) a person who has known absolutely nothing about the deceased or the cause of action. In those circumstances, it could be argued that time would not run under s 11(5) until letters of administration are granted or, at least, the person to whom they are granted acquires relevant knowledge. If a death occurs in July 2000 and no letters of administration are granted or court action is commenced, it may be submitted that if a hitherto ignorant person is informed of the material facts within s 14 in July 2005 and is granted letters of administration in September 2005, time under s 11(5) only begins to run from his date of knowledge in July 2005 and will not expire until July 2008.

Such a result can hardly have been intended by Parliament. Yet it may take considerable judicial ingenuity to avoid. The most obvious route is for the court to seek to impose constructive knowledge on such a personal representative pursuant to s 14(3). By s 14(3), 'a person's knowledge includes knowledge which he might reasonably have been expected to acquire'. It would be straining this wording considerably to apply it to fix a stranger who is appointed as a personal representative, such as a financial adviser, with knowledge of facts 'which he might reasonably have been expected to acquire' before he had even heard of the deceased. Perhaps this problem was not considered when Parliament passed the Limitation Act 1980. A different result from that outlined above can only be achieved by judicial interpretation or statutory amendment.

(D)   SECTION 33 AND THE LAW REFORM ACT CLAIM

Section 33(1) states that:

'If it appears to the court that it would be equitable to allow an action to proceed having regard to the degree to which:

(a)   the provisions of section 11 (or 11A) or 12 of this Act prejudice the plaintiff or any person whom he represents; and

(b)   any decision of the court under this subsection would prejudice the defendant or any person whom he represents;

the court may direct that those provisions shall not apply to the action, or shall not apply to any specified cause of action to which the action relates.'

The reference to the provisions of s 11 applies equally to the deceased's limitation period under s 11(4) and the personal representative's limitation period under s 11(5). Thus the provisions of s 33 apply to Law Reform Act claims in two different ways. The first is where the injured person is prima facie statute barred under s 11(4) at the date of his death. The second is where the personal representative has become statute barred after the death under s 11(5). In each case, the action can only proceed if the court's discretion to disapply s 11(4) or (5) is exercised in the claimant's favour.

In the exercise of the court's discretion, the normal principles governing s 33 cases apply with some minor modifications. First, the prejudice referred to in s 33(1) (a) is not that of the deceased but that of the claimant or the person(s) whom the claimant represents, eg legatees of the estate if there is a will, or the next of kin if the deceased died intestate. In exceptional circumstances, such a claimant could also represent creditors.

The second main difference concerns the length of, and the reasons for, the delay on the part of the claimant. Under s 33(3)(a), any delay on the part of the claimant's personal representative will be considered. However, s 33(4) also provides:

'In a case where the person injured died when, because of section 11 (or subsection (4) of section 11A), he could no longer maintain an action and recover damages in respect of the injury, the court shall have regard in particular to the length of, and the reasons for, the delay on the part of the deceased.'

Where s 33 applies because the claimant is outside the personal representative's limitation period under s 11(5), it is the claimant's delay that must be considered. Where s 33 applies because the deceased's limitation period under s 11(4) has been exceeded, it is the length of and reasons for the deceased's delay that are relevant.

The third modification concerns other conduct relevant under s 33(3). Section 33(5) states that:

'In a case under subsection (4) above, or any other case where the time limit, or one of the time limits, depends on the date of knowledge of a person other than the plaintiff, subsection (3) above shall have effect with appropriate modifications, and shall have effect in particular as if references to the plaintiff included references to any person whose date of knowledge is or was relevant in determining a time limit.'

Section 33(5) normally applies to a case where the deceased's limitation period has been exceeded under s 11(4), ie where the case is statute barred by his death. In that event, it will be the duration of any disability of the deceased that will be considered under s 33(3)(d), the extent to which the deceased acted promptly and reasonably that will be considered under s 33(3)(e) and the steps, if any, taken by the deceased to obtain medical, legal or other expert advice that will be considered under s 33(3)(f). In such a case, it is the deceased's delay, knowledge and conduct that is primarily relevant.

Therefore, the reality in a Law Reform Act claim to which s 33 applies is that the court will be concerned with the knowledge and conduct of both the deceased and the personal representative(s). Moreover, with s 33(3)(b) in mind, it is important where a deceased is prima facie statute barred at the date of his death for the estate to institute proceedings as soon as possible thereafter, in order to minimise any additional impairment of the cogency of the evidence and, for the purposes of s 33(1) (b), to minimise any additional prejudice to the defendant which might tilt the balance in favour of the defendant in the exercise of the court's discretion.

(E)   CASES

An example of a Law Reform Act claim that failed under s 33 is *Cotton v General Electric Co Ltd* (p388). In 1964, the Pneumoconiosis Medical Panel had assessed Mr Cotton as 50% disabled with industrial chest disease. In 1971 he died without having commenced proceedings. Therefore the case was prima facie statute barred. In his widow's action against the defendants, the Court of Appeal upheld the trial judge's refusal to exercise his discretion in her favour under s 2D of the Limitation Act 1939 as amended. One of the major reasons for this was that, as the Pneumoconiosis Medical Panel records had been destroyed in the meantime, it had become much harder to determine the extent to which Mr Cotton's disability was due to industrial disease and how much was due to pre-existing bronchitis from which he had suffered since the 1940s. A similar refusal to grant a dispensation occurred in *Hinchcliffe v Corus UK Ltd* (p475), where a deceased's date of knowledge in respect of an asbestos injury was held to be 2002 and proceedings had not been issued before his death in 2009. The claim brought in 2010 was therefore statute barred and the prejudice to the defendant meant that the s 33 discretion was not exercised in the claimant's favour.

The Court of Appeal upheld a contrary decision in the case of *Reynolds v Spousal (London) Ltd and others* (p620). Mr Reynolds, a former lagger, was diagnosed as suffering from asbestosis in 1966 and was awarded DSS industrial disablement benefit then. He promptly instructed a solicitor who failed to recover damages for him over the next 10 years and abandoned the case in 1977. In 1983 the unfortunate Mr Reynolds contracted the further asbestos-related disease of mesothelioma from which he died in April 1984 without having commenced proceedings. His widow consulted a different solicitor who issued her writ in December 1985. The case was prima facie statute barred under s 11(4). However, the Court of Appeal upheld the trial judge's decision to exercise discretion in the claimant widow's favour against three of four defendants, partly because, although the delay on the part of the deceased had been long, the reasons for it were good. Moreover, considering all the accrued complications, his widow had commenced proceedings reasonably promptly after his death.

The cases above were prima facie statute barred under s 11(4) by the date of death. The alternative circumstance where s 33 applies to a Law Reform Act claim is where the personal representatives have exceeded their limitation period under s 11(5) by starting court action more than three years after the death and their date of knowledge. In such cases, the court will be concerned with the delay of the personal representatives rather than the deceased. In *Halford v Brookes* (p453), the claimant mother sued the two men who appeared to have combined to murder her daughter in April 1978. She was held to have acquired the requisite knowledge by the end of the criminal trial of one of the defendants in November 1978. Thus her case was prima facie statute barred under s 11(5). Her writ was finally issued in April 1987. The Court of Appeal held that the court's discretion under s 33 should be exercised in her favour, since her first solicitors had not advised her that she could claim damages from the defendants (as distinct from compensation from the Criminal Injuries Compensation Board) and she was not aware that a civil remedy was open to her until she consulted new solicitors whereupon she acted promptly.

In *Hammond v West Lancashire Health Authority* (p456) a widower sued in January 1994 in respect of the death of his wife from lung cancer on 9 August 1988 on the basis that she was initially wrongly diagnosed and treated for Hodgkin's Disease in December 2007. The claim asserted that, had the correct diagnosis been made earlier than when it was in March 1988, she would have survived two years longer. The deceased's claim was not statute barred at the date of her death, so the claimant had three years to bring his action from his date of knowledge. His claim was held to be statute barred as he had supportive medical opinion in September 1988. The trial judge allowed the action to proceed by granting a s 33 discretion dismissing the claim of evidential prejudice by the defendant on the basis of the destruction of the relevant x-rays as something that they brought upon themselves, as they were aware of a potential claim in 1988).)

2   Fatal Accidents Act claims

(A)   SECTION 12(1)

Section 12(1) of the Limitation Act 1980 states that:

> 'An action under the Fatal Accidents Act 1976 shall not be brought if the death occurred when the person injured could no longer maintain an action and recover damages in respect of the injury (whether because of a time limit in this Act or in any other Act, or for any other reason).
>
> Where any such action by the injured person would have been barred by the time limit in section 11 or 11A of this Act, no account shall be taken of the possibility of that time limit being overridden under section 33 of this Act.'

Through the words 'or for any other reason', s 12(1) confirms that a fatal action cannot be brought if, for instance, the deceased had already finally settled his claim. So far as limitation is concerned, its significance lies in confirming that the case is prima facie statute barred if the deceased had exceeded his limitation period during his life. This applies not only to time limits under s 11 of the 1980 Act but also those imposed by other statutes such as the Carriage by Air Act 1961. In making this assessment under s 12(1), no account is to be taken of the possibility of the court's discretion being exercised under s 33.

There can be no clearer example of death occurring 'when the person injured could no longer maintain an action and recover damages in respect of the injury' than a case such as *Young v Western Power Distribution (South West) plc* (p733), where the deceased's court action for mesothelioma had been discontinued during his life. He learned of his mesothelioma in 1993, started court action in 1995 and discontinued it in 1997 when the diagnosis was doubted. After he died in 1999, it was discovered that he had indeed been suffering from mesothelioma. His widow started her own court proceedings in 2002. The Court of Appeal held that s 12(1) operated to bar her claim, since the subsequent negative expert opinion could not retrospectively cause the deceased not to have known that he had mesothelioma. At the time of the hearing of the appeal in *Young*, no s 33 dispensation was available in a second action because of the rule in *Walkley v Precision Forgings* (p705). Following the abolition of this fetter in *Horton v Sadler* (p482), a case like Mrs Young's would now permit the court to exercise its discretion to allow the Fatal Accidents Act claim to proceed.

(B)   SECTION 12(2)

Section 12(2) of the 1980 Act provides that:

'None of the time limits given in the preceding provisions of this Act shall apply to an action under the Fatal Accidents Act 1976, but no such action shall be brought after the expiration of three years from:

(a)   the date of death; or
(b)   the date of knowledge of the person for whose benefit the action is brought;

whichever is the later.'

Thus, s 12(2) creates what may be termed a dependant's limitation period. Dependants are defined by s 1(3) of the Fatal Accidents Act 1976 and principally include spouses or former spouses, 'common law partners' of at least two years' standing, parents and grandparents, children and grandchildren, brothers and sisters, uncles and aunts, nephews and nieces. Although a number of these disparate persons may have a claim as a dependant on a deceased, s 2(3) of the 1976 Act provides that only one action shall be brought in respect of the same subject matter of the complaint. Accordingly, it is imperative that all named dependants are included in that action.

A dependant's date of knowledge may be much later than the date of death. In *Smith v Ministry of Defence* (p661), the claimant's husband had worked with asbestos in the defendant's employment between 1960 and 1992. However, she was unaware of this because she first met him in 1964, and when he was finally diagnosed as suffering from mesothelioma he was too ill to be questioned about it. Following his death in May 1991, she only learned of his asbestos work for the defendants in May 1995 when she met a former workmate who told her about it. It was held that time started to run then, four years after the death, so that the limitation period expired in May 1998, seven years after his death.

In *Brooks v Boots Company plc* (p348), a mother died due to mesothelioma in 1967, and her daughter's case was that she did not connect the mesothelioma with her mother's asbestos work on gas masks until 1992 or 1993. This, however, was undermined by her 1994 statement to the *Nottinghamshire Evening Post* that 'If I had been older at the time I would have done something about it ' and 'All along I thought my dad should have had some compensation'. Her court action commenced in 1997 was held to be statute barred.

Section 12(1) and (2) combine to operate in the following way. If the deceased's limitation period under s 11(4) has been exceeded, the case is prima facie statute barred by s 12(1), and s 12(2) will not apply. If it has not been exceeded, however, the case is governed by the dependant's limitation period under s 12(2). Thus, there are in effect two relevant limitation periods that have to be considered in turn: that of the deceased under s 11(4); and that of the dependant(s) under s 12(2). If either is exceeded, the case is prima facie statute barred and can only be rescued by the favourable exercise of the court's discretion under s 33.

An example may serve to illustrate this. Suppose that the deceased learns of his industrial disease and other material facts in April 2001. He dies due to it in April 2003, and the claimant (his widow) acquires the relevant knowledge within s 14 in October 2003. The deceased's limitation period under s 11(4) will not have been exceeded at his death, so the Fatal Accidents Act 1976 action may be brought under s 12(1). Accordingly the case is governed by the dependant's limitation period under s 12(2), which starts to run from the date of knowledge in October 2003 and expires in October 2006, five and a half years after the deceased's date of knowledge. As in Law Reform Act claims, it is important to avoid the fallacy of applying a single three-year limitation period starting from the deceased's date of knowledge. In this example, a lawyer advising the widow in 2005 that the limitation period had expired in April 2004 would be not only mistaken but at risk of a negligence action, if the result of his erroneous advice was to dissuade the widow from bringing a valid action timeously.

(C)   SECTION 12(3)

Section 12(3) of the Limitation Act 1980 states that:

'An action under the Fatal Accidents Act 1976 shall be one to which sections 28, 33 and 35 of this Act apply, and the application to any such action of the time limit under subsection (2) above shall be subject to section 39; but otherwise Parts II and III of this Act shall not apply to any such action.'

With respect to s 28, this means that time does not run against an infant dependant until he reaches his majority, so that he has three years after the age of 18 within which to bring a dependency action. The same applies to a brain damaged dependant, for whom the three-year limitation period will only start to run from the cessation of his disability. In practice, lengthy delays in bringing infant dependency actions are rare, because only one action for dependency can be brought and this is usually done by the surviving spouse who also claims on behalf of the dependent child.

An example of how s 12(3) can benefit an infant dependant was furnished by the case of *Straw v Hicks* (CA, 13 October 1983). In that case, the mother of an 18-month-old daughter was killed in a road accident in May 1979. In August 1982 a writ was issued claiming (a) damages under the Law Reform Act 1934 on behalf of her estate and (b) damages under the Fatal Accidents Act 1976 on behalf of her daughter. The Court of Appeal upheld the trial judge's refusal to exercise his discretion under s 33 in favour of the mother's personal representative, with the result that the Law Reform Act claim was conclusively statute barred, but it was of course accepted by all concerned that there was no limitation defence to the infant daughter's dependency claim under the Fatal Accidents Act.

By omission, s 12(3) makes it clear that s 32 of the Limitation Act 1980, which postpones the limitation period in cases of fraud, disability and concealment, does not apply to an action under the Fatal Accidents Act 1976. It confirms that ss 33 and 35 do apply. The reference to s 39 means that the dependant's time limit as defined in s 12(2) does not apply where a limitation period is prescribed under any other enactment: eg the strict two-year period for actions against carriers provided by the Carriage by Air Act 1961.

(D)   SECTION 13

Section 13 of the Limitation Act 1980 deals with the operation of the time limit under s 12 when there are two or more dependants. By s 13(1):

'Where there is more than one person for whose benefit an action under the Fatal Accidents Act 1976 is brought, section 12(2)(b) of this Act shall be applied separately to each of them.'

This will be considered further in the next section of this chapter on knowledge.

In brief, its effect is to create potentially different limitation periods for different dependants. Suppose that a deceased dies of lung cancer in December 2000 and leaves two dependants: a wife who lived with him, and a mother living abroad to whom he occasionally sent money. The wife knew all the material facts within s 14 at the date of his death, but his mother did not learn them until October 2001. The wife's limitation period would expire in December 2003, whereas the mother's limitation period would not expire until October 2004. Consequently, in a court action commenced in May 2004, the wife's claim would be prima facie statute barred, whereas the mother's claim would still be in time.

Section 13(2) states that:

'Subject to subsection (3) below, if by virtue of subsection (1) above the action would be outside the time limit given by section 12(2) as regards one or more, but not all, of the persons for whose benefit it is brought, the court shall direct that any person as regards whom the action would be outside that limit shall be excluded from those for whom the action is brought.'

Section 13(3) adds that:

'The court shall not give such a direction if it is shown that if the action were brought exclusively for the benefit of the person in question it would not be defeated by a defence of limitation (whether in consequence of section 28 of this Act or an agreement between the parties not to raise the defence, or otherwise).'

The meaning of s 13(2) is clear. In the last example, the court is empowered to direct that the wife be excluded from the action which would then be pursued on behalf of the mother alone. Section 13(3) would prohibit the court from making such direction if s 28 applies to the dependent wife because, for instance, she is a person under a disability. It is difficult in this context to ascertain precisely what s 13(3) usefully adds, because s 12(3) has already stated that, in the event of disability, s 28 would apply to extend the limitation period. Continuing with the last example, s 13(3) would prevent the wife from being excluded from the action, if the defendant had already agreed not to raise a limitation defence. Again, s 13(3) may be rather otiose, since in that event the defendants would be estopped from pleading limitation even without it. The final words 'or otherwise' probably refer to a successful application under s 33 to disapply s 12. Reverting to the same example, if the court's discretion under s 33 had been exercised in the wife's favour so as to allow the case to proceed, naturally the court could not direct under s 13(2) that the wife should be excluded from the action. Consequently, it seems that the court should not give a direction under s 13(2) until it has determined not to exercise its discretion in favour of the dependant concerned under s 33. Overall, the effect of s 13(3) is that it makes explicit certain specified exceptions to the operation of s 13(2).

(E)   KNOWLEDGE AND FATAL ACCIDENTS ACT CLAIMS

As seen above, s 12 of the 1980 Act allows a claim to be brought within three years of a dependant's date of knowledge. Section 13 states that, where there is more than one dependant, this limitation period must be applied separately to each. Accordingly, in applying the principles contained in s 14 concerning a person's date of knowledge, specific attention must be paid to each dependant, in order to ascertain whether the claim has been brought within a period of three years from when the particular dependant obtained the required knowledge within the meaning of s 14. When to these considerations is added the fact that s 12 also applies to the Fatal Accidents actions the provisions of s 28, namely the extension of the limitation period in cases of disability, it is clear that circumstances of considerable complexity may arise. These are illustrated by the following example.

Suppose that A contracts cancer in April 1996. In January 1997 he discovers the existence of the cancer and that it was the negligence of B that caused it. He dies from the disease in January 1999. A's widow is C. His dependent children are D, born in January 1987, and E who was born in January 1981. C, D and E all know the material facts under s 14 at the time of A's death. F and G are A's personal representatives. They discover in March 1999 that the cause of A's death was B's negligence. They institute proceedings in February 2002 under the Fatal Accidents Act on behalf of C, D and E. The action in respect of C and E is prima facie statute barred, as it has been brought more than three years after the date of death and their date of knowledge (s 12(2)). The court may exercise its discretion in their favour under s 33, if it considers it equitable to do so. If not, the court may direct under s 13(2) that C and E be excluded from the action. D's claim is within time in any event by virtue of ss 12(3) and 28.

(F)   SECTION 33 AND FATAL ACCIDENTS ACT CLAIMS

(i)   General principles

At first glance, the second paragraph of s 12(1) of the Limitation Act 1980 might be misconstrued as meaning that s 33 does not apply to Fatal Accidents Act claims:

> 'Where any such action by the injured person would have been barred by the time limit in section 11 or 11A of this Act, no account shall be taken of the possibility of that time limit being overridden under section 33 of this Act.'

In fact, however, these words merely appear to mean that, in assessing whether the deceased's claim was prima facie statute barred at the date of his death, no account shall be taken of s 33 in the course of that preliminary assessment. Three subsequent subsections of the Limitation Act 1980 put the matter beyond doubt. Section 12(3) states that an action under the Fatal Accidents Act 1976 shall be one to which s 33 applies. Section 33(1) itself empowers the court to direct that s 12 shall not apply to the action, or to any specified course of action to which the action relates. Moreover, s 33(6) states that: 'A direction by the court disapplying the provisions of section 12(1) shall operate to disapply the provisions to the same effect in section 1(1) of the Fatal Accidents Act 1976'.

The general principle that s 33 of the Limitation Act 1980 applies to Fatal Accidents Act claims is, however, subject to the exceptions created by s 33(2):

'The court shall not under this section disapply section 12(1) except where the reason why the person injured could no longer maintain an action was because of the time limit in section 11 … If, for example, the person injured could at his death no longer maintain an action under the Fatal Accidents Act 1976 because of the time limit in Article 29 in Schedule 1 to the Carriage by Air Act 1961, the court has no power to direct that section 12(1) shall not apply.'

As seen above, s 12(1) in effect provides, inter alia, that where the deceased has exceeded the limitation period before his death, the case is prima facie statute barred. In general, this is subject to the discretion of the court to disapply s 12(1) under s 33. Where, however, the limitation period is imposed by some other statute such as the Carriage by Air Act 1961, the court has no power under s 33 to disapply that limitation period. Suppose that the deceased is seriously injured in an air crash in January 2009 and dies of his injuries in February 2011, without having taken court action against the carrier within the strict two-year time limit imposed for such actions. A subsequent Fatal Accidents Act claim would be conclusively statute barred, because the court would have no power under s 33 to direct that s 12(1) should not apply.

The same result is reached where the limitation period that has been exceeded is the dependant's limitation period under s 12(2). This is because s 12(3) provides that 'the application to any such action of the time limit under subsection (2) above shall be subject to section 39' which states that the Limitation Act 1980 shall not apply to any action for which a period of limitation is prescribed under any other enactment. Again, the Carriage by Air Act 1961 is one of these. Suppose in the above example that the deceased had died instantaneously in the air crash in January 2009 and that his dependent widow had sought to start court proceedings against the airline in February 2011. She would have been conclusively statute barred from doing so, since s 33 does not apply to such a case.

(ii) Practical application

It has already been seen that the Fatal Accidents Act action may be prima facie statute barred (a) by s 12(1) if the deceased was out of time at the date of his death or (b) by s 12(2) if his dependants fail to start court action within three years of whichever is later of the death and their date of knowledge. Subject to the exceptions arising when other statutes such as the Carriage by Air Act 1961 apply, s 33 covers both situations. Consequently, if it appears to the court that it would be equitable to allow an action to proceed, it may do so whether the exceeding of the limitation period was due to delay on the part of the deceased or on the part of his dependants.

In the former case, the enquiry under s 33(3) is concerned with the deceased's conduct and his delay. This is explicitly provided by s 33(4), which states that in such a case the court shall have regard in particular to the length of, and the reasons for, the delay on the part of the deceased, and s 33(5) which provides that, in such a case, s 33(3) shall have effect as if references to the claimant included references to any person whose state of knowledge is or was relevant in determining a time limit.

Even in a case in which it is the deceased's limitation period that has been exceeded, the conduct and the knowledge of the claimant and/or the dependants may still be relevant for the purposes of s 33. In such a case, it is always desirable to commence court action after the death as soon as is reasonably possible, in order to minimise the reduction of the cogency of the evidence which the court is directed to consider under s 33(3)(b). Also, reasonably prompt commencement of such an action will limit the prejudice to the defendant to which the court is directed to have regard under s 33(1)(b). In cases where it is the dependant's time limit under s 12(2) that has been exceeded, it is on the dependants that the enquiry under s 33(3) is concentrated. Where, for instance, the claimant is a dependent widow who commences court action more than three years after the date of death and her date of knowledge, the court will have regard to the length of and reasons for her delay, the duration of any disability she may have suffered arising after the date of the accrual of the cause of action, the extent to which she acted promptly and reasonably once she knew that she might have a claim for damages, and the steps, if any, taken by her to obtain medical, legal or other expert advice and the nature of any such advice she may have received.

The other distinguishing feature of the s 33 enquiry in a fatal case is that, where the delay was due to the deceased exceeding his own limitation period, the court can have regard under s 33(3)(b) to the extent to which, having regard to this delay, the evidence adduced or likely to be adduced by the claimant or the defendant is or is likely to be less cogent than if the action had been brought within the primary limitation period. In most fatal cases, the death of the deceased is likely to diminish the cogency of the evidence to be adduced by the claimant. If liability is not seriously in dispute, the reduction in cogency of the evidence may be relatively minor. Even where liability is an issue, provided that there are a number of other witnesses the evidence may still be reasonably cogent. After all, in cases of instantaneous death in which no limitation defence arises, the court usually finds itself able to hold a fair trial and do justice between the parties. In cases where the deceased is the only material eye witness on liability, however, and due to delay on his part the trial takes place without the advantage of his testimony, the defendant is obviously able to argue that the evidence has become less cogent by reason of the delay. Case law shows that this argument has a much greater impact in accident cases.

(iii) Case law

The significance of a death is illustrated by the clinical negligence case of *Forbes v Wandsworth Health Authority* (p434) in which the Court of Appeal held that time had started to run within 12–18 months of unsuccessful surgery in October 1982. The court action commenced in December 1992 was therefore several years out of time. The claimant died in February 1995 between the preliminary trial on limitation and the Court of Appeal hearing. The court held that this created a new situation which affected the exercise of discretion under s 33, if for no other reason than that it reduced the value of the claim. Exercising its discretion afresh, the Court of Appeal declined to allow the case to proceed under s 33 for a variety of reasons: the delay was long, the case was weak, the evidence was impaired, and the defendant health authority would have had to pay a greater proportion of the claim than before.

Another fatal clinical negligence case in which the Court of Appeal refused to exercise s 33 discretion was *Skitt v Khan and Wakefield Health Authority* (p654) which concerned an omission to diagnose cancer between 1982 and 1986. The Court of Appeal held that Mr Skitt had sufficient knowledge to set time running in November 1986 when he consulted solicitors who sent a letter of claim. After legal aid was refused, he decided in June 1998 that he could not afford to pursue the claim. Following his death from the cancer in July 1992, his widow was able to obtain legal aid in her own right in 1993 and started High Court proceedings in January 1994. Noting that, after Mr Skitt's decision in 1988, an important medical witness had died in 1990 and the first defendant's health had deteriorated to the point where it was unlikely that he could give evidence, Roch LJ held that it was equitable that the claimant should be bound by her husband's decision. This line of thought is consistent with the reasoning of Potter LJ in the later non-fatal case of *Buckler v Sheffield Forest Borough Council* (p354) discussed on page 134.

Where the death is due to industrial disease resulting from a system of work over many years, any diminution in cogency of the evidence tends to be much less marked than in accident cases. So also, in principle, is the prejudice to the defendants where they have settled similar claims on a full liability basis. The case of *Buck v English Electric Co Ltd* (p353) illustrates both these points. From 1947 to 1957 the late Mr Buck was exposed to clouds of dust in the course of his employment by the defendants at their iron foundry. He knew by 1963 that his disease was sufficiently serious to justify his issuing proceedings. Yet he felt that this would be sponging and only commenced court action in February 1975, after his disability had increased to the point where he had to give up work. In April 1975 he died. At least six claims against the defendants arising out of similar working conditions had been settled by them for substantial sums. Kilner Brown J held that the extent to which the evidence likely to be adduced by the defendants was likely to be less cogent than in 1963 was small. He decided that it would be equitable to allow the claimant widow's action to proceed, both on behalf of the estate and in respect of her own claim as a dependant under the Fatal Accidents Act 1976.

The continued cogency of evidence available to the defendants also proved influential in another industrial lung disease case: *Whittaker v Westinghouse Brake and Signal Holdings* (p715). Mr Whittaker had worked for the defendants from 1926 until his retirement at the age of 65. Silicosis resulting from his work in the fettling shop was diagnosed in 1965, and the DHSS awarded him an industrial injuries disablement pension for it. He was not aware that he could claim damages. His silicosis deteriorated over the years and he died from associated lung cancer on 15 December 1991. The claimant widow learned of her right to claim in 1993 and issued High Court proceedings on 12 December 1994. Although the foundry had closed down, witnesses were still available. Exercising his discretion to allow the widow's claim to proceed, HH Judge Dyer QC found that her husband had not been blameworthy, that further efforts could be made by the defendants to obtain evidence and that they had not been seriously prejudiced. Such favourable decisions as *Buck* and *Whittaker* would almost certainly not have been reached in cases of industrial accidents as distinct from diseases.

In the cases of *Buck* and *Whittaker*, the delay was due to the deceased. A similar decision was reached in *Rule v Atlas Stone Co* (p634), where the delay was due to the dependant. The late Mrs Rule worked with asbestos for the defendants in 1954 and died due to the asbestos tumour of mesothelioma in April 1979 shortly after it was diagnosed. Her claimant husband took no steps to claim damages, partly because he was upset and depressed and partly because he was preoccupied with looking after four children and working as a long-distance lorry driver. Court action was only started on his behalf in October 1983. Simon Brown J found that his reasons for the 18 month delay to issue of the writ were understandable and that this delay was insignificant when considering the cogency of evidence likely to be adduced by both parties upon liability. Accordingly, he held under s 33(1) that the defendants had not been prejudiced by the delay and that it was equitable to allow the case to proceed.

A longer, but also sympathetic, example of a bereaved spouse's delay is to be found in *Smith v Ministry of Defence* (p661). Following her husband's death due to mesothelioma in May 1991, time began to run against the claimant widow in May 1995 when she was told how and where her husband was exposed to asbestos. After unfortunate and discouraging dealings with a local firm of solicitors over the next few months, she abandoned her attempt to claim damages and only resumed it in

May 2002 after learning of the House of Lords decision in the *Fairchild* appeals. She was then referred to specialist solicitors who commenced High Court proceedings in May 2004. Silber J held that she had good reason for her delay and that the cogency of the defendant's oral and documentary evidence had not been reduced by it, so he exercised his discretion under s 33 to allow her case to proceed.

Unfortunate legal advice also featured in the case of *Clack v Thames Television Ltd* (p374). During his employment as a carpenter and assistant scenery manager from 1968 to 1991, Mr Rolfe breathed asbestos during the cutting of asbestos sheets. He contracted mesothelioma from which he died in July 1993. In March 1994 his widow consulted a solicitor who emphasised difficulties that lay in her path. She was deterred not only by this but by the thought of having to go to court with which at the time she felt unable to cope. Like Mrs Smith, she learned of the House of Lords decision in the *Fairchild* appeals in the summer of 2002, and consulted different solicitors who started her court action in August 2003. Detailed evidence was available from three supporting witnesses. The defendants had destroyed personnel files in 1997, but it is unlikely that they contained evidence on the issue of liability. HH Judge Hawkesworth QC held that, although the widow's court action was seven years out of time, she had acted reasonably and a fair trial would still be possible, so he allowed her action to proceed.

It is clear, therefore, that it is possible for fatal industrial disease cases to succeed under s 33, even in cases of long delay. However each case turns on its own facts. Some fail, especially where the cogency of the evidence has been reduced. In *Brooks and others v Boots Company plc* (p348), which arose out of the use of asbestos in the manufacture of gas masks during the Second World War between 1939 and 1945, the deaths due to mesothelioma in five of the six cases occurred between 1967 and 1988, many years before the issue of the writs in 1997. The judge observed that:

> 'it is very difficult to think that a truly fair trial of a case of this kind can be had when the material events occurred more than 50 years ago, furthermore at a time when the country was engaged in a most perilous war: almost all witnesses to the event of the war will either be dead or of an age and a memory that they can be of little or no assistance.'

He considered that the balance of prejudice was firmly in favour of the defendants and concluded that it would not be equitable to allow the five claims to proceed. Nevertheless he made an exception of the sixth case (*Lord*), since Mrs Lord was only informed in the autumn of 1991 that she had asbestos-related pleural thickening before subsequently contracting mesothelioma. She commenced court action in March 1997, a delay of no more than two and a half years from the end of the limitation period, before dying in July 1998. Since the period of delay was relatively short and during much of it she was mortally ill, he allowed her court action to continue.

In general, therefore, s 33 of the Limitation Act 1980 applies to Fatal Accidents Act claims, but not those for which a separate limitation period is prescribed by another statute. In general, also, the principles to be applied to the exercise of the court's discretion are similar in fatal cases to surviving cases. Nevertheless, a difference arises in fatal cases, in that the delay and conduct to be considered under s 33 is not simply that of the surviving injured claimant, but will instead be that of the deceased or/and the claimant dependant(s). Moreover, in cases where it is the deceased's delay that has created the need for s 33 to be considered, the absence of his testimony due to his death is a circumstance to be taken into account, although this is likely to be accorded much more weight in a split second accident case where liability is in dispute than in a case involving a system of work spanning several months or years.

3   Combined 1934 Act/1976 Act claims

In summary, where a death occurs, court action may be brought either or both:

(i)   on behalf of the deceased's estate, under the Law Reform (Miscellaneous Provisions) Act 1934;

(ii) on behalf of his dependant(s), under the Fatal Accidents Act 1976.

An action on behalf of the estate requires consideration of:

(i)   the deceased's limitation period, under s 11(4) of the Limitation Act 1980; and

(ii) the personal representative(s) limitation period, under s 11(5).

An action on behalf of the dependant(s) requires consideration of:

(i)   the deceased's limitation period under s 11(4), by s 12(1);

(ii) the dependant(s) limitation period under s 12(2).

Each of the above limitation periods is apt to involve the definition of the date of knowledge in s 14. In addition, each is subject to s 28 (extension for disability) and s 33 (discretion to disapply).

The only exceptions to the above, created by s 39, are cases where another limitation period is prescribed by a separate statute.

Consequently, the limitation law of fatal claims is capable of giving rise to considerable complexity. The preceding sections have considered Law Reform Act claims and Fatal Accidents Act claims separately. This concluding section considers them in combination, illustrating their operation by means of the following examples.

EXAMPLE 1

On 10 October 1998, A was seriously injured in a road accident due to D's driving. On 3 January 1999 he died due to his injuries, leaving a widow W who knew all the material facts by his death. He also left two dependent children: B who was born on 10 June 1980 and who learned all the relevant facts on 25 April 1999, and C who was born on 25 November 1981 and knew all the material facts by A's death. A's will appointed two executors: E whose date of knowledge was 24 February 1999, and F whose date of knowledge was 31 July 1999. E and F issued a claim form on 11 February 2002, claiming damages on behalf of A's estate under the Law Reform (Miscellaneous Provisions) Act 1934 and on behalf of W, B and C as dependants under the Fatal Accidents Act 1976.

So far as the Law Reform Act claim is concerned, A was not statute barred at death: s 11(4). The relevant personal representative's date of knowledge is the earlier, that of E on 24 February 1999: s 11(7). Thus the Law Reform Act limitation period expired on 24 February 2002, so the estate's action on 11 February 1992 was commenced in time: s 11(5).

So far as the Fatal Accidents Act claim is concerned, A was not statute barred at death: s 12(1). Each dependant's date of knowledge must be considered separately: s 13(1). W's date of knowledge was 3 January 1999, so the action is prima facie statute barred in respect of her claim: s 12(2). B's date of knowledge was 25 April 1999, so the action in respect of his claim is in time: s 12(2). Since C was only born on 25 November 1981, time does not start to run against her until 25 November 1999, so her claim is within time as well: s 28.

Therefore, all the claims brought by the claim form under both statutes are within time, except that of W who can apply for the court's discretion under s 33: s 12(3). In deciding whether to exercise this discretion in her favour, the court will have regard to all the circumstances under s 33(3), including the fact that a court action against D will be proceeding in any event in respect of the other claims. Particular factors that the court will consider include the length of and the reasons for E and F's delay (s 33(3)(a)), the extent to which the evidence is likely to be less cogent (s 33(3)(b)), the extent to which E and F acted promptly once they knew they might have a claim for damages (s 33(3)(e)), and any steps taken by them to obtain medical, legal or other advice and the nature of any such advice they may have received (s 33(3)(f)). By s 33(5), W's delay and conduct is to be analysed alongside that of E and F.

The court will then consider the extent to which the provisions of s 12 prejudice any person whom E and F represent, namely W: s 33(1)(a). It will also consider the extent to which their decision would prejudice D or any person whom he represents, in effect D's insurers: s 33(1)(b). It may then direct that s 12 shall not apply to the action, in which case W's claim can proceed with the others: s 33(1). If the court refuses to exercise its discretion in W's favour, it shall direct that she be excluded from those for whom the action is brought: s 13(2).

EXAMPLE 2

In January 1995, A was informed that he had contracted asbestosis. He immediately knew that this was due to the negligence of D Insulation Co Ltd by whom he had been employed as a larger from 1965 to 1980. He decided not to claim damages, because he was still working and did not wish to 'sponge'. In June 2000 he died of his asbestosis, leaving a wife W and a dependent child C. E, his executor, immediately consulted S, a solicitor, who told him that any action against D was statute barred. In doing so, S overlooked the chance of the primary limitation period being disapplied under s 33. W learned of the existence of the s 33 discretion and told E who in July 2002 issued a claim form against D Insulation Co Ltd claiming damages (i) on behalf of A's estate under the Law Reform (Miscellaneous Provisions) Act 1934 and (ii) on behalf of W and C as dependants under the Fatal Accidents Act 1976.

A's limitation period expired in January 1998, so both actions were prima facie statute barred by his death in June 2000: ss 11(4) and 12(1). Accordingly, ss 11(5) and 12(2) do not apply. E must invoke s 33 and apply for the provisions of ss 11(4) and 12(1) to be disapplied: s 33(1). In deciding how to exercise its discretion, the court will have regard to all the circumstances including:

  (i) the length of, and the reasons for, A's delay: s 33(4);

 (ii) the length of, and the reasons for, W's delay: s 33(5);

(iii) the length of, and the reasons for, E's delay: s 33(3)(a);

(iv) the extent to which, having regard to the delay, the evidence likely to be adduced by either side is likely to be less cogent than if the action had been brought within time (four and a half years earlier, in January 1998): s 33(3)(b);

 (v) the extent to which E acted promptly and reasonably once he knew that D's acts or omissions might give rise to a claim for damages: s 33(3)(e);

(vi) any steps taken by E to obtain medical legal or other expert advice, and the nature of any such advice: s 33(3)(f);

(vii) the extent to which A and W respectively acted promptly and reasonably, once each knew that a claim for damages might be possible, and any steps taken by A or W to obtain medical, legal or other expert advice, and the nature of any such advice: s 33(5); and

173

(viii) the possible negligence by S, and the prospects of recovering damages from S instead of D Insulation Co Ltd.

Many and various are the factors that may need to be considered when a limitation defence arises in a fatal accident or disease claim. Further examples are to be found in the cases of *Taylor v Taylor* (p685), *Ward v Foss* (p708) and *Bansil v Northampton Health Authority* (p319).

The interaction of the two causes of action and their differing limitation periods was crucial to the outcome in a solicitor's negligence action in *Reader v Molesworths Bright Clegg* [2007] EWCA Civ 169. Mr Reader was injured in a road traffic accident in November 1989 for which liability was not in issue and he instructed the defendant solicitors who commenced proceedings within time in July 1989. Due to depression induced by the injuries sustained in the accident, Mr Reader committed suicide on 24 December 1994. His cause of action passed to his estate and his widow became the administratrix in February 2005. The defendant solicitors negligently discontinued the deceased's claim without instructions from the widow. The defendants accepted they were negligent and settled with the claimant in respect of her husband's personal injury claim which had become the Law Reform Act estate claim after his death. The claimant, however, contended that the defendants were also liable for the loss of her Fatal Accidents Act dependency claim and she sued in respect of this. The court held that, as soon as Mr Reader died, a new cause of action under the 1976 Act accrued and this was not extinguished by discontinuance of the Law Reform Act claim which was a separate cause of action for the estate. Further, different limitation periods governed the two causes of action. Mrs Reader had three years to sue from the death of her husband (that is, to 24 December 1997). Her children's claims had longer (namely, to when they became 21). Because Mrs Reader changed solicitors in June 1995, her new solicitors had over two years within which to bring her dependency claim; and, accordingly, the defendants' negligence had caused her no loss as her cause of action remained intact long after their retainer had been concluded. The new solicitors and their counsel did not bring separate proceedings, as they erroneously believed discontinuance of the estate claim also ended the dependency claim.

In *Booker v Associated British Ports* (p338) a widow took over her husband's claim started in time during his lifetime in October 1990 following his diagnosis in 1989 of asbestos-induced mesothelioma. Mr Booker died in January 1991 and the Law Reform Act claim passed to the widow as her husband's personal representative. The claimant failed, however, to add a dependency claim within the three-year period following the death, and applied in February 1991 to amend the writ to add a dependency action under the Fatal Accidents Act 1976, relying not on s 33 discretion but on the power to amend contained in s 35 of the Limitation Act. The court upheld the decision to allow the amendment and to add the new claim on the basis that a 'new cause of action arises out of the same facts or substantially the same facts as are already in issue on any claim previously made in the original action'. The principles of permitting amendments after expiry of the limitation period are discussed in the next chapter.

7 Amendments/new claims in pending actions (section 35)

Introduction

Frequently, after proceedings are issued and served and pleadings have been exchanged, parties to an action may wish to amend their cases. The claimant may wish to add another defendant because facts have become available that indicate a cause of action exists against him. Occasionally, as occurred in *Howe v David Brown Tractors (Retail) Ltd* (p483), another claimant may wish to be added to an existing action. In other cases, the claimant may wish to amend his case to allege new or different facts which may found a different cause of action, for example, based in contract and breach of statutory duty as well as in negligence against the original defendant. Conversely, a defendant may wish to implicate another party or parties and seek to join them as a third or subsequent party in the action. CPR 20 now describes a claim brought by a defendant against another party as a Part 20 claimant. If the defendant adds a Part 20 defendant, the claimant may wish to involve that party as a further co-defendant.

All these forms of amendment, whether they add or substitute a party, or whether they add a new or extend an existing cause of action, can give rise to limitation difficulties if the amendment is sought after the expiry of the primary limitation period. A new defendant, for example, may claim that the claimant's action against him is statute barred and an existing defendant may object that the fresh cause of action sought to be added to the existing proceedings is out of time. The CPR provisions on amending claims and parties are contained in CPR 17 and CPR 19. The general principles applicable when considering whether an amendment should be granted where there is no limitation issue derive principally from the overriding objective in CPR 1.1.

Peter Gibson LJ in *Cobbold v Greenwich London Borough Council*, unreported, 9 August 1999, CA, stated:

> 'The overriding objective is that the courts should deal with cases justly. This includes, so far as is practical, ensuring that each case is dealt with not only expeditiously but also fairly. Amendments in general ought to be allowed so that the real dispute between the parties can be adjudicated upon provided that any prejudice to the other party caused by the amendment can be compensated for in costs, and the public interest in the administration of justice is not significantly harmed.'

Conversely, those amendments which involve adding or substituting new parties or new causes of action after the expiry of the primary limitation period will generally not be allowed. There are, however, certain statutory exceptions provided by s 35 of the Limitation Act 1980 which together with the specific provisions of CPR 17.3(2), 17.4 and 19.5 allow certain types of amendment after the expiry of the primary limitation period. This chapter looks at the more significant of these permissible forms of amendment concerning new claims by looking in turn at (1) the addition of new parties and then (2) the addition of new causes of action.

1 Amendments relating to new parties

For the relevant statutory provisions and rules, see s 35(1), (2)(b), (3), (5)(b), (6), (7) and (8) of the Limitation Act 1980 and CPR 17.3(2), 17.4 and 19.5.

Section 35(2) defines a new claim made in the course of an existing action as either the addition or substitution of a new cause of action (s 35(2)(a)) or the addition or substitution of a new party (s 35(2)(b)). In addition, a new claim may also be a claim by way of set-off or counterclaim. By s 35(1) a new claim made in the course of any action is deemed to be a separate action and is determined to have been commenced on the same date as the original action. The only exception is the case of third party proceedings. Third party proceedings are defined in the Act as proceedings brought in the course of an action by any party to the action against a person not previously a party to the action. However, if a claimant joins a third party as a defendant, that is not deemed to be a third party action. Unlike new claims by way of new parties and new causes of action, third party proceedings are deemed to commence on the date when they are begun (s 35(1)(a)).

The effect of s 35(1) is of paramount importance with respect to adding new parties or new causes of action after the limitation period has expired, because it gives statutory effect to the so-called relation-back theory which dates amendments not from the date when the amendment takes place but from the same date as the commencement of the action. If, therefore, a new claim (whether by adding a new party or a new cause of action) is allowed by s 35, it has the effect of defeating an accrued limitation defence. Section 35 therefore reverses the previous line of cases governed by the Limitation Act 1939 which favoured the view that amendment took effect from the date of the order amending rather than from the date of the original commencement of the action (cf *Liff v Peasley* [1980] 1 WLR 781, *Leadbitter v Hodge Finance Ltd* (p529) and *Ketteman v Hansel Properties Ltd* (p517)). As stated, the exception relates to third party proceedings which are deemed to start at the date of the order joining the third party, and any accrued limitation defence will therefore be preserved. Third party proceedings are now described as Part 20 proceedings. CPR 20 does not contain any additional procedural rules governing limitation issues save that, pursuant to CPR 20.7(2), the date at which a Part 20 claim is made is when the court issues a Part 20 claim form.

Having defined what a new claim is, and when it is deemed to commence, s 35(3) specifically prohibits any new claim, other than a third party proceeding or an original counterclaim, from being initiated after the expiry of the limitation period unless there has been a s 33 dispensation with respect to personal injury cases or unless permitted by the rules of the court. Section 35(5) lays down the parameters within which the rules of court can be made. In the case of a claim involving a new party, s 35(5)(b) stipulates that such a claim will only be allowed if it is 'necessary for the determination of the original action'. Necessity is further defined by s 35(6) as where either:

'(a) the new party is substituted for a party whose name was given in any claim made in the original action in mistake of the new party's name; or

(b)   any claim already made in the original action cannot be maintained by
        or against an existing party unless the new party is joined or substituted
        as a plaintiff or defendant in that action.'

Further, by s 35(7), rules of court are also permitted to allow a party to an action to
claim relief in a new capacity in respect of a new cause of action, even though that
party had no title to make the claim when that action was first commenced; as, for
example, in a claim under the Fatal Accidents Act previously started by an injured
party who subsequently died.

Finally, by s 35(8), the same rules are deemed to apply to new claims brought
within existing third party actions.

The main effect of these complex provisions in respect of adding or substituting
parties is to restrict amendments after the expiry of the limitation period to:

(i)   those circumstances where the court exercises its discretion within s 33 of the
        Act, or
(ii)   where the amendment comes within the restrictive exceptions of mistake,
        necessity and capacity.

Each of these forms of exception will be examined below.

(A)   SECTIONS 33 AND 35: ADDING A PARTY OUTSIDE THE PRIMARY LIMITATION PERIOD

The rules of court referred to in s 35(5) which regulate the conditions under which
a new claim, both in respect of joining a party or adding a new cause of action, may
be brought are to be found in CPR 17.3(2), 17.4 and 19.5. With respect to joinder
of parties based on a s 33 application, CPR 19.5(4) provides:

'In addition, in a claim for personal injuries the court may add or substitute a
party where it directs that–

(a)   (i)   Section 11 (special time limit for claims for personal injuries); or
      (ii)   Section 12 (special time limit for claims under fatal accidents
             legislation), of the Limitation Act 1980 shall not apply to the claim
             by or against the new party; or
(b)   the issue of whether those sections apply shall be determined at trial.'

The previous equivalent rule, contained in RSC Ord 15 r 6(5)(b), was specifically
considered in the case of *Howe v David Brown Tractors (Retail) Ltd* (p483). The
Court of Appeal held in *Howe* that if a person seeks to be added as a party to
existing proceedings after the expiry of the limitation period, then the exercise of the
court's discretion under s 33 should take place prior to, or at the same time, as the
application for leave to amend the writ. In *Howe* the claimant started his own action
for personal injury out of time but the defendant consented to a s 33 application and
no difficulty arose at that stage. In his action he claimed damages in respect of the
loss of his leg which was amputated allegedly due to defective equipment provided
by the defendant. The writ was issued on 8 July 1988, the accident having occurred
on 23 January 1985. In November 1989 the claimant sought to add to the action
his father and his firm, effectively a farm consisting of himself and his father. The
Court of Appeal held that the firm's cause of action, based on economic loss, if it
existed at all, was one to which s 11 of the Limitation Act 1980 applied. This was
so because, although it was a claim for loss of profit, it was a claim which consisted
of, or included, damages for personal injury, arising as it did from the same facts
which caused the claimant's injury. The court further held that, because the addition

of the father was a new party seeking to be added after the expiry of the primary limitation period, it would be necessary to make a s 33 application prior to or at the same time as the application to amend. The claimant had argued that, pursuant to the Court of Appeal's reasoning in an earlier decision in *Kennett v Brown* (p516), the s 33 application could be held over to a later date after a decision on the amendment had been made.

In *Kennett* the claimant sustained personal injury in a road traffic accident and sued the first defendant who was the rider of a motorcycle on which the claimant had been a pillion passenger. The first defendant blamed the driver of another vehicle, and the claimant duly amended her proceedings to name him as a second defendant. The second defendant then issued a contribution notice against the first defendant. After the expiry of the limitation period, the first defendant served his own contribution notice against the second defendant which consisted of a claim for his own personal injury.

Pursuant to the provisions of s 35(1)(b), that was a claim which related back to the original action if leave to amend was given. The Registrar in a directions hearing indicated that the first defendant could not bring such a claim unless he applied for a s 33 dispensation first. However, the Court of Appeal held that the first defendant could make such a claim and, if the second defendant decided to rely upon his accrued limitation defence, a s 33 application could be subsequently heard. Helpfully this doubt as to when such an application should be made is now clarified by CPR 19.5(4)(a) and (b) which provide that the court may add a new party when it determines the s 33 dispensation or it can put over that issue to be determined at trial.

Examples of the court's discretion include the case of *Gibbons v London Borough of Greenwich* (p441) where a claimant sought to join out of time a third party as the fifth defendant and alleged that he was not statute barred because his date of knowledge of the identity of the respective defendant arose within three years from his attempt to join the third party as the fifth defendant. In the alternative, the claimant invited the court to exercise its discretion under s 33 on his behalf. The Court of Appeal with obvious reluctance upheld the leave to join which had been granted, indicating that it would be a more circuitous route to insist that the claimant started a fresh action where the issue of limitation could be determined and then, if successful, consolidate the two actions. In *Davies v Reed Stock & Co Ltd* (p401) the Court of Appeal held that, in a simple case where the limitation issue raised by the defendants was of no substance, a s 35 application to amend to add a new party would be appropriate. However, in a more complex case where the defence of limitation was an arguable issue, it would be appropriate to have a preliminary trial on the matter before consideration of the amendment (see also *Fowell v National Coal Board* (p437)).

In *Broome v Rotheray* (p350) a claimant failed to serve an amended writ within time. The Court of Appeal set aside the service of the writ on the grounds that no person should be added or substituted as a party after the expiry of any relevant period of limitation. The claimant contended that he had a s 14 date of knowledge argument, but this was dispensed with by the Court of Appeal as having no substance. Clearly, where there is an issue as to a s 14 date of knowledge and where s 33 dispensation would be required in the alternative, it is appropriate to have a preliminary trial on the issue of limitation.

An example of the court's refusal to allow the addition of a party outside the primary limitation period is to be found in the case of *Carlisle v Associated British Ports* (p365). Here, a docker attempted to add his employers as a second defendant after they had been blamed by the first defendant in their defence. The claimant's solicitors had failed to join the employers within the primary limitation period and, when the amended writ was served on the second defendants, they applied to set aside the order adding them to the proceedings. At a trial on the preliminary hearing the judge refused to exercise his discretion under s 33 in the claimant's favour predominantly on the grounds that the second defendants would face evidential difficulties in investigating the claim against them (see also *Bansil v Northampton Health Authority* (p319), *Liff v Peasley* [1980] 1 WLR 781, cf *Farnsworth v Bott* (p425)).

(B)   SECTION 35 AND THE ADDITION OF NEW PARTIES BASED ON NECESSITY: MISTAKE AND CAPACITY

In addition to the s 33 procedure, a party may also be added pursuant to s 35(5)(b) if the new party is necessary for the determination of the original action. Necessity is defined in s 35(6) as arising when the new party is to be substituted for a party whose name was given in the original action by mistake or where the claim made in the original action cannot be maintained by or against an existing party unless the new party is joined or substituted as a claimant or as a defendant in that action. By far the most significant of these provisions concerns the issue of mistake, and two rules of court deal with this matter.

First, CPR 17.4(3) and (4) state:

'(3)   The court may allow an amendment to correct a mistake as to the name of a party, but only where the mistake was genuine and not one which would cause reasonable doubt as to the identity of the party in question.

(4)   The court may allow an amendment to alter the capacity in which a party claims if the new capacity is one which that party had when the proceedings started or has since required.'

Further, CPR 19.5 effectively mirrors the provisions of s 35 of the Limitation Act by stating:

'(3)   The addition or substitution of a party is necessary only if the court is satisfied that –

'(a)   the new party is to be substituted for a party who was named in the claim form in mistake for the new party;

(b)   the claim cannot properly be carried on by or against the original party unless the new party is added or substituted as claimant or defendant; or

(c)   the original party has died or had a bankruptcy order made against him and his interest or liability has passed to the new party.'

Mistake as to the name of a party can be concerned with the name of the intended party where the correction does not require a substitution or addition of a new party but merely a change of name because the identity of the defendant is not an issue. Here, CPR 17.4(3) is applicable (see *Adelson v Associated Newspapers Ltd* [2007] EWCA Civ 701 and *Gregson v Channel 4 Television Corporation* (p449), so-called mistakes of nomenclature).

Alternatively, the mistake may go to the actual identity of the party, ie X is sued rather than Y, which would require a complete substitution. Mistakes as to identity may be those where a claimant intended to sue an employer but sued the wrong company. They may, however, also include a more fundamental error where, say, one motorist is sued in the belief that he caused an accident, but it later emerges that it was another who was responsible for the collision. It is in the former type of 'identity' case where substantial case law, under both the old and the new rules of court, has arisen. It will be seen below that the current law, as set out in the case of *Adelson*, regards this former type of 'identity' case as actually a nomenclature case and within the power of the section and rules. The latter type of identity case is considered as outside the ambit of s 35 and the associated rules.

It is instructive to consider the court's route to *Adelson*. In the case of *Evans Construction Co Ltd v Charrington & Co Ltd* (p425) the Court of Appeal allowed an amendment to substitute Bass Holdings Ltd for Charrington & Co Ltd in circumstances where the claimant had intended to issue against his landlords but issued instead against the original landlords who had assigned the reversion of their lease to another company within the same corporate group. The Court of Appeal held that no one had been misled by the mistake and allowed the amendment. (For an earlier personal injury case, see *Whittam v W J Daniel & Co Ltd* (p715).) The approach taken by the court in *Evans* was applied in the *Sardinia Sulcis* ([1999] 1 Lloyd's Rep 201), where the court held that the appropriate test was whether it was possible to identify the intended defendant by reference to a description specific to the case such as landlord, employer, or ship owner.

The leading personal injury case post-CPR is *Horne-Roberts v Smithkline Beecham plc* (p481) which applied the principles laid down in the *Sardinia Sulcis*. The claimant in *Horne-Roberts* sued Merck & Co Inc in error, believing them to be the manufacturers of the batch of MMR vaccines which were administered to the claimant and which it was contended caused his autism. The claimant was limited to a 10-year longstop provision under the Consumer Protection Act 1987 pursuant to s 11A of the Limitation Act 1980. When the true identity of the manufacturers came to light, the claimant sought to substitute Smithkline Beecham for the original defendants. Smithkline Beecham contended that there was no power to substitute the defendant after the expiry of the 10-year longstop provision, as a person who did not claim within that period of 10 years had no right to claim thereafter (see *Payabi v Armstel Shipping Corporation* [1992] 1 QB 907). The court found that the Limitation Act, whilst incorporating s 11A(3) with respect to the 10-year provision, did not disapply s 35. Accordingly, the court had power under s 35 to substitute the party even after the expiry of the 10-year period. The Court of Appeal upheld the first instance judge's decision, confirming that the test to be applied was essentially that under the *Sardinia Sulcis*, namely that the claimant had sought to issue against a party of a particular description (that is, the manufacturers). In the action, the claimant had always intended to sue the manufacturers of the batch with which he was treated, and he came within this principle.

However, in a similar subsequent action (*O'Byrne (by his mother and litigation friend) (FC) v Aventis Pasteur SA* (p587)), where a claimant also sought to add the manufacturer of a vaccine in substitution for the producer after the 10-year period had expired, the Supreme Court and both parties concurred that, following two references to the European Court of Justice (*O'Byrne v Sanofi Pasteur MSD Ltd (formerly Aventis Pasteur MSD Ltd) (Case C-127/04)* [2006] 1 WLR 1606 and *Aventis Pasteur SA v OB (Case C-358/08)* (unreported) given 2 December 2009), the court was prohibited from extending the fixed 10-year period by its domestic law, thus excluding s 35. The ECJ did permit a very restrictive exception:

> 'However ... Article 11 must be interpreted as not precluding a national court from holding that, in the proceedings instituted within the period prescribed by that article against the wholly-owned subsidiary of the "producer", within the

meaning of Article 3(1) of Directive 85/374, that producer can be substituted for that subsidiary if that court finds that the putting into circulation of the product in question was, in fact, determined by that producer.'

The claimant's contention that they fell within this exception was dismissed and, accordingly, the substitution of the party was disallowed. The result of this case is that the domestic court does not have the power to override the strict 10-year period in product liability cases by invoking s 35.

In 2005 in *Morgan Est (Scotland) Ltd v Hanson Concrete Products Ltd* (p564) the Court of Appeal's decision, albeit briefly, further extended the ambit of s 35 and CPR 19.5. In *Morgan* the claimant sought to add two further claimants to the action to whom the benefit of assignments of the cause of action had been made. The Court of Appeal disapproved that the test under the CPR provisions was as laid down in the *Sardinia Sulcis* because it did not specifically take into account the overriding objective and was not determinative of the limits of CPR 19.5. In a comprehensive review of authorities both pre- and post-CPR, the court examined the limits of CPR 19.5 and its interaction with CPR 17.4. Specifically the court held:

'35.   I have come to the clear conclusion that the *Sardinia Sulcis* right description/wrong name test does not set the limits of rule 19.5. It was devised for a wholly different rule and not for section 35 of the 1980 Act under which rule 19.5 was made. If anything it is more relevant to rule 17.4 with its requirement that mistake be "not one which would cause reasonable doubt as to the identity of the party in question". It is those words which echo the former Ord 20 r 5 "not misleading or such as to cause any reasonable doubt as to the identity of the person intending to sue or, as the case may be, intended to be sued".

36.   In so holding I have of course considered whether I am bound by the use of the *Sardinia Sulcis* test in the trinity of post-CPR cases, *Horne-Roberts*, *Parsons* and *Kesslar*. I do not think I am for the following reasons:

(i)   They each make the fundamentally wrong assumption that the *Sardinia Sulcis* test was framed to apply a rule implementing section 35 of the 1980 Act. It was not.

(ii)   In fact the use of that test made no difference, the words of the rule are at least wide enough to include it;

(iii) No member of any of the courts held explicitly that the limits of the rule were embodied by the test;

(iv)   In the last of these cases, *Kesslar*, two members of the court reserved their position;

(v)   The first of these cases, *Gregson*, made it clear that the decisions under either rule 17.4 or 19.5 should turn on the new rules and not older authorities;

(vi)   The *Sardinia Sulcis* test does not take into account the overriding objective.

37.   I conclude that the right approach is to apply the words of rule 19.5 without regard to the *Sardinia Sulcis* but with regard to the overriding objective, bearing in mind however that the limit of the rule must be the limit set by the empowering section, s 35. Much the better approach is that set out in *Gregson*. Citation of old authorities under different rules simply obscures the debate. The *Sardinia Sulcis* should be allowed to sink back to the ocean bottom. It muddies the waters.

38.   The same goes for the application of Rule 17.4 – though the wording here is much closer to the old rule. And it should be remembered that there may be overlap between the two rules (see *Gregson*). It does not matter if there is, save possibly on some point of discretion or service, neither of which arise here.

39.   With that I turn to see whether rule 19.5 applies to this case. One goes through a series of steps:

(a)   Has the limitation period expired (19.5(1))? Answer: Yes.
(b)   Is the addition of A or C "necessary"(19.5(2)(a))?
(c)   That depends on whether the court is satisfied that "the new party is to be substituted for a party who is named in the claim form in mistake for the new party".
(d)   So was company B named "in mistake" for A or C?

40.   There is no reason to construe "in mistake" restrictively. On the contrary it is important to remember that the source of the rule is the 1980 Act which had the obvious intention of liberalising the position from that under the 1939 Act. Likewise the overriding objective of doing justice is likely to be undermined if one gets finicky about different sorts of mistakes. The jurisdiction is for putting things right.

41.   In the present case there was clearly a mistake about naming B. The very form of the particulars of claim suggests that it was A that was intended to be named ... accordingly I would allow the substitution of B by A.' (per Jacob LJ)

The ambit of CPR 19.5 was accordingly seen as wider than the previous authorities considered. The test from *Morgan Est* appeared to be that, within the limits set by s 35, the court should consider whether the mistake was unintentional and what prejudice occurred to the intended defendant.

However, in a subsequent Court of Appeal decision, just two years later, this approach was strongly deprecated and the *Sardinia Sulcis* was refloated from the muddy waters. In *Adelson v Associated Newspapers Ltd* [2007] EWCA Civ 701 the claimant sought to add two further corporate claimants out of time in a defamation action. The court reviewed all the previous case law and rules, and stated that the decision in *Morgan Est* should not be followed and it was necessary to have regard to the jurisprudence in relation to RSC Ord 20 r 5, and the test in *Owners of the Sardinia Sulcis v Owners of the Al Tawwab* 1990 remained good law. Lord Phillips stated:

'22.   It can be seen that the provisions of section 35 of the Limitation Act 1980 and of CPR 17.4(3) and CPR 19.5(3) cover the same ground as RSC Ord 20, r 5 and bear some similarity to it. In a number of instances this court has applied decisions on Ord 20, r 5 as being relevant to the interpretation of CPR 19.5(3). In *Morgan Est (Scotland) Ltd v Hanson Concrete Products Ltd* [2005] 1 WLR 2557 Jacob LJ, giving the leading judgment of a two-judge court, deprecated this course. He stated that:

"the 1980 Act had the obvious intention of liberalising the position from that under the Limitation Act 1939."

This *obiter* observation was made without the court having been referred to the legislative history of the 1980 Act or to a number of judgments that had analysed this. The observation was not correct and the reasoning in *Morgan Est* should not be followed.'

The court held that the mistake envisaged in CPR 17.4 and 19.5 was one of nomenclature. This included simple errors as to name but would also include cases where the claimant knew the category of person intended to be sued such as landlord, employer, or manufacturer. Where a person had made enquiries as to who that person was and had been erroneously told that the defendant was that person, the mistake was likely to be classified as one of nomenclature and not identity. The difference was defined as follows:

'29. Before turning to these questions we would make some general observations, using the current descriptions of claimant and defendant to describe the parties to an action. Most of the problems in this area arise out of the difference, sometimes elusive, between an error of identification and an error of nomenclature. An error of identification will occur where a claimant identifies an individual as the person who has caused him an injury, intends to sue that person, describes him in the pleadings by the correct name, but then discovers that he has identified the wrong person as the person who has injured him. An error of nomenclature occurs where the claimant identifies the correct person as having caused him the injury, but describes him in the pleadings by the wrong name.'

Following a review of the cases, the court concluded:

'43. These authorities have led us to the following conclusions about the principles applicable to Ord 20, r 5.

(i) The mistake must be as to the name of the party in question and not as to the identity of that party. Such a mistake can be demonstrated where the pleading gives a description of the party that identifies the party, but gives the party the wrong name. In such circumstances a "mistake as to name" is given a generous interpretation.

(ii) The mistake will be made by the person who issues the process bearing the wrong name. The person intending to sue will be the person who, or whose agent, has authorised the person issuing the process to start proceedings on his behalf.

(iii) The true identity of the person intending to sue and the person intended to be sued must be apparent to the latter although the wrong name has been used.

(iv) Most if not all the cases seem to have proceeded on the basis that the effect of the amendment was to substitute a new party for the party named.'

The court further concluded that:

'56. The nature of the mistake required by the rule is not spelt out. This court has held that the mistake must be as to the name of the party rather than as to the identity of the party, applying the generous test of this type of mistake laid down in the *Sardinia Sulcis*. The "working test" suggested in *Weston v Gribben* [2007] CP Rep 10, in as much as it extends wider than the *Sardinia Sulcis* test, should not be relied upon.

57. Almost all the cases involve circumstances in which (i) there was a connection between the party whose name was used in the claim form and the party intending to sue, or intended to be sued and (ii) where the party intended to be sued, or his agent, was aware of the proceedings and of the mistake so that no injustice was caused by the amendment. In the *SmithKline*

case [2002] 1 WLR 1662, however, Keene LJ accepted that the *Sardinia Sulcis* test could be satisfied where the correct defendant was unaware of the claim until the limitation period had expired. We agree with Keene LJ's comment that, in such a case, the court will be likely to exercise its discretion against giving permission to make the amendment.'

The ambit of the court's discretion is now clearly limited to cases of nomenclature, and even then may well not be exercised if the correct defendant was unaware of the claim until after the expiry of the limitation period (see *Lockheed Martin Corporation v Willis Group Ltd* (p536), *Parkinson Engineering Services Plc (in Liquidation) v Swan* (p594), *Irwin v Lynch* (p491) and *Insight Group Ltd v Kingston Smith (A Firm)* (p489)).

The remaining two examples provided by CPR 19.5(3) of necessity have generated little authority with respect to personal injury claims.

CPR 19.5(3)(b) permits the addition or substitution of a party as necessary if 'the claim cannot properly be carried on by or against the original party unless the new party is added or substituted as a claimant or defendant.' (For examples of this in a non-personal injury case, see *Merrett v Babb* [2001] QB 1174, where a new party in a professional negligence action to whom a defendant owed a duty of care jointly with the original claimant was permitted to be added under these provisions (per May LJ at paras 53–55), and *Roberts v Gill* [2010] UKSC 22, where a beneficiary under a will who sued solicitors in a personal capacity was not permitted after the expiry of the limitation period to sue as a derivative action on behalf of the estate.) In *Nemeti v Sabre Insurance Company Limited* (p579) the claimant accepted that there was no direct claim against the insurers for an accident that occurred in Romania and sought to substitute the estate of the negligent driver who died in the accident. On appeal from the master who permitted the amendment, the court held that the restrictive conditions of CPR 19.5(3) were not met and the amendment was not necessary for the determination of the original action against the insurer who had insured the car but not the defendant driver who was uninsured.

Finally, CPR 19.5(3)(c) permits the addition or substitution of a party where the original party has died or had a bankruptcy order made against him and his interests or liabilities have passed to the new party. The obvious relevance for personal injury cases would be where the injured claimant died and the claim is continued on behalf of the estate and/or on behalf of the dependants under the Fatal Accidents Act 1976.

2   Amending to add a new cause of action

As with the addition or substitution of a party, the court also has a discretionary power to allow a new cause of action to be added after the expiry of the limitation period. A new cause of action is a new claim within the meaning of s 35(1)(b) which, if allowed, dates back to the original commencement of the action. Section 35 and rules of court impose, however, very restrictive conditions on the granting of such amendments. Section 35(3) prohibits amendments adding causes of action after the expiry of the limitation period unless there has been a s 33 dispensation or pursuant to s 35(5)(a) '… if the new cause of action arises out of the same facts or substantially the same facts as are already in issue on any claim previously made in the original action'.

Accordingly, in certain circumstances the party seeking to add a new cause of action may need to rely on the provisions of s 33, as with the addition or substitution of a new party.

If a party does not rely on s 33 or fails to bring the case within s 33, the determination as to whether the new cause of action arises out of the same or substantially the same facts will be determined by the provisions of CPR 17.4(2), which provides:

'The court may allow an amendment whose effect will be it to add or substitute a new claim, but only if the new claim arises out of the same facts or substantially the same facts as the claim in respect of which the party applying for permission has already claimed a remedy in the proceedings.'

An illustration of these principles found in pre-CPR cases include *Grewal v National Hospital for Nervous Diseases* (p450), where an amendment to add an allegation of assault in a clinical negligence action was allowed to be added to an existing claim in negligence in respect of treatment received in the operating theatre. The alleged assault took place in the ward and it was held that both causes of action were deemed to arise out of substantially the same facts. Similarly, in *Sayer v Kingston and Esher Health Authority* (p642), new allegations concerning want of care arising out of the birth of the claimant's second child were allowed in circumstances where the defendants still had medical records and witnesses to deal with the fresh complaint. In *Sion v Hampstead HA* [1994] 5 Med LR 170, a father's claim for psychiatric injury arising out of witnessing his son's death over a period of 14 days following a motorcycle accident was struck out as disclosing no cause of action, as it failed to arise out of 'shock', as was required by the case of *Alcock v Chief Constable of South Yorkshire Police* [1992] 1 AC 310. The claimant sought to amend to plead a new cause of action and, in principle, the Court of Appeal agreed that, if a pleaded case showed no cause of action but a cause of action could be properly pleaded on the same or substantially the same facts, it should be permitted. On analysis of the amended cause of action in *Sion*, however, there was also no case in law, and so the action, being 'doomed to fail', was dismissed.

What constitutes a new cause of action is itself a mixed question of law and fact (cf *Steamship Mutual v Trollope and Colles* (1986) Con LR 11, *Crown Estate Commissioners v Whitfield Partners* March 30 1990, unreported, CA, *Hoechst UK v Inland Revenue Commissioners* [2003] All ER (D) 198 and *Berezovsky v Abramovich* (2011) (p329)).

In *Barrow v Consignia* (p322) a claimant obtained judgment on liability in respect of an injury at work and, by the trial of the issue of quantum, sought to add a claim for psychiatric injury which was permitted on the basis that it was an aggravation of the original injury. The Court of Appeal disagreed and considered this to be a new cause of action. In *Pledger v Martin* (p608) the claimant sued for injuries sustained in a fall at work said to be due to breach of statutory duties by a failure to provide a platform. The defendant contended that it did provide a platform. Outside the limitation period the claimant sought to argue that, if a platform was provided, it failed to comply with other statutory duties and sought to amend the particulars. The court refused, saying that the alternative case did not arise out of similar facts as the pleaded case, and was in fact inconsistent with it.

In *Dowson v Chief Constable of Northumbria* (p415) the court found some proposed amendments in respect of claims for harassment as constituting new causes of action to those already pleaded, and allowed some and rejected others which did not arise out of facts already pleaded.

If the amendment is one which seeks only to clarify the existing cause of action, it will not be necessary to refer to the s 35 of the 1980 Act. For example, in *Hay v London Brick Co Ltd* (p468) an application to substitute the date of an accident was allowed as it was held not to be a material part of the cause of action. In *Dornan v*

J W Ellis and Co Ltd (p413) a fresh allegation of vicarious liability was added to existing allegations of lack of care in the workplace and this was considered not to be a new cause of action.

The test that the court is likely to apply, in considering whether a new cause of action is being alleged, is whether the new facts in the amendments are the same or substantially the same as those which would be required to support the allegations contained in the original pleaded case. An amendment is likely to be deemed to give rise to a new cause of the action if it involves consideration of factual material which did not arise on the original claim (cf *Hydrocarbons Great Britain Ltd v Cammell Laird Shipbuilders Ltd* (1991) 25 Con LR 131, *Fannon v Backhouse* (1987) Times 22 August, *Aldi Stores Ltd v Holmes Buildings plc* [2002] EWCA Civ 1882 and *Harland v Wolff Pension Trustees Ltd v Aon Consulting Financial Services Ltd* (p460)).

In *Evans v Cig Mon Cymru Ltd* (p424), the Court of Appeal readily permitted an appeal and reinstated an action struck out following a refusal to amend a claim form. A clerical error led to a claim form describing the claimant's action as based on 'abuse at work' but the particulars of claim sought damages for a hand injury. The error occurred as the claimant had originally considered suing for both an injury to his hand and bullying at the work place, but had indicated to the defendant that the bullying claim was not currently being pursued. In addition to serving the claim form and particulars, the claimant had also served a supportive medical report dealing with the hand injury.

Toulson LJ dealt with the defendants' submission that there was no power in CPR 17.4 to permit the required amendment:

'23. However, Mr Grace had a further argument why the court does not have such a discretion. The argument runs in this way. For the court to disregard the error in the claim form as an irregularity, causing no prejudice, in respect of which the court could therefore grant relief under its general powers under Rule 3.10, would be tantamount to treating the claim form as though it referred to an accident at work, rather than to abuse at work. Were an application to be made by the claimant to make such an amendment (as the claimant in response to this application went on to do) such an application would, in his submission, be bound to fail by reason of the provisions of Rule 17.4. Therefore, if the court could not cure the mismatch by granting an amendment under Rule 17.4, it would be wrong to deal with the matter by simply refusing the application to strike out under Rule 3.4.

24. That argument brings me directly to the question of whether an application to amend the claim form would necessarily fail under Rule 17.4. It would be most unfortunate if that were the case in circumstances where, as mentioned, it is common ground that the alteration could have been made immediately before the service and nobody has been misled by it. But if the rules on their proper construction preclude such an amendment being allowed, then the rules must be applied. In applying Rule 17.4 in these circumstances, Mr Grace submits that the court should concentrate, purely and simply, on the claim form, which is the foundation document on which the proceedings depend. So viewed, it is self-evident, he submits, that to change the claim form, so as to alter the word "abuse" to "an accident", is to substitute a new cause of action. The matter has to be viewed objectively, and the judges below were right to conclude that the rules allowed no escape for the claimant.

25. That brings me to the point raised by Jacob and Mummery LJJ in granting leave to appeal, whether that is not an over-narrow way of viewing the matter,

when the claim form and particulars of claim and supporting documents were all served together. I have already made reference to the definition of the term "statement of case" in the rules.

26. In my view the just approach is to look at the totality of the documents served. These documents together set out the claimant's pleaded case. There was an obvious mismatch, but in asking whether the proposed amendment was, in truth, an amendment to raise a new cause of action or merely to clarify an internal inconsistency in the pleaded case is, it is proper to look at the pleaded case as a whole. When one does so, it is clear, in my judgment, that what was sought to be done by the subsequent application to amend was not, in substance, to raise any new claim at all, but merely to correct an obvious formal error. I reject the argument that an amendment to correct that clerical error was prohibited by Rule 17.4 and, in my judgment, there was nothing to prevent the court from exercising its general discretion to do justice in response to the application to strike out the particulars of claim. If the circuit judge had considered that he had such a discretion, it is plain how he would have exercised it and, in my judgment, rightly so. I would therefore allow this appeal and restore the action.'

In *Goode v Martin* (p445) the Court of Appeal construed CPR 17.4(2) to make it compatible with s 3 of the Human Rights Act 1998 and Article 6 of the ECHR. In *Goode* the claimant sustained severe head injuries on 24 August 1996 when onboard the defendant's yacht. Her injuries were such that she had no recollection of the accident. Her pleaded case was based upon an allegation of faulty equipment on the yacht. The defence alleged, however, that the claimant had leant into the path of the boom. The claimant sought to amend her claim over a year outside the limitation period alleging that, if the accident occurred as the defendant described, the defendant was negligent in failing to take steps to protect her as she was an inexperienced sailor. Both the master and the judge refused the application to amend. The judge said that the new cause of action did not arise from the original claim and CPR 17.4 prevented the claimant from relying on the facts as alleged by the defendant. The judge found that, if the claimant wished to rely on the new cause of action, she would have to start fresh proceedings, and date of knowledge arguments under ss 11 and 14 could be heard together with a s 33 application if appropriate. The Court of Appeal allowed the claimant's appeal. The Court of Appeal concurred that the judge was correct in finding that, on the wording of the sub-rules, CPR 17.4 prohibited an amendment. However, the rule had to be read purposefully so as to allow the claimant to have access to the court within the meaning of s 3 of the Human Rights Act 1998 and Article 6 of the Convention. Lord Justice Brooke stated:

'35. We now possess more tools for enabling us to do justice that were available before April 1999. Since then, the Civil Procedure Rules and the provisions of the Human Rights Act 1998 have come into force. By the former, we must seek to give effect to the overriding objective of dealing with the cases justly when we interpret any rule (CPR 1.2(b)). By the latter we must read and give effect to support the legislation, so far as it is possible to do so, in a way which is compatible with the Convention rights set out in, Schedule 1 of the Act (Human Rights Act of 1998), Section F3(1).

36. It is commonplace that the claimant must not be impeded in her right of access to a court for a determination of her civil rights unless any hindrance

to such access can be justified in a way recognised by the relevant Strasbourg jurisprudence (for the general principle *Cachia v Faluyi* [2001] EWCA Civ 998 at [17]–[20], [2001] 1 WLR 1996). All she wants to do is to say that even if the accident happened in the way in which Mr Martin says it happened, he was nevertheless negligent in failing to take the appropriate steps as an experienced yachtmaster, to protect her safety as a novice sailor. She does not want to rely on any facts which will not flow naturally from the way Mr Martin sets up the evidential basis of his defence at the trial ...

46.   Mr Ralls contended that we should interpret CPR 17.4(2) as if it contains the additional words "are already in issue on". It would therefore read, so far as is material:

> "The Court may allow an amendment whose effect will be to add ... a new claim, but only if the new claim arises out of the same facts or substantially the same facts as *are already in issue* on a claim in respect of which the party applying for permission has already claimed a remedy in the proceedings." (emphasis added)

This would bring the sense of the rule in line with the language of the 1980 Act, which is the source of authority to make the rules contained in CPR 17.4.

47.   In my judgment it is possible, using the techniques identified by Lord Steyn in *R v A*, to interpret the rule in the manner for which Mr Ralls contends.'

3   Original counter-claims and set-offs

A significant exception to the s 35 procedure exists in relation to a defendant's original counterclaim or set off. Section 35(3) provides:

> 'Except as provided by section 33 of the Act or by rules of court, neither the High Court nor any county court shall allow a new claim within subsection (1)(b) above, other than an original set-off or counter-claim, to be made in the course of any action after the expiry of any time limit under this Act which would affect a new action to enforce that claim.'

This subsection then defines an original set-off or counterclaim as a claim by a party who has not previously made any claim in the action. An example would be where in a road traffic accident both the claimant and the defendant are injured. If the claimant sues inside the limitation period, the defendant may allow the period to expire before he amends his defence to add a counterclaim for his own personal injury. Effectively there is no limitation period for the defendant in these circumstances. However, any amendment to the original counterclaim would need to comply with the s 35 requirements of obtaining a s 33 dispensation if the amended counterclaim did not arise out of the same or substantially the same facts already in issue (*Jfs (UK) Ltd v Dwr Cymru Cyf (No 1)* [1999] 1 WLR 23).

In *Kennett v Brown* (p516) the then Master of the Rolls, Lord Donaldson, construed the subsection as referring to a set-off or counterclaim by an original defendant as against an original claimant. The subsection did not therefore apply in *Kennett* where the new claim was brought by the first defendant in a contribution notice against a second defendant. This was so, despite the fact that no claim had been previously made by him in the action (see also *Law Society v Douglas Weymss* [2008] EWHC 2515 (Ch).

4   Third party and Part 20 proceedings and s 10 of the Limitation Act 1980

Section 35(2) defines third party proceedings as:

> '"third party proceedings" means any proceedings brought in the course of any action by any party to the action against a person not previously a party, other than proceedings brought by joining any such person as a defendant to any claim already made in the original action by the party bringing the proceedings.'

Third party proceedings, as defined in the Limitation Act 1980, brought after the expiry of the primary limitation period are deemed by s 35(1)(a) to be commenced on the date upon which they are sealed by an officer of the court and not from the commencement of the original action (cf *College Street Market Gardens v Stuart* (5 October 1989, unreported)). As seen, CPR 20 now calls such contribution claims 'Part 20 claims'. However, Part 20 claims also include (pursuant to CPR 20.2) a counterclaim by a defendant against a claimant, and a claim where a defendant is added to the action by an existing claimant.

These latter two types of Part 20 claims are not third party actions within the meaning of s 35(2) of the Limitation Act 1980. CPR 20 contains no procedural requirement with respect to limitation save that it does state (pursuant to CPR 20.7(2)) that a Part 20 claim is made when the court issues a Part 20 claim form.

Part 20 actions (within the meaning of the Limitation Act) typically arise when a defendant seeks contribution or indemnity in respect of its own potential liability to a claimant from another party. That third party might be liable directly to the claimant but the claimant, for a variety of reasons, chooses not to sue him. Alternatively, the third party may be directly liable to the defendant under contract, apart from any separate common law liability arising out of being a joint tortfeasor. If a defendant fails to issue against a third party within the relevant period of limitation in a clear case, the third party may take out a summons seeking to dismiss the third party action as being frivolous, vexatious or an abuse of process (*Ronex Properties Ltd v John Laing Contract Ltd* [1983] QB 398).

However, in *Howe v David Brown Tractors (Retail) Ltd* (p483), dicta of Nichols LJ concerning certain third party actions would indicate that a defendant himself may rely on the provisions of both ss 14 and 33 of the Limitation Act in third party proceedings. This was because certain third party proceedings were deemed to consist of, or include, damages in respect of personal injuries within the meaning of s 11(4) 'to the plaintiff or any other person'. Lord Justice Nichols gave the following example:

> 'My third example is of a case where P buys a defective product from D and in consequence P's employee is injured whilst using it in the course of his employment. The employee recovers damages from his employer P for breach of statutory duty or negligence. P then brings proceedings against D by way of third party proceedings in the employer's action or by way of a separate action. P seeks to recover from D the damages for breach of contract and indemnity in respect of P's liability in damages to his employee. In my view, P's claim in contract against D falls within section 11. The crucial feature is that the breach of contract upon which P founded his action caused the personal injuries in respect of which the damages claim arises. P is claiming damages to compensate him for the loss suffered by him as a result of breach of contract which caused personal injury. The consequence of D's supply of the defective

189

tool or whatever was personal injury to the employee. True, in this example, the personal injuries were sustained by P's employee and not by P himself. But section 11 expressly caters for this possibility when providing that the damages claimed consist of and include damages in respect of personal injury "to the Plaintiff or any other person".' ([1991] 4 All ER 30 at 41H–42A)

If this analysis is correct in respect of such third party actions, the defendant will be able to raise questions of knowledge concerning attribution and identity and also seek to persuade the court, if necessary, to disapply the provisions of s 11 pursuant to the powers contained in s 33 of the 1980 Act. This is a rather surprising extension of the ambit of ss 33 and 14 of the 1980 Act, but it is a logical extension of the Court of Appeal's indication that certain third party actions consist of and include damages for personal injury. This would have the effect of limiting to three years the limitation period in respect of any contract that the defendant has with the third party, for example, over the supply of a defective product. In those circumstances, it would be quite a frequent occurrence that third party proceedings will be statute barred where the claimant had used most of the primary limitation period before issuing proceedings and where the defendant had delayed for a short period only before attempting to bring in the supplier. Moreover, in any case where the claimant himself seeks to rely on s 33, the defendant's cause of action against the third party is also likely to be statute barred.

5   Claims under the Civil Liability (Contribution) Act 1978

A defendant who is statute barred in respect of a third party claim may still have available a separate statutory cause of action under s 1 of the Civil Liability (Contribution) Act 1978. It is important to emphasise that this is an entirely separate cause of action from any common law cause of action arising out of contract or tort which might of itself be statute barred. Section 1(1) of the 1978 Act provides:

> 'Subject to the following provisions of this section, any person liable in respect of any damage suffered by another person may recover contribution from any other person liable in respect of the same damage (whether jointly with him or otherwise).'

This provision therefore requires that both the defendant and the third party have a legal liability to the claimant. In the simple case of joint tortfeasors, no difficulty arises, because here the claimant has sued only one defendant who simply brings proceedings to recover contribution against the third party. In the example given by Lord Justice Nichols in *Howe*, the situation might be more complicated. The employer would need to show that the manufacturer who produced the defective tool was in breach of a legal liability directly to the employee who was injured. That legal liability would not arise in contract because it would be the employer not the employee with whom the contract was made. The legal liability could arise in tort but if, as is often the case, the equipment had a latent defect, the manufacturer may well have a good defence in negligence. Since, however, the passing of the Consumer Protection Act 1987, a legal liability to a claimant may be more easily established.

In *Royal Brompton Hospital NHS Trust v Hammond and others (Taylor Woodrow Construction (Holdings) Ltd)* [2002] 2 All ER 801, the court held that the words 'liable in respect of the same damage' did not mean substantially or materially similar, as the words had to be given their ordinary and natural meaning, and same means same.

By s 10 of the Limitation Act 1980 a defendant has a two-year period to bring a claim for contribution. Under the 1978 Act, time runs in respect of this two years from either the date of judgment given in civil proceedings or arbitration or two years from the date when an agreement to make a payment to the claimant is made (see s 10(3), (4)). In *Knight v Rochdale Health NHS Trust* (p523) the court held that, in the case of a settlement, time ran from the date when a firm agreement was reached and not the later date when a consent order was made. The claimant, a surgeon, had settled a personal injury action against him brought by a former patient. He then brought contribution proceedings within the two years from the date of the consent order but outside the two years from the date of the agreement to pay damages. The court struck out the case as statute barred.

In *Aerlingus v Gildacroft and Sentinel Lifts Ltd* (p295) the court was required to determine whether judgment or award within the meaning of s 10(3) meant a judgment or award in relation to liability or in relation to quantum. Mr Smyth was injured whilst working for the claimant and entered judgment on liability against them on 9 May 2001; and later, having agreed damages in the sum of £490,000, he entered judgment on quantum on 3 October 2003. The claimant brought contribution proceedings against both defendants on 4 February 2004. The first defendant had contracted to do work on a lift which had malfunctioned and caused the claimant's injury. The second defendants actually undertook the works on a subcontract. Both defendants contended that time ran from the first of the two dates on judgment and succeeded at first instance in having the claim struck out as statute barred. The Court of Appeal reversed the decision, holding that the two-year period ran from the judgment on quantum and the claim was accordingly in time. The Court of Appeal stated that, because the relevant date with respect to settlements was when quantum was agreed (pursuant to s 10(4)), then by a parity of reasoning, the same date should apply with respect to judgments under s 10(3). Dicta in others cases (*Royal Brompton NHS Trust v Hammond* [2002] 2 All ER 801 and *Ronex Properties Ltd v John Laing Construction Ltd* [1983] QB 398) tended to support this interpretation.

By s 1(2) of the Civil Liability (Contribution) Act 1978, a *defendant* is entitled to recover contribution even though, at the time when he makes the claim against the contributor, his own liability to the claimant would have been statute barred. The only requirement is that the defendant was not statute barred immediately before he made (or was ordered or agreed to make) the payment in respect of which contribution was sought. A contributor would, however, have a good defence to contribution if he was able to demonstrate that, at the time the defendant made his payment, the claimant was in fact statute barred against him and presumably the defendant failed to take the defence.

A more complex issue arises in respect of the question of the *contributor's* liability to the claimant being barred by limitation. Section 1(3) of the 1978 Act provides:

'A person shall be liable to make a contribution by virtue of subsection (1) above notwithstanding that he has ceased to be liable in respect of the damage in question since the time when the damage occurred, unless he ceased to be liable by virtue of the expiry of a period of limitation or prescription which extinguished the right on which the claim against him in respect of the damage was based.'

This provision stipulates that the contributor may only rely on a limitation defence if it is one which would have extinguished the claimant's right to bring an action against him. The time for determining whether the contributor had such a limitation defence would be immediately before the defendant's liability to the claimant was established. The vast majority of actions governed by the Limitation Act 1980 in respect of personal injuries are not those whereby a claimant's right is extinguished but are those where the claimant's remedy is barred. The major exception arises under the Consumer Protection Act 1987 which has a 10-year longstop provision from the first supply of the defective product. In non-personal injury actions, a similar 15-year longstop applies under the provisions of the Latent Damage Act 1986.

Section 1(3) of the 1978 Act was specifically designed to reverse the situation that arose in *Wimpey v BOAC* [1955] AC 169 under the earlier but similar provisions of s 6 of the Law Reform (Married Women and Tortfeasors) Act 1935. In that action a claimant sued a defendant who successfully argued a limitation defence. The claimant then sued a further defendant who claimed contribution against the defendant in the first action. The successful first defendant resisted the claim for contribution on the basis that he was not a person liable to the claimant because he had been successful in his own limitation defence. The Law Commission Report (No 79 1977), which examined this case, submitted a draft Bill which would have, if enacted, reversed *Wimpey* (see clause 13(7) Law Commission's draft Bill) in that it determined a contributor would only be liable to defeat a defendant's claim against him if he was able to establish that he had defeated the claimant's claim on the merits of the case and not on a limitation defence. However, s 1(5) of the 1978 Act was not drafted in the same terms as the Law Commission's own clause. Section 1(5) provides:

> 'A judgment given in any action brought in any part of the United Kingdom by or on behalf of the person who suffered the damage in question against any person from whom contribution is sought under this section shall be conclusive in the proceedings for contribution as to any issue determined by the judgment in favour of the person from whom the contribution is sought.'

The Law Commission's draft clause was in the following terms:

> 'In any proceedings for contribution under this section the fact that a person had been held not liable in respect of any damage in any action brought by for or on behalf of the person who incurred it shall be conclusive evidence that he was not liable in respect of the damage at the time when it occurred, provided that the judgment in his favour rested on a determination of the merits of the claim against him in respect of the damage (and not for example, on the fact that the action was brought after the expiration of any period of limitation applicable thereto).'

On the actual wording of s 1(5) of the 1978 Act, a contributor may reasonably argue that a judgment obtained in an earlier action, even if it was based on limitation, is still a judgment within the meaning of the section. In cases where there has been no judgment between a contributor and the claimant, s 1(3) will obviously prevail.

Section 10 of the Limitation Act 1980 provides that ss 28, 32 and 35 of the Act apply and, accordingly, the provisions concerning disability, fraud, concealment and mistake apply, as do the provisions within s 35 concerning new claims and new parties within the contribution action itself. Section 33 is specifically excluded, which is perhaps some small indication that Parliament had not intended the provisions of ss 14 and 33 of the 1980 Act to be applied to third party proceedings, as might now be possible given the Court of Appeal's dicta in *Howe*. It is not entirely clear as to why a third party action consolidated with the claimant's action allows a defendant to take advantage of ss 14 and 33 of the 1980 Act but, if a separate action for contribution is started (relying on the 1978 Act) after the claimant's claim has been settled or determined, the defendant is no longer permitted to take advantage of ss 14 and 33 of the Act.

8 Special time limits (section 39, CICB, MIB)

Introduction

Section 39 of the Limitation Act 1980 provides a saving for those periods of limitation prescribed in other statutes:

> 'This Act shall not apply to any action or arbitration for which a period of limitation is prescribed by or under any other enactment (whether passed before or after the passing of this Act ...'

There are very many enactments which prescribe special periods of limitation, but most are not relevant to personal injury actions (cf Halsbury's Statutes, Volume 24, notes to s 39; A McGee *Limitation Periods*, -6th edn, chs 24–28). The principal exceptions include those Acts which incorporate international conventions on the carriage of persons and goods by sea, air, road and rail. These Acts generally impose shorter periods of limitation. This chapter will briefly discuss the legislation which is likely to be pertinent to personal injury cases. It will also briefly outline the provisions of the Foreign Limitation Periods Act 1984, which governs the law of limitation where a cause of action has arisen in a foreign jurisdiction.

1 Statutes governing transport

(A)   WATER TRANSPORT

(i)   *Section 190 of the Merchant Shipping Act 1995*

Section 190 of the Merchant Shipping Act 1995 replaced s 8 of the Maritime Conventions Act 1911 in an unaltered form. Section 190 imposes a two-year limitation period in respect of an action against a vessel or her owners and permits a lien for damages against the offending vessel. The period of two years applies to an action against an offending vessel used in navigation where damage or loss to another vessel, the travelling vessel, occurs either to it, or its cargo freight or property, or when personal injury or death is sustained by a person on the travelling vessel. An action may be brought against the offending vessel's owners or any person responsible for her.

A vessel will include a hovercraft pursuant to the Hovercraft (Civil Liability) Order 1979 (SI 1979/305) but will exclude a jet ski on the basis that it is not a vessel used in navigation (see *Steadman v Scholfield* (p673), approved in *R v Goodwin (Mark)*

193

[2005] EWCA Crim 3184, (2006) Times, 4 January). A ship or vessel includes a rigid inflatable boat used for pleasure trips around the Anglesey coast (*Michael v Musgrove (t/a YNYS Ribs, 'The Sea Eagle')* (p557)).

In *Curtis v Wild* (p393), a collision between two sailing dinghies that occurred on Belmont Reservoir was held not to be covered by the ambit of the previous Maritime Conventions Act 1911 because neither of the boats used were for navigation purposes. Navigation requires a vessel to be proceeding from an originating place to a place of destination for the discharge of cargo or passengers. Although the vessel must be used in navigation, the cause of action is not dependent on their being a fault in navigation which causes a collision. In *The Norwhale* (p583), HMS Eagle discharged so much oily water onto the Norwhale that it sank. Brandon J held that fault within s 1 of the Act was not restricted to navigational fault but covered fault in general, such as the negligent discharge of water causing a capsize.

Where a claimant is injured on board in a collision and sues his travelling vessel but does not sue the other offending vessel, the Act does not apply. This is because the wording of the Act requires the action to be against *another vessel*. Accordingly, in *The Niceto de Larrinaga* (p582) a mother who sued as administratrix of her son's estate in respect of his death on board a ship on 23 September 1961 was held not to be statute barred when she brought proceedings on 8 September 1964. Her son was on The Niceto when it collided with the Sitala but, as the Sitala was not being sued, the action was not against another *vessel* and was not therefore governed by the Act. An action *in personam* against any individual responsible for the collision or tort which causes personal injury is probably available outside the provisions of the Act when that person is not the master of the vessel, because in those circumstances the wrongdoer might not be a person responsible for the vessel within the meaning of the Act (cf *The Danube II* [1921] P 183 but see also *HMS Archer* [1919] P 1 and *Santos v Owner of Baltic Carrier and Owner of Flinterdam* (p640)).

Section 190 of the Merchant Shipping Act 1995 imposes the two-year period of limitation from the date when the damage occurs. In the case of a death, it is likely that the two-year period will run from the date of death if that occurs later than the accident. At a time when a Fatal Accident Act action had to be brought within one year from the date of death (under the 1846 Fatal Accidents Act), a widow was held to be in time in respect of an action arising out of her husband's death which was brought within the two-year period from when his ketch collided with the defendant's steam trawler (see *The Caliph* (p365), decided under the Maritime Conventions Act 1911). In *Sweet v Owners of Blyth Lifeboat (The Edward Duke of Windsor)* ((2002) 2 January, unreported), Tomlinson J found that time ran from the date when the injury was suffered by the claimant and not when the incident occurred.

Section 190(5) and (6) of the Merchant Shipping Act 1995 contains provisions analogous to s 33 of the Limitation Act 1980 permitting the court to extend the primary limitation period in certain circumstances. Unlike the provisions of s 33 of the 1980 Act, however, no guidelines are given within the Act itself for the exercise of discretion. Section 190 contains two sets of circumstances where an extension arises.

First, the court is *required* to extend the two-year limitation period pursuant to s 190(6) if it is satisfied that there has not arisen within the two-year primary limitation period any reasonable opportunity of arresting the defendant ship and bringing it within the jurisdiction of the court or the territorial sea of the country where the claimant's travelling ship belongs or in which the claimant resides or has his principal place of business. Once satisfied that no such reasonable opportunity has been available, the court must extend the limitation period for a time long enough to give a reasonable opportunity of arresting the ship and bringing proceedings in the relevant jurisdiction.

Secondly, the court also has a *discretionary* power to extend the time limit under s 190(5) on such conditions and to such extent as it thinks fit. This is an entirely unfettered discretion. The earlier authorities, under the Maritime Conventions Act 1911, emphasise that the onus was on the claimant to satisfy the court that there was 'some good and substantial reason' to extend the limitation period. In *The Kashmir* (p514) a mother sued nearly four years after her son's death as a result of a marine collision. Her delay was explained in terms of not knowing that she had a cause of action until approximately three and a half years after the collision. The Court of Appeal upheld the first instance judge's refusal to extend the limitation period, on the grounds that ignorance of her legal rights was not a good and substantial reason (see also *The Hesselmoor and The Sergeant* [1951] 1 Lloyd's 146). In *The Sunoak* (p680) an Italian widow was also shut out by the provisions of the 1911 Act when she sued two months out of time. The court did not accept that her impecuniosity, which made it difficult to raise legal fees, together with complexities that had arisen over taking instructions for the purposes of the administration of her husband's estate, constituted special circumstances. Alternatively, in *The Alnwick* (p302) a widow was allowed to proceed out of time against a second Norwegian ship, the Braemar, which had been blamed for a collision in the Alnwick's defence. The deceased foy-boat had collided with the Alnwick. The court took the view that the Alnwick had caused the delay, in that it did not in advance intimate that the Braemar was to blame. In addition, the court thought it fit that the Braemar's owners should be in the action, so it rather than the widow would have the burden of obtaining the relevant evidence from Norway concerning the ship's navigation.

In *The Gaz Fountain* [1987] 1 FTLR 423, Sheen J emphasised that, for the court to exercise its discretion in favour of the claimant, the conduct of the defendants in causing or contributing to the delay was likely to be crucial. Proceedings in *The Gaz Fountain* started 16 days after the end of the last of a series of voluntary extensions. The trial judge refused to allow the matter to proceed, indicating that the special circumstances required under the Act would nearly always come from the conduct of the defendant. The judge further stipulated that special circumstances would not arise out of the mere fact that a claimant would be without remedy, because that was the necessary consequence of the limitation period being invoked. Nor could special circumstances arise from the fact the defendants knew of the dispute and were in a position to ascertain relevant facts. The judge went so far as to indicate that demonstrating that the defendants suffered no prejudice could not amount to a special circumstance either. (See also *The Al Tabith and Alanfushi* [1983] Lloyd's Rep 195 where the same trial judge also refused an extension where proceedings had been issued 17 days too late due to the claimant's solicitors believing that an extension was likely to be granted.)

This restrictive approach was softened in *The Zirje* (p735) where Sheen J determined that the relevant test had shifted away from the claimant needing to show exceptional special circumstances to merely demonstrating a good reason. In *The Zirje*, Sheen J was influenced by the House of Lords' reasoning in *Waddon v Whitecroft–Scovill* [1988] 1 WLR 309, a case concerned with the renewal of a writ in an action for personal injury due to the contraction of dermatitis by the claimant at work. Sheen J thought that, by parity of reasoning, the discretion under s 8 of the Maritime Conventions Act 1911 was analogous to discretion to renew a writ where the primary limitation period expired. In *The Zirje*, particular attention was given to the facts that the defendants had agreed not to contest liability, the required extension was only for three days and the defendants had, during negotiations, been willing to extend voluntarily the limitation period for one year. By contrast, in *The Vita* (p702), Sheen J found no good reasons for extending the validity of the writ which had not been promptly served and which went astray because the claimant had decided to use the British Document Exchange.

In *Santos v Owner of Baltic Carrier and Owners of Flinterdam* (p640) a Filipino seaman on board the Baltic Carrier was injured in a collision between the two vessels on 16 March 1998. The limitation period was two years under the Merchant Shipping Act 1995 against the second defendant, the owner of the Flinterdam, but was three years against the travelling vessel, the Baltic Carrier. The claimant's solicitors misunderstood the position and believed that they had three years in which to sue the second defendant. The claimant's solicitors put the second defendant ship on their internal ship watch system but chose UK Watch Only. They missed an opportunity to arrest the ship on 19 August 1999. The limitation period against the second defendant expired on 16 March 2000. The claimant had commenced two actions, the first against both defendants and the second against the second defendant only. The second defendant applied to set aside an order that the claim form in the first action be renewed against them and simultaneously the claimant applied for an extension of time for issuing proceedings in the second action pursuant to s 190 of the Act. The trial judge, Steel J, found firstly that pursuant to s 190(6) because there had objectively been an opportunity to arrest the vessel there was no question of a mandatory extension. The court's discretion to extend time under s 190(5) was engaged and he concluded that the practice had emerged of exercising such a discretionary power on similar principles to applications to extend the validity of the claim form pursuant to the relevant rules of court (cf *The Sea Speed America* [1990] 1 Lloyd's Rep 150, *The Myrto (No 3)* [1987] AC 597). The judge accordingly considered the provisions of CPR 7.6 and noted the substantial difference between the current provisions and the predecessor RSC Ord 6 r8. The judge concurred with the observations of Rix J in *The Hai Hing* [2000] 1 Lloyd's Rep 300 that the previous jurisprudence may be illuminating but he did not regard it as binding in the new procedural circumstances. The judge then exercised his discretion in favour of the claimants on the basis that it had not been incompetent of the claimant's solicitors not to place the second defendant's vessel on worldwide watch and, in any event, it probably would have made little difference. The judge was of the view that the claimant had taken all reasonable steps to serve the claim form during its validity and the application to extend had been made properly. He also found that there was no material hardship to the second defendant.

The principle which appears to emerge from the authorities, both under the Maritime Conventions Act 1911 and s 190 of the Merchant Shipping Act 1995, is that the court is more likely to follow the principles applied when considering the extension of the validity of a claim form pursuant to CPR 7.6 than the principles involved in weighing the respective prejudices to each party under s 33 of the Limitation Act 1980.

(ii) Section 183 of, and Schedule 6 to, the Merchant Shipping Act 1995

Section 183 of the Merchant Shipping Act 1995 governs the international carriage of passengers and their luggage by sea through incorporating into domestic law the Convention Relating to the Carriage of Passengers and their Luggage by Sea ('the Athens Convention') (see Schedule 6 to the 1995 Act; Schedule 3 to the Merchant Shipping Act 1979 formerly fulfilled this function). The Convention makes the carrier liable for the death or personal injury to a passenger and for the loss or damage to their baggage, caused by the fault or neglect of the carrier or his servants or agents acting in the course of their employment. By Article 16(2) and (3) the limitation period is two years, and time runs in the case of personal injuries from the date when the passenger disembarks:

'Article 16

Time-bar for actions

1. Any action for damages arising out of the death of or personal injury to a passenger or for the loss of or damage to luggage shall be time-barred after a period of two years.

2. The limitation period shall be calculated as follows:

    (a) In the case of personal injury, from the date of disembarkation of the passenger;

    (b) In the case of death occurring during carriage, from the date when the passenger should have disembarked, and in the case of personal injury occurring during carriage and resulting in the death of the passenger after disembarkation, from the date of death, provided that this period shall not exceed three years from the date of disembarkation;

    (c) In the case of loss of or damage to luggage, from the date of disembarkation or from the date when disembarkation should have taken place, whichever is later.

3. The law of the court seised of the case shall govern the grounds of suspension and interruption of limitation periods, but in no case shall an action under this Convention be brought after the expiration of a period of three years from the date of disembarkation of the passenger or from the date when disembarkation should have taken place, whichever is later.

4. Notwithstanding paragraphs 1, 2 and 3 of this Article, the period of limitation may be extended by a declaration of the carrier or by agreement of the parties after the cause of action has arisen.'

In fatal cases, time runs from when the deceased should have disembarked if he dies on board. If he survives but dies later because of the injury sustained on board, time will run from the date of death. However, Article 16(3) imposes a three-year limitation in such cases. Time for the three years runs from when the deceased would have disembarked or, if later, when he should have disembarked (as, for example, when the ship is lost). The Convention provides for the suspension or interruption of the time limits to be governed by the domestic law of the country in which proceedings are initiated. It is likely, therefore, that ss 28 and 32 of the Limitation Act 1980 will apply in cases of disability, fraud or concealment but only to the extent of the longstop provision of three years within Article 16(3).

Section 33 of the Limitation Act 1980 would not apply, however, because the prejudice which would have been suffered would not have arisen from the provisions of s 11 or 12 of the Limitation Act 1980 but from the provisions of the Merchant Shipping Act 1995 itself.

Moreover, s 33(2) specifically excludes a fatal claim, if it is limited by a time provision under the Carriage by Air Act 1961. The Carriage by Air Act 1961 is merely referred to in the subsection as an example and, accordingly, s 33 will not apply to other such examples including the Merchant Shipping Act 1995. In addition, in *Higham v Stena Sealink Ltd* (p474) the Court of Appeal held that s 33 dispensations involve extensions of the primary limitation period rather than an interruption or suspension and, accordingly, s 33 does not apply. In *Higham* the claimant slipped on broken glass while on the defendant's ferry on 16 August 1991 and issued proceedings on 2 September 1993. The defendant applied to strike the claim out on the basis that the two-year period applied, but the district judge exercised a s 33 discretion under the Limitation Act 1980. On appeal, the circuit judge held that s 33 did not apply and struck the claim out. The Court of Appeal agreed, noting that Article 16(3) reincorporated domestic law with respect to suspension or interruption but that did not include setting aside the limitation period which is effectively what s 33 achieves.

In *Norfolk v My Travel Going Places* [2004] 1 Lloyd's Rep 106, a claimant was injured whilst on holiday on a cruise ship. She sued pursuant to the Package Holidays and Package Tour Regulations 1992, claiming that the tour operator was in breach of contractual duty as imposed by the regulations and that her limitation period was three years. The court disagreed, holding that the claim was essentially a claim within the Convention, and the regulations and the contract did not displace the Convention. However, a different decision was made by another county court judge in *Lee v Airtours Holidays* [2004] 1 Lloyd's Rep 683 where a claimant sued for the loss of luggage involved in the sinking of a cruise liner. Here the court held that reg 15 of the Package Holidays and Package Tour Regulations did have the effect of supplanting the Convention. *Lee* was not specifically concerned with limitation or personal injury but whether Article 5 of the Convention was engaged, namely whether the luggage had been deposited with the carrier for the agreed purpose of safekeeping.

In *Adams v Thomson Holidays Ltd* (p293) the court held that s 183 and the Athens Convention did not exclude the court substituting a defendant after the two-year period pursuant to CPR 19.5.

(B)   AIR TRANSPORT

The Carriage by Air Act 1961 applies to all international air carriage of persons, as well as goods or cargo, as is implied by the title. The Act incorporates the Warsaw Convention and, by amendment through the Carriage by Air and Road Act 1979, incorporates changes to the Warsaw Convention brought about by The Hague Protocol and, later, the Montreal Protocol (Schedule 1). The cause of action lies against a carrier or its servants or agents. The relevant article on limitation is Article 29, which provides:

'Article 29
(1)   The right to damages shall be extinguished if an action is not brought within two years, reckoned from the date of arrival at the destination, or from the date on which the aircraft ought to have arrived, or from the date on which the carriage stopped.
(2)   The method of calculating the period of limitation shall be determined by the law of the Court seised of the case.'

The time limit is accordingly two years running from the date when the aircraft arrived at its destination or, alternatively, if it crashes, the date when it should have arrived or when the carriage stopped. After two years the cause of action is extinguished, as opposed to the remedy merely being barred. The method of calculating time by Article 29 is to be determined by the *lex fori* (that is, the domestic law of the tribunal where proceedings are instigated). The method of calculating time is not the same as allowing for extensions or interruptions of time. Questions of calculation will only refer to, for example, whether the day of the accident counts or whether time is extended if process cannot be served because, on the final day of the primary limitation period, the court is closed (see eg *Marren v Dawson Bentley* (p543) and *Pritam Kaur v S Russell & Sons Ltd* (p613)). Accordingly, the provisions of ss 28 and 32 of the Limitation Act 1980 will not apply and neither will the provisions of s 33. Therefore, even a child's claim or the claim of a person under a mental disability will be conclusively barred against the carrier after the two-year period.

The event giving rise to the carrier's statutory liability is required to take place in the course of embarkation, whilst on board, or during the process of disembarkation. In *Adatia v Air Canada* [1992] PIQR P238 the Court of Appeal found that an injury occurring to a claimant who had got off a plane but who was hurt whilst on a travelator at Heathrow Airport (but before the claimant had gone through Immigration and Customs) was not one occurring in the process of disembarking and the Convention did not apply. The court applied a three-fold test as to where the location of the injured party was, the nature of the activity being undertaken, and whether at that time the claimant was under the control of the carriers.

Conversely, in *Phillips v Air New Zealand Ltd* (p604), the claimant was being pushed in a wheelchair on an escalator towards the departure area at Nadi International Airport at Fiji when the wheelchair fell backwards causing her injury. The accident occurred on 22 March 1997 but proceedings were issued on 16 March 2000. The court held that the Convention was engaged because the claimant was in the process of embarkation, having already completed the checking-in. Her claim accordingly was dismissed as being time barred.

Notification of a claim is required under Article 26 within the two-year period, but only the institution of proceedings will stop time running against a prospective claimant.

The two-year period also applies to hot air balloons. In *Laroche v Spirit of Adventure (UK) Ltd* (p526) a claimant brought an action outside the two-year period in respect of injuries sustained when the basket of an air balloon crashed. The claimant contended that the purpose of the flight was recreational, the balloon was not an aircraft, there was no carriage as there was no specific place of departure or arrival, and he was not a passenger within the meaning of Article 17 of Schedule 1 to the Carriage by Air Acts (Application of Provisions) Order 1967. The court found to the contrary on all grounds and that the 1967 Order applied, and so the action was statute barred.

(C)   LAND TRANSPORT

(i)   Rail

The International Transport Convention Act 1983 (which repealed the Carriage by Railway Act 1972) governs the liability of a railway carrier for injury to passengers and/or damage to their luggage caused by an accident during an international journey that occurs within the territory of a state which is a party to the Convention on International Carriage by Rail. The limitation period is three years, with time running from the day after the accident. Where death occurs, the period is three years from the date of death, but a longstop provision limits any action to a five-year period from the date of the accident. (See Article 55 of Appendix A to the Convention, Cmnd 8535.) A claim needs to be made in writing (Article 49) and, when this is done, time is suspended until the railway rejects the claim in writing (Article 55, paragraph 4). Thereafter, time begins to run again (see also Article 53 for claims in respect of death). By Article 3 of Appendix A to the Convention, a state which is a party to the Convention may contract out of the provisions of the Convention in respect of an accident which occurs within its own territory and causes injury or loss to a passenger who is a national of that state.

By paragraph 6 of Article 55 of Appendix A, questions of suspension or interruption to periods of limitation are to be determined by the national law. It is, therefore, likely that the provisions of ss 28 and 32 on disability, fraud or concealment will apply. However, s 33 of the Limitation Act 1980 will not apply, because any prejudice caused to a claimant is not caused by s 11 of the 1980 Act but by the provision of the International Transport Convention Act 1983. In addition, a s 33 dispensation does not involve a suspension or interruption of a period of limitation (see *Higham v Stena Sealink Ltd* (p474) for analogous reasoning based on the Merchant Shipping Act 1995).

(ii) Road

The Carriage of Passengers by Road Act 1974 enacts the provisions of the Convention on the Contract for the International Carriage of Passengers and Luggage by Road. The relevant contract must be one in which transport takes place within the territory of more than one state and the departure or destinations or both are within a contracting state territory. The relevant article on limitation is Article 22, which provides:

'Article 22

1. The period of limitation for actions arising out of the death or wounding of or out of any other bodily or mental injury to a passenger shall be three years.

The period of the limitation shall run from the date on which the person suffering the loss or damage had or should have had knowledge of it. However, the period of limitation shall not exceed five years from the date of the accident.

2. The period of limitation for actions arising out of carriage under this Convention other than those referred to in paragraph 1 of this Article shall in all cases be one year.

The period of limitation shall run from the date on which the vehicle arrived at the place of destination of the passenger or, in the case of a non-arrival from the date on which the vehicle ought to have arrived at the place of destination of the passenger.

3. A written claim shall suspend the period of limitation until the date on which the carrier rejects the claim by notification in writing and returns any documents handed to him in support of the claim. If a part of the claim is admitted, the period of limitation shall start to run again only in respect of that part of the claim which is still in dispute. The burden of proof of the receipt of a claim or of the reply and of the return of the documents shall rest with the party relying upon those facts. Further claims having the same object shall not suspend the running of the period of the limitation unless the carrier agrees to consider them.

4. Subject to the provisions of the preceding paragraph, the extension of the period of limitation shall be governed by the provisions of the law of the Court or tribunal seized of the case not including the rules relating to conflict of laws. That law shall also govern the fresh accrual of rights of action.'

The limitation period for personal injury actions is, accordingly, the later of three years from the date of the injury and three years from the date when the claimant has or should have had knowledge of the injury. Conversely, time in respect of property loss or damage runs from either when the vehicle arrived or when it should have arrived. The limitation period of three years has a longstop provision of five years for cases based on the discoverability of the injury. Property actions are limited to a one-year period. Article 22(4) makes extension of the limitation period a matter for domestic law. Extension probably does not include the postponement of a limitation period and, accordingly, it is unlikely that the provisions of ss 28 and 32 of the Limitation Act 1980 concerning disability, fraud and concealment will apply. For reasons which are discussed above in respect of the International Transport Convention Act 1983 and the Merchant Shipping Act 1995, it is also unlikely that the provisions of s 33 of the Limitation Act will apply, as s 33 may be seen to be not extending a limitation period but setting aside the limitation period contained in ss 11 and 14 of the Limitation Act 1980.

2   Miscellaneous statutes

(A)   THE CONSUMER PROTECTION ACT 1987

The Consumer Protection Act 1987 makes direct amendments to the Limitation Act 1980 principally by s 11A and consequential amendments to ss 14, 28, 32 and 33 (for a discussion of the Consumer Protection Act, see **Chapter 2**). The Act determines that the primary limitation period in respect of an action arising out of the supply of a defective product is either three years from the date when the cause of action accrued or three years from the injured person's date of knowledge (see ss 11A(4) and 14(1A) of the Limitation Act 1980). In fatal cases the period is the later of three years from the date of death and three years from the personal representative's date of knowledge (s 11A(5)). If there is more than one personal representative, the date of knowledge is the earliest (s 11A(7); see **Chapter 3**). There is, however, a longstop provision extinguishing the cause of action after 10 years from the date when the offending product was last supplied (s 11A(3)). Section 28 on disability and s 32 on fraud and concealment will apply to the Act, as will the provisions of s 33, but all extensions and postponements will be subject to the longstop of 10 years (see s 33(1A)(a)). This longstop provision could, therefore, extinguish a cause of action under the Act in a case of latent damage even before an injured person knew or could have known of his injury. It would also prevent, for example, a five-year-old child suing after the age of 15 in respect of any injury sustained due to a defective product. Other causes of action in negligence or breach of contract that might exist would, however, be unaffected.

In *Horne-Roberts v Smithkline Beecham* (p481) the court permitted a substitution of a new party pursuant to s 35 of the Limitation Act 1980 after the 10-year period in a case where a claimant sued the wrong manufacturer of the MMR vaccine. The claimant was given the vaccine in June 1990 and proceedings were issued on 25 August 1999, eight months within the longstop period but against the wrong manufacturers. The claimant sought to substitute the correct manufacturers after the expiry of the 10-year period. The Court of Appeal upheld the first instance decision, which had permitted the claimant to amend on the basis that the claimant's mistake had been one of identity only, and CPR 19.5 together with s 35(6)(a) permitted the substitution. The court was of the opinion that such an interpretation was not contrary to Council Directive 85/374, and that Parliament had incorporated the 10-year period into the Act and could have expressly excluded s 35 from applying to it if that had been its intention. However, in a similar subsequent action (*O'Byrne (by his mother and litigation friend) (FC) v Aventis Pasteur SA* (p587)), where a claimant also sought to add the manufacturer of a vaccine in substitution for the producer after the 10-year period had expired, the Supreme Court and both parties concurred that, following two references to the European Court of Justice (*O'Byrne v Sanofi Pasteur MSD Ltd (formerly Aventis Pasteur MSD Ltd) (Case C-127/04)* [2006] 1 WLR 1606 and *Aventis Pasteur SA v OB (Case C-358/08)* (unreported) given 2 December 2009), the court was prohibited from extending the fixed 10-year period by its domestic law, thus excluding s 35 (see **Chapter 7**).

(B)   THE NUCLEAR INSTALLATIONS ACT 1965

By s 15 of the Nuclear Installations Act 1965, an action for personal injury or death resulting from the radioactive properties of nuclear matter or from ionising radiation is barred if made after 30 years from the occurrence which gave rise to the claim. If the injury was as a result of a series of occurrences or as a result of a continued occurrence, the date of 30 years is from the last occurrence or the cessation of the continuing occurrence. If, however, the claim arises out of nuclear matter which has been stolen, lost, jettisoned or abandoned, the limitation period is shortened to 20 years from the date when it was stolen, lost, jettisoned or abandoned.

3   The Criminal Injuries Compensation Authority

An ex-gratia scheme came into force on 1 August 1964 designed to compensate the victims of crimes of violence with damages principally based upon common law principles but subject to various provisions of the scheme. The Board was eventually put on a statutory footing by the Criminal Injuries Compensation Act 1995, which currently operates a tariff-based system awarding damages in the range of £1,000–£500,000. The new tariff scheme applies to applications received on or after 1 April 2001. The scheme cannot apply to injuries before 1 August 1964, nor will it apply to injuries before 1 October 1979 if, at the time of the injury, the claimant was living in the same household as the perpetrator. The initial scheme went through a number of transformations and the last scheme in 1990 before the tariff system had a limitation period of three years from the date of the incident giving rise to the injury. Paragraph 4 of the 1990 Scheme allowed the Criminal Injuries Compensation Board, as it was then called, to waive that time limit, but the decision of the chairman not to waive it was deemed to be final. The scheme's guidelines indicated that the Board would give sympathetic consideration to late claims if they came from minors, from those who have difficulty in helping themselves in formulating a claim, and from those who do not immediately attribute their injury to the incident.

Under the new tariff scheme, the limitation period has been shortened to two years pursuant to paragraph 18. This allows a claims officer to waive the two-year time limit if it is considered, by reason of the particular circumstances of the case, that it is reasonable and in the interests of justice to do so. If the applicant is not content with the decision made by the claims officer, the applicant can ask for a review of the decision within 90 days of the decision being made. This period may also be extended if it is in the interests of justice to do so. Following that determination, an applicant may seek an appeal to the Criminal Injuries Compensation Appeals Panel within 90 days of the review decision. In *Hutton v First Tier Tribunal (Criminal Injuries Compensation* (p487) the wife and two children of a man murdered on 4 December 1966 sought to claim an award in respect of his death some 42 years later in June 2008. The delay was due to the mother having a nervous breakdown and the children being brought into care. The claims officer, the CICA, the First Tier judge and the Upper Tribunal all refused to exercise the discretion in para 18 to waive the time limit. The Court of Appeal permitted a judicial review of that decision on the basis that the Tribunal judge had applied the wrong test. Aikens LJ explained why:

'41. In my view Judge Ward undoubtedly erred in law in his construction of paragraph 18 of the Scheme terms. He considered that the first question he had to ask was whether there were any relevant "particular circumstances" in this case and the second question was whether or not it was in the "interests of justice" to waive the time limit. That misreads the last sentence of paragraph 18. That states that a Claims Officer "may waive" the 2 year time limit where he considers that "by reason of the particular circumstances of the case, it is reasonable and in the interests of justice to do so". To my mind the words "particular circumstances" mean the actual or distinct circumstances of this individual case. They do not mean "special" circumstances in the sense of being unusual or extraordinary circumstances. So the task of the Claims Officer or Reviewing Officer is to establish the actual circumstances of this particular case. Having done so he then has to ask: given the circumstances of this particular case, is it reasonable and in the interests of justice to waive the time limit.

42. In performing that exercise, I think that the wording requires that the Claims Officer must consider all relevant factors. These may include the length of the delay in making the claim, the reasons for the delay and the nature of the claim itself. The relative importance of particular factors will depend on the particular circumstances of the case being considered. The Claims Officer has to make an overall decision bearing all those circumstances in mind. In doing so he will have to take account of the fact that the general rule is that claims should be brought as soon as possible and, in any event, within two years of the incident giving rise to the claim.

43. So, I move on to the second question: assuming Judge Ward erred in law, is it arguable that he might reasonably have concluded that the time limit should be waived in this case. In my view it is. I accept that the period of the delay was very long indeed; it is nominally some 20 times greater than the maximum allowed. I also accept that the approach of Mr Hutton was to gather all the information he could find before making the claims and that this may have been a mistaken approach. I also take the point, made by Mr Thomas, that this delay may make the assessment of compensation (even the "standard" amounts under paragraphs 39 and 42) more difficult. But it seems to me to be reasonably arguable that on the particular facts of this case, the FTT could reasonably come to the conclusion that the time limit should have been waived by the Claims Officer. For reasons I give in [46] below, I have decided I should not go into this issue in further detail.

44. For these reasons I would grant permission to bring Judicial Review of Judge Ward's decision in relation to all three applicants. The case for Mr Hutton's mother and sister is even stronger, because they are both suffering

from mental problems and they cannot be blamed for any delays which may have resulted from the way Mr Hutton has gone about researching and presenting the claims.'

4   The Motor Insurers' Bureau

The Motor Insurers' Bureau (MIB) is a company limited by guarantee incorporated under the Companies Act 1929 and composed of representatives of insurers engaged in motor insurance. Pursuant to Agreements between it and initially the Minister of Transport, the MIB holds and administers funds to compensate victims of uninsured and untraced drivers who have suffered personal injury and damage in road traffic accidents. There are two Agreements: one concerned with uninsured drivers; and the other concerned with untraced drivers.

(i)   The Uninsured Drivers Agreement dated 13 August 1999

This Agreement concerns victims of personal injuries sustained by drivers driving whilst uninsured and was made between the MIB and the Secretary of State for the Environment, Transport and the Regions on 13 August 1999 and concerns accidents occurring on or after 1 October 1999. The Agreement supersedes the 1988 and 1972 Agreements and is supplemental to the original Agreement made on 31 December 1945. The 1988 Agreement governs any incident occurring between 31 December 1988 and 30 September 1999, and the 1972 Agreement governs any incident occurring between 1 December 1972 and 30 December 1988. Clause 5.1 of the 1999 Agreement provides that the MIB will, subject to clauses 6 and 17, satisfy a judgment for damages of a relevant liability to a claimant who has obtained a judgment against an uninsured driver.

The normal principles of limitation law apply in respect of any action against the uninsured defendant, and paragraph 2.3 of the explanatory notes contends that nothing in the Agreement is intended to vary the limitation rules applying to claimants not of full age or capacity and that the limitation period remains three years from the date of full age or capacity. Any such judgment against an uninsured driver is without limit in respect of personal injury claims but is limited to £250,000 with respect to property damage. The claimant's cause of action is not against the MIB but against the uninsured driver. The MIB may, however, be joined as a party in certain circumstances and prejudice to it is a relevant consideration under s 33 applications to disapply a limitation period (see *Straw v Hicks* 13 October 1983, CA, *Davis v Saltenpar* (p405) and *Liff v Peasley* [1980] 1 WLR 781). The 1999 Agreement contains a number of conditions precedent to the MIB's obligation and can constitute a procedural minefield for the unwary. By clause 7 the Agreement provides:

'(1)   MIB shall incur no liability under MIB's obligation unless an application is made to the person specified in clause 9(1)–

(a)   in such form,

(b)   giving such information about the relevant proceedings and other matters relevant to this Agreement, and

(c)   accompanied by such documents as MIB may reasonably require.'

Clause 9 provides:

'(1)   MIB shall incur no liability under MIB's obligation unless proper notice of the bringing of the relevant proceedings has been given by the Claimant not later than 14 days after the commencement of those proceedings –

(a)   In the case of proceedings in respect of a relevant liability which is covered by a contract of insurance with an insurer whose identity can be ascertained, to that insurer;

(b)   in any other case, to MIB.

(2)   In this clause "proper notice" means, except insofar as any part of such information or any copy document or other things already been supplied under clause 7 –

(a)   Notice in writing that proceedings have been commenced by a Claim Form, Writ or other means,

(b)   a copy of the sealed Claim Form, Writ or other official document providing evidence of the commencement of the proceedings and, in Scotland, a statement of the means of service,

(c)   a copy or details of any insurance policy providing benefits in the case of the death, bodily injury or damage to the property to which the proceedings relate where the claimant is the insured party and the benefits are available to him,

(d)   copies of all correspondence in the possession of the Claimant or (as the case may be) his solicitor or agent to or from the Defendant or the Defender or (as the case may be) his solicitor, insurers or agent which is relevant to –

(i)   the death, bodily injury or damage for which the Defendant or Defender is alleged to be responsible;
or

(ii)   any contract of insurance which covers, or which may or has been alleged to cover, liability for such death, injury or damage, the benefit of which is, or is claimed to be, available to Defendant or Defender,

(e)   subject to paragraph (3), a copy of the Particulars of Claim whether or not endorsed on the Claim Form, Writ or other originating process, and whether or not served (in England and Wales) on any Defendant or (in Scotland) on any Defender, and

(f)   a copy of all other documents which are required under the appropriate rules of procedure to be served on a Defendant or Defender with the Claim Form, Writ or other originating process or with the Particulars of Claim;

(g)   such other information about the relevant proceedings as MIB may reasonably specify.

(3)   If, in the case of proceedings commenced in England or Wales, the Particulars of Claim (including any document required to be served therewith) has not yet been served with the Claim Form or other originating process. paragraph (2)(e) shall be sufficiently complied with if a copy thereof is served on MIB not later than 7 days after it is served on the Defendant.'

Further, clause 10 requires service of the notice of proceedings:

'(1)   This clause applies where relevant proceedings are commenced in England or Wales.

(2)   MIB shall incur no liability under MIB's obligation unless the Claimant has, no later than the appropriate date, given notice in writing to the person specified in clause 9(1) of the date of service of the Claim Form or other originating process in the relevant proceedings.

(3)   In this clause, 'the appropriate date' means the day falling –

(a)   seven days after –
  (i)   the date when the Claimant receives notification from the court that service of the Claim Form or other originating process has occurred;
  (ii)   the date when the Claimant receives notification from the Defendant that service of the Claim Form or other originating process has occurred, or
  (iii)   the date of personal service, or
(b)   fourteen days after the date when service is deemed to have occurred in accordance with the Civil Procedure Rules, whichever of those days occur first.'

There are also further procedural requirements contained in clauses 11 and 12 such as the claimant being required to give notice to the MIB not less than 35 days before an application for judgment is made. Certain concessions are made with respect to these strict notice requirements in the explanatory notes at paragraphs 6.4 and 7.2.

Prior to the House of Lords' decision in *Horton v Sadler* (p482) a failure to comply with these onerous procedural conditions by a claimant's solicitors was likely to leave the claimant without a remedy from the MIB if the limitation period had expired. This was because, under the rule in *Walkley v Precision Forgings Ltd* (p705), any new proceedings begun after the expiry of the limitation period (in an effort to comply a second time around with the MIB conditions) were previously excluded from a s 33 dispensation. However, following the abolition of the *Walkley* decision in *Horton*, a claimant is now permitted to seek a s 33 discretion which, on the facts in *Horton*, was exercised against the MIB who were therefore required to satisfy the judgment against an uninsured defendant – notwithstanding a non-compliance with conditions precedent to liability in a first action (see **Chapter 5**). *Horton* was followed in the case of *Richardson v Watson* (p621).

(ii)   The Untraced Drivers' Agreement dated 14 February 2003

The second Agreement, concerning untraced drivers, was made between the MIB and the Department of Transport on 14 February 2003 and replaces the agreement between the MIB and the Secretary of State for Environment made on 22 November 1972 and a similar agreement in 1996. The 2003 Agreement covers death and bodily injury or damage to property occurring after 14 February 2003. Awards of damages are made in respect of applicants who sustain injury due to the negligent driving of an unidentified person who remains untraced. Pursuant to clause 4(3), conditions for the payment of an award before a Supplementary Agreement taking effect from 1 February 2009 included:

'(3)   The conditions referred to in paragraph (1)(f) are that –

(a)   Except in a case to which sub-paragraph (b) applies, the application must be made not later than –

(i)   three years after the date of the event which is the subject of the application in the case of a claim for compensation for death or bodily injury (whether or not damage to property has also arisen from the same event); or

(ii)   nine months after that event in the case of a claim for compensation for damage to property (whether or not death or bodily injury has also arisen from the same event);

(b)   in a case where the applicant could not reasonably have been expected to have become aware of the existence of bodily injury or damage to property, the application must have been made as soon as practicable after he did become (or ought reasonably to have become) aware of it and in any case not later than:–

(i)   fifteen years after the date of the event which is the subject of the application in the case of a claim for compensation for death or bodily injury (whether or not damage to property has also arisen from the same event); or

(ii)   two years after the date of that event in the case of a claim for compensation for damage to property (whether or not death or bodily injury has also arisen from the same event).'

In addition, the applicant or a person acting on the applicant's behalf must have reported the event to the police within 14 days of the occurrence in respect of death or bodily injury or five days after occurrence with respect to property damage.

The limitation period under the unamended Agreement was accordingly three years after the injury was sustained for a personal injury claim but nine months for property damage. The period was extendable until that time when the applicant became aware or ought to have become aware of the existence of the bodily injury or damage to property, but there was a longstop of 15 years with respect to personal injury and two years with respect to property damage. The applicant had a right of appeal pursuant to clause 18 if he did not accept the determination made by the MIB under clause 7 and had six weeks to give notice of his appeal. The appeal was determined by an arbitrator who, pursuant to clause 22, would give a preliminary decision. Not later than 28 days after the date of sending that preliminary decision, the parties could accept it or submit written observations upon it or request an oral hearing. The 2003 scheme also provided that the MIB could make awards of compensation on a provisional damages basis or by way of periodical payments. Similar limitation periods within the 1972 Agreement (and, by parity of reasoning, the 2003 Agreement) were subjected to an attack in *Byrne v Motor Insurers' Bureau* (p357). A claim was advanced under the 1972 Agreement by a 12-year-old boy who had suffered injury when he was aged three. The MIB rejected the application on the basis that it was out of time. The court held that the failure to have an extended period of limitation similar to s 28 of the Limitation Act 1980 (which would have preserved the limitation period until the applicant was 21) meant the Agreement failed to implement the relevant EC Directive 84/5 and gave rise to a *Francovich* claim against the UK state.

This led the MIB to issue a Memorandum of Understanding:

'Following the Court of Appeal ruling in the court case of Byrne and the Secretary of State for Transport the government has asked the Motor Insurers' Bureau to reconsider those cases that were summarily rejected because the claim had not been made within the three years as required by the relevant Untraced Drivers Agreement and which fulfil certain conditions. The conditions are:

- The Claimant must have been the victim of an untraced driver in an accident occurring no earlier than 31 December 1988 (the deadline for the implementation of the Second Motor Insurance Directive – 84/5 EEC).
- The Claimant, the issue of limitation apart, must be entitled to an award under the relevant Untraced Drivers' Agreement.
- The Claimant must be or have been unable to claim compensation because of the 3 year time limit contained in the relevant Untraced Drivers' Agreement. For the avoidance of doubt, the MIB will not process a Claimant's application if any other exclusion applies or applied.
- Had the driver of the accident been traced, the limitation period (as provided for in the 1980 Act or in the 1973 Act as appropriate) for bringing a claim against that driver would have expired after 4 December 2003.
- The Claimant must be in time to bring a *Francovich* action against the Secretary of State, ie within 6 years from the date of accrual of the cause of action after the relevant limitation period under the 1980 Act or the 1973 Act as appropriate had expired. (For example, this would mean 6 years from age 21 in cases of personal injury sustained by a minor).'

In *Spencer v Secretary of State for Work and Pensions* (p669) the Court of Appeal confirmed that the limitation period for a *Francovich* claim was six years from the date of the accident and not from the refusal of the MIB to make an award.

The MIB then produced, in 2008, a Supplementary Agreement to the 2003 Agreement which effectively brings MIB applications within the Limitation Act. The wording of clause 4(3)(a)(i) (set out above) is replaced so that the application must have been made within:

'subject to paragraph (a)(ii), the time limits provided for the victims of traced drivers bringing actions in tort by the Limitation Act 1980 …'

Paragraph (a)(ii) does, however, preserve the two-year period for property damage claims.

In addition, a new clause 23(f) permits an arbitrator on appeal to determine if a s 33 discretion should be exercised where the MIB refuses an award on limitation grounds and the applicant appeals.

Accordingly, both the uninsured and untraced drivers Agreements more closely approximate to the principles under the Limitation Act 1980.

5 The Foreign Limitation Periods Act 1984

The Foreign Limitation Periods Act 1984, which came into force on 1 October 1985, provides for the effective reversal of much of the common law position concerning which limitation law applies when an English court is dealing with a cause of action that occurred in a foreign jurisdiction. At common law, the English court might entertain a foreign action if it were not statute barred in English law, even though it might be statute barred under the relevant foreign law jurisdiction. Conversely, an English court would refuse to determine an action which was statute barred under English law, even if it was not barred under the law of the foreign relevant jurisdiction. The common law position was complicated by an exception that the English court would not entertain a foreign action, if the effect of the limitation period was to extinguish the claimant's right as a matter of substantive law rather than bar his remedy as a matter of procedural law (*Huber v Steiner* (1835) 2 Bing NC 202). In such circumstances, the foreign law period would apply.

The 1984 Act provides by s 1 that, where in any action in England the law of another country falls to be considered, it is the law of that other country relating to limitation which is to be applied and not the English law on limitation. The only exception is where a case requires the substantive law of England and of the foreign country to be considered. In such cases, both sets of limitation laws have to be applied. This situation, where the two sets of limitation laws are relevant, principally arises in cases based on tort which are brought in an English court but where the substantive law of England and of the foreign country are applicable. To be actionable in the English court, the case at common law must be actionable both under the law of the territory where the tort took place as well as being actionable under English law (see *Philips v Eyre* (1870) LR6 QB 1, *Chaplin v Boys* [1971] AC 356). In these types of case, the effect of the Act is to enquire whether the action is in time both within the English law of limitation and the relevant foreign jurisdiction law on limitation. The Act further provides that, if the foreign rules on limitation being applied by the court give the court a discretion, the English court, so far as is practicable, is required to exercise that discretion as it would be exercised by the court of the other country (s 1(4)).

However, whether an action has been started in time – in terms of the initiating of proceedings – is a matter which falls to be determined by the law of England and Wales rather than the law of the foreign jurisdiction, principally the law relating to the issue and service of proceedings. Moreover, the provisions of s 35 of the Limitation Act 1980, concerned with new claims in pending actions, are also deemed to apply rather than any equivalent law of a foreign jurisdiction.

Section 2(1) creates an exception to the general rule that the foreign limitation law will apply. If the foreign limitation law period conflicts with public policy, it is not applicable. Public policy is not defined in the Act. In *Durham v T & N plc* (p418) a widow's claim for compensation arising out of the death of her husband from mesothelioma, brought against the defendants as occupiers of a Canadian factory which negligently exposed the deceased to asbestos, was held to be statute barred under Quebec law. The relevant limitation law was the law of Quebec and, accordingly, the claim was statute barred pursuant to s 1 of the Foreign Limitation Periods Act 1984. The effect of the provision was to exclude the law of English limitation. The court held that there was no conflict with public policy simply because there was a less generous limitation provision in Quebec than in England.

Similar sentiments were expressed in *Connelly v RTZ Corporation* (p384), where the absence of any equivalent of a s 33 discretion to disapply the limitation period in Namibian limitation law was held not to conflict with public policy. The relevant Namibian law allowed three years for a limitation period in a personal injury case from the date of discoverability of the injury. An extensive discussion of what might constitute a conflict with public policy is to be found in the non-personal injury case of *Gotha City (a body corporate) v Sotheby's (an unlimited company); Federal Republic of Germany v Sotheby's* (1998) Times, 8 October. In this case an early seventeenth century painting went missing from an art collection in Germany at the end of the Second World War but appeared for sale in a Sotheby's auction in 1992. Part of the dispute concerned whether certain features of German limitation law conflicted with English public policy. The trial judge indicated that public policy should be used only in exceptional circumstances to disapply a foreign limitation period and where the foreign limitation law was contrary to a fundamental principle of justice.

By s 2(2) a conflict with public policy is established if the person who is statute barred under the foreign limitation period will suffer undue hardship. An example of this provision is to be found in the personal injury claim of *Jones v Trollope Colls Cementation Overseas Ltd* (p504). Miss Jones was injured in a road traffic accident on 8 May 1984 in Karachi, whilst being driven by the servant or agent of the defendants. A collision took place which, it was alleged, was due to the excessive speed of the defendants' employee. The relevant foreign law to be applied was Pakistani law on limitation, which provided for a 12-month period. The claimant issued proceedings in England on 26 July 1986 outside that period but within the primary limitation period for English law. Her case, however, was statute barred under the provisions of the Act, but the court did disapply the Pakistani law provisions on the grounds that her case fell within s 2(2) because the claimant would suffer undue hardship. The court was of the view that undue hardship must be excessive hardship, namely something greater than the circumstances warranted. On the facts of that case, Miss Jones spent a long time in hospital and the defendants had said that their insurers would deal with her case, and the court accordingly was of the view that undue hardship had been sustained.

Hardship in this context must be that which arises from the disadvantageous provisions of the foreign limitation law rather than from English law (see *Arab Monetary Fund v Hashim* [1993] 1 Lloyd's Rep 843, *Chagos Islanders v Attorney General* [2003] EWHC 2222 (QB), [2000] All ER (D) 166).

In *Harley v Smith* (p461), divers working in Saudi territorial waters suffered personal injuries due to the water being contaminated with chemicals, and they brought claims in England just within a three-year period. The law of the Kingdom of Saudi Arabia applied under the Foreign Limitation Periods Act 1984. The parties disputed whether the domestic law was governed by Shari'ah law, in which case the claims would not be statute barred as Shari'ah law did not have a time limitation, or whether it was governed by Saudi Labour Law Article 222, which imposed a period of 12 months from the accident or termination of the work relationship. The claimants' case was put on three grounds: first, Shari'ah law applied; secondly, if Art 222 applied because the claimants were paid for a further three years, the working relationship had not determined until pay stopped and the case had been brought in time; and, thirdly, the s 2 threshold was crossed as the claimants would suffer undue hardship. The trial judge found for the claimants on grounds 2 and 3. On appeal, the court reversed these decisions and found for the claimants on the basis of ground 1, as the defendants had not produced sufficient evidence to demonstrate that Shari'ah law would have been displaced in circumstances where the expert evidence on the applicable law was contradictory. The court took a further opportunity to reinforce the stringent requirements of the 'undue hardship' test. The trial judge's view was summarised by the court as follows:

'29. The judge reminded himself of the observations of this Court in *Jones v Trollope Colls Cement Overseas Limited and another* (24 January 1990, unreported), *Arab Monetary Fund v Hashim and others* [1996] 1 Lloyd's Rep 589 and *Durham v T & N PLC and others* (1 May 1996, unreported). He held (at paragraph [94] of his judgment) that the following propositions could be deduced from those authorities:

"(i) That it is not sufficient to cross the 'undue hardship' threshold [posed by section 2(2) of the 1984 Act] by reason only of the fact that the foreign limitation period is less generous than that of the English jurisdiction.

(ii) That the claimant must satisfy the court that he or she will suffer greater hardship in the particular circumstances than would normally be the case.

(iii) That in considering (ii) the focus is on the interests of the individual claimant or claimants and is not upon a balancing exercise between the interests of the claimants on one hand and the defendant on the other."

30. The judge went on to say this:

"[95] Applying these principles on the basis that the Saudi limitation period was either 12 months from the date of the incident or somewhat longer, but no longer than the expiration of the fixed term contracts that each claimant had, I would be satisfied that the 'undue hardship' threshold had been crossed in respect of each claimant in this case. On the premise to which I have referred the following factors would persuade me that this is so:

(i) Each claimant was impeded in obtaining local advice and representation in the KSA in the manner I referred to in paragraphs 33–35 above.

(ii) Had each of them obtained such advice or representation at the time, their respective interests would probably have been protected.

(iii) Each sought advice in the UK as soon as it was practicable to do so upon their return.

(iv) Each was misled by advice that was received to the effect that the limitation period did not begin until June 2006.

(v) Those giving the advice, whether in the UK or in the KSA, were disadvantaged because of the uncertainty of the legal position in the KSA and, as a result, the claimants were victims of that uncertainty.

(vi) Through no fault of their own they will be deprived of any opportunity of seeking any kind of redress as a result of the incident unless the limitation period is disapplied."

It may be said that none of those factors had been relied upon by the claimants in paragraph 7 of their amended replies; and that the judge did not find persuasive the factor which was advanced in that paragraph (the payment of wages throughout the one year period).'

The Court of Appeal disagreed with the judge's analysis and stated:

'51. I think there is force, also, in the criticism that, in holding that he would have disapplied the twelve month limitation period under article 222(1) of the Labour Law (had that period commenced at or earlier than the end of the strict contractual period), the judge exercised his discretion on a false basis.

52. The judge appreciated that that each of the claimants consulted lawyers shortly after they returned to the United Kingdom in June 2003: paragraph 95(iii) of his judgment. Each had accepted that in his oral evidence: (transcript:

15 December 2008, page 36 (Mr Harley), page 73 (Mr Hopley), page 83 (Mr Iles)). It was not in dispute – but, in any event, it was plainly to be inferred – that they had done so with a view to making a claim against their employer in respect of the incident on 7 May 2003. It is clear that, by the time the claimants returned to the United Kingdom in June 2003, they knew the circumstances in which the incident had occurred, they knew that they had suffered injury as a result, and they knew that Mr Smith (and ADAMS, as the common employer) might have some responsibility for the incident. By the end of June 2003, the difficulties which the claimants had encountered in obtaining access to a lawyer while they had remained in Saudi Arabia, to which the judge referred in paragraph [95(i)] of his judgment – had ceased to be of relevance. The real question was why no steps were taken – either in the United Kingdom or in Saudi Arabia – to commence proceedings within, say twelve months of June 2003 (which would have been within any limitation period applicable under article 222(1) of the Labour Law).

53.   The judge held (at paragraph [95](iv) of his judgment) that "each was misled by advice that was received to the effect that the limitation period did not begin until June 2006". If that is a finding as to the position under Saudi law, I have found no evidential basis to support it. The advice as to Saudi law – in a letter dated 3 May 2004 to Mr Hopley's solicitors from the Al-Sohaibani law office – was that a limitation period of one year was provided in labour laws regarding claims against the employer "for rights and entitlements arising out of and resulted from the employment contract between the parties": if the claim had no connection with the employment contract, there would be no relevant limitation period. Be that as it may, the factor relied upon by the judge is not that undue hardship arose from the fact that the relevant limitation period under Saudi law was twelve months (if that was, indeed the case); but rather from the fact that the lawyers in the United Kingdom whom the claimants consulted in June 2003 did not appreciate that that was, or might be, the position. But that cannot be a relevant factor. The question is not whether undue hardship is caused by wrong advice; but whether it is caused by the application of the foreign limitation period. There is nothing to suggest that, on the basis of the advice which they had received, the claimants chose to delay the commencement of proceedings until after the period of twelve months had expired; or that, if they had appreciated the need to commence proceedings within the twelve month period, there would have been any difficulty, in the present case, in doing so.

54.   The judge went on to hold (at paragraph [95](v) of his judgment) that those giving advice to the claimants, whether in the United Kingdom or in Saudi Arabia, "were disadvantaged because of the uncertainty of the legal position in the KSA" and "as a result, the victims were victims of that uncertainty". But, again, if that were correct, it would not be the application of the Saudi law relating to limitation that caused undue hardship. The uncertainty of the legal position, if it been known to be uncertain, would have made it necessary to bring proceedings sooner rather than later in order to avoid the risk, to which the uncertainty gives rise, of being out of time: the uncertainty does not add to the hardship (if any) caused by the need to bring the proceedings within twelve months. And, as I have said, there is nothing to suggest that, if the lawyers had appreciated the need to commence proceedings within twelve months in order

to avoid the risk of being out of time, there would have been any difficulty, in the present case, in doing so.

55. It follows, in my view, that the judge was in error in thinking that any of the matters to which he referred in sub-paragraphs (i), (iii), (iv) and (v) of paragraph [95] of his judgment led to a conclusion that application of a twelve month limitation period under Saudi law would cause undue hardship to the claimants for the purposes of section 2(2) of the Foreign Limitation Periods Act 1984. The judge failed to apply the propositions which (correctly, at paragraph [94] of his judgment) he had derived from the authorities to which he had referred. He should have appreciated that it was not sufficient to cross the threshold by reason only that the period of twelve months is less generous than the period of three years allowed under English law: and he should have appreciated that the application of a limitation period of twelve months (instead of three years) led to no greater hardship in the particular circumstances than would normally be the case.'

6   The Protection from Harassment Act 1997

Claims brought under this Act are specifically excluded from the personal injury regime under s 11 of the Limitation Act 1980, pursuant to an amendment to the Act under s 11(1A) which specifically excludes an action brought under s 3 of the Protection from Harassment Act 1997. Accordingly, the time limit is six years, being an action brought under statute pursuant to s 9 of the Limitation Act 1980 and is not one to which s 14 or s 33 applies (see *Saha v Imperial College of Science, Technology and Medicine* (p638) for the interaction of a personal injury claim held to be statute barred and a harassment claim brought in time).

9 Bringing and serving proceedings

Authors' note – CPR changes

Since the publication of the previous edition of this book, the rules regarding service of claim forms in CPR Part 6 have been substantially replaced with a new set.

Whilst the narrative below relates to the new (current) rules, much of the relevant jurisprudence relates to the old.

We have not sought to alter references to the old rules, either in this chapter (when citing from authorities relating to them) or when summarising such authorities in **Part 2**. We instead refer to the table below for any necessary cross-referencing.

References to the old service rules are listed in italics in the Table of Statutory Instruments at the beginning of this book. The old service rules are also reproduced in the **Appendix**, again italicised.

Please also note that CPR 7.5, which governs the time when a claim form is considered served, was replaced at the same time. The new (current) rule 7.5 provides that a claim form is served for the purposes of the four-month validity period when a claimant takes the relevant step under the rules; previous questions of later deemed service arise.

Subject matter	Old rule (pre-1 October 2008)	Corresponding current rule
Methods of service	*6.2*	6.3
Who is to serve	*6.3*	6.4
Personal service	*6.4*	6.5
Address for service	*6.5*	6.6–6.10
Service on children and patients	*6.6*	6.13
Alternative service	*6.8*	6.15
Dispensing with service	*6.9*	6.16

Introduction

This chapter deals with the mechanics of commencing proceedings in time. There are two elements to this: first, the claim must be brought within the relevant limitation period; and, secondly, it must be served in time.

Historically, the second of these, service, has represented the area of highest risk for claimants and their solicitors. There were two main reasons for this.

The first, as will be seen in **Chapter 10**, is that retrospective applications to extend the period of the validity of an unserved claim form are seldom successful. This is clear from a series of Court of Appeal decisions: *Vinos v Marks & Spencer plc* (p701), *Kaur v CTP Coil Ltd* (p514), *Godwin v Swindon Borough Council* (p444), *Anderton v Clwyd County Council (No 2)* (p303) and *Hashtroodi v Hancock* (p466).

The second was the House of Lords' 1979 decision in *Walkley v Precision Forgings Ltd* (p705). In that case, the claimant had issued and served a writ in 1971, and later discontinued this action. After issuing a second writ in 1977, he needed leave under s 2D of the Limitation Act 1939, as amended (the forerunner of s 33 of the 1980 Act), for the primary limitation period under s 2A to be disapplied. This was refused on the grounds that s 2D was not even applicable, since it was not s 2A that had prejudiced the plaintiff, who within the period provided by it had commenced an action for damages for the same injuries. Accordingly, his second action was struck out as being vexatious and an abuse of the process of court.

The result of this was that failure to serve court proceedings in time, once the limitation period has expired, was almost always fatal to the claimant's case against the original defendants. In consequence, a claimant who failed to serve in time, after expiry of the limitation period, was invariably in a worse position than the claimant who failed to issue in time. The latter can apply for the court's discretion to be exercised in his favour under s 33 of the 1980 Act, whereas the former, if unable to renew, would hardly ever have any remedy except against his former solicitors.

The effect of *Horton v (1) Sadler and (2) MIB* (p482), in which the House of Lords has departed from its earlier decision in *Walkley* (that is, it has overruled it), has been, however, to take much of the sting out of technical service failures. It is certain that the judiciary is now empowered to permit second actions brought out of time to be pursued by the granting of s 33 discretion in deserving cases; an attempt to argue that such duplicate proceedings constitute an abuse of process was roundly rejected in *Aktas v Adepta* (p296). This development – in conjunction with the clarification that, in the absence of any material prejudice to the defendant, the s 33 discretion should normally be exercised in the claimant's favour (*Cain v Francis* (p360)) – means that service failures will often not have the catastrophic consequences that they did previously.

It must not be assumed, however, that judges will always be willing to exercise this discretion in cases of failure to serve a first action in time after the limitation period has already expired. By definition, the second claim will be potentially susceptible to a limitation defence. There would, moreover, almost certainly be adverse costs consequences from the earlier debacle. Therefore, it might be prudent of practitioners to continue to heed the following observations of Mummery LJ in *Anderton v Clwyd County Council (No 2)*:

'The consequences of failure to comply with the rules governing service of a claim form are extremely serious for a claimant and his legal advisers. The situation becomes fraught with procedural perils when a claimant or his solicitor leaves the service of a claim form, which has been issued just before the end of the relevant statutory limitation period, until the last day or two of the period of 4 months allowed for service by rule 7.5(2) or, even worse, almost to the end of an extension of time granted by the court. If the claim form is then served by first class post, by fax or in another manner permitted by the CPR there is high risk, demonstrated by *Godwin* and by the cases under appeal, of a successful application by the defendant to strike out the claim on the ground of non-compliance with the rules and of the cause of action then being statute barred. The risks never need to be run: they can easily be avoided by progressing the proceedings in accordance with the spirit and letter of the CPR. Now that the disputed interpretations of the CPR have been resolved by *Godwin* and by this judgment, there will be very few (if any) acceptable excuses for future failures to observe the rules for service of a claim form. The courts will be entitled to adopt a strict approach, even though the consequences may sometimes appear to be harsh in individual cases.'

PRACTICAL ADVICE

Such is the peril in which claimant lawyers are placed that it may be helpful to suggest some practical tips at the outset:

1.   Claim forms are for serving. Unless the purpose of the claim form is purely protective, to preserve the claimant's position under limitation law, the claim form and the particulars of claim should almost always be served as soon as is reasonably possible.
2.   It is necessary to select a single method of service under the rules and to be sure to achieve it. It is therefore necessary to ascertain in advance the appropriate address. Merely posting a copy claim form to a defendant's solicitor who has not been authorised or nominated to accept service of it does not constitute service under either CPR 6.3(1)(b) (postal service on defendants) or CPR 6.7 (service on defendant's solicitors).
3.   It is important to keep control of service during the fourth month of validity. Consequently, there is a strong case during this vital last month for claimant's solicitors to effect service themselves rather than leave it to the court.
4.   Allow time for things to go wrong, for example through a defendant having gone abroad or through letters attempting postal service being returned undelivered. Save in exceptional and compelling circumstances, do not leave service until late in the last month.
5.   It is desirable to check that the defendant has received the proceedings (for example, in postal service, that they have reached him). Sometimes it may be suitable to arrange an appointment for personal service.
6.   Keep good evidence of when proceedings were brought and the claim form served.
7.   If all else fails, serve the claim form in time without the particulars of claim.

BRINGING PROCEEDINGS WITHIN THE LIMITATION PERIOD

To avoid a potential limitation defence, proceedings must be brought within the relevant period (in most personal injury cases, three years from the date of the accrual of the cause of action or date of knowledge, whichever is later). Therefore, in respect of a simple accident on 31 January 2010 of which the claimant immediately has knowledge, proceedings must be brought no later than 31 January 2013: *Dodds v Walker* (p411). If they are brought on 1 February 2013, they will be out of time. Note, however, that, if the day on which limitation expires is not a working day (ie it is a weekend or bank holiday), a claimant has until the next working day to bring his claim: CPR 2.8(5), *Pritam Kaur v S Russell & Sons Ltd* (p613), *The Clifford Maersk* (p377). Thus, if the same hypothetical accident were to have occurred on 2

February 2010, the claimant would have until 4 February 2013 to bring proceedings (the 2nd and the 3rd being Saturday and Sunday).

The use of the word 'brought' rather than 'issued' is deliberate and important. Practitioners (and judges) often talk about whether not proceedings have been issued in time, but this is not strictly correct. The issuing of proceedings is an act of the court. Bringing proceedings is an act of the claimant preparatory to the court issuing. Proceedings can therefore be brought on a date earlier than that on which they are issued.

The distinction is potentially crucial, as it is the bringing rather than issuing of proceedings that stops the limitation clock. It follows that the limitation clock can be stopped before proceedings have been issued. It follows again that a claim can be brought in time for the purposes of limitation, even if actually issued outside the limitation period.

This is made explicit by CPR PD 7A:

'Start of proceedings

5.1   Proceedings are started when the court issues a claim form at the request of the claimant (see rule 7.2) *but where the claim form as issued was received in the court office on a date earlier than the date on which it was issued by the court, the claim is "brought" for the purposes of the Limitation Act 1980 and any other relevant statute on that earlier date.*

5.2   The date on which the claim form was received by the court will be recorded by a date stamp either on the claim form held on the court file or on the letter that accompanied the claim form when it was received by the court.

5.3   An enquiry as to the date on which the claim form was received by the court should be directed to a court officer.

5.4   Parties proposing to start a claim which is approaching the expiry of the limitation period should recognise the potential importance of establishing the date the claim form was received by the court and should themselves make arrangements to record the date.

5.5   Where it is sought to start proceedings against the estate of a deceased defendant where probate or letters of administration have not been granted, the claimant should issue the claim against "the personal representatives of A.B. deceased". The claimant should then, before the expiry of the period for service of the claim form, apply to the court for the appointment of a person to represent the estate of the deceased.' (emphasis added)

The effect of this was made clear in *Barnes v St Helens MBC* (p321). The claimant suffered personal injury before he turned 18, which he did on 5 November 2001. He delivered the claim form and appropriate cheque (personally via his solicitor) to the county court on 4 November 2004 (the day prior to the expiry of the limitation period) with a request that the claim be issued and then returned for service. However, due to industrial action by staff, the court did not issue the claim form until four days later, on 8 November. The defendant argued that the claim was 'brought' at the date of issue and was therefore out of time.

The Court of Appeal held that, where the claimant took any necessary step required to enable the proceedings to be started, he did not take the risk that the court might be closed or would not process the claim properly. It reasoned that expiry of the limitation period was fixed by reference to something that the claimant had to do, rather than something which someone else such as the court has to do. Thus, the time at which a claimant 'brought' his claim to the court with a request that it be issued was something that he had to do; the time at which his request was complied with by the court was not within his control. In this context, 'to bring' did not mean the same as 'to start'. The Act could properly be construed so that, in the context of the CPR, a claim was 'brought' when the claimant's request for the issue of a claim form was delivered to the correct court office during its opening hours. Receipt of a claim form by the court did not involve a transactional act; it was a unilateral act of the claimant to deliver it. The court staff who received the documents were not performing any judicial function and had no power to reject the claim form. A claimant was to be given the full period of limitation in which to bring the claim and does not take the risk that the court will fail to process it in time. There was, therefore, a distinction between when a claim was 'brought' for the purposes of the 1980 Act and when it 'started' for the purpose of CPR 7.2. The latter was the date of issue on the claim form, fixed as the time within which the proceedings had to be served. The former could be an earlier date. In the instant case, it was earlier, and the proceedings were brought in time.

It should be noted, however, that the ratio of *Barnes* was explicitly confined to the situation contemplated by the Practice Direction (that is to say, receipt by the court office of the claim form). This necessarily entails actual delivery by whatever means permitted by the Rules to the correct court office during the hours in which that office is open (paras 2 and 3 of CPR PD2A). The court made it clear that different considerations might apply if delivery was made to the wrong place or outside office hours.

As regards these unresolved considerations, the better authority is probably to the effect that, when the claim form is delivered to a proper court office (even if, strictly speaking, the wrong one for that claim: *Sharma v Knight* [1986] 1 WLR 757) on a given day, even if after hours, the claim was 'brought' on that day for the purposes of limitation: *Van Aken v Camden LBC* (p699), *Whealing Horton & Toms Ltd v Riverside Housing Association Ltd* (p710). However, there is authority pointing the other way (*Barker v Hambleton DC* (p320)), and claimants and their solicitors would be well advised not to seek to test this theory.

Thus, whilst a claim form is always 'issued' for the purposes of starting the claim and calculating the time for service on the date endorsed by the court, that is not necessarily the date on which proceedings are brought for the purposes of limitation. The date on which proceedings are brought for the purposes of limitation may often be days earlier, sometimes weeks earlier, and occasionally months earlier.

This distinction is becoming increasingly important, as court resources become more stretched and bulk issue centres and the like become more frequent. The days of being able to walk up to the counter of the local court and have the claim form issued there and then are long gone in most areas.

It follows that (1) claimants and their advisers should be astute to ensure that they have evidence when proceedings were actually brought, lest they are issued at a later date outside the limitation period, and (2) defendants and their advisers should not assume that the date of issue on the claim form is determinative for the purposes of limitation.

Both these points are well illustrated by the recent professional negligence case of *Page v Hewetts Solicitors* (p592). Time started running in respect of the cause of action in question on 6 February 2003. As this was subject to a fixed six-year period (with no s 33 discretion), if the claim was brought after 6 February 2009 it was irredeemably statue barred. Proceedings were issued, although the precise circumstances surrounding that were in dispute. The claimant's solicitor (L) gave evidence that the drafting of the claim form and particulars of claim was completed in December 2008 and that bundles were sent to the court by document exchange at that time. L claimed that the reason the claim form showed a date of 17 February 2009 was that the forms were lost by the court and a fresh claim had to be issued. The defendants successfully applied for summary judgment on the basis that the proceedings were issued on 17 February 2009 and therefore were statute barred. The master held that he was not satisfied, on the balance of probabilities, that the claim form did not reach the post room or the registry, bringing the claim outwith the Limitation Act 1980 by 11 days. The claimant appealed, but the judge upheld the master's findings and dismissed the claim. The claimants appealed again, this time successfully. The Court of Appeal held that the master had applied the wrong test. The question was not whether he was satisfied on the balance of probabilities, but whether the claimants had no real prospect of showing that the documents arrived at the court office. The master and judge also erred in assuming that the systems that should have been followed were in fact followed when it was not unknown for the court to mislay important documents. On an application for summary judgment the court was required to consider not merely the current state of the evidence but also what evidence might reasonably be expected to be adduced at trial. The court had to approach the question on the footing that there was a real prospect that the claimants would show that documents put into the document exchange were delivered at least as far as the court's post room and perhaps as far as the registry. The judges below were also in error in holding that the 'claim form as issued' must be the same piece of paper as that received in the court office within the limitation period, with the consequence that the claimants could not rely on the 'lost' claim as bringing forward the date on which the action was brought. The Court of Appeal held that this was the wrong subject matter to debate. When an action was 'brought' for the purpose of the Act was a question of construction of the Act. It was not a question of construction of the CPR, or of a practice direction. Taken literally, the ratio of *Barnes v St Helens MBC* was that, once the claimant had delivered his request for the issue of a claim form to the court office, he had 'brought' his action. If L's evidence was correct, the claimants had done so. A purposive interpretation of the relevant provision supported this same conclusion. The construction of the Act favoured in *Barnes v St Helens MBC* was based on risk allocation. A claimant's risk stopped once he had delivered his request to the court office. It would be unjust for a claimant to be held responsible for any failings thereafter, such being beyond his control. CPR PD7 could not alter the correct construction of the Act, and a would-be litigant was not responsible for any shortcomings of the court: *Aly v Aly* (1984) 81 LSG 283 and *Riniker v University College London* (1999) Times, 17 April, considered. Therefore, if the claimants established that the claim form was delivered in due time to the court office, accompanied by a request to issue and the appropriate fee, the action would not be statute barred.

In the result, the court ordered that the matter be determined by trial of it as a preliminary issue. Whilst the ultimate outcome of this issue is not known, it can be seen that the claimant's difficulties arose because the evidence of when proceedings were brought was less than clear, and that the defendant's application failed (with the result that they had to pay 75% of the costs of the application and of the appeal – [2012] EWCA Civ 879) because it was predicated on an assumption that date of issue of the claim form was determinative for the purposes of limitation.

SERVICE – ROADS TO RUIN

There are two roads to ruin. The first is simply to fail to make any effort to serve the proceedings in time. This is a time-related failure and is considered under the heading

'Time for service' below. The second is to attempt to serve the proceedings in time, but for the attempt to fail because the rules have not been followed correctly. This is a method-related failure and is considered under the heading 'Methods of service', which leads to the associated section headed 'Special types of defendant' for whom particular procedures have been specified.

The rules on service underwent considerable revision on 1 October 2008 (and thus since the previous edition of this book). Many of these are beneficial to claimants. However, not all of them are, and pitfalls remain aplenty.

This chapter does not consider methods of attempting to return to the right road, such as applications for extensions. These form the subject of the next chapter.

Time for service

SERVICE OF CLAIM FORM

The service of a claim form is governed by CPR 7.5 which provides that:

'(1)   Where the claim form is served within the jurisdiction, the claimant must complete the step required by the following table in relation to the particular method of service chosen, before 12.00 midnight on the calendar day four months after the date of issue of the claim form.

(2)   Where the claim form is to be served out of the jurisdiction, the claim form must be served in accordance with Section IV of Part within 6 months of the date of issue.'

The table for CPR 7.5(1) provides as follows:

'Method of service	Step required
First class post, document exchange or other service which provides for delivery on the next business day	Posting, leaving with, delivering to or collection by the relevant service provider
Delivery of the document to or leaving it at the relevant place	Delivering to or leaving the document at the relevant place
Personal service under rule 6.5	Completing the relevant step required by rule 6.5(3)
Fax	Completing the transmission of the fax
Other electronic method	Sending the e-mail or other electronic transmission'

It can thus be seen that, in crucial distinction to the previous rules, service is complete when the claimant takes the relevant step under the rules, irrespective of when the claim form is actually received or delivered or when it would be deemed to be served or delivered under the normal rules for service of documents.

This section should be read in conjunction with CPR 2.10, which states that, 'Where "month" occurs in any judgment, order, direction or other document, it means a calendar month'.

Therefore (in line with what has previously been discussed as regards computation of time), a claim form issued on 10 June 2005 must be served by (that is, dispatched no later than) 10 October 2005. In *Dodds v Walker* (p411) the House of Lords confirmed the application of the corresponding date rule. When the relevant period is a specified number of months, the general rule is that the period ends on the corresponding date in the appropriate subsequent month, ie the day of that month that bears the same number as the day of the earlier month on which the notice was given. Thus, a Landlord and Tenant Act application that had to be made not more than four months after 30 September 1978 was held to be out of time when made on 31 January 1979. Had it been a claim form issued on 30 September 2005, it would have had to be served by 30 January 2006.

The House of Lords observed in *Dodds* that the corresponding date rule was modified for periods starting on the 31st day of a month and expiring in a 30-day month or in February, and for periods expiring in February and starting on a higher date than the 28th (except in leap years) of any other month of the year. Thus a claim form issued on 31 October 2005 must be served by 28 February 2006.

A simple example of failure to (or even an attempt to) serve in time is the case of *Vinos v Marks & Spencer plc* (p701). The claimant was injured at work on 28 May 1996. He issued proceedings on 20 May 1999 and should have served them by 20 September 1999. Owing to his solicitors' oversight, they were not served until 29 September 1999. Therefore, his claim form was set aside.

Where the claim form is to be served outside the jurisdiction, the period for service is six months: CPR 7.5(2). Special provisions about service of the claim form out of the jurisdiction, and the circumstances in which the permission of the court is required, are set out in Section IV of Part 6 (CPR 6.30 to 6.47). Detailed consideration of these complex rules is beyond the scope of this chapter, although they will be touched upon briefly below.

Valid service of proceedings on one of two or more defendants within the appropriate period does not make them valid for service on any of the other defendants outside that period. This was established in *Jones v Jones* [1970] 2 QB 576, where a writ issued in June 1968 was served on the first defendant within the 12 months then allowed, but purported service on the second defendant outside that period was held to be invalid.

It is vital to reiterate that the different rules apply to the date of service of claim forms compared to the normal class of documents. For the vast majority of documents the time service is effected is when the document is *deemed to have been delivered* under the rules. By contrast, service of a claim form is effected as soon as it is *actually dispatched* under the rules.

EXTENSION OF TIME

CPR 2.11 provides that, 'Unless these Rules or a practice direction provide otherwise or the court orders otherwise, the time specified by a rule or by the court for a person to do any act may be varied by the written agreement of the parties'.

The word 'written' is crucial. In *Thomas v Home Office* (p687), the respective solicitors orally agreed a number of extensions of time for service of the claim form and usually recorded these agreements in file notes. The Court of Appeal held that this was invalid. The written agreement had to be contained either in a single document or in an exchange or letters of other documents. It was not sufficient for:

(a) one solicitor to record the agreement in a letter that was not answered by the other; or

(b) for each side to note their oral agreement, unless the notes were exchanged.

SERVICE OF PARTICULARS OF CLAIM

CPR 7.4 states that:

'(1)   Particulars of claim must–

(a)   be contained in or served with the claim form; or

(b)   subject to paragraph (2), be served on the defendant by the claimant within 14 days after service of the claim form.

(2)   Particulars of claim must be served on the defendants no later than the latest time for serving a claim form.'

Particulars of claim may be included in the claim form, but this is rare in personal injury cases. Much more often, they constitute a separate document which may be served either with or after the claim form.

CPR 2.8(3)(iii) gives the example that, if the claim form is served on 2 October, the last day for service of the particulars of claim is 16 October. This is subject to paragraph (2) above. Therefore, if the claim form was issued on 9 June 2005 and was served on 2 October 2005, the last day for service of the particulars of claim would have been 9 October 2005. A practical illustration of this principle is to be found in the case of *Totty v Snowden* (p694), where proceedings were issued on 26 September 1999 and the claim form was served on 26 January 2000. The particulars of claim served 14 days later, on 9 February 2000, were out of time. However, as illustrated in this and several other cases, and as discussed in **Chapter 10**, the court's discretion with regard to late service of particulars is much wider than as regards late service of the claim form. The Court of Appeal has, indeed, made clear that the absence of an expert report or the like is not a good reason for delaying the service of the claim form as opposed to the particulars, and that claimants finding themselves in such difficulties should serve the claim form in time, with particulars to follow.

CPR 7.8 provides that:

'(1)   When particulars of claim are served on the defendant, whether they are contained in the claim form, served with it or served subsequently, they must be accompanied by–

(a)   a form for defending the claim;

(b)   a form for admitting the claim; and

(c)   a form for acknowledging service.'

These documents are collectively known as the 'response pack'. They are to be served with the particulars of claim. Only then is the defendant required to acknowledge service, because he is acknowledging service of the particulars of claim and not merely the claim form.

The learned authors of the White Book (2012 Edition) have noted at 7.8.1 that 'if the claimant elects to serve the claim form and particulars of claim (rather than allowing the court to do so) but fails to enclose the "response pack" for the defendant, this is a technical error which does not justify a strike out – see *Hannigan v Hannigan*' (p458).

Note, however, that the time for service of the particulars of claim (if separate from the claim form) is probably governed by the normal rules for service of documents rather than the special ones applying to claim forms; service is effected when documents are deemed to have been delivered under the rules, rather than when dispatched.

The date of deemed service is decisive. It prevails over the date of any apparently earlier service. This was first established by the Court of Appeal in *Godwin v Swindon Borough Council* (p444) where the period for service (as extended) expired on 8 September 2000. On 7 September the claimant posted by first class post to the defendants the claim form, response pack and particulars of claim, which they duly received on 8 September. Notwithstanding this receipt, the deemed date of service was 9 September so the proceedings were served out of time.

The superiority of the deemed date of service is symmetrical. It can rescue as well as condemn. As May LJ explained in *Godwin*:

> '... uncertainties in the postal system ... make it sensible that there should be a date of service which is certain and not subject to challenge on the grounds of uncertain and potentially contentious fact ... This particularly applies to claimants wanting to serve a claim form at the very end of the period available to do so. The deemed day of service is finite and they will not be caught by a limitation defence where the last day of service is a Friday, if they post the claim form by first class post on the proceeding Wednesday, whenever it in fact arrives.'

This approach was authoritatively confirmed by the Court of Appeal in the case of *Anderton v Clwyd County Council (No 2)* (p303) and the appeals linked to it.

Paragraph 4 of CPR PD16 provides that:

> '4.2   The claimant must attach to his particulars of claim a schedule of the details of any past and future expenses and losses which he claims.

> 4.3   Where the claimant is relying on the evidence of a medical practitioner the claimant must attach to or serve with his particulars of claim a report from a medical practitioner about the personal injuries which he alleges in his claim.'

It is submitted that, in contrast to the response pack, service of the schedule of loss and, where reliance is placed on it, medical evidence is an essential accompaniment to service of the particulars of claim and is, therefore, subject to the '14 days within four months' requirement set out in CPR 7.4.

DOCUMENTS TO BE SERVED

In summary, the documents to be served within four months after the date of issue of the claim form (or six months where the claim form is to be served out of the jurisdiction) are:

  (i)   the claim form (CPR 7.5);
 (ii)   the particulars of claim (CPR 7.4);
(iii)   the response pack (CPR 7.8);
 (iv)   the schedule of loss (para 4.2 of CPR PD16); and
  (v)   medical evidence (para 4.3 of CPR PD16).

In addition, a notice of funding must be served in cases where the claimant is funded by a conditional fee agreement, but the consequences of failure to do so lie in costs rather than limitation.

Methods of service

Introduction

In order to serve proceedings in time, it is necessary to serve them correctly. Incorrect service cannot be timely service; strictly speaking, it is not service at all. Therefore, this section is devoted to the main methods of service.

The five general methods of service are set out in CPR 6.1(1):

'(1) A document may be served by any of the following methods:

(a) personal service, in accordance with rule 6.5;

(b) first class post, document exchange or other service which provides for delivery on the next working business day in accordance with Practice Direction 6A;

(c) leaving the document at a place specified in rule 6.7, 6.8, 6.9 or 6.10;

(d) by fax or other means of electronic communication in accordance with Practice Direction 6A;

(e) any method authorised by the court under rule 6.15.'

To these may be added service on solicitors (CPR 6.7) and consensual service. Each of these methods will be considered in turn, save that alternative service under CPR 6.15 is considered in **Chapter 10**.

CPR 6.11 also provides for service of a claim form by a method set out in a contract, but this will seldom (if ever) apply to a personal injury action. More significant is CPR 6.1 which provides:

'This Part applies to the service of documents, except where–

(a) another Part, any other enactment or a practice direction makes a different provision ...'

This allows for special rules for particular categories of defendant, such as the Crown or children, which are considered separately in the section headed 'Special types of defendant'.

Attempted service outside the rules is invalid. The most common error in this respect is to send the proceedings to the defendants' insurers. Examples of such ineffective service are *McManus v Sharif* (p556), in which the claimant's solicitors sent a draft claim form to the defendant's insurers, and *Elmes v Hygrade Food Products plc* (p423) in which the correct documents were sent in time but to the defendant's insurers instead of to the defendants themselves. The *McManus* case also illustrates a second type of breach, in that it is essential to serve the sealed copy of the claim form. Sending a photocopy or a draft does not suffice.

Before analysing the various methods, it is desirable to deal with two fundamental issues: first, who is to serve the proceedings; and, second, the address at which the proceedings are to be served.

WHO IS TO SERVE

This is governed by CPR 6.4:

'(1) Subject to Section IV of this Part and the rules in this Section relating to service out of jurisdiction on solicitors, European Lawyers and parties, the court will serve the claim form except where–

(a)   a rule or practice direction provides that the claimant must serve it;

(b)   the claimant notifies the court that the claimant wishes to serve it; or

(c)   the court orders or directs otherwise.

(2)   Where the court is to serve the claim form, it is for the court to decide which method of service is to be used.

(3)   Where the court is to serve the claim form, the claimant must, in addition to filing a copy for the court, provide a copy for each defendant to be served.

(4)   Where the court has sent–

(a)   a notification of outcome of postal service to the claimant in accordance with rule 6.18; or

(b)   a notification of non-service by a bailiff in accordance with rule 6.19,

the court will not try to serve the claim form again.'

CPR 6.6(2) provides that, where a claim form is to be served by the court, it must include the defendant's address for service. Under CPR 6.18, if the court serves proceedings but they are returned, it must send a notice of the non-delivery to the party who requested service.

Service by the court is now the general rule. It will occur unless the claimant's solicitor volunteers to serve the proceedings instead. In the latter stages of a claim form's validity, he or she would be well advised to do so, especially if any difficulty in achieving service is anticipated.

The question arises as to the position if the court retains responsibility for service and fails to serve the proceedings. In *Cranfield v Bridgegrove Ltd* (p389), this occurred due to court staff putting the claim forms for service on the court file by mistake and erroneously informing the claimant's solicitors that they had been posted to the defendants. In the conjoined appeal of *Claussen v Yeates*, most of the fault lay with the claimant's solicitors who only supplied the court with confirmation that the defendant's solicitors should be served on 1 February 2000, a mere four days before the claim form expired, and did not communicate any sense of urgency in their letter. In both cases, the proceedings were deemed unserved. This was not altered in the *Cranfield* case by the fact that the non-service was caused by the court's administrative error. The difference between court neglect and claimant's solicitor's fault only operated in the consequent applications to extend time for service, which will be considered in the next chapter.

ADDRESS FOR SERVICE – WHERE THE DEFENDANT GIVES AN ADDRESS

This is governed by CPR 6.8:

'Subject to rules 6.5(1) and 6.7 and the provisions of Section IV of this Part, and except where any other rule or practice direction makes different provision–

(a)   the defendant may be served with the claim form at an address at which the defendant resides or carries on business within the UK or any other EEA state and which the defendant has given for the purpose of being served with the proceedings; or

(b)   in any claim by a tenant against a landlord, the claim form may be served at an address given by the landlord under section 48 of the Landlord and Tenant Act 1987.'

There are several points to note here:

(1) This provision is permissive rather than mandatory. If the defendant gives an appropriate address for service, the claimant may serve that address, but is not required to do so. The claimant would be entitled nevertheless to use a different proper method of service.

(2) This provision is, however, subject to CPR 6.5(1); where personal service is required by 'another Part, any other enactment, a practice direction or a court order', it matters not that the defendant has volunteered an address for service.

(3) Much more importantly, by application of CPR 6.5(1), this provision is subject to CPR 6.7. As discussed below, if that rule applies, service must be on the defendant's solicitor, regardless of whether the defendant might also have volunteered another address for service.

ADDRESS FOR SERVICE – WHERE THE DEFENDANT DOES NOT GIVE AN ADDRESS

This is governed by CPR 6.9:

'(1) This rule applies where–

(a) rule 6.5(1) (personal service);
(b) rule 6.7 (service of claim form on solicitor or European Lawyer); and
(c) rule 6.8 (defendant gives address at which the defendant may be served),

do not apply and the claimant does not wish to effect personal service under rule 6.5(2).

(2) Subject to paragraphs (3) to (6), the claim form must be served on the defendant at the place shown in the following table.

Nature of defendant to be served	Place of service
1. Individual	• Usual or last known residence.
2. Individual being sued in the name of a business	• Usual or last known residence of the individual; or • principal or last known place of business.
3. Individual being sued in the business name of a partnership	• Usual or last known residence of the individual; or • principal or last known place of business of the partnership.
4. Limited liability partnership	• Principal office of the partnership; or • any place of business of the partnership within the jurisdiction which has a real connection with the claim.

5. Corporation (other than a company) incorporated in England and Wales	• Principal office of the corporation; or • any place within the jurisdiction where the corporation carries on its activities and which has a real connection with the claim.
6. Company registered in England and Wales	• Principal office of the company; or • any place of business of the company within the jurisdiction which has a real connection with the claim.
7. Any other company or corporation	• Any place within the jurisdiction where the corporation carries on its activities; or • any place of business of the company within the jurisdiction

(3)   Where a claimant has reason to believe that the address of the defendant referred to in entries 1, 2 or 3 in the table in paragraph (2) is an address at which the defendant no longer resides or carries on business, the claimant must take reasonable steps to ascertain the address of the defendant's current residence or place of business ("current address").

(4)   Where, having taken the reasonable steps required by paragraph (3), the claimant–

(a)   ascertains the defendant's current address, the claim form must be served at that address; or

(b)   is unable to ascertain the defendant's current address, the claimant must consider whether there is–
(i)   an alternative place where; or
(ii)   an alternative method by which,
service may be effected.

(5)   If, under paragraph (4)(b), there is such a place where or a method by which service may be effected, the claimant must make an application under rule 6.15.

(6)   Where paragraph (3) applies, the claimant may serve on the defendant's usual or last known address in accordance with the table in paragraph (2) where the claimant–

(a)   cannot ascertain the defendant's current residence or place of business; and

(b)   cannot ascertain an alternative place or an alternative method under paragraph (4)(b).'

The Court of Appeal has recently confirmed (*Varsani v Relfo Ltd (In Liquidation)* (p700)) that whether an address constitutes a person's usual residence is an open-textured qualitative question, and that a person could have more than one 'usual residence'.

In *Marshall Rankine v Maggs* (p543), the Court of Appeal decided that an address could not be a defendant's 'last known residence' if he had never resided there at all. It is only possible to know that which is true.

In *O'Hara v McDougall* (p589), the Court of Appeal held that a property rented out by the defendant could not become his 'place of business' within CPR Part 5 merely because he either personally, or through an agent, collected the rent by visiting the tenant from time to time.

The Court of Appeal also considered the meaning of 'last known residence' in *Smith v (1) Hughes and (2) MIB* (p659). Enquiry agents reported that Mr Hughes had left his address on the electoral register in February 1999. No new address was found. In April 2001 the proceedings were sent by first class post to his old address and were not returned by the Royal Mail. The Court of Appeal stated that there are two conditions precedent for the operation of the old CPR 6.5(6), namely that: (a) no solicitor is acting for the party to be served; and (b) the party has not given an address for service. If these conditions are satisfied, the proceedings must be sent to the individual at his usual or last known address. The rule is plain and unqualified. Nowhere does it say that it was not good service if the defendant did not in fact receive the document. Therefore, service on Mr Hughes was valid.

His Honour Judge Toulmin reached a different conclusion when interpreting the words 'last known place of business' in *Mersey Docks Property Holdings Ltd v Kilgour* (p557). Mr Kilgour was an architect who, until April 1998, carried on business under the title of Michael Kilgour Associates from an address in East Peckham. Thereafter he practised as MKA Chartered Architects from an address in Hadlow. An internet search against his old practice name disclosed only his old practice address. The judge found that the claimant's solicitors could have ascertained Mr Kilgour's new practice through the RIBA or by other measures and had failed to take reasonable steps to do so. Therefore, without referring to *Smith v Hughes*, he held that good service had not been effected.

Any conflict between these last two decisions has probably been rendered obsolete by the innovation of CPR 6.9(3)–(6) which, when the claimant has reason to believe that the defendant's last known address is not current, places a burden on the claimant to make enquiries to ascertain the defendant's current address. If the current address is identified, that is the address for service. If not, the claimant must consider whether service can be effected at any alternative address or by any alternative method. If so, the claimant is obliged to apply to the court for an order of alternative service. Only if no current address has been discovered, and no other means or place of service exists whereby the defendant may be served, can the claimant simply serve at the usual or last known address. It will be apparent that there is now a heavy onus on a claimant to exhaust these avenues, and doing so doubtless has the potential to seriously eat into the four-month period for service.

PERSONAL SERVICE

CPR 6.5(2) states that a document to be served may be served personally. The exceptions are contained in CPR 6.5(2)(a), where CPR 6.7 applies and a solicitor (or equivalent) is to be served, and CPR 6.5(2)(b), in any proceedings against the Crown.

Rule 6.5(3) provides that 'a document is served personally on an individual by leaving it with that individual'. The remainder of CPR 6.5 contains specific provisions concerning service on companies or other corporations and partnerships.

The authors assume that the previous case law on personal service continues to apply. To effect personal service, the person entrusted with the task should first satisfy himself that he has found the correct person. He should then hand, or leave with, the person to be served the sealed copy claim form and other documents. If the person served will not take them, he should tell him what they contain and leave them as nearly in his possession or control as he can.

The claim form and other documents should not be inserted in an envelope. When they are, whether the envelope is sealed up or not, if the defendant is not informed of its contents and has no knowledge that an action is to be commenced against him, this is not good service: *Banque Russe et Francaise v Clark* (1894) WN 204, CA.

The word 'leaving' is important. The sealed copy claim form and other documents must be left with, and not merely shown to, the defendant (*Worley v Glover* (1731) 2 Stra 887) even though he refuses to take it. Where the person serving them brought them away, the service was held under the circumstances to be defective (*Pigeon v Bruce* (1818) 8 Taunt 410).

Also important are the words 'that individual'. Service on the wife, or even on a known agent, of the defendant is not per se good service (*Frith v Lord Donegal* (1834) 2 Dowl 527). This is so, even though the other person undertakes to hand it to the defendant (*Davies v Morgan* (1832) 2 CR & J 237).

SERVICE ON SOLICITORS

By CPR 6.7(1):

'**Solicitor within the jurisdiction**: Subject to rule 6.5(1), where–

(a)   the defendant has given in writing the business address within the jurisdiction of a solicitor as an address at which the defendant may be served with the claim form; or

(b)   a solicitor acting for the defendant has notified the claimant in writing that the solicitor is instructed by the defendant to accept service of the claim form on behalf of the defendant at a business address within the jurisdiction,

the claim form must be served at the business address of that solicitor.

("Solicitor" has the extended meaning set out in rule 6.2(d).)'

Read in conjunction with CPR 6.5(2)(a), this means that personal service is prohibited in such circumstances, save where by CPR 6.5(1) some personal service is required by 'another Part, any other enactment, a practice direction or a court order'. Where the requirements of CPR 6.7(1) are satisfied, the only valid method of service is on the defendant's solicitor.

This was confirmed by the Court of Appeal in *Nanglegan v Royal Free Hampstead NHS Trust* (p567). On 4 May 1999, proceedings were issued. On 5 July the defendant's solicitors wrote confirming that they were instructed to accept service. On 31 August the claimant's solicitors served them on the defendant instead. The court held that there had not been valid service.

A steady stream of cases shows the problems to which these (and their predecessor) provisions have given rise. In chronological order, the first is *Smyth v Probyn* (p664) in which the defendants' solicitors wrote before proceedings that they acted for the defendants and 'if you intend to commence proceedings for defamation they will be vigorously defended'. The defendants' solicitors never stated that, and the claimant's solicitors never asked, whether they were authorised to accept service of proceedings. After issuing the claim form on 30 July 1999, the claimant's solicitors sent it to the defendants' solicitors by DX on 29 November 1999. Morland J held that there was no effective service, since the defendants' solicitors had never stated that they were authorised to accept service.

In *James v First Bristol Buses Ltd* (p494), the defendants' loss adjusters wrote to the claimant's solicitors indicating that they wished to instruct a named solicitor to accept service of proceedings. However, in contrast to the *Nanglegan* case, the solicitor never wrote to confirm that he was so authorised. Consequently, the claimant's solicitors served the proceedings directly on the defendants. The district judge held that this service was valid, since (i) the letter nominating solicitors came not from the defendants but from their loss adjusters, (ii) the letter was written before proceedings when the defendants were not yet a party, (iii) the solicitors never confirmed that they were prepared to accept service, and (iv) the letter had never come to the attention of the claimant's solicitors.

Considerable uncertainty has arisen about the inter-relationship of CPR 6.4(2) with CPR 6.5, set out in full in the 'Address for service' section above. This has, it is hoped, finally been resolved by the Court of Appeal decisions in the linked cases of *Collier v Williams* and *Marshall Rankine v Maggs* (p380). Dyson LJ introduced the court's judgment with the following observations, with which the authors respectfully concur:

> 'We heard over three days six appeals which raised points on CPR Part 6 (the rule relating to service), and CPR Part 7.6 (the rule relating to the extending of time for service of the claim form). These rules have generated an inordinate amount of jurisprudence. This is greatly to be regretted. The CPR were intended to be simple and straightforward and not susceptible to frequent satellite litigation. In this area, that intention has not been fulfilled. As a result, the explicit aims of the Woolf reforms to reduce cost, complexity and delays in litigation have been frustrated. We understand that the Civil Procedure Rule Committee will shortly embark on a review of the rules relating to service. This is a welcome development. These appeals have revealed yet again that these rules are difficult to understand and apply.'

Collier v Williams raised the question whether a claim form had been validly served on a firm of solicitors nominated by an insurance company for that purpose. Relying on CPR 6.4(2)(b), the insurers argued that, because the nominated solicitors did not themselves notify the serving solicitors that they were authorised to accept service, this service was invalid. Dyson LJ dealt with this submission as follows:

> 'It seems surprising that it is even arguable that, where a defendant (or his insurer) has nominated a solicitor for service, the business address of that solicitor should not be the defendant's address for service unless the solicitor has notified the claimant in writing that he is authorised to accept service. CPR 6.5(2) and (4) are plain and unqualified on their face. A party must give an address for service within the jurisdiction (CPR 6.5(2)); and any document to be served by post or one of the other methods stated in CPR 6.5(4) must be sent or transmitted to, or left at, the address for service given by the defendant (CPR 6.5(4)). Why should these words not be given their natural meaning?'

After analysing the defendants' arguments, he stated that 'the language of the rules compels the conclusion that, where a defendant gives the claimant a solicitor's address for service, the claim form may validly be served at that address by one of the permitted methods of service'. 'Defendant', for this purpose, clearly includes an insurer acting on his behalf. Dyson LJ added that:

'if a defendant has given an address for service, including that of a solicitor, it is still open to the claimant to serve personally on the defendant unless he has received a notification in accordance with CPR 6.4(2). But if a claimant wishes to use one of the types of service referred to in CPR 6.5(4), for example, first class post, then if he has been provided with a solicitor's address as the address for service, he will not be able to post the document to the defendant himself: he must post it to the address of the solicitor.'

In *Marshall Rankine v Maggs*, points of principle that arose included (i) the meaning of 'solicitor is acting for the party to be served' in old CPR 6.5(5) and (6) (the predecessors to 6.7), and (ii) when a solicitor is acting but does not confirm that he is authorised to accept service, whether the methods of service contemplated by old CPR 6.5(6) are available to the claimant. The facts of the case were that:

(i) the claimant's solicitors sent a letter before action to the defendants;
(ii) the defendant's solicitors wrote that they were acting for him;
(iii) the claimant's solicitors asked the defendants' solicitors whether they were instructed to accept service;
(iv) the defendants' solicitors did not respond;
(v) the claimant's solicitors sent to the defendant by first class post the claim form, particulars of claim and response pack; and
(vi) the defendant applied for a declaration that the proceedings had not been validly served and that they be struck out.

The defendant submitted that, in such circumstances, the claimant was compelled to serve personally rather than use one of the methods set out in CPR 6.5(6). Rejecting this submission, Dyson LJ stated:

'We do not believe that this is what was intended. In our view, this unsatisfactory result can be avoided by interpreting the phrase "no solicitor acting" as meaning "no solicitor acting so that he can be served". We put it that way because, unless the claimant has been made aware by the defendant or his solicitor that the solicitor is authorised to accept service, the claimant would be ill-advised to serve on the solicitor. It is this factor that led Gray J. back to CPR 6.4(2) and personal service, but, as we have already said, where CPR 6.4(2) applies it *prevents* personal service. CPR 6.5(6) was not intended to be a trap for the unwary. If the claimant knows that a solicitor is authorised to accept service, then it is right that the methods of service set out in CPR 6.5(5) should not be available. But if the claimant is told that a solicitor is "acting", but that he is not authorised to accept service, it makes no sense to insist that personal service be used. It must have been intended that in these circumstances CPR 6.5(6) could be used. Even more obviously must it have been intended that CPR 6.5(6) could be used where the claimant does not even know that a solicitor is acting for the defendant.'

It is submitted that the following approach is suitable for claimant's solicitors deciding whether to serve a defendant direct or the defendant's solicitors:

(1) Consider first under CPR 6.7(1)(a) whether the defendant has given his solicitors' address as the address for service. If so, serve the proceedings on the defendant's solicitors.
(2) If not, consider next under CPR 6.7(1)(b) whether the defendant's solicitors have written that they are authorised to accept service. If so, serve the proceedings on the defendant's solicitors.

(3)   If neither of the above apply, serve the proceedings on the defendant direct under CPR 6.5(6), and do so even if there is a solicitor corresponding on his behalf.

This approach would have saved the claimant's solicitors in the case of *Horn v Dorset Healthcare NHS Trust (No 1)* (p480). The defendant nominated solicitors to accept service and gave their address. Since the defendant's solicitors did not write to confirm that they were authorised to accept service, the claimant's solicitors sent the claim form and associated documents to the defendant direct. It was held that service had not been validly effected.

A subsidiary point in *Horn* was that there was a small typographical error in the DX address that the defendant gave for its solicitors: DX 83091 Exeter instead of DX 8309 Exeter 1. This prompted the claimant's counsel to argue that the correct business address of the defendant's solicitors had not been given, a submission which the judge rejected in the following terms:

'This was in truth a mere typographical error and there is no evidence before me at all that the Document Exchange system is so constructed that such a typographical error would mean that the documents were incapable of delivery. Furthermore I note that that was the address that the defendant chose to give in the letter dated 17 June and any subsequent problems would be their sole responsibility. It seems to me that this is not an error of such materiality to remove the case from the ambit of CPR 6.5 I hold that the correct business address, being the Document Exchange address, for the solicitors had been given in this letter.'

The *Horn* case was decided before the rule which states that a party must give an address for service within the jurisdiction was amended to add that the address must include a full postcode, unless the court orders otherwise.

The fact that the defendant itself is a solicitors' firm does not by itself mean that it is acting as a solicitor in the litigation for the purposes of service: *Thorne v Lass Salt Garvin (A Firm)* (p692).

POSTAL SERVICE

CPR 6.2(1)(b) provides for service by first class post or equivalent method. This must be construed literally. Sending proceedings by second class post does not constitute valid service, even if they arrive in time. In *Godwin v Swindon Borough Council* (p444), May LJ made it clear that, if he had upheld the judge's finding that he could not infer that the posting was by first class post, the claimant's appeal would have failed on that ground alone.

The additional requirement in CPR 6.6(2), that a party's address must include a full postcode unless the court orders otherwise, is supplemented by paragraph 2 of CPR PD16, which provides as follows:

'2.2   The claim form must include an address at which the claimant resides or carries on business. This paragraph applies even though the claimant's address for service is the business address of his solicitor.

2.3   Where the defendant is an individual, the claimant should (if he is able to do so) include in the claim form an address at which the defendant resides or carries on business. This paragraph applies even though the defendant's solicitors have agreed to accept service on the defendant's behalf.

2.4   Any address which is provided for the purpose of these provisions must include a postcode, unless the court orders otherwise. Postcode information may be obtained from www.royalmail.com or the Royal Mail Address Management Guide.

2.5   If the claim does not show a full address, including postcode, at which the claimant(s) and defendant(s) reside or carry on business, the claim form will be issued but will be retained by the court and will not be served until the claimant has supplied a full address, including postcode, or the court has dispensed with the requirement to do so. The court will notify the claimant.'

A danger is created by the court's retention of the claim form: the four-month period of service will continue to run while the court waits for the postcode. It is easy to envisage circumstances in which precious time elapses whilst nothing occurs or, still worse, despite the direction that the court will notify the claimant, whilst claimant's solicitors think that the court is serving the claim form when it is not even attempting to do so. Claimant's solicitors must therefore take great care to:

(a)   insert the defendant's postcode on the claim form whenever possible, using the www.royalmail.com website where appropriate to ascertain it; and

(b)   if the court is to serve a claim form that lacks a defendant's postcode, to be diligent in informing the court of the postcode in good time or, where it cannot be ascertained, to apply in even better time for an order dispensing with the postcode requirement.

DOCUMENT EXCHANGE SERVICE

Paragraph 2 of CPR PD6A provides that:

'2.1   Service by document exchange (DX) may take place only where–

(1)   the party's address for service includes a numbered box at a DX, or

(2)   the writing paper of the party who is to be served or of his legal representative sets out the DX box number, and

(3)   the party or his legal representative has not indicated in writing that they are unwilling to accept service by DX.'

Paragraph 3 of CPR PD6A provides that:

'3.1   Service by post, DX or other service which provides for delivery on the next business day is effected by–

(1)   placing the document in a post box;

(2)   leaving the document with or delivering the document to the relevant service provider; or

(3)   having the document collected by the relevant service provider.'

The elementary requirement under paragraph 2.1 that 'the party's address for service includes a numbered box at a DX' was overlooked in *Chaudhri v The Post Office* (p372), when the claimant's solicitors sent the proceedings by DX to the Post Office which was not even a member of the document exchange. Consequently, there was no valid service.

A different type of error occurred in *Infantino v MacLean* (p488), where the claimant's solicitors sent the proceedings in a DX intended for the Medical Protection Society to the DX number of the Medical Defence Union. By the time they were returned, it was too late to effect valid service. This breached the requirement that the documents must be addressed to the numbered box at the DX of the party who is to be served, since unfortunately the documents were addressed to a different numbered box.

LEAVING SERVICE

CPR 6.3(1)(c) states that a document may be served by 'leaving the document at a place specified in rule 6.7, 6.8, 6.9 or 6.10'. This type of service is to be distinguished from personal service in which the document is tendered to (and left with) the defendant. It envisages instead the defendant being absent and the court documents being left at the appropriate place.

The issue of what is 'a place specified in rule 6.7, 6.8, or 6.9' is extensively discussed under the 'Address for service' heading above. The place specified in 6.10 is addressed under the 'The Crown' heading below.

ELECTRONIC SERVICE

CPR 6.3(1)(d) provides for service of documents 'by fax or other means of electronic communication in accordance with the relevant practice direction'. Paragraph 4 of CPR PD6A states as follows:

'Service by fax or other electronic means

4.1   Subject to the provisions of rule 6.23(5) and (6) *[which are not applicable to service of the claim form]*, where a document is to be served by fax or other electronic means-

(1)   the party who is to be served or the solicitor acting for that party must previously have indicated in writing to the party serving–
   (a)   that the party to be served or the solicitor is willing to accept service by fax or other electronic means; and
   (b)   the fax number, e-mail address or other electronic identification to which it must be sent; and
(2)   the following are to be taken as sufficient written indications for the purposes of paragraph 4.1(1)–
   (a)   a fax number set out on the writing paper of the solicitor acting for the party to be served;
   (b)   an e-mail address set out on the writing paper of the solicitor acting for the party to be served but only where it is stated that the e-mail address may be used for service; or
   (c)   a fax number, e-mail address or electronic identification set out on a statement of case or a response to a claim filed with the court.

4.2   Where a party intends to serve a document by electronic means (other than by fax) that party must first ask the party who is to be served whether there are any limitations to the recipient's agreement to accept service by such means (for example, the format in which documents are to be sent and the maximum size of attachments that may be received).

4.3   Where a document is served by electronic means, the party serving the document need not in addition send or deliver a hard copy.'

The rules for electronic service are more demanding than for DX service. With DX, the presumption is that those with DX box numbers on their writing paper can be served by DX, unless they indicate to the contrary in writing. With electronic service, however, the presumption is reversed. A defendant who is to be served must previously have indicated in writing to the party serving that he is willing to accept service by electronic means.

In *Molins plc v GD SpA* (p563), Molins sent in August 1998 a routine letter to GD on notepaper which included their fax number. In July 1999, GD purported to serve proceedings on Molins by fax. The Court of Appeal rejected the submission that this amounted to valid service. Aldous LJ stated:

> 'The suggestion that the inclusion of a fax number in a heading on writing paper amounts to an indication in writing of willingness to accept service of legal documents by fax is contrary to the clear meaning of the practice direction and commonsense. If inclusion of a fax number on writing paper were to be sufficient, then the practice direction would have said so without more ado. Further the meaning of paragraph 3.1(1) is confirmed by paragraph 3.1(3), which expressly provides that a fax number on writing paper of a legal representative of a party to be served is sufficient. If that were to be the case for the party itself, then there would be no need to make such specific provision in the case of a legal representative.'

The White Book advises that 'where a document is served by fax or email the Practice Direction says that a hard copy does not have to be sent, but that may not be prudent unless there has been acknowledgment of receipt of the electronic version'.

ALTERNATIVE SERVICE

This is dealt with in **Chapter 10**.

CONSENSUAL SERVICE

Consensual service used to occur when the parties agreed on a mode of service outside the former court rules. For instance, in *Kenneth Allison Ltd v A E Limehouse & Co* (p516), service on the senior partner's former assistant did not satisfy RSC Ord 81 r 3. However, since a partner had authorised this, the House of Lords held that valid consensual service had been achieved.

CPR Part 6 is silent on the subject of consensual service. It neither permits it nor prohibits it. Consequently, it is impossible to be certain whether, in circumstances governed by CPR Part 6, consensual service outside its rules would positively count as good service. It is, perhaps, easier to be sure of the converse, that a defendant would almost always be estopped from complaining of a method of service to which he had consented.

Where alternative rules to CPR Part 6 apply, for instance under s 725 of the Companies Act 1985, it may be assumed that the former law condoning consensual service will continue to operate. For example, if a director of a limited company asked for a claim form to be posted to him at a hotel where he happened to be staying that week, it is submitted that valid service would be achieved by sending it to him there.

Special types of defendant

INTRODUCTION

CPR 6.1 provides that the rules on service in CPR Part 6 apply subject to any other enactment or rule or practice direction. This section examines the main types of defendant to whom special provisions apply. Frequently sued categories, such as limited companies and partnerships, are considered at length; rarer defendants, such as overseas companies and children, are dealt with more briefly.

LIMITED COMPANIES

In the general methods of service under CPR 6.3, CPR Part 6 contains two special provisions for companies. Under CPR 6.5(3)(b), a document is served personally on a company by leaving it with a person holding a senior position within the company. The table attached to CPR 6.9(2) provides that, where no solicitor is acting for the party to be served and the party has not given an address for service, the place for service of a company registered in England and Wales is either the principal office of the company or any place of business of the company within the jurisdiction which has a real connection with the claim. Paragraph 6.2 of CPR PD6A provides that each of the following is a person holding a senior position: 'a director, the treasurer, secretary, chief executive, manager or other officer'.

In *Lakah Group v Al Jazeera Satellite Channel* (p525), the claimant was unable to refute evidence that the person to whom the claim form was handed was an employee of a separate (though associated) company. Accordingly, Gray J ruled that service was invalid.

CPR 6.3(2)(b) provides that 'A company may be served by any method permitted under this Part as an alternative to the methods of service permitted by the Companies Act 2006'. Thus, service under the Companies Act remains as a valid alternative to service under the CPR.

This is, however, a permissive provision. Thus, whilst under the Act it is desirable to serve proceedings at the company's registered office, in *Singh v Atombrook Ltd* (p651), the Court of Appeal (per Kerr LJ) held that service on the company elsewhere is at worst an irregularity, which does not render the proceedings a nullity.

Given the breadth of service options on companies under the CPR, it is difficult to see many advantages in the provision of service under the 2006 Act. Perhaps the only major one is that certain concepts under the Act would be less restrictively defined than under the CPR. By s 7 of the Interpretation Act 1978, service by post is 'deemed to be effected by properly addressing, prepaying, and posting a letter containing the document'. The word 'post' is wide enough to cover both ordinary first and second class and registered post. Therefore a company was properly served with a writ that was sent by registered post (*T O Supplies (London) Ltd v Jerry Creighton Ltd* (p682)). By s 1(1) of the Recorded Delivery Service Act 1962, registered post in such a context includes the recorded delivery service. Thus, postal service on a limited company may be effected by ordinary prepaid post, registered post or recorded delivery.

Section 7 of the Interpretation Act 1978 further states that service by post is deemed 'unless the contrary is proved, to have been effected at the time at which the letter would be delivered in the ordinary course of post'. In the Practice Direction at [1985] 1 WLR 489, it is provided that:

'To avoid uncertainty as to the date of service it will be taken (subject to proof to the contrary) that delivery in the ordinary course of post was effected: (a) in the case of first class mail, on the second working day after posting; (b) in the case of second class mail, on the fourth working day after posting. "Working days" are Monday to Friday, excluding any Bank Holiday.'

The operation of these provisions is neatly illustrated by *Harris v Lopen Group Ltd* [1993] PIQR P1. A copy of the writ issued on 8 January 1991 was sent by first class post to the defendants on Friday 3 May 1991. Saturday 4 May and Sunday 5 May were not working days. Monday 6 May was a bank holiday. Tuesday 7 May was a working day. The writ reached the defendants' office on Wednesday 8 May. It was held that:

(i)   service took place on 8 May, the proved date of receipt;
(ii)   if this date had not been proved, service would be deemed to have taken place on 7 May which the plaintiff's solicitor had shown was when the letter containing the writ would have been delivered in the usual course of post; and
(iii) if it had not been possible to establish either of the above, service would be deemed to have been effected on 8 May which was the second working day after posting by first class mail.

Therefore, there is one set of rules under CPR Part 6 and a second, alternative, set of rules under the 2006 Act (successor to the Companies Act 1985). An example of inter-connection between the two is the case of *Murphy v Staples Ltd* (reported under the associated appeal of *Cranfield v Bridgegrove Ltd* (p389)). The claimant served the proceedings on the defendant through sending them by first class post to the defendant's registered office. Since their solicitors had confirmed that they had instructions to accept service, this did not amount to valid service under the CPR. Giving the judgment of the Court of Appeal, Dyson LJ analysed the inter-relation between the two alternatives as follows:

'Where a choice or election is made as to the method of service to be employed, then both parties are bound by it. Once the CPR is engaged by an effective election, the parties know when the court timetable will start to run, because the claimant will have served a certificate of service specifying the deemed date of service. In this way, certainty is achieved. On the facts of the present case, the claimant by his solicitors elected to proceed by way of service on the defendant's solicitors under the CPR, rather than under section 725(1). At no time prior did the claimant seek to resile from the election. The defendant also relies on *Nanglegan*.'

Our conclusion on this issue is as follows. A claimant may serve the claim form on a defendant company either by leaving it at, or by sending it by post to, the company's registered office, or by serving it in accordance with one of the methods permitted by the CPR. They are true alternatives. That is made clear by CPR 6.3. There are differences between the two methods. For example, service under the Act may be by second class post. CPR Part 6 provides for service by first class post. Service under Act is deemed to have been effected at the time at which the letter would be delivered 'in the ordinary course of post' (s 7 of the Interpretation Act), unless the contrary is proved.

If a defendant has not given an address for service, a claimant may choose whether to follow the 2006 Act or the CPR route for service. In *Nanglegan*, it was held that, where a defendant elects to give his address for service, and nominates his solicitor to accept service, the CPR requires personal service to be effected upon the nominated solicitor, and not on the defendant. As Thorpe LJ put it (at page 1047F), 'there will be many cases in which a defendant does not want service either at his residence or at his place of business'. But in that case, the court was not concerned with the interplay between the Act and the CPR, which expressly recognise alternative methods.

The Court of Appeal in *Murphy* held that, although it is possible for parties to make a binding contract whereby the claimant agrees to serve the claim form under CPR Part 6 rather than the Act, or vice versa, the correspondence in this case had not amounted to a binding promise by the claimant to serve on the defendants' solicitors under CPR 6.4(2). Therefore, service on the company's registered office was good service.

LIMITED LIABILITY PARTNERSHIPS

The table attached to CPR 6.9(2) provides that, where no solicitor is acting for the party to be served and the party has not given an address for service, the place for service of a limited liability partnership is either the principal office of the company or any place of business of the company within the jurisdiction which has a real connection with the claim. Paragraph 6.2 of CPR PD6A provides that each of the following is a person holding a senior position: 'a director, the treasurer, secretary, chief executive, manager or other officer'.

CPR 6.3(2)(c) provides that 'A limited liability partnership may be served by any method permitted under this Part as an alternative to the methods of service permitted by the Companies Act 2006 as applied with modification under the Limited Liability Partnership Act 2000'. Thus, service under the Companies Act remains as a valid alternative to service under the CPR. The analysis above in relation to the interplay between these regimes applies equally to limited liability partnerships.

OTHER CORPORATIONS

CPR Part 6 contains two special provisions for other corporations. Under CPR 6.3(b), a document is served personally on a corporation by leaving it with a person holding a senior position within the corporation. The table attached to CPR 6.9 provides that, where no solicitor is acting for the party to be served and the party has not given an address for service, the place for service for a corporation incorporated in England and Wales other than a company is either the principal office of the corporation or any place within the jurisdiction where the corporation carries on its activities and which has a real connection with the claim.

CPR PD6A at paragraph 6.2 states that:

'Each of the following persons is a person holding a senior position:

(1)   in respect of a registered company or corporation, a director, the treasurer, secretary, chief executive, manager or other officer of the company or corporation, and

(2)   in respect of a corporation which is not a registered company, in addition to those persons set out in (1), the mayor, chairman, president, town clerk or similar officer of the corporation.'

Major examples of corporations governed by the above rules are local councils and NHS trusts.

THE CROWN

This is governed by 6.10 which provides that:

'In proceedings against the Crown–

(a) service on the Attorney General must be effected on the Treasury Solicitor; and

(b) service on a government department must be effected on the solicitor acting for that department.

(Practice Direction 66 gives the list published under section 17 of the Crown Proceedings Act 1947 of the solicitors acting in civil proceedings (as defined in that Act) for the different government departments on whom service is to be effected, and of their addresses.)'

These mandatory provisions must be read in conjunction with CPR 6.5(2), which prohibits personal service on the Crown.

Therefore it does not constitute effective service to leave the proceedings at a government department. Service must be effected instead on the solicitors acting for the department.

PARTNERSHIPS

A partnership is not a separate legal entity with a distinct legal personality for the purpose of proceedings. It is thus necessary to direct proceedings (at least notionally) to one or more of the partners. Item 3 of the table at CPR 6.9(2) provides that an 'Individual being sued in the business name of a partnership' can be served at the 'Usual or last known residence of the individual; or principal or last known place of business'.

The service regime for such a person is therefore the same as that for an individual *simpliciter*, save that, in addition to that person's usual or last known residence, they can also be served at their principal or last known place of business. Note that this has the potential to considerably widen the options a claimant may be obliged to explore and exhaust under CPR 6.9(3)–(5).

Provided one partner who was sued in the name of a firm has the proceedings properly served upon him, that is good service on the firm, and therefore upon his co-partners: *Lexi Holdings Plc v Luqman* (p535).

Regarding personal service on partnerships, CPR 6.5(3)(c) provides that a claim form is served personally on:

'a partnership (where partners are being sued in the name of their firm) by leaving it with–

(i) a partner; or

(ii) a person who, at the time of service, has the control or management of the partnership business at its principal place of business.'

AN INDIVIDUAL BEING SUED IN THE NAME OF A BUSINESS

The position is the same as for an individual being sued in the name of a partnership, save that there is no special provision for personal service. This is instead governed by the general rule for personal service on individuals at CPR 6.5(3)(a) that the claim form must be left with the individual.

CHILDREN AND PROTECTED PARTIES

Service on children and protected parties is governed by CPR 6.13:

'(1)   Where the defendant is a child who is not also a protected party, the claim form must be served on–

(a)   one of the child's parents or guardians; or

(b)   if there is no parent or guardian, an adult with whom the child resides or in whose care the child is.

(2)   Where the defendant is a protected party, the claim form must be served on–

(a)   one of the following persons with authority in relation to the protected party as–
       (i)   the attorney under a registered enduring power of attorney;
       (ii)   the donee of a lasting power of attorney; or
       (iii) the deputy appointed by the Court of Protection; or

(b)   if there is no such person, an adult with whom the protected party resides or in whose care the protected party is.

(3)   Any reference in this Section to a defendant or a party to be served includes the person to be served with the claim form on behalf of a child or protected party under paragraph (1) or (2).

(4)   The court may make an order permitting a claim form to be served on a child or protected party, or on a person other than the person specified in paragraph (1) or (2).

(5)   An application for an order under paragraph (4) may be made without notice.

(6)   The court may order that, although a claim form has been sent or given to someone other than the person specified in paragraph (1) or (2), it is to be treated as if it had been properly served.

(7)   This rule does not apply where the court has made an order under CPR 21.2(3) allowing a child to conduct proceedings without a litigation friend.

(Part 21 contains rules about the appointment of a litigation friend and "child" and "protected party" have the same meaning as in rule 21.1.)'

A 'child' is a person under 18 years of age. A 'protected party' is a person who lacks capacity within the meaning of the Mental Capacity Act 2005 to conduct the proceedings.

CPR Part 21 provides that, in general, the interest of a child or patient must be represented by a litigation friend, and it contains rules about the appointment of litigation friends.

ADDITIONAL OR SUBSTITUTED DEFENDANTS

CPR Part 19 provides for new parties to be added or substituted in proceedings, although as a general rule this would not be permitted after expiry of the limitation period. The practical rules about service on the new defendant are set out in paragraph 3 of CPR PD19A:

'3.2   Where the court has made an order adding or substituting a defendant whether on its own initiative or on an application, the court may direct:

(1)   the claimant to file with the court within 14 days (or as ordered) an amended claim form and particulars of claim for the court file,

(2)   a copy of the order to be served on all parties to the proceedings and any other person affected by it,

(3)   the amended claim form and particulars of claim, forms for admitting, defending and acknowledging the claim and copies of the statements of case and other documents referred to in any statement of case to be served on the new defendant.

(4)   unless the court orders otherwise, the amended claim form and particulars of claim to be served on any other defendants.

3.3   A new defendant does not become a party to the proceedings until the amended claim form has been served on him.'

Therefore, where an order is made for a new defendant to be added or substituted, he becomes a party to the action, not when the order is made, but only when the amended claim form is served on him. This creates a potential pitfall for claimants' lawyers, which is illustrated by the case of *Braniff v Holland & Hannen and Cubitts (Southern) Ltd* (p342). The accident occurred on 4 October 1965. The order to add second defendants was made in July 1968. Only on 23 October 1968, after obtaining an ex parte extension, was a copy of the amended writ served on the second defendant who applied for the amended writ and service of it to be set aside. This was granted since, although the order to amend was made within the limitation period, the service that made them a party occurred outside it.

ESTATES

CPR 19.8 stipulates that:

'(1)   Where a person who had an interest in a claim has died and that person has no personal representative the court may order–

(a)   the claim to proceed in the absence of a person representing the estate of the deceased; or

(b)   a person to be appointed to represent the estate of the deceased.

(2)   Where a defendant against whom a claim could have been brought has died and–

(a)   grant of probate or administration has been made, the claim must be brought against the persons who are the personal representatives of the deceased;

(b)   a grant of probate or administration has not been made–

(i)   the claim must be brought against "the estate of" the deceased; and

(ii)   the claimant must apply to the court for an order appointing a person to represent the estate of the deceased in the claim.

(3)   A claim shall be treated as having been brought against "the estate of" the deceased in accordance with paragraph (2)(b)(i) where–

(a)   the claim is brought against the "personal representatives" of the deceased but a grant of probate or administration has not been made; or

(b) the person against whom the claim was brought was dead when the claim was started.'

It is essential for the claimant to make the above application during the period of validity of the claim form. Otherwise, any service will be invalid because the proceedings are a nullity. This was confirmed in the case of *Foster v Turnbull* (p436), in which a writ issued in May 1986 named two dead men, one of whom had been riding the motor cycle that crashed, as defendants, as well as one living person (the owner of the motor cycle). In June 1986, solicitors acknowledged service on behalf of all three defendants on the insurers' instructions. In May 1987 the period of validity of the writ expired. In June 1988, new solicitors for the insurers pointed out that no order had been obtained. The Court of Appeal ruled that it was too late to appoint the insurers to represent the first two defendants' estates, since the writ had not been validly served on them and steps taken in the proceedings after the issue of the writ were nullities.

The point arose in a different form in the case of *Piggott v Aulton* [2003] EWCA Civ 24. On 14 June 1997 the claimant was injured in a road traffic accident in which the defendant was killed. She issued proceedings on 13 June 2000 but never obtained an order appointing a representative of the deceased's estate and discontinued proceedings. The Court of Appeal held that her new proceedings issued on 4 June 2001 were not barred by the rule of *Walkley v Precision Forgings Ltd* (p705) since the original proceedings had been a nullity.

The position where claims are brought against the estate of a deceased driver who was uninsured are governed by a procedure agreed between the Official Solicitor and the Motor Insurers' Bureau (MIB) and approved by the Senior Master. In brief, where no grant of probate or administration has been obtained, the claimant should invite the MIB to be appointed to represent the deceased's estate. If the MIB decline, the Official Solicitor should be approached and will usually accept the appointment. The procedure is set out in full in the White Book as a note to CPR 19.8.

DEFENDANTS ABROAD

Section IV of CPR Part 6 contains the rules about service out of the jurisdiction. CPR 6.32 states when the permission of the court is not required, and CPR 6.33 states when it is required. When leave is required, service without leave is invalid.

This is illustrated by the case of *Leal v Dunlop Bio-Processes International Ltd* (p530). Where the English plaintiff was injured in Malaya whilst working for a company registered in Jersey, it was held that the failure to obtain leave did not render the writ a nullity, but that instead it was an irregularity, and the judge had power to give leave retroactively. However, such leave was refused, and May LJ commented: 'I hope and expect that it will only be in the exceptional case that the court will validate after the event the purported service in a foreign country without leave of process issued by an English court'.

The method of service is set out in CPR 6.40:

'(1) This rule contains general provisions about the method of service of a claim form or other document on a party out of the jurisdiction.

Where service is to be effected on a party in Scotland or Northern Ireland

(2) Where a party serves any document on a party in Scotland or Northern Ireland, it must be served by a method permitted by Section II (and references

to "jurisdiction" in that Section are modified accordingly) or Section III of this Part and rule 6.23(4) applies.

Where service is to be effected on a defendant out of the United Kingdom

(3) Where the claimant wishes to serve a claim form or any other document on a defendant out of the United Kingdom, it may be served–

(a) by any method provided for by–
  (i)   rule 6.41 (service in accordance with the Service Regulation);
  (ii) rule 6.42 (service through foreign governments, judicial authorities and British Consular authorities); or
  (iii) rule 6.44 (service of claim form or other document on a State);
(b) by any method permitted by a Civil Procedure Convention; or
(c) by any other method permitted by the law of the country in which it is to be served.

(4) Nothing in paragraph (3) or in any court order authorises or requires any person to do anything which is contrary to the law of the country where the claim form or other document is to be served.'

As has already been indicated, however, detailed consideration of this complex area of law is beyond the scope of this book.

Conclusion

This chapter has set out the circumstances in which proceedings are, or are not, validly served. The next chapter covers the available attempts to rescue the position when valid service in time appears impossible or, much worse, has not been achieved.

10 Remedies under the CPR: extending time for service and dismissing claims

1 Introduction

The provisions of the Civil Procedure Rules 1998, as amended by the Civil Procedure (Amendment) Rules 2008, contain a new code for how the court deals with procedural time limits. These range from the service of claim forms (CPR 7.5), service of the particulars of claim (CPR 7.4), extensions of time to serve claim forms (CPR 7.6), dispensations with service of the claim form (CPR 6.16), service of the claim form by an alternative method or at an alternative place(CPR 6.15), a general power to extend or bridge time (CPR 3.1(2)(a)), relief from sanctions (CPR 3.9), power to rectify an error (CPR 3.10) and the power to strike out a statement of case which includes a claim form, particulars of claim or defence (CPR 3.4).

The interpretation of these provisions and how they interconnect has created a new jurisprudence to replace previous authorities concerning the extension of a writ or summons and those derived from striking out cases for want of prosecution. Reference to previous authorities is largely deprecated because the new code has to be construed in the light of the overriding objective to deal with cases justly (CPR 1.1). In *Biguzzi v Rank Leisure plc* (p335), Lord Woolf MR stated:

> 'The whole purpose of making the CPR a self-contained code was to send the message which now generally applies. Earlier Authorities are no longer generally of any relevance once the CPR applies.' (at 1934G)

Similarly, Lord Justice May in *Godwin v Swindon Borough Council* (p444) stated:

> '... it is not, in my view, generally helpful to seek to interpret the Civil Procedure Rules by reference to the rules which they replaced and to cases decided under former rules.' (at para 42)

Care is also needed in considering authorities decided under the earlier CPR 7.5 before the substantial amendments to the rules on service of the claim form which now achieve service within the jurisdiction by completing the steps required within the amended CPR 7.5 before midnight on the calendar day four months after the date of issue of the claim form.

This chapter will look at the remedies available to claimant's solicitors who have had difficulty in serving proceedings or who have failed to serve proceedings during the period of the validity of the claim form. It will then discuss the remedies open to defendants seeking to dismiss an action for non-compliance with procedural rules. In the vast majority of the cases discussed in this chapter, these rules are crucial because the primary limitation period will have expired and, although since the case of *Horton v Sadler* (p482) the rule in *Walkley v Precision Forgings Ltd* (p705) has been abolished, the claimant will still need a s 33 dispensation in a second action if the first is ineffective.

2   Extending the time for serving a claim form: CPR 7.6

In English law, the issuing of a claim form stops time running against a claimant for the purposes of limitation. Pursuant to CPR 7.2(1) and (2), proceedings are started when the court issues a claim form at the request of the claimant, and the date of the proceedings is as entered on the claim form by the court. However, pursuant to paragraph 5.1 of CPR PD7A, where the claim form, as issued, was received in the court office on a date earlier than the date on which it was issued, the claim is deemed to be 'brought' for the purposes of the Limitation Act 1980 on that earlier date. This earlier date is recorded by the court and obviously may be crucial in determining whether the case is statute barred or not. In *Salford City Council v Garner* [2004] EWCA Civ 364, a non-personal injury case, the court emphasised that this power only applied when the expiry of a limitation period was imminent. In *Barnes v St Helens Metropolitan Borough Council* (p321) the court confirmed the decision in *Salford* and held that a personal injury action was brought when it was delivered to the court during opening hours on 4 November and not when it was officially issued some four days later because of industrial action. *Barnes* was followed in *Page v Hewetts Solicitors* (p592).

In *Barker v Hambleton District Council* (p320), these cases were distinguished where the document seeking a claim form was put under the door of the court when closed for business. (Subsequently, the Court of Appeal in *Barker* found that the claim form, even if issued properly that day, was out of time as the relevant statutory period under the provisions of s 113 of the Planning and Compulsory Purchase Act 2004 specified that the period 'started' from the relevant date, and time therefore did not run from the first day after the relevant date as it does where the provisions require compliance 'from' the relevant date; see [2012] EWCA Civ 610 at para 12.)

CPR 2.11 permits parties to vary time limits within the Rules, unless otherwise prohibited; and in *Thomas v Home Office* (p687) the Court of Appeal found this included parties agreeing to extend time for service of the claim form, as long as the agreement was in writing. Written agreement included an exchange of correspondence in which the variation is agreed or an oral agreement later confirmed in writing.

The claim form, once issued, must be served pursuant to CPR 7.5(1) by completing the steps set out in the rule, depending on the mode of service chosen, before 12 midnight on the calendar day four months after the date of issue of the claim form. This means that the day of the actual issuing does not count so that, for example, as in the case of *Smyth v Probyn & PGA European Tour Ltd* (p664) an action issued on 30 July 1999 is still valid for service within a four-month period and therefore was properly served on 30 November 1999. The new rule on service from October 2008 has made it easier for a claimant's solicitor to comply with the service rules, as there is one method for all modes of service, namely simply taking the step required such as posting, faxing, e-mailing, personally serving or leaving the document at the relevant place before midnight on the calendar day four months after the date of issue. There is, therefore, no need to be concerned over the actual or deemed date of service, as the crucial date for complying with service of the claim form is when the procedural step was taken and not the deemed date in CPR 6.14.

For cases served outside the jurisdiction, the period is extended by CPR 7.5(2) to 'within six months of the date of issue'.

For a variety of reasons, a solicitor may not immediately serve a claim form. Occasionally, a solicitor may be instructed very close to the expiry of a limitation period and needs to issue to protect the cause of action, but may not be in a position to assess whether the claimant has a good case and so does not serve immediately. The delay is caused by obtaining supportive often expert evidence. In other cases, there may be a reasonable belief that the case is likely to settle, and a desire not to incur unnecessary costs results in the proceedings not being served. On other occasions, proceedings are not served because they are simply overlooked. In some cases, solicitors have difficulty in serving. Rules of court provide for an extension of the time permitted for serving a claim form in two separate situations: the first is where an application is made within the four-month period or any previously extended period (CPR 7.6(2)); and the second is where the application is made after the period of validity of the claim form has expired. Further, in very exceptional circumstances, the court may make an order dispensing with service pursuant to CPR 6.16, or where there is good reason to authorise service by an alternative method or at an alternative place (CPR 6.15); or, where there has been a procedural error, the court may give relief from sanctions under CPR 3.10. Each of these circumstances will be discussed.

3   The general rule: prospective applications

CPR 7.6(2) states:

'(2)   The general rule is that an application to extend the time for service must be made–

(a)   within the period for serving the claim form specified by Rule 7.5; or

(b)   where an order has been made under this rule, within the period for service specified by that order.'

In addition to the rule, paragraph 8 of CPR PD7A requires that an application to extend time should be accompanied by evidence including a full explanation as to why the claim has not been served. The evidence should contain details of all the circumstances relied on, the date of issue of the claim and the expiry date of any CPR 7.6 extension. The application may be made without notice but is subject to retrospective attack by the defendant subsequently seeking to appeal any successful extension.

The Court of Appeal has held that, for any period of extension to be granted, the claimant must explain the reason for the failure. If there is a very good reason, the extension will normally be allowed; the weaker the reason, the less likely it will be that an extension is granted. In *Hashtroodi v Hancock* (p466) the claimant was rendered tetraplegic in a road traffic accident on 21 January 2000. A claim was intimated and a claims management company acting for the defendant's insurers indicated that liability was in issue. The claim form was issued on 13 January 2003, some eight days before the expiry of the limitation period. On 25 April 2003 the claimant's solicitors wrote to the claims management company, not to their place of business but to their registered office, indicating that proceedings had been issued and the papers would shortly be served and asked whether solicitors could be nominated to accept service on behalf of the defendant. The letter was not received by the claims management company until 8 May. On 9 May, one clear working day before the expiry of the validity of the claim form, the claimant's solicitors made an application without notice for a three-week extension of time for service of the claim form until 3 June. The master granted that extension. On 23 May the claimant's solicitors purported to serve the claim form and response pack through the DX, but the documents were not received and the court found they were probably lost. The defendant took out an application to set aside the order extending time. Because of the importance of the case, the Master of the Rolls determined that the re-hearing should be heard by the Court of Appeal rather than the High Court. The Court of Appeal firstly reaffirmed that the previous jurisprudence under RSC Ord 6 r 8 was of limited relevance, affirming *Biguzzi v Rank Leisure plc* (p335) and *Godwin v Swindon Borough Council* (p444), by stating that it would normally be possible to interpret the CPR without recourse to case law under the former rules.

The court further stated that CPR 7.6(2) should not be construed as being subject to a condition that 'a good reason' must be shown for failure to serve in the specified period, or indeed subject to any implied condition. The court then laid down some guidelines stating that it would always be relevant for the court to determine and then evaluate the reason why the claimant had not served the claim form in the specified period:

'19.   Whereas under the previous law, a plaintiff who was unable to show a good reason for not serving in time failed at the threshold, under the CPR, a more calibrated approach is to be adopted. If there is a very good reason for the failure to serve a claim form within the specified period, then an extension of time will usually be granted. Thus, where the court has been unable to serve the claim form, or the claimant has taken all reasonable steps to serve the claim form but has been unable to do so (the CPR 7.6(3) conditions), the court will have no difficulty in deciding that there is a very good reason for the failure to serve. The weaker the reason, the more likely the court will be to refuse to grant the extension.

20.   If the reason why the claimant does not serve the claim form within the specified period is that he (or his legal representative) simply overlooked the matter, that will be a strong reason for the court refusing to grant an extension of time for service. One of the important aims of the Woolf Reforms was to introduce more discipline into the conduct of civil litigation. One of the ways of achieving this is to insist that time limits be adhered to unless there is good reason for a departure. In *Biguzzi*, Lord Woolf said at p 1933D:

"If the Court were to ignore delays which occur, then undoubtedly they will be returned to the previous culture regarding time limits as being unimportant."

21.   It is easy enough to take the view that justice requires a short extension of time to be granted even where the reason for the failure to serve is the incompetence of the claimant's solicitors, especially if the claim is substantial. But it should not be overlooked that there is a three year limitation period for personal injury claims, and a claimant has four months in which to have served his or her claim form. Moreover the claim form does not have to contain full details of the claim, all that is required is a concise statement of the nature of the claim: See CPR 16.2(1)(a). These are generous time limits.'

The court refused to give a checklist of relevant factors but, in applying the general principles to Mr Hashtroodi's case, it found that the reason why the claim form had not been served was the incompetence of the claimant's solicitors. On the material presented to the court, the Court of Appeal said it could see no answer to an allegation of negligence against the claimant's solicitors. The court emphasised that, if a solicitor leaves the issue of a claim form almost until the expiry of the limitation period and then leaves service of the claim form until the expiry of the period for service, imminent disaster is courted. Accordingly, notwithstanding that the claim was very substantial, the issues in the case had been identified early on, a short extension of time would not undermine the case management process or substantially increase the cost of litigation, the defendant's appeal was allowed and the claim was struck out.

By contrast, in *Steele v Mooney* (p675) the Court of Appeal accepted *obiter* that, where a solicitor had been instructed in a clinical negligence action shortly before the expiry of the limitation period, there were good reasons for seeking and granting an extension of time within which to serve a claim form because of difficulties in preparing the case. These included delays, not induced by the claimant, in getting medical records and the need to obtain both expert and legal opinion as to the merits of proceeding against a particular defendant (see para 33 per Dyson LJ). Difficulties in compiling a schedule of special damages will, however, be unlikely to constitute reasons to grant an extension (cf *Kaur v CTP Coil Ltd* (p514)).

In Marshall Rankine v Maggs & others (p543, reported under *Collier v Williams*), the Court of Appeal considered four separate actions (*Collier, Marshall, Leeson* and *Glass*) raising points of construction of CPR Parts 6 and 7, and restated and reaffirmed *Hashtroodi v Hancock* (p466).

In *Leeson v Marsden* the claimant's solicitors delayed service in a clinical negligence action because the doctor failed to respond to a pre-action protocol letter. The court dismissed this as not a good reason for failing to serve and queried whether it would even have been a good reason to extend time to serve the particulars of claim. In *Glass v Surrendran*, solicitors for a claimant in a road traffic accident delayed because they were waiting for an accountant's report; again, this was dismissed as not a sufficient reason to extend the period for service.

In the light of both *Hashtroodi* and *Marshall*, it is to be doubted whether *Mason v First Leisure Corporation plc* (p546) would now be decided the same way. In *Mason* the court held that it would be disproportionate to set aside a claim form where an extension of time had been granted without notice, even though there was no good reason, on the basis that there was no prejudice to the defendant who had received a pre-action protocol letter of claim. Under the pre-CPR case law, good reasons had included an express or implied agreement to defer service, cases where the defendant was difficult to serve or was obstructing service, and cases where there had been substantial difficulties investigating a claim.

For further non-personal injury cases where the relevant principles are helpfully set out, see *Imperial Cancer Research Fund v Ove Arup* [2009] EWHC 1453 (TCC), *City & General (Holborn) Ltd v Structure Tone Limited* (p373).

In *Cecil (and others) v Bayat (and others)* (p367) the court rejected, as a sufficient reason to give a prospective extension, difficulties in obtaining funding:

'42. In my judgment, it was not for the Claimants unilaterally to decide to postpone service of their claim form. They should have served it in the period of its initial validity, and, if they were not in a financial position to proceed immediately with the claim, they should have issued an application seeking a stay, or an extension of the time for procedural steps to be taken. I do not accept that this would necessarily have involved great legal costs. The nature of their application would have been apparent. It would have been for the court to ensure that those costs were kept within acceptable limits, and if necessary an order limiting the Claimants' cost exposure in respect of that application could have been sought under CPR r 44.18. The court would, in my view, have been astute to prevent the Claimants being unduly prejudiced by any attempt by the Defendants to seek to proliferate costs at that very early stage.

43. In other words, any forensic difficulties caused by the financial constraints of the Claimants should have been the subject of case management by the Court. I would respectfully endorse what was said in the judgment of this Court in *Hoddinott v Persimmon Homes (Wessex) Ltd* [2007] EWCA Civ 1203 [2008] 1 WLR 806:

> "54. It is tempting to ask: what is the point in refusing to extend the time for service if the claimant can issue fresh proceedings? But service of the claim form serves three purposes. The first is to notify the defendant that the claimant has embarked on the formal process of litigation and to inform him of the nature of the claim. The second is to enable the defendant to participate in the process and have some say in the way in which the claim is prosecuted: until he has been served, the defendant may know that proceedings are likely to be issued, but he does not know for certain and he can do nothing to move things along. The third is to enable the court to control the litigation process. If extensions of time for serving pleadings or taking other steps are justified, they will be granted by the court. But until the claim form is served, the court has no part to play in the proceedings. A key element of the Woolf reforms was to entrust the court with far more control over proceedings than it had exercised under the previous regime. The rules must be applied so as to give effect to the overriding objective: this includes dealing with a case so as to ensure so far as is practicable that cases are dealt with expeditiously and fairly (CPR 1.1(2)(d)). That is why the court is unlikely to grant an extension of time for service of the claim form under CPR 7.6(2) if no good reason has been shown for the failure to serve within the four months' period."

In *Hoddinott v Persimmon Homes (Wessex) Ltd* (p477), the Court of Appeal was of the view that an extension had been inappropriately given; but, because the defendant had been sent the claim form and did not dispute jurisdiction within the 14 days as required by CPR 11, the defendant was deemed to have accepted that the claim should proceed. CPR 11 can create a trap for an unwary defendant who wishes to dispute service as being in time. The rule requires the defendant to file an acknowledgement of service in accordance with Part 10 and then to issue an application contesting service within 14 days. If the application is not taken out, the defendant is treated by CPR 11(5) to have accepted the court's jurisdiction to try the claim.

4 Retrospective applications: CPR 7.6(3)

In *Marshall Rankine v Maggs* (p543) the court emphasised that there was a substantial difference between the court's discretion under CPR 7.6(2) and under CPR 7.6(3). Where the application is made before time had expired, the court must make a judgment about the reason why service was not effected; whereas, where an application is made after time for service has expired, the court is involved in a less subtle exercise and is simply determining whether the conditions under CPR 7.6(3) have been met.

CPR 7.6(3) as amended now states:

'(3)   If the claimant applies for an order to extend the time for compliance after the end of the period specified by rule 7.5 or by an order made under this rule, the court may make such an order only if–

(a)   the court has failed to serve the claim form; or

(b)   the claimant has taken all reasonable steps to comply with rule 7.5 but has been unable to do so; and

(c)   in either case, the claimant has acted promptly in making the application.

(4)   An application for an order extending the time for compliance with rule 7.5–

(a)   must be supported by evidence; and

(b)   may be made without notice.'

With respect to the first condition, where the court has been unable to serve the claim form, it was held in *Cranfield v Bridgegrove* (p389) that a failure by the court to take any steps at all to attempt to serve would fall within the condition. In *Cranfield* the court dealt with five linked appeals concerning CPR 7.6. Two of the cases, *Cranfield* and *Claussen*, concerned actions where the claimant's solicitors had asked the court to serve the claim form. In both cases the court failed to do so through administrative neglect. The Court of Appeal held that 'unable to serve' in CPR 7.6(3)(a) included those cases where no attempt at all had been made by the court. In *Cranfield* the Court of Appeal upheld the judge's decision to extend time. However, in *Claussen* the court refused the claimant an extension to serve the claim form. This was because, on analysis, the real reason for the failure by the court to serve in time was that the claimant's solicitors failed to inform the court that the defendant's solicitors were willing to accept service and that the court should serve urgently rather than 'in due course'.

Most of the reported cases have concerned condition (b), namely whether the claimant has taken all reasonable steps to serve the claim form but has been unable to do so. Cases where the claimant's solicitors have simply served the wrong person are unlikely to satisfy this condition. In *Smyth v Probyn & PGA European Tour Ltd* (p664), proceedings were served on the defendant's solicitors, who pointed out that they had no instructions to accept service and had never indicated that they had. The Court of Appeal declined to extend time to serve the claim form on the simple basis that the defendant could have been served personally, and clarification as to whether the defendant's solicitors had authority to accept service could have been sought. Similarly, a failure to serve the right person in *Nanglegan v Royal Free Hampstead NHS Trust* (p567), where the defendant was served, even though solicitors had been nominated, resulted in the Court of Appeal refusing an extension. In *Nanglegan* the Court of Appeal pointed out that the claim form could have been faxed to the defendant in time in any event. The claimant's errors were said to come against a background of 'a catalogue of risk taking' where proceedings had been issued on the last day of the limitation period followed by three months of dilatory behaviour. Serving the defendant's insurers, instead of the defendant, on the last day of the validity of the claim form also resulted in a failure to obtain an extension in *Elmes v Hygrade Food Products plc* (p423).

In *Vinos v Marks & Spencer plc* (p701) the claimant's solicitors failed to serve in time due to an oversight. It was accepted in the Court of Appeal that the extension could not be made under CPR 7.6(3) or under CPR 3.1(2)(a), but the claimant sought relief under CPR 3.10 which gave the court a power to rectify an error of procedure which, it was contended, a failure to serve in time constituted. The court rejected this submission:

> '20.   The meaning of rule 7.6(3) is plain. The court has power to extend the time for serving the claim form after the period for its service has run out "only if" the stipulated conditions are fulfilled. That means that the court does not have powers to do so otherwise. The discretionary power in the rules to extend time period – Rule 3.1(2)(a) – does not apply because of the introductory words "except where these rules provide otherwise". The general words of rule 3.10 cannot extend to enable the court to do what rule 7.6(3) specifically forbids, nor to extend time when the specific provisions of the rules which enables extensions of time specifically does not extend to making this extension of time. What Mr Vinos in substance needs is an extension of time – calling it correctly an error does not change its substance. Interpretation to achieve the overriding objectives does not enable the court to say that provisions which are quite plain mean what they do not mean, nor that the plain meaning should be ignored. It would be erroneous to say that, because Mr Vinos's case is a deserving case, the rules must be interpreted to accommodate his particular case. The first question for this court is, not whether Mr Vinos should have the discretionary extension of time, but whether there is power under the Civil Procedure Rules to extend the period for service of a claim form if the application is made after the period has run out and the conditions of Rule 7.6(3) do not apply. The merits of Mr Vinos's particular case are not relevant to that question. Rule 3.10 concerns correcting errors which the parties have made, but it does not, by itself, contribute to the interpretation of other explicit rules. If you then look up from the wording the Rule, at a broader horizon, one of the main aims of the Civil Procedure Rules and their overriding objective is that civil litigation should be undertaken and pursued with proper expedition. Criticism of Mr Vinos's solicitors in this case may be muted and limited to one error capable of being represented as small; but there are statutory limitation period for bringing proceedings. It is unsatisfactory with a personal injury claim to allow almost three years to elapse and to start proceedings at the very last moment. If you do, it is in my judgment, generally in accordance with the overriding objective that you should be required to progress the proceedings speedily and within the time limit. Four months is in most cases more than adequate for serving a claim form. There is nothing unjust in a system which says that, if you leave issuing proceedings to the last moment and then do not comply with this particular time requirement and do not satisfy the conditions in Rule 7.6(3), your claim is lost and a new claim will be statute barred. You have had three years and four months to get things in order. Sensible negotiations are to be encouraged, but protracted negotiations generally are not. In the present case, there may have been an acknowledged position between the parties that defendant's insurers will pay compensation; but it is not suggested that they acted in any way which disabled the defendant in law or equity on relying on the statutory limitation provisions and on the Civil Procedure Rules as properly interpreted.' (per May LJ)

In *Chaudhry v Post Office* (p372) an attempt to serve the defendants through the DX was bound to fail as they were not members of it. The court held, unsurprisingly, that this was a self-inflicted wound and refused an extension. In *Spade Lane Cool Stores v Kilgour* (p667) the court also refused an extension where it found that the claimant's solicitors had made insufficient attempts to identify the last known place of business of the defendant who was an architect. The solicitors had undertaken an internet search and had looked at an RIBA directory, but the court held that was insufficient. A further search through the yellow pages and contact with the RIBA should have been made. Similarly, in *Marshall Rankine v Maggs* (p543) the Court of Appeal emphasised that it was incumbent on a claimant to take reasonable steps to ascertain a defendant's last known residence (see paras 102–105).

The final condition in CPR 7.6(3)(c), that the application to extend has to be made promptly, is self-explanatory and requires the claimant's advisers to make an application probably within days.

5   Service by an alternative method or place

CPR 6.15 provides as follows:

'(1)   Where it appears to the court that there is a good reason to authorise service by a method or at a place not otherwise permitted by this Part, the court may make an order permitting service by an alternative method or at an alternative place.

(2)   On an application under this rule, the court may order that steps already taken to bring the claim form to the attention of the defendant by an alternative method or at an alternative place is good service.

(3)   An application for an order under this rule–

(a)   must be supported by evidence; and
(b)   may be made without notice.

(4)   An order under this rule must specify–

(a)   the method or place of service;
(b)   the date on which the claim form is deemed served; and
(c)   the period for–
    (i)   filing an acknowledgment of service;
    (ii)   filing an admission; or
    (iii) filing a defence.'

One of the objects of this rule was to give the court a discretion to mitigate the effects of decisions such as *Elmes v Hygrade Food Products plc* (p423), where the court had no power to remedy a solicitor's error in serving the wrong party (namely the insurers rather than the defendant), or *Nanglegan v Royal Free Hampstead NHS Trust* (p567), where the claim form was served on the defendant instead of the nominated solicitors.

In *Brown v Innovatorone plc* (p352) the court refused to sanction service by fax because the claimant's solicitors had not been told by the solicitors served that they would accept service. The judge indicated that the power should be exercised rigorously, although there was no requirement to show exceptional reasons why the designated mode of service was not used.

In *Bethell Construction v Deloitte and Touche* (p332) the parties had agreed extensions of time for serving the claim form which was sent to the defendants but explicitly not by way of service. After terminating the extension by notice, the particulars of claim (but not the claim form) were served on the defendant. The Court of Appeal upheld the decision not to treat the delivery of the claim form as service or to dispense with service under CPR 6.16. The court accepted that the test was, first, to see whether there was good reason to apply the rule, and then to see if the discretion should be exercised. The first instance judge's approach was set out and endorsed by the Chancellor:

'23. ... The order Bethells seek is that the possession of the copy of the claim form by Deloittes since 2007 and the sending of the letter dated 14th October by Bethells' solicitors should be treated as an alternative method of service. It was suggested that the facts relied on for the establishment of a waiver or an estoppel, if not sufficient for that purpose, constitute good reason for the purposes of this rule to justify the order sought.

24. This was rejected by the judge. He held (paragraphs 40 and 41):

"40. I do not accept those submissions. I do so principally because it seems to me that it would subvert the whole basis of the agreement reached between the parties as to the extension of time for service of the claim form and particulars of claim. It seems to me that it is in the interest of the overriding objective for parties to be able to reach agreement for an extension of time for service of the claim form if this enables them to achieve a resolution of litigation without over-extensive resort to the courts, with a consequent expenditure of legal costs and use of court time. However, for the parties to proceed in this way, it is also important that the court is seen to be upholding the basis upon which they have agreed that they will proceed. Mr Dagnall's approach, it seems to me, would operate to subvert the parties' contractual autonomy, and it would fail to give effect to the important principle of freedom of contract ...

41. Adopting the language employed by Lord Justice Neuberger in the case of *Kuenyehia and others v International Hospitals Group Ltd.* [2006] EWCA Civ 21 at paragraph 36, this was not a case of 'a minor departure from a permitted method of service or an ineffective attempt to serve by a permitted method within the time limit'. This was not a case of mis-service but one of non-service. The claim form had been delivered in 2007 expressly 'not by way of service'. The defendants agreed to that; and the parties agreed that either party could determine what was effectively the standstill agreement by giving 14 days' notice for service of the claim form. That is what the defendants' solicitors did by their letter of 22nd October. The Heatons letter of 14th October had said absolutely nothing about service of the claim form. It seems to me that the parties should be held to what they had agreed; and, after all, it was the claimants' solicitors who had originally proposed it back in 2007. For those reasons, to hold that there was good service would be to subvert the express agreement between the parties, and fail to give effect to the important principle of freedom of contract and the contractual autonomy of the parties. It would be a wholly inappropriate exercise of the court's discretion to effectively allow the claimants to rewrite the agreement between the parties. It does not seem to me here that there is any good reason to authorise service contrary to what the parties had agreed."

Counsel for Bethells submits that there are two issues (a) whether there is good reason shown sufficient to engage the rule, and if so (b) whether the judicial discretion which then arises should be exercised in favour of making the order Bethells seek. He submits that the judge was wrong on both points.

253

25. I accept that that is the correct approach to the rule in that they are cumulative conditions. I also accept, as counsel submitted, that "the good reason" needed is something less than the exceptional circumstances required by CPR Rule 6.16. For my part I do not accept that either condition was satisfied. In the events which happened and in the light of my conclusions so far Deloittes is entitled to rely on the Limitation Act as a bar to all further proceedings. Given that, as I would hold, they have not waived the requirement for service of the claim form and are not estopped from requiring it I cannot see any reason, whether good or not, why the court should exercise any discretion it might have so as to deny Deloittes their accrued right.

26. The judge relied on the sanctity of the extension of time agreement. In addition I can see nothing in the correspondence of 2010 to justify penalising Deloittes. Even accepting, as the judge found, that they had set a trap, the cause of Bethells' problem was that Mr Austin fell into it. I do not understand why or how the mistake of one party can justify denying so substantial a lawful consequence to the other. I would reject this ground too.'

In the light of the restrictive application of the power demonstrated to date, it remains to be seen whether the rule will be used to mitigate situations as occurred in *Elmes* and *Nanglegan*.

6   Dispensing with service: pre-amendment CPR 6.9 and post-amendment CPR 6.16

CPR 6.16 provides:

'(1)   The court may dispense with service of a claim form in exceptional circumstances.

(2)   An application for an order to dispense with service may be made at any time and–

(a)   must be supported by evidence; and
(b)   may be made without notice.'

CPR 6.9 CASES

From 1 October 2008, CPR 6.16 replaced the previous CPR 6.9, which gave the court a power to dispense with service of any 'document', which was held in *Anderton v Clwyd County Council* (p303) to include a claim form. However, the court has been asked to exercise that power in relation to cases where a claim form has not been served timeously and where the provisions of CPR 7.6 concerning an application to extend time for serving a claim form were unlikely to be granted. The precise ambit of the discretion within the previous CPR 6.9 took some time to be determined by the courts, but it became clear that the power would only rarely be exercised.

One of the first examples where the power was used is to be found in *Infantino v MacLean* (p488), where a claim form was delivered a day late because it had been sent to the wrong DX number. The court followed *Vinos* and *Kaur* and held that the conditions specified in CPR 7.6(3) were not satisfied. However, the judge exercised his discretion within CPR 6.9 on the basis that the pre-action clinical negligence protocol had been fully complied with and the defendants had suffered no prejudice. *Infantino* did not go to appeal and was reluctantly followed shortly afterwards at first instance by McCombe J in *Anderton v Clwyd County Council* (p303) on the issue of the court having such a discretion. The judge in *Anderton* did not, however, exercise the discretion in the claimant's favour.

In *Godwin v Swindon Borough Council* (p444) the Court of Appeal (10 October 2001) held that CPR 6.9 could not displace CPR 7.6(3) to permit the court to dispense with service entirely, and overruled *Infantino*. Lord Justice May stated:

'50. ... The heart of the matter, in my view, is that a person who, by mistake, failed to serve the claim form within the time period, permitted by rule 7.5(2) in substance needs an extension of time to do so. If an application for an extension is not made before the current time period expired, rule 7.6(3) prescribes the only circumstances in which the court has power to grant such an extension. Just as *Vinos v Marks & Spencer* decides that the general words of rule 3.10 cannot extend to enable the court to do what rule 7.6(3) specifically forbids, I do not consider that rule 6.1(b) or 6.9 can extend to enable the court to dispense with service when what would be done is in substance that which rule 7.6(3) forbids. If rule 6.9 did so extend, it would be tantamount to giving the court a discretionary power to dispense with statutory limitation provisions ... I ... consider that rule 6.9 does not extend to extricate a claimant from the consequences of late service of the claim form where limitation is critical and rule 7.6(3) does not avail a claimant.'

Anderton v Clwyd County Council (p303) was subsequently appealed and the Court of Appeal modified the *Godwin* decision and determined that the power under CPR 6.9 to dispense with service, both prospectively and retrospectively, did exist. The power, however, should be exercised retrospectively only in exceptional circumstances. In particular, the Court of Appeal in *Anderton* made a distinction, not analysed in *Godwin*, between category 1 cases – where there had been no attempt to serve the claim form in time by any of the permitted methods in CPR 2.3 – and category 2 cases – where there had been an ineffective attempt. The court held that the first type of case was indeed caught by the ruling in *Godwin*. However, the second category of cases, where there had been an ineffective attempt to serve the claim form by an appropriate method, was different in kind. In such cases, where the defendant had in reality received the claim form within the relevant period but, because of deeming provisions, the claim form was held to have been received out of time, the claimant did not need an extension to serve out of time but needed to be excused service. Such examples are to be found in *Chambers* and *Dorgan*, two of the consolidated appeals in *Anderton*. In *Chambers* the claimant's husband was killed in a road traffic accident and liability was admitted. The claim form was sent by first class post on 12 July and in fact arrived on 13 July which was the last day of the validity of the claim form. However, the deeming provisions meant that the claim form was deemed to have arrived on the second day after posting and accordingly the claim form was held to have been served out of time and the claim was struck out. The Court of Appeal said that, in reality, the claim form had been brought to the defendant's attention within the four-month period. In addition, the defendant had made an offer to settle the case after it had received the claim form. Accordingly, the court considered that this was an exceptional case and dispensed with the need for service. In *Dorgan* the claim form was faxed at 4.02pm on Friday, 10 August 2001. Being after 4pm, it was deemed to have arrived on the business day after the day it was transmitted, namely on the following Monday. Had it been transmitted before 4pm it would have been deemed delivered that day. The claim form's validity in fact expired on Saturday, 11 August. The defendant had already been notified of the claim. The judge exercised his discretion under CPR 6.9 to dispense with the service of the claim form and this was upheld by the Court of Appeal. The court in *Anderton* stated that, since the rules on deemed service have now been clarified both in *Godwin* and in *Anderton*, there will be fewer cases where a failure to observe service rules would give rise to an acceptable excuse warranting the exercise of discretion under CPR 6.9. In *Wilkey v BBC* (p717) the Court of Appeal confirmed that, in post-*Anderton* cases, a different attitude to dispensing with service was appropriate. Whereas, in pre-*Anderton* cases, there was a prescription in favour of dispensing with service where the claimant had sought to serve and the defendants had in fact received the claim form within the period of validity, the position post-*Anderton* would be quite different. Now that the rules concerning deemed service were clear, it would only be in exceptional cases that CPR 6.9 would be exercised to dispense with service of a claim form.

Lord Justice Simon Brown stated:

'18.   The solution I would propose to the problem is this. In category 2 cases which, like the present (and, as I am led to believe, like a number of other appeals now awaiting hearing in this court), involve deemed late service before this court's decision in *Anderton*, the Rule 6.9 dispensing power should ordinarily be exercised in a claimant's favour unless the defendant can establish either that he would suffer prejudice (apart, obviously, from the loss of his limitation act defence) or some other good reason why the power should not be exercised. Merely to establish that the claimant has been guilty of avoidable delay in either the issue, or the service, of the claim form, or both, would not generally constitute such good reason. There will always have been some avoidable delay. Similarly, the fact that the claim looks unpromising will not generally be a good reason for refusing to exercise the dispensing power in a pre-*Anderton* category 2 case. In a post-*Anderton* case, however, the dispensing power should, in my judgment, ordinarily not be exercised in the claimant's favour. These cases, albeit within category 2, and therefore in one sense to be regarded as exceptional, in my mind fall foul of paragraph 2 of the court's judgment in *Anderton*. In these cases "the strict approach" should generally be adopted.'

In *Wilkey*, a pre-*Anderton* case, the court said that the power should be exercised to dispense with service, but had it been a post-*Anderton* case it would have failed. (The claim form was in fact delivered to the defendant but was deemed one day late.) Lord Justice Carnwath stated in *Wilkey*:

'It is now clear that, in the respects relevant to this case, the rules of service in the CPR constitute a strict regime, introduced in the interests of certainty … the matter now having been exhaustively reviewed in three judgments of this court, the transition period must be taken to have come to an end.' (at para 28)

In *Cranfield v Bridgegrove* (p389) the Court of Appeal confirmed that, unless a case fell squarely within the exceptional category identified in *Anderton*, CPR 6.9 should not be exercised to dispense with service. Accordingly, it refused to dispense with service in the cases of *Claussen* and *McManus* but did state that it would have, if necessary, permitted a dispensation in the case of *Murphy*. In *McManus* the solicitors served the insurers rather than the defendant, and accordingly the *Anderton* conditions were not engaged because at no time had the claim form been received by the defendants or their solicitors. In *Murphy* the claimant served the defendant company personally instead of nominated solicitors. Service was held in fact to be valid as the claimant had elected to serve under s 725 of the Companies Act 1985. The court did state, openly, that the facts fell within *Anderton* and the judge would have been correct to dispense with service under CPR 6.9.

The strict approach in post-*Anderton* cases is illustrated in *Horn v Dorset Healthcare NHS Trust* (p480), where the court applied both *Anderton* and *Cranfield* in a case where the claimant's solicitors served the defendant health authority rather than nominated solicitors. The claimant's solicitors did so because they had received no confirmation from the defendant's solicitors that they were authorised to accept service, even though the defendant itself had indicated so. The court held that the solicitors did not need to confirm their authority and the claimant was bound once solicitors were nominated to serve on them (see *Nanglegan v Royal Free Hampstead NHS Trust* (p567)). Although the case came within the second category of *Anderton* (the claimant had effected service by a permitted method and the defendant had in fact received the claim form), the court found that there were no exceptional circumstances and refused to dispense with service. (See also *Lakah v Al-Jazeera Satellite Channel* (p525).)

In *Olafsson v Gissurarson* [2008] EWCA Civ 152 the Court of Appeal confirmed that the old CPR 6.9 provision should only ever be invoked in exceptional cases (see also *Thorne v Lass Salt Garvin* (p692).

CPR 6.16 CASES

It was therefore unsurprising that the new power to dispense with service specifically states that the power will be used exceptionally. This in part reflects the decided cases on the earlier rule, but it also reflects the advantages that the new rules on service have given to a claimant's solicitors which make service, even at the last moment, easier to effect. There is no longer a concern for a claimant's solicitors as to when actual or deemed service takes place, as the crucial date is the date when the required steps in CPR 7.5 were taken.

In *Bethell Construction Ltd v Deloitte and Touche* (p332), where a claim form was sent specifically not by way of service, the court declined to exercise its power in CPR 6.15 and allow it to stand as service by an alternative method. It therefore logically followed that, if there were no good reasons under CPR 6.15, it would be difficult to cross the higher threshold of exceptional circumstances in CPR 6.16. The Lord Chancellor stated:

'27. … Bethells sought to persuade the judge that he should make an order in this case dispensing with service of the claim form. The judge refused. He said (paragraph 42):

"… this is not a case where the claim form was delivered to the defendants within the period for service by a method of service which the claimants and their solicitors thought was a reasonable method of service. The claim form had been delivered expressly not by way of service, and was never delivered to the defendants again; nor was any statement made that by serving the particulars of claim the claimants were treating the claim form as having, by that act, been served. There was nothing to suggest that the claimants were regarding the not-by-way-of-service condition attached to the previous delivery of the claim form as in any way having been extinguished. Again, it seems to me that it would be an impermissible exercise of the power under the rule to dispense with service of the claim form in those circumstances."

28.   Counsel for Bethells submitted that the judge was wrong. I can only say that I reject that submission. If the facts of this case do not reveal a "good reason" to make the order regarding service of the claim form sought under CPR Rule 6.15 they cannot possibly disclose "exceptional circumstances" sufficient to justify dispensing with service altogether. Nor could they provide any sufficient reason to make the order sought. And, for good measure, Bethells have entirely failed to show any ground on which this court could interfere with the discretion of the judge.'

7   Rectifying an error of procedure: CPR 3.10

CPR 3.10 provides:

'3.10   Where there has been an error of procedure such as a failure to comply with a rule or practice direction–

(a)   the error does not invalidate any step taken in the proceedings unless the court so orders; and

(b)   the court may make an order to remedy the error.'

As discussed in *Vinos* above, the Court of Appeal has specifically stated that the provisions of CPR 3.10 do not give the court power to do what the provisions of CPR 7.6 prohibit (see also *Kaur v CTP Coil Ltd* (p514) and *Elmes v Hygrade Food Products* (p423)). However, on the special facts of *Steele v Mooney* (p675) the Court of Appeal distinguished *Vinos* and *Elmes* and permitted an order rectifying an application to extend the period of time permitted for serving the particulars of claim and supporting documentation to include an additional reference to the claim form. In *Steele* the claimant underwent a hysterectomy on 9 May 2000 and contended that she received further surgery to which she had not consented. She pursued complaints for a period of two years but only instructed solicitors on 22 May 2003. Those solicitors issued protective proceedings on 6 May 2003 three days within the limitation period. On 13 August the solicitors issued an application for an extension of time to serve the particulars of claim and 'supporting documents' but did not include a specific reference to the claim form. However, the solicitor acting for the claimant had sent a draft consent order which referred to leave to serve the particulars of claim and supporting documentation including the claim form. The applications themselves, however, did not include that reference. The solicitor obtained two extensions on the basis that she needed more time, because she had great difficulty in obtaining the claimant's records and the expert instructed felt unable to comment until the missing records were obtained. In addition, she also required the opinion of counsel to determine whether there was a reasonable cause of action. The extensions were granted until 29 January 2004. On 18 February the claimant's solicitors realised their previous errors and applied under CPR 3.10 to rectify the extensions to include extension of time for service of the claim form. The Court of Appeal allowed this rectification on the basis that, on a true analysis, the application was to correct a procedural error to include the word 'Claim Form' in the applications and was not a renewed application for further time to serve and therefore not an attempt to circumvent the prohibition in CPR 7.6(3). The court distinguished *Vinos* on the basis that there was a difference between making an application which contained an error and erroneously not making an application at all:

'28.   In our judgment, the error made in the present case falls into the first of these two categories. The applications for an extension of time was clearly intended to be an application for an extension of time for service of the claim form but by mistake they referred to the wrong, albeit closely related, document, ie the particulars of claim … If the error were a failure to make an application for an extension of time at all within the period specified by Rule 7.5(2), then an application to remedy that error would in substance be an application for an extension of time after the expiry of the specified period, and would fail for the reasons stated in *Vinos*: it would in substance be an application for an extension of time for service of the claim form after the expiry of the time for service in circumstances where such an extension of time would be prohibited by Rule 7.6(3) … the application of 18 February 2004 was not in substance an application for an extension of time for service of the claim form. It was in substance an application to correct the applications for an extension of time which were made within the time specified for service by Rule 7.5(2) and which by mistake did not refer to the claim form. To remedy the error contained in the applications (and the resultant orders) does not circumvent the prohibition in Rule 7.6(3).'

It is apparent that the ambit of CPR 3.10 in this context is closely circumscribed. There is, for example, no power to extend time where a statute imposes a limit, unless found within the same statute (*Mucelli v Albania* [2009] UKHL 2, [2009] 1 WLR 276).

8   Extension of time to serve a particulars of claim

The court has a more extended discretion under CPR 3.10 to extend time for service of the particulars of claim. In *Totty v Snowden* (p694) the claimant failed to serve his particulars of claim within the time limits imposed by CPR 7.4(2); that is, no later than the latest time available for serving the claim form itself. This period will always be less than the 14 days permitted under CPR 7.4(1) after serving the claim form in those cases where the claim form was served in the period within 14 days of its expiry. This is a frequent trap for a claimant's solicitors to fall into. The Court of Appeal acknowledged that the particulars of claim were not an integral part of the claim form and that the provisions of CPR 7.6 did not apply to applications to extend time to serve the particulars of claim as they did to serve the claim form itself. The court was satisfied, both in *Totty* and in the conjoined appeal of *Hewitt v Wirral Cheshire Community NHS Trust*, that the exercise of discretion within CPR 3.10 should be in the claimant's favour.

In *Price v Price* (p611) the Court of Appeal was faced with an action where the delay in serving the particulars of claim was 14 months. The particulars were served with a schedule indicating, for the first time, a substantial claim for loss of earnings. Insurers had estimated the value of the claim at £10,000 but the schedule claimed £500,000. The judge at first instance struck the claim out because of substantial breaches of compliance with the court timetable. On appeal, the Court of Appeal permitted the action to proceed notwithstanding that the solicitors' conduct put them very much on the wrong side of the checklist of factors set out in CPR 3.9 which govern how the court grants relief from sanctions. In addition the defendants had behaved entirely properly. The court was of the opinion that to strike out the claim was disproportionate. Instead, the court imposed a number of sanctions by limiting the claim to damages that could be supported by medical evidence available in April 2000 and required the claimant to pay costs off-set against damages.

In *Gregory v Benham* (p447), a failure to serve particulars of claim two months out of time led to the court refusing to extend time for service, and the claim for defamation was struck out in circumstances where there had also been failures to comply with the relevant pre-action protocol.

In *UK Highways A55 Ltd v Hyder Consulting (UK) Ltd* (p698), an extension to allow service of the particulars of claim was permitted in circumstances where the parties had agreed four stays and the claimant could no longer comply with the rule of service of the particulars within 14 days of service of the claim form. However, an additional allegation of failing to supervise the construction of a road designed by the defendants was not permitted to be added some 12 years after the original allegations limited to negligent design.

In *Roberts v Momentum Services Ltd* (p623) a prospective application for an extension of time to serve the particulars of claim was made. Proceedings had been issued on 1 March 2001 but the claimant's solicitors feared they would not be ready to serve the particulars of claim by 1 July 2001 due to a lack of medical evidence. They accordingly applied under CPR 3.1(2)(a) to extend the time permitted for serving the particulars of claim. The district judge allowed the application but, on appeal, the circuit judge allowed the defendant's appeal. The Court of Appeal reinstated the district judge's decision, saying that he had not erred in the exercise of his discretion. The court held that a prospective application to extend time did not require the judge to go through the checklist of factors in CPR 3.9 (*Sayers v Clarke-Walker* [2002] 3 All ER 490 distinguished).

9 Striking out a statement of case: CPR 3.4

CPR 3.4 provides:

'(1)   In this rule and rule 3.5 reference to a statement of case includes a reference to part of a statement of case.

(2)   The court may strike out a statement of case if it appears to the court–

(a)   that the statement of case discloses no reasonable grounds for bringing or defending the claim;

(b)   that the statement of case is an abuse of the court's process or is otherwise likely to obstruct the just disposal of the proceedings; or

(c)   that here has been a failure to comply with a rule, practice direction or court order.'

The provisions of the CPR have imposed a court-based case management structure on litigation, which has restored to the court control over the length of time it takes an action, once issued, to reach trial. The success of the CPR in this respect has rendered largely irrelevant the substantial jurisprudence that arose between 1960 and 1998 concerning the court's inherent powers to strike out a case for want of prosecution. Further, the court has developed a new body of case law governing how it sanctions failures to comply with the court timetable or a court order pursuant to CPR 3.4(2)(c). This approach has seen the court more reluctant to strike out cases and more inclined to impose sanctions on failures to comply with orders.

The court's approach under the CPR was initially set out in *Biguzzi v Rank Leisure plc* (p335), a case where the claimant was injured in November 1993, issued proceedings in October 1995 and had his case struck out by a district judge in 1999 for failing to comply with a number of court requirements. The circuit judge reinstated the case on the basis that he thought that a fair trial could still be heard. The defendant appealed to the Court of Appeal. Lord Woolf stated that the judge had an unfettered discretion under CPR 3.4(2)(c) and that earlier authorities would have little relevance. The court also stated that, although the court had an unfettered power to strike out, that did not mean that that should be the initial approach. Lord Woolf stated:

> 'The advantage of the CPR over the previous rules is that the court's powers are much broader than they were. In many cases there will be alternatives which will enable a case to be dealt with justly without taking the draconian step of striking the case out.
>
> Under the court's duty to manage cases, delays such as has occurred in this case, should, it is hoped, no longer happen. The court's management powers should ensure that this does not occur. But if the court exercises those powers with circumspection, it is also essential that parties do not disregard timetables laid down. If they do so, then the court must make sure that the default does not go unmarked. If the court were to ignore delays which occur, then undoubtedly they will be returned to the previous culture of regarding time limits as being unimportant.'

Lord Woolf mentioned some of the alternative sanctions, such as adverse costs orders including orders for indemnity costs, a deprivation of interest or the imposition of enhanced rates of interest, and orders that money should be paid into court. On the facts in *Biguzzi* the court was of the view that the trial judge had properly exercised his discretion.

In 1999 in *Purdy v Cambran* (p614) the Court of Appeal upheld the decision to strike out a claim which arose out of a road traffic accident in 1989 and where liability had been admitted. In *Purdy* the defendant suffered a specific form of prejudice in that their medical expert had died in 1998. The court stated that, while it was inappropriate to refer to the large body of authority that arose under the previous jurisprudence, the underlying thought processes of previous decisions could still be relevant and should not be completely thrown overboard.

The more measured approach of imposing conditions on permitting a claim to continue is illustrated in the case of *Stacey v Joint Mission Hospital Equipment Board* (p672). Mr Stacey suffered a head injury in 1987 which rendered him a patient. Because of procedural delays his case became automatically stayed in 2000 under the provisions of CPR 51. Mr Stacey applied to have the stay lifted and it was granted on condition that he was precluded from claiming losses beyond those set out in a schedule served on 21 January 1998 and that he was precluded from claiming interest from 1 January 2000. A similar approach was taken in *Price v Price* (see above), where an extension of time to serve particulars of claim was granted on the basis that damages would be limited to those that could be substantiated by medical evidence that was already in existence in April 2001. In *Price* the Court of Appeal relied on an earlier decision in *Walsh v Misseldine* (p706), where the Court of Appeal restricted the claimant's claim to that which could still be subject to a fair trial. In *Walsh* the Court of Appeal considered the cases of *Biguzzi* and *Purdy* and confirmed the more calibrated approach open to it under the CPR:

> '82.   I would add that the court is no longer necessarily faced, in a case in which liability is not in issue, with making the decision wholly in favour of one side or the other on a strike out application. It may be able to take a middle

course if this is more consistent with the overriding objective of doing justice.'
(per Brooke LJ)

and:

'99. It is clear that the court is now able to adopt the much more flexible
approach to the question of striking out for delay or non-compliance of an
order, than was possible under the somewhat rigid rules of the old law. In
Biguzzi v Rank Leisure plc [1999] 1 WLR 1926 this court made it clear that
references should no longer be made to the old cases (see per Lord Woolf
MR at 1932). But some of the considerations which were relevant before
are obviously relevant now. For example the length of, explanation for and
responsibility for the delay; whether the defendant has suffered prejudice as
a result and if so whether it can be compensated for by some order relating
to costs or interest or is it so serious that it would be unjust to the Defendant
to require the case to be tried. Moreover, the delay may be such that it is no
longer possible to have a fair trial.' (per Stuart-Smith LJ)

The court, on the facts of that case, permitted the action to proceed to trial on the
basis that the judge assessed compensation which would have been payable to Mr
Walsh at a trial conducted on 15 March 1995. In addition, the court ordered that he
would not be entitled to any interest on those damages between that date and the
date of the court order allowing his appeal.

Orders such as those made in *Walsh* and in *Price* may create a degree of artificiality
in the assessment of damages but, obviously, so far as the claimant is concerned, have
the benefits of preserving something of value in the cause of action. Cases concerning
the new strike-out provisions have been mainly concerned with transitional cases
between the pre-CPR and CPR periods, and it is to be anticipated that striking out a
case for want of prosecution will be something of an increasing rarity now that the
CPR provisions are fully in force and properly case managed.

In *Aktas v Adepta* (p296) the court examined in great detail whether the issuing
of a second personal injury action after the first was not served and whether seeking
a s 33 discretion (following the abolition of the rule in *Walkley v Precision Forging*)
amounted to an abuse of process so that the second action should be struck out. After
a lengthy discourse on the jurisprudence of abuse of process, service under both RSC
and CPR, and s 33 discretion, the court concluded there was no abuse:

'89. It is time to draw the strings together. In my judgment, the abuse of
process argument relied upon by the defendants to deny the claimants an
opportunity to rely on section 33 of the 1980 Act for the purpose of bringing
within time a second action which would otherwise be time barred under
section 11 of that Act fails. It does so for the following reasons, which have
been more or less anticipated in the preceding analysis.

90. A mere negligent failure to serve a claim form in time for the purposes
of CPR 7.5/6 is not an abuse of process. It has never been held to be in any of
the many cases cited to this court, nor in my judgment should it be described
as such, nor as being tantamount to such. I say a "mere" negligent failure to
serve in time in order to distinguish the typical case of such failure to be found
in these appeals and many other cases in the reports from any more serious
disregard of the rules; but not in order to be in any way dismissive of the proper
strictness with which a failure to serve in time, without good reason for doing
so, is and has been rigorously dealt with by the courts, whether under the CPR
or under the previous regime of the RSC. However, all the cases make clear that

for a matter to be an abuse of process, something more than a single negligent oversight in timely service is required: the various expressions which have been used are inordinate and inexcusable delay, intentional and contumelious default, or at least wholesale disregard of the rules.

91. The reason why failure to serve in time has always been dealt with strictly (even if CPR 7.6(3) represents a still further tightening of the rules where a retrospective request for an extension is made out of time) is in my judgment bound up with the fact that in England, unlike (all or most) civil law jurisdictions, proceedings are commenced when issued and not when served. However, it is not until service that a defendant has been given proper notice of the proceedings in question. Therefore, the additional time between issue and service is, in a way, an extension of the limitation period. A claimant can issue proceedings on the last day of the limitation period and can still, whatever risks he takes in doing so, enjoy a further four month period until service, and his proceedings will still be in time. In such a system, it is important therefore that the courts strictly regulate the period granted for service. If it were otherwise, the statutory limitation period could be made elastic at the whim or sloppiness of the claimant or his solicitors. For the same reason, the argument that if late service were not permitted, the claimant would lose his claim, because it would become time barred, becomes a barren excuse. But even where the claimant is well within the limitation period despite his delay in serving, there is a clear public interest in the rules and the courts curtailing the efficacy of a claim form which, because it has not been served, is not very different from an unposted letter. Therefore, the strictness with which the time for service is supervised has entirely valid public interest underpinnings which are quite separate from the doctrine of abuse of process. It is sufficient for the rules to provide for service within a specified time and for the courts to require claimants to adhere strictly to that time limit or else timeously provide a good reason for some dispensation. There is no need for that procedure to be muddled up with the different doctrine of abuse of process.

92. There is of course the (possibly) new argument in the era of the CPR which emphasises the importance of any misuse of court resources. It is well to be aware of the important public interest bound up in the efficient use of those limited resources. However, to seek to turn that proper concern, in such a case as these, into a surrogate for the doctrine of abuse of process is to my mind a disciplinarian view of the law of civil procedure which risks overlooking the overriding need to do justice. Certainly, the authorities have not gone that far, and there is nothing in the CPR themselves to indicate that a mere failure to serve in time is to be regarded as an abuse requiring or deserving anything further than the failure of the claim form itself – with the vital consequence in the absence of section 33 of losing a claim which has become time barred. Moreover, it should not be forgotten that one of the great virtues of the CPR is that, by providing more flexible remedies for breaches of rules as well as a stricter regulatory environment, the courts are given the powers and the opportunities to make the sanction fit the breach. That is the teaching of one of the most important early decisions on the CPR to be found in *Biguzzi v. Rank Leisure Plc* [1999] 1 WLR 1926 (CA).

93. Be that as it may, however, Parliament has in any event enacted that personal injury claims should be treated in a special way. They have a shorter limitation period than the general run of tortious and contractual claims, but,

at the same time, there is a special discretion, now to be found in section 33 of the 1980 Act, to displace the three year time limit. That discretion arises, if invoked, whenever a personal injury claim is commenced outside that three year limit. For these purposes it does not matter whether the claim in question is brought in an action for the first time commenced outside the three year limit, or is brought outside that limit in a second action after the first action has failed because, although commenced in time, the claim form was served too late or indeed never served: that is the teaching of *Horton*. In these circumstances, to say that a second action can never reach the section 33 discretion because the mere bringing of it is an abuse of process is to ignore the will of Parliament: that is what *Firman* taught in the era of the RSC and *Horton* has reverted to *Firman* in the era of the CPR. Moreover, the disputed submission would have the effect of resurrecting the *Walkley* anomaly.

94.   By seeking to apply the *Janov* line of authority to a mere failure to effect timely service, the respondents acknowledge that it should make no difference, on the logic of their submission, whether there is still time, after the failure of the first action, to commence a second action before the expiry of a relevant limitation period. However, dicta in *Gardner*, *Anderton*, and *Hoddinott* are inconsistent with the view that a second action could not be started within a limitation period which was still running after the failure of a first action for lack of timely service. *Gardner* is particularly interesting in this respect, for the automatic strike-out generated by a failure to apply for a hearing after a delay of no less than 15 months from close of pleadings would appear to arise out of a much more serious breach than a failure to serve within four months of issue. The submission which was rejected in that case was very close to the submission which the respondents make in these appeals.

95.   It is suggested that it is a sufficient reason to ignore the will of Parliament that otherwise there is no or no sufficient sanction for the failure to serve a claim form within the lime allowed. The submission is misconceived. It is for Parliament to say that the section 33 discretion cannot be invoked in a second action after the failure to serve in time in a first action. In *Walkley* the House of Lords considered that that was what Parliament had enacted: but in *Horton* the House ruled that that interpretation was in error and had, in justice, to be corrected. In any event, the failure of the first action is a sufficient sanction in itself, for it comes accompanied by costs, and, where a claim has in the meantime become time barred and is not covered by section 33, the loss of the claim itself.

96.   It is suggested that the alternative remedy against a negligent solicitor supports the respondents' doctrine. That may be an argument about the balance of prejudice, and it is clear from *Horton* itself that it is relevant to the section 33 discretion: but it cannot turn what is not an abuse of process into some kind of quasi-abuse. In any event, a remedy against negligent solicitors, although a necessary long-stop for the victim of negligence, is a generally unsatisfactory way of litigating the claimant's claim, and does little or nothing for the courts' limited resources.'

Part 2

Index to cases in Part 2

Causation

Civil Procedure Rules

Companies Act 1948

Companies Act 1985

Computation of time

Consumer Protection Act 1987

Costs

Criminal Injuries Compensation Scheme

Declaratory relief

Discovery

Dismissal for abuse of process of court

Limitations Acts 1837 and 1874

Limitation Act 1938, s 32

Limitation Act 1939

Limitation Act 1963

Limitation Act 1975, s 3

Limitation Act 1980, s 2

Limitation Act 1980, s 5

Limitation Act 1980, s 9

Limitation Act 1980, s 10

Limitation Act 1939, s 2A/Limitation Act 1980, ss 11, 14

Limitation Act 1939, s 2D/Limitation Act 1980, s 33

Limitation Act 1980, s 35

Limitation Act 1980, s 38

Case summaries

A v Hoare; C v Middlesbrough Council; X & Anor v Wandsworth LBC; H v Suffolk County Council; Young v Catholic Care (Diocese of Leeds)

Limitation Act 1980, s 2, s 11, s 14, s 33

House of Lords [2008] UKHL 6; [2008] 1 AC 844; [2008] 2 WLR 311;
[2008] 2 All ER 1; [2008] 1 FLR 771; [2008] 1 FCR 507;
(2008) 11 CCL Rep 249; (2008) 100 BMLR 1;
[2008] Fam Law 402; (2008) 105(6) LSG 27;
(2008) 158 NLJ 218; (2008) 152(6) SJLB 28;
(2008) Times, 31 January

Six appellants in unrelated cases, all of whom alleged that they had been victims of sexual abuse, appealed against decisions that their claims were statute barred. In each case, the respective judges, following *Stubbings v Webb* (p677), had concluded that the claim failed on limitation grounds. The issues for determination were: (1) whether *Stubbings* was wrongly decided and whether the court should depart from it; and (2) whether the definition of 'significant' injury in s 14(2) of the Limitation Act 1980 allowed account to be taken of a claimant's personal characteristics, either pre-existing or consequent upon the injury suffered.

Held:

(i) *Stubbings* was wrongly decided, and the right thing was to depart from it and reaffirm the law laid down in *Letang v Cooper* (p533).

(ii) *Stubbings* had placed more weight upon the Report of the Committee on the Limitation of Actions 1949 (Cmd 7740) under the chairmanship of Tucker LJ and on Hansard than they could properly bear. Although the decision had not initially given rise to much difficulty until 2002 and the widening of the concept of vicarious liability in *Lister v Hesley Hall Ltd* (p535), after that the observation in *Jones v Secretary of State for Social Services* [1972] AC 944, HL, that unsatisfactory decisions of the highest court could cause uncertainty because lower courts tended to distinguish them on inadequate grounds, became particularly pertinent as the consequences of *Stubbings* were that victims of sexual abuse seeking the discretion of the court under s 33 were driven to alleging that abuse was the result of some other breach of duty, which could be brought within the language of s 11.

(iii) The test in s 14(2) was an entirely impersonal standard. It was not whether the claimant himself would have considered the injury sufficiently serious to justify proceedings, but whether he would 'reasonably' have done so. The correct approach was to ask what the claimant knew about his injury, add any 'objective' knowledge which might be imputed to him under s 14(3), and then ask whether a reasonable person in the claimant's circumstances with that knowledge would have considered the injury sufficiently serious to justify his instituting proceedings for damages.

(iv)   Having ascertained what the claimant knew and what he should be treated as having known, the actual claimant dropped out of the picture, and judges should not have to consider the claimant's intelligence. Standards were, by their nature, impersonal and did not vary with the person to whom they were applied. Section 14 made time run from when the claimant had knowledge of certain facts, not from when he could have been expected to take certain steps, and s 14(2) merely defined one of those facts by reference to a standard of seriousness.

(v)   Applying and doubting *Adams v Bracknell Forest BC* (p292) and partially distinguishing *KR v Bryn Alyn Community (Holdings) Ltd* (p505), the effect of the claimant's injuries upon what he could reasonably have been expected to do was irrelevant. A victim of serious abuse immediately suffered a significant injury within the meaning of s 14.

(vi)   In Y's case, if the Court of Appeal had not been bound by *Bryn Alyn*, the date of knowledge would have been 1977; the later date determined by the court below could not be justified. That did not mean that the law regarded as irrelevant the question whether the actual claimant, taking into account his psychological state in consequence of the injury, could reasonably have been expected to start proceedings, but it dealt with that question under s 33. That was the right place to consider it until Parliament decided whether to give effect to the Law Commission's recommendation of a more precise definition of psychological incapacity suffered by victims of sexual abuse. Thus a more restrictive approach to s 14 was balanced by a more generous approach to s 33.

(vii)   The approach to the exercise of discretion remained as described in *Horton v Sadler* (p482), but the court commented on the sort of considerations which ought clearly to be in mind in sexual abuse cases. These included: the inhibiting nature of such abuse so as to effectively prevent a claimant bringing a claim; the prejudice to the defendant and whether or not delay has rendered a fair trial impossible; the impact upon the ability to have a fair trial of the fact that there would often be no need to prove systemic negligence; whether a complaint was made at the time; and whether the assailant was convicted or, conversely, whether the complaint is unsupported and comes out of the blue, depriving the defendant of an opportunity to investigate.

(viii) The case of A – where the rapist defendant had become worth suing when he won the lottery – was remitted to the Queen's Bench Division to decide whether the discretion under s 33 should be exercised in the claimant's favour. In respect of the cases, all of which concerned sexual abuse, orders that the trial judge said he would have made in C's case had he been free to decide that the action came within s 11 of the Act were made; H's appeal allowed on the issue of limitation only and case remitted for decision whether to exercise discretion under s 33 of the Act; damages awarded to X and Y as if the previous limitation defence had failed; Y's case remitted.

Appeals allowed.

Per Lord Hoffmann: '35. It follows that I cannot accept that one must consider whether someone "with [the] plaintiff's intelligence" would have been reasonable if he did not regard the injury as sufficiently serious. That seems to me to destroy the effect of the word "reasonably". Judges should not have to grapple with the notion of the reasonable unintelligent person. Once you have ascertained what the claimant knew and what he should be treated as having known, the actual claimant drops out of the picture. Section 14(2) is, after all, simply a standard of the seriousness of the injury and nothing more. Standards are in their nature impersonal and do not vary with the person to whom they are applied.

37. [The *Bryn Alyn*] approach treats the statute as if it had said that time should run from the date on which it would have been reasonable to expect the claimant to institute proceedings. If it had said that, the question posed in *Bryn Alyn* would have been correct. But section 14 makes time runs from when the claimant has knowledge of certain facts, not from when he could have been expected to take certain steps. Section 14(2) does no more than define one of those facts by reference to a standard of seriousness.

38. The Court of Appeal said that there was some "tension" between the *Bryn Alyn* test and the recent decision of the House of Lords in *Adams v Bracknell Forest Borough Council* [2005] 1 AC 76. I suppose that this is true in the sense that the House in *Adams* said that one had to take words like "reasonable" and "reasonably" seriously and the *Bryn Alyn* test does not. But *Adams* was dealing with section 14(3), which is very different in its purpose from section 14(2). The test for imputing knowledge in section 14(3) is by reference to what the claimant ought reasonably to have *done*. It asks whether he ought reasonably to have acquired certain knowledge from observable or ascertainable facts or to have obtained expert advice. But section 14(2) is simply a standard of seriousness applied to what the claimant knew or must be treated as having known. It involves no inquiry into what the claimant ought to have done. A conclusion that the injury would reasonably have been considered sufficiently serious to justify the issue of proceedings implies no finding that the claimant ought reasonably to have issued proceedings. He may have had perfectly good reasons for not doing so. It is a standard to determine one thing and one thing only, namely whether the injury was sufficiently serious to count as significant.

39. The difference between section 14(2) and 14(3) emerges very clearly if one considers the relevance in each case of the claimant's injury. Because section 14(3) turns on what the claimant ought reasonably to have done, one must take into account the injury which the claimant has suffered. You do not assume that a person who has been blinded could reasonably have acquired knowledge by seeing things. In section 14(2), on the other hand, the test is external to the claimant and involves no inquiry into what he ought reasonably to have done. It is applied to what the claimant knew or was deemed to have known but the standard itself is impersonal. The effect of the claimant's injuries upon what he could reasonably have been expected to do is therefore irrelevant ...

44. This does not mean that the law regards as irrelevant the question of whether the actual claimant, taking into account his psychological state in consequence of the injury, could reasonably have been expected to institute proceedings. But it deals with that question under section 33, which specifically says in subsection (3)(a) that one of the matters to be taken into account in the exercise of the discretion is "the reasons for ... the delay on the part of the plaintiff".'

Per Lord Brown of Eaton-under-Heywood: '84. With regard to the exercise of the court's discretion under section 33 of the 1980 Act, however, I would make just three brief comments – not, let it be clear, in any way to fetter a discretion which the House in *Horton v Sadler* [2007] 1 AC 307 recently confirmed to be unfettered, but rather to suggest the sort of considerations which ought clearly to be in mind in sexual abuse cases in the new era which your Lordships are now ushering in, firstly, by departing from *Stubbings v Webb* and, secondly, by construing section 14(2) so as to transfer from that provision to section 33 consideration of the inhibiting effect of sexual abuse upon certain victims' preparedness to bring proceedings in respect of it.

85. First, insofar as future claims may be expected to be brought against employers (or others allegedly responsible for abusers) on the basis of vicarious liability for sexual assaults rather than for systemic negligence in failing to prevent them, they will probably involve altogether narrower factual disputes than hitherto. As Lord Hoffmann suggests, at para 52, that is likely to bear significantly upon the possibility of having a fair trial.

86. Secondly, through the combined effects of *Lister v Hesley Hall Ltd* and departing from *Stubbings v Webb*, a substantially greater number of allegations (not all of which will be true) are now likely to be made many years after the abuse complained of. Whether or not it will be possible for defendants to investigate these sufficiently for there to be a reasonable prospect of a fair trial will depend upon a number of factors, not least when the complaint was first made and with what effect. If a complaint has been made and recorded, and more obviously still if the accused has been convicted of the abuse complained of, that will be one thing; if, however, a complaint comes out of the blue with no apparent support for it (other perhaps than that the alleged abuser has been accused or even convicted of similar abuse in the past), that would be quite another thing. By no means everyone who brings

a late claim for damages for sexual abuse, however genuine his complaint may in fact be, can reasonably expect the court to exercise the section 33 discretion in his favour. On the contrary, a fair trial (which must surely include a fair opportunity for the defendant to investigate the allegations – see section 33(3)(b)) is in many cases likely to be found quite simply impossible after a long delay.

87. Hitherto the misconstruction of section 14(2) has given an absolute right to proceed, however long out of time, to anyone able to say that he would not reasonably have turned his mind to litigation (more than three years) earlier (the *Bryn Alyn* test described by Lord Hoffmann at paragraph 36). It is not to be supposed that the exercise of the court's section 33 discretion will invariably replicate that position.

88. My third and final comment relates most directly to A's appeal and it is this. The definition of "significant injury" in section 14(2) refers to the justifiability of bringing proceedings against a defendant "able to satisfy a judgment". That surely is unsurprising. It would not ordinarily be sensible to sue an indigent defendant. How then should the court approach the exercise of its section 33 discretion in a case like A where suddenly, after many years, the prospective defendant becomes rich. The House is not, of course, itself exercising this discretion. I would, however, suggest that it would be most unfortunate if people felt obliged (often at public expense) to bring proceedings for sexual abuse against indigent defendants simply with a view to their possible future enforcement. (Judgments, although interest-bearing for only six years, are enforceable without limit of time.)'

Abala v Surrey Oaklands NHS Trust

Limitation Act 1980, s 33

Mayor's and City of London Court (HHJ Simpson)   [2000] CLY 527

The claimant was involved in an accident during the course of her employment and issued proceedings on 27 April 1998. The defendant contended that the cause of action arose on 29 March 1995 and that the claim was therefore statute barred. It was confirmed by the claimant, following disclosure of accident documentation, that the accident occurred on that date. The court accepted that the claimant's solicitors had received late instructions and were required to issue court proceedings at short notice. The claimant did not have a good command of English and would have required the services of an interpreter. Unfortunately, one of the crucial forms for legal assistance had been incorrectly completed on the claimant's behalf with the accident date set out as 29 April 1995. The claimant argued that the court should exercise its s 33 discretion to allow the claim to proceed. The defendant argued that the mistake lay either with the claimant herself or with those from whom she sought legal assistance and that a great deal of delay had occurred prior to the eventual issue of proceedings.

Held: There was no evidence of prejudice to the defendant in allowing the claim to proceed (*Hartley v Birmingham City Council* (p465) applied). The period from the end of limitation to the issue of claim was 29 days, which was not a very long time.

The judge accordingly disapplied the time limit.

Abouchalache v Hilton International Hotels (UK) Ltd

Cappucci v Same; Ladki v Same

Dismissal for want of prosecution

Court of Appeal   (1982) 126 SJ 857

In 1975 a bomb exploded at the defendants' hotel in London. The claimants were injured by it and sued for negligence in New York. It was there held that England was the forum conveniens. Consequently the New York actions were dismissed, after the defendants undertook not to plead a limitation defence in England if the actions were started there before 12 December 1979. The claimants issued the writs by this date and served them, but took no further steps for two years.

The master dismissed the actions for want of prosecution. A judge allowed the claimant's appeals. The defendants appealed, contending that when a writ was issued after the expiry of the standard limitation period and injurious delay had already occurred, the action might be dismissed even though the further delay had not significantly added to the previous prejudice.

Held: the judge was right to find that no additional prejudice had been caused by the delay after the issue of the English writs. The defendants, as part of a large international concern, did not fear the outcome of the litigation. Such records as were necessary and had not been destroyed could be preserved without causing trouble. Fresh prejudice could not be presumed where all the relevant facts showed its absence.

The appeal was dismissed.

Ackbar v C F Green & Co Ltd

Limitation Act 1939, s 2(1)

Croom-Johnson J   **[1975] 2 All ER 65; [1975] 1 Lloyd's Rep 673; [1975] QB 582**

On 19 September 1966 the claimant (Ali Ackbar) bought a lorry. He contracted with the defendant insurance brokers that they would advise him as to necessary insurance. Two days later he instructed them to obtain cover for passenger liability. The defendants did not communicate this to the insurance company who issued a policy which did not cover passenger liability. On 15 May 1967 the claimant was a passenger in the lorry when it was involved in an accident. The driver was not covered against passenger liability either, so the claimant was unable to recover damages for his injuries from any insurer.

On 3 May 1972 he issued a writ against the defendants for breach of their duty to have the lorry insured against passenger liability. He claimed as damages the sum that the driver would have been liable to pay him for his injuries. The defendants alleged that the claim was statute barred under the proviso to s 2(1) of the Limitation Act 1939, on the grounds that more than three years had elapsed before issue of the writ and the damages claimed 'consist of or include damages in respect of personal injuries'.

Held: the case was about an alleged breach of contract by the defendants, due to which the claimant lost the chance to recover damages either from the driver or his own insurers. The damages did not consist of or include damages in respect of personal injuries. Those damages were merely the measure of the damages now claimed. Accordingly, the limitation period was six years and the action was not statute barred.

McGahie v Union of Shop Distributive & Allied Workers (p552) applied.

See *Howe v David Brown Tractors (Retail) Ltd* (p483).

Adam and Adam v Hemming

Limitation Act 1980, s 35   **RSC Ord 20, r 5**

Court of Appeal   **(1991) Times, 20 March**

On 2 April 1979 Mrs Alice Smith and her daughter Mrs Joyce Adam were passengers in a car driven by her husband Mr Adam when a car driven by the defendant collided with the back of it. The defendant was convicted of careless driving. Claims in respect of both women's injuries were notified. During the subsequent negotiations with the defendant's insurers, Mrs Smith died of natural causes. The medical report on Mrs Adam at that stage stated that she was suffering from a mild whiplash injury and that her loss of disc space was unrelated to the accident.

On 26 March 1982 a writ was issued with the title:

Joyce Adam and Stanley Kessock Adam
(as administrator of the estate of Alice Maud Smith deceased)   Claimant
and
Eric John Francis Hemming   Defendant

The writ was endorsed: 'The claimants claim is for damages pursuant to the Law Reform (Miscellaneous Provisions) Act 1934 and to the Fatal Accidents Act 1846–1959 consequent on the death of Alice Maud Smith deceased by reason of the negligence of the defendant on or about 2nd April 1979'. It thus claimed in respect of Mrs Smith's injuries but not those of Mrs Adam.

The writ was served. Mrs Adam's claim was pursued in negotiations with the insurers who obtained a medical report on her in 1983. The last letter in the negotiations was sent in January 1984. Following further medical reports on Mrs Adam in 1985 and 1986, an orthopaedic surgeon reported in 1987 that she had suffered a lesion of a lumbar intervertebral disc in the 1979 accident. None of these reports was disclosed.

No further steps in the action were taken until February 1989 when notice of intention to proceed was served. In April 1989 the claimants' solicitors issued a summons under RSC Ord 20, r 5 for leave to amend the writ. Patrick Bennett QC, sitting as a deputy High Court judge, upheld the district registrar's order granting this leave. The defendant appealed.

Held:

(i)   The effect of the amendment was to add a new cause of action within s 35(1) of the Limitation Act 1980. Mrs Adam's claim for personal injury damages was a different and new cause.

(ii)   Her new claim arose out of substantially the same facts, namely the same collision. Thus there was power to give leave under RSC Ord 20, r 5(5) to make the amendment.

(iii)   Under RSC Order 20, r 5(2), leave for the amendment could only be granted if just to do so. If the defendant could show that by reason of the claimant's inordinate and inexcusable delay a substantial risk had been created that a fair trial would be impossible, it would not be just to grant leave.

(iv)   There was no issue on liability. The insurers' medical expert who reported in 1983 was still available. The claimant had agreed to disclose all her medical reports and records. The defendant had not proved that a fair trial would be impossible.

(v)   It was just to allow the amendment. The defendant's appeal must be dismissed.

Adams v Bracknell Forest Borough Council

Limitation Act 1980, s 14, s 33

House of Lords   **[2005] 1 AC 76; [2004] 3 All ER 897; [2005] PIQR P2**

The claimant attended the defendant's schools between 1977 and 1988. He alleged a failure to address severe dyslexia. Proceedings were issued on 25 June 2002 when he was thirty. The judge found that the claimant did not have actual knowledge of the cause of his difficulties until he spoke to an educational psychologist at a social event in 1999. He found that the claimant did not have constructive knowledge more than three years before issue as a reasonable person with undiagnosed dyslexia was unlikely to have sought help or deduced the source of the problem for themselves. The defendant appealed. The Court of Appeal held that the judge was entitled to make the findings that he did. The defendant appealed again.

Held:

(i) The test for constructive knowledge is objective. The question is what a reasonable man in the claimant's position should have done. The claimant's particular characteristics and intelligence are irrelevant (*Forbes v Wandsworth Health Authority* (p434) applied, *Smith v Central Asbestos Co Ltd* (p658) and *Nash v Eli Lilly* (p568) overruled).

(ii) It was correct to say that negligent failure to ameliorate dyslexia could constitute a personal injury. It was analogous to a defendant failing to treat a physical injury which he did not himself cause (*Robinson v St Helens MBC* (p628) approved).

(iii) There was no reason why the normal expectation that a person suffering a significant injury would be curious about its origins should not apply to dyslexics. The absence of such an expectation would extend the limitation period indefinitely and burden defendants with impossibly stale claims.

(iv) The judge was correct in applying the standard of reasonable behaviour in a person suffering from untreated dyslexia. However, although the judge would have been correct to have held that the injury itself had inhibited the taking of advice so as delay constructive knowledge if that had been the evidence, he was wrong to hold that extreme reticence was the natural consequence of undiagnosed dyslexia. In the absence of any special inhibiting factor, the claimant should reasonably have sought medical advice years before. Proceedings were therefore issued out of time.

(v) The principles in *Robinson* applied to the exercise of the s 33 discretion. The claimant's award if he succeeded was likely to be modest, the defendant were in great evidential difficulties. There were no special circumstances tilting the balance in the claimant's favour. It would not be equitable to allow the claim to proceed.

Appeal allowed.

Adams v Thomson Holidays Ltd

Merchant Shipping Act 1995, s 183, s 190   **CPR 16.4, 19**

QBD (Comm) (Judge Waksman QC)   **[2009] EWHC 2559 (QB)**

The claimant had paid for a holiday on a cruise ship. She had been injured and brought a claim in negligence. The claim was brought against T as defendant. It was common ground that the claim should have been brought against another company (T2), which was part of the same group. The fact that the proper defendant was T2 was pleaded in the defence. The defence also asserted that the only claim which could be made was a claim under the Athens Convention 1974, which had not been mentioned in the particulars of claim.

T then applied to strike out on the basis that the claim was brought against the wrong defendant and that the claim was fatally defective since it did not mention the Athens Convention. By cross-application the claimant sought an order for T2 to be substituted as defendant under CPR 19.5 and, if necessary, for the particulars of claim to be amended to refer to the Athens Convention. The proceedings against T had been issued within the two-year period for bringing proceedings under the Convention but that period had since expired. T submitted that CPR 19.5 did not apply because the Athens Convention, which was given the force of law by s 183 of the Merchant Shipping Act 1995, was an enactment which did not allow a change of parties after the end of the limitation period.

Held:

(i) There was nothing in the Athens Convention which expressly permitted a change of parties after the end of the limitation period, but neither did it prohibit such a change.

It was therefore an enactment which fell within CPR 19.5 (*Parsons v George* [2004] EWCA Civ 912 followed).

(ii) It would be surprising if the result were otherwise, given that the parallel right to claim damages for personal injuries under s 190 of the 1995 Act would clearly be regarded as falling within the rule, because under previous versions of the rule that section had been expressly mentioned. No material distinction could be drawn between the type of claim made under the Athens Convention, and given the force of law by s 183, and a claim such as that made under the 1995 Act. That was sufficient to bring the Convention within the rule.

(iii) The court therefore had jurisdiction to allow substitution under CPR 19.5. The same reasoning would have applied to substitution under CPR 17.4.

(iv) As a matter of discretion the change of party should be permitted. No possible prejudice could have been suffered by T or T2. The claimant's solicitors had made a mistake but T's solicitors had conducted correspondence in substantive terms without making a specific point about it. The fact that the claimant would have a claim against her own solicitor was not by itself a reason to refuse the amendment.

(v) The particulars of claim as they stood were not liable to be struck out. They contained a concise statement of the facts on which the claimant relied, as required by CPR 16.4.

(vi) If that was wrong, so that amendment was required, permission to amend to plead the Athens Convention would be granted. That would come as no surprise to the defendant because the Convention had already been referred to in the defence.

Judgment accordingly.

Re Advance Insulation Ltd

Companies Act 1985, s 653

Limitation Act 1980, s 33

Hoffmann J   **(1988) 5 BCC 55**

From 1954 Ronald Crouch worked as a labourer in the building industry. Asbestos pleural disease was diagnosed in 1978. He consulted solicitors who recovered £4,750 damages from one of his former employers, Standard Flat Roofing Ltd.

Advance Insulation Ltd had employed Mr Crouch for six months between May 1955 and December 1956. In May 1968 it was struck off the Companies Register.

In 1986, his condition having worsened, Mr Crouch instructed new solicitors. They found that Advance had an employers' liability policy with the Prudential Assurance Co Ltd. After notifying a prospective claim to the Prudential, they issued an originating summons in the Companies Court. This was served on Advance and the Treasury Solicitor but not on the Prudential. In July 1987 Mr Registrar Bradburn ordered that Advance be restored to the Register and that the period between dissolution and restoration should not be counted for the purposes of the Limitation Act 1980.

High Court action (*Crouch v Advance Insulation Ltd*) was started in August 1987. A defence pleading limitation was served in October 1987. In March 1988 a reply relying on Mr Registrar Bradburn's order and if necessary s 33 of the Limitation Act 1980 was served. The action was set down for hearing and marked KP 7 November 1988.

On 21 September 1988 the Prudential issued a notice of motion on behalf of Advance for an order setting aside that part of Mr Registrar Bradburn's order which referred to limitation. By consent, the motion was treated as an application for leave to appeal against the order out of time.

Held: until the motion was issued a few weeks before the trial, the parties were proceeding upon the assumption that the Registrar's order had been validly made. It was too late to overturn that assumption. Accordingly, the Prudential's submission that the jurisdiction under s 33 to disapply s 11 of the Limitation Act 1980 made it wrong in principle for the Registrar to make an order depriving the insurers of a limitation defence did not fall to be considered.

Aerlingus v (1) Gildacroft Ltd (2) Sentinel Lifts Ltd

Limitation Act 1980, s 10

Court of Appeal   **[2006] 1 WLR 1173; [2006] 2 All ER 290**

Under a contract between the claimant and the first defendant, the first defendant carried out refurbishment work at the claimant's building including the refurbishment/alteration of a lift. Under a sub-contract between the first defendant and the second defendant, the second defendant carried out work on the lift from 23–27 January 1998.

On 27 January 1998, Mr Smyth, an employee of the claimant, suffered an accident when the lift malfunctioned, trapping his left arm and causing him serious injury. He brought proceedings against the claimant, for damages for personal injury. On 9 May 2001, he obtained consent judgment on liability.

Subsequently, by an agreement between Mr Smyth and the claimant, made in about September 2003 and embodied in a consent judgment on quantum dated 3 October 2003, Mr Smyth's claim was settled for £490,000 plus costs.

On 4 February 2004, the claimant commenced proceedings against the defendants, claiming an indemnity or contribution under the Civil Liability (Contribution) Act 1978 in respect of that settlement. The defendant pleaded that these claims were statute barred by the two-year time limit: s 10 of the Limitation Act 1980. This was heard as a preliminary issue.

The judge held that 'judgment or award' in s 10(3) meant a judgment or award in relation to liability, not quantum. The claim was thus statute barred. The claimant appealed.

Held:

(i)   There was no decisive authority on the point.

(ii)   Persuasive authority and the language of the relevant provisions tended towards deferring the running of limitation period (*Knight v Rochdale Healthcare NHS Trust* (p523) considered and approved).

(iii)   Limitation did not start to run until there was a judgment or award that ascertained the quantum, not merely the existence, of the tortfeasor's liability.

Appeal allowed.

Akram v Adam

European Convention on Human Rights 1950, Art 6   **CPR 6**

Court of Appeal   **[2004] EWCA Civ 1601; [2005] 1 All ER 741;
(2005) HLR 14**

The claimant was the defendant's landlord. There was a history of problems with the defendant's receiving letters and in earlier proceedings a judge had informally remarked that service on the defendant's sister's address would constitute good service in those earlier proceedings.

The claimant in any event issued fresh possession proceedings and sent the claim form and particulars by first class post to the property where the defendant lived. There was no response and the court duly made a possession order. The defendant had been at his sister's tending their sick mother and first learned of the proceedings when he returned to the property to find that the warrant for possession had been executed.

The defendant successfully applied to have the order set aside. The claimant successfully appealed this decision. The defendant then appealed.

Held (as regards the service point):

(i)   Under CPR 6.5(6), where no solicitor was acting for a party, service is effected by sending, transmitting or leaving a document at his last known residence. The rule did not say that service was not good if the party did not in fact receive the document (*Cranfield v Bridgegrove* (*Smith v Hughes* therein) (p389) applied).

(ii)   The rules of service provided an accessible, fair and efficient way of administering justice and did not contravene the ECHR. If the defendant did not know about proceedings he could apply to have judgment set aside (*Godwin v Swindon BC* (p444) considered).

(iii)   There was no doubt that the property in question was the defendant's usual residence. The claim form had been posted to the defendant's address, even if it was not delivered to his room. It was therefore properly served.

Appeal dismissed.

Aktas v Adepta

Dixie v British Polythene Ltd

Limitation Act 1980, s 33   **CPR 3.4, 6.9, 7.5, 7.6**

Abuse of process, Striking out

Court of Appeal   **[2010] EWCA Civ 1170; [2011] QB 894; [2011] 2 WLR 945; [2011] 2 All ER 536; [2011] CP Rep 9; [2011] PIQR P4**

In conjoined appeals, the claimants appealed against decisions striking out their personal injury claims.

Both claimants were injured in accidents at work. Both claims were intimated swiftly and liability admitted, but in both cases quantum remained in dispute. Claim forms were therefore issued just before the expiry of the limitation period. However, both claimants (or rather their solicitors) failed properly to serve in time. Their respective claims were therefore struck out.

The claimants both issued second duplicate claims but these were also struck out as an abuse of process. In *Dixie*'s case the judge at first instance indicated that, had he not struck the claim out as abusive, he would in any event have declined to exercise his discretion under s 33 to allow the claim to continue. This issue was not argued at that stage in the case of *Aktas*. The claimants appealed.

Held:

(i)   A mere negligent failure to serve a claim form in time for the purposes of CPR 7.5 and 7.6 was not an abuse of process. Something more than a single negligent oversight in timely service was required (*Johnson v Gore Wood & Co (No 1)* [2002] 2 AC 1, HL, followed, *Janov v Morris* [1981] 1 WLR 1389 and *Arbuthnot Latham Bank Ltd v Trafalgar Holdings Ltd* [1998] 1 WLR 1426 applied, *Vinos v Marks & Spencer Plc* (p701) and *Hashtroodi v Hancock* (p466) considered).

(ii)   Proceedings in England were commenced when issued and not when served, but it was not until service that a defendant was given proper notice of them. The additional time between issue and service was effectively an extension of the limitation period; a claimant could issue proceedings on the last day of the limitation period and still enjoy a further four-month period until service. It was therefore important that the courts strictly regulated the time granted for service, as otherwise the statutory limitation period could be extended at the whim or sloppiness of the claimant or his solicitors. Even where the claimant was well within the limitation period despite delay in serving, there was a clear public interest in the rules and the court curtailing the efficacy of a claim which, because it had not been served, was not very different from an unposted letter. The strictness with which time for service was supervised had entirely valid public interest underpinnings which were quite separate from the doctrine of abuse of process. It was sufficient for the rules to provide for service within a specified time and for the courts to require claimants to adhere strictly to that time limit or provide a good reason for dispensation. There was no need for that procedure to be muddled up with the doctrine of abuse of process.

(iii)   The CPR emphasised the importance of misuse of court resources, but to seek to turn proper concern regarding efficient use of those resources into a surrogate for the doctrine of abuse of process was a disciplinarian view of the law of civil procedure which risked overlooking the overriding need to do justice. There was nothing in the CPR to indicate that a mere failure to serve in time was to be regarded as an abuse. Parliament had in any event enacted that personal injury claims should be treated in a special way. Such claims had a shorter limitation period than tortious and contractual claims but there was a special discretion under s 33 to displace the three-year limit. That discretion arose whenever a personal injury claim was issued outside the three-year limit or had been brought outside that limit in a second action after an action had been issued in time but the claim form was served too late or not at all (*Horton v Sadler* (p482) and *Firman v Ellis* (p433) followed). To say that a second action could never reach the s 33 discretion because it was an abuse of process was to ignore the will of Parliament.

(iv)   The suggestion that it was sufficient reason to ignore the will of Parliament that there would otherwise be no sufficient sanction for the failure to serve a claim form within time was misconceived. It was for Parliament to say that the discretion under s 33 could not be invoked in a second action after a failure to serve in time (*Horton* followed). The failure of the first action was a sufficient sanction in itself, for it came accompanied by costs, and, where a claim had become time barred and was not covered by s 33, the loss of the claim itself.

(v)   The possibility of an alternative remedy against a negligent solicitor might be an argument about the balance of prejudice and relevant to the s 33 discretion, but it could not turn what was not an abuse of process into some kind of quasi-abuse. In any event, such a remedy was a generally unsatisfactory way of litigating a claim.

(vi)   Regarding s 33 in the case of *Dixie*, there was no forensic prejudice to the defendant and the loss of a limitation defence could properly be described as a windfall (*Cain v Francis* (p360) applied, *McDonnell v Walker* (p550) considered). The discretion would therefore be exercised in the claimant's favour.

(vii)   The question of s 33 in the case of *Aktas* would be remitted to the county court.

Appeals allowed.

Albon (t/a NA Carriage Co) v Naza Motor Trading Sdn Bhd

CPR 6.8, 7.2

Ch D (Lightman J)   **[2007] EWHC 327 (Ch); [2007] 1 All ER (Comm) 813**

The claimant English motor car dealer had had business dealings in the motor trade with the defendants, a Malaysian company and its principal shareholder, over a number of years in three separate jurisdictions. A dispute arose between the parties, and the claimant commenced proceedings in respect of sums that he alleged the defendants owed him pursuant to various agreements. The claimant obtained an order from a judge permitting service on the defendants outside the jurisdiction. Thereafter the claimant obtained an alternative service order pursuant to CPR 6.8 authorising service on the defendants by an alternative method. The alternative service order was sought and granted on the basis that the claimant had been unable to effect service on the defendants in Malaysia, that the claim form was due to expire, and that the defendants' Malaysian legal representatives had raised a fresh complaint that service at the defendants' registered office in Malaysia was not good service. The second defendant subsequently applied to have both orders set aside.

Held:

(i)   The provisions of CPR 6.8 and the requirement of a good reason for authorising an alternative method of service had to be interpreted and applied in a manner that gave effect to the overriding objective. In particular the court had to have in mind the cost of litigation, the hurdles thereby created in the way of obtaining justice on the part of those with limited means (in particular, those when facing litigants with abundant means), and the need to ensure that cases proceeded expeditiously.

(ii)   The question as to whether there was good reason was a matter to be determined by the judge at the date of the application on the particular facts of the case before him. It was not a precondition of the making of the order that service by a method permitted by the CPR was impracticable: it was only necessary that there was a good reason to make the order. In deciding what was a good reason the court would have in mind the overriding objective and whether the making of the order would enable the court to deal with the case justly.

(iii)   There was no good reason if the application was made to achieve a collateral object that the rule was not designed to confer, namely a step ahead in a race to commence proceedings in the instant jurisdiction before they were commenced elsewhere. The court would have in mind, in circumscribing the ambit of what was a good reason, that a finding of its existence was only the first stage in the process: the second stage then had to be gone through of deciding whether the court's discretion should be exercised, having regard to all the facts including the parties' conduct.

(iv)   In the instant case the master was correct in exercising his discretion to make the alternative service order; it was the order that the overriding objective practically dictated. A reasonable interpretation of the conduct of the first defendant company was a desire to make life as difficult as possible for the claimant while protesting the contrary. The case was very important for the claimant in particular, as the sums at stake were critical to his financial survival. The order saved further expense and time, promoted the objective of dealing with the case justly, and was necessary to protect the claimant whose financial position called for such protection.

Application dismissed.

Albonetti v Wirral MBC

Limitation Act 1980, s 14

Court of Appeal   **[2008] EWCA Civ 783**

The claimant, who was born in 1955, had suffered sexual abuse, including anal rape, at the age of 15 while living in a children's home operated by the defendant local authority. The claimant was admitted to a psychiatric hospital in 1986 following the breakdown of his marriage. In 1996 he told his partner about the abuse he suffered as a child, and in 1999 he contacted the police. He issued proceedings in 2001, and shortly after that a psychiatrist provided an expert opinion to the effect that he was suffering from post-traumatic stress disorder caused by the abuse and that that condition accounted substantially for his previous psychiatric symptoms.

The defendant pleaded that the claim was time barred. Limitation was heard as a preliminary issue. The claimant contended that, at the time of the abuse, he did not know that he had suffered a significant injury. The judge, directing himself by reference to *KR v Bryn Alyn Community (Holdings) Ltd (In Liquidation)* (p505), held that the claimant had not known that the injury was significant and attributable to the abuse until he saw the psychiatrist in 2001.

The defendant appealed, arguing that the 'injury in question' for the purposes of s 14 was the whole injury which the claimant had suffered, including any psychiatric harm which later manifested itself. It further argued that the claimant had knowledge that he had a significant injury at the time it was happening, and he had to bring his claim by 1976, namely three years after he attained his majority. The defendant submitted that the acts of anal intercourse in particular must have been so painful and humiliating that the claimant must have known that he had suffered a significant injury, not merely a significant wrong. The claimant argued that, in 1976, he did not know that he had suffered a significant injury in the sense required by s 14(2), namely that it would have been worth bringing an action for damages against a defendant who would admit liability and could pay the damages; in 1976, damages were not available for humiliation or distress. The claimant further argued that it would only have been in about 1989 or 1990 that he could have known he had suffered a significant injury, since before that time, if he had consulted a solicitor, he would have been advised that he had not suffered any such.

The resolution appeal was stayed pending the outcome of *A v Hoare* (p287).

Held:

(i)   In *A v Hoare* the House of Lords had disapproved the partly subjective test applied in *Bryn Alyn*. It was now clear that the test of whether a claimant knew at any particular date that he had suffered a significant injury was an objective one. In the light of that, the approach of the judge below to s 14(2) had been wrong.

(ii)   The 'injury in question' for the purposes of s 14 must be the injury which the claimant knew about at the material time. In the instant case, the injury to be considered was the immediate effect of the abuse, namely the pain, distress and humiliation which the claimant experienced at the time.

(iii)   A person who had been raped whether vaginally or anally must know that she or he had suffered not only a grave wrong but also a significant injury (*Stubbings v Webb* (p677) considered).

(iv)   It could not be accepted that if the claimant had consulted a solicitor in the mid-1970s, shortly before the primary limitation period ran out, he would have been advised that he had not suffered a significant injury and that the damages at common law would be so small as not to be worth pursuing. The argument that damages were not awarded for distress and humiliation was misconceived: in a case of rape or buggery, there was a sufficient physical injury on which to found a claim for distress and humiliation, even where no actual psychiatric harm had been caused.

(v)   The claimant knew at all times after it had occurred that the abuse amounted to a significant injury. He would not know of his own knowledge whether it was worth bringing an action, but would at least know enough to make it reasonable to expect him to consult a solicitor. Had he done so, he would have discovered that substantial damages could in theory be awarded for such abuse. Although he might well have been advised not to proceed, that would have been for other reasons, not because he had not suffered a significant injury. Thus time began to run from the date of his majority and ran out in 1976.

(vi)   The issue of whether the court should exercise its discretion under s 33 to disapply the limitation provisions was remitted for determination by the judge.

Appeal allowed.

Per Smith LJ: '24 … In my view, a person who has been raped whether vaginally or anally must know that she or he has suffered not only a grave wrong but also a significant injury. That was the view expressed obiter by Lord Griffiths in *Stubbings v Webb* at page 506B and I respectfully agree. He drew a distinction between an allegation of rape and lesser forms of sexual abuse, such as fondling, which might not amount to a significant injury. Here, the allegation of anal rape by more than one man on more than one occasion cannot in my view sensibly be regarded as anything other than a significant injury …

32. For the avoidance of doubt, I wish to make it plain that I am not suggesting that, in every case of abuse, the victim must be taken to have known at the time that he has suffered a significant injury. I quite accept that, where the abuse is of a less obviously intrusive nature, a different conclusion might be reached.'

Albonetti v Wirral MBC

Limitation Act 1980, s 33

QBD (McKinnon J)   **[2009] EWHC 832 (QB)**

Following the Court of Appeal decision immediately above, the court was required to determine whether to exercise its discretion and not apply the limitation period in relation to a claim for damages for personal injury by the claimant against the defendant local authority.

The claimant had brought a claim in relation to alleged sexual abuse suffered while he was resident in a children's home over 30 years previously. He alleged that he was sexually assaulted by a friend (N) of the couple who managed the home. A psychiatric report supported his contention that the abuse had caused him to suffer post-traumatic stress disorder which had led to his psychiatric problems. The claimant submitted that the effect of the decision in *A v Hoare* (p287) was to transfer a claimant's subjective belief from a consideration of s 14 to s 33, which made the approach to the exercise of discretion under s 33 more generous, and that it would be fair to allow his claim to continue because his conduct in not commencing proceedings earlier was reasonable. The defendant argued that it was important to remember that the claim was in negligence and not for vicarious liability, and that it was unsafe for the court to make any meaningful assessment of the nature and/or extent of any alleged abuse so long after the event, and that the chances of a fair trial were therefore remote.

Held:

(i)   The fundamental question was whether it would be fair to allow this action to go to trial. There were two issues to be considered: the very long delay and the explanations for it, and whether it would be fair to allow a trial to proceed.

(ii)   Although the delay was understandable and it was not disputed that the claimant had acted reasonably in not instituting proceedings earlier, the very great delay of almost 40 years was decisive because it was difficult to imagine a case where there could be more prejudice to a defendant.

(iii)   N had died many years ago, and it was important to note that the local authority had not contributed to the delay in any way. N had not been convicted of abuse in respect of the claimant, and there had been no similar claims made against him. It was quite impossible to have a fair trial now regarding whether the alleged abuse had taken place. There had been no complaint made by the claimant at the time of the alleged abuse, and his claim had come completely out of the blue. It would also be very difficult for the parties to adduce reliable expert evidence regarding the relevant standards of the day, including in relation to the propriety of visitors having access to the home, particularly given that more was now known about the potential for abuse.

(iv)   The court would further be faced with the further significant difficulty of attempting to disentangle the causative effect of the alleged abuse from other damaging life events suffered by the claimant before and after the alleged abuse. A fair trial was quite simply impossible after such a long delay.

(v)   A balancing exercise had to be performed and it was not appropriate to exercise the court's discretion under s 33 not to apply the limitation period (*Hoare* followed and *Dobbie v Medway HA* (p411) considered).

Claim dismissed.

Allen and others v British Rail Engineering Ltd and RFS Industries Ltd

Limitation Act 1980, s 33

Court of Appeal   **[2001] EWCA Civ 242; (2001) ICR 942; LTL 26/6/01**

The four claimants worked as platers or welders for the first defendant up to 1987 and thereafter for second defendant in the same capacity. They suffered from vibration white finger. The judge found that the claimants had actual knowledge when they consulted doctors more than three years before proceedings were issued and constructive knowledge before that. However, the judge exercised her discretion under s 33 to allow the claims to continue on the basis that (a) the claimants did not appreciate that they had good claims (b) the delay was not blameworthy (c) the delay had not affected the cogency of the defendant's evidence (d) the case had been prosecuted expeditiously once it was started. She found for the claimants and awarded damages. One of the claimants appealed on quantum, and the defendants cross-appealed on the exercise of discretion in two of the cases.

Held: there was no unambiguous evidence of culpable delay on the part of the claimants or their advisers. The judge had not exercised her discretion wrongly.

Appeal dismissed.

Ali v Courtaulds Textiles Ltd

Limitation Act 1980, s 11, s 14

Court of Appeal   **(2000) 52 BMLR 129; (1999) Lloyd's Rep Med 301**

The claimant worked at the defendant's mill until 1988. In 1986 he consulted a GP who diagnosed deafness in his right ear. He was given ear drops. On 12 October 1990 he consulted an ENT registrar. The registrar wrote to the claimant's GP on 23 May 1991 diagnosing bilateral sensory neuro-deafness. In November 1991 a community worker advised the claimant to consult solicitors as he might have a claim against the defendant. The claimant did so later that same month. The claimant was examined by an ENT consultant who on 9 September 1992 communicated his opinion that the claimant was suffering from noise-induced deafness. A letter before action was sent on 30 April 1993 and proceedings issued on 5 May 1995. The defendant pleaded limitation. The judge held that the claimant had the requisite knowledge immediately following his conversation with the community worker and dismissed the claim. The claimant appealed.

Held:

(i)   Regard was needed as to the claimant's circumstances; his English was poor, he could not read or write in any language and was not a member of a union.

(ii)   The claimant knew he was deaf but neither he, his solicitors nor the community worker could have known whether this was attributable to ageing or noise.

(iii)   The claimant did not possess the relevant medical advice until September 1992. The judge's finding that the mere seeking of this advice fixed him with knowledge was contrary to s 14(3). At the time the judge fixed the claimant with constructive knowledge he had taken all reasonable steps to obtain advice.

(iv)   Where the cause of an injury was beyond the scope of even an informed and intelligent layman expert evidence was needed (*Davis v MOD* (p405), *Nash v Eli Lilly & Co* (p568) and *Spargo v North Essex DA* (p667) applied).

Appeal allowed.

Allistone v North Leicester Motors Ltd

Striking out for delay

Court of Appeal   **LTL 29/4/99**

The claimant was injured in a road traffic accident on 11 October 1993. She suffered whiplash and an injury to her left knee. Proceedings were issued on 26 September 1994. She succeeded in a trial on liability only on 26 January 1996. Each side by this stage had instructed two medical experts each. Thereafter there was minimal progress until 15 May 1998 when the defendant issued an application to strike out for want of prosecution. The judge found that the delay of two years and two months was inexcusable and had prejudiced the defendant. He therefore struck the claim out. The claimant appealed.

Held:

(i)   It was clear by May 1998 that the claim for damages had substantially increased from that pleaded.

(ii)   There was no reason why a trial on quantum had not been set down within a year of the liability trial. The defendant had been prejudiced both financially and evidentially by the delay. A fair trial was now almost impossible.

(iii)   The court had to consider the totality of the delay between January 1996 and May 1998. The judge was right to characterise it as inordinate.

(iv)   The claimant's argument that the reason for the delay was to improve her position by awaiting a change in the CRU laws was not accepted. Whilst there might be certain circumstances in which a party could legitimately use delaying tactics to their benefit, that was not the case here.

(v)   The claimant's solicitors, if they believed the case not to be ready for trial, should have explained to the defendant their reasons and disclosed their medical evidence.

Appeal dismissed.

The Alnwick

Limitation   **Maritime Conventions Act 1911, s 8**

Court of Appeal   **[1965] 2 All ER 569; [1965] P 357**

On 28 April 1962 Ronald Robinson was crossing the Tyne as a passenger in a foy-boat (a mooring vessel). The foy-boat was passing between the sterns of the Alnwick and of a Norwegian packet vessel called the Braemar. The foy-boat collided with the Alnwick, and Mr Robinson was killed.

In March 1963 the claimant (his widow) was granted legal aid. In December 1963 her writ was issued against the Alnwick. In February 1964 a statement of claim was served. On 2 May 1964 the Alnwick served a defence blaming the Braemar.

On 8 July 1964 the claimant added the Braemar to the claim as second defendants. In August 1964 the amended writ was served. In December 1964 the Braemar's solicitors sought an order that the action against the Braemar was not maintainable, as proceedings had not been commenced against the Braemar within two years, as required by s 8 of the Maritime Conventions Act 1911. Hewson J granted this order. The claimant appealed.

Held:

(i)   An action against a vessel, including a claim in respect of 'loss of life' was governed by the two-year time limit under s 8 of the Maritime Conventions Act 1911. The three-year limit under s 3 of the Law Reform (Limitation of Actions etc.) Act 1954 did not apply.

(ii)   The two-year time limit should be extended so as to allow the action to proceed against the Braemar because:

    (a)   the real responsibility for the delay lay with the Alnwick for not serving her defence in time without having given any advance indication that it would blame the Braemar;

    (b)   it the action were to be tried against the Alnwick alone, the claimant's widow, instead of the Braemar's owners, would have to obtain evidence from a Norwegian ship and deal with allegations of bad look-out, wrong engine or helm movements or the like; and

    (c)   if the claimant succeeded against the Alnwick, the Alnwick would be entitled to seek contribution against the Braemar, and it was desirable that one trial should establish the facts between the claimant and the Alnwick and the Alnwick and the Braemar.

Anderton v Clwyd County Council and linked appeals

CPR 6.7   **Human Rights Act 1998, s 3**
ECHR, Art 6

Court of Appeal   **[2002] EWCA Civ 933; [2002] 1 WLR 3174;**
[2002] 3 All ER 813

Five appeals concerning service.

Held (general):

(i)   The deemed day of service under the rules was not rebuttable by evidence of the actual day of service (*Godwin v Swindon BC* (p444) followed). This did not contravene Article 6 of the ECHR.

(ii)   Saturday and Sunday were not excluded from the calculation when service was by post (dicta in *Godwin* disapproved). CPR 2.8 did not apply to CPR 6.7. If that had been the intention the provision would have specifically stated 'business day'.

(iii)   As a result of the fiction of deemed service, CPR 6.7 could produce incongruous results. There was an argument that the section should be amended.

(iv)   There was a power under CPR 6.9 to dispense with service of the claim form both prospectively and retrospectively. However, this power should only be exercised retrospectively in exceptional circumstances.

(v) There was a distinction, not analysed in *Godwin*, between two types of cases:

  (a) cases where there had been no attempt to serve the claim form in time by one of the methods authorised by CPR 2.3; such cases were clearly caught by *Godwin* and service in these circumstances could not be dispensed with; and

  (b) cases were there had been an ineffective attempt to serve the claim form in time by an appropriate method. A claimant in this case did not require permission to serve out of time but rather to be excused from service altogether. Where the defendant had in reality received the claim form within the requisite period there would usually be no prejudice.

(vi) In exercising the discretion to dispense with service it might be legitimate to consider other relevant circumstances such as the explanation for late service, any criticism of the claimant or his advisers and any possible prejudice to the defendant.

(vii) Now that the disputed interpretations of the CPR had been clarified in *Godwin* and this appeal there will be very few (if any) acceptable excuses for future failures to observe the rules for service of the claim form. The courts were entitled to adopt a strict approach even if it produced harsh results in individual cases.

(A) BRYANT

On 27 July 1998 the claimant was injured in a road traffic accident. On 9 August 2000 liability was agreed 65/35% in his favour. Proceedings were issued on 18 July 2001. The validity period was due to expire on Sunday 18 November 2001. The claim form was sent by first class post and recorded delivery on Thursday 15 November 2001 and received by the defendant the following day. The defendant applied for service to be set aide as out of time. The judge held that Saturday and Sunday were excluded from the calculation of the deemed day of service and refused to dispense with service. The claimant appealed.

Held: Saturday should have been taken into account. If it had been the deemed day of service would have been within the four month period. Appeal allowed.

(B) CHAMBERS

The claimant's husband was killed in a road traffic accident on 25 February 1998. Liability was admitted following the defendant's conviction in the magistrates' court and quantum reports had been exchanged by the time of issue of proceedings on 15 February 2001. The claimant claimed slightly under £500,000. On 14 June 2001 time for service was extended to 13 July 2001. On Thursday 12 July the claimant sent the claim form to the defendant by first class post. It actually arrived the following day, the last day for service. The judge struck out the claim for late service refused to dispense with service. The claimant appealed.

Held:

(i) The claim form was in reality received by and brought to the attention of the defendant within the four-month period.

(ii) When the claim form had been received the defendant had made an offer to settle. The prejudice to the claimant would be great if service were not dispensed with. Conversely, the only prejudice to the defendant was that contemplated by the power to dispense with service.

(iii) This could be regarded as an exceptional case where it would be appropriate to dispense with service.

Appeal allowed.

(C) ANDERTON

The claimant alleged negligence against the defendant's teachers for a failure to ameliorate learning difficulties when she was at school between 1983 and 1990. Proceedings were issued on 5 July 2000, a day before limitation expired. On 27 July 2000 the House of Lords gave judgment in the claimant's favour in relation to pre-action disclosure. The period for service expired on Sunday 5 November 2000. The defendant applied to strike out. The judge held that as there was no evidence that service was by first rather than by second class post he could not find that service had been effected by a permissible method. In the alternative, he found the deemed date of service to have been Monday 6 November 2000. The claimant appealed.

Held:

(i)   In light of further evidence adduced that the claimant's solicitors always used first class post, the judge was wrong to hold that the claim form was not sent by first class post on Friday 3 November 2000.

(ii)   The deemed day of service was Sunday 5 November 2000, the last day of service, not the following Monday.

Appeal allowed.

(D) DORGAN

This was a claim by a prison inmate for an assault by prison officers. Proceedings were issued on 11 April 2001, just inside the limitation period. The period for service expired on Saturday 11 August 2001. At 4.02pm on Friday 10 August 2001 the claimant's solicitor faxed the claim form and particulars to the defendant's solicitors. The defendant's solicitors, upon receiving the fax, replied that deemed date of service was not until the following Monday. The judge granted an application to dispense with service under CPR 6.9.

Held:

(i)   The list of permitted methods of service in CPR 6.2 was exhaustive unless the court permitted an alternative method under CPR 6.8(2).

(ii)   The defendant's actual receipt of the claim form within the validity period did not displace the deemed day of service, Monday 14 August 2001. The claim form was therefore not served in time.

(iii)   The judge was entitled in the exceptional circumstances of the case to make the order he did. The defendant had already been notified of the details of the claim and its only prejudice was a time point under the rules. If service was not dispensed with the claimant would be statute barred and suffer the serious prejudice of a trial on the merits.

Appeal dismissed.

(E) CUMMINS

The issue here was whether service outside the jurisdiction was governed by CPR 7.6.

Held: Service outside the jurisdiction was governed by Section III of CPR Part 6. CPR 7.6 had no application. Appeal allowed.

Appleby v Walsall Health Authority

Limitation Act 1980, s 11, s 14, s 33

QBD (Popplewell J)   **[1999] Lloyd's Rep Med 154**

The claimant was born on 15 October 1971 suffering from cerebral palsy arising from a lack of oxygen to his brain during delivery. The claimant's case was that his mother first learned that the cerebral palsy was attributable to the defendant in 1977, but did not convey his information to him and was reluctant to discuss the issue. In early 1996, the claimant gave birth to his first son. Concerned with her son's health, the claimant's wife extracted the cause of the claimant's injury from the mother. He issued proceedings on 2 May 1997. The defendant pleaded limitation which was heard as a preliminary issue.

Held:

(i)   There was no basis for imputing the mother's knowledge to the claimant, and to do so would be contrary to the purpose of the Act. The claimant did not have actual knowledge until June 1996.

(ii)   Knowledge of the possibility of a claim was not enough to have required the claimant to press for more information about his birth. On the facts, the claimant's mother would not have disclosed this information until after the birth of her grandson in any event. He was therefore not fixed with an earlier date of constructive knowledge.

(iii)   As regards s 33:

    (a)   the treating registrar had returned to India. Due to ill-health he was unable to return for a trial. Although he could still make a statement or give evidence by video link, the defendant may be caused some difficulties by the inability of its witnesses to discuss the case with lawyers in the absence of notes;

    (b)   the claimant's ability to prove his case was equally affected by the lack of live witnesses. The experts would be almost entirely reliant on contemporaneous notes; and

    (c)   the prejudice to the defendant was not such as to prevent a fair trial and a s 33 discretion would have been exercised if required.

Preliminary issue decided in favour of the claimant.

NB: A different approach would probably now be taken to constructive knowledge: *Whiston v London SHA* (p710).

Arnold v Central Electricity Generating Board

Public Authorities Protection Act 1893, s 1

Limitation Act 1939, s 21

House of Lords   **[1987] 3 All ER 694; [1988] AC 228**

Between April 1938 and April 1943 Albert Arnold was employed by the Birmingham Corporation at Hams Hall power station. He contracted mesothelioma which was first diagnosed in October 1981 and caused his death in May 1982.

In 1984 the claimant (his widow) started court action against the Corporation's successors in title on the grounds that it had failed to protect Mr Arnold from inhalation of asbestos dust. The defence pleaded that the claim was statute barred, and a preliminary trial was ordered.

The Court of Appeal allowed the defendant's appeal against the judgment of Michael Ogden QC that the case was not statute barred. The claimant appealed.

Held:

(i)   As s 21 of the Limitation Act 1939 prescribed a one-year limitation period for actions against public authorities to which the Public Authorities Protection Act 1893 applied, by April 1944 any cause of action which the deceased may have had in respect of his mesothelioma was statute barred.

(ii)   Section 7(1) of the Law Reform (Limitation of Actions etc) Act 1954 did not revive any cause of action which was already time barred.

(iii)   Section 6 of the Limitation Act 1963 did not operate to deprive any defendant of a time bar which had accrued on the expiry of the six-year limitation period prescribed by s 2(1) of the Limitation Act 1939, and s 1(4)(a) of the 1963 Act preserved any relevant limitation defence available by virtue of any enactment other than s 2(1) of the 1939 Act, eg s 21 of the Limitation Act 1939 which applied in this case.

(iv)   A statute affecting substantive rights is not to be construed as having retrospective operation unless it clearly appears to have been so intended, and nothing in s 3 of the Limitation Act 1975 led clearly to the conclusion that defendants previously entitled to rely on accrued six-year and one-year time-bars under the 1939 Act were intended to be deprived of those accrued rights by the 1975 Act.

(v)   Paragraph 9 of Schedule 2 to the Limitation Act 1980 provides that nothing in the 1980 Act shall enable any action to be brought which was barred by the Limitation Act 1939.

Accordingly, the claimant's appeal was dismissed.

But see *Keenan v Miller Insulation & Engineering Ltd* (p515).

Asia Pacific (HK) Ltd and others v (1) Hanjin Shipping Co Ltd (2) Owners of The MV Hanjin Pennsylvania

CPR 7.5, 7.6, 6.9

Christopher Clarke J   **[2005] EWHC 2443 (Comm); LTL 15/11/2005**

A number of cargo owners including the claimant issued proceedings against the defendant for damages arising from an explosion on the defendant's ship. (The defendant began a limitation action and obtained a limitation decree). The claimant instructed his solicitors to serve the claim form. The defendant's solicitors asked for confirmation that proceedings had been issued, enquired as to the possibility of consolidation and stated that they were authorised to accept service of proceedings. The claimant's solicitors replied by fax attaching a copy of the claimant's claim form.

After expiry of the four-month validity period for service, the defendant took the point that the claim form had never been served as service involved delivery of a document in circumstances that conveyed to the objective knowledgeable observer that delivery was intended by way of service rather than merely for information, whereas the instant circumstances conveyed the converse impression.

The claimant sought a declaration that service was validly effective service of the claim form within time.

Held:

(i)   The CPR did not define service beyond prescribing how it might be done. The common thread was that the serving party delivered it into the recipient's possession or control or took steps to do so.

(ii)   The claimant did not indicate that the claim form was for information only or that its delivery was not to be regarded as service.

(iii) None of the lack of a response pack, the fact that the claim form was marked 'Claimant's copy' or the omission of the words 'by way of service' demonstrated that service was not intended.

(iv)   The substance of the position was that the claimant had delivered the claim form to the defendant thereby not only providing the defendant with notice of its issue but also providing a copy of it.

(v)   When a claim form was delivered to a recipient in the manner provided by the rules it was served unless the sending party made clear that the delivery was not in fact service.

(vi)   If the recipient was unsure whether a document was being served or provided for information only he could simply enquire of the sender.

(vii)   If service had not been valid, there could have been no extension of time under CPR 7.6, but the facts of the case were exceptional so as to dispense with service under CPR 6.9.

Declaration granted.

Atha v ATV Network and others

Limitation Act 1980, s 33

Talbot J   **Lexis, 28 June 1983**

The claimant (Ms Atha) was a television stage manager. She was working for the first defendants, in a hall which they had hired from the second defendants, in which was an upright piano provided by the third defendants. On 3 April 1979 the piano fell and struck her left hand, causing her quite severe injuries. Her case was that the piano was unstable.

She immediately placed the matter in the hands of her union's legal officer. He promptly notified her claim to the first defendants whose insurers by 1981 had involved the insurers for the other defendants. Owing to an oversight, no writ was issued until 14 September 1982. The writ and statement of claim were served on the first defendants on 15 September. An amended statement of claim was served on the other defendants on 8 March 1983. A preliminary trial on limitation was ordered.

Held:

(i)   The length of delay (just over five months) was short. There was no valid reason for it: s 33(3)(a).

(ii)   The accident was simple, and the main facts did not admit of much dispute. The passage of time would not vitally affect the cogency of the evidence: s 33(3)(b).

(iii)   The claimant claimed promptly and was entitled to leave the matter thereafter in the hands of her trade union: s 33(3)(e).

(iv)   While she would have a clear cause of action against her union, she would have to begin proceedings entirely afresh with obvious consequences and difficulties: s 33(3).

(v)   On balance it would be equitable to permit the matter to proceed and to disapply the provisions of s 11 of the Limitation Act 1980: s 33(1).

Atkinson v Oxfordshire Health Authority

Limitation Act 1980, s 14, s 33

S Tuckey QC   **[1993] 4 Med LR 18**

In 1967 the claimant (Keith Atkinson), then aged 17, was complaining of progressive deafness. The Radcliffe Infirmary confirmed that he suffered from bilateral acoustic neuromas. On 2 May 1967 the tumour on the left side of the head was removed. On 16 May 1967 he underwent a second operation to evacuate the tumour on the right side of the brain. Following this operation the claimant was in a bad way. He had great difficulty in communicating with people outside the family. He suffered from double vision, although his balance improved. Described by his mother as 'intelligent but unable to fight', he was entirely reliant on her.

When he was 21 solicitors were instructed. Attention focused on late referral to the Radcliffe and, after a medical expert reported that no-one was to blame, negative legal advice was given. In 1972 Mrs Atkinson consulted a second firm of solicitors who gave negative advice, as did a third firm in 1980. Subsequently some concrete evidence emerged in the shape of a letter to the claimant's GP, a copy of which was also sent to the claimant, which referred to a pre-operative respiratory arrest. Mrs Atkinson then instructed a fourth firm of solicitors who obtained pre-trial disclosure revealing the respiratory problems in the operation and then favourable expert medical advice. The grounds of claim were that either the second operation was unnecessary or it was negligently performed and should have been stopped when it was seen that the claimant was suffering from distress.

The writ was issued on 6 July 1989. A preliminary trial on the issues under s 14 and s 33 of the Limitation Act 1980 was held before Mr Tuckey QC sitting as a deputy judge of the Queen's Bench Division.

Held:

(i)   The claimant and his mother understandably felt that they had been up against a brick wall. Looking at their conduct in obtaining advice over the years, neither had acted unreasonably: s 14(3). The claimant was not to be fixed with relevant knowledge before 6 July 1986: s 14(1). His claim was not time barred.

(ii)   Under s 33, were that relevant, the fact that if not allowed to proceed the claimant would be denied compensation for his serious condition was nearly balanced by the prejudice to the defendants of having to defend allegations of negligence so long ago when the anaesthetist had died and the surgeon had retired. However, the balance just tipped in favour of the claimant, since to a large extent the delay was of the defendants' own making in that it would not have occurred if the claimant or his mother had been told at the time exactly what had happened during the operation. Had he needed it, discretion under s 33 would have been exercised to allow his action to proceed.

Austin v Newcastle Chronicle & Journal Ltd

CPR 3.1, 3.4, 7.5, 7.6

Court of Appeal   **[2001] EWCA Civ 834**

On 28 February 1999, the Sunday Sun newspaper, published by the defendant, ran an article upon which claimant was suing for libel. On 1 March 1999, an article was published in another North East regional newspaper, the Sunderland Echo, published by North East Press and concerning the same subject matter. The action against North East Press was settled in December 2000 by way of acceptance of a payment into court. A letter before action was sent to the editor of the Sunday Sun on 10 February 2000. The delay in sending this was caused because he was awaiting the outcome of the decision in a landmark case at the House of Lords (*Reynolds v Times Newspapers Ltd & Ors* [1999] 3 WLR 1010). Proceedings were issued naming the editor of the Sunday Sun as defendant on 25 February 2000 and served on 1 February 2000. They were therefore issued and served in time.

On 7 March 2000, solicitors for the Sunday Sun wrote to the claimant's solicitors informing them that the purported editor was the wrongly named defendant, submitting that he was neither the editor, author nor publisher of that article. The Sunday Sun's solicitors invited an amendment and agreed that they would not withhold the claim form and would reply to proceedings upon amendment of the defendant's name and service of particulars of claim. The appropriate amendments were made and were returned to the Sunday Sun on 10 May 2000 although, through the error of the claimant's solicitors, the enclosures in fact related to the action against the Sunderland Echo. On 19 May and 2 June 2000, the defendant wrote to the claimant pointing out the error. On 8 June 2000, the claimant's solicitors acknowledged their mistake and wrote to the defendant's solicitors proposing a further extension of time in which to serve a corrected claim form and particulars of claim. That period expired on 26 June 2000. On 21 July 2000, the claimant's solicitors served an amended claim form and particulars of claim but, on 27 July 2000, the defendant's solicitors wrote advising the claimant's solicitors that it was unable to accept service because the time in which to serve the amended documents had expired.

The claimant's solicitors filed a notice to amend on 10 August 2000. In a subsequent hearing on 13 September 2000, a new timetable in which to serve and reply was established. The defendant successfully appealed that decision to Holland J, submitting that the crucial point was that the claim form was not served within the period that it should have been, and that the amendment was not carried out within the appropriate time frame. Further, the judge held that the claimant had utilised the full one-year period within which to initiate proceedings and had not made good use of the time extensions readily granted to him.

The claimant made a second tier appeal, submitting that, in the exercise of his discretion not to extend time for service as the district judge had so ordered, Holland J failed to have regard to important and relevant considerations and erred in principle in relation to facts in reaching the conclusion that he did in dismissing the claimant's action against the defendant.

Held:

(i) To suggest that the claimant had not put in process the steps to amend was plainly wrong. An attempt was made on 10 May 2000, albeit that the wrong papers were sent to the defendant.

(ii) The jurisprudence relating to service (such as *Vinos v Marks & Spencer* (p701)) had little relevance to the general discretion to extend time under CPR 3.1.

(iii) The defendant was fully aware of the claim that was being made against it from as early as 10 February 2000. There was no evidence that it had suffered any prejudice. The relevance of the action, the prejudice to the claimant, and the need to have the case tried were all factors that needed to be considered in determining whether this case should fail due to an error by the claimant's solicitors. The need for a quick resolution in defamation cases had to be weighed in the balance.

(iv) There was no doubt that the delay in bringing this case prevented the claimant from vindicating his character and there was no doubt that the delay offended the proper administration of justice. However, that delay, coupled with the solicitors' error should not have prevented the claimant from pursuing his claim. Accordingly, the district judge's findings would be adopted and a new time frame in which to serve an amended claim form and particulars of claim would be set.

Appeal allowed.

Azaz v Denton

[2009] EWHC 1759 (QB)

QBD (Judge Richard Seymour QC)   **Limitation Act 1980, s 11, s 32, s 33**

The claimant brought proceedings alleging undue influence by the defendants (D1 and D2). D2 was a healing center which had been established by D1, who was its spiritual leader attributed with the status of 'guru'. D2's activities included teaching meditation and healing and it operated as a residence for those who wished to participate in communal living. The claimant had left his career as a medical doctor and he and his wife decided, or were persuaded, to become resident at D2, and to earn their keep through teaching meditation and healing activities. Upon joining, the claimant (in January 1993) transferred all his assets, both in cash and property comprising furniture, books and miscellaneous items, to D2. The claimant later left the center in December 2003. In May 2007 he requested the return of his assets. This did not happen, and in April 2008 he issued proceedings alleging, inter alia, that D1, as his spiritual leader, had exercised undue influence over him as a result of which he had handed over and allowed the use of all his personal possessions (the 'possessions' and 'cash' claims), worked for D1 and D2 without receiving proper remuneration (the 'work' claim), and developed episodes of severe dissociative mental illness beginning in around 1996 (the 'personal injury' claim). The claimant sought equitable compensation or damages or both.

By their defence, D1 and D2 alleged that the claimant's equitable claim was barred by the doctrine of laches and that the other claims were statute barred pursuant to the Limitation Act 1980. The court ordered the trial of preliminary issues concerning: whether all or any part of the claimant's claim was an action for personal injuries within s 11 and, if so, whether the primary limitation period had expired when the claim was issued and the court should exercise its discretion to disapply the primary limitation period under s 33; whether all or any part of the claimant's claim was otherwise statute barred; whether the claimant was entitled to rely upon s 32; and whether all or any part of the claimant's claim for equitable relief was barred by the equitable defence of laches. The claimant also made a later claim for delivery up of the possessions (the 'later possessions' claim) on the ground that they had been provided to D1 and D2 on a long-term loan and it was common ground between the parties that that claim was not susceptible to a defence of limitation or laches.

Held:

(i)   It was accepted on behalf of the claimant that he had the relevant knowledge for the purposes of s 14 in April 2004 when he received a psychiatric report setting out his illness. The personal injury claim was therefore prima facie statute barred.

(ii)   Part of the claim amounted to a personal injury claim which had been issued after the expiry period. In multiple claims, the effect of s 11(1) was to render claims which were not for damages for personal injury (such as claims for breach of contract or alleged breaches of duties of care) vulnerable to limitation defences to which they would not be vulnerable but for being packaged with the personal injury claim. Subject to the effect of s 33, the personal injury claim, and the cash, possessions and work claims, insofar as based on some alleged breach of duty, whether in contract, tort or otherwise, should be dismissed as statute barred.

(iii)   There was no satisfactory reason why the claimant had not issued his claim form prior to the expiry of the limitation period relevant to the personal injury claim, and no explanation at all for the delay between the expiry of that limitation period and the issue of the claim form. The provisions of s 33(3)(b) required attention to be given to the impact of the passage of time since the expiry of the limitation period on the quality of the evidence available to each of the claimant and the defendants.

(iv)   The prospects of success were also relevant to s 33. Here, the claimant's case was very weak. This was a particularly weighty consideration where, as here, there was little or no prospect of the defendants recovering their costs from the claimant if ultimately successful.

(v)   In the circumstances, it was not appropriate for the court to exercise its discretion under s 33(1) in favour of the claimant.

(vi)   The alleged exercise of undue influence was irrelevant to the question whether the conditions set out in s 32(1), concerning fraudulent concealment, were satisfied. It was implicit in the analysis that the person the subject of the undue influence was aware of the relevant facts, but was dissuaded by the influence from doing anything in consequence of that knowledge. Whether that was so or not, there was just no connection in logic between the exercise of undue influence and knowledge, or ignorance, of facts relevant to a cause of action. It followed that the claimant was not entitled to rely on s 32.

(vii)   The issue of laches was also determined against the claimant.

(viii) Whilst the claimant would face considerable difficulty in establishing the facts alleged to found the later possessions claim, that action remained live and was transferred to the county court for determination. All of the claimant's other claims were dismissed.

Preliminary issues determined.

B v Ministry of Defence

Limitation Act 1980, s 11, s 14, s 33

Supreme Court   [2012] UKSC 9

Ten lead claimants (in the 'atomic veterans litigation') represented over 1,000 veteran servicemen who had been involved in thermonuclear tests carried out by the defendant in the South Pacific in the 1950s. They claimed that during the testing they had been exposed to radiation and that as a result they had suffered illness, disability or death.

The defendant denied that they had been exposed to radiation and denied that their injuries had been caused by exposure to radiation. Most of the claims in the group action had been issued in 2004, by which time the veterans had come to believe that they had been exposed to radiation, a minority being added in 2007–2008. However, the claimants all asserted that it was not until 2007, when an expert's report provided some evidence of their having been exposed to radiation to support their prior belief of exposure, that they acquired the knowledge required by s 11(4) and s 14(1). Limitation was determined as a preliminary issue.

At first instance, the judge held that in five of the cases the claims had been issued in time, and that the other five cases, although barred by the expiry of the primary limitation period, should be permitted to continue under s 33.

The defendant accepted that one case had been brought in time but appealed in respect of the others. The Court of Appeal reversed the judge's decision, holding that all but one of the claimants had acquired the relevant knowledge more than three years before issuing their claims. It declined to exercise its discretion under s 33 of the Act to disapply s 11 in relation to the remaining nine claimants, holding that the claims had no real prospect of success on causation.

The nine claimants appealed. The issues were (i) whether it was possible for a claimant to begin proceedings before having acquired the knowledge required by s 14(1)(b) that his injuries were attributable to the defendant's negligence; (ii) what 'knowledge' meant for the for the purposes of s 14(1)(b); and (iii) if the claimant's claims were time barred, whether the court should exercise its s 33 discretion.

Held (Lord Phillips of Worth Matravers PSC, Baroness Hale of Richmond and Lord Kerr of Tonaghmore JJSC dissenting):

(i)   By the time a claimant issued proceedings he had, pursuant to s 14(1)(b), to have knowledge of the fact that his injuries were attributable to the defendant's breach of duty. It was a legal impossibility for a claimant to lack such knowledge after he had issued proceedings. The statement of truth could be regarded as an explicit recognition by the claimant that he had knowledge that his injuries were attributable to the defendant. It was clear that the inquiry mandated by s 14(1) was retrospective and was aimed at discovering whether the claimant first had the requisite knowledge within the three years prior to the date of issue (*Whitfield v North Durham HA* (p713) and *Nash v Eli Lilly & Co* (p568) considered).

(ii)   It was thus heretical to assert that a claimant could escape the time bar by establishing that, even after his claim had been issued, he remained in a state of ignorance as to whether his injuries were attributable to the defendant.

(iii)   As to the meaning of 'knowledge' for the purposes of s 14(1)(b), Lord Donaldson's formulation in *Halford v Brookes* (p453) was to be endorsed: a claimant was likely to have acquired knowledge of the required facts when he first came reasonably to believe them (*Halford* approved). His belief had to have been held with sufficient confidence to justify embarking on the preliminaries to the issue of proceedings.

(iv)   Lord Donaldson envisaged that the collection of evidence to support the claim would normally come after the claimant first knew that he had a possible claim. There was a distinction between a claimant's knowledge that he had a real possibility of a claim, and the assembly by him and his legal team, with the help of experts, of material justifying the commencement of proceedings with a reasonable prospect of success. While it did not automatically follow that a claimant would have acquired the requisite knowledge by the date he first took legal advice, such an inference might well be justified.

(v)   However, the date upon which he first consulted an expert was not, of itself, likely to assist in determining whether he had the requisite knowledge by then. Rather, the court would have regard to the confidence with which he held the belief, the substance it carried prior to his consulting the expert, and the effect of the expert's report.

(vi)   Applying those principles to the instant case, the Court of Appeal had been correct to conclude that the claimants had the requisite knowledge more than three years before the issue of proceedings.

(vii)   While it was undesirable for a court deciding a limitation issue to have detailed regard to the evidence which the claimant put forward as supporting his substantive case, the Court of Appeal had been in the unusual position of having before it a mass of material which enabled it to assess with confidence the claimants' prospects of establishing causation. As the claims had no real prospect of success, it would have been absurd for the Court of Appeal to have exercised its discretion under s 33 so as to allow them to proceed.

Appeals dismissed.

Per Lord Wilson JSC: '2. What is the nature of the exercise which the court conducts when asked by a defendant to rule that an action in respect of personal injuries is time barred under section 11 of the Act? Subsection (4) provides that the action shall not be brought after the expiration of three years from "(a) the date on which the cause of action accrued; or (b) the date of knowledge (if later) of the person injured." The subsection refers, at (a), to "the cause of action" notwithstanding that, if the action is to continue, it may well transpire that the claimant has no cause of action. When the subsection turns, at (b), to "the date of knowledge (if later)" and so requires the court to appraise the claimant's knowledge of the four "facts" specified in section 14(1), which relate to, although do not comprise all elements of, his cause of action, the assumption that indeed he has a cause of action remains. That explains why sections 11(4)(b) and 14(1) refer to "knowledge" (which can be only of matters which are true) rather than to "belief" (which can be in matters which are untrue as well as in those which are true). Knowledge of the second of the four facts specified in section 14(1) is "that the injury was attributable in whole or in part to the act or omission which is alleged to constitute negligence, nuisance or breach of duty". This knowledge of attributability (as it is convenient to describe it) is predicated upon the assumption that the claimant has a valid cause of action and thus would be able to establish among other things, even in the teeth of opposition from the defendant, not just attributability (which means only that there is a real possibility that the act or omission caused the injury: *Spargo v North Essex District Health Authority* [1997] PIQR P235 at P242, Brooke LJ) but, rather, that his act or omission actually caused the injury in the legally requisite sense. In the decision of the Court of Appeal in *Halford v Brookes* [1991] 1 WLR 428 the trial judge, Schiemann J, is quoted, at p 442H, as having referred to "the bizarre situation when a defendant asserts that the plaintiff had knowledge of a fact which the plaintiff asserts as a fact but which the defendant denies is a fact". The situation may indeed seem bizarre until one remembers that, at the stage of an inquiry under section 11, the exercise requires the existence of the fact to be assumed. Were the action to continue, the defendant might well deny it; but he does not do so at that stage ...

3. ... In my view, however, it is a legal impossibility for a claimant to lack knowledge of attributability for the purpose of section 14(1) at a time after the date of issue of his claim. By that date he must in law have had knowledge of it ...

6. ...It is in my view heretical that a claimant can escape the conventional requirement to assert his cause of action for personal injuries within three years of its accrual by establishing that, even after his claim was brought, he remained in a state of ignorance entirely inconsistent with it ...

11. ...So I consider that this court should reiterate endorsement for Lord Donaldson's proposition that a claimant is likely to have acquired knowledge of the facts specified in section 14 when he first came reasonably to believe them. I certainly accept that the basis of his belief plays a part in the inquiry; and so, to that limited extent, I respectfully agree with para 170 of Lady Hale's judgment. What I do not accept is that he lacks knowledge until he has the evidence with which to substantiate his belief in court ...

12. What then is the degree of confidence with which a belief should be held, and of the substance which it should carry, before it is to amount to knowledge for the purpose of the subsection? It was, again, Lord Donaldson in the *Halford* case, cited above, who, in the passage quoted by Lord Phillips in para 115 below, offered guidance in this respect which Lord Nicholls in the *Haward* case, cited above, was, at para 9, to describe as valuable and upon which, at this level of generality, no judge has in my view yet managed to improve: it is that the belief must be held "with sufficient confidence to justify embarking on the preliminaries to the issue of a writ, such as submitting a claim to the proposed defendant, taking legal and other advice and collecting evidence". In *Broadley v Guy Clapham & Co* [1994] 4 All ER 439 Hoffmann LJ, in the passage quoted by Lord Phillips at para 118 below, paraphrased Lord Donaldson's guidance in terms of a search for the moment at which the claimant knows enough to make it reasonable for him to begin to investigate whether he has a "case" against the defendant. I respectfully agree with the analysis by Lord Phillips of what Hoffmann LJ meant. The investigation upon which the claimant should reasonably embark is into whether in law he has a valid claim (in particular whether the act or omission of the defendant involves negligence or other breach of duty, being a matter of which the claimant is specifically not required to have had knowledge under section 14(1)) and, if so, how that claim can be established in court. So it is an investigation likely to be conducted with the assistance of lawyers; but, in the light of their advice, it may well also embrace a search for evidence, including from experts. The focus is upon the moment when it is *reasonable* for the claimant to embark on such an investigation. It is possible that a claimant will take legal advice before his belief is held with sufficient confidence and carries sufficient substance to make it reasonable for him to do so. Thus, as Judge LJ pointed out in the *Sniezek* case, cited above, at P229 and P232, it does not automatically follow that, by the date when he first took legal advice, the claimant will have acquired the requisite knowledge; but such an inference may well be justified.

13. I hasten however to attach an obvious rider. From the fact that a claimant may well need to consult experts *after* he has acquired the requisite knowledge, it in no way follows that he will have acquired such knowledge by the date when he first consults an expert. Section 14(3) expressly recognises that the facts which he is required to know may be ascertainable by the claimant only with the help of experts and deems him to have acquired such knowledge at the point at which he might, with their help, reasonably have been expected to acquire it. In my view the date upon which the claimant first consulted an expert is not, on its own, likely to assist the court in determining whether by then he had the requisite knowledge. Instead the court will have regard – broadly – to the confidence with which the claimant held the belief, and to the substance which it carried, prior to his consulting the expert (and in particular, no doubt, the reasons which induced the claimant to consult him) and also, if the conclusion is that at that prior stage the claimant lacked belief of the requisite character, the effect upon the claimant's belief of his receipt of the expert's report.

14. In short the assistance given to a claimant by an expert in this respect can be of two kinds. One is assistance in his acquiring "knowledge" of the "facts" required by section 14. He may, for example, advise the claimant that he has a medical condition, of which he was previously unaware, which provides him with a substantive basis for believing that his injury is attributable to an act or omission of the defendant. The other is the provision of evidence which will, in court, help him to substantiate the claim which, in the light (among other things) of his knowledge of the limited matters specified by section 14(1), he proposes to bring.'

Per Lord Walker JSC: '63. Our judgments on this appeal will not, I fear, be an ideal source of guidance to lower courts which regularly have to deal with these difficult problems.

There are two reasons for that: the extreme complexity of this group litigation, and the division of opinion in the court. For my part I would suggest that short summaries like that of Brooke LJ in *Spargo* (which Lord Phillips rightly describes as a "valiant attempt") may be unhelpful if treated as if they were statutory texts. The words of the 1980 Act themselves must be the starting-point, illuminated where necessary by judicial exposition, of which the opinion of Lord Nicholls in *Haward v Fawcett* [2006] 1 WLR 682, paras 8 to 15, is the most authoritative. To that guidance I would tentatively add two points. In a complex case section 14(3) is an essential part of the statutory scheme, not an occasional add-on. And the date of a claimant's first visit to a solicitor is (without more) of very little significance in most cases.'

B and others v Nugent Care Society

Limitation Act 1980, s 14, s 33, s 38

Court of Appeal   **[2009] EWCA Civ 827; [2010] 1 WLR 516;**
[2010] 1 FLR 707; [2010] PIQR P3;
[2009] LS Law Medical 524; [2009] Fam Law 1045;
(2009) 153(30) SJLB 28

Three claimants (JB, JPM, DVB) were part of a group action of 50 claimants who had all allegedly suffered sexual abuse at St Aiden's children's home in Widnes (which closed in 1982) and St Vincent's home in Formby (which closed in 1989). The defendant was responsible for these homes.

Proceedings were issued on 22 January 1998, 30 March 2001 and 8 October 2001 by JB, DVB and JPM respectively, many years after the expiry of the primary limitation period. Limitation was raised as a preliminary issue. At first instance, Holland J that the claims were well out of time and refused to exercise his s 33 discretion in the claimants' favour.

The claimants appealed. The appeals were heard on 17 June 2008, after the House of Lords' decision in *A v Hoare* (p287). The Court of Appeal upheld the decision of Holland J in part, but, based on *A v Hoare*, it held that it was incorrect and incomplete in relation to aspects of the approach to s 33 of the 1980 Act. The matter was therefore remitted to Irwin J, as Holland J had now retired. Irwin J used some of the findings by Holland J as a basis for his decision on limitation.

Irwin J held that JPM had been abused. Under the approach set out by *A v Hoare* the decision of Holland J had to be modified. As the abuse was proved and 'system evidence' was no longer relevant, it was proper to exercise his discretion under s 33 in his favour. The judge also held that JB had been abused, but his date of knowledge was about November 1995. Based on the passing of time and that the alleged abuser could not have a fair trial, he refused to exercise his discretion under s 33 of the 1980 Act in JB's favour.

The case of DVB was considered by Irwin J afresh. DVB was placed at St Aiden's in the 1970s and claimed sexual abuse in or about 1975/6. His housemaster was convicted of significant sexual offending in 1995. Although not a complainant at the criminal trial of the abuser, DVB reported his abuse to the police in 1995 and claimed a late date of knowledge of injury in 2000. He commenced proceedings in March 2001. Irwin J rejected the claim of a late date of knowledge but exercised his discretion in DVB's favour.

In the conjoined case of *GR v Wirral Metropolitan Borough Council* at first instance, the claim was brought in assault and trespass to the person. The claimant resided at one of the defendant's care homes, known as Shackleton Road, in Wallesley. From about 1974–1976 he was allegedly sexually abused by one of the employees. The home was closed in 1985 and the claim became time barred in January 1985. A claim form was issued on 20 June 2003. HHJ Main QC held that the claimant had significant knowledge under s 14 of the Act more than three years before issue of proceedings, but having considered the relevant factors he exercised his discretion in the claimant's favour under s 33.

All these findings were subject to appeals and cross-appeal. They raised questions as to the correct approach to the application of s 33 of the Limitation Act 1980 in the light of the decision in *A v Hoare* and to what extent the reasoning of *KR v Bryn Alyn Community (Holdings) Ltd* (p505) survived *Hoare*.

Held:

(i) *Hoare* established that a claim for damages for trespass to the person was a claim for damages for breach of duty, and that the limitation period was three years, but was subject to the court's discretion to extend it under s 33. *Lister v Hesley Hall Ltd* (p535) made it clear that, where there was a sufficient connection between the work of an employee and the acts of abuse committed by him, such as would arise from employment in a care home or a school, vicarious liability was likely to be established. That was a significant development because it meant that it was often no longer necessary for a claimant to establish systemic negligence and thus direct liability.

(ii) The starting points set out in *KR v Bryn Alyn Community (Holdings) Ltd* (p505) (at para 74) for the exercise of discretion under s 33 remained valid, subject to appropriate amendment in the light of *Hoare*.

(iii) There were two important points of distinction between the questions being considered in *Bryn Alyn* and those being considered in *Hoare* and the instant appeals.

(iv) Firstly, previously it was necessary for the evidence to cover the whole system being operated in the relevant home over a long period, and for the court to consider whether there was a relevant breach of duty. Now the claimant only had to show: (a) that the alleged abuse occurred; (b) that the defendant was vicariously liable for it; (c) that it caused the alleged psychological or physical damage; and (d) quantum.

(v) Secondly, the exercise under s 33 was significantly different now. The question whether the claimant, taking into account his psychological state in consequence of the injury and any consequential inhibition, could reasonably have been expected to institute proceedings was now to be considered under s 33, whereas previously this had gone to s 14 knowledge.

(vi) In relation to point 2 in para 74 of *Bryn Alyn*, it was correct to describe the exercise of the discretion as an exceptional indulgence to the claimant only in that, but for the exercise of the discretion, his claim would be time barred. It was exceptional only for that reason; the authorities stressed that the discretion was wide and unfettered.

(vii) In relation to point 6 in para 74 of *Bryn Alyn*, it was now likely that there would be many cases where a judge would consider it unfeasible to decide the issues simply by reference to the pleadings, written witness statements and the extent and content of discovery. Oral evidence might be desirable; the strength of the claimant's evidence was relevant to the way in which the discretion should be exercised.

(viii) In undertaking the s 33 exercise, the judge must consider all the circumstances, including any prejudice to the defendant. That involved considering what evidence might have been available to the defendant if a trial had taken place earlier or the defendant had learned of the claim earlier (*Bryn Alyn* considered).

(ix) Irwin J below had been wrong to hold that the original trial judge had found proven abuse in the cases of JB and JPM. He was wrong simply to hold that the fact of abuse was established without considering, in the context of s 33, what effect the passage of time would have on the question whether the defendant was prejudiced and, if so, balancing any prejudice against other factors, including the evidence accepted by the original trial judge that JB and JPM had been inhibited from reporting the abuse any earlier than they did.

(x) However, considering the matter afresh, Irwin J had made no error of principle in reaching the conclusion that the discretion should be exercised in favour of JPM and

DVB, but not in favour of JB. Nor had HHJ Main QC below made any error of principle in exercising the discretion in favour of GR in order to allow his claim to proceed.

(xi) Two of the claimants, DVB and GR, cross-appealed on s 14, arguing that they did not acquire the relevant knowledge until many years after the abuse when the consequential psychiatric injuries manifested themselves. They did so on the basis that the sexual assaults were not violent and no physical injury occurred. These arguments were rejected. The lack of immediate physical or psychiatric damage did not mean that the injury was insignificant when the claimant's feelings of defilement, humiliation and so forth were brought into account. Following *Stubbings v Webb* (p677) and the Court of Appeal in *Albonetti v Wirral MBC* (p298) 'a practical and relatively unsophisticated approach to the question of knowledge' was appropriate, which entailed a broad interpretation of 'personal injuries' within the meaning of s 38(1). The abuse here fell within that definition.

Appeals and cross-appeals dismissed.

The defendants were subsequently refused permission to appeal to the House of Lords.

Per Lord Clarke of Stone-cum-Ebony MR: '11. We consider the correct approach to knowledge further below but will consider first the principles relevant to the exercise of the discretion under s 33. In that regard the critical point is that the effect of the decision of the House of Lords is to transfer the relevance of the question whether the actual claimant, taking into account his psychological state in consequence of the injury, could reasonably have been expected to institute proceedings from the enquiry whether he had sufficient knowledge for the purpose of s 14 to the consideration of the question whether the court should exercise its discretion to extend time under s 33. As Lord Hoffmann put it at [44] and [45], s 33(3) (a) expressly says that one of the matters to be taken into account in that regard is "the reasons ... for the delay" on the part of the claimant and s 33 enables the judge to look at the matter broadly ...

20. In the light of the considerations in *A v Hoare* to which we have referred we conclude that the "starting points" taken from [74] of *Bryn Alyn* and quoted above remain valid subject to these considerations. As to ii), it is correct to describe the exercise of the discretion as an exceptional indulgence to the claimant because, but for the exercise of the discretion, his claim will be time barred. But it is only exceptional for that reason. The cases stress that the discretion is wide and unfettered.'

B and others v Nugent Care Society (formerly Catholic Social Services (Liverpool))

Limitation Act 1980, s 33

QBD (Manchester) (Irwin J)   [2010] EWHC 1005 (QB); (2010) 116 BMLR 84

This was the remitted hearing following the appeal summarised directly above. The court was required to determine issues of limitation, liability, causation and quantum in relation to claims of historic physical and sexual abuse at children's homes. The claimants (JA, JPM and RM) had all allegedly suffered abuse in children's homes run by the defendant (N) in the 1960s and 1970s. Claims for damages were issued over 20 years later, following a police investigation. The court had already decided to exercise its discretion under s 33 to allow JPM's claim to proceed out of time. It fell to be determined whether (i) the s 33 discretion should also be exercised in the case of JA, and if so, whether he had suffered any identifiable damage for which the defendant was responsible, and the correct approach to compensating assault claims where the consequences fell short of any psychiatric diagnosis; (ii) JPM was entitled to damages on his claim; and (iii) the limitation period should be extended also in RM's case.

Held (in respect of limitation):

(i)   In exercising the s 33 discretion to extend time for bringing claims for child abuse that had taken place many years earlier, some real significance had to be attached to the specific factor arising in sex abuse cases that the tort had itself the tendency to inhibit the victim from complaining, reporting or suing.

(ii)   JA's case was one where, for practical purposes, he had been disabled from commencing proceedings by the psychological consequences of the abuse he had suffered (*A v Hoare* (p287) considered). In the circumstances, given the corroborative evidence, there was little loss of cogency in the evidence by reason of the delay, and no significant delay in commencing proceedings once JA had in fact realised that he could do so, albeit reluctantly. JA had acted promptly once the police investigation had brought the abuse to the forefront of his mind. The claim was proportionate, in that, if proved, the abuse had made a significant contribution to ongoing problems experienced by JA. The limitation period would, therefore, be extended to allow JA's claim to proceed.

(iii)   A striking feature of RM's case was the inconsistency of his successive accounts of the alleged abuse, and it was difficult to see how the truth could now properly be established. RM might have been abused whilst in institutions run by the defendant, but there was a significant loss of cogency by reason of the delay in issuing proceedings, in a context where more evidence would be particularly desirable. Given the discrepancies and conflicts in the accounts given by RM, and the significant loss of evidence of potential aid to the defendant, there was a real risk of injustice were the claim to proceed. The exercise of the discretion to extend the limitation period had, therefore, to be declined and RM's action dismissed as being out of time.

Judgment for claimants in part.

Baig v City and Hackney HA

Limitation Act 1980, s 14, s 33

QBD (Rougier J)   **[1994] 5 Med LR 221**

The claimant suffered from partial deafness and had an operation in August 1973 to treat his condition. He had been assured that the operation was virtually certain of success, but several weeks later developed total deafness. He was told that his ear would take some time to settle down, but by 1977 he had abandoned all hope of improvement. The claimant accused the defendant of negligence in 1985 and consulted solicitors in 1986. He did not, however, obtain a medical report until March 1987. He issued proceedings in May 1991. The defendant argued that the action was time barred.

Held:

(i)   The claimant had constructive knowledge at some time during the early 1980s. He was intelligent, and the fact that the operation had proved a disaster rather than the success promised should have put him on inquiry that something had gone amiss. As he had not sought professional help until 1985, his action was time barred.

(ii)   It would not be equitable to allow the action to proceed under s 33. The claimant had been guilty of inordinate delay, leading to a deterioration in the personal recollection of the witnesses. During the intervening period the defendant's insurance arrangements had changed so that, if the claim were successful, it would have to be met in full by the defendant itself (*Antcliffe v Gloucester HA* [1992] 1 WLR 1044 applied).

Claim dismissed.

Bailey v T J Frames

Limitation Act 1980, s 33

Boreham J   **Lexis, 18 May 1984**

On 25 July 1978 the claimant (Mr Bailey) sustained injury in the course of his employment by the defendants. He was using a staple gun and somehow, instead of firing the staple into the furniture under construction, fired it into his knee where it became embedded. He was taken to hospital and was off work for five months. He claimed disablement pension which the DHSS awarded him in 1981.

After seeing a television programme, he consulted solicitors in late 1982. His writ was issued on 29 March 1983, and his statement of claim alleged that the safety catch on the staple gun was not in good working order due to lack of oil. The defendants still had the same four staple guns in use, but by then it was impossible to identify which if any was defective as alleged. A preliminary trial of their limitation defence was ordered.

Held:

(i)   The claimant was not entirely unaware that if his employers were at fault they could be sued. The main reason why he did not take any proceedings until 20 months after the primary three-year period was that it never occurred to him that his employers were to blame: s 33(3)(a).

(ii)   The cogency of the evidence was impaired because neither the claimant nor the defendants were able to identify the particular gun which was alleged to have been defective. This was compounded by the difficulties of trying an accident case six years after the event: s 33(3)(b).

(iii)   The greater prejudice would fall on the defendants if the action was to proceed. Section 11 of the Limitation Act 1980 should be applied in their favour: s 33(1).

Bansil v Northampton Health Authority

Amendment of writ   **Limitation Act 1980, s 33**

Court of Appeal   **Lexis, 30 March 1987**

Philip Bansil was attacked by his stepson Stephen Bansil who struck him on the head with an object. He was admitted to hospital and died on 23 January 1978. Stephen Bansil pleaded guilty to manslaughter. The claimant (Mrs Doreen Bansil) alleged that negligent hospital treatment caused or contributed to the death.

Her writ under the Fatal Accidents Act 1976 was issued on 26 November 1980. The dependants were the claimant, her son Stephen born in August 1959, and the two children of the claimant and the deceased: Patricia, born in June 1963 and Gary, born in October 1964. In addition, an action under the Law Reform (Miscellaneous Provisions) Act 1934 was commenced by two parties in the claimant's firm of solicitors.

Although the claimant went through a ceremony of marriage with Philip Bansil in 1961, he was already married to another woman. Thus the claimant was neither his widow nor a dependant under the Fatal Accidents Act 1976 (which had not then been amended by the Administration of Justice Act 1982). This was communicated by the claimant's counsel to the defendant's counsel in July 1982.

In September 1985 the defendants amended their defence so as specifically to deny that the claimant was the widow. The claimant's solicitors promptly gave notice that they wished to apply to add the three children as claimants to the Fatal Accidents Act action, but the application was not formally made until 6 November 1985 after all three had reached the age of 21.

When the defendants' successful appeal against the district registrar's grant of the application was heard before Alliott J, it was accepted that the relevant principles to be adopted were those appropriate to applications under s 33 of the Limitation Act 1980. During argument on the claimants' subsequent appeal it was accepted that, as Stephen Bansil had been responsible for the injury which led to the death, he could not be allowed to benefit from it. The appeal proceeded in relation to Patricia and Gary alone.

Held: despite the fact that for the two potential claimants the periods of limitation were respectively over six years and over seven years from their father's death, no effective steps were taken during these periods to ensure that an action on their behalf was properly constituted. They stood to receive substantial compensation under the Law Reform Act action if successful, because as formerly dependent children they could claim from the estate under the Family Inheritance Act. The judge had correctly exercised his discretion.

The claimants' appeal was dismissed.

Barker v Hambleton DC

CPR 7.2

QBD (HHJ Shaun Spencer QC)   **[2011] EWHC 1707 (Admin)**

The court was required to decide as a preliminary issue whether it had jurisdiction to entertain an application made by the claimant under s 113 of the Planning and Compulsory Purchase Act 2004 to quash the allocations of certain land and the failure to allocate other land by the defendant local planning authority.

The defendant had accepted the relevant development plan document on 21 December 2010. That was the 'relevant date' as defined by s 113(11)(c) which began the six-week period provided by s 113(4) in which anyone aggrieved by the document could make an application. Therefore, that period expired at midnight on 1 February 2011. The claimant's application was posted under the courthouse outer door at 7.46pm on 1 February, the doors having been locked at 5.45pm and the issue counters having closed at 4pm. The papers were recovered the following morning and the claim form was sealed with the date of issue of 2 February. The issue for determination was whether the application was made in time.

The claimant submitted that an application to the court implied a unilateral act to be performed by the maker; it did not necessarily connote some form of reciprocity by way of receipt from the court. The defendant argued that, to make an application under s 113(3), proceedings had to be started which meant, under CPR 7.2, that the court had to issue a claim form and that it was issued on the date written on the form by the court.

Held: The question of whether the claimant had been making an application when he pushed the envelope under the outer locked door of the court building, when the court office was closed and the building was locked, depended on how ordinary language was used. On that basis, the claimant's action did not involve making an application within time (*Van Aken v Camden LBC* (p699) and *Barnes v St Helens MBC* (p321) considered, *Mucelli v Albania* [2009] UKHL 2, [2009] 1 WLR 276 applied).

Application refused.

Barnes v St Helens MBC

Limitation Act 1980, s 11   **CPR 7.2, PD7.5**

Court of Appeal   **[2006] EWCA Civ 1372; [2007] 1 WLR 879;**
[2007] 3 All ER 525; [2007] CP Rep 7; [2007] PIQR P10;
(2006) Times, 17 November; (2006) Independent, 27 October

The claimant suffered personal injury before he turned 18, which he did on 5 November 2001. He sought to bring proceedings against the defendant. He delivered the claim form and appropriate cheque (personally via his solicitor) to the county court on 4 November 2004 (the day prior to the expiry of the limitation period) with a request that the claim be issued and then returned for service. However, due to industrial action, the court did not issue the claim form until four days later on 8 November. The defendant argued that the claim was 'brought' at date of issue and was therefore out of time. The judge held that there was no difference between 'bringing' and 'starting' proceedings, but that the wording of CPR 7.2 about when proceedings were started was ambiguous. He resolved that ambiguity by reference to para 5 of CPR PD 7A in favour of the date on which the claim form was delivered to the court, if that was earlier than the date it was issued by the court. The defendant appealed, arguing that proceedings started when the claim form was issued by the court, the date of which appeared on the face of the claim form, and that was the same date on which proceedings were 'brought' for the purposes of the expiry of the limitation period.

Held:

(i)   Provided that the claimant took any necessary step required to enable the proceedings to be started, he did not take the risk that the court might be closed or would not process the claim properly, and para 5.1 of the Practice Direction reflected that (*Pritam Kaur v S Russell & Sons Ltd* (p613) and *Riniker v University College London* (1999) Times, 17 April considered).

(ii)   The expiry of the limitation period was fixed by reference to something that the claimant had to do, rather than something which someone else such as the court has to do. The time at which a claimant 'brought' his claim to the court with a request that it be issued was something that he had to do; the time at which his request was complied with by the court was not within his control. In this context 'to bring' did not mean the same as 'to start'. The Act could properly be construed so that, in the context of the CPR, a claim was 'brought' when the claimant's request for the issue of a claim form was delivered to the correct court office during its opening hours. A claimant is given the full period of limitation in which to bring the claim and does not take the risk that the court will fail to process it in time.

(iii)   The receipt of a claim form by the court did not involve a transactional act; it was a unilateral act of the claimant to deliver it. The court staff who received the documents were not performing any judicial function and had no power to reject them. Paragraph 5 of the Practice Direction gave guidance to ensure that the actual date of delivery was readily ascertainable by recording the date of receipt.

(iv)   There was therefore a distinction between when a claim was 'brought' for the purposes of the 1980 Act and when it 'started' for the purpose of CPR 7.2. The latter was the date of issue on the claim form; fixed the time within which the proceedings had to be served. The former could be an earlier date.

(v)   This reasoning was confined to the situation contemplated by the Practice Direction, that is to say receipt by the court office of the claim form. This necessarily involves actual delivery by whatever means permitted by the Rules to the correct court office during the hours in which that office is open (paras 2 and 3 of CPR PD 2A). That is what happened in this case. Different considerations might apply if delivery was made to the wrong place or outside office hours. They would have to be considered if they arise.

Appeal dismissed.

Barrow v Consignia Plc (formerly known as the Post Office)

Limitation Act 1980, s 33   **CPR 17.4**

Court of Appeal   **[2003] EWCA Civ 249**

On 23 November 1995 the claimant sustained injuries whilst working for the defendant when another fork lift truck driver (S) drove his truck into collision with the claimant's truck. The claimant alleged that S was drunk at the time. On 10 November 1998, a few days before the expiry of the limitation period, the claimant brought proceedings in respect of this accident. Paragraph 3 of the particulars of claim alleged that the collision was caused by the negligence of S. Paragraph 4 gave particulars of the physical injuries alleged to have been sustained. These were not very serious. Paragraph 4 added, however, '… it is possible that the Plaintiff has developed a psychological pain syndrome'. Paragraph 5 alleged that the claimant had been 'harassed, discriminated against and victimised as a result of his complaints [relating to the accident]. Full particulars will be given as soon as is practicable.'

Liability was tried as preliminary issue on 2 July 1999. It was adjudged that 'The sole cause of the accident … was the negligence alleged in paragraph 3 of the Particulars of Claim'. Quantum then advanced slowly. On 7 November 2001, the claimant sought permission to amend his particulars of claim. The amendment added to paragraph 3 details of the injuries alleged to have been sustained as a result of the accident to include alleged psychiatric injuries. It added to paragraph 5 that the claimant's 'medical state has been maintained and/or exacerbated by reason of his continued exposure to drunkenness amongst fellow employees in circumstances which could have exposed him to further injury and/or that the defendants have negligently failed to have regard to the claimant's medical condition since the 23rd of November 1995'.

The defendant successfully resisted the amendments on the grounds that they amounted to fresh claims of breach of duty that were advanced after the trial on liability had been concluded. The claimant's application was dismissed on 11 February 2002. However, on 15 February 2002 the claimant commencing a second action, alleging that the defendant had treated him negligently after his accident with the result that he developed a depressive disorder. The particulars of claim concluded the allegations which formed the subject matter of the unsuccessful application to amend. As regards limitation, the claimant pleaded that the cause of the psychiatric illness which he developed in 1998 only became apparent on 3 April 2002 on receipt of a joint medical report in the earlier action. Alternatively, he relied on s 33.

An appeal from the order refusing permission in the first action was heard at the same time as the issue of limitation in the second action. The judge held that the amendment at paragraph 5 did not constitute a new cause of action under CPR 17.4, but represented rather an aggravation of the original injury. He therefore allowed the appeal in respect of the first action. As regards the second action, he held that the claimant possessed the relevant knowledge from the time of the commencement of proceedings in the first action in November 1998. It followed that (subject to s 33) no claim in the second action could be based on any events between 11 November 1995, when the accident occurred, and 15 February 1999. However, the overlap between these events and those in the first action was such that they would have to be investigated anyway, so it was equitable to exercise the s 33 discretion in the claimant's favour, notwithstanding that, absent this factor, it would not be.

The defendant appealed.

Held:

(i)   It was agreed that the judge's characterisation of subsequent wrongs aggravating the original injury was inaccurate. If a claimant needed to rely upon a specific breach of duty in order to establish his right to relief in whole or in part, that breach of duty will constitute a discrete cause of action to which the provisions of the Act will apply. The claimant therefore conceded that the appeal in relation to the first action had to be allowed, insofar as the pleadings sought to found liability on breaches of duty that occurred after the claimant's accident. Although the amendments to paragraph 5 were inept, that is what they purported to do.

(ii)   The claimant's request for permission to reformulate the amended paragraph 5, so as to rely on the matters there pleaded as 'elements of the post-accident history which maintained or exacerbated [the claimant]'s condition', was refused. The amendments could not appropriately be treated as particulars of injury and the appeal was not about an application to amend particulars of injury. If the claimant wished to particularise his case on causation, he could do so in the normal manner without objection from the defendant or the need for the intervention of the court.

(iii)   As regards the second action, although there had been culpable delay on the part of the claimant, it was not likely to have resulted in significant additional problems in meeting the allegations made in relation to the time-barred period. Whilst that would not in itself be sufficient to determine the issue in the claimant's favour, the overlap factor made all the difference. The two actions would be tried together. The primary issue will be whether the 1995 accident was the cause of the psychiatric illness which the claimant subsequently developed. It was his case that the effects of his accident, in conjunction with his subsequent treatment at work, combined to produce the illness. That would inevitably require the court to focus on events in the time-barred period. Such events would also have to be considered in respect of the non-time barred allegations in the second action.

(iv)   There would be a danger of injustice if the claimant were barred from relying upon the earlier time-barred allegations. The defendant could rely upon victimisation and harassment by its own employees in the time-barred period as (i) breaking the chain of causation after the accident; and (ii) so damaging the claimant's mental health that the events after February 1999 added little, if anything, to his condition.

(v)   If the s 33 discretion were not exercised, the consolidated actions would be 'a mess to try'. The two actions could not be properly or fairly tried with a black hole of some three years in the middle, in respect of which, however the evidence emerges, the judge is precluded from making any finding of breach of duty against the defendant.

Appeal allowed in part.

Bater v Newbold (sued as Newbold Builders, a firm)

Limitation Act 1980, s 33

Court of Appeal   Lexis, 30 July 1991

The claimant (Mr Bater) alleged that on 27 November 1978 he was employed by the defendant as a plasterer when he fell from a scaffold which was being used in construction work on flats and sustained injury. He consulted solicitors in 1980, but his writ was not issued until 18 August 1988. By then no witnesses could be traced. The defendant was unable to trace the contractors who erected the scaffolding. The claimant could not remember the specific circumstances of the accident. The site foreman had died. Moreover the defendant denied that in 1978 he was trading in his own name or as Newbold Buildings, stating that any liability would rest with F Newbold Building Contractors Limited which was dissolved in 1984.

The claimant's application for a direction under s 33 of the Limitation Act 1980 that s 11 should be disapplied was granted by Master Turner and upheld on appeal by Sir Peter Pain. The defendant appealed.

Held: the appeal should be allowed because:

(i)   The length of the delay was very great and inordinate: s 33(3)(a).

(ii)   The delay had greatly reduced the cogency of the evidence available to the defendant, and the claimant would have great difficulty in establishing that the defendant was a proper party to the action and in proving his claim: s 33(3)(b).

(iii)   An inability to remember dates and some details of the accident was not a disability within s 33(3)(d).

(iv)   Having regard to the appalling length of delay, the very grave prejudice to the defendant and the inherent weakness of the case, it would be most inequitable for the action to be allowed to proceed: s 33(1).

Per Parker LJ: 'Subsection (d) refers to "the duration of any disability of the plaintiff arising after the date of the accrual of the cause of action". It is suggested on behalf of the plaintiff that his loss of memory can constitute a disability within that paragraph. The disability in that paragraph, although it is not necessary finally to decide it, appears to me not to be a disability as defined in section 38, which refers, as I see it, to section 28, which prevents, in the event of the defined disability, the time running until the disability ceases. If that be the case, it does not appear to me that the disability referred to in sub-paragraph (d) of subsection (3) can be that form of disability: it could be something less. But the disability which is relied upon here, is in my judgement of no weight. It is a disability to remember dates, it is a disability to remember some details, and it is a disability to remember the details of the accident. But that does not appear to me to be a disability which can possibly, in the circumstances, come within (d).'

cf Lord Diplock's statement in *Thompson v Brown Construction (Ebbw Vale) Ltd* (p690) that: 'Paragraph (d) is restricted to cases where plaintiffs have been under a disability, a class of reasons that equity has always been zealous to protect'.

Bates v Leicester Health Authority

Limitation Act 1980, s 14, s 33

QBD (Dyson J)   **[1997] 8 Med LR 243; [1997] PIQR P1**

The claimant was born on 10 January 1968 with severe cerebral palsy. This left him with no useful limb function, although his mental faculties were unaffected. Using a computer, his fastest speed of communication was four words per minute. His case was that this was the result of the defendant's mismanagement of his birth in that labour had been allowed to continue for more than four hours. The claimant asked his parents if he could claim against the hospital but was forcefully told no.

In September 1992 a solicitor was contacted, the course of action having been suggested by a care worker with no knowledge of the facts of claimant's birth following the claimant's father's death. Legal aid was obtained in April 1993 and a letter of claim was sent on 9 June 1993. An expert's report opining that the defendant had been negligent was received on 16 February 1994. Proceedings were issued on 10 February 1995 and limitation was heard as a preliminary issue.

Held:

Actual knowledge

(i)   The onus was on the claimant to prove that first had knowledge within three years of issuing proceedings. The onus was on the defendant to establish any earlier date on which they sought to rely (*Nash v Eli Lilly* (p568) applied).

(ii)   The claimant's knowledge that his injury was caused by the duration of his mother's labour was insufficient to start time running. It did not fix him with knowledge of the relevant omission.

(iii)   As the relevant omission was the failure to intervene, an essential element of the claimant's knowledge under s 14 was that intervention was possible. When told of the duration of the labour, the claimant did not understand this to mean that there had been a failure to intervene.

(iv)   At this point therefore the claimant knew that his injury was the result of a long labour but believed that this was a natural part of the birth process outside the control of the medical staff.

(v)   Knowledge that a failure to intervene was avoidable was relevant to actual knowledge. Knowledge that the failure was negligent was not (*Forbes v Wandsworth HA* (p434) applied).

(vi)   The claimant did not know until he received the expert's report that his injury was capable of being attributed to the defendant's failure to intervene.

Constructive knowledge

(i)   Although the issue was what would be expected by a claimant of average intelligence and without unusual personal characteristics, it was highly relevant in the present case that the claimant had extreme communication problems and that the potential source of knowledge was a parent whom the claimant trusted and relied upon heavily in important areas of his life.

(ii)   The defendant's primary contention that the claimant should have consulted solicitors when he achieved his majority in 1986 was rejected. There was nothing in or about 1986 which would have put the claimant on notice that he should have taken that step at that time.

(iii)   Faced with his mother's forceful dismissal of the idea of claiming, it was reasonable for the claimant not to pursue the matter further.

(iv)   Even if the claimant had pressed his mother, the defendant had not established on the balance of probabilities that this would have produced sufficient information to make it reasonable for him to have sought legal or expert advice. If asked, the mother would probably have said that she knew of nothing the defendant could have done to have prevented the injury. Even if she had felt that something could have been done, it was not established that she would have communicated this to her son.

Section 33

(i)   The claimant's claim was a strong one, supported by impressive expert evidence, and he was likely to recover substantial damages if he succeeded.

(ii)   This was not a case where, if the action was statute barred, the claimant would have a claim against his solicitor or anyone else. He would therefore suffer great prejudice if the claim were barred.

(iii)   The introduction of Crown Indemnity on 1 January 1990 was of no relevance as, even taking an earlier date of knowledge, the limitation period did not begin to run until after this date.

(iv)   The length of delay went against allowing the claim to continue but the claimant was to blame for none of it, bearing in mind his communication difficulties and his reliance on his mother.

(v)   The trial would turn on expert opinion rather than the evidence of those present at the time.

(vi)   Even if the action had been brought by 1993, it was difficult to see how the defendant's evidence would be much more cogent. Even if there were contemporaneous witnesses who could have assisted the defendant, it was difficult to imagine what they could have usefully said in 1992 or thereabouts.

(vii)   The claimant had been under a disability until 1986. Eighteen years passed before then, although nine years passed from then to the date of issue.

(viii)   On balance it would be equitable to allow the action to continue. If it had been necessary, the judge would have exercised his discretion under s 33 to this end.

Preliminary issues decided in the claimant's favour.

Barrand v British Cellophane Ltd

Limitation Act 1980, s 33

Court of Appeal   **LTL 26/1/95**

The claimant worked for the defendant as a mechanic between 1958-1980. He alleged hearing damage and tinnitus due to exposure to excessive noise. There was a trial on liability and whether discretion under s 33 should be exercised. The claimant succeeded on both points. The defendant appealed.

Held:

(i)   The judge's finding on liability could not stand.

(ii)   (obiter) The burden to show that discretion should be exercised is a heavy one on the claimant (*Thompson v Brown Construction (Ebbw Vale) Ltd* (p690) applied, *Buck v English Electrical Co Ltd* (p353) disapproved).

(iii)   Having found that the delay was extensive and largely the claimant's own fault the judge was wrong to exercise his discretion simply because the defendant had been unable to show prejudice.

(iv)   In any event it was clear from the judge's other findings that the defendant had suffered prejudice which outweighed that to the claimant. It was therefore not equitable to have allowed the claim to proceed.

Appeal allowed.

NB: It is no longer correct to say that there is a heavy burden on a claimant to show that that the limitation period should be disapplied: *A v Hoare* (p287), *Cain v Francis* (p360), *B v Nugent Care Society* (p315) and *Sayers v Chelwood* (p642).

Batchelor v Hull & East Riding Community Health NHS Trust

Limitation Act 1980, s 11, s 33

Kingston upon Hull CC (HHJ Heppel QC)   **LTL 4/11/2003**

Between October and November 1994 and January and February 1995 the claimant underwent a series of electro convulsive therapy sessions for psychiatric conditions. She claimed cognitive impairment as a result. In February 1997 she contacted solicitors investigating a group action for ECT treatment. This did not proceeded because of poor merits. The claimant then pursued an individual claim, issuing proceedings on 6 November 2000. Limitation was tried as a preliminary issue:

Held:

(i)   The claimant had the requisite knowledge to start time running by the time that she first contacted solicitors. She firmly believed that her condition was attributable to ECT treatment and did not require confirmation from a medical expert. Proceedings were therefore issued outside the limitation period.

(ii)   The claimant's case was exceptionally weak on the merits. Her own medical expert was unable to say that her treatment was negligent. Had there been an application for summary judgment the judge would have found that there were no prospects of success at all. It would therefore not be appropriate to exercise a s 33 discretion.

Claim struck out.

Beattie v British Steel plc

Monk v British Steel plc

Limitation Act 1980, s 33

Court of Appeal   **LTL 18/8/97**

Mr Beattie was employed by the defendant between 1960 and 1980. He alleged loss of hearing and tinnitus due to excessive noise. He first became aware of poor hearing in the mid-70s, his condition worsening with time. The judge fixed him with knowledge from the mid-70s. The proceedings were thus statute barred and, notwithstanding a very strong case on liability, the judge declined to exercise his discretion under s 33, citing the length of the delay.

Mr Monk worked for the defendant between 1967 and 1980. He also alleged hearing loss and tinnitus due to excessive noise. The judge found that he had knowledge for limitation purposes in 1968 when he consulted a doctor or, if he was wrong about that, in 1978 or 1979. Although again finding that the claimant had an extremely strong case, he refused to exercise his s 33 discretion.

Both claimants appealed. The appeals were heard together.

Held:

(i)   The judge was correct to emphasise the lengths of the delays (*Thompson v Brown Construction (Ebbw Vale) Ltd* (p690) applied).

(ii)   The defendant was prejudiced by having to meet claims it had never expected to meet there was no need to show evidential prejudice. The fact that it had settled other similar claims did not prevent it from being prejudiced.

(iii)   Section 33(c) required consideration of the blameworthiness of the defendant as regards the ability of the claimant to pursue its action. It does not refer to wider culpability. It was of no assistance to the claimants that the defendant might have been highly and reprehensibly negligent.

(iv)   The delay was inordinate and not adequately explained. The judge's decision was correct.

Appeals dismissed.

Beer v London Borough of Waltham Forest

Limitation Act 1980, s 33

Hodgson J   **16 December 1987**

On 28 September 1981, when the claimant (Mrs Beer) was pregnant, she fell on a defective paving stone in the forecourt between her house and the main road. Her child was born on 18 November 1981. Around mid-February 1982 she was pushing the child in a buggy when she had another accident caused by the same defective paving stone. Her case was that this caused further injury to her back.

Her main concerns at the time were the state of housing in which she was accommodated by the local authority and her general state of health, so she did not consider claiming damages. In 1984 a hospital physiotherapist told her that she was silly not to have reported the accidents. In October 1984 she consulted her local Citizens Advice Bureau about her housing. The lady whom she initially saw about it learned of her falls and passed her on to a subsequent meeting with a colleague who knew about such matters. The CAB then referred the claimant to a solicitor who issued a writ on 22 February 1985.

The matter came on for a preliminary trial on whether s 11 of the Limitation Act 1980 should be disapplied.

Held:

(i)   The delay on the claimant's part was short: about five months from the first accident and about one week from the second. During this time she was overwhelmed by worries and difficulties which seemed to her much more important than claiming damages: s 33(3)(a).

(ii)   The evidence on each side was not likely to be less cogent than if the action had been brought within the time allowed by s 11: s 33(3)(b).

(iii)   Once the claimant was alerted by the CAB to the possibility that she had a claim against the local authority, she and the solicitor whom she consulted acted as promptly as possible: s 33(3)(e)(f).

(iv)   Everything with the possible exception of the strength of claimant's case, lay on her side of the balance. Section 11 should be disapplied in respect of both accidents: s 33(1).

Bentley v Bristol & Western Health Authority

Limitation Act 1980, s 14(1)(b), s 33

Hirst J   **[1991] 2 Med LR 359**

On 15 June 1981 the claimant (Mrs Elsa Bentley) underwent an operation for replacement of her left hip. During the course of this her sciatic nerve sustained serious damage, noted by the surgeon on 16 June 1981. This was confirmed through an exploratory operation on 10 August 1981 and explained to the claimant shortly afterwards. She suffered severe pain combined with permanent loss of feeling and mobility in her left leg and foot.

In Autumn 1981 she consulted the community health council. In April 1982 she instructed solicitor 1, but after a negative medical report and counsel's opinion her legal aid certificate was discharged. In February 1984 she instructed solicitor 2 who obtained a report from Mr R F Winkworth FRCS which was sent to the claimant on 16 September 1985. Although this report raised a number of possible causes of her injury including 'injudicious retraction', a second counsel gave pessimistic advice. In October 1986 she consulted AVMA who referred her to solicitor 3 who issued a writ on 12 September 1988. A subsequent expert's report stated that the surgeon was negligent in applying undue traction and taking inadequate steps to protect the sciatic nerve.

Held: the claimant's action was not statute barred because:

(i)   The relevant act or omission was not the mere performance of the operation but the alleged excessive traction of the nerve and failure reasonably to safeguard it from damage. The broad knowledge that her injury was capable of being attributed to this was only acquired by the claimant at the earliest when she received Mr Winkworth's report on or shortly after 16 September 1985, within three years of issue of the writ: s 14(1)(b).

(ii)   If necessary, s 33 of the Limitation Act 1980 would have been applied in the claimant's favour because otherwise she would suffer very severe prejudice and the defendants would not suffer material prejudice: s 33(1). Delays by her advisers should not count significantly against her, since she was vigorously striving at all times to carry her claim forward: s 33(3)(a). All the hospital notes were available, including those of both the initial and subsequent exploratory operation, and there were before the court detailed witness statements from both surgeons: s 33(3)(b).

NB: Held (i) was overruled by *Broadley v Guy Clapham & Co* (p345).

Bennett v Greenland Houchen & Co

Solicitors' negligence   **Limitation Act 1980, s 11**

Court of Appeal   **(1998) 4 PNLR 458; LTL 11/11/9**

The claimant instructed the defendant, a firm of solicitors, to act for him in an employment matter. The action was compromised in terms which were tantamount to a discontinuance. In 1994 he brought a claim against the defendant for professional negligence. He alleged that the mishandling of the employment claim had resulted in clinical depression. The defendant denied liability and pleaded limitation. The judge found the defendant negligent. On the latter point he held that the action was for economic losses arising from professional negligence and s 2 rather than s 11 applied. The action was therefore not statute barred. The defendant appealed.

Held:

(i)   The claimant's distress was a personal injury within s 38 of Limitation Act 1980.

(ii)   Although the judge had asked the right question in seeking to categorise the action 'What was the case all about?' (*Ackbar v Green* (p291)), the conclusion he drew was wrong in law. He was wrong to approach the question with a need to limit s 11(1).

(iii)   The judge attached undue importance to the *Ackbar* question. This question was merely a useful tool for reaching a commonsense result. The current claim clearly included damages for personal injury and fell with s 11 (*Ackbar* distinguished).

(iv)   Limitation therefore expired around June 1991, three years from the date upon which the claim accrued.

Appeal allowed.

Berezovsky v Abramovich

Limitation Act 1980, s 35   **CPR 17.4**

Court of Appeal   **[2011] EWCA Civ 153; [2011] 1 WLR 2290;**
                    [2011] 1 CLC 359; (2011) 108(10) LSG 23

The claimant alleged that he had once had disposable interests in a Russian oil and gas company (S) and in a Russian aluminium company (C). He claimed that he had been intimidated by threats emanating from the defendant, who had the legal title to the shares in S, into disposing of his interest in S to companies controlled by the defendant at an undervalue. He sought to recover his loss as compensation for the tort of intimidation. He also claimed that the defendant, who had legal title to the shares in C, had disposed of a large number of shares to companies controlled by a third party (D) in breach of fiduciary or contractual duty, thus rendering his remaining shares much less valuable than before. The claimant sought to recover that loss as compensation for the alleged breaches of duty also.

The claimant originally pleaded that his interest in S was a beneficial interest. The defence was that the arrangement made was between Russian citizens in Russia and was governed by Russian law which did not recognise the concepts of a trust or a beneficial interest. The claimant then applied for permission to amend his particulars of claim to plead only that he had an interest arising from a joint activity or other *sui generis* agreement with the defendant. In relation to the shares in C, the allegation of a beneficial interest was maintained because the claimant asserted that the relevant arrangements were not governed by Russian law but impliedly by English or British Virgin Islands law. The claimant also sought to amend to plead an express agreement that English law applied. The judge refused an application by the defendant for summary judgment or to strike out and gave the claimant permission to amend. The defendant appealed.

Held:

(i)   The proposed amendments in the case of S did not raise a new and time-barred claim or cause of action for the purposes of s 35 or CPR 17.4(2). The new claim merely claimed the same loss as originally claimed albeit under a different label, namely loss arising from the requirement that he dispose of his contractual interests rather than, as originally, his beneficial interests.

(ii)   Alternatively, if it was a new loss, different in kind from the old loss, there was no substitution of a new cause of action for loss caused by intimidation for the original cause of action for loss caused by intimidation. If a loss stemmed from an already pleaded breach of duty, the fact that the loss might be measured by a different law from that already pleaded did not necessarily mean that there was a new claim (*Latreefers Inc v Hobson* [2002] EWHC 1586 (Ch), (2002) 146 SJLB 209 and *Steamship Mutual Underwriting Association Ltd v Trollope & Colls* (City) Ltd 33 BLR 77 CA (Civ Div) distinguished).

(iii)   The claimant should have permission to plead a restitution claim as an alternative to his main claim and parasitic upon it, to the effect that, if he could not recover the value of any beneficial or contractual or other interest merely because Russian law did not recognise such interest, he was nevertheless entitled to recover the value of whatever he had.

(iv)   However, the claimant should not have permission to plead a second restitution claim on the basis that, if Russian law negated the claim completely because it recognised no right of the claimant in relation to any interest of any kind in S, he was nevertheless entitled to be rewarded on a *quantum meruit* basis for the work done by him in relation to the receipt by the defendant of the benefit of the majority shareholding in S. That was a new claim which did not arise from the same or substantially the same facts as the old claim. The pleading sufficiently alleged not only the threat of expropriation but impliedly that the defendant would do what he could to bring about the threatened expropriation if the claimant did not agree to dispose of his interest in S for the supposed undervalue.

(v)   The act of state principle did not apply to allegations by the claimant about what the Russian state had done since he did not allege that those acts were invalid, only that they had taken place (*A Ltd v B Bank* (1997) 6 Bank LR 85 CA (Civ Div) followed).

(vi)   The court could not be sure at the interim stage that the law governing the alleged fiduciary or contractual relationship of the claimant and the defendant with regard to the shareholdings in C was Russian law so that all claims were time barred; it was arguable that English law applied, in which case no question of time bar arose. The judge was entitled to allow the claimant's amendment to allege that there was an express agreement that the relationship was to be governed by English law.

Appeal allowed in part.

Berger v Eli Lilly & Co and others

Limitation Act 1980, s 11, s 14

Court of Appeal   **[1992] 3 Med LR 395**

See *Nash v Eli Lilly & Co* (N) (p568)

Berry v Calderdale HA

Limitation Act 1980, s 11, s 33

Court of Appeal   **[1998] Lloyd's Rep Med 179**

The claimant sustained a Colles fracture to her wrist on 24 March 1989 and had been treated by the defendants. Because of the way she had been treated, her wrist required a re-manipulation in April 1989 and a further operation in September 1991. Whilst in hospital for that operation the claimant had been advised that she might have a claim against the defendants for the initial treatment in 1989. In consequence of that, she sought advice from a Citizens Advice Bureau later that month, who advised her to consult a solicitor. However it was not until six months later in March 1992 that she did so. On 24 March 1992 the solicitors wrote to the defendants outlining the allegations of negligence and on 21 September 1992 sent a letter before action. Nothing further was done until the defendants raised the issue of limitation on 29 June 1993 which prompted the solicitors to issue proceedings on 16 July 1993. At the trial in December 1996 the judge found that the plaintiff's date of knowledge was sometime in June 1989. Accordingly, the judge found that her claim was statute barred but exercised his discretion under s 33 to disapply s 11. He found the defendants liable in negligence and the plaintiff guilty of contributory negligence as a result of having failed to undergo a full course of physiotherapy. The claimant appealed against the judge's finding of contributory negligence and the defendants cross-appealed inter alia against the judge's exercise of his s 33 discretion.

Held:

(i)   The judge was entitled to find that the claimant had knowledge by June 1989, when her symptoms, rather than resolving, had seriously deteriorated.

(ii)   In exercising his s 33 discretion the judge stated that he had taken into account the whole history of the matter and concluded that, as there was no prejudice to the defendants, he would disapply s 11. In fact the judge had failed to address himself to the provisions contained in s 33(3) and in particular to s 33(3)(a) as to the reasons for the delay. Accordingly, the judge had not exercised his discretion properly and the Court of Appeal would intervene.

(iii)   In the circumstances of the case, where solicitors had been consulted in time and had been in a position to settle a letter before action, they ought to have applied for emergency legal aid if that was appropriate and ought to have issued protective proceedings if necessary. It might have been possible to forgive the claimant's initial delay, but after she had consulted the Citizens Advice Bureau she had delayed for a further six months before consulting solicitors who had delayed for a further ten months. There was thus culpable and unexplained delay.

(iv)   The judge had wrongly exercised his discretion to disapply s 11 and the claim was statute barred. Accordingly, it was unnecessary to consider the claimant's appeal or the other grounds of the cross-appeal.

Appeal dismissed. Cross-appeal allowed.

NB: In light of *Cain v Francis* (p360), s 33 on these facts would now almost certainly be decided in the claimant's favour, given the finding of the lack of any prejudice to the defendant. None of the relevant prior authorities in this regard appear to have been cited to the court.

Berry v Stone Manganese & Marine Ltd

Limitation Act 1963, s 7

Ashworth J   **[1972] 1 Lloyd's Rep 182; (1971) 115 SJ 966; 12 KIR 13**

In 1957 the claimant (Mr F R Berry) commenced employment with the defendants in the chipping shop at their Charlton factory. As several men might be using pneumatic hammers on metal at the same time, the resulting noise was enormous. The claimant became aware of loss of hearing by the end of 1960 and knew that this was due to the noise at work. He had known since 1957 that other men in the chipping shop were going deaf. His hearing continued to deteriorate. In 1968 he consulted his trade union. On 2 April 1970 his writ was issued.

Held:

(i) He had all necessary knowledge of facts of a decisive character before 2 April 1967. Accordingly, his claim in respect of matters before that date was statute barred.

(ii) Damages for his deafness and discomfort since 1960 would have been £2,500. It would not be right to award him only four-elevenths, on the basis that he had had 11 years of deafness since 1960 of which only the four since 1967 were compensatable. Such a course would not give sufficient weight to the fact that to make a man already deaf still deafer is to increase his hardship very considerably, as he has fewer decibels to spare. The right award was £1,250.

Newton v Cammell Laird & Co (Shipbuilders & Engineers) Ltd (p581) applied.

Bethell Construction Ltd v Deloitte and Touche

CPR 6.15, 6.16   **Estoppel**

Court of Appeal   **[2011] EWCA Civ 1321**

The claimant brought a claim for professional negligence. Protective proceedings were issued on 22 February 2007. On 9 March 2007 the claim form was sent, but expressly not by way of service, to the defendant with what purported to be a letter of claim. There were thereafter numerous agreements to extend time for service. On 18 June 2007 the defendant requested a further month's extension for provision of its letter of response.

The claimant proposed 'to agree a two-week extension of time (to 4pm on 3 July) on condition that you agree extensions of time for service of the claim form and particulars of claim to 2nd August or 14 days after written notice is given by one party to the other (such notice to be given after 2nd August) whichever is the later'. The defendant accepted this proposal and the parties over the next two years explored settlement, but without success.

On 14 October 2010 the claimant sent a letter to the defendant, enclosing by way of service the particulars of claim, but without the claim form. On 22 October 2010 the defendant wrote to the claimant giving the requisite 14 days' formal notice of determination agreement to stay time for service. When the claim form was not served by the expiry of the 14 days, the defendant asserted that the claims were time barred.

The claimant applied for orders: (1) that the original claim form had been validly served and/ or that the defendant had waived such service or was estopped from contending otherwise; (2) that delivery of a copy of the claim form to the defendant on 9 March 2007 together with the letter from the claimant dated 14 October 2010 should be held to constitute due service under CPR 6.15; and (3) dispensing with service of the claim form under CPR 6.16.

The judge held that the claim form had not been validly served within time and that service should not be dispensed with. The claimant appealed on the grounds that: (1) the letter dated 14 October 2010 from the claimant constituted 'constructive' service of the claim form sent to and possessed by the defendant since 9 March 2007 'not by way of service'; (2) the letter from the defendant dated 22 October 2010 was not effective to determine the extension of time agreed by the emails dated 18 June 2007, so that service in the week commencing 16 November was not out of time; (3) the defendant waived entitlement to proper service of the claim form and/or was estopped from insisting on it; (4) the judge was wrong to have refused to make an order under CPR 6.15 deeming due service of the claim form from its original delivery to the defendant on 9 March 2007 and the letter from the claimant solicitors dated 14 October 2010; (5) the judge was wrong not to dispense with service of the claim form under CPR 6.16; and (6) given his conclusions on the foregoing issues, the judge had no jurisdiction to order the claimant to pay the defendant's costs of the claim in addition to their costs of the applications.

Held:

(i) The first ground relied upon the proposition that a claimant may unilaterally determine a method of service of the claim form not authorised by the rules. The short answer was that a claimant was not so entitled. The rules were there to be complied with. They were capable of amendment in accordance with the Civil Procedure Act 1997 but not by the unilateral act of the claimant.

(ii) The 22 October letter was effective to terminate the extension of time agreed by the emails in June 2007. Any semantic difference between lifting a stay (as had been referred to) and determining an extension was irrelevant; the defendant's meaning was clear.

(iii) The letter of 22 October did not constitute a positive representation that the defendant accepted that the claim form had been duly served or waived its entitlement to require its proper service (*The Stolt Loyalty* [1993] 2 Lloyd's Rep 281 considered). Although that might have been the case had the defendant simply replied acknowledging the 14 October letter, it had gone further and within the same communication given 14 days' notice that could only have referred to the claim form. That being so, although the defendant had set a trap, the letter contained sufficient information for the claimant's experienced solicitor to understand that there was no waiver of the need to serve the claim form.

(iv) There was no reason why the court should exercise any discretion it might have under CPR 6.15 so as to deny the defendant its accrued right to limitation defence. The claimant was (through its solicitors) the author of its own misfortune.

(v) If the facts did not reveal a good reason to make the order regarding service of the claim form sought under CPR 6.15, they could not possibly disclose exceptional circumstances sufficient to justify dispensing with service altogether under CPR 6.16. Nor could they provide any sufficient reason to make the order sought. Moreover, the claimant had entirely failed to show any ground on which the court could interfere with the discretion of the judge.

(vi) The claim form had been issued and proceedings were extant. The judge therefore had jurisdiction to make the order he did as to the costs of the action.

Appeal dismissed.

Biddle & Co v Tetra Pak Ltd and others

Limitation Act 1980, s 14A, s 35	CPR 7.4, 16.2, 16.4, 17.4
Ch D (Warren J)	**[2010] EWHC 54 (Ch); [2010] 1 WLR 1466**

The claimant claimed against a firm of solicitors (D1) and a firm of actuaries (D2) in respect of an alleged failure to advise adequately concerning the claimant's pension scheme. A claim form was issued against both defendants giving brief details of claim some 15 years after the relevant events, the claimant relying upon the date of knowledge extension in s 14A of the Limitation Act 1980.

D2 did not agree to a stay that the claimant had proposed to allow compliance with the relevant pre-action protocol, so the claimant served it with the claim form and with particulars of claim relating only to D2. Shortly afterwards, the claimant served the same claim form on D1 along with draft amended particulars which referred to D1. D2 refused consent to the amendment on the grounds that it would introduce a new claim outside the limitation period.

The court gave permission to the claimant to serve particulars on D1, not by way of amendment to the original particulars but as separate particulars, those being the first particulars of claim against D1.

D1 appealed against the decision to allow service of the particulars of claim despite the expiry of a relevant limitation period. The claimant cross-appealed against a refusal of permission to amend its original particulars. D1 argued that it was not open to a claimant who had joined two defendants to serve separate particulars of claim on each of them, since the CPR did not contemplate more than one set of particulars being served. Allegations against one defendant different from those in the original particulars had to be made by amendment, and if no amendment was possible, no new allegations could be raised. D1 also argued that the judge had been right to refuse permission to amend the original particulars, since they raised a new claim outside the limitation period and the new claim did not arise out of substantially the same facts as the original claim.

Held:

(i)   It was open to the claimant to serve separate particulars of claim on D1 and so obviating the need for amendment to the original particulars. The CPR, most relevantly 7.4 and 16.4, could be operated consistently in the context of separate particulars in respect of different defendants against whom different causes of action were asserted. The fact that the court could order separate particulars showed that there was no prohibition on separate particulars, and in the absence of a prohibition there was no reason why a claimant should not serve separate particulars without the court's direction, especially when that might enable the overriding objective to be better achieved.

(ii)   Neither the separate particulars nor an amendment to the original particulars would be the addition of a new claim or a new cause of action for the purposes of s 35 of the 1980 Act or CPR 17.4. Although the claim form, under CPR 16.2(1)(a), only had to set out the nature of the claim, and the facts on which the claimant relied had to be set out in the particulars under CPR 16.4(1)(a), it did not follow that the claim that a defendant had to meet was not to be found in the claim form. If the particulars of claim did not confine the claim against a particular defendant, the cause of action remained seated in the claim form in the same way that it remained seated as against all defendants before the service of any particulars (*Steamship Mutual Underwriting Association Ltd v Trollope & Colls (City) Ltd* 33 BLR 77 CA (Civ Div) considered). Thus the fact that the particulars served on D2 by the claimant had only related to D2 did not mean that the claimant could be taken as confining or abandoning its claim against D1.

(iii)   If there had been a new claim, the claim against D1 would not arise out of substantially the same facts as that against D2, since the duties imposed on them as solicitors and actuaries were markedly different. However, the claimant would still be allowed to amend its particulars to maintain its claims against D1 insofar as they related to breaches within the 15-year period before service of the amended particulars, as specified in s 14B. Although the focus of those claims would be breaches of duty within that period, it would be necessary to establish the scope of the retainer, which would necessitate going back prior to the start of the period. Accordingly, a further amendment allowing claims dating back to the beginning of the 15 years before the issue of the claim form would arise out of substantially the same facts, as would a claim dating back to the beginning of 15 years before the service of the amended particulars. Accordingly, such an amendment would not be time barred (*Harland & Wolff Pension Trustees Ltd v Aon Consulting Financial Services Ltd* (p460) considered).

Appeal dismissed, cross-appeal allowed.

Biguzzi v Rank Leisure plc

CPR – Striking out

Non-compliance with time limits

Court of Appeal   **[1999] 1 WLR 1926; [1999] 4 All ER 934;**
[2000] CP Rep 6

In November 1993 the claimant suffered an injury when working for the defendant. Almost two years later he issued proceedings. In March 1999, before the implementation of the civil procedural rules, the claim was struck out for wholesale disregard of the court's orders. The claimant appealed successfully shortly after the CPR came into force. The defendant made a further appeal.

Held:

(i)   Time limits were important under the CPR and the court had an unqualified discretion to under rule 3.4(2)(c) for non-compliance. However, in many cases a less draconian punishment would be appropriate.

(ii)   The court had to take into account the broader interests of other litigants than the parties.

(iii) The CPR was a new procedural code and authorities pertaining to the old rules were of little relevance.

(iv)   The judge was entitled to take the view that both parties were at fault and that a strike out was unjustified.

Appeal dismissed.

Birnie v Oxfordshire Health Authority and Another

Limitation Act 1980, s 33

Glidewell J   **(1982) 2 Lancet 281**

In December 1972 the claimant (Mr Birnie), who had severe pain in his side and legs, was admitted to a pain clinic under the care of Mr Lloyd, a specialist in pain relief. Mr Lloyd carried out barbotage on two occasions. After the second barbotage, on 19 December 1972, the claimant was permanently paralysed in his two lower limbs.

He became severely depressed and on 6 October 1973 he attempted suicide. He was in hospital between 6 October and 23 December 1973 during which period severe bedsores and gangrene developed.

The claimant needed further surgery, including a chordotomy in November 1974 and, due to gangrenous sores, the amputation of his right leg in July 1975. In 1977 he spent a week in a Scottish hospital where the doctor and nurses were critical of those who had allowed the bedsores to develop. In August 1977 he consulted solicitors. His depressive state continued until 1978.

The writ was issued in August 1979. It was accepted that the three-year limitation periods covered by it expired not later than 19 December 1975 and 23 December 1976 respectively. The claimant relied on s 33 Limitation Act 1980.

Held:

(i)   In considering the delay, the claimant's state of health and state of mind had to be taken into account. For much of the time he was sunk in depression which produced inertia of will. The delay before he consulted solicitors was understandable. After he had consulted solicitors there had been a two-year delay before the writ was issued, and 10 to 12 months of this delay were without valid excuse.

(ii) So far as prejudice to the defendants was concerned, there was substantial documentation, although recollection was needed with regard to the barbotage and this was affected by the passage of time. Mr Lloyd was prejudiced in that he had the claim hanging over his head and was not insured. The nursing notes on the claimant's bedsores were available.

(iii) The prejudice to the claimant outweighed the prejudice to the defendants or the effect of delay on the cogency of evidence. The scale tipped in the claimant's favour even when the inexcusable delay by the solicitors was added. He was granted leave to proceed under s 33 of the Limitation Act 1980.

Biss v Lambeth, Southwark and Lewisham Area Health Authority (Teaching)

Dismissal for want of prosecution

Court of Appeal   **[1978] 2 All ER 125; [1978] 1 WLR 382**

In March 1965 the claimant (Mrs Biss) contracted multiple sclerosis. She awoke at home to find that she could not move her legs. She was taken to Lewisham Hospital where she lay paralysed and helpless on her back. Bedsores developed and were very painful. She accused the nursing staff of negligence.

In 1966 she made an abortive attempt to claim damages, but her legal aid certificate was discharged after negative advice from counsel. In 1973 she was encouraged through the Multiple Sclerosis Society to renew her claim. She obtained legal aid again.

In February 1975 she was granted leave to proceed under the Limitation Act 1963 and issued a writ alleging negligence by Lewisham Hospital. Pleadings were closed in July 1975.

In November 1975 the hospital gave particulars of its defence and served on the claimant a request for further and better particulars. These were never supplied. Nine months later, in September 1976, she changed her solicitors. Subsequently she declined to travel to see her medical expert at Stoke Mandeville Hospital. The case was not set down for trial.

In March 1977 the defendants issued a summons to dismiss for want of prosecution. The master granted it, but on appeal the judge (Sir Norman Richards) allowed the action to proceed.

Held: the defendants' appeal was allowed.

Per Lord Denning MR: 'Prejudice to a defendant by delay is not to be found solely in the death or disappearance of witnesses or their fading memories or in the loss or destruction of records. There is much prejudice to a defendant in having an action hanging over his head indefinitely, not knowing when it is going to be brought to trial. Like the prejudice to Damocles when the sword was suspended over his head at the banquet ...

Likewise the hospital here. There comes a time when it is entitled to have some peace of mind and to regard the incident as closed. It should not have to keep in touch with the nurses, saying: "We may need you to give evidence"; or to say to the finance department: "We ought to keep some funds in reserve in case this claim is persisted in"; or to say to the keepers of records: "Keep these files in a safe place and don't destroy them as we may need them". It seems to me that in these cases this kind of prejudice is a very real prejudice to a defendant when the plaintiff is guilty of inordinate and inexcusable delay since the issue of the writ: and that it can properly be regarded as more than minimal. And when this prejudice is added to the great and prejudicial delay before writ (as the House of Lords says it may be: see *Birkett v James*) then there is sufficient ground on which to dismiss the action for want of prosecution.

Applying this principle, I am clearly of opinion that this action should be dismissed for want of prosecution. It would be an intolerable injustice to the hospital, and to the nurses and staff, to have to fight it out twelve years after the incident, when they quite reasonably regarded it as closed eleven years ago …

One word more. It is, I believe, accepted on all hands, that if the plaintiff is guilty of inordinate and inexcusable delay before issuing the writ, then it is his duty to proceed with it with expedition after the issue of the writ. He must comply with the rules of court and do everything that is reasonable to bring the case quickly for trial. Even a short delay after the writ may in many circumstances be regarded as inordinate and inexcusable, and give a basis for an application to dismiss for want of prosecution. So in the present case the delay of nine months was properly admitted to be inordinate and inexcusable. It is a serious prejudice to the hospital to have the action hanging over its head even for that time. On this simple ground I think this action should be dismissed for want of prosecution. I would allow the appeal, accordingly.'

Bond v Livingstone & Co

Solicitors' negligence

Limitation Act 1980, s 33

Bellamy QC (sitting as a deputy High Court judge)   **[2001] PNLR 30**

On 31 July 1990 the claimant entered into a contract with company called MRL for hair implant treatment. He paid by credit card. His first implant session in August 1990 caused pain and bleeding. His course of treatment finished in early 1991. He began to lose hair fibres at an alarming rate and suffered a scalp infection. The claimant consulted the defendant firm of solicitors in June 1993 with a view to claiming against MRL.

In June 1994 counsel was instructed to advise, inter alia, on limitation. Counsel stated that as the claim arose out of breach of contract it was clearly not statute barred. Proceedings were issued in September 1995. However, the defendant was insolvent. The claimant sought advice from a second counsel who advised that there was a good cause of action against the credit card providers under s 75 of the Consumer Credit Act 1974. He also took the view that because the matter was contractual the limitation period was six years. The claimant therefore on 29 July 1996 issued against the credit card providers.

The credit card companies pleaded limitation. There was a preliminary hearing on 18 December 1998 where it was conceded that a s 33 discretion was required. This was not granted as the credit card companies, who were not party to the negligence itself, were unable to carry out meaningful investigations and because the claimant had a strong case against the defendant.

The claimant brought an action in professional negligence against the defendant. Summary judgment was entered for the claimant. The defendant appealed.

Held:

(i)   The defendant knew by at least 28 June 2003 that the action included a claim for personal injuries, otherwise a medical report would not have been commissioned.

(ii)   A solicitor specialising in personal injury who overlooks s 11 makes a mistake of the most basic kind. It was incumbent upon the defendant to protect the claimant's position.

(iii) Reliance on counsel did not excuse the claimant from so basic a mistake of failing to be familiar with such a mainstream statute. The defendant should have appreciated that counsel's advice was glaringly wrong.

(iv)   The defendant's conduct was clearly causatively negligent and summary judgment was appropriate.

Appeal dismissed.

Booker v Associated British Ports

Limitation Act 1980, s 12, s 35

Court of Appeal   **[1995] PIQR P375**

The claimant was employed by the defendant at intervals between 1970 and 1984. His duties included the handling of cargoes of asbestos. In 1989, at the age of 44, he developed symptoms of mesothelioma. On 5 October 1990, he issued proceedings against the defendant for negligent asbestos exposure. His particulars of injury included a pleading that: 'His life expectancy is very limited. There is no prospect of recovery.' He died in January 1991, and in February 1993 his widow obtained leave to carry on the action as his personal representative of his estate under the Law Reform (Miscellaneous Provisions) Act 1934. She did not, however, at that time assert any claim to damages for her own benefit as a dependant under the Fatal Accidents Act 1976. Her claim under that Act therefore became statute barred in January 1994.

In February 1994 the widow applied for leave to amend in order to add the 1976 Act claim. Leave was granted by the district judge and upheld on appeal by the judge. The defendant appealed, arguing: (i) that a claim arising out of death could not be raised at the same time as a lifetime claim founded on loss of expectation of life; the two could not be deemed to arise together, and, in enacting s 35, Parliament could never have intended that they should; and (ii) that, in the alternative, if s 35 did apply, the facts proposed to be introduced were substantially different from the facts from which the original action arose, and therefore the condition in s 35(5)(a) was not satisfied.

Held:

(i)   What was introduced by s 35 was a limited exception, laid down in subsection (5), to the old rule of practice that a proceeding cannot be amended to introduce a cause of action which did not exist at the date of the writ; s 35 was not to be construed restrictively so as to apply merely to remediable defects of form and procedure.

(ii)   The requirement was not for identity or similarity between the new claim and the old; it was for substantial identity between the facts from which the old and new claims arise. The relevant degree of substantial identity which has to be established lies between the facts of the new claim and those facts which are 'already in issue' in the original action. The facts from which the first claim in this case arose, and which were in issue in the original action, were that the claimant was suffering from an incurable disease which was expected to lead to his premature death. The facts from which the second claim arose were that this expectation had become realised in his death from the same fatal illness. To that extent the facts of the two cases, when regarded generally, were different. But the facts which matter were the facts that were in issue in the original action, namely the facts going to causation and those relating to the adequacy of the precautions taken by the defendant to protect its dockers from contact with asbestos dust.

(iii)   In the instant case, the facts in issue in the new claim, so far as they affected liability, would be precisely the same as the facts in issue in the original action, except for the very minor difference that the defendants would not acknowledge that the plaintiff's cause of death was his mesothelioma. So far as the facts of the Fatal Accidents Act claim affected the quantum of damages, they would be very closely related to the facts relevant to quantum that were in issue in the original action.

Appeal dismissed.

Bothwell v University of Greenwich

Limitation Act 1980, s 33

Queen's Bench Division, Wright J   **4 October 2000, unreported**

The claimant, who worked as a part-time security officer, sought damages from his employer in respect of an attack on 8 January 1996 by an intruder. The claimant, who was subsequently made redundant, recovered from the physical scars of the attack, but suffered from post-traumatic stress disorder. Proceedings were issued on 13 January 1999, five days out of time, the claimant having taken no steps to pursue the claim until the third anniversary of the assault itself (although he had lodged a claim with the Criminal Injuries Compensation Board, he rejected the initial award offered and fail to pursue an intended appeal). The claimant therefore applied for the limitation to be disapplied pursuant to s 33. He submitted that he had complained to his line manager about the lack of self-locking devices on doors entering the building through which he alleged the intruder must have entered. The defendant contended that it had been prejudiced by the delay, given that it no longer occupied the building where the incident took place, and the security officers who worked there had been disbanded.

Held:

(i)   Although the claimant was responsible for the delay in bringing the proceedings, he did have substantial mitigation in his favour for doing so, including the state of anxiety that he suffered as a result of the incident.

(ii)   Furthermore, there was no evidence that the defendant had been significantly prejudiced by the delay, given the insurance company's attitude to the matter. It was relevant in this regard that the defendant's insurers had indicated a willingness to settle.

(iii)   Although the merits of the claim were speculative, given the fact that there was no evidence that the intruder entered through one of the doors of which the claimant complained, and the identity of the intruder was vague, a failure to disapply s 11 would leave no other avenue for the claimant to seek compensation.

(iv)   It was therefore (by a small margin) equitable to disapply the time bar.

Preliminary issue determined in favour of the claimant.

Bournemouth & Boscombe AFC Ltd v Lloyds TSB Bank plc

CPR 3, 7

Court of Appeal   **[2003] EWCA Civ 1755; LTL 10/12/2003**

The parties had been in long-running dispute regarding a complicated loan agreement. On 28 June 2002 the claimant issued proceedings. The claim form was served on 28 October 2002 but the particulars of claim were not served until 11 days later, notwithstanding that CPR 7.4(2) required them to be served by the same date.

The defendant applied to strike out on the alternative bases of failure to serve the Particulars or having no real prospect of success. In response the claimant applied under CPR 3.9 for an extension of time. This was unsuccessful, the judge holding that the failure to serve Particulars in time was deliberate and that in any event the claim was bound to fail. The claim was thus struck out. The claimant appealed.

Held:

(i)   There was no satisfactory basis for the judge's conclusion that the failure had been deliberate. The overwhelming probability was that it arose out of misunderstanding of the rules. The court's discretion therefore fell to be exercised afresh.

(ii)   However, the claim was bound to fail on the merits and should be struck out in any event.

Appeal dismissed on those grounds.

Boxall v Eli Lilly & Co and others

Limitation Act 1980, s 11, s 14, s 33

Court of Appeal   **[1992] 3 Med LR 381**

See *Nash v Eli Lilly & Co* (C) (p568)

Bradley v Hanseatic Shipping Co Ltd

Limitation Act 1980, s 33

Court of Appeal   **[1986] 2 Lloyd's Rep 34**

The claimant (John Bradley) was an officer in the Merchant Navy. Early in April 1980 a ship belonging to the defendant and registered in Panama was off Abidjan on the Ivory Coast of Africa. The company was registered in Cyprus. Its English agents hired the claimant as chief officer over the telephone. He was told that the defendants had an insurance arrangement to cover their crew against accident or death, but he was never shown any contract.

On 5 April 1980, as the ship was leaving port at Abidjan, one of the staylines snapped. The probable cause was that the ship was going astern while the stayline was still attached to a bollard. It recoiled and struck the claimant, causing him fairly serious injury.

In May 1980 the claimant instructed solicitors to collect the insurance moneys he had been told would be available. In January 1982 they sent a letter before action claiming personal injury damages. The claimant changed solicitors who eventually obtained a copy form of contract. It excused the defendants from liability for accidents, in the absence of wilful default, and stated that the contract was to be governed by Cypriot law.

In October 1982 the claimant's solicitors wrote to Cypriot lawyers for advice on Cypriot law. Despite reminders, they only received this advice in October 1983. Meanwhile, they had overlooked the expiry of the primary limitation period on 5 April 1983. After getting the Cypriot opinion, they issued a writ and got leave to serve it out of the jurisdiction.

Sheen J granted their application for leave under s 33 of the Limitation Act 1980 to be exercised in the claimant's favour. The defendants appealed.

Held:

(i)   The words 'all the circumstances of the case' in s 33 are very wide and would include the insurance position of either of the parties and the possibility of the claimant having a cause of action against his solicitors if the delay had been attributable to any mistake made by them: s 33 (1).

(ii)   Although at one stage the defendants had not been as helpful as they could have been, they had not behaved unfairly towards the claimant: s 33(3)(c). The claimant had acted promptly and reasonably: s 33(3)(e). He had taken appropriate steps to obtain legal advice: s 33(3)(f).

(iii)   The judge weighed all the matters which had to be taken into account and, in particular, the problem of getting an opinion about Cypriot law. He acted in a way in which the court might not have acted had it dealt with the matter in the first instance, but what he did was clearly within the bracket of what was reasonable.

The defendants' appeal was dismissed.

Conry v Simpson and Others (p385) followed.

Brady v Wirral HA

Limitation Act 1980, s 14, s 33

Court of Appeal   **[1996] CLY 834**

The claimant was anaesthetised for the purposes of a laparoscopy on 31 January 1984. Afterwards, Neostigmine was administered to reverse the effect of a muscle relaxant drug. The Neostigmine was administered subcutaneously rather than intravenously, with the effect that the claimant remained paralysed after the anaesthetic had worn off and she regained consciousness. She was then subjected to emergency resuscitation procedures whilst she was still awake but unable to move or even open her eyes. The trauma of the incident caused the claimant psychiatric problems. Proceedings were issued in around 1995. Limitation was ordered to be tried as a preliminary issue. The judge held that the claimant had no knowledge of relevant matters until August 1991 when the hospital records were received by her solicitors, and that, in the event that she did have knowledge before then, an extension should be granted under s 33. The defendant appealed arguing that the claimant had knowledge by June 1984 at the latest. Additionally, the defendant contended that the judge should not have granted an extension under s 33.

Held:

(i)   Knowledge was acquired when the claimant knew that she had suffered a significant injury and knew that the injury was attributable to the acts or omissions of the defendant. The claimant did not have to know whether or not the acts or omissions were capable of amounting to negligence or breach of duty.

(ii)   The judge's decision to believe the evidence of the claimant was clearly wrong as it meant disbelieving evidence from two doctors, taken from contemporaneous notes, that they had explained exactly what had happened to her the day after the incident and conveyed that something had gone wrong. It also meant disbelieving the evidence of the claimant's general practitioner and a former solicitor who had inquired into the incident for the claimant's own peace of mind. The solicitor had told the claimant that there was nothing to worry about. That suggested that the claimant's worry, that she was allergic to anaesthetic, had not proved to be true and demonstrated that the incident had been the fault of the hospital.

(iii)   The judge assessed the s 33 application on the wrong basis as he relied upon his own conclusions in relation to the evidence which, in order to entertain a s 33 application, he should have assumed was wrong because he was working on the hypothetical basis that the claim was made out of time and his conclusions obviously pointed to the fact that the claim was made within the time limit.

(iv)   On a reassessment of the s 33 application, the defendant would have suffered prejudice in defending a claim 12 years after the incident. In addition, the claimant admitted to a 15-month delay before consulting her solicitors after having knowledge of the claim and there was no explanation for that delay. The court observed that the problems in this case were caused by the defendant's solicitors failing to appreciate the correct procedure for adducing evidence in a preliminary trial in a case of medical negligence and merely supplying affidavits of hearsay evidence. It had to be appreciated that determination of a preliminary issue was the first stage of the trial and not a hearing of an interlocutory matter.

Appeal allowed.

Braniff v Holland & Hannen and Cubitts (Southern) Ltd and another

Amendment of writ   **RSC Ord 15, r 8; Ord 20, r 5**

Court of Appeal   **[1969] 3 All ER 959; [1969] 1 WLR 1533**

On 4 October 1965 the claimant (James Braniff) was injured at work by the fall of a hoist. In October 1966 he issued a writ against the first defendants, his employers. In May 1968 they decided that the true fault lay with Barfords of Belton Ltd who had made or maintained the hoist. In July 1968 the claimant obtained leave to amend the writ and statement of claim in order to join Barfords as second defendants.

The claimant's solicitors duly amended the statement of claim but neglected to amend the writ pursuant to RSC Order 15, r 8(1). In August 1968 they sent to the second defendants a copy of the amended statement of claim and a copy of the unamended writ. On 18 October 1968 the second defendant's solicitors wrote to point out that the writ had not been amended and, therefore, the amended writ had not been served pursuant to RSC Ord 15, r 8(4). After obtaining ex parte an extension of time from the master, the claimant formally amended the writ on 23 October 1968 and served a copy on the second defendants.

The second defendants applied under RSC Ord 12, r 8 for the amended writ and service of it to be set aside. Chapman J allowed their appeal against the master's refusal to grant this. The claimant appealed.

Held:

(i)   The fact that in certain cases under the new RSC Ord 20, r 5 amendments are to be permitted although the statutory period has run does not mean that there was any relaxation of the former strict principle. When specific exemption is made by RSC Ord 20, r 5(3), (4) and (5) in cases where the statute has run, it is not then legitimate to interpret the rule as making similar provision and excuses available in other cases.

(ii)   Under RSC Ord 15, r 8(4), the added defendant is not a party until the amendment is duly completed in accordance with the rule. Prior to that, there is no writ available against the added defendant. This case was in the same class as that in which a claimant seeks to renew a writ which has expired. The judge exercised his discretion rightly.

The claimant's appeal was dismissed.

Heaven v Road and Rail Wagons Ltd [1965] 2 QB 355 applied.

Brazier v Ministry of Defence

Law Reform (Limitation of Actions) Act 1954   **Accrual of cause of action**

McNair J   **[1965] 1 Lloyd's Rep 26**

On 16 December 1956 the claimant (Reginald Brazier), a deep sea diver, contracted an infected right hand while cleaning up wrecks in the Suez Canal. He was treated in the sick bay of HMS Forth. When the attendant there gave him an injection, the needle broke and lodged in the claimant's right buttock. An operation to extract it failed.

On 27 January 1957 the claimant took the precaution of putting this on record in a 'hurt note'. On 29 January 1957 he wrote to the Commander of the Boom Defence Depot 'that in the event of any serious complications ensuing from the above incident, I will have documentary proof to substantiate it'. From 1957 to 1960 he suffered occasional pain, as if somebody had rammed him with a hat pin in his buttock. In October 1960 the needle shifted to such a position in his groin that it caused him very severe pain and compelled him to give up his diving work. On 20 July 1962 he issued a writ against the Ministry of Defence.

Held:

(i) The cause of action occurred when real, as distinct from purely minimal, damage was suffered. His occasional pain from 1957 went beyond such negligible discomfort as the court would disregard.

(ii) Moreover he had suffered by January 1957 more than a remote possibility of serious complications ensuing and that factor alone, combined with his body having been invaded by a foreign body, was sufficient in itself to complete the accrual of the cause of action.

His case was statute barred.

NB: The court would now have a discretion to allow such a case to proceed under s 33 of the Limitation Act 1980.

Brewer v North Tees Health NHS Trust

Limitation Act 1980, s 33

Manchester County Court (HHJ Charles James)   **CLY 98/555**

The claimant attended her GP in June 1989 suspecting that she might be pregnant. She was referred to the defendant's hospital for an ultrasound. The results of this were interpreted as indicating a fibroid condition, and a hysterectomy was advised. This was duly performed in July 1989. The claimant was advised in September 1989 that, although the operation was successful, she had in fact been pregnant. However, she did not instruct a solicitor until November 1994. A letter of claim was sent in May 1995 and proceedings issued in October 1995. The defendant applied for the claim to be struck out as statute barred. The claimant conceded that she had knowledge to start time running from autumn of 1989, but sought a s 33 discretion.

Held:

(i) The medical records were complete and contemporaneous and would be of great assistance to the defendant (*Forbes v Wandsworth HA* (p434) distinguished).

(ii) The defendant had produced no evidence to suggest that any witness it might wish to call had difficulty in recollecting the relevant events.

(iii) There was no particular prejudice to the defendant and it would be equitable to allow the claim to proceed. Application dismissed.

Bridgeman v McAlpine-Brown

Limitation Act 1980, s 33   **CPR 3.4, 19**

Court of Appeal   **LTL19/1/2000**

The claimant was injured in a road traffic accident on 29 February 1996. Her insurers wrote to the defendant's insurers, who conceded liability. Proceedings were issued on 19 February 1999. The defence denied liability on the basis that is was not the defendant but the defendant's wife who had been driving. The defendant applied to strike out whilst simultaneously the claimant applied to join the wife to proceedings. The judge did not hear oral evidence but concluded that Mrs Brown had clearly been driving. Given that the primary limitation period had expired, the claimant would have required an adjournment to make a s 33 application before joining Mrs Brown. The judge held that this would be disproportionate to the size of the claim and so struck it out. The claimant appealed.

Held:

(i)   The judge had failed to consider the provisions of CPR 3.4(2).

(ii)   As regards proportionality, there was nothing to stop the claimant issuing fresh proceedings against Mrs Brown and seeking a s 33 discretion. This would indeed be disproportionate.

(iii)   The identity of the driver needed proper resolution. The result achieved was unpalatable.

Appeal allowed. Case remitted for a joint trial on the identity of the driver and the exercise of s 33.

Briggs v Pitt-Payne and Lias

Limitation Act 1980, s 11, s 33

Court of Appeal   **(1999) 46 BMLR 132; (1999) 1 Lloyd's Rep Med 1; LTL 20/11/98**

The claimant issued proceedings in September 1994 against the defendants (both GPs) for negligent prescription of valium from 1983 to September 1991, when the claimant abruptly discontinued the course because of its injurious effect. The claimant alleged 'zombification' as a result of the drug. The judge found that the claimant had knowledge in January 1991 having read an article in the *Law Society Gazette*. He declined to exercise his s 33 discretion so the claim was statute barred. The claimant appealed.

Held:

(i)   The judge had been entitled to make the finding that he did as regards actual knowledge.

(ii)   The question of significance was more straightforward than the claimant contended. His symptoms were more serious than side-effects and were thus significant and an injury within s 38 (*Nash v Eli Lilly & Co* (p568) considered).

(iii)   Knowing that his injuries were attributable to the valium, it followed that the claimant knew his injuries might have been attributable to the doctors who prescribed him the valium. Any question of fault was irrelevant.

(iv)   The judge was entitled not to exercise his discretion given the shadowy merits of the claim. The claimant had previously been advised that his prospects were not more than 10%.

Appeal dismissed.

Briody v St Helen's & Knowsley Health Authority

Limitation Act 1980, s 33

Court of Appeal   **(1999) Lloyd's Rep Med 185; LTL 21/4/99**

In 1973 the claimant suffered a stillbirth. She had a history of one other stillbirth. She alleged that the obstetrician was negligent in failing to offer or perform an elective caesarean section. On 8 September 1995 there was a preliminary hearing on limitation where the judge exercised his s 33 discretion to allow the claim to continue in part. The judge held that the first category of allegations, relating to the decision to try labour, could be fairly tried as the evidence was not particularly time dependent, but the second category, regarding the management of the labour, could not be tried fairly and would be struck out. The claimant succeeded in establishing negligence at trial on 24 April 1998. The defendant appealed this finding and simultaneously sought leave to appeal the limitation decision out of time, arguing that the course of the evidence at trial had demonstrated that the defendant had been prejudiced by the delay.

Held (on the limitation issue):

(i)   The defendant's application for leave to appeal years out of time on the Limitation Act discretion had to be considered against the interests of justice in its broader sense which demanded a finality of judgment and an end to litigation. The defendant had also consented at the time to the resolution of limitation as a preliminary point.

(ii)   Although the result might be hard on the defendant, injustice would be done to the claimant and to the administration of justice itself if, so late in the day, a fair trial was to be set aside. The application for leave was dismissed.

Appeal dismissed (appeal on liability also dismissed).

Bristow v Grout

Limitation Act 1980, s 14(1)

Jupp J   **(1986) Times, 3 November**

In 1982 the claimant (Philip Bristow) was struck by the defendant's car and sustained facial injuries. His claim in respect of these was settled. In 1985 he discovered a far more serious hip injury which he ascribed to the same accident. In 1986 he commenced court action in respect of this.

Held:

(i)   Where s 14(1) of the Limitation Act 1980 provided that the claimant's date of knowledge was the date on which he first knew, inter alia, that the 'injury in question' was significant, this injury was the first of the injuries which the claimant had known to be significant. Therefore the limitation period had begun to run when the claimant had first known that his facial injuries were significant in 1982.

(ii)   Accordingly, the action brought in respect of the hip injury more than three years after that date was barred by s 11 of the Limitation Act 1980.

This decision was confirmed by the Court of Appeal (1987) Times, 9 November.

Broadley v Guy Clapham & Co

Limitation Act 1980, s 11, s 14

Court of Appeal   **(1993) Times, 6 July**

On 13 August 1980 the claimant (Mrs Maureen Broadley) underwent an operation for the removal of a foreign body from her knee. The next day nerve palsy of the left lateral popliteal nerve was noted. She suffered left foot drop. Her post-operative treatment ceased in October 1980.

In June 1983, as a result of a conversation with nurses from a hostel near where she was working, she instructed the defendant solicitor. He arranged for her to be seen in July 1983 by an independent surgeon who told her that the operation might have been negligently conducted. No report was received from this surgeon, and no writ was ever issued by the defendant.

The claimant subsequently instructed new solicitors who issued her writ against her former solicitor on 17 August 1990. The defence pleaded limitation, ie that her cause of action against the defendant occurred before 18 August 1984. Consequently a preliminary trial was ordered as to whether her date of knowledge against the surgeon and health authority under s 11 and s 14 of the Limitation Act 1980 was before 19 August 1981.

Turner J held that it was. The claimant appealed. It was argued that her date of knowledge was not reached until she knew of some act or omission, 'such as unreasonable interference with the nerve or failure reasonably to safeguard it from damage, or failure properly to investigate and/or repair the nerve lesion in time'.

Held:

(i)   The use of the words 'unreasonable', 'reasonably' and 'properly' could only be justified if s 14(1)(b) required knowledge that the injury was attributable to negligence. However, it was plain from the concluding words of s 14(1) that knowledge of negligence was irrelevant.

(ii)   It followed that the judge was wrong in *Bentley v Bristol and Western Health Authority* to hold that knowledge must be proved of the mechanics of damage to a nerve.

(iii)   The claimant in this case knew before August 1981, or could have known with the help of reasonably obtainable medical advice, that her injury had been caused by damage to the nerve resulting from some act or omission of the surgeon during the operation. This was all the knowledge or imputed knowledge which she needed to have.

Per Balcombe LJ: 'In the course of his argument Mr Fenwick, QC for the defendant submitted that the knowledge of the plaintiff necessary for the purposes of section 14 could be considered under four heads:

(1) Broad knowledge

Carrying out the operation to her knee in such a way that something went wrong, namely that it caused foot drop (an injury to her foot).

The judge's findings of fact set out above establish that the plaintiff herself had this broad knowledge by February.

(2) Specific knowledge

Carrying out the operation in such a way as to damage a nerve thereby causing foot drop (an injury to her foot).

The judge's findings, which in my judgment are correct, establish that the plaintiff constructively had specific knowledge by 19 August 1981.

(3) Qualitative knowledge

Carrying out the operation in such a way as unreasonably to cause injury to a nerve (unreasonably to expose a nerve to a risk of injury).

(4) Detailed knowledge

(which I take it to be knowledge sufficiently detailed to enable the plaintiff's advisers to draft a statement of claim).

In my judgment qualitative or detailed knowledge goes beyond the standard necessary for the purposes of section 14 of the 1980 Act.

The judge came to the right answer for the right reasons. I would dismiss this appeal.'

Bentley v Bristol and Western Health Authority (p328) overruled.

Brooks v AH Brooks & Co (A Firm)

CPR 6.9, 6.5, 10, 11

Ch D (Birmingham) (Judge David Cooke)

[2010] EWHC 2720 (Ch);
[2011] 3 All ER 982;
(2010) 160 NLJ 1615

The defendant solicitors' firm (D1) was a partnership in which D2 and D3 had been partners. The claimant alleged that on the advice of D3, given whilst D3 was allegedly acting in the course of D1's business, he had given D1 money to invest. The claimant later issued proceedings concerning how the money was used and related matters which were said to have taken place over approximately 17 years. However, during that period D3 had ceased to be a partner and, after the 17-year period, D2 had sold D1 and later stopped working there. The claimant's claim form and particulars of claim were later sent to D1 with a letter addressed to 'the Managing Partner'. The defendant's name on the claim form was D2. A firm of solicitors who had been instructed on behalf of the underwriters of D1's insurance policy sent a letter stating that it acted on behalf of the defendant, D1, and it enclosed an acknowledgment of service, signed by a person identified as 'defendant's solicitor'. The later partners of D1 commenced proceedings under CPR Part 20 against the former partners, seeking an indemnity or contribution. By the date of the hearing to determine whether the claim form had been served on D2 and D3 (in their capacity as partners of D1 and thus defendants in the main action), the claimant had accepted that it had no claim against the present partners of D1. The issue of costs in this respect also fell to be determined.

D2 argued that the intention and effect of the service was only to serve the present partners of D1. She further contended that the acknowledgment of service had no effect if she had not been served. The claimant argued that, as the present partners were not partners when the pleaded causes of action accrued, the claim was never brought against them and so did not stand to be dismissed; further, the costs they sought had been incurred by them voluntarily and unnecessarily involving themselves in the proceedings and so they should not be entitled to recover them.

Held:

(i)   Service was intended to be on all persons who were partners in D1 when the causes of action accrued. As it was not suggested that D3 was then carrying on business at D1's address, the claimant was required, in accordance with CPR 6.9(3), to take reasonable steps to ascertain a current address at which D3 could be served.

(ii)   D2 was known no longer to have been D1's employee. D1's address was thus known to be that at which she no longer carried on business, so the claimant should also have considered an alternative address at which to serve her.

(iii)   However, under para 4 of CPR PD 10, if an acknowledgment of service was signed by a person who was a partner at the time a cause of action accrued, or by a person who was authorised by any such partner, it was effective on behalf of those who were partners at that time, notwithstanding any lack of actual authority as between themselves, unless and until any of them were given permission to withdraw it. In the instant case, the firm of solicitors acting for the underwriters of D1's insurance policy had been authorised by D2 to sign the acknowledgment of service; and the effect of para 4.4(2) of CPR PD 10 was that it was also authorised to sign on behalf of all other partners, including D3. It therefore acknowledged service on D2 and D3's behalf and they were both bound by that acknowledgment, which waived any defects in service. The proceedings were therefore deemed to be properly served.

(iv)   In any event, had it been necessary to do so the court would have acceded to the claimant's application for an order pursuant to CPR 16.15(2) that the steps taken to bring the claim form to the attention of D2 and D3 be deemed to be good service. D3 accepted that she knew the proceedings had been issued in April 2009, and that she had been sent a copy of the claim form and particulars of claim. Given that the particulars of claim make clear that the claim was intended to be brought against D2 and D3, that D2 was well aware that a claim was in the offing, having engaged over several months in some rather ill-tempered correspondence with the claimant's solicitors about it, and that D2 and D3 have at all times lived together at the same address, it is impossible to believe that the claim did not come to his attention at the same time. The business address of the present partnership was not a place at which service on D2 and D3 was authorised by the rules. The fact that such service nevertheless had the effect of bringing it to D2 and D3's attention within a very short time, so that they had every opportunity to participate in its defence since then, constituted both good reason to make an order permitting service at that address and sufficient reason to direct that the steps already taken by way of posting to D2 and D3 constituted good service.

(v)   The claimant's advisers did everything they could to hold out the possibility that a claim would be pursued against the present partners, until they could no longer do so. It was therefore reasonable for D1's present partners to take steps to ensure that a defence was filed that would protect their position. The claimant had also sought directions that those partners should become parties to the action, so he could not later complain that costs were incurred in doing so. In relation to the Part 20 proceedings, it was reasonable for the present partners to seek an indemnity or contribution from those who were equity partners when the relevant causes of action accrued. The claimant therefore had to pay those costs of the present partners which were reasonably incurred in relation to the claim, on a standard basis.

Judgment accordingly.

Brooks and others v Boots Company plc

Limitation Act 1980, s 14, s 33

Collender QC, sitting as a deputy High Court judge   **23 October 1998, unreported**

Shortly before the Second World War the defendant were required by the government to assemble gas masks. The gas masks contained asbestos. The health risks from these gas masks gained some notoriety through a variety of channels from 1965 onwards.

This action involved six claims under the Law Reform (Miscellaneous Provisions) Act 1934 arising from mesothelioma (an asbestos related cancer). Mrs Brooks claimed to be within the primary limitation period. The others accepted that they were outside it and applied for s 33 discretions.

Mrs Brooks, who was born 10 March 1953, claim arose from the death of her mother on 31 December 1967. Proceedings were issued on 19 March 1997.

Held (generally):

(i)   The primary burden of proof lies on the claimant to show that knowledge only arose within three years of date of issue. Once that has been met an evidential burden may exist to rebut this, for example by proving an earlier date of constructive knowledge (*Nash v Eli Lilly & Co* (p568) and *Crocker v British Coal Corporation* (p392) followed).

(ii)   The fact that the defendant has to defend other similar cases did not prevent them claiming prejudice. The cases had to be considered individually.

(iii)   The merits of the claims were relevant (*Forbes v Wandsworth HA* (p434) applied). However, the most that could be said for the claimants was that there was a serious issue to be tried.

(iv)   The costs of defending against legally aided claimants was a relevant factor (*Lye v Marks & Spencer* (p538) applied) but not a weighty one.

(v)   Account needed to be taken of how much delay was attributable to the latency period of mesothelioma.

(vi)   As regards prejudice to the claimants, none of the people bringing or benefiting from the claim actually suffered from the disease.

(vii)   It would be difficult to have a fair trial of events over 50 years ago during wartime. The cogency of evidence had greatly deteriorated.

(A) THOMPSON

Mrs Thompson died on 31 December 1967. Her daughter, who brought the claim behalf of the estate, was nearly 15 at the time. She conceded that she knew from the late 1960s that her mother had died of mesothelioma but maintained that she did not have the requisite knowledge until she saw a television programme linking mesothelioma to asbestos and made some investigations. Proceedings were issued on 17 March 1997.

Held:

(i)   The daughter possessed the requisite knowledge shortly after her mother's death and the subsequent inquest. In the balance of probabilities the coroner would have told her or she would have made enquiries.

(ii)   The delay was enormous and the balance of prejudice firmly in favour of the defendant. The claim was therefore statute barred and s 33 would not be exercised.

(B) HEATH

Mrs Heath died on 15 May 1986 having been diagnosed in January 1986. A letter of claim was written on 17 June 1986 but proceedings not issued until 17 March 1997.

Held: The delay of eight years was substantial. The balance of equity was firmly in the defendant's favour and the discretion would not be exercised.

(C) GOODWIN

Mrs Goodwin died on 4 September 1981, her first symptoms having developed in the spring of 1980. Proceedings were issued on 17 March 1997.

Held: Given the delay of 12½ years the claim must remain statute barred.

(D) MILLINGTON

Mrs Millington died on 26 March 1988, her symptoms having first developed in December 1985. A letter of claim was sent on 25 January 1989 but proceedings were not issued until 17 March 1997.

Held: Balancing the delay of six years and the prejudice to the defendant, it would not be equitable to disapply s 11.

(E) LORD

Mrs Lord died on 20 July 1998, having first had knowledge of her condition in late 1991. A letter of claim was written on 14 February 1995 and proceedings issued on 17 March 1997.

Held: The delay was a modest one of 2½ years, and partly attributable to illness. Although finely balanced, it was equitable to allow the claim to proceed. s 33 exercised.

(F) SPENSLEY

Mrs Spensley died on 6 June 1970, having developed symptoms the previous year. A letter before action was sent on 24 September 1970 but proceedings were not issued until 18 July 1997.

Held: The delay was 24 years. It would be inequitable to allow the claim to continue.

Judgments accordingly.

Brooks v J & P Coates (UK) Ltd

Limitation Act 1980, s 11, s 33

Boreham J   **[1984] 1 All ER 702; [1984] ICR 158**

The claimant (Thomas Brooks) was exposed to cotton dust during the course of his employment by the defendants at their Bolton Mill from 1935 to 1940 and from 1940 to 1965. He left on medical advice because he had become breathless on exertion and had symptoms of coughing and wheeziness. In 1979 he applied for and was awarded industrial disablement pension for byssinosis which was diagnosed for the first time by the Pneumoconiosis Medical Panel in October 1979. In March 1980 he consulted solicitors who issued his writ on 19 September 1980. A full trial took place in 1983.

The claimant had not realised until 1980 that he had a cause of action. He did not know of anyone having a similar claim, certainly at this mill. Indeed it was not until 1976 that such a claim was settled. The mills where he worked had closed, the records were no longer available, and the work force had dispersed. The general practitioner's records were intact, and the family doctor who advised the claimant in 1965 was able to testify.

Held:

(i)   In 1965 the claimant knew that he had serious symptoms due to cotton dust, even though he had not been told of the disease of byssinosis. Accordingly, his action was prima facie statute barred by s 11 of the Limitation Act 1980.

(ii)   (a) the long delay of 15 years to issue of the writ in 1980 was due to the claimant not realising that he might have a cause of action. His attitude was reasonable and not blameworthy: s 33(3)(a);

      (b)   the case involved a system of work rather than a particular incident, and general conditions may be comparatively readily recalled even after a long period of time. There was some real prejudice to the defendants, but a fair trial had been possible: s 33(3)(b);

      (c)   there could be no criticism of the defendant's conduct in the action: s 33(3)(c);

      (d)   the claimant acted promptly and reasonably once he realised that he might have a cause of action: s 33(3)(e); and

      (e)   the claimant's claim was very substantial and the prejudice in denying him the chance to litigate it substantially outweighed such prejudice as the defendants had suffered by reason of the delay. It was equitable to allow the action to proceed: s 33(1).

The claimant established liability and recovered £22,688 damages.

Broome v Rotheray and others

Amendment of writ   **RSC Ord 15, r 6; Ord 20, r 9**

Court of Appeal   **Lexis, 30 July 1992**

On 16 September 1987 the claimant (Trevor Broome) was moving some steel angles which had been left with one end on a flat bed articulated lorry and with one end on the ground when one of the engines slid and fell, injuring his left leg and ankle.

On 4 September 1989 he issued a writ against three defendants: the company that employed him, and two of its directors. In October 1989 they served a defence alleging that the accident was caused by the negligence of the lorry owners.

In August 1990 the claimant applied to amend the writ by adding the lorry owners as fourth defendants. On 3 September 1990 the district registrar granted leave for this. He did not specify any time within which the writ was to be amended so that, under RSC Ord 20, r 9, his order ceased to have effect on 17 September 1990. The claimant's solicitors did not purport to amend the writ, by re-sealing it, until 2 October 1990. They purported to serve it on the fourth defendants on 15 December 1990.

The fourth defendants applied to set aside the purported amendment of the writ and all subsequent proceedings thereunder. Douglas Brown J granted this. The claimant appealed. RSC Ord 15, r 6(5) provides that 'no person shall be added or substituted as a party after the expiry of any relevant period of limitation ...' subject to two exceptions which did not apply in this case.

Held:

(i)   The claimant knew from the outset who was the lorry driver, how the steel angles were loaded, and that he had been given no help in their unloading by the lorry driver. There was no foundation for holding that under s 14(1) of the Limitation Act 1980 time only started to run from service of the first three defendants' defence in October 1989.

(ii)   The three-year limitation period expired on 16 September 1990. Even if the court had power to validate the writ retrospectively, the earliest date from which it could have been retrospectively validated was 2 October 1990, by which time the limitation period had expired.

(iii)   By reason of the application of RSC Ord 15, r 6, the claimant's appeal must necessarily fail.

Braniff v Holland & Hannen and Cubitts (Southern) Ltd (p342) followed.

Brown v Goldsmith (trading as Steyning Homecrafts)

Limitation Act 1980, s 33

Court of Appeal   Lexis, 17 March 1987

On 8 December 1979 the claimant (Mr Brown), whose 18th birthday was on 17 December 1979, fell from the first floor balcony of the defendant employer's do-it-yourself shop, apparently because the rail of the balcony was unsafe, and broke one of the vertebrae of his neck. In September 1980 he went to see Mr Blackie, an insurance broker, who advised him on claiming certain DHSS benefits, the last of which was a final award in August 1983 of an industrial disablement gratuity assessed at 12% for life. This prompted the claimant to instruct solicitors in September 1983. After an application for legal aid, his writ was issued on 21 May 1984.

At a preliminary trial, B Hytner QC sitting as a deputy judge of the Queen's Bench Division rejected the claimant's evidence that Mr Blackie had erroneously advised him that his claim against his employers was barred six months after the accident. He further found that, by the time the claimant came out of hospital in January 1980, he had all the requisite knowledge to enable him to bring an action and that, for a period of over three years, he took no step whatever to pursue it and that, as there was no satisfactory explanation for this inactivity, it would not be equitable to disapply s 11 of the Limitation Act 1980. The claimant appealed.

Held: there was a conflict of evidence between the claimant and Mr Blackie, which the judge had resolved against the claimant. There was ample evidence to support the judge's findings, and there was no basis on which the court could properly interfere with the judge's exercise of his discretion under s 33 of the Limitation Act 1980. The appeal was hopeless and should be dismissed.

Brown v Innovatorone Plc

CPR 6.3, 6.4, 6.5, 6.7, 6.8, 6.9, 6.15, 7.6, PD 6A para 4.1

QBD (Comm) (Andrew Smith J)   **[2009] EWHC 1376 (Comm);**
[2010] 2 All ER (Comm) 80;
[2010] CP Rep 2; (2009) 153(25) SJLB 27

The defendants applied for declarations that the claim forms that were sent via fax to their respective solicitors by the claimants were not validly and effectively served upon them. In the alternative, the claimant applied under CPR 6.15 for an order that their intended service should stand as good service by an alternative method.

The claimant on 17 October 2008 issued proceedings against a number of defendants in relation to alleged sham investment schemes. In December 2008, the claimant served the claim form on all the defendants except the seventh and eighth defendants. The claimant's solicitors informed the seventh and eighth defendants that they were intending to bring proceedings against them. They enclosed copies of the claim form, but stated that they were not yet served, but would be served within the four-month validity period. The seventh and eighth defendants' solicitors confirmed to the claimant's solicitors that they were acting. In correspondence, the seventh and eighth defendants' solicitors had written to the claimant's solicitors on writing paper that set out their fax numbers. The claimant's solicitors sent amended claim forms by fax to the seventh and eighth defendants' solicitors at 10pm on 17 February 2009, shortly before the end of the validity period. The transmissions of both faxes were received by the solicitors before the midnight deadline, but they did not forward the faxed claim forms to their clients before the deadline. The claimant's solicitors had not asked the seventh and eighth defendants' solicitors whether they were instructed to accept service, nor had they been advised by either the seventh and eighth defendants or the solicitors that the latter were instructed to accept service.

The seventh and eighth defendants applied for declarations that the claim forms were not validly and effectively served upon them. In the alternative, the claimant applied under CPR 6.15 for an order that their intended service should stand as good service by an alternative method. The claimant submitted that CPR and PD 6A para 4.1 meant that, when a claimant's solicitor had received correspondence from a solicitor acting for a defendant on writing paper setting out the solicitor's fax number, a claim form could be validly served by transmitting it to the fax number. The defendants submitted that CPR 6.3 and PD 6A were concerned with the method of service, and were not about the circumstances where there could be valid service on a defendant's solicitor. They contended that a claim form could not be served on a solicitor unless CPR 6.7 required it; in other words, unless either the defendant had given in writing the business address of a solicitor as an address that could receive service, or the solicitor in question had notified the claimant in writing that he had been instructed to accept service of the claim form.

Held:

(i)   The defendants' formulation gave Part 6 a coherent and sensible structure. There was no apparent reason why the fact that a defendant's solicitors had a fax number on their writing paper would mean that they could be validly served, but it made perfect sense for that to mean that, if the claimant had been told that the solicitors could be served, then service upon them could be by fax. If a claimant has been informed that a solicitor is instructed to accept service of the claim form, service must be effected on the solicitor. Conversely, if the solicitor has not confirmed that they are so instructed, service on a solicitor is not valid service.

(ii)   The wording of PD 6A made it clear that para 4 applied as far as service on a solicitor was concerned only where the solicitor was 'acting for' the party to be served. It was necessary to qualify that statement, as it was clear that it would not apply where a solicitor was acting for a defendant in relation to an entirely separate matter, and therefore it could not be said that PD 6A required merely that the solicitor had been instructed by a defendant. It followed that PD 6A referred to the situation when a solicitor was to be served under CPR 6.7. That qualification was supported by the fact that a solicitor upon whom service was required by CPR 6.7 might not have been authorised to accept it. There was also authoritative support for such a contention from the decision in *Collier v Williams* (p380), which stated that, unless a claimant had been made aware by the defendant or his solicitor that the solicitor was authorised to accept service, the claimant would be ill-advised to serve on the solicitor. Accordingly, the claim forms had not been validly or effectively served upon the defendants.

(iii)   It was not appropriate to exercise the power under CPR 6.15 to permit service by an alternative method. That rule expressly required that there be a good reason for the court to exercise the power and did not simply confer a discretion; that emphasised that the power should not be exercised over-readily. There was no evidence that suggested a reason why the claimant could not have served the claim form in accordance with the rules (*Marconi Communications International Ltd v PT Pan Indonesia Bank TBK* [2004] EWHC 129 (Comm); [2004] 1 Lloyd's Rep 594; [2004] 2 CLC 570 considered). Although the defendants had suffered no prejudice as a result of the proceedings being served on their solicitors rather than upon them personally, the mere absence of prejudice to a defendant was not sufficient reason to make an order under CPR 6.15 (*Kuenyehia v International Hospitals Group Ltd* (p524) applied). Although the objective of the rules about service was to enable the court to be satisfied that the method used either had put the recipient in a position to ascertain its contents or was reasonably likely to enable him to do so within any relevant time period, that did not mean that the court should indulge a claimant who had devised his own method outside the rules for achieving that purpose. The rules stipulated how the objective was to be achieved, and it was necessary in the interests of certainty that the courts allowed a litigant to depart from them only where there was a sufficiently compelling case to do so (*Anderton v Clwyd CC* (p303) applied). That was supported by the fact that CPR 6.15 had to be interpreted in accordance with the overriding objective.

Judgment accordingly.

Bryant v Mike Beer Transport Ltd

CPR 6.7   **Human Rights Act 1998, s 3**

ECHR, Art 6

Court of Appeal   **[2002] EWCA Civ 933; [2002] 1 WLR 3174;**
[2002] 3 All ER 813

See *Anderton v Clwyd County Council* (A) (p303)

Buck v English Electric Co Ltd

Limitation Act 1939, s 2A, s 2D

Kilner Brown J   **[1977] 1 WLR 806; [1977] ICR 629;**
[1978] 1 All ER 271

From 1947 to 1957 Edward Buck was employed by the defendants at their iron foundry in Rugby. He knew throughout that his work created clouds of dust for which the masks supplied were inadequate. The Pneumoconiosis Medical Panel assessed his disability at 10% in August 1959 and at 20% in July 1963. It was in 1963 that he first realised that he might be able to claim. He deposed that 'I did not think it worth my while to do so. I was only assessed at 20% disabled then and was working and earning a full wage as well as receiving a disability pension. I felt I would be sponging if I tried to take up their suggestions ...'. His disability rose to 40% in July 1964 and gradually increased until it reached 100% in September 1970. He struggled on until finally in 1973 he had to give up work. Only then did he yield to his wife's advice and go to his trade union for help.

In January 1975 he was given leave to sue the defendants pursuant to s 1 of the Limitation Act 1963. On 5 February 1975 his writ was issued. In April 1975 he died of his pneumoconiosis. The claimant (his widow) continued the action.

A preliminary trial on limitation took place in autumn 1976. Evidence was given by a solicitor who had acted in eight claims against the defendants arising out of similar work at the Rugby factory. The first two writs were issued in 1963, and by 1966 four cases had been settled. Three further court actions were issued between 1973 and 1976, two of which had already led to settlements at substantial sums. The solicitor had preserved all the files.

Held:

(i)   The deceased knew by 1963 that his disease was sufficiently serious to justify his issuing proceedings. His claim was prima facie statute barred under s 2A of the Limitation Act 1939 as amended.

(ii)   The delay of 12 years from 1963 to the issue of the writ in 1975 was plainly inordinate, and the deceased did not act promptly once he knew he could claim. However, he was a man in the best tradition of dignified responsible workmen, and he had acted reasonably. The extent to which the evidence likely to be adduced by the defendants was likely to be less cogent than in 1963 was small. It would be equitable to allow the action to proceed under s 2D of the 1939 Act as amended.

Per Kilner Brown J: '... a delay in excess of five years raises a presumption of prejudice to the defendants ... it is a rebuttable presumption.'

NB: It would now be a misdirection to say that there was any such presumption: *A v Hoare* (p287), *Cain v Francis* (p360) and *B v Nugent Care Society* (p315).

Buckler v Sheffield Forest Borough Council

Limitation Act 1980, s 11, s 14, s 33

Court of Appeal   **[2004] EWCA Civ 920; LTL 21/6/2004;**
[2005] PIQR P3

The claimant was employed by the defendant in the early seventies when he was exposed to asbestos. In April 1991 he was informed that he had pleural thickening to the left lung, the condition being described at the time as slight scarring with the risk of lung cancer. He was informed that he could claim against the defendant. His view at this time was that the condition was too mild to justify making a claim. Further screenings during the 1990s showed no change. In 1999 he was advised that he had pleural plaques. He mistakenly believed that this synonym meant that his condition had deteriorated.

He issued proceedings on April 2003. Limitation was heard as a preliminary issue. The judge held that the claimant had both actual and constructive knowledge in 1991. However, the judge found that the claimant had real and substantial reasons for his inactivity between 1991 and 1999, this being the subjective belief that his condition had deteriorated, and exercised her discretion under s 33 to allow the claim to continue. The defendant appealed.

Held:

(i)   Under s 33 the court had to consider the length of and reasons for the delay. Having identified the reason, the court had to decide whether it was a good or a bad one, which meant considering whether the reasons given for the delay had any real or decisive weight.

(ii) In this case, the claimant had the relevant knowledge from 1991 but consciously chosen not to sue. The question was whether he should be allowed to bring an action many years later because of a mistaken belief that his health had deteriorated.

(iii) The claimant's misapprehension that his condition had changed could not answer his conscious decision not to sue earlier. This was a clear case of the claimant failing to show a good reason for the delay.

(iv) The judge had not adequately address the delay in terms of s 33(3)(a). The reason for the delay had been weak. The exercise of her discretion would therefore be set aside. The claimant had failed to discharge the heavy burden of showing sufficient or satisfactory reasons for the long delay. There was no equitable reason justifying the setting aside of s 11.

Appeal allowed.

Burgin v Sheffield City Council

Limitation Act 1980, s 33

Court of Appeal   [2005] EWCA Civ 482

The claimant had been employed between 1964 and 1992 by the first defendant local authority and then between 1994 and 2001 by the second defendant private company. He had used vibratory tools which, it was well-known, could cause vibration white finger ('VWF') if used for any length of time without any kind of protection. By 1989, and perhaps as early as 1986, the claimant first had symptoms of tingling and numbness in his fingers in cold weather. By 1992 he was suffering from all the symptoms of VWF. In the mid-1990s, in around 1995, he was talking to a fellow employee of the second defendant when he first heard of VWF as such. The description of VWF given to him matched his symptoms. He therefore thought that he might have VWF and that it was caused by his using vibratory tools. It may be that, since he was using such tools by working for the second defendant, his condition had worsened. In 2000 he heard some more from another of the second defendant's employees, who suggested to him that he apply to the Department of Social Security for benefit. He decided to do so and was examined by a doctor for that purpose. In his account, as noted by the doctor on 30 November 2000, he said that he first noted 'this May' that his hands were cold when he was on holiday. He then described the symptoms of VWF, although not including vascular symptoms. The claimant's application for benefits was refused, apparently on the footing that he was not sufficiently suffering from VWF in order to be entitled to benefit. He appealed, but his appeal failed in 2001. This decision was communicated to him in May 2001. The claimant then went to solicitors, having seen an advertisement which they had put in a newspaper, and he was subsequently seen by Dr Anne Hicks in December 2001. She diagnosed 'Hand/Arm Vibration Syndrome Stage 3'. On 20 March 2003 he issued proceedings.

The first defendant pleaded limitation, which was heard as a preliminary issue. The second defendant took no limitation point and played no part in that hearing. The second defendant pleaded that it intended to adopt the claimant's allegations against the first defendant. The judge held that the claimant had the relevant knowledge by 1992 or, in any event, by 1995. He went on to hold, however, that there would be no prejudice to the first defendant and allowed the claim to proceed. The first defendant appealed, arguing that the judge had failed to heed or properly apply the heavy burden of proof in relation to prejudice. By reason of the delay in bringing proceedings, it had lost the opportunity to use the evidence of the claimant's former supervisor in relation to working practices as the supervisor had died. It had also lost the opportunity to make an earlier medical examination of the claimant in order to determine liability as between it and the second defendant.

Held:

(i) The judge had not made any error in disapplying s 11 and allowing the claim to proceed. He had correctly directed himself and had stressed that he was required to have regard to all the circumstances.

(ii)   In relation to the reasons for the delay, the judge expressly directed himself by reference to s 33(3)(a) and said that the reasons for delay were essentially a disinclination on the part of the respondent to take action until he was sufficiently motivated to do so. He therefore identified this as a factor going against the claimant.

(iii) In relation to prejudice, the effect of delay on a defendant's ability to defend the claim was of paramount importance. Whilst it was true that the ultimate burden was on the claimant, the evidential burden of showing that the evidence was less cogent by reason of delay was on the first defendant. In the instant case, it was unclear what the nature of any prejudice was as regards the evidence of the supervisor. There was no question of any change in working practices and there was no reason to believe that the second defendant could not itself adduce evidence as to that or provide witness statements in that regard. Equally there was no prejudice by reason of difficulties in the apportionment of liability as between the defendants that could be attributed to delay. Since the second defendant intended to adopt the claimant's allegations against the first defendant, the company would only be liable to the extent that it had contributed towards an existing medical condition. It followed that the court would have to consider issues of apportionment in any event and it was desirable that those issues should be fairly resolved as between all three parties.

(iv)   The judge had recognised potential prejudice but in all the circumstances had concluded that it was equitable to allow the claim to proceed. In so concluding the judge had not exceeded the generous ambit of discretion in which reasonable disagreement was possible and, accordingly, he had not erred in the exercise of his discretion.

Appeal dismissed.

Burke v Ash Construction

Limitation Act 1980, s 33

Court of Appeal   **[2003] EWHC Civ 717; [2004] PIQR P11; LTL 23/5/2003**

On 1 July 1994 the claimant, whilst working for the defendant, fell through a temporary storage platform whilst renovating houses and suffered serious injury. In June 1997 counsel advised that the prospects of success were worse than evens but also that different counsel might advise more favourably and that proceedings should be issued before July 1997. Legal aid to do so was denied.

After favourable advice from different counsel, proceedings were issued on 19 June 2001. The judge exercised his discretion under s 33 to allow the claim to continue as, although the evidence was likely to be less cogent as it depended on personal testimony and a simple personal injury case should not be fought over eight years after the event, a fair trial was still possible and the reason for the delay was that the claimant's legal advisers were incompetent and/or dilatory, although probably not quite to the point of negligence. The defendant appealed.

Held:

(i)   The judge undertook a careful balancing exercise with regard to all the relevant factors and made no error of law.

(ii)   The prejudice pleaded by the defendant was potential rather than actual. This was a case of whether a system of work was safe rather than one involving substantial dispute of fact. The actual prejudice was slight and a fair trial could still take place.

(iii) The judge's decision, although at the extremity of the permitted margins, was not obviously wrong given the wide ambit of his discretion.

Appeal dismissed.

Busuttill-Reynaud v Eli Lilly & Co and others

Limitation Act 1980, s 11, s 14

Court of Appeal   **[1992] 3 Med LR 396**

See *Nash v Eli Lilly & Co* (O) (p568)

Byrne v Motor Insurers' Bureau

Limitation Act 1980, s 28   **MIB Untraced Drivers Agreement**

Court of Appeal   **[2008] EWCA Civ 574; [2009] QB 66;**
[2008] 3 WLR 1421; [2008] 4 All ER 476;
[2008] RTR 26; [2008] 3 CMLR 4; [2008] Eu LR 732;
[2008] Lloyd's Rep IR 705; [2008] PIQR P14;
(2008) 158 NLJ 860; (2008) 152(22) SJLB 31;
(2008) Times, 2 July

The claimant had been injured by a car in a hit-and-run incident in June 1993 when he was three years old. The car did not stop and the driver was never traced. Some eight years later the claimant's parents became aware of the possibility of claiming compensation from the MIB and submitted a claim on his behalf.

The claim was rejected as outside the three-year time limit in the Untraced Drivers Agreement. When he was 16 the claimant began proceedings against the MIB and the Secretary of State claiming that the Agreement, interpreted in accordance with Community law, conferred a right to make an application to the MIB within time limits no less favourable than those in the Limitation Act 1980, which contained a provision suspending the limitation period during a claimant's minority.

The judge made declarations that, on the true construction of Directive 84/5 and/or by virtue of the Community principle of equivalence, the MIB procedure should be subject to a limitation period no less favourable than that which applied to the commencement of actions in the courts in respect of claims brought by minors for personal injury in tort against a traced driver. He held that the United Kingdom was in sufficiently serious breach of its obligations under Community law to give rise in principle to liability in damages for failure to ensure conformity with the Directive in that respect.

The MIB and Secretary of State appealed, submitting that the requirement to provide protection equivalent to that provided in respect of identified and insured drivers under the court system was concerned only with the amount of compensation.

Held:

(i)   The European Court of Justice had ruled that the protection provided by the national scheme had to be equivalent to and as effective as the protection available under the national legal system to victims of insured drivers (*Evans v Secretary of State for the Environment, Transport and the Regions* (C-63/01) [2005] All ER (EC) 763 ECJ (5th Chamber) applied). There was no reason to adopt a more restrictive meaning.

(ii)   Clause 1(1)(f) of the Untraced Drivers Agreement precluded any application made more than three years after the accident. By contrast, a claim in tort in court proceedings against an insured driver could have been brought by the claimant at any time prior to his 21st birthday, by virtue of s 28 of the 1980 Act. The same would have applied to a claim against an identified but uninsured driver whose liability was covered by the Uninsured Drivers Agreement. Once that was accepted as the appropriate comparison, the conclusion was unavoidable that the Untraced Drivers Agreement gave less favourable treatment.

(iii)   It did not make any material difference that there might be other procedural advantages to the MIB scheme. The competing procedures needed to be looked at as a whole but the claimed advantages of the MIB scheme did not justify the much shorter time limit. In order to meet its intended role as implementing the Directive, the MIB Agreement should be subject to a limitation period no less favourable than that which applied to the commencement of court proceedings by a minor under s 28.

(iv)   The UK's failure to comply with the Directive was sufficiently serious to expose it to a claim for *Francovich* damages. The ECJ judgment in *Evans* was an authoritative statement of the legal context in which the Untraced Drivers Agreement had to be considered and contained an unambiguous statement of the need to ensure equivalence with the system for insured drivers. The 'sufficiently serious' criterion laid down by the ECJ for *Francovich* liability required a value judgment by the national court, taking account of the various factors summarised by the court in *Evans*.

(v)   In the instant case the important points which established liability in principle were: the relative precision of the requirement, following *Evans*; the serious consequences of failure to comply; and the clear warning given in *Evans* of the need to make the comparison.

Appeal dismissed.

NB: This decision is reflected in a subsequent Memorandum to the Untraced Drivers Agreement.

Bytheway v British Steel

Alternative dispute resolution – waiver   **Limitation Act 1980, s 33**

Court of Appeal   **LTL 26/6/97**

The claimant worked for the defendant between 1963 and 1975. He was exposed to daily noise and an explosion occurred a few feet from him in 1970. He became aware of deterioration in hearing in 1975. He sent a letter of claim in 1990. The defendant's insurers had a voluntary arrangement for the settlement of claims such as this. The insurers formally confirmed that limitation periods would be extended for cases under the arrangement. Either side could terminate the arrangement without notice. The consequences of termination were not stipulated, although it was implicit that a claimant's rights in subsequent litigation would not be prejudiced.

The insurer terminated the arrangement in 1993. The claimant issued proceedings in 1994. The defendant pleaded limitation. The judge found that (a) the defendant had waived its limitation rights, and (b) if they had not he would have exercised his discretion under s 33 to allow the claim to proceed. The defendant appealed.

Held:

(i)   The insurer did not waive limitation rights. Claims pending ADR resolution were not entitled to the double benefit of moving on to judicially assessed quantum free from limitation defences.

(ii)   The logical conclusion of the claimant's argument was that he was entitled to abandon the arrangement in favour of formal litigation, but that the defendant was tied to its obligations under the arrangement. This could not be right.

(iii)   The defendant had not waived the right to raise a limitation defence.

(iv)   Any detriment to the claimant flowed from his willing participation in the scheme. The insurer's termination was not a breach of the agreement but the exercise of a right under it.

(v)   The judge misdirected himself by approaching s 33 on the basis of waiver and the overriding importance of the scheme.

(vi) Considering the discretion afresh, it would not be equitable to allow the claim to proceed. The delay was between 15 and 20 years and attributable to the claimant's inactivity. The defendant was blameless and the delay had reduced the cogency of the evidence.

Appeal allowed.

C v D

Limitation Act 1980, s 2, s 11, s 33

Sir Michael Wright   **[2004] All ER (D) 92 (Mar); LTL 4/3/2004**

The defendant was a Roman Catholic order which provided pastoral care for young people. The claimant, who came from a religious family, as a teenager became distressed at his homosexuality and was bullied at school. His mother took him to see a priest of the defendant's order. The priest offered treatment which included a 'therapeutic massage', entailing the priest rubbing his hands over the claimant's naked body. This occurred from 1983 to 1989. In 1992 the claimant complained to the police about the priest's behaviour. The claimant suffered from severe depression. In 1995 he met with the defendant's representatives and told them that he intended to issue proceedings. In 1996 he instructed solicitors but they considered that the claim was bound to fail. In 2002 he instructed new solicitors and issued proceedings claiming that the defendant was liable both vicariously and directly. Limitation was heard as a preliminary issue. The master struck out the vicarious liability claim as being irredeemably barred by the flat six-year period under s 2, it being a claim for trespass to the person. He held however that the claim for direct liability, being a claim for negligence, came within s 11 and thus a s 33 discretion was available. The master decided that it would be equitable to allow the claim to continue and exercised his discretion in the claimant's favour. The claimant appealed and the defendant cross-appealed.

Held:

(i) The master had been correct to strike out the vicarious liability claim. It was settled that the priest's trespass to the person could not also constitute a breach of duty of care (*Lister v Hesley Hall* (p535) and *KR v Bryn Alyn Community Holdings Ltd* (p505) applied).

(ii) It was appropriate to disapply the limitation period in respect of the direct liability claim. On the evidence, the claimant had the requisite knowledge of the causal link between the abuse and his depression in 1995. Although there was extreme delay on the claimant's part, there were exceptional circumstances in his favour. It was not in dispute that the claimant had been sexually abused, and given that concession, the delay did not seriously hamper the defendant's ability to defend the action. Further, it would be unjust not to allow the claimant an opportunity to seek recompense for so serious a wrong.

Appeal and cross-appeal dismissed.

NB: The vicarious liability claim would now also be considered under s 11/s 14/s 33: *A v Hoare* (p287).

C v Middlesbrough Council

Limitation Act 1980, s 2, s 11

Court of Appeal   **[2004] EWCA Civ 1746; LTL 21/12/2004**

The claimant had as a child been placed in a school run by the defendant. He remained there until 1988. Shortly after he left he complained to a social worker that he had been sexually abused by a teacher. In May 2002 he issued proceedings claiming damages for psychiatric injury and subsequent losses. He made his claim on two bases: (a) that the defendant was directly negligent for failing to properly assess his need and for failing to provide proper supervision, and (b) that the defendant was vicariously liable for the teacher's actions.

The judge found that the claimant had knowledge for the purposes of s 14 by 1996 at the latest, but allowed the direct liability claim to proceed under s 33. However he found that, although the defendant had been in breach of its duty, no harm flowed from that breach. He further found that vicarious liability claim was claim for trespass to the person and thus barred by the non-extendable six-year period set down by s 2. The claimant appealed.

Held:

(i) The judge had been entitled to dismiss the direct negligence claim.

(ii) Where the action for which an employer was vicariously liable was deliberate abuse, the cause of action fell within s 2 (*Stubbings v Webb* (p677), *KR v Bryn Alyn Community (Holdings) Ltd* (p505) applied).

Appeal dismissed.

NB: The vicarious liability claim would now also be considered under s 11/s 14/s 33: *A v Hoare* (p287).

CD v Bryn Alyn Community Holdings Ltd

Limitation Act 1980, s 2, s 11, s 14, s 33

Court of Appeal   **[2003] EWCA Civ 783;
[2003] 3 WLR 107; [2003] 1 FLR 1203**

See *KR v Bryn Alyn Community Holdings Ltd* (M) (p505)

CGE v Bryn Alyn Community Holdings Ltd

Limitation Act 1980, s 2, s 11, s 14, s 33

Court of Appeal   **[2003] EWCA Civ 783; [2003] 3 WLR 107;
[2003] 1 FLR 1203**

See *KR v Bryn Alyn Community Holdings Ltd* (C) (p505)

Cain v Francis; Hamlani v Direct Line Insurance plc

Limitation Act 1980, s 33

Court of Appeal   **[2008] EWCA Civ 1451; [2009] QB 754;
[2009] 3 WLR 551; [2009] 2 All ER 579;
[2009] CP Rep 19; [2009] RTR 18;
[2009] LS Law Medical 82; (2009) 106(2) LSG 20**

The appellant in the first appeal (C1) and the respondent in the second appeal (C2) had been injured in road traffic accidents and liability had been admitted. In both cases, through the fault of their solicitors, proceedings had been issued outside the primary limitation period and limitation defences had been raised. In both cases the issue had been whether the court should exercise its discretion under s 33 to disapply the time limits, and in exercising that discretion the effect of any prejudice to the respective defendants if they lost the opportunity to rely on the limitation defence.

In C1's case the delay was one day. The judge held that the defendant, the respondent in the first appeal, would be prejudiced by the loss of the limitation defence and he refused to disapply the limitation period.

In C2's case the delay was one year. The judge held that he should ignore any prejudice to the defendants, the appellants in the second appeal, from the loss of the 'windfall' of the limitation defence, and he disapplied the time limits.

Held:

(i)   There should be consistency of approach between judges on an issue as fundamental as whether the loss of a limitation defence amounted to real prejudice where the defendant had no defence to liability on the merits.

(ii)   There was now a long line of authority to support the proposition that, in a case where the defendant had had early notice of the claim, the accrual of a limitation defence should be regarded as a windfall and the prospect of its loss, by the exercise of the s 33 discretion, should be regarded as either no prejudice at all, as in the case of *Firman v Ellis* (p433), or only a slight degree of prejudice, as in the case of *Donovan v Gwentoys Ltd* (p412) (*Thompson v Brown (t/a George Albert Brown (Builders) & Co)* (p690), *Hartley v Birmingham City Council* (p465) and *Horton v Sadler* (p482) applied).

(iii)   However, all the authorities had arrived at the same result but by different reasoning and it was helpful to advance some rational explanation for the authorities. Whether it would be equitable, meaning fair and just, to allow an action to proceed was at the heart of s 33. In fairness and justice, a tortfeasor only deserved to have his obligation to pay damages removed if the passage of time had significantly diminished his opportunity to defend himself on liability and/or quantum. The disapplication of the limitation period, which would restore his obligation to pay damages, was only prejudicial to him if his right to a fair opportunity to defend himself had been compromised.

(iv)   Although, on a literal construction of s 33, it appeared to be relevant to the exercise of the discretion that the defendant would suffer the financial prejudice of having to pay damages if the arbitrary time limit were to be disapplied, Parliament cannot have intended that the financial prejudice, as such, should be taken into account. If having to pay the damages was not a relevant prejudice under s 33, it could not be relevant either as one of the circumstances of the case.

(v)   Any prejudice to the claimant in being prevented from proceeding with his claim would be greatly reduced if he had a good claim against his solicitor. In a case where the defendant had suffered some forensic or procedural prejudice that would diminish his ability to defend himself, it would be relevant to consider that the claimant had another remedy. But the fact that the claimant has a possible claim against his solicitor would not necessarily mean that the time limit should not be disapplied.

(vi)   The basic question to be asked was whether it was fair and just in all the circumstances to expect the defendant to meet the claim on the merits, notwithstanding the delay in commencement. The length of the delay, of itself, was not a deciding factor. It was whether the defendant had suffered any evidential or other forensic prejudice which should make the difference. The reason for the delay might be relevant. Although the delay referred to in s 33 was delay after the expiry of the limitation period, it would also be relevant to consider when the defendant knew that a claim was to be made against him and the opportunities he had had to investigate the claim and collect evidence.

(vii)   Applying those principles, C1's appeal was allowed, and C2's appeal was dismissed.

Judgment accordingly.

Per Smith LJ: '63. ...I do not think one can infer much from the six factors in s 33(3) which, as Lord Diplock said, are "a curious hotchpotch". I agree with the Chancellor that the phrase "it would be equitable to allow the action to proceed" is at the heart of the section. Equitable here means "fair and just". With that in mind, I think that the rationale underlying the provision must be found in a consideration of the background to limitation law as a whole.

64. It is a fundamental precept of the common law that a tortfeasor should compensate the victim of the tort. At common law, the victim, now the claimant, could sue the tortfeasor at any time, without limitation. It is also a fundamental precept that any person who is sued in respect of a tort should have a fair opportunity to defend himself. In 1623, a uniform limitation period of six years was introduced for all actions. The rationale behind the limit was to protect defendants from stale claims. It was not fair and just to impose liability on a defendant who had not had a proper opportunity to investigate the allegations against him and to assemble the evidence necessary to defend himself. There may have been other policy reasons for the provision, such as the desirability of finality but, as between the parties, the reason was to protect the defendant from a stale claim.

65. The effect of the limitation provision was not to extinguish the claimant's right of action, only to bar his remedy. The Act did not provide a defence on the merits; the defendant was ex hypothesi still a tortfeasor; but he could not be sued. The six-year period must have been Parliament's best estimate of when it would be unfair or unjust to the defendant to allow the claimant to enforce his right of action.

66. So far as personal injury actions were concerned, the limit remained at six years until the Limitation Act 1954, when it was reduced to three. I infer that Parliament must have thought that, in the context of that kind of action, unfairness to the defendant was likely to arise at an earlier date than in other actions.

67. Any limitation bar is arbitrary. It cannot always be fair and just to permit a claimant to proceed with his action if he commences it two years and 364 days after the relevant injury. Significant prejudice and unfairness might already have arisen, even long before the expiry of three years, for example by the death of an important witness. But the rule is that the claimant can proceed, notwithstanding any unfairness to the defendant. On the other hand, the expiry of the three-year term does not automatically create unfairness. Yet what was deemed fair on Tuesday is deemed unfair on Wednesday. There might be no unfairness to the defendant even if he is required to answer the claim, say, five years after the accident. The three-year limit is Parliament's best guess as to when prejudice can be expected to have arisen such that it is unfair to expose the defendant to the claim. The imposition of an arbitrary limit could only ever hope to do rough justice ...

68. ... The only rationale which could have underlain the introduction of this provision [the predecessor to s 33] was a desire to refine the rough justice of the old arbitrary provision. Instead of a limitation rule of thumb, the courts would be required to consider what was fair and just in all the circumstances of the individual case.

69. In my view, the words of section 33 must be construed against that background. The context is that the claimant had the right to pursue his cause of action which he has lost by the operation of section 11. The defendant, on the other hand, had an obligation to pay the damages due; his right was the right to a fair opportunity to defend himself against the claim. The operation of section 11 has given him a complete procedural defence which removes his obligation to pay. In fairness and justice, he only deserves to have that obligation removed if the passage of time has significantly diminished his opportunity to defend himself (on liability and/or quantum). So the making of a direction, which would restore the defendant's obligation to pay damages, is only prejudicial to him if his right to a fair opportunity to defend himself has been compromised.

70. Thus, although on a literal construction of section 33(1), it appears to be relevant to the exercise of the discretion that the defendant would suffer the financial prejudice of having to pay damages if the arbitrary time limit were to be disapplied, Parliament cannot have intended that that financial prejudice, as such, should be taken into account. That is because, in fairness and justice, the defendant ought to pay the damages if, having had

a fair opportunity to defend himself, he is found liable. If having to pay the damages is not a relevant prejudice under section 33(1), it cannot be relevant either as one of the circumstances of the case ...

72. A claimant's position is different. He has a substantive right, his cause of action, but he cannot proceed with it because of the operation of section 11. He has therefore been prejudiced by the loss of the right to enforce his cause of action. That prejudice is greatly reduced if he has a good claim over against his solicitor. In a case where the defendant has suffered some forensic or procedural prejudice, which will diminish his ability to defend himself, it will be relevant to consider that the claimant has another remedy. But the fact that the claimant has a claim over will not necessarily mean that the direction should be refused. It might still be fair and just that the defendant remains in the frame. It is the defendant who has, ex hypothesi, committed the tort and, as Lord Denning MR pointed out in *Firman v Ellis* [1978] QB 886, 906, it is his insurer who has received the premiums in respect of the relevant risk. So the fact that the claimant will not suffer financially in the end is relevant but not determinative.

73. It seems to me that, in the exercise of the discretion, the basic question to be asked is whether it is fair and just in all the circumstances to expect the defendant to meet this claim on the merits, notwithstanding the delay in commencement. The length of the delay will be important, not so much for itself as to the effect it has had. To what extent has the defendant been disadvantaged in his investigation of the claim and/or the assembly of evidence, in respect of the issues of both liability and quantum? But it will also be important to consider the reasons for the delay. Thus, there may be some unfairness to the defendant due to the delay in issue but the delay may have arisen for so excusable a reason, that, looking at the matter in the round, on balance, it is fair and just that the action should proceed. On the other hand, the balance may go in the opposite direction, partly because the delay has caused procedural disadvantage and unfairness to the defendant and partly because the reasons for the delay (or its length) are not good ones.

74. Although the delay referred to in section 33(3) is the delay after the expiry of the primary limitation period, it will always be relevant to consider when the defendant knew that a claim was to be made against him and also the opportunities he has had to investigate the claim and collect evidence: see *Donovan v Gwentoys Ltd* [1990] 1 WLR 472. If, as here, a defendant has had early notification of a claim and every possible opportunity to investigate and to collect evidence, some delay after the expiry of three years will have had no prejudicial effect.'

Per Sir Andrew Morritt VC: '81. The consequence of the disapplication of section 11 will be that there may be a trial of the claimant's claim on its merits notwithstanding the delay in commencing the proceedings. Has that delay caused prejudice to the defendant in its defence? If so, does it outweigh the prejudice to the claimant of being denied a trial at all? In addition the court will need to consider all the circumstances of the case and in particular the other aspects of the case enumerated in subsection (3).

82. In that context it does not appear to me that the loss of a limitation defence is regarded as a head of prejudice to the defendant at all; it is merely the obverse of the disapplication of section 11 which is assumed. It is this consideration which, in my view, accounts for and justifies the marked reluctance of the courts, as demonstrated by the judgments to which Smith LJ has referred in detail, to have regard to the loss of a limitation defence.'

Cairns-Jones and others v Christie Tyler South Wales West Division Ltd

Limitation Act 1980, s 11, s 14, s 33

Court of Appeal   [2010] EWCA Civ 1642

The claimants had been employed by the defendant in upholstery work involving the use of staple guns. They had developed High Alarm Vibration Syndrome, which they claimed had resulted from using the guns. A further three claimants had brought similar claims against the defendant. It was accepted that two of those claims had been brought in time. A further 26 such claims had been notified to the defendant but not yet litigated. The defendant had ceased trading and gone into administrative receivership in 2005.

C1, who was 66 at the time of the hearing before the judge, was employed until November 2003. He was found to have actual knowledge by way of a medical report dated May 2007 but constructive knowledge in 1998. He issued his claim form on 18 December 2007. C2, aged 57 at the time of the hearing, was employed until July/August 2005. He moved away from upholstery for a short period. He was found to have actual knowledge by way of a medical report dated August 2007 but constructive knowledge in 1998 at the latest. His claim was deemed issued on 24 September 2008. C3, aged 43 at the time of hearing, was employed until the early summer 2001 as an upholsterer. He was found to have actual knowledge by way of a medical report dated 22 June 2007 but constructive knowledge in early 1999. His claim was deemed issued on 24 September 2008.

The judge declined to exercise his discretion to allow the claims to continue. He held that, whilst the extent of delay was variable, it was in all three cases unexplained. Although the delay between times of actual knowledge and expiration of the limitation period was limited, there was considerable delay from the times of constructive knowledge. He held that the defendant would have great difficulty in locating witnesses of fact and his conclusion was: 'it will be intensely difficult for the defendant fairly to meet the claims brought against it'. He took the view that, as the claims were of dubious prospects on liability and of modest value as to quantum, proportionality told against allowing them to continue.

The claimants appealed contending that the judge had: (1) failed to take the appropriate period of time for considering the question of delay under s 33(3)(a) as the time from the expiry of the limitation period and not the date of actual or constructive knowledge; (2) underestimated the strength of the claims; (3) overestimated the difficulty that the defendant would face in defending the claims; and (4) erred in his approach to proportionality in failing to attach weight to the fact that the claims were lead cases in a group action.

Held:

(i)   It was accepted that the judgment did not specifically focus on the period of delay from the expiry of the limitation period. Insofar as the judgment suggested that the judge thought the issue of delay had to be considered from the date of actual or constructive knowledge for the purposes of s 33(3)(a), that was an error of the most technical kind. The delay with respect to those periods was highly material in assessing the forensic prejudice to the defendant, and the judge was entitled to take account of it in his consideration of all the circumstances in s 33(3) (*Donovan v Gwentoys Ltd* (p412) applied). The judge had recognised, when considering s 33(3)(b), that the relatively limited delay between the expiry of the limitation period and the commencement of the action was of no real significance in the instant case and it did not prejudice the defendant.

(ii)   The judge had concluded that the overwhelming measure of liability would turn on detailed evidence relating to the nature, degree and frequency of exposure to vibrating tools. He had been entitled to conclude that there was considerable uncertainty as to whether the claims would succeed, supported by the claimants' expert's preliminary view that the claimants were in a low risk category. The judge had been entitled to distinguish between a claim which was intrinsically strong and one which depended on the uncertainties of description of detail as to each claimant's system of work many years after the cause of action arose.

(iii)   The judge had uncontradicted evidence that the delay would cause serious problems in investigating the claims. He had been entitled to draw on his own experience to conclude that the difficulties would be very substantial.

(iv)   The judge had recognised that two cases would be going forward in any event, and had weighed that in the balance. The fact that the claimants represented the lead cases was not central to the issue of proportionality. The judge was considering the costs of the claims against the prospect of substantial damages. He rejected the argument that the lead cases would not require significant further expenditure on the basis that each claim was very much dependent on its own facts and the defendant would have to identify particular witnesses with respect to each claim. Balanced against the value of the claims, his conclusion on the issue was a legitimate one.

Appeal dismissed.

The Caliph

Limitation   **Maritime Conventions Act 1911**

Bargrave Deane J   **[1912] P 213; 82 LJP 27; 107 LT 274;**
28 TLR 597; 12 Asp MLC 244

On 16 December 1910, Joseph Williams, owner and master of the ketch Glyndwr, was drowned in a collision that took place between the Glyndwr and the defendant's steam trawler Caliph. On 12 May 1912 the claimant (his widow) issued a writ for damages (1) for the loss of the ketch and (2) on behalf of her children as dependants under the Fatal Accidents Act 1846.

The defendants admitted liability for the value of the ketch, but pleaded that the dependency claim was statute barred as the writ had not been issued within the one year time limit set by the 1846 Act. The Maritime Conventions Act 1911 came into force on 16 December 1911.

Held: s 8 of the Maritime Conventions Act 1911, where it applied as in this case, effectively extended to two years the one-year time limit otherwise applicable under s 3 of the Fatal Accidents Act 1846.

Carlisle v Associated British Ports and another

Limitation Act 1980, s 33

Court of Appeal   **Lexis, 18 November 1987**

The claimant (Mr Carlisle) was employed by Sutcliffes as a decker. On 24 February 1983 sets of steel were being loaded on to a ship by a crane operated by a servant of the first defendants, Associated British Ports. One of the sets became entangled and then fell, trapping the claimant's right foot. Two of his toes had to be amputated.

His statement of claim against the first defendants was served in November 1984. Their defence in January 1985 blamed Sutcliffes. A summons to add Sutcliffes as second defendants was issued on 11 November 1986. The file was overlooked on being passed to a trainee legal executive, and the summons was not served on Sutcliffes. When the amended writ was served on them on 30 March 1987, they applied to set aside the order adding them to the proceedings. At a preliminary trial, it was accepted that the claimant's solicitors would be liable to him in negligence for failing to add Sutcliffes as defendants within time. It was argued that this delay had caused to prejudice to them, because they had been made parties to third party proceedings. Sutcliffes asserted that they would face evidential difficulties in investigating the more wide-ranging claim pleaded by the claimant, alleging not only vicarious liability but also primary negligence over failures to provide a platform or proper supervision or a safe place and system of work. At a preliminary trial, French J in effect refused to exercise discretion under s 33 of the Limitation Act 1980 against Sutcliffes in favour of the claimant who appealed.

Held:

(i)   It could not be contended that the judge wrongly had regard to a matter which possessed no weight when he decided that there was substance in the second defendants' evidential difficulties: s 33(3)(b).

(ii) (per Ralph Gibson LJ) '... some judges might have been persuaded that it was equitable to take a different course with reference to section 33. But, as the Court of Appeal has said many times, the fact that each one of the judges there sitting would have taken a different view does not entitle the court to hear in substance an appeal on an issue of fact from the exercise of the judge's discretion': s 33(1).

Cartledge and others v E Jopling & Sons Ltd

Limitation Act 1939, s 2   **Accrual of cause of action**

House of Lords   **[1963] 1 All ER 341; [1963] AC 758;**
[1963] 2 WLR 210; 107 SJ 73;
[1963] 1 Lloyd's Rep 1

For many years, Fred Cartledge and six others were employed as steel dressers at the defendants' steel works. The atmosphere became laden with dust from the particles of fractured sand or silica. From 1939 until October 1950 the defendants failed to provide effective ventilation. Without most of them knowing or suspecting it then, the seven men all had pneumoconiosis before October 1950. Between 1950 and 1955 they were informed of this on various dates. The seven claimants (the dressers or their personal representatives) commenced court action on 1 October 1956.

The Court of Appeal upheld the decision of Glyn-Jones J that the cases were statute barred. The claimants appealed.

Held:

(i) A cause of action accrues as soon as a wrongful act causes personal injury beyond what can be regarded as negligible – that is, real damage as distinct from purely minimal damage. Further injury arising at a later date from the same act does not give rise to a further cause of action.

(ii) Time under s 2 of the Limitation Act 1939 ran from 'the date on which the cause of action accrued', even where this was before the injury was known to, or could have been discovered by, the sufferer.

(iii) As all the seven steel dressers had sustained lung damage before October 1950, the claimants' cases were statute barred.

Casey v J Murphy & Sons

Limitation Act 1939, s 2A, s 2D

Court of Appeal   **[1979] CLY 1668**

From 1972 to 1974 the claimant (Mr Casey) was a labourer employed by the defendants in work that brought him into contact with epoxy resin. By December 1973 he knew that he had dermatitis, and by May 1974 he knew that this was due to his contact with epoxy resin during this work. He did not know until February 1979 that he might in law have a cause of action. His writ was promptly issued then.

At a preliminary trial on limitation, Boreham J held that the claim was statute barred. The claimant appealed.

Held:

(i) His lack of knowledge that in law he had a claim did not prevent the running of the three-year period under s 2A of the Limitation Act 1939.

(ii)   The court could take this lack of knowledge into account under s 2D. However the claimant's knowledge of the nature and cause of his dermatitis, (in respect of which, generally, there had been previous litigation) and the fact that as a member of a trade union he had access to legal advice even if he did not take it, meant that it would be inequitable to allow the action to proceed. The prejudice to the claimant was outweighed by the prejudice to the defendants because of the delay.

Cecil v Bayat

CPR 6.5, 7.6

Court of Appeal   **[2011] EWCA Civ 135;**
[2011] 1 WLR 3086; [2011] CP Rep 25

Most of the parties had been involved in proceedings in the United States arising out of a project to set up a telecommunications network in Afghanistan. The US proceedings had been dismissed of the court's own motion. The claimants later issued a claim form in England regarding the same dispute, claiming substantial damages for breach of contract, fraudulent misrepresentation and conspiracy. The claimants sought an extension of time for service of the claim form under CPR 7.6(2) on the basis that they needed to arrange funding for the proceedings, having exhausted their funds during the US proceedings. A six-month extension was granted, which took the time for service beyond the limitation period. Near the end of that period the claimants' application for permission to serve out of the jurisdiction was refused, and a further six-month extension of time for service was granted. Three weeks before that period expired, the claimants obtained permission to serve out of the jurisdiction and permission under CPR 6.15 to serve by electronic means.

The defendants unsuccessfully applied to set aside the orders extending time for service and to set aside permission for the claimants to serve the claim form by alternative means. The judge held that, in the unusual circumstances, the claimants' lack of funding was a good reason for an extension of time, and that service through official channels under the Hague Convention on the Service Abroad of Judicial and Extrajudicial Documents in Civil or Commercial Matters 1965 or by normal means would not bring the proceedings to the defendants' attention promptly.

Held:

(i)   It was not for the claimants to unilaterally decide to postpone service of their claim form; they should have served it in the period of its initial validity, and, if they were not in a financial position to proceed immediately, they should have applied for a stay. Any forensic difficulties caused by the financial constraints of the claimants should have been the subject of case management by the court (*Hoddinott v Persimmon Homes (Wessex) Ltd* (p477) considered).

(ii)   The position was analogous to where a claimant was waiting for an expert's report, as in *Glass v Surrendran* (one of the four appeals in *Collier v Williams* (p380). These were reasons to extend time for service of the particulars of claim, not the claim itself. Nor was the absence of negligence on behalf of a claimant's solicitors in itself a reason to extend time for service.

(iii)   A claimant applying under CPR 7.6(2) for an extension of time made within the period of validity, in a case in which the limitation defence of the defendant would or might be prejudiced, should have to show that he had taken reasonable steps, as was required under CPR 7.6(3) on an application for an extension made outside the period of validity of the claim form; it would be curious if a different test were to apply (*Hoddinott* considered, *Aktas v Adepta* (p296) applied).

(iv)   The judge had been wrong to find that it was not financially viable for the claimant to commence and serve proceedings without having funding in place for the whole proceedings. Further, the judge had not addressed appropriately the limitation consequences of his order; the primary question was whether, if an extension of time was granted, the defendant would or might be deprived of a limitation defence. It was relevant that a refusal to extend time might deprive a claimant of a good claim, but the stronger that claim, the more important was the defendant's limitation defence, which should not be circumvented by an extension of time for serving a claim form save in exceptional circumstances. If an extension is sought beyond four months after the expiry of the limitation period, the claimant is effectively asking the court to disturb a defendant who is by now entitled to assume that his rights can no longer be disputed. A defendant's right only to be sued within this period was fundamental.

(v) There had been no good reason to grant either extension of time. The judges below had erred in doing so.

(vi) Service of proceedings was more than a means of bringing proceedings to a defendant's attention; it was an exercise of the court's power, and in a case involving service out of the jurisdiction was an exercise of sovereignty within a foreign state. As that amounted to interference with the sovereignty of that state, service on a party to the Hague Convention by an alternative method under CPR 6.15 should be regarded as exceptional. Therefore, whilst it might be a relevant consideration that service by an alternative method would be speedier than service under the Hague Convention, it was generally not a sufficient reason for granting service by an alternative method. In the instant case, the only reason for urgency arose from the claimant's delay in seeking and obtaining permission to serve out of the jurisdiction, which was not a good reason for granting permission to use alternative methods of service.

Appeal allowed.

Chambers v Southern Domestic Electrical Services Ltd

CPR 6.7 **Human Rights Act 1998, s 3**

ECHR, Art 6

Court of Appeal **[2002] EWCA Civ 933; [2002] 1 WLR 3174;**
[2002] 3 All ER 813

See *Anderton v Clwyd County Council* (B) (p303)

Chantrey Vellacott v The Convergence Group plc and another

CPR 17.4

Court of Appeal **[2005] EWCA Civ 290; LTL 16/03/2005;**
(2005) Times 25 April

The defendant had retained the claimant to provide tax and accountancy advice in relation to a proposed restructuring. The claimant brought proceedings for its fees. The defendant pleaded a defence and counterclaim on the basis that the claimant had performed its duties prior to but pursuant to the retainer negligently. It subsequently applied to re-amend to plead numerous allegations of negligence relating to the 12-month period after the admitted date of the claimant's original retention. The master rejected the application and the defendant appealed. The judge held that the proposed allegations introduced a 'new claim' within the meaning of CPR 17.4.2 and declined to allow the re-amendments as they did not arise from the same or substantially the same facts as the matters already in issue. The defendant appealed again.

Held:

(i) The pleading before re-amendment did not disclose a claim in relation to the later 12-month period. The expression 'at all material times' meant material to the period of breach set out in the pleading as was then, and did not include the later period. CPR 17.4.2 therefore applied.

(ii) The question of whether or not the new claim arose out of the same facts as the old claim was essentially a qualitative judgment for the court.

(iii) Whilst the appeal court should be slow to interfere with a judge's decision on a matter of this kind, which was essentially a question of impression, that impression nevertheless had to be informed by a reasoned assessment of the relevant factors.

(iv) It was not clear that in the present case the judge had taken account of the relevant matters (*Welsh Development Agency v Redpath* (p709) considered).

(v) The pleading described a continuous course of action over a period of three years prior to the retainer, and in particular cumulative delay. In this context, although the proposed re amendments inevitably alleged facts not already pleaded, they rose out of essentially the same facts as they stemmed from the same retainer and arose in relation to the same matter, the proposed restructuring. It would be artificial to consider the later advice without considering the earlier advice.

Appeal allowed.

Chappell v Cooper

Player v Bruguiere

Limitation Act 1939, s 2D

Renewal of writ **RSC Ord 6, r 8(2)**

Court of Appeal **[1980] 2 All ER 463; [1980] 1 WLR 958; 124 SJ 544**

CHAPPELL

On 11 August 1971 the claimant (Ronald Chappell) sustained personal injuries when the motorcycle he was riding collided with a car driven by the defendant. His writ was issued on 25 June 1974 but not served. In December 1976 his solicitors obtained an ex parte order extending the validity of the writ, but after service the defendant's solicitors obtained an order setting aside the writ and dismissing the action.

On 24 May 1978 the claimant's second solicitors issued a second writ against the defendant who pleaded a limitation defence which was tried as a preliminary issue. Bush J ordered that this second action should continue pursuant to s 2D of the Limitation Act 1939 as amended. The defendant appealed.

PLAYER

On 9 December 1971 the claimant (Marjorie Player) was injured when she was knocked down by a car driven by the defendant. Her writ was issued on 6 December 1974 but not served.

On 4 April 1978 the claimant's new solicitors issued a second writ against the defendant who pleaded limitation and applied pursuant to RSC Ord 18, r 19 for the second writ to be struck out. The defendant appealed against the decision of Park J who, following the Court of Appeal decision in *Walkley v Precision Forgings Ltd* (p705), had directed pursuant to s 2D of the 1939 Act that s 2A should not apply.

After the Court of Appeal's decision in *Walkley*'s case was reversed by the House of Lords, on 13 June 1979 the claimant made an ex parte application for leave to extend the validity of the first writ. Kenneth Jones J upheld the district registrar's refusal to grant the application. The claimant appealed.

Held: (both cases) the House of Lords had decided in *Walkley*'s case that if a claimant starts but then does not proceed with an action, it is not open to him thereafter to seek to take advantage of the provisions of s 2D of the Limitation Act 1939 in a second action. Thus the court's discretion under s 2D is not wholly unfettered. The defendants' appeals must be allowed, and in both cases the directives that the provisions of s 2A be disapplied must be set aside.

Held: (*Player* only) the writ expired on 6 December 1975. The second period of 12 months, the maximum for which a timeous extension might be allowed under RSC Ord 6, r 8(2), would have run out on 5 December 1976. As the affidavit in support of the application to renew was not sworn until 3½ years after the expiry date, there was no power to grant the extension sought.

Per Roskill LJ: 'But it has been strenuously argued that as a result of the introduction of the Limitation Act 1975 *Heaven*'s case is no longer binding, and that it is open to this court, and indeed necessary for this court, wholly to reconsider its practice (for this is basically a matter of practice rather than substantive law) regarding granting leave to extend the time for service of the writ which has ceased to be valid because it has not been timeously served. It is said that it is now open to us to reconsider the position and to grant the requisite extension of time in any case where it seems equitable for us to do so, notwithstanding that so to do would be to deprive a defendant of the accrued benefit of a period of limitation prescribed by the Limitation Act 1939, as subsequently amended. The argument is designed to put a claimant who has failed timeously to serve his writ and who ex hypothesi is unable to obtain the benefit of s 2D in the same position as if he had obtained that benefit, because although he cannot successfully pursue a second action, as he cannot have the relevant limitation provisions "disapplied", he nonetheless, so the argument runs, can be allowed to go on with his first action and serve that writ many, many months, or indeed years, after that writ ought to have been but was not served.

There is one short answer to this submission. That was given by counsel for the defendant at the outset of his submissions. That answer turns on the true construction of RSC Ord 6, r 8(2) which provides:

"Where a writ has not been served on a defendant the Court may by order extend the validity of the writ from time to time for such period, not exceeding twelve months at any one time, beginning with the day next following that on which it would otherwise expire, as may be specified in the order, if an application for extension is made to the Court before that day or such later day (if any) as the Court may allow."

Let me give the dates. The writ in the action of *Player v Bruguiere* was issued on 6th December 1974. The 12 months therefore expired on 5th December 1975, and the second period of 12 months, which would be the maximum for which a timeous extension might be allowed, would have run out on 5th December 1976. But the affidavit in support of this application was not sworn until 13th June 1979, some 3½ years after that last date. In view of those dates it seems to me clear, with all respect to counsel for the plaintiff, beyond doubt that we have no power under the rules to grant the extension sought.

That is enough to dispose of this appeal, but having regard to the importance of the issue I think it right not only to rest my judgment on that conclusion. It was strenuously argued that the foundation of Megaw J's decision was that in 1965 there was an absolute entitlement (save only for the provisions of the Limitation Act 1963 which are not presently relevant) on the part of a defendant to a three year limitation period, and that, save in very exceptional circumstances, the court would not at that date grant an extension the effect of which would be to deprive him of that accrued right. That, it is said, was the foundation of the judge's decision. It is argued that since 1975 and because of the provisions of s 2D there is now no absolute entitlement on the part of a defendant to the period of limitation. The court has, subject to the decision in *Walkley*'s case, a discretion to "disapply" the relevant limitation period. Therefore it is argued that the foundation for *Heaven*'s case having gone we are free to reconsider, and should reconsider, the practice of the court ...

It is not and would not be right for this court to by-pass their Lordships' decision by altering the practice that has long existed both before and since *Heaven*'s case by granting long extensions of time to serve a writ which has not been timeously served, even if that were permissible under RSC Ord 6, r 8(2). The principles on which extensions of time for the service of a writ beyond the initial 12 months can be granted have long been laid down. Those principles seem to me to remain unaffected. Accordingly, if a plaintiff who has failed timeously to issue and serve his writ wishes to obtain an extension under RSC Ord 6, r 8, he must comply with the principles and the practice under which the court grants such extensions. If he cannot do so, and also cannot avail himself of the benefits and privileges extended by the 1975 Act that is his misfortune and he must look for redress elsewhere than to the proposed defendant, if indeed such other redress is open to him.'

Walkley v Precision Forgings Ltd (p705) and *Heaven v Road and Rail Wagons Ltd* [1965] 2 All ER 409 applied.

NB: *Walkley* was overruled in *Horton v Sadler* (p482).

Chare v Fairclough and another

CPR 7

Treacy J   **[2003] EWHC 180 (QB)**

The claimant's husband was killed in a road traffic accident in Saudi Arabia in June 1997. The claimant brought proceedings against the first defendant (the driver of the vehicle in which he husband was travelling) and the second defendant (the first defendant's employer). In March 1999 the claimant invited the second defendant to nominate an English address for service, but it declined to do so. On 26 October 1999 permission was given to the claimant to issue and serve proceedings out of the jurisdiction. An order was also made for an acknowledgement of service to be filed 24 days after service was also made. In mid-November 1999 she lodged the relevant documents with the High Court to effect service in Saudi Arabia through the Foreign Office using the British Consular. In May 2000 she reminded the Foreign Office that she had yet to receive confirmation of service. She did so again in July 2000. Service was not actually effected until June 2002.

The second defendant applied to have service set aside and the claim struck out. The master refused the application, holding that the claimant satisfied the criteria for extension of time for service at CPR 7.6(3). The second defendant appealed:

Held:

(i)   It was for the claimant to effect service, not the court. Although service was to be through the Consular, the responsibility to effect it remained on the claimant. CPR 7.6(3)(a) was therefore not applicable.

(ii)   CPR 7.6(3)(b) needed to be considered in the context of the entirety of the time frame from when permission to serve outside the jurisdiction was given.

(iii)   In this case the claimant had not taken all reasonable steps to serve the claim form as required by CPR 7.6(3)(b). She took no step at all until 10 days after the expiry of the period for service. This failure was particularly glaring when the claimant had been advised by her agents to expect an acknowledgment of service by February 2000.

(iv)   'Promptness' in CPR 7.6(3)(c) should be given its ordinary meaning of 'readily, quickly, at once'; the term conveyed a substantial degree of urgency. To assess it the court needed to look at all the circumstances of the case, including the history prior to the expiry of the validity period.

(v) The master had given insufficient weight to the criterion of promptness when properly construed and had erred in limiting himself to considering the claimant's actions only after expiry of the validity period.

(vi) The claimant therefore failed to satisfy any of the relevant criteria.

Appeal allowed. Claim dismissed.

Chaudhri v Post Office

CPR 6.7

Jack J   **LTL 26/4/2001**

The claimant suffered a back injury on 15 May 1997 whilst working for the defendant. Proceedings were issued on 12 May 2000. The court was requested not to serve the claim form until the particulars of claim were available. In the event, the claimant's solicitor chose to serve the claim form himself via DX. The defendant was not in fact a member of DX. Realising the DX might not have worked, he served the particulars without the claim form. The claim form was set aside as it had been served late. The claimant appealed.

Held:

(i) The time limit in CPR 6.3 applied.

(ii) On the evidence the judge had been correct to find that the court had not served the claim form.

(iii) Neither 7.6(3)(a) or (b) were satisfied. It could not be said that the claimant had taken all reasonable steps to serve the claim form but had been unable to do so. The problems with service were self-inflicted. Further, the application to extend time was not made promptly.

(iv) There were no grounds to extend time. Claim dismissed.

Chellaram and another v Chellaram and others

CPR 6

Lawrence Collins J   **[2002] EWHC 632 (Ch);**
[2003] 3 All ER 17; LTL 17/4/2002

The claimants claimed for various breaches of trust. They received permission to serve outside the jurisdiction in respect of some defendants, but in the case of the fourth defendant purported to serve upon his last known address in England. The defendants applied for alternative orders that (a) the orders for permission for service outside the jurisdiction be set aside, (b) that service had no been properly effected, (c) the court had no jurisdiction over the defendants, or should not exercise it.

Held:

(i) All defendants were all domiciled and resident outside England.

(ii) The fourth defendant could not be validly served at his last known address in England as he had no such residence. Further, it remained a fundamental principle of English procedure and jurisprudence, surviving the advent of the CPR, that a defendant could only be served with an originating process within the jurisdiction if he was present in the jurisdiction at the time of actual or deemed service.

(iii)   Service out of the jurisdiction could not be justified.

(iv)   In any event India was a more appropriate forum.

Orders for service set aside.

City & General (Holborn) Ltd v Structure Tone Ltd

Limitation Act 1980, s 29(5)	**CPR 7**
Court of Appeal	**[2010] EWCA Civ 911;**
	[2010] BLR 639; 131 Con LR 1

On 16 January 2009 the claimant, the developer of a building in London, issued proceedings against the defendant, his insurers, in respect of damage allegedly suffered as a result of flooding in the basement discovered in April 2002, the collapse of a crane on an adjoining site on 18 January 2003, and the infestation of water systems with bacteria which was discovered in May 2004. It followed from this chronology that any cause of action in respect of the flooding was likely to be statute barred; any cause of action in respect of the crane collapse was just in time when proceedings were issued; and any cause of action in respect of the infestation was in time if it was a separate cause of action and time ran from the discovery of the infestation. The claimant did not serve the claim form within the permitted four-month period, instead successfully applying within that period to extend time for service. The reason given by the claimant was that it could not establish with any certainty the proper extent of its loss and damage until the building contractor's claim had been determined by arbitration.

The extension was granted on a without notice basis. However, the defendant successfully applied for it to be set aside, the court holding that there was no good reason for failing to serve the claim form in time and that it was arguable that if an extension was granted the defendant would be deprived of a limitation defence.

The claimant appealed, submitting that (1) the judge should have considered each of the three claims separately and come to a separate conclusion about limitation in respect of each claim; (2) the judge was wrong to hold that the flood claim was statute barred, because a new cause of action arose every time more water entered the construction site causing fresh damage; and (3) the defendant had acknowledged the flood and crane claims for the purposes of s 29(5) by a letter in which it had made offers in relation to those claims.

Held:

(i)   The judge was never asked to consider each head of claim separately and it was too late on appeal to ask the court to do so for the first time. Both parties contended for an all or nothing approach and the judge could not possibly be criticised for adopting the same approach.

(ii)   In any event, it was enough for a defendant to show that he might be deprived of a defence of limitation if time for service of a claim form was extended (*Hashtroodi v Hancock* (p466) and *Hoddinott v Persimmon Homes (Wessex) Ltd* (p477) followed). It was inappropriate to attempt to decide debatable issues of limitation on an interlocutory application for an extension of time for service of a claim form. A claimant could always begin a fresh action in which, if a time bar was asserted, it could be adjudicated upon.

(iii)   The question whether successive water ingresses causing fresh damage would give rise to successive causes of action against a tortfeasor and its insurers was not straightforward (*Darley Main Colliery Co v Mitchell* (1886) LR 11 App Cas 127 HL and *Homburg Houtimport BV v Agrosin Private Ltd (The Starsin)* [2003] UKHL 12, [2004] 1 AC

715 considered). However, it was clear that the judge did not purport to come to any conclusion on that issue and therefore the claimant was not precluded, whether by issue estoppel or otherwise, from making that point in any second action in respect of water ingress if the defendant took the limitation point in such a second action. There was no reason for interfering with the judge's exercise of discretion.

(iv)   The defendant's letter made an open offer of £25,000 in respect of the water ingress claim of £1,197,638.89 and an open offer of £24,022 in respect of the crane damage claim of £552,291. It was not immediately obvious that an open offer of a small amount, in response to a claim of a much larger amount, was an acknowledgment of a claim in that much larger amount. It might be said that it was at least an acknowledgment of the claim in the smaller amount, but the question remained whether it would be right to extend time for service of a claim form merely to enable that much smaller amount to be claimed. Further, s 29(5) only applied where a right of action had accrued 'to recover any debt or other liquidated pecuniary claim' and these claims were not, on the face of it, claims for a debt or other liquidated claims. Again, it would not be appropriate to extend the time for service of the claim form in the instant case so as to enable a doubtful response to the limitation defence to be taken. If it was correct, it could be taken in any second action which the claimant wished to pursue.

(v)   The points regarding limitation were additional to the judge's central reasoning which was that there was no good reason for the claim form not to have been served in time. The judge was right about this.

Appeal dismissed.

Clack v Thames Television Ltd

Limitation Act 1980, s 33

Hawksworth J   LTL 16/9/204

This was a claim brought on behalf of a deceased's estate. The deceased worked for the defendant from 1968 to 1991 and in doing so came into contact with asbestos. He became ill and died from mesothelioma in 1993. His widow knew in July 1993 that this was a result from asbestos exposure and that he was exposed by the defendant and possibly two other employers. In 1994 she sought advice from solicitors, who advised her that it might be difficult to sue multiple employers. This, coupled with her fragile mental state consequent to having dealt with her husband's illness and death, deterred her from pursuing a claim. In 2002, following publicity of the House of Lords decision in *Fairchild v Glenhaven Funeral Services Ltd* [2002] UKLH 22, she became aware that she could pursue one employer notwithstanding exposure by several. She then consulted solicitors and proceedings were issued in August 2003.

A preliminary hearing was ordered to deal with the issue of whether the court should disapply the limitation period under s 33.

Held:

(i)   The primary limitation period expired in July 1996. The claimant had sought legal advice well before then.

(ii)   There were several factors in the instant case in the claimant's favour:

(a)   although the delay was substantial, issue of proceedings within the limitation period would still have involved investigating matters that had occurred 20–30 years before. The defendant's evidence failed to show that the effect of the delay on the cogency of the evidence was more than negligible and a fair trial as still possible;

(b)   the delay was mainly due to the poor advice the claimant received in combination with her emotional state at the time; and

(c)   the claim was instituted promptly and reasonably once the merits of the action against the defendant were discovered.

(iii)   On the evidence the defendant had not suffered any prejudice in relation to potential joint tortfeasors.

(iv)   The defendant was not prejudiced by the possibility of a larger award of interest, which could in any event be reduced to reflect the delay.

(v)   The increase in damages generally following *Heil v Rankin* and *Wells v Wells* could not legitimately be put in the defendant's favour.

(vi)   The fact that the defendant was now potentially liable for an uplift on conditional fee agreement costs could not assist it. It could be argued that the withdrawal of legal aid benefited defendants by discouraging claims from the start and removing a situation where the defendant could not recover costs even if the succeeded on liability.

(vii)   If the claim remained barred the claimant would suffer substantial prejudice in losing an apparently strong claim of substantial value when it was far from clear that she had a remedy against her previous solicitors.

(viii) In the circumstances it was equitable to disapply the limitation period.

Re Clark v Forbes Stuart (Thames Street) Ltd (intended action)

Limitation Act 1963, s 1, s 7

Court of Appeal   **[1964] 2 All ER 282; [1964] 1 WLR 836**

On 12 October 1960 the claimant (Francis Clark) slipped on some premises at Billingsgate Market where he had gone to collect a load of fish. He alleged that his injuries were due to the floor being worn, smooth and slippery. In May 1961 his solicitors notified his claim to Forbes Stuart (Billingsgate), Ltd whose solicitors entered into negotiations without taking the point that their clients were not the occupiers. On 7 February 1963 the claimant's solicitors issued a writ against Forbes Stuart (Billingsgate), Ltd. After serving it, they were telephoned by solicitors who said: 'Forbes Stuart (Billingsgate), Ltd are not the occupiers; the occupiers really are an associated company, Forbes Stuart (Thames Street), Ltd. You have got the wrong defendants'.

Mocatta J refused the claimant's ex parte application under the Limitation Act 1963 for leave to start a new action against Forbes Stuart (Thames Street), Ltd. The claimant appealed.

Held:

(i)   As this was an ex parte application, the decision could be only provisional.

(ii)   The identity of the occupier was a material fact of a decisive character within s 7(3)(c) of the Limitation Act 1963.

(iii)   While there was doubt as to whether the claimant 'had taken all such action as it was reasonable to have taken for the purpose of ascertaining' this fact in compliance with s 7(5)(b), there was enough evidence for the purpose of this ex parte application to enable leave to be granted.

NB: It is submitted that a similar result would now be reached under s 11(4) and s 14 of the Limitation Act 1980. See *Simpson v Norwest Holst Southern Limited* (p648).

Clarke v Barber

Limitation Act 1980, s 11   **Animals Act 1971, s 2(2)**

Manchester County Court (Recorder Berkley QC)   **CLY 02/464**

The claimant was injured when a dog bit off the top of his finger. Proceedings were issued three years and nine months after the incident. The claim was pleaded in negligence and under the 1971 Act. The defendant raised limitation at trial. The claimant conceded that proceedings in relation to the claim in negligence were out of time, but argued that a six-year limit applied to the statutory claim.

Held:

(i)   Section 11 applied to actions involving a breach of duty, negligence or nuisance. This implied a requirement of a breach of duty causing the injury rather than merely the infringement of a legal right (*Stubbings v Webb* (p677) applied).

(ii) The cause of action under the 1971 Act was one of strict liability. Once a claimant had established the three requirements in s 2(2) liability followed. It did not involve the defendant breaching any duty as the 1971 Act imposed none. The applicable period was therefore six rather than three years.

Preliminary issue decided in the claimant's favour.

NB: The authors would respectfully question the correctness of this decision.

Clarkson v Modern Foundries Ltd

Limitation Act 1939, s 2   **Causation**

Donovan J   **[1958] 1 All ER 33; [1957] 1 WLR 1210**

From 1940 to 1951 the claimant (John Clarkson) was employed as a metal dresser in the defendants' iron foundry. He breathed silica particles from the atmosphere of the fettling and dressing shop. In May 1951 he was found to be suffering from pneumoconiosis. In September 1951 he went into hospital.

His writ was issued on 19 August 1955. The defendants pleaded that any cause of action which accrued prior to 19 August 1949 was statute barred. A full trial was held at which the defendants were found to have been in breach of statutory duty. The medical evidence was that each year from 1940 to 1951 played its part in producing his diseases and that the two years between August 1949 and August 1951 made a material contribution, which could not be arithmetically assessed, to the severity of the disease which probably already existed.

Held:

(i)   The whole injury had been caused by the defendants' default. The onus was on them to plead successfully limitation as to part of it. All they could show was that an unascertainable part of the injury was inflicted by August 1949.

(ii) The claimant, having established that the last two years of dust exposure had materially contributed to his disease, was entitled to recover damages in full, because it was impossible in this case to distinguish between innocent dust and guilty dust in the quantum of damages.

Claussen v Yeates

Companies Act 1985, s 725(1)   **CPR 6.9, 7.6**

**[2003] EWCA Civ 656;
[2003] 1 WLR 2441; [2003] 3 All ER 129**

See *Cranfield and anor v Bridgegrove* (B) (p389)

Clay v Chamberlain

Limitation Act 1980, s 11, s 33

Cox J   **Unreported**

On 8 July 1997 the claimant suffered serious injuries as a passenger in the defendant's car. The defendant died as a result of the same action. Proceedings were validly issued on 8 July 1997. However, to proceed with the action it was necessary for the claimant to apply within four months for an order that someone represent the defendant's estate. No such application was made and thus the subsequent steps in the litigation were entirely invalid and ineffective. The insurers of the defendant's father (who was the relevant policyholder) also failed to notice the error. They entered a defence and continued to progress the litigation, negotiating a liability settlement of 95/5 in the claimant's favour and making interim payments. A quantum trial was fixed for January 2001 but some six weeks before this the insurers came to appreciate the fact and consequences of the non-appointment of personal representatives. The action was struck out for incurable irregularity.

The claimant issued fresh proceedings in April 2002. On this occasion personal representatives were appointed. The defendant applied to strike out the claim as being statute barred, arguing that *Walkley v Precision Forgings Ltd* (p705) precluded any s 33 discretion. The master distinguished *Walkley* on the grounds that (a) the first action in the present instance was invalid; (b) the parties were not the same in the present first and second actions, appointed personal representatives being distinct from pleaded but non-existent personal representatives; and (c) the defendant's conduct in carrying on the litigation and thus encouraging the claimant to believe that she had a valid action was analogous to an estoppel. He exercised his s 33 discretion in the claimant's favour, finding that the delay was neither reprehensible, long or prejudicial and that the insurers merited criticism for taking the point at so late a stage. The defendant appealed.

Held:

(i)   The master erred in law in holding that there was a difference in the parties that enabled him to distinguish *Walkley*. In each case the defendant was the personal representatives of the deceased.

(ii)   This case could not be said to be plainly indistinguishable from *Walkley* as, whereas *Walkley* referred to a self-inflicted wound, here the insurers materially contributed to the problem.

(iii)   As the first proceedings were ineffective (although not an nullity), this case could not be said to be plainly indistinguishable from *Walkley*.

(iv)   The master was correct in finding that the insurer's conduct fell within the ambit of exceptional circumstances so as to displace the *Walkley* principle. Such circumstances were not limited to misrepresentation or improper conduct. The master was entitled to find that the defendant's conduct, whilst not improper, was sufficiently blameworthy to bring it within the exception.

(v)   There was no basis to interfere with the master's exercise of his discretion.

Appeal dismissed.

NB: *Walkley* was overruled by *Horton v Sadler* (p482).

The Clifford Maersk

Computation of time

Sheen J   [1982] 3 All ER 905; [1982] 1 WLR 1292;
                                                       [1982] LS Gaz R 988; 126 SJ 446;
                                                                      [1982] 2 Lloyd's Rep 251

The claimants were the owners of a cargo of timber carried in the ship Clifford Maersk in June and July 1979. The Hague Rules provided that an action in respect of damage to cargo had to be brought within one year after delivery. The defendants granted a series of extensions, the last of which was 'up to and including 21st June 1981'. 21 June 1981 was a Sunday. The writ was issued on Monday 22 June 1981.

The defendants applied to have it set aside, on the grounds that the extended limitation period had expired.

Held: the rule in the *Pritam Kaur* case – that when a time is prescribed by statute for doing any act, and that act can only be done if the court office is open on the day when the time expires, then if the court office is closed the time is extended to the next day on which the court office is open – should also be applied to cases where the time limit is extended by agreement. Accordingly, the writ had been issued in time.

Pritam Kaur v S Russell & Sons Ltd (p613) applied.

Coad v Cornwall & Isles of Scilly Health Authority

Limitation Act 1980, s 33

Court of Appeal   **[1997] 1 WLR 189; [1997] PIQR P92; [1997] 8 Med LR 154**

On 29 August 1983 the claimant, a nurse, injured her back lifting a patient. A CT scan in 1990 revealed a serious back injury which could prevent her from working again. She contacted solicitors in February 1991. Proceedings were issued in January 1993. Limitation was heard as a preliminary issue. The judge found that the claimant's date of knowledge was at the time of the accident itself. However, having accepted the claimant's evidence that for a long time she did not know that she had a case against the defendant, he held that it was equitable to disapply s 11, not withstanding the significant prejudice to the defendant. The defendant appealed.

Held:

(i)   The assessment of s 33(3)(a) (the length of and reasons for the delay on the part of a claimant) was subjective. There was no basis for inserting a requirement of objectivity into the subsection.

(ii)   There was no statutory requirement that a claimant need provide a reasonable explanation for the delay in issuing proceedings.

(iii) Although there were reservations by two Lord Justices about the decision, the judge was not so plainly wrong the court was bound to interfere.

Appeal dismissed.

Cockburn v Eli Lilly & Co and others (No 1)

Limitation Act 1980, s 11, s 14

Hidden J   **[1991] 1 Med LR 196**

The claimant (Timothy Cockburn), a young man, was first prescribed Opren in March 1981 by his consultant. He continued to take it until it was withdrawn from the market in August 1982, but he could not remember seeing or hearing anything about its withdrawal. He suffered from photosensitivity in his eyes and skin from the summer of 1982 onwards. Neither his consultant nor his general practitioner told him that this was attributable to Opren.

His reading was limited to the sports and TV pages of the *Sun* and the *Daily Mirror*, so he did not read any newspaper articles about Opren. On 19 January 1988, because the racing had just finished on Channel 4, he found himself watching a programme about Opren called 'The

Years Ahead'. Subsequently his mother wrote off for a fact sheet about it. On 2 March 1988 she and he wrote a joint letter to his general practitioner to verify that he had been on Opren.

In April 1988 he consulted solicitors. His writ was issued on 12 August 1988.

Held:

(i)   Accepting his evidence, his actual knowledge of the relevant facts only started in January 1988 when he saw the television programme and was completed in April 1988 when he instructed solicitors: s 11(4).

(ii)   He was a young man of limited intelligence and interest, the width of whose life had been badly contracted by his general ill health since early childhood. He could not reasonably be expected to have acquired such knowledge at any earlier time: s 14(3).

(iii)   Accordingly, his claim was not statute barred: s 11(4).

See *Cockburn v Eli Lilly & Co* (No 2) (below) and *Nash v Eli Lilly & Co* (p568).

Cockburn v Eli Lilly & Co and others (No 2)

Limitation Costs	**RSC Ord 62, r 3(3)**
Court of Appeal	**[1992] 3 Med LR 374**

See *Nash v Eli Lilly & Co* (I) (p568)

Colk v Firth Brown Ltd

Limitation Act 1980, s 14, s 33

Sheffield County Court (Judge Bowers)	**[1999] CLY 463**

The claimant brought an action claiming damages for industrial deafness which he alleged was caused by the high noise levels he experienced whilst working for the defendant from May 1968 to June 1973. He contended that the relevant date of knowledge was November 1995 when he first consulted his GP and a connection between his hearing problem and noise levels at work was realised. The defendant claimed the action was statute barred because the claimant should have realised there was a connection between hearing loss and noise levels, as a result of ear protection being issued by the defendant shortly before termination of his employment in 1973. Further, the defendant contended that the claimant was suffering from hearing difficulties prior to 1995 and, if he had visited his GP, the connection between his deafness and the noise levels would have been made.

Held:

(i)   The claimant could not by reference to s 14 delay the commencement of the primary limitation period beyond the mid-1980s, as any reasonable man in his position would have made the connection between the risk of damage to hearing and the exposure to noise when the ear protection was issued. The date of knowledge was actually in the mid-1980s when the claimant was suffering hearing difficulties, because if he had approached his GP he would have realised his deafness could have been linked to the noise levels at work.

(ii)   Although the claimant could not be criticised for the conduct of his claim after 1995, the claim was now 20 years old and the evidence would be uncertain and changeable. The claimant would be unable to identify any witnesses to corroborate the evidence and it would be impossible to obtain reliable evidence of the level of noise and the effect of the ear protection provided at the time. As a result, discretion would not be exercised under s 33.

Claim dismissed.

Colley v Bard Ltd

Limitation Act 1980, s 33

Court of Appeal   **10 November 1992**

From 1976 to 1980 the claimant (Mrs Catherine Colley) was continuously exposed to noise from industrial sewing machines and other mechanical equipment at the defendants' factory. In 1983 she consulted her doctor about her hearing problems and was referred to a specialist, and in November 1983 she was fitted with a hearing aid. She suffered industrial bilateral deafness to a degree that ultimately her disability was assessed at 10%. The factory closed in 1983.

The claimant did nothing to make a claim until she read a newspaper in 1988 which indicated that industrial deafness could be compensated through the courts. She then consulted solicitors who notified her claim. Her writ was issued on 2 June 1989.

At a preliminary trial, Mr Recorder Briggs sitting in the Sunderland County Court ruled under s 33 of the Limitation Act 1980 that s 11 be disapplied and the action allowed to proceed. At the subsequent trial, he found in favour of the claimant and awarded her agreed damages of £1,750. The defendants appealed.

Held:

(i)   The claimant's explanations for delay, when she had the requisite knowledge to set time running by November 1983 at the latest, of ignorance that a claim was possible and the idea that legal aid was confined to the criminal field, were to be taken into account: s 33(3)(a).

(ii)   The closure of the factory plainly prejudiced the defendants in defending the claim, since the working conditions and noise levels could not be reproduced for scientific assessment. However the case basically turned on whether the recorder was prepared to accept from the claimant and her witness that it was impossible for them to make themselves heard without shouting, even when standing shoulder to shoulder with the person being addressed: s 33(3)(b).

(iii) While some judges might have declined to disapply the provisions of s 11, the recorder's decision did not exceed the generous ambit within which reasonable agreement was possible. It was open to him on the facts: s 33(1).

The defendants' appeal was dismissed.

Collier v Williams

Marshall Rankine and another v Maggs

Leeson v Marsden and another

Glass v Surrendran

                                                              CPR 6, 7

Court of Appeal   **[2006] EWCA Civ 20;**
                              (2006) Times, 3 February; LTL 25/1/2006

These conjoined appeals concerned interpretation of the CPR service provisions.

COLLIER

The claimant in *Collier* suffered personal injury in an accident on 9 April 2001. Proceedings were issued on 1 April 2004. On 23 July 2001 the claimant served on solicitors nominated by the defendant's insurers. The defendant unsuccessfully argued that because the solicitors had not themselves notified the claimant that they were authorised to accept service, service was invalid. The defendant then appealed.

MARSHALL RANKINE

The claimants in *Marshall Rankine* were stockbrokers, and assignees of a commercial debt against the defendant. The claimants' solicitors sent a letter of claim to a London address. This provoked a repudiatory response by the defendant's solicitors, who in that letter specifically stated that they were acting for the defendant. Proceedings were issued on 28 January 2004. On 27 April 2004 the claimants wrote canvassing the possibility of settlement, and asking for a response within seven days, given the service deadline. The defendant's solicitors replied asking for 14 days. This was accepted. On 20 May 2004, there having been no response, the claimant wrote to the defendant's solicitors asking for confirmation of their instructions to accept service, failing which they would serve at the address to which the letter of claim was sent. There was no response and the claimant sent the claim form to that address, a copy also being sent to the defendant's solicitors. The defendant's solicitors wrote on 26 May stating that the defendant had not resided at that address for some months. On 27 May the claimant unsuccessfully sought confirmation from the defendant's solicitors that the claimant had been properly served. On the same day they applied without notice for an order that service had been properly effected or alternatively for a 21-day extension of service. The master ordered (wrongly, as was conceded at appeal) that the receipt by the defendant's solicitors was to be deemed good service.

On 28 May the claimant served the order on the defendant's solicitors. On 17 June the defendant applied to set the order aside. In response the claimant renewed its order in essentially the same terms, but also seeking extension of time under CPR 7.6(3), and that if service were extended under either CPR 7.6(2) or (3), that it be dispensed with under CPR 6.9. The master allowed the claimants' application and dismissed the defendant's application, on the bases that, whilst there was no solicitor acting for the defendant, the London address was his last known address as per CPR 6.5(6), and in any event the claimant was entitled to succeed under CPR 7.6(3) and 6.(9). The defendant successfully appealed. It was held on appeal that the order of 27 May was wrong, that the defendant had never lived at the London address, that the defendant had solicitors acting for him, and that it was not appropriate to extend time. The claimant appealed against the last two of these.

LEESON

The claimant in *Leeson* alleged that the defendants (a GP and a hospital trust) had between 27 November and 14 December 2000 negligently failed to diagnose a neurological condition. The claimant sent a letter of claim on 27 August 2002. The hospital delayed responding for a year, and the GP failed to respond at all. Proceedings were issued on 24 November 2003. On 9 February 2004 the claimant requested from the defendants a six-month extension of time for service. The hospital agreed to a three-month extension. The GP wrote on 24 February agreeing an extension of time for the service of particulars, schedule and medical evidence. There was no mention of extension of time for service of the claim form. On 9 March the claimant applied without notice for extension of time for service of the claim form until 20 September on the basis that she required the GP's response to the letter of claim before finalising particulars. The claimant requested a paper determination. On 16 March the hospital agreed a further three-month extension, offering to sign a consent order in support of a without notice application to that effect. On 22 March the claimant telephoned the court to enquire about the progress of the application, to be informed that there had been an administrative error. The application was sent again, and indicated as very urgent. On 23 March the court, without a hearing, extended time for service of the particulars by four months but refused to extend time to serve the claim form. The claimant was informed of the terms of this order on 24 March.

The hospital then took the point that there had been no valid service. On 1 April the claimant wrote to the court stating that the order of 23 March had put her in an impossible position and inviting the court to rectify the position by retrospectively granting a 7-day extension of time for service. On 6 April this was granted, again without a hearing. Upon receipt of the order the following day, the claimant wrote to the court requesting a further extension to 15 April. This was again granted on paper. The claim form was sent on 8 April. On 15 April the hospital applied for the order of 8 April to be set aside and for the claim to be struck out on the basis that there was no jurisdiction for the late orders (the claimant's only remedy being an appeal against the 23 March order), or alternatively that the discretion had been wrongly exercised. The application was refused. The defendants successfully appealed. The claimants then appealed this order.

GLASS

The claimant in *Glass* suffered neck and back injuries in a road traffic accident on 5 September 2001. Liability was admitted in December 2001. Proceedings were issued on 3 September 2004. On 21 December the claimant issued an application to extend time for service. This was refused on paper, but the claimant reapplied successfully under CPR 3.3(5), relying upon the admission of liability, the lateness of accountancy evidence arriving and counsel's consequent inability to draft particulars in time. Time was extended for a month. The defendant unsuccessfully appealed to the circuit judge, and then renewed its appeal.

Held:

(i)   Where a defendant had given the claimant a solicitor's address for service the claim form may be validly served by delivering it to that address by one of the permitted methods.

(ii)   CPR 6.4(2) served a single purpose, to prevent personal service when a solicitor had been nominated. If a claimant knew that a solicitor was acting then the methods set out in 6.5 were not available.

(iii) However, if a claimant was told that a solicitor was not authorised to accept service, it was not mandatory that personal service be used. The other methods set out in CPR 6.5(6) were valid in these circumstances.

(iv)   CPR 3.3(5) only applied where the court had made an order of its own initiative. This was quite distinct from considering a without notice application on paper. There was thus no direct route of reconsideration under this rule.

(v)   The court could nevertheless indirectly reconsider by electing to deal with an application without a hearing under CPR 23.8. This was proportionate and unobjectionable, giving any party affected the opportunity to apply to set aside, vary or stay.

(vi)   However, if the court had dismissed an application under CPR 3.3(5), whether on paper or at a hearing, any further application would be struck out as an abuse of process unless it were based on substantially different material from the earlier application.

(vii) Similarly CPR 3.1(7) only applied where there had been a material change in circumstances or where the judge making the initial order had in effect been misled (innocently or otherwise) as to the correct factual position. It could not be used an alternative route of appeal.

(viii) As a matter of practice, applications for extension of time for should generally not be disposed of on paper.

(ix)   Although the requirements of CPR 7.6(3) were relevant to the exercise of discretion under CPR 7.6(2), satisfaction of the pre-conditions set out at CPR 7.6(3)(b) and (c) was not necessarily determinative either way.

(x)   When considering whether to grant an extension of time the court had to consider how good a reason there was for the failure to serve in time. The stronger the reason the more likely the prospect of an extension being granted (*Hashtroodi v Hancock* (p466) applied). This in turn involved evaluating why service had not been effected in the four months provided. This was a more subtle exercise than that under CPR 7.6(3), which allowed the court to extend time only if all reasonable steps had been taken

(xi)   Therefore:

  (a)   in *Collier*, there was no requirement that the solicitors confirmed instructions to accept service. Appeal dismissed;

(b)　in *Marshall Rankine*, it would not be right to extend time as there was no reasonable basis for concluding that the claim form had been served at the defendant's last known residence. As he had never resided there, it could not be. Appeal ultimately dismissed, although the claimant succeeding on the point that there was no solicitor acting for the defendant;

(c)　in *Leeson*, the further applications constituted abuses of process. Further, there was no reason, or at best a very weak reason, for the failure to serve in time. Appeal ultimately dismissed; and

(d)　in *Glass*, there was no basis for the delay. The claimant was unable to identify anything that could properly be characterised as a reason for extending time. Even if there had been justification for extending time for service of particulars, this would not necessarily have been sufficient.

Appeal allowed.

Collins v Tesco

Limitation Act 1980, s 11, s 14

Court of Appeal   LTL 24/7/2003

The claimant was employed by the defendant as an assistant in a petrol kiosk. This involved collecting goods from a nearby store using a metal cage. She claimed to have suffered injury as a result of this activity, which she blamed on the defendant's breach of duty. She first experienced shoulder pain in late 1996. She continued to work until 26 June 1998 but thereafter only returned to work for short periods. On 14 January 1998 she consulted a rheumatologist. On 28 January 1998 she consulted a physiotherapist, who told her that her shoulder problems were caused by heavy lifting. On 26 June 1998 a physiotherapist told her that she was suffering from a strain injury caused by heavy lifting.

The claimant issued proceedings on 26 January 2001. The defendant pleaded limitation, which was heard at the final hearing. The judge awarded damages to the claimant. As regards limitation he held: (a) the test for claimant's knowledge under s 14 was both subjective and objective; (b) it was reasonable for the claimant to adopt a wait-and-see approach to give the injury a chance to subside; (c) following her meeting with the rheumatologist, the claimant expected her symptoms to subside with rest; (d) the claimant's awareness that moving the metal cages caused her pain did not mean that she knew her injury was attributable to her work; (e) the claimant did not become aware that her injury was significant before her meeting with the physiotherapist. The defendant appealed.

Held:

(i)　The judge had adopted an inappropriately over-elaborate approach to the question of knowledge. This question had to be approached in a common sense manner.

(ii)　Whilst the effect on a particular claimant might be relevant, the question of knowledge was an objective one (*McCafferty v Metropolitan Police District Receiver* (p546) followed). The willingness of a given claimant to resort to litigation was not material.

(iii)　The only proper conclusion on the evidence was that the claimant knew that she had a significant injury more than three years before the issue of proceedings.

(iv)　The necessary link to establish attributability was also present by January 1998 (*Spargo v North Essex DHA* (p667) applied). Irrespective of whether or not he applied the correct test, the judge's finding on this question was not one that he could properly reach.

(v)　(per Laws LJ) 'The question identifying significance is: is the injury bad enough, to the putative claimant's knowledge, for it to be reasonable for him or her at the point of time under consideration to start proceedings against a defendant who is able to pay the claim and will not dispute liability?'

Appeal allowed.

Common v Crofts

Limitation Act 1980, s 11, s 14, s 33

Court of Appeal   **1980 CAT 041**

On 4 November 1975 the claimant (Mr Common) was seriously injured in a road accident. On 10 November 1975 the police gave him the name and address of the defendant. He was not fit enough to appreciate what they said and mislaid it. On 12 April 1976 both he and the defendant were convicted at the same court of driving without due care and attention.

The claimant believed that, as he had been convicted of an offence arising out of the accident, he was not entitled to any damages. As a result of hearing a radio programme, he eventually consulted solicitors. Shortly afterwards, they issued his writ against the defendant on 3 April 1979.

The trial judge accepted that, in view of his condition, the claimant had no knowledge of the defendant's identity until 12 April 1976 and that therefore the action had been started in time. He added that if necessary he would have exercised his discretion under s 33 of the Limitation Act 1980 in the claimant's favour. The defendant appealed.

Held:

(i)   (a)   The claimant might reasonably have been expected to make enquiries of the police as to the defendant's identity, as soon as he got notice of the intended prosecution, which was before 3 April 1976: s 14(3); and

      (b)   accordingly, the writ issued on 3 April 1979 was out of time: s 11(4).

(ii) However, there were no grounds for interfering with the exercise of the trial judge's discretion under s 33(1) because:

      (a)   there was a strong probability that the claimant would be able to establish liability on the part of the defendant: s 33(3);

      (b)   the claimant had been seriously injured: s 33(3);

      (c)   the relevant delay was a short one: s 33(3)(a);

      (d)   it would not cause the evidence to be less cogent: s 33(3)(b); and

      (e)   the claimant's mistaken belief about the law was not altogether unreasonable: s 33(3)(e).

Connelly v RTZ Corporation

Limitation Act 1980, s 11, s 14, s 33

Wright J   **[1999] CLC 533; LTL 4/12/1998**

The claimant, a British citizen, emigrated to South Africa in the 1970s to work in an open case uranium mine. In 1985, having returned to Scotland, he discovered that he had cancer. He was advised that this might have been caused by exposure to uranium. A complex litigation history ensued against the defendant (his employers' English parent company) and a foreign subsidiary. Proceedings were issued on 7 September 1994. The defendant applied for the action to be struck out on the grounds of no reasonable prospects of success and limitation.

Held:

(i)   The case, although weak, was not so weak so as to be appropriate to strike out on lack of merit alone.

(ii) However, the weak merits were relevant in considering limitation.

(iii)   It was clear that by 1986 the claimant believed that his injury was attributable to his employer. At this point, however, he did not appreciate the relationship between his employers and the relevant defendant.

(iv)   The question was therefore when the defendant should have realised that the defendant itself was a possible target.

(v)   It appeared that the claimant's current solicitors perceived the possibility of proceeding against the defendant between. May 1993 and September 1994. However, his previous solicitors may have had a similar inkling in 1989.

(vi)   The claimant had constructive knowledge eighteen months from September 1988, the date when he received the necessary information from his employer's insurers to make enquiries. Proceedings were therefore issued out of time.

(vii)   As to s 33:

(a)   a balancing exercise was required between the claimant's loss of a claim and the defendant's having to meet what was a stale claim;

(b)   the cogency of both sides evidence was significantly reduced but there was greater evidential prejudice to the defendant. It faced great difficulties in tracing witnesses given that the mine in question depended largely on migrant labour;

(c)   the fact that the claimant had initially intimated fruitless claims in foreign jurisdictions was not a good reason for the delay;

(d)   the prospect of an unrecoverable bill of costs was a relevant factor, although it was less so in the case of a multi-national company such as the defendant compared with a more modest claimant; and

(e)   on balance it would not be equitable to allow the action to continue.

Claim struck out.

Conry v Simpson and others

Limitation Act 1980, s 33

Court of Appeal   **[1983] 3 All ER 369**

On 12 January 1973 the claimant (Roy Conry) got out of a van that belonged to the third defendant and was being driven by the second defendant. While he was standing by the nearside of the van, he was struck by a car driven by the first defendant which was coming in the opposite direction. He suffered injury to his left knee which became unstable.

In May 1974 the claimant's left hand was injured in an accident at work. Questions of fact arose as to the relative contributions of the two accidents to his ability to work as a steel erector.

After the first accident, the claimant had promptly consulted a solicitor. His claim was notified to the first defendant whose insurers never denied liability, although they alleged contributory negligence, and asked the claimant's solicitor to quantify his claim. He subsequently wrote to inform the claimant that he had become too busy to deal with it. By the time they met to discuss this, the three-year limitation period had expired.

In 1977 the claimant instructed fresh solicitors who issued a writ against his first solicitor. The first defendant's insurers destroyed their file, including a medical report they had obtained in April 1974.

After the decision in *Firman v Ellis*, the claimant's new solicitors switched from pursuing his former solicitor. On 22 November 1979 they issued a writ against all three defendants. At a preliminary trial, Skinner J held that (a) the claimant had a strong case in negligence against the first defendant, to whom his claim had been promptly notified, and disapplied s 11 of the Limitation Act 1980 to allow the claimant's action to proceed against him, but (b) the claimant had an arguable case only against the second and third defendants, to whom the claim had not been notified until much later, so he dismissed the second and third defendants from the action. The first defendant appealed.

Held:

(i)   The judge was not wrong in thinking that the destruction of the first defendant's insurer's file and Mr Redwood's report had not seriously prejudiced them because 'the claimant still has his knee available for examination by the first defendant, and the prognosis will now be clearer'.

(ii)   The first defendant was not necessarily condemned by the judge's order to pay all the claimant's damages, as he could still bring third party proceedings against the second and third defendants if so advised.

(iii)   The judge had rightly concluded that the claimant did not have a cast-iron case against his former solicitor. While the existence of a good claim in negligence against a solicitor was a highly relevant consideration, it was very seldom that a remedy against a solicitor was as satisfactory as a remedy against the original tortfeasor.

(iv)   Section 33 of the Limitation Act 1980 confers on judges an almost unfettered discretion. Provided that a High Court judge follows the directions in that section and has regard to the degree to which the imposition of the primary period of limitation prejudices the claimant and his decision would prejudice the defendant, and provided he has regard to all the circumstances of the case and in particular those six circumstances specified in s 33(3), the Court of Appeal will not interfere with the exercise of his discretion.

The first defendant's appeal was dismissed.

Firman v Ellis (p433) and *Thompson v Brown Construction (Ebbw Vale) Ltd* (p690) followed.

Constantinides v C Birnbaum & Co

Limitation Act 1939, s 2D

HH Judge Dow   **[1980] CLY 1680**

The claimants (Mr and Mrs Constantinides) were both employed by the defendants. She alleged injury in an accident at work in October 1974. He was injured in an accident at work in April 1975. Four days later, he instructed a Law Centre to notify their claims. By October 1978, the Law Centre had still not done so.

The claimants consulted new solicitors. Proceedings for both were commenced in May 1979. The defendants denied that the claimant's wife had had an accident at all. They admitted the husband's accident but denied liability for it.

The defendants applied to dismiss both actions.

Held:

(i)   If the actions were dismissed, the claimants would suffer little or no prejudice because they each appeared to have an unassailable action in negligence against the Law Centre.

(ii)   Moreover in the case of the claimant's husband there were witnesses whose evidence would be less cogent because of the delay.

(iii)   Accordingly, it would be inequitable to allow the actions to proceed under s 2D of the Limitation Act 1939 as amended.

Firman v Ellis (p433) applied.

Copeland v Smith and Goodwin

Limitation Act 1980, s 14

Court of Appeal   **[2000] 1 WLR 1371; [2000] 1 All ER 457;**
[2000] CP Rep 14

The claimant was injured in a road traffic accident on 24 September 1993. He was knocked off his motorbike in a multi-vehicle pile-up, but was unable to identify which vehicle had struck him. A police report was obtained on 14 January 1994. This failed to provide the necessary details of the accident itself, but it did give details of witnesses and officers involved in the investigation. However the claimant's solicitors took no steps to interview any of these. Proceedings were issued against the first defendant alone. A complete police report was received in April 1998, which revealed that a bolt from the claimant's motorbike was found embedded in the second defendant's car. The claimant applied successfully in November 1998 for permission to join the second defendant. The second defendant applied for this order to be set aside on limitation grounds. This application was refused, the claimant successfully arguing that for the purposes of s 14 he was not to be fixed with the failings of his solicitors. The second defendant appealed.

Held:

(i)   The judge had been wrong to hold that the claimant was not fixed with the responsibility of the actions or inactions of his legal advisers (*Henderson v Temple Pier* (p471) applied).

(ii)   However, the judge was entitled to hold, in the alternative, that the actions of the claimant's solicitors were not unreasonable without the benefit of hindsight. The standard of investigation required by a competent solicitor was very much a question for the trial judge.

(iii)   Even fixing the claimant with his solicitors' actions, he did not have constructive knowledge before April 1998.

Appeal dismissed.

Corbin v Penfold Metalising

Limitation Act 1980, s 14, s 33

Court of Appeal   **[2000] Lloyd's Rep Med 247;**
(2000) 97(17) LSG 35; (2000) 144 SJLB 203

The claimant worked for the defendant, a metal finishing company, from 1979 until 1992. His job was air blasting and metal spraying. He gave up work because of a chest complaint; he was told at this time that he had iron deposits in his lungs. In February and March 1993 the treating specialist wrote letters confirming that the claimant was suffering from an 'inhaled' or 'industrial' disease. The claimant consulted solicitors in September 1993 but it was not until 1994 that causation of the injury was confirmed by a medical expert.

Proceedings were issued in August 1996 and limitation heard as a preliminary issue. The judge held that the claimant had knowledge for limitation purposes more before August 1993 and declined to exercise his discretion under s 33. The claimant appealed.

Held:

(i)   The judge was entirely correct on the issue of knowledge. The claimant had the requisite knowledge when he knew enough to begin investigating the claim (*Spargo v North Essex DA* (p667) applied and identified as authoritative).

(ii)   The specialist had told the claimant in clear terms in 1993 that the injury was an inhaled or industrial injury. Its only source could have been working for the defendant. The claimant had the requisite knowledge at this time.

(iii)   The judge had been wrong in the exercise of his discretion to entirely attribute to the claimant the delay on the part of his solicitors. There was no rule of law that he should do so (*Das v Ganju* (p398), *Whitfield v North Durham HA* (p713)).

(iv)   Exercising the discretion afresh, it was equitable to allow the claim to proceed. The following factors were particularly important in this respect:

(a)   the delay was short: just over five months;

(b)   the claimant had instructed solicitors promptly; and

(c)   the claim was a strong one.

Appeal allowed.

NB: This decision was doubted by the House of Lords in *Horton v Sadler* (p482).

Cornish v Kearley & Tonge Ltd

Limitation Act 1980, s 33

Hirst J   **(1983) 133 NLJ 870**

The claimant (Mr Cornish) was employed in a wholesale butchery owned by the defendants. In July 1975 he and two other employees were manoeuvring a large piece of beef, in order to try to get it on to a hook, when the beef fell on him. He felt pains from time to time, and knew by January 1976 that his injury was significant and attributable to the incident in question. His writ was issued in December 1981.

Held: his action would be allowed to proceed under s 33(1) of the Limitation Act 1980 because:

(a)   although the delay was long, the reasons for it were reasonable: s 33(3)(a);

(b)   although there was some reduction of cogency of evidence, this was not of a high degree: s 33(3)(b);

(c)   the claimant and his advisers acted promptly and reasonably: s 33(3)(e); and

(d)   it was not unreasonable for him not to have taken legal advice until 1981: s 33(3)(f).

McCafferty v Metropolitan Police District Receiver (p546) followed.

Cotton v General Electric Co Ltd

Limitation Act 1939, s 2D

Court of Appeal   **(1979) 129 NLJ 737**

From 1941 to 1951 Mr Cotton had been employed as a sand blaster by another company. From 1951 to 1963 he worked for the defendants as a room blaster in very dusty conditions.

In the early 1940s he suffered from bronchitis. In 1964 the Pneumoconiosis Medical Panel assessed him as 50% disabled. In 1971 he died.

The claimant (his widow) commenced proceedings against the defendants. The judge held the action to be statute barred, refusing to exercise his discretion under s 2D of the Limitation Act 1939 as amended on the ground that since Mr Cotton had been exposed to dust in other employments it would be impossible to investigate the true cause of the beginnings of the disease. The claimant appealed.

Held:

(i) It was impossible to investigate the true cause and original inception of the disease as effectively as might have been done in the late 1960s.

(ii) As the Pneumoconiosis Medical Panel records were no longer available, it was harder to determine the extent to which the disability had been due to bronchitis.

(iii) The prejudice to the defendants from the continuance of the action substantially outweighed the prejudice to the claimant from its discontinuance.

The claimant's appeal was dismissed.

Cranfield and anor v Bridgegrove and linked appeals

Companies Act 1985, s 725(1) **CPR 6.9, 7.6**

Court of Appeal **[2003] EWCA Civ 656;**
[2003] 1 WLR 2441; [2003] 3 All ER 129

Five linked appeals concerning CPR 6.9 (dispensing with service) and 7.6 (extending time for service).

(A) CRANFIELD v BRIDGEGROVE

The claimant requested that the court serve the claim form but by administrative error it failed to do so. The judge granted an extension of time under CPR 7.6(3), holding that the court's failure to serve by mistake satisfied the criterion of the court's being unable to serve with in the permitted time. The defendant appealed.

Held:

(i) There was jurisdiction to extend time under CPR 7.6(3) where the court's neglect led to a failure to serve in time. 'Unable to serve' did not require an unsuccessful attempt at service.

(ii) The judge was therefore correct in his interpretation of CPR 7.6(3). Given that the failure in service was the court's neglect the judge did not err in his discretion. By allowing the extension of time.

Appeal dismissed.

(B) CLAUSSEN

The claimant requested that the court serve the claim form but by administrative error it failed to do so. The judge held that it could not be said that the court had been unable to serve the claim form in time and therefore there was no jurisdiction under 7.6(3) to extend time for service. The claimant appealed.

Held:

(i) There was jurisdiction to extend time under CPR 7.6(3) where the court's neglect led to a failure to serve in time (as in *Cranfield*).

(ii) The judge was therefore misdirected himself in holding that he had no power to extend time and the discretion to do so fell to be reconsidered.

(iii) The real reason for the failure in service in this case was not the court's neglect but rather the claimant's failures to timeously notify the court that the defendant's solicitors were willing to accept service and to request that the court serve proceedings urgently rather than 'in due course'. It would therefore not be appropriate to extend the validity period.

(iv)   Service should not dispensed with under CPR 6.9 unless the facts of the case fell squarely within the exceptional category identified in *Anderton v Clwyd County Council* (p303). These facts did not.

Appeal dismissed.

(C) McMANUS

The claimant served proceedings on the defendant's insurers when they should have been served on the defendant personally. The judge dispensed with the need for service under CPR 6.9. The defendant appealed.

Held:

(i)   The judge took too liberal a view of the scope of CPR 6.9. It was only to be exercised in exceptional cases.

(ii)   The decision in *Anderton* was based upon timeous receipt by the defendant or his solicitor of proceedings deemed to be served out of time.

(iii)   Here a draft claim form had been sent to insurers who had no authority to accept service. There were therefore significant departures from the rules governing service which went beyond the technical.

(iv)   The facts of this case did not fall squarely within the exceptional criteria of Anderton, as they needed to for CPR 6.9 to apply.

Appeal allowed.

(D) MURPHY

The claimant served proceedings upon the defendant personally when the defendant had nominated solicitors to accept service under CPR 6.4(2). The judge, relying upon *Anderton*, dispensed with service under CPR 6.9. The defendant appealed, arguing that *Anderton* did not apply as there had been no unsuccessful attempt to serve at the correct address. On appeal an issue arose as to whether service at the defendant's registered office was good under s 725(1) of the 1985 Act.

Held:

(i)   Service on the company's registered office was valid service under s 725 of the 1985 Act.

(ii)   CPR 6.2(2) made clear that service under the CPR was an elective alternative to service under the 1985 Act. Once the choice of method of service is made both parties are bound by it. The claimant having complied with the relevant provisions of that Act, compliance or otherwise with CPR rules of service was irrelevant.

(iii)   (obiter) The circumstances of this case fell within *Anderton* and the judge would have been right to dispense with service under CPR 6.9 had he needed to do so.

Appeal dismissed.

(E) SMITH

The claimant served proceedings on the first defendant in 2001 at his last known address in accordance with CPR 6.5(6). The Motor Insurers' Bureau had in 1999 informed the claimant that the defendant had left that address. The district judge held that the first defendant had not been properly served as the claimant had sent the claim form to an address knowing the defendant would not receive it. The claimant appealed.

Held: CPR 6.5(6) clearly stated that where there was no solicitor acting for a party and that party had given no address for service, service had to be to that party's last known address. There was no qualification or basis for adding any other requirement.

Appeal allowed.

Crawford v Dalley and Royal Marsden Hospital

Limitation Act 1980, s 33   **Res judicata**

Ebsworth J   **[1995] 6 Med LR 343**

In October 1980 the claimant was diagnosed with carcinoma of the right breast. Following successful surgery she began a course of radiotherapy on 15 December 1980 at the second defendant's private hospital. This was undertaken by the first defendant, a doctor working there. The claimant was dissatisfied with the results of the treatment and consulted several doctors in this regard during 1980. The claimant's husband withheld payment to the second defendant on the basis, set out in a letter of 12 August 1981, that the treatment had severely damaged the claimant's right arm and shoulder. The hospital replied denying this allegation and pressing for payment of the £278.60 owing.

This sum remained unpaid and in February 1983 the second defendant issued county court proceedings in respect of it. On 1 March 1983 the claimant filed a defence and counterclaim limited to £500 for 'medical expenses incurred in consultations and treatments as a result of treatment at the Royal Marsden Hospital'. The counterclaim fell as the result of a debarring order in October 1983 and judgment entered in January 1984. The claim was not decided on its merits and no evidence was heard.

In October 1991 the claimant became seriously ill with radionecrosis (tissue death caused by radiation). She issued proceedings claiming medical negligence on 9 September 1994.

The defendant applied for the claim to be struck as (a) an abuse of process, and (b) statute barred.

Held:

(i)   The claim was an abuse of process. The issues could and should have been litigated 12 years earlier.

(ii)   In such a case of both cause of action and issue estoppel it would be wrong in principle to allow the claim to continue.

Cressey v E Timm & Son Ltd and E Timm & Son Holdings Ltd

Limitation Act 1980, s 11, s 14

Court of Appeal   **[2005] EWCA Civ 763;**
                                            (2005) 1 WLR 3926; LTL 24/06/05

The claimant suffered a broken leg in a accident at work on 2 December 2000. He worked for the first defendant but his pay slips were in the name of an associated company, the second defendant. The claimant instructed solicitors who sent a letter of claim to the first defendant on 20 March 2001. The first defendant passed the letter to its insurers, who confirmed themselves as insurers of the second defendant and its subsidiary companies. Following redundancy in April 2001 the claimant received a letter of reference from the first defendant on its headed paper.

The insurers admitted primary liability subject to contributory negligence on 9 October 2001. On 7 May 2002 it was agreed that the second defendant would pay 75% of any damages awarded.

On 18 November 2003 the claimant indicated that protective proceedings would be issued and asked for confirmation of the 'correct identity of the defendant'. The insurers replied saying that the second defendant was the correct defendant. A claim form had in fact been prepared naming both defendants. This was issued on 27 November 2003. However it was not served within the four-month validity period. The claimant therefore issued a second claim form, again naming both defendants, on 30 March 2003 and served it on the same day (the first claim form was undeniably ineffective). The defendants applied to strike out on the grounds that this second claim was statute barred.

The essential issue was whether the date of the claimant's knowledge of the identity of the second defendant was 2 December 2000 or 30 April 2001. The district judge at first instance found in favour of the later date and refused the application. The second defendant appealed unsuccessfully to the circuit judge.

The second defendant appealed again.

Held:

(i)   In most cases of accidents at work, the employee would have immediate knowledge of the identity of his employee and therefore the defendant. However, in a minority of cases where the identity of the employer was uncertain or even wrongly stated the date of knowledge could be postponed (*Simpson v Norwest Holst Southern Ltd* (p648) applied).

(ii)   How long the date of knowledge would be postponed would depend on the facts of the individual case. Normally it would only be postponed for the shortest reasonable length of time needed to complete appropriate enquiries. In the absence of a positively misleading response it would be wise for claimants to work on the basis that the date of knowledge was the date of accident.

(iii)   (obiter) Knowledge of a defendant's identity and knowledge of its actual name are not the same. If a claimant knew the identity of the defendant that would probably constitute the requisite knowledge even if he was labouring under a misnomer, although in some cases where a description of identity can only be ascertained in a general way identity for the purposes of knowledge will not be known until a name has been or could have been attached. In this case, however, there was no misnomer; the defendants were separate companies.

(iv)   In the instant case the claimant had been misinformed about the identity of his employer. His payslips identified the second defendant and he had no reason to think that any other company was his employer until receipt of the insurers' letter. It was not suggested that he should have clarified the name of his employer sooner.

(v)   The second claim was therefore brought within the limitation period and was not statute barred.

Appeal dismissed.

Crocker v British Coal Corporation

Limitation Act 1980, s 11, s 14, s 33

Mance J   **(1996) 29 BMLR 159;**
(1995) Times, 5 July; LTL 7/6/1995

The claimant was eleven years old when she suffered psychiatric injuries as a result of being involved in the Aberfan coal tip disaster on 21 October 1966. Around 1976 she saw a television programme about the disaster. That night she experienced unusual and sharp psychosomatic pains in her fingers, which developed into a longterm problem. She also developed depression and anxiety. She attended her GP about these problems on 1 March 1978. She continued to make

GP visits thereafter, and there was a GP note from around October 1978 records a link with the disaster, the television programme and the symptoms. Her psychiatric wellbeing continued to deteriorate, and it was noted that she was reliving childhood trauma. Abreaction therapy in 1988–1989 ameliorated her problems. The claimant issued proceedings on 18 September 1990 and applied for s 11 to be disapplied by s 33 if s 14 did not bring the claim within time.

Held:

(i)   The burden of proving that proceedings were issued in time was on the claimant.

(ii)   The claimant knew by October 1979 that she had a significant injury and that it was attributable to the defendant. The claim was therefore issued out of time and required s 33 to save it.

(iii)   The primary purpose of the limitation period is to protect a defendant against stale claims.

(iv)   The claimant did not have knowledge and could not be expected to bring an action until around 1978–1979.

(v)   The staleness of the claim arose from the delay between then and the issue of proceedings.

(vi)   One of the reasons for the delay was that the claimant's psychiatric symptoms were not continuous. Another reason was that the abreaction therapy focused her attention very strongly upon the accident from 1988 onwards.

(vii)   As a matter of common sense a delay of 11 years would have reduced the cogency of the evidence. Overall, the defendant would be placed in the greater evidential difficulty.

(viii) It would not be equitable to disapply the limitation period.

Application dismissed.

Cummins v Shell International Manning Services Ltd

	CPR 6.7
Human Rights Act 1998, s 3	**ECHR, Art 6**
Court of Appeal	**[2002] EWCA Civ 933;**
	[2002] 1 WLR 3174; [2002] 3 All ER 813

See *Anderton v Clwyd County Council* (E) (p303)

Curtis v Wild

Maritime Conventions Act 1911, s 8

Henry J   **[1991] 4 All ER 172**

On 2 August 1987 the claimant (Marjorie Curtis) was in a Lark dinghy sailing on Belmont Reservoir when it capsized and she was thrown into the water. The defendant was sailing another dinghy some distance behind. She alleged that he negligently permitted his dinghy to strike her.

Her writ was issued on 11 June 1990. The defendant sought by summons a declaration that s 8 of the Maritime Conventions Act 1911 applied and statute barred the action.

Held:

(i)   The waters of Belmont Reservoir were simply used for pleasure purposes by people who were messing about in boats. They were not used as navigable waters in which to proceed from an originating place to a destination point for the purpose of discharging people or cargo.

(ii)   Accordingly, the dinghies were not vessels 'used in navigation' for the purposes of s 8 of the Maritime Conventions Act 1911, so its special two-year time limit did not apply. The case was governed by the standard three-year limit and had been commenced in time.

Cyster v Council of the City of Manchester

Limitation Act 1980, s 11, s 33

Court of Appeal   **Lexis, 23 October 1990**

The claimant (Miss Cyster) alleged that on 27 September 1977 a health inspector sprayed linoleum at her place of work, advising that it would take 1 minute to dry and that 'after 1 minute I slipped on the linoleum attempting to rescue a dish of cat food which the said employee should have carried out prior to commencing his spraying'. Her injuries included severe bruising on the left main hip joint and lower spine, the loss of power in her hands one week later and, from 1982 onwards, numbness and paralysis.

In October 1977 she instructed a firm of solicitors. In October 1978 she moved to Tunbridge Wells where she instructed two further firms. Subsequently she moved to Eastbourne and Hailsham where she instructed two more firms. On 27 March 1985 her writ was issued by a sixth firm. It was served on 19 March 1986. These solicitors having come off the record, the claimant served her statement of claim in December 1987.

At a preliminary trial of the limitation defence, Mr A T May QC, sitting as a deputy judge of the High Court, dismissed the action as statute barred. The claimant appealed.

Held:

(i)   She appreciated that her injuries were significant by October 1977. The action was statute barred by s 11 of the Limitation Act 1980.

(ii)   (a) The length of the delay was considerable: 7½ years from accident to writ. Difficulty in obtaining medical advice as the claimant moved homes and changed solicitors was no reason for not issuing the writ in time: s 33(3)(a);

         (b)   as the defendants could not find the health inspector and all records of that period had gone, the cogency of their evidence was reduced: s 33(3)(b);

         (c)   there was no lack of endeavour on the claimant's part to obtain legal advice, but this was combined with a failure to obtain disclosable medical advice: s 33(3) (f);

         (d)   the deputy judge was right not to exercise his discretion to exclude the primary limitation period: s 33(1).

D v Harrow LBC and others

Limitation Act 1980, s 11, s 33

QBD (Eady J)   **[2008] EWHC 3048 (QB);**
[2009] 1 FLR 719; [2009] 2 FCR 297;
[2009] Fam Law 203

The claimant was born on 28 January 1967. In 1973, when aged six, she had been adopted by a man (H) and his wife who lived within the jurisdiction of the first defendant. H first assaulted the claimant on her eighth birthday in 1975 and pleaded guilty to indecently assaulting her two years later in 1977. He was put on probation for two years and shortly thereafter returned to the family home. A few weeks later, however, H left his wife to live with another woman in Birmingham. Over the following year or so, the claimant stayed with H and his new partner from time to time in the course of access visits until, in February 1979, she went to live with them permanently. Her case was that the abuse was resumed almost immediately and she was later raped on a number of occasions. She finally plucked up courage and reported the matter in October 1981, whereupon H was convicted of rape in July 1982 following a contested hearing at which she had to give evidence before the court. On this occasion, H was sentenced to five years' imprisonment.

The claimant's suffering from the abuse extended well into adulthood. There was evidence that each of the defendant local authorities permitted the claimant to have contact with H or to live in his care despite knowing of one or more of his convictions for assault. In particular, the second and third defendants allowed it in the knowledge that he had pleaded guilty to indecently assaulting her. In December 2006 (following an agreed 'limitation holiday') the claimant, then aged 42, issued proceedings alleging that the defendants had failed to protect her from H's predations in the period between 1975 and 1981 (over the period when she ranged from 8 to 14 years of age). Limitation was heard as preliminary issue.

Held:

(i)   On the facts, the claimant was fixed with knowledge, at least from the time of attaining her majority in 1988, of the relevant facts for the purposes of s 14. By that time, she knew that (1) she had been abused from her eighth birthday by her adoptive father and later raped, (2) he had already been convicted of indecently assaulting her in December 1977, (3) there were at least family rumours to the effect that H had committed some form of sexual offence(s) in respect of other people before she had been abused; (4) the judge at the rape trial in 1982 highlighted the shortcomings of at least one social services department as to her protection and welfare, (5) she had not been removed from H's care and placed in a safe environment until October 1981, (6) she was suffering continuing psychological trauma as a result of the abuse over a long period of time, and (7) she had lived at various addresses and could have established, without difficulty, which were the relevant local authorities. Moreover in 1985 that she was awarded compensation by the Criminal Injuries Compensation Board. She therefore knew enough to make it reasonable for her to begin to investigate whether or not she had a case against any of the relevant local authorities (*Broadley v Guy Clapham & Co* (p345) applied).

(ii)   There would be very serious prejudice to the first defendant, largely caused by long delay on the claimant part in bringing proceedings, and a fair trial was not possible. The claimant knew many years ago of at least rumours of H's sexual offending and knew, or could have established, that she was living within the jurisdiction of the first defendant. Although the claimant could not be blamed for suppressing the abuse, that was not a complete answer. Not everyone bringing a late claim for damages, however genuine their complaint might be, could reasonably expect the court to exercise the s 33 discretion in their favour (*A v Hoare* (p287) applied).

(iii)   Although the discretion was unfettered and had to be addressed in the light of all the circumstances, the court should never lose sight of the public policy considerations on limitation periods. There was a public interest in legal certainty and finality that should not lightly be discounted, especially not out of sympathy for an individual litigant with a strong case on liability and causation. Fairness required a balance of interests.

(iv)   The second defendant's involvement with the claimant was shorter and records showed that the claimant's interests were monitored regularly. There was no evidential basis for suggesting that the claimant should have been taken into care during that time. There was an absence of a realistic prospect of success in respect of the claim against the second defendant. There was no sufficient evidence of a breach of duty such that justice required disapplication of the limitation period.

(v)   Decided case law suggested that the law recognised that there could be a duty of care owed to children in relation to suspected child abuse (*JD v East Berkshire Community*

Health NHS Trust [2003] EWCA Civ 1151, [2004] QB 558 considered). On the assumption that there was such a duty, it was necessary to decide whether a fair trial was still possible in the case of the third defendant. It was accepted that, while within its jurisdiction, the claimant was abused and raped by H and that H was ultimately convicted. The relevant events took place between 27 and 30 years before the claimant brought proceedings. There were significant gaps in documentation and there were witnesses who were untraceable. After so long, a fair trial of the issues would not be possible, and the court would not exercise the s 33 discretion in respect of any of the claims.

Judgment for defendants.

DHM v Bryn Alyn Community Holdings Ltd

Limitation Act 1980, s 2, s 11, s 14, s 33

Court of Appeal   **[2003] EWCA Civ 783;
[2003] 3 WLR 107; [2003] 1 FLR 1203**

See *KR v Bryn Alyn Community Holdings Ltd* (K) (p505)

DJ v Bryn Alyn Community Holdings Ltd

Limitation Act 1980, s 2, s 11, s 14, s 33

Court of Appeal   **[2003] EWCA Civ 783;
[2003] 3 WLR 107; [2003] 1 FLR 1203**

See *KR v Bryn Alyn Community Holdings Ltd* (G) (p505)

DK v Bryn Alyn Community Holdings Ltd

Limitation Act 1980, s 2, s 11, s 14, s 33

Court of Appeal   **[2003] EWCA Civ 783;
[2003] 3 WLR 107; [2003] 1 FLR 1203**

See *KR v Bryn Alyn Community Holdings Ltd* (B) (p505)

Dale v British Coal Corporation (No 2)

Limitation Act 1980, s 33

Court of Appeal   **(1992) 136 Sol Jo LB 199**

The claimant (Donald Dale), a diabetic since the age of five, was a welder at Lofthouse Colliery. On 25 June 1972 a spark had entered his boot and caused a burn which had subsequently ulcerated. He had not been wearing spats. As a result of the ulceration, his left leg had to be amputated.

He received £500 from a medical tribunal where he was represented by the National Union of Mineworkers. In November 1975 he wrote to the union's president, Arthur Scargill, who replied that he might have a case at common law and advised him to contact his branch secretary immediately. The claimant did not do so.

In July 1981 the colliery closed. In September 1985 the claimant's right leg was also amputated. On 3 September 1987 he saw a solicitor who issued a writ and served a statement of claim. At a preliminary trial on limitation, Blofield J directed that s 11 of the Limitation Act 1980 should not apply. The defendants appealed.

Held:

(i)   Where the existence of a claim and sufficient particulars were notified so late that it was virtually impossible for the defendants to investigate, the defendants were gravely prejudiced and it would require exceptional circumstances for the court to disapply s 11: s 33(3)(b).

(ii)   The judge had erred in applying a wholly subjective test of reasonableness to the conduct of the claimant in not acting on Mr Scargill's advice and bringing the case late. The test was an objective one: what would a reasonable man in the claimant's position have done. A trade union member could usually be said to act reasonably if he followed union advice: s 33(3)(f).

(iii)   In the circumstances, the court was free to exercise its discretion afresh and would do so in favour of the defendants: s 33(1).

Dale v Michelin Tyre plc

Limitation Act 1980, s 33

Court of Appeal   LTL 3/3/1999

The claimant worked for the defendant from 1955 to 1985, when the defendant's factory closed down. During this period he was exposed to various chemicals which caused anosmia (total loss of smell). A letter of claim was sent on 17 September 1993 and proceedings issued on 29 September 1994. The defendant denied liability and pleaded limitation. This was heard at the final trial. The judge held that the claim was brought outside the relevant period, the claimant having the requisite knowledge in the 1970s when, as health and safety representative he complained to management. However, the judge, finding the claimant's reasons for the delay acceptable, exercised his s 33 discretion in the claimant's favour and awarded damages to the claimant. The defendant appealed.

Held:

(i)   There must have been prejudice to the defendant. The factory had closed down in 1985, records were no longer available and the defendant had no inkling of a potential claim until 1993. The judge overlooked the inevitable consequences of the extensive delays both before and after the factory's closure.

(ii)   The judge was probably influenced by hearing Limitation Act 1980 after other issues which he found in the claimant's favour.

(iii)   The finding of fact that the claimant had knowledge in the 1970s could not be reconciled with the finding that the claimant had acted reasonably in accepting the condition was something he had to live with.

(iv)   The judge had erred in his discretion.

Appeal allowed.

Das v Ganju

Limitation Act 1980, s 11, s 33

Court of Appeal   **[1999] PIQR P260; [1999] Lloyd's Rep Med 198;**
(1999) 96(19) LSG 28

On 28 February 1978 the claimant attended her GP, the defendant, complaining of a rash on her face and allegedly stating that she thought that she might be pregnant. The defendant took no action. On 24 October 1978 she gave birth to a daughter consequently diagnosed with congenital rubella syndrome. The child was blind and severely handicapped. The defendant first became aware that she had a potential claim in negligence in June 1987. She received a favourable medical report and applied for legal aid. An offer of legal aid, subject to a contribution, was made on 21 April 1999. However, she was wrongly advised by counsel that as a matter of law she could not bring a claim for wrongful birth (inconsistently, counsel also advised on limitation). The claimant declined the legal aid offer and on 11 September 1999 her solicitors wrote for their fees, but also advising (incorrectly) that the daughter could bring a claim in her own right when she turned sixteen. The claimant replied confirming that she did not wish to pursue the claim. On 7 July 1993 she instructed new solicitors and acquired a legal aid certificate. Proceedings were issued on 17 September 1996. On trial of preliminary issue the judge held that the claim was issued out of time, but exercised his discretion to allow it to nevertheless continue. The defendant appealed.

Held:

(i)   The court had to consider the reason for the claimant's delay after the limitation period expired. It was clear that the reason here was the misleading advice the she had received from her lawyers.

(ii)   There were no grounds for criticising the claimant personally.

(iii)   There was no rule of law requiring legal advisers' failures to be visited upon a claimant (*Whitfield v North Durham HA* (p713) found to be wrongly decided as it conflicted with *Thompson v Brown* (p690) and *Halford v Brooks* (p453)).

(iv)   There was little evidential prejudice to the defendant because of the delay. It was not accepted that the need for expert witnesses to judge the standards of 18 years previously was significant.

(v)   It would be clearly wrong for claimant's action to be struck out as a result of receiving incorrect legal advice. Her claim against her lawyers would be speculative and she would be severely prejudiced if she were not allowed to pursue her claim against the defendant.

(vi)   The judge was wrong to give weight to criticism of the defendant's conduct at the time of the pregnancy. However, this was not a significant error.

(vii)   The judge gave strong reasons for the exercise of his discretion and his decision was not to be interfered with.

Appeal dismissed.

NB: This decision was doubted by the House of Lords in *Horton v Sadler* (p482).

Davie v RWE Npower Plc

Limitation Act 1980, s 14, s 33

Newport, Gwent County Court (Recorder Hartley-Davies)   **[2009] CLY 2854**

The claimant claimed damages for hearing loss and tinnitus that he alleged he suffered as a result of his employment at the defendant. The claimant, aged 63, worked for the defendant at Aberthaw power station from 1973 until 1999. There was excessive noise at the power station from machines in operation. The claimant was not provided with effective ear protection in the form of ear muffs until 1988. He knew by that date that he had been exposed to noise which could cause damage to his hearing for 14 years. His hearing was initially tested by the defendant, probably in the 1980s, when he was not told that there was anything wrong with his hearing. It was further tested in the 1990s when he was told that his hearing was what was 'to be expected of a man of [his] age and the time [he had] spent in the industry'. The claimant thought he was being told that his hearing was all right. However he gave evidence that he began to experience temporary hearing problems from 1974 onwards. By the 1980s he began to suffer permanent hearing problems, which over the years became progressively worse. Despite that, the claimant took no steps to obtain any expert advice or opinion about his hearing. He knew a possible cause for his problems, from the time they started, was noise at work and nothing different occurred in 2006, when he sought legal advice, to prompt his claim. He had simply received a leaflet advertising a no win, no fee legal service. The claimant's letter of claim was dated September 2006 and his claim was issued in March 2008. Days before the claim was issued, the defendant admitted liability for the early period of the claimant's employment up until 1980 when it alleged that the claimant was provided with protection. The principal issues were (1) whether the date of the claimant's knowledge for the purposes of s 14 was within the three years preceding the issue of the claim, and (2) if it was outside that period, whether the court should exercise its discretion pursuant to s 33.

Held:

(i)   The claimant first had knowledge that he had sustained a significant injury in the sense of s 14(1) by 1988 at the latest when he knew that he had a significant hearing impairment and his hearing loss and tinnitus had moved from temporary to permanent. Further, as the claimant said, he always knew that his hearing loss was due to noise at his place of work, and he knew that the significant injury was 'attributable' to something done or not done by the defendant pursuant to s 14(1)(b) again by 1988 at the latest. Thus the action was commenced outside the limitation period and was prima facie statute barred.

(ii)   There were no factors in s 33(3) that pointed to the discretion being exercised in the claimant's favour. There was a delay of 20 years in issuing proceedings. After instructing solicitors in about September 2006, the claimant still took 18 months to issue his claim. The defendant was first notified of the claim 18 years after the date on which the cause of action arose. There was no good explanation for the delay. The claimant was only prompted to make his claim because of a leaflet he received advertising a no win, no fee legal service. There was no reason why the claim could not have been brought within the limitation period. The evidence which the claimant was likely to be able to adduce was bound to be less cogent by reason of a 20-year delay. There had been no criticism of the defendant's conduct after the cause of action arose. The claimant took no steps to obtain medical, legal or expert advice prior to seeking legal advice in 2006.

(iii)   Whilst the defendant originally admitted liability for the early part of the claimant's employment, that did not prevent it from raising the limitation defence (*Cain v Francis* (p360) applied). It was abundantly clear that the admission was made without any investigation of the case and for commercial reasons only.

Judgment for defendant.

Davies v Babcock Energy Ltd

Limitation Act 1980, s 14, s 33

QBD (Swansea District Registry) (DJ Gray Hughes)   **Unreported**

The claimant was employed by the defendant between 1956 and 1957 as an electrical welder. The claimant alleged that during this period he was exposed to asbestos which later caused pleural disease. In 1972, 1982 and 1983 he applied for disablement benefit in relation to pneumoconiosis but was rejected. He reapplied successfully in 1986. His evidence was that he did not realise that the DSS would only deal with part of his claim and at that at that time he was preoccupied by caring for his ill mother. Shortly after she died in April 1990 he contacted the Citizens Advice Bureau and then a solicitor. The claimant instructed his current solicitors on 29 March 2003, who wrote to the defendant three months later. Proceedings were issued on 7 January 1994. The defendant applied to strike the claim out as statute barred.

Held:

(i)   The claimant did not have knowledge until 1986. Before then he had in effect been told by doctors that his injury was not significant. He was entitled to accept that view. Proceedings were therefore issued four years and five months late, not 12 years as contended by the defendant.

(ii)   As regards s 33:

    (a)   there is no long stop requiring the court to automatically refuse a s 33 discretion;

    (b)   the claimant suffered from a severe disability and it could not be said that the claim is weak. He would therefore be severely prejudiced if the action was not allowed to proceed;

    (c)   the defendant was able to pinpoint precise dates of employment;

    (d)   the defendant made no attempt to respond to the detailed statements of the claimant's solicitor as regards prejudice;

    (e)   the allegations relate to a system of work rather than an isolated incident;

    (f)   the defendant was dealing with 12 similar claims and had obtained engineering evidence in relation to them; and

    (g)   there was no allegation of contributory negligence. Therefore, if the claimant succeeded, he would succeed in full.

(iii)   It would therefore be equitable to allow the action to proceed. Obiter, the district judge stated that his decision would have been the same had he found for the defendant on date of knowledge.

Application dismissed. Costs in the case.

Davies v British Insulated Callender's Cables Ltd

Limitation Act 1939, s 2D

Thesiger J   **(1977) 121 SJ 203; (1979) Times, 15 February**

On 3 November 1970 the claimant (Mr Davies) was working with a gang of men clearing a long pipe. Their aim was to pull a brush through it with a rope. They held the rope over their shoulders and walked away from the pipe. An obstruction in the pipe caused the rope to stop and the claimant fell down.

His case was that the fall caused him a back injury which manifested itself a few days later. The accident was not reported, and no witness statements were taken. He did not seek legal advice until 1975. His writ was issued on 1 March 1976. He applied for the court's discretion under s 2D of the Limitation Act 1939 as amended to allow the action to continue.

Held:

(i)   The claimant had done nothing for five years. As he had been employed in the mines for about 40 years, it was hard to believe that he did not know that he could claim against his employers: s 2D(3)(a).

(ii) It was often difficult to pinpoint when a back injury occurred. The case was quite different from *Buck v English Electric Co Ltd*, a pneumoconiosis case where the defendants had been dealing with a series of similar claims. The defendants would find it extremely difficult to obtain evidence about this minor incident: s 2D(3)(b).

(iii) The defendants would be greatly prejudiced. It would not be equitable to allow the claimant's action to proceed: s 2D(1).

Buck v English Electric Co Ltd (p353) distinguished.

Davies v Reed Stock & Co Ltd and another

Limitation Act 1980, s 11, s 14, s 35

Court of Appeal   **Lexis, 26 July 1984**

On 16 October 1978 the claimant (Mr Davies) was injured in an accident which occurred on steps leading to the office of his employers, Reed Stock & Co Ltd. On 17 September 1981 his writ was issued against them. His statement of claim alleged that Reed Stock were the occupiers, and their defence admitted this.

In November 1982 Reed Stock's solicitors wrote to the claimant's solicitors with a proposed amended defence and third party notice. These withdrew the admission that Reed Stock were the occupiers and alleged that they held the premises under a lease whereby Lovells Shipping & Transport Group Ltd were the landlords and that Lovells had certain obligations as to the repairs of the steps.

Park J granted the claimant leave to amend his statement of claim so as to join Lovells as second defendants. Lovells appealed on the ground that s 35(1) of the Limitation Act 1980 produced the effect that, if leave to amend was given, the action against Lovells would be deemed to have started at the date of the original action against Reed Stock and that therefore Lovells would have no opportunity to pursue a limitation defence.

Held:

(i)   If there is a real question arising that the claim against the party sought to be joined may well be statute barred, it would be wrong to amend so as to permit the joinder of that party. In that sort of case, it may be necessary (a) to direct a preliminary trial to determine whether the action is statute barred or (b), in a complicated case, for the claimant to start a separate action and then consolidate it.

(ii) In this case, however, there was no serious question on limitation to be tried at all. The claimant was not aware of a possible claim against Lovells until November 1982: s 14(1)(d). In view of Reed Stock's previous admission, there had been nothing to put his solicitors on enquiry: s 14(3). Lovells had no triable limitation defence: s 11(4).

Their appeal was dismissed.

Davies and others v Secretary of State for Energy and Climate Change

Limitation Act 1980, s 33

Court of Appeal   **[2012] EWCA Civ 1380**

The claimants, eight representative former miners in a group action, had worked between 1954 and 1993 for British Coal, for whom the defendant was the successor in liability. They alleged that, negligently and in breach of statutory duty, they had been exposed to working conditions which were responsible in due course for the onset and development of osteoarthritis of the knee. Their primary allegation was that they were required to work using unsuitable roadways which caused repeated jarring and minor trauma to their knees.

It was impossible to say with any precision when injury was actually caused. The date of first diagnosis was therefore in each case bound to be later than the date on which the cause of action accrued, and none of the claimants could have had the relevant knowledge before first diagnosis of the condition. However, even on that basis, the shortest period of delay between the expiry of the limitation period and the issue of proceedings was 10 years, and the longest was 21 years. On a trial of the preliminary issues, the judge refused to exercise his discretion to disapply the primary limitation period. He found evidence of substantial prejudice to the defendant in three respects. First, he found the documentary evidence now available could only go so far to create the kind of picture necessary to show a case of repeated failures amounting to negligence and breach of statutory duty. The documentation which survived tended to concentrate upon major accidents. Secondly, he found that there was now a dearth of available and willing witnesses at the managerial level, the level at which would have lain the responsibility for arranging repairs to the roadways and so on. Thirdly, the judge was mindful of the impact of delay on recollection. The level of generality of the evidence given by the claimants tended to prove the point that recollection as to the cause of deteriorating conditions, and as to what was or could have been done about them and within what timescale, was severely impaired and imperfect. He also held that there was culpable delay on the part of the claimants.

The claimants appealed, submitting that (1) the judge had wrongly applied what he termed the 'broad merits' test; (2) the judge's assessment of the impact of the delay on the cogency of the evidence was clearly wrong; and (3) the judge's analysis of the reasons for the delay was at fault, and his treatment of those reasons, in particular in failing to give weight for those reasons for delay, was wrong.

Held:

(i)   The judge did not determine that the claims had no reasonable prospect of success. He recognised that the claimants' descriptions of the conditions of identified roadways over which they were obliged to walk for identifiable periods of their service underground might have been sufficient of itself to have established a prima facie case of breach of statutory duty. He identified the issues which were likely to arise at any substantive trial and the evidence which would be required to attempt to prove the case and to attempt to defend the claims. Both were equally important in assessing the broad view merits of the litigation. What the judge was rightly concerned to identify was the extent to which the enquiry would be hampered by the diminished cogency of the evidence available as a result of the long delay in bringing the claims. His approach to the assessment of the broad merits was careful, conscientious and impeccable.

(ii)   There was a clear distinction between the industrial disease cases, which concerned continuous exposure to a dangerous state of affairs or toxic substance, and the instant case where the injury was essentially traumatic. The judge was correct to regard the case as more akin to an accident case or to a case concerned with a series of accidents.

(iii)   It was accepted by the claimants that repeated jarring of and stressing to the knee joint was at all material times an inherent and inevitable concomitant of working in an underground mine. It was also accepted that there were numerous other possible causes of osteoarthritis. The substantive issues therefore were whether the employers were at any given time in respect of any given roadway in breach of their duty, which could only be resolved by a detailed examination of the circumstances in which a roadway came to be obstructed and the opportunity and resources available to the employers to remedy the situation, and then by detailed expert consideration of whether and to what extent such breach caused the osteoarthritis. The criticism that the judge had focused too much on the need to distinguish avoidable harm from the unavoidable was rejected: that distinction was at the heart of the case.

(iv)   In looking at all the circumstances of the case the judge was entitled to look at the totality of the delay and the impact of the delay (*Donovan v Gwentoys Ltd* (p412) and *Roebuck v Mungovin* [1994] 2 AC 224 considered). The judge recorded a positive conclusion that post-limitation period delay had caused additional substantial prejudice to the employers and had had a serious impact upon the cogency of the evidence. He gave careful and principled consideration to the impact of delay upon the cogency of evidence bearing upon the issues in the litigation and there was no error in his approach. His conclusion was well within the ambit of reasonable decision-making and indeed was clearly correct.

(v)   As at their date of knowledge the claimants had a firm belief that the knee conditions were as a result of their work as miners. There was a wholesale failure on their part to initiate an enquiry, to go to see a solicitor, to lobby their unions or to seek expert advice. The situation called out for consideration and enquiry. If any consideration was given the evidence did not reveal it, and the judge was presented with a case in which there was simply inaction on the part of both the claimants and their unions. The judge was correct to regard the claimants' failure to make enquiries as not telling in their favour when he came to exercise his discretion.

(vi)   The arguments advanced on behalf of the claimants, to the effect that they were dependent on the actions of their union and of other potential funders before they could contemplate the pursuit of any proceedings, were not well founded. There is no special privilege that attaches to a potential claimant just because he happened to be a member of a union. To hold otherwise would place him in a special position which has no basis in the terms of s 33.

Appeal dismissed.

Davis v City and Hackney Health Authority

Limitation Act 1980, s 11, s 14

Jowitt J   [1989] 2 Med LR 366

The claimant (Martin Davis) was born a spastic on 15 June 1963. He could only move with considerable difficulty, and his speech was seriously affected. When he was about 17, he asked his mother what caused this. She replied that she thought his delivery might have been mishandled but discouraged him from claiming damages. In February 1983 he left home to live with other disabled people. In August 1985 he met in a pub a law student who advised him that he might still be able to claim damages.

Consequently in September 1985 he consulted solicitors who received a report from Professor Taylor on 26 November 1986. This report criticised, not the delivery, but an injection of Ovametrin to his mother before his birth. The writ was issued on 1 April 1987. There was a preliminary trial on limitation.

Held:

(i)   The act alleged to constitute negligence was the injection of Ovametrin: s 14(1)(b). The claimant did not learn about this until the expert's report was available.

(ii)   In view of his disability and his heavy dependence on his parents, the claimant had not delayed unreasonably in failing to take legal advice earlier. He should not be fixed with any earlier date of constructive knowledge: s 14(3).

(iii)   Accordingly, the date of the claimant's knowledge was 26 November 1986 or a few days later when the contents of Professor Taylor's report were communicated to him. His claim was not statute barred: s 11(4).

Davis v (1) Jacobs (2) Camden & Islington Health Authority (3) Novartis Pharmaceuticals Ltd (4) Smith

Limitation Act 1980, s 33

Court of Appeal   **[1999] Lloyd's Rep Med 72;**
                                       (2000) 51 BMLR 42; LTL 5/3/1999

In 1971 the claimant set up a publishing business, which traded profitably until 1989. 1987 he began to suffer from persistent nasal congestion. His GP referred him to an ENT specialist who in turn referred him to the fourth defendant who prescribed Bromocriptine ('BC'). On 11 May 1989 the claimant attended the first defendant, a professor of medicine, complaining of side-effects from the drug. The dose was reduced and a different drug 'CV' recommended. CV was at the time in the process of clinical trials. The claimant signed a consent form, but one of the main controversies was whether or not he was given an information sheet. The claimant began CV treatment on 28 October 1989 and in June 1990 the dose was increased. The claimant's case was that BC had turned him psychotic and hypomanic and that these conditions were aggravated by CV. He was convicted for several criminal offences, his libido increased alarmingly and he lost a significant amount of weight.

On 28 September 1992 the claimant's solicitors wrote to the first defendant enquiring whether CV could account for this behaviour. On 17 December 1992 the first defendant gave evidence that CV could induce psychosis. In July 1993 the claimant told police that the drugs had turned him into a manic depressive. In April 1994 he informed his solicitors that he was concerned as to the effects of BC as well as CV. Proceedings were issued on 9 February 1995.

The claimant sought to amend his particulars in March 1997 to enlarge the time frame for the events he said constituted negligence. At a preliminary hearing the judge, attaching no credibility to the claimant as a witness, found that he had knowledge more than three years before the issue of proceedings. The judge declined to exercise his discretion under s 33. The claimant appealed.

Held:

(i)   An important factor as to knowledge was the degree of insight a hypomanic would have into his condition. Although the court would normally be very slow to interfere with a trial judge's findings of fact, the fact here that the trial judge, having seen the claimant, roundly disbelieved him, left the issue open to review. There was no evidence for it to be safe to conclude that the claimant had the relevant knowledge in relation to BC before May 1994.

(ii)   The only parts of the claim that were statute barred were therefore the amendments.

(iii)   The judge erred in attaching importance to an inapplicable non-statutory compensation scheme. The s 33 discretion should therefore be exercised afresh.

(iv)   Section 33 should be exercised in the claimant's favour. The relevant periods of delay were quite short. The claimant's solicitors had acted diligently, and some delay was unavoidable due to the factual complexity of the case. The defendants had failed to fully comply with pre-action disclosure. Although the judge had been entitled to take the merits of the claim into account, this should be done with great care. It would be inequitable to deny the claimant access to the court, notwithstanding that the defendant faced unrecoverable costs due to his being legally aided. However, the claimant's advisers should reconsider the pleadings in the light of their obligations to the Legal Aid Board and advise the Board to withdraw its support from those parts of the case lacking reasonable prospects of success.

Appeal allowed.

Davis v Ministry of Defence

Limitation Act 1980, s 14   **RSC Ord 18, r 19**

Court of Appeal   **[1985] CLY 2017**

The claimant (Henry Davis) was employed by the defendants from 1955. He worked as a welder until April 1969 when he contracted a localised attack of dermatitis. He suffered similar outbreaks up to August 1971 when he had a serious generalised outbreak and left the defendants' employment.

The claimant and his general practitioner had always believed that his dermatitis was due to contact with dust at his place of work. However, his solicitors obtained various negative medical reports and counsel's opinions, as a result of which the claimant was advised and accepted that there were no reasonable grounds for continuing his original claim. His writ which was issued in October 1973 was allowed to lapse.

A fresh writ was issued on 10 November 1981. The statement of claim pleaded that the claimant was unaware before 10 November 1978 that the general outbreak of dermatitis and his subsequent symptoms were attributable to the defendants' acts and omissions. The defendants pleaded limitation in their defence and applied to strike out the action under the inherent jurisdiction of the court. Sir Neil Lawson allowed their appeal against the master's refusal to grant this. The claimant appealed.

Held:

(i)   As the defendants' application was summarily to strike out the action in limine, the court should only accede to it if the answer to the question about the claimant's date of knowledge was clear and obvious and the contrary unarguable.

(ii)   'Knowledge' was an ordinary English word with a clear meaning to which full effect must be given. 'Reasonable belief' or 'suspicion' was not enough.

(iii)   The combined state of mind of the claimant himself, as a layman, and that of his medical and legal advisers, which must be attributed to him under s 14(3) of the Limitation Act 1980, could not so surely be said to have been such that he and they knew, prior to 10 November 1988, that his dermatitis was capable of being attributed to his working conditions in the defendant's employment: s 14(1)(b).

The claimant's appeal was allowed.

Davis v Saltenpar

Limitation Act 1939, s 2D

Hobhouse J   **(1983) 133 NLJ 720**

On 10 October 1977 the claimant (Mr Davis), a pedestrian, was struck by a car driven by the uninsured defendant. He was severely injured. His solicitors notified his claim to the Motor Insurers' Bureau who appointed an insurance company as their agents. Considerable correspondence ensued between the solicitors and the insurers.

The writ was issued on 3 November 1980. The defendant pleaded limitation. The claimant's application for an order that the primary limitation period should not apply was tried as a preliminary issue.

Held:

the application was refused because:

(i)   If a trial were to take place, it was never going to be a very satisfactory one in view of the defendant's character and the injuries (including amnesia) suffered by the claimant: s 33(3)(b).

(ii) The balance of advantage to the claimant was that he could sue his solicitors for damages for negligence: s 33(1).

(iii) The prejudice to the defendant was that he would continue to be involved in the action. It was appropriate for the court to take into account the position of the Motor Insurers' Bureau, for the insurers and the defendant should be viewed as a composite unit: s 33(1).

Davis v Union Insulation Co Ltd and another

Limitation Act 1980, s 33

Central London County Court (HHJ Hallgarten QC)　　　**29 February 2000, unreported**

The claimant worked for the defendant between 1965 and 1971. It was admitted that during that time he was negligently exposed to asbestos. This lead to pleural thickening. It was agreed that he had knowledge for limitation purposes by 19 June 1990 but did not issue proceedings until 22 December 1998. The defendant applied for the action to be struck out and the claimant sought relief under s 33.

Held:

(i) The reason for the first three years of delay was the collecting of evidence. However, the reason for the delay thereafter was:

(a) the claimant did not act on his solicitor's advice;

(b) he only reconsidered his position when his condition materially worsened in 1996/1997;

(c) there was a five-month gap between seeking and receiving the papers from previous solicitors;

(d) there was a 15-month delay after this before proceedings were started.

(ii) Although at first difficult to credit, having heard the claimant the judge accepted his evidence that he was under the misapprehension that a material deterioration in his condition would set the clock back to zero.

(iii) As the defendant admitted liability, there was no evidential prejudice arising from the post 1993 delay.

(iv) There was potentially some prejudice to the defendant in that the delay had led to the late discovery of a third possible defendant to whom damages can be apportioned. However, on the evidence, the chances of this new party being liable were quite remote.

(v) The claimant's employment record was not relevant.

(vi) The claimant's failures had to be weighed against the lack of prejudice to the defendant. The matter was very finely balanced, but overall it would be just equitable to allow the claim to proceed.

Claim allowed to continue. No order as to costs.

Dawson v Scott-Brown

Limitation Act 1980, s 28(1), s 32(1)　　　　　　　**RSC Ord 18, r 19(1)**

Court of Appeal　　　　　　　　　　　　　　　　**18 October 1988**

The claimant (Richard Dawson) was an able-seaman in the Royal Navy. Surgeon-Commander Scott-Brown reported on his medical condition. His reports led to the claimant being discharged from the Royal Navy on the grounds of mental ill-health in October 1974.

In July 1987 the claimant issued a writ, alleging negligence in relation to Surgeon-Commander Scott-Brown's reports and treatment. The master struck out his statement of claim and dismissed the action pursuant to RSC Ord 18, r 19(1).

Held:

(i)   The fact that the claimant was invalided out of the Navy on the ground of mental ill-health did not mean that he was incapable of managing his affairs, so the extension of time in s 28(1) Limitation Act 1980 did not apply;

(ii)   The Surgeon-Commander took no steps to conceal what he was reporting. While he did not disclose the reports to the claimant, this was because it was to the Navy that the reports were made. Thus the claimant could not rely on s 32(1)(b) Limitation Act 1980;

(iii)   The master was entitled to conclude that, since the limitation defence was almost inevitably bound to succeed, the action was an abuse of the process of the court and should be dismissed.

Day v Eli Lilly & Co and others

Limitation Act 1980, s 11, s 14, s 33

Court of Appeal   **[1992] 3 Med LR 382**

See *Nash v Eli Lilly & Co* (D) (p568)

Deeming v British Steel Corporation

Limitation Act 1939, s 2D

Court of Appeal   **(1978) 123 SJ 303**

On 26 June 1973 the claimant (Mr Deeming) sustained severe injuries when he was knocked down by a motor vehicle driven by L at the defendants' premises. He sued L and obtained judgment in default of defence. On applying to set this aside, L swore an affidavit that he was the defendants' employee, that at the time of the accident he had been travelling to work in a vehicle which belonged to someone else, that he had been examined during an internal inquiry by the defendants' work police, and that he had been a disqualified driver and was not covered by any insurance.

On 8 December 1976 the claimant issued a writ against the defendants. At the hearing of cross-appeals from a decision of Swanwick J, it was accepted that the case was prima facie statute barred because the claimant's solicitors had received a copy of the report of the defendants' internal inquiry which contained information about L's position. Thus the appeal hearing was confined to the claimant's appeal under s 2D of the Limitation Act 1939 as amended.

Held:

(i)   The delay that was relevant was the 5½-month delay between 26 June and 8 December 1976. It did not affect the cogency of the defendant's evidence. The judge had come to the wrong conclusion about this: s 2D(3)(b).

(ii)   The judge was right in not attaching too much weight to the fact that the prejudice to the claimant, if not permitted to proceed, was reduced to some extent by the claim that he had against L: s 2D(1).

The claimant's cross-appeal was allowed.

Deerness v John R Keeble & Son (Brantham) Ltd and another

Limitation Act 1980, s 33

House of Lords   **[1983] 2 Lloyd's Rep 260;
133 NLJ 641; [1983] Com LR 221**

On 7 October 1977 the claimant (Lorna Deerness), a 19-year-old prospective professional showjumper, was a passenger in a car driven by the second defendant which ran into a lamp standard on a motorway. She sustained very serious injuries which left her a paraplegic. The first defendant was convicted on her plea of guilty of a charge of careless driving.

The claimant's solicitors notified her claim to the two defendants both of whom were insured by Cornhill Insurance. Negotiations proceeded in a desultory fashion. A writ was issued on 23 August 1979 but was not served. In August 1980 the Cornhill made an interim payment of £5,000.

On 23 April 1981, the first writ having expired due to oversight on the part of the claimant's solicitors, a fresh writ was issued. Comyn J gave the claimant leave to proceed under s 33 of the Limitation Act 1980 through finding 'exceptional circumstances' to justify avoiding the application of the decision in *Walkley v Precision Forgings Ltd*. The Court of Appeal reversed the judge's decision. The claimant appealed.

Held:

(i)   None of the matters relied on by the judge as exceptional circumstances could overcome the fatal obstacle caused by the fact that a writ was issued within the primary limitation period. Consequently the prejudice to the claimant had been caused by her solicitors' inaction, not by the operation of the Limitation Act 1980.

(ii)   Neither the interim payment nor anything else in the correspondence amounted to an agreement or representation by the Cornhill that it would not rely on a limitation defence. The failure to serve or renew the writ was due to the solicitors' oversight, not the Cornhill's conduct.

(iii)   The claimant would not suffer, since by now she had already received £100,000 and would proceed to recover the balance from her solicitors' insurers.

Her appeal was dismissed.

Walkley v Precision Forgings Ltd (p705) applied.

NB: *Walkley* was overruled in *Horton v Sadler* (p482).

Denford v Redbridge and Waltham Forest HA

Limitation Act 1980, s 11, s 33

QBD (Tucker J)   **[1996] 7 Med LR 376**

In November 1973, at the defendant's hospital, the claimant was wrongly diagnosed as suffering from coeliac disease. After his readmission to the hospital in August 1974 with abdominal acute pain, his doctor wished to repeat tests carried out in 1973. The claimant refused and discharged himself. His symptoms continued, and in March 1991 he was admitted to another hospital and diagnosed as having cholecystitis and gallstones. After a cholecystectomy the claimant was told in August 1991 that he had never suffered from coeliac disease. He issued proceedings in February 1994 alleging negligent medical treatment between April 1973 and August 1974. Limitation was heard as preliminary issue.

Held:

(i)   It could not be said that the original diagnosis was not questioned in 1974; it was because the doctor was unsure about it that he ordered further tests.

(ii)   The claimant ought to have realised that the diagnosis was provisional; by discharging himself and refusing further tests in the unreasonable belief that it would serve no useful purpose, he had deprived both those treating him and himself from acquiring the knowledge which would have revealed the true nature of his complaint.

(iii)   By virtue of s 14(3) the date of the claimant's constructive knowledge could be fixed at 1975 at the latest, as by then he could have been reasonably expected to acquire such knowledge from facts ascertainable by him with the help of medical advice which it was reasonable for him to seek.

(iv)   The action was therefore out of time. The court would not exercise its discretion under s 33 of the Act as it would be inequitable to do so in light of the serious prejudice which would be caused to the defendant by a total delay of over 20 years.

Claim dismissed.

De Martell v Merton and Sutton HA

Limitation Act 1980, s 14

QBD (HHJ Simpson QC)   **[1995] 6 Med LR 234**

The claimant alleged that negligence by the defendant had caused his condition of athetoid cerebral palsy in the 40 minutes immediately prior to his birth. The defendant denied this and argued that the claim was time barred as proceedings were not issued until more than three years after his 18th birthday. Substantive and limitation issues were heard together.

Held:

(i)   It was reasonable for the claimant not to enquire into the circumstances of his birth as his mother had become pregnant by her uncle. In those special circumstances his contention that he had not acquired actual knowledge until over two years after his 18th birthday was credible.

(ii)   If the claimant did have constructive knowledge, the court would exercise its discretion under s 33 and allow the claim to proceed. This was because no prejudice had been caused to the defendant and the special circumstances provided good mitigation for the claimant not investigating his birth.

(iii)   Although a competent registrar would not have allowed the labour to proceed but would have ordered a Caesarean section, the claimant had not established that his condition had been caused during the short period prior to his birth.

Limitation decided in the claimant's favour, but claim dismissed.

Devonport v A V Wright (Builders) Ltd

Limitation Act 1980, s 14, s 33

Webster J   **Lexis, 23 April 1985**

On 18 January 1980 the claimant (Mr Devonport) suffered an injury to his back as a result of an accident at work. The next day he could not move, so he was taken by ambulance to hospital where he was an inpatient from 19 January for one day and from 22 January for a fortnight. He still suffered back pains after his discharge and underwent traction and a six week course of physiotherapy. His second course of traction started in late April or early May 1980. When it failed, he became despondent about his injury and thought that it might be more serious.

On 5 February 1980 he took to the defendants' contracts manager a DHSS form to complete about the accident. Apart from that, the claimant's main priority was getting back to work. In September 1982 he first saw a solicitor who advised him that he might have a good claim. However, he was uncertain that he wished to proceed, and no legal aid forms were completed. The solicitor omitted to enter the third anniversary of the accident in his diary. When he realised this, he immediately sought instructions from the claimant and issued the writ on 20 April 1983. A preliminary trial of the limitation defence was ordered.

Held:

(i) The claimant would not reasonably have considered the injury sufficiently serious to justify his instituting proceedings for damages until May 1980 or thereafter: s 14(2). Accordingly, the writ was issued in time within the Limitation Act 1980: s 11(4).

(ii) (a) The reasons for the claimant's delay were not really explained or entirely clear: s 33(3)(a);

(b) there was evidence that the three-month delay from January 1983 to April 1983 did not have any effect on the cogency of the evidence: s 33(3)(b);

(c) the claimant did not act promptly on learning in September 1982 that he had a good claim. However, he did not act unreasonably because he could assume his solicitor would protect his interests: s 33(3)(e);

(d) in principle he would have a claim against his solicitors, but in the circumstances any claim against them would be, if not speculative, by no means certain of success: s 33(3);

(e) even if the limitation period ran from 18 January 1980, it would be equitable to allow the action to proceed, because the prejudice to the claimant if it did not would be greater than the prejudice to the defendants if it did: s 33(1).

NB: The authors express respectful surprise at the learned judge's ruling under ss 11 and 14 of the Limitation Act 1980. However, it is clear that he was acting well within the exercise of his discretion when deciding in favour of the claimant under s 33.

Dickins v Solicitors Indemnity Fund

CPR 7.5

Sir Andrew Morritt (C)   **[2005] EWHC 2754 (Ch); LTL 26/10/2005**

The claimant issued proceedings against the defendant seeking declaration of entitlement to an indemnity. He did so three days before the expiry of the limitation period. He then applied without notice for a four-month extension of the validity period for service. This was refused but a seven-day extension granted. The claimant had given the defendant no notice of either the application or its result. The defendant applied unsuccessfully set aside the order. The defendant appealed. The claimant accepted that the order should not have been made, but argued that it would be unjust and disproportionate to dismiss the claim for relying upon it.

Held:

(i) If in these circumstances there was no justification for a four-month extension then there was no justification for a seven-day extension.

(ii) The master had incorrectly considered that the discussions between the deputy master and the claimant constituted an arrangement and that it would have been unjust to nullify.

(iii) The master had also asked himself the wrong question and had failed to adequately consider the implications for the defendant. The hearing to set aside was a rehearing and he ought to have asked himself if the order should have been made at all.

(iv)   The deputy master had failed to determine the application in accordance with well-established principles. His order was wrong and both ought to be set aside.

Appeal allowed.

Dobbie v Medway Health Authority

Limitation Act 1980, s 11, s 14, s 33, s 38

Court of Appeal   **[1994] 1 WLR 1234;**
[1994] 4 All ER 450; [1994] 5 Med LR 160

In April 1973 the claimant attended the defendant's hospital for the excision of a lump on her breast. The surgeon took the view that the lump was cancerous and, without further investigation, removed the claimant's breast. It was subsequently established that the lump had been benign and this was communicated to the claimant shortly after the accident. The claimant suffered devastating psychological consequences as a result of the mastectomy. In 1988 she became aware that the breast need not have been removed. On 5 May 1989 she issued proceedings. The defendant pleaded limitation which was heard as a preliminary issue. The judge held that the claim was statute barred and declined to exercise his discretion under s 33. The claimant appealed.

Held:

(i)   Section 14 did not require knowledge that the defendant's action was negligent. Attributability referred to causation rather than legal responsibility.

(ii)   The claimant had known within a short time of the operation that her injury – the removal of a healthy breast, irrespective of whether or not that removal was necessary – was significant and attributable to the defendant's acts or omissions. The lack of knowledge of arguable negligence was irrelevant and time began to run in 1973. The claim was therefore statute barred.

(iii) The definition of 'injury' in s 38(1) could not be qualified by reference to its source or aetiology. Nor was there any need, in a medical context, to import any concept of a reasonable patient. Where a doctor attempts to cure an affliction but fails to do so, the patient will continue to suffer an 'injury' as he would be suffering an impairment to his health requiring further medical intervention.

(iv)   Given the extent of the delay, it would not be equitable to exercise discretion under s 33 to allow the claim to continue.

(v)   (obiter) There was no prejudice to a doctor in having an action hanging over his head for a long period of time when the doctor is not in fact aware that an action is contemplated against him (*Biss v Lambeth, Southwark and Lewisham HA* (p336) distinguished).

Appeal dismissed.

Dodds v Walker

Computation of time

House of Lords   **[1981] 2 All ER 609; [1981] 1 WLR 1027;**
125 SJ 463; 42 P&CR 131

Under s 29(3) of the Landlord and Tenant Act 1954 the claimant (Robert Dodds) had to apply for a new business tenancy 'not … more than four months after the giving of the landlord's notice'. The landlord's notice was given on 30 September 1978. The claimant's application was made on 31 January 1979.

The claimant appealed against the majority decision of the Court of Appeal that his application was out of time.

Held: the general rule is the corresponding date rule. When the relevant period is a month or a specified number of months after the giving of a notice, the general rule is that the period ends on the corresponding date in the appropriate subsequent month, ie the day of that month that bears the same number as the day of the earlier month on which the notice was given. Accordingly, the claimant's application was out of time. His appeal was dismissed.

Per curiam: the corresponding date rule is modified for notices given on the 31st day of a month and expiring in a 30-day month or in February, and notices expiring in February and given on the 30th or 29th (except in leap years) of any other month of the year. In these exceptional cases, the period given by the notice ends on the last day of the month in which the notice expires.

Re Donald Kenyon Ltd

Companies Act 1948, s 353

Roxburgh J **[1956] 3 All ER 596; [1956] 1 WLR 1397**

On or about 1 March 1949, pursuant to s 353 of the Companies Act 1948, Donald Kenyon Ltd was struck off the register of companies. In 1956 the petitioner (Mabel Kenyon), a director, applied for the company to be restored to the register. Her petition stated that the company's debts had all become statute barred.

Held: when a company has been dissolved and cannot be sued without being restored to the register, it is only common fairness that, if the contributories for their own purposes want to have its name restored to the register years later, the position of legitimate creditors should be protected. Accordingly, the order for restoration must contain a proviso that, in the case of creditors whose debts were not statute barred at the date of dissolution, the period between the date of dissolution and the date of restoration to the register should not be counted for the purpose of any statute of limitation.

Donovan v Gwentoys Ltd

Limitation Act 1980, s 33

House of Lords **[1990] 1 All ER 1018; [1990] 1 WLR 472**

On 25 April 1963 the claimant (Lorraine Donovan) was born. On 3 December 1979 she had an accident at work. Her case was that she slipped on a plastic bag on the floor of the defendants' factory, as a result of which she strained her right wrist and suffered an aggravation to a pre-existing condition in her right knee. She received industrial injury benefit from the DHSS for the injury to her wrist but did not claim damages.

On 6 April 1984 she consulted a solicitor who filed a legal aid application but took no steps to issue a protective writ by 25 April 1984. A vaguely worded letter before action was sent in September 1984. The writ was issued on 10 October 1984. Only when the statement of claim was served in January 1985 did the defendants know that they were being blamed for the claimant having slipped on a plastic bag. Not until a medical report was disclosed in January 1986 did they learn that the claimant's claim focused on injury to her right knee.

The Court of Appeal upheld the judgment of HH Judge Francis that the claimant should be allowed to proceed with her claim under s 33 of the Limitation Act 1980, on the grounds that the judge was right to have regard only to the 5½ month delay after the expiry of the limitation period. The defendants appealed.

Held:

(i)   The delay referred to in s 33(3)(b) is delay subsequent to the expiry of the limitation period.

(ii)   It does not, however, follow that, in weighing the prejudice to the defendant under s 33(1), the court is not entitled to take into account the date on which the claim is first made. This is always relevant. The defendants were faced with a truly stale claim and would be seriously prejudiced if it were allowed to proceed.

(iii)   It was very difficult to envisage circumstances which would acquit the claimant's solicitors of negligence. She would suffer only slight prejudice if required to pursue her remedy against them: s 33(1).

The defendants' appeal was allowed.

Dorgan v Home Office

CPR 6.7

Human Rights Act 1998, s 3   **ECHR, Art 6**

Court of Appeal   **[2002] EWCA Civ 933;**
[2002] 1 WLR 3174; [2002] 3 All ER 813

See *Anderton v Clwyd County Council* (D) (p303)

Dornan v J W Ellis & Co Ltd

Amendment of statement of claim

Court of Appeal   **1962] 1 All ER 303; [1962] 1 QB 583;**
[1962] 2 WLR 250

On 10 April 1957 the claimant (Patrick Dornan) lost the sight of an eye through flying metal from a broken drill in the defendants' factory. His writ was issued in February 1960 and served in January 1961.

In March 1961 the statement of claim was served. It alleged that the drill was defective and that the defendants failed to fence it securely or to supply the claimant with goggles.

In October 1961 the claimants' solicitors applied to amend the statement of claim by alleging that a fellow employee failed to ensure that the drill was firmly held in the machine and failed to use reasonable care in its manipulation.

Winn J refused the amendment, not as a matter of discretion, but because he considered that he had no authority to allow it. The claimant appealed.

Held:

(i)   Although the fresh allegations added the element of vicarious liability, they did not introduce a new cause of action. They were all part of the allegation that the claimant suffered injury through lack of proper care by the defendants, their servants or agents. The allegation against the fellow workman was an extension of the existing case rather than a new case.

(ii) As the judge did not exercise his discretion, because he thought that he did not possess any, the appeal would be allowed.

NB: The same set of facts would now be governed by s 35 of the Limitation Act 1980 and CPR Part 19. It is submitted that the same conclusion would be reached.

Doughty v North Staffordshire Health Authority

Limitation Act 1980, s 11, s 14, s 33

Henry J   **[1992] 3 Med LR 81**

On 20 April 1957 the claimant (Mrs Doughty) was born with an extensive birth mark, known as a port wine stain, on the right side of her face. A plastic surgeon, Mr Growcott, operated twice on her when she was five. Thereafter there was no turning back. She had had 12 operations by his retirement in 1974. His successor then advised that no significant improvement was possible and questioned whether it had been right to embark on the long course of surgery. Her face had been significantly scarred by the operations, and some of the port wine stain remained.

In 1976 she consulted solicitors who obtained a limited legal aid certificate. In 1978, after a discouraging expert's opinion, counsel advised that there was no case and the certificate was discharged. In 1982 she gave birth to a severely handicapped daughter and became preoccupied with looking after her. In 1985 she was put in touch with AVMA. Around this time she was divorcing her husband who had blamed her for their daughter's genetic disorder and walked out on her. AVMA referred her to a solicitor who contacted her in April 1986. He let the case go to sleep until he issued a writ on 2 December 1987. After an expert's report, there was a conference with counsel in March 1989. The statement of claim was not served until February 1990. The defence pleaded limitation.

Held:

(i) The claimant knew when she saw her surgeon's successor in 1974 that her injury was significant and that it was attributable to the course of surgery: s 14(1). Therefore her case was prima facie statute barred by s 11 of the Limitation Act 1980.

(ii) (a) The length of the delay was considerable. The reasons were discouraging professional advice, compounded by the limitations on the legal aid certificate: s 33(3)(a);

     (b) the reality of the delay was a trial in 1991 rather than 1980. The most serious effect on evidence was that the surgeon had a stroke in 1989 that left him unable to testify. This distinctly reduced the cogency of the defendants' evidence, but the basic medical records were still available: s 33(3)(b);

     (c) the claimant's present solicitors did not act promptly, but in view of all her other problems the claimant could not be blamed for any failure to chivvy or activate them: s 33(3)(e);

     (d) the course of treatment had blighted the claimant's childhood and affected her whole life. She was not to blame for the delay. Although there was prejudice to the defendants, as a fair trial was still possible it was equitable to disapply s 11 of the Limitation Act 1980: s 33(1).

The defendants were found negligent, and the claimant was awarded £30,000.

Down v Harvey and others

Limitation Act 1939, s 2D

Court of Appeal

**[1978] 2 All ER 851; [1978] QB 886;
[1978] 2 WLR 1; 122 SJ 147**

See *Firman v Ellis* (p433)

Dowson and others v Chief Constable of Northumbria

CPR 17.4

QBD (Manchester) Coulson J

[2009] EWHC 907 (QB)

The claimant police officers, in nine linked cases, applied for permission to amend their particulars of claim in proceedings for harassment brought against the defendant chief constable. The chief constable applied to strike out the claims of three of the respondents. The central features of the proceedings were illustrated by reference to the lead claim (C1). The allegations of harassment concerned the conduct of a chief inspector (P), who had been responsible for a team to which all the applicants belonged. The chief constable was said to be vicariously liable for P's conduct. In the case of C1, the pleaded particulars of harassment dealt with a series of events covering at least two police operations. C1 alleged that, through a combination of P's aggressive manner and his use of inappropriate, and at times unlawful, policing techniques, P had caused problems in what had previously been a cohesive team. C1 alleged that he had been bullied by P, had been required to act in an unprofessional and unlawful way, had received negative appraisals and that, when he had complained, he had been removed from the team. He maintained that he had suffered severe stress, loss of status and loss of income and benefits as a result. The allegations of harassment were repeated in a variety of permutations in the other claims. The chief constable submitted that (1) certain proposed amendments raised new claims or causes of action outside the limitation period and those claims did not arise out of the same facts as those already pleaded so the court should refuse permission to amend them; and (2) the conduct complained of was pursued for the purposes of preventing or detecting crime and so the exception under s 1(3)(a) of the Protection from Harassment Act 1997 applied.

Held (in relation to the amendments):

(i) The court has to consider the proposed amendments by reference to the overriding objective (CPR 1.1), to maintain a balance between the desirability of an adjudication on all the issues, and the need to ensure that late amendments do not cause irredeemable prejudice to the recipient. It is important not to take too legalistic an approach, particularly in circumstances such as these, where many of the particulars of claim allege a considerable number of different events. The court should seek to avoid hobbling the trial process by interlocutory rulings to the effect that conduct at a meeting on one day can be legitimately the subject of evidence, whilst evidence about conduct at a meeting on the next day must be excluded because it was only raised after the limitation period had expired.

(ii) Whilst it will often be a question of fact and degree, not each alleged incident of harassment necessarily gives rise to a separate claim or cause of action. Harassment arises out of a course of conduct. If a course of conduct has originally been pleaded, and by way of amendment a claimant seeks to add one or two other factual events said to be part of that course of conduct, then those amendments may not themselves give rise to a separate claim. Depending on the precise nature of the amendments, they may constitute further particulars of a claim which has already been pleaded. Alternatively, even if the amendment does raise a new claim or cause of action, if it is similar in nature, chronology and effect to matters already in issue, it may well be found to arise out of the same or substantially the same facts and matters as those already pleaded.

(iii)   Save for three specific matters relating to the claims pursued by C1 and another, all the proposed amendments to the particulars of claim relating to P's conduct, including the conduct during the two police operations, were allowed either because they were entirely a matter of factual background or they were not new claims and, if they were, they arose out of the same or substantially the same facts as those already pleaded (*Cobbold v Greenwich LBC* unreported, 9 August 1999, CA, applied, *Savings & Investment Bank Ltd (In Liquidation) v Fincken* [2003] EWCA Civ 1630, [2004] 1 WLR 667, *Brickfield Properties v Newton* [1971] 1 WLR 862 CA (Civ Div) and *Chantrey Vellacott v Convergence Group Plc* (p368) followed).

(iv)   As regards the three specific matters, two of them were new claims, which were statute barred and which did not arise out of the same or substantially the same facts as those already pleaded.

(v)   The third matter did not appear to be a proper allegation. More information was required before that amendment could be ruled upon.

Driscoll-Varley v Parkside Health Authority

Limitation Act 1980, s 11, s 14

Hidden J   [1991] 2 Med LR 346

On 18 April 1984 the claimant (Ann Driscoll-Varley) was assaulted by her then husband who kicked her and caused her to fall downstairs. She was taken straight to St Mary's Hospital in Paddington where she was treated by traction, with a pin through her right heel, until 30 April. On 1 May the pin was removed and plaster encased round her leg. On 2 May a supervised attempt at walking showed this to be unsuccessful. On 3 May her leg was fixed by the insertion of a nail. The wound improved, and by spring 1985 she was able to walk normally.

After the Kunschner nail was removed on 28 July 1985, her leg became hot, swollen, painful and blistered. In September 1985 Mr Johnson, the new consultant, advised that a sinogram be carried out and then informed her that he felt that there was a piece of dead bone floating around, causing infection. She had great faith in Mr Johnson who performed nine operations on her over the next 12 months to September 1986 in an effort to obtain satisfactory union. She was also terrified of losing her leg.

In August 1986 she instructed solicitors who issued a writ in April 1987. She instructed them not to serve it, for fear of alienating Mr Johnson who continued to treat her. In June 1987 he referred her to another specialist who fixed her right tibia using a Gross-Kempf nail with two cross screws and discharged her from his care in November 1987. She instructed new solicitors who received expert advice on 30 June 1988 that the cause of her problem was that her leg had been removed from traction too early. They obtained an ex parte order extending the validity of the writ and served it in July 1988. In early May 1989 the defendants on appeal obtained an order setting aside the renewal and service.

On 4 May 1989 a fresh writ was issued. After close of pleadings, a preliminary trial of the limitation defence was ordered.

Held:

(i)   The claimant knew that her injury was significant by September 1985 when the sinogram showed that her leg had not correctly set and that there was dead bone: s 14(1)(a).

(ii)   It was only on 30 June 1988 that the claimant learned that her injury, in the sense of failure of the damaged leg to respond to treatment in a normal and satisfactory manner, was capable of being attributed to the act or omission alleged to constitute negligence, namely prematurely taking her off traction and mobilising her limb: s 14(1)(b).

(iii)   The burden of establishing any earlier date of constructive knowledge under s 14(3) was upon the defendants.

(iv)   It was perfectly reasonable for the claimant, with her burning desire to keep her leg and her firm faith that the best way to do so was to continue with treatment by Mr Johnson, to act as she did. The defendants had not discharged the burden of fixing her with any earlier constructive knowledge: s 14(3).

(v)   Accordingly, the action was not statute barred under s 11 of the Limitation Act 1980.

Drury v Grimsby HA

Limitation Act 1980, s 14, s 33

QBD (HHJ Bentley QC)   **[1997] 8 Med LR 38; (1998) 42 BMLR 208**

The claimant was admitted to the defendant's hospital in November 1976 for an operation to remove a suspected rodent ulcer on his nose. The excised tissue was shown by histological examination to include part of a carcinoma, local excision of which was not complete. The claimant alleged that he was not told to attend for a follow-up examination, and a blue mark reappeared on the nose shortly after surgery. The tip of the nose became irregular and wart-like, and by the time the claimant was again admitted for surgery in January 1978, the cancer was so extensive that the whole of the nose had to be removed. After a number of operations to reconstruct his nose, the claimant underwent prosthesis in July 1990. He instructed solicitors in November 1990 and medical records were obtained by August 1991. Proceedings alleging the defendant to have been negligent in failing to recall the claimant following receipt of the histology report in November 1976 was issued in December 1992. Limitation was heard as preliminary issue.

Held:

(i)   The cause of action accrued in early 1977 when the blue mark reappeared.

(ii)   The claimant knew that he had suffered a significant injury within the meaning of s 14 when he came round from the operation in 1978 and was told his nose had been removed. However, he did not learn of the omission of which he now complained until he learnt of the contents of an expert's report in January 1992. Until that date his dissatisfaction with the medical treatment received had centred around the unsatisfactory result achieved by reconstructive surgery. He therefore did not have actual knowledge until that date.

(iii)   The claimant was told that the second operation was to remove a cancerous lesion. On the facts then within his knowledge, he ought reasonably to have drawn the conclusion that the first lesion may also have been cancerous, and that his problems in 1978 may have stemmed from the manner in which the first lesion was dealt with in 1976. He ought reasonably to have sought advice on this question, and had he done so, the fact that the contents of the histology report had not been acted upon would have been discovered by 1982 at the latest. He therefore had constructive knowledge that the injury was capable of being attributable to the omission by 1982 and the claim was primarily statute barred.

(iv)   The delay was due to the plaintiff's ignorance, to which the defendant had contributed by its lack of candour and especially by withholding from him information about the histology report.

(v)   The evidence that the defendant could now call on was possibly less cogent than it would have been had proceedings been issued in time, but there was a strong probability that the defendant was in no worse position now than it would have been; the clinical records survived and showed no record of recall action.

(vi)   Once the claimant knew he had a possible claim, he had acted promptly in pursuing it.

(vii)   It would be equitable to disapply the limitation period under s 33.

Preliminary issue determined in the claimant's favour.

Durham v T & N plc

Foreign Limitation Periods Act 1984, s 1

Court of Appeal   **LTL 2/5/1996**

The claimant's husband worked for the defendant from 1955 to 1956, during which time he was exposed to asbestos. In 1992 he discovered he had mesothelioma. On 26 November 1993 he issued proceedings. In September 1993 he had recovered Can$44,000 from a Quebec Government authority whereby an employee who suffers disease or injury at work in entitled to compensation from his employer without proof of fault. This was not disclosed to the defendant until late in proceedings. The defendant then amended its defence to plead jurisdictional issues. It was admitted that the defendant was negligent in exposing the claimant to asbestos. It was also agreed that they were occupiers of the Canadian factory where the negligence occurred. At a preliminary hearing the judge held that the cause of action was extinguished; Quebec law required a claim to be brought within a year of discovery of injury and, as the claimant could not recover under Quebec law, he could not be in a better position under English law. The claimant appealed.

Held:

(i)   The cause of action clearly arose in Quebec.

(ii)   There was no reason on the facts to depart from the rule that the defendant must be liable under both English and foreign systems of law for the claimant to maintain an action in the English courts for a wrong committed outside the country.

(iii) The one-year time limit therefore extinguished the claimant's claim in both jurisdictions.

(iv)   Section 1 of the 1984 Act excluded the English law of limitation; s 1(2) did not apply.

(v)   It would be wrong to treat a foreign limitation period as contrary to public policy simply on the basis that it was less generous than was provided under English law.

Appeal dismissed.

EB v Haughton

Limitation Act 1980, s 33

QBD (Slade J)   **[2011] EWHC 279 (QB)**

The claimant, who was born August 1982, sought damages from the defendant for psychological injuries caused by his sexual abuse of her. She claimed that the defendant had sexually abused her over the course of a year in 1993 when she was between 10 and 11 years old. She claimed that he had stroked her legs and breasts, and that he had once digitally penetrated her vagina under the guise of giving her a massage. In 1994 she had told social services that she was uncomfortable around the defendant. At around the same time she told a friend and a foster carer about some of the assaults. In 2003 the defendant pleaded guilty to the indecent assault of another young girl and, in December 2004, the claimant made a statement to the police about her own abuse. This led to the defendant being prosecuted. In August 2006, under the law as it then was (*Stubbings v Webb* (p677)) the fixed six-year limitation period expired.

In September 2006 the defendant was acquitted of the offences forming the basis of the claimant's civil action. In May 2007 the claimant successfully claimed compensation from the CICA. In January 2008 the House of Lords in *A v Hoare* (p287) reversed *Stubbings v Webb* so that the s 33 discretion became available in respect of claims for intentionally inflicted injuries.

The claimant intimated civil proceedings by way of a letter of claim in February 2008, issuing a claim form in December 2009. Limitation was heard at trial alongside the substantive issues. The claimant submitted that her claim had been conclusively statute barred until the decision in

Hoare, that she had been a minor for some of the time since the accrual of the cause of action, and that a fair trial was possible. The defendant argued that the claimant had not shown any good reason for her delay in issuing proceedings and that requiring him to face stale allegations more than seven years after the expiry of the limitation period constituted prejudice.

Held:

(i)   The evidence in support of the claimant's allegations was cogent. The types of assault she alleged were unusual; she maintained, credibly, that her recollection of them was clear; and she had mentioned them to others. In addition, some weight was to be given to the defendant's plea of guilty to a strikingly similar offence.

(ii)   Save for the period between early 2008 and late 2009, for which no good explanation had been given, the claimant's delay in issuing the proceedings was explicable. She would have been satisfied if the defendant had been convicted for the assaults, it was only after his acquittal that she thought about bringing civil proceedings, and it was not unreasonable for her to await the outcome of the criminal trial. While a precautionary claim could have been lodged, it was not unreasonable for her to await the decision of the House of Lords in *Hoare*.

(iii)   The defendant would suffer little or no prejudice if the limitation period were extended. The allegations were the same as those made in the criminal proceedings and he had been made fully aware of them in 2005. While he had not been notified of the possibility of civil proceedings for more than a year after his acquittal, he did not suggest that any evidence was lost by reason of the delay. The issue was one of recollection, and the assessment of the claimant's recollection as against defendant's would be central.

(iv)   While the authorities did not go so far as to state that lack of prejudice to the defendant would trump all other considerations, it was a factor that was to be given considerable weight (*A v Hoare* (p287), *B v Nugent Care Society* (p315) and *Cain v Francis* (p360) followed).

(v)   The limitation period would therefore be disapplied.

(vi)   As to substantive issues, the claimant's evidence was to be preferred to that of the defendant. Her allegations were found proved. The psychiatric evidence was that in the years since the assaults she had suffered from an emotional disorder, a generalised anxiety disorder and post-traumatic stress disorder. The assaults were the principal cause of her continuing mental health problems. The guidelines on psychiatric damage issued by the Judicial Studies Board were to be taken into consideration in valuing such claims, and general damages would be awarded in the sum of £28,000. An award of aggravated damages was not appropriate.

Judgment for claimant.

EL v Children's Society

Limitation Act 1980, s 33

QBD (Haddon-Cave J)   **[2012] EWHC 365 (QB)**

The claimant (born November 1944) claimed damages for the sexual abuse he had suffered in childhood whilst living in a children's home run by the defendant charity.

The claimant had been taken into the defendant's care and had lived at the children's home for various periods between 1949 and 1959. In mid-2008, he contacted the defendant complaining that, between 1956 and 1959, he had been sexually assaulted by the houseparents' son (B) when B was at the home either on leave from National Service or on vacation from university. The defendant referred the matter to the police in accordance with its procedures, and the claimant was interviewed by the police in November 2008. He gave an account of the alleged abuse, including two instances of anal rape.

In July 2009, B was arrested on a charge of buggery. He admitted that he had been involved in masturbation with three boys at the home but denied having raped the claimant or ever having been involved in anal sex. In February 2010, the claimant issued proceedings against the defendant and B. B committed suicide in July 2010, and his relatives settled the claimant's claim against his estate. The claimant maintained his claim against the defendant.

It being admitted that the claim was brought out of time, the court determined as preliminary issues whether the defendant was vicariously liable for the abuse perpetrated by B and, if so, whether the court should exercise its discretion under s 33 to allow the claim to proceed.

Held:

(i)   The defendant was not vicariously liable for B's abuse.

(ii)   (obiter) Even if a different conclusion had been reached on vicarious liability, it would not be appropriate to disapply the limitation period. Although there was no criticism to be made of the claimant for not bringing proceedings earlier, the delay had resulted in severe deterioration in the cogency of the evidence.

(iii)   The factual inquiry necessarily required to determine the question of vicarious liability for the abuse is much broader than that relating to the relatively narrow question as to the nature and extent of the abuse itself. Whilst it might not be as extensive as the sort of 'systemic negligence' inquiry that Lord Hoffmann mentioned at paragraph [52] in *A v Hoare* (p287), an inquiry into vicarious liability in this case would inevitably include an investigation as to the systems and organisation in place and how the house was run in practice by B's parents from day to day. Vicarious liability is a fact-sensitive matter, particularly here given that B had no formal position within the defendant organisation.

(iv)   The parents themselves were no longer alive, most of the other staff were no longer available to give evidence, and those who were available were now elderly and the half-century that had passed would have impaired their recollections. B himself was also dead. Contemporaneous documents were likely to have been long lost. The defendant would thus be seriously prejudiced by the delay: first, by being unable satisfactorily to investigate the factual contentions advanced by the claimant and his witnesses in relation to vicarious liability; and secondly, by being unable properly to test the assertions of fact upon which the allegation of vicarious liability is based. A fair trial of the issue of vicarious responsibility would not have been possible.

(v)   The claimant's argument that it would have been impossible to bring a claim prior to the decisions of the House of Lords in *Lister v Hesley Hall* (p535) in 2002 and *Hoare* (p287) in 2008, and therefore that the delay before 2002 or 2008 was irrelevant, was not well founded. *Lister* returned the law to the position which the courts had adopted prior to *Trotman v North Yorkshire County Council* [1999] LGR 584. The claimant's cause of action pre-dated *Trotman* by decades and so there was no legal bar to him bringing a claim earlier. *Hoare* reversed *Stubbings v Webb* (p677) and extended s 33 to claims for wilful assault. The claimant's cause of action pre-dated *Stubbings* by decades. It was always open to the claimant, in law, to bring the claim earlier.

Judgment for defendant.

Eastman v London Country Bus Services Ltd

Limitation Act 1980, s 33   **Costs**

Court of Appeal   **(1985) Times, 23 November**

On 24 November 1978 the claimant (Earnest Eastman), a general hand employed by the defendants, had been bailing out an inspection pit at their St Albans bus depot. When he straightened up, he struck his head on a grating which was lying across the top of an inspection pit. On 21 November 1981 he sent the defendants a detailed letter of claim. He consulted solicitors around February 1982. They issued his writ on 29 September 1982. All potential witnesses, both factual and medical, were still alive and able to testify.

At the preliminary trial on limitation Mr J M Collins QC, sitting as a deputy judge of the Queen's Bench Division, held that the claimant's date of knowledge for the purposes of s 11(4) of the Limitation Act 1980 was 28 February 1979. He refused to exercise discretion under s 33 in the claimant's favour because of the 'substantial delay' of 'three years or so' from after the time 'when the claimant first had the relevant knowledge'. The claimant appealed.

Held:

(i)   The accepted date of knowledge was 28 February 1979. The writ was issued on 29 September 1982. The relevant period of delay under s 33(3)(a) was the period after expiry of the limitation period, namely about seven months.

(ii)   The delay referred to in s 33(3)(b) was the same period of seven months after expiry of the limitation period. It was not suggested on behalf of the defendants that there had been any deterioration in the cogency of the evidence during this period.

(iii)   There is a material difference in language between s 14(1)(b) and s 33(3)(e). Knowledge whether any acts or omissions as a matter of law involved negligence was irrelevant under s 14(1) but critical under s 33(3)(e). Accordingly, the date from which the claimant's promptness will be assessed under s 33(3)(e) will, in some cases at least, be later than the date of knowledge under s 14(1).

(iv)   In all these matters, the judge fell into error and miscalculated the relevant periods. The exercise of his discretion could not be allowed to stand.

(v)   This was a case where all the evidence came from the side of the claimant, and the defendants had decided to call no evidence and argue the exercise of the discretion on the basis of the claimant's evidence. Therefore a new trial was unnecessary. The court could substitute its own discretion.

(vi)   The claimant would not be able to sue his solicitors. The defendants had not made out any, or at any rate any substantial, case of prejudice in relation to the seven-month period after expiry of the limitation period. Accordingly, discretion should be exercised in favour of the claimant: s 33(1).

(vii) It is not the case that, whenever a claimant ultimately has to invoke s 33, even if he succeeds on that, the fact that he had been compelled to invoke that section, because he is outside the primary limitation period, ought to be reflected in an order for costs. Section 33 is part of the entire statutory framework dealing with limitation in claims for personal injuries and death, and is not to be separated from the other limitation provisions for cost purposes. The order for costs should follow the event.

The claimant's appeal was allowed.

Thompson v Brown Construction (Ebbw Vale) Ltd (p690) applied.

Eaton v Eli Lilly & Co and others

Limitation Act 1980, s 11, s 14, s 33

Court of Appeal   **[1992] 3 Med LR 383**

See *Nash v Eli Lilly & Co* (E) (p568)

Eidi v Service Dowell Schlumberger SA

Limitation Act 1980, s 11, s 14, s 33

T Morrison QC   **December 1989**

In December 1984 the claimant (Mr Eidi) was injured in the course of his employment. At that time, he was not sure which company within his employer's group employed him. Until March 1986 he was paid salary under his contract. Thereafter he received further sums under a health insurance scheme.

In September 1988 his court action was commenced. The limitation defence was heard before T Morrison QC sitting as a deputy High Court judge.

Held:

(i)   So long as he was receiving full pay, the claimant had acted reasonably in not seeking to ascertain the exact identity of his employer: s 14(3).

(ii)   Accordingly, his action had been commenced in time: s 11(4).

(iii)   Otherwise a relevant factor would have been the uncertainty over the claimant's entitlement to benefits under the health insurance scheme, even though he had accepted such benefits: s 33(3).

(iv)   Consequently if necessary the court's decision would have been exercised in his favour, so as to allow his action to proceed: s 33(1).

NB: The authors would respectfully question the correctness of the s 14(3) ruling.

Eidha v Toropdar

Declaratory relief

QBD (McCombe J)   **[2008] EWHC 1219 (QB)**

On 22 June 2002 the claimant, a 10-year-old boy, was injured after being struck by a car driven by the defendant. The claimant sustained head injuries which were so severe that there was a possibility that he might never regain full mental capacity. A letter of claim was sent in April 2005 but, whilst the claimant's solicitors had indicated an intention to issue proceedings, they never in fact did so. In December 2006 the defendant began proceedings (in which technically he was the claimant, but still referred to hereafter as the defendant) for a declaration that he was not liable to the claimant (technically the defendant, but still referred to hereafter as the claimant) for any injury or loss sustained as a result of the accident. He claimed that the accident had occurred wholly as a result of the claimant's negligence, alleging that, as he had been passing a bus that was stationary at a bus stop, the claimant had run out in front of the bus in such a manner as to render a collision unavoidable.

The claimant requested that the court try as a preliminary issue the question of whether a claim for negative declaratory relief was available in an action in respect of personal injuries where the time limit for the commencement of an action had not expired. The master declined to make such an order and gave directions for a trial of all the issues save quantum. The claimant submitted that the issue of whether declaratory relief was appropriate ought to be decided as a preliminary issue; otherwise, the injured victim would be forced to litigate an issue before he had made a claim and before the limitation period had expired. The defendant submitted that, absent the declaration proceedings, it was highly probable that the limitation period would never expire, given the claimant's lack of capacity. In those circumstances he argued that he had a real and pressing need to have a determination of his potential liability.

The master accepted the defendant's arguments and refused to order the trial of a preliminary issue. The claimant appealed.

Held:

(i)   The court's decision as to whether to grant a negative declaration was a matter of discretion and not of jurisdiction (*Messier Dowty Ltd v Sabena SA* [2000] 1 WLR 2040 followed).

(ii)   It was also a matter of discretion for the court to decide whether or not to direct the trial of a preliminary issue, in advance of the trial of the main issue, as to whether it was appropriate to make such a declaration in the particular proceedings before it.

(iii)   The question was simply whether justice was served by permitting the action for a negative declaration to proceed to trial, and the court could not see how the arguments on that question could be substantially different on a future hearing of the proposed preliminary issue or at a trial on all the issues including liability.

(iv)   Once it was recognised that a negative declaration had value in certain cases, it seemed inevitably to follow that, in most cases, the limitation period would not have expired. If it had expired, the alleged wrongdoer would have the security of knowing that the action was time barred, and a declaration would be unnecessary.

(v)   The important matter for the court was to ensure that justice was done fairly between the parties. A material factor for the court to consider was how the quality of the evidence was likely to be affected with the passage of time. In the instant case, extensive investigations into the accident had been carried out and there was a possibility of prejudice if witnesses were lost or the quality of their recollection deteriorated with time. From that point of view, justice required that liability be determined sooner rather than later.

(vi)   In terms of funding, the claimant had a conditional fee agreement to allow him to pursue a claim, and it was hard to see any reason why that arrangement could not be extended to a counterclaim in the defendant's action.

(vii)   The negative declaration procedure was appropriate given that there had been a very long delay, that threats of proceedings had been made without action having been taken, and that there was a real danger that the trial of the action would become less and less satisfactory as time went on.

Appeal dismissed.

Elmes v Hygrade Food Products plc

CPR Parts 3, 6 and 7

Court of Appeal   **[2001] EWCA Civ 121;**
[2001] CP Rep 71; LTL 27/2/2001

The claimant was injured whilst working for the defendant on 28 September 1996. Proceedings were issued on 28 September 1999. On the last day of service the claimant's solicitors faxed the claim form to the defendant's insurers in error. The district judge ordered that service be deemed to have been effective in time. The defendant appealed. The circuit judge allowed the appeal. The claimant appealed this decision.

Held:

(i)   CPR 6.8 could not apply retrospectively. The failure to serve could not be thus remedied (*Nanglegan v Royal Free Hospital* (p567) followed).

(ii)   The claimant did not meet the criteria in CPR 7.6, and neither CPR 3.9 nor 3.10 could assist him (*Vinos v Marks & Spencer* (p701) and *Kaur v CTP Coil Ltd* (p514) applied).

(iii)   The court had no power the correct the mistake.

Appeal dismissed.

See also *Anderton v Clwyd County Council and linked appeals* (p303).

Evans v Cig Mon Cymru Ltd

CPR 17.4

Court of Appeal   **[2008] EWCA Civ 390;**
[2008] 1 WLR 2675; [2008] PIQR P17

In summer 2001 the claimant (then 16) suffered a hand injury whilst working for the defendant. He consulted solicitors and intended to bring a personal injury claim in relation to the accident and in respect of alleged workplace bullying. The letter of claim in respect of the accident was sent in March 2003, a letter of claim in respect of the bullying having been sent three months earlier. In April 2004 the claimant intimated that the bullying claim was not being currently pursued, although it might later be revived. The claimant turned 18 on 24 December 2002, and on 7 December 2005 (before the expiry of the limitation period) he issued a claim form in relation to the accident.

Owing to a clerical error, the claim form described the action as one for 'loss and damage arising out of abuse at work'. The claim form, particulars of claim (which set out the claim in respect of the hand injury) and a medical report (which was also solely in respect of the hand injury) were subsequently served on 16 March 2006. The defendant noticed the inconsistency between the description of the claim that appeared on the claim form and the nature of the claim contained within the accompanying documents and applied to strike out the particulars on the ground that they were irrelevant to the matter described by the claim form. The claimant, having confirmed to the defendant that the discrepancy was a clerical error, cross-applied to amend the claim form with the effect that the words 'an accident' be substituted for the word 'abuse'. The district judge granted the defendant's application to strike out, and rejected the claimant's application to amend on the ground that the proposed amendment, when compared with the original claim form, constituted a new claim that fell foul of CPR 17.4. The circuit judge dismissed the claimant's appeal, albeit in the most reluctant terms, remarking: 'The position we are in has no merit whatever. This is an obvious minor error, which has had drastic consequences for the solicitors responsible for drafting the document and it is a pity that I have not got the power to relieve them of the consequences of such a minor error; nevertheless I have not, and I so hold'. The claimant appealed again.

Held:

(i)   Given the lack of prejudice to the defendant, if the court had a discretion, there was no reason not to exercise it in the claimant's favour. The discrepancy was, by common understanding, an error which caused no detriment to anybody.

(ii)   There was an obvious mismatch between the claim form and the accompanying documents but, when the court was deciding whether the proposed amendment raised a new cause of action or simply clarified an inconsistency, it was proper to look not just at the claim form but at the pleadings as a whole. It was the totality of the documents served together that set out the claimant's pleaded case.

(iii)   When looked at that way, it was clear that what the claimant sought was not to raise a new claim but to correct an obvious error. It followed that the court had a discretion both to decline to strike out and to allow the amendment. The claim form was therefore to be amended as sought and the action was restored.

(iv)   (per Arden LJ) The normal rules of construction applied to pleadings. They fell to be interpreted contextually in light of the factual matrix (an accident at work) and with reference to the background of communications between the parties. When that was done here, the clear objective interpretation was that the reference to 'abuse' was a clerical error.

Appeal allowed.

Per Laws LJ: 'The decisions below represent a stark surrender of substance to form. We should not allow such a thing unless irresistibly driven to do so.'

Evans Construction Co Ltd v Charrington & Co Ltd and another

Amendment of application   **RSC Ord 20, r 5; CCR Ord 15, r 3**

Court of Appeal   **[1983] 1 All ER 310; [1983] QB 810;**
[1983] 2 WLR 117

In August 1970 Evans Construction Co Ltd entered into a lease of a piece of land from Charrington & Co Ltd. Charringtons assigned the reversion to Bass Ltd, another company in the same group. In April 1977 the claimants entered into a fresh lease with Bass Ltd who subsequently changed their name to Bass Holdings Ltd. In January 1982, pursuant to s 24 of the Landlord and Tenant Act 1954, the claimant's solicitors filed an application for a new tenancy in the Slough County Court. By mistake, thinking that Charringtons were still the landlords, they named the respondents as Charrington & Company Limited.

In March 1982 Charringtons successfully applied to the deputy registrar for the application to be struck out, on the grounds that they were not the landlord. The lessees appealed and applied to join Bass Holdings Ltd as additional respondents. Charringtons appealed against the decision of HH Judge Baker granting this.

Held:

(i)   As there was no issue between the lessees and Charringtons, there was no point in joining Bass as additional respondents. The only question was whether it was right to substitute the name 'Bass Holdings Ltd' for 'Charrington & Company Limited'.

(ii)   The only possible basis for so amending the name of the respondents was RSC Ord 20, r 5 which the County Court would follow under CCR Ord 15, r 3. RSC Ord 20, r 5 is not to be limited to mere misspelling or some other slip such as leaving out one word in the long title of a company.

(iii)   There is a real distinction between (a) suing A in the mistaken belief that A is the party who is responsible for the matters complained of and (b) seeking to sue B, but mistakenly describing or naming him as A, and thereby ending up suing A instead of B. The rule is designed to correct the latter and not the former category of mistake. A genuine mistake of the latter category had been made in this case.

(iv)   The applicant for leave has also to satisfy the court that the mistake was not misleading or such as to cause reasonable doubt as to the identity of the person intended to be sued. Neither Charringtons or Bass could have been misled or could have had any real doubt.

(v)   There remained a discretion whether to permit the amendment. Charringtons could have no complaint, and Bass's only regret would be having been deprived of a wholly adventitious chance of obtaining possession of the land without regard to the merits of their claim.

(vi)   The three criteria above will of themselves make a successful application under RSC Ord 20, r 5(3) something of a rarity. If leave to amend or correct would otherwise be given under that rule, the court should not hesitate to grant any necessary extension of time for service.

(vii)   Accordingly, Charringtons' name should be deleted as respondent, leaving only that of Bass Holdings Ltd, and the time for service on Bass should be extended until the expiration of 14 days.

Farnsworth v Bott and others

Limitation Act 1980, s 33

Court of Appeal   **Lexis, 14 January 1986**

On 10 August 1979 the claimants (Mrs Farnsworth and Miss Farnsworth) were passengers in a car driven by Mr Farnsworth which collided with a car driven by Mr Bott. Mr Farnsworth was convicted of careless driving.

All three Farnsworths were initially represented by the same firm of solicitors. In July 1982 claimants commenced court proceedings against Mr Bott. Mr Farnsworth commenced a separate action against him.

After a considerable lapse of time, Mr Bott joined Mr Farnsworth as a third party to the claimant's claim. The claimants instructed fresh solicitors and were advised in April 1983 to join Mr Farnsworth. In April 1984 Mr Farnsworth instructed new solicitors who indicated that there would be no objection to his being joined as second defendant. Then they received a change in their instructions and refused to consent.

In January 1985 the registrar refused the claimants' applications to join the third party Mr Farnsworth as defendant. The claimants' appeal, which relied on s 33 of the Limitation Act 1980, was dismissed by HH Judge Mott. They appealed further.

Held:

(i) the judge was wrong to hold that there was no prejudice to the claimants, if their application was refused, because otherwise they would be unable to proceed against a party who was plainly a potential defendant with prospective liability for the accident: s 33(1).

(ii) Also he was wrong to find that s 33(3)(e) was fatal. The extent to which the claimants acted reasonably and properly once they realised they had a course of action was only one of the matters to which the court was enjoined to have regard.

(iii) He failed to take into account the very unusual circumstances of the case and the need to unravel the complication caused by the claimants and the third party being represented by the same firm of solicitors: s 33(1).

(iv) There had been a wrong exercise of discretion. The claimants' appeal was allowed.

FG Hawkes (Western) Ltd v Beli Shipping Co Ltd ('The Katarina')

CPR 7.6

QBD (Comm) (Gross J)   **[2009] EWHC 1740 (Comm);**
[2010] 1 Lloyd's Rep 449

Pursuant to a straight consigned bill of lading, the claimant was the consignee of a parcel of plywood shipped on the defendant's vessel in China for carriage to Swansea. During discharge on 22 February 2007 the cargo was found to be damaged by mould. The terms of the bill of lading provided for a one-year time limit for the bringing of proceedings in respect of loss or damage to the cargo. On 29 January 2008 (some 11 months after the completion of discharge), the claimant informed the defendant's insurers of a potential claim against and sought to agree an extension of time. The claimant also indicated that a claim against the cargo insurers was under consideration. Two extensions of time were agreed: the first up to 10 March 2008; and the second up to and including 10 April 2008. The claim form was issued on 10 April itself, the very last day of the second period of extension. As the claim form was to be served out of the jurisdiction the claimant had six months within which to do so. That period accordingly expired on the 10 October 2008. On 19 September 2008, three weeks before the end of the period for service the claimant asked the insurers to confirm the defendant's address or whether the claim form could be served on the vessel's managers in Croatia. The insurers declined to give that information. The claimant then on 2 October 2008 sought the same information from the managers, who did not reply. On 3 October 2008 the claimant applied an ex parte order for the extension of time to 10 February 2009. This was granted on 10 October 2008. The claim form was served on the defendant on 21 January 2009 at its registered office in St Vincent.

The defendant applied for the ex parte extension to be set aside on the basis that: the claimant's failure to serve the claim form within the permitted six-month period was attributable to its solicitors' neglect; they had left it until the end of the period before starting to make enquiries as to the defendant's address for service; and, on the authorities, such neglect did not constitute a good reason for extending time.

Held:

(i)   Where there was no reason for the failure to serve the claim form within the time allowed other than incompetence, neglect or oversight on the part of the claimant or his legal representative, that would be a powerful reason for refusing to grant an extension of time, though not an absolute bar (*Hashtroodi v Hancock* (p466) applied).

(ii)   It was incumbent upon a claimant to take reasonable steps to ascertain a defendant's address for service and the fact that a claimant was giving priority to another claim was not a good reason for the grant of an extension (*Collier v Williams* (p380) considered).

(iii)   In the instant case the claimant's solicitors did nothing for five months while they were focusing on the claim against the cargo insurers. That was a strong reason for not extending time. When the claim form had itself been issued on the very last day of an agreed extension period, to leave enquiries as to service until 21 days before the period for service expired was leaving it very late indeed. The solicitors might hope for a helpful response from the insurers or ship managers but were not entitled to expect or assume that they would co-operate.

(iv)   There were a number of points in favour of the claimant, which was assumed to have a good arguable case: the defendant knew that the proceedings had been issued and knew of their nature; the defendant would not be prejudiced by a short extension of time; and the application was made before the expiry of the six-month period. However, those matters, whether considered individually or cumulatively, did not outweigh the strong reason for not extending time emphasised in the authorities, namely neglect or oversight in getting on with service until too late and for reasons solely attributable to the claimant or its legal representatives. Discovering the defendant's address was not a task giving rise to any or undue difficulty; what was required was timely attention to that matter. In the circumstances, the order extending time should be set aside. A refusal to extend time was appropriate and not disproportionate.

Application granted.

Farraj and Farraj v Kings Healthcare NHS Trust and Cytogenetic DNA Services Ltd

Limitation Act 1980, s 11, s 14, s 33

QBD (Swift J)   [2006] EWHC 1228 (QB); LTL 2/6/2006

The claimants, a Jordanian couple, had a propensity for passing on a rare hereditary condition, beta-thalassemia, to their children. This had already happened in the case of their second child. When therefore in 1995 the first claimant fell pregnant for the third time, the first defendant was asked to assess whether or not the child would have beta-thalassemia by analysis of a tissue sample. The first defendant contracted with the second defendant laboratory for the culturing of this sample. At no time was there any direct contact between the claimant and the second defendant. The claimants were subsequently advised that the child would not have suffer from beta-thalassemia and thus proceeded with the pregnancy. This proved incorrect. The claimants' son was born with beta-thalassemia on 14 April 1995. The condition was discovered on 24 April 1999.

Proceedings for wrongful birth were issued against the first defendant on 14 April 1999, the claimants having instructed English solicitors on 23 March 1999. The first defendant's defence blamed the second defendant (not at this time a party). Various problems with evidence, disclosure, jurisdiction and logistics served to complicate an already difficult case. In February or March 2004 the claimants instructed new counsel. This led to amended particulars of claim alleging that the first defendant's duty was non-delegable. This was denied by an amended defence which was served on 25 July 2004 simultaneously with Part 20 proceedings against the second defendant for a contribution or indemnity. The second defendant denied this.

In August 2004 the second defendant indicated that it would not consent to the claimants joining it as second defendant to bring their case against it directly. The amended defence to the Part 20 claim were not served until October 2004. Simultaneously an embargo was placed on the claimants' public funding following representations by the second defendant's solicitors. Full finding was restored on 13 April 2005. On 6 May 2005 the claimants applied to join the second defendant. There was a preliminary hearing, inter alia, on the limitation point.

Held (in relation to the limitation point):

(i)   Notwithstanding that this was an action for economic loss, it was to be treated as a personal injury action (*Walkin v South Manchester HA* (p705) applied by consent).

(ii)   The key question was when the claimants knew that the injury might have been attributable to the second defendant, applying *Spargo v North Essex District HA* (p667), *Whitfield v North Durham HA* (p713) and *Haward v Fawcetts* (p469).

(iii)   There was no suggestion that the claimants or their Jordanian lawyers ever knew of the second defendant's involvement, nor would that knowledge, without more, have been sufficient. There was nothing prior to the first defendant's defence in March 2001 that should have put the claimants on notice.

(iv)   However, the defence did put them on notice of a possible case against the second defendant. They therefore had the requisite knowledge in March 2001. This was over four years before the application to join, which was therefore out of time. With regard to the exercise of the court's discretion under s 33 the period was around 15 months.

(v)   The claimants' counsel had taken a conscious decision not to delay following the expiry of the primary limitation to join the second defendant until they gauged the first defendant's reaction to the allegation of a non-delegable duty. They could not be criticised for doing so. Thereafter the delays were mainly due to funding problems, having initially had no permission from the Legal Services Commission to purse the second defendant, and then having been under a complete embargo.

(vi)   The prior delays in the litigation were mainly due to factors (such as problems with disclosure and expert evidence and the master managing the case falling ill) which could not be held against the claimants. There had been no long periods of inactivity.

(vii)   The cogency of the evidence had not been significantly affected by the delay. It did not follow from the fact that one of the second defendant's key employees had retired that he would be unwilling to give evidence. Some relevant documents had been destroyed, but this occurred in 1997, well before the claimants' date of knowledge and at a time when the second defendant knew there had been a problem and might have been expected to retain them. There was no suggestion that the cogency of the claimants' evidence was affected and a fair trial was still possible.

(viii) The claimants had taken all proper steps to obtain advice.

(ix)   Given the complexity and difficulty of the case there was an understandable reluctance to proceed against the second defendant without clear supporting evidence.

(x)   The claimants would clearly be prejudiced if the application was refused and the claim against the first defendant failed on the basis that the fault lay purely with the second defendant.

(xi)   Although the second defendant would inevitably prejudiced by the deprivation of the limitation defence, they would be involved in the litigation as a Part 20 defendant in any event. The position was thus significantly different from the usual position. In the circumstances it was equitable to allow the claim to proceed.

Claimants' application granted.

Farthing v North Essex District Health Authority

Limitation Act 1980, s 33

Court of Appeal   **[1998] Lloyd's Rep Med 37; LTL 3/12/1997**

In December 1980 a consultant wrote to the claimant's GP recommending a hysterectomy, which was undertaken on 28 July 1981 at the defendant's hospital. During the operation the right ureter was damaged, which led to a triple fistula. The claimant suffered only minor problems from 1981-1989. In February 1989 she was admitted as an emergency with a pelvic abscess. Since then she suffered urinary tract infections and other problems. She was told in August 1993 that her problems were related to the hysterectomy, which the GP said had been performed negligently. The claimant instructed solicitors the next month, but it took considerable time to find supportive medical evidence. Proceedings were issued on August 1995. Limitation was heard as a preliminary issue. The judge found that the claimant had the requisite knowledge on 1981, but exercised his s 33 discretion to allow the claim to proceed despite the defendant's contentions that one of the treating doctors had died, another emigrated, and a third lacking recollection. The defendant appealed.

Held:

(i)   In cases such as this where experts are able to interpret contemporaneous records more will turn on documentation than witness recollection. The prejudice to a defendant in these circumstances is very much reduced.

(ii)   Whilst there was some prejudice to the defendant, the earliest the case could realistically have been heard was five or six years after the event, again highlighting the importance of the records.

(iii)   The judge's exercise of his discretion could not be criticised.

Appeal dismissed.

Fell v Eli Lilly & Co and others

Limitation Act 1980, s 11, s 14

Court of Appeal   **[1992] 3 Med LR 398**

See *Nash v Eli Lilly & Co* (Q) (p568)

Fenech v East London & City Health Authority

Limitation Act 1980, s 14

[2000] Lloyd's Rep Med 35; [2000] PNLR 205; LTL   **19/10/1999**

The claimant gave birth to her first child in July 1960. She experienced severe pain in the perineum in the following weeks and lesser pain thereafter, particularly during sexual intercourse. The claimant did not mention this to her male GP, but complained of pelvic pain to a female GP who took over in 1983. Investigations were undertaken but did not reveal the source of the pain. In April 1991 an x-ray was taken of the claimant's hip which showed a two inch needle fragment lodged in the perineum. However, the claimant was not informed of this discovery until February 1994. She consulted solicitors and proceedings were issued on 29 January 1997. Limitation was heard as a preliminary issue. The judge held that the claimant did not have actual knowledge until February 1994, but had constructive knowledge under s 14(3) long before then, citing the lack of enquiry up to 1983. The claimant appealed.

Held:

(i)   A degree of objectivity must apply to s 14(3), otherwise it would only bite when a claimant acted out of character. However much weight was given to the claimant's reticence, it was clear that she should have sought advice long before she did.

(ii)   It had not been established that the claimant had been misled by the defendant into thinking that there was nothing wrong with the episcotomy that was performed.

(iii)   The defendant had established that, had the claimant properly sought advice, the presence of the pin would have been discovered. Had the claimant informed doctors at the relevant time that her pain dated back to the birth, targeted investigations could have been carried out.

Appeal dismissed.

Feveyear v Cole and others

Limitation Act 1980, s 33

Court of Appeal   **(1993) PIQR P42**

On 29 November 1985 two motor vehicles, driven by Mr Feveyear and Mr Callaway respectively, collided with each other on the A2 near Sittingbourne. Both drivers were injured, as were three passengers in Mr Feveyear's car. Within the limitation period, Mr Feveyear sued Mr Cole on the basis that his bad driving, coming over to the wrong side of the road to pass another vehicle, had forced Mr Feveyear to take avoiding action, as a result of which his car collided with Mr Callaway's car. On 25 November 1988 Mr Feveyear's three passengers issued a separate writ against Messrs Cole, Feveyear and Callaway. As Mr Cole was apparently uninsured, the Motor Insurers' Bureau was added as second defendant in Mr Feveyear's action.

In October 1990 both actions came before HH Judge Russell-Vick in the Medway County Court where they were remitted. In Mr Feveyear's action he (a) gave Mr Cole leave to amend his defence to allege negligence against Mr Callaway, (b) gave Mr Cole leave to serve a contribution notice against Mr Callaway and (c) gave Mr Feveyear leave to add Mr Callaway as third defendant. Mr Cole's contribution notice was within the time permitted by s 10 of the Limitation Act 1980. Mr Feveyear required and was granted leave under s 33 to proceed against Mr Callaway.

In his pleadings, Mr Callaway counterclaimed for damages for his own personal injuries. His counterclaim against Mr Feveyear was permitted by s 35 of the Limitation Act 1980. However, he required leave under s 33 to proceed with the counterclaim against Mr Cole. The judge heard this application before the main trial and refused it. The basis of his decision was that in September 1989 solicitors had issued a writ against Mr Cole on behalf of Mr Callaway who had decided not to proceed with it.

At the trials on liability, HH Judge Russell-Vick concluded that Mr Cole was solely liable for the accident. He therefore gave judgment against Mr Cole in favour of Mr Feveyear and his passengers and dismissed all the proceedings against Mr Feveyear and Mr Callaway, including Mr Callaway's counterclaim against Mr Feveyear. Mr Callaway appealed against the decision that his case against Mr Cole was statute barred.

Held:

(i)   The fact that Mr Callaway had made a deliberate decision in 1989 not to litigate for his own damages against Mr Cole, although he was a party to the passengers' action against him, could have been a very valid reason for refusing to allow him to change his mind at a later date if there had been no other change in the circumstances: s 33(3)(a).

(ii)   However, the situation had entirely changed in 1990 starting off from Mr Cole's own change of mind. The delay from accident to trial was not a relevant consideration, because Mr Cole had himself to thank for the fact that he had sought to blame Mr Callaway with all the consequences which followed from that: s 33(3)(c).

(iii)   The consequence of the judge's decision was that Mr Callaway was entitled to make his counterclaim against Mr Feveyear but was not entitled to make an identical counterclaim, arising out of the same facts as to the accident, against Mr Cole. That was plainly unfair and wrong. Everyone else in October 1990 had changed their minds and been given the necessary permission to do so: s 33(3).

(iv)   There was no valid reason for refusing Mr Callaway the order that he sought, disapplying s 11 of the Limitation Act 1980 in his counterclaim against Mr Cole: s 33(1).

Mr Callaway's appeal was allowed.

Field v British Coal Corporation

Limitation Act 1980, s 14

Court of Appeal   **[2008] EWCA Civ 912**

The claimant had started working for the defendant at a colliery in 1982. He had a variety of jobs. In 1985 he consulted his doctor complaining of minor hearing loss and build-up of ear wax and infections. The defendant ceased to employ the claimant when it disposed of its business in 1995. However, the claimant continued to work at the colliery. Audiograms were carried out to test his hearing, notably in March 1998 and August 2000. In the early part of 2003 the claimant began to notice a slight ringing in his ears when he left work which would clear by the time he got home. He also found that his wife started to complain that he had the television on too loud. Eventually, in October 2003 he spoke to his union and as a result in November 2003 he was referred to a consultant ENT surgeon who carried out further tests and diagnosed mild noise-induced hearing loss. Proceedings were issued in August 2006. The defendant pleaded limitation, which has heard as a preliminary issue. The claimant maintained that for the purposes of s 14 he had no knowledge of his injury until he was diagnosed in November 2003.

The judge held that, in March 1998, following the examination that detected no abnormality with his ears, the claimant had been in a position to know that he had had some hearing impairment not explicable by wax or infection and he could then reasonably have taken steps to enquire into the matter, even though the claimant himself had not been aware that he had a hearing problem not attributable to wax or infection. The judge concluded that the claimant was fixed in 1998 with constructive knowledge that his injury was significant within the meaning of s 14(2) and consequently his claim was time barred. The judge declined to exercise his discretion under s 33.

The claimant appealed, submitting the judge had been wrong to hold that the state of his knowledge for the purposes of s 14(2) was to be determined by reference to an objective evaluation of the facts and without regard to whether he had been aware that he had suffered an injury. The claimant argued that the judge had found that he had no subjective knowledge of his injury until November 2003 and before that time he had no reason to attribute his hearing problems to anything other than wax and infections, and therefore he could not be fixed with constructive knowledge of his condition.

Held:

(i)   It was not easy to reconcile the judge's conclusions. On the one hand, he appeared to be saying that the claimant had been aware in March 1998 that he had a minor problem with his hearing that was not caused by wax or infection, such that a reasonable person in his position would have taken steps to investigate the problem; and, on the other hand, he had made clear findings that until November 2003 the claimant had not known that his reduced sense of hearing was due to anything other than wax and infections.

(ii)   This confusion could be explained by the judge's direction that it was necessary for him to make an objective evaluation of the facts without regard to the claimant's individual history and circumstances. The judge had wrongly thought that he was required to attribute to the claimant knowledge of the facts that he did not actually possess, as well as the additional knowledge that a reasonable man possessed of that knowledge would have discovered (*A v Hoare* (p287) applied).

(iii)   If the claimant had been aware of the fact that the medical examiner had detected no abnormality with his ears, he could reasonably have been expected to have taken some steps to obtain further medical advice. However, he could not reasonably have been expected to seek further medical advice in March 1998 or in August 2000, while he had reason to ascribe his symptoms to recurrent problems with wax and infections, especially when those who had carried out the tests had caused him to believe that there was nothing much wrong with his hearing and that he was fit to continue work.

(iv)   It was apparent that the claimant had not been aware in 1998 that he had suffered an injury and his knowledge of his condition was not such as would lead a reasonable man in his position to seek further medical advice. Accordingly, the claimant had not known that the injury in respect of which he sought compensation was significant until November 2003. Consequently, his claim was brought within time.

Appeal allowed.

Firstdale Ltd v Quinton

CPR 6.4, 6.5

QBD (Comm) (Colman J)   **[2004] EWHC 1926 (Comm);**
[2005] 1 All ER 639; LTL 05/08/2004

The claimant sued the defendant, a self-employed stockbroker working for a subsidiary company of the claimant ('Q'), for breach of contract. Q went into liquidation in August 1998. Its liquidators instructed solicitors to prepare proceedings and the defendant instructed solicitors to accept service of proceedings. Some correspondence subsequently passed between solicitors. In November 2003 the same solicitors as for the liquidators wrote directly to the defendant serving a deed of assignment of the claim fro Q to the claimant. Proceedings were issued on 1 December 2003, less than two weeks before the expiry of limitation. The claimant's solicitors (the same as those who had acted for Q through its liquidators) served the claim from directly on the defendant on 24 March 2004. The defendant's solicitors (the same who had been acting previously) wrote on 8 April 2004, after expiry of the claim form's validity period, stating that the claim form should have been served on them.

The defendant applied for the claim form to be struck out as having not been validly served and/or that it as defective in form as it provided no description beyond asserting the sum owed for breach of contract.

Held:

(i)   For the purposes of CPR 6.4 and 6.5, an indication by a potential defendant's solicitors that they were authorised to accept service of already proposed proceedings could not normally be taken to indicate their authority to accept service relating to different proceedings or a different claim.

(ii)   The party to whom the address for service was given was Q through its liquidators. It did not follow that the solicitors were authorised to accept service from an assignee. Although a statutory assignee takes subject to equities going to the substance of the assigned debt, he did not take subject to the procedural status of the assignee at the time of assignment.

(iii) The claim was thus validly served. Had it not been, the claimant's application under CPR 6.9 to dispense with service would have been refused.

(iv) Although the claim form was in some ways deficient, the defendant knew everything that ought to be included in the brief description of the claim. The lack of descriptive detail was thus not in any way prejudicial, and to strike the claim form out because of it would be an excessively strict response.

Application dismissed.

Firman v Ellis

Ince and others v Rogers

Down v Harvey and others

Limitation Act 1939, s 2D

Court of Appeal	**[1978] 2 All ER 851; [1978] QB 866;**
	[1978] 3 WLR 1

On 23 May 1973 Michael Firman, aged 17, was a passenger in a car driven by Diane Ellis. She drove too fast and collided with an on-coming lorry. She pleaded guilty to driving without due care and attention. He suffered injuries to his head, neck and spine. Solicitors notified his claim within three months. On 26 July 1974 they issued a writ but failed to serve it. In December 1976 they applied to renew it. This application was rejected. Consequently on 21 March 1977 they issued a new writ. Kerr J granted the application for an order under s 2D of the Limitation Act 1939 as amended that the primary limitation period should be disapplied. The defendant appealed.

On 22 February 1973 Mrs Pamela Ince was driving two of her children to school. A car driven by Mr Rogers came up fast from the opposite direction on the wrong side of the road and collided head-on with her car. He was convicted of careless driving. She was badly injured. Her claim was notified within two months. On 24 June 1975 her solicitors issued a writ. They failed to serve it within a year. An order for renewal and service of the writ was set aside on appeal. Consequently on 8 July 1977 a new writ was issued. Talbot J granted an application under s 2D that Mrs Ince's case should not be barred by the primary limitation period. The defendant appealed.

On 16 February 1973 Frederick Down, an employee of O Nicklin & Sons Ltd, was sent by them in a van to deliver a piano to Mr Harvey. The van got stuck in a muddy track. Mr Harvey got a Land Rover to pull it out. Whilst Mr Down was helping, his leg caught in a rope and he was badly injured. After many operations, his left foot was amputated. His claim was notified the next month. On 9 February 1976 solicitors issued his writ. They failed to serve it within a year. The order for renewal that they obtained on 8 February 1977 was subsequently set aside. On 19 July 1979 they issued a fresh writ. Lawson J ordered pursuant to s 2D that s 2A of the Limitation Act 1939 as amended be disapplied. The defendants appealed.

Held:

(i) Section 2D conferred on the court an unfettered discretion to extend the three-year limitation period in any case in which it considers it equitable to do so. This discretion is not limited to exceptional cases.

(ii) Delay on the part of the claimants was purely formal in each case, as the claims were made in good time: s 2D(3)(a). It was conceded that the effect of the delay on cogency of the evidence was nil: s 2D(3)(b). There was no criticism of the promptness of the claimants, s 2D(3)(e), or the steps taken by them: s 2D(3)(f).

(iii)   The court is not concerned solely with prejudice to the claimant that is financial. It is prejudicial to be forced to start another set of proceedings against an original solicitor whom one does not particularly wish to sue and to be deprived of a good cause of action against the original tortfeasor. This may not amount to serious prejudice, but it has to be balanced against no prejudice to the defendant personally and the mere loss of a fortuitous bonus to his insurers: s 2D(1).

(iv)   The judges were clearly right to have exercised discretion in favour of the claimants. The defendants appeals were dismissed.

The case of *Pheasant v Smith* (p602) was heard and decided at the same time as these three cases. As it raises some different issues, it has been summarised separately.

Fletcher v Containerbase (Manchester) Ltd

Limitation Act 1980, s 33

Court of Appeal   **LTL 31/10/2003**

The claimant worked for the defendant from 1977 to 1981. His job involved working with hazardous chemicals. He developed cancer of the bladder, but did not link his condition to his previous employment. By 1995 the claimant knew that another employee of the defendant had been diagnosed with cancer of the bladder. He issued proceedings on 17 December 2002, having in the interim learned of a third employee with bladder cancer. The defendant pleaded limitation which was heard as a preliminary issue. The judge found that the claimant had knowledge for the purposes of limitation in 1995. However, on the basis that the claim was fundamentally based upon the occurrence of a cluster of cancers and the defendant's ability to defend had not been effected by the passage of time, he exercised his discretion under s 33 to allow the claim to continue. The defendant appealed.

Held:

(i)   The judge had considered all the relevant facts and issues. In particular he had compared the defendant's position in 1998 when the claim should have been brought with its position in 2002 when it was brought.

(ii)   The judge's decision was not unreasonable.

Appeal dismissed.

Forbes v Wandsworth Health Authority

Limitation Act 1980, s 11, s 14, s 33

Court of Appeal   **[1997] QB 402; [1996] 3 WLR 1108;**
[1996] 4 All ER 881

The claimant was admitted to the defendant's hospital on 16 October 1982. He had a long history of circulation problems and had undergone successful bypass operations in 1975 and 1978. His wish was that the same surgeon should treat him on this occasion and this was granted. On this occasion two attempted bypass operations were unsuccessful and the claimant's leg was amputated. The claimant first sought professional advice in 1991. In October 1992 the claimant received medical advice that the amputation was due to a failure to perform the second bypass in 1982 earlier. Proceedings were issued on 10 December 1992. The defendant pleaded limitation which was heard as a preliminary issue. The judge found that the claimant had neither actual nor constructive knowledge until 1992. On the latter point the judge placed emphasis on the claimant's confidence in his treating surgeon. Alternatively, the judge would have exercised his s 33 discretion if it had been necessary. The defendant appealed, and the claimant died on 5 February 1995 pending the appeal.

Held (Roch LJ dissenting):

(i) The judge's finding of date of actual knowledge was correct. Until he was so told by an expert, he did not know as a matter of science that there was an opportunity to prevent the amputation, albeit that it was irrelevant as a matter of practice that the failure to take this opportunity might be negligent.

(ii) The amputation was clearly a significant injury. It could not be interpreted as simply an outcome of medical treatment.

(iii) The claimant expected or at least hoped for a successful outcome from the operation and that had manifestly not occurred. The amputation was such a serious injury and its repercussions on the claimant and his family so dramatic that the claimant could reasonably be expected to take expert advice more than three years before proceedings were issued.

(iv) This was not a case were there had been any event or alteration in circumstances which increased the onus on the claimant to seek advice. He was in the same position when he eventually consulted a solicitor as he had been for some years previously.

(v) This lack of any significant occurrence in the intervening period in no way excused the claimant's failure to seek advice. Any other construction would, contrary to the purpose of the Act, as it allow a claimant to delay indefinitely before seeking expert advice yet remain within time.

(vi) The claimant's individual characteristics were not relevant to s 14(3) (*Nash v Eli Lilly* (p568) on this point doubted and distinguished as obiter by Stuart-Smith and Evans LLJ, doubted but held to be binding by Roch LJ).

(vii) It was reasonable to allow the claimant 12–18 months from the amputation to get over the shock, take stock of his situation and take advice. He was therefore fixed with constructive knowledge in 1984 and proceedings were issued out of time.

(viii) The death of the claimant significantly altered the position as regards s 33 and required the court to reconsider the discretion afresh.

(ix) Section 33 applied to claims under the Law Reform (Miscellaneous Provisions) Act 1974 when the original claimant had died.

(x) The defendant would suffer prejudice in the following ways if the discretion were exercised:

(xi) A change in insurance arrangements during the period of delay meant that it would pay a greater proportion of any damages awarded.

(xii) The operating notes could not be found. This was potentially a very serious prejudice.

(xiii) The operating surgeon had no clear recollection of the relevant events.

(xiv) Delay in medical negligence cases causes particular problems in that it is difficult to judge what constituted acceptable practice many years ago when practices will almost inevitably have progressed significantly in the interim. This tends to create more problems for defendants.

(xv) The merits of the claimant's case appeared very poor. This was particularly pertinent when a claimant was impecunious and the defendant very unlikely to recover costs.

(xvi) It would not be appropriate to exercise a s 33 discretion.

Appeal allowed.

NB: The majority reasoning was subsequently approved by the House of Lords in *Adams v Bracknell Forest BC* (p292).

Forster v Eli Lilly & Co and others

Limitation Act 1980, s 11, s 14

Court of Appeal   **[1992] 3 Med LR 386**

See *Nash v Eli Lilly & Co* (H) (p568)

Foster v Mall Builders Ltd

Limitation Act 1980, s 11, s 14

Beldam J   **Lexis, 17 March 1983**

On 19 July 1978 the claimant (Christopher Foster), then aged 19, was working as an apprentice gas fitter at a house in Hammersmith when he stepped on rubble that had been left on the stairs by contractors and fell injuring his left leg. He was off work for about three weeks and continued to have some pain and trouble with his left knee. He concentrated on completing his apprenticeship studies and passed his City and Guilds course. In September 1979 his leg played him up and he had to be given a special job, that of delivering pre-assembled cookers. The arduous nature of this work caused him to realise that his knee was not serviceable. In May 1980 his cartilage was removed, but this operation did not cure him.

Later in 1980, in the course of seeing his union branch secretary, the claimant realised for the first time that he could claim. In January 1981 his trade union instructed solicitors who wrote in March to Hammersmith Borough Council who replied that the contractors were Contact Services Ltd. In July 1981 a writ against this company was issued. In August Contact Services Ltd told the claimant's solicitors that the house had been sold in January 1978 to the Notting Hill Trust from whom the claimant's solicitors ascertained in September 1981 that the contractors in question were in fact Mall Builders Ltd. After discussion with the senior master, who told them that it was inappropriate to substitute Mall Builders Ltd as defendants in the original action, the claimant's solicitors issued a fresh writ against them on 13 January 1982. A preliminary trial of the limitation defence was ordered.

Held:

(i)   The claimant did not have any actual knowledge of the identity of the defendants until September 1981: s 14(1).

(ii)   Accordingly, the issue was constructive knowledge under s 14(3) of the Limitation Act 1980 and the relevant question was 'would he have been unreasonable if he did not make enquiries to discover the identity of the defendant prior to the 12th February 1979?'. As the injury did not immediately seem serious, as the claimant hoped with the natural optimism of a young person that it would clear up, as he did not return to the same site, and as he was engaged on studies, the question should be answered in his favour: s 14(3).

(iii)   Therefore his action was brought within three years of his date of knowledge and was not statute barred: s 11(4).

Foster v Turnbull and others

Service of writ

Court of Appeal   **(1990) Times, 22 May**

In May 1983 the claimant (Mrs Foster) was being driven by her husband when their car collided with a motor cycle ridden by either Mr Turnbull or Mr Kennett, with the other as pillion passenger. All three men were killed. Norwich Union, insurers of the motor cycle, which had been ridden without the owner's consent, dealt with the claim as representatives of the Motor Insurers' Bureau and agreed that liability was not in doubt.

On 22 May 1986 a writ was issued naming the two dead men as defendants as well as the living motor cycle owner. In June 1986 local solicitors acknowledged service on behalf of all three defendants on the Norwich Union's instructions. On 22 May 1987 the period of validity for service of the writ expired. In June 1988 Norwich Union instructed new solicitors who pointed out to the claimant's solicitors that they had failed to obtain an order under RSC Ord 15, r 6A(4).

On appeal from the district registrar, Nolan J ordered that pursuant to Ord 15, r 6A(4)(b) Norwich Union be appointed to represent the first and second defendants' estates for the purpose of the proceedings and extended the validity of the writ. Norwich Union appealed.

Held:

(i)   Service of a writ was not at large. It had to be on a legal person. As the first two defendants were dead, the writ was not validly served on them.

(ii)   Since the steps taken after the issue of the writ were nullities, none could create an estoppel binding on Norwich Union. The action had therefore died.

In allowing the appeal, Leggatt LJ observed that, notwithstanding this opportunity to shed their responsibility, it was still open to Norwich Union to safeguard their reputation by meeting the claim.

Fowell v National Coal Board

Limitation Act 1980, s 11, s 14, s 35

Court of Appeal   **(1986) Times, 28 May**

On 13 February 1977 the claimant (James Fowell) sustained injuries when a ceiling in the public house managed by him collapsed because of subsidence caused by mining operations. On 8 February 1980 he initiated proceedings against the defendant. In May 1983 his amended statement of claim alleged that the defendants had negligently carried out repairs. In October 1983, when the amended defence was served, the claimant became aware that the repairs had been performed by a third party.

In May 1985 he applied for leave to re-amend his claim and to add the third party, William Plowman & Co Ltd, as second defendant. Cantley J dismissed his appeal from the refusal of the district registrar to allow this. The claimant appealed.

Held:

(i)   The claimant could not have ascertained the existence of a claim against the third party: s 14(3)(a).

(ii)   Nor could such knowledge be presumed against him on the basis that his solicitors ought to have made enquiries. It was reasonable for solicitors to proceed on the assumption that their instructions were correct unless and until something occurred to indicate to a prudent solicitor that he should make further enquiries.

(iii)   A party's solicitor was not an expert within the meaning of s 14(3)(b). That provision was directed to experts in the sense of expert witnesses.

(iv)   The claimant was not statute barred from adding the third party as second defendant: s 11(4), s 35(3).

Fox v Wallace

Limitation Act 1980, s 33

Court of Appeal   **26 June 1989**

On 18 June 1981 the body of claimant (Mr Fox) came into contact with the working parts of a rotavator on the defendant's farm. The defendant's insurers inspected the equipment shortly afterwards. The claimant was off work for a time, but then returned to the defendant's employment. In April 1986, on his doctor's advice, he consulted a solicitor who sent a letter before action. The writ was issued on 10 April 1987, and the statement of claim was served in July 1987.

At the preliminary trial on limitation in October 1988, the claimant said that he had not sought legal advice earlier because (a) until his back caused him to consult his doctor in 1986 he was content to go on working and (b) shortly after the accident the defendant told him that he was not insured. When he testified that it was a defect in the power shaft of the rotavator that had caused the accident, this altered the case erroneously pleaded in the statement of claim that the accident was due to damage to the power shaft of the tractor. The eye witness and the defendant's foreman were available to testify.

HH Judge Martin, sitting as a deputy High Court judge, preferred the claimant's evidence to the defendant's contrary evidence on the reasons for his delay. He exercised his discretion under s 33 of the Limitation Act 1980 in the claimant's favour. The defendant appealed.

Held:

(i)   The cause of the claimant's delay was essentially a question of fact to be determined by the trial judge, and was not a matter in which the court could properly intervene.

(ii)   Although it was regrettable that an error appeared in the statement of claim, an inspection after its service in July 1987 would not have revealed evidence that was not available in October 1988. The defendant had not been seriously prejudiced by the error.

The defendant's appeal was dismissed.

Freeman v Home Office (No 1)

Limitation Act 1939, s 2D

Court of Appeal   **31 July 1981**

The claimant (David Freeman) was serving a life sentence at Wakefield Prison. He behaved in a disruptive way, suffered from bouts of depression and attempted suicide on a number of occasions. In August 1972 Dr Xavier, a prison medical officer, prescribed Stelazine to be taken orally. The claimant refused to take it.

He alleged that subsequently he was taken to a cell, forcibly divested of his trousers by prison hospital orderlies and injected in his buttocks with a drug called Serenace. Between September 1972 and January 1973 he was given further forcible injections of Serenace and Modecate. He suffered unwelcome side effects and was driven to a further attempt at suicide.

The claimant stated that he wrote to a solicitor in autumn 1972 after the first series of injections, that his letter was intercepted by the prison authorities, that he completed a petition asking consent to instruct the solicitor to take action but was later told that the Home Secretary had refused this. In February 1977 the defendants were notified of his allegation that he had been punished by the forcible administration of drugs, and Dr Xavier prepared a memorandum commenting on his treatment and stating that it was conducted with the patient's consent. Dr Xavier died in October 1977.

On 15 October 1979 the claimant's writ was issued. It claimed damages for (i) negligence in the administration of the drugs and (ii) assault, battery and trespass to the person. Taylor J refused the defendants' application for, inter alia, the action to be dismissed or stayed on the grounds that it was statute barred. The defendants appealed. The case turned on s 2D of the Limitation Act 1939 as amended.

Held:

(i)   The death of Dr Xavier had the result that the defendants were gravely prejudiced in relation to the claim founded on his alleged medical negligence: s 2D(3)(b). It would not be equitable to allow this to proceed: s 2D(1).

(ii)   The situation was different in regard to the claim for assault, battery and trespass. There was no suggestion that the hospital officers referred to by the claimant were not available to give their recollection of events at the material time, albeit that they occurred many years ago: s 2D(3)(b). It was equitable to allow the action to proceed in regard to this claim: s 2D(1).

NB: In view of the House of Lords' decisions in *Stubbings v Webb* (p677), the case on the second claim might now be decided differently.

Furniss v Firth Brown Tools Ltd

Limitation Act 1980, s 14

Court of Appeal   **[2008] EWCA Civ 182**

The claimant had worked for the defendant from 1976 until about 1982. His case was that he had been exposed to loud noise at work and had never been provided with hearing protection. He maintained that he visited his doctor to report a deterioration in his hearing and was told that it was due to a build-up of wax. A medical examination in 2004 revealed that he had hearing loss and tinnitus, which were, according to a consultant, probably caused by exposure to loud noise. He issued proceedings in June 2006. The defendant pleaded limitation, which was tried as a preliminary issue.

In cross-examination, the claimant agreed that his first problems were that he could not hear the telephone and needed to have the television sound turned up and that he experienced those problems around 1996 but asserted that they were due to his ear wax and that he thought the tinnitus was hereditary. The judge held that the claimant knew around 1996, and well before 1998, that he had a hearing loss independent of the wax and that he had enough knowledge of the possibility of noise affecting hearing for him to have associated that with his work. The judge therefore ruled that the claim was time barred, and declined to exercise his discretion under s 33 to allow the claim to continue.

The claimant appealed, submitting that (1) the judge's crucial finding of fact that he knew around 1996 that he had hearing loss independent of wax had been unsupported by evidence, and (2) the only evidence on the question of seriousness for the purposes of s 14 was that, when the symptoms first began, they were fairly insignificant.

Held:

(i)   It was apparent that the judge had not dealt with the question of when the claimant knew or ought (with expert advice that it was reasonable for him to seek) to have known that his injury was significant as defined by s 14(2).

(ii)   If the judge had dealt with that question, he would not have been bound to find that, by 1998, the claimant knew or ought to have known that his hearing loss was significant. There was little evidence to support the proposition. It was not clear from the evidence that the claimant was agreeing that he had hearing problems, namely that he could not hear the telephone and needed to have the television sound turned up, as early as 1996.

In any event, those hearing problems did not sufficiently support the conclusion that the injury was significant to justify the commencement of an action for damages.

(iii)   It was difficult to reach a firm conclusion on the date by which the claimant had knowledge that his injury was significant; the point was not sufficiently explored in evidence. Accordingly, the burden of proof under s 14, which lay on the defendant, had not been discharged and the claim was in time.

Appeal allowed.

GOM v Bryn Alyn Community Holdings Ltd

Limitation Act 1980, s 2, s 11, s 14, s 33

Court of Appeal   **[2003] EWCA Civ 783; [2003] 3 WLR 107; [2003] 1 FLR 1203**

See *KR v Bryn Alyn Community Holdings Ltd* (J) (p505)

GS v Bryn Alyn Community Holdings Ltd

Limitation Act 1980, s 2, s 11, s 14, s 33

Court of Appeal   **[2003] EWCA Civ 783; [2003] 3 WLR 107; [2003] 1 FLR 1203**

See *KR v Bryn Alyn Community Holdings Ltd* (E) (p505)

Gaud v Leeds Health Authority

Limitation Act 1980, s 11, s 33

Court of Appeal   **(1999) 49 BMLR 105; (1999) Times, 14 May; LTL 27/4/999**

On 1 February 1989 the claimant began working for the defendant as a cardio-thoracic surgeon on six month contracts. On 23 August 1990 he was diagnosed as suffering from hepatitis B and tuberculosis. His work with the defendant concluded at the end of the same month. However, he continued to practice surgery and in 1994 he was pleaded guilty to charges of being a nuisance by endangering the health of the public. He served a prison sentence and was released in March 1996. On 29 August 1996, more than six years after diagnosis but less than six years after he left the defendant's employment, he issued proceedings against the defendant. He alleged that he had contracted the diseases whilst working for the defendant and that the defendant was responsible for them. He also alleged that the defendant had been had been negligent in failing to advise him in the areas he could practice in once he had been diagnosed and in failing to advise him of his benefits rights. The judge refused to exercise his discretion under s 33. The claimant sought permission to appeal.

Held:

(i)   The claimant's claim for contracting the disease was statute barred by s 11 unless a s 33 discretion was exercised. This claim had no prospect of success. This was a relevant matter to the exercise of the s 33 discretion. The judge had been correct on this ground to refuse to allow the claim to proceed.

(ii)   The claimant's other claims did not fall under s 11, but were likewise bound to fail. The judge was right to strike them out.

Permission to appeal refused.

Gelder v British Steel Plc

Limitation Act 1980, s 11, s 33

Bury County Court (Recorder Sycamore)   **[2000] CLY 523**

The claimant worked for the defendant as a pole pit driver from January 1971 to April 1973. For the majority of the time he was protected from the factory noise by virtue of being sheltered in his cab. In March 1999 he issued proceedings for noise-induced hearing loss. The preliminary issues to be determined by the court were (1) the date of knowledge under s 14, and (2) whether the court should exercise its discretion under s 33. The defendant contended that the claimant had a possibility of a claim against his solicitors, which would diminish any prejudice suffered by him in the event of the court exercising its discretion in favour of the defendant.

Held:

(i)   It was not until the examination of the claimant by a medical expert in October 1995 that he realised that the damage was permanent and that his hearing problems, or at least some of them, were noise induced.

(ii)   Section 33 required the court to have regard to all the circumstances of the case, therefore the onus was on the claimant to satisfy the court that it would be equitable to exercise the discretion in his favour (*Price v United Engineering Steels Ltd* (p612) followed). The general prejudice likely to be caused to the defendant by the passage of time was that it would have to find witnesses and obtain evidence from them. Quantum was not likely to be substantial. In a case of this age there was clearly an onus on the claimant and his legal advisers to progress quickly after appropriate expert evidence has been obtained. The present solicitors had been dealing with the matter since 1996 and no acceptable reason had been put forward for the delay.

(iii)   Whilst it was undesirable to embark on a detailed enquiry of the conduct of the matter by the claimant's present solicitors, it was likely that they had been negligent. The possibility of a claim against the claimant's legal advisers was clearly a significant feature. This was a case which it would not be equitable to require the defendant to meet. The claimant would only suffer a slight prejudice if he was left with pursuing a remedy against his solicitors and, on that basis, it would not be equitable for the court to exercise the discretion in his favour.

Preliminary issue determined in favour of the defendant.

Gibbons v London Borough of Greenwich and others

Amendment of writ   **RSC Ord 15, r 6; Ord 20, r 5**

Court of Appeal   **16 July 1980**

On 22 June 1976 the claimant (David Gibbons) fell down a scaffold on a building site and was left a paraplegic. On 16 June 1977 he issued a writ against four defendants. On 30 August 1977 the second defendants served a defence blaming, inter alios, a site foreman named Anthony Weller. On 10 November 1977 the fourth defendants issued a third party notice against him.

On 12 July 1979 the claimant applied for leave to add Mr Weller as fifth defendant, with the necessary amendment to the writ and statement of claim. The master refused.

On 9 June 1980 Smith J on appeal ordered that the claimant have leave to amend the writ by adding Anthony Weller as fifth defendant. Mr Weller appealed. The claimant's counsel accepted that it was wrong to join a defendant against whom the primary period of limitation had expired, but submitted that time only began to run from service of the second defendants' defence naming Weller on 30 August 1977 so that the primary limitation period was still running.

Held:

(i)   In general, where a cause of action has accrued more than three years earlier, the proper course for the claimant to take is to start a fresh action against the further defendant, in which any limitation defence can be investigated and, if necessary, tried as a preliminary issue.

(ii)   This case was exceptional, however, in that there were already third party proceedings against Mr Weller, the proposed fifth defendant. Little purpose would be served by forcing the claimant to incur the extra expense and delay of a further action, and there was a risk of injustice to the claimant if at the hearing of the original action Mr Weller alone was held responsible for his injuries.

The appeal was dismissed.

Gibson v Jobcentre Plus (Secretary of State for Work and Pensions)

Limitation Act 1980, s 14

Court of Appeal   **6 December 2012, unreported**

The claimant had been employed by the defendant for many years in a number of roles. In September 2006 she claimed damages for repetitive strain injury (RSI) sustained as a result of her employment. Her particulars of claim alleged that she had developed symptoms from September 2003. The defendant challenged the claim on the bases that it was statute barred and that there was no relevant breach of statutory duty or negligence to have caused such injury. It referred to documentary evidence in the form of a number of medical reports which referred to the claimant experiencing symptoms from 1998, possibly attributable to RSI. A joint expert report stated that she had a past history of neck, upper back and arm pain from 1998 onwards. At the hearing, the claimant raised for the first time the case that her symptoms from 1998 onwards were wholly separate and different from those notified in 2003. That was supported by oral evidence from her medical expert. The judge rejected that submission and found that the claimant had the requisite knowledge under s 14 before September 2003, so that her claim was statute barred, and that there had been no breach of statutory duty or negligence on the defendant's part after September 2003.

The claimant appealed, contending that the judge had erred in failing to express clear reasons for rejecting the medical expert's oral opinion or address the question whether the defendant had breached its duties to her prior to 2003.

Held:

(i)   The judge had been entitled to look at the medical expert's evidence with caution, given the late stage at which the claimant's amended claim had been made and in particular because of the abundant documentary evidence in respect of her condition over the relevant period. There was overwhelming evidence of relevant and persistent symptoms over many years, and the submission that a separate condition had emerged in 2003 could not be sustained.

(ii)   Although the judge had made no express finding that he rejected the expert's oral opinion, he had considered the medical evidence in detail and referred to the documentary evidence. Whilst there might be conditions which a patient was aware of earlier which were different to the subsequent condition on which a claim was based, in the instant case, the claimant's symptoms and conditions were plainly connected. The judge had put his finding in a shorthand form but there was abundant evidence for his finding that the claim was statute barred. That conclusion was sufficient to dispose of the appeal.

(iii)   (obiter) The judge was justified in finding that there had been no breach of statutory duty or negligence from 2003 onwards and, given the conclusion on limitation, any earlier breaches were irrelevant.

Gibson v Metropolitan Police Commissioner

CPR 3

Cooke J   **[2002] EWHC 584; LTL 28/11/2002**

The claimant claimed damages for wrongful arrest. Although the relevant incident occurred in September 1994, proceedings were not issued until September 1997. Thereafter there were numerous delays and breaches of rules and orders on the part of the claimant, which he accepted were inexcusable. On the defendant's application, the master struck out the claim on 26 July 2001. The claimant appealed.

Held:

(i)   The master was entitled to come to the conclusions he did that the defendant was massively prejudiced and that a fair trial was impossible. Having done so, he had no choice but to strike out.

(ii)   The claimant was in the driving seat of his litigation. It was particularly incumbent upon him to move the matter forward expeditiously as he had tarried before issuing proceedings.

(iii)   In these circumstances, and in the context of the claimant's many breaches and failure to conduct litigation expeditiously, it could not be said that striking out was unreasonable or disproportionate.

Appeal dismissed.

Glass v Surrendran

CPR 6, 7

Court of Appeal   **[2006] EWCA Civ 20;**
(2006) Times, 3 February; LTL 25/1/2006

See *Collier v Williams* (p380)

Godfrey v Gloucestershire Royal Infirmary

Limitation Act 1980, s 11, s 14, s 33

Leveson J   **[2003] EWHC (QB) 549;**
[2003] Lloyd's Rep Med 398; LTL 1/5/2003

The claimant's daughter was born on 1 March 1995 with significant brain damage and cerebral palsy. She died on 5 February 2003. Abnormalities had been discovered during a prenatal ultrasound. Further investigations were undertaken and termination canvassed but the claimant elected against it. A letter of claim was sent on 8 March 1996, although medico-legal investigations proceeded slowly thereafter. The claimant issued proceedings on 25 April 2002 alleging that the defendant's failure to accurately assess the ultrasound scans lead to her wrongly electing to continue the pregnancy. The defendant pleaded limitation which was heard as a preliminary issue. The defence alleged that as no claim for personal injury was advanced the claim was for pure economic loss and the limitation period was six years. Alternatively the defence contended that the claimant's date of knowledge was in 1995.

Held:

(i)   The claimant knew of the relevant acts or omissions from the outset. She therefore had the requisite knowledge before the birth of her daughter.

(ii)   The claim included a claim for personal injuries, and the claim for economic loss for negligent misrepresentation could not be severed for limitation purposes (*Walkin v South Manchester HA* (p705) applied). s 11 and s 33 therefore applied.

(iii)   Given the early notification of the complaint and the prejudice to the claimant if s 11 were not disapplied, notwithstanding the lack of explanation for the delay and modest prejudice to the defendant, it would be equitable to allow the claim to continue. A significant factor was the level of emotional, physical and financial constraint imposed upon the claimant by the need to care for her severely disabled child.

Preliminary issue decided in the claimant's favour.

Godwin v Swindon Borough Council

CPR 6, 7

Court of Appeal   **[2001] EWCA Civ 1478; [2002] 1 WLR 997;
[2001] 4 All ER 641**

The claimant sustained a back injury on 26 February 1997 working as a roadman for the defendant. He issued proceedings on 17 February 2000. He was granted two extensions of time for service so that the period for service expired on 8 September 2000. On 7 September 2000 the claimant posted the claim form to the defendant. Although the defendant received this the next day, by CPR 6.7(1) this service was deemed effective on 9 September 2000. The district judge struck the claim form out as out of time on the basis that the deemed date of service was not rebuttable. The claimant appealed and the circuit judge held that proof of the actual date of service displaced the deemed date of service. The defendant appealed this decision.

Held:

(i)   The deemed date of service must be treated as the date of service, irrespective of proof of the actual date of service. The wording of CPR 6.7(1) was clear.

(ii)   It was not generally helpful to seek to interpret the CPR by reference to the rules it replaced.

(iii)   (obiter, per Pill LJ and Rimer J) Although a claimant could not adduce evidence to prove that the claim form was served before the deemed date of service, a defendant might be able to prove that it was not in fact served until later.

(iv)   An extension of time was not available as the claimant did not satisfy the criteria in CPR 7.6(3).

(v)   CPR 6.9 could not displace CPR 7.6 to allow the court to dispense with service entirely (*Infantino v MacLean* (p488) overruled).

Appeal allowed. Claim struck out.

See also *Anderton v Clwyd County Council and Linked Appeals* (p303), *Cranfield v Bridgegrove* (p389) and *Wilkey v BBC* (p717).

Goodchild v Greatness Timber Company Ltd

Limitation Act 1963, s 7

Court of Appeal   **[1968] 2 QB 372; [1968] 2 WLR 1283;**
[1968] 2 All ER 255

On 1 April 1961 the claimant (Albert Goodchild), an office manager employed by the defendants at their timber yard in Kent, was crossing a concrete bridge on the premises when he tripped and fell. He sustained injuries, including a comminuted fracture of the right humerus, and was unable to work for three months. From December 1965 his right shoulder became increasingly painful, with permanent restriction of movement, a deterioration which his orthopaedic surgeon stated that the claimant could not have foreseen.

In November 1966 his ex parte application for leave to proceed pursuant to s 1 of the Limitation Act 1963 was granted. The defence pleaded limitation. The master ordered a preliminary trial without evidence of the issue of whether 'the fact that the said condition of the claimant's right arm would deteriorate was at all times until December 1965 outside the actual or constructive knowledge of the claimant' was 'a fact of a decisive character as defined in subsection (4) of section 7 of the Limitation Act 1963'. Cantley J on appeal set aside the master's order. The defendants appealed.

Held: the master's order should be restored. The point was so short that it was advantageous to deal with it as a preliminary issue. This would enable the defendants to be heard at an early stage without all the expenses of witnesses.

The defendants' appeal was allowed.

Per Lord Denning: 'In this case the plaintiff knew all the material facts relating to his accident and injuries within the first three years, save this: that he says that he did not know the "extent of the personal injuries" within section 7(3)(b) of the Act of 1963. These words, however, are intended to apply to cases where a man has an injury which he reasonably believes is trifling (for example, a knock on the head) and is not worth while to bring an action for it, but then after three years it is found to be far more serious than anyone realised (for instance, to cause a tumour). In such a case the newly found "extent of the injuries" is a fact of a material and decisive character. His time will be extended. But if the injury was from the beginning fairly serious, or at any rate sufficiently serious to make it worth while to bring an action, then he must bring it within the first three years. The time will not be extended simply because it turns out after three years to be more serious than he first thought.'

NB: Lord Denning's words above are equally applicable to the knowledge 'that the injury in question was significant' within s 14(1)(a) and s 14(2) of the Limitation Act 1980, although there is now the additional factor of the court's discretion under s 33 of the 1980 Act.

Goode v Martin

Limitation Act 1980, s 11, s 14, s 33, s 35   **CPR 17**

Human Rights Act 1998, s 3   **ECHR, Art 6**

Court of Appeal   **[2001] EWCA Civ 1899;**
[2002] 1 WLR 1828; [2002] 1 All ER 620

The claimant suffered catastrophic head injuries on 24 August 1996 on the defendant's yacht. She had no recollection of the accident. The defendant did not reply to her pre-action correspondence and the claimant issued proceedings on 16 October 1997 alleging that a car had come free from its guide-rail. In a draft amended defence the defendant claimed that the claimant, an inexperienced sailor, had leaned into the path of the boom. The claimant obtained leave to amend her particulars within 21 days of service of the amended defence, but failed to do so. Over a year outside the limitation period (on 14 April 2000), the claimant applied to amend her particulars to allege that, if the accident happened as the defendant described, he was negligent in failing to take steps to protect the claimant's safety. The master refused the application, holding that, as limitation had expired and the new claim did not arise out the same facts as the old, he had no jurisdiction to allow the amendment.

The claimant appealed. Colman J held that (a) the factual basis for the proposed amendment was not the same as that for the original claim and CPR 17.4 prevent the claimant from relying on new facts not pleaded before limitation expired; (b) the claimant had not shown that the defendant had no arguable case that time did not run under s 11 and s 14 until the claimant learned of the defendant's version of events; (c) the claimant had not shown that the defendant had no arguable case that a s 33 should be refused; (d) to rely on the new cause of action the claimant would have to start fresh proceedings and the s 11, s 14 and s 33 issues could be fully heard. The claimant appealed again.

Held:

(i)   Section 35 of the 1980 Act applied. The new cause of action arose out the same facts as were in issue on the original claim form. s 35(4) was not intended to add any further restrictions.

(ii)   The defendant's argument that CPR 17.4 prohibited an amendment in these circumstances would have been soundly based but for the Human Rights Act 1998. The interpretation suggested by the defendant would impede the claimant's access to court. The court was bound to interpret CPR 17.4 purposively so as to allow the claimant access to the court.

(iii)   The judge was correct to hold that the defendant would have had an arguable case on the limitation points.

Appeal allowed.

Goodman v Fletcher and others

Limitation Act 1980, s 11, s 33

Court of Appeal   **4 October 1982**

The claimant (Miss Goodman) suffered from a number of allergies. In June and July 1973 she consulted Dr Buisseret who advised her to go on a gluten-free diet. In September 1974 she learned that he had recommended this on an empirical basis, that is, he wanted to see what was going to happen. In February 1975 she was discharged from the Peace Memorial Hospital with a dietary recommendation that included gluten.

In March 1978 she issued a writ against Dr Buisseret (among others). In April 1981 she served an inadequate statement of claim. A substitute statement of claim was served in November 1981, alleging that Dr Buisseret's advice was negligent and wrong. In April 1982 her case was struck out as statute barred.

Held:

(i)   The claimant knew in September 1974 that Dr Buisseret's diagnosis and advice were in error, and she certainly knew it by February 1975. Thus her case was prima facie statute barred by s 11 of the Limitation Act 1980;

(ii)   The delays had been great, and it would be impossible for Dr Buisseret at a trial in 1983 to have an accurate recollection of the consultations 10 years earlier in 1973. The delay was fatal to any exercise of discretion under s 33 of the 1980 Act.

Goodwin v Boots Company plc

Limitation Act 1980, s 14, s 33

QBD   **23 October 1998, unreported**

See *Brooks and others v Boots Company plc* (C) (p348)

Grattage v Home Office

CPR 6

Liverpool CC (DDJ O'Neill)   **CLY03/456 237269**

The claimant was injured working for the defendant on 9 November 1998. He issued proceedings on 8 November 2001. He served proceedings on the Treasury Solicitor by fax around noon on 8 March 2002. The defendant applied to strike out on the basis that service by fax was impermissible on the Crown under CPR 6 and 50 and Sch2 CCR Ord42 r 7(2).

Held:

(i)   Service by fax was not permissible on the Crown. The rules were clear and not ultra vires.

(ii)   The defendant's previous acceptance of communication by fax did render it estopped from raising this point.

(iii)   However, this fact, coupled with the peculiar service rules pertaining to the Crown, constituted exceptional circumstances justifying dispensation with service under CPR 6.9 (*Anderton v Clwyd CC* (p303) applied).

Application dismissed.

Gregory v Benham

CPR 3, 7, 16

QBD (Eady J)   **[2012] EWHC 2971 (QB)**

This claimant alleged that emails sent on 27 January 2010 were defamatory. He issued proceedings on 25 January 2011, thus just within the 12-month limitation period. Although he served the claim form on 9 May 2011, he failed to serve his particulars of claim within 14 days thereafter, instead serving them over two months late on 15 July 2011. The master refused his application for an extension of time and struck out his claim. The master mistakenly said in his judgment that the claim had been brought outside the limitation period and that the particulars of claim were filed nearly three months late. He also said that, if he exercised his discretion to allow an extension of time, he would be 'flying in the face of authority' and he would be 'depriving the defendant of his accrued rights' which had accrued to him because of the claimant's 'wholesale failure to comply with the rules'. The claimant appealed.

Held:

(i)   The master was not taken to have concluded that he was bound by authority to strike out the claim or to have believed that he was deprived of any discretion. When he said that extending time would fly in the face of authority, the master was referring to the numerous cases in which it had been urged, specifically in defamation claims, that claimants should act with expedition. The master did not believe that he had no discretion and was bound to strike the claim out; he was merely pointing out that there had been a failure to comply with the CPR and there was no proper explanation why.

(ii)   Further, the master's statement as to the defendant's accrued rights was not a reference to his mistaken belief that the claimant's claim had been issued outside the limitation period. Although it was unclear what the master meant by the defendant's 'accrued rights', there was nothing to justify granting an extension other than the barren excuse that, otherwise, the claimant would lose his claim (*Aktas v Adepta* (p296) considered).

(iii)   In referring to the 'wholesale failure to comply with the rules', which the master undoubtedly took into account, he was taken to have had in mind the claimant's failure to comply with the relevant pre-action protocol, the omission of details required on the claim form by para 2.2(1) of CPR PD 53, and the long delay in serving the particulars of claim. The master was entitled to characterise those failures as he did. The defendant did not know the nature of the complaint he faced until receipt of the particulars of claim nearly 16 months after the emails were sent. The master had not erred in fact or law in any material sense so as to vitiate the exercise of his discretion, nor had he stepped outside the bounds of the generous ambit within which reasonable disagreement was possible.

(iv)   Even if the instant court had misinterpreted the master's comments and he had made a material error of law such that it had exercised its discretion afresh, it would have come to the same conclusion on the claimant's application for an extension of time.

Appeal dismissed.

Gregory v Ferro (GB) Ltd and Jones and Wolverhampton Health Authority

Limitation Act 1980, s 14, s 33

Court of Appeal
[1995] 6 Med LR 321;
(1996) 30 BMLR 57; LTL 25/5/1995

On 7 August 1985 the claimant injured her right foot in an accident at work in the employ of the first defendant. She had a long history of rheumatoid arthritis. She was treated at the third defendant's hospital. On 13 August 1985 she attended her GP, the second defendant, who told her that the continued pain and swelling was a recurrence of her arthritis, but nevertheless referred her to the third defendant with a letter requesting that her left (uninjured) foot be x-rayed. This was done, although the claimant alleged that she had told hospital staff that it was her right foot that was injured. The second defendant reiterated his diagnosis of arthritic recurrence.

In early 1988 the claimant was making an unrelated visit to the hospital when she felt a sharp pain in her right foot. She was referred to a surgeon who on 29 June 1988 provisionally diagnosed a rupture to the Achilles tendon. This was confirmed on 20 April 1989. Following surgery to repair the rupture the claimant sought legal advice on 18 October 1989. She issued proceedings on 28 June 1991, whereupon the defendants pleaded limitation. This was tried as a preliminary issue. The judge held that the claimant had actual knowledge in June 1988. However, she had constructive knowledge under s 14(3) by March 1986 at the latest as by that point she should have changed doctors or voiced concerns that her symptoms had not subsided after six months. The claimant's own evidence was that by this time she had lost all faith in the second defendant. Proceedings were therefore issued out of time. The judge declined to exercise his discretion under s 33 to allow the action to continue, due in particular to the evidential prejudice of the delay to the second and third defendants, who had not been notified of a potential claim until 1991. The claimant appealed.

Held:

(i)   The judge had considered the evidence carefully and applied the law correctly. The court was not entitled to interfere with his findings on constructive knowledge.

(ii)   The claimant had not shown that, when exercising his discretion, the judge had failed to consider relevant matters or placed excessive weight on any matter.

Appeal dismissed.

Gregson v Channel 4 Television

CPR 17.4(3), 19.5(2)

Court of Appeal   **[2000] CP Rep 60;**
(2000) Times, 11 August; LTL 11/7/2000

On 23 June 1999, within a few days of the expiry of the limitation period, the claimant issued proceedings for libel. The claim form misstated the name of the defendant. It was served on 22 October 1999, the final day of the validity period. An application to amend was made on 5 November 1999. The judge allowed the application, holding that as the claim form had already been served an extension of time was not needed and the application therefore came within CPR 17.4(3). He rejected the defendant's contentions that the claimant also had to satisfy CPR 19.5 (change of parties after the end of a limitation period) and that an extension of time was needed but should be refused as granting it would deprive the defendant of an accrued limitation defence or, alternatively the necessary extension of time should not be granted as the requirements of CPR 7.6 were not met. The defendant appealed.

Held:

(i)   Given that it was conceded that the mistake was genuine and would not have caused reasonable doubt as to the identity of the party in question, CPR 17.4 applied. This was sufficient to provide the discretion to rectify the mistake and there was no need to go to CPR 19.5.

(ii)   CPR 19.5 applied when a claimant sought to substitute a new party when the wrong party was named on the claim form. This was distinct from the ambit of 17.4, which applied when the correct party was misnamed on the claim form.

(iii)   CPR 19.5 had no application to this case, and applying it would produce an insensible and unjust result. Even if it did apply, the accrued limitation defence would not have decided the point in the defendant's favour.

(iv)   If a new party was to be added or substituted, a consequential order for service of the claim form was not strictly bound by the requirements of CPR 7.6.

Appeal dismissed.

Grenville v Waltham Forest Health Authority

Limitation Act 1980, s 33

Court of Appeal   **18 November 1992**

On 4 May 1988 the claimant (Anne Grenville) underwent a sterilisation operation at a hospital operated by the defendants. Within the next two days, she noticed a burn on her right buttock. She consulted her general practitioner about it on 14 May and saw a doctor at the hospital about it on 16 June. Her solicitors sent a letter before action on 21 June 1988. Legal aid was granted. From October 1988 they tried to find a medical expert to report, but due to practical difficulties the claimant was not seen by one until March 1991.

On 2 May 1991 a clerk from the claimant's solicitors attended Bow County Court with particulars of claim and asked that a summons be issued as a matter of urgency. The court failed to issue the summons until 9 May. The defence pleaded limitation. The claimant's application under s 33 of the Limitation Act 1980 for the limitation period under s 11 to be disapplied was dismissed by the district judge whose decision was upheld on appeal by Mr Assistant Recorder Roberts. The claimant appealed and was allowed to adduce fresh affidavit evidence.

Held:

(i)   The most striking feature of the case was that the limitation period expired at a time when the claimant's solicitors had sought to issue process.

(ii)   The consequence might well be that an action by the claimant against her solicitors for negligence might fail, in which event she would have no redress.

(iii)   It was pertinent that the claimant's solicitors were not, as the assistant recorder believed on the information before him, inactive between October 1988 and March 1991.

(iv)   The assistant recorder did not appear to have taken into account the degree of prejudice, albeit small, which would necessarily accrue to the claimant if she had to sue her solicitors in negligence.

(v)   The assistant recorder, having regard to events at Bow County Court and to the history of the case, did not appropriately assess the prospects of success against the claimant's solicitors in an action for negligence.

The claimant's appeal was allowed.

Grewal v National Hospital for Nervous Diseases and another

Amendment of Statement of Claim   **RSC Ord 20, r 5**

Court of Appeal   **(1982) Times, 15 October**

On 15th June 1973 the claimant (Kuljinder Grewal) underwent a dorsal laminectomy at the first defendants' hospital. He was left completely paraplegic.

The writ was issued on 17 May 1976. His statement of claim served in November 1977 pleaded that the operation was unnecessary and negligently performed. It was amended in May 1979 to add allegations of delay in diagnosis and wrong diagnosis.

In 1982 the claimant applied to reamend his statement of claim to plead that he only consented to a biopsy, thereby adding a new cause of action of trespass to the person, and that the defendants negligently failed to inform him of the risks of the operation.

Sir Douglas Franks QC upheld the master's refusal to allow the reamendment. He considered that what was or was not said to the claimant in the ward before the operating depended on an entirely different set of facts from what took place in the operation theatre and held that he therefore had no jurisdiction to allow the reamendment. The claimant appealed.

Held:

(i)   RSC Ord 20, r 5(5) adds specifically to the wide terms of Ord 20, r 5(1). Where an amendment adds a new cause of action, it should only be made if the new cause arises out of the same facts or substantially the same facts as the cause of action already pleaded.

(ii)   The issue of trespass was different from the issue of negligence, but that was not the question under Ord 20, r 5(5). The question was whether the causes of action arose out of (substantially) the same facts.

(iii)   It was artificial to distinguish between what happened in the ward and what happened in the operating theatre. The new cause of action raised by the reamendment arose out of substantially the same facts as the original cause of action.

(iv)   No attempt had really been made by the defendants to make out a case of prejudice. On the other hand, the claimant suffered the most disastrous consequences from this operation and might be very much at risk if the amendment was not allowed. The court's discretion should be exercised in his favour.

The claimant's appeal was allowed.

Griffin and others v Clwyd Health Authority and others

Limitation Act 1980, s 33

Court of Appeal   LTL 14/5/2001

The first, second and third claimants were employed by the first defendant at Broughton Hospital until 1990-1992 respectively. The second to fifth defendants had been contracted by the defendant to undertake pest control. The claimants issued proceedings on 14 January 1997, alleging that they suffered from multi-chemical sensitivity due to exposure to pesticides used in the first defendant's hospital. The claimants addressed limitation in their particulars of claim stating that, notwithstanding that their ill health had manifested itself by 1990–1992, they did not have the requisite knowledge until August 1994 when they received medical treatment. The defendants denied liability and pleaded limitation which was heard as a preliminary issue.

The judge held that proceedings were issued out of time, stressing that the claimants had consulted solicitors as early as 1991. He declined to exercise his discretion under s 33. The first and second claimant's appealed.

Held:

(i)   The judge correctly directed himself and followed the principles in *Spargo v North Essex DHA* (p667). These principles were not merely guidelines but a binding set of rules. His finding that the claim was brought outside the primary limitation period was correct.

(ii)   As regards s 33, the delay was not reasonable and required explanation. As none had been provided, despite the judge's request for one, the judge was entitled to strike the claims out.

Appeal dismissed.

Guidera v NEI Projects (India) Limited

Limitation Act 1939, s 2   Limitation Act 1980, s 11, s 14

Court of Appeal   30 January 1990

From September 1952 to March 1953 the claimant (Thomas Guidera) was employed by the defendants as a steel erector at Poplar Power Station where he came into contact with asbestos. In April 1976 he was referred to the East Ham Chest Clinic because of an abnormal x-ray but did not tell Dr Hanson, the consultant there, in answer to her questions that he had been exposed to asbestos because it was so long ago. When he told her in May 1982, she advised him to apply to the Pneumoconiosis Medical Panel to see whether he had a prescribed disease for DSS benefit. In February 1983 the PMP examined him and decided 'there is insufficient evidence to diagnose asbestosis', so the claimant instructed his trade union to take no action. In June 1983, following a further scan, Dr Hanson advised him to reapply, but he did not do so because he did not think he had good grounds. In February 1985 Dr Rudd diagnosed probable asbestosis and discussed with the claimant claims for benefit through the PMP and for damages through the courts. In April 1986 the claimant instructed his trade union to proceed, and his writ was issued on 12 January 1987.

At a preliminary trial on limitation Dr Rudd testified that when asbestos fibres are inhaled the body's defence mechanism operates and that, in the process, enzymes attack lung cells but when the enzymes are released the cells are replaced and the body is not impaired. He said that these attempts by the body's defence mechanism persist, but that if fibre remains after a period fibrosis occurs. McCullough J held that the destruction of the lung cells was not damage and that moreover any fibrosis suffered by the claimant up to 4 June 1954 would have been so minimal as not to constitute damage. Accordingly, his cause of action had not arisen by then and was not barred by s 2 of the Limitation Act 1939. The defendants did not appeal against this finding.

However McCullough J also found that the defendants, on whom the burden lay, had not established on the balance of probabilities that had the claimant taken reasonable steps he would have been fixed with appropriate knowledge before 12 January 1984. He held that his action had been begun in time and ordered that the costs of the preliminary trial should be the claimant's in any event. The defendants appealed.

Held:

(i)   (a)   The judge should not have introduced the word 'reasonably' into s 14(1)(b) of the Limitation Act 1980 when it was not there. Interpreting the word 'attributable' as 'capable of being attributed', that phrase means that attribution is a real possibility and not a fanciful one;

       (b)   'reasonableness' becomes relevant to attribution when knowledge is to be imputed under s 14(3). It was not for the claimant to refuse to answer Dr Hanson's questions properly in 1976, notwithstanding his mistaken belief that his asbestos exposure was irrelevant. She would then have told him that his x-ray changes were probably caused by his asbestos work;

       (c)   consequently time started to run against the claimant in April 1976: s 14(1). His action was commenced out of time: s 11(4).

(ii)   (a)   The delay from the limitation period expiring in April 1979 to issue of the writ in January 1987 was 7½ years. Within that, the period of delay which the judge considered to be unreasonable was from July 1983 to April 1986, a period of 2½ years: s 33(3)(a);

       (b)   it appears that the defendants never had, even by 1976, any evidence of any value so far as the claimant's working conditions and their own precautions (or lack of them) were concerned. Moreover the medical evidence since 1979 had become more rather than less cogent: s 33(3)(b);

       (c)   initially, in 1976 and thereafter, the claimant's silence was innocent if misguided. He did not withhold the information from any wrong motive, and his injury was in 1976 symptomless and in its early stages: s 33(3)(e);

       (d)   the court's discretion should be exercised in the claimant's favour: s 33(1);

       (e)   on the basis that the claimant's action was prima facie statute barred and that he succeeded only by virtue of s 33, the proper order for costs was to reserve the costs of the preliminary trial to the trial judge. The costs of the appeal should be costs in cause.

The defendants' appeal was dismissed on the limitation issue but allowed in relation to costs.

Gurtner v Circuit

Substituted service and renewal of writ

Court of Appeal   **[1968] 1 All ER 328; [1968] 2 QB 587;**
                                                 [1968] 2 WLR 668

On 29 June 1961 the claimant (Frederick Gurtner) was run down and severely injured by a motor cycle on the Kingston by-pass. The motor cyclist gave his name to the police as John Christopher Circuit and gave his address as 45 Alpine Avenue, Tolworth. He supplied them with details of his insurance which they failed to record properly. Subsequently he went out to Canada and married there.

On 26 June 1964 the claimant's solicitors issued a writ against Mr Circuit. On 24 June 1965, when a process server tried to serve it at his Tolworth address, neighbours said that he had gone to Canada about three years ago. On 25 June 1965 the writ was renewed ex parte for 12 months.

In November 1965 the claimant's new solicitors wrote to the Motor Insurers' Bureau who asked the Royal Insurance to investigate the matter. Neither the defendant nor his insurers could be traced. Three further renewals were obtained, extending the validity of the writ to 14 September 1967.

On 22 June 1967, on the claimant's ex parte application, the master ordered substituted service by sending the writ by ordinary prepaid post addressed to John Christopher Circuit c/o Royal Insurance Co Ltd, 24/28 Lombard Street, London EC3. MIB applied to be added as defendants. The master granted this and set aside the orders for substituted service and renewal of the writ. Chapman J on appeal held that MIB could not be added as defendants and restored the orders for substituted service and renewal.

Held:

(i)   MIB should be added as defendants, on their undertaking to pay any damages that might be awarded to the claimant, since they would be directly affected by the determination of the case.

(ii)   The order for substituted service was unwarranted, since the writ was not likely to reach the defendant and he was not insured with Royal Insurance. However, no useful purpose would be served by setting it aside. Service should be allowed to stand.

(iii)   The defendant was away in Canada and could not be traced so as to be served. That was good reason for not serving the writ, so the orders for renewals should stand as well.

Per Lord Denning MR: 'Once they are added as defendants, they would be in a position to urge that the order for substituted service was not properly made and should be set aside. It seems to me not to have been properly made. The affidavit in support was insufficient to warrant the order, for the simple reason that it did not show that the writ was likely to reach the defendant, nor to come to his knowledge. All that it showed was that, if the writ were sent to the Royal Insurance Co Ltd, it would reach the Motor Insurers' Bureau; but the Motor Insurers' Bureau were not defendants at that time. So that would not suffice. It would be different if the defendant were insured with Royal Insurance Co Ltd, but that was not suggested. In my opinion, therefore, the order for substituted service made on June 22, 1967, could be set aside if that would serve any useful purpose. If there were any possibility of tracing the defendant in Canada, substituted service should be ordered by advertisement; but that seems to be a useless procedure here. The practical course is to allow the order for substituted service to stand without incurring any further costs; and to allow the service to stand.'

Per Diplock LJ: 'In a case like this, however, which must be rare, where there is strong prima facie evidence that the defendant is insured but it is not possible to ascertain the identity of his insurers, an order for substituted service might properly be made on the defendant at the address of the Motor Insurers' Bureau. Such an order, of course, should not be made except on evidence that all reasonable efforts have been made by the claimant to trace the defendant and effect personal service. It is now common ground, however, that the defendant has left this country and that there is no real prospect of tracing him.'

Halford v Brookes and another

Limitation Act 1980, s 11, s 14, s 33

Court of Appeal   **[1991] 3 All ER 559; [1991] 1 WLR 428**

On 3 April 1978 Lynn Siddons, aged 16, went for a walk with the second defendant (Michael Brookes), then aged 15. On 9 April she was found strangled and stabbed to death in open countryside in Derbyshire. The second defendant confessed to the police that he had attacked the girl with a knife and was charged with her murder. The first defendant (Fitzroy Brookes), his stepfather, denied any involvement. In October 1978 the second defendant alleged that the first defendant had planned the killing, strangled and repeatedly stabbed the girl and that he (the second defendant) had only inflicted superficial wounds. The first defendant was cross-examined to this effect at the second defendant's trial in November 1978.

Through hearing the trial evidence the claimant (Mrs Gail Halford) formed the firm belief that both defendants were responsible for her daughter's death. Her then solicitors advised her about claiming compensation from the Criminal Injuries Compensation Board, but not about claiming damages from the defendants. She continued to campaign for the first defendant to be prosecuted. Between 1980 and 1984, evidence that he had made various confessions to the murder came to light. In July 1985 she consulted new solicitors, and in October 1985 counsel advised that a civil claim for damages was feasible and limited legal aid was granted. After investigations, full legal aid was granted in March 1987 and the writ was issued on 1 April 1987.

At a preliminary trial, Schiemann J ruled that her claim was statute barred and would be dismissed on the grounds that it was brought after the expiration of the three-year limitation period under s 11 of the Limitation Act 1980. The claimant appealed.

Held:

(i)   'Knowledge' does not mean 'know for certain'. It does, however, mean 'know with sufficient confidence to justify embarking on the preliminaries to the issue of a writ, such as submitting a claim to the proposed defendant, taking legal and other advice and collecting evidence'. Suspicion will not be enough, but reasonable belief will normally suffice. The claimant had this knowledge by November 1978. It would not make any difference if her 'knowledge' had been that the injuries were caused by one or other of the defendants, but could not have been caused by both and she did not know which was responsible. This is a common situation in which the claimant would be expected to sue in the alternative. The only knowledge that she did not have was that the killing gave rise to a civil cause of action, but that is specifically declared by s 14(1) to be irrelevant. The primary time limit expired not more than three years later in November 1981: s 11(5), s 14.

(ii)   (a)   The claimant was not to blame for the delay, since she was not aware that a civil remedy was open to her until she consulted new solicitors: s 33(3)(a);

        (b)   the answer to the question 'who killed Lynn Siddons' did not depend on the accuracy of anyone's recollection. It essentially depended on the extent to which the first and second defendants were telling the truth or lying. A fair trial was still possible: s 33(3)(b);

        (c)   the claimant acted promptly once she knew that she might have a claim for damages: s 33(3)(e);

        (d)   the alleged inability of a defendant to meet a judgment after a finding of intentional tort is not a legitimate reason from preventing a blameless claimant from pursuing a civil claim for damages. Moreover there was some evidence that both defendants were in gainful employment: s 33(3);

        (e)   in all the circumstances, it would be equitable to allow the action to proceed: s 33(i).

The claimant's appeal was allowed.

In view of the House of Lords' decision in *Stubbings v Webb* (p677), this case would now be decided differently under s 2 of the Limitation Act 1980.

Hall v John Laing Plc

Limitation Act 1980, s 33

Bishop Auckland County Court (HHJ Brigs)   22 December 2008, unreported

The claimant worked for the defendant between 1954 and 1961. Following a medical diagnosis on 12 March 2002 that he suffered from asbestosis, the claimant on 11 March 2005 issued proceedings, a letter of claim having been sent in August 2004 but never answered. However, the claimant (or rather his solicitors) failed to serve proceedings in time and the claim was struck out. At that time, the rule in *Walkley v Precision Forgings Ltd* (p705) would have precluded bringing duplicate proceedings. That rule, however, was abolished in June 2006 by *Horton v Sadler* (p482). On 14 November 2007 the claimant issued duplicate proceedings. Limitation was heard as preliminary issue. The defendant contended that it was inappropriate to remove the limitation bar as to do so would unfairly remove their only defence, namely the limitation defence. It had no positive defence on the merits, beyond requiring the claimant to prove his case.

Held:

(i)   The court's discretion under s 33 was wide and unfettered, but the burden of persuading the court to exercise it was a heavy one that rested on the claimant and discretion should be exercised where equity between the parties demanded it (*Horton v Sadler* (p482) and *KR v Bryn Alyn Community (Holdings) Ltd (In Liquidation)* (p505) applied). Before exercising the discretion the court was required to carry out a balancing exercise on a consideration of all relevant circumstances (*Long v Tolchard & Sons Ltd* (p537) applied).

(ii)   The existence of an alternative remedy was an important, relevant factor to consider but it could never be decisive on its own and its existence did not necessarily mean that a party who could avail itself of such a remedy would suffer no prejudice (*Thompson v Brown (t/a George Albert Brown (Builders) & Co)* (p690) and *Steeds v Peverel Management Services Ltd* (p674) applied).

(iii)   In the instant case, whilst the claimant clearly had a claim against his former solicitors on which he was likely to succeed, there was a significant risk that the damages that he would recover would be less than those from the defendant. Moreover, the further delay of having to start a third set of proceedings would be prejudicial, especially as the claimant was in poor health.

(iv)   The defendant's defence only arose through the failure of the claimant's former solicitors to serve his original claim in time. In the context of the case, that failure was a tiny delay that caused the defendant no prejudice at all. The real delay that was prejudicial to the defendant was the long delay between the end of the claimant's employment and the commencement of the original claim. However, that delay was not attributable to the claimant as he was unaware of his condition until the medical diagnosis that identified that he suffered from asbestosis. The delay in the first proceedings was also not attributable to the claimant directly, and he had acted promptly once it became possible to bring a second claim.

(v)   The defendant's conduct in not responding to or even acknowledging correspondence sent under the Pre-Action Protocol, and in not doing anything to respond to the claim other than to take procedural points as and when they occurred, counted against it under s 33(3)(c).

(vi)   Accordingly, in all the circumstances, it was clear that the claimant would suffer a greater prejudice than the defendant if his claim was not allowed to proceed, and equity between the parties required the court to exercise its discretion under s 33.

Judgment for claimant.

Hallam Estates Ltd v Baker

CPR 6, 7

QBD (Tugendhat J)   **[2012] EWHC 1046 (QB)**

The claimant issued a libel action against the defendant six days before the one-year limitation period expired. The claim form was issued on 11 May 2011; the time for its service expired on 11 September 2011. However, on 30 August, upon the claimant's application, the master extended the time for service until 11 November 2011. On 18 and 25 August, the claimant's solicitors wrote to the defendant's solicitors asking whether they had instructions to accept service; by then, the claimant had learnt that the defendant had left the address they had for her. On 23 August, the defendant's solicitors wrote to say that they were seeking instructions; they did not say that they were instructed to accept service. The claim form was served on 9 November, and upon receipt the defendant applied to set aside the order granting the claimant an extension of time. Refusing the application, the master held that it was necessary to identify why the claim form had not been served; he held that the reason was that the defendant had left her known address and that the claimant was not aware of her new address. The defendant appealed.

Held:

(i)   The master had erred by confining his consideration of the reason why the claim form had not been served in time to the period in late August when the claimant became aware that defendant had left her known address. The whole of the four-month period starting in mid-May should have been looked at (*Hashtroodi v Hancock* (p466) considered).

(ii)   Further, the claimant should not have been granted an extension of time which would or might have the effect of depriving the defendant of a limitation defence. It would be therefore be appropriate to exercise the court's discretion afresh.

(iii)   Having regard to the availability to the defendant of a limitation defence and to the lack of evidence as to why the claimant had failed to pursue their defamation claim with the expedition required, the order granting an extension of time would be set aside.

(iv)   It was not open for the claimant to argue that the defendant's failure to apply to set aside the order made within the seven-day period prescribed by CPR 23.10 was fatal to its application. That point had not been raised before the master.

Appeal allowed.

Hammond v West Lancashire HA

Limitation Act 1980, s 33

Court of Appeal   **[1998] Lloyd's Rep Med 146;**
(1998) 95(14) LSG 23; (1998) Times, 5 March

The claimant was the widower of a woman who had been admitted to hospital on 2 December 1987. A diagnosis of Hodgkin's disease was made and she was given chemotherapy for that condition. In fact, she was suffering from small cell lung cancer, diagnosis of which was made in March 1988. She died on 9 August 1988 and the claimant, as administrator of her estate, commenced proceedings on 20 January 1994 alleging that the wrongful diagnosis and treatment had caused the deceased injury, namely that her symptoms were worse than they should have been and that her life was shortened by 24 months. Limitation was heard as preliminary issue. As regards s 14, the judge found that the report dated 15 September 1988 from a consultant physician to the claimant's solicitors sufficiently conveyed the information necessary to fix the knowledge of a significant injury attributable wholly or in part to a failure to undertake a differential diagnosis. In exercising his discretion the learned judge concluded that, in all the circumstances, taking into account any prejudice that might be suffered by the defendant, it was equitable to disapply the three-year limitation period. The defendant appealed on the principal ground that the judge had not taken sufficient account of the fact that x-rays taken of the deceased had been destroyed and that these would have shown that the original diagnosis of Hodgkin's disease was justified.

Held:

(i) The judge had been entitled to conclude that the defendant brought any potential prejudice upon itself by its practice of destroying all x-rays after three years, particularly in the light of medical notes which suggested that they were put on notice of a potential claim in March 1988. The procedure of not informing radiology about the possibility of a claim, because radiographs were not considered part of the medical notes, was inexplicable.

(ii) Since the defendant's primary case was that a differential diagnosis should have been undertaken and that it ought to have been obvious to a competent medical practitioner that Hodgkin's disease may not have been the only condition present, the x-rays were not particularly significant in this case. If anything, their destruction caused prejudice to the claimant in that there was no evidence to refute the defendant's view that their diagnosis was justified.

(iii) Although there was no explanation for the delay, it was clear that the judge had taken that matter into account when he struck the balance. This was not a matter so plainly wrong that the Court of Appeal could interfere.

Appeal dismissed.

Hands v Coleridge-Smith and Horsburgh

Limitation Act 1980, s 33

Court of Appeal   **14 May 1992**

On 1 September 1981 Ronald Hands, who was suffering from a severe pain in the stomach, was admitted to hospital. On 11 September 1981 he died.

On 29 April 1985 the claimant (his widow) issued a writ against the health authority. She never served it. On 4 October 1988 she applied to amend the writ by adding the present defendants. On 7 October 1988 the amended writ was served on them. This was the first notification of her claim. In December 1988 she obtained a favourable expert's report. In April 1989 she supplied details of the alleged negligence.

She applied under s 33 of the Limitation Act 1980 for the time limit in s 11 to be disapplied. Mr J Crowley QC, sitting as a deputy high court judge, upheld the master's refusal to grant this. The claimant applied for leave to appeal.

Held:

(i) As the defendants were totally unaware that they might have to meet a claim until October 1988, and as they had no details of the alleged negligence until April 1989, some 7½ years after dealing with the case, the judge was almost bound to reach the conclusion which he did.

(ii) The truth was that the claimant had left it too late to bring these defendants into the proceedings, and the reason for that, no doubt, was because the earlier medical opinion was unfavourable.

The claimant's application was dismissed.

Hannigan v Hannigan and others

CPR 3, 7

Court of Appeal   **(2000) Independent, 3 July; LTL 18/5/2000**

The claimant brought proceedings under the Inheritance Act 1975 against the executors and beneficiaries of her later husband's estate. Proceedings were issues, shortly after the advent of the CPR, using the wrong form (in effect a Part 8 Claim Form). There were other errors; the pleading was not endorsed with a statement of truth, the first defendant was incorrectly named, no Acknowledgment of Service was served and numerous other matters of form were awry.

The defendants applied to strike the claim out under CPR 3.4(2)(c). The district judge allowed this application, refusing the claimant permission to remedy the defects by amendment. The claimant appealed but the circuit judge was equally critical of the claimant's solicitors and, having regard to the factors set out at CPR 3.9, dismissed the appeal. The claimant appealed again.

Held:

(i)   The petition provided the defendants with all the information needed to understand the claim being made. The complaints were thus purely about form rather than substance.

(ii)   The makers of the CPR had not intended a reversion to the arid pre-1965 technicalities.

(iii) CPR 7.5(5) embodied Lord Woolf MR's recommendation that all claims should be started on a single claim form.

(iv)   The county court staff should never have permitted the claim to be issued in the form done.

(v)   The problem here was a technical one in that the correct claim form had not been used.

(vi)   The judge's exercise of his discretion was seriously flawed. He failed to take into account the availability of all the regular information, instead focusing on technicalities such as the lack of the Royal Coat of Arms and the width of the margins.

(vii) It was therefore appropriate to consider the discretion afresh.

(viii) Refusing to allow the necessary corrections would be the antithesis of justice; the claim would be struck out and the defendants would receive a windfall. The balance was overwhelmingly in the claimant's favour. Notwithstanding the number of errors, striking out would be a disproportionate response.

(ix)   The judgment was not to be taken as a green light for sloppy and inefficient behaviour by lawyers, for which sanctions existed.

Appeal allowed.

Harding v People's Dispensary For Sick Animals

Limitation Act 1980, s 14

Court of Appeal   **[1994] PIQR P270; [1994] JPIL 152**

On 19 October 1988 the claimant suffered a strain to her back at work. She had sustained a previous similar injury in 1982 which had resolved itself within five weeks. It had not occurred to her then to take proceedings against her employers. After the injury in 1988 she consulted her general practitioner, who diagnosed lumbar strain, but did not refer the claimant to an orthopaedic surgeon. She returned to work on 9 December 1988 and continued until August 1990 when her back was causing her considerable trouble. In April 1990 she went to see solicitors because she feared, accurately, that she was likely to be dismissed because, in the opinion of her employers, she was failing to carry out the work that she was employed to do. She was dismissed on grounds of ill-health in August 1990. She subsequently began proceedings on 7 October 1992, claiming that her date of knowledge for the purposes of s 14 was no earlier than October 1990. Limitation was heard as preliminary issue. The judge held that the date of knowledge was April 1990, when the claimant first consulted solicitors, indicating that he would not have exercised his s 33 discretion in the claimant's favour had this been necessary. The defendant appealed.

Held:

(i)   The question of significant injury was pre-eminently a matter for the trial judge.

(ii)   The judge was entitled to take the objective view that it was reasonable for the claimant not to realise that her injury was significant or sufficiently serious to justify her instituting proceedings for damages until April 1990, in view of the previous similar injury which had resolved itself within five weeks, and of the fact that she had not been referred to a consultant.

Appeal dismissed.

Harding v Richard Costain Ltd

Limitation Act 1980, s 33

QBD (Judge Mackie QC)   **[2009] EWHC 1348 (QB)**

The claimant acted on behalf of the estate of his deceased father (D) who had suffered from asbestosis. In 1995, D successfully applied for industrial disablement benefit. This followed an x-ray in 1990 showing pleural fibrosis and calcification and a discussion in 1995 with his GP regarding asbestosis. D then contacted solicitors regarding a potential claim for damages for the asbestosis. The solicitors advised him by letter in 1997 that the asbestosis was very likely to have been contracted during his employment with the defendant in 1961–1962 and 1966–1968. The letter further stated that pursuing the claim would be arduous, protracted and that, relative to its length and complexity, the rewards would not be great. The letter also stated that further instructions would be required from D and referred to the possibility of a conditional fee agreement (CFA) being set up. D did not pursue a claim. D died on 19 April 2005. The subsequent inquest found that he had died from an industrial disease. The coroner referred to the prospect of a claim and encouraged the bringing of such a claim. A letter of claim was sent in October 2007 and proceedings issued on 11 April 2008, the claimant applying under s 33 for the statute bar to be disapplied. The claimant contended that D's decision not to pursue a claim was reasonable given the tone of the solicitors' letter and that it was, in all the circumstances, appropriate to disapply the three-year limit to the claim.

Held:

(i)   D did not possess the relevant knowledge until August 1995. The evidence pointing towards an earlier date was too thin.

(ii)   It was appropriate for the court to exercise its discretion and exclude the three-year time limit (*Cain v Francis* (p360) applied). Having regard to the provisions of s 33(3)(b) it could not be said that the evidence available had become less cogent as a result of the delay. Although it was not good enough simply to say that 30 years went by before the cause of action accrued, so another year or so was neither here nor there, the fact remained that many of the difficulties for the defendant, and indeed the claimant, sprang from the period of 30-plus years and, given that length of time, the parties were not in any event going to obtain much evidence about quite what was happening during D's period of employment with the defendant.

(iii)   There was no real prejudice to the defendant as regards quantum. D would not have been a realistic target for surveillance, and any difficulties in proof counted against the claimant, upon whom the burden lay.

(iv) Further, when looking at reasons for the delay it was necessary to stand back from close analysis of the paperwork and look at the practicalities as they had faced D and his family. D was not an educated man. It was important not to look at the solicitors' letter in terms of its literal text, nor indeed to consider how it would be analysed, for example, by an educated person. It was clear that D, from what he told his family and the fact that he did not pursue a claim, thought he had a difficult case for limited potential reward and that he might put his life savings at risk in the process. It was also apparent that D was put off by the context of the legal advice that he obtained. It was not an answer to say that D had been advised about a CFA, as there was no evidence that a CFA had been explained to him.

(v) Accordingly, the period from the solicitors' letter until after D's death was one in which neither D nor anyone else had a reason to change the view that they reasonably but erroneously held about the chances of a claim's success. The claim only began to be formulated after the inquest. To people in the position of D's family, advice from a respected authority figure such as a coroner would be something to count on and something which would reasonably lead them to pursue a claim. The coroner's advice amounted to a change of circumstances.

(vi) Having regard to the broad principle of equity, it was appropriate to exclude the three-year time limit as the application of the bar would unfairly prejudice the claimant.

Application granted.

Harland & Wolff Pension Trustees Ltd v Aon Consulting Financial Services Ltd

Limitation Act 1980, s 35   **CPR 17.4**

Ch D (Warren J)   **[2009] EWHC 1557 (Ch); [2010] ICR 121**

Following the decision in *Barber v Guardian Royal Exchange Assurance Group* (C-262/88) [1991] 1 QB 344, ECJ, the defendant had given the claimant trustees pension and actuarial advice on the equalisation of normal retirement dates. The defendant advised that the normal retirement date for women should be increased with retrospective effect, which, it transpired, was ineffective under European law. The claimant issued proceedings for professional negligence on the basis that, as a result of the defendant's advice, the claimant had thought the retrospective change was a legal and effective way of equalising retirement ages for male and female members of the pension scheme. As a result of the wrong advice the true cost to the scheme was much larger than the defendant had advised.

Following the trial of a preliminary issue the claimant applied to amend the particulars of claim to plead that the defendant had wrongly valued the surplus of the pension scheme, as it had assumed that equalisation had been carried out effectively. The defendant objected to the amendments on the basis that they related to a new cause of action that was time barred. The master held that the proposed amendments gave rise to a new cause of action, as matters now alleged constituted an allegation of a breach of duty by the defendant that was different to that already pleaded. The claimant appealed.

Held:

(i) The new claim that the claimant was seeking to raise could be pleaded as a consequential loss flowing from the original advice given in relation to the equalisation. That would not introduce a new cause of action but would simply introduce a new head of damage (*Aldi Stores Ltd v Holmes Buildings Plc* [2003] EWCA Civ 1882, (2005) PNLR 9 considered). Accordingly, an amendment to add a new head of loss was caught by either s 35 or CPR 17.4.

(ii)   The particulars of claim could not be amended so as to introduce any allegation of a new breach of duty. However, in the exercise of discretion, amendments would be allowed to introduce a new claim as a further head of loss or damage arising out of the original breach. That amendment would be permitted on condition that the claimant gave undertakings not to seek at any time to further amend the particulars of claim to rely on any breach of duty in order to recover the new head of loss.

Appeal allowed in part.

Harley v Smith

Foreign Limitation Periods Act 1984, s 2

Court of Appeal   **[2010] EWCA Civ 78; [2010] CP Rep 33**

The claimant had sustained personal injuries whilst working as a professional diver for D1 (a Saudi-based company) in Saudi territorial waters. D2 was the claimant's co-employee and diving supervisor. The month after the accident, the claimant returned to the United Kingdom and, just less than three years later, commenced proceedings against D1 and D2. A dispute arose as to whether Sharia law applied, whether the claims were time barred under art 222 of Saudi labour law, as they had been made more than 12 months after the accident or after the termination of the work relationship, or whether, under s 2 of the Foreign Limitation Periods Act 1984, the limitation period did not apply, as undue hardship would be caused to the claimant. The judge found that the claimant had continued to be paid as if still employed by D1 for approximately three years after returning to the UK and so 'work relations' under art 222 had not ended until the end of that month and the claims were not time barred. After considering the availability and content of the claimant's legal advice, the judge further found that the undue hardship threshold under s 2 was crossed and so the 12-month period could have been disapplied. The defendants appealed, submitting that (1) there was no factual basis upon which the judge could conclude that the limitation period under art 222(1) did not end until the effective termination of the relationship of the employer and employee, which did not necessarily mean when the strict contractual period ended; and (2) the judge had erred in holding that he would have disapplied that limitation period.

Held:

(i)   In the absence of evidence that recognised principles of interpretation under Sharia law would require an extended meaning to be given to the phrase 'work relation' in art 222(1), the judge effectively decided for himself what Sharia law would require. In that respect he went beyond what he could properly do (*Bumper Development Corp v Commissioner of Police of the Metropolis* [1991] 1 WLR 1362 considered). He purported to construe foreign legislation by applying principles of interpretation which had not been established by evidence.

(ii)   In holding that he would have disapplied the limitation period, the judge relied upon undue hardship arising from the fact that lawyers in the UK whom the claimant had consulted the month after the accident had not appreciated that the relevant limitation period under Saudi law was, or might be, 12 months. That could not be a relevant factor. The question was not whether undue hardship was caused by wrong advice but whether it was caused by the application of the foreign limitation period. There was nothing to suggest that, on the basis of the advice which they had received, the claimant had chosen to delay the commencement of proceedings until after the 12 months had expired or that, if they had appreciated the need to commence proceedings within that period, there would have been any difficulty in doing so.

(iii)   The judge further found that those giving advice to the claimant were disadvantaged because of the uncertainty of the legal position in Saudi Arabia and so were victims of that uncertainty. However, the uncertainty of the legal position, if known to be uncertain, would have made it necessary to bring proceedings sooner rather than later to avoid the risk to which the uncertainty gave rise of being out of time: the uncertainty did not add to any hardship caused by the need to bring the proceedings within the 12 months.

(iv)   The judge should have appreciated that it was not sufficient to cross the threshold of undue hardship by reason only that the period of 12 months was less generous than the period of three years allowed under English law, and he should have appreciated that the application of the limitation period of 12 months, rather than three years, led to no greater hardship in the circumstances than would normally be so.

Appeal dismissed, but order varied.

Harnett v Fisher

Limitation Act 1623

House of Lords   [1927] AC 573

The claimant (Mr Harnett) was a Kentish farmer. On 10 November 1912, Dr Fisher, a country doctor, was asked by another doctor to examine him. From a window, he watched the claimant for a short time in the street and took note of his demeanour. As a result he signed a certificate in the form required by the Lunacy Act 1890, in which he pronounced the claimant to be of unsound mind. On the petition of the claimant's brother, a justice of the peace made a reception order on the same day. The claimant was confined in a lunatic asylum and licensed houses for lunatics until he escaped in October 1921.

On 31 May 1922 he started court action against Dr Fisher. At the trial the jury found that, at the date of the certificate, the claimant was not of unsound mind and that Dr Fisher did not act with reasonable care. The judge dismissed the case as statute barred, and this was affirmed by the Court of Appeal. The claimant appealed.

Held:

(i)   As the claimant was never insane, time was not prevented from running by reason of disability.

(ii)   The six-year limitation period ran from his detention on 10 November 1912, so he was debarred from recovering damages by the Limitation Act 1623.

His appeal was dismissed.

Harris v CDMR Purfleet Ltd (formerly Purfleet Thames Terminal Ltd)

Limitation Act 1980, s 14, s 33

Court of Appeal   [2009] EWCA Civ 1645

From September 2001 the claimant had worked for the defendant as a cargo operative, which involved driving a truck. He alleged that he had suffered from a repetitive strain injury in his left shoulder as a result of the prolonged use of the truck's steering wheel which had caused him to remain off work from February 2003. Proceedings were issued in January 2006. Although the claim form stated that the action was in respect of an accident in February 2003, the particulars of claim pleaded a repetitive strain injury. The defendant pleaded limitation, which was tried alongside liability.

In a witness statement, the claimant said that, in about April 2002, he had complained to his supervisor that the driving was causing him pain, but the issue was not resolved. The claimant's medical records first made reference to pain in his left shoulder in August 2002 when he was given a steroid injection. A further three references were made before March 2003, at which point the medical records noted that the problem was attributable to the operating of a heavy locking truck. The claimant conceded that he knew that the injury was significant for the purposes of s 14 in August 2002, but maintained that the date of his knowledge that the injury was attributable to the acts or omissions of the defendant was when he received medical advice in March 2003 and that his claim was, accordingly, within the relevant time limit. In the alternative he argued for s 33 (that application being raised for the first time in closing written submissions).

The judge concluded that the claim was time barred under s 14, the claimant's date of knowledge being October 2002. In respect of s 33, the judge held that the balance of prejudice lay in the defendant's favour. He also found against the claimant on liability.

The claimant appealed, submitting that the judge's analysis as to limitation was inadequate and that he was required to give more substantial reasons for his decision. He also argued that the judge had not explained why his date of knowledge was October 2002 and contended that he did not know why he had lost his claim.

Held:

(i)   It was always desirable that a judgment should be comprehensible upon first reading, and the judgment in the instant case was not. However, that was not the test of adequacy of reasons. Adequacy must be tested in the context of the knowledge and understanding of the evidence and submissions at trial (*English v Emery Reimbold & Strick Ltd* [2002] EWCA Civ 605, [2002] 1 WLR 2409 applied).

(ii)   After one had read the pleadings and the evidence, the judgment could be understood, and it was reasonably clear why the judge had decided as he did.

(iii)   Insofar as there were any doubts about the judge's reasons, there were none in respect of his conclusions. Regarding his conclusion that the claimant's date of knowledge was October 2002, one possible explanation was that he had found that, although it was not clear that the claimant knew the injury was significant in August, he must have known by October.

(iv)   In truth, it did not matter whether the judge thought it was August or October. On any view, the claimant had knowledge well before the date relevant for the limitation. With regard to the judge's findings as to the date on which the claimant knew that his injury was attributable to the defendant, the judgment on that issue was unclear. However, the claimant's witness statement clearly suggested that he knew to what his injuries were attributable in April 2002. A finding against the claimant on that matter was, therefore, inevitable.

(v)   Accordingly, the judge was right to hold that the claim was statute barred.

(vi)   The judge was entitled to hold that the balance of prejudice lay in the defendant's favour. There was no sign that he misdirected himself in respect of s 33.

Appeal dismissed.

Harris v Newcastle Health Authority

Supreme Court Act 1981, s 33   **Discovery**

Court of Appeal   **[1989] 2 All ER 273; [1989] 1 WLR 96**

The claimant (Veronica Harris) was born in October 1959. She suffered from a squint in her left eye. Around April 1961 her parents consulted Mr Lake who conducted an operation either at the Fleming Memorial Hospital or at the Royal Victoria Infirmary. The result was that her eyelid became nearly closed.

In 1965 Mr Howard was consulted. He performed a further operation. This resulted in some cosmetic improvement, with the eyelid opening more. However, she since suffered pain which became progressively worse.

In February 1987 a nurse suggested to the claimant that the problem was not of natural origin. Indeed, the claimant had always connected it with the operation which she had had as a small child. She consulted solicitors who applied for pre-action disclosure of the hospital records under s 33(2) of the Senior Courts Act 1981. Staughton J upheld the district registrar's refusal to grant this on the ground that there was no point in ordering pre-action discovery when a limitation defence was virtually bound to succeed. The claimant appealed.

Held: the claimant's counsel had stated that proceedings were likely to be instituted, so the jurisdictional requirements of s 33(2) were satisfied. Although there was a strong limitation defence, the claimant's case was not clearly doomed to failure. The application for pre-action discovery should be granted.

Per Kerr LJ: 'If it is plain beyond doubt that a defence of limitation will be raised and will succeed, then it seems to me that the court must be entitled to take that matter into account … But I would accept that in the normal run of cases, even where a defence of limitation has a strong prospect of success, like here, it is very difficult for a court, on limited material, before pleadings and discovery, to conclude at that stage that the situation is such that the proposed action is bound to fail and therefore frivolous, vexatious or otherwise ill-founded. So in general I would accept the submission of counsel that issues relevant to limitation should not enter into consideration on applications for pre-trial discovery.'

Hart v British Leyland Cars Ltd

Limitation Act 1980, s 11, s 14, s 33

Lawson J   **Lexis, 22 March 1983**

The claimant (Frederick Hart) was employed by the defendants as a fitter at the Abingdon factory. His work brought him into contact with (synthetic) rubber which contained a chemical called neophrene. In January 1969 he suffered rashes on both hands and forearms and was found to be sensitive to neophrene. The defendants' doctors gave him strong advice about skin care and included his case in an article they wrote in August 1969 which was subsequently published in the British Journal of Industrial Medicine.

The claimant was off work for 8 weeks in 1969. Thereafter he continued in the same work until the end of 1979, using the ointment with which he was supplied and wearing gloves when he could. He had occasional explosion of rashes but only needed two further short periods of absence from work. In February 1980 he was allowed to take voluntary redundancy because of his condition.

While he was in work, his shop steward had told him he could not make a claim against the defendants. After his redundancy, he took legal advice and his writ was issued on 26 January 1981. The defendants' doctors and safety officer were still available to testify. Their foreman and works manager, referred to in the medical notes, had died but the claimant accepted those passages in the notes. A preliminary trial on the limitation issue was ordered.

Held:

(i) By February 1969 the claimant must have known that he had a significant injury attributable to contact with soft sealing rubber at work: s 14(1). Accordingly, the three-year limitation period expired by February 1972: s 11(4).

(ii) (a) The reason for the long delay was that, until he took voluntary redundancy, the claimant had lost very little time off work and very little money as a result of his dermatitis. That reason was not adverse to his case: s 33(3)(a);

(b)   the delay had not caused any significant reduction in the cogency of either the claimant's or the defendant's evidence: s 33(3)(b);

(c)   the claimant acted promptly and reasonably once he was told that he might have a claim for damages: s 33(3)(e);

(d)   the claimant followed the medical advice given him by the defendants' doctors. This did not include any suggestion that he had a case against his employees: s 33(3)(f);

(e)   the prejudice to the claimant from applying s 11 would be overwhelmingly greater than the prejudice to the defendants from disapplying it. Accordingly, it was equitable to allow his case to proceed: s 33(1).

Hartley v Birmingham City District Council

Limitation Act 1980, s 33

Court of Appeal   **[1992] 2 All ER 213**

On 10 December 1986 the claimant (Mrs Carmel Hartley) was injured in an accident while visiting a primary school owned by the defendants. In January 1987 her husband notified her claim to the defendants whose insurers made an offer in October 1987 and increased this to £350 in November 1987. The claimant instructed solicitors in January 1988. The third anniversary of her accident fell on a Saturday, so the last day for issue of the writ was Monday 11 December 1989. The file came to the solicitor's attention at 5.15pm that evening, with the result that the writ was issued one day late on 12 December 1989.

On a preliminary trial over limitation, Owen J dismissed her appeal against the deputy registrar's refusal to disapply the provisions of s 11 of the Limitation Act 1980. At the hearing of her further appeal, it was accepted (a) that the defendants were liable for her injuries and (b) that if the action did not proceed she would have an unanswerable claim against her solicitors.

Held:

(i)   The actual delay was a matter of hours only, from the close of the writ office on 11 December until shortly after it opened on 12 December. The reason for the delay was a slip on the part of the claimant's solicitors: s 33(3)(a).

(ii)   The cogency of the evidence from both sides was totally unaffected by the delay: s 33(3)(b).

(iii)   The claimant acted with unusual promptness. Her claim was notified in the month after the accident: s 33(3)(e).

(iv)   There was no criticism as to when the claimant took legal and medical advice: s 33(3)(e).

(v)   If there is a delay, which is due to a slip on the part of the claimant's solicitors and does not affect the defendant's ability to defend the case because there has been early notification of the claim, the exercise of discretion in favour of the claimant is justified even if the claimant, if not allowed to proceed, would have a cast-iron action against her solicitors.

(vi)   A defendant will normally suffer prejudice if discretion is exercised in favour of a claimant, but he will only have lost a windfall unless his ability to defend has been affected by the delay. Consequently if the delay does not seriously affect the evidence, such power will generally be exercised.

(vii)   If ever there was a case for discretion to be exercised in favour of the claimant, this was it: s 33(1). The judge erred in regarding the windfall concept 'as of little value'. The claimant's appeal was allowed.

Per Parker LJ: 'In view of their Lordships' indication that this court might provide some guidelines and also because the exercise of the discretion under s 33 is of considerable importance I venture, however, upon some general observations with regard to the matter.

It appears to me to be apparent that in all, or nearly all, cases the prejudice to the plaintiff by the operation of the relevant limitation provision and the prejudice which would result to the defendant if the relevant provision were disapplied will be equal and opposite. The stronger the plaintiff's case the greater is the prejudice to him from the operation of the provision and the greater will be the prejudice to the defendant if the provision is disapplied. Likewise the weaker the case of the plaintiff the less is he prejudiced by the operation of the provision and the less the defendant prejudiced if it is disapplied.

This might lead one to suppose that the prejudice referred to in s 33(1)(b) was not the deprivation of the fortuitous defence as such but prejudice to the defence on the merits caused by the delay. Both Lord Denning MR and Ormrod LJ appear to have assumed that this was so. That this was the parliamentary intent appears to be indicated by the fact that, as Lord Diplock pointed out, only s 33(3)(a) and (b) appear to go to prejudice and both are dealing with the merits. The decisions of their Lordships preclude such a construction of the section. In my view, however, as the prejudice resulting from the loss of the limitation defence will always or almost always be balanced by the prejudice to the plaintiff from the operation of the limitation provision the loss of the defence *as such* will be of little importance. What is of paramount importance is the effect of the delay on the defendant's ability to defend. The specific example given in s 33(3)(b) so indicates.

Next, it appears to me that if it is, as it is, legitimate to take into account, when considering prejudice to the claimant, that he will have a claim against his solicitors, it must in my judgment follow that it is legitimate to take into account that the defendant is insured. If he is deprived of his fortuitous defence he will have a claim on his insurers.

Finally, I would add to the items of prejudice which a plaintiff will suffer even if he has a cast-iron claim against his solicitors and which were indicated by both Lord Diplock and Ormrod LJ, the fact that, if the plaintiff has to change from an action against a tortfeasor, who may know little or nothing of the weak points of his case, to an action against his solicitor, who will know a great deal about them, the prejudice may well be major rather than minor.

I do not consider that, apart from the foregoing, it is either useful or desirable to attempt to lay down guidelines, for circumstances are infinitely variable.'

Firman v Ellis (p433), *Thompson v Brown Construction (Ebbw Vale) Ltd* (p690) and *Donovan v Gwentoys Ltd* (p412) applied.

Hashtroodi v Hancock

CPR 7

Court of Appeal   **[2004] EWCA Civ 652;**
(2004) 3 All ER 530; LTL 25/5/2004

The claimant suffered tetraplegia when his motorbike collided with the defendant's taxi. The claimant instructed solicitors and the defendant alleged substantial contributory negligence. Proceedings were issued eight days before limitation expired. The claimant attempted to serve the claim form but failed, sending it to the wrong address. One working day before the expiry of the validity period the claimant successfully applied without notice for 3 week extension. The claimant then purported to serve the claim form but it was lost. The defendant made an application to set aside the extending order on the basis that there were no grounds under CPR 7.6 for extending time. This was coupled with an application to strike out for failure to serve. The deputy master refused these applications. The defendant appealed. The appeal was heard a rehearing.

Held:

(i) CPR 7 should not be interpreted by reference to authorities applicable to the previous rules (*Biguzzi v Rank Leisure* (p335) followed).

(ii) The lack of a good reason for the failure in service was not necessarily determinative of the issue. However, it will always be relevant to evaluate the reason for the failure. The weaker the reason, the more likely that the extension will be refused. Conversely, if there is a very good reason an extension would normally be granted.

(iii) There was a distinction between a claimant who requires the court's help in overcoming a genuine problem he has encountered in trying to serve one seeking relief from the consequences of his own neglect.

(iv) The only reason for the failure in service was the incompetence of the claimant's solicitors. This in itself, although not an absolute bar, was a strong reason for refusing to grant an extension.

(v) A solicitor who did not issue until near the end of the limitation period and then did not attempt service until near the end of the validity period courted disaster.

(vi) If the court were to extend time in this case the rule in CPR 7.5 that a claim form must be served within four months would cease to be the general rule. There was also a real risk that the Court of Appeal's statements about the importance of observing time limits would not be taken seriously.

(vii) It was not appropriate to extend time in this case.

Appeal allowed.

Hattam v National Coal Board

Limitation Act 1939, s 2A, s 2D   **Dismissal for want of prosecution**

Court of Appeal   **(1978) 122 SJ 777; (1978) Times, 28 October**

In 1953 the claimant (Mr Hattam) was working as a trainee miner for the defendants when his arm was crushed in an accident. He claimed and received all the relevant DHSS industrial benefits. 20 years later, when consulting a solicitor about an unrelated matter, he was advised that he might have a claim for damages against the defendants. By then, all their evidence had been lost.

The claimant's writ was issued in 1976 and served a year later. The defendants applied to have the action dismissed for want of prosecution on the ground of prolonged or inordinate and inexcusable delay. HH Judge Johnson, sitting in the Queen's Bench Division, held that, although it was impossible to have a fair trial, the action could not be dismissed for want of prosecution as there had been no breach of the Supreme Court Rules. The defendants appealed.

Held:

(i) The claimant's knowledge of the facts must have been clear at the time of the accident in 1953, so the primary period prescribed by s 2A of the Limitation Act 1939, as amended, expired in 1956. However, s 2D gave the court a discretion to disapply that time bar.

(ii) Determination of that matter need not be deferred until the trial of the action itself but could be dealt with on a simple summons to dismiss the action on the ground that it was not equitable to allow it to proceed, with affidavits on either side. In some cases the matter might have to be deferred for further evidence, but in most cases it could be dealt with summarily.

(iii) In the present case, it was clear that it would not be equitable to allow the action to proceed, as the defendants' evidence had been lost and the claimant had been receiving full DHSS benefits.

The defendants' appeal was allowed.

Hay v London Brick Co Ltd

Amendment of writ   **RSC Ord 20, r 5**

Court of Appeal   **(1981) 131 NLJ 657; (1981) Times, 12 May**

The claimant (Mr Hay) was employed by the defendants as a blocker. In July 1977 he issued a writ. His statement of claim alleged that on 18 November 1974 he was dismantling the top part of a stacked pile of bricks when the head of bricks on which he was standing broke and collapsed, so that he was injured. The defendants searched their records and found that an accident had occurred on 3 December 1975, not on 18 November 1974.

It was in respect of the accident on 3 December 1975 that the claimant was claiming. He had been involved in another accident on 18 November 1974, and had given particulars of it in an accident form submitted to his trade union. From that form, the date of 18 November 1974 had mistakenly been inserted into the writ and the statement of claim.

In 1979–80 he applied for leave to amend the writ so that 3 December 1975 could be substituted as the date of the accident. The defendants opposed this on the ground that it would be introducing a new cause of action out of time.

Held: the claimant was claiming in respect of the same accident as before; only the date was different. He was not seeking to substitute a new cause of action for the existing cause pleaded in his original statement of claim. Leave to amend the writ would be granted.

Hayes v Bowman

Dismissal for want of prosecution   **RSC Ord 25, r 1**

Court of Appeal   **[1989] 1 WLR 456**

On 2 August 1981 the claimant (Brian Hayes), then aged 39, was riding a motor cycle when he was in collision with the defendant's motor car. He suffered bad injuries and was left with permanent loss of use of his right arm, coupled with some neck pain. His writ was issued in April 1984, and his statement of claim served in July 1984. Immediately a defence was served admitting liability. The claimant's medical evidence was disclosed in August 1984. No schedule of special damages was ever served, despite a request from the defendant's solicitors. In July 1985 they served a request for further and better particulars of the statement of claim, seeking to ascertain how the claimant's case on loss of earnings was put. This went unanswered until after the defendants issued in March 1987 a summons to dismiss for want of prosecution.

The registrar granted the application. Before the adjourned hearing of the appeal before Otton J, the claimant's solicitors served an accountant's report, based on his assertion that at the time of the accident he had been about to start work as a self-employed carpenter, claiming total loss of earnings of £124,574. Otton J held that the claimant's delay had been gross and inordinate but that the defendant had not established sufficient prejudice, so he allowed the claimant's appeal.

Held:

(i)   The judge was correct in holding that the delay had been inordinate and inexcusable.

(ii)   He had erred in finding that there were still medical difficulties whereas the medical position had not changed since 1984.

(iii)   Delay in bringing a case on for trial may lead to a larger award for damages. One reason why this may occur is the multiplicand becoming larger due to increases in wage rates. In the present case, the net value of the claim, even allowing for interest earned by the insurers on the retained damages, was arguably £16,637 more at a trial in 1988 then in 1985.

(iv)   That could be considered significant prejudice, but the point about the multiplicand had not been before the judge. It would not be appropriate to interfere with the exercise of his discretion, so the appeal should be dismissed.

Per Slade J: 'I would, however, add this warning. On the particular facts of other future cases, where there has been inordinate and inexcusable delay in prosecuting a claim for personal injuries by a living plaintiff, defendants may be in a position to produce compelling evidence of substantial financial prejudice due to the delay (more compelling than that available in the present case) sufficient to justify the dismissal of the proceedings for want of prosecution. This could provide a salutary precedent.'

Haward v Fawcetts

Limitation Act 1980, s 14, s 14A

House of Lords   **[2006] UKHL 9**

The claimant had been advised by his accountants, the defendant, in relation to a business interest acquired in 1994. This business failed in 1998. In May 1999 the claimant for the first time began to question the soundness of the defendant's advice. Proceedings were issued in December 2001. The defendant pleaded that the claim in respect of the initial investment in 1994 to 1995 was statute barred. This was heard as a preliminary issue. The claimant successfully argued at first instance and before the Court of Appeal that he did not have the requisite actual knowledge under s 14A.

Held:

(i)   The observations to be made in relation to s 14A applied equally to the corresponding provisions of s 14.

(ii)   Knowledge entailed knowing with sufficient certainty to embark upon preliminary enquiries; it did not entail knowing for certain beyond all possible conviction (*Halford v Brookes* (p453) approved).

(iii) It was not necessary for the claimant to have sufficient knowledge to support a fully particularised statement of case (*Wilkinson v Ancliff* (p718) approved). A broad knowledge of attribution may suffice even if the precise mechanism of what went wrong is not known (*Hendy v Milton Keynes HA* (p472) approved). This could be described as a broad knowledge of the essence or essential thrust of the relevant acts or omissions (*Nash v Eli Lilly & Co* (p568), *Spargo v North Essex District HA* (p667) approved). To the same effect one should look at the way the claimant puts his case, distil what he is complaining about and ask whether he had in broad terms knowledge of the facts upon which the complaint is based (*Broadley v Guy Clapham & Co* (p345) approved).

(iv)   The criterion of attribution was met by a real rather than fanciful possibility that the damage was attributable in whole or in part to the relevant act or omission. It thus need only be a possible rather than a probable cause (*Nash v Eli Lilly & Co* approved). Therefore time does not begin to run against a claimant until he knows that there is a real possibility that his damage was caused by the act or omission in question.

(v)   Although knowledge of negligence itself was irrelevant, describing the act or omission in terms suggesting culpability was often unavoidable and not objectionable providing there was no blurring of the necessary distinction between the relevant and irrelevant. The facts themselves were relevant, the legal consequences of the facts irrelevant ((*Hallam-Eames v Merrett Syndicates Ltd* [1995] 7 Med LR 122 approved, *Dobbie v Medway HA* (p411) doubted in part).

(vi)   In the present case the claimant knew all the material facts – the terms of the retainer, the fact of the defendant's advice, his reliance upon the defendant's advice and the consequential losses – as they occurred. He therefore had the requisite knowledge.

Appeal allowed.

Hayward v Sharrard

Limitation Act 1980, s 11, s 14, s 33

Court of Appeal   **(2000) 56 BMLR 155; LTL 28/7/1998**

The claimant was born in 1965 with congenital dwarfism, the main consequence of which was that her legs were too short. In July 1986 the claimant consulted the defendant, a professor, who advised that her legs could be lengthened by 15cm. An operation to this effect was performed on 13 October 1986. An x-ray was taken on 3 November 1986; the claimant alleged that this revealed a problem, an allegation the defendant denied. The claimant underwent an operation on 12 October 1987. This resulted in orthopaedic problems which the claimant alleged should have been diagnosed in November of that year. In October 1988 was advised that yet a further operation was necessary. This was performed on 30 January 1989 and in October of that year the claimant was discharged from further treatment. On 29 August 1990 the claimant's GP informed her that there was a possibility that the bone was dying. She consulted solicitors on 18 October 1990. An expert was instructed but he did not report in until June 1992 when he gave an adverse opinion based upon a lack of access to the relevant x-rays. A different expert, with the benefit of the x-rays, produced a favourable report on November 1994.

Proceedings were issued on May 1995. Limitation was heard as a preliminary issue. The judge found that the claimant had the relevant knowledge for more than three years before issue of proceedings and refused to exercise his s 33 discretion as the prejudice to the defendant, by then 75 and in poor health, whose oral evidence would be crucial, was too great. The claimant appealed.

Held:

(i)   The judge had been correct in his findings on actual knowledge (18 October 1990).

(ii)   Even if this were not the case, the claimant faced insurmountable difficulties on constructive knowledge. The claimant had sought expert advice in October 1990. Her solicitors knew that limitation was due to expire by October 1992. They did not request x-rays until after this date. Constructive knowledge was fixed by 17 May 2005.

(iii)   The absence in a short judgement on the s 33 to several specific factors did not mean that the judge did not have them in his mind. There were no grounds for interfering with the judge's exercise of his discretion.

Appeal dismissed.

Headford v Bristol and District Health Authority

Limitation Act 1980, s 28

Court of Appeal   **[1995] PIQR P180; (1995) 139 SJLB 17;**
                                                                    LTL 24/11/1994

The claimant, who was born on 31 October 1963, underwent an operation at the defendant's hospital on 1 September 1964. He suffered cardiac arrest and severe brain damage. Solicitors were not instructed until 19 May 1989. A letter before action was sent to the defendant in July

1990. Proceedings were eventually issued on 13 July 1992 alleging negligent administration of anaesthetics. The defendant denied liability and defendant applied to strike the action out under the court's inherent jurisdiction on the grounds that the delay was unreasonable, prejudicial and an abuse of process. The judge granted the application, finding that there was no acceptable excuse for the delay which had greatly prejudiced the defendant. The claimant appealed.

Held:

(i)   The claimant had been under a disability for the entire 28 years.

(ii)   Section 28(1) made no mention of prejudice and, in contrast with s 28(4) (concerning recovery of land or money charged on land) contained no longstop. There was therefore no time bar on the action.

(iii)   Although there might be circumstances were a claim by a claimant under a disability could be struck out within the limitation period, there was nothing so exceptional here (*Hogg v Hamilton* (p479) considered).

(iv)   The appearance of a new allegation after issue of proceedings could not make the action an abuse of process.

Heath v Boots Company plc

Limitation Act 1980, s 14, s 33

QBD   **23 October 1998, unreported**

See *Brooks and others v Boots Company plc* (B) (p348)

Henderson v Temple Pier Co Ltd

Limitation Act 1980, s 14

Court of Appeal   **[1998] 1 WLR 1540; [1998] 3 All ER 324;**
[1999] PIQR P61

The claimant alleged that she was injured on 28 January 1993 when she slipped and fell whilst boarding a hip moored on the Thames which was owned and occupied by the defendant. In February 1993 she instructed solicitors, who erred by failing to discover the identity of the ship's owner. On April 1997, having instructed different solicitors, the claimant issued proceedings. The defendant applied to strike the claim out as being statute barred. The judge found that the solicitors originally instructed by the claimant had not provided a competent service, and on this basis held that the claimant did not have constructive knowledge of the identity of the defendant under s 14(3) before July 1994. The defendant appealed.

Held:

(i)   Advice given by a solicitor fell within s 14(3)(b) (a claimant not being fixed with knowledge ascertainable only by expert advice) only if it related to matters of fact on which expert advice was required. Knowledge under s 14 is knowledge exclusively of matters of fact, not of matters of law.

(ii)   Although it was conceivable that a claimant could require expert legal advice in identifying a defendant, in the sense of identifying the person legally responsible for the injuries (ie occupier, employer, etc), this would only be in the most exceptional circumstances.

(iii)   The name of the occupier of the ship was knowledge which the claimant might reasonably have been expected to ascertain for herself without expert assistance.

(iv)   Section 14(3)(b) did not extend the limitation period for a claimant whose solicitor had acted dilatorily in acquiring facts, the acquisition of which entailed no particular expertise.

(v)   The claimant was consequently fixed with the constructive knowledge as the identity of the defendant which her solicitors ought to have had before April 1994.

Appeal allowed.

Hendy v Milton Keynes Health Authority

Limitation Act 1980, s 11, s 14, s 33

Blofield J   **[1992] 3 Med LR 114; (1991) Times, 8 March**

On 25 February 1985 the claimant (Mrs Hendy) underwent a hysterectomy and a bilateral salpingo-oophorectomy performed by Dr Dua. Afterwards she felt very low, became incontinent and suffered from diarrhoea. On 26 March 1985 a further operation was performed by Mr Walker and her health improved.

On 12 November 1985, in the course of a follow-up, she saw Dr Didier who told her that in the operation performed by Dr Dua there had been adhesions around the bladder and uterus with the result that her right ureter had become caught up in the operation and injured. Owing to her imperfect recovery from the operation combined with concern over her daughter's marital problems and the death of her pet dog, it was not until September 1986 that she went to a Citizens Advice Bureau.

They referred her to solicitors who obtained medical records and in 1987 instructed Dr Huntingford who finally reported in July 1988. He criticised Dr Dua's use of sutures and concluded that if the adhesions of the bladder to the uterus were such as to increase the risk of damage to the ureter, Dr Dua should have positively identified the ureter to avoid damage and/or he should have asked for his supervisor's assistance.

On 21 November 1988 the writ was issued. A preliminary trial on limitation was ordered.

Held:

(i)   (a) The claimant could be held to have sufficient knowledge within s 14 of the Limitation Act 1980 if she appreciated that her problem was capable of being attributed to the first operation, even when the particular facts of what specifically went wrong were not known to her. She received sufficient information from Dr Didier who was giving an expert opinion: s 14;

         (b)   accordingly, the three-year limitation period expired on 12 November 1988 and her case was prima facie statute barred: s 11(4).

(ii)   (a) The length of the delay was only nine days: s 33(3)(a);

         (b)   all the witnesses and all the notes were available: s 33(3)(b);

         (c)   taking into account the other concerns, the claimant acted reasonably and promptly once she knew that she might have a claim. Her solicitors as her agents could have acted more promptly, but that was not a major factor: s 33(3)(e);

         (d)   some small criticism could be levelled at her solicitors, but she did not have a cast-iron case against them: s 33(3);

         (e)   she would be substantially prejudiced if unable to bring the action. The defendants accepted that there was no prejudice to them. It was right to exercise the discretion on the claimant's behalf: s 33(1).

Wilkinson v Ancliff (BLT) Ltd (p718) applied.

Bentley v Bristol & Western Health Authority (No 1) (p328) distinguished.

Hewitt v Wirral Cheshire Community NHS Trust

CPR 3, 7, 16

Court of Appeal   **[2002] 1 WLR 1384; [2001] 4 All ER 577;**
[2002] CP Rep 4

See *Totty v Snowden* (p694)

Heyes v Pilkington Glass Ltd

Limitation Act 1980, s 14

Court of Appeal   **[1998] PIQR P303**

The claimant was employed by the defendant as a crane driver on two occasions: first, in the mid-1960s, and then continuously between 1967 and 1985. As a result of the vibration experienced when operating the defendant's cranes, he contracted vibration-induced white finger ('VWF'). The claimant ceased work in 1987. He knew when he left that he was experiencing numbness and loss of sensation in his fingers and that he had suffered from this condition since about 1980. In about 1990 he had a conversation with a friend as a result of which he consulted solicitors. The claimant did not give evidence of what advice he received. Some time later he was examined by a consultant neurological surgeon, who gave as his diagnosis digital neurovascular injury as a consequence of exposure to pathological vibration frequencies during the course of the claimant's working life mainly as a crane driver with the defendants. Proceedings were issued in October 1993. Limitation was tried along with the substantive issues.

The defendant conceded that, from 1976 onwards, it knew or ought to have known that excessive exposure to vibration could cause VWF. This was in accordance with the conventional date of knowledge within industry generally, but confined to hand-operated tools. In cross-examination the claimant was asked about his state of knowledge before the proceedings were instituted. He conceded that he thought he had a work-related injury when he consulted his solicitor, before being examined by the surgeon. The Recorder found as a fact that (1) the claimant suffered from occupationally induced rather than constitutional white finger, and (2) the white finger was suffered in consequence of his employment with the defendants and, although not expressly but by inference, his exposure to vibration while operating their cranes. Neither of these findings was disputed, nor was the award of damages. The defendant appealed on both limitation and liability.

Held:

(i)   On the limitation issue (Staughton LJ dissenting): whilst it could be said that the claimant could be deemed to have had knowledge earlier, it was only in recent years that upper limb disorders have become more frequently attributed to repeated movements of the hands and arms. Litigation in that field often centred on the issue whether the condition complained of was caused by the work conditions or was constitutional in origin. VWF could be, but is not necessarily, caused by exposure of the hand and arm to vibration. It was true that the claimant gave an unfortunate answer in cross-examination, but it would be unjust to deprive him of his cause of action on the strength of that answer alone. The claimant did not have the requisite knowledge within s 14 that his condition was not constitutional, but was attributable to his employment with the defendants until shortly after he received the report in 1991. Hence the action was commenced in time. Consequently, the balancing exercise under s 33 did not need to be considered.

(ii)   The liability appeal, however, succeeded.

Appeal allowed.

Higgins v Eli Lilly & Co and others

Limitation Act 1980, s 11, s 14, s 33

Court of Appeal   **[1992] 3 Med LR 385**

See *Nash v Eli Lilly & Co* (G) (p568)

Higham v Stena Sealink Ltd

Athens Convention 1974, Art 16   **Merchant Shipping Act 1979, s 14, Sch 3**

Merchant Shipping Act 1980, s 186, Sch 6   **Limitation Act 1980, s 33, s 39**

Merchant Shipping Act 1995, s 183, Sch 6

Court of Appeal   **[1996] 1 WLR 1107; [1996] 3 All ER 660;**
                                               [1996] 2 Lloyd's Rep 26

The claimant was injured on 16 August 1991 when she slipped on some broken glass on the defendant's ferry. She issued proceedings on 2 September 1993. Article 16 of the 1974 Convention, incorporated by the 1979 Act and afterwards the 1995 Act, provided a two-year time limit. The defendant applied to strike the claim out on this basis. The district judge held that s 33 of the 1980 Act applied and exercised his discretion under that section to disapply the time limit. The defendant appealed to Bernstein J who held that s 33 did not apply and that there was no discretion to allow the action to proceed. The claimant then appealed.

Held:

(i)   Section 39 of the 1980 Act provides that the 1980 Act does not apply to an action where the limitation period is prescribed by another enactment. However, Article 16(3) of the 1974 Convention reincorporates domestic law insofar as in involves the suspension or interruption.

(ii)   However, s 33 did not involve the suspension or interruption of the limitation period, but rather its setting aside. It was therefore not applicable and there was no discretion to set aside the time limit. Appeal dismissed.

Hills v Potter and others

Limitation Act 1939, s 2A, s 2D

Hirst J   **[1983] 3 All ER 716; 128 SJ 224**

On 10 January 1974 the claimant (Mrs Sylvia Hills) underwent an operation at the Radcliffe Infirmary which was performed by Mr Potter for spasmodic torticollis, a deformity of the neck. Although the operation was performed with due care, it left her paralysed from the neck downwards.

On 12 August 1980 her writ was issued. The claimant's case was that Mr Potter had failed to provide her with all appropriate information as to the nature of the operation, its prospects and its inherent risks. A full hearing took place.

Held:

(i)   The claimant knew by mid-1974 at the latest that her injury was significant, and she knew the identity of the potential defendants. By then, or very shortly afterwards, she had constructive knowledge that her injury was or might be attributable to an act or omission by the defendants, in the sense that by that date it was reasonable for her to take legal advice. Thus her writ was issued out of time: s 2A.

(ii)   The defendants accepted that they had suffered no prejudice by reason of the delay, and that no factors that might tell against exercising discretion in the claimant's favour applied. Accordingly, the limitation bar was dis-applied: s 2D.

However, judgment was given for the defendants on the merits of the case.

Hinchcliffe v Corus UK Ltd

Limitation Act 1980, s 14, s 33

QBD (Roger Ter Haar QC)   **[2010] EWHC 2871 (QB)**

The claimant was the personal representative of the deceased (D). D had worked for a company, whose liabilities the defendant had succeeded, between 1950 and 1966. It was D's opinion that, whilst in that employment, he had been exposed to asbestos in sufficient quantities to cause asbestosis. In January 2002, D was referred to a specialist because of breathing difficulties. Following investigations, exposure to asbestosis was canvassed with his doctors in April 2002. In December 2004, D (then aged 77) instructed solicitors, who took a witness statement from him in January 2005 and intimated a claim in April 2005. Thereafter, there were unsuccessful efforts to obtain supportive medical evidence from D's treating doctors. The solicitors eventually abandoned these attempts and in June 2008 instructed a medico-legal expert, who in turn provided an unsupportive preliminary desktop opinion. D died on 15 February 2009, four days before he was due to be examined by the expert. Proceedings were issued in January 2010. The defendant pleaded limitation, which was heard as a preliminary issue.

Held:

(i)   As D had died on 15 February 2009 the first consideration was whether any cause of action he might have had was statute barred under the Limitation Act 1980 by 16 February 2006. On the evidence, D's date of knowledge for the purposes of s 14 was April 2002. D knew he had an injury by the time he consulted his doctor and a specialist in early 2002 because of his shortness of breath. He knew the injury was significant at that time. The knowledge which D had, that he was suffering from fibrosis which was debilitating, was knowledge sufficient to satisfy the requirements of s 14(1)(a) in April 2002. By April 2002, D knew that, if the fibrosis was caused by exposure to asbestos, the exposure had occurred during the course of his employment; so, by that date, s 14(1) (c) was also satisfied. Accordingly, time started to run in April 2002, and the action was statute barred by approximately April 2005.

(ii)   If that conclusion was wrong, the time started to run from December 2004, being the date that solicitors were instructed.

(iii)   On the evidence, taking into account all the factors in s 33(3), the court declined to exercise its discretion to allow the claim to proceed. The time taken overall to pursue the claim was greater than the primary limitation period and contained within that period were substantial periods of inactivity. Although there were mitigating factors, D's solicitors failed to properly expedite matters. Had they done so by instructing a medico-legal expert in 2005 the matter would have come to trial in around September 2007, long before D died.

(iv)   Given D's age when the solicitors were instructed, it was obviously important to proceed with the claim. Had due expedition been used, proceedings would have been commenced by the beginning of 2006 and come to trial before D died. Had the action been brought to trial before D's death, it would have been possible for the defendant to test his evidence. The inability of the defendant to do so was significantly prejudicial.

Preliminary issue determined in favour of defendant.

Hind v York Health Authority

Limitation Act 1980, s 11, s 14, s 33

Mitchell J   **[1998] PIQR P235; [1997] 8 Med LR 377**

The claimant suffered an anal sphincter injury consequential to an episiotomy performed during childbirth on 14 September 1988. The treating surgeon was unaware of any problem at the time, but the claimant suffered considerable pain and lack of bowel control. She was repeatedly assured by the defendant's staff that these problems would settle in time. Six months after the birth her GP referred her to a consultant surgeon who, in May 1989, informed her of the injury and advised an operation to repair it. Nothing was said to indicate that the injury was anything other than a natural complication of childbirth. The operation was performed in August 1989. She became pregnant again, and was advised that the problems could reoccur, as the original pregnancy had been the cause of her symptoms. On the defendant's staff's advice, the claimant elected a caesarean delivery. In March 1991 she fell pregnant again, and was again advised to have a caesarean section. It was at this point that the claimant realised that the doctors were of the view that her condition would not improve. She consulted solicitors in June 1991. In December 1991 the solicitors wrote to the defendant stating that the claimant had concerns about her 1988 post-natal treatment and requesting release of the medical records. In May 1993 the claimant received an expert report opining that the failure of the surgeon who attended the birth to identify the injury had been negligent. Proceedings were issued that same month. Limitation was heard as a preliminary issue.

Held:

(i)   The claimant knew very quickly that her injury was significant.

(ii)   Although an explanation for the injury must have been apparent to the defendant following the operation in August 1989, they did not inform the claimant of it.

(iii)   The claimant was in regular contact with, and acted upon the advice of, the defendant's staff who assured her that the injury would settle.

(iv)   The claimant was never told that the sphincter injury should have been repaired immediately. The defendant's failure to act aggravated the injury by retarding the prospects of recovery. Merely telling the claimant that she had an injury which required surgery did not equate to imbuing her with knowledge of a immediate post-natal failure to rectify it. The act or omission of which the claimant must have knowledge for s 14(1) was that which was causally relevant for the purposes of negligence (*Smith v West Lancashire HA* (p657) applied).

(v)   The claimant did not have actual knowledge until she received the expert's report in May 1993.

(vi)   The claimant did not have constructive knowledge more than three years before issue. An objective standard applied. Until 1991 the claimant remained under the claimant's care for a problem she thought had occurred naturally rather than through medical intervention.

(vii)   Alternatively, it would be equitable to disapply s 11 by way of s 33. The defendant had been put on notice three months following the expiry of the primary limitation period from the accrual of the cause of action. Although the defendant was unable to trace the treating surgeon, this appeared to be a self-inflicted prejudice resulting from inadequate procedures for keeping track of junior doctors when they moved jobs. The claimant had a reasonable prospect of success, the defendant having placed no contradicting medical evidence before the court, and the there was no suggestion that the relevant records were not available. The case was in truth a simple one.

Preliminary issues decided in the claimant's favour. Costs in the case.

Hoddinott v Persimmon Homes (Wessex) Ltd

CPR 7, 7.6, 11

Court of Appeal   **[2007] EWCA Civ 1203;**
[2008] 1 WLR 806; [2008] CP Rep 9;
(2007) 104(47) LSG 25; (2007) Times, 28 December

The defendant had entered onto the claimant's land, pursuant to a deed of transfer, to construct a sewer and thereafter reinstate the land. The claimant issued proceedings alleging that the defendant did not reinstate the land properly and issued a claim form claiming damages for breach of the terms of the deed of transfer, trespass, nuisance and negligence. Particulars of claim were not attached to the claim form.

Before the four-month period for service of the claim form expired, the claimant applied without notice and obtained a two-month extension of time to permit the claim to be fully particularised which, it was said, would promote the chances of the claim being settled. The claimant then sent a copy of the claim form to the defendant for information only and explicitly not by way of service. The defendant applied to set aside the extension of time on the ground that there had been no good reason for it. The claim form and particulars were then served and the defendant filed an acknowledgment of service indicating that it intended to defend the claim but not to contest the jurisdiction. The judge set aside the order extending time and held that the defendant did not have to make an application under CPR 11 since it had made an application disputing service before the proceedings had been served. The defendant successfully argued that CPR 11 had no relevance in the context; alternatively that the application to set aside the order extending time for service rendered an application under CPR 11 unnecessary. The claimant appealed, submitting that in exercising his discretion the judge should have taken into account the facts that the 'without notice' order extending time had given the claimant a false sense of security that it could safely serve the claim form within the extended period, that the claim was not statute barred and that delay had not caused any prejudice to the defendant which had been sent a copy of the claim form for information. The claimant also argued that the mandatory provisions of CPR 11 were engaged, and that by not following the procedure to dispute jurisdiction the defendant was deemed to have waived any service point.

Held:

(i)   CPR 11 was engaged. The word 'jurisdiction' was used in two different senses in the CPR: one meaning was territorial jurisdiction, but in CPR 11(1) the word did not denote territorial jurisdiction but the court's power or authority to try a claim. Even if the court had jurisdiction to try a claim where the claim form had not been served in time, it was open to a defendant to argue that the court should not exercise its jurisdiction to do so and CPR 11(1)(b) was engaged in such a case.

(ii)   The application to set aside the order extending time for service did not render an application under CPR 11 unnecessary. Rule 11(5) provided that, if the defendant filed an acknowledgment of service and did not make an application within the period specified, he was to be treated as having accepted that the court had jurisdiction. The meaning of that rule was clear and unqualified. There was no warrant for holding that, if an application was made before the filing of an acknowledgment of service to set aside an order extending the time for service, that had the effect of disapplying the requirement for an application under CPR 11(1).

(iii)   The reference to disputing the court's jurisdiction in CPR 11(3) and accepting that the court had jurisdiction in CPR 11(5) encompassed both limbs of CPR 11(1). The reference to the court's jurisdiction was shorthand for both the court's jurisdiction to try the claim and the court's exercise of its jurisdiction to try the claim. The effect of CPR 11(5) was that the defendant was to be treated as having abandoned its application to set aside the order extending the time for service.

(iv)   That conclusion was reinforced by the fact that the defendant indicated on the acknowledgment of service that it did not intend to contest jurisdiction.

(v)   There was no good reason for the claimant's failure to serve the claim form within the four-month period (*Collier v Williams* (p380) applied). The false sense of security given by the 'without notice' order was not a relevant factor to be taken into account under CPR 7.6(1) (*Jones v Telford and Wrekin Council* (1999) Times, 29 July considered and *Mason v First Leisure Corp Plc* (p546) disapproved). If a claimant obtained an extension of time without notice to the defendant, he did so at his peril.

(vi)   The claimant's claim for breach of the terms of the deed of transfer was not statute barred and that was a relevant consideration. Although there was no good reason for the failure to serve in time, the unusual combination of facts, namely that the claim was not statute barred and that a copy of the claim form had been sent to the defendant within the four-month period, led to the conclusion that the order extending time should not have been set aside.

Appeal allowed.

Hodgson and others v Imperial Tobacco Co Ltd and others

Limitation Act 1980, s 11, s 33

Wright J   LTL 26/2/1999

This was a group action by 52 claimants against defendant tobacco companies for diseases allegedly caused by smoking. Eight of the ten lead claimants sought s 33 discretions in their favour, it been agreed that their claims were prima facie barred by s 11 and s 14.

Held:

(i)   As the merits of the claims were dubious, the likely level of damages small, and the costs liability of a given claimant high if he lost, the prejudice to any given claimant if the discretion were not exercised might not be as great as otherwise it might have been.

(ii)   As there would be 16 surviving claims in any event, it was relevant that the defendants would inevitably bear substantial costs from the larger action (*Nash v Eli Lilly* (p568) applied).

(iii) Conversely, the defendant could validly respond to this that:

(a)   they would still bear increased costs in respect of claimants whose claims were allowed to continue out of time;

(b)   if the number of claimants were reduced from 52 to 16 there was a real prospect that the remaining claimants would discontinue because of the increased share of the costs they would be required to bear; and

(c)   a s 33 direction would greatly encourage an unidentifiably large number of lung cancer sufferers diagnosed more than three years ago to issue against the defendants.

(iv)   The only factor which had a material impact upon individual decisions to proceed was the readiness of lawyers to work under a CFA.

(v)   The claimants' allegations of deliberate or reckless concealment were more difficult to assess as a result of the delay as defendant witnesses and experts might now be unavailable.

(vi)   Having considered each of the individual cases, the judge declined to exercise his discretion in respect of any of them. This was not only because of the problematic nature of the claims but also because none of the claimants had acted promptly or reasonably once they had the requisite knowledge. The purpose of the Act as a whole was to encourage prompt litigation and discourage stale claims. The purpose of s 33 was to ameliorate unfairness, not to enable a claimant to lie in wait for a good moment to come forward.

Applications dismissed.

Hogg v Hamilton and another

Dismissal as abuse of process of court

Court of Appeal   **[1992] PIQR P387**

On 29 June 1976 the claimant (Michael Hogg, suing by his father and next friend) underwent a vagostomy and gastroenterostomy at a hospital operated by Northumberland Health Authority. The anaesthetist was Dr Hamilton. Afterwards, as a result of hypoxia and cardiac arrest which occurred when he was in a recovery room, he suffered permanent brain damage and remained under a serious disability.

In December 1978 his first solicitors issued a writ against the health authority. Second solicitors who took over the case were unable to obtain supporting medical evidence. In January 1982, at a hearing in which no mention was made of the claimant's disability, his action was dismissed for want of prosecution.

Later in 1982, Dr Hamilton retired. Knowing that the claim had been struck out, he destroyed his anaesthetic record cards. Similarly, by 1985 the health authority's solicitors destroyed their files. So did Dr Hamilton's defence union.

From 1982 to 1986, a third firm of solicitors was investigating a possible professional negligence claim against the second firm. In 1987 a fourth firm wrote for the hospital records to the health authority which initially declined to disclose them. On 4 December 1987 the fourth firm wrote a further letter, explaining that the records were required with a view to issuing proceedings against the second firm and ending 'we would again stress that there is no intention to attempt to resurrect the proceedings against your Health Authority'. In reliance on this, the authority sent them not only the full medical records but also privileged witness statements.

After obtaining reports, the fourth firm issued a writ against Dr Hamilton alone on 13 March 1989. In November 1990, when his application to strike out this action was dismissed, leave was given to the claimant to join the health authority as second defendants. The amended statement of claim was served in January 1991.

The health authority's application to strike out the action was refused by the district judge. Brooke J allowed the appeals of both defendants. The claimant appealed.

Held:

(i)   Proceedings can be struck out as being an abuse of the process of the court, even though the claimant is a person to whom an extended and unexpired limitation period is applicable.

(ii)   A person under a disability cannot in all circumstances disavow and relieve himself of responsible actions within the process of litigation by those representing him if they are, at the time, apparently in his interest and which it is open to the court to consider as having had an impact on the mind of the defendants.

(iii)   The judge was fully entitled to conclude that the commencement of the second action, in the context of prejudice which had undoubtedly been suffered by the defendants and the assurance that had been given to the authority, was an abuse of the process which entitled him to strike out the action against both defendants.

The claimant's appeals were dismissed.

Holland and another v Yates Building Co Ltd and others

Limitation Act 1980, s 35

Court of Appeal   **(1989) Times, 5 December**

The claimants sought to join Mr Good, an architect, in the action commenced by them against the defendant builders. Their application was made after the expiry of the limitation period, if that period had started to run from the time of completion of the building, but not if it started on discovery of the alleged defects in the building.

Judge Lloyd Jones, sitting as an official referee in the Chester District Registry, concluded that the limitation period started to run from the date of the building's completion and that Mr Good should not be joined. He had never pleaded a defence under the Limitation Act 1980. The claimants appealed.

Held:

(i)   Consideration of whether a claim against a defendant was time barred should not be considered until that point had been pleaded by that defendant.

(ii)   The proper approach to a case where the issue was whether or not an action against a person whom it was sought to join as a party was statute barred was for the court to ask itself: 'if at the time when the writ was amended, the claimant had instead issued a fresh writ against the same defendant, could that defendant have successfully applied to strike out the action on the ground that the limitation period had expired and the action was thus an abuse of the process of the court'.

(iii)   The onus was on the defendant to establish this. It was not for the claimant to prove that the limitation period did not apply.

(iv)   The judge had erred and the appeal should be allowed.

NB: Compare *Howe v David Brown Tractors (Retail) Ltd* (p483).

Horn v Dorset Healthcare NHS Trust (No 1)

CPR 6.5

Southampton CC (HHJ Hughes QC)   **LTL 17/09/2004**

The claimant, an employee of the defendant, injured herself in a manual handling operation. Shortly before the primary limitation period expired, the claimant wrote to the defendant inviting it to nominate solicitors to accept service of proceedings. The defendant did so, providing a document exchange address containing a typographical error of one digit. The claimant replied that they had received no notification from the solicitors that they were instructed to accept service and in light of this served the claim form directly on the defendant. They did so, and the defendant applied to strike the claim form out. The deputy district judge held that the claim form had not been validly served.

The claimant appealed.

Held:

(i)   The error in the document exchange number was not material. The documents were still capable of delivery. The defendant had therefore given its solicitors correct business address in accordance with CPR 6.5(2).

(ii)   The validity of service ought not to and did not depend upon whether at the moment of service a defendant's solicitors had actual rather than ostensible authority to accept service. The defendant's letter constituted a representation that these solicitors acted for the defendant giving them ostensible authority to accept service. The claimant was thereafter obliged to follow CPR 6.5 (*Nanglegan v Royal Free Hospital* (p567) applied and *Smyth v Probyn & anor* (p664) distinguished).

(iii)   CPR 6.5 imposed no obligation on the solicitors to confirm that they were nominated to accept service.

Appeal dismissed.

Horn v Dorset Healthcare NHS Trust (No 2)

CPR 6.9

Southampton CC (HHJ Hughes QC)   **LTL 17/09/2004**

See above for the relevant facts. Following the ruling that the claim form had not been properly served the claimant applied for relief from the need for service under CPR 6.9.

Held:

(i)   This case fell into the second category identified in *Anderton v Clwyd County Council* (p303) as the claimant had sought to effect service by a permitted method and the defendant had in fact received the claim form during the service period. The court could therefore only dispense with service if the case were truly exceptional.

(ii)   The claimant had had simply served on the wrong person. None of the facts she relied upon showed the case to be exceptional (*Cranfield v Bridgegrove Ltd* (p389) applied).

Application refused.

Horne-Roberts v Smithkline Beecham

Limitation Act 1980, s 11, s 35   **CPR 19**

Court of Appeal   **[2001] EWCA Civ 2006; [2002] CP Rep 20;**
(2002) 65 BMLR 79

The claimant was administered the MMR vaccine in June 1990. He claimed to have suffered injuries as a result. His parents instructed solicitors to pursue a claim against the manufacturers. The time limit for such a claim was a flat 10 years (s 11A, s 28(7), s 33(1A)). Due to an error the claimant's solicitors proceeded under the misapprehension that the batch in question was produced by a different manufacturer to the defendant, who was in fact the producer. Proceedings were therefore issued on 25 August 1999 against the wrong defendant. When the mistake came to light the claimant applied to substitute the defendant. The defendant contested the application on the grounds that the judge had no power to substitute a party after the expiry of the 10-year limit. The judge permitted the substitution on the basis that s 35 of the Act applied and the claimant's mistake had been of identity only. The defendant appealed the judge's finding that he had a discretion but not his exercise of it.

Held:

(i)   Section 35 applied. Parliament had incorporated the 10-year period into the Act and could have expressly excluded s 35 from applying to it if that had been the intention.

(ii)   The test for substitution under s 35(6)(a) and CPR 19.5 was whether the party could be identified by a case-specific description (*The Sardinia Sulcis and The Al Tawwab* [1991] 1 Lloyds LR 2001 followed). In this case the claimant had always intended to sue the manufacturer of the batch with which he was treated. He therefore met the criterion.

Appeal dismissed.

NB: Doubted by *Morgan Est (Scotland) Ltd v Hanson Concrete Products Ltd* (p564).

NNB: This case would now be decided in favour of the defendant in light of *O'Byrne v Aventis Pasteur MSD Ltd* (p587).

Horton v (1) Sadler (2) MIB

Limitation Act 1980, s 11, s 33

European Convention on Human Rights, Art 6

House of Lords **[2006] UKHL 27**

On 12 April 1998 the claimant was injured in an accident which was entirely the first defendant's fault. The first defendant was uninsured, thus the involvement of the second defendant. In October 2000 the second defendant made an interim payment. On 10 April 2001 the claimant issued proceedings but failed comply with the condition precedent to the second defendant's liability that it be given notice of proceedings. The second defendant took this point in its defence and counterclaimed for the return of the interim payment.

In September 2001 the claimant issued what were essentially duplicate proceedings, this time giving the requisite notice to the second defendant. The second defendant pleaded limitation, which was heard as a preliminary issue. In respect of the first proceedings, the judge ruled that the second defendant had no liability. In respect of the second proceedings he ruled that *Walkley v Precision Forgings Ltd* (p705) precluded any discretion under s 33 and that these proceedings were thus statute barred. However, he indicated that if he had possessed a discretion, he would have exercised it in the claimant's favour on the basis that the second defendant had had notice of the claim, there was no evidential problem and the prejudice to the second defendant of losing a windfall defence was outweighed by the prejudice to the claimant of having to bring a further action against a different defendant.

The claimant appealed on the basis that *Walkley* was wrongly decided. As *Walkley* was binding on the Court of Appeal, the point was subject only to a cursory appeal at that level which was dismissed as expected. The House of Lords then gave permission to appeal. The second defendant cross-appealed on the question of the judge's exercise of his discretion on the basis that the loss should fall on the insurers of the claimant's solicitors, who had accepted a premium, rather than the second defendant, which was a insurer of last resort funded by the motoring public.

Held:

(i)   *Walkley*:

    (a)   was wrongly reasoned as a matter of construction;

    (b)   had given rise to indefensible distinctions and much unsatisfactory jurisprudence and

    (c)   deprived the court of the wide discretion that the legislation had intended to give it (*Firman v Ellis* (p433) approved).

    It was therefore right and proper that the rule should be done away with (*Walkley* and subsequent authorities overruled).

(ii)   *Walkley* did not, however, violate the claimant's rights under ECHR Art 6.

(iii)   There was thus a discretion to be exercised.

(iv)   As regards the exercise of that discretion:

    (a)   the prejudice to the parties of disapplying the limitation defence per se tended to be equal, so the effect of the delay on the ability of the defendant to defend was of paramount importance (*Hartley v Birmingham City DC* (p465) approved);

(b)   the prejudice to the claimant may be reduced if he has a claim against his own solicitors. A claimant's claim over against his solicitor is important but not necessarily determinative (*Thompson v Brown* (p690) applied, *Das v Ganju* (p398), *Corbin v Penfold Metalising Co Ltd* (p387) doubted); and

(c)   there was no reason for the loss to fall on insurers who had accepted a premium. The MIB should not be regarded differently from a road traffic or professional liability insurer for these purposes.

(v)   Although the claimant's solicitors had made a very basic error, the judge's exercise of his discretion was permissible one.

Appeal allowed, cross-appeal dismissed.

Howe and others v David Brown Tractors (Retail) Ltd

Limitation Act 1980, s 11   **RSC Ord 15, r 6**

Court of Appeal   **[1991] 4 All ER 30**

The claimant (Neville Howe) and his father were farmers trading under the name of W O J Howe (a firm). On 10 August 1982 the firm bought from the defendants a tractor and a recotiller. On 23 January 1985 the claimant was standing on the recotiller when the guard gave way and one of his legs came into contact with the machinery which was in motion. As a result of his injuries, the leg had to be amputated.

On 8 July 1988 he issued a writ claiming damages for negligence and/or breach of statutory duty. His statement of claim also pleaded breach of contract. The defence pleaded, inter alia, that (1) the machine was supplied to the firm and not to the claimant, (2) that the claimant was not entitled to advance a claim for breach of contract since such a claim was not endorsed on the writ, and (3) that the claimants' claim was statute barred. In December 1988 the registrar ordered by consent pursuant to s 33 that the provisions of s 11 of the Limitation Act 1980 be disapplied.

In November 1989 the claimant applied by summons to add his father and/or the firm as second claimants and for leave to amend the writ and statement of claim. The amendment to the writ was to include the following claim by the firm: 'The second claimant's claim is for damages for breach of contract of sale made on the 10th day of August 1982 between the second claimant and the defendants, their servants or agents and/or as a result of their negligence'. The firm's claim was for the whole, as distinct from the claimant's 50%, of the loss of profits, and certain additional expenditure on machinery, labour and outside contractors was itemised.

Evans J upheld the district registrar's order granting leave. The defendants appealed.

Held:

(i)   The alleged breach of duty in contract had caused the claimant's injuries. The firm's addition of a claim in respect of its own losses resulting from the injuries did not take it outside s 11(1) of the Limitation Act 1980 which applied where the damages claimed 'consist of or include damages in respect of personal injuries to the claimant *or any other person*'. The relevant limitation period was therefore three years from the accident or date of knowledge: s 11(4). Accordingly, it was not current at the date of the proposed amendment of proceedings, and the application fell to be considered under RSC Ord 15, r 6(5)(b).

(ii)   The words of Ord 15, r 6(5) were clear and unambiguous: 'No person shall be added or substituted as a party after the expiry of any relevant period of limitation unless ... (b) the relevant period arises under the provisions of section 11 or 12 of the Limitation Act 1980 and the Court directs that these provisions should not apply to the action by or against the new party'. Accordingly, for the second claimant to be added as a party, it would have been necessary to make an application under s 33 of the Limitation Act 1980 before or at the same time as the application for leave to amend. The order for the addition of the firm as an additional claimant was premature. The defendants' appeal must be allowed.

Per Stuart-Smith LJ: 'It may well be that if and when the court disapplies s 11 of the Limitation Act 1980 pursuant to an application made by the father and/or the firm under s 33 of that Act, the court will also permit the writ to be amended under Ord 20, r 5(5) to include a claim in contract by the firm. This is because the new cause of action arises out of substantially the same facts as the original claim in negligence.'

Per Nicholls LJ (on s 11(1)): 'It is helpful to approach by stages the question posed in the present case. Take first the simple case of a patient who is treated privately by a doctor or a dentist. The doctor and the dentist owe to him a duty to exercise reasonable skill and care in their treatment of him. There is an implied term to that effect in the contract between the patient and the doctor or dentist: see s 3 of the Supply of Goods and Services Act 1982. There is also a duty to that effect quite apart from the contract. If the patient suffers physical injury as a result of negligent treatment by his doctor or dentist, he may bring an action in negligence or for breach of contract. The damages recoverable will include general damages in respect of the physical injury and pain and suffering. They will also include damages for financial loss resulting from the physical injury, such as loss of future earnings. In such a case the claim for financial loss is as much a claim for "damages in respect of personal injuries" as is the claim for damages in respect of the physical injury itself. The plaintiff could not step outside the three-year limitation period prescribed by s 11 by abandoning any claim for damages in respect of the physical injury and claiming only damages in respect of his loss of earnings.

Take next the case of a plaintiff who buys from a retailer a defective product which subsequently injures him. He brings an action claiming damages for breach of implied terms as to merchantable quality and fitness for purpose. Is such an action for breach of contract within s 11? ... the words in parentheses in sub-s(1) seem to me to leave no room for doubt. The section applies to "any action for damages for ... breach of duty (whether the duty exists by virtue of a contract ... or independently of any contract ...)". I do not think it is possible to say that s 11 applies to an action for breach of contract where the term breached is to exercise reasonable skill and care, but that s 11 does not apply to an action for breach of contract where the term breached is one as to merchantable quality or fitness for purpose. The phrase "breach of duty" must apply in both cases or neither. In my view, and the contrary was not argued before us, it applies in both cases.

My third example is of a case where P buys a defective product from D and in consequence P's employee is injured while using it in the course of his employment. The employee recovers damages from his employer P for breach of statutory duty or negligence. P then brings proceedings against D, by way of third party proceedings in the employee's action or by way of a separate action. P seeks to recover from D as damages for breach of contract an indemnity in respect of P's liability in damages to his employee. In my view, P's claim in contract against D falls within s 11. The crucial feature is that the breach of contract upon which P founds his action caused the personal injuries in respect of which the damages claim arises. P is claiming damages to compensate him for the loss suffered by him as a result of a breach of contract which caused personal injuries. The consequence of D's supply of the defective tool or whatever was personal injury to the employee. True, in this example, the personal injuries were sustained by P's employee and not by P himself. But s 11 expressly caters for this possibility when providing that the damages claimed consist of or include damages in respect of personal injuries "to the plaintiff or any other person".

My third example is to be contrasted with a case where, although the recoverable damages fall to be measured or assessed by reference to the loss flowing from personal injuries, the personal injuries were not caused by the negligence or breach of duty which is the subject of the action. If a solicitor negligently fails to launch a personal injuries action on behalf of his client within the three-year period, the client may bring an action in negligence against the solicitor. The damages recoverable will fall to be assessed by reference to the damages which the client could be expected to have recovered in the action, making any appropriate discount to reflect the chances that the action might not have succeeded. In such a case, the action against the solicitor for damages for professional negligence is not within s 11, because the damages claimed do not consist of or include damages in respect of personal injuries. The damages claimed comprise damages in respect of the solicitor's failure to issue a writ in time. That failure did not cause any personal injuries.'

Hughes v Jones

Limitation Act 1980, s 33

Court of Appeal   **[1996] PIQR P380;
(1996) Times, 18 July; LTL 24/6/1996**

The claimant suffered whiplash in a road traffic accident on 22 October 1991. The defendant was notified of the claim in December 1991 but proceedings were not issued until 8 February 1995. The claimant applied for s 11 of the Act to be disapplied under s 33. The deputy district judge declined on account of the prejudice to the defendant arising from the delay. The claimant appealed to the circuit judge who dismissed the appeal, believing it to be an final matter and therefore not subject to rehearing but to a review of the district judge's exercise of discretion. The claimant appealed again.

Held:

(i)   The determination of a limitation point was a final rather than an interim manner.

(ii)   The district judge would have given a more reasoned judgment if he had appreciated the above. As it was, his judgment could not stand.

(iii)   Unless the parties consented or the claim was for less than £5,000 a district judge did not have jurisdiction to hear a s 33 application as it was a final hearing.

Appeal allowed. Case remitted to the county court.

NB: The relevant provisions of the CPR regarding allocation of cases to different levels of judges are frequently subject to change and should be checked at the time of the matter under consideration.

Hunt v Yorke

Limitation Act 1980, s 11, s 14, s 33

HH Judge Lewis Hawser   **Lexis, 26 November 1985**

The claimant (Mr Hunt) was employed by the defendant (Major Yorke) as an estate man. On 16 January 1980 the flooring in the circular saw shed collapsed and he fell into the void underneath, injuring his back and leg. The accident was reported the same day. The claimant visited his general practitioner with the defendant's approval on about six occasions in 1980. His back and leg got worse. In May 1982 he became unable to work, as a result of which he underwent a laminectomy.

When the matter arose from time to time, the defendant assured him, 'I always look after my estate workers. We look after our employees'. However, on 7 January 1983 the defendant wrote to the claimant that his employment was terminated and that he would have to give up the tied cottage in which he had been living. Consequently the claimant consulted solicitors on 26 January 1983 and, after obtaining limited and then more extensive legal aid, his writ was issued on 9 September 1983. After close of pleadings, a preliminary trial on limitation was ordered.

Held:

(i) The claimant ought to and did in fact have knowledge that the injury in question was significant, and he must have had this knowledge in the early period up until September 1980: s 14. Accordingly, his action was started out of time: s 11(4).

(ii) (a) It was suggested that the claimant's solicitors ought to have issued the writ at the end of January 1983 but not served it until the legal aid position had been cleared up. Had they taken that step, the writ would have been issued very shortly after the three-year period was up: s 33(3)(a);

    (b) however, the result, so far as the defendant was concerned, would have been nil, because the defendant would not have been in a better position in any respect to have conducted the matter: s 33(3)(b);

    (c) the claimant acted reasonably in relying upon assurances given by the defendant, and he only took steps to bring legal proceedings when he was dismissed from his employment and lost his tied cottage: s 33(3)(e);

(iii) The claimant had made out his case for the exercise of discretion in his favour: s 33(1).

Re Huntingdon Poultry Ltd

Companies Act 1948, s 353

Buckley J   **[1969] 1 All ER 328; [1969] 1 WLR 204**

Huntingdon Poultry, Ltd was dissolved in May 1968. Six or seven months later the Ministry of Social Security petitioned for an order that the company be restored to the register of companies, so that it could attempt to recover contributions due under the National Insurance Act 1965.

The Ministry also applied for a direction that in the case of creditors who were not statute barred at the date of dissolution of Huntingdon Poultry Ltd, the period between the date of such dissolution and the date of restoration should not be counted for the purpose of any statute of limitations.

Held:

(i) None of the company's liabilities to the Ministry was statute barred when the company was dissolved or when it was due to be restored.

(ii) Nor was there anything to suggest that any other creditor would be benefited by inserting in the order for restoration the special provision sought.

(iii) Accordingly, the order for restoration should not contain any direction relating to limitation.

Re Donald Kenyon Ltd (p412) distinguished.

Hutcheson v Pontinental (Holiday Services) Ltd

Limitation Act 1980, s 33

Court of Appeal   **[1987] BTLC 81**

On 16 September 1979 the claimant (Mrs Rebecca Hutcheson) and her husband went on a 14-day holiday which they had booked with the defendants to the Holiday Club M'Diq in Morocco. She alleged that the food there caused her to contract salmonella and her husband to become ill. She promptly claimed under her insurance policy, and the loss adjusters referred their correspondence with her to the defendants in early December 1979. Correspondence continued until August 1981.

On 27 June 1984, over a year after her husband's death, the claimant commenced proceedings in the Shoreditch County Court. At the preliminary trial on limitation, evidence was given that the defendants had lost their file but that the hotel's records, although incomplete, still existed in part. HH Judge Stucley held that the claim for damages for personal injuries was barred by s 11 of the Limitation Act 1980 but disapplied that provision under s 33. The defendants appealed.

Held:

(i) The proceedings were started 20 months late, but it was accepted that 12 months of this period was due to the illness of the claimant's husband and his subsequent death: s 33(3)(a).

(ii) The comparison to be made under s 33(3)(b) is between the cogency of the evidence if the action had been brought in time and the cogency of the evidence at the time when the action is finally brought. It had not been shown that the defendants' file would have been available had the action been brought in time. Nor had they shown that any particular witness who was available had become unavailable, although their evidence would be less precise: s 33(3)(b).

(iii) It would be equitable to allow the action to proceed. The judge's decision should be upheld: s 33(1).

Per Parker LJ: 'It is equally clear that the plaintiff must always suffer some prejudice if s 11 applies, for the action will be barred, and that in every case the defendants must suffer some prejudice if an action, prima facie barred, is restored. Neither of those matters can therefore, by themselves, really amount to anything. It is only when some additional delay in bringing the action is a delay which has caused prejudice or for some other reason is so excessive that the court comes to the conclusion that such prejudice as there is to the claimant is outweighed by the prejudice to the defendant, which, as the delay grows, clearly increases.'

Hutton v First Tier Tribunal (Criminal Injuries Compensation)

Criminal Injuries Compensation Scheme

Court of Appeal   **[2012] EWCA Civ 806**

When the claimant was an infant his father had been stabbed to death in the street after an argument in a pub. His attacker was found guilty of manslaughter and sentenced to 18 months' imprisonment. After the attack, the claimant's mother had a nervous breakdown, and the claimant and his sister were taken into care. Both children knew of their father's death from about the age of eight but were not told any of the details. Once the claimant reached adulthood, he tried to find out details of the circumstances of his father's death. He had little or no success until he discovered relevant documents in the National Archive. He then made a claim for compensation to the Criminal Injuries Compensation Authority under the Criminal Injuries Compensation Scheme on behalf of himself, his mother and his sister. This was 42 years after the death of his father. The authority's claims officer refused the claim. He refused to exercise the discretion under para 18 of the scheme terms to extend the two-year time limit for making claims. That was because the authority had asked the relevant police force for information in connection with the death and had been told that any relevant papers had been destroyed. The authority upheld that decision on review and the claimant appealed. The First-tier Tribunal dismissed his appeal and the Upper Tribunal refused judicial review of that decision. The claimant appealed again.

Held:

(i) The judge in the First-tier Tribunal erred in law in his construction of para 18. He had first considered whether there were 'particular circumstances', meaning 'special circumstances', in the claimant's case. That was a misreading of para 18, which permitted a claims officer to waive the time limit where, by reason of the particular circumstances of the case, it was reasonable and in the interests of justice to do so. The words 'particular circumstances' simply meant the actual circumstances of the particular case.

(ii) The task of the claims officer was to establish the actual circumstances of the particular case and then ask whether it was reasonable and in the interests of justice to waive the time limit given those circumstances. In performing that exercise, the claims officer had to consider all relevant factors, including the length of any delay, the reasons for it and the nature of the claim itself.

(iii) It was arguable that the judge applying the correct test might reasonably have concluded that the time limit should be waived in the instant case. The period of delay was very long and the claimant's approach in gathering all the information he could find before making a claim might have been mistaken. The delay might make the assessment of compensation more difficult. Nevertheless the First-tier Tribunal could reasonably come to the conclusion that the time limit should have been waived.

(iv) The court granted permission to apply for judicial review of the decision of the First-tier Tribunal in respect of all three applicants. The case for the claimant's mother and sister was even stronger because they were suffering from mental health problems and could not be blamed for any delay.

(v) It was not appropriate for the appeal court to decide whether to grant judicial review. That matter was remitted to the Upper Tribunal to reconsider all the relevant factors to see whether or not it was in the interests of justice to waive the time limit.

Appeal allowed.

Ince and others v Rogers

Limitation Act 1939, s 2D

Court of Appeal   **[1978] 2 All ER 851; [1978] QB 886;**
[1978] 2 WLR 1

See *Firman v Ellis* (p433)

Infantino v MacLean

CPR 6.9, 7.6

Douglas Brown J   **[2001] 3 All ER 802;**
[2001] CP Rep 99; LTL 14/6/2001

In 1995 the defendant, a medical professor, carried out a radical hysterectomy on the claimant to remove a cancerous tumour. The date of knowledge for limitation purposes was agreed as being 14 September 1997. Proceedings were issued on 31 August 2000 but not served. The parties agreed to an extension of time in that the service by DX was to be no later than 26 January 2001, thus giving a deemed service date of 30 January 2001. The claim form was served on the wrong DX address in error on 26 January 2001. The mistake was discovered and the form was sent by DX on 30 January 2001 but was a day late. The defendant refused to accept service. The claimant applied successfully to extend time for service. The defendant appealed.

Held:

(i)   The claimant had not satisfied the conditions of CPR 7.6 (*Vinos v Marks & Spencer* (p701) and *Kaur v CTP Coil* (p514) followed).

(ii)   CPR 6.9 gave the court a general power to dispense with re-service and this service (*Elmes v Hygrade Food Products Ltd* (p423) distinguished).

(iii)   There was no prejudice to the defendant. Service should be dispensed with. Appeal dismissed.

NB: This decision was overruled in *Godwin v Swindon BC* (p444).

Insight Group Ltd v Kingston Smith (A Firm)

Limitation Act 1980, s 35   **CPR 19**

QBD (Leggatt J)   **[2012] EWHC 3644 (QB)**

The claimant sought damages for professional negligence against its former accountants in respect of advice given in the period 1999 to 2006. At the time proceedings were issued the accountants were an LLP. However, nearly all the alleged breaches occurred before 1 May 2006 when the LLP's members had practised as a partnership under the name of Kingston Smith ('the Firm'). The claimant brought the proceedings against the LLP when they should have been brought against the former partnership. Before the error was recognised, the limitation period for starting a new action had expired, rendering the majority of the allegations statute barred. The claimant applied to correct the error by substituting the former partnership for the LLP as the defendant to the claim. This was granted without notice, but set aside on the defendants' application with the result that the claim was struck out. The master held that the relevant statutory criteria were not satisfied, and that if even if they were she would not have exercised her discretion in the claimant's favour. In relation to the latter she noted that: (i) that both parties appeared to proceed on the same basis, namely that the distinction between the Firm and the LLP was immaterial, and there was no prejudice to the Firm, the relevant personnel having been aware of the claim, for all practical purposes, since July 2008; (ii) that it was the duty of a claimant's legal representatives to identify the correct party or parties against whom to make particular claims, and this was not properly done; (iii) that there were obvious difficulties on the merits of the pleaded case; and (iv) the claimants' conduct of the claim, including delay. She held that factor (i) was outweighed by factors (ii)–(iv), noting that the majority of the difficulties that the application faced were as a consequence of errors of law in properly identifying the claims, the limitation periods and the correct defendants, and that the court should be generally unwilling to excuse such mistakes, unless there is a very good explanation, the claimant having a remedy against its legal representatives.

The claimant appealed. It relied primarily on s 35(6)(a) and CPR 19.5(3)(a), arguing that the LLP had been named by mistake. In the alternative, they relied on s 35(6)(b) and CPR 19.5(3)(b), arguing that the relevant claims could not properly be carried on by them unless the Firm were substituted as defendant.

Held:

(i)   The *Sardinia Sulcis* test, whilst still important, did not fully survive the advent of the CPR. As per *Adelson v Associated Newspapers Ltd* [2008] EWHC 278 (QB) the criteria for substitution under CPR 19.5(3)(a) were that (1) the person who has made the mistake must be the person responsible, directly or through an agent, for the issue of the claim form; (2) it must be shown that, had the mistake not been made, the new party would have been named; and (3) the mistake must be as to the name of the party, applying the *Sardinia Sulcis* test. However, it was no longer necessary to show that the mistake was not misleading or such as to cause any reasonable doubt as to the identity of the person intended to be sued; *Horne-Roberts v Smithkline Beecham plc* (p481) and *Lockheed Martin Corp v Willis Group* (p536).

(ii)   Applying the *Sardinia Sulcis* test as modified, the relevant description of the defendant in a case of this kind was that of professional adviser. It was the fact that the defendant had provided professional services and had allegedly done so negligently, which potentially gave rise to legal liability.

(iii)   In order to decide whether the claimant's mistake here could be regarded as one of name rather than description, it was thus necessary to distinguish between (1) the claimant suing the LLP in the mistaken belief that the LLP provided the services which are said to have been performed negligently, failing to recognise that the services were provided by the former partnership and not the LLP, and (2) the claimant knowing that the services were provided by the former partnership but mistakenly believing that the LLP is legally liable for the negligence of the earlier firm. The court had the power to grant relief in case (1) but not in case (2).

(iv)   Given the brief and general description of the claim given in the claim form and the absence of contemporaneous particulars of claim, the pre-action correspondence was of particular importance in resolving this question in this case, because it formed the background to the issue of the claim form and in the light of which the claim form is to be understood.

(v)   On the evidence, this was a mistake as to name rather than identity. All the allegations made by the claimants' solicitors in the pre-action correspondence were directed solely at the LLP. All the pre-action correspondence, including that from the defendant's representatives, proceeded on the basis that the LLP had provided all the professional services which were the subject of the claim. The claim form was intended to allege that the LLP had been negligent in the course of acting as auditor and professional adviser to the claimants throughout the period 1999–2006 referred to in the Protocol letters. It followed that the court had power to substitute under s 35(6)(a) and CPR 19.5(2)(a).

(vi)   The court would have power to order substitution under section 35(6)(b) and CPR 19.5(3)(b) if: (1) a claim made in the original action is not sustainable by or against the existing party; and (2) it is the same claim which will be carried on by or against the new party; *Irwin v Lynch* (p491) and *Parkinson Engineering Services plc v Swan* (p595).

(vii)   It was common ground that the claims were unsustainable against the LLP. The first requirement was therefore satisfied. However, the second requirement was not satisfied, as the claims which the claimants sought to carry on against the Firm were not the same claims as were made against the LLP. It followed from the earlier conclusion that the claims originally made against the LLP alleged that the LLP had been negligent in auditing the accounts of the second claimant and providing administrative and fiduciary services during the relevant period. In contrast, the claims asserted against the Firm after the claimants had realised their mistake alleged that the Firm (and not the LLP) acted as auditor and provided the relevant services. The new claims, therefore, alleged different facts and were not identical to the original claims. However, if the court had upheld the master's ruling that s 35(6)(a) and CPR 19.5(2)(a) were not satisfied due to the nature of the mistake, the original and new claims would have been identical, with the result that 35(6)(b) and CPR 19.5(3)(b) would have been satisfied.

(viii)   The master's exercise of discretion was flawed in a number of respects. The court should generally be willing to excuse such mistakes in correctly identifying the defendant when there is no prejudice to the party who is substituted. A potential claim against legal representatives was not an adequate substitute for the loss of the original claim. The master was wrong to treat the hearing as an occasion to investigate the merits of the claim, unless it could be said (as it was not) that it had no real prospect of success.

(ix) Accordingly, none of the factors identified by the master were reasonably capable of justifying the court's refusal to permit substitution. The error in naming the LLP as defendant had caused no prejudice. It was reasonable to assume, in the absence of any contrary suggestion, that the former partners of the Firm would have the benefit of an indemnity from the LLP for any liability which they may incur as well as the same insurance cover and the same legal representation. In commercial reality, therefore, even though not in law, the change of party had made no difference to the defence of the claim. The point taken by the Firm was thus a purely technical one which, if successful, would give a windfall to the Firm and the LLP. Given that there was power to order substitution, the justice of the case was overwhelmingly in favour of doing so.

Appeal allowed.

Irwin v Lynch

Limitation Act 1980, s 35   **CPR 17.4, 19.5**

Court of Appeal   **[2010] EWCA Civ 1153;**
[2011] 1 WLR 1364; [2011] Bus LR 504;
[2011] BPIR 158

The defendant had engaged a company to carry out substantial building works at their home. The company went into liquidation. The administrator brought proceedings alleging that the agreement to carry out the works was a transaction at an undervalue and brought a claim against the company alleging that they were guilty of misfeasance and were liable to compensate the company. The defendant claimed that s 212 of the Insolvency Act 1986 prevented the administrator from bringing the claim, and applied to strike out. The administrator subsequently applied to add or substitute the company as a claimant, but that application was refused on the basis that the addition would be outside the limitation period.

The administrator appealed, submitting that the judge had misapplied CPR 19.5(3)(b). The defendant submitted that the judge had applied the correct statutory interpretation, which was a narrow one, and that the administrator had no standing to bring the claim so that the company could not be substituted as claimant; and if substitution was allowed there was a danger that claims could be pursued by complete strangers with parties later being substituted outside the limitation period.

Held:

(i) It was apparent that under s 212(3) of the 1986 Act the administrator did not have the necessary locus standi to bring a claim for misfeasance against the defendant, whereas the company did. CPR 19.5(2) and 19.5(3)(b) had to be construed in the light of s 35 of the Limitation Act 1980. When that was done it could not be said that the claim was vitiated so that one party could not be substituted for another simply because the original party did not have the standing to bring the claim.

(ii) It was possible and appropriate in the circumstances to allow the company to be substituted for the administrator, as the substitution was necessary for the determination of the original claim, which was the same in every respect (*Parkinson Engineering Services Plc (In Liquidation) v Swan* (p595) applied). Furthermore, the administrator was not a complete stranger; his task was to collect in the assets of the company and the claim which he asserted was avowedly brought on the part of the company.

(iii) (obiter) If a party sought to use r 19(5)(3)(b) in what was really a case of mistake but in which CPR 19.5(3)(a) or 17.4 could not be satisfied, the court would take a dim view of an attempt to escape the limits imposed in the express provisions dealing with mistake cases.

Appeal allowed.

J and others v Birmingham Roman Catholic Archdiocese Trustees

Procedure – whether limitation as a preliminary issue appropriate

QBD (Master Fontaine)   **25 July 2008, unreported**

The claimants alleged that during their childhood they had been victims of sexual abuse apparently committed by a priest. They issued proceedings against the defendants after the expiry of the limitation period, claiming that the defendants were vicariously liable for the priest's actions and were negligent in failing to act upon information allegedly given to the priest's supervisor. They applied for orders that the limitation period should be disapplied under s 33. The defendants applied for an order that limitation should be dealt with as a preliminary issue. They submitted that, if limitation was considered as a preliminary issue, there was likely to be a substantial saving of time and costs if it was determined in their favour. They contended that, if a judge had to determine the limitation issue within the trial, he might experience difficulties in separating out issues of limitation in circumstances where he or she may have formed a view as to liability.

Held:

(i)   There would be a large degree of overlap between the evidence that would have to be given in respect of the limitation issues and in respect of the liability and quantum issues. It would be difficult to 'hive off' the issue of limitation in the instant cases and would not result in any significant saving of costs (*KR v Bryn Alyn Community (Holdings) Ltd (In Liquidation)* (p505) considered).

(ii)   It would be more stressful for the claimants to have to attend court and give evidence twice. The evidence at the hearing of a preliminary issue would relate to issues surrounding the period of abuse and how they subsequently dealt with the fact of the abuse. On balance, the possibility of having to give evidence about those distressing events twice outweighed the possibility that they would never have to give direct evidence if they did not succeed on the limitation issues or they did succeed and settlement was achieved.

(iii)   It would be very difficult for a judge to exercise his discretion under s 33 in the instant cases without considering the merits of the claim (*Forbes v Wandsworth HA* (p434) applied). There was such a large amount of factual and expert evidence that the judge would have to consider in making the s 33 determination that it would not be appropriate to deal with limitation as a preliminary issue.

(iv)   The difference in costs if the trial lasted an additional day because the limitation issue was determined within the trial was not such that the saving would be the major factor. Furthermore, if the claimants were successful on the limitation issue, there would also be an increase in costs where two trials had to be prepared for.

(v)   The s 14 issues and the s 33 exercise of discretion would have to be considered separately in respect of each of the causes of action.

(vi)   Considering the matter overall and the claimants' strong objections to the ordering of a trial of preliminary issues, it would not be just to make the order.

Application refused.

JM v Bryn Alyn Community Holdings Ltd

Limitation Act 1980, s 2, s 11, s 14, s 33

Court of Appeal   **[2003] EWCA Civ 783;**
                                                       [2003] 3 WLR 107; [2003] 1 FLR 1203

See *KR v Bryn Alyn Community Holdings Ltd* (N) (p505)

JS v Bryn Alyn Community Holdings Ltd

Limitation Act 1980, s 2, s 11, s 14, s 33

Court of Appeal   **[2003] EWCA Civ 783;**
[2003] 3 WLR 107; [2003] 1 FLR 1203

See *KR v Bryn Alyn Community Holdings Ltd* (I) (p505)

James v East Dorset Health Authority

Limitation Act 1980, s 14, s 33

Court of Appeal   **(2001) 59 BMLR 196;**
(1999) Times, 7 December; LTL 24/11/1999

The claimant suffered from chronic piles. He underwent surgery in 1987 but his condition deteriorated. He underwent a second operation in December 1990, whereupon his condition deteriorated further. In August 1992 he underwent an independent examination which alerted him to the possibility that he might have suffered injury in the 1987 operation.

In September 1993 he consulted a solicitor and in July 1995 he received an expert's report confirming that he had suffered damage in the first operation. He issued proceedings on 17 January 1997 claiming that (a) he had sustained injury in the 1987 operation, and (b) the 1990 operation was undertaken ill-advisedly and without his informed consent. Limitation was heard as a preliminary issue. As regards the 1987 operation, the judge found that the claimant had actual knowledge in August 1992. The judge held that the claimant had knowledge in respect of the 1990 operation almost immediately after it failed. He therefore held that both claims were statute barred and declined to exercise his s 33 discretion to allow them to continue. The claimant appealed.

Held (Sir Christopher Staughton dissenting):

(i)   The judge's finding that the claimant was before 1992 well aware that his injury resulted from the 1987 operation was not justified on the evidence.

(ii)   The judge's conclusion as to knowledge in respect of the 1987 operation was based on a false premise. This was a rare case where the claimant had to know that he suffered an injury before time could run. He could not know that the injury was significant until he knew that he was injured.

(iii)   Until 1992 the claimant had been entitled to assume merely that the 1987 operation had not been a success. s 14 was not intended to reward those ever alert to the presumption that any misfortune could be blamed on another party. He was only put on enquiry to the possibility that he had sustained injury in the first operation in August 1992. He did not have actual knowledge until July 1995.

(iv)   As regards constructive knowledge under s 14(3), although the claimant could reasonably have obtained the relevant information earlier, even if he had moved with proper speed his date of knowledge would not have been accelerated to a date more than three years before the issue of proceedings. Although the claimant's solicitors delays were at law his, the same could not be said of the delays of the medical expert instructed. The claim arising from the 1987 operation was therefore not statute barred.

(v)   The 1990 palliative operation was statute barred. The claimant knew in relation to the 1987 operation by the end of 1990 that that operation had made his symptoms worse and had been undertaken on the doctor's advice without warning as to the risks involved.

(vi)   There was no basis for interfering with any other aspect of the judge's decision. As regards s 33, it could be difficult to reconstruct the standards of a decade ago in a specialised field, and litigation of this kind casts a long shadow over the personal and professional lives of those involved.

Appeal allowed in part.

James v First Bristol Buses

CPR 6.5

Sheffield CC (DJ Hawksworth)   **CLY 03/454**

The claimant informed the loss adjusters acting for the defendant that the claimant intended to claim damages for personal injuries. The loss adjusters wrote to the claimant indicating that they wished to instruct named solicitors to accept service of proceedings. The claimant, alleging that he had never received this letter, served proceedings directly upon the defendant. The defendant applied to strike out the claim on the basis that service was defective.

Held: The claimant was entitled to served directly upon the defendant because:

(a)   the letter nominating solicitors did not come from the defendant himself;

(b)   the letter was written before proceedings were issued and therefore before the defendant was a party to proceeding;

(c)   the named solicitors had not confirmed that they were prepared to accept service; and

(d)   the letter had never come to the claimant's attention (*Nanglegan v Royal Free Hampstead NHS Trust* (p567) distinguished).

Application dismissed.

Janov v Morris

Dismissal as abuse of process of court   **RSC Ord 18, r 19**

Court of Appeal   **[1981] 3 All ER 780; [1981] 1 WLR 1389**

On 7 August 1978 the claimant (Arthur Janov) issued a writ against the defendant in which he claimed damages for breach of a contract for the sale of a yacht. Pleadings were exchanged. In March 1980 the master made an order that the action be struck out unless the claimant served his summons for directions by 1 April 1980. The claimant failed to do so, and judgment on his claim was duly entered by the defendant.

On 9 September 1980 the claimant issued a fresh writ claiming the same relief. The defendant issued a summons under RSC Ord 18, r 19 to strike out the new writ on the grounds that it was an abuse of the process of the court. The master granted this order. Smith J rescinded it on appeal. The defendant appealed.

Held:

(i)   It was necessary to distinguish between cases such as *Birkett v James* [1977] 2 All ER 801 and *Tolley v Morris* (p693), where the first action had been struck out for want of prosecution on the ground of inordinate and inexcusable delay, and a case such as this in which the first action had been struck out because the claimant had failed to comply with a peremptory order.

(ii)   In this latter category, the court has to consider whether in the exercise of its discretion under Ord 18, r 19 the second action should be struck out. The court should be cautious in allowing the second action to continue and should have due regard to the necessity of maintaining the principle that orders are made to be complied with and not ignored.

(iii)   The judge was in error in not approaching the matter as one of discretion in that way. In the absence of any explanation as to why the peremptory order was not complied with in the previous action or any assurance as to the conduct of this action, this was a case in which the necessity for maintaining the principle that orders are made to be complied with should be upheld. The action should be struck out.

The defendant's appeal was allowed.

Jeffrey v Bolton Textile Mill Co plc

Limitation Act 1980, s 33

Garland J   6 March 1989

The claimant (Mrs Florence Jeffrey) was the widow of James Jeffrey who worked successively as a side piecer, cross piecer and mule spinner for Bolton Textile Mill Co Ltd between (except for the war years) 1919 and 1957 when he retired due to ill health. Her case was that he suffered from byssinosis which materially contributed to his death.

She commenced court action outside the primary limitation period and applied for an order under s 33 of the Limitation Act 1980. There were complications and doubts over the company structure of the defendants, and the mill had closed down in 1959.

Held:

(i)   The immediate consequence of the difficulty over the company structure was the question of insurance, because the relevant employer might be covered through a block insurance entered into through a trade association, but for that purpose the correct company would have to be identified. That difficulty might be more prejudicial to the defendants: s 33(3).

(ii)   Since the mill had closed 30 years ago, the number of witnesses who could testify to working conditions there was rather limited. However, a number of former employees had been able to testify and a fair trial was still possible: s 33(3)(b).

(iii)   Discretion would be exercised in favour of the claimant, in the knowledge that she had an uphill but not impossible task. The onus was on her to prove her case, not for the defendants to disprove it, and if she could not do so she would fail: s 33(1).

Brooks v J & P Coates Ltd (p350) applied.

Jeffrey v CMB Speciality Packaging (UK) Ltd

Limitation Act 1980, s 14, s 33

Court of Appeal   [2000] CP Rep 1

The claimant was exposed to high levels of noise in the defendant's employment. He began to experience tinnitus in 1969 but did not issue proceedings until 1993. On trial of limitation, the judge accepted the claimant's evidence that he did not attribute his problems to his work until 1992. However, he fixed the claimant with constructive knowledge under s 14(3) of the Act from 1970, holding that he should have made further inquiries of medical staff who provided him with the results of hearing tests. He declined to exercise his s 33 discretion. The claimant appealed.

Held:

(i)   The judge required an unrealistically inquisitive disposition from the claimant. The consultant to whom he was referred on 1970 indicated that a natural cause was being investigated. The claimant could not be expected to go behind this.

(ii)   Similarly, the claimant could not be expected to quiz the nurses who had performed audiograms in 1979.

(iii) There was no evidence that, had the claimant made the enquiries suggested, he would have received information constitutive of knowledge.

(iv)   The claimant did not have constructive knowledge until less than three years before the issue of proceedings.

Appeal allowed.

Jenkins v Eli Lilly & Co and others

Limitation Act 1980, s 11, s 14, s 33

Court of Appeal   **[1992] 3 Med LR 388**

See *Nash v Eli Lilly & Co* (J) (p568)

Johnson v Busfield

Limitation Act 1980, s 14, s 33

Nelson J   **(1997) 38 BMLR 29; LTL 29/7/1996**

The claimant suffered from a foot condition. On 1 July 1988 the defendant, a surgeon, carried out a Mayo's excision of the first metatarsal head. The allegation was that the procedure utilised was negligently obsolete. Complications ensued, but the claimant did not attribute them to the nature of the operation. Further operations were carried out and the operating surgeons condemned the defendant's approach.

In March 1989 the claimant was told that the operation had exacerbated her condition. However, she did not make the connection until she was told that the operation was obsolete in September 1990. Proceedings were issued on 19 February 1993. The defendant pleaded limitation which was heard as preliminary issue.

Held:

(i)   The claimant did not have actual knowledge for limitation purposes until September 1990 when she appreciated that the effects of the operation went beyond a normal complication.

(ii)   A reasonable person would have discovered the defendant's fault within six months of being told that the operation had exacerbated her condition. Constructive knowledge was therefore present in September 1989. The claim was therefore out of time.

(iii) Proceedings were issued five months late. The delay had not greatly affected the cogency of the defendant's evidence. The defendant had set out his position prior to his death on 5 June 1994. The question of whether or not the operation was obsolete was a matter of expert opinion that did not involve a close examination of the facts as recalled.

(iv)   It would be equitable to allow the action to proceed.

Johnson v Chief Constable of Surrey

Limitation Act 1980, s 32

Court of Appeal   **(1992) Times, 23 November**

The claimant (Francis Johnson) was arrested by the Surrey police. His writ was issued long after the standard limitation period. He claimed that new facts had emerged which had been deliberately concealed by the defendant.

Otton J struck out his claim as statute barred. The claimant appealed.

Held:

(i)   Section 32(1)(b) of the Limitation Act 1980 only operated to postpone the limitation period if the new facts allegedly concealed affected the claimant's right of action. Facts which merely improved his chance of success were not relevant for this purpose.

(ii)   The claimant's right of action was complete at the moment of his arrest. The new facts did not affect it. His appeal was dismissed.

NB: In a personal injury action, concealment that is not sufficient to postpone the limitation period under s 32(1)(b) may nevertheless be relevant under s 33(3)(c) when seeking its discretionary disapplication.

Johnson v Ministry of Defence and another

Limitation Act 1980, s 14

Court of Appeal   **[2012] EWCA Civ 1505**

The claimant was born in 1940. For periods between 1965 and 1979, he had been employed by the defendants in jobs where he was exposed to very loud noise. The claimant indicated that he had become aware of his hearing problem in about 2001, but it did not occur to him that it might have been caused by noise, or that he might have a claim against his previous employers. He did not consult his doctor about his hearing until 2006, when he asked whether there was any wax in his ears during a consultation about another matter. The doctor pronounced his ears to be clear and advised that any hearing difficulty was probably due to his age, which was then 66. The claimant maintained that it was not until 2009, when he consulted an expert, that he knew that he had a significant injury or that it was attributable to noise exposure. He commenced his claim in June 2010. The judge found that the claimant had failed to establish that his date of knowledge was after June 2007 because he had been aware that he had worked in noisy environments which could cause hearing difficulties and had actual knowledge of the onset and development of symptoms in 2001. The judge further declined to exercise his s 33 discretion to disapply the limitation period.

The claimant appealed, submitting that the judge had erred in moving straight from his findings of fact to the conclusion that, by 2001, he had actual knowledge of his cause of action because he could not have known that his deafness might have been caused by noise without expert advice.

Held:

(i)   The judge had erred in concluding that, by 2001, without the benefit of expert advice, the claimant had actual knowledge that his significant deafness might be attributable to noise exposure at work. Knowledge that his deafness was significant, coupled with knowledge that he had in the past been exposed to loud noise which he knew was capable of causing deafness, did not, of itself, amount to knowledge that his deafness might be attributable to noise or knowledge of that possibility.

(ii)   The judge's alternative conclusion that, even if the claimant did not have actual knowledge by 2001, he had it by 2006, was something of a mystery. Nothing had changed in the interim save that the deafness had become worse. As it was established that knowledge of significant injury was already present in 2001 in any event, nothing occurred between 2001 and 2006 which could have contributed to the claimant's knowledge.

(iii) The judge should have considered whether the claimant had constructive knowledge within the meaning of s 14(3). He had not, however, done so. It was necessary to consider objectively whether the claimant could reasonably have been expected to seek expert advice.

(iv)   Lord Hoffmann's judgment in *Adams v Bracknell Forest BC* (p292) appeared to say that anyone who had suffered a significant injury had to be assumed to be sufficiently curious that he would seek expert advice. However, it was not certain that this assumption had to apply in every case. The degree of curiosity to be expected would depend upon the context, and in particular the seriousness of the condition and the way it manifested itself. Lord Hoffmann must have meant that there would be an assumption that a person who had suffered a significant injury would be sufficiently curious to seek advice unless there were reasons why a reasonable person in his position would not have done. Such a reason might be that the condition was something that the claimant had become so used to that a reasonable person would not be expected to be curious about its cause. However, for good policy reasons, the House of Lords had intended to impose a fairly demanding test on claimants.

(v)   In the instant case, the claimant's hearing loss had developed over a period of time and its realisation must have dawned on him gradually. The question of whether a reasonable man in his situation and with his knowledge would be curious to know the cause was not easy; this was a case close to the line. Applying the demanding test required since *Adams*, a reasonable man in the 21st century would be curious about the onset of quite serious deafness at the relatively early age of 61 and would wish to find out its cause. In the claimant's circumstances, the reasonable man would have consulted his GP by the end of 2002, allowing one year's 'thinking time' for the realisation of serious symptoms in 2001.

(vi)   It was probable that, if the GP had been asked about the cause of deafness, as an open question, in 2001 or shortly thereafter, he would have considered the possibility of noise deafness and asked the claimant about his working history. Although there was no evidence on the point, it was a matter of which the court could take judicial notice. The claimant should be deemed to have had knowledge, by the end of 2002, that his deafness might be attributable to exposure to noise during his employment.

(vii) The primary limitation period had expired by the end of 2005. The appeal on s 33 having been abandoned, the claim was statute barred.

Appeal dismissed.

Johnston v Chief Constable of Merseyside

Limitation Act 1980, s 33

QBD (Coulson J)   **[2009] EWHC 2969 (QB); [2009] MHLR 343**

The claimant had a history of mental health problems, including schizophrenia. On 8 January 2006 as a result of his behaviour and at his request, a third party called the emergency services. When the police arrived an incident occurred and the claimant was sprayed with CS gas by an officer, which resulted in severe skin blistering and damage to the face, ear, neck and chest region. The claimant was put in handcuffs, detained and taken to hospital. He was not subsequently charged with any criminal offence. The police officer alleged that he had acted in accordance with s 136 of the Mental Health Act 1983, as he had found the claimant in a public place, apparently suffering from a mental disorder and in immediate need of care or control.

The claimant issued proceedings on 21 October 2008 for assault and false imprisonment. The defence on 12 December 2008 alleged that the proceedings were a nullity, as the claimant had failed to apply for permission to bring proceedings under s 139(2) of the Mental Health Act. The claimant's solicitors on 23 December 2008 issued an application for retrospective leave to proceed which was later discontinued by agreement. The claimant on 24 March 2009 applied for permission to bring fresh proceedings and, if that were granted, for the time bar to be disapplied pursuant to s 33.

Held:

(i)　　The claimant's claim passed the necessary threshold to be allowed to proceed under the 1983 Act: it was not frivolous, vexatious or an abuse of process and it had a real prospect of success. Permission under s 139 was to be granted.

(ii)　　Although the claim for false imprisonment was the subject of the six-year limitation period under s 2 of the 1980 Act, the claim for assault was subject to s 11(4) which provided for a three-year limitation period (*A v Hoare* (p287) followed). However, pursuant to s 33(1) of the 1980 Act, on the balance it was fair and just to disapply the relevant limitation period (*Cain v Francis* (p360) followed). The longer the delay, the more likely and greater the prejudice to the defendant (*KR v Bryn Alyn Community (Holdings) Ltd (In Liquidation)* (p505) followed). In the instant case the delay was only two and a half months, which was a relatively short period. Moreover, the only reason for the delay was that the claimant's solicitors had failed to follow the correct procedure. Further, the claimant's position in equity was strong, given that the original proceedings were commenced within the limitation period. Finally, no prejudice flowed to the defendants from that comparatively short delay, and it had no effect on the cogency of the evidence on either side.

Applications granted.

Jones v G D Searle & Co Ltd

Limitation Act 1939, s 2D　　　　　　　　　　　　　　　　**Interrogatories**

Court of Appeal　　　　　　　　　　　　　　**[1978] 3 All ER 654; 122 SJ 435**

Between February 1966 and September 1969 the claimant (Mrs Lavinia Jones) took Ovulen, an oral contraceptive drug manufactured by the defendants. In September 1969 she developed venous thrombosis in her legs. Her writ was issued on 8 June 1976. Her statement of claim relied inter alia on s 2D of the Limitation Act 1939 as amended 'in particular having regard to the fact that the claimant was unable to obtain legal aid to commence proceedings herein until after 15 March 1976. On the said date the claimant obtained the opinion of leading counsel, given in the light of documentary evidence from the United States of America'.

After close of pleadings the defendants served interrogatories, the seventh of which asked the claimant in respect of counsel's opinions that she had received before 15 March 1976: 'in the case of each advice was the same favourable or unfavourable to your prospects of success in an action against the defendants herein?'. Mais J upheld the district registrar's refusal to order the claimant to answer this. The defendants appealed.

Held:　　　under s 2D(3)(f) of the Limitation Act 1939 as amended, the court is enjoined to consider not only the steps if any taken by a claimant to obtain medical, legal or other expert advice but also the 'nature of any such advice' he or she may have received. Therefore it was right that the claimant should be required to state, since it was relevant, whether each advice was favourable or unfavourable to her case. The defendant's appeal was allowed.

Per Roskill LJ: 'nothing in this judgment is intended to suggest that as a consequence of giving that answer ... those opinions are liable to discovery or production. That question must await decision until it arises, if it does.'

Jones v G R Smith & Co

Limitation Act 1980, s 2, s 5   **Solicitors' negligence**

Court of Appeal   **8 February 1993**

On 17 June 1982 the claimant (Mrs Dorothy Jones) tripped on a pavement in West Bromwich and damaged her sacrum. She claimed damages against the local council. In a telephone conversation on 11 May 1984 the defendants (her solicitors) discussed her claim with the council's insurers. On 14 May 1984 they wrote to them 'without prejudice', 'We refer to our telephone conversation on Friday afternoon and accept on behalf of our client an offer of £6,500 in full and final settlement of our claim on the understanding that all our costs and disbursements are discharged'. The letter proceeded to justify profit costs of £750 plus VAT and disbursements. When the insurers sought by their letter of 22 May to deal separately with damages and costs, the defendants wrote on 25 May that it was 'part of the settlement' that their costs were to be discharged in full. When the insurers sent the damages cheque on 12 June, the defendants wrote on 15 June, 'we cannot accept this cheque in full and final settlement of our clients' claim until our costs have been paid in full'. These costs were finally agreed by 28 June 1984.

On 30 May 1990 the claimant issued a writ against the defendants, alleging that by reason of their negligence her claim was settled for less than it was worth. At a preliminary trial, McCullough J decided that her action was not statute barred. The defendants appealed. If her claim was settled on 11 or 14 May 1984, her action was statute barred. If the claim was not settled until 16–28 June 1984, the action was not statute barred.

Held:

(i)   The language of the defendants' letter of 14 May 1984 was inconsistent with any enforceable agreement having been made. It was only when the amount of the costs was resolved and the insurers agreed to pay them that a settlement was concluded between the parties.

(ii)   Since that did not happen until after 15 June 1984, the judge's conclusion that the claimant's action against the defendants was not statute barred was correct.

The defendants' appeal was dismissed.

Jones v Liverpool Health Authority

Limitation Act 1980, s 11, s 14, s 33

Court of Appeal   **[1996] PIQR P251;**
                                                                                       (1996) 30 BMLR 1; LTL 19/7/1995

The claimant was treated at the defendant's hospital between 1974 and 1983. He alleged negligence in respect of the insertion of a catheter into his femoral artery on 5 September 1974 and a failure to repair the damage by use of anti-coagulants on 30 October 1974. The claimant through solicitors sent a letter of complaint about his treatment to the defendant on 6 January 1976. Proceedings were issued on 24 October 1987. Limitation was heard as a preliminary issue. The judge found that the claimant had knowledge for limitation purposes in January 1977. Finding that there was no substantial explanation for the claimant's delay, which had reduced the cogency of the evidence, he declined to exercise his s 33 discretion. The claimant appealed.

Held:

(i) The claimant had the requisite knowledge by January 1977. He knew the damage had been caused by the catheter. He knew what treatment he had and had not received, including that anti-coagulants had not been administered until November 1974. He also knew that they should have been.

(ii) The claimant had been advised by one consultant on 3 January 1977 of the same facts that, when stated by another consultant in 1991, led him to believe he had a cause of action. A claimant in these circumstances could not claim that he did not have knowledge on the earlier date.

(iii) The judge's exercise of his discretion could not be said to be obviously wrong. Appeal dismissed.

Jones v Norfolk CC

Limitation Act 1980, s 14, s 33

QBD (Judge Eccles QC)   **[2010] EWHC 1313 (QB)**

Between August 1982 and June 1985 the claimant had been employed as a technician at a college run by the defendant. His job involved handling large quantities of lead. During that time he began to suffer some respiratory problems and, at his request, the level of lead fumes to which he was exposed was assessed but found not to be dangerous. He also consulted his doctor on various occasions and had some time off work.

When the claimant went to give blood in February 2006 his haemoglobin level was too low and his donation was refused. This prompted extensive medical investigation and in July 2006 he was diagnosed with chronic severe lead poisoning. He believed that it must have been caused by exposure to dangerous levels of lead dust and fumes when he was working for the defendant. The defendant denied liability and the claimant issued proceedings in June 2009. Limitation was heard as preliminary issue. The claimant's case was that his date of knowledge was in July 2006 when he received the diagnosis. In the alternative he sought relief under s 33. The defendant contended that the claimant had actual knowledge during his employment at the college, or constructive knowledge in either 1986 or 1997, when he was concerned enough about various ailments that he had to make lifestyle changes.

Held:

(i) On the evidence, the claimant would have taken steps when he was the defendant's employee if he had known that his symptoms were being caused by lead poisoning. When he was found to be anaemic in 2006 he went to considerable lengths not only to a get a confirmed diagnosis, but also to set in train enquiries about what had happened when he was at the college. His state of mind in 1982 was that he had suspected that his symptoms might be caused by dust and lead, despite the protective mask that he wore, and in that state of mind he asked the chief medical officer to investigate. That investigation reassured him and his suspicion went away.

(ii) However, his symptoms did not go away and so he went to the doctor again with a degree of renewed suspicion but was not advised that there might be any real or urgent cause for concern. When he next saw the doctor in 1984, although lead exposure was discussed, he was told that he had influenza. Therefore his state of knowledge did not rise above a vague suspicion, which in 1982 was met with positive reassurance and in the next two years with an absence of medical advice, that he might be affected by lead poisoning or other possibly serious condition. It was not credible that he would have let matters rest back in the 1980s if he had firmly believed that he was suffering from lead poisoning (*Spargo v North Essex DHA* (p667) followed).

(iii)   The claimant did not know enough in the period 1982 to 1985 to make it reasonable to have expected him to investigate whether he had a case against the defendant, or indeed to take any steps other than those that he did. His state of mind at that time did not amount to actual knowledge for the purposes of s 14(1).

(iv)   As to constructive knowledge, the court had to add to those facts of which the claimant was actually aware those facts of which he ought objectively to have become aware, applying the test of 'heightened curiosity' about his 'injury', in the claimant's case his persistent symptoms, but taking into account relevant circumstances other than his personal characteristics (*Whiston v London SHA* (p710) and *Adams v Bracknell Forest BC* (p292) followed). It was plainly a very relevant circumstance that it was almost 25 years since the claimant had left the college and that over the years he had suffered a very wide variety of symptoms which, over time, could well lead a person with his history away from concluding that there had to be an overarching diagnosis. His view that his symptoms were caused variously by age, manual work in early life, stress or just being prone to aches and pains was not unreasonably uncurious, given the steps he had taken in the 1980s to seek medical assistance. Furthermore, his curiosity to find out whether his exposure to lead might have had anything to do with the symptoms he had in 1982 and 1983 had been satisfied by the chief medical officer's assurance and by his doctor's apparent lack of urgent concern. It was also relevant that he had been a regular blood donor for many years, as he was thereby less likely to think that there was something serious underlying his symptoms potentially capable of being attributed to some omission by somebody in his past when his blood continued to be acceptable to the donor service.

(v)   The burden of proving constructive knowledge lay upon the defendant (*Lennon v Alvis Industries* (p532) followed). The defendant here faced the further hurdle of showing that, on the balance of probability, further investigations in 1986 or 1997 would have resulted in a diagnosis of lead poisoning. The defendant had not discharged that burden; the results of any further investigations were speculative.

(vi)   (obiter) If the claimant's date of knowledge was either in 1986 or 1997, because he should have sought expert advice then about the cause of his symptoms and been given a correct diagnosis, it would not have been appropriate to apply s 33 in his favour. The delay in bringing the action would (a) have been very substantial; (b) have been substantially his fault; and (c) be such as to cause the defendant a significant degree of prejudice in defending this action, most of the relevant evidence having been lost.

Preliminary issue decided in favour of the claimant.

Jones v Patel

Limitation Act 1980, s 33

Court of Appeal   **5 July 1988**

On 18 May 1984 the claimant (Doriel Jones) was bitten by the defendant's dog as she passed his shop. In June 1984 a letter before action was written. In March 1985 the defendant was convicted of having an unmuzzled, ferocious dog. Negotiations took place. An offer made by the defendant's insurers in December 1986 was rejected. Nothing further happened until proceedings were commenced on 4 August 1987.

At a preliminary trial on limitation, HH Judge Goldstein directed that the provisions of s 11 of the Limitation Act 1980 should not apply to the action. The defendant applied for leave to appeal.

Held:

the judge was justified in concluding that:

(i)   The defendant would suffer no prejudice beyond the loss of a windfall defence, since there was no defence on liability, no witness who had ceased to be available and no delay which had prevented the defendant from investigating what had happened;

(ii) The claimant would suffer precisely the prejudice outlined by Lord Diplock in *Thompson v Brown* (p690), were the case to have to start again by her suing her solicitors in negligence to judgment.

Permission to appeal was refused.

Jones and others v Secretary of State for Energy and Climate Change and another

Limitation Act 1980, s 14, s 33

QBD (Swift J)   **[2012] EWHC 2936 (QB)**

The eight lead claimants in the Phurnacite Workers Group Litigation sought damages for negligence and breach of statutory duty in relation to respiratory disease and/or various types of cancer alleged to have been contracted during the course of their work at a Phurnacite plant in South Wales. Their periods of employment collectively spanned between 1948 and 1991.

Phurnacite was a popular and profitable domestic fuel made by binding fragments of waste coal with pitch to form briquettes, which were carbonised at high temperatures to drive off the volatile constituents. During carbonisation, gases and fumes containing volatile polycyclic aromatic hydrocarbons (PAHs) were produced. As they cooled, they attached to dust particles emitted from the ovens. The plant opened in 1942, by which time it was well-known that exposure to high levels of coal dust could cause pneumoconiosis, and awareness of the hazards associated with PAHs was starting to develop. The plant reached its height in the late 1960s and early 1970s, during which time health concerns in the surrounding community grew and there was significant pressure on the operators to take remedial action. By 1972, there were uncertainties about the long-term future of the product and capital expenditure was curtailed. Conditions deteriorated. Between 1976 and 1982, the plant operated twice-yearly dust sampling, which was reduced to one sample in 1983. Thereafter, there were no sampling results available. The plant closed in 1991.

The claimants submitted that, if the defendants had complied with the Patent Fuel Manufacture (Health and Welfare) Special Regulations 1946, many of the dust sources would have been entirely eliminated. They also alleged poor cleaning and housekeeping systems and a failure to take practicable measures such as the provision of respiratory protective equipment. The defendants argued that, even if all practicable measures had been taken to reduce dust and fume levels, there was nevertheless an irreducible minimum level which would inevitably have been generated, which was non-tortious, and that any damages should be apportioned.

The defendants also alleged that all but two of the claims were statute barred. The defendants highlighted the length of the periods of delay, difficulty in tracing witnesses, the fact that many of the workers in respect of whom claims were advanced were dead, the death and non-availability of witnesses, and the paucity of documentation. Limitation was tried alongside issues of liability and causation.

Held:

On limitation

(i)   The claimants accepted that workers at the Phurnacite plant would have been aware from the outset of their employment at the plant that the inhalation of coal dust in underground mining could cause respiratory disease. The claimants also accepted that workers at the Phurnacite plant would have been aware of the potential for skin lesions (including skin cancer) as a result of exposure to pitch. However, the awareness that there was a link between lung and/or bladder cancer would have come significantly later, around 1990. There was also general and long-standing local concern as to the plant with regard to health and safety.

(ii) The claims in question were therefore all brought out of time. They could only proceed if the court exercised its discretion under s 33.

(iii) In favour of the claimants was the difficulty that all would have experienced in obtaining funding for unitary actions, and therefore the need, effectively, for there to be a Group Litigation Order. None of the delay in bringing proceedings arose as a result of any fault on the part of the claimants or their advisers.

(iv) As regards evidential prejudice to the defendants in witnesses being unavailable, the attempts made by the defendants to identify and trace witnesses were very superficial. They did not employ the obvious expedient of attempting to communicate with former supervisory and management staff through the relevant pension schemes. Furthermore, even when they became aware of the availability of a potential witness of management grade, they elected not to interview him. In the event, the defendants chose to rely on the evidence of only five of the nine witnesses from whom they had obtained witness statements. Thus, even when the defendants had been able to trace and interview witnesses, they judged that it was not in their interests to rely on them.

(v) In any event, there was copious evidence as to the relevant matters, both in terms of documents and 30 lay witnesses who gave generally clear and consistent accounts. Whenever the defendants had begun their search for witnesses and however thorough that search had been, it was in the highest degree improbable that it would have identified a witness or witnesses who would have given evidence about the working conditions such as to change the outcome of the issues in the litigation.

(vi) The defendants' ability to defend the claim had not been compromised as a result of the delay, and it was fair and just to permit the action to proceed.

On substantive issues

(i) The defendants were in wholesale breach of statutory duty.

(ii) The causation issues were complicated, both legally and factually. Success for the claimants as a whole was mixed. No bladder, lung or skin cancer case succeeded. However, causation was established in respect of non-malignant respiratory disease.

Jones v Trollope Colls Cementation Overseas Ltd and another

Foreign Limitation Periods Act 1984

Court of Appeal   **(1990) Times, 26 January**

On 8 May 1984 the claimant (Frances Jones), a US citizen employed by the US government in Karachi, Pakistan, was given a lift there by the second defendant, an employee of the first defendant. Owing, she alleged, to the speed at which he drove, an accident occurred in which she suffered injuries that included the fracture of both her legs. She spent a long time in hospital. She notified a claim to the first defendants who assured her that their insurers would be dealing with the case.

On 26 July 1986 she issued a writ against the defendants in England. On 1 October 1985 the Foreign Limitation Periods Act 1984 came into force. Section 1(1)(a) stated that in such a case the limitation law of the country in which the accident occurred would apply. By Pakistani law this was 12 months.

Sir Peter Pain upheld the master's refusal to dismiss the proceedings. The defendants appealed.

Held:

(i)   Section 7(3)(a) of the 1984 Act made an express exemption for actions commenced before the appointed day. The unavoidable inference was that the Act applied to actions begun on or after 1 October 1985.

(ii)   Section 2(2) provided that an exception was to be made where the application of the 1984 Act would cause undue hardship to any party to the proceedings. The word 'undue' added something to normal hardship. It meant excessive hardship or a greater hardship than the circumstances warranted.

(iii)   Undue hardship to the claimant had been caused by her long hospitalisation and by the belief that her claim would be met. Accordingly, she could rely on the s 2(2) exception.

The defendants' appeal was dismissed.

KJM v Bryn Alyn Community Holdings Ltd

Limitation Act 1980, s 2, s 11, s 14, s 33

Court of Appeal   **[2003] EWCA Civ 783;**
[2003] 3 WLR 107; [2003] 1 FLR 1203

See *KR v Bryn Alyn Community Holdings Ltd* (H) (p505)

KR v Bryn Alyn Community Holdings Ltd

Limitation Act 1980, s 2, s 11, s 14, s 33

Court of Appeal   **[2003] EWCA Civ 783;**
[2003] 3 WLR 107; [2003] 1 FLR 1203

This was a consolidated action brought by 14 claimants. The claimants had been physically and/or sexually abused in the defendant's children's homes in 1973–1991. The abuse ranged from beatings to buggery. The claimants were all adults when they issued proceedings, primarily for psychiatric injury, with between 8 and 24 years having passed since the abuses ended. All consulted psychiatrists less than three years before the issue of proceedings. The defendant pleaded limitation and required the claimants to prove liability. All the issues were heard together. The judge found that the defendant had been negligent in respect of all but one claimant, the last having a cause of action in trespass to the person only and thus barred by the flat six-year limit in s 2 (see *Stubbings v Webb* (p677)). He found that all the claimants had the requisite knowledge for s 14 at the time of the abuse and that the claims were therefore all statute barred. However, he exercised his s 33 discretion in favour of the claimants in all the negligence claims and awarded damages accordingly. The defendant appealed and the claimants cross-appealed.

Held:

1.   Knowledge

(i)   The judge had erred on s 14 significance, which was a pragmatic, fact-sensitive question requiring the court to decide when a particular claimant would reasonably turn his mind to litigation as a remedy. The judge was therefore wrong to decide the knowledge of all 14 claimants together without considering them discretely.

(ii) The word 'significant' in s 14 had a special and partly subjective meaning (*McCafferty v Metropolitan Police* (p546) applied). Cases of child abuse required the court, on a case by case basis, to ask when an already damaged child would reasonably turn his mind to litigation as a solution to his problems. A psychiatrist's intervention could be the trigger to knowledge. Such injuries should be treated, in terms of latency and knowledge of significance, like industrial diseases (*Nash v Eli Lilly* (p568) and *Stubbings v Webb* [1992] QB 197 (part of the Court of Appeal judgment not disturbed by the House of Lords) followed, dicta in *Stubbings v Webb* (House of Lords (p677)) not followed).

(iii) The judge therefore erred by focusing knowledge of the immediate impact rather than knowledge of the long term psychiatric harm. The immediate impact was not the injury for which damages were sought ('the injury in question').

(iv) The socio-historical context was important in judging whether a claimant would be likely to resort to litigation. Previously, ill-treatment in children's homes was little discussed, its effects little understood, and it would have been accepted by the victims, the idea of claiming would not have occurred to them. Conversely, the increased awareness of abuse and society's increasingly litigious nature means that injuries will likely to become 'significant' at increasingly shorter intervals from the original torts.

(v) Damages can be claimed from injuries present before the claimant knew his injury was significant if they arise from the same cause of action, the otherwise barred claim 'piggy-backing' the valid claim.

(vi) Conversely, if a claim is made for the initial injury, any subsequent claim for aggravation or development of the initial injury is likely to be statute barred in the normal way (*Bristow v Grout* (p345) affirmed).

NB: The Court of Appeal in *Catholic Care (Diocese of Leeds) and another v Young* [2006] EWCA Civ 1534 held that the definition of knowledge set out at (ii) could not survive the House of Lords' decision in *Adams v Bracknell Forest BC* (p292).

2. *Section 33*

(i) Although the discretionary nature of s 33 was central to its function, there were nevertheless general guidelines that applied. It should not be determined simply by assessing comparative scales of hardship. Rather, the central question was whether, stripping away legal niceties, given the delays the judge could fairly try the claims.

(ii) The following uncontroversial principles were apparent from the leading cases:

   (a) in multiple claims, the judge should consider s 33 separately in relation to each claimant;

   (b) the claimant has a heavy burden in showing that it would be equitable to disapply the limitation period;

   (c) generally, the longer the delay, the less likely discretion will be exercised;

   (d) where a judge is minded to grant a long extension, he should take meticulous care to give reasons;

   (e) a judge should not reach a decision by effectively concluding the matter on any one circumstance. A balancing exercise of all the factors was required;

   (f) evidential prejudice to the defendant is crucial.

(iii) The court should not form a concluded view of the validity of allegations of abuse to determine the extent of the claimant's prejudice under s 33. This was especially so in cases of old and supported allegations as such allegations were easy to make and difficult to refute. In these circumstances the cogency of the claimant's evidence, insofar as it support the claimant, was neutral.

(iv) Limitation should be decided distinctly as a preliminary issue if practicable. It appeared in this case that the order of treatment (dealing with limitation last) appears to have affected the judge's reasoning on the limitation issues.

(v)   Alternatively, if limitation is to be determined at trial, this should be done before determining the substantive issues. To do otherwise would unfairly require the defendant to prove a negative: that the judge would not have found against him on the substantive issues had the case been heard earlier.

(vi)   In cases such as these, the correct application of the date of knowledge test to extend time in favour of the claimant necessarily means that limited weight should be given for the claimant's reasons for delay.

(vii)   A judge's s 33 discretion could only be disturbed if it was outside the ambit of reasonable disagreement. This included the exercise of wrong principles, taking account of irrelevant factors, ignoring relevant factor or making a decision that was plainly wrong. If the appeal court intervened on any such ground the matter should be treated as at large and the discretion exercised afresh.

(viii)   The judge's exercise of his s 33 discretion was flawed. He gave far too much weight to the fact that much delay was caused by the abuse itself; this factor went rather towards s 14. Conversely, he gave insufficient weight to the length of delays, the varying gravity of abuse and the evidential prejudice to the defendant. The defendant was severely limited in its ability to defend the claim.

(ix)   The judge also failed to direct himself that the cogency of the claimants' evidence, to the extent that it favoured their claims, was a neutral factor (*Hartley v Birmingham City Council* (p465) followed).

(x)   The judge erred in his use of the findings of an independent report into the abuses. This report itself was made long after the relevant events.

(xi)   In any event, the judge's exercise of his discretion was plainly wrong and predicated on incorrect findings as to date of knowledge. The court would therefore consider the discretion afresh.

3.   Applicability of s 2

(i)   Applying *Lister v Hesley Hall Ltd* (p535) there was a two-stage test. Firstly, is the tortious act sufficiently closely connected with employment so as to give rise to vicarious liability? If so, the employer will be liable for the deliberate acts of the employee for trespass to the person but the limitation period will be six years. Secondly, has the claimant proven systemic negligence of the part of the employer? If so, a claimant will also be able to relay on the extended limitation period in s 11, s 14 and s 33.

(ii)   In the absence of some provable allegation of negligence, the six-year time limit applied.

(iii)   Inspection of the individual decisions makes it clear that the central question on negligence is whether due diligence on the defendant's part could have prevented a particular abuse. s 2 applied to deliberate acts by the defendant's employees that could not have been so prevented.

(iv)   The fact that a tort can be characterised as another tort does not exclude characterisation as negligence for limitation purposes. The House of Lords in *Stubbings v Webb* did not hold that deliberate assault was not capable of constituting a breach of duty.

(v)   The cause of an injury is not defined by the pleader's label but by the factual situation that entitles the claimant to a remedy. It is therefore necessary to look at each case individually and consider whether the facts met the s 11 criteria.

(A) KR

(i)   KR was just under 14 years old when he was taken into the defendant's care, following an appearance in front of the juvenile court. He remained there from 1973 to 1975.

(ii)   During his time at Bryn Alyn, he was sexually abused by the head of the home, John Allen, and physically abuse by other staff. John Allen attempted to bugger him but he resisted. The judge found that the abuse occurred because the staff were used to hitting children and did not look into what John Allen was doing despite clear warning signs.

(iii) It was clear from KR's 1993 social security records that he did not at that time appreciate that he had a psychiatric injury. The disabling long-term effect of the abuse caused him to put the events to the back of his mind.

(iv) For the reasons given in the main judgment, the judge erred in his finding on date of knowledge. The claimant did not have knowledge more than three years before the issue of proceedings in September 1999.

(v) If the judge had been correct in finding that the date of knowledge was 1979, it would not have been equitable to disapply the limitation period. The sheer length of the twenty year delay was strongly against it. Further, the evidential prejudice to the defendant was correspondingly great.

(vi) Quantum should be increased to award damages for the immediate impact of the abuse.

(B) DK

(i) DK was in the defendant's care from 1979, at which time he was 14, to 1982. He arrived as a difficult child needing specialist care and understanding. Instead he suffered physical violence at the hands of the staff, as was the norm in the home's regime.

(ii) DK blocked out all thoughts of Bryn Alyn until he consulted the police, solicitors and a psychiatrist between 1997 and 1998.

(iii) For the reasons given in the main judgment, the judge erred in his finding on date of knowledge. The claimant did not have knowledge more than three years before the issue of proceedings in July 1999. The initial physical abuse, although serious, was not significant for the purposes of s 14.

(iv) If the judge had been correct in finding that the date of knowledge was 1983, it would not have been equitable to disapply the limitation period. The sheer length of the 17-year delay was strongly against it. Further, the evidential prejudice to the defendant was correspondingly great.

(v) Quantum should be increased to award damages for the immediate impact of the abuse.

(C) CGE

(i) CGE came to Bryn Alyn in 1980 when he was 13 and stayed until 1983. He suffered numerous assaults of varying degrees of gravity.

(ii) Although CGE made a statement to the police in 1993 about the abuse and also made a claim to the Criminal Injuries Compensation Board, he was not at that time aware of its long-term psychiatric effect. This was not apparent until he consulted solicitors and a psychiatrist.

(iii) For the reasons given in the main judgment, the judge erred in his finding on date of knowledge. The claimant did not have knowledge more than three years before the issue of proceedings in July 1999. The initial physical abuse, although serious, was not significant for the purposes of s 14.

(iv) If the judge had been correct in finding that the date of knowledge was 1987, it would not have been equitable to disapply the limitation period. The sheer length of the 12-year delay was strongly against it. Further, the evidential prejudice to the defendant was correspondingly great. This was especially so as there were large question marks over CGE's truthfulness as a witness.

(v) Quantum should be increased to award damages for the immediate impact of the abuse.

(D) RM

(i) RM spent just under two years at Bryn Alyn between 1988 and 1990, between the ages of 15 and 17. She arrived as a very needy girl. She suffered numerous assaults.

(ii)   For the reasons given in the main judgment, the judge erred in his finding on date of knowledge. The claimant did not have knowledge more than three years before the issue of proceedings in July 1999. The initial physical abuse, although serious, was not significant for the purposes of s 14. Because of her deeply troubled psychiatric history both before and after attending Bryn Alyn, it was unrealistic to expect her to have attributed her problems to the defendant.

(iii)   Alternatively, it would have been equitable under s 33 to disapply the limitation period. Although there was a long delay – proceedings on the judge's findings were issued five years after the limitation period expired and nine years after the relevant events – it was significantly shorter than in the other cases. Secondly, there was some documentary evidence of her time in the defendant's care. Thirdly, the difficulties in reliving the unhappy experiences at Bryn Alyn were, as the judge found, a relevant circumstance to s 33.

(E) GS

(i)   GS came to Bryn Alyn in 1988 when aged 15 and stayed there for nine months. He came from a troubled background. Whilst at Bryn Alyn he was assaulted on an almost daily basis.

(ii)   For the reasons given in the main judgment, the judge erred in his finding on date of knowledge. The claimant did not have knowledge more than three years before the issue of proceedings in July 1999. The initial physical abuse, although serious, was not significant for the purposes of s 14 in the context of his difficult past.

(iii)   Alternatively, it would have been equitable under s 33 to disapply the limitation period. Although there was a long delay – proceedings on the judge's findings were issued five years after the limitation period expired and 10 years after the relevant events – it was significantly shorter than in the other cases. Secondly, there was some documentary evidence of her time in the defendant's care. Thirdly, the difficulties in reliving the unhappy experiences at Bryn Alyn were, as the judge found, a relevant circumstance to s 33.

(F) MCK

(i)   MCK was abused at Bryn Alyn over a period of six months between 1982 and 1983. She issued proceedings in 1999.

(ii)   The judge held:

(a)   MCK had been indecently assaulted by John Allen, but without her protesting or complaining and without the knowledge of the staff;

(b)   there was no systematic negligence on the part of the defendant. To suggest otherwise would be a counsel of perfection;

(c)   although the defendant was vicariously responsible for John Allen's acts, the non-extendable six-year limit under s 2 applied and the claim was statute barred.

(iii)   The judge's rulings were correct.

(iv)   If this had been a negligence claim, for the same reasons as above, it would have been issued in time but if not it would not have been equitable to disapply the time limit.

(G) DJ

(i)   DJ was in the defendant's care from 1975, when he was 10, to 1981. He arrived a very troubled child, having previously been sexually abused.

(ii)   Whilst at Bryn Alyn he was buggered by two members of staff and offered as a sexual plaything. He was also physically abused. He later suffered delayed post-traumatic stress disorder.

(iii) For the reasons given in the main judgment, the judge erred in his finding on date of knowledge. The claimant did not have knowledge more than three years before the issue of proceedings in January 1998. The initial physical abuse, although serious, was not significant for the purposes of s 14 in the context of his difficult past and public opinion at the time.

(iv) If the judge had been correct in finding that the date of knowledge was 1981, it would not have been equitable to disapply the limitation period. The sheer length of the 17-year delay was strongly against it. Further, the evidential prejudice to the defendant was correspondingly great. This was especially so as there were large question marks over DJ's truthfulness as a witness and no documentary evidence.

(v) Quantum should be increased to award damages for the immediate impact of the abuse.

(H) KJM

(i) KJM was at Bryn Alyn between 1973 and 1975 between the ages of 13 and 15. He arrived as a difficult and needy child. He was buggered by John Allen.

(ii) For the reasons given in the main judgment, the judge erred in his finding on date of knowledge. The claimant did not have knowledge more than three years before the issue of proceedings in July 1999. The initial physical abuse, although serious, was not significant for the purposes of s 14. He was ambivalent about his psychiatric injuries and its attributability to the defendant's conduct from 1992 onwards, although he claimed compensation from the Criminal Injuries Compensation Board. His belief was insufficiently firm to qualify as knowledge.

(iii) if the judge had been correct in finding that the date of knowledge was 1975, it Would not have been equitable to disapply the limitation period. The sheer length of the 24-year delay was strongly against it. Further, the evidential prejudice to the defendant was correspondingly great. This was especially so as there were large question marks over KJM's truthfulness as a witness and no documentary evidence.

(I) JS

(i) JS was first taken into care at the age of 5. She was a difficult child when she arrived at Bryn Alyn in 1982 aged 12. She stayed for three years during which time she was sexually abused by three members of staff, one of whom had intercourse with her. She commenced proceedings in January 1994.

(ii) The judge found the defendant vicariously liable in negligence save for one act for which it was vicariously liable in trespass only. However, although this was overlooked at first instance, the limitation period in respect of this act did not expire until six years after JS attained her majority, and proceedings were in fact issued before this date.

(iii) As regards the proceedings founded in negligence, for the reasons given in the preceding cases where the delay had been relatively short, it was likely that JS did not have the requisite knowledge more than three years before proceedings were issued or, if she did, it would be equitable to allow the claim to continue by way of s 33.

(J) GOM

(i) GOM was in the defendant's care from 1984 to 1986, between the ages of 13 and 15. He came from a very troubled background and had developed a non-trusting attitude to adults.

(ii) During his time at Bryn Alyn, GOM was repeatedly buggered and indecently assaulted by John Allen. He was also forced to masturbate him. This was accompanied by money and presents. There was also physical abuse.

(iii) GOM was not for a long time willing to give a full account of these events. He did not discuss the abuse at all until 1986. He did not admit to having been buggered until 3 weeks before trial.

(iv)   By 2000, when he was seen by two psychiatrists, GOM was a mess. His psychiatric problems included post-traumatic stress disorder.

(v)   The judge found that GOM had knowledge for limitation purposes 13 years before issuing proceedings in July 1999.

(vi)   Despite the duration and gravity of the abuse GOM suffered, it did not fix him with knowledge under s 14. The immediate effect was of confusion and shame, and his injury did not become 'significant' until he began many years later to face up to its long term effects. The claimant did not have knowledge more than three years before the issue of proceedings.

(vii)   If the judge had been correct in finding that the date of knowledge was 1975, it would not have been equitable to disapply the limitation period. The sheer length of the 24-year delay was strongly against it. Further, the evidential prejudice to the defendant was correspondingly great. This was especially so as there were large question marks over GOM's truthfulness as a witness and very little documentary evidence.

(K) DHM

(i)   DHM attended Bryn Alyn for just over three years from 1977 to 1981, between the ages of 13 and 16. Like many others, he arrived a troubled child.

(ii)   DHM suffered prolonged and serious sexual and physical abuse at Bryn Alyn, although he made no complaint of it until January 1997 when he was visited by the police.

(iii)   After leaving Bryn Alyn he became an alcoholic and was prosecuted for crimes of dishonesty and violence. He was later also diagnosed with delay onset post-traumatic stress disorder.

(iv)   For the reasons given in the main judgment, the judge erred in his finding on date of knowledge. The claimant did not have knowledge more than three years before the issue of proceedings in July 1999. The initial abuse, although serious, was not significant for the purposes of s 14 in the context of his difficult past and the subsequent development of his symptoms.

(v)   If the judge had been correct in finding that the date of knowledge was 1981, it would not have been equitable to disapply the limitation period. The sheer length of the 18-year delay was strongly against it. Further, the evidential prejudice to the defendant was correspondingly great. This was especially so as there were large question marks over DHM's truthfulness as a witness.

(vi)   Quantum should be increased to award damages for the immediate impact of the abuse.

(L) PS

(i)   PS was first taken into care at aged 6, whereupon he suffered physical abuse. He arrived at Bryn Alyn in 1976 aged 13 and stayed for nearly 3½ years. During this time he was subjected to serious physical abuse.

(ii)   On leaving Bryn Alyn, PS joined the army, serving 8½ years. By the time of his discharge he was suffering from acute depression and was drinking too much.

(iii)   In 1986, PS saw a newspaper article about John Allen and Bryn Alyn. This prompted him to see a psychiatrist who diagnosed chronic post-traumatic stress disorder.

(iv)   For the reasons given in the main judgment, the judge erred in his finding on date of knowledge. The claimant did not have knowledge more than three years before the issue of proceedings in January 1998. The initial abuse, although serious, was not significant for the purposes of s 14.

(v)   If the judge had been correct in finding that the date of knowledge was 1979, it would not have been equitable to disapply the limitation period. The sheer length of the 18-year delay was strongly against it. Further, the evidential prejudice to the defendant was correspondingly great. Although there was merit in the argument that the evidence in joined cases added generally to the cogency of the evidential picture, there is a corresponding danger that a given claimant could be 'jumping on the bandwagon'.

(M) CD

(i) CD first entered care aged nine months and was overall moved more than 20 times. He suffered serious physical and sexual abuse in many of these placements. He therefore arrived at Bryn Alyn in 1990, aged 15, with severe problems.

(ii) CD remained at Bryn Alyn for a year. During this time he was repeatedly buggered by a member of staff. This mostly occurred in the claimant's bedroom but on 3 occasions elsewhere and outside the care home. He was also subjected to lesser, albeit very serious, sexual and physical abuse. On 2 occasions he attempted suicide and he ran away several times.

(iii) CD told the police in 1993 of the physical assaults but denied any sexual abuse. He did not reveal the sexual abuse until 1995, when he did so to his partner.

(iv) CD was diagnosed with a range of serious psychiatric problems, including post-traumatic stress disorder.

(v) The judge found that there was no negligence proved against the defendant in relation to those acts of buggery that took place outside the care home. However, the judge found that the defendant had been negligent in relation to those acts which occurred in the claimant's bedroom. It should have been apparent that the member of staff in question was making to many visits to this bedroom. The judge was entitled to make the distinction that he did and it would not be disturbed. The practical consequences of the finding of no negligence in relation to 3 incidents were in any event minimal.

(vi) As regards the proceedings founded in negligence, for the reasons given in the preceding cases where the delay had been relatively short, it was likely that CD did not have the requisite knowledge more than three years before proceedings were issued or, if he did, it would be equitable to allow the claim to continue by way of s 33.

(N) JM

(i) This claimant again came from a troubled background. He was in the defendant's care for two periods totalling about three years between the ages of 13 and 16, from 1985 to 1989. Even before this he had been the victim of extensive physical and sexual abuse. Whilst in the defendant's care he was subjected to buggery and sexual and physical abuse. As a result he suffered several psychiatric problems including post-traumatic stress disorder.

(ii) For the reasons given in the main judgment, the judge erred in his finding on date of knowledge. The claimant did not have knowledge more than three years before the issue of proceedings in July 1999. The initial abuse, although serious, was not significant for the purposes of s 14 in the context of his difficult past and the subsequent development of his symptoms.

(iii) Alternatively, although it was very finely balanced given the delay of 10 years, it would have been equitable to allow the claim to continue under s 33.

The claimants' appeals on s 14 allowed. The defendant's cross-appeals dismissed. Appeals of MCK and CD dismissed. JS appeals on limitation and liability allowed.

NB: Much of this reasoning has since been disapproved: *B v Nugent Care Society* (p315). The vicarious liability claims for trespass would now also be considered under s 11/s 14/s 33: *A v Hoare* (p287). The approach to knowledge is no longer good law: *Adams v Bracknell Forest BC* (p292); *McCoubrey v Ministry of Defence*. It is also no longer correct to say that there is a heavy burden on a claimant to show that the limitation period should be disapplied: *A v Hoare* (p287), *Cain v Francis* (p360), *B v Nugent Care Society* (p315) and *Sayers v Chelwood* (p642). Finally, the heavy presumption in favour of a trial of limitation as preliminary issue is now doubtful: *Raggett v Society of Jesus Trust 1929 for Roman Catholic Purposes* (p617).

Kamar v Nightingale

Limitation Act 1980, s 33

QBD (Eady J) **[2007] EWHC 2982 (QB); [2008] PNLR 15**

The claimant had been sentenced to five years' imprisonment for grievous bodily harm, together with four years to run concurrently for threats to kill, as a result of a criminal trial which had concluded in December 1997. He had also been charged with an offence of obtaining a passport and opening a bank account under a false name. The convictions were subsequently set aside by the Court of Appeal in March 2009 because there was no good character direction in the summing up. The court commented that the defendant, who was the barrister who represented the claimant at the trial, should have introduced the claimant's good character in the course of the proceedings.

The claimant brought a claim for personal injury on the basis that the defendant's negligence had led him to suffer serious mental health problems. The claim was intimated to the defendant in January 2006. Proceedings issued in December 2006 and were served in March 2007. Limitation was tried as a preliminary issue. The judge, whilst holding that the claimant possessed the relevant knowledge by October 2008 and that the claim was thus six years out of time, allowed it to proceed under s 33. The defendant appealed. He submitted that the judge gave no reason for concluding that he would not be prejudiced on issues of causation and quantum by extending the limitation period as he did; and, in seeking to rebut the claimant's case that the negligence led to serious mental health problems, he would wish to argue that there were other contributing factors, and that he would wish to instruct an expert to assess the claimant's mental state as it was nine years previously.

Held:

(i) The circumstances of this case (in contrast to others in which the limitation period had only been extended by a small margin) engaged the primary public policy consideration underlying the limitation regime that people should not find themselves vexed by stale claims. Nor could the deprivation of the limitation defence be described as a windfall.

(ii) It was plain that there would be enormous difficulties for the defendant to reconstruct the claimant's mental state at the material times, yet that point was not addressed by the judge. It was also clear that at least two other sources of stress and anxiety had been removed in the intervening years. That would make it extremely difficult for the court, or for any expert psychiatrist, to assess the impact of negligence at that time in the light of the position as it then stood.

(iii) The other important issue on delay was how to assess the significance of the omission to introduce good character. If the defendant had referred to the claimant's good character at the trial, it might have led the Crown to refer to other charges which lay in the background at the time, namely those related to the bank account and passport. The judge concluded that a good character direction would have been quite likely to result in an acquittal, but what he did not address was the issue of what the Crown would have done if character had been introduced.

(iv) For those reasons, the judge's conclusions were flawed. Those were plainly relevant matters, both as to mental health and the impact of the pending criminal charges, which were required to be weighed and taken into account in deciding what was equitable.

(v) There was nothing to outweigh the prejudice faced by the defendant. The claimant was aware of his mental health problems many years previously and could have consulted a doctor much nearer the time with a view to assessing his chances of bringing proceedings for negligence. The delay was culpable and there was no reasonable excuse for it. Moreover, the claimant's causation case appeared weak.

Appeal allowed.

The Kashmir

Maritime Conventions Act 1911, s 8

Court of Appeal [1923] P 85; 39 TLR 197

The claimant (Mrs Mary Trimpe) was the mother of Julius Trimpe, an American soldier who lost his life on 6 October 1918 in a collision between the Otranto and the Kashmir in which 400 drowned. In 1920, in an action between the Admiralty (which had requisitioned the Otranto) and P&O (owners of the Kashmir) it was decided that both vessels were equally to blame. In April 1921 a decree was made that limited the liability of P&O for claims for death and personal injuries and limited the time for bringing in claims to three months.

The claimant's writ was issued 5 September 1922. She issued a summons asking that the time for bringing her action be extended, notwithstanding that both the two years allowed under the Maritime Conventions Act 1911 and the two months fixed by the decree in the limitation proceedings had expired.

Hill J dismissed her summons. The only ground on which her claim for indulgence was based was that it was not until shortly before May 1922 that she had become aware that she had a right of action against the owners of the Kashmir. But she must have known that her son had lost his life in the collision. The claimant appealed. More than 350 claims depended on the outcome.

Held: the mere fact that she was ignorant of her legal rights was not sufficient ground for extending the time. The judge had not acted on any wrong principle in exercising his discretion. The appeal must be dismissed.

Kaur and another v CTP Coil Ltd

CPR 3, 7

Court of Appeal [2001] CP Rep 34; LTL 10/7/2000

The claimant's claimed damages for injuries allegedly suffered whilst working for the defendant. It was agreed that the date of knowledge in both cases was 28 July 1996. The claim forms and particulars were sent to the court for issue on 13 July 1999 and returned to the solicitor on 22 July 1999. The solicitor mistakenly thought that they had been issued on 21 July 1999 despite the forms clearly stating that they had been issued on the 14 July 1999. Proceedings were not served until 18 November 1999, outside the four-month period allowed, in part because of difficulties with the schedules of special damages. The judge held that the claimants had taken all reasonable steps to serve the claim forms but had been unable to do so and therefore fell within CPR 7.6(3)(b). He extended time for service. The defendant appealed.

Held:

(i) The judge had erred in finding that the claimants fell within CPR 7.6(3)(b). Problems with collating a schedule of special damages did not go to the actual process of service. In any event, the reason for the failure was the solicitor's mistake as to the date.

(ii) A claimant in these circumstances could no more rely on CPR 3.9 to mitigate the rules of service than on CPR 3.10 (*Vinos v Marks & Spencer* (p701) followed).

Appeal allowed.

Keenan v Miller Insulation & Engineering Ltd

Limitation Act 1939, s 2   **Accrual of cause of action**

Piers Ashworth QC   **8 December 1987**

From August 1952 to May 1953 the claimant (Thomas Keenan) worked with substantial quantities of asbestos in the defendants' employment. In 1985 he was diagnosed as suffering from fibrosis. His writ was issued in 1986. The defendants' case was that his cause of action accrued before 6 June 1954 and was statute barred.

At a trial of the limitation issue, evidence was given that as part of the body's defence mechanisms polymorph neutrofils attack asbestos particles and in the process create chemicals which may cause some local internal inflammation. In many cases the inflammation might be transient, but in some it would eventually occur in sufficient quantities to result subsequently in fibrosis.

It was found that there must be an individual susceptibility for this to occur, and that there was no damage to the claimant's lungs of any significance (nothing that a doctor would describe as damage) until well after June 1954.

Held:

(i)   Damage was something different from the defence mechanisms activated by the inhalation of asbestos fibres and different from the claimant's inherent susceptibility. Damage occurs when more than minimal changes occur in the lung, even though that time may be well before x-ray examination would reveal them.

(ii)   No damage occurred to the claimant until many years after June 1954. Therefore the defendants could not rely on the Limitation Act 1939.

(iii)   Accordingly, the claimant could rely on s 11 of the Limitation Act 1980, the requirements of which he had satisfied. His case had been brought in time.

Arnold v Central Electricity Generating Board (p306) distinguished.

Kelly v Bastible

Limitation Act 1980, s 33

Court of Appeal   **[1997] 8 Med LR 15;**
                                                [1997] PNLR 227; (1997) 36 BMLR 51

The claimant was born on 5 February 1965. He suffered cerebral palsy during a very difficult delivery. Proceedings were issued on 22 March 1990 and limitation heard as a preliminary issue. The judge held that the claimant had knowledge from early 1984 at the latest. The claim was thus statute barred. On the basis of *Hartley v Birmingham City District Council* (p465), the judge felt obliged to exercise his s 33 discretion because the Medical Defence Union had been prejudiced as 'insurers' and not the defendant himself. The defendant appealed.

Held:

(i)   Defendant and insurers were for the purposes of limitation to be treated as a composite entity (*Hartley* considered). Nil weight should be attached to the bare fact that the defendant is insured.

(ii)   A defendant's lack of insurance can be a relevant factor.

(iii)   If the judge had not felt himself bound by his misinterpretation of the insurance point he would not have allowed the action to proceed due to the effect of the delay on the cogency of evidence. There was no reason to interfere with that decision.

Appeal allowed.

Kenneth Allison Ltd and others v A E Limehouse & Co (A Firm)

Service of writ   **RSC Ord 10, r(1); Ord 65, r 2; Ord 81, r 3**

House of Lords   **[1991] 3 WLR 671**

On 5 October 1987 the claimants issued a writ claiming damages for negligence against the defendants, a firm of chartered accountants. On 4 October 1988 Mr Swann, on the instructions of the claimants' solicitors, went to the defendants' office. The receptionist called Mrs Morgan, the senior partner's personal assistant. Mr Swann showed her the writ. She went to speak to Mr Hall, a partner, who told her that she might accept it. She returned to the reception area and told Mr Swann that she had been authorised to accept the writ. He handed her a sealed copy of the writ together with an acknowledgement of service form.

The defendants subsequently applied for an order setting aside service of the writ. This application was allowed on appeal by McCullough J who declared that it had not been duly served. The claimants' appeal was dismissed by the Court of Appeal. They appealed to the House of Lords.

Held:

(i)   The writ had not been served personally on Mr Hall in accordance with RSC Ord 10, r 1(1), Ord 65, r 2 and Ord 81, r 3. Personal service requires that the document be handed to the person to be served or, if he will not accept it, that he be told what the document contains and the document be left with or near him.

(ii)   However, the ad hoc agreement in question achieved valid service. If one party, knowing that another wishes to serve notice upon him, requests or authorises the other to do so in a particular way which is outside the rules and the other does so, then, since nothing in Ord 10 prohibits such consensual service, the party so served cannot be heard to say that the service was not valid.

NB: The continuing validity of these observations under the CPR has yet to be tested.

Kennett v Brown and another

Limitation Act 1980, s 35

Court of Appeal   **[1988] 2 All ER 600;**
[1988] 1 WLR 582; 132 SJ 752

On 15 July 1983 the claimant (Karen Kennett) was a pillion passenger on a motor cycle ridden by Mr Brown when it came into collision with another ridden by Mr Teagle. Within three years the claimant sued Brown and, when he blamed Teagle, joined Teagle as second defendant. Teagle made a claim for contribution against Brown.

Later, a short time after the third anniversary of the accident, Brown served a contribution notice on Teagle in which he claimed (a) an indemnity and (b) damages for his (Brown's) own personal injuries. At the hearing of Brown's application for directions, the district registrar referred to s 35 of the Limitation Act 1980 and held that Brown's claim in respect of his own injuries could not proceed unless and until there was an application under s 33 to disapply the ordinary limitation period.

Sir Douglas Frank reversed the registrar's decision on appeal, directing that it was for Teagle to raise the issue of limitation by pleading in the contribution proceedings, at which stage it would be for Brown to make his application under s 33. Teagle appealed.

Held:

(i)   Brown's claim against Teagle fell within s 35(1)(b) of the Limitation Act 1980. The effect of s 35(1) was to cause that claim to relate back, so far as its commencement date was concerned, to the date of the original action.

(ii)   Whilst s 35(1) would prevent Teagle ever pleading s 11, it did not prevent his relying on s 35(3). His case would be that, subject to any application under s 33, Brown's claim could not succeed.

(iii)   The provision in s 35(3) that the court shall not 'allow a new claim within subsection (1)(b) above, other than an original set-off or counterclaim, to be made in the course of any action after the expiry of any time limit under this Act ...' did not stop such a claim from being started. It simply stopped it from succeeding.

(iv)   Accordingly, the district registrar was in error in trying to intervene at the stage in which he did. The judge's directions should stand.

Distinguished in *Howe v David Brown Tractors (Retail) Ltd* (p483).

Ketteman and others v Hansel Properties Ltd

Limitation Act 1939, s 2   **Amendment of defence**

House of Lords   **[1988] 1 All ER 38; [1987] AC 189;**
[1987] 2 WLR 312

In 1973–75 the five claimants purchased houses with faulty foundations. Between 11 August and 9 September 1976 these began to show signs of structural damage, in the form of cracks to the walls. On 27 May 1980 the claimants issued a writ against the builders. On 25 June 1982 they obtained leave to join the architects as defendants, but never served a copy of the reissued writ on them. However, they sent them a copy of the statement of claim, and on 6 October 1982 the architects served a defence and thereafter acted as if they had been properly joined.

In the course of closing speeches at the trial, the architects applied for and were granted leave to amend their defence to plead, inter alia, that they had not been effectively joined until 6 October 1982 which was more than six years after the cracks in the walls had occurred. HH Judge Hayman hearing official referees' business also granted an application by the claimant for the order of 25 June 1982 to be amended to provide for the joinder of the architects as defendants to take effect from 30 July 1982 and gave judgment for three of the claimants against the architects. The Court of Appeal upheld the judge's decision on different grounds. The architects appealed.

Held:

(i)   A latent defect in a building did not give rise to a cause of action until damage occurred. The limitation period began to run when the cracks in the walls occurred in August and September 1976.

(ii)   Although the amended writ had never been served on the architects, they waived the necessity for such service by serving a defence and thus became parties to the action on 6 October 1982.

(iii)   When the claimant's action against the architects was brought, it was time barred.

(iv)   However, when a defendant decided not to plead a procedural bar, such as a limitation defence, before trial and fought the case on its merits, it was not open to him to amend his defence during the final stages of the trial in order to plead the procedural defence when it had become apparent that he was likely to lose.

(v)   Accordingly, the architects should not have been allowed to amend their defence to plead they had not been joined until 6 October 1982. In the absence of that defence, the claimants were entitled to succeed on their claim.

NB: This case was governed by s 2 of the Limitation Act 1939, not ss 2 and 35 of the Limitation Act 1980.

Kew v Bettamix Ltd and others

Limitation Act 1980, s 11, s 14, s 33

Court of Appeal **[2006] EWCA Civ 1535**

The claimant claimed for vibration white finger against his employers. In the early 1990s he had experienced numbness in his fingers but attributed it to age. By the late 1990s he had appreciated that age might not have been the only cause. Following a routine occupational health assessment in March 2000, the claimant's doctor informed him that his symptoms might be attributable to work. This was confirmed in July 2000. Proceedings were issued in April 2004. Limitation was heard as a preliminary issue.

The judge identified the relevant date of knowledge as being July 2000 but exercised her discretion to disapply the limitation period, finding that the defendant would not be unduly prejudiced by the delay and that it was equitable to allow the claim continue taking into account the financial value of the claim to the claimant and the potential cost to the defendant. She also ordered the defendant to pay all the costs of the limitation issue notwithstanding their success on primary limitation.

The defendant appealed.

Held:

(i) An injured person had to have sufficient knowledge to make it reasonable for him acquire further knowledge of the link between his injury and his prior working conditions (*Haward v Fawcetts* (p469) considered).

(ii) In the early 1990s there was no basis for suggesting that the claimant had considered, or should have considered, that his symptoms were attributable to anything other than ageing.

(iii) In the late 1990s there was no evidence that the claimant had any idea of the link between his working conditions and his condition. His concession that he knew that his condition might not have been caused solely by age did not constitute evidence that he knew what the other cause might have been.

(iv) However, the claimant had constructive knowledge from March 2000 following the discussion with his doctor. Although the claimant was not expressly told of the link, the doctor's conclusions demonstrated that there was a real possibility that working conditions caused his injury and, for a reasonable man, required investigation (*Adams v Bracknell Forest BC* (p292) considered).

(v) The judge's exercise of her s 33 discretion had been open to her. Proportionality was a relevant factor (*Robinson v St Helens MBC* (p628), *McGhie v British Telecommunications plc* (p553) and *Adams* considered).

(vi) Section 33(3)(c) (the defendant's conduct) included forensic tactics but did not exclude other conduct (*Hodgson v Imperial Tobacco* (p478) doubted).

(vii) There was no reason for the defendant to bear the entire costs of the preliminary issue. The hearing had largely been concerned with the issues of knowledge and the identity of the employers, both of which the claimant lost. The order would be varied to one requiring the defendant to pay 65% of the claimant's costs of and incidental to the primary issue.

Appeal allowed in part.

Khairule v North West SHA

Limitation Act 1980, s 14, s 33

QBD (Cox J) **[2008] EWHC 1537 (QB)**

The claimant had been born by emergency caesarean section in June 1981 and was subsequently diagnosed as suffering from athetoid cerebral palsy with preservation of intellect. In March

2006, at age 25, he issued proceedings against the defendant health authority alleging that his brain damage was caused by the staff attending his mother's labour. The defendant pleaded limitation, which was heard as a preliminary issue.

The claimant had experienced a difficult home life, leaving at the age of 16 to become a resident college student. He was told very little about the circumstances of his birth or any possible reason for his disability. Although his physical disabilities were severe, his intellect was fully intact. He moved into his own flat in November 2002, when he bought his own computer. He struggled with independent living. He was alerted to the possibility of bringing a claim during discussions with friends also suffering from cerebral palsy but benefiting from a better lifestyle due to compensation received. This was in 2002. Having conducted his own internet searches, he consulted solicitors in February 2004. A request for medical records was made in August 2004.

The defendant conceded that the claimant did not have actual knowledge of the relevant s 14 matters until within three years of proceedings commencing, but contended that he had constructive knowledge before that. The claimant's case was that his date of both actual and constructive knowledge was in November 2005, when he received supportive expert opinion confirming that his injury was capable of being attributed to acts or omissions relied on by him as constituting negligence. In the alternative, he sought relief under s 33.

Held:

(i)   The person contemplated in s 14(3) is a person who is in the same position, in objective terms, as the claimant. Whilst the test for knowledge was objective, that did not prevent the claimant's objective circumstances being taken into account in asking when a reasonable person in his circumstances, suffering from athetoid cerebral palsy and with the same level of disability and intellect, would have had the curiosity to begin investigating with expert help whether his injury could be considered capable of being attributed to something the hospital staff did or did not do at the time of his birth.

(ii)   Personal, subjective characteristics were to be disregarded, save to the extent that any such characteristic was a direct result of the injury (*McCoubrey v Ministry of Defence* (p548) and *A v Hoare* (p287) applied, *Adams v Bracknell Forest BC* (p292) and *Catholic Care (Diocese of Leeds) v Y (Kevin Raymond)* [2006] EWCA Civ 1534 considered).

(iii)   When assessing the extent to which someone was reasonably to be expected to be curious as to the cause of his particular disability, it was appropriate to distinguish between someone who had lived with disability from birth and someone who suffered injury in his later years. The claimant's condition could not be regarded as a trigger for fixing the date of knowledge of attribution. His cerebral palsy was part of him and he had lived with it for as long as he could remember. However, gradually over time the claimant gained independence, experience and, by the end of 2002, unrestricted access to the internet.

(iv)   As a result, pursuant to s 14(3), taking into account the claimant's circumstances in asking the question set out above, he had constructive knowledge of attribution by the end of 2002 and his claim was statute barred unless it could be saved by s 33.

(v)   In deciding whether it would be equitable for an action to proceed pursuant to s 33, the overall question was whether it would be equitable to disapply the limitation provisions, having regard to the balance of potential prejudice in all the circumstances of the case (*Horton v Sadler* (p482) and *A v Hoare* applied). The nature of the burden of proof on a claimant for the court to exercise its s 33 discretion depended on the strength or weakness of the evidence available, and to exercise that discretion in a claimant's favour was not to be viewed as an 'exceptional indulgence' (*KR v Bryn Alyn Community (Holdings) Ltd (In Liquidation)* (p505) doubted).

(vi)   In the instant case, the delay which occurred outside the limitation period, considered pursuant to s 33(3)(a), was understandable given the claimant's particular characteristics and general circumstances. Further, when considering the effects of the passage of time generally and the s 33 discretion, the crucial question was whether it was still possible to have a fair trial of the issues on the available evidence.

(vii)   In the instant case, the expert evidence suggested that the matters of factual dispute were capable of being resolved on the available material, with the assistance of witnesses and reconstructions by medical experts. There was no evidence from the defendant for the purposes of the limitation hearing to make good the assertion that the cogency of the witness evidence was compromised by the further delay. To the contrary, the defence set out a positive factual case. The reality was that the factual witnesses would rely at trial upon both the contents of the hospital records and what was then their usual practice. This was standard territory for clinical negligence disputes, and this would have been the position even if the claimant's claim was not statute barred. The loss of the CTG trace, whilst a serious problem, was not an insurmountable one.

(viii) On all the available evidence, it would be equitable to disapply the limitation period and allow the claim to proceed.

Preliminary issue determined in favour of claimant.

Khan v Ainslie and others

Limitation Act 1980, s 11, s 14

Waterhouse J   **19 February 1992**

On 13 June 1983 the claimant (Mr Khan) was examined by the first defendant, an ophthalmic medical practitioner. She inserted mydriatic drops in his left eye. He felt considerable pain in it and reported to the other effective defendant, a locum general practitioner, who gave him painkillers. Another doctor subsequently referred him to the local hospital where on 27 June 1983 a left iridectomy operation was performed. It proved to be unsuccessful, and the claimant was left without sight in his left eye.

In December 1983 he complained to the Family Practitioner Committee that the drops had caused his injury. In January 1984 he consulted solicitors who in January 1985 received a negative expert report that praised the first defendant. After his solicitors' supplementary questions were answered by the expert, his legal aid certificate was discharged in March 1985.

At the end of 1987, the claimant saw a television programme featuring AVMA. He contacted them and they referred him to new solicitors who issued a protective writ on 30 November 1988. In February 1989 they obtained an expert opinion that the claimant had lost the sight of his left eye totally 'as the result of closed angle glaucoma and of the delay in its treatment.' In June 1989 they received a further favourable report from a professor in general practice.

The writ was subsequently served. A preliminary trial was ordered.

Held:

(i)   It was only when the first favourable expert's report was received in February 1989 that the claimant first had knowledge that the injury to his left eye was attributable to the defendants' acts or omissions (delay, not drops) that were alleged to constitute negligence: s 14(1).

(ii)   There was no unreasonable failure by the claimant's first solicitors to follow up the first expert's negative report. Having regard to the general tenor of this report, there was no reason to infer that this expert would have reported favourably if different questions had been put to him. The claimant should not be fixed with constructive knowledge in early 1985: s 14(3).

(iii) Accordingly, his action had been commenced in time: s 11(4).

Kirby v Eli Lilly & Co and others

Limitation Act 1980, s 11, s 14

Court of Appeal   **[1992] 3 Med LR 394**

See *Nash v Eli Lilly & Co* (M) (p568)

Kirby v Leather

Limitation Act 1939, s 22

Court of Appeal   **[1965] 2 WLR 1318;**
[1965] 2 All ER 441; [1965] 2 QB 367

On 15 May 1959 the claimant (David Kirby), then aged 24, was riding his motor scooter when he collided with a van and was thrown on to his head. After he recovered consciousness several days later, he was badly affected mentally and his behaviour was extremely abnormal. After a time he was able to some extent to appreciate (from being told by others) something of what had happened to him. However, he could not concentrate on it long enough to understand the nature and extent of any claim that he might have. He had no insight into his own mental state. He was incapable of instructing a solicitor properly or of exercising any reasonable judgment on a possible settlement.

In August 1963 he went to a firm of solicitors and told a managing clerk there that he wanted to know where his scooter was. He could not remember about the accident. The managing clerk made enquiries and took up the case. On 2 October 1963 a writ for personal injury damages was issued. The defendant pleaded that the action was statute barred.

Payne J found in favour of the claimant on limitation but held that the accident had been due to his own fault. The Court of Appeal found that the defendant was two-thirds to blame and considered his respondent's notice on limitation.

Held: the claimant had been of unsound mind and under a disability from the moment of his accident onwards. There was ample evidence on which the judge was entitled so to hold. Accordingly, the action was not statute barred.

NB: The same result would now be reached under s 28 of the Limitation Act 1980.

Per Denning LJ: 'Under the statutes of limitation an action for personal injuries "shall not be brought after the expiration of three years from the date on which the cause of action accrued"; see s 2(1) of the Limitation Act 1939, as amended by s 2(1) of the Law Reform (Limitation of Actions &c.) Act 1954. In calculating the three years, one excludes the day of the accident itself; see *Marren v Dawson Bentley & Co Ltd* (p543). The accident here took place on May 15, 1959. The cause of action accrued on that date. The three years started at midnight on May 15–16, 1959 and ran up to midnight on May 15–16, 1962, and then expired. There is an extension of time when a person is under a disability:

"If on the date when any right of action accrued ... the person to whom it accrued was under a disability, the action may be brought at any time before the expiration of three years ... from the date when the person ceased to be under a disability" (s 22 of the Act of 1939 as amended by s 2(2) and s 8(3) of the Act of 1954).

A person is deemed to be under a disability "while he is an infant or of unsound mind"; see s 31(2) of the Act of 1939. In this particular case, the right of action accrued at 8.05pm on May 15 1959. If on that date David Kirby was under a disability, the period of three years would not begin to run until he had ceased to be under a disability. "On the date" means, I think, at any time before the end of the day, because the law takes no account of fractions of a day.'

Per Winn LJ: '... care must be taken not to confuse the decision which has been announced in these judgments with any such proposition (as was indeed advanced to the court in argument) as that there can be a suspension of the running of the statutory limitation period during such time as an injured person is unconscious or ill or in a state of delirium without more being shown. In this case I am satisfied, as are my lords, that from the moment when David Kirby suffered these injuries to his head, he then became, and thereafter at all material times remained, of unsound mind in the sense in which my lords have defined that term for the present purpose. Had he merely been unconscious, as indeed he was for some three weeks, unable to recognise any member of his family, as indeed he was for some six weeks, but had there been lacking cogent and convincing medical evidence that throughout that period of unconsciousness and amnesia his mental powers had been so affected as to make him in the relevant sense of unsound mind, I would not have thought that there would have been any suspension of the running of the statutory period of limitation.

In *Re Martin's Trusts, Land, Building, Investment and Cottage Improvement Co v Martin, Re Martin (5)*, Cotton, LJ, concerned then with the question whether there should be a fresh trustee appointed on the ground of unsoundness of mind of an existing trustee, said this:

"He could not be considered of unsound mind within the Act [the Trustee Act 1850] if his incapacity was a temporary one, arising from an accident – as, for instance, concussion of the brain, or from illness of a temporary character; but he is to be so considered where he is subject to a permanent incapacity of mind, rendering him incapable of attending to business."

As I see it, there may be cases, bearing in mind the great advances made by medical skill nowadays and by modern science, where, following on a prolonged period of delirium or unconsciousness involving factual inability to attend to any material matters, a victim of an accident may recover and it may be impossible to postulate that throughout his period of functional incapacity due to those conditions of illness, he was of unsound mind.'

Kitchen v Royal Air Forces Association and others

Limitation Act 1939, s 26   **Solicitors' negligence**

Court of Appeal   **[1958] 2 All ER 241; [1958] 1 WLR 563**

On 22 May 1945 Mr Kitchen, a leading aircraftman in the RAF, turned on the main switch at the control box at his home. He was electrocuted and died. The case of the claimant (his widow, Mrs Hilda Kitchen) was forwarded to the second defendants, a firm of solicitors, who allowed the one year limitation period under the Fatal Accidents Act 1846 to expire without informing the claimant of it and without having obtained expert evidence in accordance with counsel's advice.

In October 1946 the claimant herself wrote to the electricity company whose solicitor telephoned the second defendants. They agreed that the company would make a donation of £100 to the first defendants on the understanding that they would distribute it to the claimant. A condition was that she should not know the originator of the donation. The transaction duly took place, subject to the second defendants deducting five guineas for their charges.

On 30 September 1955 the claimant sued the second defendants for damages for professional negligence. They pleaded that her action was statute barred under s 2 of the Limitation Act 1939. She relied on s 26 as the basis that her right of action had been concealed by their fraud. Lloyd-Jacob J found in her favour. The second defendants appealed.

Held:

(i)   A necessary consequence of the concealment of the original donor, as the second defendants must have realised, was that it also concealed from the claimant the real effect of their having thrown away in May 1946 any case which she may have possessed under the Fatal Accidents Acts.

(ii)   Fraud is not limited to common law fraud or deceit. No degree of moral turpitude was necessary to establish fraud within s 26.

(iii)   The concealment was intentional and did, in fact, benefit and save the interests of the second defendants. It was sufficient to prevent them from relying on the defence of the Limitation Act 1939.

NB: The same outcome would today be more simply reached through s 32(1)(b) of the Limitation Act 1980.

Kitt v South West Peninsula Health Authority

CPR 6

Exeter County Court (HHJ Overend)   **LTL 10/1/2005**

The claimant claimed for psychiatric damage arising out of a misdiagnosis of a heart condition. Proceedings were issued on 12 September 2003. On 25 September 2003 the claimant sent a letter of claim to the defendant's solicitors, who responded by stating that they had no instructions to accept service. The claim form was sent to the defendant's solicitors on 6 January 2004, who replied on 12 January 2004 by reiterating that they had no authority to accept service.

The claimant then served the claim form directly on the defendant outside the validity period and simultaneously applied for service to dispensed with under CPR 6.9. The district judge granted the application on the basis that as the defendant's solicitors had received the claim form no-one had been prejudiced. The defendant appealed.

Held:

(i)   The claimant had made an ineffective attempt to effect service by one of the permitted methods, first class post. This case therefore fell into category 2 as identified in *Anderton v Clwyd CC* (p303). The matter was brought to the defendant's attention within the relevant period. The only reason service was not effective was because the solicitors were not authorised to accept it, although they were authorised to act for the defendant in all other respects.

(ii)   The district judge did not apply the guidance given by the Court of Appeal in *Wilkey v BBC* (p717) and *Cranfield v Bridgegrove* (p389) that a strict approach was to be taken to dispensation of service, which should only be allowed in exceptional circumstances. His discretion was therefore flawed and had to be reconsidered anew.

(iii)   None of the matters raised by the claimant either singly or cumulatively amounted to exceptional circumstances. This case therefore did not fall within the limited discretionary power contemplated by the Court of Appeal.

Appeal allowed.

Knight v Rochdale Healthcare NHS Trust

Limitation Act 1980 s 10

QBD (Crane J)   **[2003] EWHC 1831;**
[2004] 1 WLR 371; [2003] 4 All ER 416

The claimant, a surgeon, settled a personal injuries action against him by a former patient on 24 October 2000. A consent order reflecting the agreement was made on 8 November 2000. The claimant brought an action against the defendant under the Civil Liability (Contributions) Act 1978. s 10 of the 1980 Act provided a two-year limitation period. Proceedings were issued on 1 November 2002. The defendant pleaded limitation which was heard as a preliminary issue.

Held: Time began to run whenever a firm settlement was reached. A consent order was not a necessary constituent of such a settlement.

Claim struck out.

NB: Approved by the Court of Appeal in *Aerlingus v Gildacroft Ltd* (p295).

Kuenyehia and others v International Hospitals Group Ltd

CPR 6, 7

**[2006] EWCA Civ 121; (2006) Times,
17 February; LTL 25/2006**

This was a commercial dispute. The claimants, having previously corresponded with the defendant by fax, issued proceedings it. The defendant's solicitors had no instructions to accept service. On the last day for service the claimants sent a copy of the claim form by courier and by fax to the defendant's legal department. The defendant argued that service had not been effected. The claimant successfully applied to dispense with service under CPR 6.9, the judge holding that the failure to obtain written consent to service by fact was a comparative minor failing. The defendant appealed.

Held:

(i) If time had expired under CPR 7.5(2) service should only be dispensed with under CPR 6.9 had expired in exceptional circumstances. Even then, discretion was unlikely to be exercised unless the claimant had either made an ineffective attempt to serve by one of the methods set down by CPR 6.2, or had served in time in a manner involving a minor departure from one of the permitted methods of service (*Vinos v Marks & Spencer* (p701), *Godwin v Swindon Borough Council* (p444), *Anderton v Clwyd CC* (p303), *Wilkey v BBC* (p717) considered).

(ii) Although the judge had posed the right question, he had given the wrong answer. The failure to obtain written consent as required by the practice direction was not a minor departure.

(iii) Further, the judge had failed to consider whether the current case was an exceptional one. It was not. The fact that the claimants had been in faxed communication with the defendant could not assist them. Firstly, every previous faxed communication appears to have been accompanied by a hard copy. Secondly, a party's willingness to receive faxed correspondence cannot support an assumption that it is willing to accept service of proceedings by fax. Thirdly, the fact of well-established lines of communication made the failure to obtain the defendant's consent less excusable. Fourthly, given that the claim form had been couriered to the defendant's solicitors in London, there was no reason it could not also been couriered to the defendant's offices on the outskirts of London.

(iv) That the claim form was received within the four-month period did not render this case exceptional.

(v) Prejudice to the defendant was a reason for not dispensing with service, but the absence of such prejudice could not usually be a reason for so dispensing, if ever.

(vi) The rules regarding service were to be strictly observed. The court would not provide relied in a case such as this where a party had waited until the very last day to serve the claim form and, despite knowing the defendant's address and being able to properly serve it, had failed to do so.

Appeal allowed.

Lakah Group v Al Jazeera Satellite Channel

CPR 6, 7

Court of Appeal
**[2003] EWCA (Civ) 1781;
(2004) BCC 703; LTL 9/12/2003**

The claimant had purported to served the claim form by leaving it with an employee of an English company that made programmes for the defendant, a Quatar broadcaster. The employee was at the English company's studio premises. The court held that the employee in question was not a person holding a senior position within the meaning of CPR PD 6.2 and that English company's studio was not a place of business of the defendant, it holding merely a transient or irregular connection with the defendant's activities. Therefore the requirements for service imposed by CPR 6.5(6) had not been met. The judge refused to the claimant's application to dispense with service, made more than three months after the expiry of the validity period set out at CPR 7.5. The claimant sought permission to appeal.

Held:

(i)   The judge had applied the correct tests for deciding whether service had been effective and his findings of fact in this regard could not be challenge.

(ii)   There was ample material to support the judge's refusal to exercise his discretion to dispense with service. The appeal did not have a real prospect of success. Application dismissed.

Langdon v Corus UK Ltd

Limitation Act 1980, s 14   **Alternative dispute resolution – waiver**

Swansea County Court (HHJ Hickinbottom)   **[2002] CLY 462**

The claimant brought a claim for damages for noise-induced hearing loss, which, he alleged, resulted from being exposed to excessive levels of noise at work due to the defendant's negligence and breach of statutory duty. The claimant had been employed as an electrician for approximately 20 years since 1982 by the defendant and its predecessor. In March 1996, he began to suspect that his hearing problems were caused by noise at work and he completed a union claim form. He was examined in July 1996 by a consultant ENT surgeon, who confirmed that he was suffering from bilateral high tone sensory neural deafness caused by noise during his employment. The claimant's claim proceeded under an agreement entered into between the defendant's insurers, Iron Trades, and various unions, including his own. Under the agreement, upon refusal of an offer of compensation made by Iron Trades, the claimant was required to serve proceedings within 12 months, in which event they would be deemed to have been served as on the date of receipt by the defendant of the letter of claim for limitation purposes. In default of service of proceedings within that time, they were to be treated as issued and served on the actual dates of those events. Various correspondence followed and, on 11 August 2000, Iron Trades wrote a letter, amounting to a rejection of the claim. The claimant issued proceedings on 11 July 2001. The preliminary issue to be decided was whether proceedings had been brought within the limitation period.

Held:

(i)   The claimant did not have the requisite knowledge for the purposes of s 14 until 13 July 1996, when he received the consultant's report.

(ii)   The Iron Trades agreement, which was effectively a form of ADR scheme allowing the parties an opportunity to replace the uncertainties of litigation with a scheme providing for relatively modest payments of compensation, was laudable, and such arrangements were endorsed by the Court of Appeal in *Bytheway v British Steel Corp Plc* (p358). It was proper to interpret the agreement as applying equally to rejections of claims as well as offers which were subsequently rejected. Iron Trades had clearly treated the claim as one under the agreement scheme. Under the provisions of the agreement, the issue and service of proceedings by July 2001, which was within 12 months of the August 2000 rejection of the claimant's claim, meant that proceedings were deemed issued and served on the date of receipt of the claim by the insured, namely 13 June 1998. As that was within three years of the date on which L became aware of the injury, the proceedings were issued properly within the primary limitation period.

Preliminary issue decided in favour of the claimant.

Laroche v Spirit of Adventure (UK) Ltd

Court of Appeal
[2009] EWCA Civ 12; [2009] QB 778;
[2009] 3 WLR 351; [2009] Bus LR 954;
[2009] 2 All ER 175; [2009] 2 All ER (Comm) 1149;
[2009] 1 Lloyd's Rep 316; [2009] 1 CLC 1;
[2009] PIQR P12; (2009) 159 NLJ 157;
(2009) Times, 24 March

In August 2003 the claimant was taken in a hot air balloon on a flight organised by the defendant. The flight route was not pre-determined. During the journey, the basket that was attached to the balloon crashed, and the claimant was injured. In June 2004 the defendant entered into voluntary liquidation and was dissolved but was in May 2006 restored to the Register of Companies so that the claimant's claim for damages could be brought. Proceedings were issued in August 2006. The defendant contended that, the claim having been brought outside the relevant two-year period, the cause of action was extinguished by virtue of art 29 of Sch 1 to the Carriage by Air Acts (Application of Provisions) Order 1967. This point was heard as a preliminary issue.

The judge held that the claimant's claim was governed by Sch 1 to the 1967 Order, that the relevant schedule provided the exclusive cause of action and sole remedy available to the claimant, and that the claimant had not brought the proceedings within the two-year period prescribed by art 29 of Sch 1.

The claimant appealed, submitting that (1) the fact that the balloon flight was for recreational purposes meant that Sch 1 to the 1967 Order and the Warsaw Convention on International Carriage by Air 1929 did not apply; (2) the hot air balloon was not an 'aircraft' within the meaning of art 1 of Sch 1 as the judge had held; (3) there was not a 'carriage' of him within the meaning of the same article because the contract of carriage involved agreement as to the point of departure and destination prior to embarkation; (4) he was not a 'passenger' within the meaning of art 17 of Sch 1; and (5) in respect of his permission to appeal, the stopping of time for bringing proceedings following the commencement of a voluntary liquidation was a long-established principle in English law and, therefore, the voluntary liquidation of S suspended the running of the two-year period under art 29.

Held:

(i)   The mere fact that the flight in the hot air balloon was for recreational purposes was not of itself a sufficient reason for concluding that the Convention and Sch 1 did not apply.

(ii)   The natural and ordinary meaning of the word 'aircraft' was wide enough to include a passenger-carrying hot air balloon. The balloon was designed for, and capable of, carrying passengers from one place to another. The fact that it was used for recreational purposes or was not a regular or obvious means of international transport did not mean that it was not an 'aircraft'. The important point was that it was capable of being used for international transport and was so used from time to time. By the terms of art 3 of the 1967 Order, it was intended to apply to 'all' carriage by air not being carriage to which the Convention applied. Accordingly, as the judge held, there was no reason for excluding from the classification of 'aircraft' a hot air balloon designed for the carriage of passengers.

(iii)   It was not necessary for a person to be carried under a contract of a particular type and a contract of carriage did not require an agreement as to departure and destination. The reference in art 1(2) of the Convention to the place of departure and the place of destination, according to the agreement between the parties, was no more than a way of defining the carriage as 'international'.

(iv)   The claimant was a passenger within the meaning of art 17 of Sch 1. He was not on board as a pilot under instruction, he did not contribute to the flight in any way, and so he was not a member of the crew.

(v)   Article 29 did not permit the two-year period to be suspended, interrupted or extended by reference to domestic law. It was (rightly) not disputed by the claimant that article 29 provided a substantive and not merely a procedural time bar. It was also (again rightly) not disputed that Schedule 1 provided a code that is exclusive of any resort to the rules of domestic law. The *travaux preparatoires* to the Warsaw Convention revealed that the proposal to enable domestic courts to suspend or interrupt the calculation of time was rejected in favour of the certainty of a fixed two-year period. The claimant's interpretation would also frustrate the purpose of the Convention that it was to be a uniform international code, which could be applied by the courts of all the high contracting parties without reference to the rules of their own domestic law.

Appeal dismissed.

Law Society and others v Shah and others

Limitation Act 1980, s 35(3)   CPR 17.2

Ch D (Norris J)   [2008] EWHC 2515 (Ch);
[2009] 1 WLR 2254; [2009] 1 All ER 752

The Law Society had issued proceedings against the solicitor defendants for their alleged involvement in the misappropriation of money from client accounts. Some of the defendants were discharged bankrupts but all were insured by the same professional liability insurer, X. The trustee in bankruptcy was joined as a defendant, and X later consented to being made a defendant, on a limited basis, to the actions concerning those of the defendants who were bankrupt. The main proceedings were not amended by the Law Society so as to make any claim against, or seek relief from, X. The defendants later issued a claim against the Law Society alleging that it had breached its duty of care owed to the defendants' clients. Approximately eight years after the Law Society had intervened in the defendants' financial affairs, the defendants and X made an application seeking to insert by re-amendment an additional and new claim alleging that the Law Society had also breached its duties owed to X.

X submitted that, as the new claim was a counterclaim for the purposes of the exception in s 35(3), it could be made outside the limitation period. The Law Society contended that the claim was incapable of being a counterclaim as it had not made a claim against X to which the new claim could run counter.

Held:

(i)   An original counterclaim under s 35(3) referred to any cause of action that might be asserted by an existing defendant against a claimant. The nature of the cause of action on which the counterclaim was founded was not integral to the concept of a counterclaim. All that mattered was that the parties asserting the cause of action were on one side of the record and one of the persons against whom the cause of action might be asserted was on the other side of the record. X's counterclaim was therefore an original counterclaim for the purposes of s 35(3).

(ii)   The court's discretion to grant permission for an amendment, pursuant to CPR 17.2 had to be applied so that a case was dealt with fairly (*Cobbold v Greenwich LBC* unreported, 9 August 1999, CA, applied). Amendment in general ought to be allowed, provided that any prejudice caused by the amendment could be compensated for in costs, and provided that the public interest in the administration of justice was not significantly harmed. In the instant case, that discretion would be exercised to refuse the amendment. The amendment proposed exploited a procedural quirk. X had only been added to the proceedings because some of the defendants had become bankrupt. X had become parties not so that any substantive relief could be claimed against them, but to afford them a real opportunity to defend the claims being brought against the defendants. X were not deploying the new claim as a weapon to defeat a claim being brought against them, but rather as an offensive weapon. That was not the basis upon which consent to the joinder had been obtained. There was no substantial merit in treating the actions in which the bankruptcy point arose so differently from those in which it did not arise.

(iii)   Furthermore, it was not fair to introduce a new claim which was radically different from anything already in the action. The alleged acts and omissions of the Law Society said to constitute breaches of its duty to the clients were significantly different from its acts and omissions which were said to constitute breaches of its duty to X. The differences were sufficiently substantial to justify the view that an already complex matter should not be further complicated and X should be left in the same position in the actions to which they were the defendants as they were in the claims which did not raise the bankruptcy point and in respect of which any claim by X against the Law Society for breach of duty was to be pursued in separate, fresh proceedings.

(iv)   Even if the additional claim did not fall within the specific exception to the general rule in s 35, and the claim sought to be advanced by X was a new action, permission to amend under CPR 17.4 would nevertheless be refused, because X did not cross the threshold clearly stated in that rule that they should already have made a claim.

Application refused.

Lea v Armitage Shanks Group Limited

Limitation Act 1939, s 2D

Swanwick J   19 July 1977

From 1922 the claimant (Harold Lea) worked as a drawer and than as a setter in pottery kilns operated by the defendants. In 1953 he consulted his doctor who diagnosed pneumoconiosis and he was granted a 30% industrial disablement pension. He had a family to support and did his best to go on working until 1962 when he had to give up due to his deteriorating pneumoconiosis. In 1965 his disability was measured at 100%.

He had long since ceased to be a trade union member. The defendants had never had a claim against them for pneumoconiosis. It never occurred to him that he could claim damages until May 1975 when he read a newspaper article. He promptly consulted the solicitors recommended therein. His writ was issued on 30 December 1975.

It was agreed that the primary limitation period expired in 1956. A preliminary trial was held on whether the court's discretion to disapply it should be exercised in his favour under s 2D of the Limitation Act 1939 as amended by the Limitation Act 1975.

Held:

(i)   The length of the delay was 19 years. It was due to the claimant not knowing that he could claim damages: s 2D(3)(a).

(ii)   The distinction between recollecting an accident and a system of work was valid. The facts in this case were absolutely basic. No one who carried out or saw the operation of the kilns could be in any doubt about any of those matters or could fail to recollect them: s 2D(3)(b).

(iii)   His disability had endured ever since the date of accrual of the cause of action and was still enduring and increasing: s 2D(3)(d).

(iv)   He acted promptly and reasonably once he knew that he could claim. The wording 'once he knew' did not extend to constructive knowledge: s 2D(3)(e).

(v)   The prejudice to the claimant of not allowing the action to proceed far outweighed any prejudice to the defendants caused by exercising discretion in the claimant's favour as it was equitable to do. The provisions of s 2A should not apply to this action: s 2D(1).

Buck v English Electric Co Ltd (p353) followed.

Leadbitter v Hodge Finance Ltd and others

Limitation Act 1939, s 2A

Bush J   **[1982] 2 All ER 167**

On 12 September 1976 the claimant (Geoffrey Leadbitter) was driving his three wheeler Reliant Robin car in heavy rain along the A695 in Newcastle upon Tyne. He lost control of the car and crashed into a lamp post. He suffered severe personal injuries and, after three weeks in intensive care, was discharged from hospital in November 1976. He attended as an out-patient until November 1977. After an abortive attempt, he finally returned to work in April 1978.

He remembered nothing about the accident. Around May 1978, due to publicity about the instability of Reliant three wheelers, he instructed solicitors to investigate on the basis that the vehicle might be defective. They obtained the police examiner's report (but not the full police accident report) and a consulting engineer's opinion, pursuant to which in July 1978 they gave negative legal advice.

A BBC programme on the Reliant Robin caused the claimant to instruct other solicitors. On 31 August 1979 counsel advised that the full police report should be obtained. On 12 September 1979 the writ was issued against the hire purchase company, the suppliers and the manufacturers. On 17 October 1979 the police accident report was received and recorded that there was a large puddle extending well into the road; the words 'road flooded' appeared. Subsequently the claimant's solicitors interviewed the attending police officer who described a massive pool of water ankle deep at the point of collision.

On 6 August 1980 an application was made to amend the writ and join the City of Newcastle upon Tyne as fourth defendant. This application was amended on 2 September 1980 when the claimant's solicitors learned that the highway authority concerned was in fact Tyne and Wear City Council. The registrar ordered that the application be adjourned to a High Court judge.

Held:

(i)   The claimant knew that his injuries were attributable to the alleged negligence on 17 October 1979. He knew the fourth defendant's identity on 29 August 1980: s 2A(4)(b).

(ii)   However, it was necessary to take into account knowledge which the claimant might reasonably have been expected to acquire. The facts concerned were not facts ascertainable only with the help of expert advice, so this included any knowledge that his solicitors ought to have acquired: s 2A(8).

(iii)   Apart from a brief spell, he did not return to work until April 1978. Allowing time thereafter for the first solicitors to make the enquiries about the road and weather conditions that they should have made, the notional date when the claimant (and his legal advisers) might reasonably have been expected to have acquired the relevant knowledge was 31 July 1978.

(iv)   Therefore the claimant's claim against the proposed fourth defendant was not statute barred. Leave to amend the writ was given.

Leal v Dunlop Bio-Processes International Ltd

Service of writ out of jurisdiction   **RSC Ord 2, r 1; Ord 11, r 1**

Court of Appeal   **[1984] 2 All ER 207;**
[1984] 1 WLR 874; [1984] LS Gaz R 1523

On 27 May 1978 the claimant (Robert Leal) was injured while working for the defendants in Malaya. Their registered office was in Jersey, outside the jurisdiction. On 20 May 1981 the claimant's writ against them was issued without leave of the court. On 18 May 1982 agents purported to serve it on the defendants in Jersey, again without leave of the court.

The defendants' solicitors issued a summons applying to set aside purported service of the writ and to dismiss the action on the ground that the claimant had failed to obtain leave to serve it out of the jurisdiction pursuant to RSC Ord 11, r 1. The claimant cross-applied for an order under RSC Ord 6, r 8(2) for the renewal of the writ and for leave under Ord 11, r 1 to serve the renewed writ out of the jurisdiction. The registrar dismissed the defendants' application. Neill J allowed the defendants' appeal and dismissed the claimant's application. The claimant appealed.

Held:

(i)   The failure to obtain leave to serve the writ out of the jurisdiction did not render it a nullity. It was an irregularity capable of being cured. RSC Ord 2, r 1 gave the court power to make good the service of the writ, and the judge had the power to give leave retroactively.

(ii)   However, he would have been wrong to do so. The mistake was serious. Correction would have deprived the defendants of a limitation defence. There was no good reason to justify it. It was by no means certain that the claimant would have been able to establish under RSC Ord 11, r 4(2) that the case was a proper one for service out of jurisdiction. It would be wrong to allow him to bypass this restriction, even by accident.

Per Stephenson LJ: 'the procedure for which Ord 11 provides is an exceptional enlargement of our courts' jurisdiction ... The court's restraining hand is an important restriction on the misuse of the procedure, and rule 4(2) underlines its importance.'

Per May LJ: 'I hope and expect that it will only be in the exceptional case that the court will validate after the event the purported service in a foreign country without leave of process issued by an English court.'

Per Slade LJ: 'When seeking the indulgence of the court under Ord 2, r 1, in circumstances such as the present, a plaintiff cannot, in my opinion, expect the court to exercise its discretion more favourably than it would be prepared to exercise it on an application under Ord 6, r 8. If he cannot properly enter through the front door of Ord 6, r 8, he should not be allowed to enter through the back door of Ord 2, r 1.'

Leeson v Marsden and another

CPR 6, 7

Court of Appeal   **[2006] EWCA Civ 20;**
(2006) Times, 3 February; LTL 25/1/2006

See *Collier v Williams* (p380)

Leeson v Marsden and another

Limitation Act 1980, s 33   **Striking out for abuse of process**

QBD (Cox J)   **[2008] EWHC 1011 (QB);**
[2008] LS Law Medical 393; (2008) 103 BMLR 49

The claimant brought clinical negligence proceedings against the first defendant GP (D1) and the second defendant NHS trust (D2). Her case was that, in December 2000, D1 negligently failed to refer her for specialist treatment, and that D2 negligently discharged her from its care. Through her solicitors instructed in January 2001 (H), she intimated the claim in August 2002. D2 admitted liability in part, but D1 failed to serve a letter of response to the letter of claim. The claimant issued a claim form within the primary limitation period on 24 November 2003 but served it one day late on 25 March 2004, by which time any fresh action was time barred. The court at first instance refused the claimant's application to extend time for service. Although her appeal against that refusal was allowed, the refusal was reinstated by the Court of Appeal in January 2006 (see the summary immediately preceding this one).

The claimant instructed solicitors in relation to a professional negligence claim against H but, after the decision in *Horton v Sadler* (p482) in June 2006, which held, contrary to the decision in *Walkley v Precision Forgings Ltd* (p705), that a claimant could issue a second claim out of time and ask the court to exercise its discretion under s 33 to disapply the limitation period, decided instead to issue a second claim against the defendants. This was issued in December 2006 and served in January 2007.

The defendants pleaded limitation and abuse of process. These were heard as preliminary issues. The defendants submitted that the court should first resolve the issue of whether there had been an abuse of process before considering s 33. They argued that the claim should be struck out as abusive because it was indistinguishable from the first claim which, because of the appeals, had used substantial court resources.

Held:

(i)   To require the court to exercise a wholly separate discretion in relation to a free-standing abuse argument, based solely on the grounds of previous deployment of court resources, would place an unwarranted fetter on the court's discretion under s 33 (*Firman v Ellis* (p433) and *Horton v Sadler* (p482) applied).

(ii)   Appropriate use of the court's resources could be considered when the court had regard to 'all the circumstances of the case' under s 33. In any event, the defendants had failed to show that the claimant had misused court resources in relation to her first claim (*Securum Finance Ltd v Ashton (No 1)* [2001] Ch 291 applied). Until the decision in *Horton*, the claimant had no prospect of successfully issuing a second claim and had been justified in pursuing her appeal.

(iii)   The nature of the burden upon a claimant to show that it would be equitable to disapply the limitation provisions would depend upon the strength or weakness of the evidence available (*A v Hoare* (p287) considered, *KR v Bryn Alyn* (p505) doubted).

(iv)   No second claim could have been successfully pursued until the law had changed. The period between the date of expiry of the primary limitation period and the decision in *Horton* should not be weighed in the balance against the claimant in relation to delay under s 33(3)(a) (*Richardson v Watson* (p621) applied).

(v)   There had been no material delay prior to the letters of claim being sent. It was reasonable for the claimant to fully investigate the claims against, and obtain expert evidence in respect of the claims against both defendants before intimating the claim to either.

(vi)   The fault of the claimant's former solicitors was not to be held against the claimant for the purposes of s 33.

(vii)   Whilst there was some prejudice to D1 in the revival of a professional negligence claim that she had thought had finished, it was not great.

(viii) The cogency of the evidence to be adduced, or likely to be adduced, by the defendants was unlikely to be adversely affected by events since the expiry of the limitation period. The continued availability of all the relevant medical records and the opportunity afforded to the defendants within the limitation period to investigate the allegations fully and to take witness statements meant that a fair trial was still possible. There was no evidence in support of the proposition that D1's memory had seriously dimmed.

(ix) D1's failure to respond to the letter of claim was a serious matter to which the court should have regard under s 33(3)(c).

(x) Although D2 had suffered forensic prejudice in disclosing to the claimant a privileged report unfavourable to it in support of the claimant's claim against H, this could be ameliorated by appropriate case management. The court would be willing in principle to make an order limiting the use of that material.

(xi) The costs prejudice to the defendants would be met by ordering that, before the action could continue, the costs of the abortive claim would be paid to the defendants by the claimant (whom H had undertaken to indemnify in this respect).

(xii) The defendants had been ready and able to meet the claim but had elected to take the opportunity that presented itself for a rapid exit from the case and for the transfer of liability from their insurers to H's insurers. In those circumstances it was appropriate for the court to have regard to the effects of that election in weighing prejudice and considering how to exercise its discretion.

(xiii) The claimant had not had an opportunity to litigate her claim. Her decision to expend resources in seeking to persuade the courts to extend time for service had not been unreasonable. Furthermore, even if the claim did not proceed, court resources would be used to pursue a claim against H. In a claim against H, it would be argued that the claimant's damages should be discounted to reflect the chance that the first claim would have failed. She could thus recover only the full value of her lost chance to bring the claim, rather than the full value of the claim if she succeeded against the defendants. The claimant would therefore suffer real and material prejudice if she could not maintain her original claim.

(xiv) Overall, the claimant had discharged the burden upon her under s 33 to satisfy the court that it would be equitable to disapply the limitation period and allow the claim to proceed (*Horton v Sadler* (p482) applied).

Preliminary issues determined in favour of claimant.

Lennon v Alvis Industries plc

Limitation Act 1980, s 11, s 14, s 33

Court of Appeal   **LTL 27/2/2000**

The claimant worked for the defendant until 1981. The claimant issued proceedings in 1998 alleging noise induced hearing loss. The judge found the claimant's actual date of knowledge to have been 1992 and his date of constructive knowledge to have been 1981. However, the judge exercised his s 33 discretion to allow the claim to continue. The defendant appealed and the claimant cross-appealed the finding of constructive knowledge.

Held:

(i) On the cross-appeal, it appeared that the judge may have erred in placing the burden on the claimant to establish date of constructive knowledge. This for the defendant to establish (*Nash v Eli Lilly* (p568) applied). The judge's finding was speculative and unsustainable. The correct date for constructive knowledge was between 1984–1986.

(ii)   On the appeal:

(a)   the 14-year delay was inordinate.

(b)   the judge did not appear to consider the consequences of such a delay.

(c)   the greater the intervening period between the relevant acts and trial, the more difficult for the court to do justice by properly assessing the evidence.

(d)   it would not be appropriate to allow the claim to proceed.

Cross-appeal allowed but appeal allowed also. Claim struck out.

Lefevre v White

Limitation Act 1980, s 9   **Third Party (Rights against Insurers) Act 1930**

Popplewell J   **[1990] 1 Lloyd's Rep 569; (1989) Times, 1 November**

On 22 July 1972 the claimant (Phillipe Lefevre) was a passenger in a Ford motor car owned and driven by Mr Evans when it went out of control and he suffered severe injuries. He sued Evans. On 16 December 1981 Bristow J gave a consent judgment in his favour for £275,000.

Evans had a motor insurance policy with KGM Motor Policies at Lloyds who repudiated liability to indemnify him. On 8 December 1987 Evans issued a writ against the defendant, a representative Lloyds underwriter who subscribed to a KGM policy. On 9 December 1987 Evans was made bankrupt on the claimant's petition.

On 3 June 1988 the claimant issued a writ claiming an indemnity against the insurers pursuant to the Third Party (Rights against Insurers) Act 1930.

Held:

(i)   The claimant was not carrying on Evans's proceedings. He was exercising his own right to claim against the insurers. Accordingly, the issue of Evans's writ did not preserve his position. The claimant's proceedings had to be issued within six years of the cause of action arising on 16 December 1981 and were therefore out of time.

(ii)   There was no logic or sense in the submission that the claimant's cause of action arose out of Evans's bankruptcy and that the limitation period was six years from the date of bankruptcy. The claimant's case was statute barred.

Judgment was given for the defendant on both limitation and the merits.

Letang v Cooper

Limitation Act 1939, s 2

Law Reform (Limitation of Actions etc) Act 1954, s 2(1)

Court of Appeal   **[1964] 2 All ER 929; [1965] 1 QB 232;**
[1964] 3 WLR 573; [1964] 2 Lloyd's Rep 339

On 10 July 1957 the claimant (Mrs Doreen Letang) was sunbathing in Cornwall on a piece of grass where cars were parked. The defendant drove his Jaguar into the car park. He did not see her. The car went over her legs and she was injured.

On 2 February 1961 she issued a writ claiming damages for (i) negligence and (ii) trespass to the person. It was conceded at trial that her cause of action in negligence was statute barred.

However, Elwes J held that she also had a cause of action in trespass which was not statute barred because the limitation period for trespass was six years.

Held:

(i)   Where personal injury is inflicted unintentionally, the only cause of action is in negligence. The claimant had no cause of action in trespass.

(ii) Accordingly, her case was statute barred, since proceedings had not been commenced within three years as required by the proviso to s 2(1)(a) of the Limitation Act 1939 inserted by s 2(1) of the Law Reform (Limitation of Actions etc) Act 1954.

Lewis v Poulton

Limitation Act 1980, s 33

Court of Appeal   **Lexis, 29 January 1982**

In August 1970 the claimant (Mrs Lewis), who was not wearing a seat belt, was driving on her correct side of the road when she was involved in a head-on collision with the defendant's motor car. She suffered at the time moderate orthopaedic injuries including a fractured left collar bone and a sprained left wrist. A full police report was compiled.

She emigrated to Australia a fortnight after the accident. One month later, she started to develop severe headaches accompanied by some blurring of vision. She consulted doctors who diagnosed sinusitis and then migraine. In December 1973 she returned to England and instructed solicitors who rightly advised that her claim was statute barred.

In 1977 she met a solicitor who told her about the Limitation Act 1975. She instructed solicitors to pursue her claim, but they proved dilatory and she instructed a new firm who, after a protracted struggle, obtained the papers from the previous firm and notified her claim in April 1979. The writ was issued later in April 1979 and served on 4 May 1979.

Two neurosurgeons failed to act on instructions to report. A third finally reported in March 1981 that the accident was responsible for the onset of the claimant's headaches and the first year of their continuance. Her solicitors issued a summons for an order under s 33 of the Limitation Act 1980 disapplying the three-year time limit in s 11. This was granted by Barry Chedlow QC sitting as a deputy judge of the Queen's Bench Division.

The defendant appealed. Meanwhile the claimant's solicitors obtained a further report from an eminent neurosurgeon that she had received an upper cervical strain in the accident and that her long lasting headaches were referred pain from these joints.

Held:

(i)   The delay of eight years and eight months from accident to writ was inordinate. It had been swelled by unexplained delay on the part of the first solicitors and the first neurosurgeon. However, the claimant had valid reasons for her own part in it and was in no way culpable: s 33(3)(a).

(ii) She had a cast-iron case on the defendant's negligence. The only issue on liability, arising out of her admitted failure to wear a seat belt, could be tried without reduced cogency of evidence. The defendant was prejudiced in having to investigate the position concerning the headaches at a late stage and with considerable expense and difficulty, but fortunately the original hospital records were still available: s 33(3)(b).

(iii) The claimant acted promptly and reasonably once she had reason to suppose that the law (the Limitation Act 1975 as it then was) and the medical view of her injuries permitted her to proceed with a claim, in respect of both her originally and her subsequently attributed injuries: s 33(3)(e).

(iv) On balance the prejudice to the claimant outweighed that to the defendant. It was impossible to say that the deputy judge's conclusion was wrong, and the fresh medical evidence confirmed the rightness of his decision: s 33(1).

The defendant's appeal was dismissed.

Lexi Holdings Plc v Luqman

CPR 6.5

Ch D (Briggs J)   **22 October 2007, unreported**

The claimant company applied for judgment in default of acknowledgment of service against the defendant partnership (M). M, which consisted of a partnership between the first defendant and another individual (B), was the sixteenth defendant in extensive litigation issued by the claimant. The claimant purported to have served M with proceedings by postal service upon the first defendant successively at his two residences or former residences. M did not file an acknowledgment of service or defence to the claim. It was common ground that the first defendant had, at the time when proceedings were sent to his two residences or former residences, been serving a substantial term of imprisonment as the result of committal proceedings taken against him in his personal capacity by the claimant.

M contended that postal service on one partner of a firm was not, under the rules, good service on all partners, whereas personal service was. M further submitted that the first defendant had not been served effectively where the first defendant's last known residence was the prison at which he was then serving, rather than his residences. M contended that a purposive interpretation of the rule designed to ensure that service of legal documents came to the attention of the person served was better achieved by interpreting the usual or last known residence of a long-term prisoner as being the prison at which he was incarcerated. The claimant argued that a prisoner's house was no less his residence when he was in prison.

Held:

(i) Under the table in CPR 6.5(6), the two places where documents might be served on an individual who was being sued in the name of a firm were 'usual or last known residence' or 'principal or last known place of business of the firm'. Provided one partner who was sued in the name of a firm had the proceedings duly sent to his usual or last known residence, that was good service on the firm, and therefore upon his co-partners.

(ii) In the absence of authority, it seemed that the M's purposive interpretation was correct. In those circumstances, service had not been effected on the partnership consisting of the first defendant and B by service on the first defendant's house when he was, to the knowledge of the claimant, serving a substantial term of imprisonment.

(iii) Even if the court was wrong in the view that, where a claimant knew that his defendant was serving a long term of imprisonment, the prison was his usual or last known place of address, the instant case was a proper one for relief from sanctions on terms that service be duly acknowledged by the end of the following day.

Application refused.

Lister and others v Hesley Hall Ltd

Vicarious liability

House of Lords   **[2001] UKHL 22; [2002] 1 AC 215;**
[2001] 2 WLR 1311; [2001] 2 All ER 769

Between 1979 and 1982 the claimants were resident at the defendant's boarding house. The warden of the boarding house was employed by the defendant. Without the defendant's knowledge, he systematically sexually abused the claimants. The claimants claimed damages for personal injuries on the basis that (a) the defendant had been negligent in the care, selection and control of the warden, and/or (b) the defendant was vicariously liable for the warden's torts. The judge dismissed the negligence claim. He held that the defendant could not be vicariously liable for the warden's torts but were vicariously liable for the warden's failure to report to them his intentions to commit harmful acts and their consequences. The defendant successfully appealed to the Court of Appeal, who held that the warden's acts were outside and contrary to his duties and could not therefore be characterised as an unauthorised mode of carrying out his authorised duties. The claimant appealed.

Held:

(i)   There was no reason for approaching the question of vicarious liability in case of sexual abuse or harassment in a different manner from any other vicarious liability case. Such cases did not fall into a special category.

(ii)   The relevant criterion for establishing vicarious liability in these circumstances was the closeness of the connection between the nature of the employment and the particular tort.

(iii)   There was a sufficient connection between the warden's work and the harm that occurred for his acts to be regarded as within the scope of his employment. It was important to consider the circumstances of his employment, in particular that it entailed close contact with pupils and then inherent risks of such close contact.

(iv)   The warden had a general authority in managing the care home. His position provided him with the opportunity to abuse. The abuse was inextricably interwoven with the carrying out of his duties. The defendant was therefore vicariously liable for the warden's torts.

Appeal allowed.

Lockheed Martin Corp v Willis Group Ltd

Limitation Act 1980, s 35   **CPR 19.5**

Court of Appeal   **[2010] EWCA Civ 927; [2010] CP Rep 44;**
                                                       [2010] PNLR 34; (2010) Times, 5 October

The claimant brought proceedings against D1 for professional negligence arising from the broking of insurance policies. The claimant believed D1 to be the holding company for its group broking operations in the United Kingdom. After service of the proceedings, the claimant was informed that D1 was a Bermudan company and could not be served in the UK without the consent of the court. The claimant obtained permission to amend its claim to substitute D2 as defendant in place of D1. D2 was a related company, and was the group's principal holding company in the UK. The amendment was made after the expiry of limitation.

D2 then successfully applied to set aside that order, and the claimant appealed. The judge commented that he was prepared to assume that the claimant had made a genuine mistake as to name rather than identity but concluded that the claimant failed the second limb of the test under CPR 19.5, namely whether the true intended party was reasonably apparent to D1. This was based upon evidence from D1's legal adviser that it had not been obvious to her which company the claimant had intended to sue.

The claimant sought a second tier appeal, submitting that the judge was wrong to apply the second limb of the test as it was not contained in CPR 19.5; and, even if it did apply, it should be applied objectively rather than subjectively.

Held:

(i)   Under s 35(6)(a) of the Limitation Act 1980 and CPR 19.5(3)(a) the claimant had to satisfy the court that the original party (D1) was named in mistake for the new defendant (D2), and that, but for the mistake, the new party would have been named.

(ii)   However, the claimant had identified no cause of action against D2. The claim form spoke of 'duties of care', but it was very difficult to see how such duties could arise against D2, which was a holding and not a broking company. It could not therefore be necessary to substitute D2 for D1 where the claimant had no cause of action against it. The renewed application for permission to appeal was refused.

(iii)   (obiter) In applying the second requirement the judge appeared to have been acting on the basis that it was a further ingredient of the overall test applied in *Owners of the Sardinia Sulcis v Owners of the Al Tawwab* [1991] 1 Lloyd's Rep 201 under RSC Ord 20 r 5 and that it continued to apply to CPR 19.5. Although Lord Philips had stated in *Adelson v Associated Newspapers Ltd* [2008] EWHC 278 (QB) that 'it was necessary to have regard to the jurisprudence in relation to Ord 20 r 5', that was not a basis for making the second requirement an additional formal condition of the CPR 19.5 jurisdiction, especially as it was not contained in that rule. His comments suggested that the second requirement was really an aspect of discretion.

(iv)   In many cases the justice of the matter would militate against a successful application under CPR 19.5 unless the correct defendant knew about the complaint at some time before the limitation period passed. However, even that could not be laid down too firmly as a principle, as the case of *Horne-Roberts v Smithkline Beecham* (p481) demonstrated. The *Sardinia Sulcis* test, as it had survived in the new world of the CPR and the altered language of CPR 19.5, did not embrace all the wording of the old RSC Ord 20 r 5, but was properly confined to the substantive test that it was possible to identify the intended claimant or intended defendant 'by reference to a description which was more or less specific to the particular case'. That would ensure that the court could be satisfied that a genuine mistake had been made and that the mistake had caused the wrong party to be named.

(v)   There was no further jurisdictional requirement that the mistake was not misleading to the other party or had not caused reasonable doubt as to the identity of the party intended to be sued. Even if such a test had to be applied, it was to be judged objectively by the court.

Application refused.

Long v Tolchard & Sons Ltd

Limitation Act 1980, s 33

Court of Appeal   **[2001] PIQR P2; (2000) Times, 5 January;**
LTL 23/11/1999

The claimant allegedly injured his back on 9 August 1983 when employed by the defendant as a drayman. The claimant did not issue proceedings until 8 February 1990, which was the defendant's first intimation of the claim. He claimed that he had only been in a position to consider proceedings after receiving an orthopaedic opinion in March 1987. Liability and limitation were heard together in December 1993. The claimant succeed on both, the judge accepting that the claimant did not have knowledge under the Act until March 1987 and indicating that that in the alternative he would have exercised his s 33 discretion.

Quantum was tried in July 1998 before a different judge. On this occasion the claimant adduced evidence from a chiropractor that he had suffered back problems from 1983 until the defendant dismissed him in 1988. However, the chiropractor's notes showed that the claimant had told him in July 1985 that his back problems were the result of an accident at work. The judge awarded the claimant reduced damages of £10,000 in light of undisclosed pre-existing back problems and due to the claimant's significant exaggeration of his symptoms which made assessment of his true disabilities difficult.

The claimant appealed and the defendant cross-appealed out of time with leave from the trial judge on limitation, who also granted permission to adduce fresh evidence.

Held:

(i)   The new evidence clearly demonstrated that the claimant had knowledge in July 1985. Proceedings were therefore issued out of time.

(ii)   The judge's exercise of his discretion was based upon a false picture. The discretion needed to be considered afresh.

(iii)   The claimant's strong case on liability was only one factor, albeit an important one.

(iv)   Taking into account the extensive delays, exacerbated by the claimant's failure to notify the defendant of the claim, and the claimant's failure to disclose relevant documents and give a true account of his condition, it would not be equitable to allow the claim to proceed.

Appeal dismissed, cross-appeal allowed.

Lord v Boots Company plc

Limitation Act 1980, s 14, s 33

QBD   **23 October 1998, unreported**

See *Brooks and others v Boots Company plc* (E) (p348)

Lye v Marks and Spencer plc

Limitation Act 1980, s 33

Court of Appeal   **(1988) Times, 15 February**

The claimant (Bettina Lye) sued out of time for personal injury damages. She was legally aided. If the action went ahead and the defendants succeeded on the merits, they would be unlikely to recover their costs from her.

Rougier J refused her application under s 33 of the Limitation Act 1980 to allow her action to proceed out of time. The claimant appealed.

Held: the fact that a claimant was legal aided and would therefore be unlikely to meet the defendants' costs could be taken into account under s 33(3), although it was not an overriding factor.

The claimant's appeal was dismissed.

M v Islington Council and another

Limitation Act 1980, s 14, s 33

Court of Appeal   **1 December 2000, unreported**

The claimant brought proceedings for psychological damage which he alleged had resulted from the failure to review his fostering arrangements so as to place him with a family that reflected his own ethnic origin. He was born in March 1965. It is believed that he was the child of a Nigerian mother and a Ghanaian father. He turned 18 on 16 March 1983. He was placed in foster care by Islington Borough Council (the first defendant) on 4 January 1966 at the age of 10 months. In December 1966 the first defendant placed him with white foster parents, Mr and Mrs S, in Lewes in Sussex. The claimant's complaint is not directed to the original placement but to the alleged failure of the authorities to review the fostering arrangements adequately after 1970 when cultural knowledge had progressed. In January 1971, East Sussex County Council (the second defendant) took over supervision of the placement. Mr S died in May 1974. The claimant remained with Mrs S until 1985. He was then 20 years of age. Proceedings were issued on 23 September 1999.

The defendants successfully applied to strike out the claim as being statute barred. The judge held that from 1996 the first defendant had made efforts to help the claimant and that their letters recognised that he had expressed a concern to the Lewes social workers about his fostering and identity problems in late 1979 and early 1980. The judge referred to the fact that the claimant had applied for legal aid as long ago as 1996 and to a probation report in 1989, which had been accompanied by a psychiatrist's report, and held that these were clear confirmation that the claimant then knew well what his psychological problems were and the cause of them. He therefore held that the claimant had the requisite knowledge long before November 1996. He declined to exercise his s 33 discretion in the claimant's favour, primarily on the basis of the evidential prejudice to the defendants. The claimant appealed.

Held:

(i)   The claimant had had the requisite knowledge for the purposes of s 14 prior to three years before the date of commencement of proceedings. By 1979 the claimant, although not able to articulate the precise nature of the fault which he alleges on the part of the first defendant, was aware that some act or omission had taken place which had adversely affected him; that was sufficient. That he was already conscious of his cultural identity crisis was apparent from reports in 1989.

(ii)   The judge had not erred in the exercise of his discretion under s 33. His concerns as regards evidential difficulties were well founded. Moreover, there was no real prospect of the claimant establishing that either local authority had been in breach of a duty of care, and the defendants had already offered amends.

Appeal dismissed.

MCK v Bryn Alyn Community Holdings Ltd

Limitation Act 1980, s 2, s 11, s 14, s 33

Court of Appeal   **[2003] EWCA Civ 783;**
[2003] 3 WLR 107; [2003] 1 FLR 1203

See *KR v Bryn Alyn Community Holdings Ltd* (F) (p505)

Mackie v Secretary of State for Trade and Industry

Limitation Act 1980, s 14

Court of Appeal   **[2007] EWCA Civ 642**

The defendant was responsible for the liabilities of the British Coal Corporation, which had employed the claimant (born 1964) as an electrician between 1981 and 1993. According to the claimant, he had experienced hearing difficulties after being exposed to loud noise at work. In

1992, he took a hearing test and was informed by a union official that he had a hearing loss of 9.98dB. The claimant maintained that the official informed him that he did not have a hearing problem or a claim. In the same year, a firm of solicitors wrote to the corporation intimating a claim on the claimant's behalf for noise-induced deafness. This was later abandoned. The claimant denied knowledge of that firm's actions. He claimed that in 1993 he became aware that other employees who had hearing loss of 10dB were bringing claims, but that he did not take any further advice to clarify his own position. In December 2003 the claimant consulted solicitors with a view to making a claim. In August 2004, the claimant was examined by a consultant who reported that he had a hearing loss of 10.8dB, attributable to noise exposure. The claimant issued proceedings on December 2005. Limitation was heard as preliminary issue.

The claimant's case was that, until December 2003 when he consulted solicitors, he did not consider that he had significant hearing loss or hearing loss caused by noise. The judge held that the claimant knew in 1992 that he had significant hearing loss but that he had not had actual or constructive knowledge that his deafness was attributable to his working conditions. He held that the claim was not statute barred because it was not until 2004 that the claimant had the knowledge necessary to commence his action.

The defendant appealed, submitting that the judge had failed to make findings of fact that were central to the whole question of knowledge, and that he should have made findings as to whether the first firm of solicitors had been instructed to advance a claim on the claimant's behalf, who had arranged the hearing test and whether that had been arranged as part of the process of pursuing a claim for noise-induced deafness. The defendant further argued that, in light of those findings, the judge should have analysed more carefully what the claimant had understood as the result of his conversation with the union official.

Held:

(i)   It was not satisfactory for the judge to leave open the factual issues about the circumstances in which the claimant came to have his hearing tested and in which the solicitors came to intimate a claim. They were plainly matters of great importance, without which the judge was not in a position to apply the law. The instant court had to resolve those factual matters before it could decide whether the judge's conclusion was sustainable.

(ii)   On the facts, the claimant went for the hearing test, probably arranged by the union or the solicitors, with a view to bringing a claim for damages. Although the judge held that the claimant had not in fact met with solicitors, it was highly likely that he completed a form provided by his trade union in which he set out his personal details, working history and noise exposure and that his trade union must have sent the form to the solicitors who then regarded themselves as instructed. The hearing test was most likely organised either by the union or the solicitors.

(iii)   The claimant plainly then had knowledge that his hearing loss was capable of being attributed to noise exposure and that was enough to fix him with knowledge for the purposes of s 14 (*Spargo v North Essex DHA* (p667) applied). The fact that afterwards he had been informed that he had no claim did not deprive him of that knowledge.

(iv)   Further, there was no basis to make a finding that the claimant had been misled or given incorrect advice by the union official and that that advice had displaced his previous assumption that his hearing loss was due to noise (*Sniezek v Bundy (Letchworth) Ltd* (p664) considered).

(v)   There was no need for the judge to consider whether it had been reasonable for the claimant to take no further steps until, more than 10 years later, he received further advice about the cause of his deafness. However, even if the judge had been right to think that the claimant's assumption had been displaced by whatever the union official had said, it was not reasonable for him to do nothing for the next 10 years. By 1993, the claimant knew he had significant injury. He had learnt that other miners at the colliery who had hearing loss of 10dB were bringing claims. Although the claimant had not realised that 9.98dB was only a little less than 10dB, a reasonable person would have made enquiries about the significance of those figures and the reliability of the information he had been given as to the cause of his deafness. Given the information and knowledge available to the claimant, it was not reasonable for him to do nothing at all to clarify his uncertain position.

(vi) In the circumstances, the claimant had had the knowledge necessary to commence an action against the Secretary of State well before December 2002.

(vii) As there was no cross-appeal in respect of the judge's indication that he would not have exercised his discretion under s 33 of the Act, the claim was statute barred.

Appeal allowed.

Maga v Birmingham Roman Catholic Archdiocese Trustees

[2009] EWHC 780 (QB)   **Limitation Act 1980, s 14, s 28, s 33, s 38**

QBD (Jack J)   **24 April 2009, unreported**

The claimant, who was born on 8 October 1963, sought damages from the defendant church trustees arising from the alleged sexual abuse suffered as a boy at the hands of an assistant priest (P) serving at a local church.

In 1972, P had been ordained priest and appointed second assistant priest at a church within the parish in which the claimant and his family lived, although they were not Catholics. The claimant suffered from learning difficulties and attended a specialist school. On 30 November 2000 the claimant made a statement to the police concerning events at the school in question. In October 2003, he learnt from a television programme that another man had recovered damages from the Catholic Church for the abuse he had suffered as a boy from P. He learnt that it had been alleged that a complaint had been made to the senior priest about sexual abuse by P in 1974. The claimant, via his social worker, contacted the police. It was not, however, until 31 July 2006 that a letter of claim was sent. On 26 September 2006 the claimant issued proceedings alleging that he too had been abused by P over a period of many months in 1976 when he was aged 12 to 13. At that time, an acquaintance had developed between P and the claimant, and P had paid the claimant for doing jobs such as cleaning P's car. The claim alleged that the defendants were vicariously liable for the assaults committed by P, and also that they were negligent because the complaint alleged to have been made concerning P in about 1974 was not followed up, so that he was left free to abuse others including the claimant.

The issues to be determined were whether the claimant's claim was statute barred and, if not, whether the claimant had suffered abuse for which the defendants were liable.

The claimant contended that, as he had at all times been under a disability within the meaning of s 28(1), the period of limitation had never begun to run. The defendants submitted that, whilst there could be circumstances in which the church would be vicariously liable for sexual assaults committed by one of its priests, the assaults by P on the claimant were not so closely connected with his 'employment' as to render the church liable.

Held:

(i) The claimant was represented in the litigation by the Official Solicitor on the ground that he was a 'patient', and he had been medically certified as such. There was evidence that the claimant did not have the mental capacity to manage his property and affairs: he had an IQ of around 70, epilepsy, inability to read or write, difficulty in remembering instructions and had a social worker and regularly attended the community learning disability team. Looking at the litigation process from when the claimant first saw solicitors, he was likely to be unable to deal rationally with the problems that had arisen or would arise in the course of it, and he did not have the capacity to conduct legal proceedings.

(ii)   The claimant was, accordingly, of 'unsound mind' for the purpose of s 38(2) as it stood prior to the issue of the proceedings and his claim was not, therefore, statute barred.

(iii)   (obiter) Even if the claimant possessed capacity, the negligence claim would have been in time under s 14 as the claimant did not know the relevant acts or omission until October 2003.

(iv)   (obiter) Had consideration of s 33 been necessary, it would have been granted in the claimant's favour.

(v)   Although the delay was very long, 30 years after the alleged abuse, the immediate reason for the claim not being brought soon after the abuse was that the claimant was a child and his family did not know of the abuse. When the claimant became an adult, he did not bring a claim because it did not occur to him that he might do so. The passage of time had not greatly disadvantaged the defendants as regards liability; they had settled other cases relating to P's abuse, and would not have called him as a witness in any event. The delay had some potential prejudicial effect on the defendants as regards the evidence of the claimant, especially as he was prone to fantasy and exaggeration. The defendants were themselves open to criticism for not investigating fully when first alerted to the possibility of P being an abuser. This was a claim by a mentally disadvantaged claimant for abuse by a priest to whom he should have been able to accord particular trust. The balance was in the claimant's favour.

(vi)   The assaults which P carried out on the claimant were not so closely connected with P's employment or quasi-employment by the church that it would be fair and just to hold the church liable. That conclusion was also fatal to the claim in respect of the church's negligence in failing to act upon earlier allegations against P.

Judgment for defendants.

NB: The judge's decision on vicarious liability was reversed by the Court of Appeal: [2010] EWCA Civ 256; [2010] 1 WLR 1441; [2010] PTSR 1618; (2010) 107(13) LSG 15; (2010) 154(11) SJLB 28; (2010) Times, 25 March.

Mann v Bournemouth District Council

Limitation Act 1939, s 2A, s 2D

Court of Appeal   **[1981] CLY 174**

In March 1975 the claimant (Mrs Marjorie Mann) fell on a pavement in Bournemouth and dislocated a shoulder. In May 1975 solicitors notified her claim. The defendants arranged an inspection showing no more than half an inch irregularity in the surface of the pavement, and by August 1975 they wrote denying liability.

In March 1979 the claimant, acting in person, commenced court proceedings. At a preliminary trial on limitation, Michael Davies J decided that the action was statute barred and refused her leave to proceed under s 2D of the Limitation Act 1939 as amended.

At the hearing of her appeal, the claimant told the court that she was not sure what caused her to trip. She alleged that she had acquired information that the cause of the pavement being defective was that heavy lorries were allowed to cross the stretch of pavement in question, a practice condoned by a councillor who had his back garden abutting on the pavement, and applied for leave to adduce fresh evidence.

Held:

(i)   If the claimant could not prove that her fall was caused by anything but a very slight irregularity, or could not say what had caused her to fall, she had no case; whereas if she could say that a dangerous defect in the pavement caused her fall, she did not need any information about the cause to mount her action. She knew enough about all material matters to bring her action well within the primary three-year period. Her case was statute barred: s 2A.

(ii)   The judge evidently concluded that, first, the claimant had no good reason for not bringing her action in time, and second, that if she had done so it was very likely to fail. He was right to decide that it would be inequitable to let the defendants be harassed by a very stale action that was unlikely to succeed: s 2D.

The claimant's appeal was dismissed.

Marren v Dawson Bentley & Co Ltd

Limitation Act 1939, s 2   **Computation of time**

Havers J   **[1961] 2 QB 135; [1961] 2 WLR 679;
[1961] 2 All ER 270**

At 1.30pm on 8 November 1954 the claimant (Martin Marren) was injured in the course of his employment with the defendants. His writ was issued on 8 November 1957.

Counsel for the defendants contended that, as the accident occurred at 1.30pm on 8 November 1954, the claimant, if he liked, could have issued his writ that day and therefore the last day on which he would be entitled to bring his action was 7 November 1957.

Held: the day on which the accident occurred was to be excluded from the computation of the three-year period (under s 2(1) of the Limitation Act 1939 as amended by s 2(1) of the Law Reform (Limitation of Actions etc) Act 1954). Accordingly, the action had been started in time.

Marshall Rankine and another v Maggs

                                        CPR 6, 7

Court of Appeal   **[2006] EWCA Civ 20; (2006) Times,
3 February; LTL 25/1/2006**

See *Collier v Williams* (p380)

Martin v (1) Kaisary (2) The Royal Free Hospital NHS Trust (No 1)

                                        CPR 19

Court of Appeal   **[2005] EWCA Civ 594; LTL 16/03/2005**

The claimant allegedly suffered personal injury when complications developed after an operation on 2 October 2000 to remove his prostate gland. These culminated in a cardiac arrest on the 3 October 2000. The first defendant was the surgeon who carried out the operation, who was employed by the (proposed) second defendant. The first defendant in fact treated the claimant as a private patient, but the second defendant provided facilities and support staff. Proceedings were issued against the first defendant on 30 September 2003. The particulars of claim pleaded, inter alia, that the first defendant failed to monitor the claimant's post-operative condition. The first defendant's defence pleaded that the second defendant's staff were not his servants or agents and that he was not vicariously liable for their failures. The limitation period having expired, the claimant applied on 29 July 2004 under CPR 19.5(2) and (3) to add the hospital as the second defendant.

The judge refused the application on the basis that the proposed addition was to pursue an alternative claim against the second defendant and was therefore not necessary to properly pursue the claim against the first defendant. The claimant appealed.

Held:

(i)   Although determination of the first defendant's liability would entail an examination of the actions of the hospital staff, it would not require a determination of their liability.

(ii)   The judge was therefore correct to find that the addition was not necessary and that the criterion for permission was not satisfied.

Appeal dismissed.

Martin v (1) Kaisary (2) The Royal Free Hospital NHS Trust (No 2)

Limitation Act 1980, s 11, s 14, s 33

Hodge J   **[2005] EWHC 531 (QB); LTL 18/04/05**

See above for the facts. Subsequent to the failed appeal, there was a preliminary hearing on whether the claim against the second defendant was outside the primary limitation period and, if it was, whether the court should exercise its discretion to allow the claim to continue (this was initially due to be heard alongside the joinder issue, but was adjourned for lack of time).

Held:

(i)   Until the results of an MRI scan where explained to him in August 2001 the claimant believed that his post-operative ill-health was attributable to the drug Heparin. He also thought that he had been cared for by nurses provided by the first defendant. He therefore did not have the requisite knowledge under s 14 until after that date as, although he thought he knew of the relevant acts and omissions, he was 'barking up the wrong tree' (*Spargo v North Essex DA* (p667) applied). As proceedings were issued against the second defendant in July 2004 the claim was not statute barred, notwithstanding that the claimant's solicitors had been mistaken in assuming that the first defendant would be vicariously liable for the hospital staff.

(ii)   Had it been necessary, the s 33 discretion would have been exercised in the claimant's favour as:

(a)   the delays could not be described as lengthy. Part of the reason for the delays were the difficulties the claimant experienced in obtaining information, some of which were the fault of the second defendant;

(b)   the prejudice to the claimant in potentially having to issue further proceedings against his solicitors weighed against the prejudice to the second defendant when it was likely to be joined as a Part 20 defendant by the first defendant in any event clearly pointed to exercising the discretion in the claimant's favour;

(c)   the delay had not in any sense reduced the cogency of the available evidence;

(d)   the claimant suffered from continuing disability;

(e)   the claimant's conduct could not be greatly criticised; and

(f)   the faults of the claimant's lawyers should not be visited on the claimant himself.

Marshall v Martin and another

Limitation Act 1980, s 33

Court of Appeal

Lexis, 10 June 1987

The claimant sued outside the primary limitation period. The second defendants had made an interim payment. Nolan J on appeal upheld the master's order granting the claimant leave to proceed under s 33 of the Limitation Act 1980. The second defendants applied for leave to appeal.

Held: s 33(3)(c) directed the court to consider the defendants' conduct. This might often be in some way discreditable or unsatisfactory. However, s 33(3)(c) could not be limited in this way. For example, if the defendants had explicitly said that liability was not to be contested, that would clearly be relevant. Accordingly, the judge had not erred in taking into account the second defendants' interim payment.

Leave to appeal was refused.

Marston v British Railways Board and another

Limitation Act 1939, s 2A, s 2D

Croom-Johnson J

[1976] ICR 124

On 3 October 1957 Gerald Marston, a relayer employed by the first defendants, was striking a metal sett with a hammer supplied by them when a piece of metal flew up from the striking surface of the hammer and lodged in his neck, severing the carotid artery. In April 1959 a consulting engineer inspected the hammer on his behalf. In July 1959 a representative of the first defendants said in terms that the hammer was new at the time of the accident. In September 1960 Mr Marston's action for damages was commenced. In June 1961 a metallurgist appointed by all three parties reported that the hardness of the hammer and the sett were satisfactory. Believing that he had been supplied with a new hammer, Mr Marston discontinued his action.

In September 1969 the chip that had come off the hammer head was finally removed from his neck. The chip itself was then subjected to metallurgical examination which showed that there had been a defect in the hammer face. In March 1970 Mr Marston died of unconnected causes. On 13 August 1970 the claimant (his widow) commenced a fresh action for damages which was heard in October 1975, just after the Limitation Act 1975 (which amended the Limitation Act 1939) had come into force. Expert evidence at the trial disclosed for the first time that the hammer had not been new.

Held:

(i)   (a) Mr Marston believed that the hammer was new. This is what he was told by other workmen and the first defendants' representative. He did not have actual knowledge that it was defective: s 2A(6);

      (b) he had obtained expert advice which simply informed him that the hardness of the hammer was adequate. The fact that the hammer was in a poor condition was undoubtedly ascertainable with the help of the expert advice, but Mr Marston should not be fixed with constructive knowledge since he had taken all reasonable steps to obtain that advice: s 2A(8);

      (c) supposing that Mr Marston were still alive, he would not have had knowledge of the relevant facts until hearing the expert evidence at the trial. That was the first time that he could have been fixed with the requisite knowledge for the purposes of s 2A.

(ii)   If it had been necessary for the claimant to rely on s 2D, the conduct of the first defendants' representative in mistakenly telling Mr Marston's representative that the hammer was new would justify exercising the court's discretion so as to allow the action to proceed: s 2D(3)(c).

Mason v First Leisure Corporation plc

CPR 7

Tugendhat J   **[2003] EWHC 1814; LTL 30/7/03**

On 24 April 1999 the claimant suffered a brain injury in a skiing accident for which the defendant was responsible. Immediately following the accident he suffered post-traumatic amnesia and it was broadly agreed that limitation probably started to run from a few weeks after the accident. On 22 April 2002 the claimant instructed solicitors. They issued proceedings the following day. On 8 August 2002 the claimant successfully applied without notice to extend the date for service to 23 December 2002 pursuant to CPR 7.6(1) and (2). Proceedings were served on 19 December 2002. The defendant successfully applied on notice to have the order extending service set aside on the grounds that there had been insufficient reason to grant it and doing so deprive the defendant of a limitation defence. Service was set aside as being out of time. The claimant appealed.

Held:

(i)   The master was mistaken in holding that the claimant had refrained from instructing solicitors until the last minute. He was also mistaken in holding that the authorities on CPR 7.6(3), *Vinos v Marks & Spencer* (p701), and *Godwin v Swindon Borough Council* (p444), applied without qualification to the wider discretionary provision CPR 7.6(2). His discretion therefore had to be exercised afresh.

(ii)   The claimant's application was in principle misconceived. He should have served the claim form and applied for an extension of time for service of particulars of claim and supporting documents. Had the defendant not received a letter of claim indicating that a claim form had been issued, it might have been denied the opportunity to contest the proceedings.

(iii)   There must be a good reason for the extension. Here there was not and the claimant was lulled into a false sense of security given the liability of the without notice order to be set aside.

(iv)   The defendant had however suffered no prejudice by the extension.

(v)   The defendant's conduct subsequent to receiving the letter of claim in August 2002 amounted to an encouragement to the claimant to pursue the action which led to an expectation that the original order would not be challenged.

(vi)   Setting aside service would be disproportionate and unjust.

Appeal allowed.

McCafferty v Metropolitan Police District Receiver

Limitation Act 1939, s 2A, s 2D

Court of Appeal   **[1977] 2 All ER 756;**
                                    [1977] 1 WLR 1073; [1977] ICR 799

In January 1965 the claimant (John McCafferty), a leading expert in ballistics, retired from the police force and was re-employed by the defendant as 'temporary senior experimental officer' in charge of the ballistics section of the laboratory which in September 1965 was moved to a small and unsuitable room in Theobalds Road, London WC1. He continually fired rounds of ammunition (usually bullets) into boxes containing cotton wool. In autumn 1967 he noticed that the ringing in his ears did not disappear as quickly as before. At the end of 1967 the cotton wool that he had been using in his ears was replaced by ear muffs. In February 1968 a specialist diagnosed a perceptive deafness in each ear resulting from acoustic trauma.

There was no substantial change in his hearing until 1973 when an audiogram in April showed 'signs of severe acoustic trauma' and the reporting doctor advised that the claimant 'should stop shooting forthwith'. Consequently his employment was terminated in October 1973. His writ was issued on 24 February 1974.

At trial the claimant described his hearing defect from autumn 1967 (the first incident) as 'an irritating nuisance'. It was agreed that the 1973 trauma and subsequent dismissal (the second incident) were caused by the noise of a shot or series of shots in the course of a few days or weeks before the April 1973 audiogram. Crichton J found that the claimant had sued in time within s 2A of the Limitation Act 1939 as amended and awarded £850 damages for the first incident. He also awarded £9,150 damages for the second incident in respect of which there was no limitation defence. The defendant appealed.

Held:

(i)   The claimant's injury from autumn 1967 was 'significant' since it justified £850 damages. By early 1968 he had full knowledge of all the relevant facts. Accordingly, his case was prima facie statute barred by s 2A of the Limitation Act 1939 as amended.

(ii)   However, under s 2D it was proper to take into consideration factors which, at least subconsciously, prevented him from starting proceedings against his employer: the nature of the injury as he regarded it then as being, his interest in his job, the insecurity of his tenure, his desire to preserve good relations, and so forth: s 2D(3). Despite some small prejudice to the defendant arising from the delay, the balance tipped in favour of the claimant: s 2D(1).

Per Geoffrey Lane LJ (on s 2A(7)): 'it is clear that the test is partly a subjective test, namely: would this plaintiff have considered the injury sufficiently serious? And partly an objective test, namely: would he have been reasonable if he did *not* regard it as sufficiently serious? It seems to be that sub-s(7) is directed at the nature of the injury as known to the plaintiff at that time. Taking *that* claimant, with *that* plaintiff's intelligence, would he have been reasonable in considering the injury not sufficiently serious to justify instituting proceedings for damages?'

Per Lawton LJ (on s 2D): 'The factor which has weighed with me is this: the plaintiff revealed himself as a man who was not anxious to litigate over something which he regarded as "an irritating nuisance". That is commendable. In my judgment the court should be understanding of men who, after taking an overall view of their situation, come to the conclusion that they would prefer to go on working rather than become involved in litigation.'

The defendant's appeal was dismissed.

NB: The partly subjective test for constructive knowledge, taking into account a claimant's individual characteristics, has since been disapproved: *Adams v Bracknell Forest BC* (p292).

McCaul v Elias Wild & Sons Ltd

Limitation Act 1939, s 2

McNeill J   **14 September 1989**

Between 1943 and 1950 the claimant (Thomas McCaul) was employed by the defendants as an apprentice in work which involved cutting, mitring and drilling asbestos sheeting. In 1985 he first experienced breathlessness. In early 1987 he was told that he had asbestos induced pleural thickening. His writ was issued on 17 October 1988.

A preliminary trial was held on the issue of whether the case was statute barred by s 2 of the Limitation Act 1939 before the Law Reform (Limitation of Actions etc) Act 1954 came into force on 4 June 1954. Dr Page testified that inhalation of asbestos fibres would have contaminated his lung at the time but that damage would have taken many years to develop.

Held:

(i)   There was no evidence of any actionable damage to the claimant's lungs prior to 4 June 1954.

(ii)   He suffered no injury to his lungs or, if he did, no more than purely minimal injury, certainly not amounting even to inconvenience, prior to three years before issue of the writ.

(iii)   Accordingly, his action was commenced in time under s 11(4) of the Limitation Act 1980.

Arnold v Central Electricity Generating Board (p306) distinguished.

Keenan v Miller Insulation & Engineering Ltd (p515) followed.

McCoubrey v Ministry of Defence

Limitation Act 1980, s 14

Court of Appeal   **[2007] EWCA Civ 17; [2007] 1 WLR 1544;
[2007] LS Law Medical 150; (2007) 151 SJLB 159;
(2007) Times, 26 January**

The claimant had suffered an impairment to his hearing on 15 October 1993, when he was on a training exercise and a thunderflash exploded near him. He noticed immediate ringing in his ears and, within a day or two, the hearing in his left ear deteriorated. He requested, and received, several medical examinations over the following months. The contemporaneous medical notes indicated that the claimant was reporting 'muffled' hearing in his left ear, and they record him as suffering from deafness, tinnitus, and pain in the left ear. A consultant who saw the claimant in early 1994 noted that he had marked sensorineural hearing loss. Audiograms over the years showed that the damage to the claimant's hearing remained fairly consistent. However, it did not affect his military career until August 2001, when his status was temporarily downgraded. By 2003 he was formally downgraded, prevented from deployment with his unit in Iraq and told that he was likely to be permanently excluded from active service. He then believed his military career was permanently blighted. He consulted solicitors in April 2003 and on 21 July 2004 he issued proceedings. Limitation was heard as preliminary issue.

The claimant sought to rely on both s 14 and s 33. The judge proceeded on the basis that, in evaluating the seriousness of the injury, the court must look not only at the severity of the injury itself but also at the effect of the injury on the claimant's quality of life and ability to participate in his chosen career. The judge held that the effect of the claimant's injury did not have a significant impact on him until the MOD restricted his activities in 2001, and so time did not run under s 14 until then. The judge therefore did not rule on s 33. The issue was the proper approach to the meaning and application of s 14(2) of the 1980 Act, which dealt with whether an injury was 'significant'.

Held:

(i)   The law as it had previously been understood and applied had changed. The test under s 14(2) was substantially objective, and not the mixture of subjective and objective in the way in which the analysis of Geoffrey Lane LJ in *McCafferty v Metropolitan Police District Receiver* (p546) suggested.

(ii)   The question of whether an injury was 'significant' within s 14(1)(a), as expanded by s 14(2), was to be decided by reference to the seriousness of the injury, and not by reference to its effect on the claimant's private life or career, and still less by reference to its subjectively perceived effect on the claimant's private life or career (*Catholic Care (Diocese of Leeds) v Y (Kevin Raymond)* [2006] EWCA Civ 1534 and *Adams v Bracknell Forest BC* (p292) applied, *KR v Bryn Alyn Community (Holdings) Ltd (In Liquidation)* (p505) distinguished).

(iii) Given that a claimant who could rely on s 11(4)(b) and s 14 could extend his limitation period, possibly by many years, as of right, s 14 should be relatively narrowly construed, considering that such a claimant would always have a fall-back position under s 33. It seemed unlikely to have been the intention of Parliament that there would be many cases where both s 14 and s 33 would be available to a claimant seeking to bring proceedings outside the three-year period.

(iv)   Accordingly, s 14(2) had a comparatively limited application. It was enacted to extend the limitation period for victims of personal injury who were effectively unaware that they had been injured at all or who were aware that they had suffered an injury which they reasonably thought to be very mild, but which subsequently turned out to be very serious.

(v)   The person contemplated in s 14 was a person who was in the same position, in objective terms, as the claimant. That test was objective, but it did not prevent the objective circumstances of the claimant being taken into account, as opposed to personal characteristics like intelligence, ambitions and personality, which could not be taken into account. The proper approach to the question raised by s 14(2) was to consider the reaction to the injury, as opposed to its possible consequences, of a reasonable person in the objective circumstances of the actual claimant, while disregarding his actual personal attributes.

(vi)   The judge below had erred in taking into account the claimant's subjective attitude to the effect of his injury, and his personal reasons for not pursuing or contemplating a claim against the defendant in 1993. The fact that the injury did not lead to any setback in the claimant's career until 2001 was not an appropriate reason for holding that time did not start running under s 11(1)(b) until 2001. The claimant had all the information he needed about the injury to set time running by early 1994. The claim was therefore primarily statute barred as of around February 1997.

(vii) The issue of s 33 was remitted to the judge below.

Appeal allowed.

McDonnell v Congregation of Christian Brothers Trustee and another

Limitation Act 1980, s 11, s 41	**Limitation Act 1939, s 1, s 21, s 22**

Law Reform (Limitation of Actions) Act 1954, s 1, s 7

Limitation Act 1963, s 1	**Limitation Act 1975, s 3**
House of Lords	**[2003] UKHL 63; [2003] 3 WLR 1627; [2004] 1 All ER 641; LTL 04/12/2003**

The claimant sought damages for alleged abuse suffered whilst attending the defendant's school between 1941 and 1951. At that time the governing statute was the 1939 Act under which the claimant's action was statute barred in January 1963 (being six years after the end of his minority). This was amended by the 1963 and 1975 Acts which introduced a date of knowledge test. In *Arnold v Central Electricity Generating Board* (p306) the House of Lords held that this did not apply retrospectively to deprive defendants of a defence under the 1939

Act. Proceedings were issued on 9 August 2001. On trial of the issue the judge, following *Arnold*, struck the claim out. On appeal, the Court of Appeal came to the same decision. The claimant appealed again.

Held:

(i)   The decision in *Arnold* was not obviously wrong and the court needed more than just doubts to justify departing from it.

(ii)   Schedule 2 para 9(1) of the 1980 Act rendered s 33 inapplicable in these circumstances.

(iii) The defendant was entitled to rely on its defence under the 1939 Act and the claim was statute barred.

Appeal dismissed.

McDonnell and another v Walker

Limitation Act 1980, s 33

Court of Appeal   **[2009] EWCA Civ 1257;**
[2010] CP Rep 14; [2010] PIQR P5;
(2009) 106(47) LSG 18; (2009) 153(45) SJLB 29

The claimants were the driver and a passenger in a car involved in a road traffic accident on 24 April 2001. The driver of the other car was killed in the accident. On 20 April 2004 the claimants issued proceedings against the driver's estate, represented by the defendant executor, claiming damages for personal injury limited to £15,000. Liability was not disputed by the defendant's insurers. The claimant's proceedings were served one day late on 21 August 2004. The insurers took the late service point and, on 21 January 2005, an application for an extension of time was refused. At that time, *Walkley v Precision Forgings Ltd* (p705) precluded any second action.

The claimants went to new solicitors who initially pursued a claim against their previous solicitors. A letter of claim was sent to them on 3 April 2007. In the interim, on 14 June 2006, the law then changed; *Horton v Sadler* (p482) overturned *Walkley* and granted to second proceedings brought out of time the potential of the s 33 discretion. On 17 April 2008 the claimants, at the urgings of their former solicitors, commenced a second action against the defendant and successfully applied under s 33 to disapply the limitation period. The claims in the second proceedings were different from and much larger than the claims in the first proceedings, including substantial claims for loss of future earnings and psychological injury. The first claimant's claim was stated to be worth over £300,000 and the second claimant's claim to be worth between £100,000 and £300,000.

The defendant appealed, contending that the judge had misunderstood important aspects of the evidence, misdirected himself in various ways including in respect of the test to be applied, failed to identify the correct period of delay, and reached a decision in the exercise of his discretion which was not open to him.

Held:

(i)   Depending on the issues and the nature of the evidence going to them, the longer the delay, the more likely and the greater the prejudice to the defendant. Moreover, a judge should not reach a decision by reference to one circumstance or without regard to all the issues; he should conduct a balancing exercise at the end of his analysis of all the relevant circumstances and with regard to all the issues, taking them all into account.

(ii)   The judge had failed to identify the correct period of delay. The 'delay' in s 33(3)(a) and (b) was the delay since expiry of the limitation period, but the overall delay was also relevant as part of all the circumstances of the case: *Donovan v Gwentoys Ltd* (p412).

The judge concentrated on the period after *Horton v Sadler* made it possible to exercise the discretion under s 33 in a second action, even though a claimant had brought an abortive action prior to the expiry of the limitation period. That wrongly suggested that, provided there was no delay post-*Horton*, a claimant should always be able to succeed in a disapplication of the limitation period in any second action. However, *Horton* was a case where there was no forensic prejudice to the defendant. *Cain v Francis* (p360) similarly supported the disapplication in a second action where there was no forensic prejudice. Conversely, if there was forensic prejudice, then where that prejudice was caused by inexcusable delay and where there was little if any prejudice to a claimant with an action against his solicitors, the position would be different.

(iii) The judge's approach to forensic prejudice was flawed. He suggested that there was correspondence during the period of three years from the accident and that it was for the defendant's insurers to investigate; but, until the insurers had details of the claim being made, they were in no position to do so. Reports relevant to general damages were only received three years after the accident, no psychological report was received at that time, and no claim for loss of present or future earnings was received at all. The claims ultimately received some seven years after the accident were of a different magnitude to those previously intimated.

(iv) Clear forensic prejudice had been suffered by the defendant's insurers who had to investigate the second claim from a standing start. Since the judge had misdirected himself in various respects, the court had to consider whether it was appropriate to disapply the limitation period under s 33.

(v) As delay had caused forensic prejudice to the defendant, the court had to consider the cause of the delay. If the delay was excusable and, on balance, it was still possible to have a fair trial, it might be just and fair to allow the action to proceed. On the other hand, if the delay had caused unfairness to the defendant in his ability to investigate the claim and there was no excuse for the delay, the action should not be allowed to proceed.

(vi) Where there has been inexcusable and lengthy delay in a claimant notifying a defendant as to his case on liability or (as in this case) quantum, and there has been negligence in issuing the proceedings or in serving them on time, that is a situation in which it almost speaks for itself that a defendant has suffered forensic disadvantage and a claimant is unlikely to suffer prejudice.

(vii) In this case, the only period of delay for which there was any kind of excuse was that between the failure of the first action and the decision in *Horton*. Thus, the defendant had been forensically disadvantaged by a substantial period of inexcusable delay. The claimants would suffer only minor prejudice if they had to proceed against the solicitors who made the error over service of the first proceedings, given that there was no loss of chance discount to be applied and some of that prejudice was their own fault in that they had failed to co-operate to arrange medico-legal appointments. In all the circumstances, it was not right to disapply the limitation period under s 33.

Appeal allowed.

McEvoy v AA Welding & Fabrication Ltd

Limitation Act 1980, s 11, s 33

Court of Appeal   **[1998] PIQR P266; LTL 5/12/1997**

On 18 October 1990 the claimant, a self-employed steel erector, was injured on a building site when a beam being hoisted by a crane fell on him. The defendant was a sub-contractor who had hired the crane from a company called Dixons. Dixons investigated the accident and agreed a statement of facts. The claimant issued proceedings against Dixons on 13 July 1992. However, on 22 September 1992 the claimant learned that Dixons were in liquidation. They wrote to

Dixons' insurers and received notification that Dixons were not insured in November 1993, after expiry of the limitation period. On 21 October 1993 the claimant had sought permission to continue against Dixons in liquidation. However, this was sought in the wrong court and not granted until 28 June 1995. On 10 October 1994 the claimant obtained permission to join the defendant and the main contractor. The order was by consent, but was nevertheless set aside on 22 February 1994 on the grounds that a limitation defence could not be pleaded.

On 27 June 1995 the claimant successfully applied to have the proceedings against Dixons struck out on the grounds that they were a nullity as Dixons were in liquidation at the date of issue and permission had not been obtained to proceed against them. The claimant issued fresh proceedings against the defendant on 21 September 1995, which was met by a limitation defence. The judge exercised his discretion under s 33 to allow the claim to continue, distinguishing the decision in *Walkley v Precision Forgings Ltd* (p705) that would otherwise have prevented him doing so. The defendant appealed.

Held:

(i) As the first action was a nullity, *Walkley* did not apply, irrespective of the fact that it was not an irretrievable nullity in that it could be retrospectively redeemed. *Walkley* did not apply when the first action was not properly constituted, notwithstanding that it could be retrospectively validated (*White v Glass* applied). The judge was correct to distinguish it.

(ii) The circumstances in this case were exceptional in that both parties believed that the earlier action was a nullity, which was sufficient to distinguish *Walkley*. *Walkley* was not intended to operate in an inflexible or technical way.

(iii) The judge was correct to hold that there was no evidence that the defendant would suffer any prejudice beyond the loss of a limitation defence, whereas the claimant, whose claim against his solicitors was uncertain, would suffer considerable prejudice if s 11 were not disapplied. The defendant had admitted liability and would therefore suffer no evidential prejudice. It was therefore equitable to allow the action to continue.

Appeal dismissed.

NB: The rule in *Walkley* was abolished in *Horton v Sadler* (p482).

McGahie v Union of Shop Distributive and Allied Workers

Law Reform (Limitation of Actions etc) Act 1954, s 6

Outer House, Scotland **1966 SLT 74**

On 18 February 1957 the pursuer (Euphemia McGahie) was injured in an accident at work. The limitation period against her former employers expired on 18 February 1960.

On 12 February 1964 she commenced court action against the defender trade union for failing, in breach of their alleged contract with her, to pursue her claim timeously.

The defenders submitted that the damages claimed in this action included damages 'in respect of personal injuries' and that the time limit for action against them therefore expired on 18 February 1963.

Held:

(i) There was only one item of loss in the damages claimed in this action, that item being the loss caused by the lapse of the pursuer's right to sue her employers. The lapse of that right did not cause her any personal injury.

(ii) Accordingly, the damages claimed by the pursuer in this action were not damages in respect of personal injuries. The action was not struck out by the three year time limit under s 6(1)(a) of the 1954 Act.

McGhie v British Telecommunications

Limitation Act 1980, s 33

Court of Appeal   **[2005] EWCA Civ 48; LTL 18/1/05**

On 26 August 1998 the claimant injured his back working for the defendant. The defendant completed an accident investigation shortly afterwards, but then heard nothing of the matter until receiving a letter of claim dated 30 May 2003. The claimant had been prompted to take legal advice in April 2003 by, in February 2003, being informed that he required an operation on a prolapsed disc and also that there were deficiencies in the defendant's working practices. Proceedings were issued more than two years outside the primary limitation period. The defendant pleaded limitation, which was tried as a preliminary issue. The judge exercised his discretion under s 33 on the basis that the claimant had acted reasonably in making a claim promptly as soon as he had reason to think that one was available to him.

The defendant appealed on the grounds that (a) the judge did not base his decision upon the balance of prejudice, (b) did not properly address the issue of proportionality as set down in *Adams v Bracknell Forest Borough Council* (p292), and (c) did not address the strength of the claimant's claim.

Held:

(i)   Although the judge mentioned the question of proportionality with reference to *Adams* he did not evaluate it. Proportionality is proportionality between the size of the claim and the costs of running it. A claimant who has a strong claim for serious injuries will be more prejudiced by a statute bar than one who has a weak claim for minor injuries.

(ii)   The judge also misdirected himself by failing to do address the balance of prejudice and by failing to address the strength of the claim as required by authority (*Forbes v Wandsworth HA* (p434), *Nash v Eli Lilly & Co* (p568)). All three criticisms of the judge were therefore made out and the discretion had to be considered afresh.

(iii)   There were several strong factors on the defendant's side of the balance:

       (a)   the length of delay was substantial and, applying the constructive knowledge precepts laid down in *Bracknell*, there was no good reason for it;

       (b)   there was evidential prejudice to the defendant;

       (c)   the claimant's case was thin (*Dale v British Coal Corp* (p396) applied); and

       (d)   the claim was for acceleration of symptoms and thus modest in financial terms so as to give rise to disproportionate legal costs.

(iv)   The claimant had nothing significant to put on his side. The balance came down firmly in the defendant's favour.

Appeal allowed.

McHugh v Gray

Limitation Act 1980, s 33

QBD (Beatson J)   **[2006] EWHC 1968 (QB);**
[2006] Lloyd's Rep Med 519;
(2006) 150 SJLB 1051

The claimant had been present at the Hillsborough football ground in April 1989 when a number of spectators died or suffered serious injury as a result of crushing in the crowd. The defendant, a consultant psychiatrist, had been instructed to examine the claimant and report on any psychiatric injuries that he had sustained. The defendant reported in November 1989 that the claimant had a moderate degree of post-traumatic stress disorder and that his symptoms should resolve within a matter of months. The claimant then settled his claim against the South Yorkshire Police in January 1990 for £2,750. His condition, however, did not resolve and led, according to him, to the breakdown of his relationship with his girlfriend, continuing depression and heavy drug use. He sought advice about Hillsborough from the solicitors who acted on his behalf in criminal proceedings thereby arising. They gave him the name of his solicitors who had held a forum for Hillsborough victims and had apparent success on behalf of one Hillsborough claimant. The claimant wrote to them on 2 March 2000. They accepted instructions and arranged medical evidence.

The claimant issued proceedings in February 2002, alleging that he had suffered personal injuries as a result of the defendant's negligent diagnosis and prognosis. Limitation was tried as a preliminary issue. (The personal injuries claim was pleaded in February 2002 but deleted in December 2002. In October 2004 the claimant applied to re-amend the particulars of claim to reinstate the personal injuries claim. This application was also before the judge but fell away in the light of his decisions on limitation.) The judge found that (1) by the time the claimant saw the defendant, he knew that his condition was very different and that it was the result of his experience at Hillsborough; (2) by the time he acted on the defendant's report, he knew that the condition which accounted for the difference was called post-traumatic stress disorder; (3) the unexpected outcome was the failure of the claimant to recover in accordance with the defendant's prognosis, that being a fact observable and in his judgment observed by the claimant without the help of expert advice; (4) once the defendant's prognosis proved to be inaccurate, the claimant had good reason to enquire when he would in fact recover and, if the answer was that he would not, the reason, and that such an enquiry would have been made by a reasonable person and post-traumatic stress disorder did not change the claimant from such a person; (5) despite having ample opportunity, the claimant made no such enquiry; and (6) although the test was objective, the claimant's circumstances were relevant. He was registered with a GP, knew the name and address of his former solicitor, was still in work and was living with someone unaffected by the trauma he suffered. The judge therefore held that the claimant had constructive knowledge of his claim in June 1992, so that the primary limitation period expired in June 1995; that the claimant had been responsible for the 'significant' seven-year delay in issuing proceedings; that, as regards any reduction in the cogency of the evidence, the prejudice was not more than minor, especially as the defendant had since died; and that, while the claimant stood to lose a potentially valuable claim, the defendant was faced with a stale claim and prejudice would be caused to those with financial responsibility for it. The claimant appealed.

Held:

(i)   The judge had been entitled not to exercise his discretion to disapply the limitation period. He had been entitled to take account of the length of the delay and to find that for the purposes of s 33(3)(a) it was significant. Further, he had not fallen into a 'plain' error either in relation to his consideration of the question of evidential prejudice under s 33(3)(b), or in the way in which he had weighed that factor in coming to his conclusion as to whether it would be equitable to allow the claim to proceed. His conclusion that the prejudice was not more than minor did not point inexorably to the disapplication of the primary limitation period.

(ii)   Moreover, in weighing the various factors, the judge had been entitled to take into account the prejudice to those with financial responsibility for claims, such as the instant, where uncertainty persisted because they were not made and dealt with promptly. The judge had also properly considered the strength of the claim and given sufficient weight to its size. He was not obliged to take account of the fact that the claimant had no case over against his own lawyers, a matter not listed in the statute nor apparently referred to at first instance.

Appeal dismissed.

McLaren v Harland and Wolff Ltd

Limitation Act 1980, s 33

Outer House, Scotland   **1991 SLT 85**

Between 1953 to 1960, apart from two years' national service, John McLaren was employed as an apprentice plumber by the defender shipbuilders. He worked near laggers and other tradesmen using asbestos materials. In 1960 he left the defenders' employment and worked as a driver. In September 1983 asbestosis was diagnosed. In 1984 he stopped work. In September 1985 he lodged a successful claim for DSS industrial disablement benefit for asbestosis. He did not claim damages. In December 1988 he died.

Three months later the claimant, his widow Mrs Agnes McLaren and their three children commenced court action. Documentary evidence of Mr McLaren's apprenticeship was still available. His foreman Harry Ridley had died in 1988 after himself claiming against the defenders for asbestosis in 1987.

At the preliminary trial on limitation, Lord Milligan found that the case was prima facie statute barred and considered the exercise of discretion under s 19A of the Prescription and Limitation (Scotland) Act 1973 which is similar (though not identical) to s 33 of the Limitation Act 1980.

Held:

(i)   Mr McLaren was unaware that he had a prospective right of action against the defenders. This was not unreasonable, since by his death he had been away from employment in the shipyards for 28 years.

(ii)   The apprenticeship documents meant that no difficulty arose in proving that he worked for the defenders as averred.

(iii)   A partial answer to the point about loss of the evidence of Mr McLaren and Harry Ridley was that this might well be more of a disadvantage to the pursuers than to the defenders.

(iv)   It was important that the action involved averments as to regular exposure to asbestosis over a lengthy period, not an allegation of a single transient event on which a witness no longer available could have provided evidence.

(v)   There was evidence that in a case such as this where employment involving exposure to asbestos dust is proved, where asbestosis is proved to be contracted many years later and where there has been no other apparent exposure to asbestos dust, liability is not a live issue.

(vi)   While, if Mr McLaren had raised an action timeously, the defenders might have had him examined medically on their behalf prior to his death, his condition was thoroughly monitored by medical experts during the several years prior to his death. Thus it was speculative whether the defenders had suffered medical prejudice.

(vii)   It was equitable to allow the claimant's action to proceed.

McManus v Mannings Marine Ltd & another

Limitation Act 1980, s 11, s 14

Court of Appeal   **[2001] EWCA Civ 1668; LTL 29/10/2001**

The claimant worked from 1968 onwards in the ship-building industry. He worked for the defendant for 12 days in June 1989 and for a further 14 days in January 1990. In September 1992 he submitted a claim for vibration white finger ('VWF') to the Department of Social Security, naming the defendant as his employer in the application form. At this time he suffered from VWF in two fingers in his left hand. He claimed for this injury through an agreed trade union/insurers scheme, but this was rejected. In pursuit of the scheme claim he attended a consultant in May 1993, who informed him that his condition would deteriorate significantly if he suffered further exposure. He resumed employment with the defendant from August 1993 to November 1999. His condition worsened to the point that it affected all his fingers and thumbs. He issued proceedings on 2 December 1999. Limitation was heard as a preliminary issue. The recorder found that the claimant had knowledge for limitation purposes by September 1992, and declined to exercise his discretion under s 33. The claimant appealed.

Held:

(i)   Considering s 14 in conjunction with s 11, 'injury in question' in s 14 meant the injury for which the action was brought.

(ii) The claimant's claim was not for the VWF before 1993 but rather for its exacerbation since then. If the claimant had been claiming only in respect of damages to the right hand the defendant would have had no argument.

(iii) The recorder erred in his approach. He should have asked himself when the exacerbation was significant.

Appeal allowed. Limitation remitted below to be heard at the trial of the substantive issues.

McManus v Sharif

Companies Act 1985, s 725(1)   **CPR 6.7**

[2003] EWCA Civ 656; [2003] 1 WLR 2441;
[2003] 3 All ER 129

See *Cranfield and anor v Bridgegrove* (C) (p389)

Meherali v Hampshire County Council

Limitation Act 1980, s 11, s 33

QBD (Zucker QC)   **[2002] EWHC 2655 (QB); [2003] ELR 338**

The claimant was born on 10 May 1976. In 1982 he entered one of the defendant's schools. It was alleged that during his schooling the defendant failed to properly ameliorate the claimant's dyslexia. Proceedings were issued on 8 December 1998. The defendant applied to strike the claim out as being statute barred. It was agreed that proceedings were issued nineteen months out of time, the claimant having knowledge when he reached majority but the claimant applied for a s 33 discretion.

Held:

(i)   There was significant evidential prejudice to the defendant in tracing witnesses with a recollection of the relevant facts. Although this would have been the case even if proceedings had been issued in time, the failure to do so exacerbated the difficulty.

(ii) The claimant had no real prospect of succeeding in his claim. This was a relevant factor for refusing to exercise the s 33 discretion (*Forbes v Wandsworth HA* (p434) applied).

(iii) There was no other compelling reason for allowing the claim to succeed.

Claim struck out.

Mersey Docks Property Holdings and others v Kilgour

CPR 6.5, 7.5

Toulmin J   **[2004] EWHC 1638 (TCC)**

This was a multi-party action arising out of a fire in a fruit storage and distribution centre. The claimants issued proceedings against the defendant architect shortly before limitation expired. Shortly before the four-month validity period expired proceedings were sent to the defendant at an address from which he had practised when the centre was built. The claimants had unsuccessfully searched for the defendant's current name and address on the internet and in the directory of the architects' professional body, RIBA. However, in the interim the defendant had changed his name and moved address. He had made no attempt to conceal these changes and had communicated them RIBA. Further the assignors of the claimants' causes of action had known of the defendant's correct current address. Proceedings were resent to the defendant at his current address after the four-month validity period had expired. The defendant maintained that proceedings had not been properly served. This was heard as a preliminary issue.

Held:

(i)   The phrase 'last known place of business' in CPR 6.5(6) meant known to the claimant in question.

(ii)   To obtain the requisite knowledge a claimant had to take reasonable steps to ascertain the current or last known address. It was a matter of evidence as to whether such steps had been taken. This was fairer than an objective test, was similar to the test under the old rules and appeared to be implied in cases such as *Cranfield v Bridgegrove and associated appeals* (p389) and *Arundel Corporation v Khoker* [2003] EWCA Civ 1784.

(iii)   In the present case the claimants had not validly served the claim form. Searches could have been made through RIBA or the Yellow Pages. The failure of a search of the RIBA directory should have prompted further enquiries.

(iv)   In any event the assignors' knowledge was imputed against the claimants.

(v)   It was not appropriate to extend the time for service under CPR 7.6. The failure in service was due to the claimants' dual failures to carry proper searches and waiting until the last moment to issue and serve proceedings. There was nothing unjust in the claims being barred for these reasons. The prejudice to the defendant was irrelevant, *Hashtroodi v Hancock* (p466) applied.

Preliminary issued decided in favour of the defendant.

Michael v Musgrove (t/a YNYS Ribs)

Merchant Shipping Act 1995, s 183, Sch 6   **Athens Convention 1974, art 16**

Admiralty Division (Jervis Kay QC)   **[2011] EWHC 1438 (Admlty);**
                                                   [2012] 2 Lloyd's Rep 37

The claimant had been injured on a boat (the Sea Eagle) owned by the defendant when it was hit by a wave. The Sea Eagle was a rigid inflatable boat (RIB) used for pleasure trips such as that undertaken by the claimant around the coast of Anglesey. The claimant alleged that the defendant was negligent for failing to provide a safety briefing prior to the trip and for failing to operate the boat safely. It was the defendant's case that passengers had been told not to stand up when the vessel was underway, but the claimant had done so and had been hit by a wave that was not part of the general swell.

The defendant applied for summary judgment on limitation, contending that the claim was outside the two-year time limit provided for by art 16 of the Athens Convention 1974, as

557

enacted by s 183 of, and Sch 6 to, the Merchant Shipping Act 1995. The claimant contended that the Sea Eagle did not qualify as a seagoing ship for the purposes of art 1 of the Convention, therefore the time-bar did not apply.

Held:

(i)   The term 'ship or vessel' within the Convention included any vessel capable of being used in navigation, whether or not it was in fact being used in navigation at the relevant time. The starting point was whether the construction of an object was capable of being a vessel which might be used in navigation (*Steadman v Scholfield* (p673) and *R v Goodwin* [2005] EWCA Crim 3184 considered). The Sea Eagle was certificated as a small commercial vessel to be used on open water, which was an indication that she was to be treated as such. Even if that had not been the case, it was clear that the RIB was of a design and construction that was intended to be capable of operating offshore. It was a permanent structure of some length with a rigid hull, internal seats and engine, fixed steering position with navigational aids and a below-deck permanent fuel tank. Moreover, the manufacturer's description of the roles for which the RIB was intended certainly characterised it as a vessel to be used in navigation. The Sea Eagle was therefore a ship in the sense of being a vessel capable of being used, and actually used, in navigation.

(ii)   The word 'seagoing' was adjectival and was intended to describe the actual use of a vessel. It was therefore intended to convey something more than the words 'used in navigation'. Thus, although a ship might be a ship for the purposes of the 1995 Act, she would not be a seagoing ship unless it was her actual business to go to sea (*Salt Union Ltd v Wood* [1893] 1 QB 370 considered). Having regard to Merchant Shipping Notice MSN 1776 issued in March 2003, which indicated which of the coastal waters of the United Kingdom were to be regarded as 'sea', it could be concluded that the trips in which the Sea Eagle were involved were sea trips. It followed that she was a seagoing vessel for the purposes of the 1995 Act and the Convention, so that the claim was statute barred.

Application granted.

Middleditch v Thames Case Ltd

Limitation Act 1980, s 33

Mr Martin-Thomas QC   **Lexis, 10 November 1987**

The claimant (Sandra Middleditch) joined the defendants' employment in 1964. The department in which she worked converted plain board into cardboard. She did stitching, feeding and packing working in rotation. In May 1979, whilst engaged in particularly heavy work, she developed pain in her left wrist and forearm. On 14 May 1979 she reported to the works surgery with a very painful and swollen left wrist. She revisited the next day when a diagnosis of tenosynovitis was recorded. On 5 June 1979 she applied to her trades union for legal assistance. The union's solicitors notified her claim in July 1979. The insurers repudiated liability. The claimant suffered fresh injuries until the end of 1981 when a new system was introduced.

On 5 August 1983 the writ was issued. It was served with the statement of claim in November 1983. There was a full trial in which it was agreed that the primary limitation period expired on 14 May 1982 and the claimant sought to rely on s 33 of the Limitation Act 1980.

Held:

(i)   No reason for the delay had been advanced. On the face of it, the claimant had an unarguable claim against her solicitors for negligence: s 33(3)(a).

(ii)   The defendants were given very early notice of the claim and had every chance to investigate it. Their witnesses did not claim any difficulties in recollection, and most had already testified in the 1984 case of *Wyatt v Thames Case Ltd*. The cogency of evidence had not been seriously affected by the delay: s 33(3)(b).

(iii)   The claimant was in any event entitled to a trial of the issues of the defendants' negligence from August 1980 (three years before the writ) to December 1981 (when the new system was introduced). The real prejudice to the defendants lay in payment of increased damages for the earlier negligence: s 33(3).

(iv)   Balancing the prejudice as between claimant and defendants, it was just to override the technical limitation defence and to direct that s 11(4) should not apply: s 33(1).

Judgment was given for the claimant in the sum of £3,750.

Miller v London Electrical Manufacturing Co Ltd

Limitation Act 1963, s 7

Court of Appeal   **[1976] 2 Lloyd's Rep 284**

The claimant (Albert Miller) was employed by the defendants to work on a machine which let off a fine cloud of powder. It caused him contact dermatitis on his hands and face and skin. In 1967 he was off work for two or three months, went to hospital for treatment and was given an ointment. In 1968 he was off work on two different occasions; again he was told to avoid the powder and given the ointment. In November 1970 he suffered further trouble with his skin and was off work for a time.

In May 1971 there was a marked deterioration in his condition. His hair fell out, and he had sores all over his body. Doctors diagnosed constitutional eczema from which he would never recover. Eventually he went to a Citizens Advice Bureau. On 30 April 1974 his writ was issued.

It was clear from his evidence at the preliminary trial on limitation that from 1967 onward he knew that his condition was due to the defendants' negligence and that he would have a remedy in damages. He testified that he did not take any action in the early years because he did not want to lose his job. O'Connor J found that his case was statute barred.

Held:

(i)   The claimant's dermatitis was sufficiently serious that he could have brought an action at any time from 1967.

(ii)   His condition turned out in May 1971 to have been much more serious than he thought, but that was not a sufficient ground for extending the time.

The claimant's appeal was dismissed.

NB: It is submitted that the same decision on (i) would be reached today under s 14(2) of the Limitation Act 1980. However, on (ii) the court would have a discretion in effect to extend time under s 33 of the 1980 Act.

Miller v Thames Valley Strategic HA

Limitation Act 1980, s 14, s 33

QBD (Butterfield J)   **[2005] EWHC 3281 (QB)**

The claimant had suffered from various neurological symptoms from around 1960, when he was aged 15. Over the following years he underwent numerous medical investigations and various forms of treatment were tried. These culminated in February 1969 in his having a brain tumour removed. This was the result of a fortuitous referral in November 1968 from the claimant's optician to a particularly alert consultant ophthalmologist. By that time, however, the claimant had lost virtually all the vision in his right eye and a substantial part of the useful vision in his left eye.

In September 1994 the claimant requested copies of his medical notes from his GP when his son presented with similar symptoms to those that the claimant had experienced a little while before he had the surgery. He was told it was not possible for him to see his notes because patients had no right to see their medical records at that time.

In 2000 the claimant was listening to the radio and learnt through so doing that he was entitled to obtain his medical records under the Data Protection Act. On 13 November 2000 he obtained copies of his records and learned that a neurologist who had examined him in 1963 had suspected he had a tumour. The claimant, acting in person, issued proceedings on 12 November 2003, alleging that, had the condition been diagnosed and treated in 1963 or 1964 as it should have been, his loss of vision would have been averted. The defendant pleaded that the claim was statute barred because, although the claimant did not have actual knowledge of the failure to diagnose the tumour and the consequences of that failure for his vision, he did have constructive knowledge from about 1969.

Held:

(i)   The defendant, upon whom the burden of proof rested, had not established on the balance of probabilities that the claimant, as a reasonable man of moderate intelligence, should have appreciated in all the circumstances that there was a real possibility that the defendant had failed to diagnose his brain tumour in 1963 and 1964 and that it should have diagnosed it at that time. Nor had it established that the claimant should have appreciated that that failure caused or contributed to his loss of vision. Although the claimant knew in 1969 that his loss of vision was caused by the brain tumour, that was insufficient. The doctors had never suggested to the claimant that they could have made their diagnosis earlier than they did, there was nothing to put him on notice to the contrary, and there was no reason why he should have reached a different conclusion.

(ii)   No reasonable man of moderate intelligence would have made the connection between his condition in 1963 to 1966 and the condition as it was found in operation three years later.

(iii)   Had the claimant possessed the relevant knowledge in 1969, any s 33 discretion would not have been exercised in his favour, as the defendants were significantly prejudiced by the very great delay.

Preliminary issue decided in favour of the claimant.

Millington v Boots Company plc

Limitation Act 1980, s 14, s 33

QBD   **23 October 1998, unreported**

See *Brooks and others v Boots Company plc* (D) (p348)

Mills v Ritchie and another

Limitation Act 1980, s 11, s 33

Bingham J   **Lexis, 12 November 1984**

On 14 May 1979 the claimant (Mr Mills), who was the owner of a one-man vehicle recovery business, was called to a breakdown on the M2 motorway. The first defendant drove an oil tanker into the back of the claimant's pick-up Land Rover with such force that the Land Rover was forced forward into the broken down car, the car driver was killed and the claimant was injured. The first defendant subsequently pleaded guilty to a number of offences, including driving without due care and attention. The claimant sustained a soft tissue injury to his right leg, which had to be put in plaster, and was unable to work fully for a time. Moreover he was gravely handicapped in the conduct of his business because his Land Rover had been written off, he no longer had the use of his mobile crane and his tools had been seriously damaged and lost.

He consulted solicitors within 10 days after the accident. They notified his claim to the defendants. As they knew, the claimant had borrowed money from a bank in order to replace his Land Rover, interest was mounting and he had every incentive to seek prompt disposal of his claim. At the urging of the bank, he periodically telephoned his solicitors to ask how the claim was going and was repeatedly assured that everything was in hand. In fact, nothing significant occurred until November 1982 when they wrote to inform him that the limitation period had expired and that he should obtain independent advice.

The claimant promptly instructed fresh solicitors who obtained legal aid and in May 1983 issued a writ against his original solicitors who pleaded that under s 33 of the Limitation Act 1980 it was still open to him to sue the defendants. Consequently a writ against the defendants was issued on 28 September 1983. A preliminary trial on limitation was ordered.

Held:

(i)   The three-year limitation period applied not only to the claimant's claim for damages for personal injuries but also to his claim for damage to property and loss of earnings, since s 11(1) applied to 'any action' for damages where, as here, the damages included damages in respect of personal injuries. Accordingly, all heads of the claimant's claim were prima facie statute barred: s 11(4).

(ii)   (a) The delay to issue of the writ was 16 months. This was due to failure on the part of the claimant's original solicitors to issue proceedings as they should have done: s 33(3)(a);

        (b)   the defendants had admitted liability, subject to limitation. Whatever difficulty there might be in determining the claimant's precise losses, they had not been worsened by the delay: s 33(3)(b);

        (c)   the claimant had acted promptly and reasonably in seeking advice from his solicitors and acting in accordance with it: s 33(3)(e)–(f);

        (d)   the claimant had already started a claim against his original solicitors and had legal aid to prosecute it. There was a real prospect that certain heads of claim, such as the cost of his overdraft, might be more readily recoverable against the solicitors, who knew of the overdraft, than against the defendants who did not: s 33(3);

        (e)   exercising discretion on the peculiar facts in this case would be tantamount to saying that any claimant with a good claim against defendants, which they either admit or are in no position to deny, would earn the exercise of discretion under s 33. That was not the intention of the legislature, and on balance the right course was not to exercise discretion in the claimant's favour.

Judgment was given for the defendants.

NB: The authors would respectfully question the correctness of this reasoning in light of *Cain v Francis* (p360).

Milner v Hepworth Heating Ltd

Limitation Act 1980, s 14

Court of Appeal   **28 July 2008, unreported**

The claimant (born 1 October 1947) contended that he suffered industrial deafness as a result of his employment with the defendant company which had begun in 1962. Hearing protection became available in the early 1970s and warning notices were posted in March 1972. The claimant began to wear ear protection in 1982. Between 1986 and 1991 he served on the works safety committee. In 1990, when he was 42, he first noticed that his hearing was impaired with occasional tinnitus but he did not perceive these as serious problems. This was against the background of his having suffered earlier unrelated wax problems, to which he also attributed these later hearing difficulties. On 8 April 1993, at work, he had a hearing test. He was told his hearing was down and was referred to a doctor. He was seen by a consultant in April 1993. He issued proceedings on 2 June 1995. Limitation was heard as preliminary issue. The critical question was whether the claimant's date of knowledge was before or after 2 June 1992; the judge had not been asked to consider s 33. The judge held that the claimant did not have the requisite knowledge before 8 April 1993. He accepted the claimant's evidence that before 1993 he did not appreciate the link between noise and hearing damage (perceiving the relevant warnings to be in regard to an uncomfortable rather than harmful working environment) and that he had no indication that the ear problems were work related until 1993. The defendant appealed.

Held:

(i)   The defendant's case had been fully argued before the judge, including an exhaustive analysis of s 14 and the surrounding case law. Not only in his judgment but also in the course of the cross-examination the judge had made it clear that the longer he heard the claimant, the more convinced he was of his honesty and truthfulness.

(ii)   There were no grounds on which the court could reach any other conclusion. The question of significant injury was a matter of fact for the judge who had not misdirected himself. The judge had accordingly reached an unimpugnable conclusion as to actual knowledge.

(iii)   On constructive knowledge, it was clear that perception of deafness was a subjective matter and it was a common experience of people whose hearing was failing not to appreciate it. It could not be said that the claimant should have been reasonably expected to have acquired knowledge that his hearing deficit was significant or that it was noise induced.

Appeal dismissed.

Mirza v Birmingham Health Authority

Limitation Act 1980, s 14

Eady J   **LTL 31/7/2001**

The claimant was born in 1972 suffering from congenital heart problems. On 3 August 1976 the claimant underwent an operation that resulted in partial paraplegia. The claimant's father was told shortly afterwards that this was merely an unfortunate complication. The claimant approached solicitors in 1993. When the claim was first intimated, medical records were sought but came in dribs and drabs and a full set was not obtained until 1997. The claimant issued proceedings on 3 September 1998. Liability and limitation were heard together.

Held (as regards limitation):

(i)   The claimant could not have known that his injury was attributable to the defendant without detailed expert advice and reasonably full knowledge of the events in 1976.

(ii)   It was not possible to obtain meaningful medical advice until the full medical records were available.

(iii)   The claimant did not have the requisite knowledge until receiving the expert's report on 19 February 1998.

(iv)   The judge would have exercised his s 33 discretion if necessary. The delay had not affected the cogency of the evidence.

Claim not statute barred, but the claimant failed on liability.

Molins plc v G D SpA

CPR 6

Court of Appeal   **[2000] 1 WLR 1741;**
[2000] 2 Lloyd's Rep 234; [2000] CP Rep 54

On 22 June 1999 the claimant sent a letter of claim to the defendant's solicitors indicating an intention to issue proceedings in respect of allegedly unpaid licence royalties, and enquiring whether the solicitors had instructions to accept service. On 20 June the defendant solicitors replied that they were seeking instructions. The claimant sent a reminder on 6 July, and on 7 July the defendant solicitors replied as before. On 13 July the claimant issued proceedings in England.

On 19 July the defendant issued proceedings (without any prior indication) in the Bologna Civil Court and applied to the Italian court for authorisation to serve the Italian writ by faxing it to the claimant's English fax number. The defendant knowingly made two false statements in its application. The Italian court gave authorisation on 20 July and the fax was sent that day.

On 21 July the defendant's solicitors wrote to the claimant stating that they were not instructed to accept service. The claimant effected service of the claim form in Italy on 30 July. On 2 September the defendant applied for the claimant's claim to be stayed on the basis that the Italian court was first seised of the action. The judge granted this application, holding that proceedings were definitively pending before the Italian court. The claimant appealed.

Held:

(i)   Under CPR 6.2(1) and para 3.1 of PD 6A, service by fax was only permitted if the receiving party indicated in writing that it was willing to thus accept service and provided the fax number to be used. The claimant had not done so. The argument that the criterion was satisfied by the inclusion of a fax number on headed paper was contrary to the wording of the provision and to common sense.

(ii)   Service under Art 15 of the Hague Convention or Art 4 of the 1930 Convention between the UK and Italy had to be in accordance with the CPR as these were the rules in England at the relevant time.

(iii)   The court first seised was the one before which the requirements for proceedings to become definitively pending were first fulfilled (*Zegler v Salinitri* [1984] ECR 2397 applied).

(iv)   A decision as to jurisdiction under Art 21 of the Brussels Convention 1961 turned upon which court was seised.

(v)   It was common ground that under English law proceedings only became definitively pending upon service. The English court was thus seised on 30 July 1999.

(vi)   Service was undoubtedly a requirement under Italian law before proceedings were definitively pending. Although irregular service could be retrospectively validated under Italian law, until that had been done the Italian court could not be seised as proceedings were not definitively pending during the interim period (*AGF v Chiyoda* (1992) 1 Lloyd's Rep 235 approved). Seisin could not turn upon future events, and as of 30 July 1999 no validation had taken place.

(vii) Once it was established that service was required before seisin, the issue was whether or not service had taken place as required by Art IV of the Protocol to the Brussels Convention 1968. It had not been. Whether or not Italian law differed was irrelevant.

(viii) The Italian court was not yet seised, the English court was thus seised first and there was therefore no basis for a stay.

Appeal allowed.

Monk v British Steel plc

Limitation Act 1980, s 33

Court of Appeal   **LTL 18/8/97**

See *Beattie v British Steel plc* (p327)

Morgan Est (Scotland) Ltd v Hanson Concrete Products Ltd

Limitation Act 1980, s 35   **CPR 17.4, 19.5**

Court of Appeal   **[2005] EWCA Civ 134;
[2005] 1 WLR 2557; [2005] 3 All ER 135**

The claimant brought a claim for breach of contract against the defendant, alleging defective manufacture of pipe sections. The original party contracting with the defendant was another company ('A'). It had transferred its benefit in the contract to the claimant's former company ('B'), which later changed its name to Morgan Est (Scotland) Ltd (the claimant as currently named). The claimant then assigned its cause of action to another company ('C'). The position was therefore that the legal title to the cause of action remained in A but the benefit for the cause of action was vested in C. The claimant erred in claiming that B was the contracting party (thus ignoring the assignment) and in overlooking the second assignment to C. The defendant's defence was that as A was the original contractor and they had never been in a contractual relationship with B, the claimant had no cause of action. The claimant then successfully applied after expiry of the limitation period to join A and C as claimants pursuant to CPR 17.4 or 19.5.

The defendant appealed on the basis that the judge had no jurisdiction to the allow the amendments or, if he did, should not have exercised his discretion in the claimant's favour.

Held:

(i)   The test in *Sardinia Sulcis*, which did not take account of the CPR or the overriding objective and was not devised for s 35, was not determinative of the limits of CPR 19.5. The court was not bound by the use of that test in other post-CPR cases (*Horne-Roberts v Smithkline Beecham* (p481), *Kesslar v Moore & Tibbits* [2004] EWCA Civ 1551 disapproved).

(ii)   The proper approach to CPR 19.5 was to apply the words of the section without regard to the *Sardinia Sulcis* test but with regard to the overriding objective, bearing in mind that the limit of the rule was set by s 35 as the empowering statutory provision (*Gregson v Channel 4 Television* (p449) applied).

(iii) The same approach applied to the application of CPR 17.4, although s 35 did not apply.

(iv)   The court in this case had to decide whether the addition of A and C was necessary depending upon whether or not the new party was to be substituted for a party who was named in mistake in the claim form for the new party.

(v)   There was no reason to construe 'in mistake' constrictively.

(vi)   In the instant case there was a clear mistake about naming the party. A was intended
        to be named. There was no prejudice to the defendant, who would only be deprived
        of an unmeritorious defence. The mistake therefore could and should be corrected by
        substitution.

(vii)   C should be joined pursuant to CPR 19.5(3)(c); as a beneficial owner it was bound by
        the result (*Three Rivers District Council v Bank of England* [1996] QB 292 applied).

Appeal dismissed.

Murphy v Staples UK Ltd

Companies Act 1985, s 725(1)   **CPR 6.9, 7.6**

[2003] EWCA Civ 656;
[2003] 1 WLR 2441; [2003] 3 All ER 129

See *Cranfield and anor v Bridgegrove* (D) (p389)

Mutua and Others v Foreign and Commonwealth Office

Limitation Act 1980, s 33

QBD (McCombe J)   **[2012] EWHC 2678 (QB); (2012) 162 NLJ 1291**

The claimants, who were Kenyan nationals, brought proceedings against the defendant for
damages for personal injuries suffered whilst in detention in Kenya in the 1950s.

Kenya was a United Kingdom colony at that time and under a state of emergency. In June
2009 the claimants issued their claim that the UK Government was directly jointly liable, with
the colonial administration and the individual perpetrators of tortious assaults, for the creation
and maintenance of the system under which the claimants were mistreated, and had owed the
claimants a duty of care in negligence. The defendant did not dispute that the claimants had
suffered torture and mistreatment but disputed the UK Government's responsibility. The fifth
claimant (N) had died with no personal representative replacing her as a claimant. In *Mutua
and Others v Foreign and Commonwealth Office* [2011] EWHC 1913 (QB) the court held that
the claimants' claims, including an amended claim regarding the UK Government's vicarious
liability, were arguable and ordered determination of the limitation issue as a preliminary issue.

The defendant contended that the claims were statute barred and that a fair trial was not
possible, as the majority of witnesses who might have given material oral evidence were dead,
and that the vicarious liability claim was a considerable extension of the law which failed the
'broad merits' test. The claimants argued that a fair trial remained possible, and that the court
should exercise its discretion under s 33.

Held:

(i)   The court was required to consider 'all the circumstances of the case' and the six factors
        set out in s 33 (*B v Ministry of Defence* (p312) applied). The Court of Appeal in *B*
        also highlighted the fact that it would be inappropriate for the court to allow a trial to
        proceed if the claimants' prospects of success were slight; the 'broad merits' test.

(ii)   It was both permissible and appropriate to consider separately the different routes to
        liability being advanced by the claimants, and to exercise the s 33 discretion separately
        in relation to each. There was no need to interpret the phrase 'any specified cause of
        action' in s 33 as referring simply to individual torts themselves, such as 'assault' or

'negligence', as opposed to alternative routes to liability in respect of such a tort or torts. Section 33 permitted the court to allow a claim to proceed on one or more routes to liability while not doing so in respect of other routes, if that appeared to be the just course.

(iii)   The difficulties advanced by the defendant in respect of vicarious liability were more illusory than real. The legal issues raised were novel ones. The bases of claim all turned on the same factual background and the legal relationship between the perpetrators of the torture and the UK Government. The law regarding vicarious liability was in a continuous state of development, and the idea that, subject to very limited exceptions, vicarious liability for a tort only arose where the primary tort was committed by an employee within the scope of his employment was far too narrow. In light of those developments, the formulation of the claimants' claims could not be characterised as so weak as to fail the broad merits test, notwithstanding that the case would involve an expensive and resource-consuming trial. A court could find that their detention was part of a joint exercise by the UK Government and the colonial administration, giving rise to duties such as those owed by the prison authorities to prisoners.

(iv)   The factual issues could be fairly and cogently resolved largely by reference to the documents: the relationship between the perpetrators and the UK Government did not depend on oral evidence, and liability would not depend upon the defendant's knowledge or intention to commit torture. There was a case on which a court might conclude that there had been instigation or procurement of torture pursuant to a common design to restore law and order. Despite the absence of witnesses to add to and explain any impression derived from the papers, the evidence remained sufficiently cogent for the court to satisfactorily complete its task.

(v)   With regard to negligence, in addition to the existence of a duty of care, there were issues regarding the standard of care, whether a breach of duty had been established, and whether any such breach caused the claimants' injuries. It would be possible to determine from surviving constitutional and documentary material whether a duty of care existed. The standard of care to be applied was a matter of law on which no factual evidence was required other than the customary test of 'reasonable care'. Regarding breach of duty, it would be necessary to look at what happened to each of the claimants and what was known to the relevant authorities at the time, and what might reasonably have been done to prevent the particular acts of torture. There was an amply sufficient document base to test what was known about excessive use of force throughout the emergency period, and what London's reaction to that knowledge was. A fair trial of any question of breach of duty was therefore possible.

(vi)   There was good evidence of attempts by both Governments to limit investigation into abuses committed and that relevant evidence had thereby been lost. That had some relevance to the exercise of the court's discretion under s 33.

(vii)   The early delay on the part of the claimants was understandable. They were people of limited education and means. The possibility of any legal claim arising out of their now admitted ill-treatment was only brought to their attention by the Kenya Human Rights Commission ('KHRC') in the case of two of the surviving claimants in 2006, and in the case of the other in 2008. It was the KHRC who made contact with the solicitors who now act for the claimants, and those solicitors travelled to Kenya to interview the claimants in May 2009. The torture itself would have had an inhibiting effect. Moreover, until 2002/03 any attempt to pursue the claims would potentially have constituted a proscribed activity.

(viii)   Two of the three remaining claimants had therefore established a case for the court to direct that s 11 should not apply. However, different considerations applied to N. In that case, there had been no admission of mistreatment, and there was no signed witness or medical report available. Moreover, no proper steps had been taken to reconstitute the action on behalf of N's estate. The application under s 33 in respect of N was refused.

Preliminary issue determined.

Nanglegan v Royal Free Hampstead NHS Trust

CPR 6, 7

Court of Appeal   **[2001] EWCA Civ 127;**
[2002] 1 WLR 1043; [2001] 3 All ER 793

The claimant was injured on 3 May 1996 working for the defendant. She issued proceedings on 4 May 1999. This was the last day of the limitation period: 3 May was a bank holiday. In prior correspondence the defendant stated that it had instructed solicitors to accept service. The defendant's solicitors confirmed this on 5 July 1999. A medical expert was not instructed until 9 August 1999 and a written report produced on the day the claimant was examined, 19 August 1999. On 31 August 1999 the claimant's solicitor instructed his secretary to serve the claim form. It was served on the defendant rather than its solicitors. On 3 September 2003 the claimant's solicitor discovered the error and left a message for the defendant's solicitors. The claim form was sent on 6 September 2003, outside the validity period. It was served the following day. The defendant applied for the claim form to be struck out. The district judge held that the service was not CPR compliant but exercised her discretion under CPR 7.6 to extend time. The defendant appealed. The circuit judge held that the service was not valid and refused to retrospectively extend time. The claimant appealed.

Held:

(i)   CPR 6.5 was a difficult provision, but the best interpretation was that once a party gave an address for service, be it his or his solicitors', service had to be to that address.

(ii)   CPR 6.5(5) restricted the general obligation to give an address for service in 6.5 and the election of service address in 6.5(3). If a party gave his personal or business address, CPR 6.5(5) required service of the claim form on that address and service on his solicitors for any other document. This reflected the fact that in some cases the defendant's first involvement would be the receipt of the claim form.

(iii)   Conversely, where the parties had corresponded pre-issue, and the defendant had nominated solicitors to accept service, CPR 6.4 demanded that service could only be effected on the solicitors. CPR 6.4(2)(b) did not alter this requirement.

(iv)   The judge was right to hold that neither CPR 7.6(3)(b) or (c) had been satisfied and that there was therefore no jurisdiction to extend time for service (*Vinos v Marks & Spencer* (p701) followed).

Appeal dismissed.

Napper v National Coal Board (British Coal)

Limitation Act 1980, s 12, s 33

Woolf LJ   **Lexis, 1 March 1990**

The claimant was the son of Mr Napper who died on 17 January 1957. He had been working for the defendants as a miner at the Murton Colliery when he was struck by a heavy boulder or stone breaking away. For some period after the accident, the claimant's mother was represented by solicitors who communicated with the defendants. An official enquiry and an inquest were held.

In August 1985 the claimant's own solicitors obtained a statement from a Mr Lawson. That statement gave a different account of how his father came to meet his death from that which was given at the enquiry. The claimant issued a writ on 17 February 1988. His particulars of claim failed to establish negligence by the defendants.

The registrar struck out the proceedings on the grounds that they showed no reasonable cause of action and were statute barred. Kennedy J refused an extension of time for the claimant to appeal. The claimant applied for leave to appeal against this refusal.

Held:

(i)   It was necessary to take into account not only matters that were known but also matters that were ascertainable by those on whose behalf the action was brought. There was no evidence to indicate that proper enquiries had been made by Mrs Napper's solicitors and that it would not have been possible for the identity of Mr Lawson to be established at that time: s 14(3). Accordingly, the case was prima facie statute barred by s 12(2) of the Limitation Act 1980.

(ii)   In the lengthy period of time that had elapsed, there had undoubtedly been changes in the availability of witnesses. Some had died, and others would have the greatest difficulty now in recalling what had happened: s 33(3)(b). It would be extremely prejudicial to the defendants if they were to be faced with an action now: s 33(1).

The claimant's application was dismissed.

Nash & others v Eli Lilly & Co and others

Limitation Act 1980, s 11, s 14, s 33

Court of Appeal   **[1993] 1 WLR 782; [1993] 4 All ER 383; [1992] 3 Med LR 353; (1992) Times, 7 October**

A non-steroidal anti-inflammatory drug, Benoxaprofen, was manufactured by Eli Lilly to relieve the pain caused by arthritis. In March 1980 it was licensed for use in the United Kingdom under the name Opren. Initially it was only available for use by consultant physicians in hospitals, but in October 1980 it was made available for prescription by general practitioners. It proved to have serious side effects, in particular photosensitivity and onycholysis. In August 1982 the English product licence was withdrawn and the drug was withdrawn by Eli Lilly throughout the world.

Later in August 1982 the Opren Action Committee was formed to encourage compensation claims by patients against Eli Lilly and others. Litigation commenced by many UK claimants in the United States was dismissed in June 1984 on the ground of forum non conveniens. Attention reverted to the United Kingdom. Well over 1,000 claimants served writs by 1 October 1986 (Group A) and subsequently by 31 January 1987 (Group B). An offer of damages made around November 1987 was accepted by solicitors acting on behalf of Groups A and B claimants in January 1988.

Meanwhile further potential claimants had come forward. Those who served their writs by 9 May 1988 were known as Group C. Hidden J ordered that certain Group C claimants should have their cases tried as lead actions on the preliminary issue of limitation. He held at the preliminary trial that with one exception these claimant's actions were statute barred. They appealed.

Held:

1 Actual knowledge: s 14(1)

(a)   Suspicion, particularly if it is vague and unsupported, will clearly not be enough. However, belief may amount to or become knowledge.

(b)   Knowledge is a condition of mind which imports a degree of certainty. The degree of certainty that is appropriate for this purpose is that which, for the particular claimant, may reasonably be regarded as sufficient to justify embarking upon the preliminaries to the making of a claim for compensation, such as the taking of legal or other advice.

(c)   Whether or not a state of mind for this purpose is to be treated as knowledge depends in the first place upon the nature of the information which the claimant has received, the extent to which he pays attention to the information as affecting him, and his capacity to understand it. There is a second stage at which the information, when received or understood, is evaluated: it may be rejected as unbelievable or regarded as unreliable or uncertain. The court must assess the intelligence of the claimant, consider and assess his assertions as to how he regarded such information as he had and determine whether he had knowledge of the facts by reason of his understanding of the information.

(d)   The relevant date from which the limitation period runs is the date on which the claimant first had knowledge. Accordingly, if a claimant is shown to have had knowledge that his injury is attributable to the act or omission of the defendant, the subsequent obtaining of expert advice, which states that his injury is not so attributable, does not retrospectively cause him never to have had such knowledge and does not prevent time from running.

(e)   If a claimant held a firm belief which was of sufficient certainty to justify the taking of preliminary steps for proceedings by obtaining advice about making a claim for compensation, then such belief is knowledge and the limitation period runs from it.

(f)   If a claimant, while believing that his injury is attributable to the act or omission of the defendant, realises that his belief requires expert confirmation before he acquires such a certainty of belief as amounts to knowledge, then he will not have knowledge until that confirmation is obtained.

(g)   In any case where a claimant has sought legal advice and taken legal proceedings, it is difficult to perceive how it can rightly be held that he did not have relevant knowledge.

(h)   It is important to remember where the onus of proof lies. If a writ is not issued within three years of the date when the cause of action arose, the onus is on the claimant to plead and prove a date within the three years preceding the date of the issue of the writ. If the defendant wishes to rely on a date prior to the three-year period immediately preceding the issue of the writ, the onus is on the defendant to prove that the claimant had or ought to have had knowledge by that date.

2   *Significance of injury: s 14(1)(a), s 14(2)*

(a)   The *McCafferty* (*v Metropolitan Police Receiver*) test is accepted as correct, involving a combination of the subjective and the objective.

Taking that claimant, with that claimant's intelligence, would he have been reasonable in considering the injury not sufficiently serious to justify instituting proceedings for damages?

(b)   The distinction between an expected or accepted side effect, and an injurious and unacceptable consequence, of taking a prescribed drug is valid. Thus until the degree of photosensitivity, for example, was sufficient to indicate that the drug was causing an effect completely outside that of an acceptable side effect, it could not reasonably be said that the patient was aware of a significant injury.

3   *Attributability of injury: s 14(1)(b)*

(a)   'Attributable' means 'capable of being attributed'. The knowledge required is that attribution is possible, a real possibility and not a fanciful one, a possible cause as opposed to a probable cause of the injury.

(b)   There must be a degree of specificity, and not a mere global or catch-all character, about the act or omission which is alleged to constitute negligence or breach of duty. What is required is knowledge of the essence of the act or omission to which the injury is attributable.

(c)   The act or omission relevant in these cases is 'providing for the use of patients a drug which was unsafe in that it was capable of causing persistent photosensitivity in those patients and/or in failing to discover that this was the case so as properly to protect such patients'.

4   *Identity of defendants: s 14(1)(c)*

(a)   In the case of a corporate entity, such as a group of companies, the law provides that the true position of the member companies of the group structure are ascertainable.

(b)   The identity of the servant of Eli Lilly who was in charge of clinical research and of submissions of applications for licenses for drugs, was ascertainable on application to the Lilly defendants.

(c)   Accordingly, once attributability was established against one or more of these defendants, the identity of the remaining defendants was reasonably ascertainable.

5   *Constructive knowledge: s 14(3)*

(a)   The proper approach under s 14(3)(a) is to determine what this claimant should have observed or ascertained, while asking of him no more than is reasonable.

(b)   It is under s 14(3)(a) that the position of a solicitor falls to be considered. Since his advice as to the law is irrelevant for this purpose, his contribution can only consist of factual information. Moreover, where constructive knowledge through a solicitor is in issue, this can only be relevant where it is established that the claimant ought reasonably to have consulted a solicitor.

(c)   Section 14(3)(b) deals not only with medical advice but clearly extends to other experts whom it would be reasonable to expect the claimant to consult. In considering whether the enquiry is reasonable, the situation, character and intelligence of the claimant must be relevant.

(d)   In many of the cases, the general practitioner or specialist consulted by the claimant concentrated upon treatment, not attributability or fault. In these circumstances it would be unreasonable to attribute to a claimant knowledge possessed by a doctor, unless it would have been reasonable to expect the claimant to have sought advice which would have produced the information.

(e)   The mere announcement of the withdrawal of the drug, without more, did not necessarily put individual claimants on notice. In many cases, all that happened is that the claimant was taken off the drug. This common experience might fall short of putting a claimant on notice that there was some act or omission on the part of the manufacturer or supplier to which the undesirable effect was attributable.

(f)   This did not dispose of the defendants' argument that the patients might well have been alerted by the extensive publicity given to the unacceptable side effects of the drug and the establishment of the Opren Action Committee. This was an area in which the onus of proving constructive knowledge was on the defendants.

6   *Exercise of discretion: s 33*

(a)   The Court of Appeal will be very slow to interfere with the exercise of discretion under this section. Where, however, it is established that the judge either took into account factors which he should have ignored, or ignored factors which he should have taken into account, or was plainly wrong, then the Court of Appeal is under a duty to interfere and, in appropriate cases, to substitute a decision based on its own discretion.

(b)   Provided that it is relevant, the judge may take into account a factor not specifically listed in the subparagraphs of s 33(3). On the other hand, if it is established that he failed to take into account any of the matters mentioned in s 33(3) which were relevant to the carrying out of the balancing exercise, then his judgment is susceptible to attack. However, a judge is not under a duty specifically to refer to each and every fact which he has found and upon which he has exercised his discretion.

(c)   In the present cases, the judge fell into error in directing himself for the purposes of the s 33 issues with reference to cogency and prejudice to the defendants. As it was impossible to identify with certainty which of the possible grounds of prejudice the judge applied in any individual appeal, it was necessary to reconsider each case under s 33.

(d) The consideration under s 33 must be broadly based. The primary purpose of the limitation period is to protect the defendant against the injustice of having to face a stale claim. Once the claimant has allowed the permitted term to elapse, the defendant is no longer subject to the disability of accepting without protest the limitation period itself. In such a situation, the court is directed to consider all the circumstances of the case, including conduct before the expiry of the limitation period, and to balance the prejudice to the parties.

(e) It is not the case that wherever the ability of the defendants to contest the issue of liability has not been affected by the delay, the benefit of the limitation defence must be regarded as a windfall. It may be inequitable to secure to a dilatory claimant, who has let the limitation period pass without action, the power to claim from the defendants a sum in settlement of a poor case, which sum would reflect as much or more the risk in costs to the defendants as the fair value of the claim.

(f) If the judge attached any weight to the settlement of claim brought by claimants in Groups A and B, he was wrong. The defendants could have accepted the approach made in August 1987 on behalf of the other claimants. In so far as any prejudice was caused to the defendants by the presence of claimants in later Groups, this was directly attributable to the conduct of the defendants and should be ignored.

(g) 'Cogency' within s 33(3)(b) is directed to the degree to which either party is prejudiced in the presentation of the claim or defence because the evidence available to them is either no longer available or has been adversely affected by the passage of time. There is no room in this subsection for the concept, apparently accepted by the judge, that lack of cogency in the case of a claimant could enure to the benefit of that claimant's case and thereby prejudice the defendant.

(h) There cannot be a different method of applying the court's discretion in multi-partite cases from that in any ordinary individual claim. The judge was right to reject the submission that, were the court to exercise discretion in favour of all or a substantial number of the claimants, the action would be contrary to public policy.

NB: The reasoning on s 14 was at least partially overruled by the House of Lords in *Adams v Bracknell Forest BC* (p292).

(A) MRS NASH

Mrs Nash started to take Opren in April 1981. Soon afterwards, she began to suffer a painful scalding sensation on her skin whenever she went out into the sun. It got worse as the summer progressed. This skin sensitivity continued for about six months after she gave up Opren in June 1982. Her eye sensitivity had continued in very strong light ever since, but there was no contemporaneous record of any complaint over the years.

In June 1982 she saw a newspaper article which stated that Opren had caused significant side effects such as photosensitivity. Her doctor told her that Opren was to be withdrawn because of the side effects it had caused. She was convinced that Opren had caused her condition. In August 1982 her husband notified her claim to the manufacturers who disclaimed any responsibility for the side effects. Thereafter she did nothing until August 1987 when she read of and contacted the Open Action Group. Her writ was issued in April 1988.

Held:

(i) The judge was right to hold that by August 1982 Mrs Nash had actual knowledge of the significance and attributability of her injury. She also had constructive knowledge of the identity of at least one of the defendants. Therefore her date of knowledge was more than three years before the issue of her writ: s 11(4).

(ii) (a) The claimant, having advanced her claim in August 1982, laid it to rest for five years: s 33(3)(a);

(b) there was an absence of any contemporaneous record of complaint: s 33(3)(b);

(c) the judge regarded her claim as a weak case: s 33(3);

(d)   there would be significant prejudice to the defendants, and it would be inequitable to allow Mrs Nash's case to proceed: s 33(1).

(B) MRS ODAM

Mrs Odam started to take Opren in February 1981. In June 1982, on a holiday in Spain, she became aware of a burning and prickly sensation affecting her exposed skin. She became aware from a television programme in August 1982 that Opren had been withdrawn. Her general practitioner testified that he could not remember any complaint ever being made by her about skin and eye sensitivity up to 1987 but that, if she had asked him in August 1982, he would have told her that her symptoms were caused by Opren.

In August 1984 and October 1984 she wrote to Eli Lilly describing her symptoms and complaining of the embarrassment and expense incurred due to Opren. Their reply denied that the side effects suffered by her had been caused by Opren. A newspaper article prompted her to go to solicitors in 1987. Her writ was issued in January 1988.

Held:

(i)   Not only did she have actual knowledge of all relevant facts by August 1984 but also she had constructive knowledge by August 1982 because if she had asked her general practitioner, as reasonably she should have done, he would have told her that her symptoms were caused by Opren and she would have ascertained the rest: s 14(3). Her case was statute barred by s 11(4).

(ii)   (a)   The judge found that the real reason for her delay was her worry over what legal action would cost: s 33(3)(a);

(b)   the delay of 2½ years had affected the cogency of her evidence, and there was no corroboration by contemporaneous record of her complaints: s 33(3)(b);

(c)   the judge was right to hold that discretion should not be exercised in her favour: s 33(1).

(C) MR BOXALL

Mr Boxall took Opren from August 1981 until October 1981. Within two weeks of starting, he experienced serious symptoms of sensitivity to sunlight and to warmth. He was promptly referred back to the consultant rheumatologist who had prescribed the drug and was at once taken off it. He believed that his symptoms were caused by Opren and, from the withdrawal of the drug in August 1982, that it was unsafe. He did nothing until July 1987 when on advice from a Citizens Advice Bureau he consulted solicitors. His writ was issued in November 1987.

Held:

(i)   The judge was right to find that Mr Boxall had knowledge of all relevant facts by August 1982: s 14(1). His case was statute barred in August 1985: s 11(4).

(ii)   The judge could not be criticised for finding that:

(a)   Mr Boxall had over the years from 1982 considered making a claim and decided against it on the ground of costs of litigation: s 33(3)(a);

(b)   the delay of more than two years made the evidence likely to be less cogent than would have been the case had the action been brought at the appropriate time;

(c)   Mr Boxall had taken no steps to obtain medical or legal advice until 1987, although he had known by August 1982 that the drug was an unsafe product: s 33(3)(f);

(d)   the court's discretion should not be exercised so as to permit the claim to proceed: s 33(1).

(D) MRS DAY

Mrs Day began taking Opren in February 1981 but, due to the onycholysis which appeared to have resulted from it, she was taken off the drug in August 1981. She resumed taking it on prescription in November 1981, but in April 1982 she suffered severe photosensitivity and her general practitioner advised her not to take it any more. By early 1983 he was certain that Opren was the cause of her disability and communicated this to her. In February 1983 she wrote to Eli Lilly. There was no written record of any complaint of photosensitivity by her after December 1983. She did not obtain any medical or legal advice until 1987. Her writ was issued in November 1987.

Held:

(i)   The judge was entitled to find that Mrs Day had actual knowledge of the relevant facts by December 1982, or very shortly thereafter, in view of her letter to the defendants in February 1983 which demonstrated her prior knowledge: s 14(1). Accordingly, her case was statute barred by s 11(4).

(ii)   (a)   The proper inference from the delay of nearly two years was that in 1983 her symptoms were such that she decided not to advance a claim: s 33(3)(a);

        (b)   that inference was supported by the fact that there was no written record of any complaint of photosensitivity after December 1982: s 33(3)(b);

        (c)   she had not established that it would be equitable to allow her claim to proceed: s 33(1).

(E) MRS EATON

Mrs Eaton first took Opren in April 1981. Within a few weeks, she suffered severe symptoms of photosensitivity. The symptoms continued throughout that summer. In May 1982, as a result of reading a newspaper article and seeing a television programme, she decided to halve her intake of Opren. When her supply ran out in July or August 1982, she did not go to her doctor for more. Each year her symptoms returned. In March 1986 she went to see her doctor. In May 1987 she went to the CAB who referred her to the Opren Action Committee. Her writ was issued in November 1987.

Held:

(i)   The judge was right to find that she had suffered a significant injury and that she had actual knowledge of the identity of Eli Lilly by May 1982: s 14(1). Further, she had by August 1982 constructive knowledge of the relevant facts in that, if she had raised the matter with her general practitioner as would have been reasonable, he would have given her all the necessary answers: s 14(3).

(ii)   (a)   Between 1982 and 1986 she did not seek medical or legal advice: s 33(3)(f);

        (b)   the judge regarded this as a truly poor case in view of the lack of written record of complaints of photosensitivity, which was startling having regard to the severity of the symptoms as described: s 33(3);

        (c)   having regard to the prejudice to the defendants at being required to defend such a claim, it would not be equitable to allow the case to proceed.

(F) MRS O'HARA

Mrs O'Hara began taking Opren in September 1980. In the summer of 1981 she began to suffer symptoms of photosensitivity all over her arms and face. She consulted her general practitioner who told her to continue to use skin cream and to take the drug. In August 1982 she saw that Opren was withdrawn from the market because of the side effects caused by it. Her general practitioner prescribed another drug in its place.

In February 1983 she wrote to the Opren Action Committee and filled in a questionnaire that they sent her. She felt that she lacked the money and the education to take the case further. From 1983 to 1988 she spent her time nursing her husband who was dying. The dim light indoors reduced the effects of her injury. In June 1987 she learned from a television programme that claims were being made for damages for the results of the side effects of Opren. She was referred by the CAB to solicitors. Her writ was issued in November 1987.

Held:

(i)   It was acknowledged that the judge was justified in finding that by February 1983, when she wrote to the Opren Action Committee, she had both actual and constructive knowledge of all the relevant facts under s 14.

(ii)   (a)   The relevant delay of some 1½ years had been caused by financial constraints and domestic circumstances: s 33(3)(a);

       (b)   the absence of any contemporaneous record of any complaint by her to her doctor might cast substantial doubt on the severity of her symptoms as now recalled by her: s 33(3)(b);

       (c)   the judge was not regarding this as a poor case in the sense discussed above: s 33(3);

       (d)   upon the judge's findings of fact, the different conclusion should be reached that it would be equitable to allow Mrs O'Hara's action to proceed: s 33(1).

(G) MRS HIGGINS

Mrs Higgins first took Opren in October 1981. Her case was that she began to suffer symptoms of photosensitivity in May 1982 and that she also had other symptoms such as growth of facial hairs, loss of head hair, and depression. In July 1982, having read reports of deaths caused by Opren, she was taken off the drug at her own request and her general practitioner commented that side effects were a normal consequence of taking drugs.

Although she continued to see her doctor on a monthly basis, she did not complain of any further side effects and neither of them mentioned Opren again. In 1987, when she learned from a newspaper of claims being made, she went to the CAB, was referred to the Opren Action Committee and consulted solicitors. Her writ was issued in November 1987.

Held:

(i)   The judge was justified in finding that by July 1982 she was aware of the significance of her injury, had actual knowledge of its attributability and constructive knowledge of the identity of the defendants: s 14. Her general practitioner's words to the effect that all drugs have side effects were said merely as a statement of fact when she mentioned press reports of Opren deaths. Her claim was therefore statute barred: s 11(4).

(ii)   (a)   The main ground of the judge's refusal to exercise discretion was the total absence of record of any complaint of symptoms to her doctor when it was clear to the judge that, if she had been suffering these symptoms, she would have informed her doctor and sought advice and help: s 33(3);

       (b)   this was another case in which there would be disproportionate prejudice to the defendants if the action were allowed to proceed: s 33(1).

(H) MRS FORSTER

Mrs Forster had suffered rheumatoid arthritis since 1976. She received a number of different treatments and experienced reactions to many, including rashes and skin irritation. In November 1980 she started to take Opren. She suffered symptoms of photosensitivity in April 1981. She thought this was due to Opren, but when she told her general practitioner he said that he did not know what had caused it. She also discussed the matter with a consultant, but he did not take it seriously and asked what was more important to her, being able to sit in the sun or being able to walk. She took his advice and carried on taking the drug until July 1982. She was aware of the withdrawal of Opren in August 1982 but had thought that this was because it caused liver problems in elderly patients. The reaction to sunlight recurred in the summer of 1983. She had had innumerable appointments with her general practitioner and various consultants, but they all seemed to believe that her continuing photosensitivity was just an unfortunate consequence of her body's reactions to drugs as a whole.

When she saw a television programme in June 1987, she was prompted to write to the Opren Action Committee. She instructed solicitors in July 1987, and her writ was issued in September 1987.

Held: the judge appeared to have accepted in general her evidence. If her account of her dealings with her doctor was correct, the judge erred in finding that she had only actual or constructive knowledge of the relevant facts under s 14 before September 1984. Accordingly, her case was not statute barred: s 11(4).

(I) MR COCKBURN

Mr Cockburn was the only one of the so-called nine lead cases to succeed on limitation. The order for directions by Hirst J had provided that, unless otherwise ordered, 'any costs which are ordered to be paid by, or which fall to be borne by, a claimant shall be paid or borne proportionately by each of the claimants whose action is included in any Schedule III Action (including those claimants who are legally aided) so that each such claimant shall bear an equal part thereof'. Hidden J ordered the defendants to pay 1/338 of Mr Cockburn's costs. It was estimated that this would amount to about £90 out of £30,000.

Held:

(i) The order for directions only provided for contribution between claimants. It was not directed to orders for costs in favour of claimants.

(ii) The trial judge's order was unjust in its effect and clearly wrong. There was no reason to make an exception to the general rule under RSC Ord 62, r 3(3) that costs should follow the event.

(iii) Accordingly, the order was set aside, and the precise terms of a fresh order left until after submissions from counsel.

(J) MISS JENKINS

Miss Jenkins started to take Opren in March 1981. She first suffered symptoms of photosensitivity in August 1981. Her general practitioner took her off Opren in May 1982 because it was making no impression on her arthritis. No further mention was made of it by him or her. In September 1982 she had a nervous breakdown with depression. In January 1983 her sister wrote to Jack Ashley MP about Miss Jenkins and Opren and received a letter with information from the Opren Action Group. In July 1987 Miss Jenkins herself wrote to Mr Ashley that 'I took Opren tablets for some time during 1981 and suffered as a result. I have not put in a claim as quite honestly I could not afford the cost'. Her writ was issued in April 1988.

Held:

(i) The judge was entitled to find that she had knowledge of significant injury at the end of 1982 or the beginning of 1983 at the latest: s 14(1)(a). As to attributability, the information in her sister's January 1983 letter must have come from her: s 14(1)(b). The identity of the defendants was ascertainable: s 14(1)(c). Her case was statute barred: s 11(4).

(ii) The proper inference was that she decided that a claim was not worth pursuing: s 33(3)(a). Her case was made weaker by her impaired memory, and she had made no contemporaneous complaint to her general practitioner of the onset and progress of her allegedly severe symptoms: s 33(3)(b). The judge regarded this as a poor claim: s 33(3). The defendants would be prejudiced, and it would not be equitable to allow the action to proceed: s 33(1).

(K) MR STANLEY

Mr Stanley started to take Opren in August 1981. His case was that from the late summer of 1981 onwards he suffered severe symptoms of photosensitivity. He ceased taking Opren in about June 1982 when another drug was prescribed. In August 1982 he told his general practitioner that he had been on Opren for several months and that he had noticed increasing stiffness in his ankles as a result. He knew of the withdrawal of Opren on the grounds of safety. In 1983 he wrote to the Opren Action Committee. In 1987 he consulted a doctor for the first time about his skin condition. After he saw a television programme about Opren, his writ was issued in November 1987.

Held:

(i)   (a)   The judge found that Mr Stanley believed that his symptoms were caused by Opren by the time he applied to the Opren Action Committee for assistance. The finding that this belief amounted to actual knowledge was of uncertain validity, since his letter to the Committee was consistent with his holding the view that he needed further information and confirmation about the attributability of his symptoms: s 14(1).

        (b)   however, the judge was entitled to hold that he had constructive knowledge by 1983, because if his account of his symptoms was correct he should reasonably have reported them to his doctors and would have acquired the knowledge available from them. His constructive knowledge was to be judged upon his evidence about his injury: s 14(3).

(ii)   The judge's refusal to exercise his discretion under s 33 in Mr Stanley's favour was not referred to in the typed judgment.

The appeal was dismissed.

(L) MR SIVYER

Mr Sivyer started to take Opren in November 1980. He began to suffer symptoms of photosensitivity and light sensitivity in the summer of 1981. On 6 August 1982 his general practitioner recovered his remaining Opren tablets from him. Mr Sivyer did not complain to him about his problems, because he did not want to waste his time. Both his general practitioner and his consultant testified that, if he had asked, they would have told him that Opren was unsafe and the probable cause of his symptoms.

In June 1987 Mr Sivyer saw a newspaper article, as a result of which he consulted solicitors. His writ was issued in March 1988.

Held:

(i)   The judge was justified in finding that Mr Sivyer had actual or/and constructive knowledge of all of the relevant facts by the end of 1983 at the latest. He was suffering allegedly severe symptoms, he must have known that Opren was the cause of them, that Opren had been withdrawn and that its nature had caused his general practitioner to call to recover from him all unused Opren tablets: s 14. Accordingly, his case was statute barred: s 11(4).

(ii)   This was another case of the judge not accepting evidence to the effect that complaints had been made of symptoms. If Mr Sivyer was suffering the symptoms which he now described, it was reasonable for him to report them to his doctors and seek advice. His appeal must be dismissed: s 33.

(M) MR KIRBY

Mr Kirby took Opren from 23 January 1981 to 3 February 1981. On the latter date his general practitioner noted: 'red hot needle feeling in the neck, sunlight, query skin sensitivity due to Opren'. Dr Myers told him that he thought that his skin symptoms were due to Opren. Indeed Mr Kirby believed this himself. In May 1983 Dr Myers referred him to a skin specialist, Dr McMillan, who advised that Opren was not the cause of the symptoms and Mr Kirby accepted what he was told.

In June 1987 his daughter sent him a newspaper article. He then saw three television programmes about Opren, which caused him to consult solicitors. In July 1987 Mr Kirby was referred again to Dr McMillan who again excluded Opren as the cause of his symptoms and advised that his skin complaint was a natural condition of seborrhoeic dermatitis. His writ was issued in January 1988.

Held: his appeal must be allowed.

Per Purchas LJ: 'The judge did not reject, and there was no apparent reason to reject, Mr Kirby's assertion that he had accepted and believed the advice of Dr McMillan. It seems to us that there was no sufficient evidence upon which Hidden J could properly hold that the belief held by Mr Kirby in 1981, that his skin condition had been caused by Opren, had become a state of mind of such degree of certainty or confidence that in 1982 or 1983 it was knowledge for the purposes of section 14 of the Act. The inescapable, or at least the better and safer, inference from his conduct is that, although he thought that Opren was the cause, he had sought advice from Dr Myers for confirmation of that belief and Dr Myers had advised him to obtain more expert advice; and Mr Kirby had accepted that advice from Dr Myers; and that Mr Kirby had accepted and acted upon the advice of Dr McMillan which was to the effect that Opren was not the cause of the symptoms. This is not a case of established knowledge being reversed or suspended by later advice but of the receipt of information by Mr Kirby in such a sequence and of such nature that, as it was understood by Mr Kirby, the information did not result at the relevant time in the acquisition of knowledge by him. It may be, in circumstances of this nature, that the actions of a claimant might provide safe grounds for inferring that, despite the receipt of adverse advice from a specialist, he still, upon the information which he had, believed that his symptoms constituted a significant injury attributable to the act or omission with such a degree of confidence that it must in those circumstances be regarded as knowledge for that purpose. We cannot regard this as such a case. The onus of proof is on the defendants and, in our judgment, it has not been discharged.'

(N) MRS BERGER

Mrs Berger started to take Opren in April 1981. Around July 1981 she developed a red rash over her face and suffered symptoms of photosensitivity. In August 1982 she saw a television programme as a result of which she consulted her general practitioner who told her to stop taking Opren. He testified that if she had complained of a photosensitive reaction, he could have told her that it might be due to Opren. Her specialist gave similar evidence. Mrs Berger mentioned in cross-examination not seeking advice because of cost. Her writ was issued in November 1987.

Held: the judge's conclusion that in 1982 she had attributed her symptoms to Opren, had known that the drug had been withdrawn on grounds of safety but had decided not to pursue the matter, could not be questioned. His conclusion that she had constructive knowledge of all relevant facts by the end of 1982 was open to him on the evidence. She described severe symptoms of photosensitivity, and it was reasonable for her to have sought advice about them from the doctors. Had she done so, she would probably have learned that such symptoms were a significant injury, not mere side effects, and that they were attributable to the act or omission of the Lilly defendants of whom the identities were ascertainable: s 14.

She had not made an application under s 33. Her appeal was dismissed.

(O) MRS BUSUTTILL-REYNAUD

Opren was first prescribed to Mrs Busuttill-Reynaud in March 1982. A few weeks later, she suffered a painful burning sensation in her skin whenever it was exposed to bright sunlight. Her scalp was affected. In August 1982 she saw publicity about Opren and returned her tablets. An intelligent woman who kept herself informed about matters to do with arthritis, she did not complain to her doctor about photosensitive reactions between March 1982 and October 1986. Her writ was issued in January 1988.

Held: the judge's finding that she ought reasonably to have reported her symptoms to her doctor was unassailable. Had she done so in 1982 or early 1983, she would have acquired knowledge of the relevant facts. While she did not have actual knowledge of the identity of all defendants by the end of 1982, there was constructive knowledge at latest by the end of 1983: s 14. Her case was statute barred.

There was no mention of s 33. Her appeal was dismissed.

(P) MRS NEWELL

Mrs Newell started to take Opren in May 1982. She consulted her general practitioner about a photosensitive rash in July 1982, and he stopped her taking Opren then. From August 1982 she suffered painful burning and irritation of her skin when exposed to bright sunlight. Before the end of 1982 she attributed her symptoms to Opren which she knew had been withdrawn. She did not complain of them to her doctor until 1987. Her writ was issued in April 1988.

Held: upon the assumption that her description of her symptoms from August 1982 was accurate, she ought reasonably to have sought the advice of her doctor. If she had done so and had reported the contribution of her symptoms into 1983, she would have acquired all relevant knowledge from her doctor very strongly: s 14. The judge was justified in concluding that her sole reason for not pursuing the matter was the question of cost. Her case was statute barred: s 11(4).

There being no mention of s 33, her appeal was dismissed.

(Q) MRS FELL

Mrs Fell first took Opren on 18 May 1981 and stopped on 1 June 1981 because of a skin rash. She took it again from 11 December 1981 until 22 April 1982 when it was stopped because of photosensitivity. She continued to suffer photosensitivity and intolerance of heat. She attributed her condition to Opren, but did not return to her doctor to complain of it. In 1987 she saw a television programme involving Jack Ashley MP and was referred to a solicitor in December 1987. Her writ was issued in March 1988.

Held: on the assumption that her description of her symptoms from 1982 was accurate, it was reasonable for her to report them to her doctor and seek his advice. If she had done so, and thus made it clear to him that the symptoms were continuing after she had ceased to take the drug, he would have provided to her the requisite knowledge: s 14. The judge's findings as to her date of knowledge were justified by the evidence. Her case was statute barred: s 11(4).

There was no reference to s 33. Her appeal was dismissed.

NB: The partly subjective test for constructive knowledge, described in *McCafferty v Metropolitan Police District Receiver* (p546), has since been disapproved: *Adams v Bracknell Forest BC* (p292).

Nathoo v Ashford & St Peter's Hospital Trust

CPR 6 **[2004] EWHC 1571; LTL 24/11/2003**

The claimant was injured in a road traffic accident on 11 November 1999. She was treated – allegedly in a negligent fashion - at the defendant's hospital on 13 November 1999. Proceedings were issued on 8 November 2002. The claimant was given permission to serve the claim form by 22 April 2003. On 25 March 2003 she sent a letter to the defendant enclosing the claim form but specifically stating that service was not being effected. On 21 April 2003 (a bank holiday) the claimant sent the claim form and particulars to the defendant by fax and first class post. The defendant had not agreed to accept service by fax. The master held that the deemed date of service was 23 or 24 April. He refused the claimant's application to dispense with service under CPR 6.9. The claimant appealed.

Held:

(i) The facts of this case did not amount to exceptional circumstances (*Anderton v Clwyd County Council* (p303) applied). The letter of 25 March was insufficient to qualify.

(ii) The master had considered all relevant factors and authorities.

Appeal dismissed.

Nawaz & another v Crowe Insurance Group

Road Traffic Act 1988, s 152

**[2003] EWCA Civ 316;
[2003] CP Rep 41; [2003] RTR 29;
[2003] Lloyd's Rep IR 471**

The claimant was injured in a road traffic accident on 25 August 1998. The claimant obtained default judgment against the driver, Mr Choudry, and then issued separate proceedings against his insurers (the defendant) to satisfy default judgment. The claimant's solicitor contacted the defendant's secretary to obtain details of the other driver, explaining that the details were needed because proceedings were about to be issued. Proceedings were issued on. The defendant argued that it had no liability as notice pursuant to s 152 of the 1988 Act had not been given. The district judge found that permission had been given. On appeal the circuit judge reversed this decision. The claimant appealed.

Held:

(i)   A legal secretary was an appropriate person to receive the notice required under s 152.

(ii)   Although the purpose of the telephone call was otherwise, it clearly communicated that proceedings were about to be commenced. This should have rung alarm bells.

(iii) The circuit judge's decision was wrong. The court exercised its discretion to set aside judgment and join the defendant.

Appeal allowed.

Nemeti & Ors v Sabre Insurance Company Ltd

Limitation Act 1980, s 35   **CPR 19.5**

Foreign Limitation Periods Act 1984, s 1

QBD (HHJ Cotter QC)   **[2012] EWHC 3355 (QB)**

On 29 December 2007 the claimants were injured in a road traffic accident in Romania in which the driver of their car (D) died. Sabre provided motor insurance to D's father in respect of the car, but D was uninsured. The claimants brought a claim against Sabre alleging that, as it was the insurer of the car, it was directly liable to them under the European Communities (Rights against Insurers) Regulations 2002. Under s 1 of the Foreign Limitation Periods Act 1984 the Romanian law of limitation applied. This stipulated a fixed three-year period; it provided no discretion to extend, as is found in s 33. The claim was therefore statute barred as of 30 December 2010. Proceedings were issued on 8 December 2010 and served on 11 February 2011.

Sabre pleaded that the claimants had no direct cause of action against it and applied to strike out. The claimants accepted that the claim against Sabre was unsustainable and so applied to substitute D's estate for Sabre in their claim. Although it was outside the relevant limitation period, the master, adopting a purposive approach to the 2002 Regulations, considered that he could order substitution pursuant to s 35(6) and CPR 19.5(3)(b) on the basis that it was necessary for the determination of the claimants' original action against Sabre. Sabre appealed.

Held:

(i)   The provisions allowing the addition or substitution of a party were necessarily restrictive as to the limited circumstances in which it was permissible to deprive a defendant of the accrued right of a limitation period. They were solely aimed at errors in the constitution or formality of the action, relating to the parties joined to it, or the capacity in which parties sued or were sued, which made the extant action unsustainable. The addition or substitution of parties had to be necessary to cure some defect.

(ii)   The relevant question was whether the substitution was necessary for the determination of the original proceedings against Sabre, and it had to be necessary for the maintenance of the existing action, and not for the assertion of a new action (*Roberts v Gill & Co* (p625) applied).

(iii)   In many instances, when well into the life of an action, a claimant might wish to pursue another party as ultimate recovery post-judgment might be more likely than with a current defendant. However, that could not of itself merit substitution outside a limitation period which would otherwise provide a defence to the proposed defendant. That would fundamentally attack the ability of any party to rely on a limitation defence.

(iv)   Whilst the powers under s 35 and CPR 19.5 permitted the addition or substitution of parties after the relevant limitation period had expired, they were properly restrictive as to the circumstances when such a course was permissible. The proposed substitution in the instant case simply did not meet the necessity test on any ordinary and natural interpretation of s 35 and CPR 19.5. It could not be said that the substitution of the estate for Sabre was necessary for the determination of the original action against Sabre. It might have been necessary for effective recovery from an insurer, but that was a very different thing. On analysis, the substitution sought to bring a new action against D's estate. A purposive interpretation in light of Article 3 of the Fourth Motor Insurance Directive (2000/26/EC) produced no different result; the language of s 35 was clear, as was that of the 2002 Regulations. If the 2002 Regulations failed to give proper effect to the Directive, that was a matter for the claimant to take up with the state by way of a *Francovich* action.

(v)   Accordingly, the master erred. The interpretation he had adopted was inconsistent with the fundamental features of the Act: it would require the necessarily restrictive elements to be simply ignored, and as a result would significantly undermine the protection afforded by a limitation period. Whilst this provided Sabre with a windfall, and left the claimants with the unsatisfactory alternative remedies of a professional negligence claim and a *Francovich* action, the problems the claimants faced were of their own making as they had left matters too late.

Appeal allowed.

Newell v Eli Lilly & Co and others

Limitation Act 1980, s 11, s 14

Court of Appeal   **[1992] 3 Med LR 398**

See *Nash v Eli Lilly & Co* (P) (p568)

Newman v Bevan Funnell Ltd

Limitation Act 1980, s 11, s 14, s 33

Court of Appeal   **Lexis, 29 October 1990**

On 6 February 1979 the claimant (Mr Newman), then aged 17, was required by his chargehand to help him lift the base of a secretaire bookcase, estimated by the claimant to weigh 500–700 lbs, onto a worktable. He complained of constant back pain from that date onwards, and from time to time consulted his general practitioner about it. His 18th birthday was on 5 October 1979. When he consulted his general practitioner in May 1984 about back pain, the doctor attributed it to some kind of muscle strain and referred him to a consultant orthopaedic surgeon, Mr Staniforth, who shared this diagnosis. Although his condition progressively deteriorated from 1984, the claimant refrained from claiming damages due to loyalty to his employers and fear of unemployment. In January 1986 Mr Staniforth caused further x-rays to be taken, as a result of which he changed the diagnosis and ascribed the claimant's pain and discomfort to a stress fracture sustained in the 1979 accident.

In July 1986 the claimant instructed solicitors who sent an explicit letter before action in September 1986. His application for legal aid was initially refused and only granted subsequently on appeal. The writ was issued on 8 December 1987. The defendants' chargehand was still alive and well. Comprehensive medical records throughout the period were available. At the preliminary trial on limitation, Judge Hammerton sitting as a judge of the High Court held that the case was prima facie statute barred but disapplied the limitation provisions under s 33 of the Limitation Act 1980. The defendants appealed.

Held:

(i)   The judge had found that the claimant had knowledge by October 1982, the trial anniversary of his 18th birthday, or alternatively by June 1984 when he consulted not only his general practitioner but also the orthopaedic surgeon. There was no appeal from that finding. The judge would have been entitled to infer that the claimant did not have knowledge of causation until Mr Staniforth changed the diagnosis in January 1986.

(ii)   (a)   The judge reasonably concluded that until it was suggested in January 1986 that there was a mechanical cause for the claimant's back condition no one could have formulated a claim on his behalf, and that the delay was caused by a faulty medical diagnosis: s 33(3)(a);

(b)   although problems would be caused by the fact that the witnesses would be giving evidence about matters over 10 years old, both parties were equally affected by this delay and prejudice to the defendants was alleviated by the simplicity of the accident as well as by the completeness of the medical records: s 33(3)(b);

(c)   the judge's exercise of his discretion in relation to the period after June 1984 was unexceptionable: s 33(1).

The defendants' appeal was dismissed.

Newton v Cammell Laird & Co (Shipbuilders and Engineers) Ltd

Limitation Act 1963, s 7

Court of Appeal   **[1969] 1 All ER 708; [1969] 1 WLR 415;**
[1969] 1 Lloyd's Rep 224

From 1943 to 1955 Ernest Newton was employed by the defendants as a ship's electrician. He was exposed to substantial quantities of asbestos arising out of insulation work carried out by laggers. In August 1964 he began to feel unwell. In October 1964 an x-ray showed a left pleural effusion. In January 1965 a hospital chest physician told him that he was suffering pleurisy due to asbestos to which he had been exposed in the course of his employment by the defendants and advised him to apply to the DHSS for industrial disablement benefit. In May 1965 he was notified that the application had been granted with his disability assessed at 50%. He was in fact suffering from the malignant asbestos related tumour of mesothelioma from which he died on 29 August 1965.

After obtaining leave under the Limitation Act 1963, the claimant (his widow) issued a writ on 25 August 1966. The defendants pleaded that the case was statute barred. Park J rejected this defence at a preliminary trial. The defendants appealed.

Held:

(i)   The claimant had actual knowledge in January 1965 that he was suffering from a serious illness due to exposure to asbestos dust.

(ii) He never had actual knowledge that the defendants were guilty of negligence or breach of duty or that his illness was attributable to their negligence or breach of duty. The question was when if at all he had constructive knowledge of these facts.

(iii) It was clear that he was fighting for his life and had neither time nor inclination to think about possible claims for damages. Even at the time of his death, the date had not arrived when it could be considered reasonable for him to take legal advice about an action for damages.

(iv) Therefore time had not begun to run against him, even by the time he died. The claimant's claim had been brought in time within 12 months thereafter.

The defendants' appeal was dismissed.

NB: By s 14(1) of the Limitation Act 1980, knowledge that any acts or omissions, as a matter of law, involved negligence or breach of duty is now irrelevant in assessing the date of knowledge. Under ss 11 and 12, such a case would not be statute barred in any event.

The Niceto de Larrinaga

(Navarro v Larrinaga Steamship Co Ltd)

Maritime Conventions Act 1911, s 8

Hewson J　　　　　　　　　　　　**[1965] 2 All ER 930; [1965] 3 WLR 573; [1965] 2 Lloyd's Rep 134**

On 23 September 1961 Bernard Navarro was a member of the crew of the defendants' steamship Niceto de Larrinaga when it collided with the steamship Sitala in the English Channel. He died on the same day.

The writ of the claimant (his mother) was issued on 18 September 1964. The defendants moved that the case be dismissed, claiming that it was statute barred by the two-year time limit in s 8 of the Maritime Conventions Act 1911.

Held:

(i) Section 8 of the 1911 Act only applied to claims against *another* vessel.

(ii) As the claimant's claim was against the owners of the same vessel in which her husband had been a passenger, s 8 did not apply and her claim was not statute barred.

Norman v Ali and Aziz

Limitation Act 1980, s 11

Court of Appeal　　　　　　　　　　**[2000] RTR 107; [2000] PIQR P72; [2000] Lloyd's Rep IR 395**

The claimant suffered personal injuries on 9 October 1992 when a car driven by the first defendant and owned by the second defendant struck her car. There was a dispute as to whether the first defendant had insurance cover. She first issued proceedings against the first defendant on 2 April 1993. There were numerous procedural complications until August 1997 when fresh proceedings were issued on the second defendant. Earlier proceedings brought against the second defendant on 20 June 1996 were discontinued as no proper notice under the Motor Insurers' Bureau agreement had been given. As a condition precedent of their potentially satisfying the claim, the Motor Insurers' Bureau required the claimant to issue proceedings against the second defendant for permitting the first defendant to drive when his (the first defendant's) car was uninsured against third party risks as in *Monk v Warbey* [1935] 1 KB 75.

At a preliminary hearing, the judge granted a declaration that the relevant limitation period was six rather than three years (if it had been three years, the claim would have been statute barred by s 11 and the rule in *Walkley v Precision Forgings* (p705)). The second defendant appealed.

Held:

(i)   The *Monk v Warbey* action was an action for breach of duty which included a claim for damages in respect of personal injury. It was distinct from the position in *Ackbar v Green* (p291) where the breach of duty was independent of the accident. It therefore fell within s 11 and the correct period was three years.

(ii)   The question 'What is the action all about?' was not a useful approach to s 11, as an action can simultaneously be about several things.

Norton v Corus UK Ltd

Limitation Act 1980, s 14(2)

Court of Appeal   **[2006] EWCA Civ 1630; LTL 13/11/2006**

The claimant had been employed by the defendant between 1969 and 1998 using vibrating tools. From about 1992 the claimant suffered symptoms of hand and arm vibration syndrome but did nothing about it until 2003 when a relative informed him of having made a successful claim against another employer. The claimant instructed solicitors and a medical diagnosis was sought. Proceedings were issued on 10 September 2004. Limitation was heard as a preliminary issue.

The judge ruled that the claimant had actual knowledge in 2003 but constructive knowledge in 1997 and probably 1992 or 1993. She declined to exercise her s 33 discretion in the claimant's favour.

The claimant appealed.

Held:

(i)   The injury was significant in 2003 and, on the evidence, no less significant in 1992. The claimant's conversation with his relative did not alter its significance or its attribution, of which the claimant was aware through the pattern of his symptoms. The judge's conclusions in relation to constructive knowledge were correct (*Adams v Bracknell Forest BC* (p292) considered).

(ii)   The judge had accepted that the onus was on the defendant to establish constructive knowledge. There was nothing objectionable in her finding that a doctor would have identified the injury if the claimant had sought his advice earlier.

(Permission to appeal the s 33 point was conditional upon the appeal court holding that knowledge was no earlier than 1997.)

Appeal dismissed.

The Norwhale

(Owners of the vessel Norwhale v Ministry of Defence)

Maritime Conventions Act 1911, s 8

Brandon J   **[1975] 2 All ER 501; [1975] QB 589;
[1975] 2 WLR 829**

The claimants were the Australian owners of the sullage barge Norwhale. The defendants owned and operated the aircraft carrier HMS Eagle. On 17 February 1968 the Norwhale was brought alongside the Eagle in Freemantle Harbour to take oily water from her. It remained alongside during the night when the Eagle discharged liquid from a number of side orifices on to the deck of the Norwhale. This caused the barge to list, so that further water from the harbour entered her and she sank.

The writ was issued on 16 August 1973. The defendants pleaded the two-year time limit in s 8 of the Maritime Conventions Act 1911. The claimants relied on the 1910 International Convention for the Unification of Certain Rules of Law with respect to Collisions between Vessels.

Held:

(i) The references in s 1(1) and s 8 of the 1911 Act to fault were entirely general. Their wording was wide enough to include not only faults of navigation but other faults as well.

(ii) This did not signify any failure on the part of the UK to fulfil its obligations in relation to the 1910 Convention which covered collisions and navigational fault respectively. It simply meant that the provisions of the Convention had been applied to other cases as well.

(iii) Accordingly, s 8 of the 1911 Act applied to the claimant's claim. It was therefore out of time and could not be maintained.

NV Proctor & Gamble and others v Gartner KG & others

CPR 7

Andrew Smith J
[2005] EWHC 90 (Comm); (2006) 1 Lloyd's Rep 82; LTL 27/5/2005

The claimants claimed from the defendants in respect of a lost cargo shipment. The first defendant was an Austrian company who had provided transport services. The claimants pursued the first defendant through recovery agents. An extension of time for service was agreed between the claimants and the first defendant, but the lack of agreement to this on the part of the fifth defendant forced the claimant to issue proceedings. The first defendant's English solicitors were not authorised to accept service. The claimants applied successfully for an extension of time to serve on the first defendant in Austria. A second extension was required, applied for and granted. Both extensions were granted on paper and without notice to the defendant. The defendant applied to have the extension orders set aside on the basis that the claimants' evidence in support of the applications had not disclosed good reasons for not serving within time.

Held:

(i) Although the claimants could be criticised to an extent for lack of urgency, they had not been entirely inert.

(ii) The first defendant had always been well aware that the claim was being pursued but had given no indication of a desire for a speedy resolution.

(iii) The first defendant had provided no explanation for wanting proceedings served in Austria when it had English solicitors.

(iv) The evidence in support of the applications was thin and did not provide detailed explanations as to the failure to serve within time as required by the Practice Direction to Part 7.

(v) The delay in service had not prejudiced the first defendant.

(vi) In the circumstances it would be disproportionate to deprive the claimants of their claim by setting the orders aside.

Application dismissed.

Oakes v Hopcroft

Limitation Act 1980, s 14A

Court of Appeal   **[2000] Lloyd's Rep Med 394; (2000) 56 BMLR 136; [2000] Lloyd's Rep PN 946**

The claimant suffered an accident at work on 27 August 1980. She was examined by the defendant, her treating orthopaedic surgeon, who in 1982 gave an optimistic diagnosis and prognosis. On the basis of the defendant's report the claimant was advised by her solicitors and counsel to settle her claim against her employer for £2,000, which she duly did in January 1983. By 1988 the claimant's physical symptoms remained severe. A medical report obtained in 1990 stated that the claimant was suffering form permanent and disabling injuries which the defendant had negligently misdiagnosed. The claimant issued proceedings on 8 March 1991 against the defendant for the difference between the settlement she accepted and the award she would have achieved with a correct diagnosis. The critical date for limitation purposes was 8 March 1988 pursuant to s 14A as added by s 1 of the Latent Damage Act 1986. Limitation was heard as a preliminary issue and the judge held that the claim was statute barred. The claimant appealed.

Held:

(i) (per Waller and Clark LJJ) The claimant did not know of any causative misdiagnosis until she received the later medical report, and time did not begin to run until then. The judge erred in concentrating of the claimant's knowledge of her physical injuries rather than her knowledge of under-settlement.

(ii) (per Woolf LCJ) Although by January 1988 the claimant knew that the defendant had significantly underestimated her injuries, she had no reason to doubt or dispute the advice of solicitors and counsel that the claim was only worth £2,000. She did not have knowledge under s 14A until she knew not only of the misdiagnosis but also that the settlement she accepted was too low due to the defendant's actions.

(iii) It was not unreasonable for the claimant to fail to seek a second opinion earlier than she did. Once a claimant acts on advice, as time passes that advice is pushed to the back of the mind until an event occurs challenging the advice.

Appeal allowed.

Oates v Harte Read & Co (a firm)

Limitation Act 1980, s 11, s 38

Singer J   **[1999] 1 FLR 1221; [1999] Lloyd's Rep PN 215; [1999] PIQR P120**

The claimant claimed damages against her former solicitors in a professional negligence action which included a claim for anxiety and stress arising from their handling of her divorce ancillary relief claim. The master held that this was an action in respect of personal injuries as defined by s 38 and therefore fell within s 11. The claim was thus statute barred. However, the master allowed the claimant to abandon the personal injuries claim by amendment. The defendant appealed and the claimant cross-appealed.

Held:

(i)   The claim for stress and anxiety was clearly a personal injury claim when viewed with a common sense approach (*Bennett v Greenland Houchen & Co* (p329) applied). It was clear that the claimant did not consider this aspect of her claim to be without substance; she alleged memory laps, slurred speech and general debilitation caused by imbalance in her thyroid condition precipitated by stress.

(ii)   The construction of the statute was determinative rather than the parties' perception of whether or not the claim was for personal injuries. The claimant had simply failed to appreciate the consequences of the applicable limitation period.

(iii)   Although there was a discretion to allow an amendment to sever the personal injuries element of the claim, it would not be appropriate to deprive the defendant of a good limitation defence by exercising it.

Appeal allowed, cross-appeal dismissed.

Obembe and Others v City and Hackney Health Authority

Limitation Act 1980, s 11, s 14, s 33

Drake J   **Lexis, 9 June 1989**

The first claimant (Geoffrey Obembe) was born on 8 July 1979. The second and third claimants (his parents) alleged that immediately after his birth he was left unattended for 10–15 minutes, during which time he ceased to breathe, in consequence of which he suffered irreversible brain damage. They claimed damages for themselves as well as him.

In July 1984 they instructed solicitors who set out the claimants' allegations of negligence in a letter to the hospital in which they requested the medical records. The hospital produced these in October 1984, and another hospital produced records in December 1984. A conference with counsel was held in July 1986. Further notes were obtained. After another conference in February 1988, the writ was issued on 21 July 1988.

A preliminary trial was held on the issue of limitation. The claimants conceded that at a very early stage they knew that the injury in question was significant. The defendants produced affidavit evidence that certain nurses or midwives could not be traced and that a doctor who had gone to Australia had not been traced either.

Held:

(i)   (a)   The fact that the second and third claimants were dealing with a severely handicapped child did not provide a good reason, viewed objectively, why nothing was done by them to seek legal advice at an earlier stage: s 14(3);

      (b)   nor did the fact that they had 21 years in which to bring an action on behalf of the first claimant provide a good reason for their not seeking legal advice and pursuing their own claim earlier: s 14(3);

      (c)   their solicitors' letter in July 1984 suggested that they knew that they had a good cause of action for the injuries that they had sustained arising out of their infant's injuries: s 14(1);

      (d)   their state of knowledge was greatly increased by the prompt production of hospital records in October and December 1984: s 14(1);

      (e)   accordingly, time began to run against them well before 21 July 1985, and their writ issued on 21 July 1988 was statute barred: s 11(4).

(ii)   (a)   The second and third claimants had not shown good reason for the delay which had occurred: s 33(3)(a);

      (b)   the cogency of the defendants' evidence had been reduced by their inability to find certain witnesses: s 33(3)(b);

      (c)   there was a completely inexplicable and inexcusable delay on the claimants' side between December 1984 and July 1988: s 33(3)(f);

      (d)   the second and third claimants would be prejudiced by not being able to pursue their action for their own injuries: s 33(1)(a);

      (e)   the long delay since the birth greatly prejudiced the defendants, even though they would still have to meet the claim of the infant first claimants: s 33(1)(b);

      (f)   it would not be equitable to disapply the provisions of s 11 in favour of the second and third claimants: s 33(1).

O'Byrne v Aventis Pasteur MSD Ltd

Consumer Protection Act 1987, s 2

Limitation Act 1980, s 35(5)(b)   **CPR 19.5(3)(a)**

Supreme Court   **[2010] UKSC 23; [2010] 1 WLR 1412;**
[2010] Bus LR 1381; [2010] 4 All ER 1;
[2010] 3 CMLR 35; [2010] ECC 19;
(2010) 114 BMLR 170; (2010) 154(21) SJLB 28;
(2010) Times, 27 May

The claimant alleged that a vaccine manufactured by D2, a French company, was defective and had caused him brain damage. D2 had sent a consignment of the vaccine to D1, its wholly owned English subsidiary, in 1992. Later that year it was used to vaccinate the claimant. In 2001 the claimant claimed damages against D1 under the Consumer Protection Act 1987. As D1 was not the manufacturer, but the distributor, of the product, the claimant successfully applied for D2 to be substituted for D1 as the defendant in 2003. The application was made after the expiry of the time limit under art 11 of Directive 85/374 of 10 years from the date on which the producer had put the product into circulation, and was founded on s 35(5)(b) of the Limitation Act 1980 and CPR 19.5(3)(a).

D2 appealed and a reference to the European Court of Justice was made. The ECJ held (*Aventis Pasteur SA v OB* (C-358/08) (2010) All ER (EC) 522, ECJ (Grand Chamber)) that art 11 prevented a producer from being sued after 10 years had expired, unless proceedings had been taken against it within the 10-year period, and that a national rule allowing the substitution of one defendant for another could not be applied in a way which allowed a producer to be sued after expiry.

The claimant therefore accepted that he could not rely on s 35. However, the ECJ stated that art 11 did not prevent a producer from being substituted for a wholly owned subsidiary which had been sued during the period, if it was found that the producer had determined the putting into circulation of the product, and that it was for the national court, in accordance with the applicable rules of national law on matters of proof, to determine whether the putting into circulation had in fact been determined by the producer. The claimant argued that D1 was a wholly owned subsidiary of D2, and D2 had determined that the product should be put into circulation by transferring it to D1, so the case fell within the qualification stated by the ECJ and the substitution could be made.

Held:

(i)   The ECJ's core ruling had been that a national rule allowing substitution could not permit a producer to be sued after expiry. In giving the qualification, it had gone on to give additional guidance which it considered might be helpful to domestic judges dealing with the case. There was nothing to suggest that in that guidance the ECJ intended to depart from the principle in its core ruling, and the guidance had to be read in the light of that principle.

(ii)   The ECJ had been concerned to show how the principle applied in relation to the substitution of D2 for D1. The only way in which the principle could be maintained and yet D2 could be substituted for D1 would be if, by suing D1, the claimant had in effect sued D2.

(iii)   The ECJ had been pointing the domestic court to the way in which it should approach that issue. The claimant's argument was internally incoherent as well as inconsistent with the ECJ's reasoning: if D2 had put the product into circulation when it supplied it to D1, that could only be because the two companies were to be regarded as operating distinctly. The fact that D1 was a wholly owned subsidiary of D2 did not point to that conclusion.

(iv)   The ECJ's reference to D1 being a wholly owned subsidiary was only consistent with it directing attention to factors which might point to a close connection between the two companies. That was to be expected in the context of seeing whether proceedings against D1 counted as proceedings against D2. The ECJ had been contemplating a situation where, to outward appearances, a supplier had decided to put a product into circulation.

(v)   The domestic court had to look at the circumstances to see whether in fact it was the manufacturing parent company which had determined that it should be put into circulation. The ECJ had indicated that the domestic court was to consider, in accordance with domestic rules of proof, whether D2 was in fact controlling D1 and determining when it put the product into circulation. There was nothing in its judgment to suggest that the fact that D1 was a wholly owned subsidiary could of itself be a reason for allowing D2 to be substituted after the expiry of the period. Rather, that fact was one factor to be taken into account by the domestic court when assessing how closely the subsidiary was involved with its parent's business as a producer.

Appeal allowed.

Odam v Eli Lilly & Co and others

Limitation Act 1980, s 11, s 14, s 33

Court of Appeal   **[1992] 3 Med LR 380**

See *Nash v Eli Lilly & Co* (B) (p568)

O'Driscoll v Dudley Health Authority

Limitation Act 1980, s 14, s 33

Court of Appeal   **[1998] Lloyd's Rep Med 210; LTL 30/4/98**

The claimant suffered from cerebral palsy, allegedly as a result of the defendant's negligence in delivering her. She was born in 1970. The family had been alerted to the possibility of mismanagement in 1985 and discussed it with the claimant in 1988. A solicitor was instructed in 1991, the family having decided to wait until the claimant turned 21 as they believed that to be the age of her legal majority. A favourable expert report was obtained in 1993. Proceedings were issued on 11 May 1994. Limitation was heard as a preliminary issue. The judge found that the claimant required expert confirmation of her belief before she could be said to have knowledge. Time therefore did not begin to run until 1993 and proceedings were issued in time. The defendant appealed.

Held:

(i)   The question here as regards knowledge was when did the claimant first know that there was a real possibility that her injury was the result of the defendant's failure to deliver her by caesarean section.

(ii)   The judge had erred by applying a higher test requiring proof of causation.

(iii)   On any view the answer to the question was a date more than three years before proceedings were issued.

(iv)   The claimant certainly had knowledge by the time she turned 21, and probably by the time she was 18.

(v)   It was not necessary to determine constructive knowledge.

(vi)   The claimant had at first instance abandoned her application for a s 33 discretion. There were no grounds for allowing that point to be taken at this late stage.

Appeal dismissed.

O'Hara v Eli Lilly & Co and others

Limitation Act 1980, s 11, s 14, s 33

Court of Appeal   **[1992] 3 Med LR 384**

See *Nash v Eli Lilly & Co* (F) (p568)

O'Hara & another v McDougall

CPR 6.5

Court of Appeal   **[2005] EWCA Civ 1623; LTL 22/11/2005**

The claimant had issued proceedings against the defendant. The address for service was a residential property owned by the defendant but rented to tenants which was stated to be the defendant's place of business. Default judgment was entered with damages to be assessed. The defendant first became aware of the proceedings when he was served with an order for sale. He applied unsuccessfully to have judgment set aside. He successfully appealed on the grounds that (a) as he was being sued personally proceedings should not have been sent to his business address, and (b) the property in question was not a 'place of business' as envisaged by CPR 6.5.

The claimant then appealed.

Held:

(i)   The mere renting out of a property could not make its address a place of business. Neither could the fact that the defendant's agent regularly visited the property to collect rent make it so.

(ii)   As a landlord the defendant had very limited rights of entry to the property. Service of proceedings on a property to which the defendant had only such limited rights was an extraordinary proposition.

(iii)   The CPR should be interpreted and applied in furtherance of clarity and certainty. To allow the claimant's contentions would to be depart from practicability.

Appeal dismissed.

Ogunsanya & another v Lambeth Area Health Authority

Limitation Act 1980, s 11, s 14

Bristow J   **Lexis, 3 July 1985**

On 25 May 1977 the claimant (Christinana Ogunsanya), the wife of the then Attorney General in Lagos, underwent as a private patient at St Thomas's Hospital an operation for the removal of gallstones and exploration of the common bile duct. On 26 May she suffered a collapse; a second operation was performed in which it was found that she had extensive internal bleeding at the operation site and the blood vessels were sewn up. Later that day she complained of a heavy feeling in her legs and was given a further transfusion. At 11.30pm on 26 May she complained of inability to move her legs, trouble in moving her arms, and absent or diminished sensation in her legs. Various doctors at St. Thomas's saw her and reached provisional diagnoses. During the afternoon of 27 May she was transferred to the National Hospital of Nervous Diseases where at an operation performed at 6pm an extra-dural haematoma was found and removed. She was left a paraplegic.

In June 1978 her solicitors asked the defendants for the hospital records. These were not produced until April 1979. The solicitors then instructed a neurological expert who reported on 16 August 1979 that her paralysis was attributable to acts or omissions by the doctors at St. Thomas's between 11.30pm on 26 May and 6pm on 27 May. On 27 February 1980 her writ was issued against the defendant Health Authority. In March 1980 a statement of claim was served which alleged that it was vicariously liable for the negligence of four of its doctors. In April 1980 the Authority served a defence pleading that as the claimant was a private patient of the surgeon it was not vicariously liable for any negligence by the doctors. In July 1980 the claimant's solicitors applied to join the doctors as defendants. On 4 December 1980 the master refused this application.

Consequently on 15 December 1980 a fresh writ was issued against the individual doctors. In early 1982 the two actions were consolidated and an amended statement of claim served. The case proceeded slowly until it was set down for trial in November 1985. All defendants applied to dismiss it for want of prosecution, and the doctors applied for a preliminary trial on limitation. The master referred both matters to a judge under RSC Ord 32, r 12.

Held:

(i)   The claimant knew well before December 1977 of the relevant act or omission, namely that the hospital doctors did not ensure that her haematoma was promptly dealt with after her complaint at 11.30pm on 26 May 1977. However, it was originally thought that her paralysis was caused by low dose subcutaneous heparin treatment. Only when Dr Kendall reported on 16 August 1979 did she learn that her injury was attributable to the doctors' delay: s 14(1).

(ii)   In view of the nature of her tragic condition and her husband's position, it was entirely reasonable that she should not have rushed into litigation. It was also reasonable for her solicitors to await the hospital records before instructing the expert. She should not be fixed with a constructive date of knowledge about the cause of her condition earlier than 16 August 1979: s 14(3).

(iii)   Accordingly, her action against the doctors was not statute barred: s 11(4).

The defendants' application to dismiss for want of prosecution was also dismissed.

Ostick v Wandsborough HA

Limitation Act 1980, s 14

County court (Recorder Serota)   [1995] 6 Med LR 338

The claimant alleged that advice that an injury to her left shoulder would heal and that it required mobilisation was negligent and contributed to the failure of the left clavicle to unite. On a preliminary issue the defendant argued that the claim was time barred.

Held:

(i)   For the claimant to have actual knowledge, it was necessary for her to know that there was a causative link between her treatment and the failure of the left clavicle to unite and not just that there was an injury which had failed to heal.

(ii)   As regards constructive knowledge, the claimant was justified in not pressing for a medical explanation from the defendant before waiting to see if her treatment was successful.

Preliminary issue decided in favour of the claimant.

PS v Bryn Alyn Community Holdings Ltd

Limitation Act 1980, s 2, s 11, s 14, s 33

Court of Appeal   [2003] EWCA Civ 783; [2003] 3 WLR 107;
[2003] 1 FLR 1203

See *KR v Bryn Alyn Community Holdings Ltd* (L) (p505)

Pacheco v Brent & Harrow Area Health Authority

Limitation Act 1980, s 11, s 14, s 33

Comyn J   Lexis, 17 April 1984

The claimant (Mrs Pacheco), a lady of Spanish origin, was employed by the defendants as a state enrolled nurse. On 13 March 1978, while helping a sister to lift a geriatric female patient into the bath at Shenfield Hospital, she felt a short hard stabbing pain in her back. She did not report the incident at the time and returned to work the next day. However, she was not able to work again after 15 March, the pain got worse and she had to spend periods in bed. On 17 March her general practitioner diagnosed a ricked back and sciatica; another subsequently suspected disc trouble. On 20 May her husband wrote to the hospital a letter signed by her, which reported the incident and explained her absence from work. On 26 May 1978 she was told at St Albans City Hospital that she had disc trouble and to await a bed as an in-patient for traction.

In October 1979 solicitors sent a letter before action on her behalf. Then they allowed the matter to go to sleep until they issued her writ on 22 May 1981. A preliminary trial on the limitation defence was held. The documents included a statement made by the Sister shortly after the accident in which she said that she could not recall any incident having taken place.

Held:

(i)   (a)   The claimant did not appreciate the significance of her injury until 26 May 1978 when a firm opinion was expressed to her at the hospital and a somewhat dramatic treatment ordered: s 14(1);

        (b)   as a state enrolled nurse of Spanish origin, whose command of English was imperfect, she was reasonable in not considering earlier that her injury was sufficiently serious to justify her instituting proceedings. A combination of subjective and objective criteria applied: s 14(2);

        (c)   accordingly, her writ was narrowly within time: s 11(4).

(ii)   If, however, s 33 of the Limitation Act 1980 were to be applicable,

        (a)   at most the delay to issue of the writ was only a matter of a couple of months: s 33(3)(a);

        (b)   the defendants got ample notice by the letter of 20 May 1978, they could still reconstruct the bathroom and any lifting machinery, and they had no live witness because the Sister said at an early stage she could not remember. Thus there was no factual prejudice to them: s 33(3)(b);

        (c)   the claimant personally acted promptly, although her solicitors were dilatory: s 33(3)(e);

        (d)   it was not certain that an action by the claimant against her solicitors would succeed. Moreover she would be further prejudiced by having to get fresh solicitors, having to make outlays of money, and having still further delay before her claim could be resolved: s 33(3);

        (e)   even if her action was out of time, it was just and equitable that she should be allowed to proceed with it: s 33(1).

Page v Hewetts Solicitors

CPR 7.2, PD 7A para 5

Court of Appeal   **[2012] EWCA Civ 805;**
[2012] CP Rep 40; [2012] WTLR 1427

The claimants were beneficiaries under a will. The defendant solicitors acted for them in the administration of the estate. In early 1998 the defendants were instructed in relation to a sale of a property in the estate. The sale was completed in March 1999. Unknown to the claimants, one of the solicitors carried on business as a property developer through a company and recommended that the claimants sell the property to a second company, which had agreed to pay the solicitor's company a share of the future profit or a fee. The claimants later discovered that the property's true value was higher than the sale value. In November 2000 they complained to the Office for the Supervision of Solicitors (OSS). They then issued proceedings. The claimant's solicitor (L) gave evidence that the drafting of the claim form and particulars was completed in December 2008 and that bundles were sent to the court by document exchange at that time. L claimed that the reason the claim form showed a date of 17 February 2009 was that the forms were lost by the court and a fresh claim had to be issued. The defendants applied for summary judgment on the basis that the proceedings were issued on 17 February 2009 and therefore were statute barred. The master held that the claimants' letter to the OSS showed that they knew enough to start time running in respect of the undervalue in December 2000, and that those proceedings were clearly barred. He further held that time began to run for the claim relating to the secret profit on 6 February 2003, and that he was not satisfied on the balance of probabilities that the claim form did not reach the post room or the registry, bringing the claim outwith the Limitation Act 1980 by 11 days. The judge upheld the master's findings and dismissed the claim. The claimants appealed again.

Held:

(i)   The judges below were correct to hold the undervalue claim out of time.

(ii)   As regards the secret profit claim, the master had applied the wrong test. The question was not whether he was satisfied on the balance of probabilities but whether the claimants had no real prospect of showing that the documents arrived at the court office. The master and judge also assumed that the systems that should have been followed were in fact followed. However, it was not unknown for the court to mislay important documents. On an application for summary judgment, the court must consider not merely the current state of the evidence but also what evidence might reasonably be expected to be adduced at trial. The court had to approach the question on the footing that there was a real prospect that the claimants would show that documents put into the document exchange were delivered at least as far as the court's post room and perhaps as far as the registry.

(iii) The main issue before the judge was whether the 'claim form as issued' must be the same piece of paper as that received in the court office within the limitation period. The master and judge held that it must, with the consequence that the claimants could not rely on the 'lost' claim as bringing forward the date on which the action was brought. This was the wrong subject matter to debate. When an action was 'brought' for the purpose of the Act was a question of construction of the Act. It was not a question of construction of the CPR, or of a practice direction.

(iv)   Taken literally, the ratio of *Barnes v St Helens MBC* (p321) was that, once the claimant had delivered his request for the issue of a claim form to the court office, he had 'brought' his action. If L's evidence was correct, the claimants had done so. A purposive interpretation of the relevant provision supported this same conclusion. The construction of the Act favoured in *Barnes v St Helens* was based on risk allocation. A claimant's risk stopped once he had delivered his request to the court office. It would be unjust for a claimant to be held responsible for any failings thereafter, such being beyond his control. PD7A could not alter the correct construction of the Act, and a would-be litigant was not responsible for any shortcomings of the court (*Aly v Aly* (1984) 81 LSG 283 and *Riniker v University College London* (1999) Times, 17 April considered).

(v)   Therefore, if the claimants established that the claim form was delivered in due time to the court office, accompanied by a request to issue and the appropriate fee, the action would not be statute barred. The master and the judge were wrong to summarily reject L's evidence in this regard.

Appeal allowed.

Parchment v Secretary of State for Defence

Assault – racial abuse   **Limitation Act 1980, s 2, s 11 applicability**

J Griffiths Williams QC   **LTL 23/2/98**

The claimant alleged that he had been the victim of racial abuse and physical violence whilst training to become a Royal Marine. He enlisted in 1988. On 26 May 1989 he went absent without leave. On 8 May 1994 he was arrested and returned to his unit. On 9 June 1994 he was discharged. On 14 December 1995 he complained to an industrial tribunal. This was withdrawn as being out of time. On 26 September 1996 he issued proceedings against the defendant, claiming negligence in failure to provide a safe system of work. On 24 October

1996 he served an amended statement of claim alleging psychiatric injury. The defendant denied liability and raised limitation, which was heard as a preliminary issue.

Held:

(i)   The claimant's claim could only be brought under the Race Relations Act 1976, which exclusively provides for remedies for racial discrimination.

(ii)   (obiter) The allegation of failing to provide a safe system of work was a disingenuous attempt to circumvent *Stubbings v Webb* (p677). The claimant's allegations were of trespass to the person and were barred by the six-year time limit (Limitation Act 1980 s 2).

(iii) (obiter) Between June 1989 and May 1994 the claimant contacted numerous solicitors as he knew that he had a significant injury. The allegations of trespass were not severable from the allegations of racial abuse and harassment. All claims based on breach of duty were barred in May 1992.

(iv)   (obiter) It was the claimant's decision not to bring proceedings earlier. The fact that he was a fugitive and thus unable to bring an action did not change this. It was his decision to remain at large when he knew his injury was significant. Any psychiatric injury he might have suffered was not prohibitive. Despite the lack of prejudice to the defendant, it would not be appropriate to exercise a s 33 discretion.

Claim struck out.

NB: The flexible limitation regime under s 11/s 14/s 33 would now apply to the alleged trespass: *A v Hoare* (p287).

Parish v Imperial Chemical Industries plc

Limitation Act 1939, s 2

Court of Appeal   26 July 1991

The claimant (Anthony Parish) was born on 6 May 1931. From around August 1945 to August 1947, in the course of his employment with Bertol Cleaners, he was exposed to the chemical Trichloroethylene (trade name Triklone) which the defendants distributed. He alleged that in consequence he suffered a progressive poisoning syndrome. Many of his symptoms were immediately apparent between 1945 and 1947, but after 1971 they became increasingly severe. He did not acquire knowledge for the purposes of the Limitation Act 1980 until 1985. His writ was issued on 23 December 1986.

Waller J dismissed the defendants' application to strike out the action as statute barred. The defendants appealed. It was common ground that damage had been caused to the claimant by the end of August 1947.

Held:

(i)   Under the Limitation Act 1939, the combined effect of s 2(1), which laid down a six-year limitation period, and s 22, which provided that this commenced at the end of a claimant's infancy, was that the limitation period would expire on 6 May 1958.

(ii)   The transitional provisions in s 7(1) of the Law Reform (Limitation of Actions etc) Act 1954 meant that the above limitation period was unaffected by the 1954 Act, since the claimant's cause of action had arisen before its passing.

(iii) Section 1(4)(a) of the Limitation Act 1963 specifically excluded from that Act's reforms 'any defence which … may be available by virtue of any enactment other than s 2(1) of the Limitation Act 1939'. Thus the 1963 Act did not affect the defendants' limitation defence arising under s 22 of the 1939 Act as preserved by s 7(1) of the 1954 Act.

(iv)   The presumption against retrospectivity meant that those causes of action, which had already become statute barred because they were governed by some period of limitation other than the three-year period under the 1954 Act, would not be reviewed by the transition provisions of s 3 of the Limitation Act 1975.

(v)   Paragraph 9 of Schedule 2 to the Limitation Act 1980 clearly and unambiguously provided that, if a cause of action had become statute barred by the 1939 Act, it could not be revived by the 1980 Act.

(vi)   Accordingly, the claimant's action must be struck out as statute barred.

The defendants' appeal was allowed.

Arnold v Central Electricity Generating Board (p306) followed.

Parkinson Engineering Services Plc (In Liquidation) v Swan

Limitation Act 1980, s 35(5)(b)   **CPR 19.5(3)(b)**

Court of Appeal   **[2009] EWCA Civ 1366; [2010] Bus LR 857;**
[2010] 1 BCLC 163; [2010] BPIR 437;
[2010] PNLR 17; (2010) Times, 13 January

The claimant company had been made the subject of an administration order in May 2003, and the defendants were appointed as joint administrators. Six months later, the order was discharged and the claimant was wound up. The administrators were released from liability under s 20 of the Insolvency Act 1986 with effect from 13 February 2004 except in relation to claims against them notified to them in writing by then. In April 2009 the claimant's liquidator caused the claimant to sue the defendants for damages for negligence in the performance of their duties as administrators. The defendants pleaded that the claim was barred by their statutory release under s 20. If the liquidator had commenced a fresh action, it would have been statute barred. He therefore then successfully applied to substitute himself as claimant in proceedings brought by the claimant company and permitting him under s 212 of the Insolvency Act 1986 to proceed against the defendants despite their earlier release from liability. The defendants appealed, submitting that the circumstances did not satisfy the test in either s 35(5)(b) or CPR 19.5(3)(b), namely whether the substitution was necessary for the determination of the original action, because the original claim was doomed by their statutory defence under s 20 of the 1986 Act. The claimant submitted that the proceedings under s 212 of the 1986 Act asserted exactly the same cause of action as the original claim, and it was therefore the same claim.

Held:

(i)   The distinctive feature of the instant case was that, on the one hand, the original proceedings could not succeed but, on the other, subject to obtaining leave under s 212(4), the liquidator could assert exactly the same cause of action on behalf of the claimant, and could thereby overcome the s 20 defence to the claimant's own proceedings. It was thus a case in which, if the court thought it appropriate to give permission, the claimant's cause of action, which would otherwise be defeated, could be asserted against the same defendants relying on exactly the same facts.

(ii)   Section 212 clearly contemplated such a situation, where a claim in the name of a company would fail because of s 20, but the same claim, on behalf of the company but in the name of the liquidator, could be asserted despite the release.

(iii)   It was appropriate to permit the substitution: it was necessary in terms of s 35(5)(b) as well as CPR 19.5(3)(b). The original action could not be determined without the substitution of the liquidator; whereas, if brought by the liquidator under s 212, it could be. Without that substitution, it was bound to be determined in favour of the defendants because of the s 20 defence. It would be struck out because of that defence, and it could not be decided on its merits. In terms of CPR 19.5(3)(b), it could not properly be carried on by the original party, whereas it could be maintained and carried on if the liquidator was substituted.

(iv) No more than minimal change was necessary to the statement of case; it was the same claim in every respect (*Adelson v Associated Newspapers Ltd* [2008] EWHC 278 (QB) and *Roberts v Gill & Co* (p625) distinguished). It was true that proceedings under s 212 would normally be brought in the Companies Court rather than the Chancery Division, and would be commenced by an application rather than by a Part 7 claim form; but those differences were not at all significant.

(v) The judge had not erred in the exercise of his discretion to grant leave under s 212(4) or in the exercise of his discretion under CPR 19.5. The defendants had been aware of the cause of action before the expiry of the limitation period. That substantially qualified any prejudice to them of not being able to assert a limitation defence in respect of the first month or so of the administration.

Appeal dismissed.

Parry v Clwyd Health Authority

Limitation Act 1980, s 14

Colman J   **[1997] 8 Med LR 243; [1997] PIQR P1**

The claimant was born on 21 July 1966. She had severe cerebral palsy which she claimed was the result of the defendant's negligent mismanagement of her birth. Her was a breach delivery and various allegations of acts and omissions were made in relation to it, in particular the failure to perform a caesarean section. The cerebral palsy was apparent from about six months after her birth, but the claimant's mother never inquired as to the cause of the injury. Her condition caused her severe communication problems. When she was about 10 years old, the claimant asked her mother for an explanation of her condition. The mother merely attributed it to the breach delivery. In October 1990 she saw a television programme which suggested that a hospital had been at fault when a child developed cerebral palsy following a breach delivery. She consulted solicitors, began investigations and on 21 December 1992 she issued proceedings. Limitation was heard as a preliminary issue.

Held:

(i) The claimant did not have actual knowledge for the purposes of the Act until 1990. Other than once with her mother, she had no discussed the cause of her injury with anyone prior to watching the television programme.

(ii) The criteria for constructive knowledge under s 14(3) should be purely objective (*Forbes v Wandsworth HA* (p434) preferred to *Nash v Eli Lilly* (p568)). However, as the claimant in this case was of average intelligence and medical knowledge, a subjective test would produce the same result. The claimant knew no more or no less than what a normal person might be expected to pick up at school, through family and friends or the media. The general public understanding of such matters was not even that of a person with a GCSE in biology.

(iii) There was no reason why an average person should have connected the injury with the birth mismanagement or begun the preliminaries of making a claim before the claimant actually did.

(iv) Section 11 and s 14 clearly referred only to the claimant's own knowledge. The actual or constructive knowledge of a parent was irrelevant.

Preliminary issue decided in favour of the claimant.

Parsonage v Fastway Steel Ltd

Limitation Act 1980, s 33

Court of Appeal   **[2001] EWCA Civ 1796; LTL 13/11/2001**

The claimant was driving the defendant's van when he was injured in a 54 car pile-up on 29 August 1992. The claimant claimed against the defendant alleging faulty tyres. However, he dropped this claim pre-issue on receipt of negative engineering advice. In October 1998 he received evidence from criminal proceedings that poor tyre quality had in fact been causative. Proceedings were issued on 16 May 2000 and the defendant raised limitation. This was tried as a preliminary issue and the judge found that the claimant had the relevant constructive knowledge shortly after receiving the engineer's report in March 1994 on the basis that he should have sought a second opinion. However, he exercised his discretion under s 33 to allow the claim to proceed as there had been no significant prejudice to the defendant. The defendant appealed.

Held:

(i)   The judge did not misdirect himself on the burden of proof. He correctly placed it on the claimant.

(ii)   The judge was correct to find that expert evidence rather than witness evidence of fact was likely to be determinative.

(iii)   The claimant's admitted exaggeration of his injuries was a relevant factor, but the judge had not erred by giving it insufficient weight. The medical evidence had not been affected.

(iv)   The judge had approached s 33 systematically and he could not be faulted in the exercise of his discretion.

Appeal dismissed.

Parsons v Warren

Limitation Act 1980, s 14, s 33

Court of Appeal   **[2002] EWCA Civ 130**

The claimant alleged that he suffered from asthma caused by the inhalation of oil mist and dust during his employment at a small private drift mine, where he was employed by the first defendant from December 1986 until a date in 1990 when the mine was purchased by the second defendant, who employed the claimant thereafter until he left the mine in March 1992.

The claimant first became aware that he was suffering from some respiratory problems in 1987. He went to see his general practitioner, who referred him to a consultant physician in June 1988. In a letter dated 15 June 1988 to his general practitioner, the consultant reported that in his opinion the claimant had developed asthma. He recorded the fact that the claimant was a smoker and by then had worked underground for a total of 14 years. Consideration was given thereafter by the consultant and his team to the question as to whether or not the respondent was suffering from pneumoconiosis. The consultant's Registrar, in a letter to the general practitioner of 27 November 1988, excluded that possibility. A diagnosis of asthma was confirmed in February 1989.

The claimant applied for disablement benefit on the basis that he was suffering from occupational asthma. In a form dated October 1991 he said: 'there is something at work that seriously affecting my breathing and I presume its the horses.' The claimant was then supplied with a flow meter to check his lung function at work and at home. The results which he recorded showed markedly reduced lung function at work as compared to home. On 17 January 1992 he wrote to the Medical Board, enclosing the charts. He stated that these showed that he was better at home than at work, and that he had been able to blow more air some 18 months previously. He referred to a conversation with someone taking air samples at the mine and having been informed of the low oxygen content. He said (sic): '... now Ive discovered that over the last 5½ years we been working in foul air ... Im convinced now that this as caused my breathing problems.' The doctor advised the claimant to give up work in the mine, which he duly did.

In 1993, solicitors acting for a fellow-employee approached the claimant for a statement in relation to a possible claim against the second defendant. Proposed proceedings were notified to the second defendant's insurers in 1995, which was in fact after the second defendant had gone into liquidation in November 1994. The proceedings were themselves commenced in 1996 and were settled in 2001 for £6,000. In May 1997 the claimant's application for disablement benefit was allowed on review. He then, for the first time, went to see solicitors on 30 June 1997. Proceedings were issued on 20 March 2000. Limitation was heard as preliminary issue.

The judge held that the claim had been brought in time, as the claimant did not have knowledge for the purposes of s 14 until he received medico-legal confirmation of occupational asthma in 1998, and that even had it not been he would have exercised his s 33 discretion in the claimant's favour. The defendants appealed.

Held:

(i)   It was insufficient for a claimant to know merely that his injury was caused by his working conditions. To say that an injury or disease is due to working conditions says in itself little or nothing about the relevant act or omission which could have caused that injury or disease.

(ii)   However, in cases such as this, where the allegation is in relation to contaminated air within the workplace, it is sufficient for the court to conclude that a claimant has knowledge if he knows that the injury or disease from which he suffers was the result of exposure to contaminated air. In other words, that injury was to do with the failure of the employers to prevent contamination of the air or, alternatively, caused by the contamination of the air as a result of the activities of the employer.

(iii)   It was not correct to restrict the relevant knowledge to the particular contaminant which is the subject matter of the claim as ultimately pleaded (in this case, the oil mist identified by the medico-legal expert in 1998). That was far too restrictive. Such an approach would permit someone in the position of the claimant, in effect, to defer the date of knowledge until the precise aetiology of his complaint had been identified.

(iv)   The knowledge which the court had to identify as relevant knowledge is broad knowledge of the essence of the causally relevant act or omission, and the extent of knowledge is that which would make it reasonable for the person to set in train the enquiries which would enable him or her to determine whether or not he or she has a claim in negligence or breach of duty. The claimant possessed the relevant knowledge at the latest in 1992. Accordingly, the primary limitation period had expired by the time the claim was brought.

(v)   However, there was no error in the judge's approach to s 33. He fairly balanced all the competing factors. He was entitled to find for the claimant.

Appeal dismissed.

Pavan v Holwill's (Oils) Ltd

Limitation Act 1980, s 33

Court of Appeal   **Lexis, 15 June 1989**

On 6 June 1983 the claimant (Mr Pavan), a manager employed by Qualby Meats Ltd, slipped and fell on oil and was seriously injured. The oil was alleged to have been spilt through the negligence of the driver of the tanker which delivered it. The firm which normally delivered the oil was Jeremy's Oil Distributors Ltd.

Following a social conversation with a solicitor, the claimant instructed solicitors in November 1985. A writ was issued against Jeremy's Oil Distributors Ltd just before the third anniversary of the accident. In November 1986 it became clear that the oil had not been delivered on this occasion by Jeremy's Oil Distributors Ltd.

In November 1986 Qualby Meats Ltd had gone into liquidation. A solicitor's search of their documents in March 1987 failed to find any trace of a delivery of oil on 6 June 1983. In May 1987 the managing director's secretary made a more extensive search and discovered a delivery note for the delivery of oil on 6 June 1983 by the defendants, Holwill's (Oils) Ltd. On 15 June 1987 a letter before action was sent. Shortly afterwards the writ was issued.

At the preliminary trial on limitation, McNeill J decided that the action had been brought out of time. However, he exercised his discretion under s 33 of the Limitation Act 1980 in the claimant's favour and gave leave for the action to proceed. The defendants applied for leave to appeal.

Held:

(i) The judge found that the length of the delay was not conclusive. Until a matter of days before issue of the writ, the claimant could theoretically have had the advantage of the primary limitation period together with the 12-month period then allowed for service of the writ. He considered that the claimant's explanation for the delay was convincing: s 33(3)(a).

(ii) The judge accepted that the cogency of the evidence had been reduced, in that the defendants had not been able to trace the tanker driver or anyone else who had first hand knowledge and it was no longer possible to inspect the locus in quo: s 33(3)(b).

(iii) The judge also took into account the gravity of the claimant's injuries and the fact that, because it was not a case in which he could sue his solicitors for any fault, the claimant would be without remedy unless s 11 was disapplied: s 33(3).

(iv) The application of the Limitation Act tends to result in injustice to one party or another. If s 11 is disapplied, the defendant often faces difficulties and prejudice. Equally a claimant who may be deserving (apart from the delay) is faced with loss of compensation for serious injury. The judge balanced these matters and did not fail to take into account any relevant consideration: s 33(1).

The defendant's application was refused.

Pavey v Ministry of Defence

Limitation Act 1980, s 33

Court of Appeal   **(1999) Lloyd's Rep Med; (1998) Times, 25 November; LTL 19/11/1998**

The claimant claimed that the defendant's military hospital had negligently treated his bunions between 1982 and 1984. Proceedings were issued on 22 November 1994. The defendant pleaded limitation. By consent the issue was tried before a master as a preliminary hearing. The master found that by April 1986 the claimant had knowledge under the Act. This finding was based upon a GP referral letter suggesting that the claimant doubted the wisdom of his previous treatment. The delay had prejudiced the defendant in that its doctors were now unable to recall any of the relevant details. It would not be equitable to exercise discretion under s 33. The claimant appealed.

Held:

(i) The parties consented to the master trying the issues and the validity of the proceedings could not be impugned on the grounds of jurisdiction. The master's order was a final order and any right of appeal was to the Court of Appeal (*Dale v British Coal Corpn* (p396) followed).

(ii)   The master's conclusion on date of knowledge was, on the evidence, correct.

(iii)   The master had not erred in the exercise of his discretion.

Appeal dismissed.

Pearse v Barnet HA

Limitation Act 1980, s 33

QBD (John Griffiths-Williams QC)   **[1998] PIQR P39**

The claimant was born on 28 December 1970, severely incapacitated by spastic cerebral palsy affecting all four limbs. He commenced proceedings on 20 June 1994 (when he was aged 23½) against the defendant, claiming negligent management of his birth. The claimant, confined to a wheelchair and almost totally dependent on others for daily living, had obtained an honours degree in psychology at Nottingham University, and said of the delay that he had found mainstream education exhausting, with exacerbations of his spasticity often incapacitating him for days. The more he studied, however, the more he came to realise that it would only be with the facilities that damages could provide that he could become independent. The claimant also adduced evidence from a prominent consultant obstetrician that the medical records were complete and that the staff would have been compelled to rely on those records rather than their recollections from about three years after the events onwards. The defendant said a doctor and midwife were untraceable, but that might not have been so within the limitation period, and that the consultant obstetrician, under whose care the claimant had been, had died in 1994.

Held:

(i)   The claimant had admitted frankly that, by the time he was 17, he knew because of what he had been told that something had gone wrong at his birth and he knew that, in the appropriate circumstances, a hospital authority could be sued in negligence. His date of knowledge within s 14 was thus before he was 18 in 1988, and so proceedings were two and a half years out of time.

(ii)   The claimant's disability was relevant, notwithstanding that he was not under a disability for the purposes of the Mental Health Act 1983. Although the claimant had not acted promptly in 1988, his disabilities were such that it would be wrong to ignore the pressure created by them. The claimant delayed litigation because he was focusing on overcoming his disabilities to pursue his studies. It would be harsh to hold him at fault for this.

(iii)   The two and a half year delay had not prejudiced the defendant, as it would be no more difficult to call evidence of 1970s medical practice in 1994 than it was in 1991, and the records were virtually complete. It was not uncommon in cases of medical negligence for the issues to be tried very much by reference to such records.

(iv)   It would be equitable to disapply the normal time limit.

Limitation period disapplied.

Penrose v Mansfield

Limitation Act 1939, s 22

Court of Appeal   **(1971) 115 SJ 309; (1971) Times, 19 March**

On 10 November 1965 the claimant (Mr Penrose) was seriously injured in a car accident. His writ was issued on 12 December 1968. The defendant admitted liability. Damages were assessed at £19,602.

The defendant alleged that the action was statute barred. The claimant by his reply pleaded that, for at least 32 days to 12 December 1965, he was under the disability of unsoundness of mind and incapable of managing his affairs in respect of the accident, and that under s 22 of the Limitation Act 1939 time did not run against him until the disability ceased.

This plea was supported at trial by evidence from the claimant and close relatives and the orthopaedic surgeon in charge of him. A neurologist who had seen him in 1967 testified that he had been suffering from an 'organic confusional state' until early January 1966, but agreed when contemporary hospital records were shown to him that if he were right the notes of two neurological opinions of 26 and 29 November 1965 would have to be wrong. The defendant's neurological expert, who had examined the notes, opined that by late 1965 the claimant was conscious and rational and capable of making business decisions.

Waller J said that it was impossible to disregard the many indications in the contemporaneous notes of the claimant's recovery of consciousness and held that the claim was statute barred. The claimant appealed.

Held:

(i)   The case threw into relief the enormous importance to be attached to contemporary records as a means of checking the recollection of those giving evidence about past events. In so far as such records in the present case cast doubt on the factual evidence of witnesses about past events, the written contemporary record must be preferred.

(ii)   The onus was on the claimant to prove the relevant disability over the whole of the relevant period. The judge was entitled to conclude that he had failed to do so.

The claimant's appeal was dismissed.

NB: The same issues would fall to be decided today under s 28 of the Limitation Act 1980.

Petford v Saw

CPR 6

Bow CC (Recorder Morris)   **CLY 02/478**

The claimant was injured in a road traffic accident for which the defendant admitted liability. There was a disputed medical issue and quantum could not be agreed within the limitation period. Protective proceedings were therefore issued on 3 July 2001. On 30 October 2001 the claimant served the claim form on defendant's nominated solicitors. As there was a Post Office strike pending, this was done by special delivery, the claimant paying an extra fee to guarantee that that the claim form would be delivered the next day. It was but, the defendant argued that special delivery was not a valid method of service under CPR Part 6. The claimant applied for a declaration that the service was valid.

Held:

(i)   The Royal Mail's special delivery was specifically designed, inter alia, for the service of legal documents. Its purpose was to achieve next day delivery as per first class post.

(ii)   The Court of Appeal in *Godwin v Swindon BC* (p444), when holding that CPR 6.2(1) did not permit any form of service beyond what was therein specified, was making the distinction between first and second class post. This distinction did not apply to services equivalent to first class post in speed and reliability of delivery.

(iii)   Special delivery was therefore valid service under CPR 6.2(1).

(iv)   Alternatively, good service had been effected under CPR 6.5 by leaving the claim form at the authorised solicitor's address.

Declaration granted.

Pheasant and others v STH Smith (Tyres) Ltd and another

Limitation Act 1939, s 2D   **Limitation Act 1975, s 3**

Court of Appeal   **[1978] 2 All ER 851; [1978] QB 886;**
[1978] 3 WLR 1

On 10 July 1970, Robert Pheasant was driving his wife and two young children along the M5 motorway. An overtaking car driven by Mr Carver came right across his path. There was a collision in which all four Pheasants were injured.

On 4 January 1972 their writ was issued against Mr Carver. In June 1972 his defence blamed the collision on sudden deflation of one of the tyres of his car due to negligent repair by Mr Smith and his company whom he joined as third parties. The claimants sought to add them as defendants by a summons returnable on 6 June 1973 which, due to a misleading entry in his diary, their solicitor did not attend. When he realised this and attended before the registrar on 11 July 1973, he produced a letter from the Smiths' solicitors stating that they would not oppose the joinder. The registrar granted leave to amend, and the Smiths were joined as defendants in August 1973. In fact, their solicitor's letter was only a consent for 6 June (within the three-year limitation period) and not for 11 July (the day after it had expired). The joinder was subsequently set aside.

On 1 September 1975 the Limitation Act 1975 came into operation. On 24 March 1976 the claimants' solicitor issued a fresh writ against the Smiths who pleaded limitation, res judicata and issue estoppel. Cusack J granted the claimants' application under s 2D of the Limitation Act 1939 as amended so that the primary limitation period be disapplied. The Smiths appealed.

Held:

(i)   While s 3 of the Limitation Act 1975 did not apply to actions in which before 1 September 1975, 'a final order or judgment had been made or given therein', the order of 11 July 1973 was a nullity and void ab initio because (a) it was made under a fundamental mistake in that the registrar was told and believed that the Smiths had agreed to do it, when they had not, and (b) it was made contrary to the rules of natural justice, since no notice of appointment had been given to the Smiths' solicitor. Thus no previous action had been commenced by the claimants against the Smiths, so there had been no final order therein. Accordingly, s 3 applied to operate the 1975 Act (and thereby the Limitation Act 1939 as amended) retrospectively.

(ii)   Once it came to discretion, it was clear that it should be exercised in favour of the claimants. There was nothing but purely formal delay on their part and no prejudice to the defendants since they had been involved in the litigation as third parties since 1972: s 2D(1).

The Smiths' appeal was dismissed.

This case was heard and decided by the Court of Appeal together with *Firman v Ellis* and the associated two cases (p433). In contrast to these three cases, the decision was unaffected by the former rule in *Walkley v Precision Forgings Ltd* (p705).

Pierce v Doncaster MBC

Limitation Act 1980, s 14, s 33

Court of Appeal   **[2008] EWCA Civ 1416; [2009] 1 FLR 1189;**
[2009] 3 FCR 572; [2009] Fam Law 202

The claimant had been born in March 1976 into an emotionally and financially unstable household. His mother (M) and father (F) were not married to one another, but were living together, although they had periods of brief separation. During a hospital visit when he was around six months old, the claimant had shown signs of neglect, and for the second time he was taken into voluntary care under the Children Act 1948. Whilst he was still in care, it was clear that M and F's situation was unsatisfactory. Their house was often dirty. F was usually out of work and went to prison at one point. F also failed to visit the claimant, and M's visits were occasional and disorganised. At about 14 months old, the claimant was returned to his family, where he lived until he left home at the age of 14 years old to fend for himself. He showed signs of personality disorder. His behaviour was sexualised and included living rough as a rent boy, and there were episodes of theft and arson. The claimant claimed that, in the years following his return to his family, he suffered indifference, neglect and periodic violence, and in his late twenties he claimed damages for the local authority's failure to keep him in care.

This claimant complained from the early 1990s onwards that the defendants had failed him by not taking him into care and thus caused him substantial injury. Agreed correspondence showed that the claimant had written to the defendants asking for his records in July 1995 (when he was 19) and, when sent a form to complete in October 1995, had returned it with a similar request in May 1996. In September 1996 he instructed solicitors who made a similar request in writing. The correspondence suggested that the defendants continued to deal directly with the claimant. After other letters, they offered him several appointments in January and March 1997 to visit to view the file, and indeed offered to pay for his train journey from London for the purpose. Three appointments were not taken up, and the correspondence ended with an open offer by the defendants to arrange another if asked.

Proceedings were commenced on 24 August 2004, when the claimant was 28, after he had sight of his care records. He alleged a continuing failure to take him into care from the age of approximately 18 months until he was 15, but as the case developed it was refined to focus on events in (1) November 1977 (aged 18 months), (2) May 1979 (aged 3) and (3) 1990–91 (aged 14–15). Limitation was tried alongside the substantive issues. The court found against the defendant, who appealed. The issues in the appeal were (a) whether there was a basis for finding a breach of duty when the claimant was returned to his home; (b) if so, whether there was a basis for finding that the breach caused the claimant to remain in his family for years when otherwise he would have not; (c) if so, whether damages for injury by violence as distinct from negligence were recoverable; and (d) s 14.

Held:

(i)   The judge had been entitled to find the defendant negligent.

(ii)   He had also been entitled to find that negligence causative.

(iii)   Although the instant case was a case of neglect rather than that of violence or abuse, the foreseeable loss had been injury through bad parenting, and it was impossible to say that the judge's award lay outside the bracket properly available to him.

(iv)   The judge had held that the claimant's knowledge of the authority's breach was through the consideration of his care records, which he had only been able to obtain shortly before he issued the proceedings, and therefore he was within the limitation period. However, the claimant had requested his file several years earlier, and the authority had offered to pay for his train fare for him to go and view them, but he failed to take up the appointments. The claimant could and should have obtained these records, and thus the relevant knowledge, earlier. It was thus clear that the claimant had had constructive knowledge under s 14(3), and his claim was out of time. It followed that the matter would be remitted to consider the issue of extension of time under s 33.

Appeal allowed.

Re Philip Powis Ltd

Limitation Act 1980, s 11, s 33

Court of Appeal   **[1998] 1 BCLC 440; [1998] BCC 756;**
(1998) 95(11) LSG 36

On 25 February 1985 the applicant injured himself whilst working for the respondent company. He issued proceedings on 28 February 1988. Various steps were taken, but the matter proceeded slowly and the respondent indicated that it was considering applying for strike out for want of prosecution. On 28 January 1993 the respondent's solicitors told the applicant correctly that the company had changed its name but incorrectly that it had ceased trading and might be in liquidation. On 14 May 1993, £5,000 was paid into court but the applicant declined to accept it. On 13 March 1995 the respondent went into voluntary liquidation and a liquidator was appointed. The company was dissolved on 7 September 1995. The company had been solvent and £10,268 was paid to creditors and £176,616 returned to members.

In December 1995 the applicant learned of the dissolution, which barred him from recovering compensation. He applied to have the company restored to the register. The company (in effect, its insurers) resisted the application on the grounds that restoration would serve no purpose as the claim was statute barred. The judge found for the company, holding that the rule in *Walkley v Precision Forgings Ltd* (p705) was an insuperable obstacle to the claim. The applicant appealed.

Held:

(i) On the date the company resolved to go into voluntary liquidation the pending action was a debt with the Insolvency Rules rr 13-12 and could be proved in the normal way. If the applicant's claim was good the liquidator had an obligation to pay.

(ii) The company could have made an earlier application to strike out but failed to do so. They could not now complain of the applicant sought to enforce his rights.

(iii) The second purpose the order declaring the dissolution to be void was so fresh proceedings could be issued against the company.

(iv) Normally s 11 would bar a fresh claim, but s 33 might provide relief. The applicant had an arguable case for estoppel so the rule in *Walkley v Precision Forgings* could not at this stage be said to be decisive. That being so, the application should be allowed for a hearing on the merits of the limitation point (*Re Workvale* (p726) applied).

Appeal allowed and restoration order made.

NB The *Walkley* rule was abolished by *Horton v Sadler* (p482).

Phillips v Air New Zealand Ltd

Warsaw Convention, Art 29	**Carriage by Air Act 1961, s 1, s 5**

Morrison J	**[2002] 1 All ER (Comm) 801;**
	[2002] 2 Lloyd's Rep 408; [2002] CLC 1199

On 22 March 1997 the claimant requested assistance from the defendant at Nadi International Airport, Fiji, because she was unfit to move her heavy luggage. She was being transported in a wheelchair on an escalator towards the departure area when the wheelchair fell backwards injuring her. Proceedings were issued inn England on 16 March 2000. The applicability of the Warsaw Convention was heard as a preliminary issue.

Held:

(i) The contract for air travel was engaged when the claimant completed checking-in. The Convention therefore applied to this claim.

(ii) As the claim had been brought outside the strict two-year time limit the claimant's right to damages was extinguished.

Claim struck out.

Phillips and another v Symes and others

CPR 6

Peter Smith J   **[2005] EWHC 1880 (Ch), LTL 26/8/2005**

The claimant sought an order that the defendants paid them substantial sums of money. Prior to the issue of proceedings a freezing order was made against the defendants which the claimant, to the defendants' knowledge, sought to enforce by an attachment of earnings order. The attachment was subsequently discharged in Switzerland. The claimant properly endorsed the claim form as required by CPR 6.19(1) but the court office on issue erroneously stamped on its form in red ink *'Not for service out of the jurisdiction'*. The error arose because the claimant had provided a certificate, verified by his solicitor, that the High Court had jurisdiction. The claimant noted the error but the court official permitted issue but did not delete the stamping or require clean copies. Identical packages including the erroneously stamped claim form were delivered to the senior master for service, which was duly arranged as per CPR 6.28. The stamp was still not removed. In the case of one of the defendants, the clerk in Switzerland, unknown to the claimant, removed the claim form and resealed the package before delivering it to the defendants. In respect of another there was a failure by the Swiss post office. There was no prejudice to the defendants, who were fully aware of the proceedings. The defendants instituted proceedings in the Zurich court against the claimant without informing him beforehand and contended that these later proceedings were those where the dispute was definitively pending. The claimant contended that the defendants had been validly served for the purposes of the Hague convention and that the English court was definitively seised. The claimant sought a declaration to this effect.

Held:

(i)   Definitive seisin for the purposes of the English courts required both issue and service. However, the court could dispense with service in exceptional circumstances.

(ii)   In the first case, it would be a gross miscarriage of justice if the lack of service of the claim form as a result of it being removed by the clerk resulted in a stay of proceedings. No such order under CPR 3.10 staying or setting aside proceedings would be made. It was appropriate to dispense with service under CPR 3.9. The English court was thus definitively seised when the package was served notwithstanding that the claim form was not included.

(iii)   In the second case, the sole reason for the service failure was the failure of the Swiss post office to comply with its obligations. However, this meant that there was no service under Swiss law. In the exceptional circumstances of this case, where communications between the co-defendants meant that there was no prejudice, it was appropriate to dispense with service. The English court definitively seised.

Declarations granted.

Pietkowicz v Smethwick Drop Forgings Ltd and British and Midlands Forgings Ltd

Limitation Act 1980, s 11, s 14, s 33

Dudley County Court (HHJ Hodgson)   **CLY 97/656**

The claimant worked from 1968-1975 with the first and second defendants. He developed industrial deafness. Proceedings were issued in 1994. The defendant pleaded limitation.

Held:

(i)   The claimant was aware during the course of his employment that not only he but also his colleagues were going deaf. He therefore had knowledge for the purposes of the Act as regards the first defendant in 1973 and as regards the second defendant in 1975. The claim was thus statute barred.

(ii)   This was not an appropriate case in which to exercise a s 33 discretion to let the claim proceed.

Claim struck out.

Pilmore v Northern Trawlers Ltd

Limitation Act 1980, s 33

Eastham J   **[1986] 1 Lloyd's Rep 552**

During the periods between January 1971 and March 1972 the claimant (Matthew Pilmore) was employed by the defendants on their fishing vessel Northern Reward. He suffered an acute attack of contact dermatitis of the hands and was unable to work from 26 May to 11 July 1971. Following two relapses in 1972, he was declared permanently unfit for further sea service on 30 October 1972.

He did nothing until he went to the branch of his union in 1980 when he was told that he was too late to claim. In December 1982 he joined the British Fishermen's Association. In November 1983 he reached solicitors. His writ was issued in August 1984. It was accepted that his action was prima facie statute barred under s 11 of the Limitation Act 1980. A preliminary trial was held on whether this should be disapplied under s 33.

Held:

(i)   The claimant knew that he was suffering from dermatitis, which he knew was due to oil during his service, since 1971 so the delay was very long indeed. The reason was that he was a simple man who needed to be told in words of one syllable that he had a claim and should go to a solicitor: s 33(3)(a).

(ii)   The defendants' evidence was likely to be much less cogent because they had parted with the relevant vessel, requisition document and gloves and barrier cream had long since been destroyed, and the crew who might have been able to give evidence as to whether there were sufficient quantities of gloves and barrier cream had dispersed: s 33(3)(b).

(iii)   The Limitation Act was introduced by Parliament for the purpose of stopping stale claims. It would not be equitable to allow the action to proceed: s 33(1).

Platt v Quaker Oats Limited

Limitation Act 1980, s 11, s 14, s 33

Rougier J   **12 July 1991**

On 23 January 1984 the claimant (Mr Platt), a lorry driver, picked up a quantity of tinned dog food in pallets which had been loaded by the defendants at their premises in Southall. When he delivered them in Barnsley one of the pallets broke in half and tins of dog food fell on his back, knocking him down.

He needed 2 weeks off work due to back pain and continued to suffer intermittent pain. In 1985 he took a total of 12 days off. The pain grew progressively worse until it deteriorated sharply in November 1986. His general practitioner referred him in February 1987 to a consultant orthopaedic surgeon in whose care he underwent a variety of treatments, including a partial laminectomy, until August 1988 when the surgeon told him that he would be unlikely to be able to work as a heavy goods driver again.

The claimant went to a local Citizens Advice Bureau and was referred to solicitors in October 1988. After legal aid was acquired, and medical reports and counsel's opinion were obtained, the writ was issued on 12 September 1989. A preliminary trial on limitation was ordered. It was conceded that the claimant had known all the requisite facts, except that the injury was significant within s 14(1)(a) of the Limitation Act 1980.

Held:

(i) (a) The test under s 14(2) was whether a decision to sue by this claimant would have been considered a reasonable one. The wording of the subsection did not allow this to be reversed by asking whether the claimant would be acting reasonably if he did not bring a claim;

(b) the question was whether such a man as the claimant would be thought reasonable if he considered it worth his while to bring a claim, balancing what he was likely to be awarded on one hand and such things as time and trouble on the other. Other considerations, such as whether or not a claim would be likely to result in the loss of his job, were outside the ambit of this particular enquiry: s 14(2);

(c) the injury had been very painful in the early stages and had cost the claimant two weeks' wages. If it had stopped there, it might not have been appropriate to penalise a robust man who decided not to claim for something he regarded as short lived: s 14(1);

(d) however, by February 1985, when the claimant had very nearly a full week off because of his back, it would have been apparent to him that it was not clearing up. On the contrary, it was getting worse. It would certainly have been reasonable for him to pursue a claim then: s 14(3);

(e) therefore the claimant's action was started outside the primary limitation period: s 11(4).

(ii) (a) The delay from accident to writ was over five years. The reasons for it were commendable, since while the claimant was able to carry on with his work he preferred to do so and did not think it worthwhile to claim until his whole livelihood was at risk: s 33(3)(a);

(b) the delay had caused substantial prejudice to the defendants in producing evidence to rebut the claim. In particular, their inward goods supervisor, who was in charge of the system, had recently died so his evidence would not be available orally. On the other hand, the site and nature of the accident were always going to place the defendants in some difficulty: s 33(3)(b);

(c) from the time he went to the Citizens Advice Bureau, it had been conceded that the claimant and his advisers acted promptly. It was reasonable of him not to go to law until he received the depressing prognosis from his consultant surgeon: s 33(3)(e);

(d) his chances of establishing liability seemed good, since the pallet broke and the defendants put the pallet into circulation. The claim would be substantial if it succeeded. The claimant did not have an alternative claim against his solicitors: s 33(3);

(e) it was a fairly finely balanced decision, but discretion under s 33 should be exercised in the claimant's favour: s 33(1).

McCafferty v Metropolitan Police District Receiver (p546) followed.

Player v Bruguiere

Limitation Act 1939, s 2D **Renewal of writ; RSC Ord 6, r 8(2)**

Court of Appeal **[1980] 2 All ER 463; [1980] 1 WLR 958; 124 SJ 544**

See *Chappell v Cooper* (p369)

Pledger v Martin

Limitation Act 1980, s 33, s 35 **CPR 19**

QBD (HHJ Coningsby QC) **[2000] PIQR P31**

The claimant, a carpenter employed by the defendant, suffered personal injury on 25 September 1995 when he fell from the roof of a garage upon which he was working. He contended that the defendant ought to have provided a platform for him to work upon, which would have avoided the need for him to balance upon the central roof support. He commenced proceedings, pleading absence of a platform in breach of the Construction (Working Places) Regulations 1966 and in breach of the common law duty of care. The defendant argued that a platform had been provided and that it was sufficient to comply with both the common law duty and the regulations.

There was some clarification of the allegations by way of further and better particulars, and the claimant maintained his case that there was a complete absence of any boards. When asked to say whether any specific breaches of the regulations were relied on, if there were boards, he said that that was not relevant. The claimant thus did not indicate the possibility of pursuing an alternative case until discussions between opposing counsel in the week before trial, the date of trial being 1 March 1999. The claimant contended that, if the court were to find there had been a platform, he was entitled to rely on the alternative case that the platform was inadequate to meet the requirements of the regulations, by virtue of RSC Ord 18, r 14 (now CPR 16.7), as a result of which assertions made in the defence are automatically put in issue. The defendant argued, relying upon *Waghorn v George Wimpey & Co Ltd* [1969] 1 WLR 1764, that the alternative case was a new claim, which had not been pleaded, and therefore could not be advanced. The claimant in response applied, if necessary, to amend. The defendant resisted this on the basis that the proposed amendments sought to plead a new cause of action outside the limitation period, and that it would not be equitable under s 33 to so permit.

Held:

(i) The deemed joinder of those issues which were pleaded in the defence did not obviate the need for an amendment. A claimant was obliged to plead the facts, including the hypothetical alternative facts, upon which he relies. It is one thing for a claimant to dispute a defence and another thing for him to set up and properly plead his own case. As a matter of general principle, there is no reason why a claimant should not plead an alternative case even though the main and alternative cases are inconsistent.

(ii) The alternative case should have been pleaded as well as the original case because the defendant's preparation of his defence was likely to have been different if specific breaches of the regulations relating to the inadequacy of the platform had been pleaded. In particular, both parties would have been likely to commission expert evidence with respect to the pleaded breaches which neither had done to date, due to the nature of the claimant's case as presently formulated (*Waghorn* followed). The claimant would not be permitted to run his alternative case without an amended pleading.

(iii) The proposed amendment raised a new cause of action, and it did not arise out of substantially the same facts as the existing claim. It was, in fact, wholly inconsistent with the existing claim.

(iv)   It would not be equitable to allow the amendment to plead the new cause of action because the requirements of s 33 were not met. The claimant could suffer no prejudice from not being able to run a case which had never been his case and which would be run only on his lawyer's advice. The fresh allegation was inconsistent with the existing plea and the amendment substantial and made at a very late stage and, as per above, there was substantial prejudice to the defendant arising from this. It was also relevant that, if successful, the defendant would have little chance of costs recovery from the legally aided claimant, and that allowing the amendment would very likely entail an adjournment and much further evidence.

Permission to advance the proposed alternative case refused and application to amend the original statement of case dismissed.

Poyner v Linde Heavy Truck Division Ltd

Limitation Act 1980, s 14

Cardiff County Court (Elias J)   **LTL 9/1/2004**

The claimant worked for the defendant as fitter from 1978-1980 and from 1987-1990 using various vibrating tools. In mid 1990 he noticed stiffness in his fingers. His condition deteriorated over the next two years and he suffered blanching, tingling and loss of function. He issued proceedings on 15 February 2002. There was a trial on limitation, liability and causation. The claim failed on liability.

Held (as regards limitation):

the claimant first knew that his condition could be attributed to his working condition in 2001 when a colleague informed him that he was making a claim. Although, other workers in the claimant's position might have been aware of a possible causal link, the judge accepted that subjectively the claimant did not. Proceedings were therefore issued in time.

NB: The partly subjective test for constructive knowledge has since been disapproved: *Adams v Bracknell Forest BC* (p292).

Preston v BBH Solicitors

Limitation Act 1980, s 11, s 14

Court of Appeal   **[2011] EWCA Civ 1429**

The claimant, a 75-year-old former shipwright, had been exposed to asbestos during his career. He visited his GP in January and February 2002 with chest problems. Chest x-rays were done and pleural plaques were found, which indicated the possibility of asbestosis. The claimant's GP advised him to seek legal advice. He consulted the defendant solicitors in March 2003. In July 2005 the claimant was referred to a consultant chest physician who agreed with the GP's diagnosis that the x-rays illustrated the possibility of mild underlying asbestosis, but he ordered a CT scan to be sure. Proceedings were not issued against his former employer in November 2005. At the time the claim was issued, pleural plaques were considered an actionable injury. However, this was under challenge in a group of test cases which culminated in the House of Lords ruling in October 2007 that they were not: *Rothwell v Chemical Insulation Co Ltd & Ors* [2007] UKHL 39; [2008] 1 AC 281; [2007] 3 WLR 876; [2007] 4 All ER 1047. The claimant's claim appears to have been effectively stayed awaiting resolution of this issue. In December 2005, the expert confirmed the presence of pleural plaques and advised the claimant that he also had mild underlying asbestosis.

In 2007, the claimant changed solicitors. The new solicitors advised him that his claim was statute barred and, in June 2009, he issued proceedings against the defendants on the basis that they had been negligent in issuing proceedings outside the limitation period. He contended that they had allowed his claim to become statute barred as his date of knowledge was February 2002 when he was advised about the possibility of asbestosis. Dismissing the claimant's claim, the judge held that, since it was not clear to the GP in February 2002 that the claimant actually had asbestosis, his date of knowledge was December 2005 and, therefore, the claim had been brought within time. Knowledge of asbestosis itself was needed. He held that, following *Rothwell*, knowledge of pleural plaques and future risks could not be sufficient. The claimant appealed.

Held:

(i)   It was plain that the first diagnosis of asbestosis was in December 2005, and not February 2002. The GP in 2002 did not have cause to find anything but the possibility of asbestosis. The judge did not make a clear finding as to what the claimant was told by the GP in 2002. If all that was known in 2002 was knowledge of pleural plaques, that in itself did not give the claimant knowledge of asbestosis, and time had not begun to run where the claimant had an asbestos-related disease which might have been actionable in the future (*Rothwell* applied). The GP had not had the benefit of a CT scan, and it was only such a scan that allowed confirmation of asbestosis. Consequently, the judge had been right to find that the claimant only had knowledge in 2005.

(ii)   The claimant's contention that the presence of pleural plaques was indicative of the possibility of asbestosis, and therefore he should be treated as having knowledge of asbestosis as in the third category listed by Brooke LJ in *Spargo v North Essex DHA* (p667), was incorrect. On the facts, he fell within the fourth category in *Spargo*, namely the need to check with an expert before the act or omission giving rise to injury could be attributed to negligence. When the diagnosis was made in 2002, the claimant had no actionable injury.

(iii)   Although the claimant considered the injury he had in 2002 sufficiently serious to initiate proceedings, no such knowledge could be imputed. The claimant took reasonable steps to investigate and did not have earlier constructive knowledge. The relevant knowledge was of having asbestosis. An action could not be brought without having proper knowledge of the facts, and the presence of pleural plaques and the possibility of asbestosis or further injury was not sufficient.

Appeal dismissed.

Price v Cornwall County Council

Limitation Act 1980, s 33

HHJ Thompson (sitting in the QBD)   **3 November 1995, unreported**

On 2 February 1984 the claimant, then aged 16, had a riding accident resulting in numerous fractures to her right leg and permanent disability. The accident occurred during a Youth Training Scheme of which the defendant was the managing agent. Liability was denied. The claimant, upon receiving unfavourable advice from counsel, did not pursue the claim. She turned 18 in July 1985. In October 1992, proceedings were issued following favourable advice from different counsel.

Held:

(i)   The only basis upon which the claimant could ask the court to exercise its discretion in her favour was that she had initially received the wrong legal advice.

(ii)   This was insufficient. The claimant had been aware of her cause of action almost immediately.

Claim struck out.

Price v Price

CPR 7.4, 3.9

Court of Appeal   **[2003] EWCA Civ 888; [2003] 3 All ER 911; LTL 26/6/2003**

In May 1998 the claimant was injured when working at his wife's shop. He instructed solicitors who intimated a claim to the defendant's insurers in November 1999. In February 2000 the insurers admitted negligence subject to medical evidence proving causation. There had been no mention of a loss of earnings claim and the insurers valued the claim at about £10,000. Nothing was heard from the claimant's solicitors until proceedings issued on 4 April 2001 were served on April 14 2001. The claim form stated the value of the claim to be over £50,000. Particulars of claim were not served within the 14 days required. The insurers pressed for more details and medical evidence. Not until August 2001 did the claimant reply stating that he was seeking an extension of his legal aid certificate (which did not in fact cover issue of proceedings). In fact, he was seeking a second medical opinion. He did not approach the Legal Services Commission until 20 December 2001, the LSC confirming an extension on 21 January 2002.

On 24 January 2002 the claimant's solicitors wrote that they were seeking an up-to-date medical report when in fact they were instructing an expert different from the one previously agreed. The defendant queried the position of the original expert but received no reply. They did not serve the second medical report until 29 July 2002, by which point they applied for an extension of time to serve particulars of claim 14 months out of time. The schedule of loss revealed to the defendant for the first time a claim for £548,170.

The district judge granted the claimant's application. The defendant appealed. The judge allowed the appeal, holding that the there was a large and unexplained delay. He was heavily critical of the claimant's solicitors and ordered that they show cause why they should not be liable for wasted costs. The claimant appealed.

Held:

(i)   The claimant and his solicitors were guilty of numerous breaches and were on the wrong side of the relevant criteria in CPR 3.9.

(ii)   Conversely, the defendant had behaved impeccably throughout.

(iii)   However, to bar the claim entirely would be disproportionately harsh to the claimant and provide an undeserved windfall to the defendant.

(iv)   The claimant was therefore permitted an extension on the condition that his claim was only for such damages as could be substantiated by medical evidence which already existed in April 2001.

(v)   The order for costs would stand and the claimant would pay the costs of the appeal to be set-off against his damages.

Appeal allowed to a limited extent.

Price v United Engineering Steels Ltd

Limitation Act 1980, s 33

Court of Appeal   **[1998] PIQR P407**

The claimant, a former steelworker, was employed by the first defendant between September 1961 and May 1964 and by the second defendant between 1969 and 1980. In the mid to late 1970s he developed hearing problems. In 1978 he was examined by a works doctor for the second defendant but he was never provided with ear protection. He did not appreciate the link between noise and deafness until shortly before he first consulted solicitors in 1986. The first defendant's premises were shut down in the 1970s and the second defendant's premises were demolished in about 1980, although the same insurers acted for both defendants and had settled many claims over many years relating to each works.

The first letter before action was written by the claimant's first solicitors in January 1987, shortly after the claimant saw a doctor who told him he had a good claim. They corresponded with the defendants' insurers until the end of 1988, but some time after this their firm closed down. When the claimant learned in 1989 what had happened, he instructed a second firm of solicitors. They obtained a report from a medical audiologist in November 1989 and then entered into correspondence with the defendants' insurers between January and November 1990 which did not result in a settlement. The claimant instructed a third firm of solicitors in 1991, who issued proceedings in November 1992.

The claimant applied for a direction under s 33 that the statute bar be disapplied. The judge found that the claimant knew he had knowledge within s 14 at the end of 1986, some six years before commencement of proceedings. It was held that, due to the delay, the defendants had suffered real prejudice in defending the claim and it would not be equitable to allow the action to proceed by disapplying s 11 of the Act. The delay was not their fault but that of the claimant and his various solicitors. The claimant appealed. Two grounds of appeal were advanced: (1) the judge was wrong to set aside a subpoena served on a Mr Tempest by the claimant's solicitors for the purposes of establishing the existence and extent of other similar claims that the defendant has settled; and (2) the judge wrongly exercised his discretion under s 33. The subpoena had been served on Mr Tempest, a senior claims manager with the insurers of both defendants, so that the claimant could ask questions relating to schemes created to compensate employees or ex-employees of insured companies for noise-induced hearing loss. The defendants claimed that the questions which the claimant wished to raise were oppressive, requiring investigation of some 75,000 settled claims. On the s 33 point the claimant argued that, if the defendants would already have been seriously prejudiced if the action had been started against them within the time before the end of 1989, any additional prejudice by an extra three years' delay would be minimal, and the defendants should have adduced positive evidence of the difficulties they faced if they wanted the judge to take those difficulties seriously.

Held:

(i)   The judge was right to set aside the subpoena. In *Beattie v British Steel Plc* (p327) the court ruled in a similar case that it was not open to a claimant to submit that because defendants or their insurers had settled other claims they were not thereby in any way prejudiced by the delay which had taken place in the two cases then before the court.

(ii)   Once a claimant's audiograph had the characteristics which are typical of noise-induced hearing loss, it was notoriously difficult for a defendant who had a noisy factory to defend a claim that the claimant was exposed to excessive amounts of noise. It was understandable why defendant insurers preferred to settle such claims under agreed schemes where the quantum of their liability could be readily determined on a tariff basis.

(iii)   A defendant is always likely to be prejudiced by the dilatoriness of a claimant in pursuing his claim; memories fade, records are lost etc. It was not essential that defendants should call evidence of the particular respects in which the witnesses' recollections were impaired. The court was entitled to draw an inference of prejudice.

(iv)   The fact that the law permits a claimant within prescribed limits to disadvantage a defendant in this way did not mean that the defendant was not prejudiced. It merely meant that he was not in a position to complain of whatever prejudice he suffered: *Donovan v Gwentoys Ltd* (p412).

Appeal dismissed.

Pritam Kaur v S Russell & Sons Ltd

Limitation Act 1939, s 2   **Computation of time**

Court of Appeal   **[1973] QB 336; [1973] 2 WLR 147;
[1973] 1 All ER 617**

On 5 September 1967 Bikar Singh was working in a pit in a foundry. A skip suddenly fell on him and killed him immediately. On Monday 7 September 1970 the claimant (Pritam Kaur), his widow, issued a writ against his defendant employers for damages under the Law Reform (Miscellaneous Provisions) Act 1934 and the Fatal Accidents Act 1846.

The defendants pleaded limitation. The question whether the writ had been issued in time was tried as a preliminary issue by Willis J who held that the action was statute barred. The claimant appealed.

Held:

(i)   In computing the three-year limitation period, the first day (on which the accident occurred) is not to be counted. Accordingly, the limitation period did not expire on 4 September 1970.

(ii)   When a time is prescribed by statute for doing any act, and that act can only be done if the court office is open on the date when the time expires, then, if it turns out in any particular case that the day is a Sunday or other dies non, the time is extended to the next day on which the court office is open.

(iii)   Therefore the claimant had until Monday 7 September 1970 in which to issue her writ. Her action was commenced in time.

The claimant's appeal was allowed.

Marren v Dawson Bentley & Co Ltd (p543) approved.

Purnell v Roche

Real Property Limitation Acts 1837 and 1874

Romer J   **[1927] 2 Ch 142; [1927] All ER Rep 560; 71 SJ 452**

By an indenture of mortgage dated 27 September 1902, James Roche assured to the claimant (Mrs Purnell) certain freehold hereditaments at Cheltenham by way of mortgage for securing payment to the claimant of the principal sum of £350 and interest subject to redemption on payment on 27 March 1903. Since the date of the mortgage, James Roche and those claiming under him remained in undisturbed occupation of the premises.

On 23 February 1907 the claimant became and thereafter continued to be of unsound mind. The last payment in respect of interest was made on 25 May 1907. On 28 January 1926 the claimant's husband was appointed receiver of her estate.

Later in 1926 a summons was issued in the claimant's name for the enforcement of the mortgage by foreclosure or sale. The defendant pleaded that her right were statute barred.

Held:

(i) The claimant's right to make her entry or bring her action first accrued either at the date of the mortgage on 27 September 1902 or, at the latest, on 27 March 1903 when the estate of the mortgagee became absolute at law.

(ii) A disability beginning after the date of action first accrued did not entitle the claimant to the protection given by s 3 of the Real Property Limitation Act 1874.

The claimant's summons was dismissed.

NB: It is submitted that the same principle would prima facie apply in a modern personal injury action by virtue of s 28 of the Limitation Act 1980. However, it would be subject to the exercise of the court's discretion under s 33 of the 1980 Act with particular regard to 'the duration of any disability of the claimant arising after the date of the accrual of the cause of action' under s 33(3)(d).

Purdy v Cambran

CPR – Striking out – delay

Court of Appeal   **LTL 17/12/99**

The claimant suffered serious orthopaedic injuries in a road traffic accident on 6 December 1989. He issued proceedings on 30 November 1992. Liability was admitted. Between 1990 and 1992 the claimant instructed four different medical experts. The defendant instructed a medical expert who contradicted the claimant's evidence. In response to this the claimant commissioned a further report from one of his experts which threw doubt on the original prognosis.

In February 1995 the claimant instructed yet a further expert which prompted the defendant to return to its expert for a supplementary report. On 24 June 1997 the defendant applied to have the claim set down for a hearing. However, on 27 July 1997 the district judge ordered a hearing to be listed on the filing of a joint certificate of readiness.

On 5 January 1998 the defendant sent a signed certificate of readiness to the claimant. The claimant did not attempt to set the matter down but rather sought a further report from his most recently instructed expert. In August 1998 the defendant's expert died. On 17 May 1999 the defendant applied to strike the claim out for want of prosecution. The application was dismissed by the district judge, but upheld on appeal to the circuit judge. The claimant made a second tier appeal.

Held:

(i) It is incumbent upon a litigant who waits until limitation has almost expired before issuing proceedings to prosecute the claim expeditiously thereafter.

(ii) The death of the defendant's expert constituted substantial prejudice. The delay for a simple assessment of damages was inordinate. A fair trial of the issues was no longer possible. The strike out was therefore not a disproportionate measure.

(iii) Whilst it was not appropriate to analyse the issues in cases such as these by reference to large numbers of authorities decided under the old rules, the older authorities were not be automatically disregarded. The underlying thought processes of previous decisions should not be completely thrown overboard (*Biguzzi v Rank Leisure* (p335) and *UCB v Halifax* (p697) considered).

Appeal dismissed.

RAR v GGC

Limitation Act 1980, s 33

QBD (Nicola Davies J)   **[2012] EWHC 2338 (QB)**

The defendant was the claimant's step-father. She alleged that between 1972 and 1977, when she was aged from 7 to 12, he physically and sexually assaulted her on many occasions, including hitting and punching her, requiring her to undress, taking indecent photographs of her, rubbing his penis against her vagina, fondling her vagina and inserting his finger and other objects into her vagina. The defendant had pleaded guilty in 1978 to one offence of indecently assaulting the claimant. The claimant subsequently suffered from mental health problems requiring hospitalisation. She had attempted suicide and self-harmed, resulting in substantial permanent scarring.

In April 2011 the claimant issued proceedings. The defendant denied the allegations and raised a limitation defence. Although the defendant had contended that limitation should be heard as a preliminary issue, the court had ordered that all issues be tried together. The claimant admitted that the claim was issued beyond the primary limitation period but invited the court to give a direction pursuant to s 33 that it would be just and equitable to allow it to proceed. The issues for determination were (1) whether the discretion conferred by s 33 should be exercised in the claimant's favour; (2) the nature and extent of the alleged assaults perpetrated by the defendant on the claimant; (3) the nature and extent of any resultant personal injury and loss; and (4) the appropriate level of damages.

Held:

(i)   It was clear that the claimant's mental health had been adversely affected by the assaults perpetrated on her. This had played a real part in the delay which had occurred in bringing such a claim. The abuse itself had been an inhibiting factor.

(ii)   The instant case depended upon the evidence of the parties themselves. Although the claimant would find it distressing to give evidence, the detail contained in her witness statement demonstrated that she was able to remember and articulate her memories, however unpleasant. There was nothing in the defendant's witness statement which demonstrated any difficulty on his part in remembering the detail of relevant periods. In 1977/78 the defendant had cause to consider allegations of sexual assault upon the claimant by reason of the criminal proceedings. The evidence of both parties remained sufficiently cogent to enable a fair trial to take place.

(iii)   It would, therefore, be fair and just to disapply the limitation period.

(iv)   The claimant's account of the abuse was accepted. Liability was established and damages assessed accordingly.

Judgment for claimant.

RM v Bryn Alyn Community Holdings Ltd

Limitation Act 1980, s 2, s 11, s 14, s 33

Court of Appeal   **[2003] EWCA Civ 783; [2003] 3 WLR 107;**
                                                  [2003] 1 FLR 1203

See *KR v Bryn Alyn Community Holdings Ltd* (D) (p505)

Rabone v Pennine Care NHS Trust

Human Rights Act 1998, s 7(5)

Supreme Court

[2012] UKSC 2; [2012] 2 WLR 381;
[2012] PTSR 497; [2012] 2 All ER 381;
[2012] HRLR 10; (2012) 15 CCL Rep 13;
[2012] Med LR 221; (2012) 124 BMLR 148;
(2012) 162 NLJ 261; (2012) 156(6) SJLB 31;
(2012) Times, 20 February

M had suffered from depression and had been informally admitted to the defendant's hospital following a suicide attempt. She was assessed as a high risk of suicide but was allowed two days' home leave during which she committed suicide on 20 April 2005. Her parents brought proceedings for negligence and breach of art 2 of the European Convention on Human Rights 1950. The claim form was issued on 11 August 2006. The defendant denied all allegations of breach. It also alleged that the human rights claim was time barred under s 7(5) of the Human Rights Act 1998, since it had been issued more than one year after M's death. By their reply, the claimants asked the court to extend the time limit by four months in the exercise of its discretion under s 7(5)(b).

The negligence claim was settled but the High Court held that there had been no duty on the hospital under art 2. The Court of Appeal dismissed the claimants' appeal. They appealed again. The issues to be determined were (1) whether the art 2 obligation could in principle be owed to a mentally ill hospital patient who was not detained under the Mental Health Act 1983; (2) if yes, whether there was a 'real and immediate' risk to M's life of which the defendant had known or ought to have known and which it failed to take reasonable steps to avoid; (3) if yes, whether the claimants were 'victims' within the meaning of art 34 of the Convention; (4) if yes, whether the claimants had lost that victim status because the defendant had made adequate redress and had sufficiently acknowledged its breach of duty; (5) if no, whether the claims were time barred under s 7(5) of the Human Rights Act 1998; and (6) if no, whether the Court of Appeal had erred in holding that it would have awarded £5,000 each to the claimants if their claims had been established.

Held:

(i)   The defendant owed an operational duty to M to take reasonable steps to protect her from the real and immediate risk of suicide.

(ii)   There was a real risk that M would take her life when allowed home. The defendant was or ought to have been aware of that risk. The decision to allow M two days' home leave was one that no reasonable psychiatric practitioner would have made. The defendant had failed to do all that could reasonably have been expected to prevent the real and immediate risk of M's suicide.

(iii)   Family members could bring claims in their own right in relation to the investigative and substantive obligations under art 2.

(iv)   The claimants had not renounced an art 2 claim by settling the negligence claim.

(v)   The grounds on which the courts below had exercised their discretion by refusing to extend time was flawed in the light of the Supreme Court's decision on the merits of the art 2 claim, and therefore the discretion had to be exercised afresh. The extension of time would be granted. The required extension was short, the defendant had suffered no prejudice by the delay, and the claimants had acted reasonably. They had made a formal complaint within five months of M's death. They were advised that their complaint would be 'put on hold' until an internal investigation had been completed. Their evidence to the judge was that they believed that the trust would produce a 'reasonably prompt report' providing a proper explanation. They said that their waiting for the report was a material factor in their decision not to issue proceedings. As the judge found, if the investigation which began in September 2005 had produced a reasonably prompt report, they might have issued proceedings sooner. The investigation report was not in fact sent to them until 16 March 2007. Most importantly, the claimants had a good claim for breach of art 2.

(vi) The claimants would be awarded £5,000 each.

Raggett v Society of Jesus Trust 1929 for Roman Catholic Purposes

Limitation Act 1980, s 14, s 33

Court of Appeal   **[2010] EWCA Civ 1002; [2010] CP Rep 45; (2010) 160 NLJ 1228; (2010) 154(34) SJLB 30**

In February 2007 the claimant issued proceedings for personal injury consequent upon sexual abuse and assaults committed on him by a teacher at a school he had attended between 1969 and 1976. The defendant governors pleaded limitation. This was heard alongside the substantive issues. The judge held, first, that the abuse had taken place. Next she held, applying the requisite test for knowledge for the purposes of s 14, that the claimant must be taken to have known the nature and extent of those acts from the time they had been committed and that therefore the claim became time barred in 1979 when he turned 21. The judge was satisfied that it would be equitable to allow the action to proceed under s 33; as to the extent that there was any prejudice in relation to the issue of causation, it was likely to operate to the detriment of the claimant, since he had the burden of proving his loss. The defendant appealed, contending that the judge erred in making findings that the abuse had occurred before determining whether it was appropriate to exercise her discretion under s 33 to extend the time limit and had applied the wrong principle in determining whether the defendant had suffered prejudice in relation to the issue of causation.

Held:

(i) When an application is made to disapply the limitation period under s 33, the judge should decide the s 33 issue not on the basis of the finding that the abuse had in fact occurred, but on an overall assessment of the factors relevant to s 33, namely an assessment of the reasons for the delay, the cogency of the claimant's case against the prejudice likely to be caused to the defendant, and other relevant considerations.

(ii) In observing that the exercise of discretion under s 33 should be decided before reaching conclusions on liability, the authorities are not seeking to prescribe a formulaic template for the construction of a judgment. It is not appropriate for an appellate court to prescribe a format for the delivery of a judgment or to decide the issue on the form of the judgment and the order in which the issues are set out.

(iii) Notwithstanding that the issue of liability was located in the judgment before the s 33 issue, it is clear from an analysis of the judgment that the judge approached the issue under s 33 entirely in accordance with principle. The evidence that the abuse had occurred was strong, particularly in light of the evidence of the claimant's contemporaries and the defendant's approach to liability, and there were ample grounds for concluding that the prejudice to the defendant, particularly the inability to adduce evidence and general effects of delay, had not materially affected its ability to defend the action.

(iv) In the circumstances of this case, the judge had not erred in concluding that the defendant was unlikely to suffer any material prejudice in relation to causation. There would undoubtedly be some small award for general damages on the basis of the judge's finding of sexual assault. The claimant's claim for very significant damages, on the basis that the abuse had affected the whole of his career at university and subsequently as a barrister, would be very difficult to establish in the instant case.

Appeal dismissed.

Ramsden v Lee

Limitation Act 1980, s 33

Court of Appeal [1992] 2 All ER 204

On 26 September 1985 the claimant (Arthur Lee) was riding his motor scooter along a major road when he was struck and knocked off by a car driven by the defendant out of a side road. He sustained injuries which caused him to be off work for a considerable period.

His solicitors notified his claim on 4 November 1985. The defendant's insurers accepted full liability. In 1986 and 1987 they made two interim payments totalling £2,400. Owing to practical delays, the claimant was not examined by the defendant's consultant until 29 September 1988. His writ was issued on 4 April 1989.

The defendant relied on s 11 of the Limitation Act 1980, so the claimant applied under s 33 for this to be disapplied. The district registrar refused. Potter J on appeal granted the requested direction under s 33. The defendant's counsel argued on appeal that the court should lay down a guideline that, subject to certain conditions, in the absence of some element of fault on the part of the defendant leading to the claimant missing a limitation period, the limitation period should be adhered to save where the delay had been minimal.

Held:

(i) It would not be appropriate for the court to approve the suggested guideline. The proposed exception for minimal delay was illogical and would itself give rise to borderline cases. Moreover, although the fact that the claimant would have a valid claim against his solicitor was highly relevant, it would be wrong to disregard the various kinds of prejudice to a claimant that were involved in having to sue his former solicitors.

(ii) A judge in applying the test under s 33(1) is required to take into account all the circumstances including those particularly specified under s 33(3). There was no evidence that the judge in this case had done anything else. The court should not interfere with his decision.

The defendant's appeal was dismissed.

Reade v Oldham Metropolitan Borough Council

Limitation Act 1980, s 33

Court of Appeal 18 October 1990

On 25 September 1982 the claimant (Shirley Reade), a tenant of a third floor council flat, was sitting on a sill cleaning the outside of a window when she lost her balance and fell backwards to the ground. She sustained serious injuries to her spine and to her right leg which had to be amputated below the knee.

Early in 1987, the premises were demolished. It was not until the summer of 1987, in a casual discussion with a hospital consultant, that the question of claiming damages was mentioned for the first time. In July 1987 she consulted a solicitor who in October sent a vaguely worded letter before action. On 10 May 1988 the writ was issued. Only in August 1988, when the writ and statement of claim were served, did the defendants learn the detail of the claim which was based on their failure to clean the windows and an implied term in the tenancy agreement that they would do so.

Their defence pleaded limitation. The claimant applied under s 33 of the Limitation Act 1980. Judge J allowed the defendants' appeal from the registrar's order disapplying the provisions of s 11. The claimant appealed.

Held:

(i) The judge correctly took into account that she would be severely prejudiced by s 11, since she did not have an alternative claim against solicitors. The only mitigating feature in this context was that the claim appeared to be arguable rather than strong: s 33(3).

(ii) The judge was right to find that the defendants had been seriously prejudiced by the delay, on the issues of both primary liability and contributory negligence, since not only had the premises been demolished but also any tenants who could be traced would be trying to recollect events a long time ago: s 33(3)(b).

(iii) There was no respect in which the judge failed properly to exercise his discretion in carrying out the balancing exercise imposed on him by s 33.

The claimant's appeal was dismissed.

Re Regent Insulation Co Ltd

Companies Act 1948, s 353

Vinelott J   **(1981) Times, 4 November**

Between 1970 and 1976 Leonard Bennett worked with asbestos as a lagger for a number of companies. One of these was Regent Insulation who employed him from November 1964 to January 1967. In May 1976 it was struck off the companies register. In summer 1976 Mr Bennett was diagnosed as suffering from asbestosis. In February 1979 a writ was issued on his behalf against seven of his former employers. Regent Insulation were omitted, as the company was dissolved and its insurers had not been traced.

In July 1980 Mr Bennett's solicitors ascertained that Regent Insulation had been insured by the National Employers Mutual (NEM). Accordingly, they applied for an order that (i) the company be restored to the register and (ii) in the case of creditors who were not statute barred at the date of dissolution, the period between dissolution and restoration should not be counted for the purpose of any statute of limitations. Mr Registrar Bradburn made an order in the terms sought.

In July 1981 an amended writ and pleadings, with Regent Insulation added as defendants, were served. The trial was fixed for 7 December 1981. The insurers purported to make an application on behalf of the company out of time for the registrar's order to be set aside.

Held:

(i) The application was hopelessly out of time. As to the main part, for restoration of the company's name, there was no hesitation in rejecting the application to extend time.

(ii) Moreover the company had given no valid authority to make the application. Purported authority had been given by a former managing director, but he was not authorised to give this without the sanction of a resolution of the company in general meeting.

(iii) Even assuming that the application relating to that part of the registrar's order which suspended the running of time was a matter which could properly be authorised by a board of directors, there was no evidence that it had been so authorised.

(iv) Apart from that defect, which might be capable of being ended by ratification, there were factors which weighed conclusively against extending the time for applying to set aside the registrar's order. It would be unfair to Mr Bennett to take any step which might delay the hearing of his action; he clearly had been prejudiced in so far as the striking off of the company made it more difficult to trace the insurers; and no good reason had been given for the delay in bringing the present application.

Reynolds v Long Ashton Research Station

CPR 6.7

Bristol County Court (HHJ Rutherford)   **[2001] CLY 640**

The claimant suffered personal injuries in March 1997. He issued proceedings in March 2000. The claim form was served by fax on the defendant's solicitors on Friday 7 July 2000 (the last day permitted for service). It was received at 4.17pm. The defendant successfully applied for the claim to be struck out due to defective service. The claimant appealed.

Held:

(i)   As the service by fax was effected after 4pm, it was deemed under CPR 6.7(1) to be served on 10 July (the next working day) and thus out of time.

(ii)   Although it was open to a defendant to show that actual service had been effected after deemed service, it was not open to a claimant to show that actual service had been effected before deemed service.

Appeal dismissed.

Reynolds v Spousal (London) Ltd & others

Limitation Act 1980, s 33

Court of Appeal   **Lexis, 13 March 1989**

Sidney Reynolds was employed to work with asbestos as a lagger by Matthew Keenan & Co Ltd (1st defendants) from 1928 to 1947, by Cork Insulation Co Ltd (2nd defendants) from 1949 to 1951, by Rex Insulation Co Ltd (3rd defendants) from 1951 to 1958 and by Dicks Asbestos Co Ltd (4th defendants) from 1958 to 1966. In 1966 he was diagnosed as suffering from asbestosis and left the thermal insulation industry. He claimed and was awarded DHSS industrial disablement benefit. He instructed a solicitor in 1966 to claim damages against his former employers and left the matter in his hands. When the solicitor wrote to him in 1977 that nothing could be done, he tore the letter up in disgust. In 1983 he contracted mesothelioma from which he died in April 1984.

The claimant (his widow) consulted a different solicitor who issued her writ in December 1985. At the preliminary trial, it was accepted that the primary limitation period had expired in 1969. Brooke J under s 33 disapplied the provisions of ss 11 and 12 of the Limitation Act 1980 against the 2nd, 3rd and 4th defendants, but declined to give a similar direction against the 1st defendants who had been in liquidation for many years and appeared to have little or no relevant insurance cover. The 2nd and 4th defendants appealed.

Held:

(i)   There was no reason to differ from the judge's finding that it was inherently unlikely that a writ had been issued by the first solicitor in 1966–77, so the judge was free to exercise his discretion under s 33 of the Limitation Act 1980.

(ii)   The judge was right to find that any cause of action against the first solicitor had almost certainly expired by 1984 and to 'largely disregard' the possibility of such a claim.

(iii)   The judge in his careful and detailed judgment had taken into account the argument that the ultimate burden of damages would fall more heavily on the remaining defendants, since the first defendant was no longer involved. This was essentially a matter for his discretion.

The 2nd and 4th defendants' appeal was dismissed.

Richardson v Watson and anor

Limitation Act 1980, s 12, s 33

Court of Appeal   **[2006] EWCA Civ 1662; LTL 6/12/2006**

The claimant's husband was killed in a road traffic accident on 24 December 2000 when his car collided with that of the uninsured defendant. The claimant issued proceedings but failed to give timely notice to the MIB. She thus failed to comply with the MIB's condition precedent to its satisfying the claim. In light of this the claimant discontinued and commenced a second set of identical proceedings outside the limitation period. The defendant successfully applied to strike out. The judge held that *Walkley v Precision Forgings Ltd* (p705) precluded any extension of time, that the second claim was an abuse of process, and that in any event the s 33 discretion should not be exercised in the claimant's favour.

The claimant appealed.

Held:

(i)   In light of *Horton v Sadler* (p482), there was no automatic bar under *Walkley*.

(ii)   It was neither objectionable nor an abuse of process for a claimant who had failed to comply with the MIB's notice requirements to seek to escape the consequences by commencing a second action. It was not unusual in the past for the MIB to have taken no objection to such a course of action, and the prejudice to the MIB would normally be met by the claimant giving timely notice in respect of the second set of proceedings.

(iii)   It had not been before the judge that the claimant's infants were also continuing to bring claims that were not out of time. In light of this material difference the discretion fell to be considered afresh.

(iv)   The MIB had suffered no prejudice and was seeking to gain a benefit that was not one of the objects of its notice requirements, the purpose of which was to enable to MIB to intervene in proceedings.

(v)   The claimant should not be blamed for the delay between the issue of the second set of proceedings and the judgment in *Horton*.

(vi)   A fair trial was possible on available evidence and the detrimental effect of the passage of time on the evidence was more likely to benefit the defence.

(vii)   That MIB would have to defend the children's claims in any event on precisely the same issues weighed in favour of the claimant.

In all the circumstances it was equitable to allow the claim to proceed.

Rigby v Smith & Johnson

Limitation Act 1939, s 2D

Mais J   **[1979] CLY 1669**

On 15 October 1974 the claimant (Mr Rigby) injured his back when moving tools at work. In June 1977 he consulted solicitors and a letter before action was sent to the defendants. By an oversight his solicitors failed to issue a protective writ. In March 1978 the defendants' insurers stated that they had completed their investigations, but they did not admit or deny liability. Correspondence continued until June 1978.

The claimant started proceedings and applied under s 2D of the Limitation Act 1939 as amended for the primary limitation period to be disapplied. He testified at trial that he did not wish to sue his solicitors, since they had done conveyancing transactions for him previously and he did not think it would be right for him to sue them. The defendants admitted that they had not been prejudiced.

Held: the court would exercise its discretion in favour of the claimant. He had been prejudiced in that he would have to start a new action against his solicitors and he did not wish to do so.

Rihani v J Wareing & Son (Wrea Green) Ltd

Limitation Act 1980, s 33

Court of Appeal   **10 February 2000, unreported**

The claimant was employed for 23 years by the defendant in a fabrication shop at its premises. The work was noisy and, as a result, the claimant suffered noise-induced deafness. The claimant sought advice from his doctor in 1986, who advised him to bring a claim against the defendant. The claimant was dismissed from his job in March 1996, but it was not until April 1997 that he issued proceedings against the defendant claiming damages for personal injury caused by the defendant's negligence. The defendant raised a limitation defence, and the claimant sought the exercise of the court's discretion under s 33 of the Limitation Act 1980.

The claimant's case was that he had been afraid to bring a claim earlier as he was the only non-Caucasian person in the defendant's employment and had experienced racial abuse in the past. The judge found that, as a result of the racial abuse, the claimant did have, on balance, a fear that further retribution would take place if he brought a claim against the defendant. The judge went on to consider whether the delay had caused the evidence in the case to be less cogent than it would have been if the claim had been made within the limitation period. He decided that it had been, on the basis that evidence for the defendant as to the provision of ear protection would no longer be available. After considering all the available evidence, the judge decided not to exercise the s 33 discretion and held the claimant's action to be limitation barred. The claimant appealed.

Held:

(i)   The real question in the case arose in relation to s 33(3)(e) of the Act and the extent to which the claimant acted promptly and reasonably once he knew the act or omission of the defendant was attributable to his injury and gave rise to an action for damages. It was clear that the claimant so knew in 1986 but failed to do anything for 11 years. That substantial delay showed that the claimant had not acted promptly.

(ii)   The Court of Appeal would only interfere with the exercise of a judge's discretion if the court was satisfied that his exercise of discretion was wrong or that he had considered irrelevant facts or failed to consider relevant matters. In the instant case, the judge heard the evidence from the parties and was justified in reaching the conclusion he had. There was nothing to link the claimant's fear of racial abuse with his actual fear that he would be dismissed if he brought a claim against the defendant. The claimant was unable to identify a single employee who had been either sacked or disciplined for bringing a compensation claim. The claimant was clearly an experienced and valued employee whom the defendants would be unlikely to sack simply in response to a modest personal injury claim covered by compulsory insurance.

(iii)   It followed that the judge was entitled to reach the conclusion that it had not been reasonable for the claimant to wait 11 years before bringing his claim. Accordingly, the court would not interfere with the judge's exercise of discretion, since the judge took account of all relevant matters, and the weight to be attached to those findings had been a matter for him.

Appeal dismissed.

Roach v Oxfordshire Health Authority

Limitation Act 1980, s 11, s 14, s 33   **Security for costs**

Court of Appeal   **Lexis, 16 January 1990**

The claimant (Ian Roach) alleged negligence by the defendants in treating his eyes between 1961 and 1981. His writ was issued on 24 March 1988. The defendants denied negligence and pleaded limitation.

At the preliminary trial on limitation, Drake J dismissed the case as statute barred. The claimant appealed. On 19 October 1989 the Court of Appeal registrar ordered the claimant to provide security in the sum of £2,500 by 16 November 1989. The claimant appealed against that decision. He made it clear that he was not in a position to meet the defendants' costs if he should continue with his appeal and lose it.

Held:

(i)   The position with regard to costs in the Court of Appeal differs from the position in the court of first instance in that if an appellant, by reason of impecuniosity, is unable to satisfy the Court of Appeal that he will be able to pay the costs of the other party should he lose the appeal, that is a valid ground upon which the Court of Appeal may order security for costs and perhaps thus effectually debar him from continuing his appeal.

(ii)   An exception to this rule arises where the claimant alleges that his impecuniosity is the result of the very actions of the defendants about which he is complaining. As the claimant alleged that the defendants' negligence had caused him to lose his earning capacity, it was appropriate to consider what were the prospects of the appeal succeeding.

(iii)   The judge's finding that there was no allegation that the defendants had been negligent within three years of the issue of the writ was clearly correct.

(iv)   The claimant's case was that he first had knowledge of some relevant facts when he received an experts' report in February 1986, but the registrar was right to conclude that all the report did was to provide the claimant with evidence in support of allegations that he had already made prior to 24 March 1985.

(v)   There was no reason to disagree with the conclusion that the limitation period should not be disapplied under s 33 of the Limitation Act 1980.

(vi)   Accordingly, the appeal against the requirement of security for costs must be dismissed. The registrar's order would be varied to allow 28 days from this dismissal for the security to be raised.

Robert v Momentum Services Ltd

CPR 3.1   **Service**

Court of Appeal   **[2003] EWCA Civ 299; [2003] 1 WLR 1577;**
                                            [2003] 2 All ER 74

On 5 March 1998 the claimant was injured whilst working for the defendant's predecessor. Proceedings were issued on 1 March 2001 but no particulars of claim were attached. There was an issue as to the instruction of an orthopaedic expert. On 13 June 2001 the claimant sought under CPR 3.1(2)(a) an extension of time for the service of particulars. The claimant foresaw that the particulars could not be served by 1 July 2004 as the medical report would not yet be ready. The district judge acceded to the application. The defendant appealed. The circuit judge allowed the appeal on the basis that the district judge had failed to follow *Bansal v Cheema*

[2001] CP Rep 6 and failed to systematically consider the factors in CPR 3.9. Exercising his discretion afresh the circuit judge refused the claimant's application and dismissed the claim. The claimant appealed.

Held:

(i)   The circuit judge had been wrong to interfere with the district judge's decision because the reasons for it were clearly discernible as required by Bansal. The district judge had fully weighed the prejudice to the defendant and his reasoning was tolerably clear.

(ii)   Similarly, the circuit judge was not entitled to interfere with the district judge's reasoning because the district judge had not gone systematically through CPR 3.9. There was no need to as an application to extend time before the deadline for service had passed was not an application for relief from sanction nor even analogous to one (*Sayers v Clerk Waller (A Firm)* [2002] 1 WLR 3095, distinguished).

(iii) It will rarely be appropriate to refuse an extension of time on the grounds that the claim is weak unless the claim would be susceptible to an application to strike out or enter summary judgment. To do so would be draconian and a possible breach of Article 6 of the European Convention of Human Rights.

(iv)   A defendant who wants to rely on a case's merits to repudiate an application for extension of time should put the claimant specifically on notice.

(v)   The district judge's approach was correct and should not have been interfered with.

Appeal allowed.

Roberts v Commissioner of Police of the Metropolis

Limitation Act 1980, s 33

Court of Appeal   **[2012] EWCA Civ 799**

On 22 April 2007, police were called to the claimant's residential premises after having received a call from his partner alleging domestic violence. The claimant agreed to leave the premises and went to his bedroom, at which point the door closed on one of the officers. The claimant was forced to the ground by two officers and handcuffed, and then allegedly kicked and punched around the chest and legs. The claimant claimed that he was pushed by the officers from the top of a staircase, falling head first down the stairs. He was taken into custody where he was charged with assault. He was subsequently acquitted. He alleged that the police had used excessive force and that their actions constituted an actionable assault. He also alleged that his arrest had been unlawful as he had not been informed of the reasons for his arrest and there had been no reasonable suspicion that he had committed an arrestable offence.

Having consulted solicitors on 1 August 2007 the claimant initially complained about the assault to the police who rejected his complaint after an internal enquiry. In January 2008 the inquiry dismissed the complaint. Public funding was applied for in March 2008 and obtained to a limited extent in August 2008. Deciding not to proceed with an appeal to the Independent Police Complaints Commission, the claimant eventually sent a letter of claim in April 2009. The defendant replied saying that the usual three-month time frame within which a response might be expected could not be adhered to as the case handler was on leave. The claimant pressed for a response, but the defendant failed to provide until 13 May 2010 after the expiry of the limitation period. Proceedings were issued on 10 August 2010. The claimant served these in December 2010, once funding had been secured. The defendant served a detailed defence detailing the events giving rise to the alleged assault. The judge refused to allow the matter to proceed by disapplying the three-year limitation period, finding that, if the limitation period were not disapplied, the claimant would be left to his remedies in negligence against his solicitors; whereas, if the limitation were disapplied and the matter went to trial, there could be serious professional and even criminal consequences for the commissioner. The trial judge reasoned that, as there had been serious prejudice arising from the allegations of assault, a fair trial would not be possible. The claimant appealed.

Held:

(i) In weighing up the prejudice that a defendant would suffer if the limitation period were disapplied, the loss of a limitation defence was not a significant prejudice in itself divorced from the ability to defend a case (*Horton v Sadler* (p482) considered). Time would in practice be extended unless a defendant was able to show that there would otherwise be an adverse impact on the ability to have the defence fairly tried, and the existence of any alternative claim in negligence against a solicitor was unlikely to be determinative. However, if a defendant were able to show real prejudice, an alternative action in negligence would be a more significant factor (*Cain v Francis* (p360) applied).

(ii) In the instant case, permission to appeal had been granted on the question whether the trial judge had been correct to find that, as the claimant's allegation of assault had been serious, it ought to have been brought promptly within the three-year limitation period, and that having failed to do so meant that a fair trial could not be had. The critical criterion was whether there could have been a fair trial: if that were possible, it would have answered the trial judge's concerns in relation to the nature of the allegations.

(iii) The trial judge's view of the seriousness of the allegation cast a special burden on the claimant inconsistent with the general discretionary power in s 33 which was to be exercised on a fair basis with regard to all of the relevant circumstances and the overriding purpose of which was to allow the court to extend time where there would be no prejudice to a defendant to have a fair trial. As a result of a misdirection, the trial judge had given undue weight to a marginal factor.

(iv) The court was unconvinced by the trial judge's treatment of the prejudice that the commissioner would suffer; he had based his finding more on assumption than evidence, and the commissioner had led no evidence on prejudice. In fact, other matters indicated to the contrary and there was nothing to indicate that the police officers' ability to recollect events would be affected. The claimant also maintained actions for malicious prosecution and unlawful imprisonment which had a six-year time limit. The relevant matters would have to be investigated in this context in any event. The trial judge's finding that a fair trial would not be possible was not justified on the evidence or for any others reasons. Accordingly, the court made an order under s 33 disapplying the limitation period.

Appeal allowed.

Roberts v Gill & Co

Limitation Act 1980, s 35   **CPR 17, 19**

Supreme Court   **[2010] UKSC 22; [2011] 1 AC 240;**
[2010] 2 WLR 1227; [2010] 4 All ER 367;
[2010] PNLR 30; [2010] WTLR 1223;
(2010) 154(20) SJLB 36; (2010) Times, 28 May

The claimant was a residuary beneficiary of his late grandmother's estate. His brother was the administrator. The claimant began proceedings, in his personal capacity as beneficiary, alleging negligence against the defendant solicitors instructed by his brother who, he alleged, had allowed the brother to dispose of land that should have formed part of the residuary estate.

Three years after the expiry of the limitation period, the claimant sought to amend the proceedings to allow him to continue the action both in his personal capacity and as a derivative action on behalf of the estate. This was in recognition of the fact that the claimant would find it difficult to establish that the defendant owed him a duty of care in his personal capacity. The High Court rejected that application, holding that there were no special circumstances entitling him to bring a derivative action. By a majority, the Court of Appeal disagreed on that point. Nevertheless, it held that the amendment was in any event time barred. It further held that, were the application to be granted, the administrator would have to be joined as a party; that, by reason of s 35(6)(b) of the Limitation Act 1980, joinder could not be permitted because it could not be said that it was necessary to enable the existing action to be pursued; and that an amendment to plead the derivative claim without joining the administrator could not be permitted because it would not enable the claimant to proceed to judgment. The claimant appealed. The issues were (1) whether the amendment could be made notwithstanding expiry of the limitation period in respect of the claimant's personal claim; and (2) if so, whether the claim was bound to fail because there were no special circumstances justifying a derivative action.

Held:

(i)   The Court of Appeal was right to conclude that the amendment to pursue a derivative claim was not permitted by the CPR after the expiry of the limitation period. The relevant provisions of the 1980 Act and the CPR meant that a 'new claim' was a claim involving either the addition or substitution of either a new party or a new cause of action. Any new claim made in the course of an action was deemed to have been commenced on the same date as the original action. No new claim could be made after the expiry of the limitation period, except as provided by rules of court.

(ii)   A new claim was permissible only if the new cause of action arose out of the same or substantially the same facts as the original claim, or if the addition or substitution of the new party was necessary for the determination of the original action. CPR 19.5(2) and (3) meant that a new party could be added only if the limitation period was current when the proceedings were started, and the addition was necessary in the sense that, without it, the claim could not properly be carried on by the original party. Under CPR 17.4(4) the court could allow an amendment to alter the capacity in which a party claimed, as long as the new capacity was one which that party either had when the proceedings began or had since acquired.

(iii) The original claim was the claimant's personal claim and the relevant limitation period was current when it was begun. The administrator could not apply to be joined as a claimant, because his joinder was not necessary for the determination of that original action.

(iv)   The amendment sought involved altering the capacity in which the claimant claimed, and the representative claim involved a new cause of action arising out of substantially the same facts as the original claim. The issue was therefore whether, under CPR 17.4(4), the claimant needed to join the administrator as a defendant. If he did, then he had to show that he could not properly carry on his claim without the addition of the administrator.

(v)   The claimant could clearly not show that. Therefore, the only way in which the action could proceed was if he could show that joinder of the administrator was either not necessary at all, or that it could be done after he had changed the capacity in which he sued, by which time joinder could be said to be necessary for the continuation of the derivative action.

(vi)   Again, the claimant could show neither of those things. The administrator had to be made a party at the outset of a beneficiary's representative action. It would be an abuse of process for amendments to be made in separate stages so as to procure the result that the addition of the administrator would be necessary for the determination of the original action and thus circumvent the limitation defence. Moreover, it would be contrary to principle for the court to grant permission to amend merely to reflect a change of capacity that would not enable the claimant to proceed to judgment.

(vii)   The judge had a wide latitude in evaluating what amounted to special circumstances such as to justify the derivative claim. In reaching his decision that there were no such circumstances, he had taken all the relevant circumstances into account and had conducted the enquiry in a way with which the Court of Appeal should not have interfered.

Appeal dismissed.

Roberts v Winbow

Limitation Act 1980, s 11, s 14, s 33

Court of Appeal   **[1999] PIQR P77; [1999] Lloyd's Rep Med 31;**
(1999) 49 BMLR 134

In 1987 the claimant, aged 19, took an overdose of aspirin. She received treatment at Basildon Hospital. In March 1987 she was diagnosed with depression. Treatment was initially successful but in December 1987 she suffered a severe relapse. Her GP referred her to the defendant, a consultant psychiatrist. The claimant was admitted on 5 January 1988, treated with various drugs and then discharged on 28 January 1988. She developed drug-induced skin problems a few days later consisting of an extremely itchy red rash over her body, but the prescriptions continued. Her general condition worsened and she developed Stevens Johnson syndrome and became dangerously ill. She was admitted to hospital on 20 May 1988.

On April 17 1989 she consulted solicitors telling them that she thought there had been a failure to identify an adverse drug reaction. Legal aid was obtained on 5 June 1989. Records were obtained by November 1990. In January 1991 a pharmacologist was instructed and his report was received on 20 June 1992. It suggested that not only the claimant's skin complaint but also a permanent and much more serious injury, an oesophageal stricture, were attributable to her drug treatment. In September 1992 a psychiatrist was instructed and a favourable report obtained in April 1993. Counsel was instructed in September 1994 and delivered a favourable advice the following month. Proceedings were issued on 5 January 1995. The defendant pleaded limitation.

The judge found the claimant's date of knowledge to have been 25 June 1992 when she first knew about the oesophageal stricture. The judge's reasoning was that the skin complaint, which would attract damages of around £2,000, was not significant as defined in the Act. He therefore did not need to consider s 33, although he indicated that his marginal inclination was to exercise the discretion in the claimant's favour. The defendant appealed.

Held:

(i)   The judge had erred in his finding of knowledge. The claimant had the broad knowledge required by the statute when she first visited solicitors in April 1989. The skin complaint was a significant injury and the Stevens Johnson syndrome serious enough to justify proceedings against a defendant who did not dispute liability and could pay damages.

(ii)   The prejudice to the claimant outweighed that to the defendant. The claimant had a reasonable prospect of establishing a high value claim against the defendant, but a claim against her own solicitors was not bound to succeed. The defendant had contemporaneous notes and pleaded to the effect that he had a clear recollection of the facts. The main issues in the case would turn on medical opinion rather than factual disputes.

(iii)   The defendant would suffer little prejudice beyond the loss of the limitation defence. It was therefore equitable to exercise the s 33 discretion in the claimant's favour.

Appeal allowed but s 33 discretion exercised in the claimant's favour.

Robinson v St Helens Metropolitan Borough Council

Limitation Act 1980, s 2, s 11, s 14, s 33

Court of Appeal [2002] EWCA Civ 1099;
[2002] EWCA Civ 1099; [2002] All ER (D) 388

The claimant attended primary school from 1972-1978 where he made no progress in reading and writing despite undergoing speech therapy. He made painfully poor literacy progress at high school from 1978-1983. In November 1992 a psychologist diagnosed him as suffering from severe dyslexia. On 1 November 2000 he issued proceedings against the defendant local education problems for failing to ameliorate his condition. The claim form, although not the particulars of claim, stated that the claim was for personal injury. The claimant claimed special damages but not for pain, suffering and loss of amenity. The defendant pleaded limitation. The judge found that the claim was not one for personal injury and therefore the strict six-year time limit applied to bar the claim, and further that the overriding time limit of 15 years from the date of alleged negligence had expired. In the alternative, if the claim was a claim for personal injuries, the claimant had knowledge by November 1992 and it would not be equitable to extend the limitation period. The claimant appealed.

Held:

(i)   Damage resulting from a failure to ameliorate congenital dyslexia was a personal injury (*Phelps v Hillingdon London Borough Council* [2001] 2 AC 619 applied). The judge was wrong to hold that psychological damage in these circumstances did not amount to a personal injury until it deteriorated into a recognised psychiatric injury.

(ii)   With considerable hesitation, and despite the lack of medical evidence, the court concluded the claimant had established that his claim was for personal injuries as defined in s 38 of the Act rather than mere economic loss.

(iii)   (obiter) A claimant's legal advisers should make efforts to identify the harm their client had suffered before embarking on a preliminary trial of this nature.

(iv)   The judge's finding on date of knowledge was correct. Upon receipt of the psychologists report the claimant knew that he was dyslexic and that he had been treated badly at school. This was sufficient to constitute knowledge under the Act.

(vi)   The claimant's challenge to the judge's exercise of his s 33 discretion was predicated upon the judge having found too early a date of knowledge. It therefore failed. Further, the claimant's case was not a particularly strong one and it would be an equitable drain on the defendant's resources to defend it.

Appeal dismissed (reasoning affirmed by the House of Lords in *Adams v Bracknell Forest Borough Council* (p292)).

Rodriguez v Parker

Amendment of Writ RSC Ord 20, r 5

Nield J [1966] 2 All ER 349; [1966] 3 WLR 546; [1967] 1 QB 116

On 30 October 1961 the claimant (Frank Rodriguez), a pedestrian, was knocked down and injured by a van owned by Robert Job Parker and driven by his son Robert Stuart Parker. In April 1962 the claimant's solicitors sent a letter before action to R S Parker. This was referred to his father's insurers who headed their correspondence R J Parker.

On 11 June 1964 the claimant's writ was issued against R J Parker (male); the endorsement complained of negligent driving on 30 October 1961 at the locus in quo. On 4 January 1965 the writ was served on R J Parker. On 14 June 1965 the statement of claim, which also alleged negligent driving, was served. The defence pleaded that 'the defendant was not driving any motor vehicle at the time or place alleged'.

Realising their mistake, the claimant's solicitors sought to amend the writ so as to substitute R S Parker (male) as defendant and to extend the validity of the writ. The master granted the requested order. The defendant appealed.

Held:

(i)   RSC Ord 20, r 5 falls within s 99(1)(a) of the Supreme Court of Judicature (Consolidation) Act 1925 as being a rule for regulating and prescribing the procedure and practice to be followed in the High Court in a matter in which the High Court has jurisdiction. It was intra vires.

(ii)   It was admitted that the claimant's solicitors' mistake was genuine. It was clear throughout to all concerned on the defendant's side that the intention was to sue the driver of the van at the time, so the mistake was not misleading and did not cause any reasonable doubt. It was just to allow the amendment, since the claim had been notified to the correct defendant within six months of the accident and he had not been prejudiced by what occurred subsequently.

(iii)   The amendment being allowed, it followed that discretion should also be exercised to extend the validity of the writ.

The defendant's appeal was dismissed.

Rogers v East Kent Hospitals NHS Trust

Limitation Act 1980, s 14, s 33

QBD (Griffith Williams J)   **[2009] EWHC 54 (QB);**
                                                         [2009] LS Law Medical 153

Between December 1995 and January 1998 the claimant received treatment at the defendant's hospital to correct a Hallux Valgus deformity (bunion) in her left foot. On 14 April 1997, she underwent amputation of the left second toe and hemi-phalangectomy of the third toe. The operation was unsuccessful and she developed progressive valgus drift of the great toe with a recurrent bunion. Consequently, she suffered severe pain in the toe and significant transfer metatarsalgia under the second and third metatarsal heads. On 13 October 2003, she was referred to an orthopaedic surgeon who discussed with her the alternatives to the 1997 surgery.

Having instructed solicitors and obtained an expert opinion, the claimant discovered that the surgeon had failed to implement the fitting of a toe spacer and surgical shoes, and that the trust had delayed when performing the necessary corrective osteotomy. The claimant issued her claim form on 31 May 2006. The judge determined that the claimant should have sought further advice in 1997 or 1998 about the failed amputation. He therefore held that the claimant was fixed with constructive knowledge in 1997/98 and that her claim was statute barred. He refused to exercise his discretion under s 33 on the basis that the claimant and her solicitors had not acted with due expedition and that there was significant prejudice to the defendant.

The claimant appealed, submitting that the judge (1) failed to make findings as to the date of the claimant's knowledge within the meaning of the Act; (2) incorrectly attributed the claimant with knowledge on the grounds that she did not visit her GP or seek expert medical opinion sufficiently promptly; and (3) refused to exercise his discretion under s 33 on the incorrect assumption that it would have caused significant prejudice to the trust.

Held:

(i)   The judge was not obliged to make a specific finding as to the claimant's date of knowledge. In some cases, such a specific finding was necessary, but there were others, particularly where the issue was one of constructive knowledge, when the evidence would make it impossible to be so exact.

(ii)   As to the issue of knowledge, the judge's conclusions were not supported by the evidence. He failed to address the issue that, after the amputation, the claimant had been reassured that the pain would go away. Moreover, she was given no explanation as to why her bunion was returning or why her pain was ongoing. The judge accepted that the claimant made regular visits to her GP and orthopaedic consultant after the amputation, so it had to follow that, in those meetings, nothing had been said or put to her regarding alternatives to amputation surgery. The judge did not have sufficient regard to the claimant's evidence that she went along with what the doctors told her, that she assumed it would take time for her condition to resolve itself, and that she had no thought of litigation in 1997 and 1998. On all of the evidence, the claimant's first date of knowledge had to be in October 2003, during the consultation with the orthopaedic consultant. The claim was therefore in time.

(iii)   Even if the judge correctly fixed the claimant with knowledge in 1997 or 1998, he should have exercised his discretion under s 33. The evidence that the defendant would suffer significant prejudice was not persuasive. The relevant treating doctors have been traced, a full set of notes were available, and the claimant's expert had experienced no difficulty in forming an opinion based upon those notes. In those circumstances, the court should ensure fairness by allowing the claimant's claim to proceed (*Horton v Sadler* (p482) applied).

(iv)   The technical point, taken by the defendant for the first time on appeal, that the proceedings were out of time in any event because the particulars of claim were served one working day late, was of no merit.

Appeal allowed.

Rogers v Finemodern Ltd and Walker

Limitation Act 1980, s 2, s 28, s 33

Morrison J   **LTL 8/11/99**

The claimant and the second defendant worked for the first defendant as painters and decorators. The claimant alleged that the second defendant seriously assaulted him whilst at work in March 1986 causing, amongst other things, a head injury. Proceedings were issued on 27 February 1998 alleging assault against the second defendant and vicariously against the first defendant, and also negligence against the first defendant for employing the second defendant knowing he was ill-tempered and had a propensity to use violence. The defendants raised limitation, which was heard as a preliminary issue.

Held:

(i)   The claimant had not demonstrated on the balance of probabilities that he was a patient incapable of managing his own affairs. He had returned to work, spoken to the police, dealt with the Criminal Injuries Compensation Board and the DHSS and attended a conference with counsel. s 28 therefore did not apply to prevent time from running.

(ii)   Section 2 imposed a strict six-year time limit for actions founded in torts such as assault, and there was no discretion under s 33 to extend this.

(iii)   In any event, it would not be equitable to allow the claim to proceed considering the length of delay, the lack of explanation for it and associated evidential difficulties.

Claim struck out.

NB: The flexible limitation regime under s 11/s 14/s 33 would now apply to the assault: *A v Hoare* (p287).

Rose v Express Welding Ltd

Limitation Act 1980, s 33   **Companies Act 1948, s 231**

Court of Appeal   **Lexis, 21 January 1986**

The claimant (Mr Rose) was injured in an accident in the course of his employment by the defendants in 1979. The three-year limitation period began to run on 19 December 1979. He consulted solicitors who negotiated with the defendants' insurers. His solicitor knew that the defendant company was in liquidation and made an enquiry to the companies registry to ascertain the true position. He issued a writ on 29 November 1982. On the same day the companies registry informed him that there had been a winding-up order, which meant that s 231 of the Companies Act 1948 required the court's leave to be obtained before any action could be commenced.

The claimant's solicitor erroneously thought that the defendants could waive any requirement for getting the court's leave. He served the writ in December 1982. The defendants' solicitors enquired in January 1983 whether leave had been obtained. The claimant's solicitor replied in the negative and asked for their consent to proceed with the action, which was not forthcoming. He then applied to the companies court for leave to proceed with it. The companies registrar held that leave to proceed could not be given in respect of an action which had been commenced without leave after the winding up, but allowed the summons to be amended and granted leave to commence an action against the defendants.

Pursuant to this, a fresh writ was issued on 16 March 1983. The claimant's solicitor applied for leave under s 33 of the Limitation Act 1980. Glidewell J granted this, finding that the delay was minimal, and it was accepted that the extra weeks made no difference. The defendants appealed.

Held:

(i)   Counsel having accepted that the effect of s 231 of the Companies Act 1948 was that no valid action could be commenced without the court's leave, the position was different from that in *Walkley v Precision Forgings Ltd* in which a valid action had been commenced within the three-year period. The judge was right to reject the submission that there was an action commenced.

(ii)   It could not be said that the prejudice had been caused, not by the expiry of the three-year time limit, but purely by the claimant's solicitor's failure to obtain the leave of the Companies Court. If so, s 33 would be of little value, because it would frequently be argued that the real reason for not starting the action in time was the failure of a solicitor to appreciate the current time limit or to discover the correct defendant or a host of other reasons. Undoubtedly the claimant had suffered prejudice by the operation of s 11.

(iii)   The judge could not be criticised for saying that the claimant did not have a cast iron case against his solicitor. It was by no means certain that the solicitor would be held to be negligent for thinking that despite s 231 the defendants could consent to the case proceeding or that he could get leave to proceed with it. The judge was entitled to find (as he did) that it was merely a better than even chance. Therefore the sole attack made upon his discretion failed.

The defendants' appeal was dismissed.

Walkley v Precision Forgings Ltd (p705) distinguished.

NB: The rule in *Walkley* was overruled in *Horton v Sadler* (p482).

Rothery v Walker and Burman

Limitation Act 1980, s 33

Court of Appeal   **12 March 1993**

On 29 January 1988 the claimant (Kenneth Rothery) was a passenger in a motor car being driven along the A104 in Humberside when a car driven by John Hoyle veered across the road and collided with it. The claimant suffered fractures of the bones of both hands and of his right foot.

He consulted a company called General Legal Protection who promptly notified his claim. In January 1990 Hoyle's insurers made an interim payment of £1,000. In May 1991 the claimant, who was wondering what was happening to his claim, instructed solicitors. In July 1991 Mr Hoyle died.

On 13 March 1992 the claimant commenced proceedings against Hoyle's personal representatives. The defence served in June 1992 pleaded limitation and alleged for the first time that Mr Hoyle had had a blackout at the time of or immediately before the collision.

The claimant's application for an order under s 33 of the Limitation Act 1980 that the provisions of s 11 be disapplied was granted by the deputy district judge. Mr Recorder Dobkin, sitting as a deputy County Court judge, dismissed the defendants' appeal. They were granted leave to appeal.

Held:

(i)   There was no great force in the submission that Mr. Hoyle's death six months after the expiry of the primary limitation period prejudiced the defendants because they were no longer able to investigate the merits of the defence. Their insurers had every opportunity of doing so at the outset. Either they failed to do so, or they thought that there was so little substance in the defence that it was not worth taking. The interim payment would have been surprising otherwise: s 33(3)(b).

(ii)   A claim against the claimant's former legal advisers was not cast iron. These advisers were not solicitors, although they appeared to have inhouse solicitors acting for them. The terms of the claimant's contract with them were not known. There would be some prejudice to the claimant in the further delay of the case: s 33(3).

(iii)   Balancing the prejudice to the claimant and the prejudice to the defendants, it was a borderline case. The court ought not to interfere with the exercise of the judge's discretion, and there was no adequate reason for doing so. The defendants' appeal should be dismissed: s 33(1).

Per Stuart-Smith LJ: 'Here the claim was notified very shortly after the accident. The defendants had every opportunity of investigating it. Mr Phillips says they did not do so and very frequently matters are not investigated until the writ is served and the matter is then put into the hands of the solicitors. It may be that cases are not investigated as fully as possible until that stage, but in my judgment it really hardly lies in the mouth of defendants, who do receive early notification of a claim and have no reasons to suppose thereafter that the claim is being dropped, that they failed to investigate the issue of liability, which is really staring them in the face on the insurance claim form itself.'

Rowbottom v Royal Masonic Hospital

Limitation Act 1980, s 11, s 14

Court of Appeal   **[2002] EWCA Civ 87; [2003] PIQR P1;**
                                             [2002] Lloyd's Rep Med 173

On 9 February 1991 the claimant underwent a hip replacement at the defendant's hospital. Shortly afterwards the wound became infected and his leg was amputated. In February 1993 he obtained an orthopaedic surgeon's opinion. On 12 May 1993 he received counsel's opinion. On

22 July 1993 he received an addendum report from the surgeon. He issued proceedings in 1992 against both the defendant and operating consultant. However, proceedings were discontinued against the defendant in November 1995 and against the consultant in February 1997. In the interim fresh proceedings were issued against the defendant alone on 12 July 1996. The hospital denied liability and pleaded limitation which was heard as a preliminary issue. The master held that the claimant had the requisite knowledge on 18 May 1993 shortly after receiving counsel's opinion. The claim was therefore statute barred and the former rule in *Walkley* (subsequently abolished by *Horton v Sadler* (p482)) precluded any s 33 discretion. The claimant appealed.

Held (Peter Gibson LJ dissenting):

(i)   The claimant did not have knowledge until he received the surgeon's second report on 22 July 1993. The relevant omission was the failure to administer antibiotics. The first report neither asserted nor assumed such a failure – it was equivocal. Until he received the second report the claimant was under the mistaken impression that antibiotics had been administered. He did not have the requisite knowledge until then.

(ii)   Although this was a borderline case, the claim was therefore brought in time.

(iii)   (per Peter Gibson LJ) The first report provided the claimant with all the requisite information to appreciate that there was a real possibility that his injury was attributable to a failure by the defendant to administer antibiotics. The claimant's date of knowledge was therefore in February 1993 and the claim was statute barred.

Appeal allowed.

Rowe v Kingston upon Hull City Council and Essex County Council

Limitation Act 1980, s 14, s 33

Court of Appeal   **[2003] EWCA Civ 1281; [2003] ELR 771;**
LTL 25/7/2003

The claimant attended the first defendant's school from 1979–1989 and the second defendant's school from 1989–1991. He turned 18 on 2 October 1992. Prompted by the first instance decision in *Phelps v Hillingdon London Borough Council* [1997] 96 LGR 1, he issued proceedings against the defendants for their failures in this respect on September 1998. The defendant pleaded limitation which was heard as a preliminary issue.

The judge held that the claimant knew before he was 18 that he suffered from dyslexia and that the defendants had failed to ameliorate it. However, the claimant could not have known that this was a significant injury until the decision of *Phelps v Hillingdon London Borough Council* [2000] 3 WLR 776. In the alternative, he exercised his discretion under s 33 to allow the claim to proceed. The defendant appealed.

Held:

(i)   The claimant knew by his 18th birthday that he was dyslexic and that he could have been helped by the defendants but was not. This was an injury irrespective of whether or not the claimant knew it could be so labelled. Time therefore ran from 2 October 1992 and proceedings had been issued outside the limitation period.

(ii)   There was no breach of Article 6 of the European Convention of Human Rights in this approach to s 14. The right of access to the courts was not absolute. The Act pursued a legitimate aim and the mere fact that the claimant did not realise he had a claim in law until *Phelps* clarified the position did not mean that the Act could be differently interpreted. The claimant could have brought the action regardless of the *Phelps* decision and himself established the precedent. To delay the attribution of knowledge to the point when the law first recognised the merits of a particular type of claim would open up defendants to a host of stale claims.

(iii) The judge had failed to adopt the correct approach to s 33 and had misdirected himself. The defendants faced great difficulties tracing teachers who could remember the claimant and there was little chance of a fair trial. They had tried but failed to find a witness able to give direct evidence of his performance. The fact that the depreciation in available evidence occurred before the expiry of the limitation period did not render it irrelevant (*Donovan v Gwentoys* (p412) applied).

(iv) Although the fact that the duty of care in this type of case had not been established in law at the pertinent time was a relevant factor, the claimant had not established that it would be equitable to disapply the time limit.

Appeal allowed.

Rule v Atlas Stone Co

Limitation Act 1980, s 11, s 14, s 33

Simon Brown J   **[1987] CLY 2335**

Mrs June Rule worked with asbestos for the defendants in 1954. She contracted mesothelioma. She and the claimant (her husband) were told that she had a cancer, probably caused by exposure to asbestos. She died at the age of 44 in April 1979.

The claimant took no steps to claim damages because he was upset and depressed. He had to look after four children and work as a long distance lorry driver. In 1982 he consulted a solicitor, and a letter before action was sent in August 1982. A legal aid certificate was granted in January 1983 but later discharged as the claimant failed to maintain his contributions to the legal aid fund. Legal aid was again granted in August 1983.

The writ was issued on 4 October 1983. The defendant denied liability and pleaded limitation. A preliminary trial was ordered.

Held:

(i) The claimant had all the relevant knowledge by the date of death, but not before May 1978 when his wife first became ill: s 14(1).

(ii) The claimant's reasons for the 18-month delay to issue of writ were understandable: s 33(3)(a).

(iii) The delay was insignificant when considering the cogency of the evidence likely to be adduced by both parties upon liability: s 33(3)(b).

(iv) The claimant did not act promptly, but this was not unreasonable: s 33(3)(e).

(v) A letter before action had been sent to the defendants 14 months before the issue of the writ: s 33(3).

(vi) The defendants had not been prejudiced by the delay. It was therefore equitable to allow the action to proceed: s 33(1).

Ryan v Carr and Marples Ridgeway & Partners Ltd

Limitation Act 1939, s 2   **Limitation Act 1963, s 1**

Eveleigh J   **(1971) 115 SJ 206**

On 20 April 1964 the claimant (Mr Ryan) was injured when travelling as a passenger in a car that was involved in a collision. Believing that the car had collided with the kerb, he sued the driver who denied liability. It was only when further and better particulars of the defence were served in June 1968 that the claimant realised that the car had collided with an obstruction left by the defendant contractors.

He was granted leave to bring an action out of time against them. They contended that the action was statute barred by s 2(1) of the Limitation Act 1939. He relied on s 1 of the Limitation Act 1963, arguing that the cause of the action was a material fact which had not been known to him within 12 months before the action was brought.

Held:

(i)   The manner in which the collision had come about was a material fact within s 1 of the Limitation Act 1963.

(ii)   The burden of proof lay on the claimant to show that he had satisfied the requirements of s 7(5) of that Act. When a defendant denied liability, a claimant was not, without more, obliged to look elsewhere to find another person responsible. In the circumstances, there had been nothing to cause him to enquire further into the cause of the collision before particulars were given in June 1968.

(iii)   Accordingly, the action was not statute barred.

NB: It would be open to a court to reach a similar decision today on the basis that the claimant did not have actual knowledge of all the relevant facts in s 14(I) of the Limitation Act 1980 until service of the particulars and that he should not be fixed with earlier constructive knowledge under s 14(3).

S v Camden LBC

Limitation Act 1980, s 33

QBD (Swift J)   **[2009] EWHC 1786 (QB); [2010] 1 FLR 100;**
[2009] 3 FCR 157; [2009] Fam Law 1040

The claimant, who was born on 25 November 1975, claimed damages for personal injury against the defendant local authority for its failure to take her into care earlier than it did, and for negligently failing to protect her from physical, emotional and sexual abuse by her mother.

The family had been well known to the local authority's social services department since before the claimant's birth. Other members of the family informed the designated social worker that the mother was violent to the claimant when she was a baby. The claimant was put on the child protection register. The defendant eventually closed the case and contact ceased when the claimant was aged 11. In the spring of 1989, when the claimant was aged 13, her aunt contacted the National Society for the Prevention of Cruelty to Children to report that the mother was still ill-treating the claimant, a fact which the mother admitted. The defendant was informed and, at the mother's request, the claimant was taken into care in November 1989. She stayed in care until she turned 18 in November 1993.

In 2004, the claimant made a complaint to the police about her mother's ill-treatment of her. A prosecution followed as a result of which, on 13 June 2005, the mother pleaded guilty to an offence of child neglect relating to her treatment of the claimant between November 1975 and November 1990. On 15 July 2005, she was sentenced to a two-year Community Rehabilitation Order. The claimant commenced proceedings on 23 May 2008, 11½ years after expiration of the limitation period on her 21st birthday.

The defendant argued, among other things, that any breach of its duty of care was not the factual cause of the claimant's damage, since such damage could only have been avoided if she had been permanently removed from the mother's care but, if there had been no breach, other measures would have been taken which would not have involved permanent removal. The defendant also argued limitation.

Held:

(i) The length of the delay in this case was very substantial indeed: 32 years from the beginning (and 19 years from the end) of the abuse to the commencement of proceedings. However, it needed to be considered in context. At the time of the abuse, the claimant was a child. She did not attain the age of 18 until November 1993. By that time, she had already begun to seek information about her early life. She had asked to see the defendant's records on her in October 1992 and she repeated that request from time to time thereafter. The records were not provided. In November 1996, just before her 21st birthday, she made a formal written request through a Legal Advice Centre. It does not appear that the defendant responded to that request. The claimant took no further active steps to pursue the matter until 2004. However, this was due to very difficult personal circumstances.

(ii) Once the claimant had reported the matter to the police, there was further delay while they attempted to obtain records from the defendant. The claimant tried to assist that process by making a written complaint to the defendant in October 2004, but the defendant decided to suspend investigation of that complaint until the police investigations had been concluded. Even when the criminal proceedings were concluded in July 2005, the records were not provided. By that time the claimant had consulted solicitors. They sent a letter of claim in August 2005. They pressed the defendant for full disclosure of the documentation and, when that was not forthcoming, made an application to the court. Meanwhile, they issued a claim form in 2007 which was allowed to lapse. It was not until April 2008 that all the relevant documents were received. The current proceedings were issued the following month.

(iii) Although the claimant had commenced proceedings 11½ years out of time, it would be equitable under s 33 to allow the action to proceed, as the ability of the defendant to defend the issues of liability and factual causation had not materially been affected. The majority of contemporaneous documents remained available. The most important missing file had been lost before 1989, well before the claimant could have brought proceedings. This loss was the defendant's own failure. It was highly unlikely that, if the other missing documentation were available, it would significantly change the picture which emerged from the existing documents. The defendant's conduct in failing to provide records also made a significant contribution to the delays that occurred.

(iv) The claimant succeeded on the substantive issues.

Judgment for claimant.

S v W (child abuse: damages)

Limitation Act 1980, s 2, s 11, s 14, s 33

Court of Appeal   **[1995] 1 FLR 862; [1995] 3 FCR 649;**
(1994) Times, 26 December

The claimant was born on 5 November 1965. She lived with her parents until the age of nineteen. Until about 1983 her father subjected her to repeated sexual and physical abuse. Her mother, the defendant, knew broadly of the abuse from an early stage. In 1985 the father admitted five counts of incest involving the claimant and was jailed.

On 10 March 1992, the claimant issued proceedings for personal injuries (psychological injuries) against both her parents. The claim against the defendant was based upon breach of her duty as a parent to protect the claimant. Both claims were struck out by the district judge as being statute barred, a flat six-year period from the claimant's majority applying by s 2 and s 28 of the 1980 Act. It was accepted that this was correct in respect of the claim against the father, as this was purely based on trespass to the person. However, the claimant appealed the striking out of the mother's claim. The circuit judge allowed the appeal. The defendant then appealed.

Held:

(i)   It was vital to appreciate that the claim against the defendant was, unlike that against the father, not based upon, direct physical contact. The claim was rather based upon an independent tort based upon breach of common law duty of care.

(ii)   The only way that s 11 would not apply was if the words 'other than breach of duty to safeguard the claimant from the deliberate infliction of injury' were read into the term 'breach of duty' in s 11(1). There was no basis for reading in so major an addition. As s 11 applied, s 2 (and thus *Stubbings v Webb* (p677)) did not.

Appeal dismissed.

NB: The flexible limitation regime under s 11/s 14/s 33 would now apply to the primary assault: *A v Hoare* (p287).

Saab v Saudi American Bank

Companies Act 1985, s 694A

Court of Appeal   **[1999] 1 WLR 1861; [1999] 4 All ER 321;**
                                                                      [1999] 2 All ER (Comm) 353

The claimant, bringing a claim in contract, purported to serve proceedings under the 1985 Act by delivering it to the defendant's London branch. There was a preliminary hearing. The judge held that service was properly effected. There was also a dispute as to the appropriate forum which again was resolved in the claimant's favour. The defendant appealed.

Held (on the service point):

'In respect of the carrying on a business' in the context of s 694A did not mean 'arising out of the operations of a branch' as in Art 5(5) of the Brussels Convention 1968. It was enough that the subject matter of the action was partly conducted in that branch. In the instant case there was a good arguable case that this requirement was met.

Appeal dismissed.

Sage v Ministry of Defence

Limitation Act 1980, s 14A

Court of Appeal   **[2001] EWCA Civ 190; LTL 9/2/2001**

The claimant served as soldier from 1972 until discharge in 1989. In 1980, 1987 and 1988 the defendant carried out tests, the result of which tallied with the claimant's own assessment of his hearing loss. In May 1996 he applied for a job at Toyota but was turned down because a medical test revealed hearing deficiencies. In October 1997 he was examined and told that his hearing loss was attributable to exposure to firearms.

He issued proceedings on 22 April 1999 claiming damages for hearing loss due to excessive exposure to firearms and the defendant's failure to inform him of his hearing loss prior to discharge to enable him to make a fully informed choice about his future. The personal injuries claim was struck out in March 2000 leaving only the claim for failure to inform. The defendant applied for the remainder of the claim to be struck out as statute barred. The recorder refused to do so and the defendant appealed.

Held:

(i)   The recorder had erred in her approach to limitation. She had adopted a two-stage test asking first, without consideration of evidence, whether s 14A applied at all and, second, whether the claimant could rely on it. This was a misdirection. Either the claimant could show that the claim was not statute barred or he could not.

(ii)   In the absence of agreed facts the question of knowledge could only be decided after a consideration of evidence.

(iii) In this case the claimant was aware of suffering hearing loss in 1987/88. The tests carried out at that time only measured its extent. It was not reasonably open to the recorder to find that the claimant was not aware of his hearing loss until 1996. The claim was statute barred.

Appeal allowed.

Saha v Imperial College of Science, Technology and Medicine

Limitation Act 1980, s 11(1)(a), s 28, s 33

Protection from Harassment Act 1997

QBD (Lang J)   **[2011] EWHC 3286 (QB)**

The claimant had been a PhD student at the defendant university from 1 October 2002 to 30 September 2005. She made a number of allegations against the man who had been her supervisor until 6 July 2004. She claimed that she had suffered a depressive illness and had been unable to complete her PhD as a result of his bullying and harassing her, and that the defendant was in breach of contract by failing to provide her with the facilities needed to complete her PhD.

The claimant made a complaint to the Office of the Independent Adjudicator on 8 May 2006, and asked for it to be stayed, in the hope that she could reach a settlement with the defendant. She did not pursue the complaint to a conclusion, mainly because of her illness, she said. She also said that the Office of the Independent Adjudicator told her they did not deal with personal injury claims and it was very unlikely they would hold a hearing as they usually dealt with complaints on the papers. They advised that she should also look at other avenues of complaint.

The claimant had sent a letter to the defendant, indicating that she was considering legal proceedings, on 18 November 2005. However, it was not until 28 May 2010 that she issued proceedings claiming damages for defamation, breach of contract, negligence, misrepresentation, harassment, breach of the Public Interest Disclosure Act 1998, breach of the Supply of Goods and Services Act 1982 and breach of the Human Rights Act 1998. She sent a letter before claim on 4 June 2010 and served proceedings on 28 September 2010. She attributed her delay in bringing proceedings to her psychiatric treatment and medication and her belief that she had a period of six years to bring her claim. The defendant successfully applied to strike out these claims, inter alia, on limitation grounds. The claimant appealed.

Held:

(i)   The Office of the Independent Adjudicator provided a valuable dispute resolution procedure for students, but was not a judicial body and had not ousted the jurisdiction of the courts. It had the power to make recommendations, but could not enforce orders against higher education institutions and did not adjudicate upon personal injury claims.

(ii)   The claimant had an arguable case that her relationship with the defendant was contractual. She was not obliged to bring her complaints by way of judicial review.

(iii) The master had been correct to strike out the personal injury claim and it would not be equitable to allow it to proceed under s 33. The claimant's psychiatric symptoms did constitute a disability under s 28. The matters complained of occurred between 2004 and 2006. The claimant had delayed considerably in issuing proceedings. She had been justified in delaying until the conclusion of the defendant's internal disciplinary and grievance procedures, and the severity of her illness provided a reasonable explanation for the delay after diagnosis. However, it would have been reasonable to expect her to issue proceedings some time not long after she returned to work in March 2008, which was within the limitation period. She had remained evidently capable of formulating formal complaints against the defendant throughout. Her failure to do so had not been adequately explained, and her apparent confusion about the limitation period was not a sufficient reason to extend time. Memories of the defendant's witnesses may have faded in the interim.

(iv) Under s 11(1)(a) of the 1980 Act the time limit for claims under the Protection from Harassment Act 1997 was six years. The claim for harassment was thus brought in time.

(v) The claims of harassment, breach of contract and breach of the 1982 Act would not be struck out because she had an arguable case and had brought her claims within time. However, her remaining claims would be struck out as they were either out of time or had no prospects of success.

Appeal allowed in part.

Sanotra v Sanotra & another

Limitation Act 1980, s 33   **RSC Ord 6, r 8**

Court of Appeal   **Lexis, 21 May 1987**

On 27 September 1981 Mr Bhamrah and Mr Sanotra, two bachelors in their twenties, were passengers in a car driven by the defendant. The car went off the road and burst into flames. Both young men were killed. The defendant, who was uninsured, survived and was convicted of causing death by dangerous driving.

In October 1981 Mr Bhamrah's administrators consulted solicitors. There were problems about the legal aid application and also about obtaining a grant of letters of administration. These were granted on 20 September 1984, a week before the third anniversary of the accident. The solicitors concentrated on obtaining counsel's opinion and pursuing contacts with the insurers nominated by the Motor Insurers' Bureau, including a meeting in December 1984. They finally issued a writ on 3 June 1985.

Mr Sanotra's personal representatives instructed the same solicitors in October 1981. Letters of administration were rapidly granted. On 31 July 1984 they notified the insurers of proceedings and sent them a copy of the draft writ. The writ was issued on 23 August 1984. On 11 July 1985 the solicitors wrote to the insurers about a discussion with their representative, to which the insurers replied on 18 July that the discussion could proceed. On 25 October 1985 the solicitors discovered to their amazement, and evidently equally to the surprise of the insurers, that by a pure oversight the writ had not been served. The insurers refused to accept service out of time.

In the *Bhamrah* case, Sir Neil Lawson upheld the master's decision to disapply s 11 of the Limitation Act 1980 by exercising his discretion under s 33. In the *Sanotra* case, he upheld the master's ex parte decision to extend the validity of the writ under RSC Ord 6, r 8(2). The defendant appealed against both decisions.

Held:

(i) In view of a move towards greater elasticity approved by the House of Lords in *Kleinwort Benson Ltd v Barbrak Ltd*, the court was not precluded from adopting a similarity of approach as between the exercise of its discretion under s 33 of the Limitation Act 1980 and under RSC Ord 6, r 8. This was particularly in point in the present cases when the relevant facts were common to both of them. Since the court had a discretion in both cases, albeit derived from separate sources, it would be strange if the discretion were to be exercised in different ways.

(ii)   So far as *Bhamrah* was concerned, the judge made it clear that he had in mind the relevant matters mentioned in s 33. Having regard to the problems in getting the grant of letters of administration, and the discussions that were nevertheless taking place after the expiry of the primary limitation period, it would have been astonishing if he had reached any other conclusion.

(iii)   So far as concerned *Sanotra*, the judge clearly considered that there was 'good reason' for exercising his discretion under RSC Ord 6, r 8. An advance copy of the writ had been sent to the insurers, they had made it clear that they were content that settlement discussions should continue, and with total indifference they failed to notice that the writ had not been served. There was no reason to conclude that the judge had exercised his discretion wrongly.

(iv)   The question whether the claimants had a remedy against their own solicitors was a relevant matter to bear in mind. But the fact that it was not mentioned by the judge in either case was not a reason for interfering with his discretion.

Kleinwort Benson Ltd v Barbrak Ltd [1987] 2 All ER 289 followed.

NB: Held (i) was qualified in *Waddon v Whitecroft-Scovill Ltd* [1988] 1 All ER 996.

Santos v Owner of Baltic Carrier and Owners of Flinterdam

Merchant Shipping Act 1995, s 190

QBD (Admiralty) (David Steel J)   **[2001] 1 Lloyd's Rep 689;**
[2001] CLC 99; LTL 21/2/2001

The claimant, a Filipino seaman, was injured in a collision between the two defendant vessels on 16 March 1998 in the Keil canal. The claimant was employed as a seaman on board the Baltic Carrier which was in collision with the Flinterdam. The relevant period of limitation was two years against the Flinterdam but three years against the Baltic Carrier. He commenced two actions, the first against both defendants, the second against the second defendant only. The claimant's solicitors had put the second defendant's ship on their internal ship-watch system, but chosen UK watch only. They missed an opportunity to arrest the ship on 19 August 1999. The limitation period against the second defendant expired on 16 March 2000 (s 190(3) of the Act), but the claimant's solicitors did not appreciate this. Under the misapprehension that they had a further year to issue proceedings, they decided to see whether the second defendant's ship returned to the jurisdiction within the 12-month period for service, and if it did not to issue another set of proceedings. This they did on 27 June 2000, serving the following day.

The second defendant applied to set aside an order that the claim form in the first action be renewed against them. Simultaneously the claimant applied for an extension of time for issuing proceedings in the second action pursuant to s 190 of the 1995 Act.

Held:

(i)   Section 190(6) of the Act required a consideration of whether objectively there was an opportunity to arrest the vessel. There had been in August 1999, and the steps actually taken were irrelevant. The precondition of a mandatory extension of time was therefore not satisfied.

(ii)   The court's discretion to extend time for issue under s 190(5) was to be treated in a similar way as an application to extend time for service under CPR 7.6. There was therefore an unfettered limitation subject to specific limitations where, as here, the application was made both after the expiration of the time limit and also after the expiration of timeous proceedings.

(iii) It was not incompetent of the claimant's solicitors not to have placed the second defendant's vessel on world-wide watch, and in any event it would have made no difference.

(iv) The claimant had taken all reasonable steps to serve the claim form during its validity. In the circumstances the application could be considered to have been made promptly.

(v) There was no material hardship to the second defendant and it was therefore appropriate to allow the claimant's application to extend time.

(vi) The claimant would only proceed in one of the actions and it was therefore unnecessary to consider the second defendant's application to set aside the earlier order.

Order accordingly.

Saxby v Morgan

Limitation Act 1980, s 14

Court of Appeal   **[1997] PIQR P531; [1997] 8 Med LR 293; (1997) BMLR 126**

The claimant, having already had two children, one of whom was autistic, decided in 1988 that she wanted no more and so began to take the contraceptive pill. In July 1991 she visited the defendant (a general practitioner) complaining of stomach pains and that her periods had ceased. She revisited the defendant in two occasions before 23 September 1991 when an ultrasound scan revealed her to be five months pregnant. The following day she was advised that her pregnancy was too developed for an abortion despite her wish to have one. She was in fact only 19-20 weeks pregnant at the time and could have aborted (this being legal up to 24 weeks into pregnancy). The child was born in February 1992.

She issued proceedings in August 1994 but missed the service deadline of December 1994. She applied to extend the period for service. The allegations of negligence were against 4 GPs and the West Sussex Family Health Services Authority for failing to diagnose her pregnancy and to provide treatment and advice regarding termination in August 1991. This was refused on the basis that the claim form was issued before limitation expired but to allow the extension would be to allow service after expiration and thus deprive the defendant of its limitation defence.

The claimant appealed to the High Court contending that she had knowledge for the purposes of the Act after the accrual of the cause of action, which by consent was agreed to have accrued after 24 September 1991. The claimant contended that she did not have the requisite knowledge until she learnt in October 1992 that she could have had a lawful termination up to 24 weeks. This was dismissed so she renewed her appeal.

Held:

(i) The claimant knew the injury was significant when she discovered the fact her pregnancy and knew that an abortion was necessary if she were not to give birth to an unwanted child.

(ii) The relevant act or omission was the defendant's advice that she could not have an abortion. The claimant knew of this as soon as it was given (*Spargo v North Essex District HA* (p667) applied).

(iii) The claimant knew that the continuation of the unwanted pregnancy was attributable to the advice when she accepted it.

(iv) The claimant therefore had knowledge of all the requisite elements by September 1991. The fact that she did not learn until a year later that the advice had been negligent was irrelevant.

Appeal dismissed.

Sayer v Kingston and Esher Health Authority

Limitation Act 1980, s 35   **RSC Ord 20, r 5**

Court of Appeal   **(1989) Independent, 27 March**

On 19 February 1980 the claimant (Pauline Sayer) gave birth to her second child by caesarean section in one of the defendants' hospitals. There were various complications, and two further operations were necessary.

In January 1983 she sued the health authority. Her writ and statement of claim were limited to complaints of what happened on 18–19 February, the period of the operation itself. In September 1988, on the eve of her trial, she applied to amend her statement of claim.

The amendment deleted the complaints about the caesarean section operation altogether. It substituted three new complaints:

(i)   That she was allowed to spend too long in the second stage of labour before the operation;

(ii) That her condition was not monitored closely enough after the operation; and

(iii) That a follow-up operation on 26 February should have been performed by a specialist urologist.

The defendants appealed against the order of Drake J granting leave to amend.

Held:

(i)   The amendments arose out of substantially the same facts, although not the same facts, as those already pleaded, so the judge had discretion to allow the amendment under s 35(5) of the Limitation Act 1980 and RSC Ord 20, r 5(5).

(ii) The judge acted within his discretion in allowing the amendment, since the defendants' main witnesses were still available and full and detailed medical records were in existence.

Sayers v Chelwood (Deceased) and another

Limitation Act 1980, s 33

Court of Appeal   **[2012] EWCA Civ 1715**

From 1981, the claimant had worked for the defendants, Lord and Lady Chelwood, as a gardener with responsibility for maintaining a large garden and forest. This entailed the use of noisy equipment. The first defendant died in 1989 but the claimant remained employed by the second defendant until May 2000, when he took up employment elsewhere. By that time, he was suffering from hearing loss and tinnitus. In 2002, the claimant was told by a nurse during an occupational health-check that he might be suffering from noise-induced industrial hearing loss. In April 2005 he consulted his general practitioner, who referred him to a specialist. The claimant was reviewed by the specialist in June 2006. On neither occasion was noise-induced hearing loss recorded. Around the summer of 2006 the claimant saw an advert encouraging claims for noise-induced hearing loss. As a consequence, he retained a firm of solicitors in October 2006 and was advised in December of that year that he was eligible to bring a claim. A letter of claim was not, however, sent until 1 July 2008, and proceedings were not issued until 29 September 2009. The defendants denied liability and pleaded limitation.

A deputy district judge found, as a preliminary issue, that the claimant's date of knowledge for the purposes of limitation was December 2006 and that his claim was therefore in time. The circuit judge allowed the defendants' appeal, concluding that the claim was out of time because the date of knowledge was 2002, when the claimant received advice from the nurse. He held that the burden on the claimant under s 33 was particularly heavy and that it would not be appropriate to exercise discretion to allow the claim to proceed because there had been unreasonable delay without explanation, the equipment used by the claimant at the relevant time was long gone, much of the complaint pre-dated the first defendant's death at a time when the second defendant had been less closely involved, and the second defendant, at the age of 88, did not have a fair opportunity to defend the claim.

The claimant appealed, arguing that the proposition in *KR v Bryn Alyn Community (Holdings) Ltd (In Liquidation)* (p505), that s 33 imposed a 'heavy burden' on a claimant, was no longer good law.

Held:

(i)   There was a wealth of conflicting authority on the question of what test should be applied under s 33. It should not be necessary for judges in the county court to engage in textual analysis of a series of appellate decisions in order to discern whether a claimant relying on s 33 had a 'burden' or a 'heavy burden' to discharge. All that could properly be said about the general approach to the section was that the burden was on the claimant, because it was he who was seeking to be exempted from the normal consequences of failing to issue proceedings in time. It was not helpful to discuss in the abstract whether that burden was a heavy one or a light one. In *Horton v Sadler* (p482) and *A v Hoare* (p287), the House of Lords stressed that the court's discretion under s 33 was broad and unfettered. Those comments made it difficult to maintain that the claimant's burden was necessarily a heavy one; every case was fact-specific (*B v Ministry of Defence* [2010] EWCA Civ 1317, (2011) 117 BMLR 101 (Supreme Court decision, p312) and *B v Nugent Care Society* (p315) followed, *KR v Bryn Alyn* disapproved).

(ii)   In the instant case, the judge had applied the wrong test; he ought simply to have said that the burden was on the claimant. The s 33 discretion therefore fell to be considered afresh.

(iii)   It would not be appropriate to exercise that discretion in the claimant's favour. The action had been commenced four years after the expiry of the limitation period with no explanation for the delay. Both the claimant and his legal advisers had progressed the claim in a leisurely manner.

(iv)   That delay made it substantially more difficult for the parties to adduce relevant evidence. The substantive issues were (a) the levels of noise emitted by the power tools, (b) how much work the claimant was required to do with the power tools, (c) whether the claimant was provided with hearing protection and, if so, whether he wore it, (d) what instructions the claimant was given by the defendant, and (e) the nature of the duty of care owed by a private or domestic as opposed to industrial employer, in relation to noise exposure and hearing protection. The delay in commencing proceedings had made it substantially more difficult for the parties to adduce relevant evidence in relation to the first four of those issues. An important witness for the claimant had died in June 2012 and would not be available for cross-examination. On the defendants' side, the only person with knowledge of relevant events was the second defendant. She was by then aged 90. With each year that passed, her ability to give relevant evidence would diminish. The specific equipment which the claimant used during his employment could no longer be identified. The noise levels generated by that equipment could not now be determined. Whilst there would have been difficulties even if the claimant had commenced his action within the limitation period, those difficulties were significantly greater and the evidence less cogent due to the four years' delay.

(v)   An important factor on the claimant's side is that he appeared to have a properly arguable claim against his employers worth around £25,000. Against that, an important factor on the defendants' side was that, because of the delay, relevant insurance documents had been lost. The defendants would have had employers' liability insurance in respect of the whole period of the claimant's employment. Now, however, the second defendant could not trace who were the insurers for the period 1 April 1981 to 1 January 1986. Thus she was exposed to personal liability in respect of 24.6% of the claim. The insurance position of the parties is a relevant factor and had to be taken into account: *Horton v Sadler*. The claimant sought to meet this point by undertaking not to enforce 24.6% of any judgment in its favour against the second defendant personally. That, however, was not a complete answer as the second defendant would remain liable for 24.6% of her own costs which were substantially higher than the damages claimed.

(vi)   Overall, the prejudice to the defendants far outweighed that to the claimants.

Appeal dismissed.

Per Jackson LJ: '20. I am bound to say that [the claimant's solicitors'] handling of this matter leaves much to be desired. Despite the fact that this was a stale claim with obvious limitation difficulties, they delayed for three years before commencing proceedings. When they did so, they named Lord Chelwood rather than his estate as first defendant. The particulars of claim, as drafted by [the solicitors], alleged numerous breaches of the Factories Act 1961, even though that Act could not possibly be applicable ...

53. There can be no doubt that if a claimant commences proceedings out of time and asks the court, in the exercise of its discretion under section 33 ... the burden is on the claimant to persuade the court by evidence and argument that such a direction is appropriate. Auld LJ was plainly correct in *KR* to say that such a claimant is seeking the indulgence of the court. Auld LJ was also correct to say that such indulgence is exceptional, in the sense that the claimant is seeking an exemption from the normal consequences of failing to commence proceedings within the limitation period. I read paragraph 74 (ii) of Auld LJ's judgment in *KR* in the same way that Leveson LJ did in *Kew v Bettamix* [(p518)].

54. Once it is established which party has the burden in relation to a particular issue, it is not helpful to discuss in the abstract whether that burden is a heavy one or a light one. [The defendant's counsel] got into difficulties in argument when we invited him to comment on hypothetical cases where it would obviously be appropriate to disapply the time bar. He submitted that in such cases the claimant's burden would still be heavy but easily discharged.

55. In *Horton v Sadler* and *A v Hoare* the House of Lords stressed that the court's discretion under section 33 of the Limitation Act is broad and unfettered. In my view these comments make it difficult to maintain that the claimant's burden under section 33 is necessarily a heavy one. How difficult or easy it is for the claimant to discharge the burden will depend upon the facts of the particular case. I therefore respectfully agree with Smith LJ's comments in paragraph 96 of *AB*. All one can say in relation to section 33 at the level of generality is that the burden is on the claimant.

56. Let me now draw the threads together. Upon reviewing the authorities cited by counsel, I prefer the view expressed by Smith LJ in paragraph 96 of *AB* rather than the earlier view expressed by Auld LJ in paragraph 74 (ii) of *KR*. All that one can properly say about the general approach to section 33 is that the burden is on the claimant. The claimant is seeking to be exempted from the normal consequences of failing to issue proceedings in time. It is for the claimant to establish by reference to the criteria set out in section 33 that it would be equitable to allow the action to proceed, despite the expiry of the prescribed limitation period.'

Scuriaga v Powell

Limitation Act 1939, s 2A

Watkins J **(1979) 123 SJ 406**

In April 1972 the claimant (Florence Scuriaga), a polio sufferer aged 22, contracted with the defendant doctor that he would terminate her pregnancy for a fee of £150. His operation failed to remove the foetus that she had been carrying for some 7 weeks. He assured her that all was well and that she could go home. She was unaware that he had found no evidence of foetal parts and thought that she had a potentially serious disorder. Several weeks later, she was examined by her general practitioner and a pregnancy test proved positive. In August 1972 the defendant told her that he had failed to terminate her pregnancy because she had a structural defect. In December 1972 she was delivered of a health baby boy by caesarean section.

In 1974 the claimant first learned that she might have a cause of action. Only when the first consultant's report was provided in October 1975, did she know that the failure to terminate her pregnancy was due to an act or omission of the defendant. Her writ was issued more than three years after the cause of action accrued. The defendant denied liability and pleaded limitation.

Held: until October 1975 the claimant believed that a defect in her had thwarted a properly conducted operation, which is what the defendant had told her. Her writ had been issued within three years thereafter (s 2A(6)), so her action had been brought in time: s 2A(4).

The judge found the defendant liable and awarded the claimant damages against him.

Sea Assets Ltd v PT Garuda Indonesia

CPR 6

QBD (Longmore J) **29 February 2000, unreported**

This was a commercial dispute. The claimant was a company incorporated in the British Virgin Islands. The defendant was a company incorporated in Indonesia, with numerous worldwide branches, including one in London. Proceedings were issued on 2 September 1999. The claimant originally sought to serve the claim form on the nominated representative for service under Part XXIII of the Companies Act 1985. This was challenged on the basis that the claim in question was not 'in respect to the carrying on of the business of' the defendant's registered branch, as per s 694A of the 1985 Act.

On 18 October the claimant obtained an order amending the defendant's address for service to that of its London branch. The claim form was duly delivered there. The defendant applied for service to be set aside.

Held:

(i) Section 694A is permissive rather than mandatory and exclusive. It does not render defective service elsewhere authorised. Service in accordance with the CPR would thus be good.

(ii) An overseas company that fully registers its branch in England does not become a company registered in England. It remains in essence an overseas company. This was the case here. There was thus no requirement to serve at its principal office or place of business within the jurisdiction which has a real connection with the claim (the London address would have met neither of these criteria).

(iii) Proceedings were therefore validly served.

Application refused.

Shade v The Compton Partnership

Limitation Act 1980, s 35   **CPR 17**

Court of Appeal   **[2000] Lloyd's Rep PN 81; LTL 22/7/99**

In April 1985 the claimant instructed solicitors for a conveyancing transaction. He became dissatisfied with their performance. In May 1991 he instructed the defendant firm of solicitors to act for him in respect of his complaint against his former solicitors. The defendant did not issue proceedings (denying having instructions to do so) and on 3 June 1993 the claimant issued proceedings against his first solicitors as a litigant in person. This claim was struck out as statute barred on 18 October 1993 and the claimant's appeal against that decision dismissed.

On 28 April 1997 the claimant issued proceedings for professional negligence against the defendant. He claimed that they had caused him severe psychiatric and physical damage. The defendant applied to have the claim struck out. This was unsuccessful, but the master did strike out the personal injuries element as being statute barred. The claimant appealed and the defendant cross-appealed. The judge struck out the entire claim. The claimant appealed again.

Held:

(i)   A pleading should not be struck out as hopeless if it could be saved by amendment.

(ii)   There was nothing in either CPR 17.4 or s 35 of the Act which prevented this claim to be saved by severing the personal injuries element (*Oates v Harte Read & Co* (p585) doubted, *Bennett v Greenland Houchen & Co* (p329) distinguished). The claimant would be entitled in any event to reissue the claim without the personal injuries element, as the six-year period had not expired.

(iii)   Commonsense had to be applied as to whether the personal injuries element of a claim was severable. This depended upon the facts of the individual case.

Appeal allowed.

Shapland v Palmer

Limitation Act 1980, s 11, s 33

Court of Appeal   **[1999] 1 WLR 2068; [1999] 3 All ER 50;**
                                                           [1999] PIQR P249

On 26 March 1993 the claimant suffered whiplash when the defendant drove into the rear of her car. The defendant was driving a company car, the insurance policy for which covered both the defendant and the company. Liability was never in doubt and an interim payment made early. Proceedings were issued against the company on the final day before limitation expired. However, the claim form was served out of time and the proceedings were struck out.

Proceedings were issued on 21 August 1998 in a second action against the driver himself. The defendant raised limitation. It was admitted that the limitation period had expired and a s 33 discretion was required. The judge held that whilst he would have been inclined to exercise any discretion in the claimant's favour, he was bound by the rule in *Walkley v Precision Forgings Ltd* (p705) (the claims being for all intents and purposes the same) and therefore had none. The claimant appealed.

Held:

(i)   There was an unwillingness to apply *Walkley* unless it was plainly indistinguishable (*Whitfield v North Durham HA* (p713) and *McEvoy v AA Welding* (p551) followed).

(ii)   *Walkley* applied only when to proceedings involving the same parties and the same cause of action as the original timeous proceedings. It did not apply here.

(iii) There was therefore a s 33 discretion to be exercised. Although there was a reluctance to allow the claimant to escape *Walkley*, and thus gain an advantage from her solicitors' failures, the court held (Waller LJ dissenting) that it was appropriate to exercise the discretion in her favour. Liability was admitted, the matter had been investigated and a fair trial on quantum could unarguably take place. Notwithstanding the claimant's cast-iron claim against her own solicitors, there was no prejudice to the defendant beyond the loss of the limitation defence itself so it was equitable to allow the case to proceed.

NB: The rule in *Walkley* was abolished in *Horton v Sadler* (p482).

Shepherd and others v Firth Brown Ltd

Limitation Act 1980, s 11

McCullough J   Lexis, 17 April 1985

The claimants (Mr Shepherd and 15 others) were employed by the defendants in their roll grinding shop at their Sheffield factory. They suffered vibration-induced white finger ('VWF') over a period of years as a result of vibration imparted from carborundum sticks which they held against rotating grinding wheels in the course of their work.

Their writs were issued on 5 October 1977 and 19 December 1977 respectively. None alleged any cause of action continuing beyond the date of the writs. Most of the claimants went on working for the defendants.

At a full hearing, the judge found that the defendants were in breach of duty after spring 1979 but not before. The defendants argued that the claimants could not recover damages for any injury caused after the date of issue of the writs and that their actions must therefore fail.

Held: the claimants did not have continuing causes of action. They had a series of causes of action accruing from day to day. It followed that no continuing causes of actions had been alleged in the writs. The writs made no allegation of any cause of action which accrued after the date of their issue. Since the defendants were not negligent before issue of the writs, judgment must be given in their favour.

Per McCullough J: 'The arguments on this part of the case have an air of unreality, since the convenience of being able to deal with all questions of damage in one action is undeniable. If Mr Woodward is right and if the claimants wish to recover damages for the injuries sustained after spring 1979, then fresh actions will have to be commenced. If the defendants' negligence thereafter continues and if further damage should result before trial, yet further writs would be needed, together with an order for consolidation. If, as has happened in this present case, the actions took more than three years to come to trial, it would be wise to issue fresh writs shortly before the third anniversary of the ones which begin the new proceedings. And so on every three years. Indeed, to have met Mr Woodward's point in the present case, this is what should have been done here. The sense of unreality is heightened by the defendants' own allegations in their amended defences that the claimants were volens "in persisting in working ... after ... the commencement of these proceedings." So, the point now taken does not seem to have occurred to them when their amended defences were drafted. Leave to serve them was only granted at trial. Nevertheless, if Mr Woodward's arguments are good, then they must carry the day, despite their technicality.'

Shiblaq v Sadikoglu

CPR 6 **Hague Convention, Art 10**

QBD (Comm)(Colman J) **[2004] EWHC 189 (Comm);**
CLC 380; LTL 16/8/2004

The claimant served proceedings in Turkey via a notary public. There was no acknowledgement and judgment was entered in default. Turkey had registered an objection under Art 10 of the Hague Convention. The defendant applied to set aside the default judgment on the basis that service had not been effected. There was conflicting expert evidence as to whether service of Turkish domestic proceedings via a notary public was permitted. The claimant argued that: (a) the reciprocity principle meant that service had complied with Art 10; (b) service was proper by Art 15; (c) any error did not invalidate any step in the proceedings unless the court so ordered, and in any event could be remedied by CPR 3.10; and (d) the court could dispense with service under CPR 6.8.

Held:

(i) Notwithstanding the expert evidence, Turkey's objection raised a very strong inference that direct service by Art 10 methods was impermissible.

(ii) Article 15 defined the minimum service criteria were judgment in default to be obtained. It did not define the available methods if service in a particular case.

(iii) The method of service in this case was not permitted under Turkish Law as required by CPR 6.24(a) nor was it a method designated by CPR 6.25(1) as appropriate for service in a convention country.

(iv) CPR 3.10 could not be used to remedy a failure to use CPR 6.8 retrospectively to retrospectively validate defective service. The court would hesitate to exercise extra-jurisdictional jurisdiction where the service formalities of local or international law had not been complied with.

(v) It was similarly inappropriate to use CPR 3.10 to create a deemed breach justifying judgment in default by retrospectively validating service. This was not discretionary; it was outside the scope of the provision (*Elmes v Hygrade Food Products Ltd* (p423) applied).

(vi) CPR 6.9 could only be applied in exceptional circumstances. It was not appropriate to apply it here. The fundamental principle of international comity was not amenable to dilution by application of the overriding objective.

Application granted, the judge noting that the claimant would have to effect service by a permitted method.

Simpson v Norwest Holst Southern Ltd

Limitation Act 1939, s 2A, s 2D

Court of Appeal **[1980] 2 All ER 471;**
[1980] 1 WLR 968; 124 SJ 313

In July 1976, when the claimant (Clive Simpson) started work as a carpenter on the Brunel Plaza building site at Swindon, his employers gave him a statement under the Contracts of Employment Act that the employing company was 'Norwest Holst Group'. His pay slips showed his employers as 'Norwest Holst'. In fact, there were at least four limited companies within the group.

On 4 August 1976 he hurt his leg at work. On 16 September 1976 his solicitors wrote notifying his claim to 'Norwest Holst Ltd', identifying the date and time and place of the accident. In subsequent correspondence, the insurers headed their letters 'Norwest Construction Co Ltd'. In October 1978 the claimant's solicitors asked Norwest's insurer at a meeting whom the defendants to any proceedings ought to be. On 11 June 1979 the claimant's solicitors wrote to the insurers asking them to confirm that the correct title was Norwest Holst Ltd. On 4 July the insurers wrote in reply that the correct title was Norwest Holst Southern Ltd. On 9 July the claimant's solicitors applied for the defendants' name on the legal aid certificate to be altered accordingly.

On 17 August 1976 the claimant's summons for personal injury damages was issued in the Swindon County Court. The defendants applied for the particulars of claim to be struck out. The registrar dismissed their application and exercised his discretion in favour of the claimant under s 2D of the Limitation Act 1939 as amended. HH Judge Vowden QC dismissed the defendants' appeal. During the hearing of the defendants' further appeal, Brightman LJ pointed out to the parties the possible applicability of s 2A(4) and (6).

Held:

(i)   The defendants hid their identity from the claimant under the words 'Norwest Holst Group'. He did not know the identity of his employers and could not before 17 August 1976 reasonably have been expected to acquire this knowledge: s 2A(6). Accordingly, his action was not barred by the effluxion of time: s 2A(4).

(ii)   If it had been, it was reasonable for the judge to disapply s 2A under s 2D because:

    (a)   s 2D should not be read in any restrictive sense so as to apply only to exceptional cases;

    (b)   the claimant's claim would have been barred by the operation of s 2A, not just his solicitors' delay in issuing the summons;

    (c)   the judge had exercised his discretion correctly because the summons would only have been two weeks out of time, the insurers had contributed to the claimant's solicitors'difficulty in identifying the defendants, the claim had been promptly notified, and the defendants were in no worse position to defend the claim then they would have been if proceedings had started two weeks earlier.

Sims v Dartford and Gravesham HA

Limitation Act 1980, s 14, s 33

Croydon County Court (HHJ Crush)   **[1996] 7 Med LR 381**

In August 1987 the claimant was prescribed the drug Tagamet by doctors at the defendant hospital. He experienced an increase in breast size in July 1988 and, in October 1988, he was diagnosed as having right-sided gynaecomastia. His treatment was changed to Ranitidine in December 1988 and his symptoms reduced. In August 1989 he consulted a solicitor with a view to issuing proceedings if his claim was meritorious. In August 1991 the claimant received an expert medical report disclosing that his condition was a known side effect of Tagamet. He issued proceedings in May 1993. The defendant contended that the action was time barred, on the basis that the claimant had knowledge that his symptoms were attributable to the act or omission of which he complained for the purposes of s 14 in December 1988, when his treatment was changed to Ranitidine.

Held:

(i)   Under s 14(1), knowledge that any act or omission did or did not, as a matter of law, involve negligence, was irrelevant. The crucial knowledge was of the act or omission to which the injury is attributable, not knowledge of a cause of action. The claimant's date of knowledge arose in December 1988 when his treatment was changed and his symptoms reduced (*Bentley v Bristol & Western Health Authority* (p328), considered).

(ii)   Having regard to the delay in bringing proceedings and the fact that evidence would be less cogent eight years or more after the event, this was not an appropriate case in which to exercise the discretion under s 33 to direct that the time limit did not apply.

Claim dismissed.

Sindall v Kirklees MBC

Limitation Act 1980, s 14, s 33

QBD (Judge Hawkesworth QC)   **29 June 2007, unreported**

The claimant (born on 31 August 1962) had been in the defendant's care in the period from 1973 to 1980, from the age of 11 until she was 18. She alleged that during that period she had been neglected and had participated in unlawful and inappropriate sexual activity. She further claimed that, on reaching 18 years old, she was discharged to live in the community without financial or social support and was obliged to take up residence in squalid conditions. In 1993 she suffered a severe mental illness for which she continued to receive treatment. She issued proceedings in 2000 alleging that she had suffered personal injury as a result of her mistreatment in care. Although she was initially part of a Group Litigation Order composed of numerous claims arising out of the same care home, the others either settled or were discontinued. The claimant's action therefore proceeded alone, with limitation being tried as a preliminary issue.

The claimant submitted that she had acquired the relevant knowledge for the purpose of s 14 of the Act in 1993 when she first suffered mental illness and that therefore the primary limitation period had expired in 1996. She contended that the delay of four years, from 1996 until she issued proceedings, was not excessively long and was excusable in light of her personal circumstances, and that it was therefore appropriate to exercise the s 33 discretion in her favour.

Held:

(i)   The defendant had had no express notice that the claimant was going to contend that the primary limitation period had expired in 1996 and, as the claimant was not called to give evidence or to be cross-examined, the court could not proceed on that basis. Whilst the claimant's psychiatric illness seriously impaired her ability to give instructions, that did not address the period prior to 1993 when the claimant was functioning without the handicap of her psychiatric illness (*Catholic Care (Diocese of Leeds) v Young* [2006] EWCA Civ 1534 considered).

(ii)   In those circumstances, it was unfair and evidentially unjustified to reach any conclusion other than that the primary limitation period expired in 1983, three years after the claimant's majority.

(iii)   The cogency of the claimant's own evidence had been seriously affected by her mental illness, and the evaluation of her evidence, particularly in relation to allegations of sexual impropriety, would be extremely difficult. The psychiatric experts agreed that it would not be safe to rely upon the claimant's uncorroborated account of the relevant matters: 'it is impossible to distinguish valid memories and complaints from persecutory delusions'. However, no supporting evidence had been served.

(iv)   Moreover, many of the defendant's relevant records no longer existed. The fact that other claims for the same care home were settled did not show that the defendant was not prejudiced by the delay in the instant case.

(v)   These evidential difficulties impacted upon all aspects of the case: liability, causation and quantum. After a lapse of 30 years, a fair trial of the claimant's allegations was no longer possible and the exercise of discretion under s 33 was declined.

Judgment for defendant.

Singh v Atombrook Ltd

Service and amendment of writ

Companies Act 1985, s 725   **RSC Ord 2, r 1, Ord 20, r 5**

Court of Appeal   **[1989] 1 WLR 810; 133 SJ 1133;**
[1989] 1 All ER 385

In June 1984 the claimant (Mrs Santosh Singh) and her husband bought three airline tickets for a flight to the United States for the claimant and her two children from a firm of travel agents trading as Sterling Travel from premises in Rupert Street, London W1. Although the company's notepaper was prominently headed 'Sterling Travel', there was a very small note at the bottom saying 'proprietors, Atombrook Ltd' whose registered office was stated to be in Goswell Road, E1.

Mr Singh died soon afterwards, so the claimant and her children were unable to travel to the USA. Sterling Travel promised a refund of the price of the tickets but never paid it. Consequently the claimant pursued a claim for £1,314 plus interest.

On 4 June 1987 her writ was issued. It was addressed to 'Sterling Travel (a firm)' at the Rupert Street address. The next day, it was posted there. Nothing was heard from the defendants. On 21 July 1987 judgment was entered in default. When steps were taken to try to execute the judgment, the claimant's solicitors were informed that there was no firm called Sterling Travel and that the defendants should have been sued as 'Atombrook Ltd, trading as Sterling Travel'.

The defendants applied for the judgment to be set aside on the grounds that it had been irregularly obtained. Hutchison J upheld the district registrar's order that the judgment be set aside, provided that the defendants pay the money claimed, and further ordered that the defendants' name be amended to read 'Atombrook Ltd trading as Sterling Travel'. The defendants appealed.

Held:

(i)   There was no reason in principle, particularly given the width of RSC Ord 2, r 1, which precluded the court in appropriate cases from amending the pleadings and proceedings even after final judgment.

(ii)   This was a case of mere misnomer. There was never the slightest doubt in the minds of the defendants that the claimant intended to sue them and that they were the persons with whom the case was concerned. The writ could be amended under Ord 20, r 5(3).

(iii)   Even assuming that there was an irregularity under s 725 of the Companies Act 1985, in that the writ had not been served at the defendants' registered office, this was insufficient to render the proceedings a nullity.

(iv)   Both the above irregularities fell plainly within the scope of Ord 2, r 1, and could be cured by it. The judgment should be amended, even though it was final. The defendants' appeal would be dismissed.

Per Sir John Megaw: '... the statutory requirement which is asserted here is s 725 of the Companies Act 1985. Subsection (1) says that a document may be served on a company by leaving it at, or sending it by post to, the company's registered office. This document, for reasons which are apparent and which really cannot be put as being in any serious way the fault of the plaintiff, was not addressed to Atombrook Ltd's registered office, but in my view that does not, in the circumstances, by itself result in invalidity; it is merely an irregularity. How serious an irregularity a failure to state a company's address accurately may be will of course depend on the circumstances. It may well be that it would in some cases be an irregularity that would justify the court, without more, in setting aside unconditionally any judgment that had been entered. But it would be absurd to suggest that any failure to send the writ to the correct address, as for example some minor error in the address which caused no conceivable prejudice to the defendant, could result in

651

the whole of the proceedings being invalid; and in this case I see no basis whatever for suggesting that there was a failure to comply with the statutory requirement such as to invalidate the proceedings.'

Whittam v W J Daniel & Co (p715) followed.

Siodlaczek v Hymatic Engineering Co

Limitation Act 1939, s 2D

Lawson J **(1980) CLY 1678**

On 21 August 1972 the claimant (Mr Siodlaczek) was injured at work when a fragment of metal entered his left eye. He consulted solicitors who sent a letter before action on 20 June 1973. Up to March 1975, there was considerable correspondence between the claimant's solicitors and the defendants' insurers and consultant metallurgist's reports were obtained by both parties. The circumstances of the accident were in dispute, and the defendants' insurers denied liability. The claimant's solicitors failed to issue a writ by 21 August 1975, although a writ had been prepared and a statement of claim settled by counsel.

The claimant then instructed a second firm of solicitors to sue his first firm in respect of their negligence. With the backing of his first firm's insurers, it was decided to commence proceedings against the defendants (his employers) in order to exhaust his remedies and mitigate his loss.

Consequently in January 1979 the claimant's third firm issued a writ against the defendant employers. After close of pleadings, the defendants applied to a judge in chambers to dismiss the action as statute barred. The claimant counter-applied for the court's discretion to be exercised in his favour under s 2D of the Limitation Act 1939 as amended so as to disapply the primary limitation period in s 2A.

Held:

(i)   There was prejudice to the claimant, in that he would have to sue his first firm of solicitors instead of his employers.

(ii)   In an action in which liability was denied, this was overwhelmingly counterbalanced by serious prejudice to the defendants on account of the delay.

(iii)   Accordingly, it would be inequitable to allow the claimant's action against the defendants to proceed.

Sir Robert Lloyd & Co Ltd v Hoey

Limitation Act 1980, s 14

Court of Appeal **[2011] EWCA Civ 1060; (2011) 155(35) SJLB 31**

The claimant was a 79-year-old man who had been exposed to asbestos in the course of his employment with the defendant. His pleaded injury was 'bilateral diffuse pleural thickening and a large area of folded lung'. He had first developed chest pains in 1984 or 1985 and was referred by his GP to a hospital chest clinic. A number of chest x-rays were taken in the course of eliminating various suspected diagnoses, such as mesothelioma. Pleural thickening was noted on certain x-rays during the period 1985 to 1987. However, that was not suspected as a cause of the chest pain. His condition improved and, in September 1987, he was discharged from the chest clinic. He continued to work until he was aged 60. In 1992 he was having difficulty breathing and retired on the grounds of ill-health. Over the years that followed, his breathing difficulties increased. In August 2007 he was again referred to the hospital, and in December 2008 a diagnosis of his later pleaded injuries was made. The claimant was advised to contact an asbestos support group. He did so, and they referred him to solicitors who commissioned expert evidence. This was to the effect that the pleural thickening, although less advanced, would have caused the chest pain in the mid-1980s. The claimant issued proceedings in August 2010. The defendant pleaded limitation, which was tried as a preliminary issue. The judge held that, although the claimant's cause of action accrued in the mid-1980s, he did not know until 2008 that he had a significant injury. He therefore held that the claim was not statute barred. The judge indicated, obiter, that if it had been he would not have exercised his discretion under s 33 to allow the claim to continue. The defendant appealed.

Held:

(i)   The judge was not constrained by the evidence to hold that the claimant's date of knowledge under s 14 occurred during the mid-1980s. On the contrary, he was right to find that what he suffered during that period was a transient bout of chest pain.

(ii)   The claimant did not know that he had suffered a significant injury within s 14(2) until 2008. In February 1984 and July to September 1985, the claimant suffered chest pains, but was unaware that these were symptomatic of any underlying injury. There was no failure by the claimant to seek professional help and so no additional knowledge could be attributed to the claimant. During that period the symptoms of which the claimant was aware would not cause a reasonable person to issue proceedings for damages against a known and solvent culprit.

(iii) Similarly, in January 1986 the claimant had been pain free for four months, but was advised of the possibility that he had developed mesothelioma as a result of encountering asbestos in his work. The claimant had not in fact developed mesothelioma and that scare soon passed. Pleural thickening and pleural shadowing had been revealed on various x-rays, but the claimant was not told about these matters and the doctors believed (wrongly, as it now turns out) that these did not constitute a significant injury. Accordingly, during 1986 the claimant was unaware of any internal injury or disability which might cause a reasonable person to issue proceedings. Again, there was no failure by the claimant to obtain professional advice and no additional knowledge should be imputed to him.

(iv)   Accordingly, the claimant commenced his action within three years of his date of knowledge (*A v Hoare* (p287) followed).

(v)   That being so, the question of knowledge of attribution under s 14(1)(b) did not arise. However, on the evidence the claimant could not be fixed with knowledge in the 1980s that his injury, namely pleural thickening, had been caused by exposure to asbestos (*Spargo v North Essex DHA* (p667) considered). The only relevant knowledge which the claimant then had was that, if he had developed mesothelioma, which he had not, that condition would be attributable to exposure to asbestos.

Appeal dismissed.

Sivyer v Eli Lilly & Co and others

Limitation Act 1980, s 11, s 14, s 33

Court of Appeal   **(1992) 3 Med LR 393**

See *Nash v Eli Lilly & Co* (I) (p568)

Skerratt v Linfax Ltd (t/a Go Karting for Fun)

Limitation Act 1980, s 11, s 32, s 33

Court of Appeal   **[2004] PIQR P10; LTL 6/5/2003**

On 4 April 1997 the claimant had an accident on the defendant's go-karting track which he blamed upon the track being unsafe. Immediately prior to using the track the claimant had signed a form which he understood to exclude the defendant from all liability for injury. He assumed that he had no cause of action until November 2001 when he spoke with a solicitor acting for a man subsequently injured on the track. This solicitor had contacted the claimant as a result of disclosure relating to the subsequent accident.

The claimant issued proceedings on 15 January 2002. The defendant pleaded limitation which was heard as a preliminary issue. The district judge found that proceedings were issued out of time, rejecting the claimant's argument that the defendant had deliberately concealed relevant facts so as to delay time running under s 32. He also declined to exercise his discretion on the bases that the claimant, an intelligent and articulate man, could with reasonable diligence have discovered that he had a cause of action by consulting lawyers and that the defendant had been prejudiced by the delay. The claimant appealed.

Held:

(i)   All the matters cited by the claimant as going to the application of s 32 occurred before the accident. It was difficult to imagine of a case of concealment under s 32 where the concealment did not occur at the time of accident or later. s 32 was to be construed narrowly. The district judge was clearly right in his finding.

(ii)   Even accepting that the claimant's evidence that he thought that he had no cause of action was honest, he could attract blame for the delay and this was a relevant factor under s 33(a).

(iii) The finding of prejudice to the defendant was merited not over-emphasised. The district judge simply recognised that there were likely to be difficulties five years down the line. A defendant will not always be able to identify precisely why they are prejudiced.

(iv)   Further, this was a case where, five years after the accident, the defendant was entitled to consider its books closed.

(v)   The district judge had not erred.

Appeal dismissed.

Skitt v Khan and Wakefield Health Authority

Limitation Act 1980, s 11, s 12, s 14, s 33

Court of Appeal   **[1997] 8 Med LR 105; LTL 10/12/1996**

The claimant's husband suffered a cut on his leg during an accident at work in 1977 that failed to heal. The first defendant was a consultant dermatologist at the second defendant's hospital to whom the husband was referred in 1982. The initial diagnosis was psoriasis and cream was accordingly prescribed. In 1984 a revised diagnosis of varicose ulcer was made. A plastic surgeon removed the ulcer in July 1986. Histology of tissue removed showed cancer, for which the husband received treatment later that year.

On 12 November 1986 the husband consulted a solicitor who sent a letter of claim on 19 November 1998 alleging failure to investigate and treat. The husband died on 4 July 1992. The claimant as his widow and administratrix issued proceedings under the Law Reform (Miscellaneous Provisions) Act 1934 and the Fatal Accidents Act 1976 alleging negligent diagnoses and treatment on 7 January 1994. The defendants denied liability and causation and raised limitation, which was heard as a preliminary issue.

The judge held that the deceased did not have the requisite knowledge so as start time running against the claim; by the time he suspected his injuries were due to the acts or omissions of the defendants he was dying and could not obtain confirmation due to his financial circumstances. The judge held that in the alternative he would exercise his discretion under s 33 to allow the claim to continue. The defendant appealed.

Held:

(i) The husband had the relevant knowledge in November 1986. The absence of expert opinion to clarify whether the acts or omissions to which his injuries were attributable constituted negligence was irrelevant.

(ii) Even allowing for the gravity of the injury and its effect and the claimant's financial circumstances it was unreasonable for him not to have sought expert medical advice. The defendants had discharged the burden of showing that the deceased had constructive knowledge.

(iii) The judge had failed to consider relevant matters in the exercise of his discretion. Particularly, he had not attached any or sufficient weight to the fact that the first defendant was now very ill and the plastic surgeon dead, nor to the husband's conduct and whether he had acted promptly.

(iv) Exercising the discretion afresh it would not be equitable to allow the claim to proceed. The husband had decided not to pursue the claim and it was equitable that the claimant was bound by that decision.

Appeal allowed.

Slevin v Southampton and South West Hampshire HA

Limitation Act 1980, s 14, s 32, s 33

QBD (Mantell J) [1997] 8 Med LR 175

The claimant was born in the first defendant's hospital on 21 April 1967. The second defendant was the consultant obstetrician and gynaecologist to whom the claimant's mother was referred. It was known before the birth that the claimant was in a transverse lie in the womb, and there was discussion of a delivery by caesarean section. However, the claimant was in fact delivered by breech extraction and her spine was damaged during the delivery, resulting in high level paraplegia.

After reading a report from an independent expert in October 1992, the claimant on 28 February 1994 issued proceedings alleging the second defendant to have been negligent in not performing a caesarean and/or that he performed the breech extraction negligently. Limitation was heard as preliminary issue. The claimant claimed that time began to run against her when she received and read the report, whereas the defendants claimed that she had earlier actual knowledge of the relevant facts, or that she could be fixed with constructive knowledge under s 14(3) of the Limitation Act 1980.

Held:

(i) By her eighteenth birthday in April 1985, when time would normally begin to run, the claimant knew as much about the circumstances of her birth as her mother did, and her mother had known from the start that there might have been an avoidable complication. The claimant knew that she should have been delivered by caesarean and that, if that course had been taken, she would not have suffered her disability. She knew that her injury occurred at the hands of the second defendant during a breech delivery.

(ii)   Those facts were sufficient to imbue her with actual knowledge that the injury was attributable wholly or partly to the act or omission alleged to constitute the negligence.

(iii)   Even if this finding was incorrect, the defendants had succeeded in showing constructive knowledge for the purposes of s 14(3), because the claimant might reasonably have been expected to acquire by April 1995, from the facts as ascertainable by her with the help of medical advice, such knowledge as would have illuminated the causal connection between the injury and the alleged negligent act or omission.

(iv)   The statement to the claimant's mother by the second defendant soon after the birth, to the effect that the claimant's condition was 'just one of those things', could not amount to deliberate concealment under s 32(1) of the Act. Also, this section could not operate where the claimant has actual or constructive knowledge. The action was therefore statute barred.

(v)   The court would not exercise its discretion under s 33, it not being equitable to do so. The delay had damaged the prospects of a fair trial and the cogency of the evidence, the second defendant was elderly and had suffered mental deterioration, and expert evidence as to what was accepted obstetric practice in 1967 would be limited.

Judgment for the defendants; claim dismissed.

Smith v Hampshire CC

Limitation Act 1980, s 14, s 33

Court of Appeal   **[2007] EWCA Civ 246; [2007] ELR 321; (2007) 151 SJLB 433**

The claimant was born on 21 October 1978. He was educated in Hampshire (which was the defendant's responsibility) between September 1986 and February 1993 (being placed in a special school in 1987), and in Knowsley between February 1993 and July 1994. He left school at 15 and became 18 on 21 October 1996. From shortly after September 1987, when the claimant began to attend Cliffdale First and Middle School, he appreciated that he had difficulties in reading and writing which were not shared by other pupils of the same age. He recognised that he had been placed in a special school on account of those difficulties, but that those difficulties were not shared (or at least not shared in the same degree he experienced) by other pupils at the school. In particular, the best reader in his class at the school at one point was a girl who suffered from Down's Syndrome. He felt that he should be doing better than the other children and that it was unfair that he could not read and write and some of the children with obvious disabilities could. The claimant turned 18 on 21 October 1996 and in September 1997 began to attend the Drop In Studies Centre run by Liverpool Community College with a view to improving his English and Mathematics for the purpose of thereafter undertaking an art course at the college.

While at the Drop In Studies Centre in 1997–98 the claimant found that he was not making the progress which he would have wished. He came to realise from discussions with other students that some students received assistance with their written work and were given more time to complete written tasks. These were students who suffered from what he then came to know as dyslexia. His understanding of the condition at that time was that it affected one's ability to read and to write and that it was a condition the effects of which could be alleviated by assistance of the type available at Liverpool Community College. In June 1998 the claimant had a meeting with a personal tutor. The possibility of dyslexia was recorded.

In October 2008 the claimant consulted his general practitioner who had referred him to a clinical psychologist. The psychologist's report stated that the claimant had a pattern of difficulties consistent with a diagnosis of severe dyslexia. The claimant received the report on 17 January 1999. He issued proceedings alleging failure on the part of the defendant to diagnose his dyslexia. These were issued on 4 January 2002, by which time he was aged 23.

Limitation was heard as preliminary issue. The claimant had also issued proceedings against Liverpool and Knowsley councils, but discontinued these before the limitation hearing.

The judge found that the claimant had had knowledge for the purpose of s 14 by the time that he had consulted his GP, alternatively that at that time his dyslexia was ascertainable with expert advice, and he had not taken reasonable steps to obtain that advice. The judge declined to disapply the limitation period under s 33 and held that the claim was statute barred.

The claimant appealed, submitting that time could not begin to run before he had received the psychologist's report because, before then, he had only been told that he might have dyslexia, and it was only when he received the report that he could be said to have had the relevant knowledge. The judge's approach to s 33 was also challenged.

Held:

(i)   The judge had been entitled to find that a reasonable person in the claimant's position, on hearing that he might have dyslexia and should seek assistance in dealing with it, would have done so sooner than the claimant in fact did.

(ii)   There was no reason why the normal expectation, that a person suffering from a significant injury would be curious about its origins, should not also apply to dyslexics. There was no reason why the claimant, who had been told before he was 21 that he should seek an assessment for dyslexia, had not obtained professional help sooner. On the evidence, the claimant himself was not inhibited from doing so. As was demonstrated by the fact that he had been to see his GP and the psychologist, his untreated dyslexia was not a special reason that had inhibited him from seeking expert advice (*Adams v Bracknell Forest BC* (p292) applied).

(iii)   Section 14(3) expressly provided that a person's knowledge included knowledge that he might reasonably have been expected to acquire from facts observable or ascertainable by him or from facts ascertainable by him with the help of appropriate expert evidence. The first relevant observable and ascertainable fact in the instant case was that the claimant was for a long time unable to read or write. The further relevant fact was that that state of affairs was attributable to his schooling, which had either failed to observe the first facts or, having observed them, did nothing about them. For that purpose the claimant did not need to be formally diagnosed as dyslexic or know that he had been so diagnosed. The judge had thus been entitled to find that, by the time the claimant consulted his GP, he had relevant knowledge for the purposes of s 14 of the Act, with the result that the proceedings were statute barred (*Spargo v North Essex DHA* (p667) considered).

(iv)   The judge had paid regard to all the relevant matters set out in s 33(3) of the Act and the prejudice to both the claimant and the local authority. He had been entitled to conclude that, while the claimant had some prospect of success at trial, the evidence of prejudice to the local authority was very strong because of the absence, after the passage of time, of relevant documentation. The judge's exercise of discretion could not be faulted (*Adams v Bracknell Forest BC* and *Robinson v St Helens MBC* (p628) considered).

Appeal dismissed.

Smith (Michael John) v West Lancashire Health Authority

Limitation Act 1980, s 14

Court of Appeal   **[1995] PIQR P514**

The claimant attended the defendant's hospital on November 12 1981, when he was 16 years old, with an injury to his right hand. He had suffered fracture dislocations and the ring and little finger metacarpals. A diagnosis of an uncomplicated fracture of the base of the ring finger was made and conservative treatment prescribed.

On 4 January 1982 the claimant was told that this treatment was not working and that an urgent operation was required. He was not informed that the operation should have been performed shortly after the initial injury. The operation was performed the following day. Thereafter the claimant consulted his GP complaining of pain in his hand and was reassured. He was dismissed from his employment in June 1989 because his loss of hand function precluded heavy lifting.

He then consulted solicitors who in February 1991 obtained a medical report stating that there had been a missed opportunity to properly treat the injury around the time of the original admission. Proceedings were issued on 23 April 1992. The defendant pleaded limitation, which was heard as a preliminary issue. The judge held that proceedings were issued out of time and declined to exercise his s 33 discretion. The claimant appealed.

Held:

(i)   It was unfortunate that the judge did not have the benefit of full medical evidence and did not permit oral evidence.

(ii)   The claimant did not have actual knowledge that his injury was attributable to the defendant's omission until February 1991 when he received the medical report. Whilst before then he knew that he had not had an operation on or about 12 November 1982 before 1991, he did not at that stage know that the absence of such an operation was the cause of his problems. Knowledge of an omission depended on knowing what was omitted and before 1991 the claimant did not know that there had been an omission to operate. Simply telling the claimant that conservative treatment had not worked did not tell him that an opportunity had been missed.

(iii)   The claimant did not have constructive knowledge under s 14(3). Having consulted his GP, it was not reasonable to expect him to seek a second opinion (*Broadley v Guy Clapham & Co* (p345) and *Dobbie v Medway HA* (p411) distinguished).

Appeal allowed.

Smith and others v Central Asbestos Co Ltd and another

Limitation Act 1963, ss 1, 7, 8

Court of Appeal   **[1972] 1 QB 244**

The claimants were workmen who had contracted asbestosis working for the defendants' asbestos factory. They applied for relief from s 2 (the primary limitation period) under s 1 (delay of the same due to lack of knowledge of material facts). The defendants alleged that they had the requisite knowledge less than 12 months before the issue of proceedings. In three of the four cases the claimants had known that they had asbestosis to varying degrees before this time, but in each case had issued within 12 months of the condition forcing them to give up work. The fourth had not issue until more than two years after being so forced. His evidence was that the defendants' manager had told him that he could not both obtain disablement benefit and bring a civil claim, and that he had elected disablement benefit on that basis. The defendants appealed limitation and quantum.

Held (on limitation):

(i)   The knowledge of the first 3 claimants as to the extent of their condition did not acquire a decisive character until they were forced to leave work because of it.

(ii)   (Edmund Davies LJ doubting) 'Attributable' meant subjectively attributable as per that specific claimant. Thus time did not run against the fourth claimant until he was disabused of his misapprehension.

Appeal dismissed.

NB: The reasoning on attribution was overruled by the House of Lords in *Adams v Bracknell Forest BC* (p292).

Smith v Donelan & Co Ltd

Limitation Act 1980, s 33

Court of Appeal   **LTL 30/7/98**

The claimant suffered an accident at work on 9 July 1991 when he fell down an unfenced manhole. He instructed solicitors in October 1991 who sent a letter of claim later that month. The claimant served medical reports in April and October 1992. Having investigated the claim through loss adjusters the defendant denied liability in December 1992. In January 1993 the claimant instructed a different solicitor's firm, which was effectively run by a sole practitioner. In May 1994 the solicitor in question suffered a heart attack, putting a temporary halt to his dealings with the claimant. Limitation expired on 9 July 1994. Proceedings were issued on 7 December 1994. The defendant applied for the action to be struck out as statute barred. The district judge exercised his s 33 discretion and directed that s 11 did not apply. The defendant appealed successfully to the circuit judge. The claimant then appealed.

Held:

(i)   The claimant's case was not poor or lacking in merit. There would be substantial prejudice to him if it were struck out.

(ii)   Although the delay was significant and the fault of the claimant's solicitor, it was largely due to that solicitors illness.

(iii)   The defendant had not been evidentially prejudiced by the delay. They knew of the claim from early stage and had the benefit of a full investigation.

(iv)   The circuit judge had misdirected himself. It was equitable to allow the action to continue.

Appeal allowed.

Smith v Hughes

Companies Act 1985, s 725(1)

CPR 6.9, 7.6   **[2003] EWCA Civ 656; [2003] 1 WLR 2441;**
[2003] 3 All ER 129

See *Cranfield and anor v Bridgegrove* (E) (p389)

Smith v Leicester Health Authority

Limitation Act 1980, s 11, s 14, s 33

Court of Appeal   **(1998) Lloyd's Rep Med 77; LTL 29/1/1998**

The claimant was born on 12 February 1943. As a yong child she had problems with her right leg, right foot and bladder. In October 1952 she was diagnosed with spina bifida occulta. She underwent extensive treatment and surgery but suffered tetraplegia as a result of the defendant's negligence during an operation performed on 9 May 1957. In 1983 she had further investigations, which revealed that her condition derived from the operation, but was told that after such a lapse of time it was impossible to say that it flowed from any act or omission. In 1984 a lay official of the Spinal Injuries Association informed her that limitation had long since expired.

She instructed solicitors in 1988, following a chance meeting with a solicitor who was attending another resident of the same care home, and in 1990 a medical expert informed her that the defendant had been negligent. Proceedings were issued on 21 May 1992 but key x-rays not found until 1995. Limitation was tried simultaneously with liability and causation. The judge held that the defendant had been causatively negligent. However, he also held the claimant had constructive knowledge in 1985, as, had she instructed solicitors then, she could have acquired all the information that was available at trial. The judge refused to exercise his s 33 discretion, holding that the delay had been enormous and prejudicial to the defendant. The claimant appealed.

Held:

(i)   The test for constructive knowledge was whether a reasonable person placed in the same position as the claimant would have acted in the same way. This includes the facts and circumstances of the case, but excludes the character traits of the individual claimant.

(ii)   *Forbes v Wandsworth HA* (p434) was not authority for the proposition that, when a patient is severely disabled following an operation they have 12 to 18 months to decide whether to investigate a claim. In this case the claimant reasonably believed that the operation, far from being a failure, had succeeded in saving her life.

(iii)   The claimant's remarkable fortitude should be disregarded. However, it was reasonable for a wheelchair bound claimant to accept the advice of a reputable national association.

(iv)   The judge had held that liability turned on the x-rays discovered in 1995. The defendant had not established constructive knowledge before then, as before then the claimant would not have been able to establish attributibility. The claim was therefore not statute barred.

(v)   The appeal court could only interfere the exercise of a s 33 discretion if the judge had (a) misdirected himself on the law, (b) taken into account a relevant consideration, or (c) failed to take into account a relevant consideration.

(vi)   The judge was wrong to say that the 'delay is enormous' in describing the passage of time between the accrual of the cause of action and the issue of proceedings. This suggested that it was the claimant's responsibility, whereas on the facts there was no proper criticism to be made of the claimant. It would be preferable to describe such periods as the passage of time rather than delay.

(vii) As the case turned on documents and x-rays, the defendant's prejudice was less than if live evidence were central. Experts could still make proper analyses many years later. The evidence that established causation was in fact that of the defendant's own expert. It was not open to the defendant to argue that it might have produced different evidence 20 years earlier. The defendant's case was doomed when the x-rays were discovered.

(viii) The prejudice to the defendant therefore paled in comparison to that to the claimant. The judge did not take account the financial prejudice to the claimant as against that of the defendant.

(ix)   The judge's exercise of his discretion was flawed. Had it been necessary, the court would have exercised it afresh in the claimant's favour.

Appeal allowed.

Smith v Liverpool CC and others

Limitation Act 1980, s 11, s 14, s 33

Richard Seymour J   **[2006] EWHC 743 (QB)**

The claimant was born on 21 October 1978. He attended schools run by the defendants where he laboured with unindentified and untreated dyslexia. He appreciated that he had difficulties in reading and writing from early on (about 1987). He later attended art college. In light of difficulties with his written work, he went to see his personal tutor on 26 June 1998. The record of the meeting suggests his tutor identified dyslexia as the problem. Around October 1998 the claimant's mother, having read an article about dyslexia and recognised the symptoms, contacted the Dyslexia Institute who advised that treatment was available. She quickly passed this information to the claimant.

Proceedings were issued on 4 January 2002. Limitation was heard as a preliminary issue.

Held:

(i)   The claimant had the requisite knowledge after the discussion with his personal tutor. From then on he knew that his condition was probably dyslexia and that help was available to ameliorate it. It was reasonable to expect claimant to draw the conclusion that if the college could have helped so could have the school (*Adams v Bracknell Forest BC* (p292) applied).

(ii)   Moreover he was told in terms by his mother that the condition should have been identified and addressed.

(iii)   The claimant's date of knowledge was therefore no later than October 1998, and the claim was brought outside the primary limitation period.

(iv)   It was relevant in cases such as this to consider the entirety of the time that had elapsed between the relevant events and the hearing (*Donovan v Gwentoys Ltd* (p412) and *Rowe v Kingston-upon-Hull CC* (p633) considered).

(v)   There was no explanation for much of the delay.

(vi)   The delay had significantly prejudiced the defendant. There were severe difficulties in identifying and tracing relevant teachers and nearly all the relevant documents were now unavailable.

(vii)   The strength of the claim was doubtful.

(viii) It was not appropriate to disapply the limitation period.

Claim dismissed.

Smith v Ministry of Defence

Limitation Act 1980, s 11, s 33

QBD (Silber J)   **[2005] EWHC 682 (QB); LTL 27/4/2005**

The claimant was the administratrix of her husband's estate. Her husband had worked for the defendant from 1960 to 1962, during which time he was exposed to asbestos. In May 1991 he died of asbestos attributable mesothelioma. It was common ground that the primary limitation period expired in 1998; although the claimant knew before then that her husband died from an asbestos associated disease, she did not until May 1995 know where he might have been exposed. At that time she contacted solicitors and gained the benefit of a legal aid certificate, albeit with the proviso of a monthly contribution that she struggled to maintain. The certificate was discharged in January 1996 for failure to pay contributions. She was simultaneously being threatened by her solicitors (who had done little to advance the claim) for non-payment of fees. At this point the claimant lost all confidence in the legal process. A TV advert in May 2002 prompted her to instruct different solicitors in June 2004. Proceedings were commenced in May 2004. A preliminary hearing was held on, inter alia, whether the court should exercise its discretion to allow the claim to continue.

Held:

(i) In regard to s 33(3)(a), the length of the delay was six years. The claimant had in the unusual circumstances of the present case a good reason for delaying in commencing proceedings from 1995 to 2004. She was unaware of her legal rights and her solicitors had failed to inform her that she had a good claim against the defendant that was not statute barred in 1995.

(ii) In regard to s 33(3)(b), the defendant was not materially prejudiced in obtaining evidence by the delay since 1995, a date some 30 years after exposure. The available evidence was no less cogent.

(iii) In the context of her restricted means, her lack of confidence in the strengths of her claim and the financial demands made by her then solicitors, the claimant had pursued the claim promptly and reasonably within the meaning of s 33(3(e).

(iv) The claimant had taken reasonable steps within the meaning of s 33(3)(f) to obtain legal advice when she first knew of her potential claim.

(v) The fact that, unlike in 1995, the claimant now had the benefit of a conditional fee agreement, constituted prejudice to the defendant.

(vi) In the circumstances the claimant had discharged the heavy burden in showing that it was equitable to disapply the limitation period (*KR v Bryn Alyn Community Holdings Ltd* (p505) applied).

Smith v NHSLA

Limitation Act 1980, s 14, s 28, s 33

QBD (Andrew Smith J)   **(2001) Lloyds Rep Med 90; LTL 28/11/2000**

The claimant had been born on 8 February 1973 with a congenitally displaced hip. This was not diagnosed until 1974 and it was complained that it should have been earlier. The claimant issued proceedings on 16 August 1996. The defendant denied liability and causation and raised limitation. The issues were tried together at a final hearing.

Held (on limitation, having found for the defendant on the question of negligence):

(i) The claimant's evidence that she had no idea that she might have been mistreated as a baby until 1996 was accepted. Hitherto she did not have the requisite knowledge and time did not begin to run against her. The claim was therefore not statute barred.

(ii) If the claim had been statute barred, it would have been equitable to have exercised s 33 discretion to lift the bar. The delay had caused the defendant no prejudice as there was nothing to suggest that the records, which were destroyed, had been in existence in 1994.

Smith v Surrey Hampshire Borders NHS Trust

Limitation Act 1980, s 2, s 11, s 32, s 33

Wilkie J   **[2004] EWHC 2101 (QB)**

The claimant brought a claim for false imprisonment and personal injury arising from his detention from April 1994 to November 1995 at the defendant's hospital under the Mental Health Act. Proceedings were issued in March 2003. Limitation was heard as a preliminary issue.

Held:

(i)   Time started to run on the claim on 14 November 1995.

(ii)   The false imprisonment claim was caught by a strict six-year limit and s 32(1) did not assist the claimant. The defendant had not concealed, deliberately or otherwise, any relevant fact. The facts relevant to the claimant's right of action were those of his detention and the lack of lawful authority for the same. The claimant had plainly been aware of these from the start; he believed his detention unlawful from the outset and unsuccessfully appealed against it several times.

(iii)   As regards to the personal injury claim based on negligence:

    (a)   there was no good reason why the claimant had not commenced proceedings in time.

    (b)   the defendant's ability to defend the case was prejudiced by the delay as the recollection of its witnesses had faded considerably.

    (c)   there was nothing in the defendant's conduct that provided a reason to exercise the discretion to disapply the statute bar.

    (d)   the claimant had failed to seek medical or legal advice.

    (e)   the claimant's prospects of success were poor (*Forbes v Wandsworth Health Authority* (p434) applied).

    (f)   it would therefore not be appropriate to allow the claim to continue.

Smith v White Knight Laundry

Limitation Act 1980, s 11, s 33   **Companies Act 1985, s 651**

Court of Appeal   **[2001] EWCA Civ 660; [2002] 1 WLR 616;
[2001] 3 All ER 862**

The claimant's husband claimed to have worked for the defendant from 1950-1956. In 1963 the defendant company was dissolved, precluding proceedings being brought against it. The husband died on 6 February 1995 from mesothelioma allegedly caused by the defendant negligently exposing him to asbestos.

On 28 January 1998 the claimant obtained an order under s 651 of the Companies Act 1985 restoring the defendant to the register in order to pursue a claim under the Law Reform (Miscellaneous Provisions) Act 1934 and the Fatal Accidents Act 1976. The restoration order also directed that the period of dissolution should not count for limitation purposes. The claimant issued proceedings on 14 April 1999. The defendant pleaded limitation and applied for a preliminary trial of this issue. The claimant unsuccessfully opposed this on the basis that the period of dissolution was to be discounted. The claimant appealed. The judge dismissed the appeal and varied the s 651 order to reflect time running for limitation purposes during then period of dissolution. The claimant appealed again.

Held:

(i)   The effect of the restoration order was as if the dissolution had never occurred. All the consequences flowing from the dissolution were thus negated and the claimant's claim was issued outside the limitation period.

(ii)   Under these circumstances, relief under s 651 was equivalent to relief under s 33 and a preliminary hearing on limitation was therefore required.

(iii)   Generally such a direction under s 651 should not be made unless;

    (a)   notice of it was served on all parties that could be expected to oppose it;

    (b)   the court was satisfied that it had all the evidence that the parties would wish to adduce for an application under s 33; and

    (c)   such an application was bound to succeed (*Re Workvale Ltd* (p726) followed). Otherwise a claimant should seek relief under s 33 in the normal manner.

Appeal dismissed.

Smyth v Probyn and PGA European Tour Ltd

Service   **CPR 6, 7**

Limitation Act 1980, s 32

Morland J   **(2000) 97(12) LSG 44; (2000) 144 SJLB 134; (2000) Times, 29 March**

The claimant, a professional golf caddie, asserted that a letter written on 3 August 1998 by the defendants was defamatory to him. In late July 1999 the claimant instructed solicitors to pursue this. They issued protective proceedings on 30 July 1999 but did not serve them immediately as they required further instructions. Proceedings were served on the defendant's solicitors on 30 November 1999 but were returned a few days later by the defendant's solicitors who pointed out that they had no instructions to accept service and had never said that they did. At a preliminary hearing the master refused to order that the service on the defendant's solicitors constituted valid service. He also declined to grant an extension of time for service or order that the one-year limitation period in respect of defamation claims did not apply. The claimant appealed.

Held:

    (i)   Had they been properly served, proceedings would have been issued just in time under CPR 7.5(2). CPR 7.5(2) adds a further day compared with RSC Ord 6 r 8(1)(c).

    (ii)   Nothing that defendant's solicitors did or failed to do could have reasonably given the claimant the impression that they were authorised to accept service. Merely corresponding with the claimant on the behalf of their client was insufficient. There is no general implied authority to accept service of a claim form on behalf of a client.

    (iii)   Under CPR 6.4(2) service on a party's solicitors was only valid if the serving party had received confirmation in writing that the solicitor was authorised to accept service.

    (iv)   The application to extend time failed because it could not be said that the claimant had taken all reasonable steps to serve the claim form but had been unable to do so. The defendants themselves could have been served.

    (v)   The application to disapply the limitation period under s 32 because of fraud was without merit. There was no misrepresentation or other improper conduct by the defendants or their solicitors.

Appeal dismissed.

Sniezek v Bundy (Letchworth) Ltd

Limitation Act 1980, s 11, s 14, s 33

Court of Appeal   **LTL 7/7/2000**

The claimant was born in Hungary and came to England in 1956. His command of English was poor. He began to work for the defendant in 1972 and from 1983 it was alleged that his work exposed him to chemical dust. He experienced burning sensations on his lips and in his throat in 1984 but initially dismissed it as an irritant. By 1988 his symptoms were severe. In 1989 his was dismissed from his employment. He had since 1984 believed that the dust was causing damage. Tests carried out between 1984 and 1988 were negative. In 1990 he consulted solicitors. They instructed an expert who reported in 1991 that there was no causal link. In 1992 an NHS doctor posited such a link, but again none was found. The claimant instructed different solicitors in 1992. They instructed an expert who reported on 20 January 1994 that there may have been some hypersensitisation. Counsel advised in May 1994 that there was a link but that more information was needed. Chromium was found in the claimant's filter mask. Engineering experts were instructed and in 1995 they asked for more information. The defendant obstructed pre-action disclosure but it was found in June 1997 that the dust in question contained a well-known sensitiser. A medical expert advised that this could be the cause of the claimant's symptoms. In June 1998 counsel advised that legal aid should be extended to the issue of proceedings.

Proceedings were finally issued in September 1998. Limitation was tried as a preliminary issue. The judge found that the claimant first had knowledge in 1994 when hypersensitisation was first suspected. However, he found a clear case to exercise his s 33 discretion based upon the conduct of the parties. The defendant appealed.

Held:

(i)   The judge had erred in his approach to the question of knowledge. A claimant could have the requisite knowledge even if medical experts told him that there was no injury. Such a claimant already has the requisite knowledge if he is seeking legal advice merely on the method of bringing a claim. There was a distinction between that person and a claimant who was not so sure and therefore required expert confirmation (*Ali v Courtaulds Textiles* (p301) doubted).

(ii)   The apparent harshness in time running against a claimant who had taken all reasonable steps to seek expert confirmation but had been rebuffed could be remedied by s 33.

(iii)   The claimant had knowledge in 1989 when he complained to his doctor of severe symptoms. His conviction that these were caused by the acts or omissions of the defendant was not shaken by contrary expert opinion.

(iv)   The claimant acted promptly and made reasonable efforts. The delay was caused by negative expert opinion and the defendant's failure to disclose. The defendant's claim that prejudice arose from the demolition of their factory was unsupported by evidence. The claim did not appear to be weak or of little value. The judge was correct to exercise his discretion in the claimant's favour.

Appeal dismissed.

Society of Lloyds v Tropp

CPR 6

Gross J   **[2004] EWHC 33 (Comm); LTL 16/2/2004**

The claimant, an assignee of a contractual benefit, claimed against the defendant for the repayment of a reinsurance premium. The defendant was a US citizen not domiciled in the UK. The contract stipulated that a name not domiciled in the UK irrevocably appointed a substitute agent to accept service of English proceedings on his behalf. The claim form was served upon this agent. The defendant applied to set aside service.

Held:

(i)   The agent clearly existed as a separate corporate entity. The fact that it had no significant assets and was controlled by the claimant was irrelevant, as was the fact that the defendant had not personally appointed it.

(ii)   The agent had authority to contract on the defendant's behalf. The service clause was within the scope of the agent's authority. The agreement as to service therefore bound the defendant. It was immaterial that the defendant had not personally appointed the agent.

(iii)   The claimant was entitled to direct the inclusion of such a service clause in the contract.

(iv)   There was no good reason to conclude that the agent's authority did not apply to claims such as these and every reason to conclude that they did.

(v)   Although the agent was under the claimant's control and direction, there was no rule that such a conflict of interest would prevent the agency from accepting service.

(vi)   In any event, in this case the agent was not affected in its capacity to accept service by such conflict as there might have been.

(vii)   Service was properly effected under CPR 6.15.

Application refused.

Sommerville v Bain and others

Limitation Act 1980, s 33

Court of Appeal   Lexis, 5 February 1985

On 12 April 1980 the claimant (Ms Sommerville) was having a driving lesson when the car she was driving mounted a kerb and collided with a tree. She sustained a laceration to her skull and severe continuing headaches. Her case was that Mrs Segui, her instructor, negligently permitted her loss of control of the car.

On 14 February 1983 the claimant commenced county court proceedings against R Bain (male) trading as Robi Driving School. A short and unrevealing defence was filed. When in due course a full defence was lodged, it took the point that Mr Bain was the manager (not the proprietor) of the driving school and that Mrs Segui was an independent contractor (not his servant).

The claimant applied promptly thereafter, but outside the three-year limitation period, to join Mrs Segui and another as defendants. Mrs Segui, who had been assisting Mr Bain with evidence, did not realise when she attended the hearing of the application on 26 March 1984 that she was there as a potential tortfeasor instead as a mere witness. Moreover the claimant's solicitor's affidavit did not focus upon the matters which it would have been essential for the judge to consider in exercising discretion under s 33 of the Limitation Act 1980.

HH Judge Dobry QC ordered that leave be given to the claimant to add Mrs Segui as a defendant. Mrs Segui appealed.

Held:

(i)   The limitation period had run out before the application to join Mrs Segui as defendant. In the circumstances, leave could only have been obtained from the judge to join her by virtue of his exercising his discretionary powers under s 33.

(ii)   The judge did not direct his mind to the provisions of s 33, or to the specified matters to which he had to have particular regard, or to the discretionary exercise that he had to perform. His order must be quashed.

(iii)   The court did not have before it all the material which should be available in order to discharge the obligation imposed upon it by s 33. Accordingly, the application would have to be reheard by another county court judge, with both sides being at liberty to put forward any additional material that they deemed to be relevant.

Spade Lane Cool Stores & others v Kilgour

CPR 6, 7

HHJ Toulmin (sitting in the QBD)   **LTL 25/6/2004**

The claimants issued proceedings just before the expiry of the limitation period against the defendant, an architect, in relation to a fire at a business premises. Shortly before the expiry of the four-month validity period stipulated in CPR 7.5, the claim form was sent to the defendant's previous business address (current at the time of the construction of the premises). The defendant had in fact moved and changed its name. There had been no attempt to conceal these changes and the defendant had informed its professional body, RIBA, of them. The defendant subsequently received correspondence form the claimants at his correct address, and a claim form was sent there after the expiry of the validity period. A preliminary hearing was ordered to decide the issue of valid service. The claimant's evidence was that they had searched for the defendant on the internet and the RIBA directory but discovered no current address.

Held:

(i)   The phrase 'last known place of business' in CPR 6.5(6) meant the last place of business know to a claimant. To obtain the requisite knowledge a claimant had take reasonable steps to ascertain a defendant's current or last known business address. It was a matter of evidence whether a claimant had discharged this test.

(ii)   In this case the claimants had not satisfied the test. The defendant was a professional architect and his current address could have been found through RIBA or the yellow pages. The failure of a search of the RIBA directory should have prompted further enquiries. The claim form had therefore not been served within the validity period.

(iii)   It was not appropriate to extend time for service under CPR 7.6. Service had failed because (a) the claimants had made insufficient attempts to identify the defendant's last known place of business, and (b) because service had only been attempted at the last moment of the limitation period. The question of prejudice to the defendant was irrelevant. The test for granting the application focused on any injustice to the claimant. In this case, the claim form would have been served in time had the claimants taken reasonable steps to do so (*Hashtroodi v Hancock* (p466) applied).

Preliminary issue decided in the defendant's favour. Claim struck out.

Spargo v North Essex District Health Authority

Limitation Act 1980, s 11, s 14

Court of Appeal   **[1997] 8 Med LR 125; (1997) 37 BMLR 99;
                                                [1997] PIQR P235**

In the early seventies the claimant began develop psychiatric problems because of family problems and the consumption of barbiturates. In 1973 she was diagnosed as suffering from drug-induced psychosis and admitted as a voluntary patient to the defendant's hospital. She was released soon afterwards but readmitted towards the end of 1974. She was discharged in March 1975. She quickly deteriorated again and was compulsorily admitted on 16 April 1975 having been found wandering about in her nightdress in a confused and emaciated state. She was detained until November 1984 despite several appeals to the Mental Health Appeals Tribunal.

Throughout her detention she was under the care of Dr Marshall, a consultant psychiatrist who died in March 1994. Dr Marshall diagnosed frontal lobe damage as the cause of the claimant's problems which had resulted from excessive purging and dieting. The defendant later admitted that this was a misdiagnosis, although not a negligent one. The parties also agreed that the claimant's behaviour justified her continued detention. However, the claimant contended that but for the misdiagnosis she would have received effective treatment leading to a much earlier release.

The claimant issued proceedings on 14 December 1993, complaining that negligent diagnosis led to her unnecessarily prolonged detention in the psychiatric award with catastrophic consequences on her life. The defendant pleaded limitation which was heard as a preliminary issue. The controversial question was when the claimant attributed her injuries to the defendant's acts or omissions so as to fix her with knowledge. The judge found that, notwithstanding that she had discovered the lack of organic brain damage in January 1986 and instructed solicitors in October of that year, the claimant did not have actual knowledge until she received an expert's report on 22 July 1991. Although the claimant's solicitors had not taken all reasonable steps, his failures were not so great as to either constitute negligence or require to the claimant to chivvy him. The claimant was therefore not fixed with constructive knowledge. The defendant appealed.

Held:

(i) Summarising previous leading authorities (*Halford v Brooks* (p453), *Nash v Eli Lilly* (p568), *Broadley v Guy Clapham* (p345), *Dobbie v Medway HA* (p411), *Smith v West Lancashire HA* (p657), *Forbes v Wandsworth HA* (p434)) the following principles applied to the question of knowledge:

    (a) the knowledge required to satisfy s 14(1)(b) was a broad knowledge of the essence of the causally relevant act or omission to which the injury is attributable;

    (b) 'attributable' in this context means 'capable of being attributed to' in the sense of being a real possibility;

    (c) a claimant has the requisite knowledge when she knows enough to make it reasonable for her to begin to investigate whether or not she has a case against the defendant. Another way of putting this is to say that she will have such knowledge if she so firmly believes that her condition is capable of being attributed to an act or omission which she can identify (in broad terms) that she goes to see a solicitor to seek advice about making a claim for compensation;

    (d) on the other hand she will not have the requisite knowledge if she thinks she knows the acts or omissions but in fact is barking up the wrong tree; or if her knowledge of what the defendant did or did not do is so vague or general that she cannot be expected to know what she should investigate; or if her state of mind is such that that she thinks her condition is capable of being attributed to the act or omission alleged to constitute negligence, but she is not sure about this, and would need to speak to an expert before she could be properly be said to know that it was.

(ii) In this case the judge erred by applying an overly sophisticated approach to the question of knowledge and by substituting the requirement of attribution with the much higher test of definite knowledge of causation. Such an approach prevented time from running until a much more advanced stage of investigation than was appropriate.

(iii) The claimant had knowledge for the purposes of the act in October 1996 when she instructed solicitors. She had a firm belief that her condition was attributable to the defendant without obtaining expert confirmation (*Nash v Eli Lilly* distinguished).

(iv) There was therefore no need to address the question of constructive knowledge. The claim was issued out of time.

Sparks v Harland

Stay   **Limitation Act 1980**

QBD (Sedley J)   **[1997] 1 WLR 143; (1996) Times, 9 August**

The claimant, who attained majority in 1986, issued proceedings against the defendant in 1995 claiming damages for personal injuries occasioned by a series of indecent assaults between 1982 and 1984. The master struck the claim out as statute barred by s 2 of the Act. The claimant appealed that the appropriate course was to stay the action.

Held:

(i)   There was nothing that required a statute barred action to be struck out when RSC Ord 18 r 9 gave the court a discretion to instead order a stay.

(ii)   There was a case awaiting determination before the ECHR (*Stubbings v UK* (p678)) which could have the effect of retrospectively relaxing the six-year rule. This was a relevant consideration.

(iii)   Given the prospect of the change in law and the difficulties in subsequently issuing new proceedings the balance of justice favoured a stay.

NB: The discretion referred to in (i) above is now contained in CPR 3.1(2)(f).

Spencer v Secretary of State for Work and Pensions

Limitation Act 1980, s 2

Court of Appeal   **[2008] EWCA Civ 750; [2009] QB 358;**
[2009] 2 WLR 593; [2009] 1 All ER 314;
[2008] CP Rep 40; [2009] RTR 5;
[2008] 3 CMLR 15; [2008] Eu LR 779;
[2008] ICR 1359; [2008] IRLR 911; [2008] PIQR P21;
(2008) 152(27) SJLB 31; (2008) Times, 24 July

The first claimant had been injured by an untraced driver in April 1995. He applied for compensation to the Motor Insurers' Bureau under the Motor Insurers' Bureau (Compensation of Victims of Untraced Drivers) Agreement 1972 and, in June 1999, was awarded damages. On 8 February 2000, on his appeal to an arbitrator, the award was increased. On 3 February 2006 the claimant brought a claim for damages against the Secretary of State, alleging that the United Kingdom had failed correctly to implement article 1(4) of Council Directive 84/5/EEC, resulting in a scheme for compensation which was inadequate. This was said to be on the bases that (1) his legal costs were not properly reimbursed under the MIB scheme; (2) interest not awarded, again alleged to be due to a defect in the MIB scheme; and (3) damages alleged to be inadequate due to an unfair procedure attributable to a defect in the MIB scheme.

The second claimant suffered a repetitive strain injury at work in 1996. He brought a claim against his employer in November 1999, seeking damages for negligence and for breach of statutory duty in failing to carry out a general risk assessment. Since the relevant regulations excluded civil liability for breach, the claim could only proceed on the basis of negligence. In March 2002 the claim was dismissed, and in October 2002 an appeal by the claimant was also dismissed. In January 2006 the claimant made a claim against the defendant for its alleged failure to implement art 6(2) of Directive 89/391 into the Management of Health and Safety at Work Regulations 1992.

The defendant obtained summary judgment in both cases on the basis that, if a cause of action accrued for '*Francovich*' damages (that is, damages against a government for failing to implement European law), it did so when the claimants suffered their personal injuries and that the claims were barred by s 2 of the Limitation Act 1980.

The claimants appealed, arguing that, until there was a decision on their case, under which they had not received that to which they asserted proper implementation would have entitled them, no cause of action had accrued. It was argued that in the first claimant's case the decision relied on was not the original decision of the adjudicating panel of the Motor Insurers' Bureau but that of an arbitrator on appeal under the 1972 agreement. In the second claimant's case it was argued that the relevant time began when the original claim against the employer was dismissed. They further argued that it was a principle of Community law that they were bound to exhaust all domestic remedies before pursuing a claim to *Francovich* damages, and no cause of action arose until all domestic remedies had been exhausted.

Held:

(i)   The *Francovich* claims fell to be treated as claims in tort in respect of which the strict period of six years from the date upon which the cause of action accrued applied. They were claims for economic loss analogous to a solicitor failing to provide an appropriate term in a contract or an insurance broker failing to provide an effective policy of insurance.

(ii)   When the second claimant suffered his personal injury, he also suffered loss in relation to his claim against the government because, although he had a claim against his employer, the claim he had was not as valuable as the claim he would say that he should have had.

(iii)   Similarly, the first claimant suffered damage as a result of the alleged failure of the government when he was injured by an untraced driver, since such claim as he had under the Motor Insurers' Bureau scheme was of less value to him than he would assert it should have been. The fact that the losses could not be quantified or were in one sense contingent was not to the point. As long as some measurable damage had been suffered, the cause of action would accrue.

(iv)   A measurable loss was suffered by both claimants in relation to their claims against the government when they suffered their injuries (*Nykredit Mortgage Bank Plc v Edward Erdman Group Ltd (Interest on Damages)* [1997] 1 WLR 1627, *Knapp v Ecclesiastical Insurance Group Plc* [1998] Lloyd's Rep IR 390 and *Law Society v Sephton & Co* [2006] UKHL 22, [2006] 2 AC 543 applied).

(v)   The United Kingdom was in breach if it failed to implement the Directive. So far as the first claimant was concerned, the UK had to be assumed to have been in continuous breach up until the moment he was injured by an untraced driver. Once the claimant suffered damage from the breach, that completed his cause of action against the government. The obligation of the government to the claimant, once he had suffered damage for its failure, was to pay damages. The instant case was not one in which there was a continuous damage (*Phonographic Performance Ltd v Department of Trade and Industry* [2004] EWHC 1795 (Ch), [200] 1 WLR 2893 distinguished). The claimant did not suffer a series of accidents, each of which would produce different damage and a fresh cause of action. His claim arose out of one accident and it was at the date of that accident that he suffered damage.

(vi)   It was not a precondition of bringing a *Francovich* claim that domestic remedies had been exhausted (*Autologic Holdings Plc v Inland Revenue Commissioners* [2005] UKHL 54, [2006] 1 AC 118 considered and *Brasserie du Pecheur SA v Germany* (C-46/93) [1996] QB 404, ECJ, applied).

(vii)   The second claimant's argument, that reasons of costs would have made it excessively difficult to bring a claim against the Secretary of State at the same time as a claim against his employers, and that that was contrary to the Community law principle of effectiveness, was not on point. There was no distinction between a *Francovich* cause of action and any other, so far as the risk of costs was concerned. Costs could not be said to make it virtually impossible to bring a *Francovich* claim at the same time as the claim against the primary tortfeasor. There were ways of mitigating that risk, for example by seeking an arrangement to stay the proceedings against one defendant while the case against the other was fought out. If such an arrangement had been offered, and it was unreasonable to refuse it, that might well have led to the court exercising its discretion as to costs against the party acting unreasonably.

Appeals dismissed.

Per Stanley Burnton LJ: '51. In a sense, Mr Spencer's *Francovich* cause of action was contingent: if well founded, it could be said to have been contingent on Boots not having been negligent and not having committed a relevant breach of the Manual Handling Operations Regulations 1992 but having been in breach of the Management of Health and Safety at Work Regulations 1992. But these are not true contingencies, in the sense of events that may or may not occur. They are facts that occurred when he suffered his injury. There may be cases where such facts are undisputed; there will be cases where they are the subject of dispute. But the existence of a dispute does not detract from the fact that they have already occurred.

52. Thus it follows that if the facts on which Mr Spencer's *Francovich* claim depends did occur, he suffered loss when he suffered his injury. He then had no cause of action against Boots because, if his allegations are well founded, the Secretary of State had failed properly to implement the Framework Health and Safety Directive.'

Spensley v Boots Company plc

Limitation Act 1980, s 14, s 33

QBD   **23 October 1998, unreported**

See *Brooks and others v Boots Company plc* (F) (p348)

St Helens Metropolitan Borough Council v Barnes

Limitation Act 1980, s 11   **CPR 7.2**

Court of Appeal   **[2006] EWCA Civ 1372; (2006)**
Times, 17 November; LTL 25/10/2006

The claimant alleged that he suffered personal injuries as a result of the local education authority's negligence in the way that he was educated. The claimant delivered the claim form to the county court on the day prior to the expiry of limitation with a request that the claim be issued. However, the claim form was not issued until four days later due to industrial action. The defendant sought to rely upon a limitation defence, arguing that under CPR 7.2 proceedings were not started until the claim form was issued. The judge, with reference to CPR 7 PD 5, held that proceedings were 'brought' pursuant to the 1980 Act and 'started' pursuant to the CPR simultaneously when the claimant delivered the claim form to the court.

The defendant appealed.

Held:

(i) Provided that a claimant took any necessary step to enable proceedings to be started, he did not take the risk that the court might be closed or would not process the claim properly.

(ii) The expiry of the limitation period was fixed by reference to something that the claimant had to do. The claimant had done all he could when he brought the claim form to court with a request that it be issued. The time the court took to comply with this request was not a matter within his control.

(iii) The proper construction was that proceedings were 'brought' when the claimant's request was for the issue of the claim form was delivered to the court during its opening hours. The receipt of the claim from by the court did not involve any transitional act. The court staff who received it were not performing a judicial function and had no power to reject it. The date stamp of receipt on the claim form will indicate when the proceedings were brought.

(iv) There was a difference between when proceedings were 'brought' and when they 'started'. The latter was the date of issue which is the date that the court staff enter on the claim form.

(v) The date of the claim form (the date the proceedings were 'started') fixed the time within which proceedings had to be served.

(vi) Different considerations might apply if delivery of the claim form was made to the wrong place or outside office hours. These issues would need to be considered if they arise.

Appeal dismissed.

Stacey v Joint Mission Hospital Equipment Board Ltd

CPR 51, 3

Owen J   **LTL 5/11/2001**

The claimant was struck on the head by a wooden pallet on 27 February 1987 whilst working for the defendant, suffering a very serious head injury. A claim was intimated three months later and proceedings issued on 15 February 1988. Thereafter the claimant's conduct was characterised by marked inactivity. On 26 April 2000 the claim became subject to an automatic stay under CPR 51. The claimant applied to lift the stay. The district judge allowed the application but imposed the following terms: the claimant was precluded from claiming losses beyond those set out in his schedule of 21 April 1998, and was precluded from claiming interest from 1 January 2000. The claimant appealed.

Held:

(i) The proper approach to lifting an automatic stay was as follows:

    (a) the application be determined with reference to the overriding objective;

    (b) the court had to consider the circumstances set out in CPR 3.9;

    (c) the onus was on the party seeking to lift the stay to show that it was just and reasonable to do so;

    (d) the rule applicable to the analogous application to strike out applied;

    (e) the court could take a middle course between refusing the application outright and lifting the stay unconditionally.

(ii) The fact that the claimant in this case was a patient who was therefore still within the limitation period was a relevant but not decisive factor (*Hogg v Hamilton* (p479) applied).

(iii) There was no conflict between the imposition of conditions and the court's duty to protect a litigant under a disability.

(iv) The delay had caused substantial prejudice to the defendant. The district judge's approach could not be faulted.

Appeal dismissed.

Stanley v Eli Lilly & Co and others

Limitation Act 1980, s 11, s 14

Court of Appeal   **[1992] 3 Med LR 390**

See *Nash v Eli Lilly & Co* (K) (p568)

Stannard v Stonar School

Limitation Act 1939, s 2D

HH Judge Hawser   **[1979] CLY 1671**

On 22 September 1974 the claimant (Mr Stannard) was injured in an accident at work. In February 1975 he consulted a solicitor who advised him that he had three years in which to decide whether to proceed. Although severely incapacitated, he returned to work and took no action in the hope that he would recover from his injures. In August 1976 he was informed by the DHSS that he had been assessed as 70% disabled. He did not tell his employers of the extent of the injuries until February 1977, because he was afraid of losing his job.

In March 1977 he saw the same solicitor and applied for legal aid. In June 1977 he instructed his solicitor 'to do whatever was necessary'. Although the solicitor sent a letter to the defendants' solicitors in June 1977, he took no further action until September 1978. The writ was issued on 10 November 1978, and the statement of claim was served in April 1979.

The defence pleaded limitation. At the preliminary trial the defendants deposed that documents had been destroyed or lost, witnesses might not be found and the locus in quo had been altered. Their insurers had inspected it in October 1974 and had taken a statement from a witness then.

Held:

(i)   The cogency of the defendants' evidence was not likely to be significantly reduced, as they had investigated the accident within five weeks of its occurrence. There was a reasonable likelihood of witnesses being traced and of them having good recollections as the accident was a memorable one: s 2D(3)(b).

(ii)   Although the claimant had not acted promptly, he had acted reasonably in all the circumstances: s 2D(3)(e).

(iii)   It was not clear that the claimant could succeed against his former solicitor, as there was the possibility of a misunderstanding: s 2D(3)(f).

(iv)   If s 2A was not disapplied, the prejudice to the claimant would be serious. As the defendants would not be so prejudiced otherwise, it would be equitable to allow the action to proceed: s 2D(1).

Steadman v Scholfield and another

Maritime Conventions Act 1911, s 8

Sheen J   **(1992) Times, 15 April; [1992] 2 Lloyd's Rep 163**

On 6 August 1988 the claimant (Mr Steadman) was riding a jet ski off Brighton. He sustained severe injuries when he collided with a speed boat driven by the first defendant and part owned by the second defendant. The jet ski was described by the manufacturers as a 'personal watercraft'.

On 20 June 1991 the writ was issued. The defendants applied to strike out the action on the ground that it was statute barred by the two-year time limit under s 8 of the Maritime Conventions Act 1911. The district judge refused the application. The defendants appealed.

Held: a jet ski was not a vessel used in navigation: s 8 of the 1911 Act did not apply. Therefore the action had been commenced in time.

The defendants' appeal was dismissed.

Steeds v Peverel Management Services Ltd

Limitation Act 1980, s 33

Court of Appeal   **[2001] EWCA Civ 419;**
(2001) Times, 16 May; LTL 30/3/2001

The claimant suffered serious injuries when he slipped on a patch of ice on 26 December 1996. Five months later he instructed solicitors to pursue the defendant for damages on the basis that the ice was a result of an overflow on the defendant's premises. They notified the defendant of the claim seven months after that. Correspondence ensued wherein the defendant indicated that they were prepared to accept primary liability subject to a reduction for contributory negligence. Due to an oversight proceedings where not issued until 49 days after 26 December 1999 when limitation expired. The claimant applied to disapply s 11 of the Act. The district judge refused on the basis that the delay had to be considered in the round and to grant the application would be to excuse the negligence of the claimant's solicitors. The claimant appealed.

The circuit judge criticised the district judge's reasoning but reached the same result on five bases: the claimant's five-month delay before instructing solicitors had not been explained, the seven months between initial instruction of solicitors and notify the defendant had not been explained, the defendant asserted prejudice arising from these delays, there was a further delay of 49 days in issuing proceedings when limitation had expired and the claimant had a cast-iron claim against his own solicitors. The claimant appealed again.

Held:

(i)   The case was indistinguishable from *Thompson v Brown* (p690). The district judge had erred in distinguishing it and also in attributing to the claimant the faults of his solicitors.

(ii)   The district judge had thus erred in treating the claimant's good claim against his solicitors as the determinative reason for dismissing the application and as a justification for teaching the claimant's solicitors a lesson (*Thompson v Brown*, *Whitfield v North Durham* (p713), *Das v Ganju* (p398) and *Corbin v Penfold Metalising* (p387) applied).

(iii) The claimant's faults were relevant but those of his solicitors were not to be attributed to him.

(iv)   Whilst not determinative, the claimant's claim against his solicitors was a highly relevant factor (*Thompson v Brown*).

(v)   Although the seven-month delay in notifying the defendant was potentially relevant, the circuit judge was wrong to hold that any evidential prejudice to the defendant flowed from it. The accident occurred in darkness during the holiday season and the defendant's chances of finding a witness after the first few weeks had passed were minimal. The circuit judge also erred in attributing the solicitor's faults to the claimant.

(vi)   The court therefore exercised the discretion afresh. This was not a thoroughly stale claim. The delay of five months before instructing solicitors was not unreasonable in the context of a claim for serious injuries. No blame could be attached to the claimant personally. The defendant had suffered no evidential prejudice and would suffer no more than the inevitable prejudice of the loss of a limitation defence. The claimant would suffer greater prejudice if the claim were barred and he had to resort to pursuing his own solicitors. It was therefore equitable to allow the claim to proceed.

Appeal allowed. The claimant's solicitors had, when obtaining leave to appeal, agreed to pay the costs of the appeal in any event.

NB: This decision must be doubted in the light of *Horton v Sadler* (p482).

Steele v Mooney

CPR 7.5, 7.6, 3.10

Court of Appeal   **[2005] 2 All ER 256; [2005] EWCA Civ 96;**
                                                        (2005) WLR 2819

The claimant was admitted on 9 May 2000 for a vaginal hysterectomy. The defendant performed the surgery. The claimant's case was that he performed a scarospinous fixation without her consent and negligently delayed in treating a haemorrhage, resulting in her suffering psychological injury. Although she tried to pursue a complaint for about two years, the claimant did not consult solicitors until 22 April 2003. Proceedings were issued on 6 May 2003, three days within the primary limitation period. The claim form was not served within the four months stipulated by CPR 7.5(2).

On 21 July 2003 the claimant unsuccessfully attempted to negotiate an extension of time for service of the particulars of claim and 'supporting documentation including the claim form'. On 13 August 2003 the issued an application for a four-month extension 'for the service of the particulars of claim and supporting documentation'; the words 'and the claim form' were omitted by mistake. On 15 August 2003 the application was allowed. On 10 December 2003 the claimant, having informed the defendant, applied for a further extension in identical terms. This was granted until 29 January 2004. On 18 February 2004 the claimant's solicitor realised her previous errors and applied under CPR 3.10 for the orders to be rectified to include extension of time for service of the claim form.

The claimant's applications succeeded at first instance, the deputy district judge distinguishing *Vinos v Marks and Spencer* (p701). The defendant appealed. The circuit judge allowed the appeal on the basis that the error was not procedural and therefore could not be remedied by CPR 3.10. The claimant appealed this decision.

Held:

(i)   The claimant's last application was an application to correct an error in an application to serve out of time properly made under CPR 7.5(2). It was not in itself actually an application to serve out of time and therefore was not caught by the strict criteria of CPR 7.6(3). There was a distinction between making an application containing an error and not making an application at all (*Vinos v Marks and Spencer* and *Elmes v Hygrade Food Products* (p423) distinguished).

(ii)   There was no reason to give the words 'procedural error' in CPR 3.10 an artificially restricted meaning or to distinguish between a procedural and a drafting error. CPR 3.10 thus applied.

(iii) The claimant had good reasons for late service; she needed further medical evidence and counsel's opinion before deciding whether the merits of her claim justified pursuing it.

Appeal allowed.

Stephen v Riverside Health Authority

Limitation Act 1980, s 11, s 14

Auld J   **[1990] 1 Med LR 261; (1989) Times, 29 November**

On 11 March 1977 the claimant (Mrs Sheila Stephen), who had worked as an unqualified radiographer in the 1950s, underwent a mammography at Charing Cross Hospital. The radiographer handled the equipment poorly and took 10 films instead of 4–6. The claimant suffered erythema in her upper chest for some three months. Her consultant at the hospital told her that she had received in the mammography a total of 34 roentgen to each breast. On 22 April 1977 she wrote a letter of complaint to the hospital administrator. On 23 May 1977 the administrator replied that the radiation dose of 34 roentgen to each breast could not cause erythema or any other adverse effects. During the next month she saw three other doctors, all of whom reassured her that she was in no danger from the effects of radiation.

The claimant was not unduly concerned about the erythema, but continued to worry over the possibility that she had received an overdose of radiation that might cause her harm in future. In early 1979 she instructed solicitors who wrote to the hospital. Its solicitors replied denying negligence. In October 1979 she instructed a second firm which obtained negative expert advice, issued a protective writ on 6 March 1980 but took no further steps. In 1983 she instructed a third firm which consulted Professor Berry. He raised in March 1984 the possibility that she could have received a very much higher dose of radiation than the 34 roentgen to each breast. His opinions during 1984 were very cautious, referring to the possibility of an excessive dose and the lack of supporting evidence. However, on 20 February 1985 he advised in conference that the 34 roentgen reading would not be reliable if the radiographer was unreliable, that to judge from her erythema the dosage was 300–1000 roentgen to each breast and that this would have increased the risk of cancer developing.

The writ was issued on 15 February 1988. A preliminary trial on limitation was ordered.

Held:

(i)   Despite all the contrary medical opinion, the claimant suspected that she was at an increased risk of cancer. However, her anxiety about this did not amount to knowledge of injury: s 14(1).

(ii)   She undoubtedly knew about her erythema and associated anxiety, but she did not regard these alone as warranting a claim for damages and she was reasonable in not regarding them as sufficiently serious to justify her instituting proceedings: s 14(1)(a), s 14(2).

(iii)   Since she had been told that she had been exposed to 34 roentgen to each breast and that hundreds or even thousands of roentgen would be needed to cause her symptoms, she did not know that her symptoms were capable of being attributed to the mammography until the conference on 20 February 1985: s 14(1)(b).

(iv)   Her past experience in radiography did not constitute her an expert in the field so as to characterise her suspicion as knowledge of attributability, to set off against the chorus of negative opinion by highly qualified experts: s 14(3).

(v)   As her writ was issued on 15 February 1988, within three years of her date of knowledge on 20 February 1985, her case was not statute barred: s 11(4).

Stevens v Nash Dredging and Reclamation Co Ltd

Limitation Act 1980, s 11, s 14, s 33

Leonard J   **Lexis, 27 July 1982**

On 16 July 1975 the claimant (Ainsley Stevens), who was employed as a greaser by the defendants, was working on board the tug Marjan in Swedish waters. The Captain, P Prins, was manoeuvring the anchor and buoy when the anchor cable slid along the gunwale on which the claimant's right hand was resting and caused it severe injury.

In November 1975 the claimant's MP, a barrister, wrote to the defendants who replied that the accident was reported immediately and a full report sent to their insurers within a week. The claimant instructed solicitors who in November 1976 met the insurers' representative who stated that the Marjan was owned, and that Captain Prins was employed by, the defendants' Dutch-based parent company Stevin Baggerin BV. The claimant's solicitors entered into lengthy correspondence with this company. In April 1978 they obtained counsel's opinion which was basically negative in relation to the defendants.

On 8 March 1979 Dutch lawyers wrote that Stevin's insurers had replied that: 'the captain of the tug Marjan was also employed by Nash Dredging & Reclamation Co Ltd ... the direction of the whole project at Lulea (Sweden) was handled by Nash Dredging'. The claimant instructed new solicitors who obtained a copy of the contract showing that Captain Prins was seconded to the defendants. His writ was issued on 31 July 1980. A preliminary trial was ordered.

Held:

(i)   Although the claimant knew from the outset 'the identity of the defendant' (s 14(1)(c)), it was only in March 1979 that he learned 'the additional facts supporting the bringing of an action against the defendant' under s 14(1)(d): ie the employment status of the captain.

(ii)   He could not reasonably have been expected to acquire this knowledge from facts observable and ascertainable by him: s 14(3). His advisers were misled by the meeting with the defendants' insurers in November 1976.

(iii) Accordingly, his action in July 1980 was commenced within three years of his date of knowledge in March 1979: s 11(4).

(iv)   Had s 33 been applicable, discretion would have been exercised in the claimant's favour because of:

    (a)   the above explanation of the delay: s 33(3)(a);

    (b)   the prompt lodging of a report on the accident: s 33(3)(b);

    (c)   the claimant acting promptly once the captain's employment position was discovered: s 33(3)(e); and

    (d)   the fact that he did not have a cast-iron case against his first solicitors: s 33(3).

Stubbings v Webb and another

Limitation Act 1980, s 2, s 28

House of Lords   **[1993] 1 All ER 322; [1993] 2 WLR 120**

The claimant (Lesley Stubbings) was born on 29 January 1957. A local authority placed her with Mr and Mrs Webb in 1959. She was adopted by them in 1960. Their eldest son was Stephen, born in July 1952.

The claimant alleged that between December 1959 (when she was aged two) and January 1971 (when she was 14) she was sexually assaulted by Mr Webb and committed acts of indecency at his instigation, and that in 1972 he punched her around the face and body, causing her nose to bleed more than once. She further alleged that Stephen Webb forced her to have sexual intercourse with him on two occasions in 1969.

In March 1984 she saw a television programme on incest in the family. This led to her introduction to a psychiatrist specialising in child abuse. On 14 September 1984 he gave her her first indication that her psychological problems might be linked with the sexual abuse in childhood.

On 18 August 1987 her writ was issued against Mr and Mrs Webb and Stephen Webb. The master struck out the case. On appeal Potter J held that her action against Mrs Webb was statute barred but not her action against Mr Webb and Stephen. The Court of Appeal upheld his decision, on the basis that the case was governed by s 11 of the Limitation Act 1980 and that the claimant did not have the requisite knowledge of attributability within s 14 before 18 August 1984. The remaining two defendants appealed.

Held:

(i)   The words 'breach of duty', which initially appeared in the proviso to s 2(1) of the Law Reform (Limitation of Actions) Act 1954, did not have the effect of including within the scope of the section all actions in which damages for personal injuries are claimed.

(ii)   The phrase 'breach of duty', lying in juxtaposition with 'negligence' and 'nuisance', carries with it the implication of a breach of duty of care not to cause personal injury; it should not be construed as including deliberate assault.

(iii)   The draftsman had used words of limitation; he had limited the section to actions for negligence, nuisance and breach of duty.

(iv)   Reference to *Hansard* made it clear that the reason he did so was to give effect to the recommendation of the Tucker Committee that the three year limitation period should not apply to a number of causes of action in which damages for personal injury might be claimed, in particular damages for trespass to the person and false imprisonment.

(v)   Rape and indecent assault fall within the category of trespass to the person. Accordingly, the case was governed by the six-year time limit in s 2 of the Limitation Act 1980, not by the provisions of ss 11, 14 and 33.

(vi)   The six-year time limit was suspended by s 28 during the claimant's infancy but started to run when she attained her majority on 29 January 1975. Her action became statute barred in January 1981.

The first and third defendants' appeal was allowed.

NB: This was overruled by *A v Hoare* (p287).

Stubbings and others v UK

Limitation Act 1980, s 2

European Convention of Human Rights, Arts 6, 8, 14

ECHR   **[1997] 1 FLR 105**

The applicants included the claimants in the case of *Stubbings v Webb* (above). They alleged that the non-extendable six-year period under s 2 breached Art 6 (right to a fair trial), Art 8 (right to personal and family life) and Art 14 (right of freedom from discrimination) of the Convention.

Held:

(i)   Limitation principles must not restrict or reduce an individual's access to the court in such a way that the very essence of the right was impaired. The English law of limitation allowed a claimant six years from their 18th birthday to commence civil proceedings. A criminal prosecution could be brought at any time and if successful a compensation order could be made. Thus the essence of the applicants' rights had not been impaired.

(ii)   There was no uniformity between member states as regards limitation periods. The contracting state properly enjoyed a margin of appreciation in deciding how to circumscribe access to the court. The UK legislature had devoted a considerable amount of time and study to the consideration of limitation issues.

(iii)   The six-year period complained of was proportionate and generous. It was longer than that set down in many international conventions applying to personal injury, such as the Warsaw and Athens Conventions (both two years).

(iv)   The UK's limitation rules pursued the legitimate aims of protecting defendants from stale claims, ensuring legal certainty and finality and preventing the injustice of courts adjudicating on events in the distant past based upon evidence degraded by the passage of time.

(v)   Allowing for the developing awareness of child abuse and its psychological effects, member states might in the future have to amend the rules or make special provision in such circumstances. However, currently, taking into account the legitimate aims of limitation rules and the margin of appreciation, there was no breach of Art 6.

(vi)   There was no separate issue under Art 8. Although the abuse clearly fell under the scope of the Article, it was prohibited under criminal law, under which such conduct was viewed very seriously indeed, and thus protected.

(vii)   Not every difference in treatment constituted a breach of Art 14. The applicants had to establish preferential treatment of other persons in a analogous or relatively similar situation where there was no objective justification for the distinction. The victims of intentional and negligently inflicted harm were not in analogous situations for the purposes of Art 14. Different factors applied. For example, it might be more readily apparent to a victim of an intentional wrongdoing that they had a cause of action.

(viii)   Even if the situations were analogous, the differential treatment was objectively justifiable again by reference to the groups' distinctive characteristics. The contracting states enjoyed a margin of appreciation in assessing whether and to what extent differences in otherwise similar situations justified differential treatment at law.

(ix)   (per Judge Foighel, partly dissenting) The right to bring a civil claim was not met by criminal procedures. The margin of appreciation should not be conceived too widely. The very essence of the applicants' access to the court had been impaired and there was a breach of Art 6.

(x)   (per Judge MacDonald, partly dissenting) (a) In the circumstances of child abuse, where the victims did not appreciate their injuries until many years later, the six year period impaired the very essence of their access to the court and breached Art 6. (b) there was also a breach of Art 14. When the positions of victims of intentional and unintentional acts were compared, the differentiating measure was unreasonable and disproportionate.

Conclusion: (by seven votes to two) no violation of Art 6; (unanimously) no violation of Art 8; (by eight votes to one) no violation of Art 14.

NB: The domestic principle was overruled by *A v Hoare* (p287). However, the ECHR ruling remains highly pertinent as to the margin of appreciation enjoyed in the implementation of limitation rules before Convention rights would be offended.

Sullivan v Devon County Council

Limitation Act 1980, s 11, s 14, s 33

Truro CC (HHJ Rucker)   **CLY 03/1163**

The claimant, who suffered from dyslexia, had been educated by at least four primary schools before moving to secondary school. The claimant's mother claimed to have notified the primary schools of the claimant's condition. The claimant left secondary school with poor qualifications and a subnormal reading age. She issued proceedings claiming that the defendant failed to ameliorate her dyslexia. The defendant applied to strike the claim out as being statute barred and on the merits.

Held:

(i) There was no evidence of negligence against the defendant.

(ii) The claimant had knowledge under the Act when she left school in 1992. This was a personal injuries action, notwithstanding the form of the pleading (*Robinson v St Helens MBC* (p628) applied) and proceedings were therefore issued out of time.

(iii) As regards s 33, there was an unexplained lapse of three years before proceedings were issued. The delay had made the evidence less cogent. Records were lost and teachers could not now be traced. The case was a weak one. It would not be appropriate to allow it to continue.

Claim struck out.

The Sunoak

Maritime Conventions Act 1911, s 8

Hewson J   **[1960] 2 Lloyd's Rep 213**

On 20 April 1958 the Norwegian motor vessel Sunoak collided with an Italian steamship, the Peppinella, in the Strait of Dover. The Peppinella sank, as a result of which the master, Giuseppe Martinolich, lost his life.

His widow consulted an Italian lawyer. In March 1959 he approached an English solicitor who pointed to the needs for a grant of representation of the deceased's estate and a payment on account of costs. The widow, who was in very strained financial circumstances, eventually scraped together £100 which was sent to the solicitor in March 1960. He issued her writ under the Fatal Accidents Acts on 12 April 1960.

Before the solicitor could issue a writ under the Law Reform (Miscellaneous Provisions) Act 1934, he had to become the administrator of the deceased's estate in the UK. Under Italian law, half the estate devolved on other relatives who in this case included nephews and nieces living in various parts of Italy and in Yugoslavia. By the time all their instructions were received, the two-year time limit under s 8 of the Maritime Conventions Act 1911 had expired. Letters of administration were finally granted on 10 June 1960.

The writ on behalf of the late master's estate under the Law Reform (Miscellaneous Provisions) Act 1934 was issued on 27 July 1960. The defendants instituted a motion for an order that this action was not sustainable, as it was commenced outside the two-year time limit.

Held:

(i) The defendants were entitled to have the benefit of this time limit, unless there were special circumstances.

(ii) The widow's impecuniosity was not a sufficient ground for the exercise of the court's discretion.

(iii) Nor were the difficulties of foreign law.

The defendants' motion was upheld.

Sweet v Royal National Lifeboat Institution

Merchant Shipping Act 1995, s 190   **Maritime Conventions Act 1911, s 8**

Tomlinson J   **[2002] EWHC 117; (2002) 99(10) LSG 32;**
(2002) Times, 22 February

The claimant was a coxswain of a pilot boat that was in collision with the defendant's lifeboat on 29 March 1998. He was not physically injured but claimed damages for psychiatric damage, specifically an adjustment order. The claimant's expert indicated that he first suffered symptoms a month after the accident but was unclear as to when these developed into a specific disorder. Proceedings were issued on 22 August 2000. The defendant applied to strike the action out as being time barred. The relevant limitation period being two years pursuant to s 190 of the Merchant Shipping Act 1995.

Held:

(i)   Section 190(3)(b) of the 1995 Act stipulated that time began to run when loss of life or injury was suffered. This contrasted with s 190(3)(a) which stipulated that for damage to ships and property time began to run when the loss or damaged was caused. It also contrasted with the position under s 8 of the predecessor 1911 Act. It was apparent from these distinctions that Parliament intended to deal with the cases differently and that s 190(3)(b) envisaged that the date when time began to run might be later than the date of the collision.

(ii)   The delayed running of time was consistent with the claimant's submission that he had no cause of action before he developed a recognised psychiatric injury.

(iii)   The claimant's evidence was confusing and contradictory as to the date when the specific disorder first occurred and the defendant had produced no evidence. It would be inappropriate in such circumstances to strike the claim out or reach a finding that the claimant's assertion that he did not develop an injury until 1999 was correct. The issued needed to be tried, and could be conveniently done so at the same time as the other medical issues.

Application dismissed.

T v Boys & Girls Welfare Service

Limitation Act 1980, s 33

Court of Appeal   **[2004] EWCA Civ 1747**

The claimant had been placed in an assisted community home managed by the defendant in 1975, when he was 12 years old. In 2002 he had initiated proceedings in negligence against the defendant, claiming damages for severe emotional and psychological damage resulting from sexual abuse allegedly committed by a member of staff of the home. At a preliminary hearing the judge determined, by reference to the relevant date of knowledge, that the limitation period for the claimant's action expired in 2000, and he decided not to exercise his discretion under s 33 of the Limitation Act 1980 to direct that that time limit should not apply. The claimant appealed, arguing that (1) the judge had made the fundamental mistake of considering the whole of the delay in bringing the claim when determining prejudice, as opposed to concentrating on the two relevant years of delay between the expiry of the limitation period and the bringing of the action, and (2) the extra two years of delay was a relatively short period of time and would not have affected the cogency of the evidence.

Held:

(i)   When considering the exercise of his discretion, the judge clearly directed himself that, for the purposes of s 33(3), the delay in s 33(3)(a) was the same as the delay in s 33(3)(b). The judge accordingly stated that the relevant period of delay was the two years after expiry of the limitation period.

(ii)   The issue was essentially a matter of discretion for the judge. A fundamental question was whether or not at the end of the day a fair trial was possible. The evidence of the abuse was uncorroborated, the records of the home had been lost or destroyed, and the evidence of the doctor who interviewed the claimant in 1997 would be less cogent because of the delay. By the time the claim was brought, 28 years had passed since the events that gave rise to the claim, and the service of the claim was the first notice that the defendant had received of those allegations.

(iii) It was no answer to say that the prejudice had only been marginally increased by the fact that the claim was made two years after the limitation period had expired. Parliament had determined in s 11 and s 14 of the Act where the balance of prejudice should normally be struck. It followed that s 33 was only available in special cases, and it was for the claimant in any particular case to establish that his claim was one of those special cases. The mere fact of being asked to deal with a stale claim was itself prejudice, and the staler the claim, the greater the prejudice. The policy of the law was to permit people and organisations to arrange their affairs on the basis that there came a time when they should not be asked to meet such claims. The judge was fully entitled to conclude that the instant case did not come within the category of those where an exception could be made under s 33 (*KR v Bryn Alyn Community (Holdings) Ltd (In Liquidation)* (p505) considered).

Appeal dismissed.

NB: In light of the later cases such as *A v Hoare* (p287), *Cain v Francis* (p360) and *B v Nugent Care Society* (p315), this reasoning is probably unsound. However, it is suggested that the result would be the same, even on the application of later authority.

T O Supplies (London) Ltd v Jerry Creighton Ltd

Service of writ   **Companies Act 1948, s 437**

Devlin J   **[1952] 1 KB 42**

On 27 July 1951 the claimants issued a writ claiming the price of goods allegedly delivered. It was sent by registered post to the defendants' registered office. The defendants did not carry on business there, so their accountants redirected the letter to the defendants' city office. A saleswoman there refused to accept it.

On 15 August 1951 the claimants signed judgment in default of appearance. On 22 August the registered letter was returned through the dead letter office. When execution of the judgment proceeded on 27 August, the defendants learned of the writ.

The master ordered that the judgment and execution be set aside, on the ground that service of the writ was bad as it was sent by registered post instead of prepaid ordinary post. The matter was governed by s 437 of the Companies Act 1948, which provided that a document may be served on a company by leaving it or sending it 'by post' to the company's registered office.

Held:

(i)   The word 'post' was wide enough to cover both registered post and ordinary post. Registration was merely one way of posting a letter.

(ii)   Accordingly, the writ had been duly served and the judgment was regular. (As there was a defence on the merits, the judgment was still set aside.)

Tan v East London and The City Health Authority

Limitation Act 1980, s 33

Chelmsford County Court (HHJ Ludlow)   [1999] Lloyd's Rep Med 389

On 10 May 1987 the claimant's wife was admitted to the defendant's hospital for an elective caesarean section. There was an overnight failure on the part of the defendant to respond to the wife's adrenal hyperplasia. The next day she was severely dehydrated and required hydrocortisone therapy. The caesarean section was delayed until the afternoon of 11 May 1997. The child was already dead. The defendant admitted that its negligence had caused the in utero death. The claimant was informed shortly after delivery that the baby was dead. He arrived at hospital approximately 90 minutes later. He comforted his wife for nearly two hours until the dead baby was delivered. He held it for a few moments after delivery and kept vigil overnight until he witnessed the dead child being placed in a metal box. He suffered psychiatric damage as a result of these events.

The wife's claim settled in 1998. In March 1993 the claimant was informed that he himself could have a claim. He issued proceedings in February 1995. The defendant denied duty of care and pleaded limitation. The issues were heard together at the final hearing.

Held (on limitation, having found for the defendant on the duty of care and dismissed the claim):

(i)   The proceedings were out of time. The claimant knew that the baby's death was caused by the defendant's negligence on 12 May 1987.

(ii)   The court would have exercised its discretion under s 33 on the following grounds:

     (a)   as the claimant's claim was based on substantially the same facts as that of his wife and the medical records were still in existence the evidence remained cogent;

     (b)   the claimant did not know that he had a possible claim until so informed by his wife's solicitors in March 1993, at which point a letter of claim was sent;

     (c)   the claimant's psychiatric evidence was disclosed and psychiatrists for both sides disclosed an expert opinion on the claimant's condition;

     (d)   the claimant relied upon solicitors to pursue his claim;

     (e)   whilst there had been considerable and undesirable delay the only prejudice to the defendant was for interest on damages, which could be remedied.

Tatlock v G P Worsley & Company Ltd

Limitation Act 1980, s 33   Discovery

Court of Appeal   Lexis, 22 June 1989

From 1954 to 1981 the claimant (Mr Tatlock) was employed as a burner by the defendants at their Merseyside factory. In 1978 or 1979 he was required to operate a profile burning machine to cut carbon steel. His case was that fumes from the machines had damaged his lungs and that he became ill in 1980.

In December 1980 he consulted his trade union who instructed solicitors on his behalf. In June 1982 the DHSS assessed him at 5% disabled for life due to 'inhalation of steel dust'. In May 1983 his solicitors obtained a medical report that his respiratory symptoms had not been caused by his work. The claimant was unwilling to accept this, so in 1984 his trade union instructed another firm of solicitors. They obtained a favourable medical report in February 1985. His writ was issued on 17 October 1985.

The district registrar granted the defendants' application for extensive discovery concerning limitation. Boreham J allowed the claimant's appeal against this. By the hearing of the defendants' appeal, the documents in respect of which discovery was disputed were the parts of the claimant's proof of evidence relating to his date of knowledge, the negative medical report in 1983, and correspondence between the medical expert who had provided it and the claimant's first solicitors.

Held:

(i)   Section 33(3)(f) of the Limitation Act 1980 referred to the steps taken by the claimant to obtain expert advice 'and the nature of any such advice he may have received'. If the legislature had intended by that section to override professional privilege entirely, other than as regards the nature of the advice, so as to extend it to the production of the document itself from which the advice was obtained, it would have said so expressly.

(ii)   In the case of *Jones v Searle*, the Court of Appeal lifted the corner of the hem of the garment of legal professional privilege. There the nature of the case was answered by the terms of the interrogatory. That did not support the proposition that there had been some sort of statutory removal of the privilege in relation to documents.

(iii)   The reference to a document or to its contents in a pleading does not waive any legal professional privilege attached to it. The claimant might well in practice have to waive the privilege subsequently in order to be able to rely effectively on the privileged document, but that was a separate matter.

The defendants' appeal was dismissed.

Jones v G D Searle (p499) considered.

Taylor v Anderson

CPR 3.4, 51   **Striking out – delay**

Court of Appeal   **[2002] EWCA Civ 1680; [2003] RTR 21;**
(2003) 100(1) LSG 25

The claimant suffered severe injuries on 18 January 1990 when his car was involved in an accident with the second defendant's vehicle. The claimant injuries rendered him a patient within the meaning of the Mental Health Act 1983 and incapable of ever giving evidence. The second defendant had pulled out to overtake the first defendant's vehicle, which was alleged to have been negligent in parking in a hazardous position. There were counter allegations against the claimant in relation to speed, failure to keep a proper lookout and failure to react in time. Shortly after the accident the police took statements from both defendant drivers as well as two drivers approaching behind the claimant. They also drew up plans setting out the positions of vehicles and indicating braking distances and skid-marks.

Proceedings were issued in October 1994 but very few steps were taken thereafter. In April 2000 the claim was automatically stayed under CPR Part 51. The defendants applied to strike the claim out for delay. The district judge held that because of the delay it was doubtful whether there could be a fair trial. On this basis she struck the action out. The claimant appealed.

Held:

(i)   Proceedings should not be struck out for delay unless an unequivocally affirmative answer could be given to the question of whether there was a substantial risk of a fair trial being impossible.

(ii)   The judge's conclusion that there was considerable doubt as to the possibility of a fair trial was insufficient to justify striking out. Her discretion therefore had to be exercised afresh.

(iii)   The trial judge in this case would have to decide three central issues. These were (a) whether the first defendant was negligent in leaving its vehicle in the position it did, (b) whether the second defendant's position at the time of the collision was a result of its negligence, and (c) whether the claimant's own negligence had contributed to the accident.

(iv)   The factors relevant to the determination of these issues could still be addressed notwithstanding the delay. In particular the trial judge would have the assistance of the contemporaneous statements.

(v)   Accordingly, it could not be said that a fair trial was impossible.

Appeal allowed.

Taylor and others v Taylor

Limitation Act 1980, s 33

Court of Appeal   **(1984) Times, 14 April; [1984] CLY 2025**

On 1 May 1978 Dr Taylor and his wife were travelling as passengers in a car driven by their son. There was an accident in which Dr Taylor was killed and Mrs Taylor was seriously injured. She instructed a firm of solicitors two of whose partners were executors of Dr Taylor's will. In August 1978 they notified her claims. In March 1979 the son's insurers wrote admitting liability.

On 28 April 1981 a writ was issued in the names of Mrs Taylor and the two executors claiming damages under the Fatal Accidents Act 1976 on behalf of Mrs Taylor and damages in respect of her injuries. In September 1982 the claimants' solicitors wrote that they had failed to serve it.

On 29 March 1983 a fresh writ was issued claiming the same relief as the first writ plus damages on behalf of the estate under the Law Reform (Miscellaneous Provisions) Act 1934. The registrar refused the claimants' application for leave to proceed under s 33 of the Limitation Act 1980. Skinner J on appeal confirmed that *Walkley v Precision Forgings Ltd* (p705) prevented leave being granted in respect of the first two claims – the Fatal Accidents Act claim and the personal injury claim – but gave the claimants leave to proceed in respect of the Law Reform Act claim. The defendant appealed.

Held:

(i)   If the judge's order stood, quantum in the first two causes of action would be assessed in an admittedly cast-iron claim for damages by Mrs Taylor against her solicitors, whereas the Law Reform Act claim would be tried in the existing action against the defendant driver, almost certainly by a different judge. Very real practical problems would arise.

(ii)   Although the judge had considered each of the lettered subparagraphs in s 33(3) of the Limitation Act 1980, he did not seem to have considered 'all the circumstances of the case'. Through failing to take into account the above matters, he fell into error.

The defendant's appeal was allowed, and the registrar's order restored.

NB: In cases of death before 1983, damages for loss of earnings (less living expenses) during the last years of life could be recovered under the Law Reform Act, subject to a complex set off against the Fatal Accidents Act. A comparable case could now arise where the death had not been instantaneous, so the estate could have a separate Law Reform Act claim.

Teague v Mersey Docks & Harbour Co and others

Limitation Act 1980, s 14

Court of Appeal [2008] EWCA Civ 1601

The claimant was employed in the Liverpool docks. Between 1967 and 1980 he was employed by the second and third defendants, and between 1980 and 1995 he was employed by the first defendant. This was a very noisy environment. On 13 January 1991 he completed a questionnaire in which he had said that, although his hearing was normal, he did have to shout to make himself heard at work and that this was for 'half the time'. He was given an audiogram at that time, administered by an occupational health nurse working in the docks. Her accepted evidence was that she gave the claimant a warning regarding right high tones, told him that he should wear ear protection, and advised him as to the length of time to be spent in a noisy environment. She also warned him that it would get worse if steps were not taken to address his loss of hearing.

A second audiogram was administered by the same nurse in 1995. It enabled a comparison to be made with the 1991 results. That comparison showed a change of 15 decibels. The previous warnings were repeated, but in stronger terms, and a medical referral indicated. On 27 August 1996 the claimant attended his general practitioner's surgery and was seen by the practice nurse. Her note recorded that the claimant was complaining of hearing problems. She examined both of his ears and found them both to be wax-free. She advised him to make an appointment to see the doctor. The claimant did not follow this advice.

In April 2004 the claimant saw a welfare rights adviser employed by the claimant's subsequent solicitor who considered him to be quite hard of hearing. That adviser asked about previous employment and brought up the subject of noise-induced hearing loss. He advised the claimant to see a doctor. On 21 June 2004 the general practitioner referred him to the ENT department at the local hospital. On 28 September 2004 the ENT doctor diagnosed noise-induced hearing loss.

On 26 August 2005 the claimant issued proceedings. The defendant pleaded limitation, which was heard as a preliminary issue. Shortly before the hearing, the claimant produced a supplementary report from his medico-legal expert to the effect that the audiogram results in 1991 and 1995 were consistent with a lower level of disability than the audiogram results in 2004 which were obtained in the course of preparation of the litigation. The judge refused to admit this additional material on the ground that, in her view, it was irrelevant, because what was important was what the appellant knew and believed in 1991 and 1995, not what an expert witness now considers to be the appropriate interpretation of the audiograms. The judge held that the claimant possessed the relevant knowledge by 1996 at the latest. It had been the claimant's decision not to follow up the advice from the nurse at the GP surgery; a reasonable person in his position would have. The judge declined to exercise her discretion under s 33.

The claimant appealed, challenging the non-admission of the supplementary report and the judge's findings generally.

Held:

(i)   The supplementary report was potentially relevant and should have been admitted. However, as it dealt with the position in 1991 to 1995, and the judge did not fix the claimant with constructive knowledge until 1996, that error did not affect her reasoning.

(ii) Although the judge had not spelt it out, by implication she had clearly found that the injury was significant by 1996. That finding was supported by evidence (*Furniss v Firth Brown* (p439) distinguished). Her conclusions on date of knowledge were sound.

(iii) A renewed application to appeal in respect of s 33 was also refused.

Appeal dismissed.

Thomas v Home Office

CPR 2.11

Court of Appeal   **[2006] EWCA Civ 1355; LTL 19/10/2006**

The claimant suffered an accident work, liability for which was agreed at 80%:20%. Proceedings were issued on 1 October 2004 and should have been served by 1 February 2005.

On 21 January 2005, the solicitors agreed a one month extension for service. The defendant's solicitor made a file note to that effect. On 24 February 2005, a further extension to 1 April 2005 was agreed. Both solicitors made file notes and the claimant's solicitor wrote to the defendant's solicitor recording this agreement that day (the defendant's solicitor made reference to the agreement in a letter to the medical expert a month later). On 30 March 2005, a further extension was agreed, although the parties' file notes differed on whether this was to 6 May or 1 May. There were further extensions given and eventually the claim form was served on 23 June 2005.

The defendant took the point that service took place outside the last agreed extension, but also took the point that there was no valid extension at all beyond 1 February 2005. The judge held that it was not open to the claimant as a matter of principle to rely upon an extension agreed between the parties. The claimant appealed.

Held:

(i)   CPR 2.11 permitted the parties to agree in writing to extend the time for performing an act without reference to the court unless there was a another provision prohibiting such an agreement. There was no explicit rule preventing variation of the four-month period for service, and that the courts should only imply an exclusion of CPR 2.11 from a time limit if it was necessary to do so or if it was obvious that CPR 2.11 was not meant to apply. Neither circumstance applied here.

(ii)   Although this meant that a series of extensions could be agreed without reference to the court, and that this would prevent the court exercises its case management powers. However, situations where a defendant would agree to a very prolonged deferral of service would be unlikely, but would be considered justified by the parties. In this case, for example, service was delayed so that negotiations about the medical evidence and settlement could take place without further escalation of costs.

(iii)   The written agreement did not have to be in a single document, and could be an exchange of correspondence. An oral agreement confirmed by both sides in writing could also qualify.

(iv)   However, there was no written agreement here since: (a) unexchanged file notes do not count; and (b) the defendant did not reply to the claimant's letter noting the agreement, and the letter to the expert did not count.

(v)   Parties would be well advised in such matters to reduce agreements to writing and precisely identify the date in question.

Appeal dismissed.

Thomas v Plaistow

Limitation Act 1980, s 33

Court of Appeal   **[1997] PIQR P540; (1997) 94(17) LSG 25; LTL 24/4/97**

On 14 July 1984 the claimant suffered serious injuries, including a significant head injury, in a road traffic accident. The defendant and the claimant were travelling on a motorcycle. There was a dispute over who was the passenger. The claimant was prosecuted for dangerous driving on the basis that she was the rider but the case collapsed due to lack of evidence, specifically the defendant withdrawing his initial statement blaming the claimant. Her employment and criminal solicitors did not advise her of the possibility of a civil claim.

Limitation expired on 13 July 1987. The claimant first became aware of the existence of the MIB, and thus a meaningful claim in 1992. In April 1994 the claimant began to get flashbacks of the accident when she had previously had no memory of it all. Proceedings were issued on 14 October 1994 and the claimant successfully applied for s 11 to be disapplied by s 33. The defendant appealed.

Held:

(i)   'Disability' for the purposes of s 33(3)(d) was the same as under s 38(2) and required that a claimant be a patient under the Mental Health Act 1983. The claimant did not meet the criterion (dicta in *Bater v Newbold* (p323) disapproved, *Re Maitland* [1995] PIQR 125 followed).

(ii)   However, the fact that the claimant's head injury, whilst not rendering her a patient, made it difficult for her take legal advice, could be a relevant consideration when looking at all the circumstances of the case.

(iii)   Despite misconstruing 'disability', the district judge had come to the right conclusion for roughly the right reasons. He had been entitled to take into account the defendant's statement and later retraction. The defendant's assertions of evidential prejudice were speculative. The claimant's claim against her former solicitors was extremely problematic. The balance of prejudice was for allowing the action to proceed. The appeal would be dismissed.

Thompson v Blenkinsopp Collieries Ltd (In Liquidation)

Limitation Act 1980, s 33

Newcastle upon Tyne County Court (Recorder Lewis)   **17 April 2008, unreported**

The claimant had worked for the defendant as a miner. He began to suffer from symptoms of hand-arm vibration. In January 1996 he acquired actual knowledge of his condition when his general practitioner confirmed that he had vibration white finger. He then instructed solicitors who corresponded with the defendant's insurers, with whom they were in agreement that his claim would be dealt with under a claims handling arrangement, a pre-condition of which was that liability was accepted. In 2000 the defendant denied liability. Under the claims handling arrangement, there was a limitation amnesty for one year after that denial. The parties continued to correspond, with the claimant's solicitors trying to persuade the defendant's representatives to alter their position and pay compensation. His solicitors did not issue proceedings until February 2007, which was over 11 years after the date of actual knowledge, meaning that his claim was over eight years outside the limitation period. Limitation was heard as preliminary issue.

Held:

(i)   There had been a substantial delay in issuing proceedings. There were some reasons for that delay: at the time of expiry of the limitation period, the claimant's solicitors were dealing with the claim under the claims handling agreement which itself had the benefit of postponing the limitation period, although in fact it had already expired. Subsequently, there was no good reason for the delay, because the claimant and his solicitors were aware that, under the scheme, the claim was being denied and yet nothing was done to institute proceedings.

(ii)   The claimant had the benefit of solicitors to investigate the claim and to pursue a claim through the courts at an early opportunity. His solicitors, it seemed, were willing to continue to correspond with the defendant's insurers with a view to forcing a settlement under the scheme. They were clearly entitled to pursue that course but not after the point when they knew the limitation amnesty had expired. There was an unacceptable delay, particularly between May 2000 and the issue of proceedings in February 2007, and a considerable part of it was unexplained.

(iii) The claimant should have had the benefit of his solicitors' advice throughout, but clearly he did not. There was evidence that there would be prejudice to the defendant if the claim were allowed to continue.

Judgment for defendant.

Thompson v Garrandale Ltd

Limitation Act 1980, s 33

Nottingham County Court (Judge MacDuff) **[2000] CLY 528**

The claimant brought proceedings alleging that he was suffering from a disabling form of vibration white finger. He was employed by the defendant during the 1980s and early 1990s, during which time he operated grinding machines. The extent of his exposure to vibration was a matter of dispute between the parties. The claimant conceded that the cause of action accrued more than three years prior to June 1997, that being the date of issue of the proceedings. Limitation was heard as preliminary issue. The claimant conceded that he had the requisite knowledge of the injury pursuant to s 14 by March 1990, but asked the judge to exercise his discretion under s 33. He contended that, although he knew the injury was significant and had been caused by his work, it was not until 1994 that he considered the condition to be sufficiently serious to justify the commencement of proceedings, being at that time more of a nuisance than a disability. As time passed, the claimant's condition deteriorated until he was experiencing constant and serious symptoms. That was supported by the fact that the claimant was assessed for benefits purposes as having two per cent disability in 1991, rising to 20 per cent in 1995.

Held:

(i) The claimant had not satisfactorily explained the delay in bringing proceedings. The evidence showed that he regarded his condition as serious by summer 1994, but did not seek further legal advice until September 1995.

(ii) The defendant would suffer very real prejudice should the claimant be permitted to pursue his claim after such delay, and the claimant had failed to establish exceptional circumstances to outweigh the prejudice to the defendant within the meaning of *Dale v British Coal Corporation (No 2)* (p396).

Claim dismissed.

Thompson and others v Smiths Shiprepairers (North Shields) Ltd and other actions

Limitation Act 1980, s 11, s 14, s 33

Mustill J **[1984] 1 All ER 881; [1984] QB 405; [1984] 2 WLR 522**

The claimants (Albert Thompson and five others) had all worked as labourers or fitters in shipyards. In Mr Thompson's case, this was from 1936 to 1941 and from 1946 to 1983. They were exposed to excessive noise which by stages progressively impaired their hearing.

Their writs were issued around 1981. At a full hearing on liability and quantum, they testified that although they were aware of a compensation scheme that the boilermakers' union had negotiated, it did not occur to them or their union representatives that they might have a cause of action against the defendant employers until a cascade of writs began to be issued.

Held:

(i)   The date of knowledge, for the purposes of ss 11 and 14 of the Limitation Act 1980 was, in the case of each claimant, more than three years before the date on which the writ was issued.

(ii)   The claimants' above testimony was accepted. They had valid claims, albeit small. Any prejudice, which had not been great, caused by the delay since the accrual of their continuing cause of action had damaged them just as much as the defendants. The interests of justice would not be properly served by holding their claims to be statute barred. The court's discretion under s 33 should be exercised in their favour.

The judge found liability established in respect of exposure to noise from (but not before) 1963 and awarded each claimant damages varying between £600 and £1,545.

Thompson v Boots Company plc

Limitation Act 1980, s 14, s 33

QBD   **23 October 1998, unreported**

See *Brooks and others v Boots Company plc* (A) (p348)

Thompson v Brown Construction (Ebbw Vale) Ltd and others

Limitation Act 1939, s 2D

House of Lords   **[1981] 2 All ER 296; [1981] 1 WLR 744;**
125 SJ 377

On 4 March 1976 the claimant (James Thompson) was working as a bricklayer's labourer for the first defendants when scaffolding that had been erected by the second defendants collapsed and he was injured. In April 1976 solicitors notified his claim. In March 1977 the scaffolders' insurers wrote that they were prepared to put forward an offer. Some time after August 1977 the solicitors mislaid and forgot the claimant's file. It was not rediscovered until spring 1979. The writ was issued on 10 April 1979, 37 days after the expiration of the primary limitation period.

It was undisputed (a) that the accident was due to the negligence of the scaffolders and (b) that the claimant would have a cast-iron case in an action for negligence against his own solicitors.

The scaffolders pleaded limitation and a preliminary trial was ordered. Phillips J held that he was bound by an unreported Court of Appeal decision to hold that the provisions of s 2A of the Limitation Act 1939 as amended had not prejudiced the claimant. He gave the appropriate certificate under s 12 of the Administration of Justice Act 1969 to enable the claimant to appeal direct to the House of Lords.

Held:

(i)   Even where, as in this case, the claimant would have a cast-iron claim for at least as much damages against his solicitor, he would suffer some prejudice if his action against the defendants was not allowed to proceed. The availability of the alternative claim against the solicitor was highly relevant but not conclusive: s 2D(3).

(ii)   The onus of showing under s 2D that it is equitable to allow him to proceed rests on the claimant. Subject to that, the court's discretion to make or refuse an order is unfettered: s 2D(1).

(iii) As the judge did not feel free to exercise his discretion, the case must be remitted to him so that he could do so.

Per Lord Diplock: 'even where, as in the instant case, and as in *Browes*, if the action were not allowed to proceed the plaintiff would have a cast-iron case against his solicitor in which the measure of damages will be no less than those that he would be able to recover against the defendant if the action were allowed to proceed, some prejudice, although it may only be minor, will have been suffered by him. He will be obliged to find and instruct new and strange solicitors; there is bound to be delay; he will incur a personal liability for costs of the action up to the date of the court's refusal to give a direction under s 2D; he may prefer to sue a stranger who is a tortfeasor with the possible consequences that may have on the tortfeasor's insurance premiums rather than to sue his former solicitors with corresponding consequences on their premiums ...

Subsection (3) requires the Court to have regard to "all the circumstances of the case", but singles out six matters for particular mention. These six present a curious hotchpotch. "The delay" referred to in para (a) must be the same delay as in para (b); so it means the delay after the primary limitation period has expired. It is the length of this delay (in the instant case 37 days), and the reasons for it, that matter under para (a). Paragraph (b) refers to the extent to which the cogency of evidence likely to be adduced by either the claimant or the defendant is likely to be less as a result of the delay. So far as the diminished cogency affects the defendant's evidence it increases the degree of prejudice he will suffer if the action is allowed to be brought despite the delay; but so far as diminished cogency affects the plaintiff's evidence and so reduces his chances of establishing cause of action if the action is allowed to be brought it lessens the degree of prejudice the claimant will suffer if he is not allowed to bring the action at this late stage.

Paragraphs (a) and (b) are the only two paragraphs which appear to be dealing with matters that affect the extent to which the plaintiff and the defendant will be prejudiced according to whether or not the action is allowed to proceed. Paragraphs (c), (e) and (f), on the other hand, deal with the conduct of the parties, a matter that is always relevant when considering whether it is "equitable" to give a direction granting a benefit to one party at the expense of the other party. Paragraph (d) is restricted to cases where plaintiffs have been under a disability, a class of persons that equity has always been zealous to protect.

Paragraph (c) requires the court to take into account the defendant's conduct ever since the action arose, not, be it noted, from what in the absence of knowledge by the plaintiff of material facts may be the later date when the primary limitation period started to run. The reference in this paragraph to response to resonable requests by the plaintiff for information, recognises an obligation on a potential defendant not to be obstructive in enabling a potential plaintiff to obtain relevant information, though not imposing any obligation to volunteer such information; but in this paragraph the conduct of the defendant must, I think, be understood as including the conduct of this solicitors and his insurers by whom in the ordinary course of things any requests for information will be dealt.

Paragraphs (e) and (f), which deal with the conduct of the plaintiff, appear to be chronologically in the wrong order, at any rate so far as the latter deals with the obtaining of legal advice. Until he has obtained legal advice a plaintiff (unless he is himself a barrister or a solicitor) will not know whether or not he has a cause of action for damages against the defendant, although under s 2A(6) the lack of this knowledge will not prevent the primary limitation from starting to run. The steps he has taken up to the point when he receives advice that he has a possible cause of action are dealt with in para (f), whereas how promptly and reasonably he acted after receiving that advice is dealt with in para (e).

In contrast to para (c), I think it is apparent that paras (e) and (f) are referring to the conduct of the plaintiff himself, as well as that of his lawyers after he has consulted them for the first time. If he has acted promptly and reasonably it is not to be counted against him, when it comes to weighing up conduct, that his lawyers have been dilatory and allowed the primary limitation to expire without issuing a writ. Nevertheless, when weighing what degree of prejudice the plaintiff has suffered, the fact that if no direction is made under s 2D he will have a claim over against his solicitor for the full damages that he could have recovered against the defendant if the action had proceeded must be a highly relevant consideration.'

Thompson v Edmeads

Limitation Act 1939, s 2D

Court of Appeal (1978) 128 NLJ 514; [1977] BLT 261

The claimant was injured in a road accident. The defendant's negligence was admitted, although there was an issue as to whether the claimant had been wearing a seat belt.

Owing to an oversight on the part of her solicitors, her county court summons was issued three months outside the three-year limitation period. The judge exercised his discretion under s 2D of the Limitation Act 1939 as amended in her favour, so as to disapply the standard limitation period. The defendant appealed.

Held: it was not wrong to extend the limitation period where the sole reason for the delay was the negligence of the claimant's solicitor. This should be taken into account in her favour, just as the receipt by her of inaccurate legal advice as to the limitation period would have been.

The defendant's appeal was dismissed.

Thorne v Lass Salt Garvin (A Firm)

CPR 6.2, 6.3, 6.9, 11, PD6

QBD (Wyn Williams J) [2009] EWHC 100 (QB)

The claimant issued a claim form against the defendant, his former solicitors, on 31 January 2008. By virtue of CPR 7.5 the final date for service was 13 May 2008. On 29 May 2008 the claimant sought an order extending time for service of the claim form. This was granted to 6 June 2008. The same order specified that the time for service of the particulars of claim should be extended to 4 July 2008. On 30 May 2008 the claimant contacted another firm of solicitors (H) with a view to instructing them in the professional negligence claim. He was advised to serve the claim immediately and to attend H's offices the following day with as many papers in the case as he could obtain. The claimant did not attend the following day. On 5 June 2008 he contacted H but was told that the solicitor dealing with the case was absent. The following day (6 June 2008) was the last day for service of the claim form. On that day, H phoned the claimant and advised that he serve the claim form and then attend H's office. The claimant did not serve the claim form, but did attend H's office at around 3pm. At around 3.15pm, H faxed a letter, the claim form and the order extending the date of service to the defendant.

The defendant signed a document entitled 'Acknowledgement of Service'. There is a box on the form in which a defendant is asked to state his full name if it is different from the name given on the claim form. The defendant wrote here 'We decline to acknowledge purported service by fax as it did not comply with the requirement of CPR 6.2 and PD 6 and the subsequent purported postal service was out of time'. The defendant ticked the box stating 'I intend to defend all of this Claim' and wrote immediately beside it: 'If it is deemed to have been served on time'. The box opposite the statement: 'I intend to contest jurisdiction' was not ticked.

On 29 July 2008, following service of the particulars of claim, the claimant issued an application for 'An Order dis-applying CPR PD 6.2 to allow for effective service of the claim form on 6 June 2008 by facsimile pursuant to 6.9'. Although this appeared to concede that service was not effective, the claimant contended that, as the defendant was a law firm, PD 6.3.1(2)(a) applied and there had therefore been good service. The judge found that the defendant had not been acting as its own legal representative when the fax was sent and where it had been unaware of the claim form and unaware that it was about to be served upon it on the afternoon concerned. The judge therefore held that the purported service by fax was invalid and ineffective, as the defendant had never indicated that it was willing to accept service by electronic means. He refused to make an order dispensing with service.

The claimant appealed on the grounds that (1) there had been effective service, as the defendant had a dual capacity as a party to the proceedings and a legal representative; and (2) the court should dispense with service as it was an exceptional case, as the defendant was also a firm of solicitors and a firm would have consented to service by fax in such a case if its consent had been sought in advance. A few days before appeal, however, the claimant issued an application to amend the notice of appeal to contend that, as the defendant had not complied with CPR 11, in that it had not (within 14 days of filing the acknowledgement of service) made an application supported by evidence for an order that the court has no jurisdiction to try the claim, it was deemed to have accepted jurisdiction and thus waived any service argument: *Hoddinott and others v Persimmon Homes (Wessex) Ltd* (p477).

Held:

(i)   The claim form had not been validly served when faxed. There was a distinction between a firm of solicitors merely being a party to proceedings and simultaneously being a party to proceedings and acting as solicitors in the litigation. The defendant could not have been acting as its own legal representative in respect of a claim of which it was wholly unaware. The reasoning of the judge was wholly correct.

(ii)   The fact that the defendant was also a firm of solicitors did not make it an exceptional case (*Kuenyehia v International Hospitals Group Ltd* (p524) applied). That fact was simply one of the factors which had to be taken into account in reaching a value judgment about whether or not the case was exceptional.

(iii)   It would be unjust to dispense with service. The attempt at service had been made on the last possible day permitted and had not been in accordance with the CPR. No prior notification of a claim had been given. The defendant had also been advised to serve the claim form seven days before the fax was sent and had not done so. He could have done so by taking it to the defendant's office, even when advised again to do so on 6 June 2008.

(iv)   Permission to amend the notice of appeal to argue the CPR 11 point was refused. The point had been raised too late. It had not been taken below and only surfaced the day before the appeal hearing itself. The reason given for this, that the claimant's advisers were unaware of *Hoddinott*, was not good enough; the decision had been reported many months before the first instance hearing.

Appeal dismissed.

Tolley v Morris

Limitation Act 1939, s 22	**Dismissal for want of prosecution**
House of Lords	**[1979] 2 All ER 561; [1979] 1 WLR 592; 123 SJ 353**

The claimant (Lynne Tolley) was born in November 1961. On 21 May 1964 she was on the pavement holding her mother's hand when she was struck by a motor car driven by the defendant. She sustained brain damage. On 3 May 1967 her writ was issued through her father. It was served on 20 April 1967. Then, through no fault of the claimant and her father, nothing happened until July 1977 when fresh solicitors who had been instructed served notice of intention to proceed. A statement of claim was delivered in August 1977. In September 1977 the defendant applied to dismiss the action for want of prosecution.

The registrar granted this, and Dunn J affirmed this decision on appeal. The Court of Appeal reversed it, relying on *Birkett v James*. It was conceded that there had been inordinate and inexcusable delay, and that this had prejudiced the defendant as all records and statements with regard to the accident had been destroyed. The defendant appealed.

Held:

(i)   Section 22 of the Limitation Act 1939, as amended by s 2 of the Limitation Act 1975, would entitle the claimant until November 1982 to issue a fresh writ for the same cause of action.

(ii)   Accordingly, it would be fruitless to dismiss the present action for want of prosecution. The defendant's appeal was dismissed.

Per Lord Diplock: '... it must not be forgotten that once an action has been started a remedy for inordinate delay by the plaintiff in proceeding lies in the defendant's hands. Under rules of court, he can take steps to compel the plaintiff to comply with the timetable of procedural requirements preliminary to setting the action down for trial; and he himself can set it down if the plaintiff fails to do so.

Where the delay by the plaintiff in taking a necessary procedural step is excessive, he may obtain a "peremptory order" which, unless it is obeyed, attracts the sanction that the plaintiff's action is dismissed. Disobedience to a peremptory order would generally amount to such "contumelious" conduct as is referred to in *Birkett v James* and would justify striking out a fresh action for the same cause of action, as an abuse of the process of the court.'

Birkett v James [1977] 2 All ER 801 followed.

Totty v Snowden
Hewitt v Wirral Cheshire Community NHS Trust

CPR 3, 7, 16

Court of Appeal   **[2002] 1 WLR 1384; [2001] 4 All ER 577;
[2002] CP Rep 4**

These were joined appeals.

In *Totty*, the claimant was severely injured in a road traffic accident on 6 June 1996. Liability was agreed at 85% in her favour on 19 August 1999. On 28 September 1999, the day before the claimant's twenty-first birthday and thus the expiration of the limitation period, proceedings were issued. The claim form was served on 26 January 2000, but particulars were not served until 9 February 2000, 14 days after the four-month period from issue of the claim form prescribed in CPR 7.4(2). The defendant applied to strike out. The district judge ruled that CPR 3.10 gave a discretion to extend time and exercised this accordingly. The defendant appealed. The judge dismissed this. The defendant appealed again.

In *Hewitt*, the claimant allegedly suffered an accident on 23 August 1996 whilst working for the defendant. She instructed solicitors in about June 1999. Proceedings were issued on 17 August 1999. Although there were general allegations on the claim form it was agreed that they did not meet the requirements in CPR 16 for statements of case. Nearly a month after time for service of particulars had passed the defendant applied to set aside service of the claim form. The district judge refused the application. The defendant appealed to the circuit judge who allowed the appeal finding that there was no discretion to allow the claim to continue. The claimant appealed this ruling.

Held:

(i) Particulars of claim were not an integral part of the claim form. This could be seen by the provision for service of the claim form before the particulars.

(ii) The claim form was not defective because of the absence of particulars. CPR 16.8 allowed the court to deal with the case without only a claim form and no statement of case.

(iii) Service of particulars of claim did not fall under CPR 7.6.

(iv) Therefore there was power under CPR 3.10 to extend time for service.

Appeal allowed in *Hewitt*, dismissed in *Totty*.

Trow v Ind Coope (West Midlands) Ltd and another

Service of writ   **RSC Ord 6, r 8**

Court of Appeal   **[1967] 2 All ER 900; [1967] 2 QB 899;**
[1967] 3 WLR 633

On 11 September 1962 the claimant (Mrs Christina Trow) was crossing the yard of an inn when she fell and hurt herself. Her writ against the inn owners and their manager was issued on 10 September 1965. The district registrar stamped on it the court seal and noted on it the time '3.05pm'. On 10 September 1966 the claimant's solicitors left a copy of the writ at 11.59am at the owner's registered office and at 12.49pm they served the other copy on the manager personally.

The defendants applied to set aside the writ as being served out of time. Blain J upheld their appeal from the refusal of the district registrar to order this. The claimant appealed.

Held:

(i) 'Date' means 'day', not 'time'. The 12-month period did not run from 3.05pm on 10 September 1965 to 3.05pm on 10 September 1966. The time of service was immaterial.

(ii) The date with which the period of the writ's validity began was the day of its issue. Beginning with that date of 10 September 1965 and counting a period of 12 months carried the period to the end of 9 September 1966, not 10 September 1966.

(iii) The time for service of this limit expired at midnight on 9 September 1966. Since it was not served until the following day, its purported service was invalid.

The claimant's appeal was dismissed.

Toumia v The Home Office

Limitation Act 1980, s 33

Court of Appeal   **LTL 9/2/1999**

On 2 June 1993 the claimant, a serving prisoner, was assaulted by several fellow inmates. The assault was serious and allegedly involved use of a chisel and other hard instruments. In early 1995 he was advised by his then solicitor that he might have a claim in negligence against the defendant. The claimant maintained that being a serving prisoner caused him difficulties progressing his claim.

In January 1996 that solicitor made an unsuccessful application for legal aid. The solicitor refused to issue proceedings without the benefit of a funding certificate. The claimant instructed further solicitors to proceed through the green form scheme. However, they failed to do so. The claimant contacted the court in mid-May 1996 and filled in various forms to attempt to issue proceedings. Unfortunately, he filled in the wrong forms and they were returned by the court on 4 June 1996.

New solicitors were instructed and proceedings properly issue on 14 August 1996. The defendant filed a defence but did not apply to strike out on limitation grounds until May 1998. The judge allowed the application and declined to exercise his s 33 discretion on the basis that the defendant had been substantially prejudiced by the delay. The claimant appealed.

Held:

(i) The claimant had adduced evidence as to the reasons for the delay and his attempts to issue proceedings in time. In the absence of contrary evidence his explanation had to be accepted as being true.

(ii) The judge had erred in that he had failed to address his mind to the reasons for the claimant's delay as s 33 required him to do. The court was therefore entitled to exercise the discretion afresh.

(iii) The difficulties facing the claimant as a serving prisoner was a relevant factor in the exercise of the court's discretion.

(iv) It was understandable that the claimant had not appreciated that a claim could be directed against the defendant, as opposed to merely against the perpetrators of the assault.

(v) The claimant had done everything within his power to advance his case and the prejudice to the defendant was minimal. It was equitable to disapply s 11.

(vi) As a general rule of practice, applications to strike out on limitation grounds should be made at an early stage in proceedings

Appeal allowed.

NB: *Stubbings v Webb* (p677) not considered.

Turner v W H Malcolm Ltd and another

Dismissal for want of prosecution   **Limitation Act 1980, s 28, s 38**

Court of Appeal   **(1992) Times, 24 August; (1992) 136 SJLB 236**

On 21 October 1980 the car of the claimant (Graham Turner) collided with an articulated vehicle, driven by the first defendants' employee, which had pulled out to overtake a parked car owned by the second defendant. He suffered devastating brain injuries and ever since the accident had been of unsound mind within the meaning of s 38 of the Limitation Act 1980.

His writ was issued in August 1981. Pleading were exchanged by December 1981. In April 1983 the order for directions provided that the case be set down for trial within 56 days. The claimant's solicitors did not comply with this order. In August 1988 his new solicitors served notice of intention to proceed.

In December 1988 both defendants applied to strike out the writ and statement of claim for want of prosecution. The district registrar dismissed their applications. Ewbank J dismissed their appeal, but on terms: 'that the claimant's will not be entitled at the hearing of the action to produce evidence that the claimant's expectation of life has increased beyond 1993 and also that the claimant is deprived of not less than 50 per of his interest on special damages since December 1985'. The claimant appealed.

Held:

(i) In s 28 of the Limitation Act 1980, Parliament had in effect provided that there was no limitation period for a claimant who since the accident was under a permanent disability as defined in s 38.

(ii) *Birkett v James* and *Tolley v Morris* were to the effect that an application to strike out an action for want of prosecution, made when the claimant was entitled under the Limitation Act to start a fresh action on the same cause, should not be granted save in exceptional circumstances.

(iii) The judge had sought by his order to remove the financial prejudice caused to the defendants by the delay. Given that he had no power to strike this action out, it was doubtful whether he had any power to make the order he did and also whether the court had an inherent jurisdiction to prohibit a claimant from calling evidence as to his likely expectation of life at the time of the trial.

(iv) The claimant could bring at any time while his disability lasted a fresh action in which he could not be inhibited, in the medical evidence that he called. Thus the effect of striking out his action, or imposing a condition on its continued progress, was likely to be an extension of time before his claim was finally resolved.

The claimant's appeal was allowed, and the judge's order set aside.

Birkett v James [1977] 2 All ER 801 and *Tolley v Morris* (p693) applied.

UCB Corporate Services Ltd v Halifax (SW) Ltd

Striking out

Court of Appeal   **[1999] CPLR 691; (2000) 97(1) LSG 24; (2000) 144 SJLB 25**

The claimant's case was that in 1989 the defendant overvalued a property which was bought with the assistance of a loan from the claimant. Proceedings were issued on 23 October 1995. A summons for directions was issued on 24 December 1996 and further directions given on 21 February 1997. The action was due to be set down on 30 July 1997 but thereafter the claimant consistently failed to comply with rules and orders of the court. On 17 May 1999 the defendant applied for the action to be struck out as an abuse of process. The application was successful, the judge finding that the claimant had been guilty of wholesale disregard of the rules of the court (*Arbuthnot Latham Bank v Trafalgar Holdings Ltd* [1998] 1 WLR 1426 applied). The claimant appealed.

Held:

(i) Although decisions under the old rules were no longer authoritative (*Biguzzi v Rank Leisure* (p335)) the underlying thought processes were potentially still applicable. The judge had not been wrong to cite *Arbuthnot*.

(ii) There was nothing to suggest that the judge was not aware of alternative sanctions short of striking out.

(iii) It would be ironic if the new rules required greater leniency towards a party in breach of its obligations to the court than did the old. Although the CPR provided a wider and more flexible range of sanctions for less serious breaches, a strike out remained the appropriate remedy in more serious cases.

(iv) The judge's decision was not plainly wrong. The appeal would be dismissed.

UK Highways A55 Ltd v Hyder Consulting (UK) Ltd

QBD (TCC) (Edwards-Stuart J)

CPR 3.1, 16   **[2012] EWHC 3505 (TCC)**

The claimant had engaged the defendant to provide design services in relation to the design of a road. The road was built between 1999 and 2001. The road soon showed signs of surface degradation. In October 2009, the claimant wrote to the defendant in accordance with the Pre-action Protocol for Construction and Engineering Disputes and asserted that the defendant had failed to use all reasonable skill, care and diligence in carrying out the design work. In May 2010, the claimant served the claim form. Before the 14-day period for serving the particulars of claim expired, the claimant invited the defendant to agree to a stay of proceedings in order to allow the protocol process to run its course. The claimant agreed to a three-month stay, and a consent order was made. The parties subsequently agreed to three further stays. The final stay expired on 23 June 2011. Mediation never took place, and the claimant eventually served particulars of claim in September 2012. The particulars of claim introduced a new allegation, described as a 'failure to supervise'.

The defendant applied for summary judgment or to strike out the claim, arguing that, if particulars of claim had to be served within 14 days of service of the claim form, and, within that period, the action was stayed for a period in excess of 14 days, it became impossible to serve the particulars of claim within the prescribed time; thus, the effect of the stay had to be to abrogate that time limit. The claimant submitted that the effect of a stay was to suspend the proceedings until the stay was lifted or until it expired, whereupon they resumed automatically from where they left off; so the effect of a stay was simply to push back any outstanding time limits by an amount of time equivalent to the length of the stay. The claimant's primary case was that it did not require an extension of time to serve the particulars of claim. In the alternative, it applied for an extension of time within which to do so.

Held:

(i)   CPR 3.1 provided that the court could stay any proceedings or judgment, either generally or until a specified date or event. If the court stayed proceedings generally, the stay remained in force until it was lifted, whereas if the court stayed proceedings until a specified date, the stay would automatically cease when that date was reached. That meant that the proceedings would start up again at the point where they left off when the stay was imposed. That approach avoided the 'impossibility' problem raised by the claimant, and had the sensible result that the proceedings could resume where they left off without any party having to go to the trouble and expense of making an application to the court. Accordingly, the defendant's submissions on the point were to be preferred.

(ii)   The time for service of the particulars of claim had expired before the second stay was imposed by consent in September 2010. However, since the parties had plainly intended that the proceedings should be stayed from the date of the first consent order until the expiry of the fourth consent order on 23 June 2011, it would be unjust if the defendant were permitted to take the point that the particulars of claim should have been served in August or September 2010. Further, by agreeing to the making of the subsequent consent orders, the defendant had probably waived its right to take such a point

(iii)   Between June 2011 and March 2012, the parties had continued to discuss the claim and to exchange information on a 'without prejudice' basis. However, by March 2012, the claimant no longer had any reasonable ground for not serving its particulars of claim and pursuing the litigation. It was therefore open to the defendant to complain about the failure to serve the particulars of claim between late April 2012 and September 2012.

(iv)   The defendant had been prejudiced by the overall delay which had occurred since the conclusion of the design some 12 years previously. That prejudice consisted of the loss of documents, the unavailability of many witnesses and the inevitable impairment of individual memories. However, much of that prejudice arose within a few years of the completion of the project. If the claimant were allowed to pursue a claim based solely on negligent design, the balancing exercise that the court had to carry out, having regard to the matters in CPR 3.9, in the context of the history and circumstances of the proceedings, fell to be resolved in favour of allowing most of the claim to proceed (*Price v Price* (p611) and *Fred Perry (Holdings) Ltd v Brands Plaza Trading Ltd (t/a Brands Plaza)* [2012] EWCA Civ 224; [2012] Costs LR 1007 applied).

(v)   However, those parts of the particulars of claim raising the issues of failure to supervise would be disallowed.

Applications granted in part.

The Vadne

(Bartlett v Admiralty and another)

Maritime Conventions Act 1911, s 8

Lord Merriman P   **[1959] 2 Lloyd's Rep 480**

On 12 July 1957 the claimant and her husband (Reginald Bartlett) were passengers in the steam ferry boat *Vadne* which collided with the frigate HMS Redpole in Portsmouth Harbour. He was killed and she was injured.

On 30 July 1957 the claimant's solicitors notified her claim to the Treasury Solicitor. In subsequent correspondence, the Treasury Solicitor repeatedly stated that liability for her claim must depend on the outcome of the action between the Admiralty and the owners of the *Vadne* and that, immediately the claimant's writ was issued, they would have to apply for a stay of her action pending a decision in the other action.

On 12 June 1959 the claimant herself wrote to the Treasury Solicitor asking when the hearing of that action was likely to commence and adding: 'for nearly two years I have waited fairly patiently for some sign that this matter was moving to its conclusion, but my patience is now completely exhausted'. On 17 June 1959 the Treasury Solicitor wrote sympathetically to explain the position, without mentioning the two-year limitation period under s 8 of the Maritime Conventions Act 1911.

On 25 August 1959 a writ was issued on behalf of the claimant against both the Admiralty and the owners of the *Vadne*. It claimed damages for her own injuries, and as administratrix of her husband's estate for damages under the Fatal Accidents Acts. The Admiralty moved for an order that the action was not maintainable, as it was out of time under s 8 of the 1911 Act.

Held:

(i)   The Treasury Solicitor's correspondence, in particular that on 17 June 1959, although not intending to mislead, was calculated to lull to sleep both the claimant and her advisers.

(ii)   The court's discretion to extend the two-year period under s 8 of the 1911 Act shall be exercised in the claimant's favour. Injustice would occur otherwise.

The Admiralty's motion was dismissed.

Van Aken v Camden LBC

Service   **CPR 2.3, PD 5A**

Court of Appeal   **[2002] EWCA Civ 1724; [2003] 1 WLR 684;**
[2003] 1 All ER 552; [2003] HLR 33;
(2002) Times, 28 October

The defendant made offers of housing to the claimant which she rejected. On 17 July 2001 the defendant notified her that it had accordingly discharged its statutory duty and on 26 November

2001 informed the claimant that it had reviewed its decision under s 202(1)(f) of the Housing Act 1996 and upheld its earlier decision. An appeal from that decision was required to be made within 21 days (see s 204(2) of the Act); accordingly, the final day for filing the notice of appeal was 17 December 2001.

On that day the claimant attempted to file the notice of appeal but the court office had closed for the day. At 6pm the claimant accordingly posted the notice of appeal through the letter box of the court building and faxed a further copy. On the following day the court office authenticated the notice as received on that day. The judge upheld the defendant's contention that the notice of appeal was filed on the 18 December 2001 and was therefore filed out of date. He found that 'deliver' as contained in CPR 2.3 meant the day on which the notice of appeal fell to be dealt with by the court office, and that anything filed after 4pm was to be determined as filed the following day. Further, the judge concluded that there was no power contained in s 204 of the Act to extend the timescale for filing the notice of appeal.

The claimant appealed arguing, inter alia, that the filing of the notice of appeal was a unilateral process that did not require the attention of the court office staff, and that the notice of appeal was filed when it was delivered to the court building. Alternatively, she argued that her failure to file the notice of appeal within the prescribed period was an error of procedure and the court accordingly had power to rectify it under CPR 3.10.

Held:

(i) This was a case that contrasted with *Swainstone v Hetton Victory Club Ltd* [1983] 1 All ER 1179 rather than *Aadan v Brent London Borough Council* (1999) Times, 3 December, in that the mere delivery of the notice of appeal to the court office was sufficient to establish filing under CPR 2.3 without an additional requirement of someone in the office to receive or authenticate it. The instant case was in fact stronger than *Swainstone* since the concept of the delivery to the office did not require any collaboration.

(ii) There were certain conditions contained in CPR PD 5A which stated that delivery could not be filed when the court office was closed. It had to be remembered, however, that the Practice Direction was subordinate to the CPR and had effect only when there was ambiguity. In the instant case the meaning of 'filing' contained in CPR 2.3(1) was clear.

(iii) The posting of the notice of appeal when the court office was closed, on the last day of the prescribed period under s 204 of the Act, was filing for the purposes of CPR 2.3 and was accordingly within the prescribed period. The appeal on that basis was allowed.

(iv) It was therefore unnecessary to determine the issue of whether the court had power to extend the prescribed period provided under s 204 of the Act.

Appeal allowed.

Varsani v Relfo Ltd (In Liquidation)

CPR 6.9

Court of Appeal   **[2010] EWCA Civ 560; [2011] 1 WLR 1402;
[2010] 3 All ER 1045; [2011] 1 All ER (Comm) 973;
[2010] CP Rep 39; [2011] 1 BCLC 71; (2010) 160 NLJ 804**

The defendant was a British citizen who had a business in Kenya. His family lived in a property owned by him and his wife in London and he visited as work permitted, staying between 27 and 53 days in each of the previous few years. The claimant brought proceedings for breach of fiduciary duty and served the claim form at the defendant's London address. The defendant unsuccessfully applied for service to be set aside on the ground that the London address was not his usual or last known residence within CPR 6.9. He then appealed, arguing that (1) the judge had wrongly found that the property in London was his 'usual' residence, the appropriate contrast being between 'usual' and 'occasional' use, and the judge had failed to apply the proper test of comparative use based on frequency and duration of residence; and (2) only a last known usual residence could be a last known residence.

Held:

(i)   The judge had been correct to hold that the property in London was the claimant's usual residence for the purposes of CPR 6.9. It was possible to have more than one usual residence. That was borne out by the distinction between 'usual residence' and 'principal' place of business and 'principal' office in CPR 6.9, which the judge had rightly taken into account.

(ii)   The test to be applied was not one of merely comparing the duration of periods of occupation, taking little account of the nature or quality of use of the premises, and ignoring altogether the fact that the premises were occupied permanently by the defendant's family and that the premises could be described as his family home. The critical test was the defendant's pattern of life (*Levene v Inland Revenue Commissioners* [1928] AC 217 applied). A test essentially of merely comparing the duration of periods of occupation, taking little account of the nature or 'quality' of use of the premises, and ignoring altogether the fact that the premises were occupied permanently by the defendant's family and that the premises could fairly be described as the family home, was too narrow and artificial.

(iii)   The settled pattern of the claimant's life was to visit his family home in London regularly each year, albeit not at the same time each year, for reasonably extensive periods. That was in marked contrast to the facts in *Cherney v Deripaska* [2007] EWHC 965 (Comm), [2007] 2 All ER (Comm) 785 and *OJSC Oil Co Yugraneft v Abramovich* [2008] EWHC 2613 (Comm). Those were cases in which the court found that the defendant had not been resident in England at all for the purposes of jurisdiction, and so the question of 'usual' residence had never arisen as a serious issue. The marked difference between the settled pattern of the claimant's life and the facts of those cases provided a good illustration of what was and was not a 'usual' residence.

(iv)   It was unnecessary to consider the 'last known residence' ground. However, where a defendant continued to reside at premises which were not his usual residence, there was doubt as to when and, if so, how the provisions of CPR 6.9(3)–(6) were engaged and operated. It would be desirable for the CPR Rules Committee to consider that matter.

Appeal dismissed.

Vinos v Marks & Spencer

CPR 1, 3, 7

Court of Appeal   **[2001] 3 All ER 784; [2001] CP Rep 12; [2000] CPLR 570**

The claimant was quite badly injured on 28 May 1996 whilst working for the defendant when a pallet fell on him. Constructive negotiations ensued and the defendant made interim payments of £5,000. The claimant issued proceedings on 20 May 1999, just within the limitation period. By oversight on the part of the claimant's solicitors, proceedings were not served until 29 September 1999, after the expiry of the validity period. The claimant applied for an extension of time for service and for an order remedying the error. The district judge rejected the application and set aside the claim form for failure to comply with CPR 7.6. The claimant appealed to the circuit judge dismissed the appeal holding that, whilst he would have been inclined to exercise any discretion in the claimant's favour, he had no power to extend time in these circumstances. The claimant appealed again, arguing that CPR 1 and CPR 3 gave the court discretion to extend time for service.

Held:

(i)   The court could extend time after the period for service had expired under CPR 7.6 only if:

    (a)   the court had been unable to serve the claim form; or

    (b)   the claimant had taken all reasonable steps to serve the claim form but had been unable to do so; and

    (c)   in either case the claimant had acted promptly.

(ii)   Although the claimant had acted promptly, neither of the other criteria were met. The court therefore had no power under CPR 7.6 to extend time.

(iii)   Neither CPR 3.1 or 3.10 gave the court the power to do what 7.6 expressly forbade. 7.6 could not be escaped to characterising an extension of time for service as a correction of an error.

(iv)   Although CPR 1.2 required the court to seek to give effect to the overriding objective, this did not allow the court to do more than was possible under the rules.

(v)   Three years and four months is entirely sufficient to get a claim in order. There is nothing unjust in a claimant who leaves the issue of proceedings to the last moment and then fails to comply with rules of service losing his claim.

(vi)   The fact that the defendant had agreed to pay compensation did not prevent it from relying on limitation and the rules of service.

(vii)   The position under the old rules was not relevant to the interpretation of the CPR.

Appeal dismissed.

The Vita

Renewal of writ   **RSC Ord 6, r 8**

Sheen J   **[1990] 1 Lloyd's Rep 528**

On 29 September 1986 the motor vessel Fordson belonging to the claimant (William Pope) was lying unmanned a short distance below Westminster Pier when the motor vessel Vita struck it. On 21 September 1988 the claimant's writ in rem for damage to the Fordson was issued. On 5 May 1989 the claimant's solicitors wrote to the defendants' solicitors to ask whether they would accept service and, in response to a request, on 16 May they sent a photocopy of the writ so that the defendants' solicitors could take instructions.

On 4 August 1989 the claimant's solicitors sent off by British Document Exchange to the defendants a letter which enclosed a sealed copy of the writ, an acknowledgement of service form and a legal aid notice. It did not arrive there. The claimant's solicitors were alerted to this by a letter of 14 November 1989 from the defendants' insurers who asked whether the proceedings had been served. The writ was then purportedly served on the defendants' solicitors on 23 November 1989.

The defendants applied to set aside service of the writ. When their motion was heard on 22 January 1990, the claimant's solicitors undertook to issue a summons seeking an order that the validity of the writ be extended. Thereupon the court heard argument on whether this relief should be granted.

Held:

(i) Solicitors who issue a writ have a duty to serve it promptly. A solicitor who deliberately takes the decision not to serve the writ for many months cannot be heard to complain if thereafter things go wrong.

(ii) The claimant's solicitors chose to use DX for transmission of documents. They took the risk of it being unreliable. It was unfortunate that the DX system let them down. But even then the claimant's solicitor should have been aware that there was no acknowledgement of service of the writ.

(iii) The main reason why the claimant was out of time was that there had been unnecessary delay, first before issuing the writ and second before attempting to serve it. There was no good reason to grant the claimant the relief sought.

Waghorn v Lewisham and North Southwark Area Health Authority

Limitation Act 1980, s 11, s 14, s 33

S N McKinnon QC   23 June 1987

The claimant (Mrs Waghorn) went to Guy's Hospital because she had a very short perineum which was causing marital problems. Her case was that she requested an operation which would lengthen the perineum and tighten the introitus, whereas instead on 31 March 1977 the surgeon performed an operation which shortened the perineum and opened the introitus further. On 4 April 1977, upon examining herself, she ascertained what had happened.

In May 1978 the claimant complained to Guy's Hospital through the Community Health Council. In September 1978 she notified the defendant health authority of her claim for damages. In May 1979 she instructed solicitors who commissioned a report from Mr Coden, a consultant obstetrician and gynaecologist. Following Mr Coden's report, counsel was instructed in December 1979 and advised that there had been no negligence in the 1977 operation.

In July 1980 Mr Coden performed a further operation on the claimant. In January 1982 he advised that if her narrative was correct the hospital might have been at fault. In February 1982 her solicitors advised her that she could have a claim. In April 1983 she changed her solicitors. Sometime in 1983 Mr Coden operated again.

Her writ was issued in April 1984. It was not served until nearly a year later. There was a preliminary trial of the limitation defence.

Held:

(i) The claimant knew that her injury was significant and attributable in April 1977. Time began to run against her then. It was immaterial for this purpose that she did not have supporting medical evidence until 1983: s 14(1).

(ii) Accordingly, her claim was commenced outside the primary three-year period specified in s 11(4) of the Limitation Act 1980.

(iii) (a) The earlier delay was due to the lack of supportive expert evidence. The later delay (from early 1982 onwards) was inexcusable: s 33(3)(a);

(b) further surgery in 1980 and 1983 had obscured the surgical procedures that were undertaken in 1977. Even so, the evidence had been rendered only marginally less cogent by the delay since April 1980: s 33(3)(b);

(c) the potential prejudice to the claimant, who would be left effectively without a remedy, outweighed that to the defendants. The court's decision should be exercised in her favour to allow her case to proceed: s 33(1).

Wake v Wylie

Road Traffic Act 1988, s 151, s 152

Court of Appeal

[2001] RTR 291; (2001) PIQR P186;
(2001) Times, 9 February

On 29 December 1993 the claimant was a passenger in a car being driven by the defendant. The car crashed as a result of the defendant's negligence, causing the claimant serious injuries. The car was insured under the defendant's mother's policy. However, the defendant himself was not covered by this policy. A letter of claim was sent to the insurers on 26 June 1995.

Proceedings were issued on 28 November 1996 but the insurers were not informed of this until 3 February 1997. In June 1999, following counsel's advice, the insurers raised the issue of notice under s 152(1)(a). They applied, under the name of the insured, for a declaration that under s 152(1)(a) they were not liable to satisfy any judgment the claimant might obtain against the defendant. The judge rejected that application. He found that *Harrington v Pinkey* (1989) 2 Lloyd's Rep 310 and *Desouza v Waterlow* (1999) RTR 71 were in conflict and held that the insurers had the requisite notice before the issue of proceedings or, alternatively, were estopped from contending otherwise. The insurers appealed.

Held:

(i) The judge was wrong to find the authorities in conflict. In *Harrington* the notice was conditional, whereas in *Desouza* the claimant, a litigant in person, told the insurers of his unconditional intention to commence proceedings and was encouraged to do so.

(ii) The following conclusions could be drawn from the authorities:

(a) to show notice, the claimant had to evidence more than a casual comment to someone who at times acted as the insurer's agent;

(b) any notification relied upon must not be subject to a condition that may or may not be fulfilled. Such notice will only be effective if the condition in question is action from the recipients which they can choose to take or not, and thus by their own choice render the notice unconditional and thus effective;

(c) the notice can be oral. It need not emanate from the claimant. It can be given before proceedings have commenced. It need not be specific as to the nature of either the proceedings or the court;

(d) the question of notice is a question of fact and degree; and

(e) the essential purpose of the notice requirement is to ensure that the insurer is not suddenly faced with a judgment it has satisfy without being given an opportunity to participate in the proceedings in which that judgment was obtained.

(iii) A letter of claim was insufficient to satisfy s 151(1)(a). It gave the insurers notice only of a claim, not of actual proceedings (*Weldrick v Essex and Suffolk Equitable Insurance Society Ltd* (1950) 83 Lloyd's Rep 91 doubted).

(iv) The fact that the essential purpose of the notice requirement was satisfied entitled neither the claimant nor the court to ignore the statutory condition precedent to an insurer's liability that the insurer had to have notice no later than seven days after the issue of proceedings.

(v) There had been no representation that could give rise to an estoppel. As the claimant's s 151 right to recover from the insurers was conditional upon his obtaining judgment against the defendant, the insurer was entitled to defend the action on the defendant's behalf up until judgment and take the s 152 point. The delay in raising the point could therefore not be construed as a waiver. Although a party entitled to rely on a statutory defence can waive it, s 152 was not a defence but a condition precedent. The unattractiveness of the insurer's failure to take the point earlier could not be determinative.

Appeal allowed.

Walkin v South Manchester Health Authority

Limitation Act 1980, s 11, s 38(1)

Court of Appeal   **[1995] 1 WLR 1543; [1995] 4 All ER 132;**
[1996] Med LR 211

In May 1986 the claimant, then 37 years old and married, was expecting her third child. She decided for economic reasons not to have any more children. In September 1986, after the third child's birth, the defendant hospital performed a sterilisation procedure on her. In February 1987 the claimant discovered that she was pregnant again and gave birth to her fourth healthy child in September of that year, having in the interim consulted solicitors who had sent a letter of claim.

In June 1989 she issued proceedings claiming damages for personal injuries and consequential losses from the failed sterilisation. These were never served. In October 1991 she issued a second writ claiming for economic losses only. The defendant pleaded limitation, which was heard as a preliminary issue. The judge held that, irrespective of the manner of pleading, the claim was one for personal injuries to which the three-year time limit under s 11 applied. The claim was therefore statute barred (the former rule in *Walkley v Precision Forgings Ltd* (p705) then precluding any s 33 discretion). The claimant appealed.

Held:

(i)   A claim for damages resulting from a failed sterilisation leading to the unwanted birth of a healthy but unwanted child was a claim for damages for personal injuries within the meaning of s 11(1). The form of pleading was irrelevant.

(ii)   In such circumstances claims for pre-natal pain and suffering and post-natal economic loss arose out of the same cause of action (*Allen v Bloomsbury Health Authority* [1993] 1 All ER 651 overruled).

(iii)   Unwanted conception, whether caused by negligent advice or negligently performed surgery, was a personal injury in the sense of an impairment under s 38(1) which arose at the moment of conception. The failed sterilisation itself did not until conception constitute an injury.

(iv)   (obiter) There was no distinction for these purposes between an action by a mother in respect of failed sterilisation and a father's in respect of a failed vasectomy (*Pattison v Hobbs* (1985) Times, 11 November doubted as the personal injury relates to the claimant 'or any other person').

(v)   The claim was therefore statute barred.

Appeal dismissed.

Walkley v Precision Forgings Ltd

Limitation Act 1939, s 2A, s 2D

House of Lords   **[1979] 2 All ER 548; [1979] 1 WLR 606;**
123 SJ 354

From 1966 to 1971 the claimant (Anthony Walkley) was employed by the defendants as a dry grinder at their factory in Monmouth. In June 1969 he started to suffer symptoms in his hands. In November 1969 he was informed that this was Raynaud's Phenomenon and had been caused by his work. On 7 October 1971 his union solicitors issued a writ and served it. Following negative advice from counsel, they took no further action.

After the claimant had consulted a second firm of solicitors, a third firm issued on 6 December 1976 a second writ claiming similar relief. When this was served in February 1977, the defendants applied to strike it out.

This succeeded before a master. Swanwick J allowed the second action to proceed on an undertaking by the claimant to discontinue the first. The Court of Appeal affirmed his decision. The defendants appealed.

Held:

(i)   It was not the provisions of s 2A of the Limitation Act 1939 as amended that prejudiced the claimant, when within the period provided by it he had brought an action for damages for the same personal injuries and in respect of the same cause of action as his second action. He was prejudiced by his delay in proceeding with the first action and by the discontinuance of that action, not by the provisions of s 2A.

(ii)   If in such circumstances a second action is started after the expiry of a limitation period without the court having directed that it may proceed, the second action may properly be regarded as vexatious and an abuse of the process of the court and may be struck out.

(iii)   Even if s 2D had been applicable, it should not be exercised in the claimant's favour because it was clear that the evidence would be considerably less cogent than if the action had been brought within the primary period. The factory was no longer occupied by the defendants, it would be difficult to simulate the claimant's working conditions, the works manager had died and a medical officer had died or was untraced.

The defendants' appeal was allowed, and the master's order was restored.

Per Lord Diplock: 'My Lords, in my opinion, once a plaintiff has started an action (the first action) within the primary limitation period it is only in the most exceptional circumstances that he would be able to bring himself within s 2D in respect of a second action brought to enforce the same cause of action ... The only exception I have been able to think of where it might be proper to give a direction under s 2D, despite the fact that the plaintiff had previously started an action within the primary limitation period but had subsequently discontinued it, would be a case in which the plaintiff had been induced to discontinue by a misrepresentation or other improper conduct by the defendant.'

NB: This rule was abolished in *Horton v Sadler* (p482).

Walsh v Misseldine

CPR 1, 3.4

Court of Appeal   **[2000] CP Rep 74; [2000] CPLR 201; LTL 1/3/2000**

The claimant was very seriously injured in a road traffic accident in July 1989. Liability was never in issue. Proceedings were issued in 1992. By the end of 1993 the only live issue was the claimant's back pain. The action, which was subject to the old automatic strike out rule (CCR Ord 17 r 11), was not progressed save for a directions hearing on 4 January 1994 and some interim payments until the claimant instructed new solicitors in 1996. There was then confusion as to whether the action was automatically struck out. There was again no action until December 1998 when the defendant sought a declaration that the action was automatically struck out. The district judge made this declaration on 21 January 1999 but reinstated the action on 26 April 1999 (coincidentally the same day the CPR came into force) following the claimant's application. The defendant did not appeal the reinstatement but on 22 June 1999 struck out the claim for want of prosecution. The claimant appealed.

The circuit judge held that an action reinstated in April could not reasonably struck out for inexcusable delay in June. He granted the defendant permission to appeal the reinstatement out of time and allowed the appeal, citing CPR Part 1. The claimant appealed with the circuit judge's permission.

Held:

(i) The circuit judge's decision could not stand and the parties consented to the appeal court considering the matter afresh.

(ii) Under the CPR the court was no longer faced with the stark choice of striking a claim out or allowing it to continue unimpeded. Where liability was not in dispute the course could take a middle course consistent with the overriding objective. That option might not be available if liability is in dispute.

(iii) Given that the claimant's case as formulated at the directions hearing in January 1994 could be fairly tried, it would be unfair to dismiss the claim entirely.

(iv) Conversely the delay would cause injustice to the defendant if the claimant were permitted to enlarge his pleaded claim as he wished. A fair trial of these additional issues was not now possible due to the elapsed time. Additionally, the defendant ability to protect itself by way of payments into court would be prejudiced.

(v) The claim would therefore be allowed to continue on the basis that damages would be assessed as what would have been payable had the trial been heard on 15 March 1995. Further, the claimant would not be entitled to interest between that date and the date of the order allowing this appeal.

Ward v British Coal Corporation and Norton plc

Limitation Act 1980, s 11, s 14

Court of Appeal   LTL 6/11/1998

The claimant was born on 18 September 1939. He worked in a deep mining pit for the first defendant from 1955 to 1984 and in the second defendant's factory thereafter until he was made redundant n 1993. In 1990 the second defendant screened its employees. An audiogram revealed that the claimant was suffering from hearing loss and he was advised to consult his GP. He did so in September 1990. The GP found nothing abnormal but referred him to an ear, nose and throat specialist. The claimant attended the ENT specialist on 10 April 1991. The specialist wrote a note to the claimant's GP the same day stating that the claimant was suffering from noise-induced deafness attributable to his work. The letter stated that nothing could be done and that the claimant should claim against his employers. The claimant next visited his GP in July 1992 following another examination at work showing marked hearing loss. He was referred to a different ENT specialist. On his return to the GP in August 1992 he insisted on referral, privately if necessary, to a different and talked about making a claim. The claimant's evidence was that he did not consider suing the defendants until his social security application was turned down. On his return proceedings were issued on 31 March 1995. The defendant pleaded limitation which was heard as a preliminary issue.

The judge accepted the claimant's evidence that the letter of 10 April 2001 was not communicated to him. She therefore found that the claimant did not have actual knowledge until July 1992. She rejected the defendant's contention that he could have placed the relevant information together so as to fix him with earlier constructive knowledge. The judge also rejected the second defendant's argument that the claimant was already suffering from marked deafness when he joined them, holding that if that had been the case they would not have employed him. The defendant appealed.

Held:

(i) The judge did not misdirect herself on the burden of proof.

(ii)   The question here was purely one of fact. The judge had seen and heard the witnesses and was entitled to come to the conclusions that she did. The claimant's evidence was not directly contradicted by any documents and the judge was entitled to conclude that he was did not see the 10 April 1991 letter. She was also entitled to conclude that if the claimant knew before 1992 that he had a claim, he would have acted the way he in fact did in 1992 by discussing and insisting on seeing another specialist.

Appeal dismissed.

Ward and another v Foss

Heathcote and another v Foss

Limitation Act 1980, s 33

Court of Appeal   **(1993) Times, 29 November**

In July 1982 Sandra and William Heathcote were killed in an accident. In November 1989 the claimants (their personal representatives) issued writs claiming damages for the benefits of their estates under the Law Reform (Miscellaneous Provisions) Act 1934 and for the benefit of the dependent children under the Fatal Accidents Act 1976.

The Administration of Justice Act 1982, which applied to causes of action accruing from 1 January 1983, provided that no damages could be recovered on behalf of a deceased's estate for loss of income in respect of any period after the death. Hitherto the interaction of the 1934 and 1976 Acts could produce some overcompensation.

By virtue of s 28 of the Limitation Act 1980, the claims on behalf of the children under the Fatal Accidents Act 1976 were brought in time. HH Judge Heald, sitting as a deputy judge of the High Court, disapplied the primary limitation period under s 33 of the 1980 Act in the actions brought on behalf of the deceased's estates under the Law Reform (Miscellaneous Provisions) Act 1934. The defendant appealed against this decision.

Held:

(i)   The cause of action might be inequitable through producing overcompensation, but that was not the point. s 33 of the 1980 Act asked, not whether the claim itself was equitable, but whether it was equitable to allow it to proceed having regard to certain specified matters.

(ii)   Section 33 was concerned with prejudice to the defendant caused by delay. The defendant's argument on this issue was unconvincing.

The defendant's appeal was dismissed.

Wasley v Vass

Limitation Act 1980, s 11, s 33

Court of Appeal   **Lexis, 1 July 1991**

On 28 September 1984 the claimant was a front-seat passenger in a car driven by the defendant which went out of control and crashed into a lamppost with no other car involved. The defendant admitted liability.

The writ was issued on 11 March 1988. At the preliminary trial, the claimant's solicitors testified that on 8 April 1986 she had spoken over the telephone to a representative of the defendant's insurers who had agreed that the defendant would not deny liability and would not plead the Limitation Act.

Otton J dismissed the case as statute barred. The claimant appealed.

Held:

(i)   The judge was fully entitled to adopt the view he did – that the telephone conversation had taken place but that there had been a misunderstanding and no agreement about not pleading the Limitation Act had been reached – and there was no basis at all on which the court could interfere with that finding. Accordingly, the case was statute barred by s 11 of the Limitation Act 1980.

(ii)   It was obvious negligence on the part of the claimant's solicitor not at once, in April 1986, to attempt to confirm in correspondence the informal oral agreement which she thought she had reached over the telephone with the insurers' representative. The claimant had a very strong case against her. The judge was fully entitled not to exercise his discretion in the claimant's favour under s 33.

The claimant's appeal was dismissed.

Welsh Development Agency v Redpath Dorman Long Ltd

Limitation Act 1980, s 35

Court of Appeal   **[1994] 1 WLR 1409; [1994] 4 All ER 10; 38 Con LR 106**

The claimant claimed for damages arising from the negligence of the defendant in designing factory units. Proceedings were issued in July 1990 and July 1990 the claimant sought to amend to claim for (a) further design faults in the same construction and (b) in respect of the defendant's negligent advice between 1985 and 1987 that the problems were not due to the design and unlikely to continue. The judge permitted the amendment to include further design faults but not as regards the defendant's misstatement, which he held to be statute barred. The claimant appealed and the defendant cross-appealed.

Held:

(i)   The judge had correctly concluded that allowing the claim for further design faults constituted a 'new claim' under RSC Ord 20 r 5(5).

(ii)   The question of whether a new claim arose out of the same facts as the original one was substantially a matter of degree and impression. Since there was no suggestion that the judge had misdirected himself or failed to take a relevant factor into account he was entitled to conclude that the facts were substantially the same.

(iii)   Section 35(1) gave a claimant an advantage of a different test to that in s 35(3). Leave to amend outside the Limitation Act 1980 period should not be given unless a claimant could show that the defendant had no arguable limitation defence or the claim came within the relevant rule of the court.

(iv)   As regards the construction of s 35, unless a new claim came within one the exceptions provided by the rules of court, leave to amend could not be given where the limitation period had expired when the court considered the matter, even if it had not expired when the application was made. The amendment was not 'made' until leave was granted.

(v)   In this case, limitation expired on 18 September 1992. As the hearing was not until May 1993 the judge was right to refuse leave, notwithstanding that the application to amend was issued on 14 July 1992.

(vi)   Section 35(3) did not create a defence but provides a mandatory direction to a court dealing either with an application to amend a new claim or an application to strike out a new claim added by amendment or way of contribution notice without leave (*Kennett v Brown* (p516) and *Holland v Yates Building Co Ltd* (p480) held to be wrongly decided).

Appeal and cross-appeal dismissed.

NB: RSC Ord 20, r 5(5) is replicated at CPR 17.4(2).

Whealing Horton & Toms Ltd v Riverside Housing Association Ltd

CPR 7.2   **Service of documents**

TCC (HHJ Stephen Davies)   **12 May 2008, unreported**

The claimant and the defendant had entered into an agreement in relation to the conversion of a building into apartments. The contract came to an end in circumstances where the defendant's head of development operations wrote a letter to the claimant giving notice that he would no longer be required to carry out further services. A notice of arbitration was given in which the claimant asserted that the termination of the contract was unlawful. One of the issues in the arbitration was whether the head of development operations was an appropriate signatory for notice of termination. The arbitrator, in making the award, found that he was.

Just after 5pm on the final day of the 28-day time limit for bringing a challenge to the award, the claimant delivered his claim form through the post box at the court district registry. Not surprisingly (because the court's offices would have closed at 4pm), when the claimant had arrived at the court just after 5pm, he had been unable to find anyone who would answer him. The form was not stamped until the following day. The claim form challenged the award on the ground of serious irregularity. The irregularity complained of was that the award was obtained by fraud or was procured in a way which was contrary to public policy. The principal issues were: (1) whether the arbitration application was issued in time; (2) whether the claimant could establish a case of serious irregularity; and (3) whether any such irregularity had caused or would cause substantial injustice to the claimant.

Held:

(i)   The arbitration application was brought in time. If an application was, as in the instant case, delivered to the court at 5pm on the last day for bringing the application, it had been brought (for the purposes of s 68 of the Arbitration Act 1996) within the 28-day period (*Barnes v St Helens MBC* (p321) applied). The bringing of the application was analogous to the bringing of proceedings for the purposes of the Limitation Act, in that it was a unilateral act rather than a transaction. The claimant was entitled to the full 28-day period.

(ii)   The claimant, however, failed on the substantive issues.

Application refused.

Whiston v London SHA

Limitation Act 1980, s 14, s 33

Court of Appeal   **[2010] EWCA Civ 195; [2010] 1 WLR 1582;**
[2010] 3 All ER 452; [2010] PIQR P12; [2010] Med LR 132;
(2010) 113 BMLR 110; (2010) 107(12) LSG 26;
(2010) Times, 4 May

The claimant suffered from cerebral palsy caused by brain damage sustained at his birth in the defendant's hospital on 6 September 1974. He issued proceedings in October 2006 (when aged 32) alleging negligence. His case was that his birth had been attended by a junior doctor, who tried for over half an hour to deliver him using forceps before summoning a more experienced registrar, who then delivered him within five minutes using different forceps. The claimant's mother (M) was a nurse and had been trained as a midwife, and was concerned about her treatment. However, she decided not to pursue or investigate these concerns, deciding it was best 'to get on with our lives and make the best of what we had'. Despite development problems the claimant did well academically, obtaining a 2:1 from Cambridge and then a PhD in Mathematics. He returned to live with his parents upon leaving Cambridge in 2001. In 2003 he found work as a quantitative analyst with the Nationwide Building Society. During this time, although his balance was not good and his speech was slightly slurred and slow, the claimant was able to walk reasonable distances unaided, was able to drive and was able to lead an independent life. In 2005, however, his condition worsened dramatically; he began to use a wheelchair constantly, his speech deteriorated, he had difficulties swallowing, he suffered from severe fatigue and was having to take time off work. M then told the claimant of her concerns, prompting him to bring the claim.

The claimant stated that he had previously known that he had been delivered by forceps and that his condition was caused by a lack of oxygen at birth, but had never investigated further as he had generally felt unimpeded by his condition and did not perceive himself to be disabled. The judge held that, for the purposes of s 14, the claimant had had neither actual nor constructive knowledge of the alleged negligence before 2005, but also that he would not have exercised his discretion under s 33 had the claim been statute barred.

The defendant appealed, arguing that (1) the judge had failed to give due weight to the claimant's benefits documentation, (2) the claimant had had actual knowledge of the alleged negligence before 2005, as he knew that he had been born using forceps; and (3) the judge had used a subjective test in determining constructive knowledge, whereas Lord Hoffmann's judgment in *Adams v Bracknell Forest BC* (p292) required an objective test under which it was assumed that, in all cases where a person had suffered serious injury, he would be sufficiently curious to ask questions about it, and he should be fixed with knowledge of the facts that he would have learned if he had asked. The claimant cross-appealed on s 33.

Held:

(i)   There was no reason to suppose that the judge had not properly taken the benefits documentation into account. Having seen the claimant give evidence, he was entitled to accept that he was a witness of truth.

(ii)   The fact that the claimant's delivery had been by forceps did not capture the essence of his claim. The essence of the case was that his injury was attributable to the junior doctor's persistence, his use of the wrong forceps, and his delay in seeking assistance. The judge had been right to determine the actual knowledge issue in the claimant's favour.

(iii)   As regards constructive knowledge, although he had purported to apply an objective test, the judge had considered subjective matters personal to this particular claimant and his decision could not stand.

(iv)   The test that the defendant relied on in *Adams* (one which assumed that a person who had suffered a serious injury would be sufficiently curious to ask questions about it) was not part of the ratio of that case. Nor was it what s 14(3) required: it did not provide that actual or constructive knowledge that the injury was significant was determinative of the constructive knowledge issue.

(v)   Instead, the issue should be determined by reference to the knowledge which a person might reasonably be expected to acquire, depending on all the circumstances of the case. *Adams* and the existence of the discretion in s 33 heightened the requirements of constructive knowledge and the degree of curiosity of the reasonable claimant.

(vi)   This claimant knew his injury was significant and, by his early 20s, he also knew that his health was deteriorating. Had he asked M at the time about his delivery, she would have told him what she told him in 2005 and he would have acquired knowledge of the alleged negligence. There would come a time when a reasonable person in the claimant's circumstances would ask his mother, particularly since she was a nurse and a midwife. He would have known that she, as a trained person, would be able to answer his questions.

(vii) In those circumstances, the claimant would have had constructive knowledge no later than around 1998, and the claim was statute barred.

(viii) The judge's consideration of s 33 was inevitably an artificial one, predicated upon a hypothetical date of knowledge, which the judge took to be in 1992. The artificiality of fixing such a notional date raised real doubts as to the utility of embarking upon the exercise at all.

(ix) The fact that a fair trial was not impossible did not necessarily determine the question of whether it would be equitable to allow the action to proceed under s 33. The judge had considered the prejudice the defendant would suffer, but had nowhere mentioned the prejudice the claimant would suffer if he could not prosecute his claim. He had also been wrong to take M's decision not to sue into account as the only reason for delay: there was no basis for finding that the claimant (as opposed to his parents) made a decision not to sue when he acquired constructive knowledge of the alleged negligence. It was therefore necessary to exercise the s 33 discretion afresh.

(x) A fair trial was still possible. However, that was not decisive: it was necessary to have regard to all the circumstances of the case, including the factors set out in s 33. It was important that the claimant had not made a decision not to start proceedings once he actually knew he had a claim. He was not to be criticised before then for wanting to get on with his life. Further, the claimant had suffered serious injury for which he would be awarded substantial damages. If he was not permitted to pursue the claim, he would lose all prospect of his future needs being provided for. Weighing all those factors, although it was a borderline case, it would be equitable to allow the claim to proceed.

Appeal allowed, and cross-appeal allowed.

Per Dyson LJ: '57. If para 47 is to be understood as Mr de Navarro contends, then if a claimant knows that he has a significant injury, he is fixed in all cases with knowledge of such facts as he would have ascertained if he had made appropriate inquiries. If knowledge that he has a significant injury is established, it necessarily follows that he should reasonably have made such inquiries and he is fixed with knowledge of all facts which he would have ascertained as a result of those inquiries.

58. But this is not what the statute says. Section 14(3) refers to knowledge which a claimant "might reasonably be expected to acquire" from facts observable or ascertainable by him or by him with appropriate expert advice which it is reasonable for him to seek. It does not say that, if a claimant has knowledge that the injury in question is significant, he is fixed with knowledge of the facts that he would ascertain if he made inquiries about the cause of his injury …

59. Thus the court should consider what is reasonably to have been expected of the claimant in all the circumstances of the case. That is not to say that the court should overlook the fact that it must apply an objective test. I also accept that, in deciding whether in all the circumstances of the case, the claimant should reasonably have made appropriate inquiries, the court should bear in mind that the House of Lords has "tightened up" the requirements of constructive knowledge in the light of the existence of the discretion in section 33 and the policy of the 1980 Act to avoid the injustice to defendants of vexing them with stale claims. I accept that the decision in Adams requires the court to expect a heightened degree of curiosity of the reasonable claimant than it would do absent section 33.

60. In my judgment, a relevant circumstance in a case such as the present is that the claimant has been suffering from the injury since he was born. I agree with the point made by Cox J in Khaiwule that, when assessing the extent to which someone is reasonably to be expected to be curious about the cause of his disability, a distinction should be drawn between someone who has lived with a disability and its effects all his life and someone who suffers an injury following an adverse incident which occurs in adulthood.'

White v Eon

Limitation Act 1980, s 14

Court of Appeal   **[2008] EWCA Civ 1463**

On 19 July 2006 the claimant issued proceedings against three defendants seeking damages for vibration white finger and carpal tunnel syndrome caused by excessive levels of vibration from tools used in his work as a lightning conductor fitter. The third defendant, for whom he had worked between 1962 and 1996, pleaded limitation which was determined as a preliminary issue.

The claimant's case was that his date of knowledge was in the summer of 2003, when he saw an advertisement for a claims company. The defendant contended that the claimant's date of knowledge was much earlier, so that his claim was statute barred. The judge found that, whilst the claimant had not actually known that his condition was attributable to negligence until 2003, he had constructive knowledge pursuant to s 14(3) by the time he left his employment with the defendant in 1996 because, by then, it had been reasonable to expect him to have sought medical advice in respect of his combination of symptoms. These symptoms, which started in the 1980s, were tingling in the fingers, blanching, intense throbbing and discomfort. The symptoms he described caused him difficulty with fine finger movements, the fastening of buttons and picking up small objects. This medical advice would have led to the necessary link between his condition and the use of vibrating tools. The judge further refused to disapply the limitation period under s 33 of the Act. The claimant appealed, arguing that the judge had erred in finding that he had constructive knowledge, and that he had applied too stringent a test.

Held:

(i)   The judge had asked himself the question whether, having regard to the symptoms the claimant was experiencing in 1996, it would have been reasonable to have expected him to seek specific advice from his doctor. It had never been suggested that that was the wrong question to ask (*Adams v Bracknell Forest BC* (p292) applied).

(ii)   It had been for the judge to decide what was or was not reasonable for the claimant to have done in the circumstances. His finding that it would have been reasonable for the claimant to have sought medical advice was a finding of fact open to him on the evidence before him and not the sort of finding that the Court of Appeal ought to interfere with. It had not been illogical to find that the claimant had constructive knowledge by the end of 1996. To the contrary, the judge's finding to that effect was both obvious and logical and could not be criticised.

Appeal dismissed.

Whitfield v North Durham Health Authority

Limitation Act 1980, s 11, s 14, s 33

Court of Appeal   **[1999] 1 WLR 2068; [1999] 3 All ER 50;**
                                                            [1999] PIQR P249

In May 1985 the claimant underwent surgery at the defendant hospital to remove a lump from her neck. As a cytology test had diagnosed the lump as malignant, the surgeon chose to remove it entirely, event though this would probably cause nerve damage. The claimant's arm was left permanently paralysed as a result. The claimant alleged negligence against both the cytologist and the surgeon because subsequent histopathological analysis showed that the lump was in fact benign. Proceedings were issued against the surgeon alone in December 1987, but these were never served nor the subject of an application for renewal, the claimant having been advised post-issue that the surgeon had not been negligent. The claimant instructed different solicitors in November 1999. She issued fresh proceedings against both the cytologist and the surgeon on 19 March 1992. The defendant pleaded limitation, which was heard as a preliminary issue.

Jowitt J found that the claimant had knowledge under the act in respect of the cytologist in June 1985, when the Association for the Victims of Medical Accidents wrote a letter on her behalf. He found that she had knowledge in respect of the surgeon on 21 December 1987 when the first writ against him was issued. He exercised his discretion under s 33 in respect of the claim against the cytologist holding that (a) the fact that it was only by the failures of her original solicitors that the claim was not caught by the former rule in *Walkley v Precision Forgings Ltd* (p705) was of little or no relevance; (b) the prejudice of the change in funding of payment for claims for hospital negligence was of reduced significance in these circumstances; (c) the claimant was not personally responsible for the delay; (d) the defendant would not be evidentially prejudiced by the delay. However he found that the rule in Walkley denied him a discretion in respect of the claim against the surgeon. The defendant appealed the exercise of the discretion and the claimant cross-appealed the *Walkley* point.

Held:

(i)   The claimant had knowledge in respect of both the cytologist and the surgeon as of the date of the AVMA letter in June 1985. The court should look at the essence of the complaint and whether the claimant had knowledge in broad terms of the relevant facts. The judge had erred in going beyond this into an anticipatory consideration of the merits.

(ii)   The judge had also erred in finding that the date of issue was itself determinative of s 14 knowledge.

(iii)   The judge was correct to hold that *Walkley* precluded his discretion in respect of the claim against the surgeon.

(iv)   The judge had misdirected himself in holding that the claimant's fortuitous advantage in escaping the *Walkley* preclusion because of her first solicitors' failure was of little or no significance. It was a highly relevant consideration.

(v)   The judge erred in assuming, when considering the effect of the change of funding, that patients would altruistically accept a that diminished NHS resources was a fair price to pay for compensation to victims of medical accidents.

(vi)   The claimant's solicitors had been responsible for the delays. The claimant's actions or inaction could not be divorced from the acts or omissions of her legal representatives. Her solicitors' delays had to be attributed against her.

(vii)   Although the judge was entitled to hold that, with histological slides remaining available, the effect of the delay on the cytologist's evidence carried minor weight, he had underestimated the impact of the delay upon the evidence. The delay made it more difficult for the cytologists to accurately reconstruct what had happened at the time in question.

(viii) Exercising the discretion afresh, on balance of prejudice it would be inequitable to allow the claim to proceed.

(ix)   Had there been a discretion to be exercised in respect of the claim against the surgeon, the court would not have exercised it. The claim involved an attack on the surgeon's clinical judgment.

Appeal allowed, cross-appeal dismissed.

NB: The rule in *Walkley* was abolished in *Horton v Sadler* (p482).

Whittaker v Westinghouse Brake and Signal Holdings

Limitation Act 1980, s 33

County Court (HHJ Dyer QC)   CLY 96/829

The claimant's husband worked for the defendant from 1926 to his retirement. He worked in the fottling shop, eventually becoming a foreman. In 1965 he was x-rayed and silicosis diagnosed. Although from this point he was aware of his condition, he did not appreciate that he had a claim against the defendant. He transferred to a lower paying job and received a state industrial diseases pension. Eventually the silicosis turned to lung cancer and he died on 15 December 1991.

The claimant herself remained unaware of a her potential claims under the Law Reform (Miscellaneous Provisions) Act 1934 and the Fatal Accidents Act 1976 until 1993 when her neighbour informed her of a radio advert for claims for the exposure to industrial dust. The claimant issued proceedings on 12 December 1994. The defendant pleaded limitation which was tried as a preliminary issue. It was conceded that the claimant required a s 33 discretion.

Held:

(i)   Notwithstanding the delay of 31 years, a fair trial was still possible. Although the foundry had closed down, there were still witnesses and the defendant could make further efforts to obtain evidence.

(ii)   The interim changes in the law (that had the claim been advanced in 1965 the husband could not have claimed provisional damages to return to court when he developed lung cancer) had not seriously prejudiced the defendant.

(iii)   The husband, being unaware of his rights, was blameless.

(iv)   It would be equitable to allow the claim to proceed.

Preliminary hearing decided in the claimant's favour with costs.

Whittam v W J Daniel & Co Ltd

Amendment of writ

Court of Appeal   [1961] 3 All ER 796; [1961] 3 WLR 1123;
                                                  [1962] 1 QB 271

On 10 September 1957 the claimant (Norma Whittam) was injured in an accident whilst working in the defendants' employment. Her claim was duly notified, and she was examined by a doctor instructed by the defendants' insurers. On every letter the defendants' name was correctly stated as W J Daniel & Co Ltd.

On 9 September 1967 her writ was issued against 'W J Daniels and Company (a firm)' claiming 'damages for personal injuries sustained by the claimant in the course of her employment by the defendants'. No such firm existed.

On 12 October 1960 the claimant was granted leave (outside the limitation period) to amend the writ by changing the name of the defendant to W J Daniel & Co Ltd. They applied for an order that the writ be set aside.

Elwes J allowed the defendants' appeal from the master's refusal to order this. At the hearing of the claimant's appeal, the defendants' counsel argued inter alios that the original description of the defendants described nothing and that it would be improper to substitute the defendants for a person that did not exist.

Held:

(i)   There was no rule of law that the mere omission of the word 'Limited' meant that no person was sued at all and that there was no defendant to the proceedings.

(ii)   This was a case of mere misnomer. The defendants were under no misapprehension as to whom the claimant intended to sue.

The claimant's appeal was allowed.

NB: The relevant rule today would be CPR 17.4(3).

Wiemer v Zone

CPR 1, 3, 7, 7.4, 7.5, 16

QBD (Silber J)   **[2012] EWHC 107 (QB)**

On 19 April 2010 the claimant issued proceedings for damages in the region of £2.325 million for breach of fiduciary duty, breach of trust, breach of contract, wrongful threats and fraudulent misrepresentation. He did not serve them immediately. Instead, on 19 August 2010 he served the claim form but applied for an extension of time to serve the particulars on the bases that: first, he needed to obtain further information from third parties fully to particularise his claim; secondly, he had not been able to serve the particulars earlier because, as a result of financial difficulties caused in part by the conduct of the defendants, the claimant had until recently been acting in person; and, thirdly, the particulars needed to be drafted by counsel but, because of their complexity, this could not be done at short notice. On 8 October this application was refused. The claimant appealed, arguing that the master had erred in finding that he did not have jurisdiction to grant the extension. The defendant argued that the master was merely 'unsure' whether he had such jurisdiction and that his decision was correct.

Held:

(i)   It did not really matter if the master refused the order on the ground that he thought that he did not have jurisdiction or whether, as the defendant argued, he was not sure if he had jurisdiction. It was common ground that the master did have jurisdiction to extend time for the service of the particulars of claim, in light of *Totty v Snowden* (p694). It followed that the master had erred in refusing the application.

(ii)   In order to determine how the master's discretion should have been exercised, it was necessary to look at the relevant facts of the case. The following factors should have been considered by the master in reaching a decision in compliance with the overriding objective of dealing with the case justly. The particulars should have been served by 19 August. Significantly, the claimant was only seeking an extension until 30 October which would have meant that there was a delay of just over 10 weeks. There was no evidence whatsoever that the defendant would have been, or indeed was, prejudiced by the delay, either during the period between 18 August and 30 October or at any time prior to those dates. If the application was not to be granted, the claimant would have lost the benefit of his claim and it would have been time barred. Those factors were of great importance and should have been considered by the master.

Appeal allowed.

Wilding v Lambeth, Southwark and Lewisham Area Health Authority

Amendment of statement of claim   **Limitation Act 1980, s 33**

McNeill J   **Lexis, 10 May 1982**

In September 1974 both the lower wisdom teeth of the claimant (Susan Wilding) were extracted in an operation by one of the defendants' surgeons. She claimed that in the operation some injury was done to the inferior dental nerve running in a canal near to the left lower wisdom tooth.

Her writ was issued in June 1977. The first allegation in the statement of claim, which was served in October 1977, was that the defendants 'removed the claimant's left lower wisdom tooth when it was not necessary to do so'. Other allegations included failure to warn of the risk of inferior dental nerve damage and negligent conduct of the operation.

When the case came on for trial in May 1982, the claimant applied to amend the statement of claim so as to add to the first allegation the words 'and/or without her consent', thereby adding a claim of trespass to the person. The claimant had signed before the operation a form consenting to the extraction of both lower wisdom teeth.

Held:

(i)   Proceeding by analogy with s 33 of the Limitation Act 1980, the real reason for the delay was that counsel who drafted the statement of claim now recognised the difficulties presented by the rest of the claimant's allegations and sought to bolster a difficult case by making a fresh averment well out of time. This was not a matter which should incline the court favourably to the application: s 33(3)(a).

(ii)   Although the majority of the relevant medical and nursing staff were still available, the real prejudice to both sides would be the trial of an oral issue as to what explanations the defendants' surgeon or registrar gave to the claimant and what consent she voiced, necessarily based, save for the medical records, on eight-year-old recollections of those who had not been asked to think about the matter until recently: s 33(3)(b).

(iii)   It would not have been appropriate to grant leave to the claimant to proceed with a fresh action in trespass under the disapplying provisions of the Limitation Act: s 33(1).

(iv)   Accordingly, the claimant's application to amend the statement of claim should be refused.

Wilkey v BBC

CPR 6.9

Court of Appeal   **[2003] 1 WLR 1; [2002] 4 All ER 1177;
[2003] CP Rep 17**

The claim form in a libel action was delivered to the defendant's legal department at 2pm on 28 February 2001, the last day of the validity period for service period, having been issued two days before the expiry of the limitation period. The defendant applied for service to be set aside on the ground that the deemed date of service was 1 March 2001. The district judge refused the application. The defendant appealed to the high court. The judge allowed the appeal. The claimant then appealed.

Held:

(i)   The defendant, having in actuality received the claim form during the validity period, had suffered no prejudice by the deemed late service. There was no good reason not to allow the action to proceed and the Court would exercise its discretion under CPR 6.9(1) (*Anderton v Clwyd CC* (p303) applied).

(ii)   A presumption in favour of dispensing with service where the claimant had sought to serve the claim form by a permitted method and the defendant had in fact received it within the validity period arose only in pre-*Anderton* cases. The deemed service rule, which provided highly desirable certainty, would apply in all but the most exceptional post-*Anderton* cases. A strict approach should generally be adopted. If this case had been post-*Anderton* the appeal would have failed.

Appeal allowed.

Wilkinson v Ancliff (BLT) Ltd

Renewal of writ   **Limitation Act 1980, s 11, s 14**

Court of Appeal   **[1986] 3 All ER 427; [1986] 1 WLR 1352; 130 SJ 766**

The claimant (Robert Wilkinson) was employed by the defendants as a road tanker driver. The tankers that he drove contained toluene di-isocyanate (TDI). In April 1981 he experienced symptoms of wheezing, coughing and shortness of breath. In August 1981 he stopped work due to ill health. In November 1981 he was admitted to hospital and, after a 'challenge test' which involved his being exposed to TDI at a steady state concentration, he became aware that his bronchial asthma resulted from his exposure to TDI in the defendants' employment.

Following a change of solicitors, his writ was issued on 7 March 1984. counsel advised that an expert's report was needed. In December 1984 a consulting chemist produced a report which detailed various failings by the defendants. Owing to an oversight by the claimant's solicitors, the writ and statement of claim were not sent to the defendants until 28 March and were received by them on 29 March 1985.

The defendants applied for service of the writ to be set aside; the claimant applied for it to be renewed. The district registrar refused the claimant's application. Caulfield J allowed the claimant's appeal and renewed the writ so as to validate service. The defendants appealed.

Held:

(i)   The real reason why the writ was not served in time was an oversight on the part of the claimant's legal advisers. An accident or mistake of this kind does not justify departure from the general principle that an order for renewal of a writ should not be granted where its effect would be to deprive the defendant of a limitation defence.

(ii)   A defendant does not have to show a cast-iron limitation defence for this purpose. It suffices if there is a real likelihood or substantial risk that renewal will deprive the defendant of a good limitation defence.

(iii)   The mere fact that a defendant seeking to set aside an order for the renewal of a writ may present argument to the effect that renewal would deprive him of a good defence based on the Limitation Acts does not prevent the court which hears the application from deciding that he has no such defence, if the evidence suffices to enable it to make the decision.

(iv)   For the purpose of s 14(1)(b) of the Limitation Act 1980, a claimant first knows that his injury is 'attributable' to the acts or omissions of the defendant when he first knows that the injury is 'capable of being attributed' to them, bearing in mind that by s 14(3)(b) he is deemed to know facts which he could ascertain from expert medical or legal advice that it was reasonable for him to seek.

(v)   The claimant knew in November 1981 that his injuries were capable of being attributed to (a) the defendants exposing him to inhalation of TDI, (b) their failure to provide him with breathing apparatus as part of the standard equipment and (c) their failure to monitor his health. Time started running against him then, not from December 1984 when greater detail was supplied by the chemist's report: s 14(1).

(vi)   Accordingly, the relevant limitation period expired in November 1984, and the effect of the judge's order was to deprive the defendants of a good limitation defence based on s 11 of the Limitation Act 1980. Purported service of the writ should be set aside, and the action dismissed.

Per Slade LJ: 'In a case such as the present, where the acts and omissions on the part of the defendants which are complained of are, in broad terms, the exposure of their employee to dangerous working conditions and their failure to take reasonable and proper steps to protect him from such conditions, I think that the employee who has this broad knowledge may well have knowledge of the nature referred to in s 14(1)(b) sufficient to set time running against him, even though he may not yet have the knowledge sufficient to enable him or his legal advisers to draft a fully and comprehensively particularised statement of claim.'

Williams v Fanshaw Porter & Hazelhurst (a firm)

Limitation Act 1938, s 32

Court of Appeal   **[2004] EWCA Civ 157; [2004] 1 WLR 3185;**
[2004] 2 All ER 616

In 1990 the claimant suffered a stroke with serious consequences as a result, on her case, of her GP's negligence. She instructed the defendant firm to pursue the doctor for damages for medical negligence. Proceedings were issued in May 1994. In August 1994 the file handler compromised the claim by way of a consent order that the claim be dismissed but did not inform the claimant of this and had not taken her instructions. The file handler unsuccessfully applied to rectify the situation by applying in December 1994 to rejoin the doctor to the (now in fact non-existent) action. He did not inform the claimant of this application. An attendance note dated July 1995 stated that the file handler explained the situation to the claimant. He advised the claimant in June 1996 to consult other solicitors.

In December 2000 the claimant issued professional negligence proceedings against the defendant, who pleaded limitation as a defence. It was common ground that the primary limitation period expired in August 2000, six years after the consent order. However, the claimant argued that s 32(1) delayed expiry of the limitation period as the defendant had deliberately concealed facts relevant to the claimant's cause of action.

Limitation was heard as a preliminary issue. The recorder held that the file handler had not known that he was negligent when the application was dismissed in December 1994 and had not deliberately concealed anything from the claimant at any material time. He accordingly held that the claim was statute barred. The claimant appealed.

Held:

(i)   The file handler must at the latest have known by the failed application in December 1994, which was not appealed and included an order that the defendant pay the original defendant's costs, that he had been negligent in agreeing to the consent order.

(ii)   (per Park J) Section 32(1)(b) did not require that the defendant must have known that the concealed fact was relevant to the right of action. However, for the concealment to be deliberate the fact must either be one the defendant was under a duty to disclose or one he would have ordinarily disclosed in the normal course of his business with the claimant but consciously chose not to. The motivation for the concealment was irrelevant.

(iii)   The file handler had deliberately concealed the fact of the consent order and of his agreeing to it. It had been his professional duty to disclose these facts to the claimant (*Cave v Robinson Jarvis and Rolf (a firm)* (2002) 19 EG 146 (CS) considered).

(iv)   These facts were indisputably relevant to the claimant's cause of action.

(v)   The claimant did not know of these facts until either June 1995 or July 1996 due to the file handler's deliberate concealment.

(vi)   The recorder was wrong on the critical issue. s 32(1)(b) applied.

(vii)   Time therefore did not begin to run against the claimant until either June 1995 or June 1996. On either date proceedings were issued within six years and the limitation defence failed.

Appeal allowed.

Williams v Johnstone's Estate

Limitation Act 1980, s 33

QBD (Judge McKenna)   **[2008] EWHC 1334 (QB)**

On 23 August 1997 the claimant was involved in a collision with an uninsured driver who was killed in the accident. She issued proceedings on 5 August 2000 against the driver and against the owner of the car who was a passenger at the time. The MIB were subsequently added as the third defendant. The MIB entered a defence admitting liability on behalf of the estate of the driver. However, the claimant's then solicitors, L, failed to serve a notice of proceedings as required under the terms of the MIB agreement, service of which was a condition precedent to the MIB's liability. As a result the claim was discontinued on 1 November 2001 and the claimant pursued a claim for professional negligence against L. Attempts to quantify the claimant's claim were complicated by the fact that, prior to the accident, she had been diagnosed as suffering from a degenerative neurological condition. A general extension in the time for service was agreed in the professional negligence claim. Extensive work had been carried out by the claimant and L to determine the extent to which the underlying condition would have impeded the claimant's mobility and independence in any event. The claimant's medical expert had used the period that had elapsed since the accident to monitor the claimant's condition. Following a change in the law (*Horton v Sadler* (p482)), L informed the claimant that she had to mitigate her loss by issuing a second set of proceedings against the original defendants (on notice to the MIB) and applying for the limitation period to be disapplied, and L undertook to indemnify the claimant in respect of any costs thereby arising. The claimant issued these futher proceedings on 31 May 2007 against both the estate of the car's driver and against the owner/passenger. The MIB was eventually joined on 12 October 2007. The MIB pleaded limitation. The claimant applied under s 33 to disapply the limitation period. Before that hearing, the claimant requested that the MIB agree to release the owner/passenger from the proceedings. When the MIB refused, the claimant discontinued the claim against the owner/passenger on the basis that it had no real prospect of success. The MIB disputed this and contended that the discontinuance constituted a further breach of one of its conditions precedent.

Held:

(i) Having regard to all the circumstances and the relevant factors set out in s 33 of the Act, it would be inequitable for the action against the MIB to be allowed to proceed. The MIB were formally joined to the second set of proceedings after almost seven years had elapsed since the primary limitation period had expired. Whilst the delay prior to the decision in *Horton v Sadler*, which changed the law, was entirely explicable, there was a further period of delay between the decision being known and the joining of the MIB to the second set of proceedings. It had taken L almost a year to act on the change and require the claimant to issue the second set of proceedings. That was a substantial delay for which there was no adequate explanation. There were also delays in agreeing the terms of the indemnity and in joining the MIB. There might be further subsequent delay in relation to any pursuit of the owner/passenger by the MIB.

(ii) The MIB would face difficulties in investigating the cost of care at such a late stage. The claimant's medical expert had had the opportunity of carrying out examinations at regular intervals and the opportunity to monitor the progress of her condition over time. He was in a far better position to give a considered view on matters of acceleration than an expert who had only examined the claimant approximately eight years ago and who would have to come to the matter afresh. The difficulties faced by L in this respect in the context of the professional negligence action were much less. Nor was there any material extra complexity to quantification in the professional negligence action.

(iii) The claimant did not have the same difficulties, as she had had the opportunity to carry out such examination since proceedings against her had been initiated. Any trial in the second proceedings was going to be significantly later than the claim against L, given the advanced state of the quantum evidence. That had to be contrasted with the absence of any such work being undertaken by the MIB since the discontinuance of the earlier proceedings.

(iv) The professional negligence claim was no less valuable than the personal injury claim. Granting the application would serve the interests of no-one other than L's insurers.

Application refused.

Williams v Lishman Sidwell Campbell & Price Ltd

Limitation Act 1980, s 14A, s 32

Court of Appeal   **[2010] EWCA Civ 418; [2010] PNLR 25;**
[2010] Pens LR 227

In 1997 the claimants were advised by the defendants to transfer their pension funds from an occupational pension scheme to personal income drawdown plans. By October 2003 at the latest, the claimants had come to the conclusion that the pension planning was not succeeding and that the defendants were probably to blame. They commenced proceedings for professional negligence in October 2006. Under the new scheme, there was an early surrender penalty of £38,000. The defendants had never mentioned this. It was the claimants' case that the penalty was deliberately concealed by the defendant and only came to light in an expert's report in July 2007. Parts of the claim were struck out on the ground that they were time barred, the judge holding that the loss occurred in 1997 and that the claimants had the requisite knowledge of damage pursuant to s 14A of the Limitation Act 1980 by mid-May 2003. The claimants appealed.

The principal issue was whether, in a claim in negligence, where the first in time loss (in this case, the surrender penalty) which completed the claimant's cause of action was deliberately concealed by the defendant, that loss remained a 'fact relevant to the plaintiff's right of action' within s 32(1) after the occurrence of a subsequent source or head of loss which the defendant had not deliberately concealed (in this case, the general underperformance of the pension scheme). The claimants submitted that the cause of action for negligent advice arose with the first loss caused by the advice in 1997, but was not statute barred pursuant to s 32 because that loss was deliberately concealed and time did not start to run until that loss first came to light in July 2007. The defendants contended that s 32 became irrelevant once the claimants suffered loss which had not been deliberately concealed. The claimants' alternative submission under s 14A(5) was that time did not start to run until they knew in October 2003 of the medium- to long-term loss involved in the ruin of their retirement strategy.

Held:

(i)   All loss, both concealed and unconcealed, was suffered at the same time, either once the new scheme was put into effect or when the claimants could no longer change their minds and stay with the original scheme (*Shore v Sedgwick Financial Services Ltd* [2008] EWCA Civ 863, [2009] Bus LR 42 followed). If the claimants had stayed with the original scheme, presumably there would have been no loss at all. Therefore, the factual premise upon which the claimants' s 32 submission was based did not exist, as there were no earlier or later losses.

(ii)   It was plain that the claimants were fixed with knowledge for the purpose of s 14A by May 2003 at the latest. It was not possible for the claimants to argue that the knowledge found by the judge related to short-term loss only and that long-term loss was only known about in October 2003, as nothing happened in that time to make a difference and the judge was completely justified on the facts in finding that it must have been abundantly clear to the claimants by May 2003 that they were in a much worse position than if they had stayed with their original investment scheme.

(iii)   (obiter, per Rix LJ) Had the £38,000 penalty preceded the loss of leaving a secure scheme for a riskier scheme, the first loss would not have been statute barred, as time would not have begun to run until the concealment was discovered, and s 14A would not apply to an action to which deliberate concealment under s 32 applied. Whilst there was force in the arguments to the contrary, particularly on the facts of the case, there was no compelling reason why a defendant responsible for deliberate concealment, which marked the original accrual of a right of action, should not have to answer for a second loss that he had not concealed and which the claimant had known about for longer than the primary limitation period, together with the first loss that he had deliberately concealed but which the claimant had only more recently discovered.

(iv)   (obiter, per Elias LJ) It might be appropriate to modify the 'statement of claim test' used in relation to s 32(1)(b) (that, in order to be a relevant fact within the meaning of s 32, any concealed fact had to be a fact that should be pleaded in a statement of claim), so that, if the fact of which a claimant was ignorant was a necessary element in the right of action itself, it would necessarily satisfy the requirement of causative relevance to the decision to pursue that right.

Appeal dismissed.

Willis v Quality Heating Services Ltd

CPR 17

Court of Appeal   **LTL 24/3/2000**

The claimant was employed by the defendant as a service engineer from June 1995 to August 1996 when he allegedly sustained a back injury that thereafter prevented him from working. The particulars of claim alleged that he was required throughout his employment with the defendant to move heavy loads but that the claim was based on two specific incidents of back trauma, in July and August 1996 respectively.

The claimant applied to re-re-amend the particulars to rely on the whole period of employment rather than merely the two cited incidents. On 8 March 2000 the judge, with reference to CPR 17.4(2), noted that the limitation period had expired and that the claimant was not relying on the same facts as those already pleaded. He held that as the trial was three weeks away it would be unfair to allow the application. The claimant appealed.

Held:

(i)   The existing particulars already alleged that the claimant had been required to carry overly heavy loads throughout his employment. It was also obvious from other documents that this was the claimant's case. The claimant was not putting forward a new case.

(ii)   Although the claimant could and should have pleaded the claim more clearly from the outset the defendant was not prejudiced.

(iii)   It would be unjust to refuse to allow the claimant to rely on the matters set out in the re-re-amended particulars and the appeal would be allowed.

Wilson v Banner Scaffolding Ltd and another

Limitation Act 1939, s 2D   **Companies Act 1948, s 231**

Milmo J   **(1982) Times, 22 June**

On 10 September 1975 the claimant (Clifford Wilson) was injured at work. Within weeks his claims were notified to both defendants who passed them on to their insurers. On 11 July 1978 his writ was issued against both defendants. In September 1978 it was served.

The claimant's solicitors subsequently learned that the second defendants had been wound up in August 1976. By s 231 of the Companies Act 1948, the making of the winding-up order prevented any claimant from commencing proceedings against the second defendants without first obtaining the leave of the court to do so. In September 1979, Leicester County Court granted the claimant's application for leave to commence an action against the second defendants notwithstanding the winding-up order.

In October 1979 the district registry gave the claimant leave to add the second defendants as defendants to the July 1978 writ. It was duly amended and served on the second defendants' solicitors who served a defence denying liability and pleading limitation. The claimant applied under s 2D of the Limitation Act 1939 as amended for an order disapplying the primary limitation period under s 2A. A preliminary trial was ordered.

Held:

(i) The writ as originally issued with the name of the second defendants upon it was a nullity as far as they were concerned. The prohibition against issue without leave of the court imposed by s 231 of the Companies Act 1948 was absolute and unqualified.

(ii) *Walkley*'s case was different, because there the initial action was perfectly valid. In the present case, there was no action in being against the second defendants until the writ was amended in October 1978 to add them. Therefore s 2D applied.

(iii) (a) Until the primary limitation period expired, neither the claimant nor his legal advisers knew or had any reason to suspect that the second defendants were in liquidation: s 2D(3)(a);

   (b) shortly after the accident, the second defendants were informed of the claimant's claim and passed it to their insurers: s 2D(3)(b);

   (c) it would be equitable to allow the action to proceed: s 2D(1).

Walkley v Precision Forgings Ltd (p705) distinguished.

NB: The rule in *Walkley* was abolished in *Horton v Sadler* (p482).

Witt v British Coal Corporation

Limitation Act 1980, s 14, s 33

Doncaster County Court (Judge Moore)   [1998] CLY 546

The claimant brought an action claiming damages in respect of deafness allegedly caused by his exposure to industrial noise during the course of his employment with the defendant. The claimant commenced employment in the coal industry in 1973 and noticed minor deafness in the late 1980s. He left the defendant's employ in 1986 or 1987. In 1990 the claimant came to appreciate that his deafness may have been caused by his employment with the defendant and he instructed solicitors on 24 November 1992. A letter of claim was sent by his solicitors to the defendant's insurers in early 1993 but, after that, they did little to progress the claim. The defendant requested details of the claimant's employment history, claims against other insurers and also requested a medical appointment. The claimant's solicitors did not respond. The claimant was informed by his solicitors that full details of his claim had been submitted although it would be a couple of years before he heard anything due to the number of claims submitted to the defendant, but that the defendant would settle his claim as soon as possible. The claimant eventually instructed new solicitors and proceedings were issued in 1997, applying under s 33 for s 11 to be disapplied.

Held:

(i) The claimant acquired knowledge pursuant to s 14 in November 1990 when he was aware that his problem was both significant and attributable to his work. His claim was therefore time barred.

(ii) The primary limitation period ended in November 1993, and the length of the consequent delay inevitably caused prejudice to the defendant, as it was now much more difficult for them to investigate his work history because of changes in the coal industry in the early 1990s.

(iii)   The discretionary powers conferred by s 33 would not be applied. The claimant's original solicitors did virtually nothing and acted wholly unreasonably. The claimant therefore had a cast iron case in negligence against them.

(iv)   In applying s 33, a balancing exercise must be conducted of the potential prejudice to each party. Relevant circumstances in assessing prejudice are the strength of a claim in negligence against legal advisers, value of the claim (which in this instance is minimal), and conduct of each party. Both parties acted reasonably and, although the claimant was misled by his solicitors, it would be wholly inequitable for the defendant to bear the burden of the claim rather than the solicitors' indemnity fund.

Claim dismissed.

Wood v Ministry of Defence

Limitation Act 1980, s 14, s 33

QBD (Middlesbrough DR, HHJ Taylor)   5 December 2008, unreported

The claimant (born in 1958) had worked as a painter and finisher of aircraft and motor vehicles between 1987 and 1995. By 1994 he was diagnosed with Parkinson's disease. This was a very unusual diagnosis given the claimant's age. He believed that his exposure to toxic chemicals used to strip paint was the cause of his neurological problems and he consulted solicitors. An application for legal aid was made and refused. Whilst appealing that decision, the claimant's solicitors on a privately instructed basis contacted the defendant investigating whether the claimant had a claim. Legal aid was never granted. During the same period the claimant acquired some information of an expert nature from two different sources which indicated that the position was not favourable to him. In 2001 he was approached by solicitors acting for another man (X), who was also pursuing a claim against the defendant. The claimant requested that the information in X's case be made available to him. He was informed that, until the conclusion of X's case, no information could be passed to him because of client confidentiality. X's case was settled in his favour in 2007. The claimant then issued proceedings in 2007. Limitation was heard as preliminary issue.

The defendant contended that, by instructing solicitors in 1994 because of his belief, the claimant was fixed with the bare minimum knowledge required for the purposes of s 14(1). The defendant submitted that 2001 was another trigger date, in that the claimant had either direct or constructive knowledge.

Held:

(i)   It was clear that the claimant did not have the relevant knowledge, either direct or constructive, in 1994. He had held a firm belief and had sought assistance from the defendant and had looked for expert medical evidence (*Nash v Eli Lilly & Co* (p568) applied). In relation to the defendant, the correspondence made it plain that the claimant was not making a claim for compensation but was making enquiries as to whether or not information might be available to bring a claim. The claimant clearly did not believe that he was taking the preliminary steps for proceedings; he was making preliminary steps to decide whether he could go that far.

(ii)   When the claimant was approached by solicitors acting for X, and he was told that no information could be provided to him, it was reasonable at that time for the claimant not to take any steps. He had taken positive steps and previously paid for enquiries which had taken him no further forward, legal aid had been rejected and, in 2001, legal aid was not available for claims such as this. Whilst he had his personal beliefs, he had no further knowledge and, given the state of his physical health, he did not want to go through the trauma of further legal enquiries unless he had some basis to go on.

(iii)   When X's case was settled, the claimant immediately instructed solicitors and proceedings were issued. As the claimant did not have knowledge in 1994 or in 2001 for the purpose of s 14, he was at liberty to pursue the action.

(iv)   If that decision was wrong, a direction under s 33 was appropriate. The experts relied on by the defendant have not been prejudiced by the delay in time. The claimant was a relatively young man, who had lost his employment and had a young family. The claim had a potential value in excess of £1 million and the prejudice to the claimant if he was not allowed to proceed was overwhelming.

Preliminary issue determined in favour of claimant.

NB: The issue date of knowledge would now almost certainly have been decided differently in light of *B v Ministry of Defence* (p312).

Woods v Attorney General

Limitation Act 1980, s 11, s 14, s 33

McPherson J   **Lexis, 18 July 1990**

From 1980 to 1982 the claimant (Rose Woods), in the course of her employment by the defendants, was required to use chemicals known as FA and FB which were heated and gave off fumes. During 1982 and 1983 she noticed a tightness in her chest and some pain in her eyes and had some time off work for what her doctor described as bronchitis and influenza. Whilst there was a suspicion in her mind, she only learned that these symptoms were connected to her work when she went to Benendon Hospital in April 1984. The treatment there made her better, but in September 1986 she suffered a nasty attack of breathlessness during a walking holiday.

On her return, she consulted her trades union who advised her to apply to the DHSS first. She did so but was not examined by the DHSS doctor until March 1988. In the summer of 1988 the DHSS doctor reported that she might be suffering from occupational asthma. She proceeded to consult solicitors who issued her writ in March 1989. A preliminary trial was ordered.

Held:

(i)   The claimant's date of knowledge was April 1984 when she knew that she had a significant injury due to her work: s 14(1). There was no reason to postpone this date to her attack of breathlessness in September 1986. Therefore her writ was prima facie out of time: s 11(4).

(ii)   (a)   The claimant's delay from April 1984 to August 1986 was because she thought she was going to be all right. From September 1986 to summer 1988 it was due to following her union's advice to take the DHSS route first. From summer 1988 to March 1989 her solicitors were investigating the case and obtaining counsel's opinion. The delay was long but gave rise at most to only minor criticisms: s 33(3)(a);

      (b)   both the defendants' main witnesses about the claimant's alleged complaints were still alive and well. It should not be difficult to go back to 1980–82 and ascertain whether noxious fumes were given off by the trade chemicals and the well known machinery and equipment provided by known suppliers. Whatever problems there might be about attributability, it was not impossible for a medical expert to deal with causation and the medical records were still available. The passage of extra time from the expiry of the limitation period in April 1987 might render the impact of some of the defendants' evidence less cogent but should not cause them serious additional trouble: s 33(3)(b).

(iii)   The equity of the situation required the claimant to be allowed to proceed with the action: s 33(1).

Woolnough v G & M Power Plant Co Ltd

Limitation Act 1939, s 2D

Court of Appeal   **3 March 1981**

On 20 October 1973 the claimant (Dennis Woolnough), a works manager employed by the defendants, slipped on oil at their factory. In December 1973 he had to go off sick with aching and numbness in his legs. The diagnosis was that he was suffering some degeneration of a disc in the C5/6 region of the spine, and an operation was performed. By March 1974 he knew that his serious spinal condition could be attributed at least in part to the accident. He returned to work in May 1974 and reported the accident to the defendants for the first time in August 1974. In December 1973 and December 1974 an eye witness, Mr Beckett, made two short written statements to him, each naming a different place as the scene of the accident. The claimant did not claim damages, because he considered that the defendants were good employers and he was content not to seek compensation as long as he was able to work.

In 1979 Mr Beckett died. In January 1980 the claimant became unfit for work and he was retired prematurely by about six years. He promptly instructed solicitors who issued his writ on 28 February 1980. They served it with a statement of claim which gave a different location of the accident from either of those in Mr Beckett's statements. The defendants served a defence pleading limitation.

At the preliminary trial, Woolf J gave the claimant leave to proceed with the action pursuant to s 2D of the Limitation Act 1939 as amended. The defendants appealed.

Held:

(i)   The claimant had decided for his own reasons not to make a claim for damages against his employers and, because it suited him to go on drawing his salary rather than claim, he had allowed a period of over six years to elapse without giving any intimation to his employers that a claim was going to come: s 33(3)(a).

(ii)   This long delay would make it very difficult for the defendants to get their evidence together. The accident had not been promptly reported. There was the problem as to where it had happened. Mr Beckett had died. The case depended on the accuracy of recollections; the longer the period of time before trial, the more difficult it was for recollection to be accurate: s 33(3)(b).

(iii)   The court can interfere on appeal if the exercise of judicial discretion is clearly wrong or is likely to lead to an injustice. That was the case here. The judge's decision would have led to an injustice to the defendants: s 33(1).

The defendants' appeal was allowed.

Re Workvale Ltd (No 2)

Limitation Act 1980, s 33   **Companies Act 1985, s 651**

Court of Appeal   **[1992] 2 All ER 627; [1992] BCLC 544**

On 27 September 1983 Donald Macdonnell fell off a ladder while working in the defendants' employment and sustained injuries. In November 1983 solicitors notified his claim. In February 1984 the defendant company went into liquidation. In January 1986 the defendants' insurers informed the claimant's solicitors of this. In April 1986 the liquidators' account and the return of the final meeting were duly registered, so in July 1986 the company was dissolved.

On 3 September 1986 the claimant's solicitors issued a writ naming the company as defendant. Although they did not realise this, it was a nullity because the company did not exist. In

January 1987 the writ and statement of claim were served on solicitors nominated by the defendants' insurers. The action proceeded to the point at which it was more or less ready for trial, when in September 1988 the defendants' solicitors ascertained and informed the claimant's solicitors that the company had been dissolved. The action was struck out in January 1990. In July 1990 Mr Macdonnell died.

In December 1990 his widow applied for a declaration that the dissolution of the company was void and for an order under s 651(5) of the Companies Act 1985 as added by s 141 of the Companies Act 1989 that the company be restored to the register and a direction under s 651(6) that the period between the dissolution of the company and its restoration to the register be disregarded for the purposes of the Limitation Act 1980. Harman J allowed the company's insurers to be added as respondent to the notice and made the order under s 651(5) that the company be restored to the register without giving the direction sought under s 651(6). The respondent insurers appealed.

Held:

(i)   It is not the case that an order under s 651(5) cannot be made, if the primary limitation period applicable to the proposed action has expired. The presence of s 33 in the Limitation Act 1980 means that it cannot be certain that such an action for personal injuries 'would fail', unless it is clear that s 33 does not apply to the case and that an order under s 33 would not be made.

(ii)   Accordingly, for the purposes of s 651(5) in a case where the primary limitation period has expired, the judge should ask himself whether the applicant has an arguable case for an order under s 33. If so, it cannot be predicted that 'the proceedings would fail'. If not, the statutory language of s 651(5) bars the making of an order thereunder. Where the primary limitation period has expired, it is for the applicant to satisfy the court that a s 33 application is arguable.

(iii)   The present case was not on all fours with *Walkley v Precision Forgings Ltd*. The action that was started in September 1986 was not an effective action. The defendant did not exist. So the claimant had been prejudiced by the three-year limitation period in s 11, and s 33 fell to be considered.

(iv)   The case for a s 33 order was very strong. The reasons for the delay involved fault on both sides s 33(3)(a). The evidence on both sides was likely to be less cogent by reason of delay, but the case had been brought to a point where it was ready for trial in 1988: s 33(3)(b). The defendants' insurers' solicitors implicitly represented from January 1987 to September 1988 that the company was in existence: s 33(3)(c). There was dilatoriness on the claimant's side after September 1988, in that the application for an order to restore the company to the register was not made until December 1990: s 33(3)(e). However, this was not enough to turn the scales against the claimant: s 33(1).

(v)   The judge was therefore right to make the order under s 651(5). The insurers' appeal should be dismissed.

Per Scott LJ: 'There is, however, an additional matter of procedural practice that I want to mention. As the case now stands, there will have to be an application in the Queen's Bench Division or in the county court, as the case may be, for a s 33 order. The material put before the court will be the same material as is now before us. There is, as I understand it, nothing extra that either side will want to adduce for the purpose of the s 33 application. So there is no point in putting the parties to the extra expense and continued delay that the further application will inevitably entail. It was, in my opinion, open to Harman J, if satisfied that a s 33 application would succeed, to exercise the power conferred on the court by s 651(6) and to allow, as asked in para 5 of the notice of motion, that "the period between 22 July 1986 and the date of restoration of the company be excluded from the limitation period in respect of the applicant's claim for damages".

In a case in which the primary limitation period had expired before the dissolution of the company, it would not be possible to avoid the necessity of a s 33 application by making a s 651(6) order. But this is not such a case. In a case in which the insurers of the proposed defendant, or the persons interested in defending the proposed action, were not the respondents to the s 651(5) application, it would not be proper to make a sub-s(6) order. To do so might prejudice the rights of absent parties. But in the present case the insurers are respondents. In a case in which either party desired to adduce evidence on the s 33 application which was not before the court on the s 651(5) application, it might not be possible for the court on hearing the s 651 application to conclude that the s 33 application would succeed. But in the present case, as I understand the position, all evidence is before the court. Finally, the judge who hears the s 651(5) application may, having regard to the particular issues which will be debated on the s 33 application, conclude that those issues ought to be dealt with in the courts, Queen's Bench Division or country court as the case might be, more accustomed to dealing with such applications. It may be that is a view which, if he had been asked to address his mind to the matter, Harman J would have adopted in the present case. However, in a case in which all the requisite evidence is before the court on the s 651(5) application and in which the judge is able to be satisfied that a s 33 application would succeed and that the right parties are represented, the judge can, in my opinion, make an appropriate order under s 651(6) and thereby avoid an unnecessary s 33 application.

Speaking for myself, I think that the present case is a case in which that course could have been taken.'

Walkley v Precision Forgings Ltd (p705) distinguished.

See *White v Glass* (1989) Times, 18 February.

NB: The rule in *Walkley* was abolished in *Horton v Sadler* (p482).

XA v YA

Limitation Act 1980, s 14, s 33

QBD (Thirlwall J)   **[2010] EWHC 1983 (QB); [2011] PIQR P1**

The claimant (born on 4 February 1978) alleged that, during his childhood, his mother (the defendant) had assaulted him directly and was jointly responsible with his father for assaults upon him by the father. He also claimed that the defendant had negligently failed to protect him from his father, as a result of which he suffered physical injury and long-term psychiatric damage. The father was a practising Catholic who had been brought up in a regime of harsh physical punishment. He adopted a similar regime in his own household, regularly striking his five children with implements including a clothes brush, a stick and a cane.

Proceedings were issued in 2009. The claimant argued that the defendant owed a common law duty of care to him to take reasonable steps to keep him safe from injury, and the standard to be applied to the duty was the standard expected of a reasonable parent judged by the standards of the day. He submitted that the defendant was negligent in failing to obtain injunctive relief to keep the father away from the family home; failing to leave the family home with the children; failing to have the children looked after under a private family arrangement; or failing to have the children taken into care. The defendant submitted that she did not encourage or instigate assaults by the father; rather, she tried to protect the children. She argued that she did not assault the claimant but only lawfully chastised him on occasion. She submitted that she owed no common law duty of care to the claimant, the duty he contended for was novel, and in any case the claim was statute barred.

Held:

(i)   In relation to the limitation issue, it was accepted that the claimant possessed the relevant knowledge at the time of his majority in February 1996 and that limitation thus expired in February 1999. The period of delay was 10 years. The claimant had suffered from anxiety and other mental health problems during his teens. The delay in bringing proceedings was partially caused by psychological factors. The claimant had a good reason for the delay. In relation to the claims in assault, the cogency of the evidence on behalf of both parties was such that the court could consider the claims without unfairness to the defendant. The court would therefore exercise its discretion under s 33 in favour of the claimant in respect of the assault claims.

(ii)   However, the position was different in relation to the negligence claim, as the defence depended almost entirely on the defendant's evidence. The defendant was genuinely bewildered by the proceedings, and was unable to assist beyond generalities. She lacked any ability to give a coherent account of the years in which she brought up her children. Her position was hopelessly prejudiced. In addition, the quality and quantity of the evidence was not sufficient to allow the court to come to any secure conclusions on the question of breach of duty. The claim in negligence was statute barred (*A v Hoare* (p287) followed and *B v Nugent Care Society* (p315) applied).

(iii)   The evidence showed that, over a period of approximately 10 years, the claimant suffered beatings from his father, sometimes several times a week. On many occasions, the punishment went beyond what was lawful and reasonable. However, the beating of the children by their father was not part of a 'joint enterprise'. The defendant was therefore not jointly responsible for those assaults.

(iv)   Although the defendant did strike the children from time to time, her conduct had been, at the most, lawful chastisement. The claimant's claim of assault against her was dismissed.

Judgment for defendant.

Yates v Thakeham Tiles Ltd

Limitation Act 1980, s 33

Court of Appeal   **[1995] PIQR P135; (1994) Times, 19 May**

On 1 October 1986 the claimant, whilst employed by the defendant, allegedly injured himself in a lifting incident. He left the defendant's employ in May 1987 and underwent a back operation in June 1987 which was apparently successful. On 19 October 1987 he applied for industrial injuries benefit and on 18 July 1989 he was awarded a disablement pension. He did not instruct solicitors until March 1991. There were legal aid difficulties and the defendant received no notification of a potential claim until 26 March 1992. The defendant appealed. Proceedings were issued on 22 May 1992, whereupon the defendant applied to strike the claim out as time barred.

Held:

(i)   Appeals against a judge's wide discretion under s 33 were inherently difficult. This was especially so when, as here, the judge had applied the statutory checklist and carefully considered each item.

(ii)   The judge did what was required and carried out a one composite exercise, identifying and weighing the material factors and then striking a balance.

(iii)   The judge erred in interpreting 'disability' in s 33(3)(d) as referring to general physical disability whereas in fact it referred to legal disability under the Mental Health Act, as in s 28 and s 38(2) of the lsolicitor. However, this was a matter that he was entitled to take into account when considering all the circumstances of the case.

(iv)   The criticism of the judge for failing to properly consider s 33(3)(e) was not made out. He was entitled to take the view that it was not unreasonable for the claimant's solicitors to gather all the relevant information before sending a letter of claim. However desirable an early letter of claim might be, it was not a requirement under the rules.

(v)   Although this was a borderline case, and there was force in the criticism of the judge's failure to give sufficient weight to the degraded cogency of evidence as required by s 33(3)(b), it was not made out that the judge would have come to a different decision if he had given appropriate weight to the cogency of evidence.

(vi)   The defendant had not demonstrated that the judge was plainly wrong.

Appeal dismissed.

NB: It is doubtful whether the observation at (iv) above remains valid under the CPR – see eg para 3.1 of the Pre-Action Protocol for Personal Injury Claims.

Yearworth and Others v North Bristol NHS Trust

Limitation Act 1980, s 38

Court of Appeal   **[2009] EWCA Civ 37; [2010] QB 1;**
[2009] 3 WLR 118; [2009] 2 All ER 986;
[2009] LS Law Medical 126; (2009) 107 BMLR 47;
(2009) 153(5) SJLB 27; (2009) Times, 10 February

The claimants were being treated at a hospital run by the trust. Due to the risk of the treatment on their fertility, they banked sperm samples at the hospital, which had a fertility unit licensed under the Human Fertilisation and Embryology Act 1990. The sperm was banked free of charge. It was damaged when the equipment storing the samples failed. The claimants alleged that, as a result of learning about the loss of their sperm samples, they subsequently suffered psychiatric injury or mental distress, and brought proceedings for negligence. The court determined preliminary issues, holding that the sperm did not amount to the claimants' property and that the damage to it did not constitute a personal injury. The claimants appealed.

Held:

(i)   It was clear that, for the purposes of claims in negligence, the claimants had ownership of their sperm. By their bodies, they alone had generated and ejaculated the sperm, and the sole object of their ejaculation was that it might later be used for their benefit.

(ii)   There was no domestic, Commonwealth or American authority that directly supported a proposition that damage to part of a person's body, including to a substance generated by it, could constitute a personal physical injury to him, even if inflicted after its removal from his body. Accordingly, damage to, and consequential loss of, the claimant's sperm did not constitute personal injury. It would be a fiction to hold that damage to a substance generated by a person's body, inflicted after its removal for storage purposes, constituted a bodily or personal injury to him.

(iii)   In addition to an action in tort, the claimants also had a distinct cause of action against the trust under the law of bailment.

(iv)   The trial judge's determination was replaced by a determination that the sperm was the claimant's property, both in tort and in bailment, and they were entitled to damages; and the matter was remitted for the determination of the remaining issues.

Appeal allowed.

Yellin v Levitt Bernstein Associates

Limitation Act 1980, s 33

Court of Appeal   **Lexis, 26 June 1986**

On 11 April 1978 the claimant (Sidney Yellin), an electrician employed by his own company, fell during a house conversion down a void which had been left by the removal of a staircase and sustained a head injury which eventually resulted in epilepsy.

Court action was initially taken against the claimant's own company, against the main contractors and against two site foremen, Alan Cook and Alexander Cook, who were shareholders in the main contractors. Judgment was given against the main contractors and Alexander Cook, but their insurance had lapsed and no damages were paid by them. The proceedings were not pursued against the claimant's own company and Alan Cook.

Both leading and junior counsel had advised that there was no cause of action against the defendant architects who were responsible for the design and supervision of the building operations. However, in July 1984 another junior counsel advised that there was an arguable case. The claimant's writ against them was issued on 21 August 1984. The defendants pleaded limitation.

The master concluded that he had no discretion to allow the action to proceed. Mr Titheridge QC, sitting as a deputy High Court judge, held on appeal that he had a discretion but that it would not be equitable to allow the action to proceed under s 33 of the Limitation Act 1980. The claimant applied for leave to appeal.

Held:

(i)   This was a case in which not only was the writ issued a long time after the accident, but in which no claim was advanced against the defendants until the writ was issued against them: s 33(3)(a).

(ii)   The judge was right in concluding that the prospects of a full and adequate investigation had been impaired by the delay since April 1981. The case could not be decided simply by drawing inferences from a report prepared very shortly after the accident by a member of the defendants' firm: s 33(3)(b).

(iii)   There was no indication of misdirection or other fault in the way in which the judge exercised his discretion. There was nothing in respect of which it would be right to grant leave to appeal: s 33(1).

The claimant's application was dismissed.

Yew Bon Tew v Kenderaan Bas Mara

Limitation   **Public Authorities Protection (Amendment)
                                       Act 1974 (Malaysia)**

Privy Council   **[1982] 3 All ER 833; [1983] 1 AC 553; [1982] 3 WLR 1026**

On 5 April 1972 the claimant (Yew Bon Tew) was injured when a bus belonging to the defendants collided with the motor cycle that he was riding along a road in the State of Selangor in Malaysia. On 5 April 1973 his cause of action became statute barred by the 12-month limitation period imposed by s 2 of the Public Authorities Protection Ordinance 1948.

In June 1974 the Public Authorities Protection (Amendment) Act 1974 was passed and came into effect. It substituted a 36-month limitation period in place of the previous 12 months. The claimant's writ was issued on 20 March 1975. The defendants admitted liability, subject to contributory negligence, but pleaded limitation.

The Federal Court of Malaysia (Appellate Jurisdiction) upheld the defendants' appeal from the decision at a preliminary trial of Azmi J who held that the 1974 act was retrospective. The claimant appealed to the Privy Council.

Held:

(i)   An accrued right to plead a time bar, which is acquired after the lapse of a statutory period, is in every sense a right, even though it arises under an Act which is procedural. It is a right which is not to be taken away by conferring on the statute a retrospective operation, unless such construction is unavoidable.

(ii)   There was no reason to conclude that the defendants acquired no 'right' when the period prescribed by the 1948 Ordinance expired, merely because the 1948 Ordinance and the 1974 Act were procedural in character. The plain purpose of the 1974 Act, read with the 1948 Ordinance, was to give and not to deprive. It was to give a potential defendant, who was not in June 1974 possessed of an accrued limitation defence, a right to plead such a defence at the expiration of the new statutory period. It was not to deprive a potential defendant of a limitation defence which he already possessed.

(iii)   Accordingly, the writ had been issued outside the applicable limitation period. The claimant's appeal was dismissed.

Per Lord Brightman: 'The briefest consideration will expose the injustice of the contrary view. When a period of limitation has expired, a potential defendant should be able to assume that he is no longer at risk from a stale claim. He should be able to part with his papers if they exist and discard any proofs of witnesses which have been taken, discharge his solicitor if he has been retained, and order his affairs on the basis that his potential liability has gone. That is the whole purpose of the limitation defence.'

Young v Chief Constable of Northumbria

Limitation Act 1980, s 33

Queen's Bench Division (Kennedy J)   **20 January 1998, unreported**

On 17 February 1994 the claimant, a police constable, slipped in the police station yard and fell, injuring her right arm. The claimant instructed solicitors to pursue a claim for damages, and papers were submitted to counsel in July 1996 to settle a statement of claim. Counsel was chased for an early return of the papers in December 1996, but only produced the statement of claim on 13 March 1997, by which time the limitation period had expired. Due to an oversight on the part of the claimant's solicitors caused by change of personnel, responsibilities and premises, proceedings had not been issued in the meantime. The defendant asserted that the claim was statute barred. The claimant requested that the court exercise its discretion under s 33, claiming that she would be prejudiced by having to instruct new solicitors to commence proceedings against her current solicitors, who would be aware of any weaknesses in her case.

Held:

(i)   The statement of claim could have been settled in a few hours, and to allow counsel to delay for such a period was a gross dereliction of duty on the solicitors' part.

(ii)   In the exercise of discretion under s 33, the principal concept was the wish to do justice between the parties. It was not a very powerful argument for the claimant to claim prejudice on the basis that her former solicitors were aware of any weaknesses in her case, whereas the defendant was not. In the circumstances, an action by the claimant against her solicitors on the grounds of negligence should not involve any argument as to their liability. The claimant might suffer prejudice because, in order to retain the goodwill of the Police Federation, the solicitors might prefer to settle the case, but on balance there was likely to be rather less prejudice than in some cases.

(iii) The prejudice which the defendant would suffer had to be seen against the existence of the discretion. In the instant case an entry was made in the accident book the day after the accident which would normally be expected to trigger some form of review of the circumstances surrounding the accident, so that those responsible for safety could take any necessary steps to improve the position. Therefore the prejudice which the defendant would suffer by the action not being brought 29 days earlier, enabling it to investigate the claim any earlier, was minimal (*Donovan v Gwentoys Ltd* (p412) considered). The defendant's claim, that he would be prejudiced by possibly having to pay an insurance excess if the claimant's claim were allowed to continue, could not carry much weight.

(iv) However, discretion ought not to be exercised under s 33, because the error in allowing counsel to delay for so long was a gross one and, in the circumstances that followed, there was prejudice to the defendant (*Hartley v Birmingham City Council* (p465) considered).

Judgment for the defendant.

NB: It is highly doubtful following *Cain v Francis* (p360) that this case would now be decided in the same way.

Young v GLC and Massey

Limitation Act 1980, s 11, s 14

Owen J   **[1987] CLY 2328**

On 14 April 1981 the claimant (Mr Young) was involved in a road traffic accident. He sustained what was considered to be a minor whiplash injury. In December 1981 he suffered a severe attack and went for an x-ray; he was told that he had arthritis in the neck and was given a soft collar. He had several days off work at irregular intervals in the three years after the accident, but he did not consider that his job was under threat.

In May 1984 he was off work again and consulted his general practitioner who declared him unfit for his job as a fireman. He remained off work. In December 1984, through a visit from his superior officer, he realised that his position at work was at risk. He took advice from his trade union. His writ was issued on 29 March 1985. He was medically retired in June 1985.

Held:

(i) The claimant knew that, having suffered an injury, he could have brought an action for damages, but reasonably at the time he did not consider it worthwhile or proper: s 14(2).

(ii) He did not know that he had a significant injury attributable to the accident until May 1984: s 14(1).

(iii) His action had been commenced in time, within three years of his date of knowledge: s 11(4).

Young v Western Power Distribution (South West) plc

Limitation Act 1980, s 11, s 12, s 33   **ECHR, Art 6**

Court of Appeal   **[2003] EWCA Civ 1034; [2003] 1 WLR 2868;**
[2004] PIQR P4

The claimant's husband worked for the defendant from 1959 to his retirement on medical grounds in 1994. His work caused him to come into occasional contact with asbestos. In December 1993 he was diagnosed with mesothelioma, an asbestos related malignant cancer.

He issued proceedings in relation to this on 6 January 1995. When the defendant investigated the claim they discovered a further report written shortly after the initial diagnosis which challenged that diagnosis and suggested that adenocarcinoma, a non-asbestos related malignant cancer, was more likely to be present. The defendant's expert adopted this view. The claimant passed the new medical evidence to his own expert who opined that it was impossible to say whether the cancer was asbestos-related or not until post-mortem. Unable to prove his case, the husband discontinued proceedings on 17 January 1997.

On 2 March 1999 the husband died. It was discovered shortly thereafter that he had in fact been suffering from mesothelioma.

The claimant issued proceedings on 22 May 2002 under the Law Reform (Miscellaneous Provisions) Act 1934 and the Fatal Accidents Act 1976. The defendant denied liability and pleaded that the claim was statute barred and that the rule in *Walkley v Precision Forgings Ltd* (p705) precluded any discretion under s 33. Limitation was tried as a preliminary issue. It was agreed that the husband's date of knowledge was December 1993 and that, despite his later altered belief, once fixed with knowledge he could not subsequently lose it (*Nash v Eli Lilly* (p568)). The judge held that (a) the claim fell within the rule in *Walkley*; (b) the claim also fell within the exception to the *Walkley* principle, that there was an estoppel or something akin to it; (c) that being so, there was no need to consider whether *Walkley* breached Art 6 of the ECHR; and (d) that any evidential prejudice to the defendant was small and it would be equitable to allow the claim to proceed. The defendant appealed findings (b) and (d) and the claimant cross-appealed findings (a) and (c).

Held:

(i)   The 1976 claim was barred by s 12(1) as the husband could no longer have maintained an action. The claimant could seek to have the section disapplied under s 33 as the reason the husband could not have maintained a claim was not the s 11 time limit itself but rather *Walkley*. The claimant could not be in a better position as regards *Walkley* than the deceased.

(ii)   The 1934 Act claim was similarly barred. There was no cause of action vested in the defendant when he died and the claimant could be in no better position. *Walkley* could not here be distinguished on the basis that either the cause of action or the parties were different.

(iii)   The rule in *Walkley* was a rule of construction and did not logically admit exceptions (*Deerness v Keeble* (p408) applied). It could only be avoided if the defendant was estopped to begin with from raising the limitation defence as unconscionable. The judge had been wrong to find an estoppel on these facts.

(iv)   The *Walkley* principle was not contrary to the ECHR. It pursued a legitimate aim and contracting states had a margin of appreciation as regards the qualified rights in Art 6 (*Stubbings v UK* (p678) applied).

(v)   Although mistaken in holding that he had a discretion, the judge could not be faulted in his exercise of it.

Appeal allowed and cross-appeal dismissed.

NB: The rule in *Walkley* was abolished in *Horton v Sadler* (p482).

Younger v Dorset and Somerset SHA

Limitation Act 1980, s 38

Southampton County Court (Recorder Blohm)   **[2006] Lloyd's Rep Med 489**

The claimant's action arose from a misinterpretation of two biopsies and a consequent misdiagnosis of coeliac disease. As a result of the diagnosis, she had been prescribed a gluten-free diet. She was later retested and given a clear result. Her medical history was investigated and it was common ground that the previous diagnosis was wrong.

She therefore issued proceedings for personal injury arising from having to eat a gluten-free diet. It was the defendant's defence that the claimant's claim was for negligent misstatement and not for damages for personal injury and that the limitation period for the claim had expired. The claimant contended that she had suffered some psychological harm from the gluten-free diet and that, whilst that harm did not amount to a recognised mental illness, it was a sufficient personal injury to bring the action within s 38. The preliminary issue that fell to be determined was whether the damages claimed by the claimant could properly be said to consist of, or include, damages in respect of personal injuries that were recoverable at law; it was agreed that, if there was no valid claim for damages for personal injury, judgment had to be entered for the defendant on the basis that the relevant limitation periods had expired and the claim was statute barred six years following the claimant's 18th birthday, and there was no discretion to disapply s 2 of the Act.

Held:

(i)   The loss claimed by the claimant for psychiatric injury, being less than a recognised psychiatric illness, was not recoverable at law, and the balance of the claim was not a claim in respect of personal injury but one of economic loss. There was no authority that permitted the recovery of the claimant's particular losses. Whilst there were circumstances where damages for anxiety were recoverable, those arose only in cases where the nature of the duty accepted by a particular person was to avoid the anxiety from arising in the first place. That was not the position in the instant case, as the defendant was not under a duty to protect the claimant's self-esteem; it was under a duty to ensure that the claimant was properly treated and received a proper diagnosis and proper treatment.

(ii)   Whilst the defendant appeared to be in breach of that duty, that did not lead to recoverability for the psychiatric harm that had been suffered as a consequence (*Robinson v St Helens MBC* (p628) and *Phelps v Hillingdon LBC* (2000) LGR 651 considered).

Preliminary issue determined in favour of defendant. Claim dismissed.

The Zirje

Maritime Conventions Act 1911, s 8

Sheen J   **[1989] 1 Lloyd's Rep 493**

On 17 October 1986 the claimants' vessel Docebarra collided with the defendants' ship Zirje in the Kiel Canal. English jurisdiction was promptly agreed. In June 1987 the defendants' insurers agreed not to contest liability and not to counterclaim.

From 16 September 1988 the claimants' solicitors made a series of requests to the defendants' agents for an extension of time for starting proceedings. On 5 October the defendants' agents answered that the defendants would grant an extension of one year provided that the claimants did likewise. On 6 October their solicitors sent a telex pointing out that the defendants had agreed not to pursue any claim and requesting an unconditional extension. The defendants' agent did not reply and swore that he did not see the telex until 20 October when he found it in a tray behind his desk after the claimants' solicitor had telephoned him.

The writ was issued on 20 October 1988. The claimants applied for an order that the two-year time limit under s 8 of the Maritime Conventions Act 1911 be extended.

Held:

(i)   A judge should grant such an extension under s 8 of the 1911 Act if there is good reason to do so. The exercise of his discretion to extend time should not be confined only to those cases where there appear to be exceptional or special circumstances.

(ii)   Discretion in this case should be exercised in the claimants' favour because:

      (a)   the defendants had agreed not to contest liability;

      (b)   the extension required was only three days;

      (c)   the defendants had been willing to grant an extension for one year. If they had not sought to impose an unreasonable condition, that extension would have been agreed; and

      (d)   if the system for incoming telexes operated by the defendants' agents had not been defective, the writ would have been issued in time.

Appendix

Index to Appendix

Limitation Act 1980

1980 c 58

An Act to consolidate the Limitation Acts 1939 to 1980

[13 November 1980]

BE IT ENACTED by the Queen's most Excellent Majesty, by and with the advice and consent of the Lords Spiritual and Temporal, and Commons, in this present Parliament assembled, and by the authority of the same, as follows:

PART I
ORDINARY TIME LIMITS FOR DIFFERENT CLASSES OF ACTION

Time limits under Part I subject to extension or exclusion under Part II

1 Time limits under Part I subject to extension or exclusion under Part II

(1) This Part of this Act gives the ordinary time limits for bringing actions of the various classes mentioned in the following provisions of this Part.

(2) The ordinary time limits given in this Part of this Act are subject to extension or exclusion in accordance with the provisions of Part II of this Act.

Annotations

Date in force: 1 May 1981.

Sub-s (2) derived from Limitation Act 1939, s 1, and Limitation Act 1963, s 4(3).

Actions founded on tort

2 Time limit for actions founded on tort

An action founded on tort shall not be brought after the expiration of six years from the date on which the cause of action accrued.

Annotations

Date in force: 1 May 1981.

This section derived from Limitation Act 1939, s 2(1)(a).

Actions founded on simple contract

5 Time limit for actions founded on simple contract

An action founded on simple contract shall not be brought after the expiration of six years from the date on which the cause of action accrued.

Annotations

Date in force: 1 May 1981.

This section derived from Limitation Act 1939, s 2(1)(a).

Actions for sums recoverable by statute

9 Time limit for actions for sums recoverable by statute

(1) An action to recover any sum recoverable by virtue of any enactment shall not be brought after the expiration of six years from the date on which the cause of action accrued.

(2)   Subsection (1) above shall not affect any action to which section 10 of this Act applies.

Annotations

Date in force: 1 May 1981.

This section derived from Limitation Act 1939, ss 2(1)(d), 32.

10   Special time limit for claiming contribution

(1)   Where under section 1 of the Civil Liability (Contribution) Act 1978 any person becomes entitled to a right to recover contribution in respect of any damage from any other person, no action to recover contribution by virtue of that right shall be brought after the expiration of two years from the date on which that right accrued.

(2)   For the purposes of this section the date on which a right to recover contribution in respect of any damage accrues to any person (referred to below in this section as 'the relevant date') shall be ascertained as provided in subsections (3) and (4) below.

(3)   If the person in question is held liable in respect of that damage–

    (a)   by a judgment given in any civil proceedings; or

    (b)   by an award made on any arbitration;

the relevant date shall be the date on which the judgment is given, or the date of the award (as the case may be).

For the purposes of this subsection no account shall be taken of any judgment or award given or made on appeal in so far as it varies the amount of damages awarded against the person in question.

(4)   If, in any case not within subsection (3) above, the person in question makes or agrees to make any payment to one or more persons in compensation for that damage (whether he admits any liability in respect of the damage or not), the relevant date shall be the earliest date on which the amount to be paid by him is agreed between him (or his representative) and the person (or each of the persons, as the case may be) to whom the payment is to be made.

(5)   An action to recover contribution shall be one to which sections 28, 32[, 33A] and 35 of this Act apply, but otherwise Parts II and III of this Act (except sections 34, 37 and 38) shall not apply for the purposes of this section.

Annotations

Date in force: 1 May 1981.

This section derived from Limitation Act 1963, ss 4, 5, 7(7).

Sub-s (5): number in square brackets inserted by SI 2011/113, regs 22, 23.

Actions in respect of wrongs causing personal injuries or death

11   Special time limit for actions in respect of personal injuries

(1)   This section applies to any action for damages for negligence, nuisance or breach of duty (whether the duty exists by virtue of a contract or of provision made by or under a statute or independently of any contract or any such provision) where the damages claimed by the plaintiff for the negligence, nuisance or breach of duty consist of or include damages in respect of personal injuries to the plaintiff or any other person.

[(1A)   This section does not apply to any action brought for damages under section 3 of the Protection from Harassment Act 1997.]

(2)   None of the time limits given in the preceding provisions of this Act shall apply to an action to which this section applies.

(3)   An action to which this section applies shall not be brought after the expiration of the period applicable in accordance with subsection (4) or (5) below.

(4)   Except where subsection (5) below applies, the period applicable is three years from–

    (a)   the date on which the cause of action accrued; or

    (b)   the date of knowledge (if later) of the person injured.

(5)   If the person injured dies before the expiration of the period mentioned in subsection (4) above, the period applicable as respects the cause of action surviving for the benefit of his estate by virtue of section 1 of the Law Reform (Miscellaneous Provisions) Act 1934 shall be three years from–

    (a)   the date of death; or

    (b)   the date of the personal representative's knowledge;

whichever is the later.

(6)   For the purposes of this section 'personal representative' includes any person who is or has been a personal representative of the deceased, including an executor who has not proved the will (whether or not he has renounced probate) but not anyone appointed only as a special personal representative in relation to settled land; and regard shall be had to any knowledge acquired by any such person while a personal representative or previously.

(7)   If there is more than one personal representative, and their dates of knowledge are different, subsection (5)(b) above shall be read as referring to the earliest of those dates.

Annotations

Date in force: 1 May 1981.

This section derived from Limitation Act 1939, ss 2(8), 2A(1)–(5), (9), (10).

Sub-s (1A): inserted by Protection from Harassment Act 1997, s 6.

[11A   Actions in respect of defective products]

(1)   This section shall apply to an action for damages by virtue of any provision of Part I of the Consumer Protection Act 1987.

(2)   None of the time limits given in the preceding provisions of this Act shall apply to an action to which this section applies.

(3)   An action to which this section applies shall not be brought after the expiration of the period of ten years from the relevant time, within the meaning of section 4 of the said act of 1987; and this subsection shall operate to extinguish a right of action and shall do so whether or not that right of action had accrued, or time under the following provisions of this Act had begun to run, at the end of the said period of ten years.

(4)   Subject to subsection (4) below, an action to which this section applies in which the damages claimed by the plaintiff consist of or include damages in respect of personal injuries to the plaintiff or any other person or loss of or damage to any property, shall not be brought after the expiration of the period of three years from whichever is the later of–

    (a)   the date on which the cause of action accrued; and

    (b)   the date of knowledge of the injured person or, in the case of loss of damage to property, the date of knowledge of the plaintiff or (if earlier) of any person in whom his cause of action was previously vested.

(5)   If in a case where the damages claimed by the plaintiff consist of or include damages in respect of personal injuries to the plaintiff or any other person the injured person died before the expiration of the period mentioned in subsection (4) above, that subsection shall have effect as respects the cause of action surviving for the benefit of his estate by virtue of section 1 of the Law Reform (Miscellaneous Provisions) Act 1934 as if for the reference to that period there were substituted a reference to the period of three years from whichever is the later of–

    (a)   the date of death; and

(b) the date of the personal representative's knowledge.

(6) For the purposes of this section 'personal representative' includes any person who is or has been a personal representative of the deceased, including an executor who has not proved the will (whether or not he has renounced probate) but not anyone appointed only as a special personal representative in relation to settled land; and regard shall be had to any knowledge acquired by any such person while a personal representative or previously.

(7) If there is more than one personal representative and their dates of knowledge are different, subsection (5)(b) above shall be read as referring to the earliest of those dates.

(8) Expressions used in this section or section 14 of this Act and in Part I of the Consumer Protection Act 1987 have the same meanings in this section or that section as in that Part; and section 1(1) of that Act (Part I to be construed as enacted for the purpose of complying with the product liability Directive) shall apply for the purpose of construing this section and the following provisions of this Act so far as they relate to an action by virtue of any provision of that Part as it applies for the purpose of construing that Part.]

Annotations

Date in force: 1 May 1981.

Inserted by Consumer Protection Act 1987, s 6, Sch 1, Part I, para 1.

12   Special time limit for actions under Fatal Accidents legislation

(1) An action under the Fatal Accidents Act 1976 shall not be brought if the death occurred when the person injured could no longer maintain an action and recover damages in respect of the injury (whether because of a time limit in this Act or in any other Act, or for any other reason).

Where any such action by the injured person would have been barred by the time limit in section 11 [or 11A] of this Act, no account shall be taken of the possibility of that time limit being overridden under section 33 of this Act.

(2) None of the time limits given in the preceding provisions of this Act shall apply to an action under the Fatal Accidents Act 1976, but no such action shall be brought after the expiration of three years from–

(a) the date of death; or

(b) the date of knowledge of the person for whose benefit the action is brought; whichever is the later.

(3) An action under the Fatal Accidents Act 1976 shall be one to which sections 28, 33[, 33A] and 35 of this Act apply, and the application to any such action of the time limit under subsection (2) above shall be subject to section 39; but otherwise Parts II and III of this Act shall not apply to any such action.

Annotations

Date in force: 1 May 1981.

This section derived from Limitation Act 1939, s 2B.

Sub-s (1): words in square brackets inserted by Consumer Protection Act 1987, s 6, Sch 1, Part I, para 2.

Sub-s (3): number in square brackets inserted by SI 2011/113, regs 22, 24.

13   Operation of time limit under section 12 in relation to different dependants

(1) Where there is more than one person for whose benefit an action under the Fatal Accidents Act 1976 is brought, section 12(2)(b) of this Act shall be applied separately to each of them.

(2) Subject to subsection (3) below, if by virtue of subsection (1) above the action would be outside the time limit given by section 12(2) as regards one or more, but not all, of the persons

for whose benefit it is brought, the court shall direct that any person as regards whom the action would be outside that limit shall be excluded from those for whom the action is brought.

(3)   The court shall not give such a direction if it is shown that if the action were brought exclusively for the benefit of the person in question it would not be defeated by a defence of limitation (whether in consequence of section 28 of this Act or an agreement between the parties not to raise the defence, or otherwise).

Annotations

Date in force: 1 May 1981.

This section derived from Limitation Act 1939, s 2C.

14   Definition of date of knowledge for purposes of sections 11 and 12

(1)   [Subject to subsection (1A) below,] In sections 11 and 12 of this Act references to a person's date of knowledge are references to the date on which he first had knowledge of the following facts–

- (a)   that the injury in question was significant; and

- (b)   that the injury was attributable in whole or in part to the act or omission which is alleged to constitute negligence, nuisance or breach of duty; and

- (c)   the identity of the defendant; and

- (d)   if it is alleged that the act or omission was that of a person other than the defendant, the identity of that person and the additional facts supporting the bringing of an action against the defendant;

and knowledge that any acts or omissions did or did not, as a matter of law, involve negligence, nuisance or breach of duty is irrelevant.

[(1A) In section 11A of this Act and in section 12 of this Act so far as that section applies to an action by virtue of section 6(1)(a) of the Consumer Protection Act 1987 (death caused by defective product) references to a person's date of knowledge are references to the date on which he first had knowledge of the following facts–

- (a)   such facts about the damage caused by the defect as would lead a reasonable person who had suffered such damage to consider it sufficiently serious to justify his instituting proceedings for damages against a defendant who did not dispute liability and was able to satisfy a judgment; and

- (b)   the damage was wholly or partly attributable to the facts and circumstances alleged to constitute the defect; and

- (c)   the identity of the defendant;

but, in determining the date on which a person first had such knowledge there shall be disregarded both the extent (if any) of that person's knowledge on any date of whether particular facts or circumstances would or would not, as a matter of law, constitute a defect and, in a case relating to loss of or damage to property, any knowledge which that person had on a date on which he had no right of action by virtue of Part I of that Act in respect of the loss or damage.]

(2)   For the purposes of this section an injury is significant if the person whose date of knowledge is in question would reasonably have considered it sufficiently serious to justify his instituting proceedings for damages against a defendant who did not dispute liability and was able to satisfy a judgment.

(3)   For the purposes of this section a person's knowledge includes knowledge which he might reasonably have been expected to acquire–

- (a)   from facts observable or ascertainable by him; or

(b) from facts ascertainable by him with the help of medical or other appropriate expert advice which it is reasonable for him to seek;

but a person shall not be fixed under this subsection with knowledge of a fact ascertainable only with the help of expert advice so long as he has taken all reasonable steps to obtain (and, where appropriate, to act on) that advice.

Annotations

Date in force: 1 March 1988 (para (1A)); 1 May 1981 (remainder).

This section derived from Limitation Act 1939, s 2A(6)–(8).

Sub-s (1): words in square brackets inserted by Consumer Protection Act 1987, s 6, Sch 1, Part I, para 3.

Sub-s (1A): inserted by Consumer Protection Act 1987, s 6, Sch 1, Part I, para 3.

Actions in respect of latent damage not involving personal injuries

[14A Special time limit for negligence actions where facts relevant to cause of action are not known at date of accrual

(1) This section applies to any action for damages for negligence, other than one to which section 11 of this Act applies, where the starting date for reckoning the period of limitation under subsection (4)(b) below falls after the date on which the cause of action accrued.

(2) Section 2 of this Act shall not apply to an action to which this section applies.

(3) An action to which this section applies shall not be brought after the expiration of the period applicable in accordance with subsection (4) below.

(4) That period is either–

(a) six years from the date on which the cause of action accrued; or

(b) three years from the starting date as defined by subsection (5) below, if that period expires later than the period mentioned in paragraph (a) above.

(5) For the purposes of this section, the starting date for reckoning the period of limitation under subsection (4)(b) above is the earliest date on which the plaintiff or any person in whom the cause of action was vested before him first had both the knowledge required for bringing an action for damages in respect of the relevant damage and a right to bring such an action.

(6) In subsection (5) above 'the knowledge required for bringing an action for damages in respect of the relevant damage' means knowledge both–

(a) of the material facts about the damage in respect of which damages are claimed; and

(b) of the other facts relevant to the current action mentioned in subsection (8) below.

(7) For the purposes of subsection (6)(a) above, the material facts about the damage are such facts about the damage as would lead a reasonable person who had suffered such damage to consider it sufficiently serious to justify his instituting proceedings for damages against a defendant who did not dispute liability and was able to satisfy a judgment.

(8) The other facts referred to in subsection (6)(b) above are–

(a) that the damage was attributable in whole or in part to the act or omission which is alleged to constitute negligence; and

(b) the identity of the defendant; and

(c) if it is alleged that the act or omission was that of a person other than the defendant, the identity of that person and the additional facts supporting the bringing of an action against the defendant.

(9)   Knowledge that any acts or omissions did or did not, as a matter of law, involve negligence is irrelevant for the purposes of subsection (5) above.

(10)   For the purposes of this section a person's knowledge includes knowledge which he might reasonably have been expected to acquire–

>   (a)   from facts observable or ascertainable by him; or
>
>   (b)   from facts ascertainable by him with the help of appropriate expert advice which it is reasonable for him to seek;

but a person shall not be taken by virtue of this subsection to have knowledge of a fact ascertainable only with the help of expert advice so long as he has taken all reasonable steps to obtain (and, where appropriate, to act on) that advice.]

Annotations

Date in force: 18 September 1986.

Inserted by Latent Damage Act 1986, s 1.

[14B   Overriding time limit for negligence actions not involving personal injuries

(1)   An action for damages for negligence, other than one to which section 11 of this Act applies, shall not be brought after the expiration of fifteen years from the date (or, if more than one, from the last of the dates) on which there occurred any act or omission–

>   (a)   which is alleged to constitute negligence; and
>
>   (b)   to which the damage in respect of which damages are claimed is alleged to be attributable (in whole or in part).

(2)   This section bars the right of action in a case to which subsection (1) above applies notwithstanding that–

>   (a)   the cause of action has not yet accrued; or
>
>   (b)   where section 14A of this Act applies to the action, the date which is for the purposes of that section the starting date for reckoning the period mentioned in subsection (4)(b) of that section has not yet occurred;

before the end of the period of limitation prescribed by this section.]

Annotations

Date in force: 18 September 1986.

Inserted by Latent Damage Act 1986, s 1.

PART II
EXTENSION OR EXCLUSION OF ORDINARY TIME LIMITS

Disability

28   Extension of limitation period in case of disability

(1)   Subject to the following provisions of this section, if on the date when any right of action accrued for which a period of limitation is prescribed by this Act, the person to whom it accrued was under a disability, the action may be brought at any time before the expiration of six years from the date when he ceased to be under a disability or died (whichever first occurred) notwithstanding that the period of limitation has expired.

(2)   This section shall not affect any case where the right of action first accrued to some person (not under a disability) through whom the person under a disability claims.

(3)   When a right of action which has accrued to a person under a disability accrues, on the death of that person while still under a disability, to another person under a disability, no further extension of time shall be allowed by reason of the disability of the second person.

(4)   No action to recover land or money charged on land shall be brought by virtue of this section by any person after the expiration of thirty years from the date on which the right of action accrued to that person or some person through whom he claims.

[(4A)   If the action is one to which section 4A of this Act applies, subsection (1) above shall have effect–

  (a)   in the case of an action for libel or slander, as if for the words from 'at any time' to 'occurred)' there were substituted the words 'by him at any time before the expiration of one year from the date on which he ceased to be under a disability'; and

  (b)   in the case of an action for slander of title, slander of goods or other malicious falsehood, as if for the words 'six years' there were substituted the words 'one year'.]

(5)   If the action is one to which section 10 of this Act applies, subsection (1) above shall have effect as if for the words 'six years' there were substituted the words 'two years'.

(6)   If the action is one to which section 11 or 12(2) of this Act applies, subsection (1) above shall have effect as if for the words 'six years' there were substituted the words 'three years'.

[(7)   If the action is one to which section 11A of this Act applies or one by virtue of section 6(1)(a) of the Consumer Protection Act 1987 (death caused by defective product), subsection (1) above–

  (a)   shall not apply to the time limit prescribed by subsection (3) of the said section 11A or to that time limit as applied by virtue of section 12(1) of this Act; and

  (b)   in relation to any other time limit prescribed by this Act shall have effect as if for the word 'six years' there were substituted the words 'three years'.]

Annotations

Date in force: 1 March 1988 (Sub-s (7)); 30 December 1985 (Sub-s (4)); 1 May 1981 (remainder).

Inserted by Latent Damage Act 1986, s 1.

Sub-s (4A): inserted by Administration of Justice Act 1985, ss 57(3), 69(5), Sch 9, para 14; substituted by Defamation Act 1996, s 5(3), (6).

Sub-s (7): inserted by Consumer Protection Act 1987, s 6, Sch 1, Part I, para 4.

[28A   Extension for cases where the limitation period is the period under section 14A(4)(b)

(1)   Subject to subsection (2) below, if in the case of any action for which a period of limitation is prescribed by section 14A of this Act–

  (a)   the period applicable in accordance with subsection (4) of that section is the period mentioned in paragraph (b) of that subsection;

  (b)   on the date which is for the purposes of that section the starting date for reckoning that period the person by reference to whose knowledge that date fell to be determined under subsection (5) of that section was under a disability; and

  (c)   section 28 of this Act does not apply to the action;

the action may be brought at any time before the expiration of three years from the date when he ceased to be under a disability or died (whichever first occurred) notwithstanding that the period mentioned above has expired.

(2)   An action may not be brought by virtue of subsection (1) above after the end of the period of limitation prescribed by section 14B of this Act.]

Annotations

Date in force: 18 September 1986.

Inserted by Latent Damage Act 1986, s 1.

Fraud, concealment and mistake

32   Postponement of limitation period in case of fraud, concealment or mistake

(1)   Subject to [subsections (3) and (4A)] below, where in the case of any action for which a period of limitation is prescribed by this Act, either–

> (a)   the action is based upon the fraud of the defendant; or
>
> (b)   any fact relevant to the plaintiff's right of action has been deliberately concealed from him by the defendant; or
>
> (c)   the action is for relief from the consequences of a mistake;

the period of limitation shall not begin to run until the plaintiff has discovered the fraud, concealment or mistake (as the case may be) or could with reasonable diligence have discovered it.

References in this subsection to the defendant include references to the defendant's agent and to any person through whom the defendant claims and his agent.

(2)   For the purposes of subsection (1) above, deliberate commission of a breach of duty in circumstances in which it is unlikely to be discovered for some time amounts to deliberate concealment of the facts involved in that breach of duty.

(3)   Nothing in this section shall enable any action–

> (a)   to recover, or recover the value of, any property; or
>
> (b)   to enforce any charge against, or set aside any transaction affecting, any property;

to be brought against the purchaser of the property or any person claiming through him in any case where the property has been purchased for valuable consideration by an innocent third party since the fraud or concealment or (as the case may be) the transaction in which the mistake was made took place.

(4)   A purchaser is an innocent third party for the purposes of this section–

> (a)   in the case of fraud or concealment of any fact relevant to the plaintiff's right of action, if he was not a party to the fraud or (as the case may be) to the concealment of that fact and did not at the time of the purchase know or have reason to believe that the fraud or concealment had taken place; and
>
> (b)   in the case of mistake, if he did not at the time of the purchase know or have reason to believe that the mistake had been made.

[(4A)   Subsection (1) above shall not apply in relation to the time limit prescribed by section 11A(3) of this Act or in relation to that time limit as applied by virtue of section 12(1) of this Act].

[(5)   Sections 14A and 14B of this Act shall not apply to any action to which subsection (1)(b) above applies (and accordingly the period of limitation referred to in that subsection, in any case to which either of those sections would otherwise apply, is the period applicable under section 2 of this Act).]

Annotations

Date in force: 1 March 1988 (Sub-s (4A)); 18 September 1986 (Sub-s (5)); 1 May 1981 (remainder).

This section derived from Limitation Act 1939, s 26.

Sub-s (1): words in square brackets substituted by Consumer Protection Act 1987, s 6, Sch 1, Part I, para 5.

Sub-s (4A): inserted by Consumer Protection Act 1987, s 6, Sch 1, Part I, para 5.

Sub-s (5): inserted by Latent Damage Act 1986, s 2(2).

Discretionary exclusion of time limit for actions in respect of personal injuries or death

33 Discretionary exclusion of time limit for actions in respect of personal injuries or death

(1)   If it appears to the court that it would be equitable to allow an action to proceed having regard to the degree to which–

> (a)   the provisions of section 11 [or 11A] or 12 of this Act prejudice the plaintiff or any person whom he represents; and
>
> (b)   any decision of the court under this subsection would prejudice the defendant or any person whom he represents;

the court may direct that those provisions shall not apply to the action, or shall not apply to any specified cause of action to which the action relates.

[(1A)   The court shall not under this section disapply–

> (a)   subsection (3) of section 11A; or
>
> (b)   where the damages claimed by the plaintiff are confined to damages for loss of or damage to any property, any other provision in its application to an action by virtue of Part I of the Consumer Protection Act 1987.]

(2)   The court shall not under this section disapply section 12(1) except where the reason why the person injured could no longer maintain an action was because of the time limit in section 11 [or subsection (4) of section 11A].

If, for example, the person injured could at his death no longer maintain an action under the Fatal Accidents Act 1976 because of the time limit in Article 29 in Schedule 1 to the Carriage by Air Act 1961, the court has no power to direct that section 12(1) shall not apply.

(3)   In acting under this section the court shall have regard to all the circumstances of the case and in particular to–

> (a)   the length of, and the reasons for, the delay on the part of the plaintiff;
>
> (b)   the extent to which, having regard to the delay, the evidence adduced or likely to be adduced by the plaintiff or the defendant is or is likely to be less cogent than if the action had been brought within the time allowed by section 11 [, by section 11A] or (as the case may be) by section 12;
>
> (c)   the conduct of the defendant after the cause of action arose, including the extent (if any) to which he responded to requests reasonably made by the plaintiff for information or inspection for the purpose of ascertaining facts which were or might be relevant to the plaintiff's cause of action against the defendant;
>
> (d)   the duration of any disability of the plaintiff arising after the date of the accrual of the cause of action;
>
> (e)   the extent to which the plaintiff acted promptly and reasonably once he knew whether or not the act or omission of the defendant, to which the injury was attributable, might be capable at that time of giving rise to an action for damages;
>
> (f)   the steps, if any, taken by the plaintiff to obtain medical, legal or other expert advice and the nature of any such advice he may have received.

(4)   In a case where the person injured died when, because of section 11 [or subsection (4) of section 11A], he could no longer maintain an action and recover damages in respect of the injury, the court shall have regard in particular to the length of, and the reasons for, the delay on the part of the deceased.

(5)   In a case under subsection (4) above, or any other case where the time limit, or one of the time limits, depends on the date of knowledge of a person other than the plaintiff, subsection (3) above shall have effect with appropriate modifications, and shall have effect in particular as if references to the plaintiff included references to any person whose date of knowledge is or was relevant in determining a time limit.

(6)   A direction by the court disapplying the provisions of section 12(1) shall operate to disapply the provisions to the same effect in section 1(1) of the Fatal Accidents Act 1976.

(7)   In this section 'the court' means the court in which the action has been brought.

(8)   References in this section to section 11 [or 11A] include references to that section as extended by any of the [provisions of this Part of this Act other than this section] or by any provision of Part III of this Act.

Annotations

Date in force: 1 March 1988 (Sub-s (1A));1 May 1981 (remainder).

This section derived from Limitation Act 1939, s 2D.

Sub-s (1): words in square brackets inserted by Consumer Protection Act 1987, s 6, Sch 1, Part I, para 6.

Sub-s (1A): inserted by Consumer Protection Act 1987, s 6, Sch 1, Part I, para 6.

Sub-ss (3), (4): words in square brackets inserted by Consumer Protection Act 1987, s 6, Sch 1, Part I, para 6.

Sub-s (8): words in first square brackets inserted by Consumer Protection Act 1987, s 6, Sch 1, Part I, para 6; words in second square brackets inserted by SI 2011/113, regs 22, 25.

PART III
MISCELLANEOUS AND GENERAL

35   New claims in pending actions: rules of court

(1)   For the purposes of this Act, any new claim made in the course of any action shall be deemed to be a separate action and to have been commenced–

    (a)   in the case of a new claim made in or by way of third party proceedings, on the date on which those proceedings were commenced; and

    (b)   in the case of any other new claim, on the same date as the original action.

(2)   In this section a new claim means any claim by way of set-off or counterclaim, and any claim involving either–

    (a)   the addition or substitution of a new cause of action; or

    (b)   the addition or substitution of a new party;

and 'third party proceedings' means any proceedings brought in the course of any action by any party to the action against a person not previously a party to the action, other than proceedings brought by joining any such person as defendant to any claim already made in the original action by the party bringing the proceedings.

(3)   Except as provided by section 33 of this Act or by rules of court, neither the High Court nor any county court shall allow a new claim within subsection (1)(b) above, other than an original set-off or counterclaim, to be made in the course of any action after the expiry of any time limit under this Act which would affect a new action to enforce that claim.

For the purposes of this subsection, a claim is an original set-off or an original counterclaim if it is a claim made by way of set-off or (as the case may be) by way of counterclaim by a party who has not previously made any claim in the action.

(4)   Rules of court may provide for allowing a new claim to which subsection (3) above applies to be made as there mentioned, but only if the conditions specified in subsection (5) below are satisfied, and subject to any further restrictions the rules may impose.

(5)   The conditions referred to in subsection (4) above are the following–

(a)   in the case of a claim involving a new cause of action, if the new cause of action arises out of the same facts or substantially the same facts as are already in issue on any claim previously made in the original action; and

(b)   in the case of a claim involving a new party, if the addition or substitution of the new party is necessary for the determination of the original action.

(6)   The addition or substitution of a new party shall not be regarded for the purposes of subsection (5)(b) above as necessary for the determination of the original action unless either–

(a)   the new party is substituted for a party whose name was given in any claim made in the original action in mistake for the new party's name; or

(b)   any claim already made in the original action cannot be maintained by or against an existing party unless the new party is joined or substituted as plaintiff or defendant in that action.

(7)   Subject to subsection (4) above, rules of court may provide for allowing a party to any action to claim relief in a new capacity in respect of a new cause of action notwithstanding that he had no title to make that claim at the date of the commencement of the action.

This subsection shall not be taken as prejudicing the power of rules of court to provide for allowing a party to claim relief in a new capacity without adding or substituting a new cause of action.

(8)   Subsections (3) to (7) above shall apply in relation to a new claim made in the course of third party proceedings as if those proceedings were the original action, and subject to such other modifications as may be prescribed by rules of court in any case or class of case.

(9)   ...

Annotations

Date in force: 1 May 1981.

Commencement order: SI 1981/588.

This section derived from Limitation Act 1939, s 28.

Sub-s (9): repealed by Senior Courts Act 1981, s 152(4), Sch 7.

38   Interpretation

(1)   In this Act, unless the context otherwise requires–

'action' includes any proceeding in a court of law, including an ecclesiastical court [(and see subsection (11) below)];

'land' includes corporeal hereditaments, tithes and rentcharges and any legal or equitable estate or interest therein ... but except as provided above in this definition does not include any incorporeal hereditament;

'personal estate' and 'personal property' do not include chattels real;

'personal injuries' includes any disease and any impairment of a person's physical or mental condition, and 'injury' and cognate expressions shall be construed accordingly;

'rent' includes a rentcharge and a rentservice; 'rentcharge' means any annuity or periodical sum of money charged upon or payable out of land, except a rent service or interest on a mortgage on land;

'settled land', 'statutory owner' and 'tenant for life' have the same meanings respectively as in the Settled Land Act 1925;

'trust' and 'trustee' have the same meanings respectively as in the Trustee Act 1925; and

...

(2)   For the purposes of this Act a person shall be treated as under a disability while he is an infant, or *of unsound mind* [lacks capacity (within the meaning of the Mental Capacity Act 2005) to conduct legal proceedings].

(3)   For the purposes of subsection (2) above a person is of unsound mind if he is a person who, by reason of mental disorder [is incapable of managing and administering his property and affairs; and in this section 'mental disorder' has the same meaning as in the Mental Health Act 1983].

(4)   Without prejudice to the generality of subsection (3) above, a person shall be conclusively presumed for the purposes of subsection (2) above to be of unsound mind–

(a)   *while he is liable to be detained or subject to guardianship under [the Mental Health Act 1983 (otherwise than by virtue of section 35 or 89)]; and*

[(b)   *while he is receiving treatment [for mental disorder] as an in-patient in any hospital within the meaning of the Mental Health Act 1983 [or independent hospital or care home within the meaning of the Care Standards Act 2000] without being liable to be detained under the said Act of 1983 (otherwise than by virtue of section 35 or 89), being treatment which follows without any interval a period during which he was liable to be detained or subject to guardianship under the Mental Health Act 1959, or the said Act of 1983 (otherwise than by virtue of section 35 or 89) or by virtue of any enactment repealed or excluded by the Mental Health Act 1959].*

(5)   Subject to subsection (6) below, a person shall be treated as claiming through another person if he became entitled by, through, under, or by the act of that other person to the right claimed, and any person whose estate or interest might have been barred by a person entitled to an entailed interest in possession shall be treated as claiming through the person so entitled.

(6)   A person becoming entitled to any estate or interest by virtue of a special power of appointment shall not be treated as claiming through the appointor.

(7)   References in this Act to a right of action to recover land shall include references to a right to enter into possession of the land or, in the case of rentcharges and tithes, to distrain for arrears of rent or tithe, and references to the bringing of such an action shall include references to the making of such an entry or distress.

(8)   References in this Act to the possession of land shall, in the case of tithes and rentcharges, be construed as references to the receipt of the tithe or rent, and references to the date of dispossession or discontinuance of possession of land shall, in the case of rent charges, be construed as references to the date of the last receipt of rent.

(9)   References in Part II of this Act to a right of action shall include references to–

(a)   a cause of action;

(b)   a right to receive money secured by a mortgage or charge on any property;

(c)   a right to recover proceeds of the sale of land; and

(d)   a right to receive a share or interest in the personal estate of a deceased person.

(10)   References in Part II to the date of the accrual of a right of action shall be construed–

(a) in the case of an action upon a judgment, as references to the date on which the judgment became enforceable; and

(b) in the case of an action to recover arrears of rent or interest, or damages in respect of arrears of rent or interest, as references to the date on which the rent or interest became due.

[(11) References in this Act to an action do not include any method of recovery of a sum recoverable under–

(a) Part 3 of the Social Security Administration Act 1992,

(b) section 127(c) of the Social Security Contributions and Benefits Act 1992, or

(c) Part 1 of the Tax Credits Act 2002,

other than a proceeding in a court of law.]

Annotations

Date in force: 1 May 1981.

This section derived from Limitation Act 1939, s 31.

Sub-s (1): words in square brackets in definition 'action' inserted by Welfare Reform Act 2012, s 108(1), (2); words omitted from definition 'land' repealed, and definition omitted repealed, by Trusts of Land and Appointment of Trustees Act 1996, s 25(2), Sch 4; for savings in relation to entailed interests created before the commencement of that Act, and savings consequential upon the abolition of the doctrine of conversion, see s 25(4), (5) thereof.

Sub-s (2): words 'of unsound mind' repealed and subsequent words in square brackets substituted by Mental Capacity Act 2005, s 67(1), Sch 6, para 25(a), as from a day to be appointed.

Sub-ss (3), (4): repealed by Mental Capacity Act 2005, s 67(1), (2), Sch 6, para 25(b), Sch 7, as from a day to be appointed.

Sub-s (3): words from 'is incapable of' to 'Mental Health Act 1983' in square brackets substituted by Care Standards Act 2000, s 116, Sch 4, para 8(a).

Sub-s (4): in para (a) words from 'the Mental Health Act 1983' to '35 or 89)' in square brackets substituted by Mental Health Act 1983, s 148, Sch 4, para 55(b)(i).

Sub-s (4): para (b) substituted by Mental Health Act 1983, s 148, Sch 4, para 55(b)(ii).

Sub-s (4) in para (b) words 'for mental disorder' in square brackets inserted by Care Standards Act 2000, s 116, Sch 4, para 8(b).

Sub-s (4): in para (b) words 'or independent hospital or care home within the meaning of the Care Standards Act 2000' in square brackets substituted by Care Standards Act 2000, s 116, Sch 4, para 8(b).

Sub-s (11): inserted by Welfare Reform Act 2012, s 108(1), (3).

39 Saving for other limitation enactments

This Act shall not apply to any action or arbitration for which a period of limitation is prescribed by or under any other enactment (whether passed before or after the passing of this Act) or to any action or arbitration to which the Crown is a party and for which, if it were between subjects, a period of limitation would be prescribed by or under any such other enactment.

Annotations

Date in force: 1 May 1981.

This section derived from Limitation Act 1939, s 32.

40 Transitional provisions, amendments and repeals

(1) Schedule 2 to this Act, which contains transitional provisions, shall have effect.

(2) The enactments specified in Schedule 3 to this Act shall have effect subject to the amendments specified in that Schedule, being amendments consequential on the provisions

of this Act; but the amendment of any enactment by that Schedule shall not be taken as prejudicing the operation of section 17(2) of the Interpretation Act 1978 (effect of repeals).

(3)   The enactments specified in Schedule 4 to this Act are hereby repealed to the extent specified in column 3 of that Schedule.

Annotations

Date in force: 1 May 1981.

41   Short title, commencement and extent

(1)   This Act may be cited as the Limitation Act 1980.

(2)   This Act, except section 35, shall come into force on 1st May 1981.

(3)   Section 35 of this Act shall come into force on 1st May 1981 to the extent (if any) that the section substituted for section 28 of the Limitation Act 1939 by section 8 of the Limitation Amendment Act 1980 is in force immediately before that date; but otherwise section 35 shall come into force on such day as the Lord Chancellor may by order made by statutory instrument appoint, and different days may be appointed for different purposes of that section (including its application in relation to different courts or proceedings).

(4)   The repeal by this Act of section 14(1) of the Limitation Act 1963 and the corresponding saving in paragraph 2 of Schedule 2 to this Act shall extend to Northern Ireland, but otherwise this Act does not extend to Scotland or to Northern Ireland.

Annotations

Date in force: 1 May 1981.

Sub-s (3) derived from Limitation Amendment Act 1980, s 14(4); Sub-s (4) derived from Limitation Act 1939, s 34(3), Limitation Act 1963, s 16(2), (3), Limitation Act 1975, s 4(3), and Limitation Amendment Act 1980, s 14(5).

SCHEDULE 2
Transitional Provisions

section 40(1)

1   Nothing in this Act shall affect the operation of section 4 of the Limitation Act 1963, as it had effect immediately before 1 January 1979 (being the date on which the Civil Liability (Contribution) Act 1978 came in to force), in relation to any case where the damage in question occurred before that date.

2   The amendment made by section 14(1) of the Limitation Act 1963 in section 5 of the Limitation (Enemies and War Prisoners) Act 1945 (which provides that section 5 shall have effect as if for the words 'in force in Northern Ireland at the date of the passing of this Act' there were substituted the words 'for the time being in force in Northern Ireland') shall continue to have effect notwithstanding the repeal by this Act of section 14(1).

3   It is hereby declared that a decision taken at any time by a court to grant, or not to grant, leave under Part I of the Limitation Act 1963 (which, so far as it related to leave, was repealed by the Limitation Act 1975) does not affect the determination of any question in proceedings under any provision of this Act which corresponds to a provision of the Limitation Act 1975, but in such proceedings account may be taken of evidence admitted in proceedings under Part I of the Limitation Act 1963.

4   (1) In section 33(6) of this Act the reference to section 1(1) of the Fatal Accidents Act 1976 shall be construed as including a reference to section 1 of the Fatal Accidents Act 1846.

(2) Any other reference in that section, or in section 12 or 13 of this Act, to the Fatal Accidents Act 1976 shall be construed as including a reference to the Fatal Accidents Act 1846.

5 Notwithstanding anything in section 29(7) of this Act or in the repeals made by this Act, the Limitation Act 1939 shall continue to have effect in relation to any acknowledgment or payment made before the coming into force of section 6 of the Limitation Amendment Act 1980 (which amended section 23 of the Limitation Act 1939 and made certain repeals in sections 23 and 25 of that Act so as to prevent the revival by acknowledgment or part payment of a right of action barred by that Act) as it had effect immediately before section 6 came into force.

6 Section 28 of the Limitation Act 1939 (provisions as to set-off or counterclaim) shall continue to apply (as originally enacted) to any claim by way of set-off or counterclaim made in an action to which section 35 of this Act does not apply, but as if the reference in section 28 to that Act were a reference to this Act; and, in relation to any such action, references in this Act to section 35 of this Act shall be construed as references to section 28 as it applies by virtue of this paragraph.

7 Section 37(2)(c) of this Act shall be treated for the purposes of the Hovercraft Act 1968 as if it were contained in an Act passed before that Act.

8 In relation to a lease granted before the coming into force of section 3(2) of the Limitation Amendment Act 1980 (which substituted 'ten pounds a year' for 'twenty shillings' in section 9(3) of the Limitation Act 1939), paragraph 6(1)(a) of Schedule 1 to this Act shall have effect as if for the words 'ten pounds a year' there were substituted the words 'twenty shillings'.

9 (1) Nothing in any provision of this Act shall–

    (a) enable any action to be brought which was barred by this Act or (as the case may be) by the Limitation Act 1939 before the relevant date; or

    (b) affect any action or arbitration commenced before that date or the title to any property which is the subject of any such action or arbitration.

(2) In sub-paragraph (1) above 'the relevant date' means–

    (a) in relation to section 35 of this Act, the date on which that section comes into force in relation to actions of the description in question or, if section 8 of the Limitation Amendment Act 1980 (which substituted the provisions reproduced in section 35 for section 28 of the Limitation Act 1939) is in force immediately before 1st May 1981 in relation to actions of that description, the date on which section 8 came into force in relation to actions of that description; and

    (b) in relation to any other provision of this Act, 1st August 1980 (being the date of coming into force of the remaining provisions of the Limitation Amendment Act 1980, apart from section 8).

Annotations

Date in force: 1 May 1981.

Para 1 derived from Civil Liability (Contribution) Act 1978, s 7(1); para 3 derived from Limitation Act 1975, s 3(3); para 4 derived from Fatal Accidents Act 1976, Sch 1, para 3; paras 5, 6, 8, 9 derived from Limitation Amendment Act 1980, ss 3(3), 6(5), 12(1), 14(4).

Latent Damage Act 1986

1986 c 37

An Act to amend the law about limitation of actions in relation to actions for damages for negligence not involving personal injuries; and to provide for a person taking an interest in property to have, in certain circumstances, a cause of action in respect of negligent damage to the property occurring before he takes that interest.

[18 July 1986]

BE IT ENACTED by the Queen's most Excellent Majesty, by and with the advice and consent of the Lords Spiritual and Temporal, and Commons, in this present Parliament assembled, and by the authority of the same, as follows:

Time limits for negligence actions in respect of latent damage not involving personal injuries

1 Time limits for negligence actions in respect of latent damage not involving personal injuries

...

Annotations

Date in force: 18 September 1986.

This section adds Limitation Act 1980, ss 14A, 14B.

2 Provisions consequential on section 1

...

Annotations

Date in force: 18 September 1986.

This section adds Limitation Act 1980, ss 28A, 32(5).

Accrual of cause of action to successive owners in respect of latent damage to property

3 Accrual of cause of action to successive owners in respect of latent damage to property

(1)   Subject to the following provisions of this section, where–

    (a)   a cause of action ('the original cause of action') has accrued to any person in respect of any negligence to which damage to any property in which he has an interest is attributable (in whole or in part); and

    (b)   another person acquires an interest in that property after the date on which the original cause of action accrued but before the material facts about the damage have become known to any person who, at the time when he first has knowledge of those facts, has any interest in the property;

a fresh cause of action in respect of that negligence shall accrue to that other person on the date on which he acquires his interest in the property.

(2)   A cause of action accruing to any person by virtue of subsection (1) above–

    (a)   shall be treated as if based on breach of a duty of care at common law owed to the person to whom it accrues; and

    (b)   shall be treated for the purposes of section 14A of the 1980 Act (special time limit for negligence actions where facts relevant to cause of action are not known at date of accrual) as having accrued on the date on which the original cause of action accrued.

(3)   Section 28 of the 1980 Act (extension of limitation period in case of disability) shall not apply in relation to any such cause of action.

(4)   Subsection (1) above shall not apply in any case where the person acquiring an interest in the damaged property is either–

    (a)   a person in whom the original cause of action vests by operation of law; or

    (b)   a person in whom the interest in that property vests by virtue of any order made by a court under section 538 of the Companies Act 1985 (vesting of company property in liquidator).

(5)   For the purposes of subsection (1)(b) above, the material facts about the damage are such facts about the damage as would lead a reasonable person who has an interest in the damaged property at the time when those facts become known to him to consider it sufficiently serious to justify his instituting proceedings for damages against a defendant who did not dispute liability and was able to satisfy a judgment.

(6)   For the purposes of this section a person's knowledge includes knowledge which he might reasonably have been expected to acquire–

    (a)   from facts observable or ascertainable by him; or

    (b)   from facts ascertainable by him with the help of appropriate expert advice which it is reasonable for him to seek;

but a person shall not be taken by virtue of this subsection to have knowledge of a fact ascertainable by him only with the help of expert advice so long as he has taken all reasonable steps to obtain (and, where appropriate, to act on) that advice.

(7)   This section shall bind the Crown, but as regards the Crown's liability in tort shall not bind the Crown further than the Crown is made liable in tort by the Crown Proceedings Act 1947.

Annotations

Date in force: 18 September 1986.

The 1980 Act: the Limitation Act 1980.

4   Transitional provisions

(1)   Nothing in section 1 or 2 of this Act shall–

    (a)   enable any action to be brought which was barred by the 1980 Act or (as the case may be) by the Limitation Act 1939 before this Act comes into force; or

    (b)   affect any action commenced before this Act comes into force.

(2)   Subject to subsection (1) above, sections 1 and 2 of this Act shall have effect in relation to causes of action accruing before, as well as in relation to causes of action accruing after, this Act comes into force.

(3)   Section 3 of this Act shall only apply in cases where an interest in damaged property is acquired after this Act comes into force but shall so apply, subject to subsection (4) below, irrespective of whether the original cause of action accrued before or after this Act comes into force.

(4)   Where–

    (a)   a person acquires an interest in damaged property in circumstances to which section 3 would apart from this subsection apply; but

(b) the original cause of action accrued more than six years before this Act comes into force;

a cause of action shall not accrue to that person by virtue of subsection (1) of that section unless section 32(1)(b) of the 1980 Act (postponement of limitation period in case of deliberate concealment of relevant facts) would apply to any action founded on the original cause of action.

Annotations

Date in force: 18 September 1986.

The 1980 Act: the Limitation Act 1980.

5   Citation, interpretation, commencement and extent

(1)   This Act may be cited as the Latent Damage Act 1986.

(2)   In this Act–

'the 1980 Act' has the meaning given by section 1; and

'action' includes any proceeding in a court of law, an arbitration and any new claim within the meaning of section 35 of the 1980 Act (new claims in pending actions).

(3)   This Act shall come into force at the end of the period of two months beginning with the date on which it is passed.

(4)   This Act extends to England and Wales only.

Annotations

Date in force: 18 September 1986.

The 1980 Act: the Limitation Act 1980.

Foreign Limitation Periods Act 1984

1984 c 16

An Act to provide for any law relating to the limitation of actions to be treated, for the purposes of cases in which effect is given to foreign law or to determinations by foreign courts, as a matter of substance rather than as a matter of procedure.

[24 May 1984]

BE IT ENACTED by the Queen's most Excellent Majesty, by and with the advice and consent of the Lords Spiritual and Temporal, and Commons, in this present Parliament assembled, and by the authority of the same, as follows:

1 Application of foreign limitation law

(1) Subject to the following provisions of this Act, where in any action or proceedings in a court in England and Wales the law of any other country falls (in accordance with rules of private international law applicable by any such court) to be taken into account in the determination of any matter–

    (a) the law of that other country relating to limitation shall apply in respect of that matter for the purposes of the action or proceedings[, subject to section 1A]; and

    (b) except where that matter falls within subsection (2) below, the law of England and Wales relating to limitation shall not so apply.

(2) A matter falls within this subsection if it is a matter in the determination of which both the law of England and Wales and the law of some other country fall to be taken into account.

(3) The law of England and Wales shall determine for the purposes of any law applicable by virtue of subsection (1)(a) above whether, and the time at which, proceedings have been commenced in respect of any matter; and, accordingly, section 35 of the Limitation Act 1980 (new claims in pending proceedings) shall apply in relation to time limits applicable by virtue of subsection (1)(a) above as it applies in relation to time limits under that Act.

(4) A court in England and Wales, in exercising in pursuance of subsection (1)(a) above any discretion conferred by the law of any other country, shall so far as practicable exercise that discretion in the manner in which it is exercised in comparable cases by the courts of that other country.

(5) In this section 'law', in relation to any country, shall not include rules of private international law applicable by the courts of that country or, in the case of England and Wales, this Act.

Annotations

Sub-s (1): in para (a) words in square brackets inserted by SI 2011/113, regs 27, 28.

[1A Extension of limitation periods because of mediation of certain cross-border disputes

(1) In this section–

    (a) 'Mediation Directive' means Directive 2008/52/EC of the European Parliament and of the Council of 21 May 2008 on certain aspects of mediation in civil and commercial matters,

    (b) 'mediation' has the meaning given by article 3(a) of the Mediation Directive,

    (c) 'mediator' has the meaning given by article 3(b) of the Mediation Directive, and

    (d) 'relevant dispute' means a dispute to which article 8(1) of the Mediation Directive applies (certain cross-border disputes).

(2)   Subsection (3) applies where–

    (a)   a limitation period prescribed by any law applicable by virtue of section 1(1)(a) relates to the subject of the whole or part of a relevant dispute,

    (b)   a mediation in relation to the relevant dispute starts before the period expires, and

    (c)   if not extended by this section, the period would expire before the mediation ends or less than eight weeks after it ends.

(3)   For the purposes of initiating judicial proceedings or arbitration, the limitation period expires instead at the end of eight weeks after the mediation ends (subject to subsection (4)).

(4)   If a limitation period has been extended by this section, subsections (2) and (3) apply to the extended limitation period as they apply to a limitation period mentioned in subsection (2)(a).

(5)   For the purposes of this section, mediation starts on the date of the agreement to mediate that is entered into by the parties and the mediator.

(6)   For the purposes of this section, a mediation ends on the date of the first of these to occur–

    (a)   the parties reach an agreement in resolution of the relevant dispute,

    (b)   a party completes the notification of the other parties that it has withdrawn from the mediation,

    (c)   a party to whom a qualifying request is made fails to give a response reaching the other parties within 14 days of the request,

    (d)   after the parties are notified that the mediator's appointment has ended (by death, resignation or otherwise), they fail to agree within 14 days to seek to appoint a replacement mediator,

    (e)   the mediation otherwise comes to an end pursuant to the terms of the agreement to mediate.

(7)   For the purpose of subsection (6), a qualifying request is a request by a party that another (A) confirm to all parties that A is continuing with the mediation.

(8)   In the case of any relevant dispute, references in this section to a mediation are references to the mediation so far as it relates to that dispute, and references to a party are to be read accordingly.

(9)   This section is without prejudice to any enactment which has effect for the purposes of provisions–

    (a)   relating to limitation or prescription periods and

    (b)   contained in an international agreement to which the United Kingdom is a party.]

Annotations

Section 1A: inserted by SI 2011/113, regs 27, 29.

2   Exceptions to section 1

(1)   In any case in which the application of section 1 above would to any extent conflict (whether under subsection (2) below or otherwise) with public policy, that section shall not apply to the extent that its application would so conflict.

(2)   The application of section 1 above in relation to any action or proceedings shall conflict with public policy to the extent that its application would cause undue hardship to a person who is, or might be made, a party to the action or proceedings.

(3)   Where, under a law applicable by virtue of section 1(1)(a) above for the purposes of any action or proceedings, a limitation period is or may be extended or interrupted in respect of

the absence of a party to the action or proceedings from any specified jurisdiction or country, so much of that law as provides for the extension or interruption shall be disregarded for those purposes.

(4) ...

Annotations

Date in force: 1 October 1985.

Commencement order: SI 1985/1276.

Sub-s (4) amends Limitation (Enemies and War Prisoners) Act 1945, s 2(1).

3   Foreign judgments on limitation points

Where a court in any country outside England and Wales has determined any matter wholly or partly by reference to the law of that or any other country (including England and Wales) relating to limitation, then, for the purposes of the law relating to the effect to be given in England and Wales to that determination, that court shall, to the extent that it has so determined the matter, be deemed to have determined it on its merits.

Annotations

Date in force: 1 October 1985.

Commencement order: SI 1985/1276.

4   Meaning of law relating to limitation

(1)   Subject to subsection (3) below, references in this Act to the law of any country (including England and Wales) relating to limitation shall, in relation to any matter, be construed as references to so much of the relevant law of that country as (in any manner) makes provision with respect to a limitation period applicable to the bringing of proceedings in respect of that matter in the courts of that country and shall include–

  (a)   references to so much of that law as relates to, and to the effect of, the application, extension, reduction or interruption of that period; and

  (b)   a reference, where under that law there is no limitation period which is so applicable, to the rule that such proceedings may be brought within an indefinite period.

(2)   In subsection (1) above 'relevant law', in relation to any country, means the procedural and substantive law applicable, apart from any rules of private international law, by the courts of that country.

(3)   References in this Act to the law of England and Wales relating to limitation shall not include the rules by virtue of which a court may, in the exercise of any discretion, refuse equitable relief on the grounds of acquiescence or otherwise; but, in applying those rules to a case in relation to which the law of any country outside England and Wales is applicable by virtue of section 1(1)(a) above (not being a law that provides for a limitation period that has expired), a court in England and Wales shall have regard, in particular, to the provisions of the law that is so applicable.

Annotations

Date in force: 1 October 1985.

Commencement order: SI 1985/1276.

5   Application of Act to arbitrations

...

Annotations

Repealed by Arbitration Act 1996, s 107(2), Sch 4.

6   Application to Crown

(1)   This Act applies in relation to any action or proceedings by or against the Crown as it applies in relation to actions and proceedings to which the Crown is not a party.

(2)   For the purposes of this section references to an action or proceedings by or against the Crown include references to–

    (a)   any action or proceedings by or against Her Majesty in right of the Duchy of Lancaster;

    (b)   any action or proceedings by or against any Government department or any officer of the Crown as such or any person acting on behalf of the Crown;

    (c)   any action or proceedings by or against the Duke of Cornwall.

Annotations

Date in force: 1 October 1985.

Commencement order: SI 1985/1276.

7   Short title, commencement, transitional provision and extent

(1)   This Act may be cited as the Foreign Limitation Periods Act 1984.

(2)   This Act shall come into force on such day as the Lord Chancellor may by order made by statutory instrument appoint.

(3)   Nothing in this Act shall–

    (a)   affect any action, proceedings or arbitration commenced in England and Wales before the day appointed under subsection (2) above; or

    (b)   apply in relation to any matter if the limitation period which, apart from this Act, would have been applied in respect of that matter in England and Wales expired before that day.

(4)   This Act extends to England and Wales only.

Annotations

Date in force: 1 October 1985.

Commencement order: SI 1985/1276.

[8   Disapplication of sections 1, 2 and 4 where [the law applicable to limitation is determined by other instruments]

(1)   Where in proceedings in England and Wales the law of a country other than England and Wales falls to be taken into account by virtue of any choice of law rule contained in [the Rome I Regulation or] the Rome II Regulation, sections 1, 2 and 4 above shall not apply in respect of that matter.

[(1A)   In subsection (1) the 'Rome I Regulation' means Regulation (EC) No 593/2008 of the European Parliament and of the Council on the law applicable to contractual obligations, including that Regulation as applied by regulation 5 of the Law Applicable to Contractual Obligations (England and Wales and Northern Ireland) Regulations 2009 (conflicts solely between the laws of different parts of the United Kingdom or between one or more parts of the United Kingdom and Gibraltar).]

(2)   In subsection (1) the 'Rome II Regulation' means Regulation (EC) No 864/2007 of the European Parliament and of the Council on the law applicable to non-contractual obligations, including that Regulation as applied by regulation 6 of the Law Applicable to Non-Contractual Obligations (England and Wales and Northern Ireland) Regulations 2008 (conflicts solely between the laws of different parts of the United Kingdom or between one or more parts of the United Kingdom and Gibraltar).]

Appendix

Annotations

Section 8: inserted by SI 2008/2986, reg 4.

Section 8 heading: words in square brackets substituted by SI 2009/3064, reg 3(1), (2).

Sub-s (1): words in square brackets inserted by SI 2009/3064, reg 3(1), (3).

Sub-s (1A): inserted by SI 2009/3064, reg 3(1), (4).

Law Reform (Miscellaneous Provisions) Act 1934

1934 c 41

An Act to amend the law as to the effect of death in relation to causes of action and as to the awarding of interest in civil proceedings.

[25 July 1934]

BE IT ENACTED by the Queen's most Excellent Majesty, by and with the advice and consent of the Lords Spiritual and Temporal, and Commons, in this present Parliament assembled, and by the authority of the same, as follows:

1 Effect of death on certain causes of action

(1) Subject to the provisions of this section, on the death of any person after the commencement of this Act all causes of action subsisting against or vested in him shall survive against, or, as the case may be, for the benefit of, his estate. Provided that this subsection shall not apply to causes of action for defamation ...

[(1A) The right of a person to claim under section 1A of the Fatal Accidents Act 1976 (bereavement) shall not survive for the benefit of his estate on his death.]

(2) Where a cause of action survives as aforesaid for the benefit of the estate of a deceased person, the damages recoverable for the benefit of the estate of that person:–

    [(a) shall not include–

        (i)   any exemplary damages;

        (ii) any damages for loss of income in respect of any period after that person's death;]

    (b) ...

    (c) where the death of that person has been caused by the act or omission which give rise to the cause of action, shall be calculated without reference to any loss or gain to his estate consequent on his death, except that a sum in respect of funeral expenses may be included.

(3) ...

(4) Where damage has been suffered by reason of any act or omission in respect of which a cause of action would have subsisted against any person if that person had not died before or at the same time as the damage was suffered, there shall be deemed, for the purposes of this Act, to have been subsisting against him before his death such cause of action in respect of that act or omission as would have subsisted if he had died after the damage was suffered.

(5) The rights conferred by this Act for the benefit of the estates of deceased persons shall be in addition to and not in derogation of any rights conferred on the dependants of deceased persons by the Fatal Accidents Acts 1846 to 1908 ... and so much of this Act as relates to causes of action against the estates of deceased persons shall apply in relation to causes of action under the said Acts as it applies in relation to other causes of action not expressly excepted from the operation of subsection (1) of this section.

(6) In the event of the insolvency of an estate against which proceedings are maintainable by virtue of this section, any liability in respect of the cause of action in respect of which the proceedings are maintainable shall be deemed to be a debt provable in the administration of the estate, notwithstanding that it is a demand in the nature of unliquidated damages arising otherwise than by a contract, promise or breach of trust.

(7) ...

Annotations

Date in force: 1 January 1983 (Sub-s (1A)); before 1 January 1970 (remainder).

Appendix

Sub-s (1): words omitted repealed by Law Reform (Miscellaneous Provisions) Act 1970, s 7, Schedule, and the Administration of Justice Act 1982, ss 4(2), 75, Sch 9, Part I.

Sub-s (1A): inserted by Administration of Justice Act 1982, ss 4(1), 73(1).

Sub-s (2): para (a) substituted by Administration of Justice Act 1982, ss 4(2), 73(3), (4); para (b) repealed by Law Reform (Miscellaneous Provisions) Act 1970, s 7, Schedule.

Sub-s (3): repealed by Proceedings Against Estates Act 1970, s 1.

Sub-s (5): words omitted repealed by Carriage by Air Act 1961, s 14(3), Sch 2.

Sub-s (7): repealed by Statute Law Revision Act 1950.

This Act does not extend to Scotland.

Fatal Accidents Acts 1846 to 1908: see now the Fatal Accidents Act 1976.

2

...

Annotations

Repealed by Fatal Accidents Act 1976, s 6(2), Sch 2.

3   Power of courts of record to award interest on debts and damages

(1)   In any proceedings tried in any court of record for the recovery of any debt or damages, the court may, if it thinks fit, order that there shall be included in the sum for which judgment is given interest at such rate as it thinks fit on the whole or any part of the debt or damages for the whole or any part of the period between the date when the cause of action arose and the date of the judgment:

Providing that nothing in this section–

(a)   shall authorise the giving of interest upon interest; or

(b)   shall apply in relation to any debt upon which interest is payable as of right whether by virtue of any agreement or otherwise; or

(c)   shall affect the damages recoverable for the dishonour of a bill of exchange.

[(1A)   Where in any such proceedings as are mentioned in subsection (1) of this section judgment is given for a sum which (apart from interest on damages) exceeds £200 and represents or includes damages in respect of personal injuries to the plaintiff or any other person, or in respect of a person's death, then (without prejudice to the exercise of the power conferred by that subsection in relation to any part of that sum which does not represent such damages) the court shall exercise that power so as to include in that sum interest on those damages or on such part of them as the court considers appropriate, unless the court is satisfied that there are special reasons why no interest should be given in respect of those damages.

(1B)   Any order under this section may provide for interest to be calculated at different rates in respect of different parts of the period for which interest is given, whether that period is the whole or part of the period mentioned in subsection (1) of this section.

(1C)   ...

(1D)   In this section 'personal injuries' includes any disease and any impairment of a person's physical or mental condition, ...]

(2)   ...

Annotations

Date in force: 1 January 1983 (Sub-s (1A)–(1D)); before 1 January 1970 (remainder).

Repealed in its application to the High Court and county courts by Administration of Justice Act 1982, s 15(4), (5).

Sub-ss (1A)–(1D): inserted by Administration of Justice Act 1969, s 22.

Sub-s (1C): repealed by Statute Law (Repeals) Act 2004.

Sub-s (1D): words omitted repealed by Statute Law (Repeals) Act 2004.

Sub-s (2): repealed by Statute Law Revision Act 1950.

4   Short title and extent

(1)   This Act may be cited as the Law Reform (Miscellaneous Provisions) Act 1934.

(2)   This Act shall not extend to Scotland or Northern Ireland.

Annotations

Date in force: before 1 January 1970.

Fatal Accidents Act 1976

1976 c 30

An Act to consolidate the Fatal Accidents Acts.

[22 July 1976]

BE IT ENACTED by the Queen's most Excellent Majesty, by and with the advice and consent of the Lords Spiritual and Temporal, and Commons, in this present Parliament assembled, and by the authority of the same, as follows:

[1   Right of action for wrongful act causing death

(1)   If death is caused by any wrongful act, neglect or default which is such as would (if death had not ensued) have entitled the person injured to maintain an action and recover damages in respect thereof, the person who would have been liable if death had not ensued shall be liable to an action for damages, notwithstanding the death of the person injured.

(2)   Subject to section 1A(2) below, every such action shall be for the benefit of the dependants of the person ('the deceased') whose death has been so caused.

(3)   In this Act 'dependant' means–

   (a)   the wife or husband or former wife or husband of the deceased;

   [(aa) the civil partner or former civil partner of the deceased;]

   (b)   any person who–

      (i)   was living with the deceased in the same household immediately before the date of the death; and

      (ii)   had been living with the deceased in the same household for at least two years before that date; and

      (iii) was living during the whole of that period as the husband or wife [or civil partner] of the deceased;

   (c)   any parent or other ascendant of the deceased;

   (d)   any person who was treated by the deceased as his parent;

   (e)   any child or other descendant of the deceased;

   (f)   any person (not being a child of the deceased) who, in the case of any marriage to which the deceased was at any time a party, was treated by the deceased as a child of the family in relation to that marriage;

   [(fa) any person (not being a child of the deceased) who, in the case of any civil partnership in which the deceased was at any time a civil partner, was treated by the deceased as a child of the family in relation to that civil partnership;]

   (g)   any person who is, or is the issue of, a brother, sister, uncle or aunt of the deceased.

(4)   The reference to the former wife or husband of the deceased in subsection (3)(a) above includes a reference to a person whose marriage to the deceased has been annulled or declared void as well as a person whose marriage to the deceased has been dissolved.

[(4A)   The reference to the former civil partner of the deceased in subsection (3)(aa) above includes a reference to a person whose civil partnership with the deceased has been annulled as well as a person whose civil partnership with the deceased has been dissolved.]

(5)   In deducing any relationship for the purposes of subsection (3) above–

(a) any relationship [by marriage or civil partnership] shall be treated as a relationship by consanguinity, any relationship of the half blood as a relationship of the whole blood, and the stepchild of any person as his child, and

(b) an illegitimate person shall be treated as the legitimate child of his mother and reputed father.

(6) Any reference in this Act to injury includes any disease and any impairment of a person's physical or mental condition.]

Annotations

Date in force: 1 January 1983.

Substituted by Administration of Justice Act 1982, s 3.

Sub-s (3): para (aa) inserted by Civil Partnership Act 2004, s 83(1), (2).

Sub-s (3): in para (b)(iii) words 'or civil partner' in square brackets inserted by Civil Partnership Act 2004, s 83(1), (3).

Sub-s (3): para (fa) inserted by Civil Partnership Act 2004, s 83(1), (4).

Sub-s (4A): inserted by Civil Partnership Act 2004, s 83(1), (5).

Sub-s (5): in para (a) words 'by marriage or civil partnership' in square brackets substituted by Civil Partnership Act 2004, s 83(1), (6).

[1A   Bereavement

(1) An action under this Act may consist of or include a claim for damages for bereavement.

(2) A claim for damages for bereavement shall only be for the benefit–

(a) of the wife or husband [or civil partner] of the deceased; and

(b) where the deceased was a minor who was never married [or a civil partner]–

(i) of his parents, if he was legitimate; and

(ii) of his mother, if he was illegitimate.

(3) Subject to subject (5) below, the sum to be awarded as damages under this section shall be [£11,800].

(4) Where there is a claim for damages under this section for the benefit of both the parents of the deceased, the sum awarded shall be divided equally between them (subject to any deduction falling to be made in respect of costs not recovered from the defendant).

(5) The Lord Chancellor may by order made by statutory instrument, subject to annulment in pursuance of a resolution of either House of Parliament, amend this section by varying the sum for the time being specified in subsection (3) above.]

Annotations

Date in force: 1 January 1983.

Inserted by Administration of Justice Act 1982, s 3.

Sub-s (2): in para (a) words 'or civil partner' in square brackets inserted by Civil Partnership Act 2004, s 83(1), (7)(a).

Sub-s (2): in para (b) words 'or a civil partner' in square brackets inserted by Civil Partnership Act 2004, s 83(1), (7)(b).

Sub-s (3): sum '£11,800' in square brackets substituted by SI 2007/3489, art 2.

[2   Persons entitled to bring the action

(1) The action shall be brought by and in the name of the executor or administrator of the deceased.

(2) If–

    (a) there is no executor or administrator of the deceased, or

    (b) no action is brought within six months after the death by and in the name of an executor or administrator of the deceased.

the action may be brought by and in the name of all or any of the persons for whose benefit an executor or administrator could have brought it.

(3) Not more than one action shall lie for and in respect of the same subject matter of complaint.

(4) The plaintiff in the action shall be required to deliver to the defendant or his solicitor full particulars of the persons for whom and on whose behalf the action is brought and of the nature of the claim in respect of which damages are sought to be recovered.]

Annotations

Date in force: 1 January 1983.

Substituted by Administration of Justice Act 1982, s 3.

Modifications: any reference to Solicitors etc modified to include references to Recognised Bodies, by Solicitors' Incorporated Practice Order, SI 1991/2684, arts 4, 5, Sch 1.

[3 Assessment of damages

[(1) In the action such damages, other than damages for bereavement, may be awarded as are proportioned to the injury resulting from the death to the dependants respectively.

(2) After deducting the costs not recovered from the defendant any amount recovered otherwise than as damages for bereavement shall be divided among the dependants in such shares as may be directed.

(3) In an action under this Act where there fall to be assessed damages payable to a widow in respect of the death of her husband there shall not be taken account the re-marriage of the widow or her prospects of re-marriage.

(4) In an action under this Act where there fall to be assessed damages payable to a person who is a dependant by virtue of section 1(3)(b) above in respect of the death of the person with whom the dependant was living as husband or wife [or civil partner] there shall be taken into account (together with any other matter that appears to the court to be relevant to the action) the fact that the dependant had no enforceable right to financial support by the deceased as a result of their living together.

(5) If the dependants have incurred funeral expenses in respect of the deceased, damages may be awarded in respect of those expenses.

(6) Money paid into court in satisfaction of a cause of action under this Act may be in one sum without specifying any person's share.]

Annotations

Date in force: 1 January 1983.

Substituted by Administration of Justice Act 1982, s 3.

Sub-s (4): words 'or civil partner' in square brackets inserted by Civil Partnership Act 2004, s 83(1), (8).

[4 Assessment of damages: disregard of benefits

In assessing damages in respect of a person's death in an action under this Act, benefits which have accrued or will or may accrue to any person from his estate or otherwise as a result of his death shall be disregarded.]

Annotations

Date in force: 1 January 1983.

Substituted by Administration of Justice Act 1982, s 3.

5   Contributory negligence

Where any person dies as the result partly of his own fault and partly of the fault of any other person or persons, and accordingly if an action were brought for the benefit of the estate under the Law Reform (Miscellaneous Provisions) Act 1934 the damages recoverable would be reduced under section 1(1) of the Law Reform (Contributory Negligence) Act 1945, any damages recoverable in an action … under this Act shall be reduced to a proportionate extent.

Annotations

Date in force: 1 September 1976.

This section derived from Law Reform (Contributory Negligence) Act 1945, s 1(4).

Words omitted repealed by Administration of Justice Act 1982, s 3, s 75, Sch 9, Part I.

6   Consequential amendments and repeals

(1)   Schedule 1 to this Act contains consequential amendments.

(2)   The enactments in Schedule 2 to this Act are repealed to the extent specified in the third column of that Schedule.

7   Short title, etc

(1)   This Act may be cited as the Fatal Accidents Act 1976.

(2)   This Act shall come into force on 1st September 1976, but shall not apply to any cause of action arising on a death before it comes into force.

(3)   This Act shall not extend to Scotland or Northern Ireland.

Annotations

Date in force: 1 September 1976.

SCHEDULE 1
CONSEQUENTIAL AMENDMENTS

section 6

General

1

(1)   Any enactment or other document whatsoever referring to any enactment repealed by this Act shall, unless the contrary intention appears, be construed as referring (or as including a reference) to the corresponding enactment in this Act.

(2)   This paragraph applies whether or not the enactment or other document was enacted, made, served or issued before the passing of this Act.

(3)   This paragraph is without prejudice to [sections 16(1) and 17(2)(a) of the Interpretation Act 1978] (effect of repeals), and the following provisions of this Schedule are without prejudice to the generality of this paragraph.

2

(1)   In the following enactments references to the Fatal Accidents Acts, or to the Fatal Accidents Act 1846, or to section 1 of that Act, include references to this Act.

(2)   The said enactments are–

section 1(5) of the Law Reform (Miscellaneous Provisions) Act 1934 (cause of action surviving death), ...

section 3 of the Carriage by Air Act 1961 (civil liability under Convention implemented by that Act),

section 14(2) of the Gas Act 1965 (civil liability under that Act),

section 10 of the Animals Act 1971 (civil liability under that Act),

section 11(2) of the Mineral Workings (Offshore Installations) Act 1971 (civil liability under that Act),

...

section 88(4)(a) of the Control of Pollution Act 1974 (civil liability under that Act),

section 6(1)(d) of the Industrial Injuries and Diseases (Old Cases) Act 1975,

...

Limitation Act 1939

3

...

Carriage by Railway Act 1972

4

...

Annotations

Date in force: 1 September 1976.

Para 1: in sub-para (3), words in square brackets substituted by virtue of Interpretation Act 1978, s 25(2).

Para 2: in sub-para (2), first words omitted repealed by Coal Mining Subsidence Act 1991, s 53(2), Sch 8, second word omitted repealed by Administration of Justice Act 1982, s 75, Sch 9, Part I.

Para 2: in sub-para (2) third words omitted repealed by Petroleum Act 1998, s 51, Sch 5, Pt I.

Para 3: repealed by Limitation Act 1980, Sch 4.

Para 4: repealed by International Transport Conventions Act 1983, s 11(2), Sch 3.

Civil Liability (Contribution) Act 1978

1978 c 47

An Act make new provision for contribution between persons who are jointly or severally, or both jointly and severally, liable for the same damage and in certain other similar cases where two or more persons have paid or may be required to pay compensation for the same damage; and to amend the law relating to proceedings against persons jointly liable for the same debt or jointly or severally, or both jointly and severally, liable for the same damage.

[31 July 1978]

BE IT ENACTED by the Queen's most Excellent Majesty, by and with the advice and consent of the Lords Spiritual and Temporal, and Commons, in this present Parliament assembled, and by the authority of the same, as follows:

Proceedings for contribution

1 Entitlement to contribution

(1) Subject to the following provisions of this section, any person liable in respect of any damage suffered by another person may recover contribution from any other person liable in respect of the same damage (whether jointly with him or otherwise).

(2) A person shall be entitled to recover contribution by virtue of subsection (1) above notwithstanding that he has ceased to be liable in respect of the damage in question since the time when the damage occurred, provided that he was so liable immediately before he made or was ordered or agreed to make the payment in respect of which the contribution is sought.

(3) A person shall be liable to make contribution by virtue of subsection (1) above notwithstanding that he has ceased to be liable in respect of the damage in question since the time when the damage occurred, unless he ceased to be liable by virtue of the expiry of a period of limitation or prescription which extinguished the right on which the claim against him in respect of the damage was based.

(4) A person who has made or agreed to make any payment in bona fide settlement or compromise of any claim made against him in respect of any damage (including a payment into court which has been accepted) shall be entitled to recover contribution in accordance with this section without regard to whether or not he himself is or ever was liable in respect of the damage, provided, however, that he would have been liable assuming that the factual basis of the claim against him could be established.

(5) A judgment given in any action brought in any part of the United Kingdom by or on behalf of the person who suffered the damage in question against any person from whom contribution is sought under this section shall be conclusive in the proceedings for contribution as to any issue determined by that judgment in favour of the person from whom the contribution is sought.

(6) References in this section to a person's liability in respect of any damage are references to any such liability which has been or could be established in an action brought against him in England and Wales by or on behalf of the person who suffered the damage; but it is immaterial whether any issue arising in any such action was or would be determined (in accordance with the rules of private international law) by reference to the law of a country outside England and Wales.

Annotations

Date in force: 1 January 1979.

2 Assessment of contribution

(1) Subject to subsection (3) below, in any proceedings for contribution under section 1 above the amount of the contribution recoverable from any person shall be such as may

be found by the court to be just and equitable having regard to the extent of that person's responsibility for the damage in question.

(2)   Subject to subsection (3) below, the court shall have power in any such proceedings to exempt any person from liability to make contribution, or to direct that the contribution to be recovered from any person shall amount to a complete indemnity.

(3)   Where the amount of the damages which have or might have been awarded in respect of the damage in question in any action brought in England and Wales by or on behalf of the person who suffered it against the person from whom the contribution is sought was or would have been subject to–

(a)   any limit imposed by or under any enactment or by any agreement made before the damage occurred;

(b)   any reduction by virtue of section 1 of the Law Reform (Contributory Negligence) Act 1945 or section 5 of the Fatal Accidents Act 1976; or

(c)   any corresponding limit or reduction under the law of a country outside England and Wales;

the person from whom the contribution is sought shall not by virtue of any contribution awarded under section 1 above be required to pay in respect of the damage a greater amount than the amount of those damages as so limited or reduced.

Annotations

Date in force: 1 January 1979.

Proceedings for the same debt or damage

3   Proceedings against persons jointly liable for the same debt or damage

Judgment recovered against any person liable in respect of any debt or damage shall not be a bar to an action, or to the continuance of an action, against any other person who is (apart from any such bar) jointly liable with him in respect of the same debt or damage.

Annotations

Date in force: 1 January 1979.

4   Successive actions against persons liable (jointly or otherwise) for the same damage

If more than one action is brought in respect of any damage by or on behalf of the person by whom it was suffered against persons liable in respect of the damage (whether jointly or otherwise) the plaintiff shall not be entitled to costs in any of those actions, other than that in which judgment is first given, unless the court is of the opinion that there was reasonable ground for bringing the action.

Annotations

Date in force: 1 January 1979.

Supplemental

5   Application to the Crown

Without prejudice to section 4(1) of the Crown Proceedings Act 1947 (indemnity and contribution), this Act shall bind the Crown, but nothing in this Act shall be construed as in any way affecting Her Majesty in Her private capacity (including in right of Her Duchy of Lancaster) or the Duchy of Cornwall.

Annotations

Date in force: 1 January 1979.

6   Interpretation

(1)   A person is liable in respect of any damage for the purposes of this Act if the person who suffered it (or anyone representing his estate or dependants) is entitled to recover compensation from him in respect of that damage (whatever the legal basis of his liability, whether tort, breach of contract, breach of trust or otherwise).

(2)   References in this Act to an action brought by or on behalf of the person who suffered any damage include references to an action brought for the benefit of his estate or dependants.

(3)   In this Act 'dependants' has the same meaning as in the Fatal Accidents Act 1976.

(4)   In this Act, except in section 1(5) above, 'action' means an action brought in England and Wales.

Annotations

Date in force: 1 January 1979.

7   Savings

(1)   Nothing in this Act shall affect any case where the debt in question became due or (as the case may be) the damage in question occurred before the date on which it comes into force.

(2)   A person shall not be entitled to recover contribution or liable to make contribution in accordance with section 1 above by reference to any liability based on breach of any obligation assumed by him before the date on which this Act comes into force.

(3)   The right to recover contribution in accordance with section 1 above supersedes any right, other than an express contractual right, to recover contribution (as distinct from indemnity) otherwise than under this Act in corresponding circumstances; but nothing in this Act shall affect–

    (a)   any express or implied contractual or other right to indemnity; or

    (b)   any express contractual provision regulating or excluding contribution;

which would be enforceable apart from this Act (or render enforceable any agreement for indemnity or contribution which would not be enforceable apart from this Act).

Annotations

Date in force: 1 January 1979.

8   Application to Northern Ireland

In the application of this Act to Northern Ireland–

    (a)   the reference in section 2(3)(b) to section 1 of the Law Reform (Contributory Negligence) Act 1945 or section 5 of the Fatal Accidents Act 1976 shall be construed as a reference to section 2 of the Law Reform (Miscellaneous Provisions) Act (Northern Ireland) 1948 or Article 7 of the Fatal Accidents (Northern Ireland) Order 1977;

    (b)   the reference in section 5 to section 4(1) of the Crown Proceedings Act 1947 shall be construed as a reference to section 4(1) of that Act as it applies in Northern Ireland;

    (c)   the reference in section 6(3) to the Fatal Accidents Act 1976 shall be construed as a reference to the Fatal Accidents (Northern Ireland) Order 1977;

    (d)   references to England and Wales shall be construed as references to Northern Ireland; and

(e) any reference to an enactment shall be construed as including a reference to an enactment of the Parliament of Northern Ireland and a Measure of the Northern Ireland Assembly.

Annotations

Date in force: 1 January 1979.

9 Consequential amendments and repeals

(1) The enactments specified in Schedule 1 to this Act shall have effect subject to the amendments set out in that Schedule, being amendments consequential on the preceding provisions of this Act.

(2) The enactments specified in Schedule 2 to this Act are hereby repealed to the extent specified in column 3 of that Schedule.

Annotations

Date in force: 1 January 1979.

10 Short title, commencement and extent

(1) This Act may be cited as the Civil Liability (Contribution) Act 1978.

(2) This Act shall come into force on 1st January next following the date on which it is passed.

(3) ...

Annotations

Date in force: 1 January 1979.

Sub-s (3): applies to Scotland only.

Merchant Shipping Act 1995

1995 c 21

An Act to consolidate the Merchant Shipping Acts 1894 to 1994 and other enactments relating to merchant shipping.

[19 July 1995]

BE IT ENACTED by the Queen's most Excellent Majesty, by and with the advice and consent of the Lords Spiritual and Temporal, and Commons, in this present Parliament assembled, and by the authority of the same, as follows:

PART VII
LIABILITY OF SHIPOWNERS AND OTHERS

Carriage of passengers and luggage by sea

183 Scheduled convention to have force of law

(1)   The provisions of the Convention relating to the Carriage of Passengers and their Luggage by Sea as set out in Part I of Schedule 6 (hereafter in this section and in Part II of that Schedule referred to as 'the Convention') shall have the force of law in the United Kingdom.

(2)   The provisions of Part II of that Schedule shall have effect in connection with the Convention and subsection (1) above shall have effect subject to the provisions of that Part.

[(2A)   But–

    (a)   subsection (1) does not give the force of law in the United Kingdom to provisions to the extent that they apply to cases in which EC Regulation No 392/2009 applies; and

    (b)   the provisions of Part 2 of that Schedule do not have effect in such cases.]

(3)   If it appears to Her Majesty in Council that there is a conflict between the provisions of this section or of Part I or II of Schedule 6 and any provisions relating to the carriage of passengers or luggage for reward by land, sea or air in–

    (a)   any convention which has been signed or ratified by or on behalf of the government of the United Kingdom before 4th April 1979 (excluding the Convention); or

    (b)   any enactment of the Parliament of the United Kingdom giving effect to such a convention,

She may by Order in Council make such modifications of this section or that Schedule or any such enactment as She considers appropriate for resolving the conflict.

(4)   If it appears to Her Majesty in Council that the government of the United Kingdom has agreed to any revision of the Convention She may by Order in Council make such modification of Parts I and II of Schedule 6 as She considers appropriate in consequence of the revision.

(5)   Nothing in subsection (1)[, (2) or (2A)] above or in any modification made by virtue of subsection (3) or (4) above shall affect any rights or liabilities arising out of an occurrence which took place before the day on which [the subsection], or as the case may be, the modification, comes into force.

(6)   This section shall bind the Crown, and any Order in Council made by virtue of this section may provide that the Order or specified provisions of it shall bind the Crown.

(7)   A draft of an Order in Council proposed to be made under subsection (3) or (4) above shall not be submitted to Her Majesty in Council unless the draft has been approved by a resolution of each House of Parliament.

[(8)   In this section 'EC Regulation No 392/2009' means Regulation (EC) No 329/2009 of the European Parliament and of the Council of 23 April 2009 on the liability of carriers of passengers by sea in the event of accidents.]

Appendix

Annotations

Date in force: 1 January 1996.

Time limit for proceedings against owners or ship

Sub-s (2A): inserted by SI 2012/3152, s 14(1), (2).

Sub-s (5): both sets of words in square brackets substituted by SI 2012/3152, s 14(1), (3).

Sub-s (8): inserted by SI 2012/3152, s 14(1), (4).

190   Time limit for proceedings against owners or ship

(1)   This section applies to any proceedings to enforce any claim or lien against a ship or her owners–

> (a)   in respect of damage or loss caused by the fault of that ship to another ship, its cargo or freight or any property on board it; or
>
> (b)   for damages for loss of life or personal injury caused by the fault of that ship to any person on board another ship.

(2)   The extent of the fault is immaterial for the purposes of this section.

(3)   Subject to subsections (5) and (6) below, no proceedings to which this section applies shall be brought after the period of two years from the date when–

> (a)   the damage or loss was caused; or
>
> (b)   the loss of life or injury was suffered.

(4)   Subject to subsections (5) and (6) below, no proceedings under any of sections 187 to 189 to enforce any contribution in respect of any overpaid proportion of any damages for loss of life or personal injury shall be brought after the period of one year from the date of payment.

(5)   Any court having jurisdiction in such proceedings may, in accordance with rules of court, extend the period allowed for bringing proceedings to such extent and on such conditions as it thinks fit.

(6)   Any such court, if satisfied that there has not been during any period allowed for bringing proceedings any reasonable opportunity of arresting the defendant ship within–

> (a)   the jurisdiction of the court, or
>
> (b)   the territorial sea of the country to which the plaintiff's ship belongs or in which the plaintiff resides or has his principal place of business,

shall extend the period allowed for bringing proceedings to an extent sufficient to give a reasonable opportunity of so arresting the ship.

Annotations

Date in force: 1 January 1996.

SCHEDULE 6

CONVENTION RELATING TO THE CARRIAGE OF PASSENGERS
AND THEIR LUGGAGE BY SEA

section 183

PART I

TEXT OF CONVENTION

Article 1
Definitions

In this Convention the following expressions have the meaning hereby assigned to them:

776

1

    (a) 'carrier' means a person by or on behalf of whom a contract of carriage has been concluded, whether the carriage is actually performed by him or by a performing carrier;

    (b) 'performing carrier' means a person other than the carrier, being the owner, charterer or operator of a ship, who actually performs the whole or a part of the carriage;

2

'contract of carriage' means a contract made by or on behalf of a carrier for the carriage by sea of a passenger or of a passenger and his luggage, as the case may be;

3

'ship' means only a seagoing vessel, excluding an air-cushion vehicle;

4

'passenger' means any person carried in a ship,

    (a) under a contract of carriage, or

    (b) who, with the consent of the carrier, is accompanying a vehicle or live animals which are covered by a contract for the carriage of goods not governed by this Convention;

5

'luggage' means any article or vehicle carried by the carrier under a contract of carriage, excluding:

    (a) articles and vehicles carried under a charter party, bill of lading or other contract primarily concerned with the carriage of goods, and

    (b) live animals;

6

'cabin luggage' means luggage which the passenger has in his cabin or is otherwise in his possession, custody or control. Except for the application of paragraph 8 of this Article and Article 8, cabin luggage includes luggage which the passenger has in or on his vehicle.

7

'loss of or damage to luggage' includes pecuniary loss resulting from the luggage not having been re-delivered to the passenger within a reasonable time after the arrival of the ship on which the luggage has been or should have been carried, but does not include delays resulting from labour disputes;

8

'carriage' covers the following periods:

    (a) with regard to the passenger and his cabin luggage, the period during which the passenger and/or his cabin luggage are on board the ship or in the course of embarkation or disembarkation, and the period during which the passenger and his cabin luggage are transported by water from land to the ship or vice versa, if the cost of such transport is included in the fare or if the vessel used for the purpose of auxiliary transport has been put at the disposal of the passenger by the carrier. However, with regard to the passenger, carriage does not include the

777

period during which he is in a marine terminal or station or on a quay or in or on any other port installation;

(b) with regard to cabin luggage, also the period during which the passenger is in a marine terminal or station or on a quay or in or on any other port installation if that luggage has been taken over by the carrier or his servant or agent and has not been re-delivered to the passenger;

(c) with regard to other luggage which is not cabin luggage, the period from the time of its taking over by the carrier or his servant or agent onshore or on board until the time of its re-delivery by the carrier or his servant or agent;

9

'international carriage' means any carriage in which, according to the contract of carriage, the place of departure and the place of destination are situated in two different States, or in a single State if, according to the contract of carriage or the scheduled itinerary, there is an intermediate port of call in another State.

Article 2
Application

1

This Convention shall apply to any international carriage if:

(a) the ship is flying the flag of or is registered in a State Party to this Convention, or

(b) the contract of carriage has been made in a State Party to this Convention, or

(c) the place of departure or destination, according to the contract of carriage, is in a State Party to this Convention.

2

Notwithstanding paragraph 1 of this Article, this Convention shall not apply when the carriage is subject, under any other international convention concerning the carriage of passengers or luggage by another mode of transport, to a civil liability regime under the provisions of such convention, in so far as those provisions have mandatory application to carriage by sea.

Article 3
Liability of the carrier

1

The carrier shall be liable for the damage suffered as a result of the death of or personal injury to a passenger and the loss of or damage to luggage if the incident which caused the damage so suffered occurred in the course of the carriage and was due to the fault or neglect of the carrier or of his servants or agents acting within the scope of their employment.

2

The burden of proving that the incident which caused the loss or damage occurred in the course of the carriage, and the extent of the loss or damage, shall lie with the claimant.

3

Fault or neglect of the carrier or of his servants or agents acting within the scope of their employment shall be presumed, unless the contrary is proved, if the death of or personal injury to the passenger or the loss of or damage to cabin luggage arose from or in connection with the shipwreck, collision, stranding, explosion or fire, or defect in the ship. In respect of loss of or damage to other luggage, such fault or neglect shall be presumed, unless the contrary is proved irrespective of the nature of the incident which caused the loss or damage. In all other cases the burden of proving fault or neglect shall lie with the claimant.

Article 4
Performing carrier

1

If the performance of the carriage or part thereof has been entrusted to a performing carrier, the carrier shall nevertheless remain liable for the entire carriage according to the provisions of this Convention. In addition, the performing carrier shall be subject and entitled to the provisions of the Convention for the part of the carriage performed by him.

2

The carrier shall, in relation to the carriage performed by the performing carrier, be liable for the acts and omissions of the performing carrier and of his servants and agents acting within the scope of their employment.

3

Any special agreement under which the carrier assumes obligations not imposed by this Convention or any waiver of rights conferred by this Convention shall affect the performing carrier only if agreed by him expressly and in writing.

4

Where and to the extent that both the carrier and the performing carrier are liable, their liability shall be joint and several.

5

Nothing in this Article shall prejudice any right of recourse as between the carrier and the performing carrier.

Article 5
Valuables

The carrier shall not be liable for the loss of or damage to monies, negotiable securities, gold, silverware, jewellery, ornaments, works of art, or other valuables, except where such valuables have been deposited with the carrier for the agreed purpose of safe-keeping in which case the carrier shall be liable up to the limit provided for in paragraph 3 of Article 8 unless a higher limit is agreed upon in accordance with paragraph 1 of Article 10.

Article 6
Contributory fault

If the carrier proves that the death of or personal injury to a passenger or the loss of or damage to his luggage was caused or contributed to by the fault or neglect of the passenger, the court seised of the case may exonerate the carrier wholly or partly from his liability in accordance with the provisions of the law of that court.

Article 7
Limit of liability personal injury

1

The liability of the carrier for the death of or personal injury to a passenger shall in no case exceed 46,666 units of account per carriage. Where in accordance with the law of the court seised of the case damages are awarded in the form of periodical income payments, the equivalent capital value of those payments shall not exceed the said limit.

2

Notwithstanding paragraph 1 of this Article, the national law of any State Party to this Convention may fix, as far as carriers who are nationals of such State are concerned, a higher *per capita* limit of liability.

Article 8
Limit of liability for loss of or damage to luggage

1

The liability of the carrier for the loss of or damage to cabin luggage shall in no case exceed 833 units of account per passenger, per carriage.

2

The liability of the carrier for the loss of or damage to vehicles including all luggage carried in or on the vehicle shall in no case exceed 3,333 units of account per vehicle, per carriage.

3

The liability of the carrier for the loss of or damage to luggage other than that mentioned in paragraphs 1 and 2 of this Article shall in no case exceed 1,200 units of account per passenger, per carriage.

4

The carrier and the passenger may agree that the liability of the carrier shall be subject to a deduction not exceeding 117 units of account in the case of damage to a vehicle and not exceeding 13 units of account per passenger in the case of loss of or damage to other luggage, such sum to be deducted from the loss or damage.

Article 9
Unit of account and conversion

The Unit of Account mentioned in this Convention is the special drawing right as defined by the International Monetary Fund. The amounts mentioned in Articles 7 and 8 shall be converted into the national currency of the State of the court seised of the case on the basis of the value of that currency on the date of the judgment or the date agreed upon by the Parties.

Article 10
Supplementary provisions on limits of liability

1

The carrier and the passenger may agree, expressly and in writing, to higher limits of liability than those prescribed in Articles 7 and 8.

2

Interest on damages and legal costs shall not be included in the limits of liability prescribed in Articles 7 and 8.

Article 11
Defences and limits for carriers' servants

If an action is brought against a servant or agent of the carrier or of the performing carrier arising out of damage covered by this Convention, such servant or agent, if he proves that he acted within the scope of his employment, shall be entitled to avail himself of the defences and limits of liability which the carrier or the performing carrier is entitled to invoke under this Convention.

Article 12
Aggregation of claims

1

Where the limits of liability prescribed in Articles 7 and 8 take effect, they shall apply to the aggregate of the amounts recoverable in all claims arising out of the death of or personal injury to any one passenger or the loss of or damage to his luggage.

2

In relation to the carriage performed by a performing carrier, the aggregate of the amounts recoverable from the carrier and the performing carrier and from their servants and agents acting within the scope of their employment shall not exceed the highest amount which could be awarded against either the carrier or the performing carrier under this Convention, but none of the persons mentioned shall be liable for a sum in excess of the limit applicable to him.

3

In any case where a servant or agent of the carrier or of the performing carrier is entitled under Article 11 of this Convention to avail himself of the limits of liability prescribed in Articles 7 and 8, the aggregate of the amounts recoverable from the carrier, or the performing carrier as the case may be, and from that servant or agent, shall not exceed those limits.

Article 13
Loss of right to limit liability

1

The carrier shall not be entitled to the benefit of the limits of liability prescribed in Articles 7 and 8 and paragraph 1 of Article 10, if it is proved that the damage resulted from an act or omission of the carrier done with the intent to cause such damage, or recklessly and with knowledge that such damage would probably result.

2

The servant or agent of the carrier or of the performing carrier shall not be entitled to the benefit of those limits if it is proved that the damage resulted from an act or omission of that servant or agent done with the intent to cause such damage, or recklessly and with knowledge that such damage would probably result.

781

Article 14
Basis for claims

No action for damages for the death of or personal injury to a passenger, or for the loss of or damage to luggage, shall be brought against a carrier or performing carrier otherwise than in accordance with this Convention.

Article 15
Notice of loss or damage to luggage

1

The passenger shall give written notice to the carrier or his agent:

    (a) in the case of apparent damage to luggage:

        (i) for cabin luggage, before or at the time of disembarkation of the passenger;

        (ii) for all other luggage, before or at the time of its re-delivery;

    (b) in the case of damage to luggage which is not apparent, or loss of luggage, within 15 days from the date of disembarkation or re-delivery or from the time when such re-delivery should have taken place.

2

If the passenger fails to comply with this Article, he shall be presumed, unless the contrary is proved, to have received the luggage undamaged.

3

The notice in writing need not be given if the condition of the luggage has at the time of its receipt been the subject of joint survey or inspection.

Article 16
Time-bar for actions

1

Any action for damages arising out of the death of or personal injury to a passenger or for the loss of or damage to luggage shall be time-barred after a period of two years.

2

The limitation period shall be calculated as follows:

    (a) in the case of personal injury, from the date of disembarkation of the passenger;

    (b) in the case of death occurring during carriage, from the date when the passenger should have disembarked, and in the case of personal injury occurring during carriage and resulting in the death of the passenger after disembarkation, from the date of death, provided that this period shall not exceed three years from the date of disembarkation;

    (c) in the case of loss of or damage to luggage, from the date of disembarkation or from the date when disembarkation should have taken place, whichever is later.

3

The law of the court seised of the case shall govern the grounds of suspension and interruption of limitation periods, but in no case shall an action under this Convention be brought after the expiration of a period of three years from the date of disembarkation of the passenger or from the date when disembarkation should have taken place, whichever is later.

4

Notwithstanding paragraphs 1, 2 and 3 of this Article, the period of limitation may be extended by a declaration of the carrier or by agreement of the parties after the cause of action has arisen. The declaration or agreement shall be in writing.

Article 17
Competent jurisdiction

1

An action arising under this Convention shall, at the option of the claimant, be brought before one of the courts listed below, provided that the court is located in a State Party to this Convention:

    (a) the court of the place of permanent residence or principal place of business of the defendant, or

    (b) the court of the place of departure or that of the destination according to the contract of carriage, or

    (c) a court of the State of the domicile or permanent residence of the claimant, if the defendant has a place of business and is subject to jurisdiction in that State, or

    (d) a court of the State where the contract of carriage was made, if the defendant has a place of business and is subject to jurisdiction in the State.

2

After the occurrence of the incident which has caused the damage, the parties may agree that the claim for damages shall be submitted to any jurisdiction or to arbitration.

Article 18
Invalidity of contractual provisions

Any contractual provision concluded before the occurrence of the incident which has caused the death of or personal injury to a passenger or the loss of or damage to his luggage, purporting to relieve the carrier of his liability towards the passenger or to prescribe a lower limit of liability than that fixed in this Convention except as provided in paragraph 4 of Article 8, and any such provision purporting to shift the burden of proof which rests on the carrier, or having the effect of restricting the option specified in paragraph 1 of Article 17, shall be null and void, but the nullity of that provision shall not render void the contract of carriage which shall remain subject to the provisions of this Convention.

Article 19
Other conventions on limitation of liability

This Convention shall not modify the rights or duties of the carrier, the performing carrier, and their servants or agents provided for in international conventions relating to the limitation of liability of owners of seagoing ships.

Article 20
Nuclear damage

No liability shall arise under this Convention for damage caused by a nuclear incident:

(a) if the operator of a nuclear installation is liable to such damage under either the Paris Convention of 29 July 1960 on Third Party Liability in the Field of Nuclear Energy as amended by its Additional Protocol of 28 January 1964, or the Vienna Convention of 21 May 1963 on Civil Liability for Nuclear Damage, or

(b) if the operator of a nuclear installation is liable for such damage by virtue of a national law governing the liability for such damage, provided that such law is in all respects as favourable to persons who may suffer damage as either the Paris or the Vienna Conventions.

Article 21
Commercial carriage by public authorities

This Convention shall apply to commercial carriage undertaken by States or Public Authorities under contracts of carriage within the meaning of Article 1.

PART II
PROVISIONS HAVING EFFECT IN CONNECTION WITH CONVENTION

Interpretation

1

In this Part of this Schedule any reference to a numbered article is a reference to the article of the Convention which is so numbered and any expression to which a meaning is assigned by article 1 of the Convention has that meaning.

Provisions adapting or supplementing specified articles of the Convention

2

For the purposes of paragraph 2 of article 2, provisions of such an international convention as is mentioned in that paragraph which apart from this paragraph do not have mandatory application to carriage by sea shall be treated as having mandatory application to carriage by sea if it is stated in the contract of carriage for the carriage in question that those provisions are to apply in connection with the carriage.

3

The reference to the law of the court in article 6 shall be construed as a reference to the Law Reform (Contributory Negligence) Act 1945 except that in relation to Northern Ireland it shall be construed as a reference to section 2 of the Law Reform (Miscellaneous Provisions) Act (Northern Ireland) 1948.

4

The Secretary of State may by order provide that, in relation to a carrier whose principal place of business is in the United Kingdom, paragraph 1 of article 7 shall have effect with the substitution for the limit for the time being specified in that paragraph of a different limit specified in the order (which shall not be lower than 46,666 units of account).

5

(1)   For the purpose of converting from special drawing rights into sterling the amounts mentioned in articles 7 and 8 of the Convention in respect of which a judgment is given, one special drawing right shall be treated as equal to such a sum in sterling as the International Monetary Fund have fixed as being the equivalent of one special drawing right for–

    (a)   the day on which the judgment is given; or

    (b)   if no sum has been so fixed for that day, the last day before that day for which a sum has been so fixed.

(2)   A certificate given by or on behalf of the Treasury stating–

    (a)   that a particular sum in sterling has been fixed as mentioned in sub-paragraph (1) above for a particular day; or

    (b)   that no sum has been so fixed for that day and a particular sum in sterling has been so fixed for a day which is the last day for which a sum has been so fixed before the particular day,

shall be conclusive evidence of those matters for the purposes of articles 7 to 9 of the Convention; and a document purporting to be such a certificate shall, in any proceedings, be received in evidence and, unless the contrary is proved, be deemed to be such a certificate.

6

It is hereby declared that by virtue of article 12 the limitations on liability there mentioned in respect of a passenger or his luggage apply to the aggregate liabilities of the persons in question in all proceedings for enforcing the liabilities or any of them which may be brought whether in the United Kingdom or elsewhere.

[7

Article 16 shall apply to arbitral proceedings as it applies to an action; and, as respects England and Wales and Northern Ireland, the provisions of section 14 of the Arbitration Act 1996 shall apply to determine for the purposes of that Article when an arbitration is commenced.]

8

The court before which proceedings are brought in pursuance of article 17 to enforce a liability which is limited by virtue of article 12 may at any stage of the proceedings make such orders as appear to the court to be just and equitable in view of the provisions of article 12 and of any other proceedings which have been or are likely to be begun in the United Kingdom or elsewhere to enforce the liability in whole or in part; and without prejudice to the generality of the preceding provisions of this paragraph such a court shall, where the liability is or may be partly enforceable in other proceedings in the United Kingdom or elsewhere, have jurisdiction to award an amount less than the court would have awarded if the limitation applied solely to the proceedings before the court or to make any part of its award conditional on the results of any other proceedings.

Other provisions adapting or supplementing the Convention

9

Any reference in the Convention to a contract of carriage excludes contract of carriage which is not for reward.

10

If Her Majesty by Order in Council declares that any State specified in the Order is a party to the Convention in respect of a particular country the Order shall, subject to the provisions of any subsequent Order made by virtue of this paragraph, be conclusive evidence that the State is a party to the Convention in respect of that country.

11

The Secretary of State may by order make provision–

    (a)   for requiring a person who is the carrier in relation to a passenger to give to the passenger, in a manner specified in the order, notice of such of the provisions of Part I of this Schedule as are so specified;

    (b)   for a person who fails to comply with a requirement imposed on him by the order to be guilty of an offence and liable on summary conviction to a fine of an amount not exceeding level 4 on the standard scale or not exceeding a lesser amount.

Application of ss 185 and 186 of this Act

12

It is hereby declared that nothing in the Convention affects the operation of section 185 of this Act (which limits a shipowner's liability in certain cases of loss of life, injury or damage).

13

Nothing in section 186 of this Act (which among other things limits a shipowner's liability for the loss or damage of goods in certain cases) shall relieve a person of any liability imposed on him by the Convention.

Annotations

Date in force: 1 January 1996.

Para 7: substituted by Arbitration Act 1996, Sch 3, para 61.

Human Rights Act 1998

1998 c 42

An Act to further give effect to rights and freedoms guaranteed under the European Convention on Human Rights; to make provision with respect to holders of certain judicial offices who become judges of the European Court of Human Rights; and for connected purposes.

[9 November 1998]

BE IT ENACTED by the Queen's most Excellent Majesty, by and with the advice and consent of the Lords Spiritual and Temporal, and Commons, in this present Parliament assembled, and by the authority of the same, as follows:

Introduction

1 The Convention Rights

(1) In this Act 'the Convention rights' means the rights and fundamental freedoms set out in–

    (a) Articles 2 to 12 and 14 of the Convention,

    (b) Articles 1 to 3 of the First Protocol, and

    (c) [Article 1 of the Thirteenth Protocol],

as read with Articles 16 to 18 of the Convention.

(2) Those Articles are to have effect for the purposes of this Act subject to any designated derogation or reservation (as to which see sections 14 and 15).

(3) The Articles are set out in Schedule 1.

(4) The [Secretary of State] may by order make such amendments to this Act as he considers appropriate to reflect the effect, in relation to the United Kingdom, of a protocol.

(5) In subsection (4) 'protocol' means a protocol to the Convention–

    (a) which the United Kingdom has ratified; or

    (b) which the United Kingdom has signed with a view to ratification.

(6) No amendment may be made by an order under subsection (4) so as to come into force before the protocol concerned is in force in relation to the United Kingdom.

Annotations

Date in force: 1 October 2000.

Sub-s (1): in para (c) words 'Article 1 of the Thirteenth Protocol' in square brackets substituted by SI 2004/1574, art 2(1).

Sub-s (4): words 'Secretary of State' in square brackets substituted by SI 2003/1887, art 9, Sch 2, para 10(1).

2 Interpretation of Convention rights

(1) A court or tribunal determining a question which has arisen in connection with a Convention right must take into account any–

    (a) judgment, decision, declaration or advisory opinion of the European Court of Human Rights,

    (b) opinion of the Commission given in a report adopted under Article 31 of the Convention,

    (c) decision of the Commission in connection with Article 26 or 27(2) of the Convention, or

    (d) decision of the Committee of Ministers taken under Article 46 of the Convention,

whenever made or given, so far as, in the opinion of the court or tribunal, it is relevant to the proceedings in which that question has arisen.

(2)   Evidence of any judgment, decision, declaration or opinion of which account may have to be taken under this section is to be given in proceedings before any court or tribunal in such manner as may be provided by rules.

(3)   In this section 'rules' means rules of court or, in the case of proceedings before a tribunal, rules made for the purposes of this section–

    (a) by ... [the Lord Chancellor or] the Secretary of State, in relation to any proceedings outside Scotland;

    (b) by the Secretary of State, in relation to proceedings in Scotland; or

    (c) by a Northern Ireland department, in relation to proceedings before a tribunal in Northern Ireland–

        (i) which deals with transferred matters; and

        (ii) for which no rules made under paragraph (a) are in force.

Annotations

Date in force: 1 October 2000.

Sub-s (3): in para (a) words omitted repealed by SI 2003/1887, art 9, Sch 2, para 10(2).

Sub-s (3): in para (a) words 'the Lord Chancellor or' in square brackets inserted by SI 2005/3429, art 8, Sch, para 3.

Legislation

4   Declaration of incompatibility

(1)   Subsection (2) applies in any proceedings in which a court determines whether a provision of primary legislation is compatible with a Convention right.

(2)   If the court is satisfied that the provision is incompatible with a Convention right, it may make a declaration of that incompatibility.

(3)   Subsection (4) applies in any proceedings in which a court determines whether a provision of subordinate legislation, made in the exercise of a power conferred by primary legislation, is compatible with a Convention right.

(4)   If the court is satisfied–

    (a) that the provision is incompatible with a Convention right, and

    (b) that (disregarding any possibility of revocation) the primary legislation concerned prevents removal of the incompatibility,

it may make a declaration of that incompatibility.

(5)   In this section 'court' means–

    [(a) the Supreme Court;]

    (b) the Judicial Committee of the Privy Council;

    (c) the [Court Martial Appeal Court];

    (d) in Scotland, the High Court of Justiciary sitting otherwise than as a trial court or the Court of Session;

(e)   in England and Wales or Northern Ireland, the High Court or the Court of Appeal;

[(f)   the Court of Protection, in any matter being dealt with by the President of the Family Division, the Vice-Chancellor or a puisne judge of the High Court].

(6)   A declaration under this section ('a declaration of incompatibility')–

(a)   does not affect the validity, continuing operation or enforcement of the provision in respect of which it is given; and

(b)   is not binding on the parties to the proceedings in which it is made.

Annotations

Date in force: 1 October 2000.

Sub-s (5): para (a) substituted by Constitutional Reform Act 2005, s 40(4), Sch 9, Pt 1, para 66(1), (2).

Sub-s (5): in para (c), words in square brackets substituted by Armed Forces Act 2006, s 378(1), Sch 16, para 156.

Sub-s (5): para (f) inserted by Mental Capacity Act 2005, s 67(1), Sch 6, para 43.

SCHEDULE 1
THE ARTICLES

section 1(3)

PART I
THE CONVENTION

Rights and Freedoms

Article 6
Right to a fair trial

1

In the determination of his civil rights and obligations or of any criminal charge against him, everyone is entitled to a fair and public hearing within a reasonable time by an independent and impartial tribunal established by law. Judgment shall be pronounced publicly but the press and public may be excluded from all or part of the trial in the interest of morals, public order or national security in a democratic society, where the interests of juveniles or the protection of the private life of the parties so require, or to the extent strictly necessary in the opinion of the court in special circumstances where publicity would prejudice the interests of justice.

2

Everyone charged with a criminal offence shall be presumed innocent until proved guilty according to law.

3

Everyone charged with a criminal offence has the following minimum rights:

(a)   to be informed promptly, in a language which he understands and in detail, of the nature and cause of the accusation against him;

(b)   to have adequate time and facilities for the preparation of his defence;

(c)   to defend himself in person or through legal assistance of his own choosing or, if he has not sufficient means to pay for legal assistance, to be given it free when the interests of justice so require;

(d) to examine or have examined witnesses against him and to obtain the attendance and examination of witnesses on his behalf under the same conditions as witnesses against him;

(e) to have the free assistance of an interpreter if he cannot understand or speak the language used in court.

Article 8
Right to respect for private and family life

1

Everyone has the right to respect for his private and family life, his home and his correspondence.

2

There shall be no interference by a public authority with the exercise of this right except such as is in accordance with the law and is necessary in a democratic society in the interests of national security, public safety or the economic well-being of the country, for the prevention of disorder or crime, for the protection of health or morals, or for the protection of the rights and freedoms of others.

Article 14
Prohibition of discrimination

The enjoyment of the rights and freedoms set forth in this Convention shall be secured without discrimination on any ground such as sex, race, colour, language, religion, political or other opinion, national or social origin, association with a national minority, property, birth or other status.

Annotations

Date in force: 1 October 2000.

Warsaw Convention as amended at the Hague, 1955 and by Protocol No 4 of Montreal, 1975

CHAPTER III
LIABILITY OF THE CARRIER

Article 17

The carrier is liable for damage sustained in the event of the death or wounding of a passenger or any other bodily injury suffered by a passenger, if the accident which caused the damage so sustained took place on board the aircraft or in the course of any of the operations of embarking or disembarking.

Article 26

1.   Receipt by the person entitled to the delivery of baggage or cargo without complaint is *prima facie* evidence that the same have been delivered in good condition and in accordance with the document of carriage.

2.   In the case of damage, the person entitled to delivery must complain to the carrier forthwith after the discovery of the damage, and, at the latest, with seven days from the date of receipt in the case of baggage and fourteen days the date of receipt in the case of cargo. In the case of delay the complaint must be made at the latest within twenty-one days from the date on which the baggage or cargo have been placed at his disposal.

3.   Every complaint must be made in writing upon the document of carriage or by separate notice in writing dispatched within the times aforesaid.

4.   Failing complaint within the times aforesaid, no action shall lie against the carrier, save in the case of fraud on his part.

Article 29

1.   The right to damages shall be extinguished if an action is not brought within 2 (two) years, reckoned from the date of arrival at the destination, or from the date on which the aircraft ought to have arrived, or from the date on which the carriage stopped.

2.   The method of calculating the period of limitation shall be determined by the law of the court seised of the case.

Civil Procedure Rules 1998

SI 1998 No 3132

PART 2

APPLICATION AND INTERPRETATION OF THE RULES

2.4 Power of judge, Master or district judge to perform functions of the court

Where these Rules provide for the court to perform any act then, except where an enactment, rule or practice direction provides otherwise, that act may be performed–

    (a)   in relation to proceedings in the High Court, by any judge, Master or district judge of that Court; and

    (b)   in relation to proceedings in a county court, by any judge or district judge.

2.6 Court documents to be sealed

(1)   The court must seal[(GL)] the following documents on issue–

    (a)   the claim form; and

    (b)   any other document which a rule or practice direction requires it to seal.

(2)   The court may place the seal[(GL)] on the document–

    (a)   by hand; or

    (b)   by printing a facsimile of the seal on the document whether electronically or otherwise.

(3)   A document purporting to bear the court's seal[(GL)] shall be admissible in evidence without further proof.

2.8 Time

(1)   This rule shows how to calculate any period of time for doing any act which is specified–

    (a)   by these Rules;

    (b)   by a practice direction; or

    (c)   by a judgment or order of the court.

(2)   A period of time expressed as a number of days shall be computed as clear days.

(3)   In this rule 'clear days' means that in computing the number of days–

    (a)   the day on which the period begins; and

    (b)   if the end of the period is defined by reference to an event, the day on which that event occurs,

are not included.

Examples–

    (i)   Notice of an application must be served at least 3 days before the hearing.

An application is to be heard on Friday 20 October.

The last date for service is Monday 16 October.

    (ii)   The court is to fix a date for a hearing.

The hearing must be at least 28 days after the date of notice.

If the court gives notice of the date of the hearing on 1 October, the earliest date for the hearing is 30 October.

(iii) Particulars of claim must be served within 14 days of service of the claim form.

The claim form is served on 2 October.

The last day for service of the particulars of claim is 16 October.

(4)   Where the specified period–

     (a)   is 5 days or less; and

     (b)   includes–

         (i)   a Saturday or Sunday; or

         (ii)   a Bank Holiday, Christmas Day or Good Friday,

that day does not count.

Example–

Notice of an application must be served at least 3 days before the hearing.

An application is to be heard on Monday 20 October.

The last date for service is Tuesday 14 October.

(5)   Subject to the provisions of Practice Direction 5C, when the period specified–

     (a)   by these Rules or a practice direction; or

     (b)   by any judgment or court order,

for doing any act at the court office ends on a day on which the office is closed, that act shall be in time if done on the next day on which the court office is open.

2.9   Dates for compliance to be calendar dates and to include time of day

(1)   Where the court gives a judgment, order or direction which imposes a time limit for doing any act, the last date for compliance must, wherever practicable–

     (a)   be expressed as a calendar date; and

     (b)   include the time of day by which the act must be done.

(2)   Where the date by which an act must be done is inserted in any document, the date must, wherever practicable, be expressed as a calendar date.

2.10   Meaning of 'month' in judgments, etc

Where 'month' occurs in any judgment, order, direction or other document, it means a calendar month.

PART 3
THE COURT'S CASE MANAGEMENT POWERS

3.1   The court's general powers of management

(1)   The list of powers in this rule is in addition to any powers given to the court by any other rule or practice direction or by any other enactment or any powers it may otherwise have.

(2)   Except where these Rules provide otherwise, the court may–

    (a)   extend or shorten the time for compliance with any rule, practice direction or court order (even if an application for extension is made after the time for compliance has expired);

    (b)   adjourn or bring forward a hearing;

    (c)   require a party or a party's legal representative to attend the court;

    (d)   hold a hearing and receive evidence by telephone or by using any other method of direct oral communication;

    (e)   direct that part of any proceedings (such as a counterclaim) be dealt with as separate proceedings;

    (f)   stay[GL] the whole or part of any proceedings or judgment either generally or until a specified date or event;

    (g)   consolidate proceedings;

    (h)   try two or more claims on the same occasion;

    (i)   direct a separate trial of any issue;

    (j)   decide the order in which issues are to be tried;

    (k)   exclude an issue from consideration;

    (l)   dismiss or give judgment on a claim after a decision on a preliminary issue;

    [(ll) order any party to file and serve an estimate of costs;]

    (m) take any other step or make any other order for the purpose of managing the case and furthering the overriding objective.

(3)   When the court makes an order, it may–

    (a)   make it subject to conditions, including a condition to pay a sum of money into court; and

    (b)   specify the consequence of failure to comply with the order or a condition.

(4)   Where the court gives directions it [will] take into account whether or not a party has complied with [the Practice Direction (Pre-Action Conduct) and] any relevant pre-action protocol[GL].

(5)   The court may order a party to pay a sum of money into court if that party has, without good reason, failed to comply with a rule, practice direction or a relevant pre-action protocol.

(6)   When exercising its power under paragraph (5) the court must have regard to–

    (a)   the amount in dispute; and

    (b)   the costs which the parties have incurred or which they may incur.

[(6A)   Where a party pays money into court following an order under paragraph (3) or (5), the money shall be security for any sum payable by that party to any other party in the proceedings ...]

(7) A power of the court under these Rules to make an order includes a power to vary or revoke the order.

3.2 Court officer's power to refer to a judge

Where a step is to be taken by a court officer–

    (a)   the court officer may consult a judge before taking that step;

    (b)   the step may be taken by a judge instead of the court officer.

3.4   Power to strike out a statement of case

(1)   In this rule and rule 3.5, reference to a statement of case includes reference to part of a statement of case.

(2)   The court may strike out^(GL) a statement of case if it appears to the court–

    (a)   that the statement of case discloses no reasonable grounds for bringing or defending the claim;

    (b)   that the statement of case is an abuse of the court's process or is otherwise likely to obstruct the just disposal of the proceedings; or

    (c)   that there has been a failure to comply with a rule, practice direction or court order.

(3)   When the court strikes out a statement of case it may make any consequential order it considers appropriate.

(4)   Where–

    (a)   the court has struck out a claimant's statement of case;

    (b)   the claimant has been ordered to pay costs to the defendant; and

    (c)   before the claimant pays those costs, he starts another claim against the same defendant, arising out of facts which are the same or substantially the same as those relating to the claim in which the statement of case was struck out,

the court may, on the application of the defendant, stay^(GL) that other claim until the costs of the first claim have been paid.

(5)   Paragraph (2) does not limit any other power of the court to strike out^(GL) a statement of case.

[(6)   If the court strikes out a claimant's statement of case and it considers that the claim is totally without merit–

    (a)   the court's order must record that fact; and

    (b)   the court must at the same time consider whether it is appropriate to make a civil restraint order.]

3.9   Relief from sanctions

(1)   On an application for relief from any sanction imposed for a failure to comply with any rule, practice direction or court order the court will consider all the circumstances including–

    (a)   the interests of the administration of justice;

    (b)   whether the application for relief has been made promptly;

    (c)   whether the failure to comply was intentional;

    (d)   whether there is a good explanation for the failure;

    (e)   the extent to which the party in default has complied with other rules, practice directions, court orders and any relevant pre-action protocol ^(GL);

    (f)   whether the failure to comply was caused by the party or his legal representative;

    (g)   whether the trial date or the likely trial date can still be met if relief is granted;

    (h)   the effect which the failure to comply had on each party; and

    (i)   the effect which the granting of relief would have on each party.

(2)   An application for relief must be supported by evidence.

3.10   General power of the court to rectify matters where there has been an error of procedure

Where there has been an error of procedure such as a failure to comply with a rule or practice direction–

(a)   the error does not invalidate any step taken in the proceedings unless the court so orders; and

(b)   the court may make an order to remedy the error.

PART 6
SERVICE OF DOCUMENTS

Authors' note

Since the publication of the previous edition of this book, the rules regarding service of claim forms in CPR Part 6 have been substantially replaced with a new set.

The old service rules are reproduced here, in italicised text, before the current rules:

'6.1   *Part 6 rules about service apply generally*

The rules in this Part apply to the service of documents, except where–

(a)   *any other enactment, a rule in another Part, or a practice direction makes a different provision; or*

(b)   *the court orders otherwise.*

(For service in possession claims, see Part 55).

6.2   *Methods of service – general*

(1)   A document may be served by any of the following methods–

(a)   *personal service, in accordance with rule 6.4;*

(b)   *first class post (or an alternative service which provides for delivery on the next working day);*

(c)   *leaving the document at a place specified in rule 6.5;*

(d)   *through a document exchange in accordance with the relevant practice direction; or*

(e)   *by fax or other means of electronic communication in accordance with the relevant practice direction.*

(Rule 6.8 provides for the court to permit service by an alternative method).

(2)   A company may be served by any method permitted under this Part as an alternative to the methods of service set out in–

(a)   *section 725 of the Companies Act 1985 (service by leaving a document at or posting it to an authorised place);*

(b)   *section 695 of that Act (service on overseas companies); and*

(c)   *section 694A of that Act (service of documents on companies incorporated outside the UK and Gibraltar and having a branch in Great Britain).*

6.3   *Who is to serve*

(1)   The court will serve a document which it has issued or prepared except where–

(a)   *a rule provides that a party must serve the document in question;*

(b)   the party on whose behalf the document is to be served notifies the court that he wishes to serve it himself;

(c)   a practice direction provides otherwise;

(d)   the court orders otherwise; or

(e)   the court has failed to serve and has sent a notice of non-service to the party on whose behalf the document is to be served in accordance with rule 6.11.

(2)   Where the court is to serve a document, it is for the court to decide which of the methods of service specified in rule 6.2 is to be used.

(3)   Where a party prepares a document which is to be served by the court, that party must file a copy for the court, and for each party to be served.

6.4   Personal service

(1)   A document to be served may be served personally, except as provided in paragraphs (2) and (2A).

(2)   Where a solicitor–

(a)   is authorised to accept service on behalf of a party; and

(b)   has notified the party serving the document in writing that he is so authorised,

a document must be served on the solicitor, unless personal service is required by an enactment, rule, practice direction or court order.

(2A)   In civil proceedings by or against the Crown, as defined in rule 66.1(2), documents required to be served on the Crown may not be served personally.

(3)   A document is served personally on an individual by leaving it with that individual.

(4)   A document is served personally on a company or other corporation by leaving it with a person holding a senior position within the company or corporation.

(The service practice direction sets out the meaning of 'senior position').

(5)   A document is served personally on a partnership where partners are being sued in the name of their firm by leaving it with–

(a)   a partner; or

(b)   a person who, at the time of service, has the control or management of the partnership business at its principal place of business.

6.5   Address for service

(1)   Except as provided by Section III of this Part (service out of the jurisdiction) a document must be served within the jurisdiction.

('Jurisdiction' is defined in rule 2.3).

(2)   A party must give an address for service within the jurisdiction.

Such address must include a full postcode, unless the court orders otherwise.

(Paragraph 2.4 of the Practice Direction to Part 16 contains provision about the content of an address for service).

(3)   Where a party–

(a)   does not give the business address of his solicitor as his address for service; and

(b)   resides or carries on business within the jurisdiction,

he must give his residence or place of business as his address for service.

(4)   Any document to be served–

    (a)   by first class post (or an alternative service which provides for delivery on the next working day);

    (b)   by leaving it at the place of service;

    (c)   through a document exchange; or

    (d)   by fax or by other means of electronic communication,

must be sent or transmitted to, or left at, the address for service given by the party to be served.

(5)   Where–

    (a)   a solicitor is acting for the party to be served; and

    (b)   the document to be served is not the claim form;

the party's address for service is the business address of his solicitor.

(Rule 6.13 specifies when the business address of a defendant's solicitor may be the defendant's address for service in relation to the claim form).

(6)   Where–

    (a)   no solicitor is acting for the party to be served; and,

    (b)   the party has not given an address for service,

the document must be sent or transmitted to, or left at, the place shown in the following table.

(Rule 6.2(2) sets out the statutory methods of service on a company).

Nature of party to be served	*Place of service*
Individual	*Usual or last known residence.*
Proprietor of a business	*Usual or last known residence; or Place of business or last known place of business.*
Individual who is suing or being sued in the name of a firm	*Usual or last known residence; or Principal or last known place of business of the firm.*
Corporation incorporated in England and Wales other than a company	*Principal office of the corporation; or Any place within the jurisdiction where the corporation carries on its activities and which has a real connection with the claim.*
Company registered in England and Wales	*Principal office of the company; or Any place of business of the company within the jurisdiction which has a real connection with the claim.*
Any other company or corporation	*Any place within the jurisdiction where the corporation carries on its activities; or Any place of business of the company within the jurisdiction.*

(7)   This rule does not apply where an order made by the court under rule 6.8 (service by an alternative method) specifies where the document in question may be served.

(Rule 42.1 provides that if the business address of his solicitor is given that solicitor will be treated as acting for that party).

(8)   In civil proceedings by or against the Crown, as defined in rule 66.1(2)–

    (a)   service on the Attorney General must be effected on the Treasury Solicitor;

    (b)   service on a government department must be effected on the solicitor acting for that department as required by section 18 of the Crown Proceedings Act 1947.

(The practice direction to Part 66 gives the list published under section 17 of that Act of the solicitors acting for the different government departments on whom service is to be effected, and of their addresses).

6.6   Service of documents on children and patients

(1)   The following table shows the person on whom a document must be served if it is a document which would otherwise be served on a child or a patient–

Type of document	Nature of party	Person to be served
Claim form	Child who is not also a patient	One of the child's parents or guardians; or if there is no parent or guardian, the person with whom the child resides or in whose care the child is.
Claim form	Patient	The person authorised under Part VII of the Mental Health Act 1983 to conduct the proceedings in the name of the patient or on his behalf; or if there is no person so authorised, the person with whom the patient resides or in whose care the patient is.
Application for an order appointing a litigation friend, where a child or patient has no litigation friend	Child or patient	See rule 21.8.
Any other document	Child or patient	The litigation friend who is conducting proceedings on behalf of the child or patient.

(2)   The court may make an order permitting a document to be served on the child or patient, or on some person other than the person specified in the table in this rule.

(3)   An application for an order under paragraph (2) may be made without notice.

(4)   The court may order that, although a document has been served on someone other than the person specified in the table, the document is to be treated as if it had been properly served.

(5)   This rule does not apply where the court has made an order under rule 21.2(3) allowing a child to conduct proceedings without a litigation friend.

(Part 21 contains rules about the appointment of a litigation friend).

6.7 Deemed service

(1) A document which is served in accordance with these rules or any relevant practice direction shall he deemed to be served on the day shown in the following table–

Method of service	Deemed day of service
First class post (or an alternative service which provides for delivery on the next working day)	The second day after it was posted.
Document exchange	The second day after it was left at the document exchange.
Delivering the document to or	The day after it was delivered to or left at the permitted address.
Fax	– If it is transmitted on a business day before 4pm, on that day; or – in any other case, on the business day after the day on which it is transmitted.
Other electronic method	The second day after the day on which it is transmitted.

...

(2) If a document is served personally–

> *(a) after 5 pm, on a business day; or*

> *(b) at any time on a Saturday, Sunday or a Bank Holiday,*

it will be treated as being served on the next business day.

(3) In this rule–

> *'business day' means any day except Saturday, Sunday or a bank holiday; and*

> *'bank holiday' includes Christmas Day and Good Friday.*

6.8 Service by an alternative method

(1) Where it appears to the court that there is a good reason to authorise service by a method not permitted by these Rules, the court may make an order permitting service by an alternative method.

(2) An application for an order permitting service by an alternative method–

> *(a) must be supported by evidence; and*

> *(b) may be made without notice.*

(3) An order permitting service by an alternative method must specify–

> *(a) the method of service; and*

> *(b) the date when the document will be deemed to be served.*

6.9 Power of court to dispense with service

(1) The court may dispense with service of a document.

(2) An application for an order to dispense with service may be made without notice.

6.10   Certificate of service

Where a rule, practice direction or court order requires a certificate of service, the certificate must state the details set out in the following table–

Method of service	Details to be certified
Post	Date of posting
Personal	Date of personal service
Document exchange	Date of delivery to the document exchange
Delivery of document to or leaving it at a permitted place	Date when the document was delivered to or left at the permitted place
Fax	Date and time of transmission
Other electronic means	Date of transmission and the means used
Alternative method permitted by the court	As required by the court

II
SPECIAL PROVISIONS ABOUT SERVICE OF THE CLAIM FORM

6.12   General rules about service subject to special rules about service of claim form

The general rules about service are subject to the special rules about service contained in rules 6.13 to 6.16.

6.13   Service of claim form by the court – defendant's address for service

(1)   Where a claim form is to be served by the court, the claim form must include the defendant's address for service.

(2)   For the purposes of paragraph (1), the defendant's address for service may be the business address of the defendant's solicitor if he is authorised to accept service on the defendant's behalf but not otherwise.

(Rule 6.5 contains general provisions about the address for service).

(Paragraph 2.4 of the Practice Direction to Part 16 contains provision about the content of an address for service).

6.14   Certificate of service relating to the claim form

(1)   Where a claim form is served by the court, the court must send the claimant a notice which will include the date when the claim form is deemed to be served under rule 6.7.

(2)   Where the claim form is served by the claimant–

  (a)   he must file a certificate of service within 7 days of service of the claim form; and

  (b)   he may not obtain judgment in default under Part 12 unless he has filed the certificate of service.

(Rule 6.10 specifies what a certificate of service must show).

6.15   Service of the claim form by contractually agreed method

(1)   Where–

> (*a*) *a contract contains a term providing that, in the event of a claim being issued in relation to the contract, the claim form may be served by a method specified in the contract; and*
>
> (*b*) *a claim form containing only a claim in respect of that contract is issued,*

the claim form shall, subject to paragraph (2), be deemed to be served on the defendant if it is served by a method specified in the contract.

(2) Where the claim form is served out of the jurisdiction in accordance with the contract, it shall not be deemed to be served on the defendant unless–

> (*a*) *permission to serve it out of the jurisdiction has been granted under rule 6.20; or*
>
> (*b*) *it may be served without permission under rule 6.19.'*

I. Scope of this Part and Interpretation

6.1 Part 6 rules about service apply generally

This Part applies to the service of documents, except where–

    (a) another Part, any other enactment or a practice direction makes different provision; or

    (b) the court orders otherwise.

(Other Parts, for example, Part 54 (Judicial Review) and Part 55 (Possession Claims) contain specific provisions about service.)

6.2 Interpretation

In this Part–

    (a) 'bank holiday' means a bank holiday under the Banking and Financial Dealings Act 1971 in the part of the United Kingdom where service is to take place;

    (b) 'business day' means any day except Saturday, Sunday, a bank holiday, Good Friday or Christmas Day;

    (c) 'claim' includes petition and any application made before action or to commence proceedings and 'claim form', 'claimant' and 'defendant' are to be construed accordingly;

    (d) 'solicitor' includes any other person who, for the purposes of the Legal Services Act 2007, is an authorised person in relation to an activity which constitutes the conduct of litigation (within the meaning of that Act); and

    (e) 'European Lawyer' has the meaning set out in article 2 of the European Communities (Services of Lawyers) Order 1978 (S. I. 1978/1910).

(The European Communities (Services of Lawyers) Order 1978 is annexed to Practice Direction 6A.)

II. Service of the Claim Form in the Jurisdiction or in specified circumstances within the EEA

6.3 Methods of service

(1) A claim form may (subject to Section IV of this Part and the rules in this Section relating to service out of the jurisdiction on solicitors, European Lawyers and parties) be served by any of the following methods–

(a) personal service in accordance with rule 6.5;

(b) first class post, document exchange or other service which provides for delivery on the next business day, in accordance with Practice Direction 6A;

(c) leaving it at a place specified in rule 6.7, 6.8, 6.9 or 6.10;

(d) fax or other means of electronic communication in accordance with Practice Direction 6A; or

(e) any method authorised by the court under rule 6.15.

(2) A company may be served–

(a) by any method permitted under this Part; or

(b) by any of the methods of service permitted under the Companies Act 2006.

(3) A limited liability partnership may be served–

(a) by any method permitted under this Part; or

(b) by any of the methods of service permitted under the Companies Act 2006 as applied with modification by regulations made under the Limited Liability Partnerships Act 2000.

6.4   Who is to serve the claim form

(1) Subject to Section IV of this Part and the rules in this Section relating to service out of the jurisdiction on solicitors, European Lawyers and parties, the court will serve the claim form except where–

(a) a rule or practice direction provides that the claimant must serve it;

(b) the claimant notifies the court that the claimant wishes to serve it; or

(c) the court orders or directs otherwise.

(2) Where the court is to serve the claim form, it is for the court to decide which method of service is to be used.

(3) Where the court is to serve the claim form, the claimant must, in addition to filing a copy for the court, provide a copy for each defendant to be served.

(4) Where the court has sent–

(a) a notification of outcome of postal service to the claimant in accordance with rule 6.18; or

(b) a notification of non-service by a bailiff in accordance with rule 6.19,

the court will not try to serve the claim form again.

6.5   Personal service

(1) Where required by another Part, any other enactment, a practice direction or a court order, a claim form must be served personally.

(2) In other cases, a claim form may be served personally except–

(a) where rule 6.7 applies; or

(b) in any proceedings against the Crown.

(Part 54 contains provisions about judicial review claims and Part 66 contains provisions about Crown proceedings.)

(3)   A claim form is served personally on–

    (a)   an individual by leaving it with that individual;

    (b)   a company or other corporation by leaving it with a person holding a senior position within the company or corporation; or

    (c)   a partnership (where partners are being sued in the name of their firm) by leaving it with–

    (i)   a partner; or

    (ii)   a person who, at the time of service, has the control or management of the partnership business at its principal place of business.

(Practice Direction 6A sets out the meaning of 'senior position'.)

6.6   Where to serve the claim form-general provisions

(1)   The claim form must be served within the jurisdiction except where rule 6.7(2), 6.7(3) or 6.11 applies or as provided by Section IV of this Part.

(2)   The claimant must include in the claim form an address at which the defendant may be served. That address must include a full postcode or its equivalent in any EEA state (if applicable), unless the court orders otherwise.

(Paragraph 2.4 of Practice Direction 16 contains provisions about postcodes.)

(3)   Paragraph (2) does not apply where an order made by the court under rule 6.15 (service by an alternative method or at an alternative place) specifies the place or method of service of the claim form.

6.7   Service on a solicitor or European Lawyer within the United Kingdom or in any other EEA state

(1)   **Solicitor within the jurisdiction:** Subject to rule 6.5(1), where–

    (a)   the defendant has given in writing the business address within the jurisdiction of a solicitor as an address at which the defendant may be served with the claim form; or

    (b)   a solicitor acting for the defendant has notified the claimant in writing that the solicitor is instructed by the defendant to accept service of the claim form on behalf of the defendant at a business address within the jurisdiction,

the claim form must be served at the business address of that solicitor.

('Solicitor' has the extended meaning set out in rule 6.2(d).)

(2)   **Solicitor in Scotland or Northern Ireland or EEA state other than the United Kingdom:** Subject to rule 6.5(1) and the provisions of Section IV of this Part, and except where any other rule or practice direction makes different provision, where–

    (a)   the defendant has given in writing the business address in Scotland or Northern Ireland of a solicitor as an address at which the defendant may be served with the claim form;

    (aa)   a solicitor acting for the defendant has notified the claimant in writing that the solicitor is instructed by the defendant to accept service of the claim form on behalf of the defendant at a business address within Scotland or Northern Ireland;

    (b)   the defendant has given in writing the business address within any other EEA state of a solicitor as an address at which the defendant may be served with the claim form; or (c)　a solicitor acting for the defendant has notified the claimant in writing that the solicitor is instructed by the defendant to accept service of the claim form on behalf of the defendant at a business address within any other EEA state,

the claim form must be served at the business address of that solicitor.

(3)　**European Lawyer in any EEA state:** Subject to rule 6.5(1) and the provisions of Section IV of this Part, and except where any other rule or practice direction makes different provision, where–

(a)　the defendant has given in writing the business address of a European Lawyer in any EEA state as an address at which the defendant may be served with the claim form; or

(b)　a European Lawyer in any EEA state has notified the claimant in writing that the European Lawyer is instructed by the defendant to accept service of the claim form on behalf of the defendant at a business address of the European Lawyer,

the claim form must be served at the business address of that European Lawyer.

(For Production Centre Claims see paragraph 2.3(7A) of Practice Direction 7C; for Money Claims Online see paragraph 4(6) of Practice Direction 7E; and for Possession Claims Online see paragraph 5.1(4) of Practice Direction 55B.)

('European Lawyer' has the meaning set out in rule 6.2(e).)

6.8　Service of the claim form where before service the defendant gives an address at which the defendant may be served

Subject to rules 6.5(1) and 6.7 and the provisions of Section IV of this Part and except where any othe rule or practice direction makes different provision–

(a)　the defendant may be served with the claim form at an address at which the defendant resides or carries on business within the UK or any other EEA state and which the defendant has given for the purpose of being served with the proceedings; or

(b)　in any claim by a tenant against a landlord, the claim form may be served at an address given by the landlord under section 48 of the Landlord and Tenant Act 1987.

(For Production Centre Claims see paragraph 2.3(7A) of Practice Direction 7C; for Money Claims Online see paragraph 4(6) of Practice Direction 7E; and for Possession Claims Online see paragraph 5.1(4) of Practice Direction 55B.)

(For service out of the jurisdiction see rules 6.40 to 6.47 .)

6.9　Service of the claim form where the defendant does not give an address at which the defendant may be served

(1)　This rule applies where–

(a)　rule 6.5(1) (personal service);

(b)　rule 6.7 (service of claim form on solicitor or European Lawyer); and

(c)　rule 6.8 (defendant gives address at which the defendant may be served),

do not apply and the claimant does not wish to effect personal service under rule 6.5(2).

(2)　Subject to paragraphs (3) to (6), the claim form must be served on the defendant at the place shown in the following table.

Nature of defendant to be served	*Place of service*
1. Individual	Usual or last known residence.
2. Individual being sued in the name of a business	Usual or last known residence of the individual; or principal or last known place of business.
3. Individual being sued in the business name of a partnership	Usual or last known residence of the individual; or principal or last known place of business of the partnership.
4. Limited liability partnership	Principal office of the partnership; or any place of business of the partnership within the jurisdiction which has a real connection with the claim.
5. Corporation (other than a company) incorporated in England and Wales	Principal office of the corporation; or any place within the jurisdiction where the corporation carries on its activities and which has a real connection with the claim.
6. Company registered in England and Wales	Principal office of the company; or any place of business of the company within the jurisdiction which has a real connection with the claim.
7. Any other company or corporation	Any place within the jurisdiction where the corporation carries on its activities; or any place of business of the company within the jurisdiction.

(3)   Where a claimant has reason to believe that the address of the defendant referred to in entries 1, 2 or 3 in the table in paragraph (2) is an address at which the defendant no longer resides or carries on business, the claimant must take reasonable steps to ascertain the address of the defendant's current residence or place of business ('current address').

(4)   Where, having taken the reasonable steps required by paragraph (3), the claimant–

    (a)   ascertains the defendant's current address, the claim form must be served at that address; or

    (b)   is unable to ascertain the defendant's current address, the claimant must consider whether there is–

        (i)   an alternative place where; or

        (ii)   an alternative method by which,

    service may be effected.

(5)   If, under paragraph (4)(b), there is such a place where or a method by which service may be effected, the claimant must make an application under rule 6.15.

(6)   Where paragraph (3) applies, the claimant may serve on the defendant's usual or last known address in accordance with the table in paragraph (2) where the claimant–

    (a)   cannot ascertain the defendant's current residence or place of business; and

    (b)   cannot ascertain an alternative place or an alternative method under paragraph (4)(b).

(For service out of the jurisdiction see rules 6.40 to 6.47.)

II. Service of the Claim Form in the Jurisdiction

6.11   Service of the claim form by contractually agreed method

(1)   Where–

    (a)   a contract contains a term providing that, in the event of a claim being started in relation to the contract, the claim form may be served by a method or at a place specified in the contract; and

    (b)   a claim solely in respect of that contract is started,

the claim form may, subject to paragraph (2), be served on the defendant by the method or at the place specified in the contract.

(2)   Where in accordance with the contract the claim form is to be served out of the jurisdiction, it may be served–

    (a)   if permission to serve it out of the jurisdiction has been granted under rule 6.36; or

    (b)   without permission under rule 6.32 or 6.33.

6.14   Deemed service

A claim form served within the United Kingdom in accordance with this Part is deemed to be served on the second business day after completion of the relevant step under rule 7.5(1).

6.15   Service of the claim form by an alternative method or at an alternative place

(1)   Where it appears to the court that there is a good reason to authorise service by a method or at a place not otherwise permitted by this Part, the court may make an order permitting service by an alternative method or at an alternative place.

(2)   On an application under this rule, the court may order that steps already taken to bring the claim form to the attention of the defendant by an alternative method or at an alternative place is good service.

(3)   An application for an order under this rule–

    (a)   must be supported by evidence; and

    (b)   may be made without notice.

(4)   An order under this rule must specify–

    (a)   the method or place of service;

    (b)   the date on which the claim form is deemed served; and

    (c)   the period for–

        (i)   filing an acknowledgment of service;

        (ii)   filing an admission; or

        (iii)   filing a defence.

6.16   Power of court to dispense with service of the claim form

(1)   The court may dispense with service of a claim form in exceptional circumstances.

(2)   An application for an order to dispense with service may be made at any time and–

    (a)   must be supported by evidence; and

    (b)   may be made without notice.

6.17 Notice and certificate of service relating to the claim form

(1) Where the court serves a claim form, the court will send to the claimant a notice which will include the date on which the claim form is deemed served under rule 6.14.

(2) Where the claimant serves the claim form, the claimant–

    (a) must file a certificate of service within 21 days of service of the particulars of claim, unless all the defendants to the proceedings have filed acknowledgments of service within that time; and

    (b) may not obtain judgment in default under Part 12 unless a certificate of service has been filed.

(3) The certificate of service must state–

    (a) where rule 6.7, 6.8, 6.9 or 6.10 applies, the category of address at which the claimant believes the claim form has been served; and

    (b) the details set out in the following table.

Method of service	*Details to be certified*
1. Personal service	Date of personal service.
2. First class post, document exchange or other service which provides for delivery on the next business day	Date of posting, or leaving with, delivering to or collection by the relevant service provider.
3. Delivery of document to or leaving it at a permitted place	Date when the document was delivered to or left at the permitted place.
4. Fax	Date of completion of the transmission.
5. Other electronic method	Date of sending the e-mail or other electronic transmission.
6. Alternative method or place	As required by the court.

III. Service of Documents other than the Claim Form in the United Kingdom or in specified circumstances within the EEA

6.20 Methods of service

(1) Subject to Section IV of this Part and the rules in this Section relating to service out of the jurisdiction on solicitors, European Lawyers and parties, a document may be served by any of the following methods–

    (a) personal service, in accordance with rule 6.22;

    (b) first class post, document exchange or other service which provides for delivery on the next business day, in accordance with Practice Direction 6A;

    (c) leaving it at a place specified in rule 6.23;

    (d) fax or other means of electronic communication in accordance with Practice Direction 6A; or

    (e) any method authorised by the court under rule 6.27.

(2) A company may be served–

    (a) by any method permitted under this Part; or

    (b) by any of the methods of service permitted under the Companies Act 2006.

(3)   A limited liability partnership may be served–

    (a)   by any method permitted under this Part; or

    (b)   by any of the methods of service permitted under the Companies Act 2006 as applied with modification by regulations made under the Limited Liability Partnerships Act 2000.

6.21   Who is to serve

(1)   Subject to Section IV of this Part and the rules in this Section relating to service out of the jurisdiction on solicitors, European Lawyers and parties, a party to proceedings will serve a document which that party has prepared except where–

    (a)   a rule or practice direction provides that the court will serve the document; or

    (b)   the court orders otherwise.

(2)   The court will serve a document which it has prepared except where–

    (a)   a rule or practice direction provides that a party must serve the document;

    (b)   the party on whose behalf the document is to be served notifies the court that the party wishes to serve it; or

    (c)   the court orders otherwise.

(3)   Where the court is to serve a document, it is for the court to decide which method of service is to be used.

(4)   Where the court is to serve a document prepared by a party, that party must provide a copy for the court and for each party to be served.

6.22   Personal service

(1)   Where required by another Part, any other enactment, a practice direction or a court order, a document must be served personally.

(2)   In other cases, a document may be served personally except–

    (a)   where the party to be served has given an address for service under rule 6.23; or

    (b)   in any proceedings by or against the Crown.

(3)   A document may be served personally as if the document were a claim form in accordance with rule 6.5(3).

(For service out of the jurisdiction see rules 6.40 to 6.47.)

PART 7
HOW TO START PROCEEDINGS – THE CLAIM FORM

7.2   How to start proceedings

(1)   Proceedings are started when the court issues a claim form at the request of the claimant.

(2)   A claim form is issued on the date entered on the form by the court.

(A person who seeks a remedy from the court before proceedings are started or in relation to proceedings which are taking place, or will take place, in another jurisdiction must make an application under Part 23.)

(Part 16 sets out what the claim form must include.)

(The Costs Practice Direction sets out the information about a funding arrangement to be provided with the claim form where the claimant intends to seek to recover an additional liability.)

('Funding arrangements' and 'additional liability' are defined in rule 43.2.)

7.2A

Practice Direction 7A makes provision for procedures to be followed when claims are brought by or against a partnership within the jurisdiction.

7.4 Particulars of claim

(1)   Particulars of claim must–

    (a)   be contained in or served with the claim form; or

    (b)   subject to paragraph (2) be served on the defendant by the claimant within 14 days after service of the claim form.

(2)   Particulars of claim must be served on the defendant no later than the latest time for serving a claim form.

(Rule 7.5 sets out the latest time for serving a claim form.)

(3)   Where the claimant serves particulars of claim separately from the claim form in accordance with paragraph (1)(b), the claimant must, within 7 days of service on the defendant, file a copy of the particulars except where–

    (a)   paragraph 5.2(4) of Practice Direction 7C applies; or

    (b)   paragraph 6.4 of Practice Direction 7E applies.

(Part 16 sets out what the particulars of claim must include.)

(Part 22 requires particulars of claim to be verified by a statement of truth.)

7.5 Service of a claim form

(1)   Where the claim form is served within the jurisdiction, the claimant must complete the step required by the following table in relation to the particular method of service chosen, before 12.00 midnight on the calendar day four months after the date of issue of the claim form.

Method of service	*Step required*
First class post, document exchange or other service which provides for delivery on the next business day	Posting, leaving with, delivering to or collection by the relevant service provider
Delivery of the document to or leaving it at the relevant place	Delivering to or leaving the document at the relevant place
Personal service under rule 6.5	Completing the relevant step required by rule 6.5(3)
Fax	Completing the transmission of the fax
Other electronic method	Sending the e-mail or other electronic transmission

(2)   Where the claim form is to be served out of the jurisdiction, the claim form must be served in accordance with Section IV of Part 6 within 6 months of the date of issue.

7.6   Extension of time for serving a claim form

(1)   The claimant may apply for an order extending the period for compliance with rule 7.5.

(2)   The general rule is that an application to extend the time for compliance with rule 7.5 must be made–

    (a)   within the period specified by rule 7.5; or

    (b)   where an order has been made under this rule, within the period for service specified by that order.

(3)   If the claimant applies for an order to extend the time for compliance after the end of the period specified by rule 7.5 or by an order made under this rule, the court may make such an order only if–

    (a)   the court has failed to serve the claim form; or

    (b)   the claimant has taken all reasonable steps to comply with rule 7.5 but has been unable to do so; and

    (c)   in either case, the claimant has acted promptly in making the application.

(4)   An application for an order extending the time for compliance with rule 7.5–

    (a)   must be supported by evidence; and

    (b)   may be made without notice.

7.7   Application by defendant for service of claim form

(1)   Where a claim form has been issued against a defendant, but has not yet been served on him, the defendant may serve a notice on the claimant requiring him to serve the claim form or discontinue the claim within a period specified in the notice.

(2)   The period specified in a notice served under paragraph (1) must be at least 14 days after service of the notice.

(3)   If the claimant fails to comply with the notice, the court may, on the application of the defendant–

    (a)   dismiss the claim; or

    (b)   make any other order it thinks just.

7.8   Form for defence etc must be served with particulars of claim

(1)   When particulars of claim are served on a defendant, whether they are contained in the claim form, served with it or served subsequently, they must be accompanied by–

    (a)   a form for defending the claim;

    (b)   a form for admitting the claim; and

    (c)   a form for acknowledging service.

(2)   Where the claimant is using the procedure set out in Part 8 (alternative procedure for claims)–

    (a)   paragraph (1) does not apply; and

    (b)   a form for acknowledging service must accompany the claim form.

PART 17
AMENDMENTS TO STATEMENTS OF CASE

17.1 Amendments to statements of case

(1) A party may amend his statement of case at any time before it has been served on any other party.

(2) If his statement of case has been served, a party may amend it only–

    (a) with the written consent of all the other parties; or

    (b) with the permission of the court.

[(3) If a statement of case has been served, an application to amend it by removing, adding or substituting a party must be made in accordance with rule 19.4.]

...

(Part 22 requires amendments to a statement of case to be verified by a statement of truth unless the court orders otherwise).

17.3 Amendments to statements of case with the permission of the court

(1) Where the court gives permission for a party to amend his statement of case, it may give directions as to–

    (a) amendments to be made to any other statement of case; and

    (b) service of any amended statement of case.

(2) The power of the court to give permission under this rule is subject to–

    (a) rule 19.1 (change of parties – general);

    (b) rule 19.4 (special provisions about adding or substituting parties after the end of a relevant limitation period(GL)); and

    (c) rule 17.4 (amendments of statement of case after the end of a relevant limitation period).

17.4 Amendments to statements of case after the end of a relevant limitation period

(1) This rule applies where–

    (a) a party applies to amend his statement of case in one of the ways mentioned in this rule; and

    (b) a period of limitation has expired under–

        (i) the Limitation Act 1980;

        (ii) the Foreign Limitation Periods Act 1984; [or]

        [(iii) any other enactment which allows such an amendment, or under which such an amendment is allowed].

(2) The court may allow an amendment whose effect will be to add or substitute a new claim, but only if the new claim arises out of the same facts or substantially the same facts as a claim in respect of which the party applying for permission has already claimed a remedy in the proceedings.

(3) The court may allow an amendment to correct a mistake as to the name of a party, but only where the mistake was genuine and not one which would cause reasonable doubt as to the identity of the party in question.

(4)   The court may allow an amendment to alter the capacity in which a party claims if the new capacity is one which that party had when the proceedings started or has since acquired.

([Rule 19.5] specifies the circumstances in which the court may allow a new party to be added or substituted after the end of a relevant limitation period(GL.)).

[PART 19
PARTIES AND GROUP LITIGATION]

19.4   Procedure for adding and substituting parties

(1)   The court's permission is required to remove, add or substitute a party, unless the claim form has not been served.

(2)   An application for permission under paragraph (1) may be made by–

    (a)   an existing party; or

    (b)   a person who wishes to become a party.

(3)   An application for an order under rule 19.2(4) (substitution of a new party where existing party's interest or liability has passed)–

    (a)   may be made without notice; and

    (b)   must be supported by evidence.

(4)   Nobody may be added or substituted as a claimant unless–

    (a)   he has given his consent in writing; and

    (b)   that consent has been filed with the court.

(4A)   The Commissioners for HM Revenue and Customs may be added as a party to proceedings only if they consent in writing.

(5)   An order for the removal, addition or substitution of a party must be served on–

    (a)   all parties to the proceedings; and

    (b)   any other person affected by the order.

(6)   When the court makes an order for the removal, addition or substitution of a party, it may give consequential directions about–

    (a)   filing and serving the claim form on any new defendant;

    (b)   serving relevant documents on the new party; and

    (c)   the management of the proceedings.

[19.4A   Human Rights

Section 4 of the Human Rights Act 1998

(1)   The court may not make a declaration of incompatibility in accordance with section 4 of the Human Rights Act 1998 unless 21 days' notice, or such other period of notice as the court directs, has been given to the Crown.

(2)   Where notice has been given to the Crown a Minister, or other person permitted by that Act, shall be joined as a party on giving notice to the court.

(Only courts specified in section 4 of the Human Rights Act 1998 can make a declaration of incompatibility)

Section 9 of the Human Rights Act 1998

(3)   Where a claim is made under that Act for damages in respect of a judicial act–

   (a)   that claim must be set out in the statement of case or the appeal notice; and

   (b)   notice must be given to the Crown.

(4)   Where paragraph (3) applies and the appropriate person has not applied to be joined as a party within 21 days, or such other period as the court directs, after the notice is served, the court may join the appropriate person as a party.

([Practice Direction 19A] makes provision for these notices)]

[19.5   Special provisions about adding or substituting parties after the end of a relevant limitation period

(1)   This rule applies to a change of parties after the end of a period of limitation under–

   (a)   the Limitation Act 1980;

   (b)   the Foreign Limitation Periods Act 1984; [or]

   [(c)   any other enactment which allows such a change, or under which such a change is allowed].

(2)   The court may add or substitute a party only if–

   (a)   the relevant limitation period$^{(GL)}$ was current when the proceedings were started; and

   (b)   the addition or substitution is necessary.

(3)   The addition or substitution of a party is necessary only if the court is satisfied that–

   (a)   the new party is to be substituted for a party who was named in the claim form in mistake for the new party;

   (b)   the claim cannot properly be carried on by or against the original party unless the new party is added or substituted as claimant or defendant; or

   (c)   the original party has died or had a bankruptcy order made against him and his interest or liability has passed to the new party.

(4)   In addition, in a claim for personal injuries the court may add or substitute a party where it directs that–

   (a)

      (i)   section 11 (special time limit for claims for personal injuries); or

      (ii)   section 12 (special time limit for claims under fatal accidents legislation),

      of the Limitation Act 1980 shall not apply to the claim by or against the new party; or

   (b)   the issue of whether those sections apply shall be determined at trial. (Rule 17.4 deals with other changes after the end of a relevant limitation period$^{(GL)}$)]

PART 20
COUNTERCLAIMS AND OTHER ADDITIONAL CLAIMS

[20.2   Scope and interpretation

(1)   This Part applies to–

   (a)   a counterclaim by a defendant against the claimant or against the claimant and some other person;

(b) an additional claim by a defendant against any person (whether or not already a party) for contribution or indemnity or some other remedy; and

(c) where an additional claim has been made against a person who is not already a party, any additional claim made by that person against any other person (whether or not already a party).

(2) In these Rules–

(a) 'additional claim' means any claim other than the claim by the claimant against the defendant; and

(b) unless the context requires otherwise, references to a claimant or defendant include a party bringing or defending an additional claim.]

CPR Practice Directions

PRACTICE DIRECTION 6A – SERVICE WITHIN THE UNITED KINGDOM

This Practice Direction supplements CPR Part 6

Scope of this Practice Direction

1.1 This Practice Direction supplements–

    (1) Section II (service of the claim form in the jurisdiction) of Part 6;

    (2) Section III (service of documents other than the claim form in the United Kingdom) of Part 6; and

    (3) rule 6.40 in relation to the method of service on a party in Scotland or Northern Ireland.

(Practice Direction 6B contains provisions relevant to service on a party in Scotland or Northern Ireland, including provisions about service out of the jurisdiction where permission is and is not required and the period for responding to an application notice.)

When service may be by document exchange

2.1 Service by document exchange (DX) may take place only where–

    (1) the address at which the party is to be served includes a numbered box at a DX, or

    (2) the writing paper of the party who is to be served or of the solicitor acting for that party sets out a DX box number, and

    (3) the party or the solicitor acting for that party has not indicated in writing that they are unwilling to accept service by DX.

How service is effected by post, an alternative service provider or DX

3.1 Service by post, DX or other service which provides for delivery on the next business day is effected by–

    (1) placing the document in a post box;

    (2) leaving the document with or delivering the document to the relevant service provider; or

    (3) having the document collected by the relevant service provider.

Service by fax or other electronic means

4.1 Subject to the provisions of rule 6.23(5) and (6), where a document is to be served by fax or other electronic means–

    (1) the party who is to be served or the solicitor acting for that party must previously have indicated in writing to the party serving–

        (a) that the party to be served or the solicitor is willing to accept service by fax or other electronic means; and

        (b) the fax number, e-mail address or other electronic identification to which it must be sent; and

    (2) the following are to be taken as sufficient written indications for the purposes of paragraph 4.1(1)–

    (a)   a fax number set out on the writing paper of the solicitor acting for the party to be served;

    (b)   an e-mail address set out on the writing paper of the solicitor acting for the party to be served but only where it is stated that the e-mail address may be used for service; or

    (c)   a fax number, e-mail address or electronic identification set out on a statement of case or a response to a claim filed with the court.

4.2   Where a party intends to serve a document by electronic means (other than by fax) that party must first ask the party who is to be served whether there are any limitations to the recipient's agreement to accept service by such means (for example, the format in which documents are to be sent and the maximum size of attachments that may be received).

4.3   Where a document is served by electronic means, the party serving the document need not in addition send or deliver a hard copy.

Service on members of the Regular Forces and United States Air Force

5.1   The provisions that apply to service on members of the regular forces (within the meaning of the Armed Forces Act 2006) and members of the United States Air Force are annexed to this practice direction.

Personal service on a company or other corporation

6.1   Personal service on a registered company or corporation in accordance with rule 6.5(3) is effected by leaving a document with a person holding a senior position.

6.2   Each of the following persons is a person holding a senior position–

    (1)   in respect of a registered company or corporation, a director, the treasurer, the secretary of the company or corporation, the chief executive, a manager or other officer of the company or corporation; and

    (2)   in respect of a corporation which is not a registered company, in addition to any of the persons set out in sub-paragraph (1), the mayor, the chairman, the president, a town clerk or similar officer of the corporation.

Certificate of service where claimant serves the claim form

7.1   Where, pursuant to rule 6.17(2), the claimant files a certificate of service, the claimant is not required to and should not file–

    (1)   a further copy of the claim form with the certificate of service; and

    (2)   a further copy of–

        (a)   the particulars of claim (where not included in the claim form); or

        (b)   any document attached to the particulars of claim,

with the certificate of service where that document has already been filed with the court.

(Rule 7.4 requires the claimant to file a copy of the particulars of claim (where served separately from the claim form) within 7 days of service on the defendant.)

Service by the court

8.1   Where the court serves a document in accordance with rule 6.4 or 6.21(2), the method will normally be first class post.

8.2   Where the court serves a claim form, delivers a defence to a claimant or notifies a claimant that the defendant has filed an acknowledgment of service, the court will also serve or deliver a copy of any notice of funding that has been filed, if–

    (1)   it was filed at the same time as the claim form, defence or acknowledgment of service, and

    (2)   copies of it were provided for service.

(Rule 44.15 deals with the provision of information about funding arrangements.)

Application for an order for service by an alternative method or at an alternative place

9.1   Where an application for an order under rule 6.15 is made before the document is served, the application must be supported by evidence stating–

    (1)   the reason why an order is sought;

    (2)   what alternative method or place is proposed, and

    (3)   why the applicant believes that the document is likely to reach the person to be served by the method or at the place proposed.

9.2   Where the application for an order is made after the applicant has taken steps to bring the document to the attention of the person to be served by an alternative method or at an alternative place, the application must be supported by evidence stating–

    (1)   the reason why the order is sought;

    (2)   what alternative method or alternative place was used;

    (3)   when the alternative method or place was used; and

    (4)   why the applicant believes that the document is likely to have reached the person to be served by the alternative method or at the alternative place.

9.3   Examples–

    (1)   an application to serve by posting or delivering to an address of a person who knows the other party must be supported by evidence that if posted or delivered to that address, the document is likely to be brought to the attention of the other party;

    (2)   an application to serve by sending a SMS text message or leaving a voicemail message at a particular telephone number saying where the document is must be accompanied by evidence that the person serving the document has taken, or will take, appropriate steps to ensure that the party being served is using that telephone number and is likely to receive the message; and

    (3)   an application to serve by e-mail to a company (where paragraph 4.1 does not apply) must be supported by evidence that the e-mail address to which the document will be sent is one which is likely to come to the attention of a person holding a senior position in that company.

Deemed service of a document other than a claim form

10.1   Rule 6.26 contains provisions about deemed service of a document other than a claim form. Examples of how deemed service is calculated are set out below.

10.2   Example 1

Where the document is posted (by first class post) on a Monday (a business day), the day of deemed service is the following Wednesday (a business day).

10.3   Example 2

Where the document is left in a numbered box at the DX on a Friday (a business day), the day of deemed service is the following Monday (a business day).

10.4   Example 3

Where the document is sent by fax on a Saturday and the transmission of that fax is completed by 4.30p.m. on that day, the day of deemed service is the following Monday (a business day).

10.5   Example 4

Where the document is served personally before 4.30p.m. on a Sunday, the day of deemed service is the next day (Monday, a business day).

10.6   Example 5

Where the document is delivered to a permitted address after 4.30p.m. on the Thursday (a business day) before Good Friday, the day of deemed service is the following Tuesday (a business day) as the Monday is a bank holiday

10.7   Example 6

Where the document is posted (by first class post) on a bank holiday Monday, the day of deemed service is the following Wednesday (a business day).

PRACTICE DIRECTION 7A – HOW TO START PROCEEDINGS – THE CLAIM FORM

This Practice Direction supplements CPR Part 7

Start of proceedings

5.1   Proceedings are started when the court issues a claim form at the request of the claimant (see rule 7.2) but where the claim form as issued was received in the court office on a date earlier than the date on which it was issued by the court, the claim is 'brought' for the purposes of the Limitation Act 1980 and any other relevant statute on that earlier date.

5.2   The date on which the claim form was received by the court will be recorded by a date stamp either on the claim form held on the court file or on the letter that accompanied the claim form when it was received by the court.

5.3   An enquiry as to the date on which the claim form was received by the court should be directed to a court officer.

5.4   Parties proposing to start a claim which is approaching the expiry of the limitation period should recognise the potential importance of establishing the date the claim form was received by the court and should themselves make arrangements to record the date.

5.5   Where it is sought to start proceedings against the estate of a deceased defendant where probate or letters of administration have not been granted, the claimant should issue the claim against 'the personal representatives of A.B. deceased'. The claimant should then, before the expiry of the period for service of the claim form, apply to the court for the appointment of a person to represent the estate of the deceased.

Claims by and against partnerships within the jurisdiction

5A.1   Paragraphs 5A and 5B apply to claims that are brought by or against two or more persons who–

(1)   were partners; and

(2)   carried on that partnership business within the jurisdiction,

at the time when the cause of action accrued.

5A.2   For the purposes of this paragraph, 'partners' includes persons claiming to be entitled as partners and persons alleged to be partners.

5A.3   Where that partnership has a name, unless it is inappropriate to do so, claims must be brought in or against the name under which that partnership carried on business at the time the cause of action accrued.

Partnership membership statements

5B.1   In this paragraph a 'partnership membership statement' is a written statement of the names and last known places of residence of all the persons who were partners in the partnership at the time when the cause of action accrued, being the date specified for this purpose in accordance with paragraph 5B.3.

5B.2   If the partners are requested to provide a copy of a partnership membership statement by any party to a claim, the partners must do so within 14 days of receipt of the request.

5B.3   In that request the party seeking a copy of a partnership membership statement must specify the date when the relevant cause of action accrued.

(Signing of the acknowledgment of service in the case of a partnership is dealt with in paragraph 4.4 of Practice Direction 10.)

Persons carrying on business in another name

5C.1   This paragraph applies where–

>   (1)   a claim is brought against an individual;
>
>   (2)   that individual carries on a business within the jurisdiction (even if not personally within the jurisdiction); and
>
>   (3)   that business is carried on in a name other than that individual's own name ('the business name').

5C.2   The claim may be brought against the business name as if it were the name of a partnership.

Particulars of claim

6.1   Where the claimant does not include the particulars of claim in the claim form, they may be served separately:

>   (1)   either at the same time as the claim form, or
>
>   (2)   within 14 days after service of the claim form provided that the service of the particulars of claim is within 4 months after the date of issue of the claim form [2] (or 6 months where the claim form is to be served out of the jurisdiction[3]).

6.2   If the particulars of claim are not included in or have not been served with the claim form, the claim form must contain a statement that particulars of claim will follow. [4]

(These paragraphs do not apply where the Part 8 procedure is being used. For information on matters to be included in the claim form or the particulars of claim, see Part 16 (statements of case) and Practice Direction 16.)

Statement of truth

7.1   Part 22 requires the claim form and, where they are not included in the claim form, the particulars of claim, to be verified by a statement of truth.

7.2   The form of the statement of truth is as follows:

'[I believe][the claimant believes] that the facts stated in [this claim form] [these particulars of claim] are true.'

7.3   Attention is drawn to rule 32.14 which sets out the consequences of verifying a statement of case containing a false statement without an honest belief in its truth.

Extension of time

8.1   An application under rule 7.6 (for an extension of time for serving a claim form under rule 7.6(1)) must be made in accordance with Part 23 and supported by evidence.

8.2   The evidence should state:

(1)   all the circumstances relied on,

(2)   the date of issue of the claim,

(3)   the expiry date of any rule 7.6 extension, and

(4)   a full explanation as to why the claim has not been served.

Index

All references are to page number.